A-Z BIRMINGHAM

CONTENTS

Key to Map Pages	2-3	Index to Streets, Towns, Villages and selected Places of Interest	171-293
Large Scale City Centres	4-5,170		
Map Pages	6-169	Index to Hospitals etc.	294-296

REFERENCE

Motorway	**M6**
A Road	**A38**
B Road	**B4284**
Dual Carriageway	
One-way Street Traffic flow on A Roads is also indicated by a heavy line on the driver's left	
Road Under Construction Opening dates are correct at time of publication.	
Proposed Road	
City Centre Ring Road & Junction Numbers	(1)
Restricted Access	
Pedestrianized Road	
Track / Footpath	
Railway	Station Heritage Station Level Crossing Tunnel
Midland Metro The boarding of Metro trams at stops may be limited to a single direction, indicated by the arrow.	Stop
Built-up Area	NEWTON PL.
Local Authority Boundary	— · — · ·
Posttown Boundary	
Postcode Boundary (within Posttown)	— — — ·
Map Continuation	**20** Large Scale City Centre **4**

Car Park (selected)	P
Church or Chapel	†
Cycleway (selected)	🚲
Fire Station	■
Hospital	H
House Numbers (A and B Roads only)	20 40
Information Centre	i
Junction Name (M6 Toll only)	BURNTWOOD JUNCTION
National Grid Reference	⁴15
Park & Ride	P+R
Police Station	▲
Post Office	★
Safety Camera with Speed Limit Fixed cameras and long term road works cameras. Symbols do not indicate camera direction.	(30)
Toilet: without facilities for the Disabled with facilities for the Disabled Disabled use only	▽ ▽ ▽
Viewpoint	☀ ☀
Educational Establishment	
Hospital or Healthcare Building	
Industrial Building	
Leisure or Recreational Facility	
Place of Interest	
Public Building	
Shopping Centre or Market	
Other Selected Buildings	

SCALE

Map Pages 6-169	Map Pages 4-5,170
1:18,103 3½ inches to 1 mile	1:9,051 7 inches to 1 mile

0   ¼   ½ Mile   0   ⅛   ¼ Mile

0   250   500   750 Met

5.52 cm to 1 km   8.89 cm to 1   1 mile

Copyright of Geographer

Fairfield Road, Borough Green, Sevenoaks, Kent TN15 8PP
Telephone: 01732 781000 (Enquiries & Trade Sales)
01732 783422 (Retail Sales)
www.az.co.uk
Copyright © Geographers' A-Z Map Co. Ltd.
EDITION 6   2013

from
Controller

7302

Speed Camera Location Database Copyright 2012 © PocketGPSWorld.com

D0061230

Every possible care has been taken to ensure that, to the best of our knowledge, the information contained in this atlas is accurate at the date of publication. However, we cannot warrant that our work is entirely error free and whilst we would be grateful to learn of any inaccuracies, we do not accept any responsibility for loss or damage resulting from reliance on information contained within this publication.

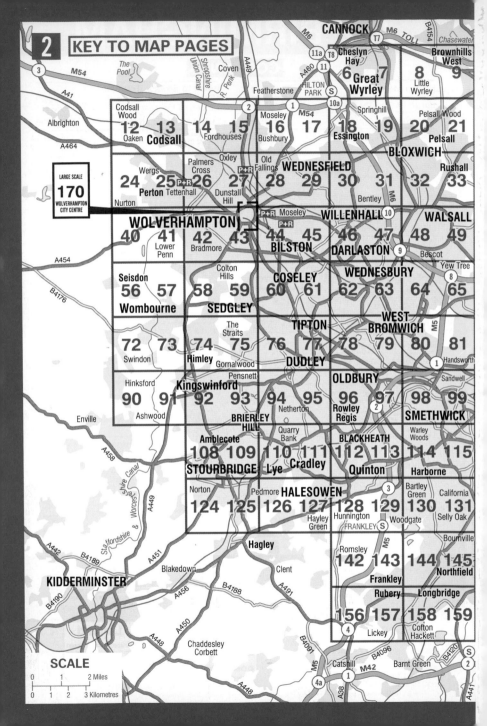

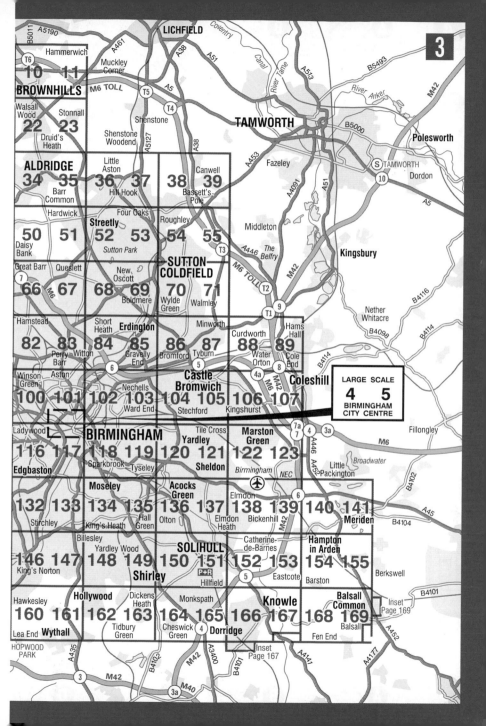

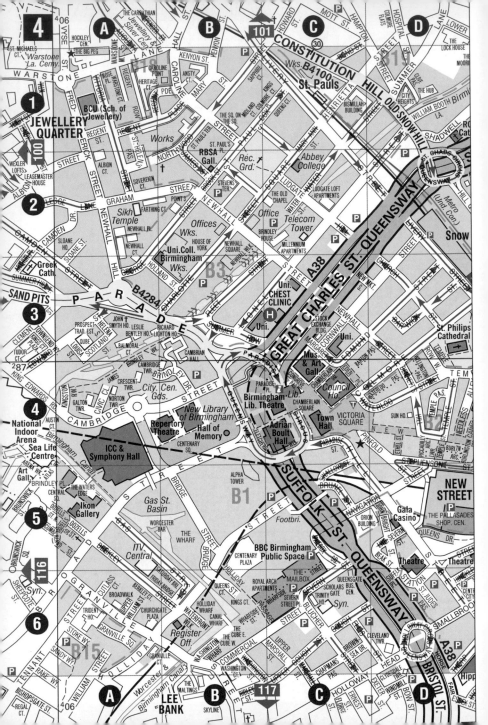

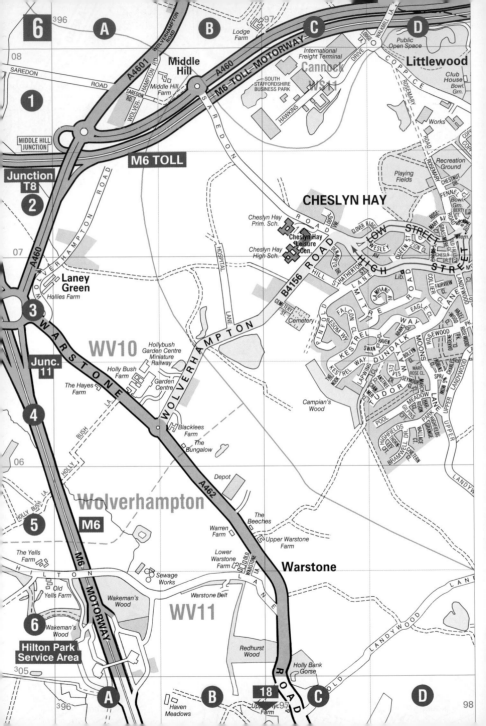

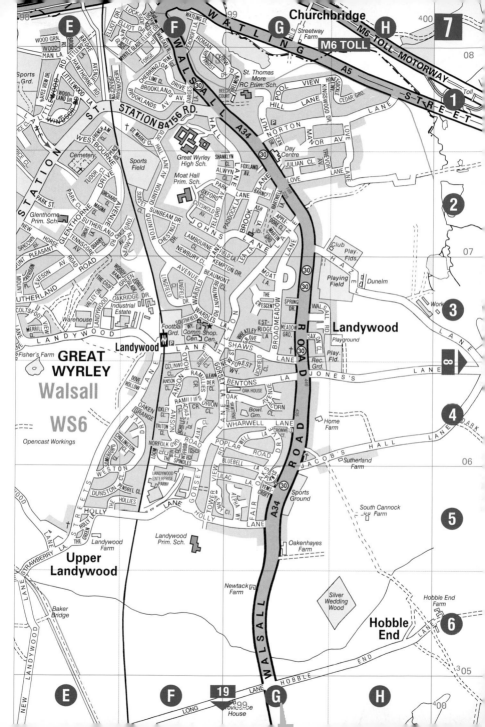

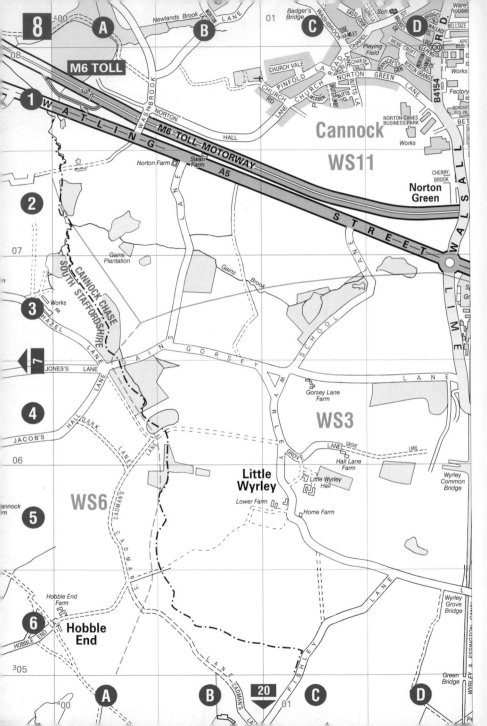

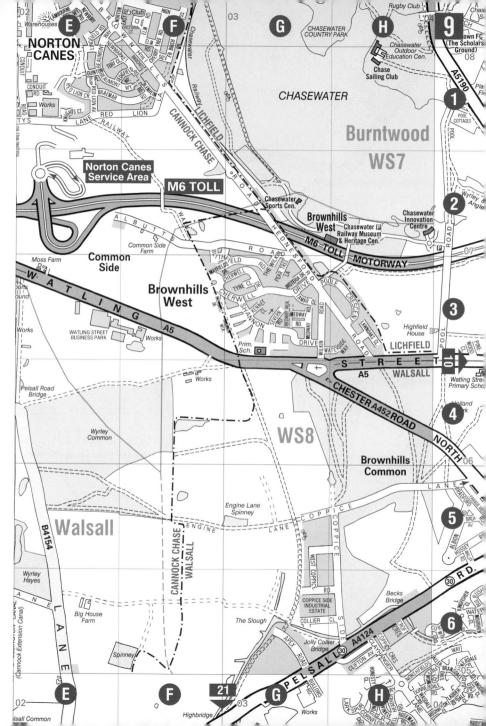

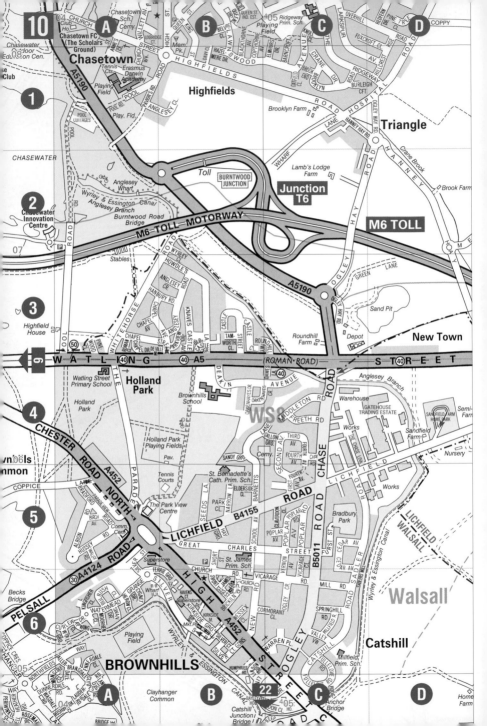

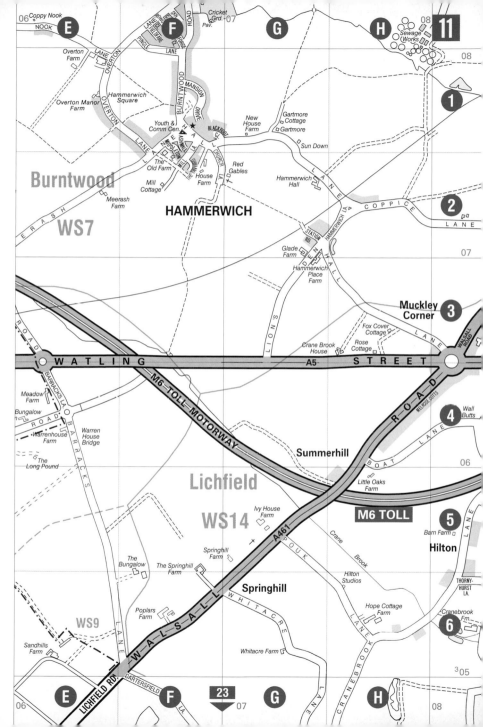

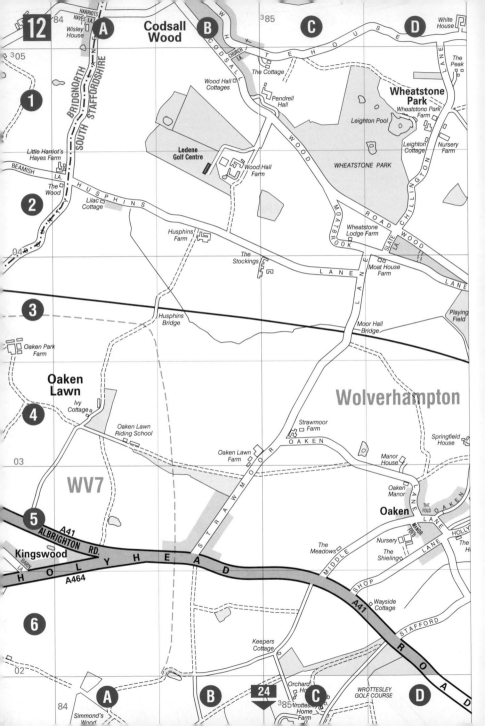

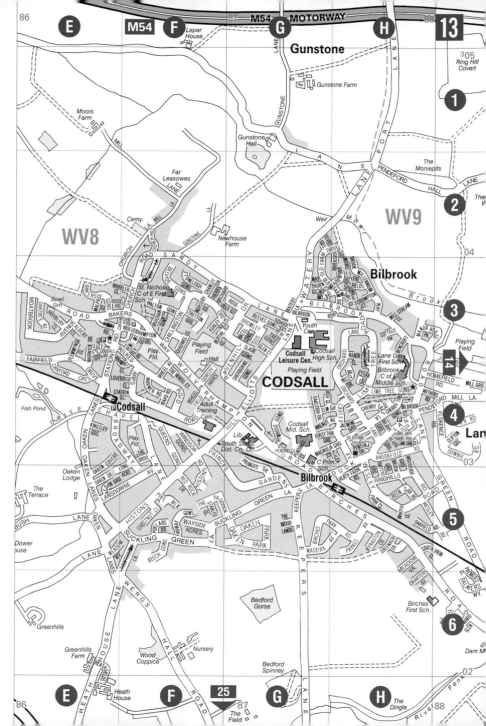

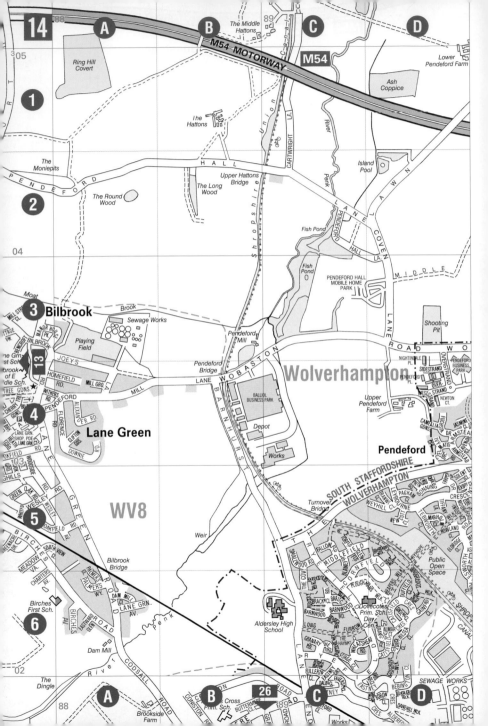

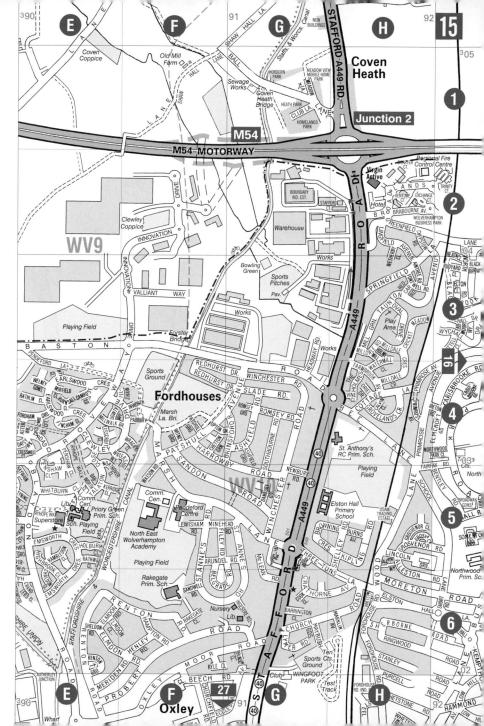

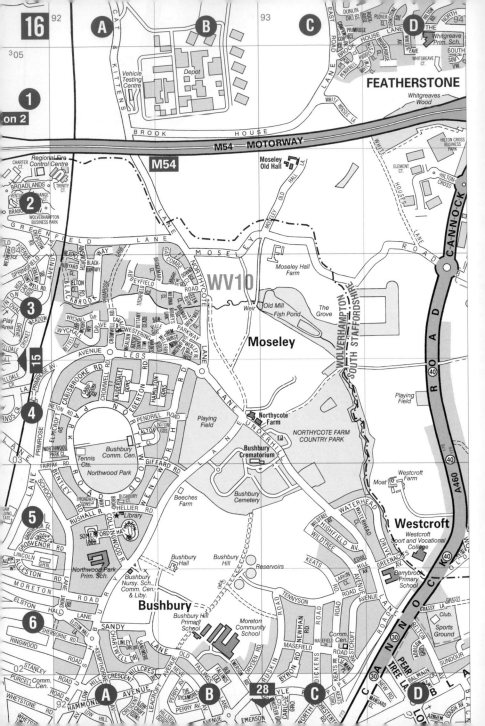

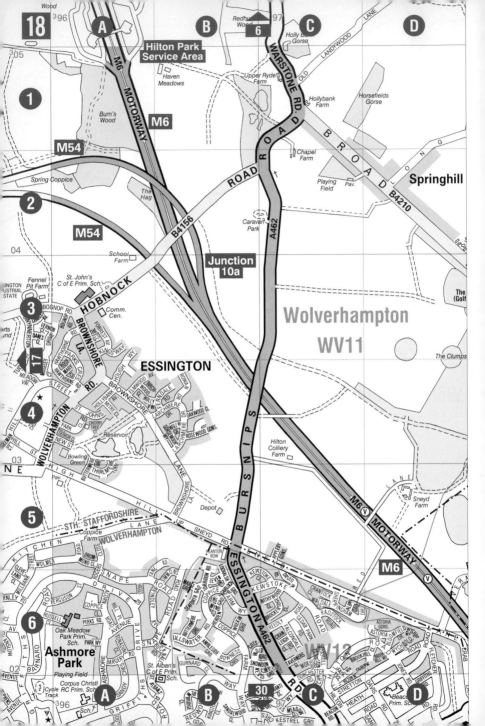

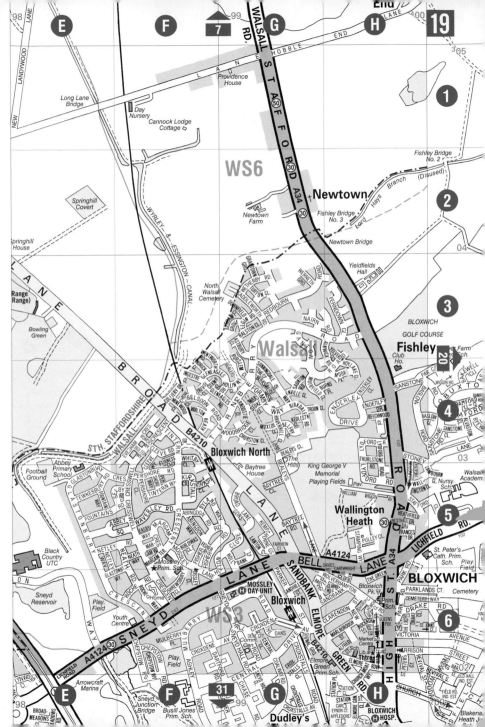

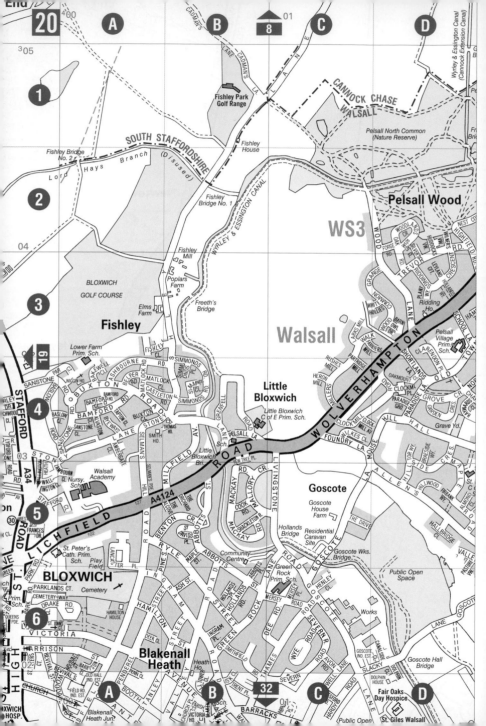

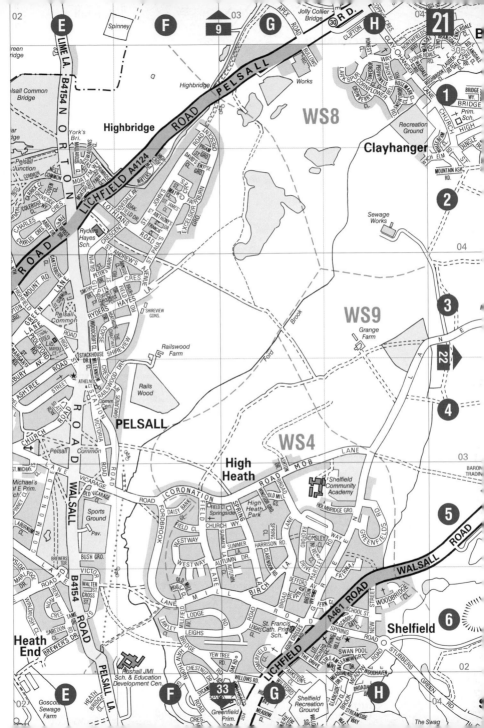

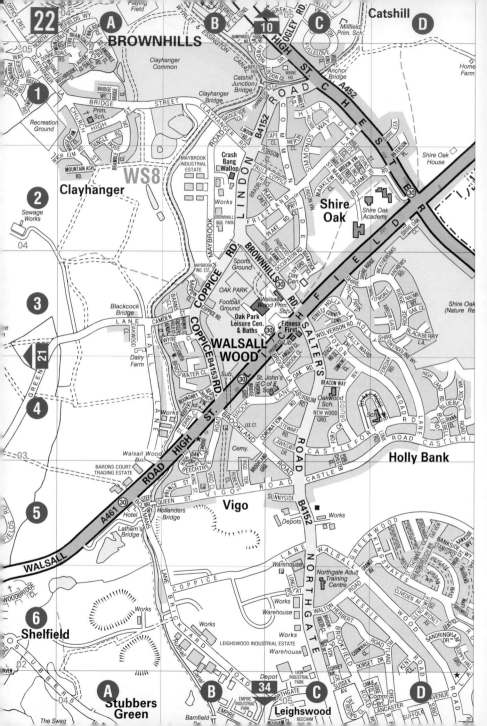

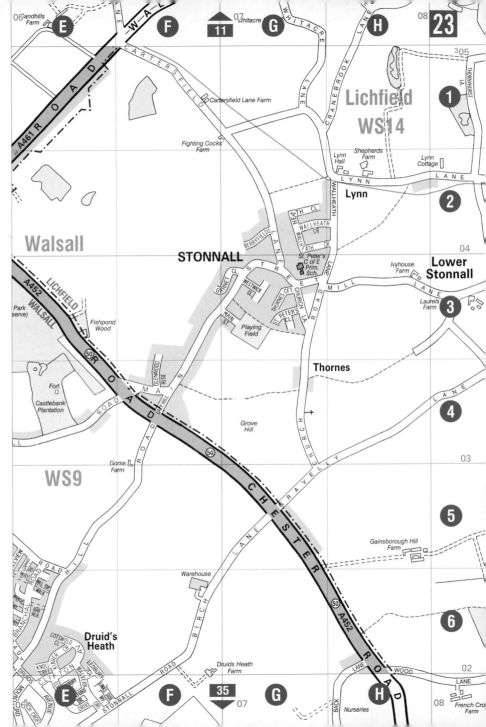

Lichfield WS14

Cartersfield Lane Farm

Fighting Cocks' Farm

Lynn Hall

Shepherds Farm

Lynn Cottage

Lynn

WALHEATH

TH. CL.

WALLHEATH CR

BERRYFIELDS

WALLI ATH CR

STONNALL

St. Peter's C of E Prim. Sch.

Walsall

GARNET CL.

WESTWICK CL.

THORNES CFT

CHURCH LANE

ST PETER'S CL.

MAIN ST.

Playing Field

Ivyhouse Farm

Lower Stonnall

Laurels Farm

MILL LANE

Thornes

GLENWOOD RISE

Park eserve)

Fishpond Wood

Fort

Castlebank Plantation

MAIN ROAD

BATH HILL

Grove Hill

Gorse Farm

ROAD HILL

WS9

CHESTER ROAD

GRAVELLY LANE

Gainsborough Hill Farm

HILLVIEW WAY

HILL TOP WALK

BRANCHAL BAR WLK.

COTSWOLD CL.

Druid's Heath

KNOLL CREST

MALVERN DR DRIVE

LILAC WAY

LEIGHBURY

STONNALL ROAD

BIRCH ROAD

Warehouse

Druids Heath Farm

BACK LANE

WOOD LANE

Nurseries

French Cro Farm

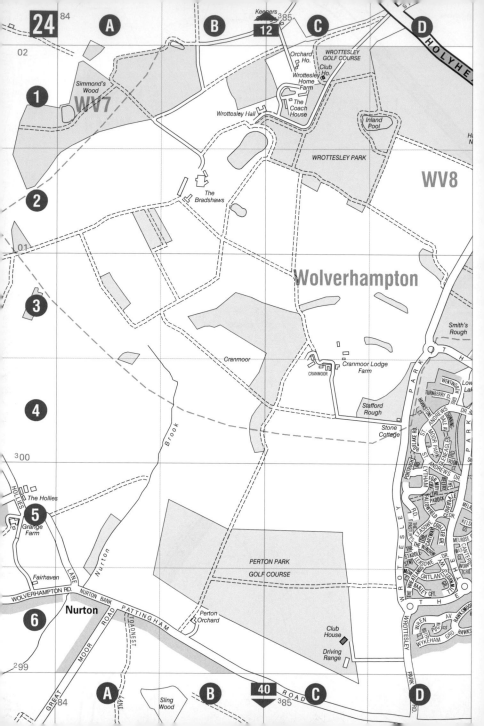

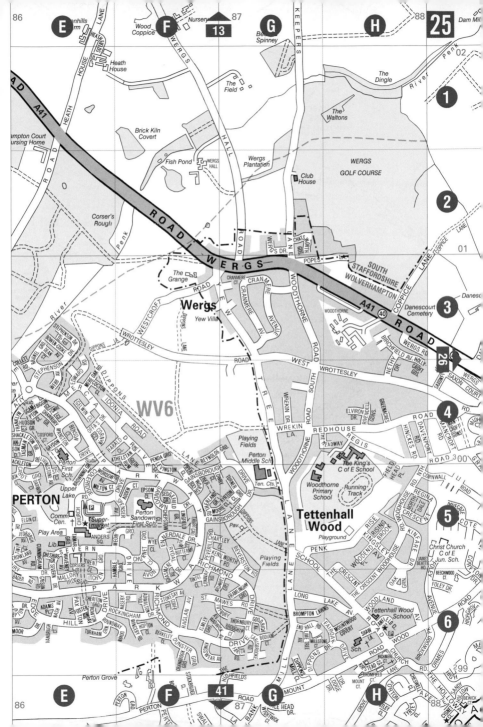

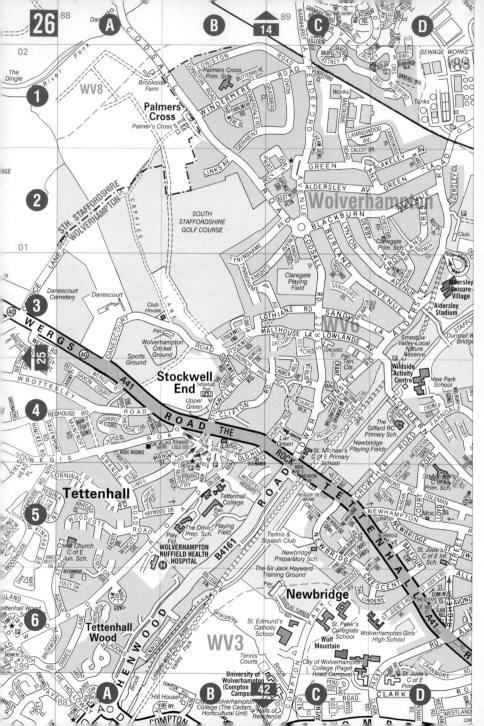

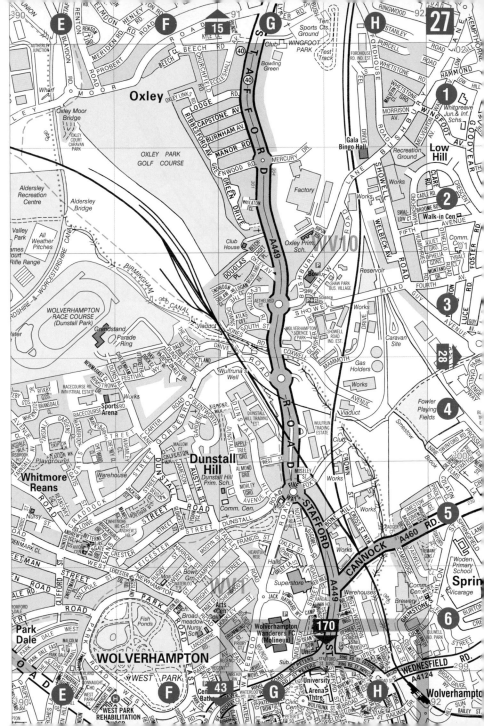

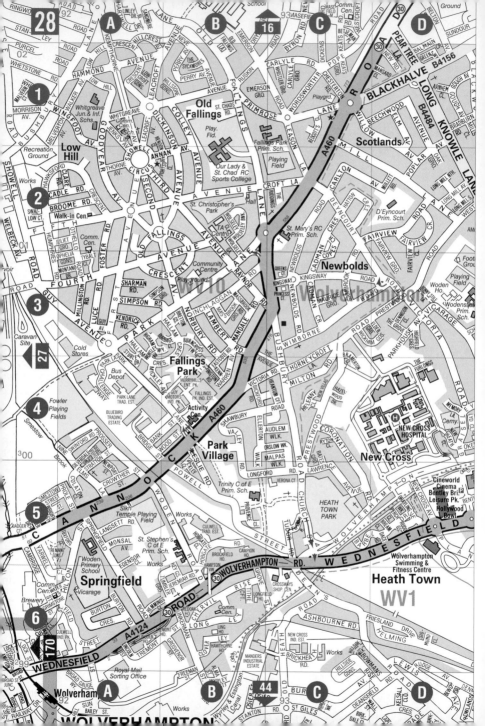

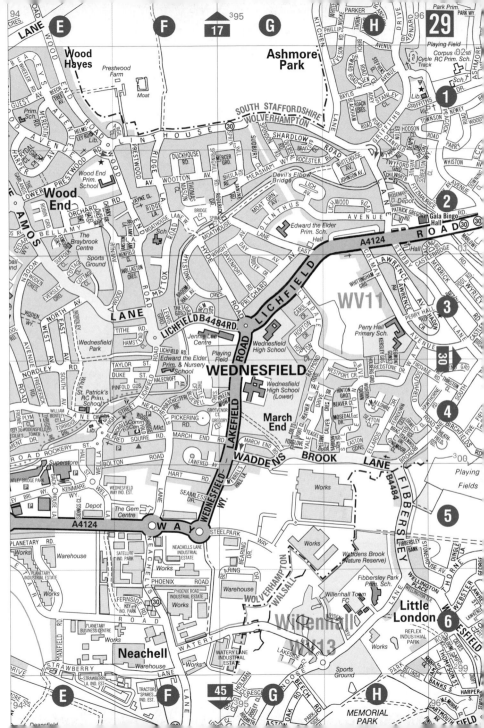

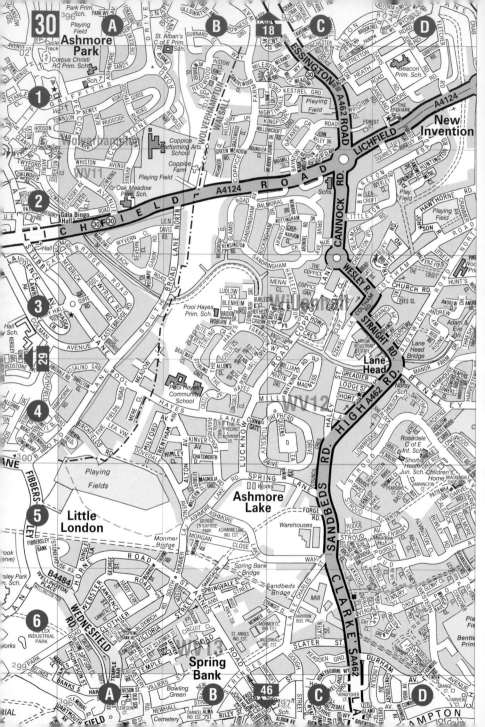

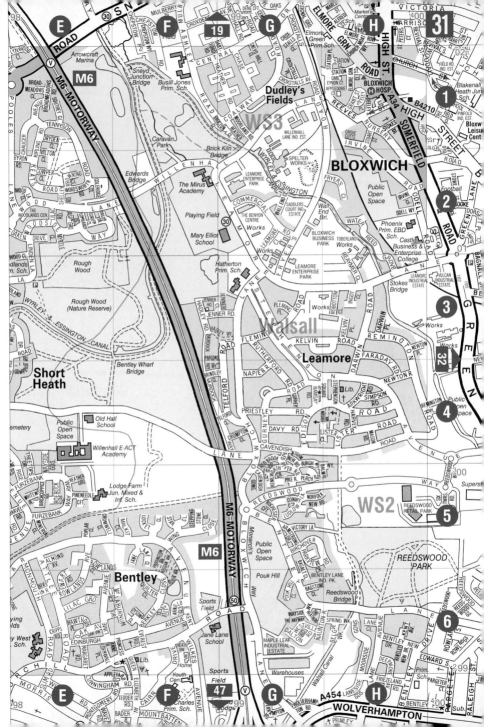

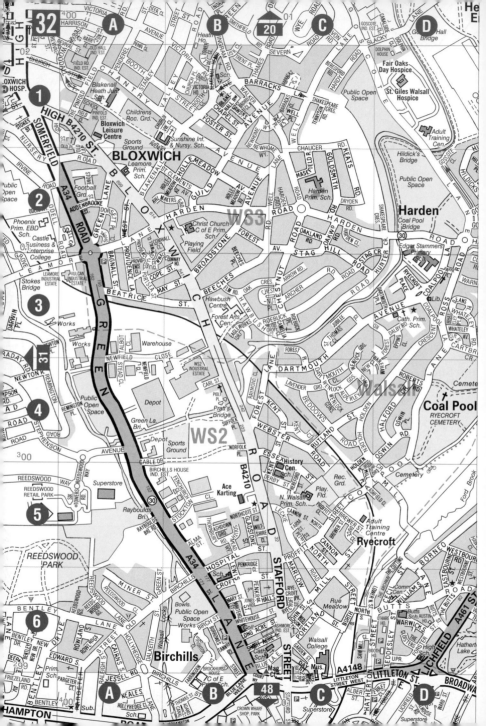

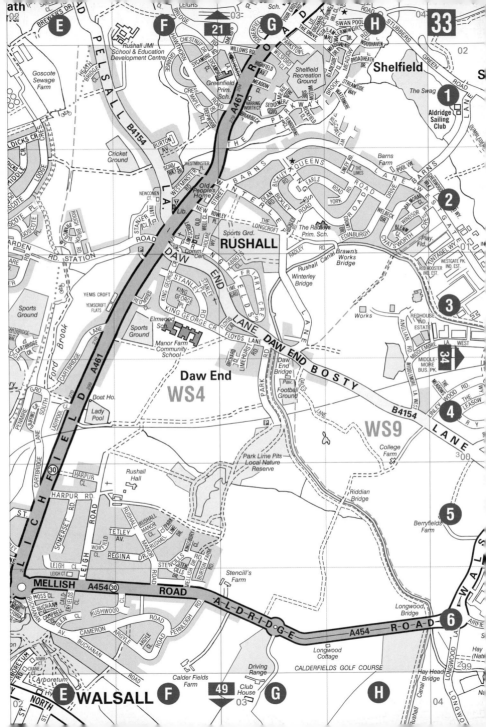

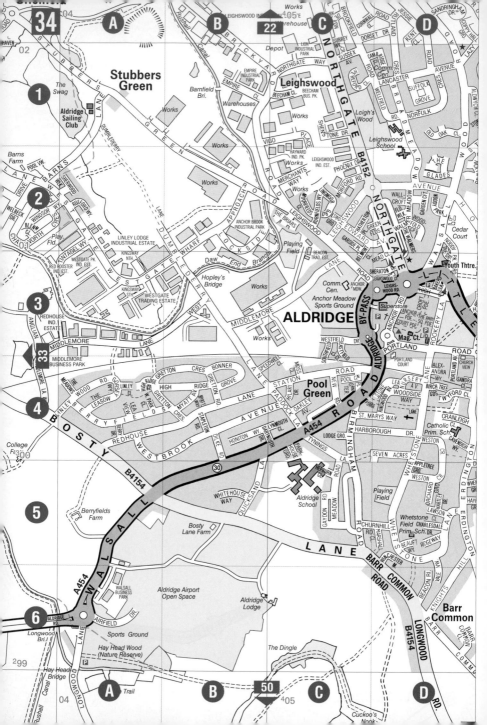

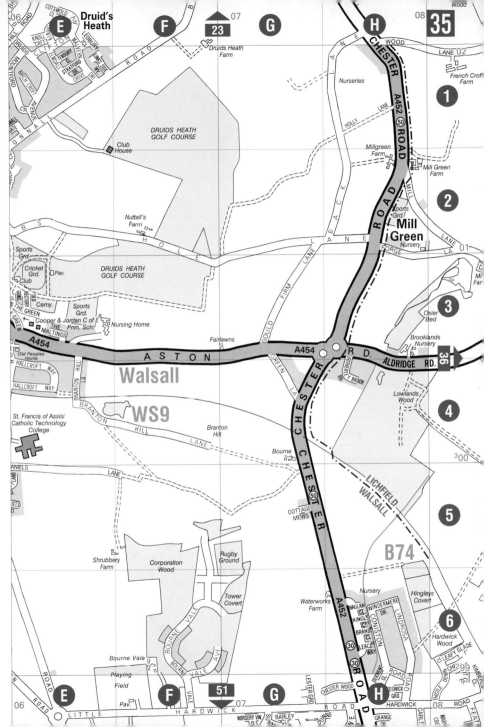

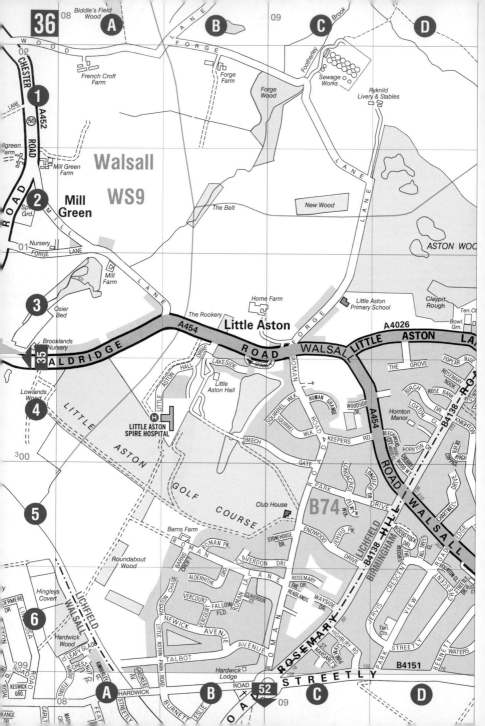

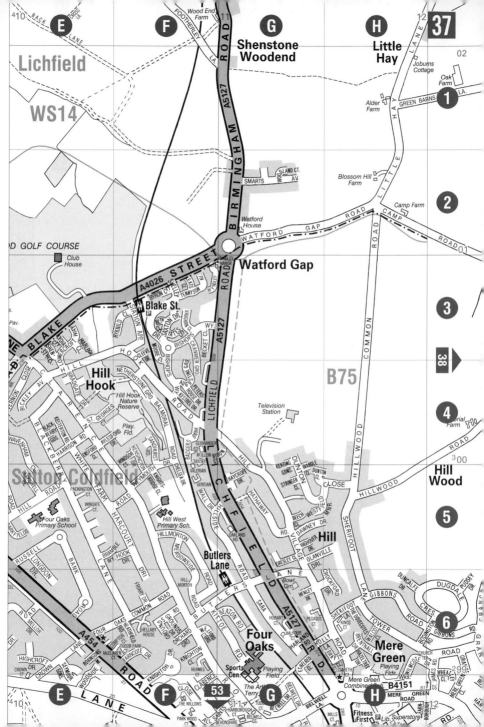

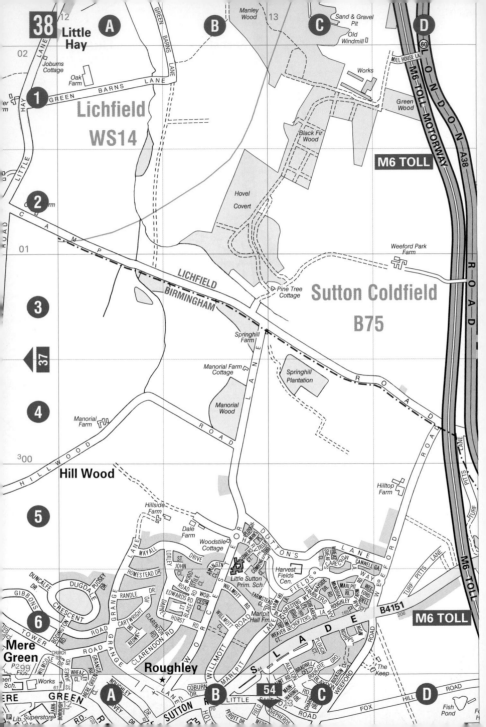

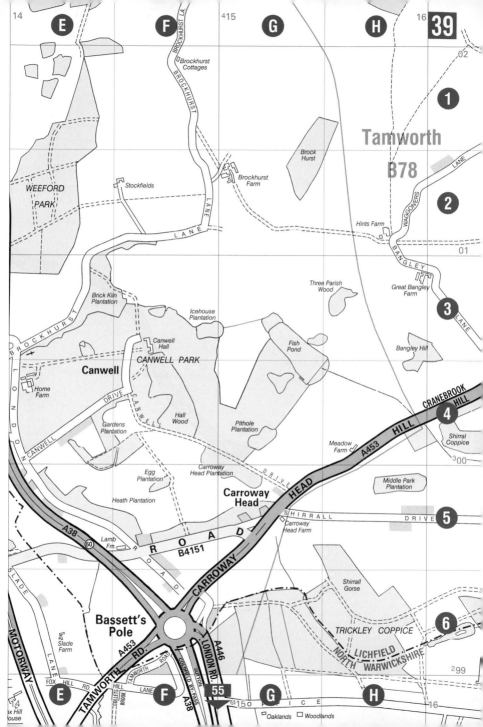

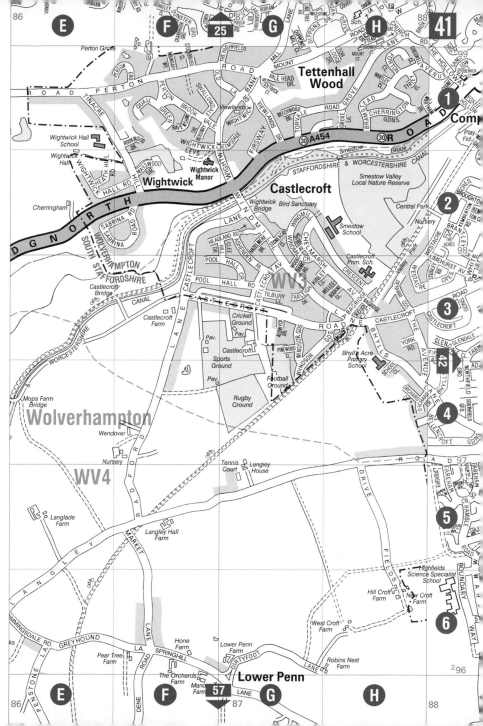

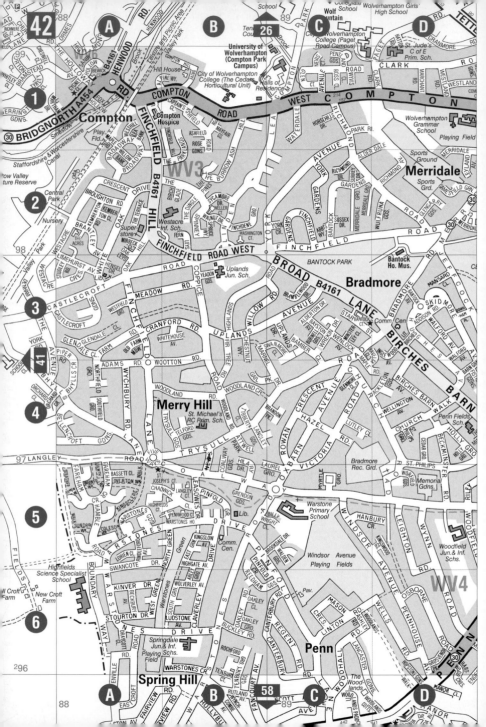

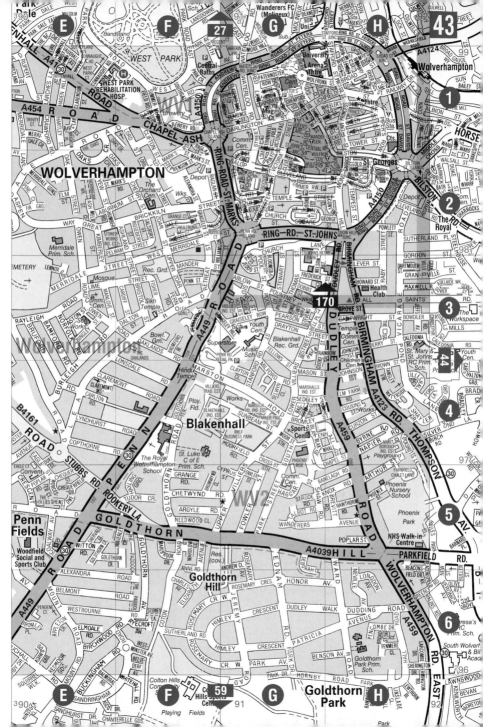

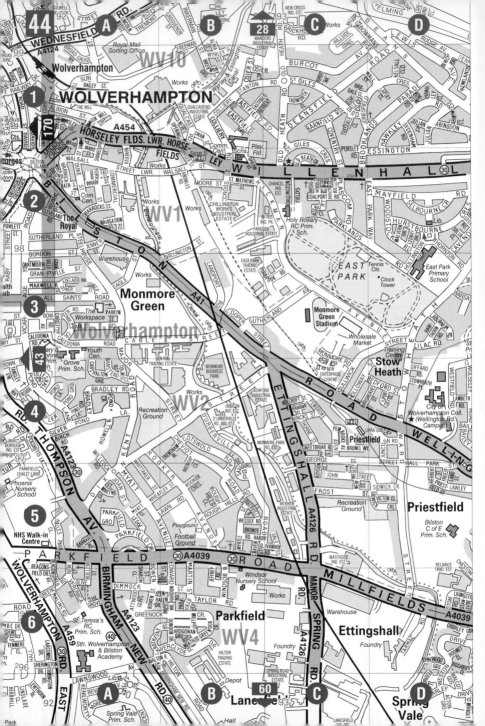

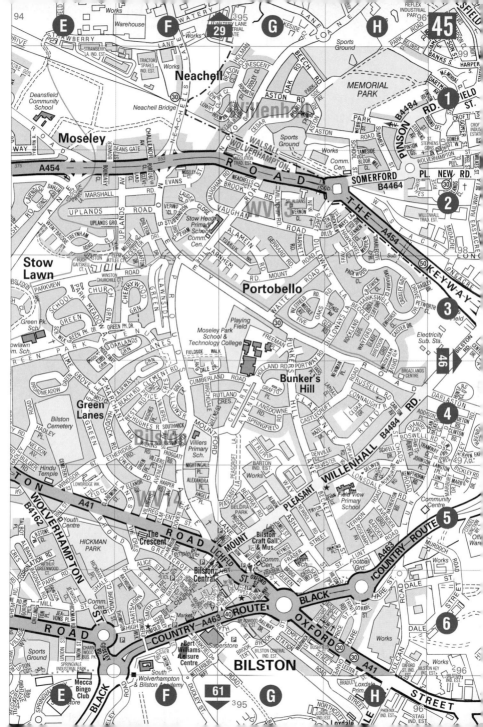

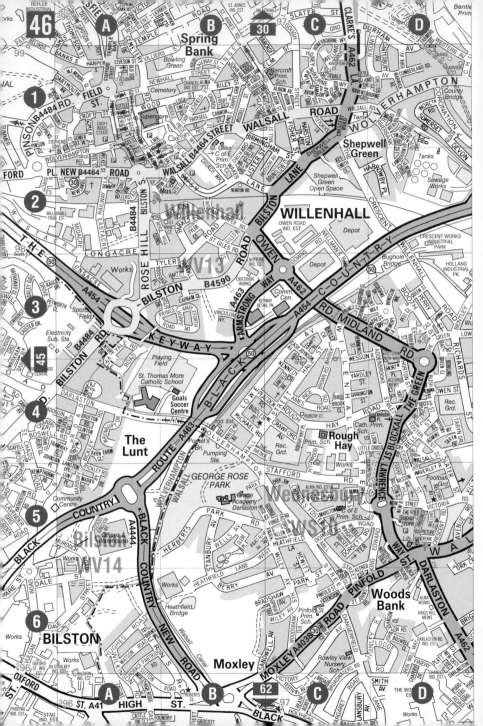

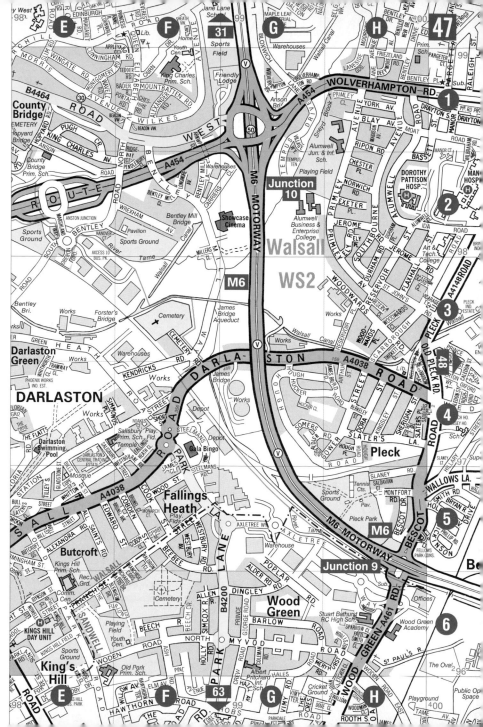

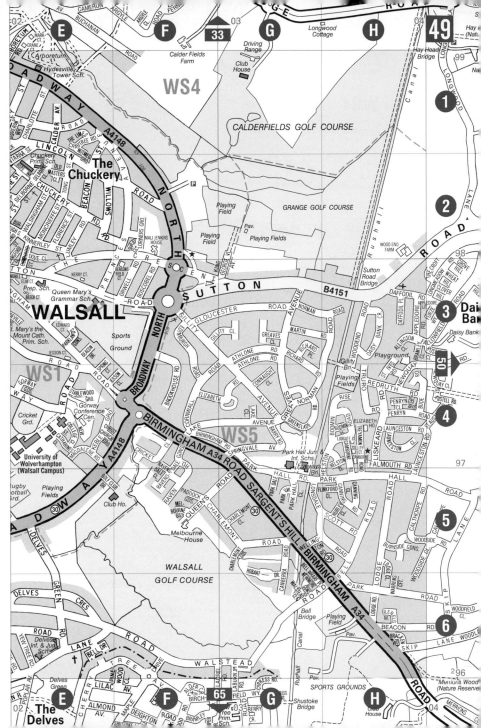

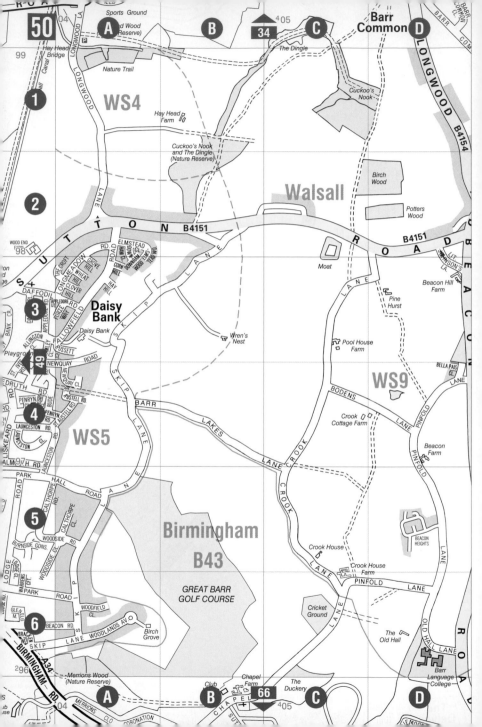

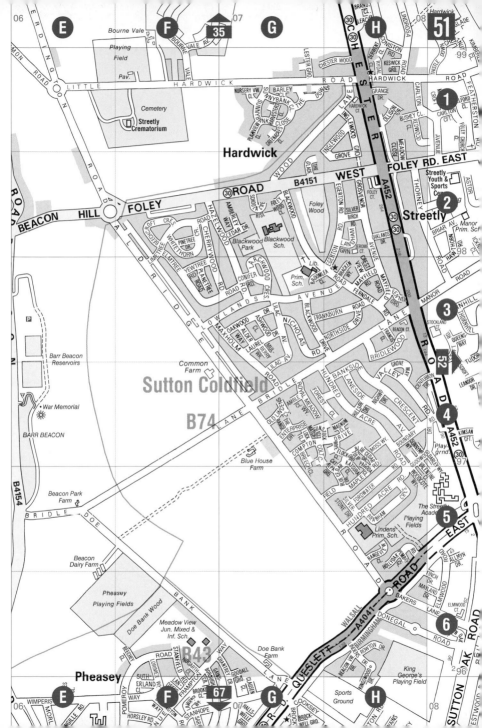

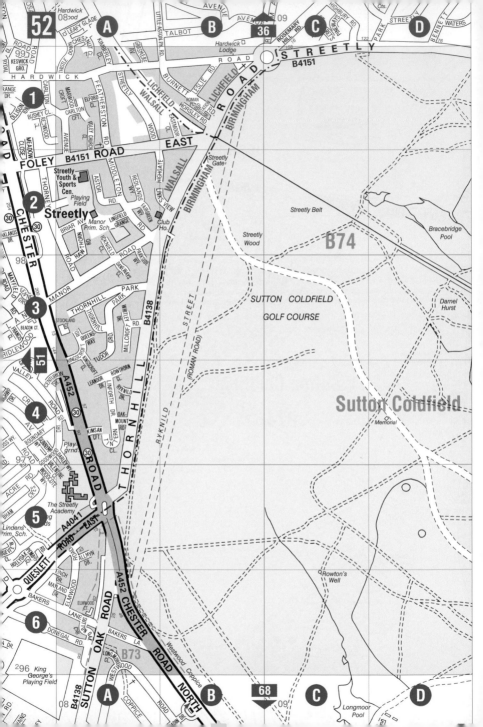

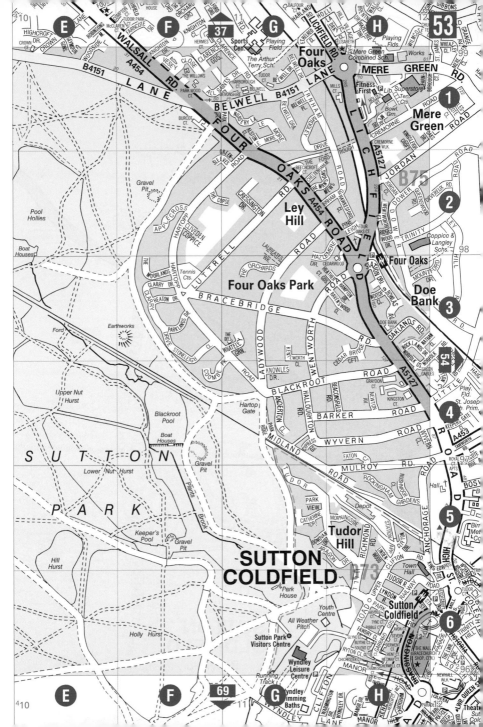

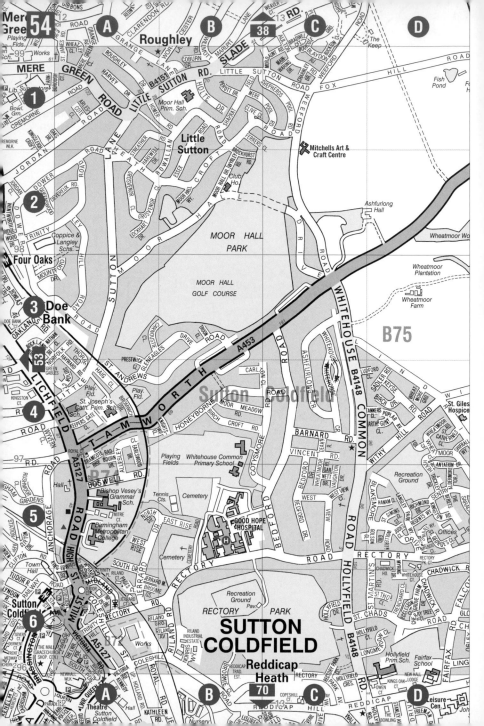

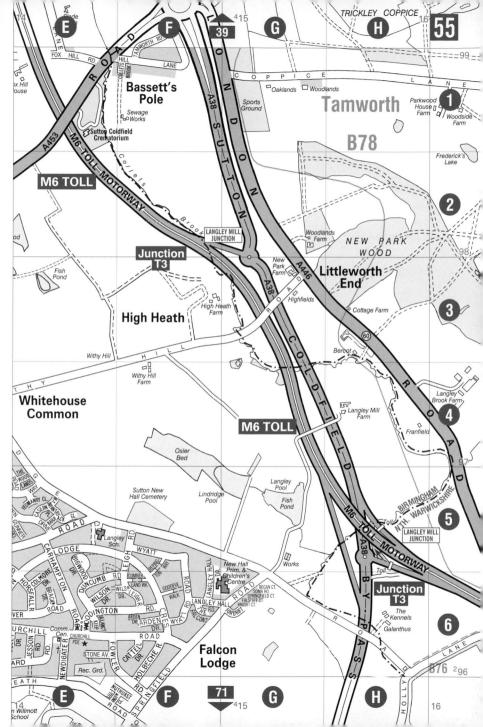

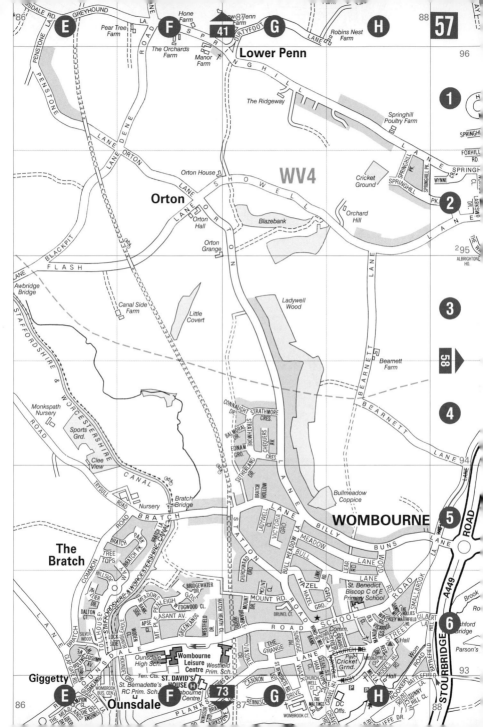

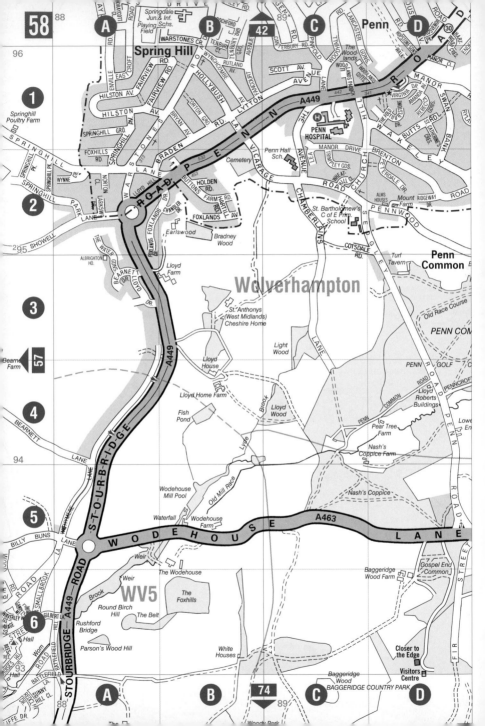

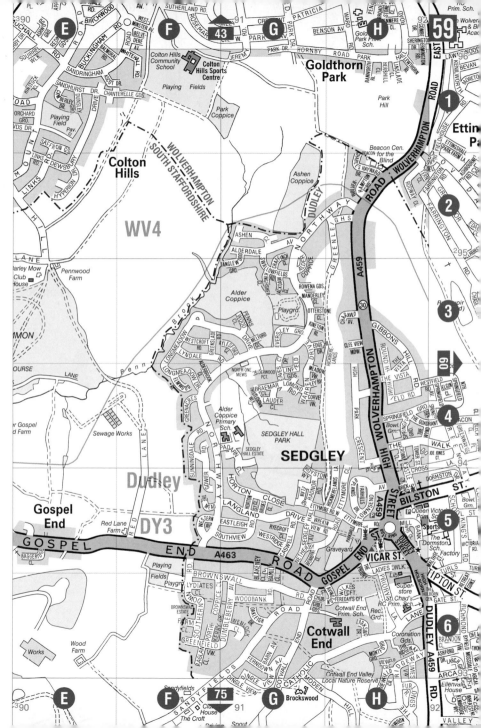

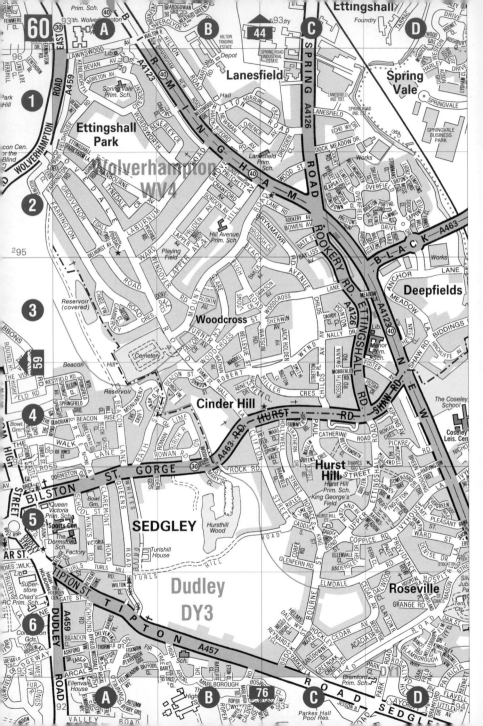

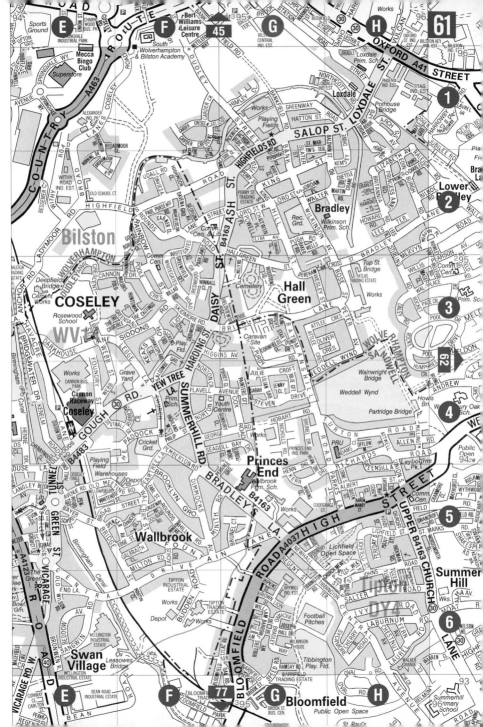

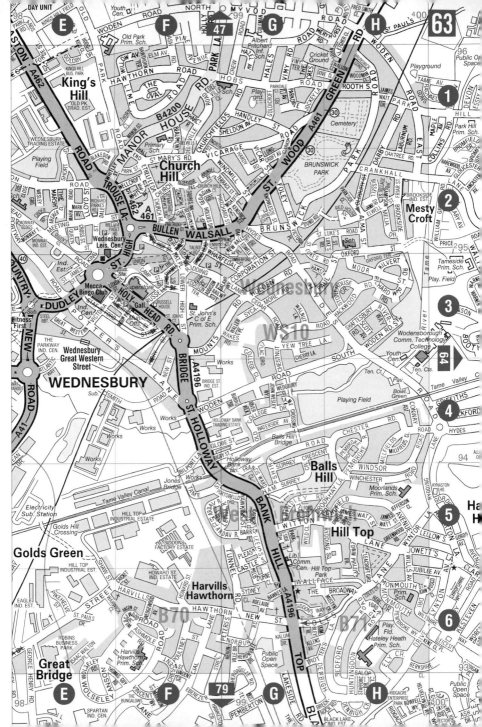

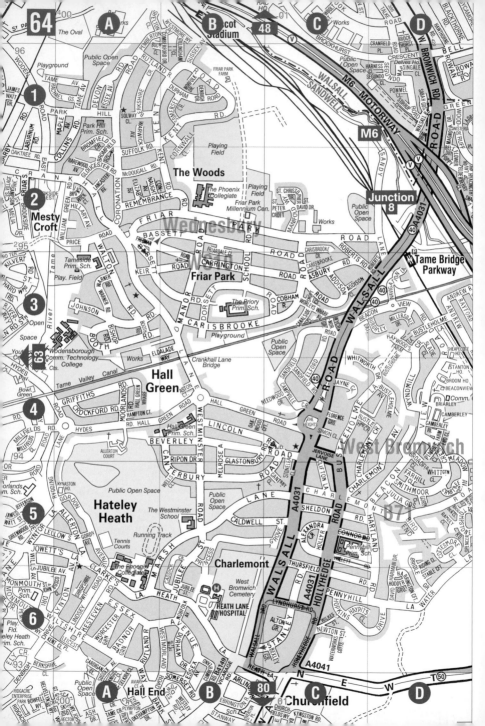

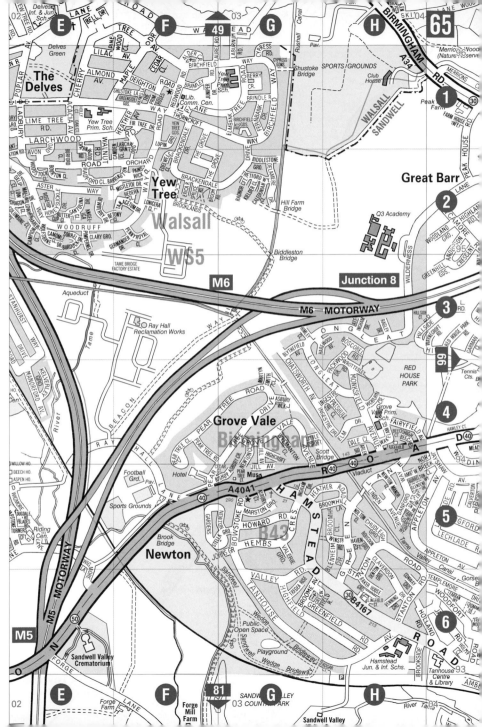

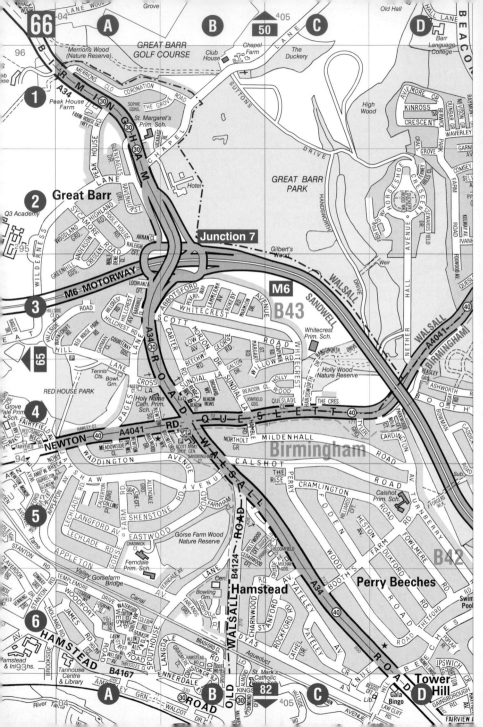

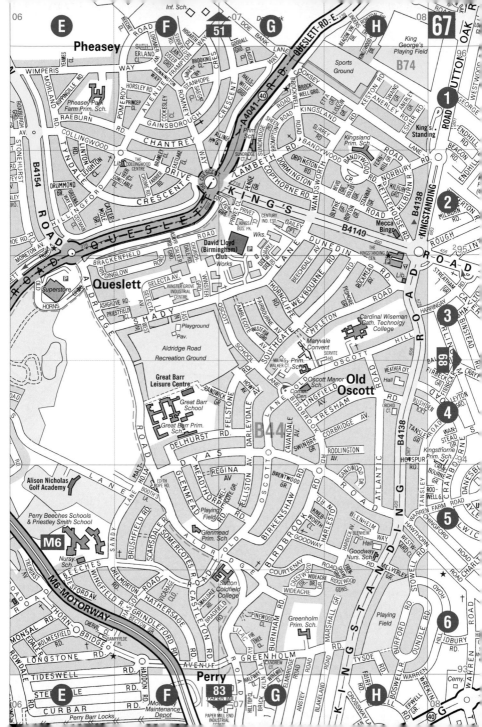

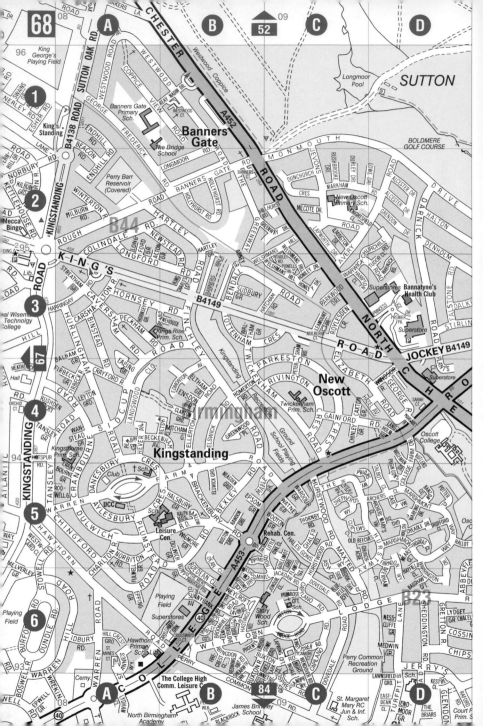

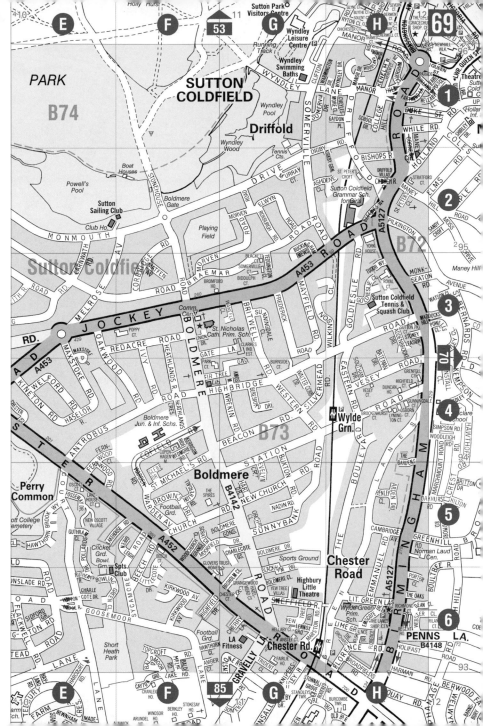

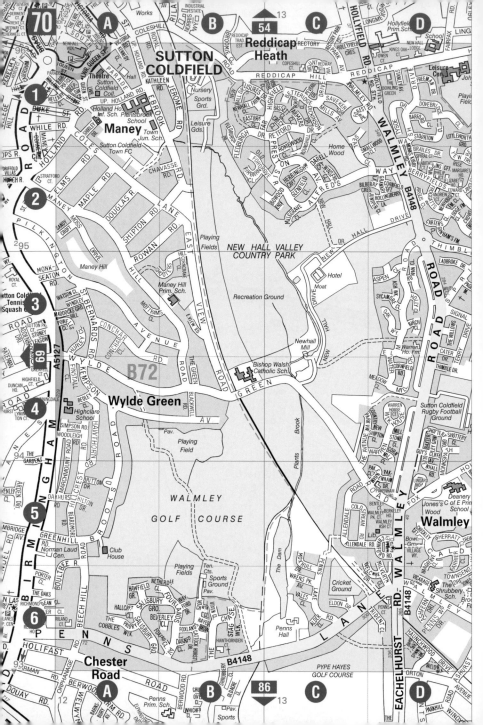

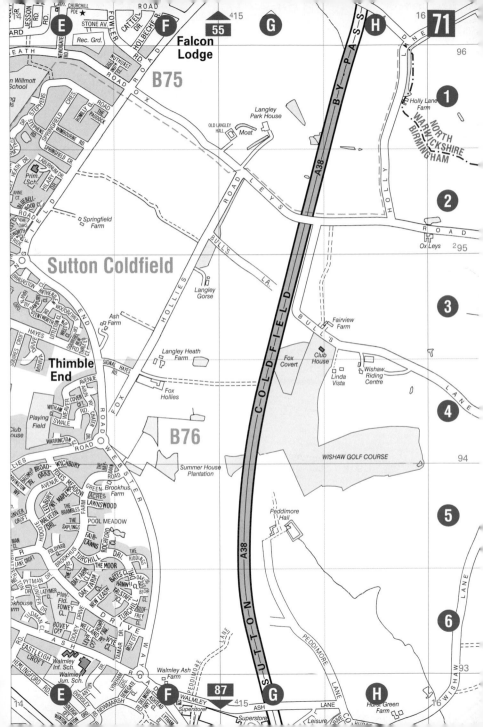

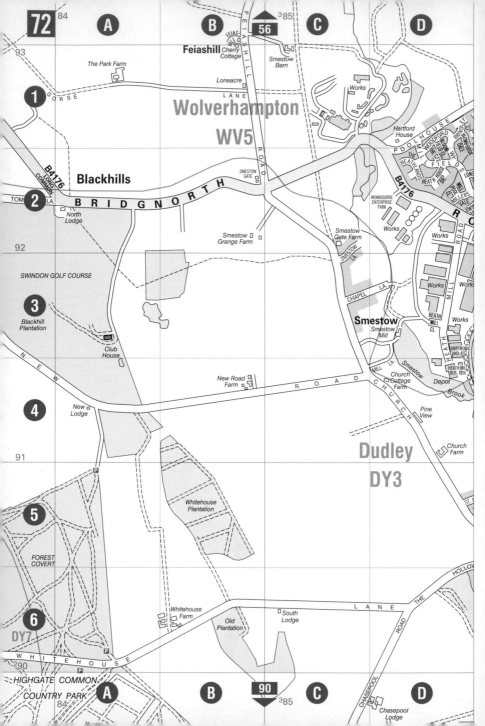

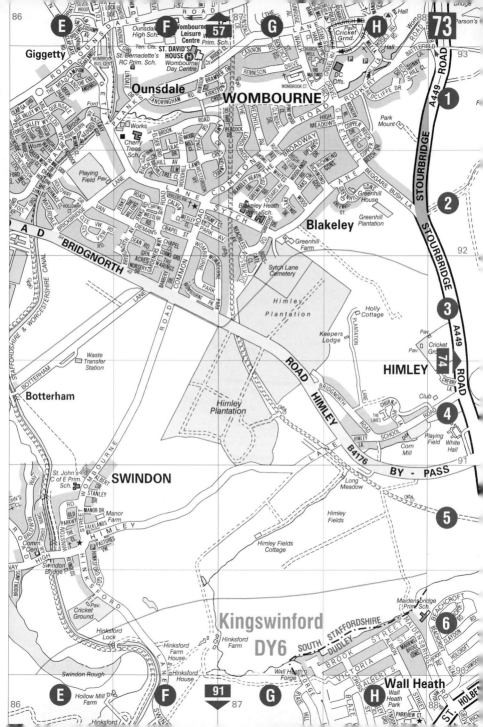

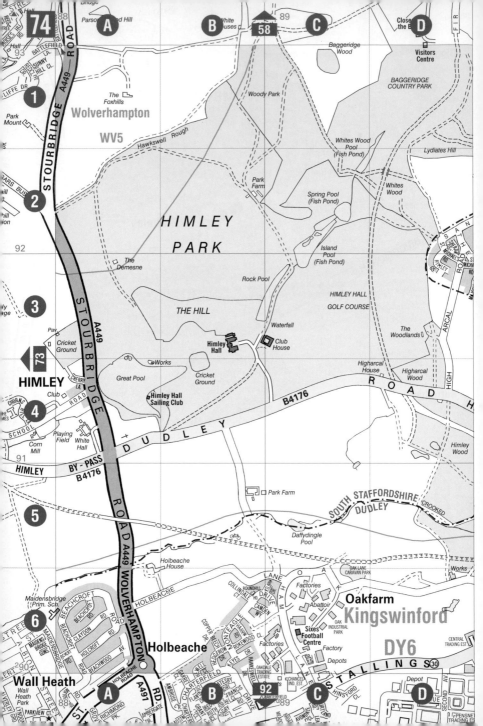

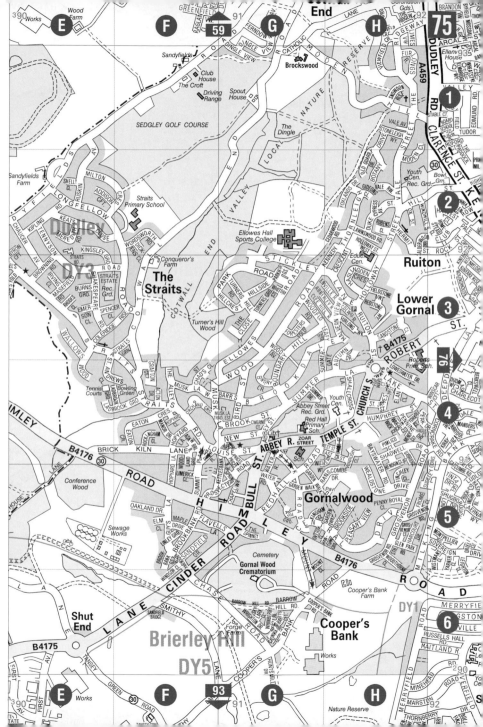

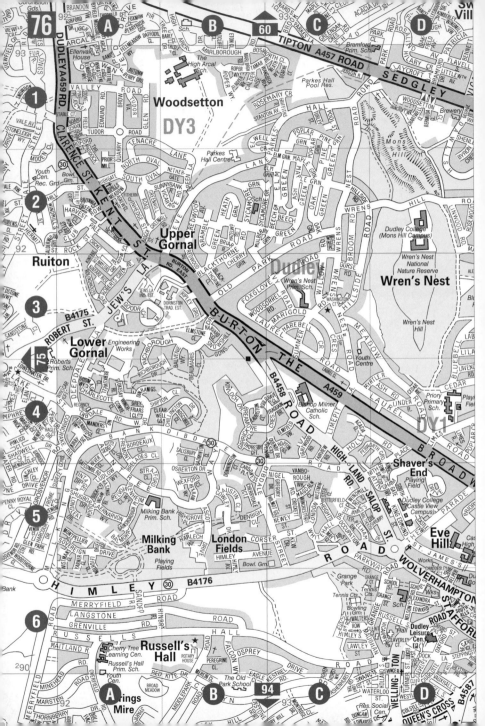

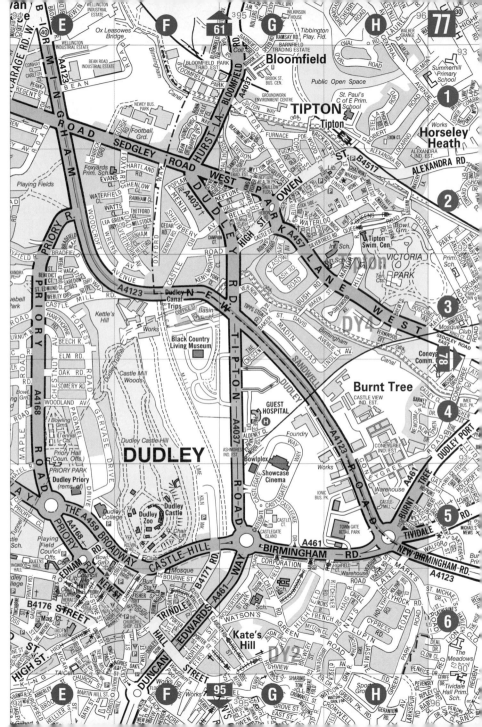

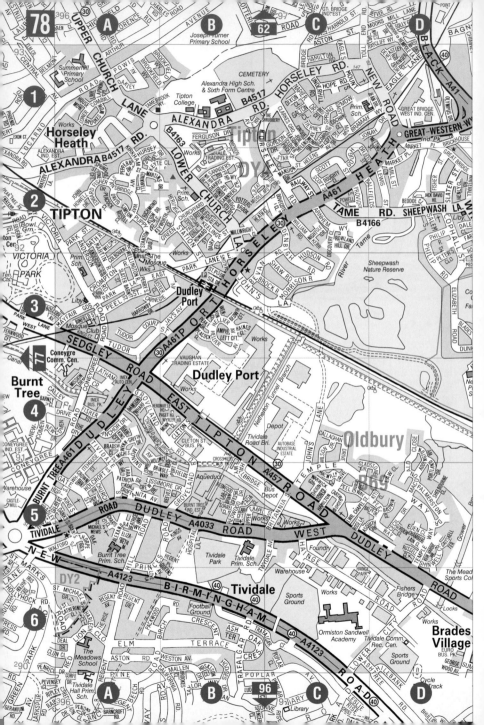

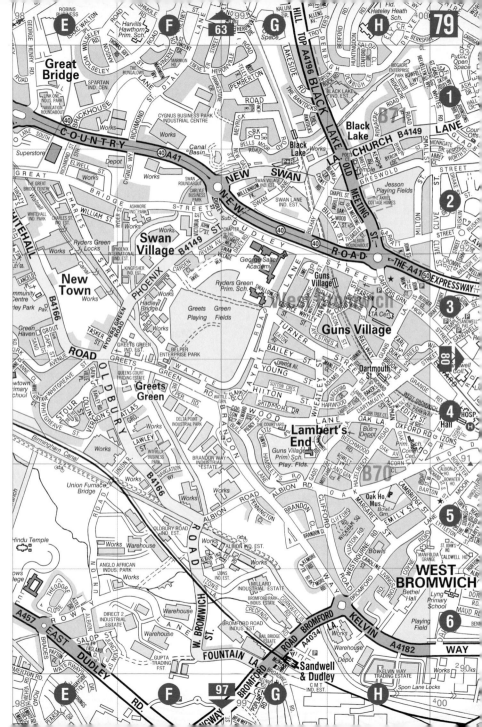

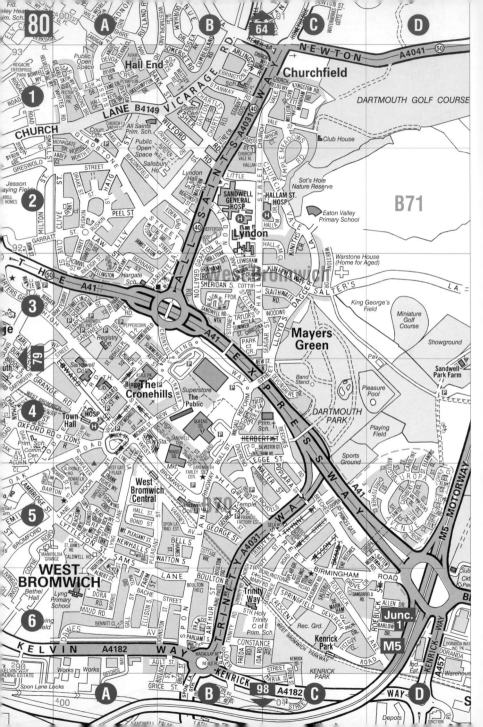

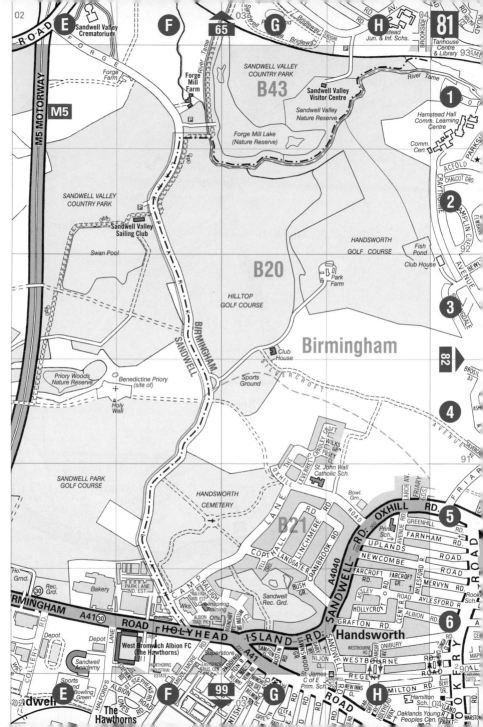

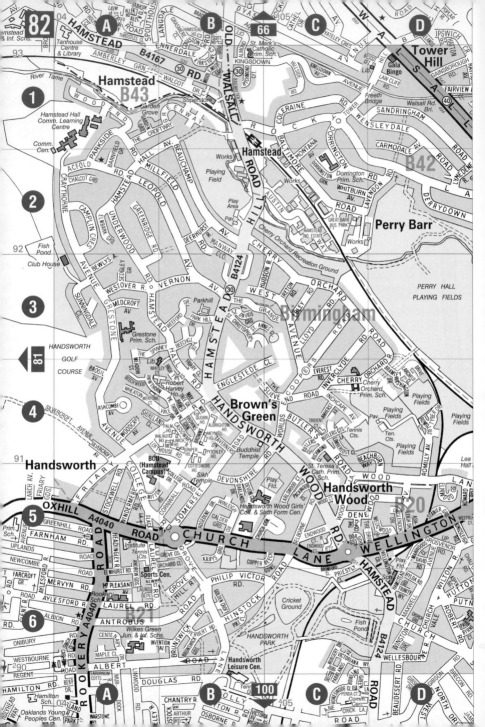

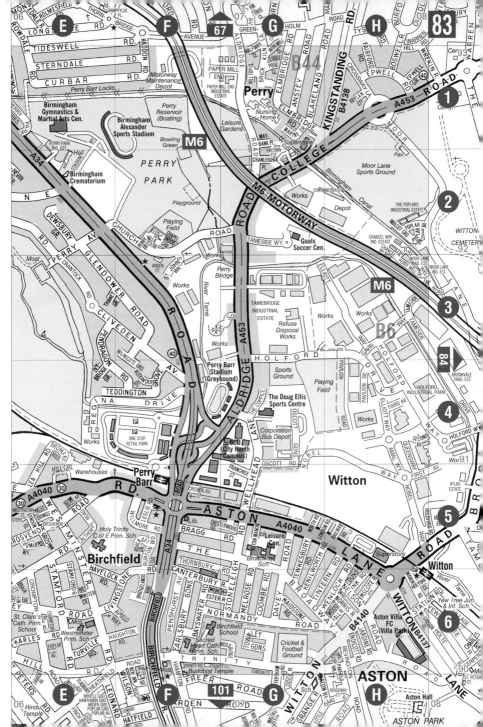

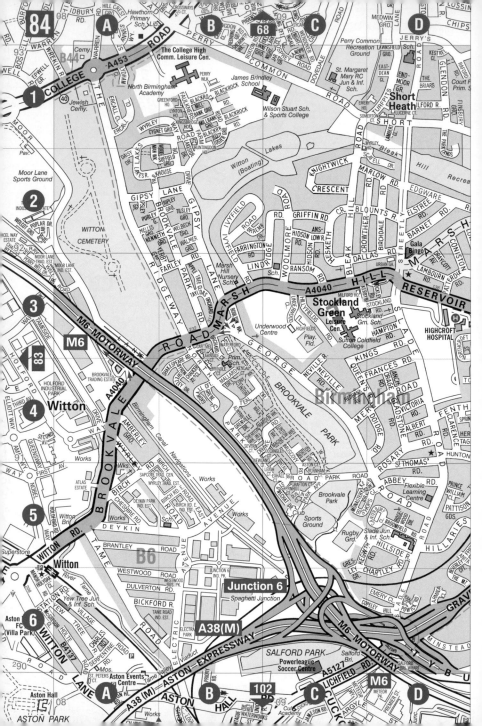

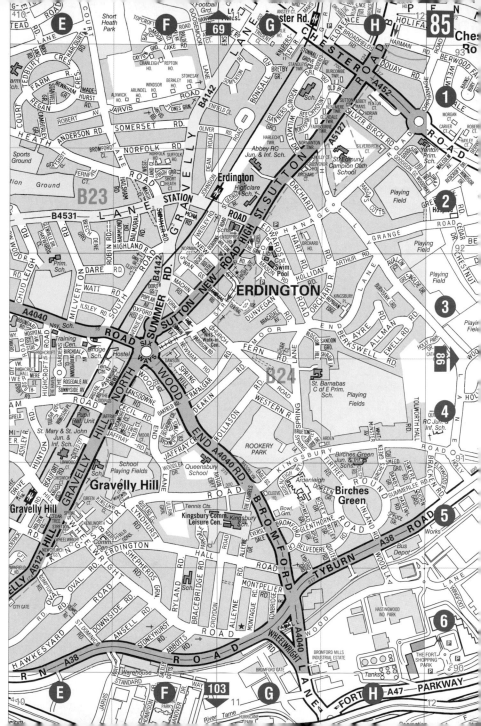

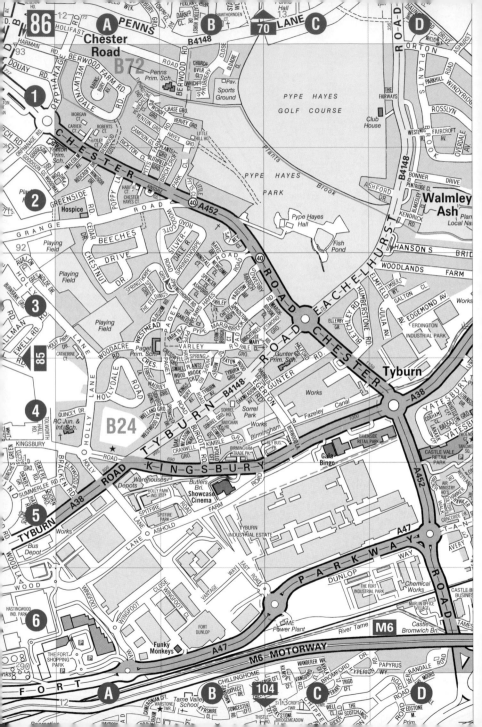

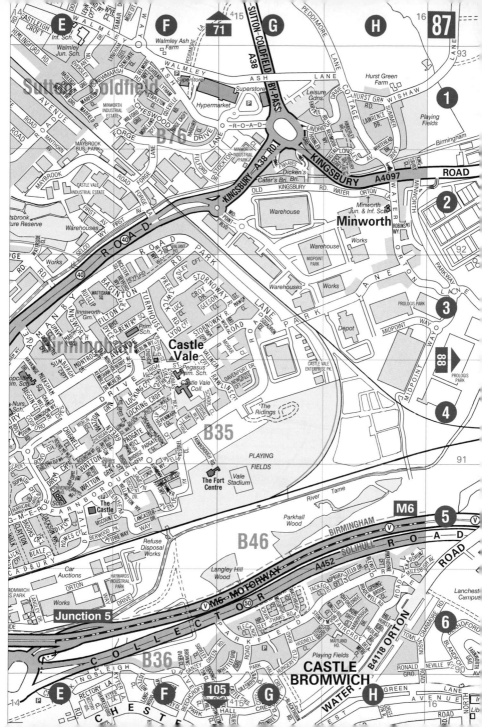

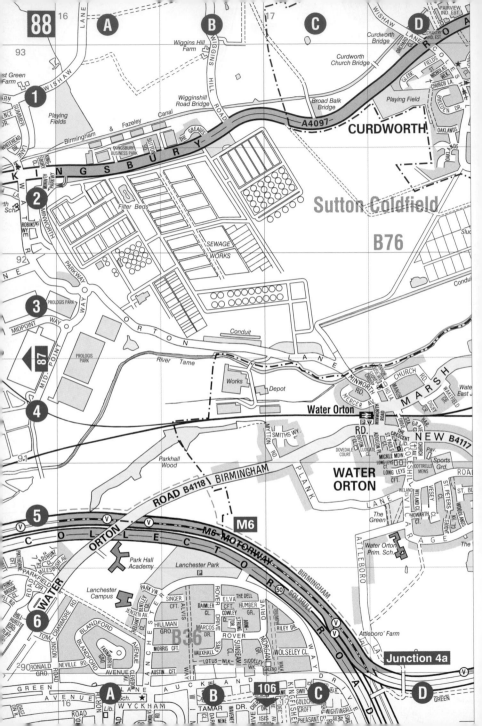

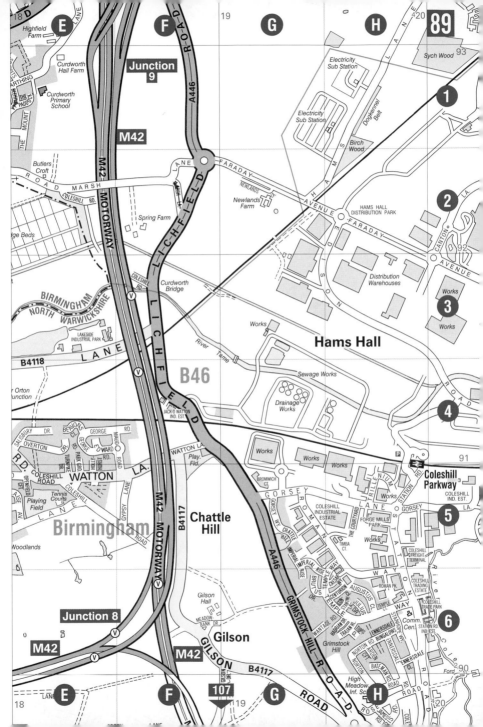

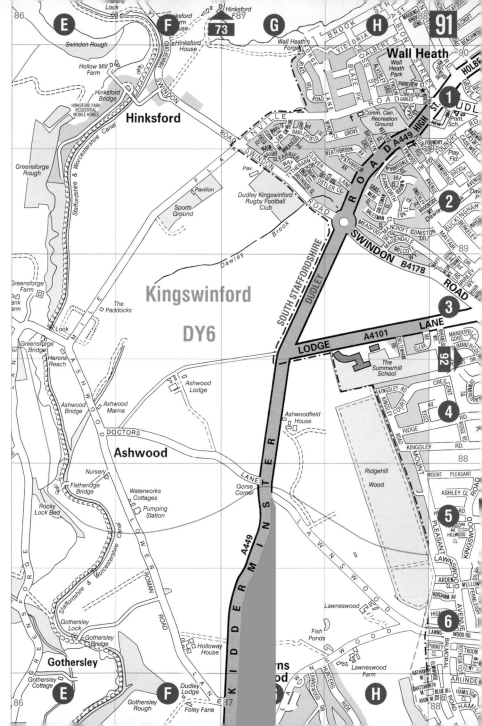

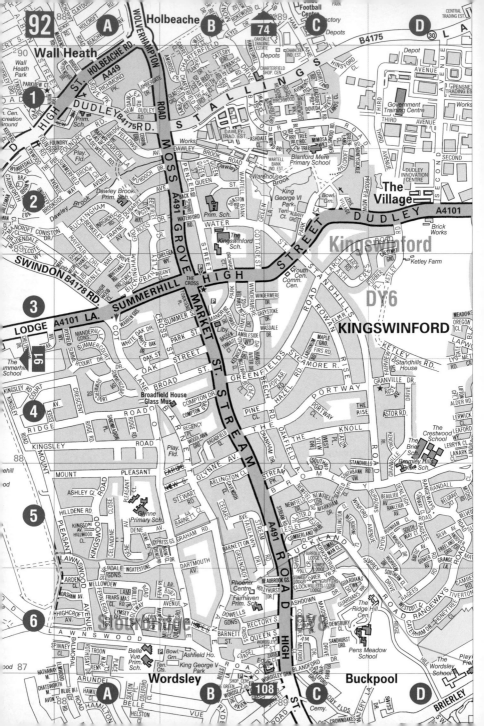

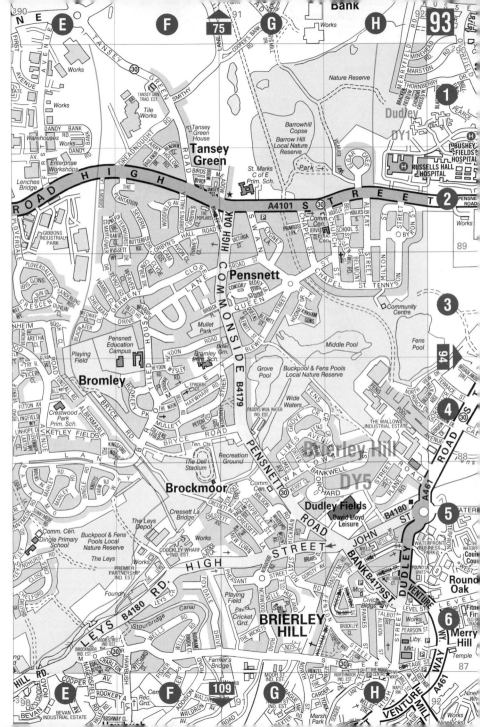

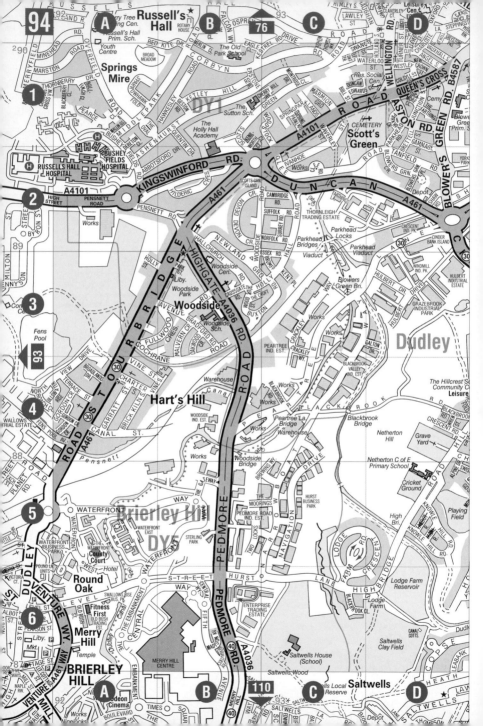

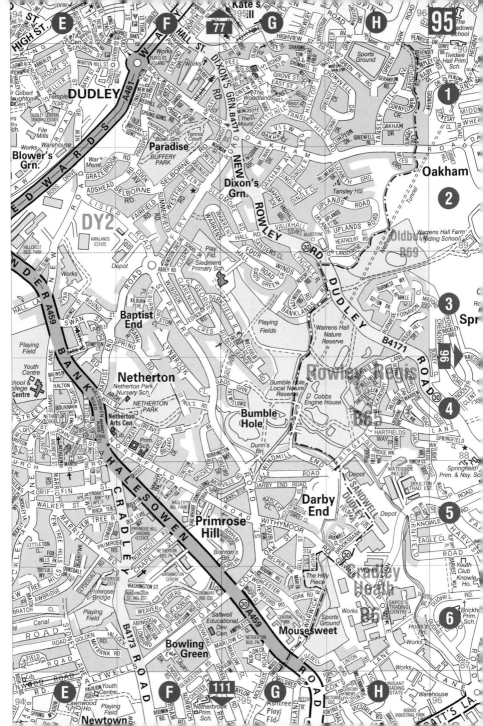

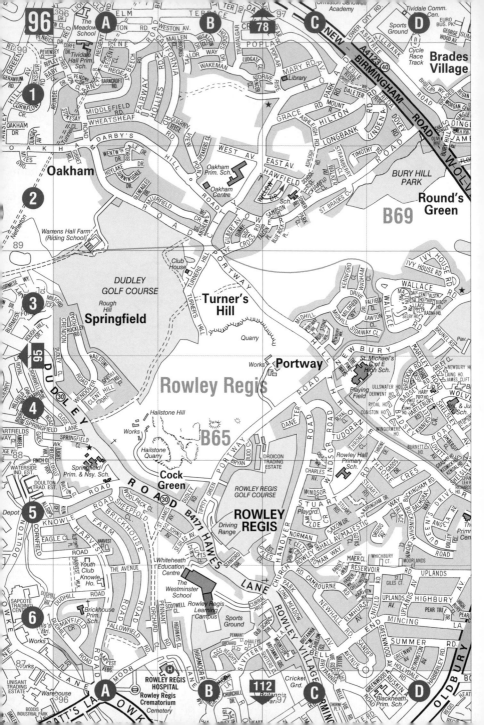

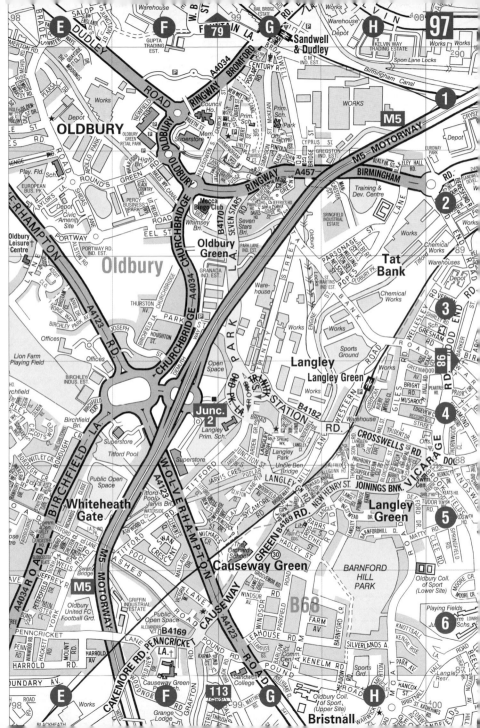

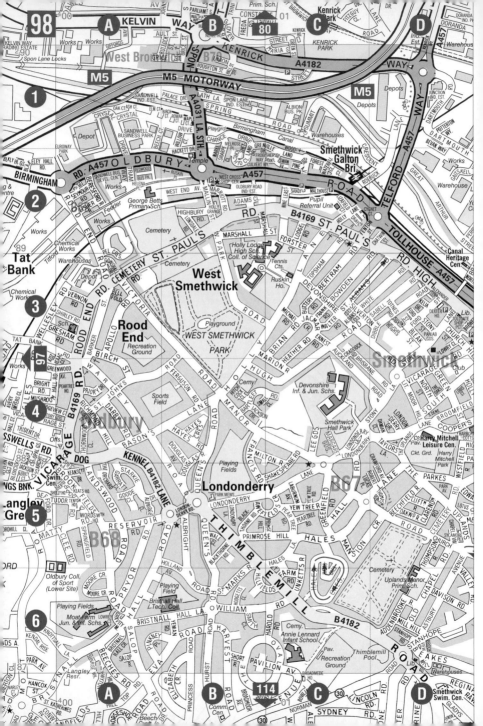

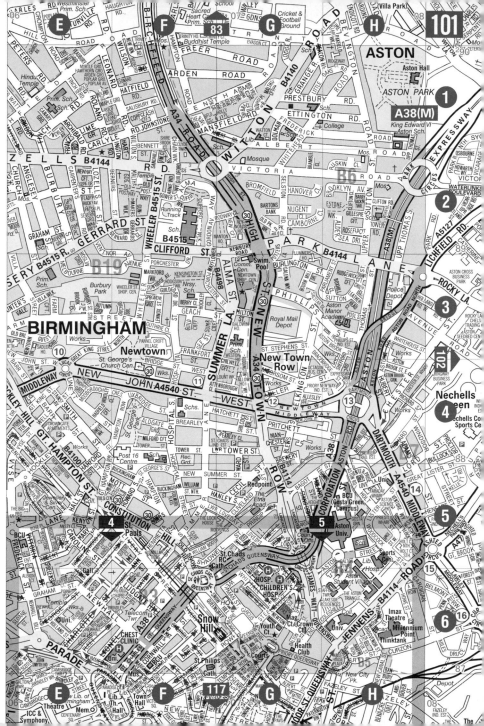

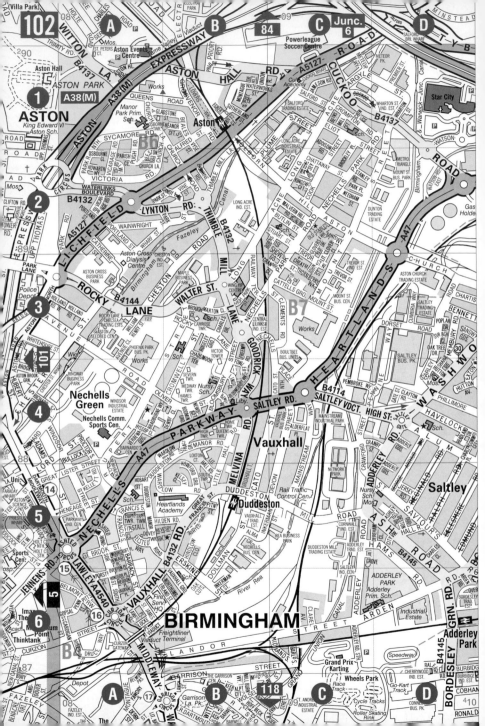

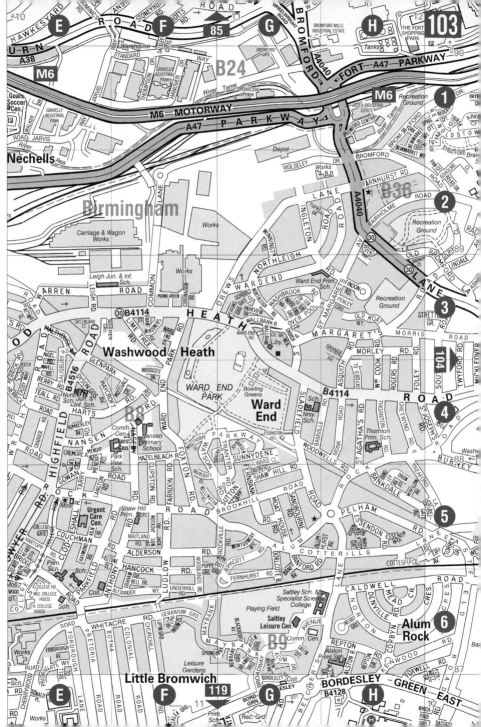

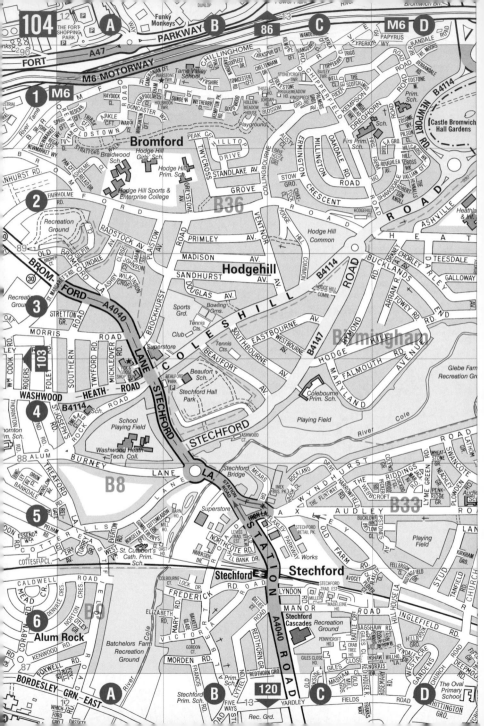

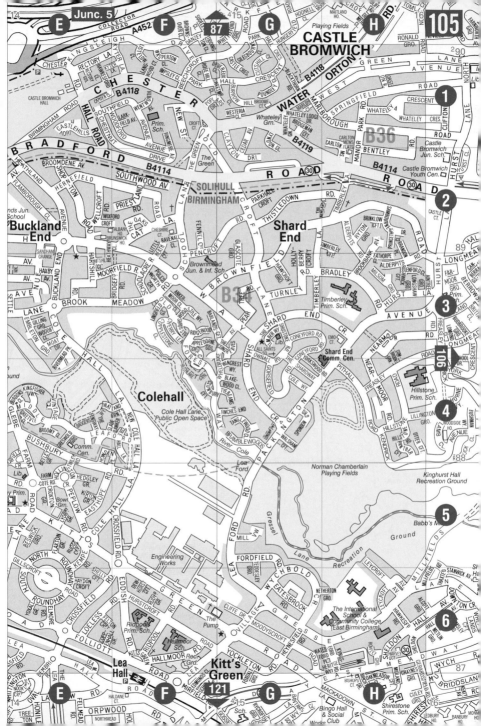

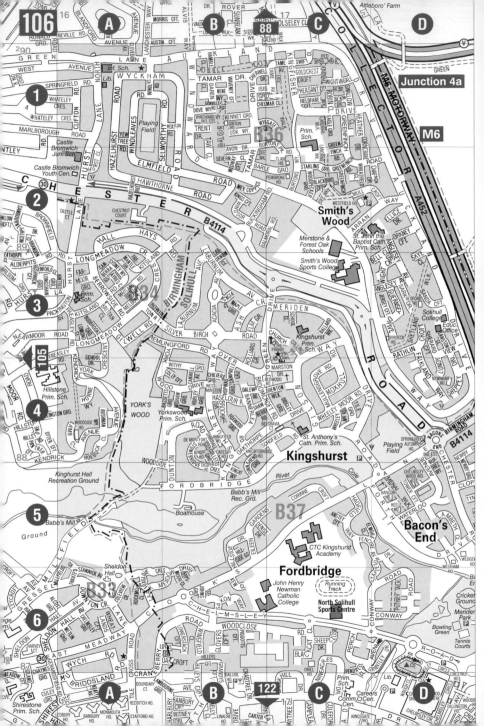

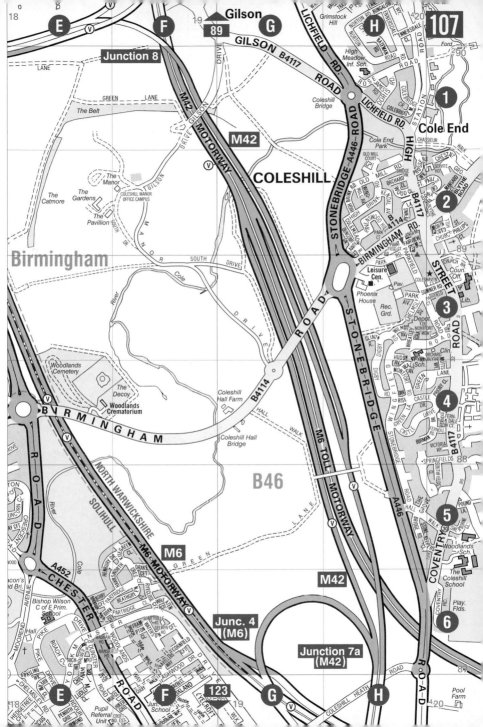

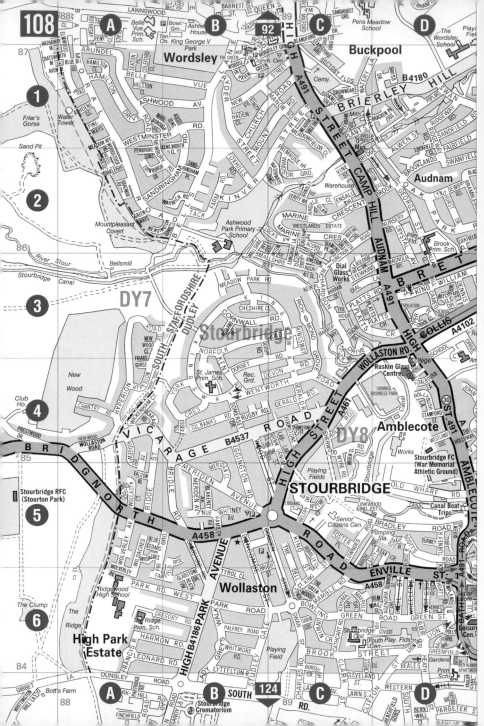

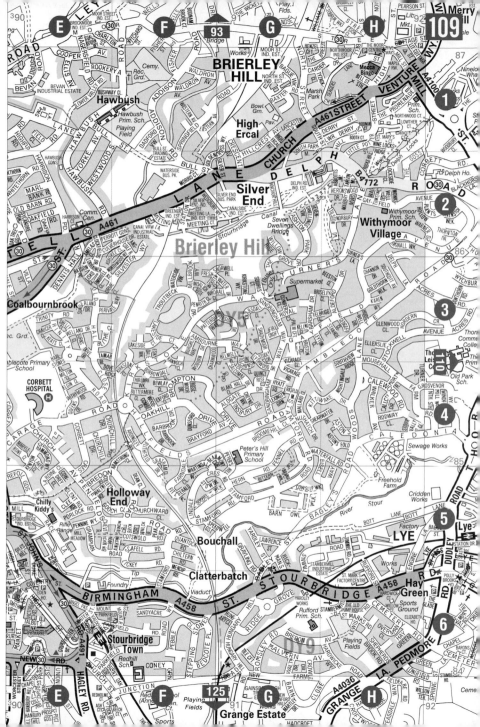

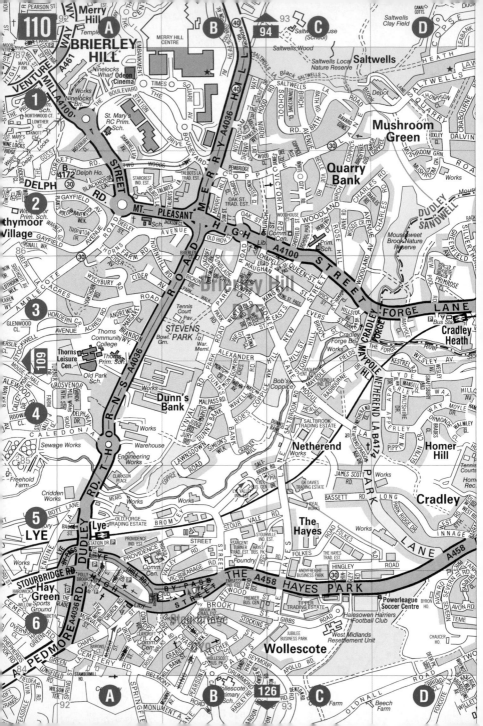

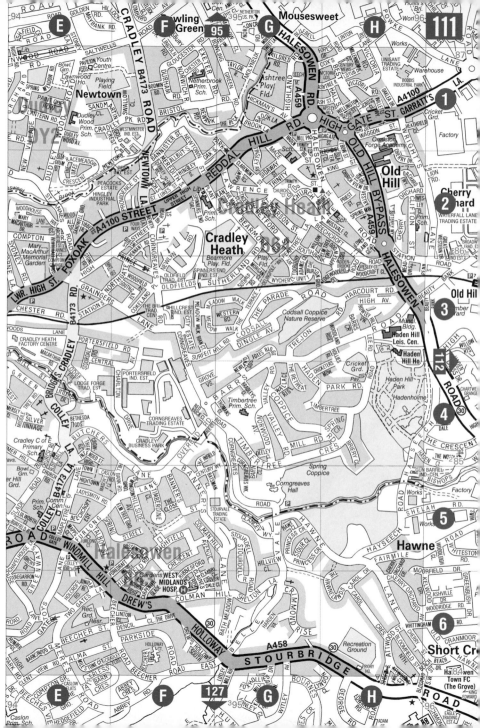

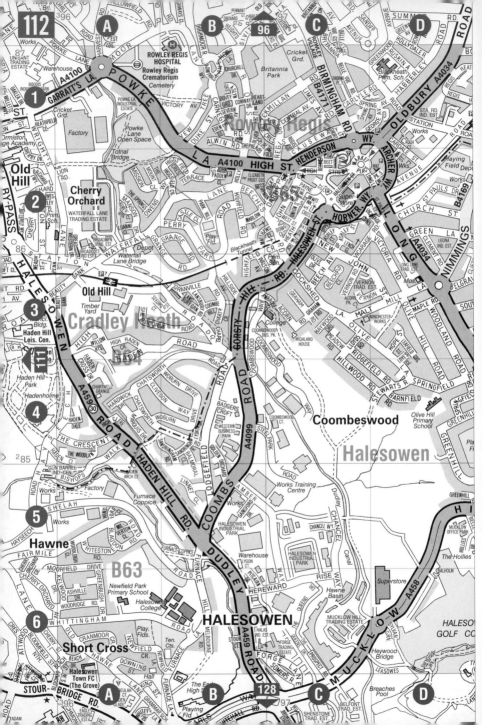

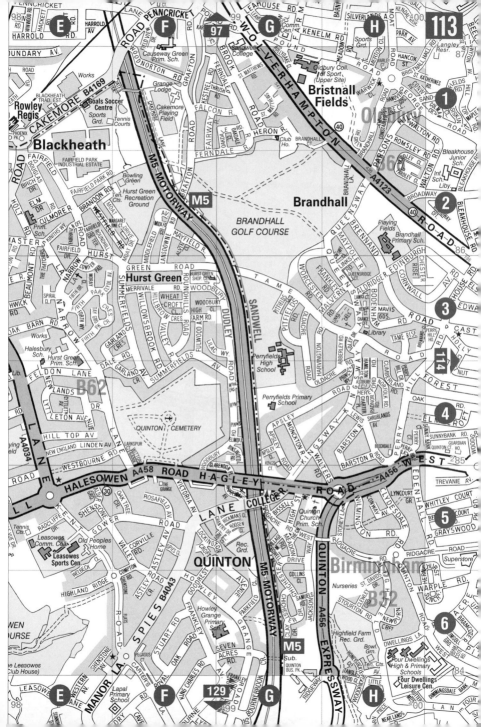

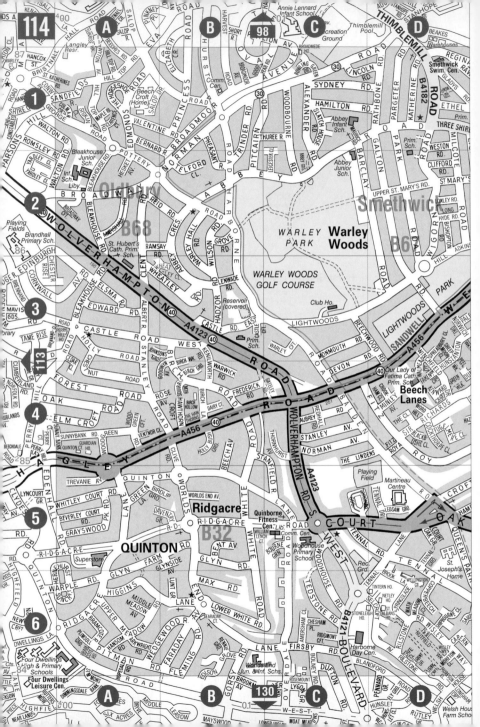

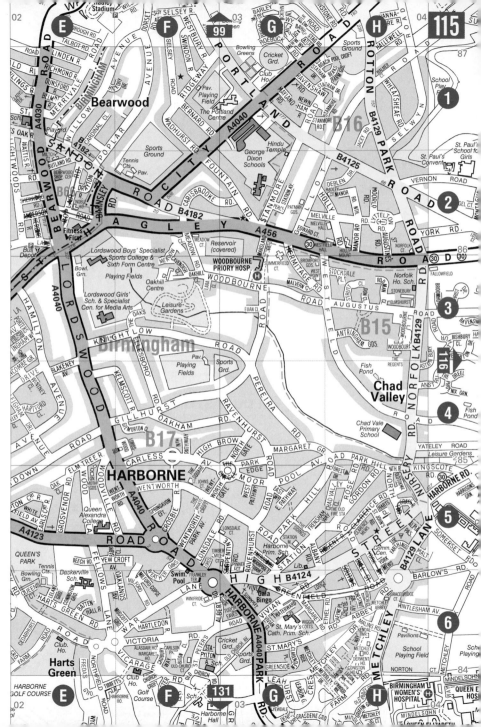

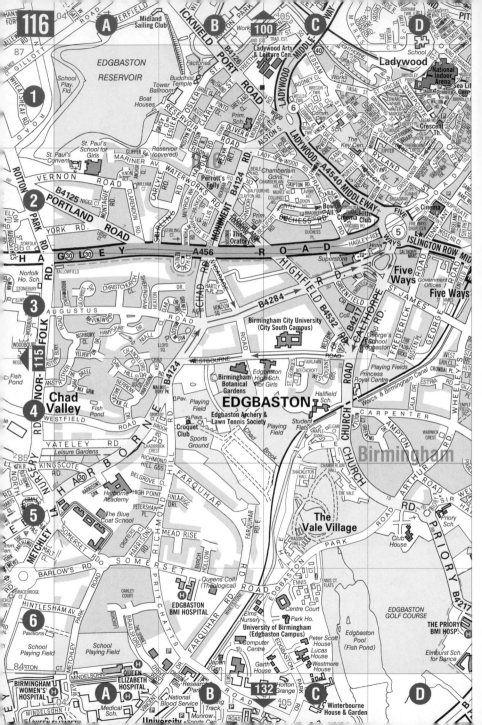

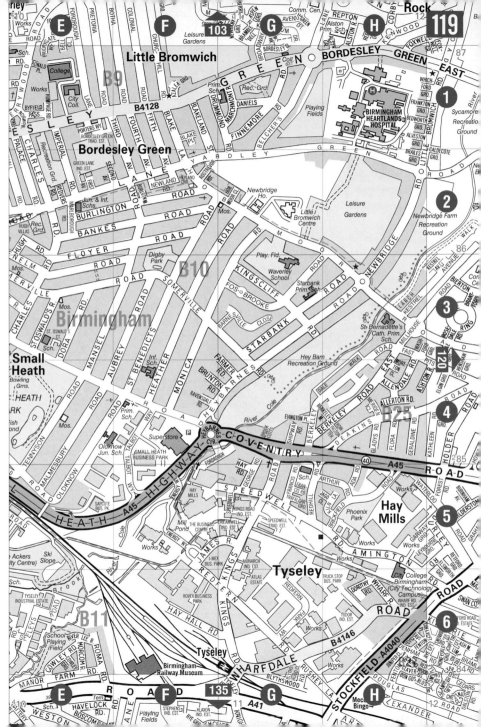

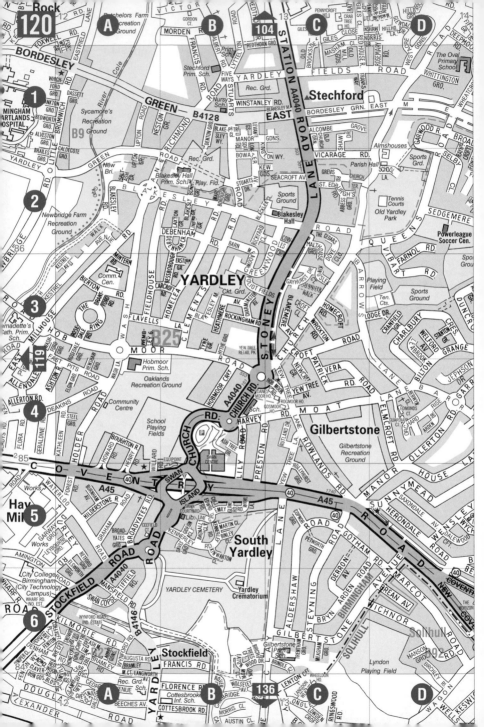

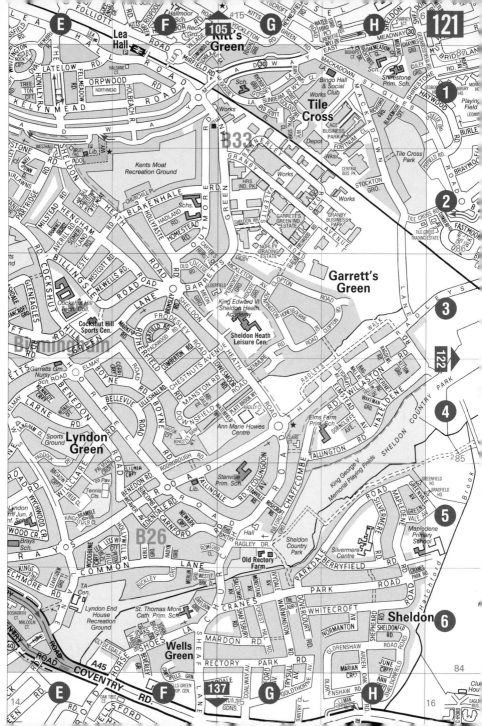

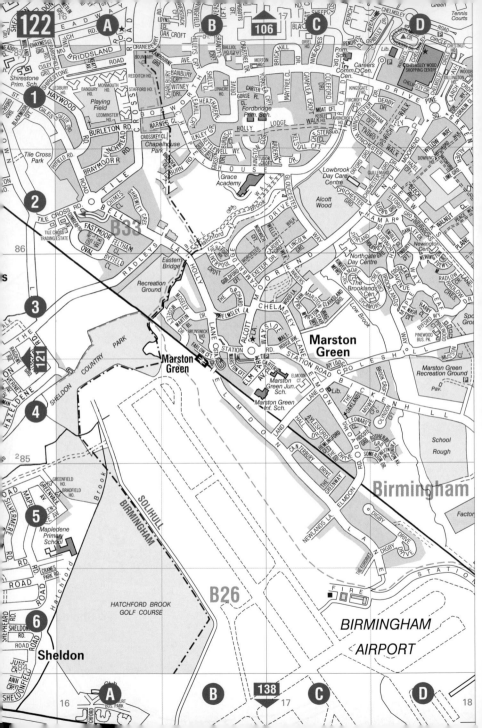

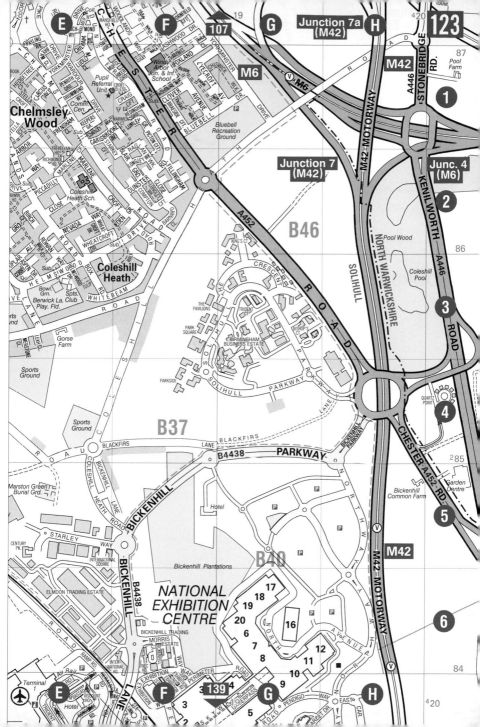

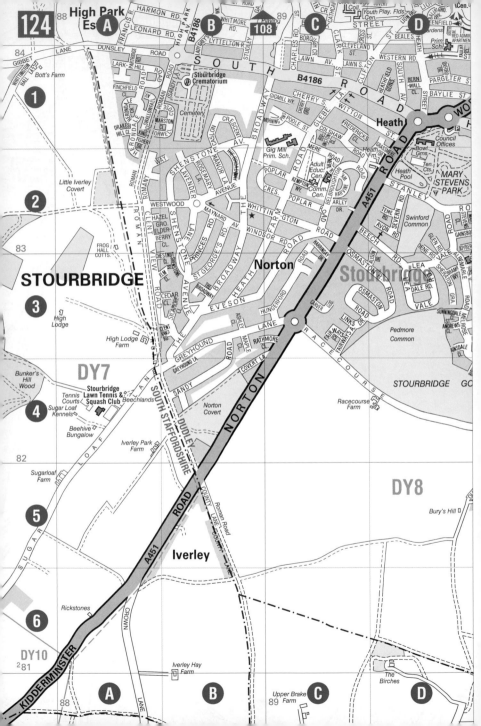

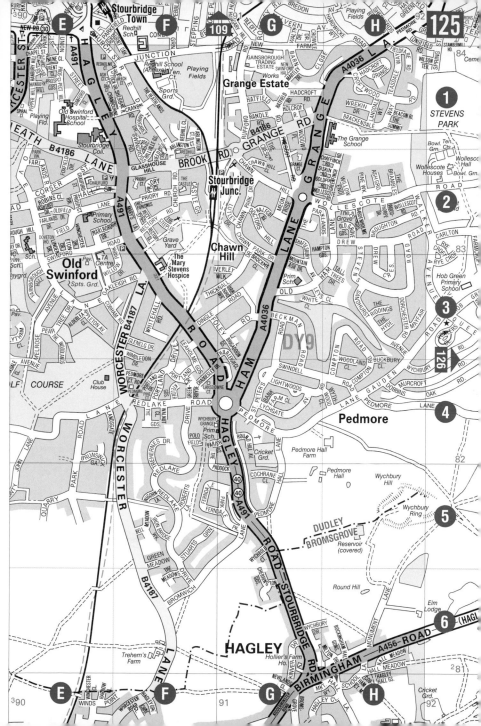

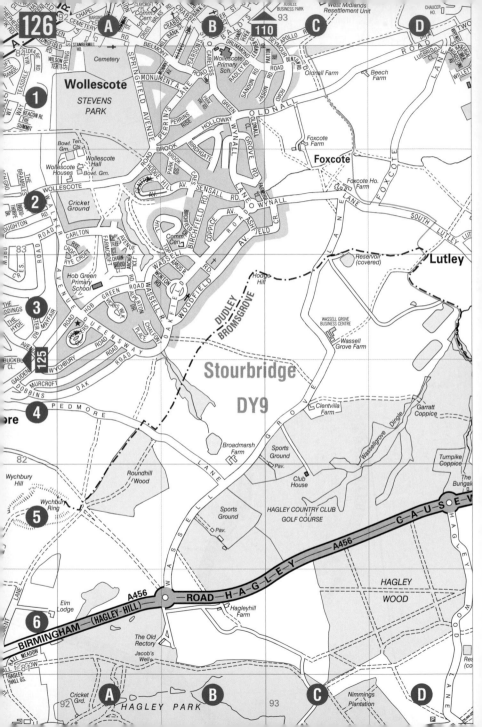

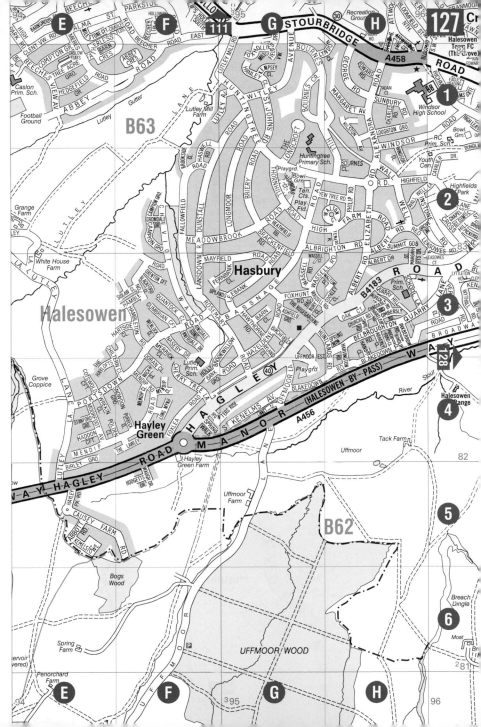

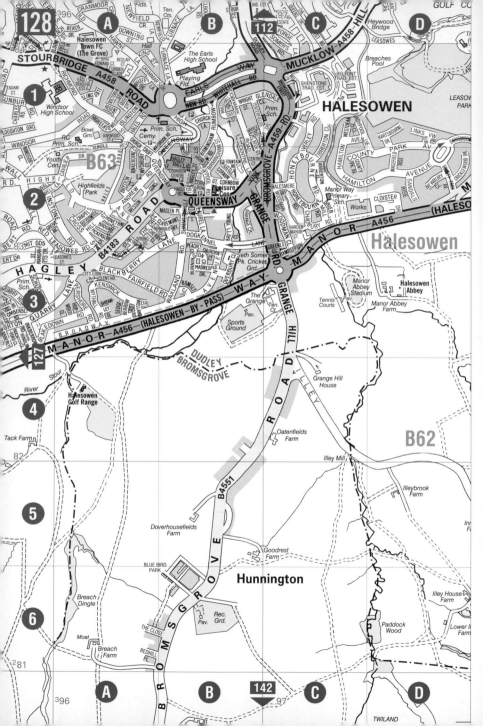

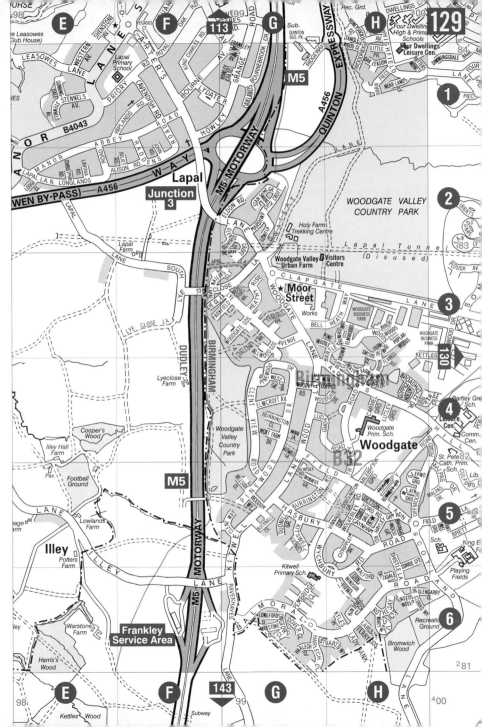

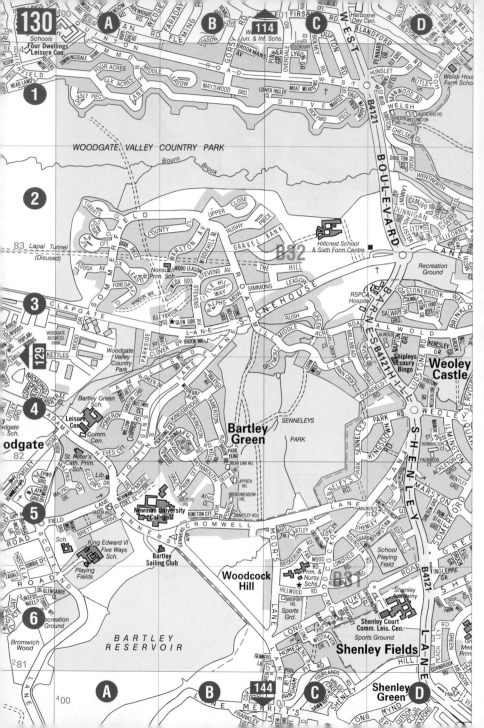

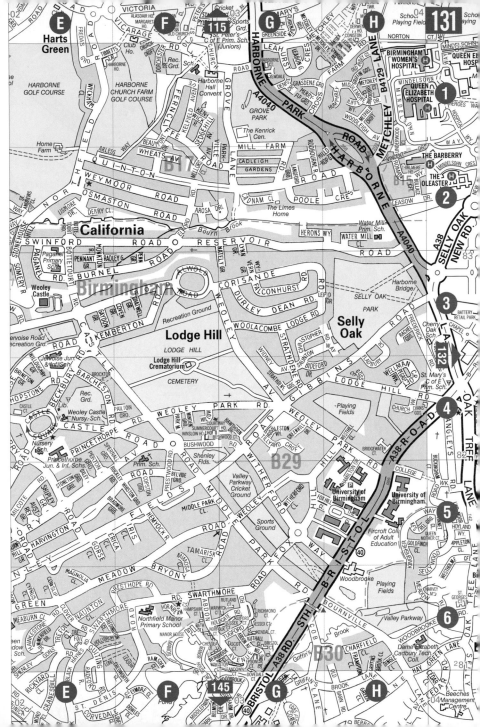

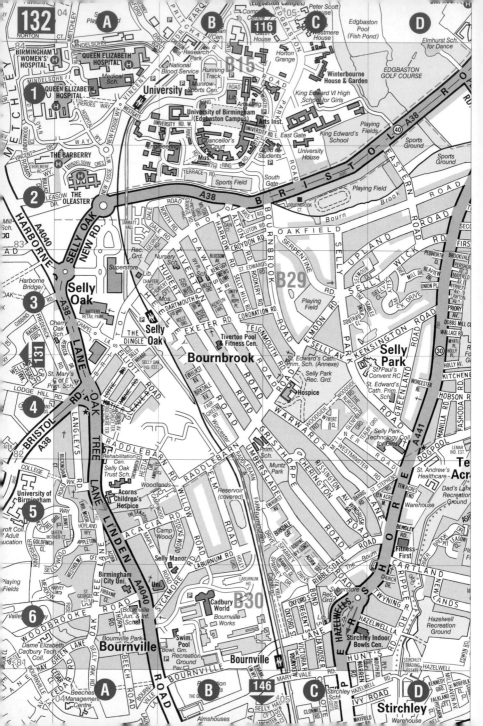

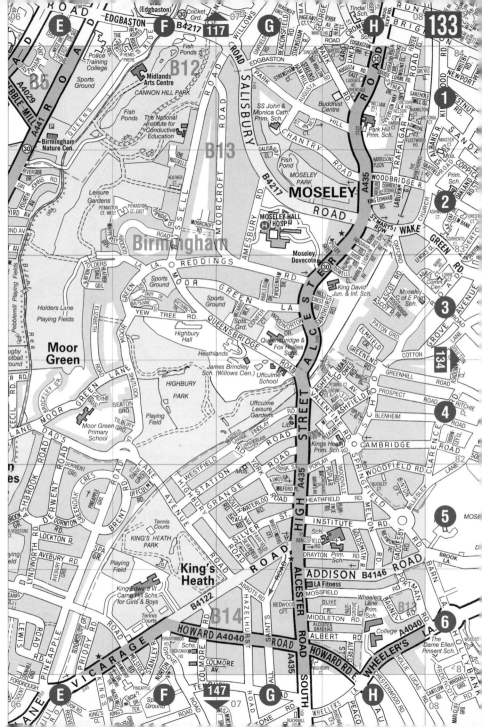

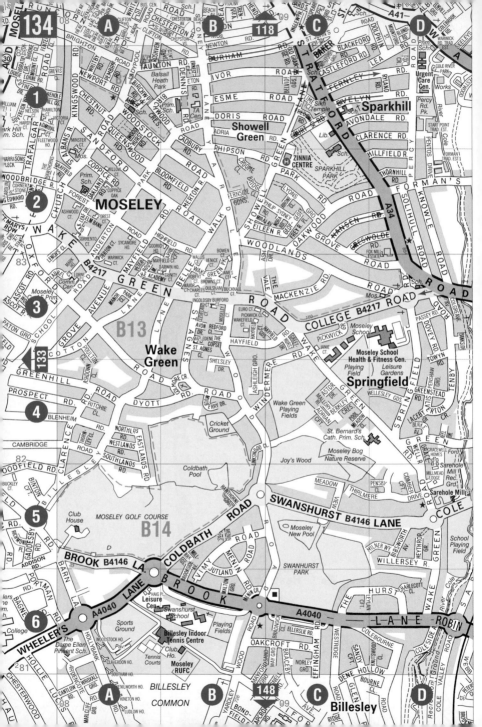

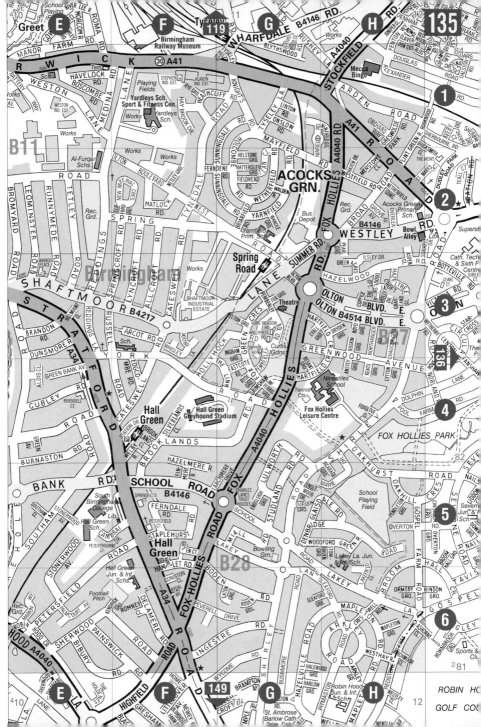

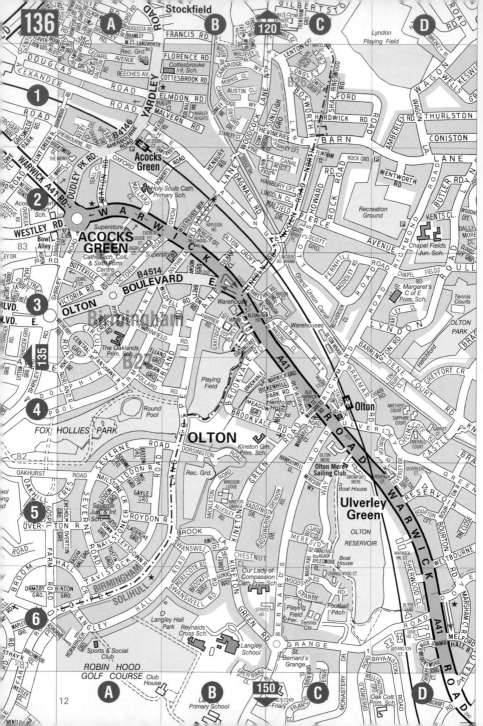

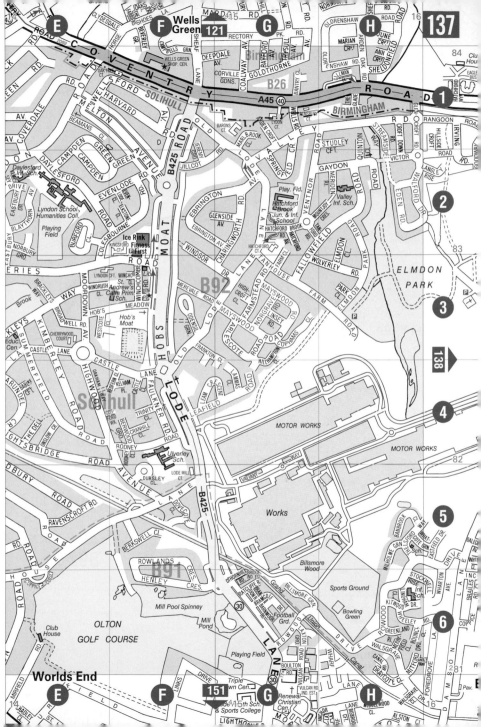

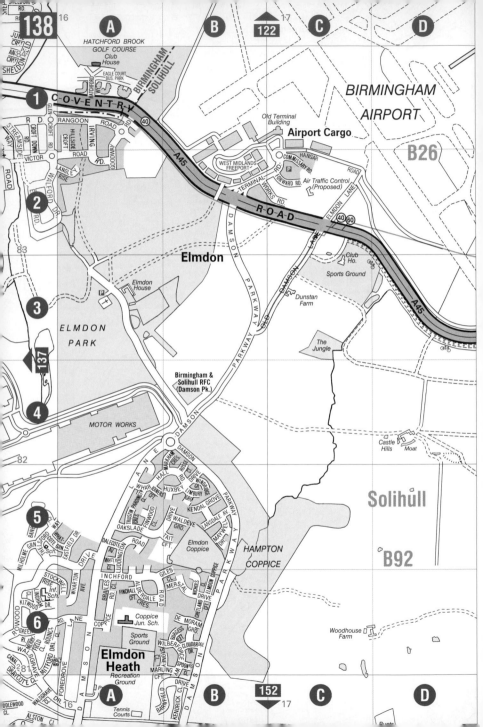

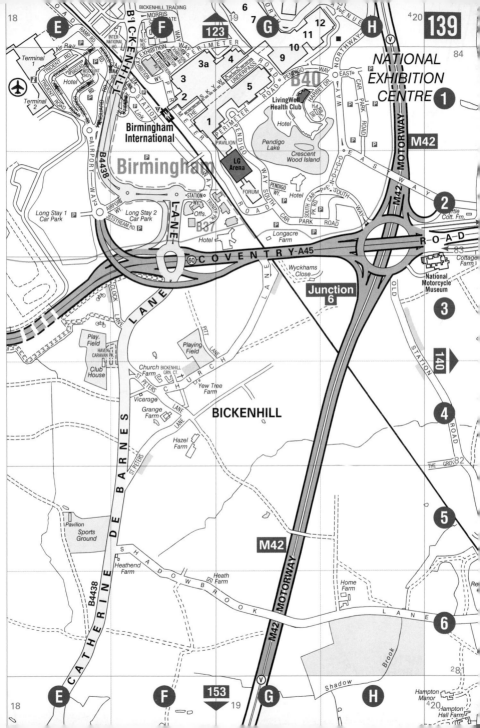

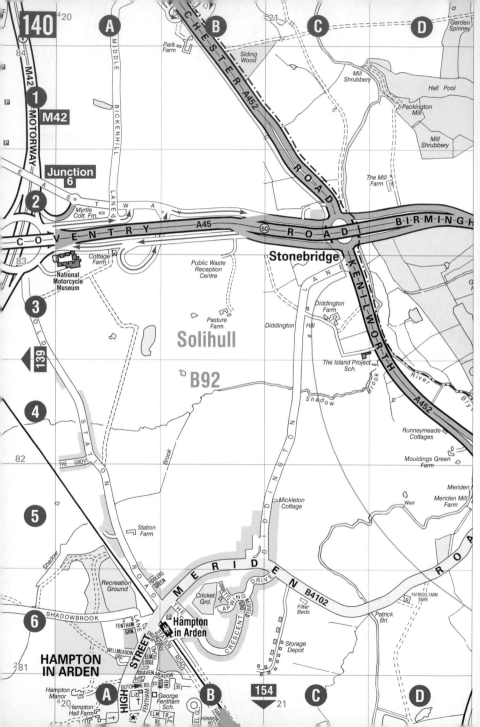

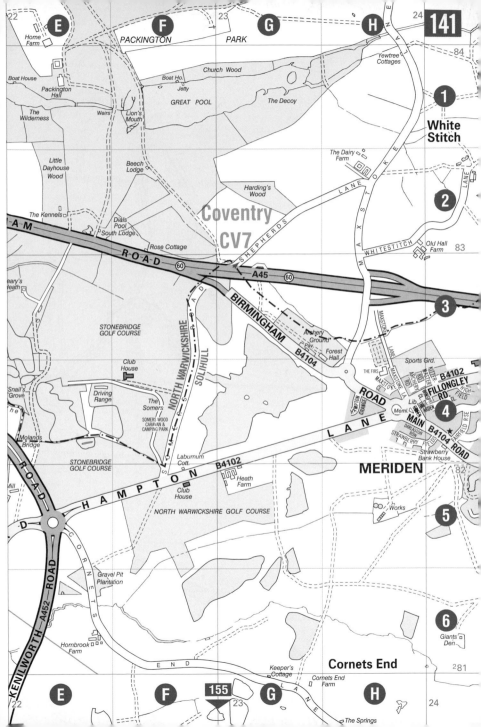

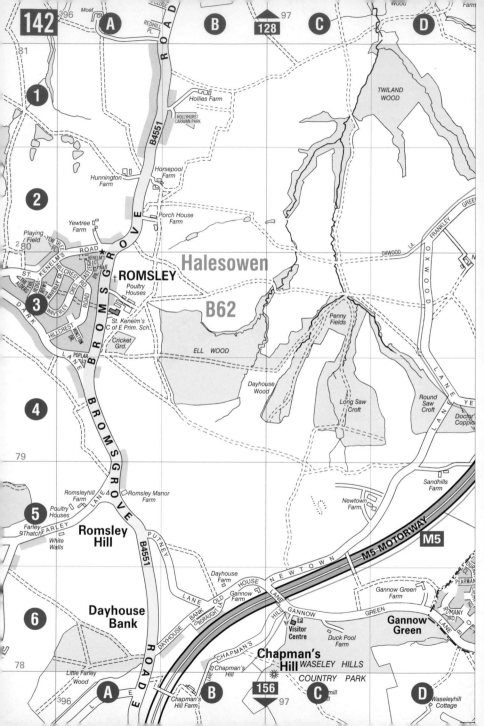

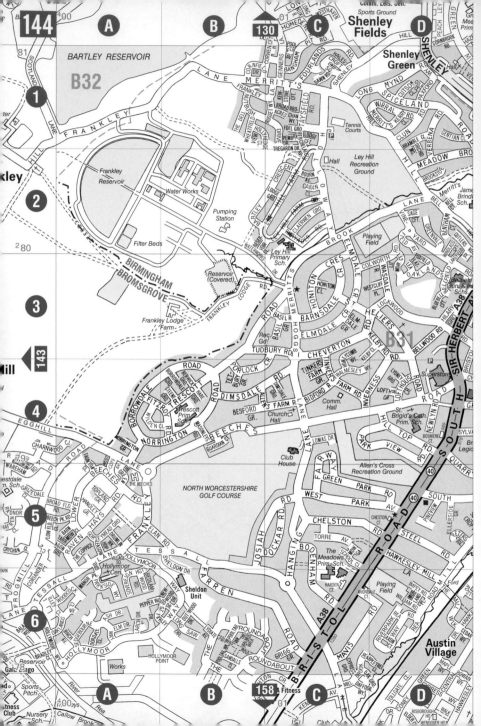

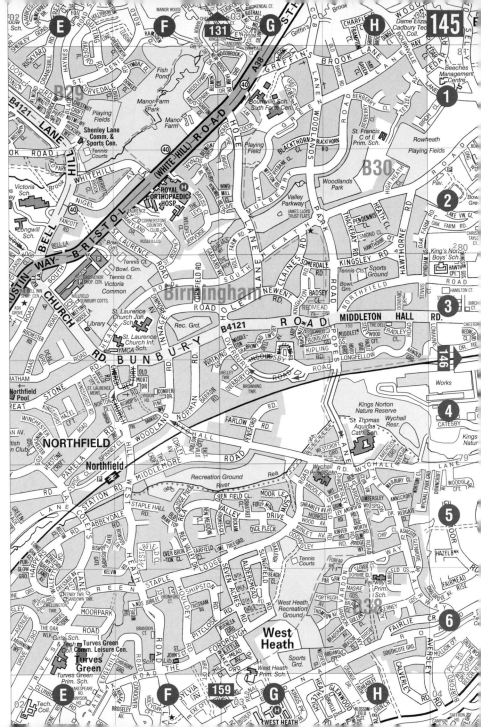

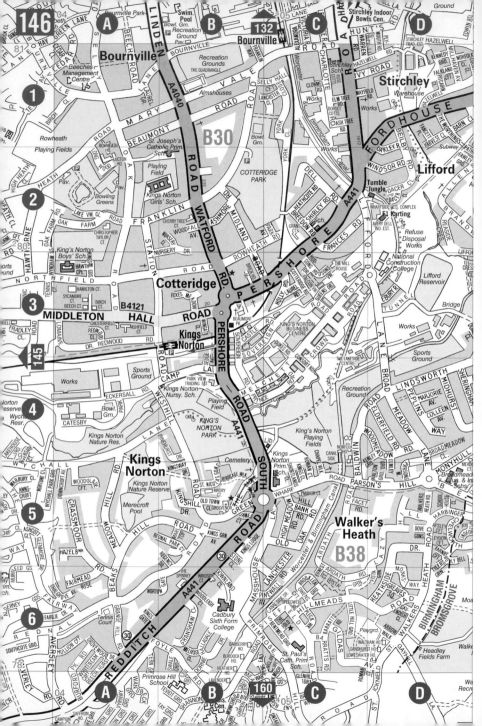

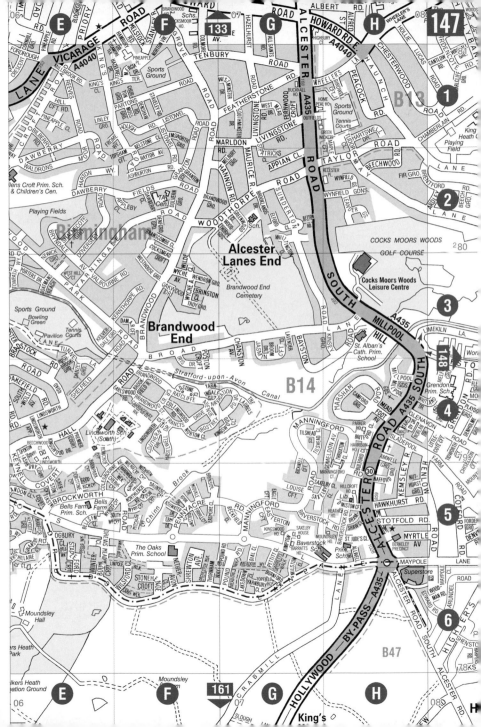

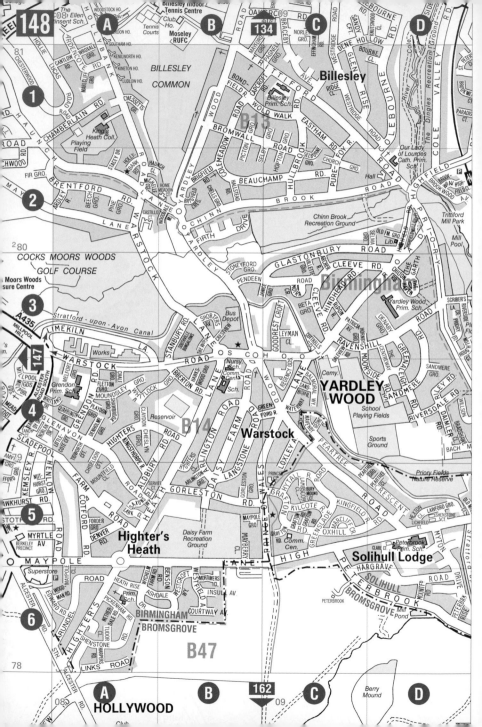

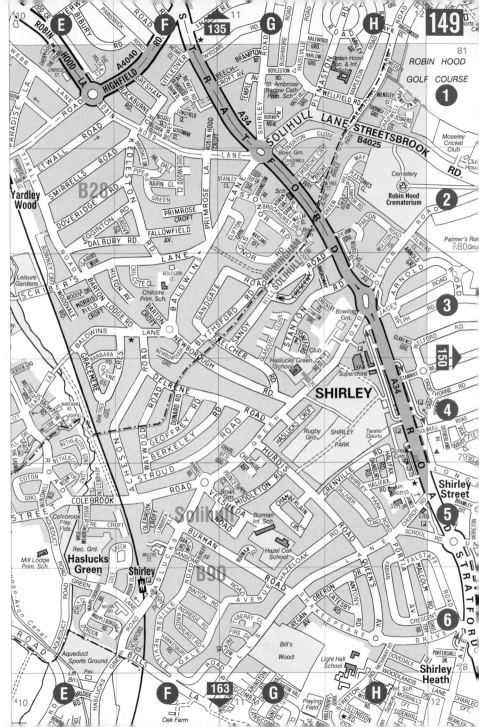

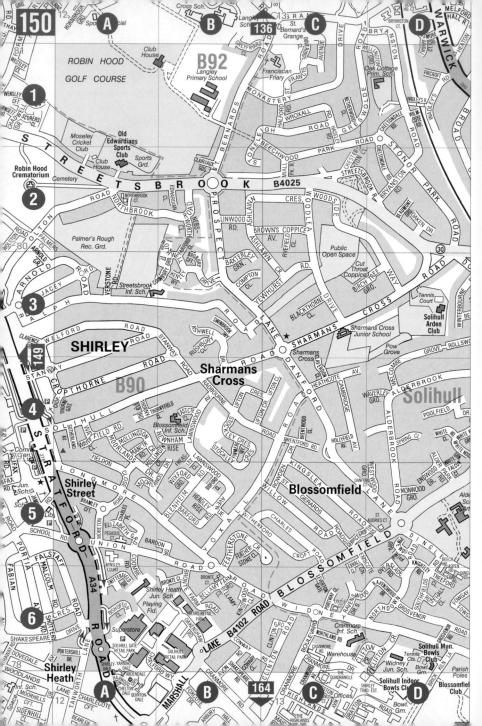

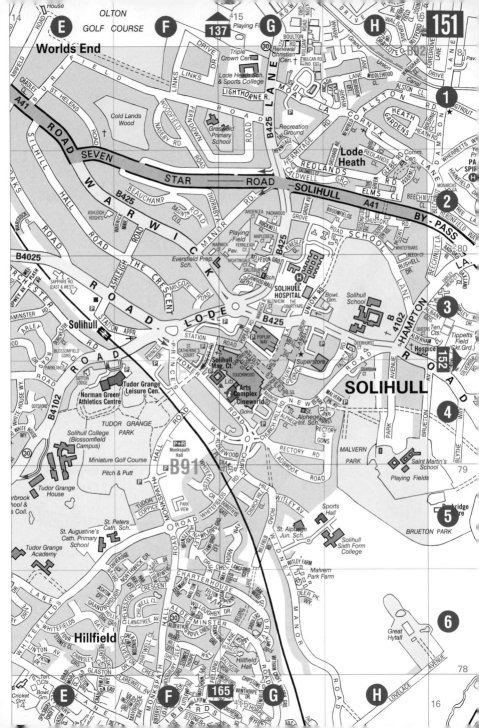

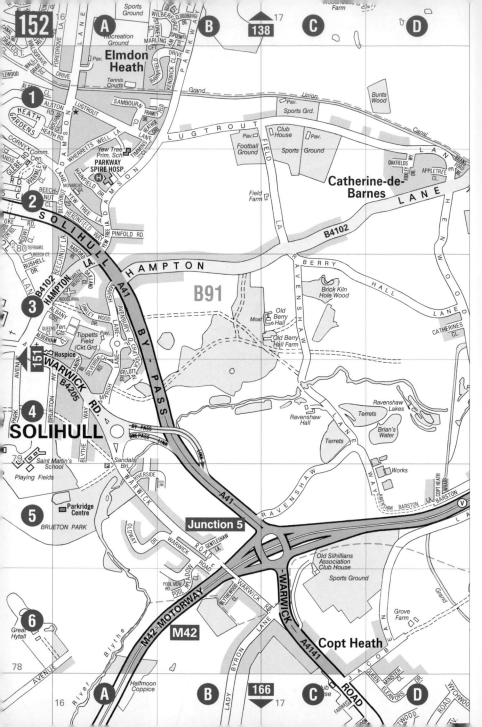

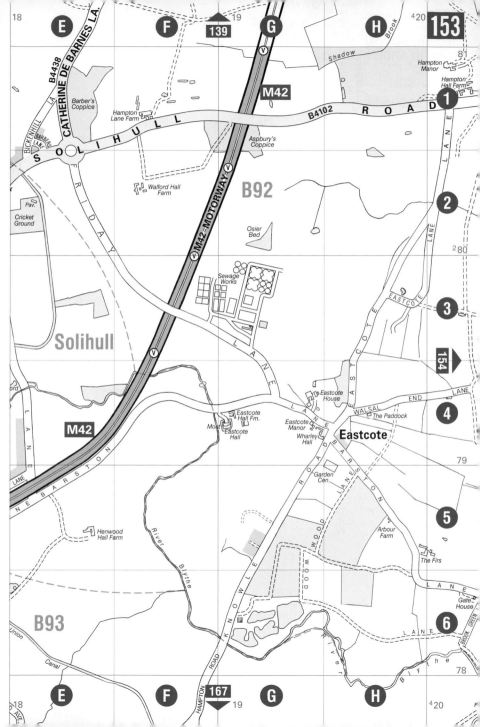

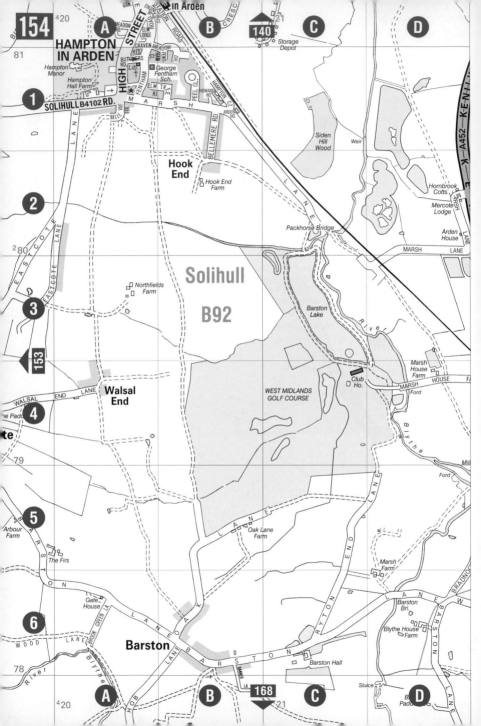

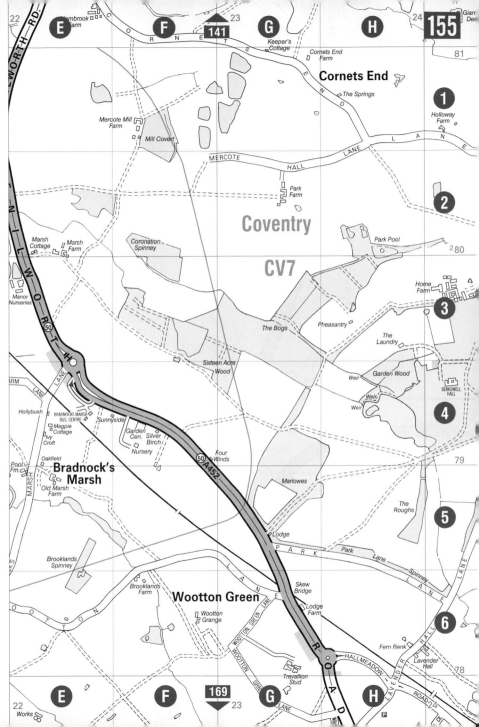

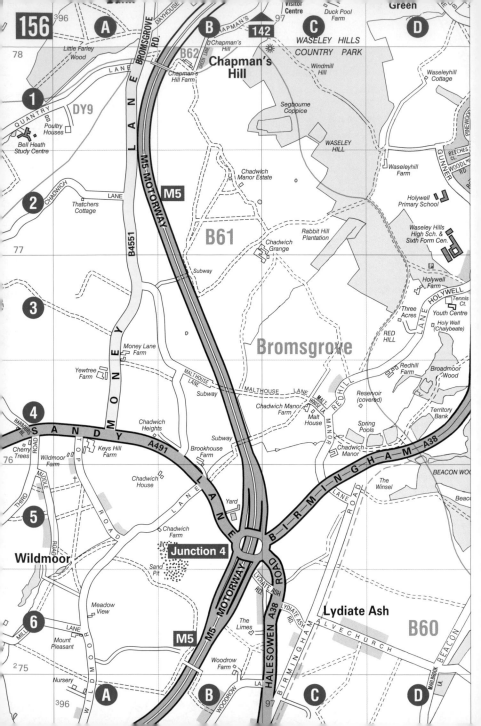

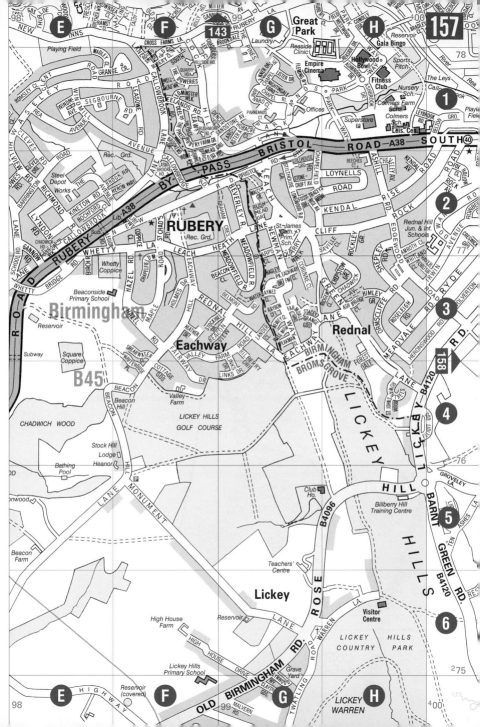

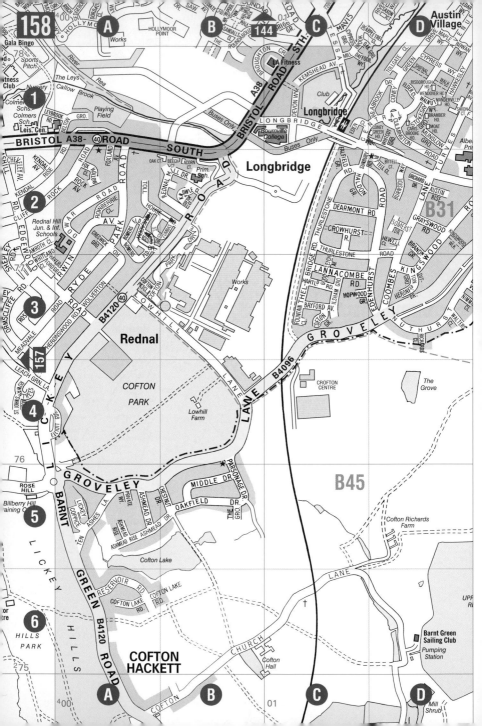

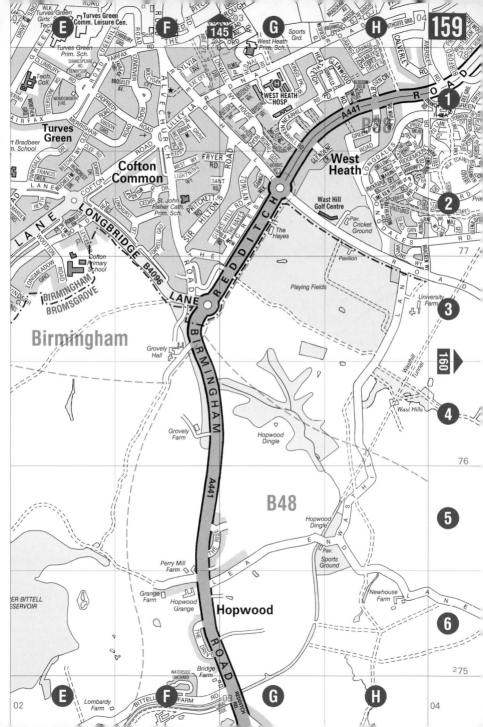

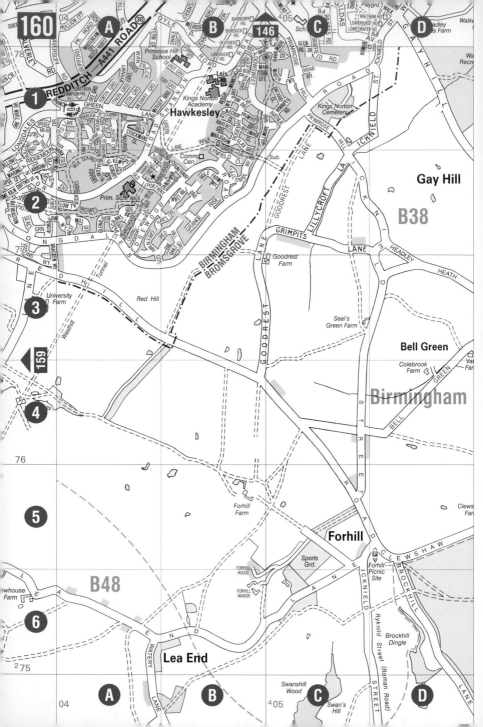

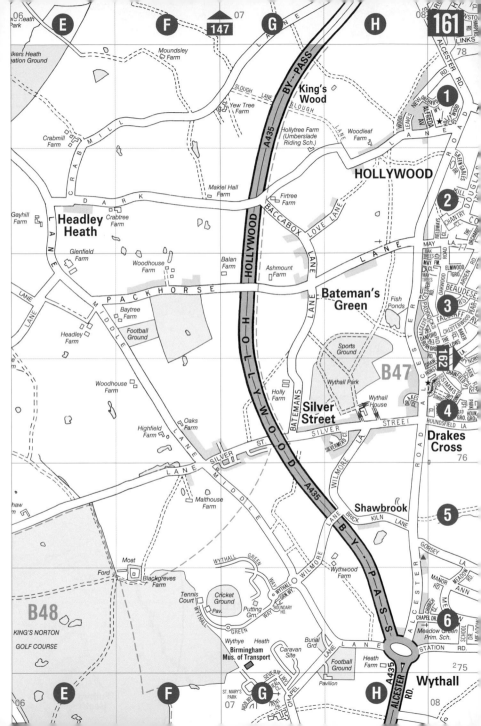

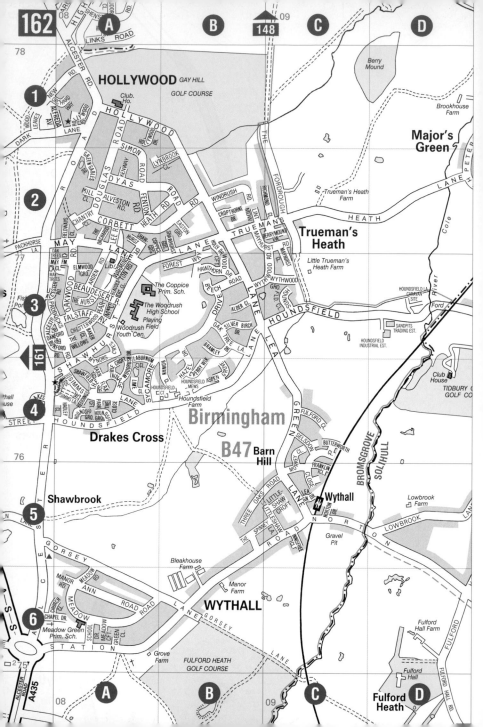

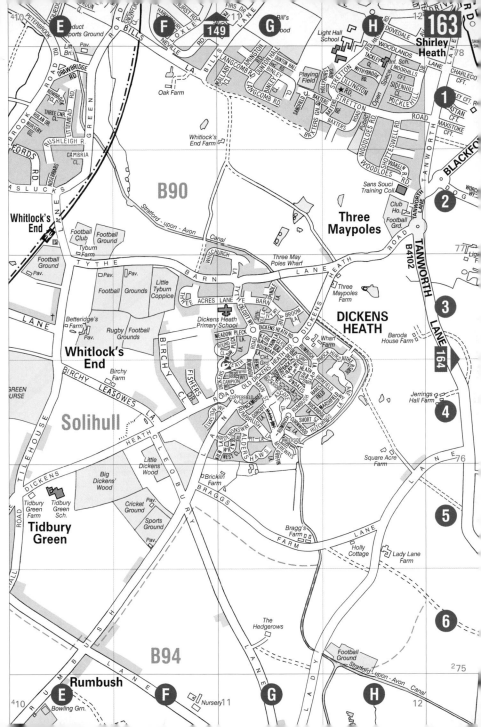

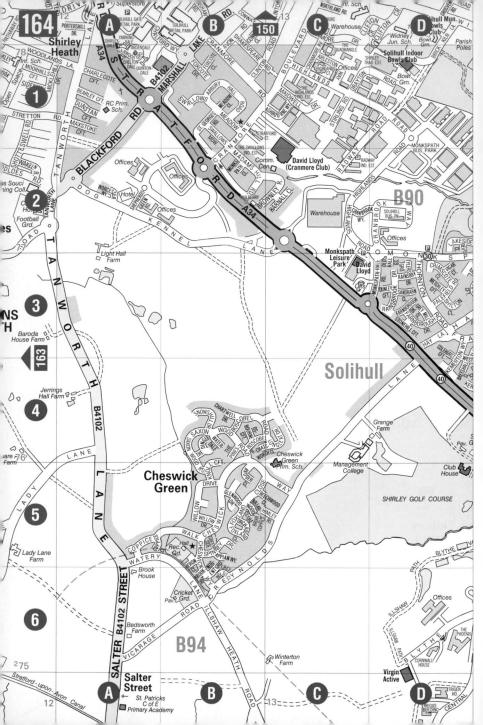

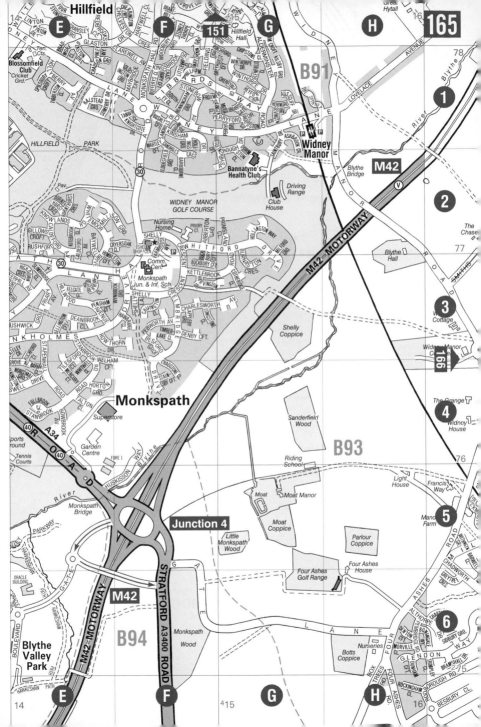

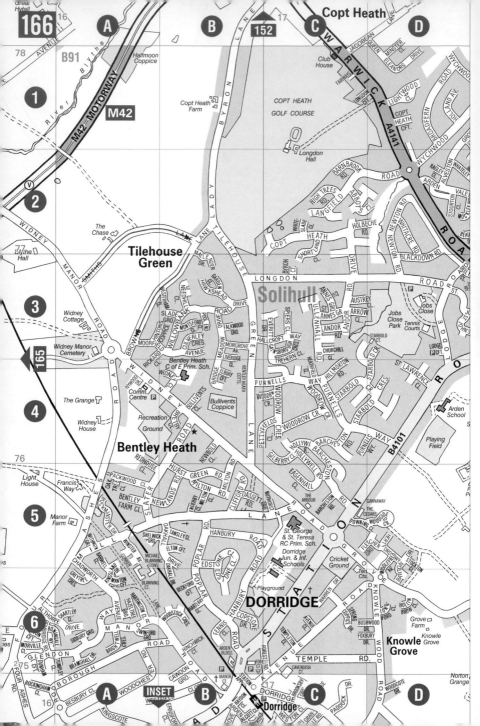

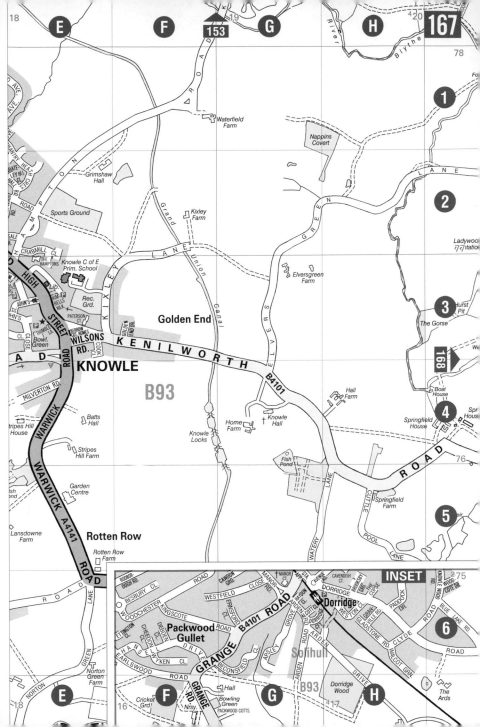

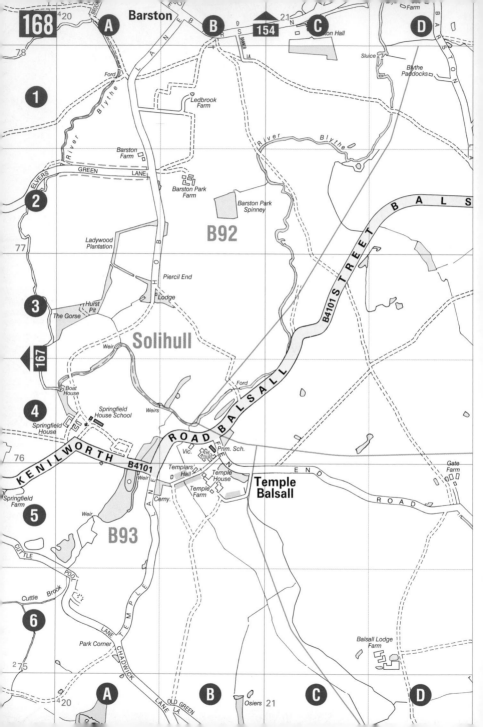

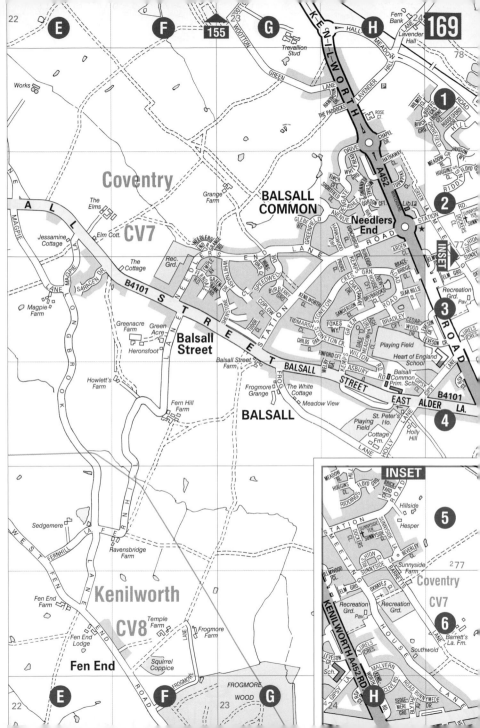

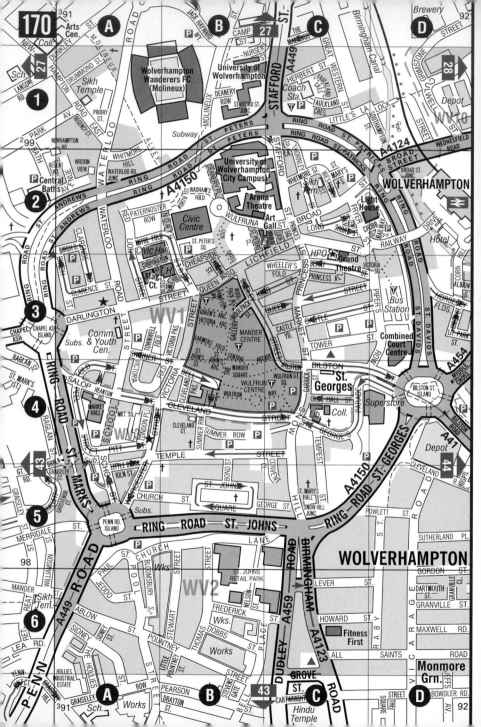

INDEX

Including Streets, Places & Areas, Industrial Estates, Selected Flats & Walkways, Junction Names & Service Areas, Stations and Selected Places of Interest.

HOW TO USE THIS INDEX

1. Each street name is followed by its Postcode District, then by its Locality abbreviation(s) and then by its map reference; e.g. **Abbey Rd.** B67: Smeth . . . .2B **114** is in the B67 Postcode District and the Smethwick Locality and is to be found in square 2B on page **114**. The page number is shown in bold type.

2. A strict alphabetical order is followed in which Av., Rd., St., etc. (though abbreviated) are read in full and as part of the street name; e.g. **Ash La.** appears after **Ashland St.** but before **Ashlawn Cres.**

3. Streets and a selection of flats and walkways that cannot be shown on the mapping, appear in the index with the thoroughfare to which they are connected shown in brackets; e.g. **Aaron Ct.** B24: Erd . . . .4F **85** (off Wood End Rd.)

4. Addresses that are in more than one part are referred to as not continuous.

5. Places and areas are shown in the index in BLUE TYPE and the map reference is to the actual map square in which the town centre or area is located and not to the place name shown on the map; e.g. **ALDRIDGE** 3D **34**

6. An example of a selected place of interest is **Bantock House Mus.** 3D **42**

7. An example of a station is **Acocks Green Station (Rail)** . . . .1A **136**. Included are Rail **(Rail)**, Midland Metro **(Metro)**, Park & Tram and Park & Ride. e.g. **Corser Street (Wolverhampton) (Park & Ride)** . . . .2B **44**.

8. Junction Names and Service Areas are shown in the index in BOLD CAPITAL TYPE; e.g. **BURNTWOOD JUNC.** 2B **10**

9. Map references for entries that appear on large scale pages **4**, **5** & **170** are shown first, with small scale map references shown in brackets; e.g. **Ablow St.** WV2: Wolv 6A **170** (3G **43**)

GENERAL ABBREVIATIONS

All. : Alley	**Est.** : Estate	**Nth.** : North
App. : Approach	**Ests.** : Estates	**Pde.** : Parade
Arc. : Arcade	**Fld.** : Field	**Pk.** : Park
Av. : Avenue	**Flds.** : Fields	**Pas.** : Passage
Blvd. : Boulevard	**Gdns.** : Gardens	**Pl.** : Place
Bri. : Bridge	**Ga.** : Gate	**Pct.** : Precinct
Bldg. : Building	**Gt.** : Great	**Res.** : Residential
Bldgs. : Buildings	**Grn.** : Green	**Ri.** : Rise
Bungs. : Bungalows	**Gro.** : Grove	**Rd.** : Road
Bus. : Business	**Hgts.** : Heights	**Rdbt.** : Roundabout
C'way. : Causeway	**Ho.** : House	**Shop.** : Shopping
Cen. : Centre	**Ho's.** : Houses	**Sth.** : South
Chu. : Church	**Ind.** : Industrial	**Sq.** : Square
Circ. : Circle	**Info.** : Information	**Sta.** : Station
Cir. : Circus	**Intl.** : International	**St.** : Street
Cl. : Close	**Junc.** : Junction	**Ter.** : Terrace
Coll. : College	**La.** : Lane	**Twr.** : Tower
Comn. : Common	**Lit.** : Little	**Trad.** : Trading
Cnr. : Corner	**Lwr.** : Lower	**Up.** : Upper
Cott. : Cottage	**Mnr.** : Manor	**Va.** : Vale
Cotts. : Cottages	**Mans.** : Mansions	**Vw.** : View
Ct. : Court	**Mkt.** : Market	**Vs.** : Villas
Cres. : Crescent	**Mdw.** : Meadow	**Vis.** : Visitors
Cft. : Croft	**Mdws.** : Meadows	**Wlk.** : Walk
Dr. : Drive	**M.** : Mews	**W.** : West
E. : East	**Mt.** : Mount	**Yd.** : Yard
Ent. : Enterprise	**Mus.** : Museum	

LOCALITY ABBREVIATIONS

A Grn : **Acock's Green**	B'hth : **Blackheath**	C Hay : **Cheslyn Hay**
Alb : **Albrighton**	Blox : **Bloxwich**	Ches G : **Cheswick Green**
A'rdge : **Aldridge**	Bly P : **Blythe Valley Park**	Clay : **Clayhanger**
A'chu : **Alvechurch**	Bold : **Boldmere**	Cod : **Codsall**
Amb : **Amblecote**	Bord G : **Bordesley Green**	Cod W : **Codsall Wood**
Aston : **Aston**	B'vlle : **Bournville**	Coft H : **Cofton Hackett**
Bal C : **Balsall Common**	Brie H : **Brierley Hill**	Col : **Coleshill**
Bal H : **Balsall Heath**	B'frd : **Brinsford**	Cose : **Coseley**
B Grn : **Barnt Green**	Bwnhls : **Brownhills**	Coven : **Coven**
Bars : **Barston**	Burn : **Burntwood**	Cov H : **Coven Heath**
Bart G : **Bartley Green**	Bush : **Bushbury**	Crad : **Cradley**
Bass P : **Bassetts Pole**	Cann : **Cannock**	Crad H : **Cradley Heath**
Belb : **Belbroughton**	Can : **Canwell**	Curd : **Curdworth**
Ben H : **Bentley Heath**	Cas B : **Castle Bromwich**	Darl : **Darlaston**
Berk : **Berkswell**	Cas V : **Castle Vale**	Dic H : **Dickens Heath**
Bick : **Bickenhill**	Cath B : **Catherine-de-Barnes**	Dorr : **Dorridge**
Bilb : **Bilbrook**	Cats : **Catshill**	Dray B : **Drayton Bassett**
Bils : **Bilston**	C'wich : **Chadwich**	Dud : **Dudley**
Birm : **Birmingham**	Chase : **Chasetown**	Earls : **Earlswood**
Birm A : **Birmingham International Airport**	Chel W : **Chelmsley Wood**	Edg : **Edgbaston**

Locality Abbreviations

Erd : **Erdington**
Ess : **Essington**
Ett : **Ettingshall**
F'stne : **Featherstone**
Fen E : **Fen End**
Foot : **Footherley**
F'bri : **Fordbridge**
F'hses : **Fordhouses**
Forh : **Forhill**
Four O : **Four Oaks**
Fran : **Frankley**
Gorn : **Gornalwood**
Gt Barr : **Great Barr**
Gt Wyr : **Great Wyrley**
Hag : **Hagley**
Hale : **Halesowen**
Hall G : **Hall Green**
Hamm : **Hammerwich**
H Ard : **Hampton in Arden**
Hand : **Handsworth**
Harb : **Harborne**
Head H : **Headley Heath**
Hilt : **Hilton**
Himl : **Himley**
Hints : **Hints**
Hock : **Hockley**
H'ley H : **Hockley Heath**
Hodg H : **Hodge Hill**
H'wd : **Hollywood**
Hopw : **Hopwood**
Hunn : **Hunnington**
I'ley : **Iverley**
King H : **King's Heath**
K'hrst : **Kingshurst**
King Nor : **King's Norton**
K'sdng : **Kingstanding**
K'wfrd : **Kingswinford**
Kinv : **Kinver**
Kitts G : **Kitt's Green**
Know : **Knowle**
Lea M : **Lea Marston**
Lick : **Lickey**
Lit As : **Little Aston**
Lit H : **Little Hay**
Lit P : **Little Packington**
Lit Wyr : **Little Wyrley**
Longb : **Longbridge**
Lwr G : **Lower Gornal**
Lwr P : **Lower Penn**
Loz : **Lozells**

Lutley : **Lutley**
L Ash : **Lydiate Ash**
Lye : **Lye**
Lynn : **Lynn**
Maj G : **Major's Green**
Marlb : **Marlbrook**
Mars G : **Marston Green**
Mer : **Meriden**
Midd : **Middleton**
Min : **Minworth**
M'path : **Monkspath**
Mose : **Moseley**
Mox : **Moxley**
Muck C : **Muckley Corner**
Nat E C : **National Exhibition Centre**
Nech : **Nechells**
Neth : **Netherton**
New O : **New Oscott**
N'fld : **Northfield**
Nort C : **Norton Canes**
Oaken : **Oaken**
O'bry : **Oldbury**
Old H : **Old Hill**
Olton : **Olton**
Oxl : **Oxley**
Patt : **Pattingham**
Pedm : **Pedmore**
Pels : **Pelsall**
Pend : **Pendeford**
Penn : **Penn**
P'ntt : **Pensnett**
P Barr : **Perry Barr**
Pert : **Perton**
Quar B : **Quarry Bank**
Quin : **Quinton**
Redn : **Rednal**
Roms : **Romsley**
R'ley : **Roughley**
Row R : **Rowley Regis**
Rub : **Rubery**
Rus : **Rushall**
Salt : **Saltley**
Sed : **Sedgley**
Seis : **Seisdon**
S Oak : **Selly Oak**
S End : **Shard End**
Share : **Shareshill**
Sheld : **Sheldon**
S'fld : **Shelfield**
Shen W : **Shenstone Woodend**

Shir : **Shirley**
Small H : **Small Heath**
Smeth : **Smethwick**
Sol : **Solihull**
S'brk : **Sparkbrook**
S'hll : **Sparkhill**
Stech : **Stechford**
Stir : **Stirchley**
Ston : **Stonnall**
Stourb : **Stourbridge**
Stourt : **Stourton**
S'tly : **Streetly**
S Cold : **Sutton Coldfield**
Swind : **Swindon**
Tett : **Tettenhall**
Tid G : **Tidbury Green**
Tip : **Tipton**
Tiv : **Tividale**
Tres : **Trescott**
Try : **Trysull**
Tys : **Tyseley**
Up Gor : **Upper Gornal**
W Hth : **Wall Heath**
Walm : **Walmley**
Wals : **Walsall**
Wals W : **Walsall Wood**
W End : **Ward End**
Wat O : **Water Orton**
W'bry : **Wednesbury**
Wed : **Wednesfield**
W'frd : **Weeford**
W Cas : **Weoley Castle**
W Brom : **West Bromwich**
Wild : **Wildmoor**
W'hall : **Willenhall**
Win G : **Winson Green**
Wis : **Wishaw**
Witt : **Witton**
Woll : **Wollaston**
W'cte : **Wollescote**
Wolv : **Wolverhampton**
Wom : **Wombourne**
Word : **Wordsley**
Wrot P : **Wrottesley Park**
W Grn : **Wylde Green**
Wyt : **Wythall**
Yard : **Yardley**
Yard W : **Yardley Wood**

1st Exhibition Av. B40: Nat E C 1F **139**
2nd Exhibition Av. B40: Nat E C 1F **139**
3B Business Village B21: Hand 2H **99**
3rd Exhibition Av. B40: Nat E C 1F **139**

A

A1 Trad. Est. B66: Smeth 2F **99**
Aaron Ct. *B24: Erd* 4F **85**
(off Wood End Rd.)
Aaron Manby Ct. DY4: Tip 5H **61**
Abacus Bldg. B12: Birm 2A **118**
Abberley Cl. B63: Hale 3H **127**
Abberley Ind. Cen. B66: Smeth 4H **99**
Abberley Rd. B68: O'bry 3H **113**
DY3: Lwr G 3G **75**
Abberley St. B66: Smeth 4H **99**
DY2: Dud 1E **95**
Abberton Cl. B63: Hale 2C **128**
Abberton Ct. *B23: Erd* 5C **84**
(off Dunlin Cl.)
Abberton Gro. B90: M'path 2F **165**
Abbess Gro. B25: Yard 2C **120**
Abbey Cl. B71: W Brom 2A **80**
Abbey Ct. B68: O'bury 5H **97**
Abbey Cres. B63: Crad 1F **127**
B68: O'bry 3B **114**
Abbeydale Rd. B31: N'fld 5E **145**
Abbey Dr. WS3: Pels 2E **21**
Abbeyfield Rd. B23: Erd 6D **68**
WV10: Bush 3A **16**

Abbey Gdns. B67: Smeth 2C **114**
Abbey Mans. B24: Erd 1H **85**
Abbey Rd. B17: Harb 6H **115**
B23: Erd 5D **84**
B63: Crad 1E **127**
B67: Smeth 2B **114**
DY2: Dud 3F **95**
DY3: Gorn 4G **75**
Abbey Sq. WS3: Blox 5E **19**
Abbey St. B18: Hock 4C **100**
DY3: Gorn 4G **75**
Abbey St. Nth. B18: Hock 4C **100**
WS4: Rus 3G **33**

Abbots Cl. B93: Know 2C **166**
Abbotsford Av.
B43: Gt Barr 3B **66**
Abbotsford Dr. DY1: Dud 2A **94**
Abbotsford Rd. B11: S'brk 5B **118**
Abbots Rd. B14: King H 6G **133**
Abbots Way B18: Hock 3D **100**
WV3: Wolv 2C **42**
Abbott Rd. B63: Hale 5E **127**
Abbotts Av. DY5: Brie H 2H **109**
Abbotts Pl. WS3: Blox 6B **20**
Abbotts Rd. B24: Erd 6F **85**
Abbotts St. WS3: Blox 5B **20**
Abdon Av. B29: W Cas 6F **131**
Aberdeen St. B18: Win G 5A **100**
Aberford Cl. WV12: W'hall 5D **30**
Abigails Cl. B26: Sheld 4F **121**
Abingdon Cl. WV1: Wolv 1D **44**
Abingdon Rd. B23: Erd 6B **68**
DY2: Neth 6F **95**
WS3: Blox 5F **19**
WV1: Wolv 1D **44**

Abingdon Way B35: Cas V 4E **87**
WS3: Blox 5F **19**
Ablewell St. WS1: Wals 2D **48**
Ablow St. WV2: Wolv 6A **170** (3G **43**)
Abney Dr. WV14: Cose 4B **60**
Abney Gro. B44: K'sdng 3B **68**
Aboyne Cl. B5: Edg 5F **117**
Ab Row B4: Birm 2H **5** (6H **101**)
Acacia Av. B37: K'hrst 3B **106**
WS5: Wals 1E **65**
Acacia Cl. B37: K'hrst 3B **106**
B69: Tiv 5B **78**
DY1: Dud 4C **76**
Acacia Cres. WV8: Bilb 3H **13**
Acacia Dr. WV14: Cose 6C **60**
Acacia Rd. B30: B'ville 5A **132**
Acacia Ter. B12: Bal H 6A **118**
Acacia, The B13: Mose 3A **134**
Accord M. WS10: Darl 4D **46**
Ace Bus. Pk. B33: Kitts G 1H **121**
Ace Karting
Walsall 5B **32**
Acfold Rd. B20: Hand 2A **82**
Acheson Rd. B28: Hall G 5F **149**
B90: Shir 5F **149**
Achilles Cl. WS6: Gt Wyr 4F **7**
Ackers, The (Activity Cen.) 5D **118**
Ackleton Gdns. WV3: Wolv 4D **42**
Ackleton Gro.
B29: W Cas 5D **130**
ACOCKS GREEN 2A **136**
Acocks Green Bowl 2H **135**
Acocks Green Station (Rail) 1A **136**
Acorn Cen. *WS1: Wals* 2D **48**
(off Ablewell St.)

Acorn Cl. B27: A Grn 6H **119**
  B30: B'ville 5A **132**
  B70: W Brom 4H **79**
  WS6: Gt Wyr 4G **7**
Acorn Ct. B45: Redn 2B **158**
Acorn Gdns. B30: Stir 5C **132**
Acorn Gro. B1: Birm 6D **100**
  DY8: Word 2C **108**
  WV8: Cod 5E **13**
Acorn Pk. B62: B'hth 3C **112**
Acorn Rd. B62: B'hth 3C **112**
  WV11: Wed 6A **18**
Acorn St. WV13: W'hall 1C **46**
Acre Ri. WV12: W'hall 4B **30**
Acres, The WV3: Wolv 2A **42**
Acres Rd. DY5: Quar B 3A **110**
Acton Dr. DY3: Lwr G 4F **75**
Acton Gro. B44: K'sdng 2A **68**
  WV14: Bils 1D **60**
Adam Ct. B63: Hale 1H **127**
Adams Brook Dr.
  B32: Bart G 4H **129**
Adams Cl. B66: Smeth 2B **98**
  DY4: Tip 4H **61**
Adams Hill B32: Bart G 4H **129**
Adams Rd. WS8: Bwnhls 2C **22**
  WV3: Wolv 4A **42**
Adams St. B7: Birm 4H **101**
  B70: W Brom 4H **79**
  WS2: Wals 1B **48**
Ada Rd. B9: Birm 1B **118**
  B25: Yard 5H **119**
  B66: Smeth 6F **99**
Ada Wrighton Cl. WV12: W'hall 2C **30**
Addenbrooke Ct. B64: Old H 3H **111**
Addenbrooke Dr. B73: W Grn 3H **69**
Addenbrooke Pl. WS10: Darl 4D **46**
Addenbrooke Rd. B67: Smeth 6D **98**
Addenbrooke St. WS3: Blox 2A **32**
  WS10: Darl 3D **46**
Addenbrook Way DY4: Tip 5D **62**
        (not continuous)
Adderley Gdns. B8: Salt 4D **102**
Adderley Pk. Cl. B8: Salt 5E **103**
Adderley Park Station (Rail) 6D **102**
Adderley Rd. B8: Salt 6C **102**
Adderley Rd. Sth. B8: Salt 6C **102**
Adderley St. B9: Birm 2A **118**
Adderley Trad. Est. B8: Salt 5C **102**
Addington Way B69: Tiv 5D **78**
Addison Cl. WS10: W'bry 3C **64**
Addison Cft. DY3: Lwr G 2E **75**
Addison Gro. WV11: Wed 6D **16**
Addison Pl. B46: Wat O 4D **88**
  WV14: Bils 4A **46**
Addison Rd. B7: Nech 1C **102**
  B14: King H 6G **133**
  DY5: Brie H 1F **109**
  WS10: W'bry 3C **64**
  WV3: Wolv 3D **42**
Addison St. WS10: W'bry 3F **63**
Addison Ter. WS10: W'bry 3F **63**
Adelaide Av. B70: W Brom 6G **63**
Adelaide St. B12: Birm 3H **117**
  DY5: Brie H 6H **93**
Adelaide Twr. B34: S End 4G **105**
       (off Packington Av.)
Adelaide Wlk. WV2: Wolv 3A **44**
Adelphi Ct. DY5: Brie H 1H **109**
       (off The Promenade)
Adey Rd. WV11: Wed 1H **29**
Adkins La. B67: Smeth 2D **114**
Admington Rd. B33: Sheld 3G **121**
Admiral Pl. B13: Mose 1H **133**
Admirals Way Rd5: Row R 1B **112**
Adrian Boult Hall 4C **4** (1F **117**)
Adrian Ct. B24: Erd 1H **85**
Adrian Cft. B13: Mose 4C **134**
Adria Rd. B11: S'hll 1B **134**
Adshead Rd. DY2: Dud 2E **95**
Adstone Gro. B31: N'fld 6D **144**
Advent Gdns. B70: W Brom 4H **79**
       (off Railway St.)
Adwalton Rd. WV6: Pert 6F **25**
Aethelred Cl. WV10: Oxl 3G **27**
Agenoria Dr. DY8: Stourb 6D **108**
Ainsdale Cl. DY8: Stourb 3D **124**

Ainsdale Gdns. B24: Erd 2A **86**
  B63: Hale 3F **127**
Ainsworth Rd. B31: N'fld 5H **145**
Aintree Cl. WV10: Bush 2A **16**
Aintree Gro. B34: S End 3A **106**
Aintree Rd. WV10: F'hses 3H **15**
Aintree Way DY1: Dud 4A **76**
Aire Cft. B31: N'fld 6F **145**
Airfield Dr. WS9: A'rdge 6A **34**
Air Ministry Ho's. B35: Cas V 5D **86**
AIRPORT CARGO 1C **138**
Airport Way B26: Birm A 1E **139**
Ajax Cl. WS6: Gt Wyr 4F **7**
Akrill Cl. B70: W Brom 2H **79**
Akrill Cott. Homes, The
  B70: W Brom 2H **79**
Alameda Gdns. WV6: Tett 3C **26**
Alamein Rd. WV13: W'hall 2G **45**
Alasdair Ho. B17: Harb 6F **115**
Albany Ct. B62: Quin 4G **113**
       (off Binswood Rd.)
Albany Cres. WV14: Bils 5E **45**
Albany Gdns. B91: Sol 3A **152**
Albany Gro. DY6: K'wfrd 2C **92**
  WV11: Ess 6C **18**
Albany Ho. B34: S End 2F **105**
Albemarle Rd. DY8: Stourb 3D **124**
Albermarle Rd. DY6: K'wfrd 4E **93**
Albert Av. B12: Bal H 5A **118**
Albert Clarke Dr. WV12: W'hall 2C **30**
Albert Cl. WV8: Cod 3E **13**
Albert Dr. B63: Hale 3H **127**
  DY3: Swind 5E **73**
Albert Ho. WS10: Darl 5C **46**
      (off Wolverhampton St.)
Albert Rd. B6: Aston 1G **101**
  B14: King H 6G **133**
  B17: Harb 6F **115**
  B21: Hand 6A **82**
  B23: Erd 4D **84**
  B33: Stech 1B **120**
  B63: Hale 3H **127**
  B68: O'bry 3A **114**
  WV6: Wolv 6D **26**
Albert Rd. E. B69: O'bry 2H **97**
Albert St. B4: Birm 4F **5** (1G **117**)
  B5: Birm 3G **5** (6H **101**)
  B69: O'bry 1G **97**
  B70: W Brom 6A **80**
  DY4: Tip 5H **61**
  DY5: P'ntt 2H **93**
  DY6: W Hth 1H **91**
  DY8: Stourb 6D **108**
  DY9: Lye 6A **110**
  WS2: Wals 1C **48**
  WS10: W'bry 3F **63**
Albert St. E. B69: O'bry 2H **97**
Albert Wlk. B17: Harb 6G **115**
Albion Av. WV13: W'hall 1C **46**
Albion Bus. Pk. B66: Smeth 1C **98**
Albion Cl. B1: Birm 2A **4** (6E **101**)
Albion Fld. Dr. B71: W Brom 3B **80**
Albion Ho. B70: W Brom 5A **80**
Albion Ind. Est. B70: W Brom 5G **79**
Albion Ind. Est. Rd. B70: W Brom 5F **79**
Albion Pde. DY6: W Hth 1H **91**
Albion Rd. B11: S'brk 6D **118**
  B21: Hand 6H **81**
  B70: W Brom 5F **79**
       (not continuous)
  B71: W Brom 1F **99**
  WS8: Bwnhls 5A **10**
  WV13: W'hall 1B **46**
Albion Rdbt. B70: W Brom 3H **79**
Albion St. B1: Birm 2A **4** (6D **100**)
  B69: O'bry 6E **79**
  DY4: Tip 2H **77**
  DY5: Brie H 6H **93**
  DY6: W Hth 6H **73**
  WV1: Wolv 3D **170** (1A **44**)
  WV13: W'hall 1B **46**
  WV14: Bils 5G **45**
Albion Ter. B46: Wat O 4D **88**
       (off St Pauls Ct.)
Albion Trad. Pk. B21: Hand 5F **81**
Alborn Cres. B38: King Nor 1H **159**

Albright Ho. B69: O'bry 5E **97**
       (off Kempsey Cl.)
Albrighton Ho. B20: Hand 4B **82**
  WV4: Lwr P 3A **58**
Albrighton Rd. B63: Hale 2G **127**
  WV7: Alb 5A **12**
Albright Rd. B68: O'bry 5B **98**
Albright Way B11: S'brk 4A **118**
Albutts Rd. WS8: Bwnhls 2F **9**
  WS11: Bwnhls 2F **9**
Alcester Dr. B73: New O 2D **68**
  WV13: W'hall 2F **45**
Alcester Gdns. B14: King H 6G **133**
ALCESTER LANES END 2G **147**
Alcester Pl. B14: King H 2H **147**
Alcester Rd. B13: Mose 3G **133**
  B47: H'wd 1A **162**
  B47: H'wd, Wyt 6H **161**
Alcester Rd. Sth. B14: King H 6G **133**
       (Addison Rd.)
  B14: King H 5H **147**
       (Maypole La.)
Alcester St. B12: Birm 6H **5** (3H **117**)
Alcombe Gro. B33: Stech 1C **120**
Alcott Cl. B93: Dorr 6G **167**
Alcott Gro. B33: Kitts G 6H **105**
Alcott La. B37: Mars G 3B **122**
Alcove, The WS3: Blox 5B **20**
Aldbourne Way B38: King Nor 2H **159**
Aldbury Rd. B14: King H 5A **148**
Aldeford Dr. DY5: Brie H 3H **109**
Aldeney Cl. DY1: Dud 4G **77**
Alderbrook Cl. DY3: Sed 4F **59**
Alderbrook Rd. B91: Sol 4D **150**
Alder Cl. B47: H'wd 3B **162**
  B76: Walm 6C **70**
Alder Coppice DY3: Sed 3G **59**
Alder Cres. WS5: Wals 1F **65**
Alder Dale WV3: Wolv 2C **42**
Alderdale Av. DY3: Sed 2G **59**
Alderdale Cres. B92: Sol 6A **138**
Alder Dr. B37: Chel W 2D **122**
Alderflat Pl. B7: Birm 4C **102**
Alderford Cl. WV8: Pend 1D **26**
Alder Gro. B62: Quin 5E **113**
Alderham Cl. B91: Sol 3H **151**
Alderhithe Gro. B74: Lit As 6B **36**
Alder La. B30: B'ville 1G **145**
  CV7: Bal C 4H **169**
Alderlea Cl. DY8: Stourb 3E **125**
Alderley Cres. WS3: Wals 4C **32**
Alderminster Rd. B91: Sol 6F **151**
Aldermoor Dr. B75: S Cold 5D **54**
Alderney Gdns. B38: King Nor 6H **145**
Alder Pk. Rd. B91: Sol 4D **150**
Alderpits Rd. B34: S End 2H **105**
       (not continuous)
Alder Rd. B12: Bal H 1A **134**
  DY6: K'wfrd 4D **92**
  WS10: W'bry 5G **47**
Alders, The B62: Roms 3A **142**
Aldersea Dr. B6: Aston 2H **101**
Aldershaw Rd. B26: Yard 6C **120**
Aldershaws B90: Dic H 4G **163**
Aldersley Av. WV6: Tett 2C **26**
Aldersley Cl. WV6: Tett 2D **26**
Aldersley Leisure Village 3D **26**
Aldersley Rd. WV6: Tett 4C **26**
Aldersley Stadium 3D **26**
Aldersmead Rd. B31: N'fld 5G **145**
Alderson Rd. B8: Salt 5F **103**
Alderton Cl. B91: Sol 6F **151**
Alderton Dr. WV3: Wolv 3C **42**
Alder Way B74: S'tly 3G **51**
Alderwood Pl. B91: Sol 4F **151**
Alderwood Pct. DY3: Sed 4C **59**
Alderwood Ri. DY3: Up Gor 2H **75**
Aldgate Dr. DY5: Brie H 4G **109**
Aldgate Gro. B19: Birm 4F **101**
Aldis Cl. B28: Hall G 4E **135**
  WS2: Wals 4G **47**
Aldis Rd. WS2: Wals 4G **47**
ALDRIDGE 3D **34**
Aldridge By-Pass WS9: A'rdge 4D **34**
Aldridge Cl. B68: O'bry 5A **98**
  DY8: Word 3C **108**

Aldridge Rd. B42: P Barr 4G 83
B44: Gt Barr, P Barr 3E 67
B68: O'bry 3H 113
B74: Lit As 4H 35
B74: S'tly 2F 51
WS4: Wals 6G 33
WS9: A'rdge 4H 35
Aldridge Sailing Club 1A 34
Aldridge St. WS10: Darl 4D 46
Aldridge Youth Theatre 3D 34
Aldwych Cl. WS9: A'rdge 1D 34
Aldwyck Dr. WV3: Wolv 3G 41
Aldwyn Av. B13: Mose 3H 133
Alexander Gdns. B42: P Barr 4F 83
Alexander Hill DY5: Quar B 3B 110
Alexander Ind. Pk. WV14: Bils 1E 61
Alexander Rd. B27: A Grn 1H 135
B67: Smeth 1C 114
WS2: Wals 1F 47
WV8: Bilb 4A 14
Alexander Ter. B67: Smeth 3D 98
Alexander Way B8: Salt 6F 103
Alexandra Av. B21: Hand 2H 99
Alexandra Ct. B65: Row R 6F 97
DY3: Gorn 4G 75
(off Redhall Rd.)
Alexandra Cres. B71: W Brom 5C 64
Alexandra Ho. B27: A Grn 3B 136
Alexandra Ind. Est. DY4: Tip 2H 77
Alexandra Pl. DY1: Dud 3D 76
WV14: Bils 5F 45
Alexandra Rd. B5: Edg 5G 117
B21: Hand 2H 99
B30: Stir 6C 132
B63: Hale 2H 127
DY4: Tip 2H 77
WS1: Wals 4C 48
WS10: Darl 5E 47
WV4: Penn 6E 43
Alexandra St. DY1: Dud 6D 76
WV3: Wolv 2F 43
Alexandra Theatre 5D 4 (1F 117)
Alexandra Way B69: Tiv 5A 78
WS9: A'rdge 4D 34
Alford Cl. B45: Redn 2A 158
Alfreda Av. B47: H'wd 1H 161
Alfred Gunn Ho. B68: O'bry 5H 97
Alfred Knight Way B15: Birm 3E 117
Alfred Rd. B11: S'hll 6B 118
B21: Hand 1A 100
Alfred Squire Rd. WV11: Wed 4E 29
Alfred St. B6: Aston 1B 102
B12: Bal H 6B 118
B14: King H 6H 133
B66: Smeth 2G 99
WS3: Blox 6H 19
WS10: Darl 6C 46
Alfryth Ct. B15: Edg 6B 117
(off Lee Cres.)
Algernon Rd. B16: Edg 5H 99
Alice St. WV14: Bils 5F 45
Alice Wlk. WV14: Bils 6F 45
Alison Cl. DY4: Tip 3A 62
Alison Dr. B73: Stourb 3D 124
Alison Nicholas Golf Academy 5E 67
Alison Rd. B62: Hale 2F 129
Allan Cl. B66: Smeth 4F 99
DY8: Word 3D 108
All Angels Wlk. B68: O'bry 5H 97
Allbut St. B64: Crad H 2F 111
Allcock St. B9: Birm 1A 118
DY4: Tip 5C 62
Allcroft Rd. B11: Tys 3F 135
Allenby Cl. DY6: K'wfrd 4E 93
Allen Cl. B43: Gt Barr 6A 66
Allendale Gro. B43: Gt Barr 5A 66
Allendale Rd. B25: Yard 4H 119
B76: Walm 5C 70
Allen Dr. B70: W Brom 6D 80
WS10: Darl 5C 46
Allen Ho. B43: Gt Barr 6A 66
Allen Rd. DY4: Tip 4H 61
WS10: W'bry 6F 47
WV6: Wolv 6D 26
Allens Av. B18: Hock 3B 100
B71: W Brom 6G 63
Allen's Cl. WV12: W'hall 4B 30

Allens Cft. Rd. B14: King H 2D 146
Allen's Farm Rd. B31: N'fld 4B 144
Allen's La. WS3: Pels 5D 20
Allen's Rd. B18: Hock 3B 100
Allen St. B70: W Brom 4H 79
Allerdale Rd. WS8: Clay 6A 10
Allerton Ct. B71: W Brom 4A 64
Allerton La. B71: W Brom 5A 64
Allerton Rd. B25: Yard 4H 119
Allesley Cl. B74: S Cold 5A 54
Allesley Rd. B92: Olton 5B 136
Allesley St. B6: Aston 4G 101
Alley, The DY3: Lwr G 4F 75
Alleyne Gro. B24: Erd 5G 85
Alleyne Rd. B24: Erd 6G 85
Allingham Gro. B43: Gt Barr 1G 67
Allington Cl. WS5: Wals 3H 49
Allison St. B5: Birm 5G 5 (1H 117)
Allman Rd. B24: Erd 3H 85
Allmyn Dr. B74: S'tly 5A 52
ALL SAINTS 4C 100
All Saints Dr. B74: Four O 1F 53
All Saints Ind. Est. B18: Hock 4C 100
All Saints Rd. B14: King H 1G 147
B18: Hock 4D 100
WS10: Darl 5E 47
WV2: Wolv 6C 170 (3H 43)
All Saints Sq. B34: S End 3G 105
All Saints St. B18: Hock 4C 100
All Saints Way B71: W Brom 3B 80
Allsops Cl. B65: Row R 5H 95
Allwell Dr. B14: King H 5H 147
Allwood Gdns. B32: Bart G 3G 129
Alma Av. DY4: Tip 6A 62
Alma Cres. B7: Birm 5B 102
Alma Ind. Est. WS10: Darl 5C 46
Alma Pas. B17: Harb 5H 115
Alma Pl. B12: Bal H 6B 118
DY2: Dud 6E 77
Almar Ct. WV8: Pend 6D 14
Alma St. B19: Hock 3G 101
B63: Crad 6E 111
B66: Smeth 3G 99
WS2: Wals 5B 32
WS10: Darl 5C 46
WS10: W'bry 2H 63
WV10: Wolv 6B 28
WV13: W'hall 1B 46
Alma Way B19: Loz 2F 101
Alma Works WS10: Darl 6D 46
Almond Av. WS2: Wals 5E 31
WS5: Wals 1E 65
Almond Cl. B29: W Cas 1E 145
WS3: Pels 5D 20
Almond Cft. B42: Gt Barr 1B 82
Almond Gro. WV6: Wolv 5G 27
Almond Rd. DY6: K'wfrd 1C 92
Alms Houses WS1: Wals 3B 48
WV4: Penn 2D 58
Almsbury Ct. B26: Sheld 1G 137
Alnwick Ho. B23: Erd 1F 85
Alnwick Rd. WS3: Blox 3H 19
Alperton Dr. DY9: W'cte 3A 126
Alpha Cl. B12: Bal H 5G 117
Alpha Twr. B1: Birm 5B 4 (1E 117)
Alpha Way WS6: Gt Wyr 5G 7
Alpine Dr. DY2: Neth 5D 94
Alpine Way WV3: Wolv 1A 42
Alport Cft. B9: Birm 1B 118
Alston Cl. B74: Four O 1G 53
B91: Sol 1H 151
Alston Gro. B9: Bord G 6H 103
Alston Ho. B69: O'bry 3D 96
Alston Rd. B9: Bord G 6H 103
B69: O'bry 2E 97
B91: Sol 1H 151
Alston St. B16: Birm 1C 116
Althorpe Dr. B93: Dorr 6H 165
Alton Av. WV12: W'hall 5B 30
Alton Cl. WV10: Bush 4A 16
Alton Gro. B71: W Brom 6C 64
DY2: Dud 6G 77
Alton Rd. B29: S Oak 2B 132
Alum Dr. B9: Bord G 6G 103
Alumhurst Av. B8: W End 5G 103

ALUM ROCK 6H 103
Alum Rock Rd. B8: Salt, W End 4D 102
Alumwell Cl. WS2: Wals 2H 47
Alumwell Rd. WS2: Wals 2H 47
Alvaston Cl. WS3: Blox 4A 20
Alvechurch Highway B60: L Ash . . .6C 156
Alvechurch Rd. B31: Longb 1F 159
B63: Hale 3H 127
Alverley Cl. DY6: W Hth 1H 91
Alverstoke Cl. WV9: Pend 5E 15
Alveston Gro. B9: Bord G 1H 119
B93: Know 2D 166
Alveston Rd. B47: H'wd 2A 162
Alvin Cl. B62: B'hth 2F 113
Alvington Cl. WV12: W'hall 5D 30
Alvis Wlk. B36: Cas B 6B 88
Alwen St. DY8: Word 1D 108
Alwin Rd. B65: Row R 1B 112
Alwold Ct. B29: W Cas 3D 130
Alwold Rd. B29: W Cas, S Oak 3D 130
Alwyn Cl. WS6: Gt Wyr 2F 7
Alwynn Wlk. B23: Erd 4B 84
Amal Way B6: Witt 4H 83
Amanda Av. WV4: Penn 1D 58
Amanda Dr. B26: Yard 2E 121
Amazon Lofts B1: Birm 6D 100
(off Tenby St.)
Ambassador Rd. B26: Birm A 1E 139
Ambell Cl. B65: Row R 4H 95
Amber Cl. B15: Edg 4F 117
(off Stone Rd.)
B23: Erd 6F 69
Amber Dr. B69: O'bry 4G 97
Ambergate Cl. WS3: Blox 4A 20
Ambergate Dr. DY6: W Hth 1A 92
Amberley Ct. B29: S Oak 5A 132
Amberley Grn. B43: Gt Barr 1A 82
Amberley Gro. B6: Witt 4A 84
Amberley Rd. B92: Olton 1D 136
Amberley Way B74: S'tly 2G 51
Amber Way B62: Hale 5B 112
Amberwood Cl. WS2: Wals 6D 30
Amble Cl. B74: S'tly 4G 51
AMBLECOTE 4D 108
Amblecote Av. B44: Gt Barr 3G 67
Amblecote Rd. DY5: Brie H 4G 109
Ambleside B32: Bart G 4A 130
Ambleside Dr. DY5: Brie H 3G 109
Ambleside Gro. WV12: W'hall 6B 18
Ambleside Way DY6: K'wfrd 3B 92
Ambrose Cl. WV13: W'hall 1G 45
Ambrose Cres. DY6: K'wfrd 1B 92
Ambury Way B43: Gt Barr 5H 65
AMC Cinema 2C 116
Amelas Cl. DY5: Brie H 2E 109
Amersham Cl. B32: Quin 6C 114
Amesbury Rd. B13: Mose 2G 133
Ames Rd. WS10: Darl 4C 46
Amethyst Ct. B15: Edg 4F 117
(off Stone Rd.)
B92: Olton 4D 136
Amherst Av. B20: Hand 4C 82
Amington Cl. B75: R'ley 5B 38
Amington Rd. B25: Yard 5H 119
B90: Shir 1G 163
Amiss Gdns. B10: Small H 3C 118
Amity Cl. B66: Smeth 4F 99
Amos Av. WV11: Wed 2D 28
Amos La. WV11: Wed 2E 28
Amos M. B73: Bold 4G 69
Amos Rd. DY9: W'cte 3B 126
Amphion Ct. DY4: Tip 1B 78
Amphlett Cft. DY4: Tip 3B 78
Amphletts Cl. DY2: Neth 6G 95
Ampleforth Dr. WV13: W'hall 3B 46
Ampton Rd. B15: Edg 4D 116
Amptronic Ind. Est. WV5: Wom 3D 72
Amroth Cl. B45: Redn 2H 157
Amwell Gro. B14: King H 4H 147
Anchorage Rd. B23: Erd 4D 84
B74: S Cold 5H 53
Anchor Brook Ind. Pk. WS9: A'rdge . .2B 34
Anchor Cl. B16: Edg 2A 116
Anchor Cres. B18: Win G 4B 100
Anchor Dr. DY4: Tip 4A 78
Anchor Hill DY5: Brie H 2G 109

Anchor La. B91: Sol 1H 151
  WV14: Cose 3D 60
Anchor Mdw. WS9: A'rdge 3C 34
Anchor Pde. WS9: A'rdge 3D 34
Anchor Rd. WS9: A'rdge 3D 34
  WV14: Cose 3E 61
Andersleigh Dr. WV14: Cose 5C 60
Anderson Cres. B43: Gt Barr 2A 66
Anderson Gdns. DY4: Tip 3A 78
Anderson Rd. B23: Erd 1E 85
  B66: Smeth 2E 115
  B67: Smeth 2E 115
  DY4: Tip 2A 78
Anders Sq. WV6: Pert 5E 25
Anderton Cl. B74: S Cold 4G 53
Anderton Ct. B13: Mose 3A 134
Anderton Pk. Rd. B13: Mose 2A 134
Anderton Rd. B11: S'brk 5B 118
Anderton St. B1: Birm 6D 100
Andover Cres. DY6: K'wfrd 5D 92
Andover St. B5: Birm 4H 5 (1H 117)
Andrew Cl. WV12: W'hall 3D 30
Andrew Ct. B44: Gt Barr 6G 67
  B76: Walm 2D 70
Andrew Dr. WV12: W'hall 3D 30
Andrew Gdns. B21: Hand 5A 82
Andrew Rd. B63: Hale 2A 128
  B71: W Brom 3D 64
  DY4: Tip 4A 62
Andrews Cl. DY5: Quar B 3A 110
Andrews Rd. WS9: Wals W 3D 22
Andyfreight Bus. Pk. DY9: Lye 6C 110
Anerley Gro. B44: Gt Barr 1H 67
Anerley Rd. B44: Gt Barr 1H 67
Angela Av. B65: Row R 5D 96
Angela Pl. WV14: Bils 5F 45
Angelica WS5: Wals 2E 65
Angelina St. B12: Birm 3H 117
Angel M. B46: Col 2H 107
Angel Pas. DY8: Stourb 6E 109
Angel St. DY1: Dud 1D 94
  WV13: W'hall 1A 46
Anglesey Av. B36: Cas B 2D 106
Anglesey Cl. WS7: Chase 1A 10
Anglesey Cres. WS8: Bwnhls 3B 10
Anglesey Rd. WS8: Bwnhls 3B 10
Anglesey St. B19: Loz 2E 101
Anglian Rd. WS9: A'rdge 3H 33
Anglo African Ind. Pk. B69: O'bry 5E 79
Angus Cl. B71: W Brom 1A 80
Anita Av. DY4: Tip 5A 78
Anita Cft. B23: Erd 5D 84
Ankadine Rd. DY8: Amb 5F 109
Ankerdine Ct. B63: Hale 2A 128
Ankermoor Cl. B34: S End 3F 105
Annan Av. WV10: Bush 2A 28
Ann Cft. B26: Sheld 1H 137
Anne Cl. B70: W Brom 4E 79
Anne Ct. B76: Walm 2E 71
Anne Gro. DY4: Tip 4B 62
Anne Rd. B66: Smeth 2G 99
  DY5: Quar B 2C 110
  WV4: Penn 5F 43
Annie Wood Way B19: Loz 2F 101
Ann Rd. B47: Wyt 6A 162
Annscroft B38: King Nor 5H 145
Ann St. WV13: W'hall 6B 30
Ansbro Cl. B18: Win G 4B 100
Ansculf Rd. DY5: Brie H 2F 109
Ansell Rd. B11: S'brk 5C 118
  B24: Erd 6F 85
Ansley Way B92: Sol 6H 137
Anslow Gdns. WV11: Wed 6H 17
Anslow Rd. B23: Erd 2C 84
Anson Cl. WS6: Gt Wyr 4F 7
  WV6: Pert 4E 25
Anson Ct. B70: W Brom 5H 79
Anson Gro. B27: A Grn 3B 136
Anson Rd. B70: W Brom 1E 79
  WS2: Wals 1E 47
  WS6: Gt Wyr 4F 7
Anstey Ct. B73: Bold 6G 69
Anstey Cft. B37: F'bri 5C 106
Anstey Gro. B27: A Grn 4H 135
Anstey Rd. B44: K'sdng 1G 83
Anston Junc. WS2: Wals 2E 47
Anston Way WV11: Wed 2F 29

Anstree Cl. WS6: C Hay 4D 6
Anstruther Rd. B15: Edg 4H 115
Ansty Ct. B18: Birm 1B 4 (5E 101)
Anthony Rd. B8: Salt 6E 103
Antler Way B16: Edg 6G 99
Anton Dr. B76: Walm 1E 87
Antony Rd. B90: Shir 6H 149
Antringham Gdns. B15: Edg 3H 115
Antrobus Rd. B21: Hand 6A 82
  B73: Bold 4E 69
Anvil Cres. WV14: Cose 3E 61
Anvil Dr. B69: O'bry 3E 97
Anvil Wlk. B70: W Brom 3F 79
Apex Bus. Pk. WS11: Nort C 1D 8
Apex Ind. Pk. DY4: Tip 5D 62
Apex Rd. WS8: Bwnhls 6G 9
Apley Rd. DY8: Woll 4C 108
Apollo Cft. B24: Erd 4B 86
Apollo Pk. B69: O'bry 2E 97
Apollo Rd. B68: O'bry 3A 98
  DY9: W'cte 6C 110
Apollo Way B20: Hand 6F 83
  B66: Smeth 4G 99
Apperley Way B63: Crad 4D 110
Appian Cl. B14: King H 2G 147
Appian Way B90: Ches G 5B 164
Appleby Cl. B14: King H 2F 147
Appleby Gdns. WV11: Ess 5C 18
Appleby Gro. B90: M'path 3F 165
Applecross B74: Four O 2F 53
Appledore Cl. WS6: Gt Wyr 2G 7
Appledore Ct. WS3: Blox 1H 31
Appledore Rd. WS5: Wals 3H 49
Appledore Ter. WS5: Wals 3H 49
Appledorne Gdns. B34: S End 3F 105
Applesham Cl. B11: S'brk 5D 118
Appleton Av. B43: Gt Barr 5H 65
  DY8: Stourb 3E 125
Appleton Cl. B30: B'ville 5A 132
Appleton Cres. WV4: Penn 6E 43
Apple Tree Cl. B23: Erd 3B 84
Appletree Cl. B31: Longb 6D 144
  B91: Cath B 2D 152
Appletree Gro. WS9: A'rdge 5D 34
  WV6: Wolv 4G 27
Applewood Gro. B64: Old H 3H 111
Appleyard Cl. WS2: Wals 6E 31
April Cft. B13: Mose 2B 134
Apse Cl. WV5: Wom 6F 57
Apsley Cl. B68: O'bry 4G 113
Apsley Cft. D30: King Nor 5D 146
Apsley Gro. B24: Erd 5G 85
  B93: Dorr 6G 167
Apsley Ho. B64: Old H 1H 111
Apsley Rd. B68: O'bry 4G 113
Aqua Cl. B65: Row R 1D 112
Aqueduct Rd. B90: Shir 5E 149
Aragon Dr. B73: S Cold 5G 53
Arbor Ct. B71: W Brom 1C 80
Arboretum Rd. WS1: Wals 1D 48
Arbor Ga. WS9: Wals W 3D 22
Arbor Way B37: Chel W 2E 123
Arbour, The B93: Know 5C 166
Arbour Dr. WV14: Bils 1H 61
Arbourtree Cl. WV5: Wom 6H 57
Arbury Dr. DY8: Word 6B 92
Arbury Hall Rd. B90: Shir 1B 164
Arbury Wlk. B76: Min 2H 87
Arcade B31: N'fld 3E 145
Arcade, The DY3: Up Gor 2A 76
  WS1: Wals 2C 48
Arcadia B70: W Brom 4A 80
  (off W. Bromwich Ringway)
Arcadian Shop. Cen.
  B5: Birm 6E 5 (2G 117)
Arcal St. DY3: Sed 6A 60
Arch, The R9: Birm 1A 118
Archer Cl. B68: O'bry 4H 97
  WS10: W'bry 2E 63
Archer Ct. DY9: W'cte 3A 126
Archer Gdns. B64: Crad H 2E 111
Archer Rd. B14: Yard W 3C 148
  WS3: Blox 3C 32
Archers Cl. B23: Erd 5D 68
Archer Way B65: B'hth 2D 112
Archery Rd. CV7: Mer 4H 141
Arches, The B10: Small H 3B 118

Arch Hill St. DY2: Neth 4E 95
Archibald Rd. B19: Loz 1E 101
Archway, The WS4: Wals 6D 32
Arcot Rd. B28: Hall G 3F 135
Ardath Rd. B38: King Nor 5C 146
Ardav Rd. B70: W Brom 5F 63
Ardedale B90: Shir 1A 164
Arden Bldgs. B93: Dorr 6B 166
Arden Bus. Pk. B45: Fran 6G 143
Arden Cl. CV7: Bal C 2H 169
  CV7: Mer 4H 141
  DY8: Woll 4C 108
  DY8: Word 6A 92
Ardencote Rd. B13: Mose 6A 134
Arden Ct. B24: Erd 4H 85
  B42: P Barr 3F 83
  B92: H Ard 6A 140
  DY3: Lwr G 4H 75
  (off Chiltern Cl.)
Arden Cft. B46: Col 6H 89
  B92: Sol 1G 137
Arden Dr. B26: Yard 4D 120
  B73: W Grn 5H 69
  B75: S Cold 6F 55
  (not continuous)
  B93: Dorr 6G 167
Arden Gro. B16: Edg 2C 116
  B19: Loz 1E 101
  B69: O'bry 4G 97
Arden Ho. B92: H Ard 1B 154
Arden Ind. Est. B8: Hodg H 1H 103
Ardenlea Ct. B91: Sol 2G 151
Ardenleigh Way B24: Erd 5G 85
Arden Oak Rd. B26: Sheld 6H 121
Arden Pl. WV14: Bils 1B 62
Arden Rd. B6: Aston 1F 101
  B8: Salt 6C 102
  B27: A Grn 1H 135
  B45: Fran 6G 143
  B47: H'wd 3A 162
  B67: Smeth 5E 99
  B93: Dorr 6G 167
Arden Va. Rd. B93: Know 2D 166
Arderne Dr. B37: F'bri 2C 122
Ardgowan Gro. WV4: Pet 6B 44
Ardingley Wlk. DY5: Brie H 4F 109
Ardley Cl. DY2: Dud 1F 95
Ardley Rd. B14: King H 2A 148
Arena Ct. B1: Birm 3A 4
  (off Clement St.)
Arena Theatre 2B 170 (1G 43)
Arena Vw. B1: Birm 3A 4
  (off Clement St.)
Arena Wlk. B1: Birm 4A 4
Aretha Cl. DY6: K'wfrd 3E 93
Argil Cl. WV11: Wed 1F 29
Argus Cl. B76: Walm 2D 70
Argyle Cl. DY8: Word 2C 108
  WS4: Wals 6F 33
Argyle Rd. WS4: Wals 6F 33
  WV2: Wolv 5F 43
Argyle St. B7: Nech 1C 102
Argyll Cl. WV12: W'hall 6C 18
Argyll Ho. WV1: Wolv 5G 27
  (off Lomas St.)
Arkle Cft. B36: Hodg H 1A 104
  B65: Row R 3H 95
Arkley Gro. B28: Hall G 6H 135
Arkley Rd. B28: Hall G 6H 135
Arkwright Rd. B32: Quin 6A 114
  WS2: Wals 4H 31
Arlen Dr. B43: Gt Barr 4H 65
Arlescote Cl. B75: Four O 1A 54
Arlescote Rd. B92: Sol 3G 137
Arless Way B17: Harb 2E 131
Arleston Way B90: Shir 1C 164
Arley Cl. B69: O'bry 4D 96
Arley Ct. DY2: Neth 3E 95
Arley Dr. DY8: Stourb 2C 124
Arley Gro. WV4: Penn 6B 42
Arley Ho. B26: Yard 2E 121
Arley Rd. B8: Salt 4D 102
  B29: S Oak 2B 132
  B91: Sol 3E 151
Arley Vs. B18: Win G 5H 99
  (off Cape St.)
Arlidge Cl. WV14: Bils 1F 61

Arlington Cl.—Aspbury Cft.

Arlington Cl. DY6: K'wfrd .5B **92**
Arlington Ct. DY8: Stourb .1F **125**
Arlington Gro. B14: King H .5B **148**
Arlington Rd. B14: King H .5B **148**
B71: W Brom .1B **80**
Armada Cl. B23: Erd .6D **84**
Armoury Rd. B11: Small H .5D **118**
Armoury Trad. Est. B11: Small H .5D **118**
Armside Cl. WS3: Pels .3F **21**
Armstead Rd. WV9: Pend .4D **14**
Armstrong Cl. DY8: Amb .4F **109**
Armstrong Dr. B36: Cas B .6B **88**
WS2: Wals .5G **31**
WV6: Wolv .4E **27**
Armstrong Way WV13: W'hall .3B **46**
Arnhem Cl. WV11: Wed .1D **28**
Arnhem Rd. WV13: W'hall .3G **45**
Arnhem Way DY4: Tip .2C **78**
Arnold Cl. WS2: Wals .6F **31**
Arnold Gro. B30: King Nor .3H **145**
B90: Shir .3H **149**
Arnold Rd. B90: Shir .3H **149**
Arnside Ct. B23: Erd .3B **84**
Arnwood Cl. WS2: Wals .1F **47**
Arosa Dr. B17: Harb .2F **131**
Arps Rd. WV8: Cod .4F **13**
Arran Cl. B43: Gt Barr .2A **66**
Arran Rd. B34: Hodg H .3D **104**
Arran Way B36: Cas B .2C **106**
Arras Rd. DY2: Dud .5G **77**
Arrow Cl. B93: Know .3C **166**
Arrowfield Grn. B38: King Nor .2H **159**
Arrow Ind. Est. WV12: W'hall .3C **30**
Arrow Rd. WS3: Blox .3C **32**
Arrow Wlk. B38: King Nor .6D **146**
Arsenal St. B9: Bord G .2C **118**
Art Ct. WS2: Wals .1B **48**
Arter St. B12: Bal H .5H **117**
Arthur Greenwood Ct. WV14: Bils .5E **45**
Arthur Gunby Cl. B75: S Cold .4D **54**
Arthur Harris Cl. B66: Smeth .6G **99**
Arthur Pl. B1: Birm .3A **4** (6D **100**)
Arthur Rd. B15: Edg .5D **116**
B21: Hand .1B **100**
B24: Erd .3H **85**
B25: Yard .5H **119**
DY4: Tip .1A **78**
Arthur St. B10: Small H .2B **118**
B70: W Brom .6B **80**
WS2: Wals .4H **47**
WV2: Wolv .5H **43**
WV14: Bils .5F **45**
Arthur Terry Sports Centre, The .6G **37**
Artillery St. B9: Birm .1B **118**
Arton Cft. B24: Erd .5F **85**
Arundel Av. WS10: W'bry .2F **63**
Arundel Ct. *B29: W Cas .6G **131***
(off Abdon Av.)
Arundel Cres. B92: Olton .4E **137**
Arundel Dr. B69: Tiv .1A **96**
Arundel Gro. WV6: Pert .6F **25**
Arundel Ho. B23: Erd .1F **85**
Arundel Pl. B11: S'brk .5A **118**
Arundel Rd. B14: King H .6A **148**
DY8: Word .1A **108**
WV10: Oxl .5F **15**
WV12: W'hall .2C **30**
Arundel St. WS1: Wals .4C **48**
(not continuous)
Arun Way B76: Walm .4E **71**
Asbury Ct. B43: Gt Barr .5G **65**
Asbury Rd. CV7: Bal C .4H **169**
WS10: W'bry .3C **64**
Asbury Wlk. B43: Gt Barr .4G **65**
Ascot Cl. B16: Birm .1B **116**
B69: O'bry .3E **97**
Ascot Ct. B29: W Cas .6G **131**
Ascot Dr. DY1: Dud .5B **76**
WV4: Penn .1E **59**
Ascote La. B90: Dic H .4G **163**
Ascot Gdns. DY8: Word .1B **108**
Ascot Rd. B13: Mose .3H **133**
Ascot Wlk. B69: O'bry .3E **97**
Ash Av. B12: Bal H .6A **118**
Ashborough Dr. B91: Sol .2G **165**
Ashbourne Gro. B6: Aston .1G **101**
Ashbourne Ridge B63: Crad .6F **111**
Ashbourne Rd. B16: Edg .6H **99**
WS3: Blox .4A **20**
WV1: Wolv .6C **28**
WV4: Ett .2A **60**
Ashbourne Way B90: Shir .1C **164**
Ash Bri. Ct. B45: Redn .3H **157**
Ashbrook Cres. B91: Sol .1G **165**
Ashbrook Dr. B45: Redn .1H **157**
Ashbrook Gro. B30: Stir .5D **132**
Ashbrook Rd. B30: Stir .5E **133**
Ashburn Gro. WV13: W'hall .1C **46**
Ashburton Rd. B14: King H .2F **147**
Ashbury Covert
B30: King Nor .4E **147**
Ashby Cl. B8: W End .3A **104**
Ashby Ct. B91: Sol .6G **151**
Ash Cl. WV8: Bilb .4G **13**
Ashcombe Av. B20: Hand .4A **82**
Ashcombe Gdns. B24: Erd .4B **86**
Ashcott Cl. B38: King Nor .5H **145**
Ash Ct. B66: Smeth .1A **98**
CV7: Bal C .4H **169**
DY8: Stourb .1E **125**
Ash Cres. B37: K'hrst .3B **106**
DY6: K'wfrd .3C **92**
Ashcroft B15: Edg .6A **116**
B66: Smeth .4G **99**
DY4: Tip .5A **78**
Ashcroft Gro. B20: Hand .5F **83**
Ashdale Cl. DY6: K'wfrd .1B **92**
Ashdale Dr. B14: King H .6B **148**
Ashdale Gro. B26: Yard .3E **121**
Ashdene Cl. B73: S Cold .2G **69**
Ashdene Gdns. DY8: Word .1A **108**
Ashdown Cl. B13: Mose .4A **134**
B45: Fran .5G **143**
Ashdown Dr. DY8: Word .6C **92**
Ashdown Gro. WS2: Wals .5B **32**
Ash Dr. B11: S'hll .3B **134**
B31: Longb .6A **144**
B71: W Brom .1A **80**
Ashen Cl. DY3: Sed .2G **59**
Ashenden Ri. WV3: Wolv .2G **41**
Ashenhurst Rd. DY1: Dud .2A **94**
Ashenhurst Wlk. DY1: Dud .1C **94**
Ashes, The B5: Edg .6F **117**
Ashes Rd. B69: O'bry .5F **97**
Ashfern Dr. B76: Walm .6D **70**
Ashfield Av. B14: King H .4G **133**
Ashfield Cl. WS3: Wals .5D **32**
Ashfield Ct. B30: King Nor .3A **146**
Ashfield Cres. DY2: Neth .6E **95**
DY9: W'cte .2B **126**
Ashfield Gdns. B14: King H .4H **133**
Ashfield Gro. B63: Hale .3G **127**
WV10: F'hses .4G **15**
Ashfield Ho. B28: Hall G .4E **149**
Ashfield Rd. B14: King H .4H **133**
WV3: Wolv .1B **42**
WV10: F'hses .4G **15**
WV14: Bils .3A **62**
Ashford Cl. B24: Erd .3B **86**
Ashford Dr. B76: Walm .2D **86**
DY3: Sed .6A **60**
Ashford Ind. Est. WV2: Ett .4B **44**
Ashford Twr. B12: Birm .3A **118**
Ash Furlong Cl. CV7: Bal C .3H **169**
Ashfurlong Cres. B75: S Cold .4C **54**
Ash Grn. DY1: Dud .2C **76**
Ash Gro. B9: Birm .1B **118**
B12: Bal H .6B **118**
B31: N'fld .3E **145**
DY3: Gorn .5G **75**
DY9: W'cte .2H **125**
Ashgrove Ho. *B45: Rub .2E **157***
(off Callowbrook La.)
Ashgrove Rd. B44: Gt Barr .3E **67**
Ash Hill WV3: Wolv .2B **42**
Ashill Rd. B45: Redn .2H **157**
Ashland St. WV3: Wolv .2F **43**
Ash La. WS6: Gt Wyr .2G **7**
Ashlawn Cres. B91: Sol .2B **150**
Ashleigh Dr. B20: Hand .5D **82**
Ashleigh Gro. B13: Mose .4B **134**
Ashleigh Hgts. B91: Sol .2E **151**
Ashleigh Rd. B69: Tiv .1C **96**
B91: Sol .3F **151**
Ashley Cl. B15: Edg .4E **117**
DY6: K'wfrd .5A **92**
DY8: Stourb .3B **124**
Ashley Gdns. B8: Salt .5D **102**
WV8: Cod .3F **13**
Ashley Mt. WV6: Tett .4B **26**
Ashley Rd. B23: Erd .4E **85**
B66: Smeth .5G **99**
WS3: Blox .6F **19**
WV4: Penn .6C **42**
Ashley St. WV14: Bils .5G **45**
Ashley Ter. B29: S Oak .4A **132**
Ashley Way CV7: Bal C .2H **169**
Ashmall WS7: Hamm .1F **11**
Ashmead Dr. B45: Coft H .5A **158**
Ashmead Gro. B24: Erd .5G **85**
Ashmead Ri. B45: Coft H .5A **158**
Ash M. B27: A Grn .6A **120**
Ashmole Rd. B70: W Brom .6F **63**
ASHMOOR LAKE .5B **30**
Ashmore Av. WV11: Wed .1A **30**
Ashmore Ind. Est. WS2: Wals .6C **32**
Ashmore Ind. Pk. B70: W Brom .2F **79**
Ashmore Lake Ind. Est.
WV12: W'hall .5B **30**
Ashmore Lake Rd. WV12: W'hall .5B **30**
Ashmore Lake Way WV12: W'hall .5B **30**
ASHMORE PARK .1H **29**
Ashmore Rd. B30: King Nor .2B **146**
Ashmores Ind. Est. DY1: Dud .4G **77**
Ashold Farm Rd. B24: Erd .5B **86**
Asholme Cl. B36: Hodg H .2A **104**
Ashorne Cl. B28: Hall G .6H **135**
Ashover Gro. *B18: Win G .5A **100***
(off Dudley Rd.)
Ashover Rd. B44: Gt Barr .2F **67**
Ash Rd. B8: Salt .5D **102**
DY1: Dud .4D **76**
DY4: Tip .3G **77**
WS10: W'bry .6F **47**
Ash St. B64: Old H .1H **111**
WS3: Blox .6B **20**
WV3: Wolv .2E **43**
WV14: Bils .2G **61**
Ashtead Cl. B76: Walm .1F **87**
Ashted Cir. B7: Birm .1H **5** (5A **102**)
Ashted Lock B7: Birm .1H **5** (5H **101**)
Ashted Row B7: Birm .5A **102**
Ashted Wlk. B7: Birm .5B **102**
Ash Ter. B69: Tiv .6B **78**
Ashton Cft. B16: Birm .1C **116**
B91: Sol .6E **151**
Ashton Dr. WS4: S'fld .4G **21**
Ashton Pk. Dr. DY5: Brie H .2G **109**
Ashton Rd. B25: Yard .4H **119**
Ashtree Cl. DY5: Brie H .3E **109**
Ash Tree Dr. B26: Yard .4B **120**
Ashtree Dr. DY8: Stourb .2E **125**
Ashtree Gro. WV14: Bils .2B **62**
Ash Tree Rd. B30: Stir .1C **146**
Ashtree Rd. B64: Old H .1H **111**
B69: Tiv .6C **78**
WS3: Pels .4E **21**
Ashurst Rd. B76: Walm .1D **86**
Ashville Av. B34: Hodg H .2D **104**
Ashville Dr. B63: Hale .6A **112**
Ash Wlk. B76: Walm .3D **70**
Ashwater Dr. B14: King H .5F **147**
Ash Way B23: Erd .5C **68**
Ashway B11: S'hll .6B **118**
Ashwell Dr. B90: Shir .3B **150**
Ashwells Gro. WV9: Pend .5E **15**
Ashwin Rd. B21: Hand .2B **100**
ASHWOOD .4E **91**
Ashwood Av. DY8: Word .1A **108**
Ashwood Cl. B69: O'bry .5F **97**
B74: S'tly .3G **51**
Ashwood Ct. B13: Mose .2A **134**
B34: Hodg H .4B **104**
Ashwood Dr. B37: Chel W .6F **107**
Ashwood Gro. WV4: Penn .6E **43**
Ashwood Lwr. La. DY6: K'wfrd .4E **91**
DY7: Stourt .4E **91**
Ashworth Rd. B42: Gt Barr .4D **66**
Askew Bri. Rd. DY3: Gorn .4F **75**
Askew Cl. DY3: Up Gor .2A **76**
Aspbury Cft. B36: Cas B .6H **87**

Aspen Cl. B27: A Grn 3H 135
  B76: Walm 3D 70
Aspen Dr. B37: Chel W 3E 123
Aspen Gdns. B20: Hand 6D 82
Aspen Gro. B9: Bord G 6G 103
  B47: Wyt 4B 162
  WV12: W'hall 2E 31
Aspen Ho. B71: W Brom 5E 65
  B91: Sol 5D 150
Aspen Way WV3: Wolv 2E 43
Asphodel B74: Four O 4F 37
    (off Badgers Bank Rd.)
Asquith Dr. B69: Tiv 5C 78
Asquith Rd. B8: W End 4H 103
Asra Cl. B66: Smeth 1E 99
Asra Ho. B66: Smeth 1E 99
    (off Oxford Rd.)
Astbury Av. B67: Smeth 6D 98
Astbury Cl. WS3: Blox 3G 19
  WV1: Wolv 2C 44
Astbury Ct. B68: O'bry 4H 113
Aster Wlk. WV9: Pend 4E 15
Aster Way WS5: Wals 2E 65
Astle Dr. B69: O'bry 6E 79
Astle Pk. B70: W Brom 4A 80
Astley Av. B62: Quin 5F 113
Astley Cl. DY4: Tip 1D 78
Astley Cres. B62: Quin 6F 113
Astley Rd. B21: Hand 6H 81
Astley Wlk. B90: Shir 2H 149
ASTON 2H 101
Aston Bri. B6: Aston 4H 101
Aston Brook Grn. B6: Aston 4H 101
Aston Brook St. B6: Aston 3H 101
Aston Brook St. E. B6: Aston 4H 101
Aston Bury B15: Edg 4H 115
Aston Chu. Rd. B7: Nech 2C 102
  B8: Salt 2C 102
Aston Chu. Trad. Est.
  B7: Nech 3D 102
Aston Cl. WV14: Bils 1B 62
Aston Ct. B23: Erd 5C 84
  B71: W Brom 4B 64
Aston Cross Bus. Pk. B6: Aston 3A 102
Aston Events Cen. 1A 102
Aston Expressway B6: Aston 4H 101
Aston Hall 1H 101
Aston Hall Rd. B6: Aston 1A 102
    (not continuous)
Aston La. B6: Aston 5F 83
  B20: Hand 5F 83
Aston Mnr. Cl. B20: Hand 5G 83
Aston Rd. B6: Aston, Birm 4H 101
  B69: Tiv 6A 78
  DY2: Dud 1D 94
  WV13: W'hall 1G 45
Aston Rd. Nth. B6: Aston 3H 101
Aston Science Pk. B7: Birm ...1H 5 (5H 101)
Aston's Cl. DY5: Brie H 4H 109
Aston Seedbed Cen. B7: Nech 3A 102
Aston's Fold DY5: Brie H 4H 109
Aston Station (Rail) 1B 102
  DY4: Tip 6C 62
  WV3: Wolv 3E 43
Aston Students Guild B4: Birm 1G 5
Aston Triangle, The
  B4: Birm 2G 5 (6H 101)
Aston University
  Aston St. 1G 5 (5H 101)
  Coleshill St. 2G 5 (6H 101)
  Engineering Academy 5H 101
Aston Villa FC 6H 83
Aston Wood Golf Course 3E 37
Astor Dr. B13: Mose 4C 134
Astoria Cl. WV12: W'hall 6D 18
Astoria Gdns. WV12: W'hall 6D 18
Astor Rd. B74: S'tly 2A 52
  DY6: K'wfrd 4D 92
Athelney Ct. WS3: Pels 4E 21
Athelstan Gro. WV6: Pert 4F 25
Atherstone Cl. B90: Shir 5E 149
Atherstone Rd. WV1: Wolv 1D 44
Athlone Rd. WS5: Wals 3G 49
    (not continuous)
Athol Cl. B32: Bart G 5B 130
Athole St. B12: Birm 4A 118

Atlantic Ct. WV13: W'hall 2A 46
    (off Cheapside)
Atlantic Rd. B44: Gt Barr 5H 67
Atlantic Way WS10: W'bry 4E 63
Atlas Cft. WV10: Oxl 3G 27
Atlas Est. B6: Witt 5A 84
  B11: Tys 6G 119
Atlas Gro. B70: W Brom 4F 79
Atlas Trad. Est. WV14: Bils 3H 61
Atlas Way B1: Birm 5A 4
Attenborough Cl. B19: Hock 4F 101
Attingham Dr. B43: Gt Barr 3H 65
  DY1: Dud 5D 76
Attleboro La. B46: Wat O 5C 88
Attlee Cl. B69: Tiv 5D 78
Attlee Cres. WV14: Bils 3G 61
Attlee Rd. WS2: Wals 5E 31
Attwell Pk. WV3: Wolv 4B 42
Attwell Rd. DY4: Tip 4H 61
Attwood Cl. B8: Salt 3E 103
Attwood Gdns. WV4: Ett 6A 44
Attwood St. B63: Hale 6H 111
  DY9: Lye 6B 110
Aubrey Rd. B10: Small H 3F 119
  B32: Harb 4C 114
Auchinleck Ho. B15: Birm 2D 116
    (within Five Ways Shop. Cen.)
Auchinleck Sq. B15: Birm 2D 116
    (within Five Ways Shop. Cen.)
Auckland Dr. B36: Cas B 1B 106
Auckland Ho. B32: Quin 1D 130
Auckland Rd. B11: S'brk 4A 118
  B67: Smeth 3C 98
  DY6: K'wfrd 5C 92
  DY8: K'wfrd 5C 92
Audleigh Ho. B15: Birm 3E 117
    (off Bell Barn Rd.)
Audlem Wlk. WV10: Wolv 4C 28
Audnam DY8: Word 2D 108
AUDNAM 2D 108
Augusta Rd. B13: Mose 1G 133
  B27: A Grn 6A 120
Augusta Rd. E. B13: Mose 1H 133
Augusta St. B18: Birm 1A 4 (5E 101)
Augustine Gro. B18: Hock 3B 100
  B74: Four O 4F 37
Augustus Cl. B46: Col 6H 89
Augustus Ct. B15: Edg 3B 116
Augustus Rd. B15: Edg 3H 115
Augustus Way WS2: Wals 2B 48
Aulton Rd. B75: R'ley 6C 38
Ault St. B70: W Brom 6B 80
Austcliff Dr. B91: Sol 1G 165
Austen Pl. B15: Edg 3D 116
Austen Wlk. B71: W Brom 2B 80
Austin Cl. B27: A Grn 1B 136
  B31: N'fld 5E 145
  DY1: Dud 5B 76
Austin Ct. B1: Birm 4A 4 (1D 116)
Austin Cft. B36: Cas B 6A 88
Austin Ho. WS4: Wals 6D 32
Austin La. B19: Hock 3G 101
    (off Alma St.)
Austin Ri. B31: Longb 2D 158
Austin Rd. B21: Hand 6G 81
Austin St. B35: Cas V 3F 87
  WV6: Wolv 5F 27
AUSTIN VILLAGE 6D 144
Austin Way B42: P Barr 2C 82
Austrey Cl. B93: Know 3C 166
Austrey Gro. B29: W Cas 5E 131
Austrey Rd. DY6: K'wfrd 4E 93
Austy Cl. B36: Hodg H 1C 104
Autherley Junc. WV9: Pend 1E 27
Autobase Ind. Est. B69: Tiv 4C 78
Automotive Components Pk.
  WS10: W'bry 2C 62
Autumn Berry Gro. DY3: Sed 1A 76
Autumn Cl. WS4: S'fld 6G 21
Autumn Dr. DY3: Lwr G 3H 75
  WS4: S'fld 5F 21
Autumn Gro. B19: Hock 3E 101
Autumn Ho. B37: K'hrst 4D 106
Avalon Cl. B24: Erd 3H 85
Avebury Gro. B30: Stir 6E 133

Avebury Rd. B30: Stir 5E 133
Ave Maria Cl. B64: Old H 2G 111
Avenbury Dr. B91: Sol 3A 152
Avenue, The B27: A Grn 1A 136
  B45: Rub 2E 157
  B65: Row R 6A 96
  B76: Walm 4C 70
  WS10: Darl 4B 46
  WV3: Wolv 3H 41
  WV4: Penn 1C 58
  WV10: F'stne 1D 16
  WV10: Wolv 4B 28
Avenue Cl. B7: Nech 3A 102
  B93: Dorr 6C 166
Avenue Rd. B6: Aston 3H 101
  B7: Nech 3H 101
  B14: King H 5F 133
  B21: Hand 5H 81
  B23: Erd 3F 85
  B65: B'hth, Row R 2D 112
  B93: Dorr 6G 167
  DY2: Dud 3B 94
  WS10: Darl 5D 46
  WV3: Wolv 1C 42
  WV14: Cose 5E 61
Averill Rd. B26: Yard 2E 121
Avern Cl. DY4: Tip 1B 78
Aversley Rd. B38: King Nor 6H 145
Avery Cft. B35: Cas V 5D 86
Avery Dell Ind. Est.
  B30: King Nor 2D 146
Avery Dr. B27: A Grn 1A 136
Avery Ho. B16: Edg 2C 116
Avery Myers Cl. B68: O'bry 4H 97
Avery Rd. B66: Smeth 3H 99
  B73: New O 3C 68
Aviary Cl. B71: W Brom 1A 80
Aviemore Cres. B43: Gt Barr 1D 66
Avington Cl. DY3: Sed 6H 59
Avion Cen. WV6: Wolv 5E 27
Avion Cl. WS1: Wals 4D 48
Avoca Cl. B12: Birm 3A 118
Avocet Cl. B33: Stech 6C 104
Avon Cl. B14: King H 6F 147
  DY5: P'ntt 2F 93
  WV6: Pert 6F 25
Avon Cl. B73: S Cold 6H 53
Avon Cres. WS3: Pels 6E 21
Avoncroft Ho. B37: Chel W 1C 122
Avon Dale B31: N'fld 6C 144
Avondale Cl. DY6: K'wfrd 1C 92
Avondale Ct. B11: S'hll 6C 144
Avondale Rd. B11: S'hll 1C 134
  WV6: Wolv 6D 26
Avon Dr. B13: Mose 3B 134
  B36: Cas B 2B 106
  WV13: W'hall 1C 46
Avon Gro. WS5: Wals 2E 65
Avon Ho. B15: Birm 3F 117
Avon M. DY8: Word 6H 91
Avon Rd. B63: Crad 6D 110
  B90: Shir 6B 150
  DY8: Stourb 2D 124
  WS3: Blox 6C 20
Avon St. B11: S'hll 6C 118
Avon Way B47: Wyt 6G 161
Avro Way B35: Cas V 5F 87
Awbridge Rd. DY2: Neth 6E 95
Awdry Ct. B38: King Nor 5B 146
Awefields Cres. B67: Smeth 5B 98
Awlmakers Gro. WS3: Blox 2A 32
Axcess 10 Bus. Pk.
  WS10: Wals 2E 47
Axletree Way WS10: W'bry 5G 47
Ayala Cft. B36: Hodg H 6C 86
Aylesbury Cres. B44: K'sdng 5A 68
Aylesford Dr. DY3: Sed 3G 59
  B74: Four O 4E 37
Aylesford Rd. B21: Hand 6H 81
Aylesmore Cl. B32: Bart G 4A 130
  B92: Olton 5C 136
Aynsley Ct. B90: Shir 5A 150
Ayre Rd. B24: Erd 3H 85
Ayres Cl. B34: S End 3A 106
Ayrshire Cl. B36: Hodg H 1B 104
Ayrton Cl. WV6: Pert 5G 25
Azalea Cl. WV8: Bilb 4H 13

Azalea Gro.—Bard St.

Azalea Gro. B9: Bord G 1F **119**
Aziz Isaac Cl. B68: O'bry 3H **97**

B

Babington Rd. B21: Hand 2A **100**
Bablake Cft. B92: Olton 4E **137**
Babors Fld. WV14: Cose 2C **60**
Babworth Cl. WV9: Pend 5E **15**
Baccabox La. B47: H'wd 2G **161**
Bacchus Rd. B18: Hock 3B **100**
B21: Hand 3B **100**
Bache St. B70: W Brom 6A **80**
Bach Mill Dr. B28: Hall G 4D **148**
Backhouse La. WV11: Wed 5E **29**
Back La. B64: Crad H 2D **110**
B90: Dic H 4G **163**
WS9: A'rdge 2H **35**
WS14: Foot 1E **37**
Back Rd. B30: King Nor 5B **146**
B38: King Nor 5B **146**
DY6: K'wfrd 2B **92**
Back to Backs ***6E 5***
(off Hurst St.)
BACONS END **5D 106**
Bacons End B37: K'hrst 4D **106**
Baddesley Rd. B92: Olton 3C **136**
Bader Rd. WS2: Wals 1F **47**
WV6: Pert 6E **25**
Bader Wlk. B35: Cas V 5D **86**
Badger Cl. B90: Ches G 5B **164**
Badger Ct. WV10: Wolv 5H **27**
Badger Dr. WV10: Wolv 5H **27**
Badgers Bank Rd. B74: Four O 4F **37**
Badgers Cl. WS3: Pels 2E **21**
Badgers Cft. B62: Hale 4B **112**
Badger St. DY3: Up Gor 2A **76**
DY9: Lye 5A **110**
Badgers Way B34: Stech 4E **105**
Badminton Cl. DY1: Dud 4B **76**
Badon Covert B14: King H 5F **147**
Badsey Cl. B31: N'fld 3G **145**
Badsey Rd. B69: O'bry 4D **96**
Baggeridge Cl. DY3: Sed 5E **59**
Baggeridge Country Pk. **1D 74**
Baggeridge Country Pk. Vis. Cen. **1D 74**
Baggott St. WV2: Wolv 4G **43**
Baginton Cl. B91: Sol 2F **151**
Baginton Rd. B35: Cas V 3E **87**
Bagley Ind. Pk. DY2: Neth 5F **95**
Bagley's Rd. DY5: Brie H 5G **109**
Bagley St. DY9: Lye 5G **109**
Bagnall Cl. B25: Yard 5B **120**
Bagnall Rd. WV14: Bils 6E **45**
Bagnall St. B70: W Brom 6D **62**
(Chimney Rd.)
B70: W Brom 5C **80**
(Jesson St.)
DY4: Tip 6D **62**
(Chimney Rd.)
DY4: Tip 4C **62**
(Seymour Rd.)
WS3: Blox 3A **32**
Bagnalls Wharf WS10: W'bry 4D **62**
Bagnall Wlk. DY5: Brie H 2H **109**
Bagnell Rd. B13: Mose 6H **133**
Bagot St. B4: Birm 5G **101**
Bagridge Cl. WV3: Wolv 3H **41**
Bagridge Rd. WV3: Wolv 3H **41**
Bagshawe Cft. B23: Erd 6D **68**
Bagshaw Rd. B33: Stech 6C **104**
Bague Wlk. DY5: Brie H 1G **109**
Bailey Rd. WV14: Bils 4D **44**
Baileys Ct. B65: Row R 6B **96**
Bailey St. B70: W Brom 3G **79**
WV10: Wolv 1A **44**
Bainbridge Rd. B66: Smeth 6G **99**
Baker Av. WV14: Cose 3B **60**
Baker Ct. *B74: Four O* *3H* ***53***
(off Lichfield Rd.)
Baker Ho. Gro. B43: Gt Barr 6H **65**
Baker Rd. WV14: Bils 2G **61**
Bakers Gdns. WV8: Cod 3E **13**
Bakers La. B73: S'tly 6A **52**
B74: S'tly 6H **51**
WS9: A'rdge 3D **34**
Baker St. B10: Small H 2D **118**
B11: S'hll 1C **134**
B21: Hand 1B **100**
B70: W Brom 4H **79**
DY4: Tip 3G **77**
(not continuous)
Bakers Way WV8: Cod 3E **13**
Bakewell Cl. WS3: Blox 4A **20**
Balaams Wood Dr. B31: Longb 6H **143**
Balaclava Rd. B14: King H 5G **133**
Balcaskie Cl. B15: Edg 4A **116**
Balden Rd. B32: Harb 4C **114**
Baldmoor Lake Rd. B23: Erd 6F **69**
Bald's La. DY9: Lye 6B **110**
Baldwin Cl. B69: Tiv 5D **78**
Baldwin Ho. B19: Hock 3G **101**
Baldwin Rd. B30: King Nor 5C **146**
Baldwins Ho. *DY5: Quar B* *3B* ***110***
(off Maughan St.)
Baldwins La. B28: Hall G 3E **149**
Baldwin St. B66: Smeth 3F **99**
WV14: Bils 1H **61**
Baldwin Way DY3: Swind 5E **73**
Balfour Ct. B74: Four O 6G **37**
WV6: Wolv *5D* ***26***
(off Balfour Cres.)
Balfour Cres. WV6: Wolv 5D **26**
Balfour Dr. B69: Tiv 5C **78**
Balfour Ho. B16: Edg 2B **116**
Balfour Rd. DY6: K'wfrd 1B **92**
Balfour St. B12: Bal H 5G **117**
Balham Gro. B44: K'sdng 3A **68**
Balholm B62: Hale 6D **112**
Balking Cl. WV14: Cose 2D **60**
Ballarat Wlk. DY8: Stourb 6D **108**
Ballard Cres. DY2: Neth 4F **95**
Ballard Rd. DY2: Neth 4F **95**
Ballard Wlk. B37: K'hrst 3C **106**
Ballfields DY4: Tip 2D **78**
Ball Ho. *WS3: Blox* *1H* ***31***
(off Somerfield Rd.)
Balliol Bus. Pk. WV9: Pend 4B **14**
Balliol Ho. B37: F'bri 1B **122**
Ball La. WV10: Cov H 1G **15**
Ballot St. B66: Smeth 4F **99**
BALLS HILL **5G 63**
Balls Hill WS1: Wals 1D **48**
Balls St. WS1: Wals 2D **48**
Balmain Cres. WV11: Wed 1D **28**
Balmoral Cl. B62: Hale 4B **112**
WS4: Rus 2H **33**
Balmoral Ct. B1: Birm 3A **4**
Balmoral Dr. WV5: Wom 4G **57**
WV12: W'hall 2B **30**
Balmoral Ho. *WV3: Wolv* *3F* ***43***
(off Pennant Ct.)
Balmoral Rd. B23: Erd 2F **85**
B32: Bart G 6G **129**
B36: Cas B 2B **106**
B74: Four O 4F **37**
DY8: Word 6A **92**
WV4: Penn 6E **43**
Balmoral Vw. DY1: Dud 5A **76**
Balmoral Way B14: Yard W 4C **148**
B65: Row R 5D **96**
WS2: Wals 5G **31**
BALSALL **4G 169**
BALSALL COMMON **3H 169**
BALSALL HEATH **6H 117**
Balsall Heath Rd. B5: Edg 4G **117**
B12: Bal H 4G **117**
BALSALL STREET **3F 169**
Balsall St. CV7: Bal C 4B **168**
Balsall St. E. CV7: Bal C 4G **169**
Baltimore Rd. B42: P Barr 1C **82**
Balvenie Way DY1: Dud 4B **76**
Bamber Cl. WV3: Wolv 3C **42**
Bamford Cl. WS3: Blox 4A **20**
Bamford Ho. WS3: Blox 4A **20**
Bamford Rd. WS3: Blox 4A **20**
WV3: Wolv 3E **43**
Bampfylde Pl. B42: Gt Barr 6E **67**
Bamville Rd. B8: W End 4G **103**
Banbery Dr. WV5: Wom 3F **73**
Banbrook Cl. B92: Sol 5H **137**
Banbury Cl. DY3: Sed 1A **76**
Banbury Cft. B37: F'bri 1B **122**
Banbury Ho. B33: Kitts G 1A **122**
Banbury St. B5: Birm 4H **5** (1H **117**)
Bancroft Cl. WV14: Cose 6D **60**
Bandywood Cres. B44: Gt Barr 2H **67**
Bandywood Rd. B44: Gt Barr 1G **67**
Banfield Av. WS10: Darl 4C **46**
Banfield Rd. WS10: Darl 1C **62**
Banford Av. B8: W End 5G **103**
Banford Rd. B8: W End 5G **103**
Bangham Pit Rd. B31: N'fld 1C **144**
Bangley La. B78: Hints 3H **39**
Bangor Ho. B37: F'bri 5D **106**
Bangor Rd. B9: Bord G 1D **118**
Bankdale Rd. B8: W End 5H **103**
Bankes Rd. B10: Small H 2E **119**
Bank Farm Cl. DY9: Pedm 4G **125**
Bankfield Rd. DY4: Tip 5C **62**
WV14: Bils 6F **45**
(not continuous)
Banklands Rd. DY2: Dud 3G **95**
Bank Rd. DY2: Neth 3F **95**
DY3: Gorn 4G **75**
(not continuous)
Bankside B13: Mose 3D **134**
B43: Gt Barr 6A **66**
WV5: Wom 6F **57**
Bankside Cres. B74: S'tly 4H **51**
Bankside Way WS9: A'rdge 5D **22**
Banks's Stadium **5B 48**
Banks St. WV13: W'hall 1A **46**
Bank St. B14: King H 5G **133**
B71: W Brom 1A **80**
DY5: Brie H 5H **93**
DY9: Lye 6B **110**
WS1: Wals 2D **48**
WV10: Wolv 4A **28**
WV14: Bils 2G **61**
WV14: Cose 5D **60**
Bankwell St. DY5: Brie H 5G **93**
Bannatyne's Health Club
Birmingham, Brunswick Arc. ***1D 116***
(off Brunswick St.)
Birmingham, The Priory Queensway
3F 5 (6G 101)
Solihull **2G 165**
Sutton Coldfield **3D 68**
Banner La. B92: Bars 6B **154**
Bannerlea Rd. B37: K'hrst 4B **106**
Bannerley Rd. B33: Sheld 2G **121**
Banners Ct. B73: S'tly 2B **68**
BANNERS GATE **1B 68**
Banners Ga. Rd. B73: S'tly 2B **68**
Banners Gro. B23: Erd 1G **85**
Banner's La. B63: Crad 5F **111**
Banner's St. B63: Crad 5F **111**
Banners Wlk. B44: K'sdng 3B **68**
Bannington Ct. WV12: W'hall 5D **30**
Bannister Rd. WS10: W'bry 3D **62**
Bannister St. B64: Crad H 2F **111**
Banstead Cl. WV2: Wolv 4A **44**
Bantams Cl. B33: Kitts G 1G **121**
Bantock Av. WV3: Wolv 3D **42**
Bantock Ct. WV3: Wolv 3C **42**
Bantock Gdns. WV3: Wolv 2C **42**
Bantock House Mus. **3D 42**
Bantocks, The B70: W Brom 1G **79**
Bantock Way B17: Harb 6H **115**
Banton Cl. B23: Erd 5D **68**
Bantry Cl. B26: Sheld 1G **137**
BAPTIST END **3E 95**
Baptist End Rd. DY2: Dud, Neth 4E **95**
Barbara Rd. B28: Hall G 3E **149**
Barbel Dr. WV10: Wolv 5C **28**
Barber Institute of Fine Arts **1C 132**
Barberry Ho. B38: King Nor 6B **146**
Barbers La. B92: Cath B 1E **153**
Barbourne Cl. B91: Sol 2F **165**
Barbrook Dr. DY5: Brie H 4F **109**
Barcheston Rd. B29: W Cas 4E **131**
B93: Know 4C **166**
Barclay Ct. WV3: Wolv 1E **43**
Barclay Rd. B67: Smeth 2C **114**
Barcroft WV13: W'hall 6B **30**
Bardenholme Gdns. DY9: W'cte 2H **125**
Bardfield Cl. B42: Gt Barr 5B **66**
Bardon Dr. B90: Shir 5A **150**
Bard St. B11: S'hll 6C **118**

178 A-Z Birmingham

Bardwell Cl. WV8: Pend 1D 26
Barford Cl. B76: Walm 1D 70
WS10: Darl 3C 46
Barford Cres. B38: King Nor 5E 147
Barford Ho. B5: Birm 4G 117
Barford Rd. B16: Birm 5A 100
B90: Shir 5B 150
Barford St. B5: Birm 3G 117
Bargate Dr. WV6: Wolv 5E 27
Bargehouse Wlk. B38: King Nor 2A 160
Bargery Rd. WV11: Wed 6A 18
Barham Cl. B90: M'path 4E 165
Barker Rd. B74: S Cold 4H 53
Barker St. B19: Loz 2D 100
B68: O'bry .3A 98
Bark Piece B32: Bart G 2A 130
Barlands Cft. B34: S End 3F 105
Barle Gro. B36: Cas B 2B 106
Barley Cl. DY3: Sed 6B 60
WS9: A'rdge 1G 51
WV8: Pend .6C 14
Barleycorn Dr. B16: Edg 5H 99
Barley Cft. WV6: Pert 6D 24
Barleyfield Ho. WS1: Wals 3C 48
(off Bath St.)
Barleyfield Ri. DY6: W Hth 1G 91
Barleyfield Row WS1: Wals 3C 48
Barley Rd. B16: Edg 6G 99
Barlow Cl. B45: Fran 5E 143
B68: O'bry .6G 97
Barlow Dr. B70: W Brom 6D 80
Barlow Rd. WS10: W'bry 6G 47
Barlow's Rd. B15: Edg 6H 115
Barmouth Cl. WV12: W'hall 3C 30
Barnabas Rd. B23: Erd 3F 85
Barnaby Sq. WV10: Bush 3B 16
Barnard Cl. B37: Chel W 2F 123
B45: Redn .1G 157
Barnardo's Cen. B7: Birm 4A 102
Barnard Pl. WV2: Wolv 5A 44
Barnard Rd. B75: S Cold 4C 54
WV11: Wed .6H 17
Barn Av. DY3: Sed 6G 59
Barnbrook Rd. B93: Know 2C 166
Barn Cl. B30: Stir 1D 146
B63: Hale 3G 127
B64: Crad H 5G 111
DY9: Lye 1G 125
Barn Cft. B32: Bart G 4C 130
Barncroft WS6: Gt Wyr 2G 7
WS7: Chase 1C 10
Barncroft Rd. B69: Tiv 1A 96
Barncroft St. B70: W Brom 5G 63
Barnes Hill B29: W Cas 3D 130
Barnesmeadow Pl. WV14: Cose 5D 60
Barnet Rd. B23: Erd 2D 84
Barnett Cl. DY6: K'wfrd 5B 92
WV14: Bils .1F 61
Barnett Grn. DY6: K'wfrd 5B 92
Barnett La. DY6: K'wfrd 4B 92
DY8: Word .4B 92
Barnett Rd. WV13: W'hall 2G 45
Barnetts La. WS8: Bwnhls 5B 10
Barnett St. B69: Tiv 5A 78
DY4: Tip 3A 78
DY8: Word .6B 92
Barney Cl. DY4: Tip 4H 77
Barn Farm Cl. WV14: Bils 4A 46
Barnfield Dr. B92: Sol 1A 152
Barnfield Gro. B20: Hand 2A 82
Barnfield Rd. B62: B'hth 4D 112
DY4: Tip 6G 61
WV1: Wolv .1C 44
Barnfield Trad. Est. DY4: Tip 6G 61
Barnford Cl. B10: Small H 2C 118
Barnford Cres. B68: O'bry 6H 97
Barntordhill Cl. B68: O'bry 5H 97
Barn Grn. WV3: Wolv 4D 42
BARN HILL 4C 162
Barn Ho. B8: W End 5B 104
Barnhurst La. WV8: Bilb, Pend 4B 14
Barn La. B13: Mose 6A 134
B21: Hand .2A 100
B92: Olton .1C 136
WV7: Alb 5A 12

Barn Mdw. B25: Yard 2B 120
Barn Mdw. Cl. B31: Longb 5A 144
Barnmoor Ri. B91: Sol 6G 137
Barn Owl Dr. WS3: Pels 3D 20
Barn Owl Wlk. DY5: Brie H 5G 109
Barnpark Covert B14: King H 5E 147
Barn Piece B32: Quin 1H 129
Barnsbury Av. B72: W Grn 1A 86
Barns Cl. WS9: Wals W 3B 22
Barns Cft. B74: Lit As 5B 36
Barnsdale Cres. B31: N'fld 3C 144
Barns La. WS4: A'rdge 2H 33
WS4: Rus 2G 33
WS9: A'rdge 2H 33
Barnsley Rd. B17: Edg 2E 115
Barn St. B5: Birm 5H 5 (1H 117)
Barnswood Cl. B63: Crad 6E 111
Barnt Grn. Rd. B45: Coft H 5A 158
Barnt Green Sailing Club 6D 158
Barnwood Rd. B32: Quin 1D 130
WV8: Pend .6C 14
Barons Cl. B17: Harb 5E 115
Barons Ct. B92: Sol 1G 137
DY9: Lye 6A 110
Barons Ct. Trad. Est. WS9: Wals W . .5A 22
Barrack Cl. B75: S Cold 5E 55
Barrack La. B63: Crad 5D 110
Barracks Cl. WS3: Blox 1C 32
Barracks La. WS3: Blox 1B 32
WS8: Bwnhls 4E 11
WS9: Bwnhls 4E 11
Barracks Pl. WS3: Blox 1C 32
Barrack St. B7: Birm 5A 102
B70: W Brom 5G 63
Barra Cft. B35: Cas V 3F 87
Barrar Cl. DY8: Amb 3C 108
Barratts Cft. DY5: P'ntt 6G 75
Barratts Ho. B14: King H 5G 147
Barratts Rd. B38: King Nor 6C 146
BARR COMMON 6D 34
Barr Comn. Cl. WS9: A'rdge 6D 34
Barr Comn. Rd. WS9: A'rdge 6D 34
Barretts La. CV7: Bal C 6H 169
Barrett St. B66: Smeth 5G 99
Barrhill Cl. B43: Gt Barr 3A 66
Barrington Cl. WS5: Wals 2E 65
WV10: Oxl 6G 15
Barrington Rd. B45: Rub 2E 157
B92: Olton .3C 136
Barr Lakes La. WS9: A'rdge 4A 50
Barron Rd. B31: N'fld 4F 145
Barrow Cl. WS9: Bwnhls 3B 22
Barrow Hill Local Nature Reserve . .1G 93
Barrow Hill Rd. DY5: P'ntt 6G 75
Barrow Ho. B16: Edg 2B 116
(off Meyrick Wlk.)
Barrows La. B26: Sheld, Yard 3H 121
(not continuous)
Barrows Rd. B11: S'brk 5C 118
Barrow Wlk. B5: Birm 4G 117
(not continuous)
Barrs Cres. B64: Crad H 3H 111
Barrs Rd. B64: Crad H 4G 111
Barrs St. B68: O'bry 5G 97
Barr St. B18: Birm 4E 101
B19: Birm, Hock 4E 101
(not continuous)
DY3: Lwr G .4G 75
Barry Jackson Twr. B6: Aston 2H 101
Barry Rd. WS5: Wals 4G 49
Barsham Cl. B5: Edg 5E 117
Barston Cl. DY5: Brie H 3G 109
BARSTON 6A 154
Barston La. B91: Sol 5D 152
(not continuous)
B92: Bars, H Ard 4H 153
CV7: Bal C .6D 154
Barston Rd. B68: O'bry 4H 113
Bartholomew Row B5: Birm . .3G 5 (6H 101)
Bartic Av. DY6: K'wfrd 5D 92
Bartleet Rd. B67: Smeth 4B 98
Bartlett Cl. DY4: Tip 4B 62
Bartley Cl. B92: Olton 3D 136
Bartley Cres. B31: N'fld 2B 144
Bartley Dr. B31: N'fld 5C 130
BARTLEY GREEN 4B 130

Bartley Green Leisure Cen. 4A 130
Bartley Ho. B32: Bart G 5B 130
Bartley M. B31: N'fld 5C 130
Bartley Sailing Club 5A 130
Bartley Woods B32: Bart G 3H 129
Barton Cft. B28: Hall G 3F 149
Barton Dr. B93: Know 6D 166
Barton Ind. Est. WV14: Bils 4G 45
Barton La. DY6: W Hth 1A 92
Barton Lodge Rd. B28: Hall G 3E 149
Barton Pas. B3: Birm 4C 4
Barton Rd. WV4: Ett 1B 60
Bartons Bank B6: Aston 2G 101
Barton St. B70: W Brom 5H 79
Bar Wlk. WS9: A'rdge 6E 23
Barwell Cl. B93: Dorr 5A 166
Barwell Ct. B9: Birm 1B 118
Barwell Rd. B9: Birm 1B 118
Barwick St. B3: Birm 3D 4 (6F 101)
Basalt Cl. WS2: Wals 5G 31
Basil Gro. B31: N'fld 3C 144
Basil Rd. B31: N'fld 3C 144
Baslow Cl. B33: Stech 5C 104
WS3: Blox 4H 19
Baslow Rd. WS3: Blox 4H 19
Bason's La. B68: O'bry 4A 98
Bassano Rd. B65: B'hth 2C 112
Bassenthwaite Ct. DY6: K'wfrd 3B 92
Bassett Cl. B76: Walm 1C 70
WV4: Penn .5A 42
WV12: W'hall 5D 30
Bassett Cres. B71: W Brom 1C 80
Bassett Rd. B63: Crad 5C 110
WS10: W'bry 2A 64
(not continuous)
Bassetts Gro. B37: K'hrst 4B 106
BASSETT'S POLE 1F 55
Bassett St. WS2: Wals 2H 47
Bassnage Rd. B63: Hale 3G 127
Batchcroft WS10: Darl 3D 46
WV14: Bils 6F 45
Batchelor Cl. DY8: Amb 3D 108
Bateman Dr. B73: W Grn 3H 69
Bateman Rd. B46: Col 6H 89
BATEMAN'S GREEN 3G 161
Batemans La. B47: H'wd, Wyt 4G 161
Bates Cl. B76: Walm 6F 71
Bates Gro. WV10: Wolv 4C 28
Bate St. WS2: Wals 6C 32
WV4: Ett 2C 60
Bath Av. WV1: Wolv 2A 170 (1F 43)
Bath Ct. B15: Birm 2E 117
B29: W Cas .6F 131
Batheaston Cl. B38: King Nor 2H 159
Bath Mdw. B63: Crad 6G 111
Bath M. DY8: Stourb 6D 108
Bath Pas. B5: Birm 6E 5 (2G 117)
Bath Rd. DY4: Tip 2A 78
DY5: Quar B 1C 110
DY8: Stourb 6D 108
WS1: Wals .3C 48
WV1: Wolv 1F 43
Bath Row B15: Birm 2E 117
B69: O'bry .1D 96
Bath St. B4: Birm 1E 5 (5G 101)
DY2: Dud 1E 95
DY3: Sed 4A 60
WS1: Wals .2C 48
WV1: Wolv .2A 44
WV13: W'hall 2B 46
WV14: Bils 6G 45
Bath Wlk. B12: Bal H 6G 117
WV14: Bils 3G 61
Batmanshill Rd. DY4: Tip 3G 61
Batman Cl. B63: Crad 5F 111
Batson Ri. DY5: Brie H 3E 109
Battenhall Rd. B17: Harb 6E 115
Battery Retail Pk. B29: S Oak 3A 132
Battery Way B11: Tys 1E 135
Battlefield Hill WV5: Wom 6A 58
Battlefield La. WV5: Wom 1H 73
Baughan Ho. B24: Erd 4E 86
Bavaro Gdns. DY5: Quar B 1C 110
Baverstock Rd. B14: King H 5G 147
Baxterley Grn. B76: Walm 4D 70
B91: Sol 3B 150

Baxter Rd. DY5: Brie H 1G 109
Baxters Grn. B90: Shir 1G 163
Baxters Rd. B90: Shir 1H 163
Bay Av. WV14: Bils 1H 61
Bayer St. WV14: Cose 5E 61
Bayford Av. B26: Sheld 1G 137
   B31: Longb 3C 158
Bayley Cres. WS10: Darl 3C 46
Bayley Ho. WS8: Bwnhls 1B 22
Bayleys La. DY4: Tip 5C 62
Bayley Twr. B36: Hodg H 1C 104
Baylie Ct. DY8: Stourb 6D 108
   (off Green St.)
Baylie St. DY8: Stourb 1D 124
Baylis Av. WV11: Wed 1H 29
Bayliss Av. WV4: Ett 2C 60
Bayliss Cl. B31: N'fld 2F 145
   WV14: Bils .4E 45
Baynton Rd. WV12: W'hall 2C 30
Bayston Av. WV3: Wolv 3C 42
Bayston Rd. B14: King H 3G 147
Bayswater Rd. B20: Hand 6F 83
   DY3: Lwr G .4H 75
Bay Tree La. B38: King Nor 1H 159
Baytree Cl. WS3: Blox 5G 19
Baytree Rd. WS3: Blox 5G 19
Baywell Cl. B90: M'path 2E 165
BBC Birmingham Public Open Space . . .5B 4
Beach Av. B12: Bal H 6B 118
   WV14: Cose .2B 60
Beach Brook Cl. B11: S'hll 6B 118
Beachburn Way B20: Hand 4C 82
Beach Cl. B31: N'fld 6G 145
Beachcroft Rd. DY6: W Hth 6A 74
Beach Dr. B63: Hale 6A 112
Beach Rd. B11: S'hll 6B 118
   WV14: Bils .4F 45
Beach St. B63: Hale 6A 112
Beach Trade Cen. B12: Bal H 6B 118
Beachwood Av. DY6: W Hth 6A 74
Beacon Cl. B43: Gt Barr 4B 66
   B45: Rub 3G 157
   B66: Smeth .2E 99
Beacon Ct. B43: Gt Barr 4B 66
   B74: S'tly 3H 51
   WV4: Sed 2H 59
Beacon Dr. WS1: Wals 3E 49
Beacon Hgts. WS9: A'rdge 5D 50
Beacon Hill B6: Aston 1G 101
   B45: Rub 4F 157
   WS9: A'rdge .2E 51
Beacon Ho. B45: Rub 2E 157
   (off Callowbrook La.)
Beacon La. B45: Lick 6D 156
   B60: L Ash .6D 156
   DY3: Sed 4A 60
Beacon M. B43: Gt Barr 4B 66
Beacon Pas. DY3: Sed 5H 59
   (off High St.)
Beacon Ri. DY3: Sed 4A 60
   DY9: W'cte .1H 125
   WS9: A'rdge .6D 34
Beacon Rd. B43: A'rdge, Gt Barr 3D 50
   B44: K'sdng .1A 68
   B73: Bold 4G 69
   WS5: Wals 6H 49
   WS9: A'rdge .3D 50
   WV12: W'hall 1C 30
Beaconsfield Av. WV4: Ett 5H 43
Beaconsfield Ct. WS1: Wals 3F 49
Beaconsfield Cres. B12: Bal H 6G 117
Beaconsfield Dr. WV4: Ett 5H 43
Beaconsfield Rd. B12: Bal H 1G 133
   B74: S Cold .4H 53
Beaconsfield St. B71: W Brom 2A 80
Beacon St. WS1: Wals 2E 49
   WV14: Cose .4B 60
Beacon Trad. Est. WS9: A'rdge 3C 34
Beacon Vw. B45: Rub 3F 157
   WS2: Wals 1F 47
   (not continuous)
Beacon Vw. Dr. B74: S'tly 6H 51
Beaconview Ho. B71: W Brom 4D 64
Beacon Vw. Rd. B71: W Brom 3C 64
Beacon Way B43: Gt Barr 4F 65
   WS9: Wals W 4C 22
Beakes Rd. B67: Smeth 6D 98

Beaks Farm Gdns. B16: Edg 1H 115
Beaks Hill Rd. B38: King Nor 6A 146
Beak St. B1: Birm 5D 4 (1F 117)
Beale Cl. B35: Cas V 5E 87
Beale Ho. B16: Edg 2B 116
Beales St. B6: Aston 1B 102
Beale St. DY8: Stourb 6D 108
Bealeys Av. WV11: Wed 1E 29
Bealeys Cl. WS3: Blox 4G 19
Bealeys Fold WV11: Wed 4F 29
   (off Aldred Squire Rd.)
Bealeys La. WS3: Blox 4G 19
Beamans Cl. B92: Olton 1E 137
Beaminster Rd. B91: Sol 3E 151
Beamish La. WV8: Cod W 2A 12
Bean Cft. B32: Bart G 2A 130
Bean Dr. DY4: Tip 1F 77
Bean Rd. DY2: Dud 1F 95
   DY4: Tip 1E 77
Bean Rd. Ind. Est. DY4: Tip 1E 77
Beard Cl. WS10: Darl 3D 46
Beardmore Rd. B72: W Grn 5A 70
Bearing Dr. WV11: Wed 5G 29
Bearley Cft. B90: Shir 1A 164
Bearmore Rd. B64: Old H 2G 111
Bearnett Dr. WV4: Penn 3A 58
Bearnett La. WV4: Lwr P 4H 57
   WV5: Wom 4H 57
BEARWOOD 2E 115
Bearwood Ho. B66: Smeth 5E 99
Bearwood Rd. B66: Smeth 2E 115
Bearwood Shop. Cen. B66: Smeth . . .2E 115
Beasley Gro. B43: Gt Barr 4D 66
Beaton Cl. WV13: W'hall 1G 45
Beaton Rd. B74: Four O 6G 37
Beatrice St. WS3: Blox 3A 32
Beatrice Wlk. B69: Tiv 5A 78
Beatty Ho. DY4: Tip 5A 62
Beaubrook Gdns. DY8: Word 6C 92
Beauchamp Av. B20: Hand 2B 82
Beauchamp Cl. B76: Walm 6F 71
Beauchamp Rd. B13: Mose 2B 148
   B91: Sol 2F 151
Beaudesert Cl. B47: H'wd 3A 162
Beaudesert Rd. B20: Hand 1D 100
   B47: H'wd 3A 162
Beaufort Av. B34: Hodg H 3B 104
Beaufort Pk. B36: Hodg H 4B 104
Beaufort Rd. B16: Edg 2B 116
   B23: Erd 5E 85
Beaufort Way WS9: A'rdge 5D 34
Beaulieu Av. DY6: K'wfrd 5D 92
Beaumaris Cl. DY1: Dud 4B 76
Beaumont Cl. DY4: Tip 1G 77
   WS6: Gt Wyr .3F 7
Beaumont Dr. B17: Harb 1F 131
   DY5: Brie H .4F 109
Beaumont Gdns. B18: Hock 3B 100
Beaumont Gro. B91: Sol 2D 150
Beaumont Pk. B30: King Nor 3B 146
Beaumont Rd. B30: B'ville 1A 146
   B62: B'hth 3E 113
   WS6: Gt Wyr .3F 7
   WS10: W'bry 1F 63
Beaumont Way WS11: Nort C 1E 9
Beausale Dr. B93: Know 2D 166
Beauty Bank B64: Crad H 3A 112
Beauty Bank Cres. DY8: Stourb 5C 108
Beaver Cl. WV11: Wed 4H 29
Beavons Cl. B46: Wat O 4E 89
Bebington Cl. WV8: Pend 1D 26
Beccles Dr. WV13: W'hall 3H 45
Beck, The DY2: Neth 1G 111
Beckbury Av. WV4: Penn 6A 42
Beckbury Rd. B29: W Cas 4E 131
Beck Cl. B66: Smeth 5E 99
Beckenham Av. B44: K'sdng 4A 68
Beckensall Cl. DY1: Dud 6D 76
Becket Cl. B74: Four O 3F 37
Beckett St. WV14: Bils 5G 45
Beckfield Cl. B14: King H 5G 147
   WS4: S'fld 1G 33
Beckford Cft. B93: Dorr 6B 166
Beckman Rd. DY9: Pedm 3G 125
Beckminster Rd. WV3: Wolv 4D 42
Beconsfield Cl. B93: Dorr 6G 167
Becton Gro. B42: Gt Barr 6F 67

Bedcote Pl. DY8: Stourb 6F 109
Beddoe Cl. DY4: Tip 2D 78
Beddow Av. WV14: Cose 6E 61
Beddows Rd. WS3: Wals 4C 32
Bedford Dr. B75: S Cold 5C 54
Bedford Ho. B36: Cas B 3D 106
   WV1: Wolv 5G 27
   (off Lomas St.)
Bedford Rd. B11: S'brk 2A 118
   B71: W Brom 6H 63
   B75: S Cold .5C 54
Bedford St. DY4: Tip 2B 78
   WV1: Wolv 4D 44
Bedford Ter. B19: Loz 1F 101
Bedlam Wood Rd. B31: Longb 6A 144
Bedworth Cft. DY4: Tip 3B 78
Bedworth Gro. B9: Bord G 1H 119
Beebee Rd. WS10: W'bry 5F 47
Beecham Bus. Pk. WS9: A'rdge 1C 34
Beecham Cl. WS9: A'rdge 1C 34
Beech Av. B12: Bal H 6A 118
   B32: Quin 4B 114
   B37: Chel W .2D 122
   B62: B'hth 3C 112
Beech Cl. B75: Four O 5G 37
   DY3: Sed 4A 60
   WV10: Oxl 1F 27
Beech Ct. B8: Salt 4E 103
   B30: King Nor 3A 146
   B43: Gt Barr .4H 65
   B45: Redn 2B 158
   B66: Smeth .1A 98
   B73: Bold 5F 69
   B91: Sol 2H 151
   DY8: Stourb .1F 125
   WS1: Wals 3E 49
   WS6: Gt Wyr .1F 7
Beech Cres. DY4: Tip 5C 62
   WS10: W'bry 6F 47
Beechcroft B15: Edg 4C 116
Beechcroft Av. B28: Hall G 1G 149
Beechcroft Ct. B74: Four O 2G 53
Beechcroft Cres. B74: S'tly 2F 51
Beechcroft Est. B63: Crad 5E 111
Beechcroft Pl. WV10: Oxl 2G 27
Beechcroft Rd. B36: Cas B 1F 105
   B64: Old H .2G 111
Beechdale B68: O'bry 4H 113
Beechdale Av. B44: Gt Barr 3G 67
Beech Dene Gro. B23: Erd 2E 85
Beecher Pl. B63: Crad 6F 111
Beecher Rd. B63: Crad 6F 111
Beecher Rd. E. B63: Crad 6F 111
Beecher St. B63: Crad 6E 111
Beeches, The B15: Edg 3E 117
   B31: Longb .5A 144
   B70: W Brom 5C 80
   B74: Four O .5D 36
   WV1: Wolv 6E 27
   WV5: Seis 3A 56
Beeches Av. B27: A Grn 1A 136
Beeches Cl. B45: Rub 2D 156
   DY6: K'wfrd .4B 92
Beeches Ct. B45: Redn 2H 157
Beeches Dr. B24: Erd 2A 86
Beeches Farm Dr. B31: Longb 2E 159
Beeches Pl. WS3: Blox 2B 32
Beeches Pool & Fitness Cen. 6D 66
Beeches Rd. B42: Gt Barr 6D 66
   (not continuous)
   B65: B'hth 2B 112
   B68: O'bry 6A 98
   B70: W Brom 4C 80
   (not continuous)
   WS3: Blox 3B 32
Beeches Rd. Pas. B70: W Brom 5C 80
Beeches Vw. Av. B63: Crad 1E 127
Beeches Wlk. B73: S Cold 2H 69
Beeches Way B31: Longb 2E 159
Beechey Cl. B43: Gt Barr 6F 51
Beech Farm Cft. B31: N'fld 4E 145
Beechfield Av. B11: S'brk 5B 118
Beechfield Cl. B62: B'hth 3C 112
Beechfield Gro. WV14: Cose 6D 60
Beechfield Rd. B11: S'brk 5B 118
   B67: Smeth .5D 98
Beech Gdns. WV8: Cod 5F 13

Beech Gate B74: Lit As 4B 36
Beechglade B20: Hand 3B 82
Beech Grn. DY1: Dud 2C 76
Beech Gro. B14: King H 2A 148
Beech Hill Ho. B32: Bart G 5A 130
Beech Hill Rd. B72: W Grn 6A 70
Beech Ho. B31: N'fld 4F 145
(off Church Rd.)
B71: W Brom 5E 65
B91: Sol 5D 150
Beech Ho. La. WV5: Seis 5A 56
Beech Hurst B38: King Nor 1A 160
Beech Hurst Gdns. WV5: Seis 3A 56
BEECH LANES 4D 114
Beech M. B64: Old H 1G 111
Beechmore Rd. B26: Sheld 6D 120
Beechmount Dr. B23: Erd 1G 85
Beechnut Cl. B91: Sol 2H 151
Beechnut La. B91: Sol 3A 152
(not continuous)
Beech Pk. Rd. B31: Longb 5A 144
B45: Fran 5H 143
Beech Rd. B17: Harb 5E 115
B23: Erd 6F 69
B30: B'ville 6A 132
B47: H'wd 3B 162
B69: Tiv 1A 96
DY1: Dud 3E 77
DY6: K'wfrd 4C 92
DY8: Stourb 2C 124
WS10: W'bry 6F 47
WV10: Oxl 1F 27
WV13: W'hall 1G 45
Beech St. WV14: Cose 5E 61
Beech Tree Av. WV11: Wed 1E 29
Beech Tree Cl. DY6: K'wfrd 1C 92
Beechtree Rd. WS9: Wals W 5B 22
Beech Wlk. B38: King Nor 1B 160
Beech Way B66: Smeth 4F 99
Beechwood B20: Hand 4A 82
Beechwood Av. WV11: Wed 1D 28
Beechwood Cl. B90: Ches G 5B 164
WS3: Blox 4H 19
Beechwood Ct. B30: King Nor 4E 147
WV6: Tett 6A 26
Beechwood Cft. B74: Lit As 4D 36
Beechwood Dr. WV6: Tett 1G 41
Beechwood Pk. Rd. B91: Sol 1C 150
Beechwood Rd. B14: King H 2H 147
B43: Gt Barr 4B 66
B67: Smeth 3C 114
B70: W Brom 4H 79
DY2: Dud 6G 77
Beehive La. B76: Curd 1E 89
Beehive Wlk. DY4: Tip 2G 77
Bee La. WV10: F'hses 4H 15
Beeston Cl. B6: Aston 2A 102
DY5: Brie H 3H 109
Beeton Rd. B18: Win G 3A 100
Beet St. B65: B'hth 2C 112
Beever Rd. DY4: Tip 6D 62
Beggars Bush La. WV5: Wom 2H 73
Beighton Cl. B74: Four O 3F 37
Beilby Rd. B30: Stir 1D 146
Belbroughton Rd. B63: Hale 3H 127
DY8: Stourb 2C 124
Belcher's La. B8: W End 1G 119
B9: Bord G 1G 119
Beldray Pk. WV14: Bils 5G 45
Beldray Rd. WV14: Bils 5G 45
Belfont Trad. Est. B62: Hale 1C 128
Belfry, The WV6: Pert 5D 24
Belfry Cl. WS3: Blox 4G 19
Belfry Dr. DY8: Woll 5C 108
Belgrade Rd. WV10: Oxl 6F 15
Belgrave Ct. DY6: K'wfrd 5D 92
Belgrave Interchange B5: Birm 4F 117
Belgrave Middleway B5: Birm 4G 117
B12: Birm 4G 117
Belgrave Rd. B12: Bal H 5H 117
(off Balsall Heath Rd.)
B62: B'hth 3D 112
Belgrave Ter. B21: Hand 2C 100
Belgrave Wlk. WS2: Wals 6H 31
Belgravia Cl. B5: Edg 4G 117
Belgravia Cl. Walkway B5: Edg 4G 117
Belgrove Cl. B37: K'hrst 4C 106

Belgrove Cl. B15: Edg 5A 116
Belinda Cl. WV13: W'hall 6H 29
Bellamy Cl. B90: Shir 6B 150
Bellamy Farm Rd. B90: Shir 6B 150
Bellamy La. WV11: Wed 2E 29
Bella Pais Cl. WS9: A'rdge 4D 50
Bell Av. WV13: W'hall 1A 46
Bell Barn Rd. B15: Birm 3E 117
Bell Cl. B9: Bord G 6E 103
B36: Cas B 3D 106
WS10: Darl 4D 46
Bell Ct. B31: N'fld 2D 144
Bellcroft B16: Birm 1D 116
Bell Dr. B8: Salt 6F 103
WS5: Wals 6E 49
Bellefield Av. B18: Win G 5A 100
Bellefield Rd. B18: Win G 5A 100
Belle Isle DY5: Brie H 6G 93
Bellemere Rd. B92: H Ard 2B 154
Bellencroft Gdns. WV3: Wolv 4A 42
Bell End B65: Row R 6C 96
Belle Va. B63: Hale 6G 111
Belle Vue DY8: Word 1A 108
Bellevue B5: Edg 4F 117
WV14: Cose 3G 61
Bellevue Av. B16: Edg 5H 99
Belle Vue Dr. B62: Hale 5D 112
Belle Vue Gdns. B65: Row R 6C 96
Belle Vue Rd. B65: Row R 1C 112
DY5: Quar B 2C 110
Bellevue Rd. B26: Sheld 4F 121
WV14: Bils 3A 62
Bellevue St. WV14: Cose 3B 60
Belle Vue Ter. B92: H Ard 1A 154
Belle Wlk. B13: Mose 3B 134
Bellfield B31: N'fld 3D 144
Bellfield Ho. B14: King H 6F 147
(off Thornham Way)
Bellflower Dr. WS5: Wals 2D 64
Bell Fold B68: O'bry 3A 98
BELL GREEN 4D 160
Bell Grn. La. B38: Head H 4D 160
Bell Heather Rd. WS8: Clay 1H 21
Bell Hill B31: N'fld 2E 145
Bell Holloway B31: N'fld 2D 144
Bellington Cft. B90: M'path 3E 165
Bell Inn Shop. Cen., The B31: N'fld . .3E 145
Bellis St. B16: Edg 2B 116
Bell La. B31: N'fld 3E 145
(not continuous)
B33: Kitts G 2A 122
WS3: Blox 5G 19
WS5: Wals 1D 64
Bellman Cl. WS10: Darl 4D 46
Bell Mdw. DY9: Pedm 5F 125
Bell Mdw. Way B14: King H 5G 147
Bell Pl. WV2: Wolv 6B 170 (3G 43)
WS5: Wals 5H 49
WV5: Try 4C 56
Bell Rd. WV2: Neth 4E 95
WS5: Wals 5H 49
WV5: Try 4C 56
Bell St. Sth. DY5: Brie H 1H 109
Bell Tower Cl. WS3: Blox 1B 32
Bell Wlk. B33: Kitts G 2B 122
B37: F'bri 2B 122
Bell Wharf Pl. WS5: Wals 5G 49
Bellwood Rd. B31: N'fld 3D 144
Belmont Cl. DY4: Tip 1H 77
WS9: A'rdge 3C 34
WS11: Cann 1G 7

Belmont Covert B31: N'fld 2F 145
Belmont Cres. B31: N'fld 1F 145
Belmont Gdns. WV14: Bils 1A 62
Belmont Pas. B9: Birm 1A 118
Belmont Rd. B21: Hand 1G 99
B45: Rub 3G 157
B66: Smeth 1E 115
DY5: Brie H 3H 93
DY9: W'cte 6A 110
WV4: Penn 6E 43
Belmont Rd. E. B21: Hand 1G 99
Belmont Row B4: Birm 2H 5 (6A 102)
Belmont St. WV14: Bils 1A 62
Belper, The DY1: Dud 6D 76
Belper Ent. Pk. B70: W Brom 3F 79
Belper Rd. B70: W Brom 4F 79
WS3: Blox 4A 20
Belper Row DY2: Neth 5G 95
Belstone Cl. B14: King H 1F 147
Belton Av. WV11: Wed 6D 16
Belton Gro. B45: Redn 1A 158
Belvedere Av. WV4: Penn 6F 43
Belvedere Cl. DY6: K'wfrd 5D 92
WS7: Chase 1B 10
Belvedere Gdns. WV6: Tett 2C 26
Belvedere Rd. B24: Erd 5G 85
Belvide Gro. B29: W Cas 5F 131
Belvidere Gdns. B11: S'hll 1C 134
Belvidere Rd. WS1: Wals 3D 48
Belvoir Cl. DY1: Dud 5A 76
Belwell Dr. B74: Four O 1G 53
Belwell Gdns. B74: Four O 1G 53
Belwell Grange B74: Four O 1G 53
Belwell La. B74: Four O 1G 53
Belwell Pl. B74: Four O 1G 53
Bembridge Cl. WV12: W'hall 1B 30
Bembridge Rd. B33: Yard 6E 105
Benacre Dr. B5: Birm 4H 5 (1H 117)
Benbeck Gro. DY4: Tip 2E 77
Bencroft WV8: Bilb 3H 13
Bendall Rd. B44: K'sdng 3B 68
Benedon Rd. B26: Sheld 4E 121
Benmore Av. B5: Edg 5F 117
Bennett Av. DY1: Dud 1D 76
Bennett Rd. B74: Four O 6D 36
Bennett's Hill B2: Birm 4D 4 (1F 117)
DY2: Dud 1G 95
Bennett's La. WV6: Patt, Tres 3A 40
Bennett's Rd. B8: Salt 3D 102
Bennett St. B19: Loz 1F 101
Ben Nevis Way DY8: Amb 5E 109
Bennitt Cl. B70: W Brom 6A 80
Benson Av. WV4: Penn 6G 43
Benson Cl. WV6: Pert 4E 25
Benson Ind. Est. B18: Hock 3B 100
Benson Rd. B14: King H 6B 148
B18: Hock 3B 100
Bent Av. B32: Quin 5B 114
Bentham Ct. B31: N'fld 2D 144
BENTLEY 6F 31
Bentley Bridge Leisure Pk. 5D 28
Bentley Bri. Pk. WV11: Wed 5E 29
Bentley Bri. Way WV11: Wed 5D 28
Bentley Cl. B36: Cas B 6A 88
Bentley Ct. B76: Walm 5D 70
Bentley Dr. WS2: Wals 1H 47
WV8: Cod 3F 13
Bentley Farm Cl. B93: Ben H 5A 166
Bentley Gro. B29: W Cas 5D 130
BENTLEY HEATH 4B 166
Bentley Heath Cotts. B93: Know 4B 166
Bentley La. WS2: Wals 5G 31
WS2: Wals, W'hall 4D 30
WV12: W'hall 4D 30
Bentley La. Ind. Pk. WS2: Wals 6G 31
Bentley Mill Cl. WS2: Wals 2F 47
Bentley Mill La. WS2: Wals 2F 47
Bentley Mill Way WS2: Wals 2F 47
Bentley New Dr. WS2: Wals 6H 31
Bentley Pl. WS2: Wals 1H 47
Bentley Rd. B36: Cas B 2H 105
WV10: Bush 5A 16
Bentley Rd. Nth. WS2: Wals 2E 47
Bentley Rd. Sth. WS10: Darl 3D 46
Bentmead Gro. B38: King Nor 6C 146
Benton Av. B11: S'hll 5C 118

Benton Cl.—Birch Cl.

Benton Cl. WV12: W'hall 5D 30
Benton Cres. WS3: Blox 5B 20
Benton Rd. B11: S'brk 5C 118
Bentons La. WS6: Gt Wyr 4G 7
Bentons Mill Cft. B7: Nech 1C 102
Bent St. DY5: Brie H 5H 93
Ben Willetts Wlk. B65: B'hth 2C 112
Benyon Cen., The WS2: Wals 2G 31
Beoley Cl. B72: W Grn 4A 70
Beoley Gro. B45: Rub 2F 157
Berberry Cl. B30: B'vlle 1H 145
Berchelai Av. B31: N'fld 1C 144
Beresford Cres. B70: W Brom 4H 79
Beresford Dr. B73: Bold 4G 69
Beresford Rd. B69: O'bry 2A 98
WS3: Blox .1C 32
Berets, The B75: S Cold 5D 54
Bericote Cft. B27: A Grn 2B 136
Berkeley Cl. WV6: Pert 6F 25
Berkeley Dr. DY6: K'wfrd 2A 92
Berkeley Ho. B76: Walm 5D 70
Berkeley M. B25: Yard 4G 119
Berkeley Pct. B14: King H 5H 147
Berkeley Rd. B25: Yard 4G 119
B90: Shir .4F 149
Berkeley Rd. E. B25: Yard 4H 119
Berkeley St. WS2: Wals 4H 47
Berkley Cl. WS2: Wals 6F 31
Berkley Ct. B1: Birm 6A 4
Berkley Cres. B13: Mose 4C 134
Berkley Ho. B23: Erd 1F 85
Berkley St. B1: Birm 5A 4 (1E 117)
Berkshire, The WS3: Blox 4G 19
Berkshire Cl. B71: W Brom 6H 63
Berkshire Cres. WS10: W'bry 1A 64
Berkswell Cl. B74: Four O 5E 37
B91: Sol 5F 137
DY1: Dud 4A 76
Berkswell Hall CV7: Berk 4H 155
Berkswell Rd. B24: Erd 3H 85
Bermuda Cl. DY1: Dud 1D 76
Bernard Pl. B18: Hock 4B 100
Bernard Rd. B17: Edg 1F 115
B68: O'bry 1A 114
DY4: Tip 6B 62
Bernard St. B71: W Brom 3A 80
WS1: Wals .3E 49
Berners St. B19: Loz 2F 101
Bernhard Dr. B21: Hand 1A 100
Bernwall Cl. DY8: Stourb 1D 124
Berrandale Rd. B36: Hodg H 1D 104
Berrington Dr. WV14: Cose 5D 60
Berrington Wlk. B5: Birm 4G 117
Berrow Cott. Homes B93: Know 3E 167
Berrow Dr. B15: Edg 4A 116
Berrowside Rd. B34: S End 3A 106
Berry Av. WS10: Darl 6B 46
Berrybush Gdns. DY3: Sed 6A 60
Berry Cl. B19: Hock 3F 101
Berry Cres. WS5: Wals 1G 65
Berry Dr. B66: Smeth 3E 99
WS9: A'rdge 4A 34
Berryfield Rd. B26: Sheld 5H 121
Berryfields WS9: A'rdge 4A 34
WS9: Ston .2G 23
Berryfields Rd. B76: Walm 2D 70
Berry Hall La. B91: Cath B, Sol 3C 152
Berrymound Vw. B47: H'wd 2C 162
Berry Rd. B8: Salt 4E 103
Berry St. B18: Hock 3B 100
WV1: Wolv 3C 170 (1H 43)
Bertha Rd. B11: S'brk 6D 118
Bertram Cl. DY4: Tip 4C 62
Bertram Rd. B10: Small H 2D 118
B67: Smeth 3C 98
Bert Williams Leisure Cen. 6F 45
Berwick Gro. B31: N'fld 4B 144
B43: Gt Barr 1D 66
Berwicks La. B37: Chel W 2D 122
(not continuous)
Berwood Farm Rd. B72: W Grn 1A 86
Berwood Gdns. B24: Erd 2A 86
Berwood Gro. B92: Olton 4F 137
Berwood La. B24: Erd 4C 86
Berwood Pk. B35: Cas V 5E 87
Berwood Rd. B72: W Grn 1B 86
Berwyn Cl. B26: Yard 4D 120
Berwyn Gro. WS6: C Hay 2F 7
Besant Gro. B27: A Grn 4G 135
Besbury Cl. B93: Dorr 6F 167
BESCOT 5A 48
Bescot Cres. WS1: Wals 5B 48
Bescot Cft. B42: Gt Barr 1D 82
Bescot Dr. WS2: Wals 5H 47
Bescot Ind. Est. WS10: W'bry 1D 62
Bescot Rd. WS2: Wals 5H 47
Bescot Stadium Station (Rail) 6B 48
Bescot St. WS1: Wals 4B 48
Besford Gro. B31: N'fld 4B 144
B90: M'path 3F 165
Besom Way WS6: C Hay 3C 6
Bessborough Rd. B25: Yard 3B 120
Bessemer Cl. WV14: Bils 2E 61
Best Rd. WV14: Bils 4F 45
Best St. B64: Old H 1H 111
Beswick Gro. B33: Kitts G 5E 105
Beta Gro. B14: Yard W 3C 148
Bethesda Gdns. B63: Crad 4E 111
Betjeman Pl. WV10: Bush 6C 16
Betley Gro. B33: Stech 4E 105
Betony Cl. WS5: Wals 2E 65
Betsham Cl. B44: K'sdng 4B 68
Bettany Glade WV10: Bush 3A 16
Betteridge Dr. B76: Walm 1C 70
Betton Rd. B14: King H 2G 147
Bett Rd. B20: Hand 4B 82
Betty's La. WS11: Nort C 1D 8
Beulah Ct. B63: Hale 1A 128
Bevan Av. WV4: Ett 1A 60
Bevan Cl. WS4: S'fld 6G 21
WV14: Bils .5H 45
Bevan Ind. Est. DY5: Brie H 1E 109
Bevan Rd. DY4: Tip 3B 78
DY5: Brie H 1E 109
Bevan Way B66: Smeth 1D 98
Beverley Cl. B72: W Grn 6A 70
CV7: Bal C 5H 169
Beverley Ct. Rd. B32: Quin 5A 114
Beverley Cres. WV4: Ett 1B 60
Beverley Cft. B23: Erd 6D 84
Beverley Dr. DY6: K'wfrd 2A 92
Beverley Gro. B26: Sheld 6F 121
Beverley Rd. B45: Rub 2G 157
B71: W Brom 4B 64
Beverston Rd. DY4: Tip 3B 62
WV6: Pert .5G 25
Bevington Rd. B6: Aston 6H 83
Bevin Rd. WS2: Wals 6E 31
Bevis Gro. B44: Gt Barr 2H 67
Bewdley Av. B12: Bal H 5A 118
Bewdley Dr. WV1: Wolv 1D 44
Bewdley Rd. B30: Stir 5D 132
Bewdley Vs. *B18: Win G 5H 99*
(off Cape St.)
Bewick Ct. WV6: Tett 1A 42
Bewlay Cl. DY5: Brie H 4F 109
Bewley Rd. WV12: W'hall 5D 30
Bewlys Av. B20: Hand 3A 82
Bexhill Gro. B15: Birm 2E 117
Bexley Gro. B71: W Brom 6C 64
Bexley Rd. B44: K'sdng 5B 68
Bhullar Way B69: O'bry 1D 96
Bhylls Cres. WV3: Wolv 4A 42
Bhylls La. WV3: Wolv 3H 41
Bibbey's Grn. WV10: Bush 3B 16
Bibsworth Av. B13: Mose 5D 134
Bibury Rd. B28: Hall G 6E 135
Bicester Sq. B35: Cas V 3F 87
BICKENHILL 4F 139
Bickenhill Grn. Ct. B92: Bick 4F 139
Bickenhill La. B37: Mars G 5E 123
(not continuous)
B40: Mars G 6F 123
B92: Cath B 1E 153
Bickenhill Pk. Rd. B92: Olton 4B 136
Bickenhill Parkway B40: Nat E C 5F 123
Bickenhill Rd. B37: Mars G 4C 122
Bickenhill Trad. Est. B37: Mars G 6F 123
Bickford Rd. B6: Witt 6A 84
WV10: Wolv 4B 28
Bickington Rd. B32: Bart G 4B 130
Bickley Av. B11: S'brk 5C 118
B74: Four O 4E 37
Bickley Gro. B26: Sheld 6F 121
Bickley Rd. WS4: Rus 2G 33
WV14: Bils .4A 46
Bicknell Cft. B14: King H 5G 147
Bickon Dr. DY5: Quar B 3B 110
Bickton Cl. B24: Erd 1A 86
Biddings La. WV14: Cose 3D 60
Biddlestone Gro. WS5: Wals 2G 65
Biddlestone Pl. WS10: Darl 4B 46
Biddulph Ct. B73: S Cold 3G 69
Bideford Dr. B29: S Oak 4G 131
Bideford Rd. B66: Smeth 4F 99
Bidford Cl. B90: Shir 5B 150
Bidford Rd. B31: N'fld 4C 144
Bierton Rd. B25: Yard 3A 120
Biggin Cl. B35: Cas V 4E 87
WV6: Pert .4E 25
Big Peg, The B18: Birm 1A 4 (5E 101)
Bigwood Dr. B32: Bart G 4B 130
B75: S Cold 5E 55
Bilberry Cres. B76: Walm 2C 70
Bilberry Dr. B45: Rub 3G 157
Bilberry Rd. B14: King H 1E 147
Bilboe Rd. WV14: Bils 2H 61
BILBROOK 4H 13
Bilbrook Ct. WV8: Bilb 4H 13
Bilbrook Gro. B29: W Cas 3D 130
WV8: Bilb .4H 13
Bilbrook Ho. WV8: Bilb 4H 13
Bilbrook Rd. WV8: Bilb, Cod 3G 13
(not continuous)
Bilbrook Station (Rail) 5H 13
Bilhay La. B70: W Brom 2G 79
Bilhay St. B70: W Brom 2G 79
Billau Rd. WV14: Cose 3F 61
BILLESLEY .1C 148
Billesley Indoor Tennis Cen. 6B 134
Billesley La. B13: Mose 5H 133
Billingham Cl. B91: Sol 1F 165
Billingsley Rd. B26: Yard 3E 121
Bills La. B90: Shir 6F 149
Billsmore Grn. B92: Sol 6G 137
Bills St. WS10: Darl 4E 47
Billy Buns La. WV5: Wom 5G 57
Billy Wright Cl. WV4: Penn 5C 42
Bilport La. WS10: W'bry 5F 63
BILSTON 6F 45
Bilston Central Ind. Est. WV14: Bils . . .6G 45
Bilston Central Stop (Metro) 6G 45
Bilston Craft Gallery & Museum 5G 45
Bilston Ind. Est. WV14: Bils 6A 46
Bilston Key Ind. Est. WV14: Bils 6H 45
Bilston La. WV13: W'hall 2B 46
Bilston Rd. DY4: Tip 3B 62
WS10: W'bry 2D 62
WV2: Ett, Wolv 4D 170 (2H 43)
WV13: W'hall 4A 46
Bilston St. DY3: Sed 5H 59
WS10: Darl 5D 46
(not continuous)
WV1: Wolv 4C 170 (2H 43)
WV13: W'hall 2A 46
Bilston St. Island
WV1: Wolv 4D 170 (2H 43)
Bilton Grange Rd. B26: Yard 4D 120
Bilton Ind. Est. B38: King Nor 1A 160
Binbrook Rd. WV12: W'hall 5D 30
Bincomb Av. B26: Sheld 5F 121
Binfield St. DY4: Tip 3A 78
Bingley Av. B8: W End 5H 103
Bingley Ent. Cen. *WV3: Wolv 3E 43*
(off Norfolk Rd.)
Bingley St. WV3: Wolv 3E 43
Binley Cl. B25: Yard 5B 120
B90: Shir .1G 163
Binstead Rd. B44: K'sdng 3A 68
Binswood Rd. B62: Quin 4G 113
Binton Cft. B13: Mose 5H 133
Binton Rd. B90: Shir 6F 149
Birbeck Ho. B36: Cas B 3D 106
Birbeck Pl. DY5: P'ntt 3F 93
Birchall St. B12: Birm 2H 117
Birch Av. B31: Longb 6A 144
DY5: Quar B 1C 110
WS8: Bwnhls 5A 10
Birch Cl. B17: Harb 6H 115
B30: B'vlle 1H 145
B76: Walm .3D 70

Birch Coppice—Black Country New Rd.

Birch Coppice DY5: Quar B 2C **110**
(not continuous)
WV5: Wom 1E **73**
Birchcoppice Gdns. WV12: W'hall 5E **31**
Birch Ct. B30: King Nor 3A **146**
B66: Smeth 1B **98**
*WS4: Wals 5E **33***
(off Lichfield Rd.)
*WV1: Wolv 5G **27***
(off Boscobel Cres.)
Birch Cres. B69: Tiv 6A **78**
Birch Cft. B24: Erd 2B **86**
B37: Chel W 2E **123**
WS9: A'rdge 1E **35**
Birchcroft B66: Smeth 4G **99**
Birch Cft. Rd. B75: S Cold 4B **54**
Birchdale WV14: Bils 4F **45**
Birchdale Av. B23: Erd 3E **85**
Birchdale Rd. B23: Erd 2D **84**
Birch Dr. B62: B'hth 2E **113**
B74: Lit As 4D **36**
B75: S Cold 4D **54**
DY8: Stourb 5C **108**
Birches Av. WV8: Bilb 6A **14**
Birches Barn Av. WV3: Wolv 4D **42**
Birches Barn Rd. WV3: Wolv 3D **42**
Birches Cl. B13: Mose 4H **133**
BIRCHES GREEN 5G **85**
Birches Grn. Rd. B24: Erd 5H **85**
Birches Pk. Rd. WV8: Cod 5G **13**
Birches Ri. WV13: W'hall 2H **45**
Birches Rd. WV8: Bilb 5G **13**
BIRCHFIELD 5D **82**
Birchfield Av. WV6: Tett 3H **25**
Birchfield Cl. B63: Hale 3G **127**
Birchfield Cres. DY9: W'cte 2B **126**
Birchfield Gdns. B6: Aston 1F **101**
WS5: Wals 1G **65**
Birchfield La. B69: O'bry 5E **97**
(not continuous)
Birchfield Rd. B19: Loz 6F **83**
B20: Hand 6F **83**
DY9: W'cte 2B **126**
Birchfields Rd. WV12: W'hall 4A **30**
Birchfield Way WS5: Wals 1F **65**
Birchgate DY9: W'cte 1B **126**
Birch Glade WV3: Wolv 2B **42**
Birch Gro. B68: O'bry 4B **114**
CV7: Bal C 1H **169**
Birch Hill Av. WV5: Wom 2F **73**
Birch Hollow B15: Edg 5B **116**
B68: O'bry 4B **114**
Birchill Pl. WV5: Wom 2F **73**
BIRCHILLS 1A **48**
Birchills Ho. Ind. Est. WS2: Wals 5A **32**
Birchills St. WS2: Wals 6A **32**
Birch La. B68: O'bry 4B **114**
WS4: S'fld 6G **21**
WS9: A'rdge 6F **23**
Birchley Ho. B69: O'bry 3D **96**
Birchley Ind. Est. B69: O'bry 4E **97**
Birchley Pk. Av. B69: O'bry 3E **97**
Birchley Ri. B92: Olton 6D **120**
Birchmoor Cl. B28: Hall G 6H **135**
Birchover Rd. WS2: Wals 5G **31**
Birch Rd. B6: Witt 5A **84**
B45: Rub 3E **157**
B68: O'bry 3B **114**
DY3: Sed 4B **60**
WV11: Wed 6H **17**
Birch Rd. E. B6: Witt 5B **84**
Birch Rd. E. Ind. Est. B6: Witt 5B **84**
Birch St. B68: O'bry 3A **98**
DY4: Tip 2H **77**
WS2: Wals 6B **32**
WV1: Wolv 2A **170** (1G **43**)
Birch Ter. DY2: Neth 5E **95**
Birch Tree Gdns. WS9: A'rdge 4D **34**
Birchtree Gdns. DY5: Quar B 2C **110**
Birch Tree Gro. B91: Sol 3C **150**
Birchtree Hollow WV12: W'hall 4D **30**
Birchtrees B24: Erd 3B **86**
Birchtrees Cft. B26: Yard 6B **120**
Birchtrees Dr. B33: Kitts G 1H **121**
Birch Wlk. B68: O'bry 4B **114**
Birchwood Cl. WV11: Ess 4A **18**
Birchwood Cres. B12: Bal H 1B **134**
Birchwood Rd. B12: Bal H 1A **134**
WV4: Penn 6E **43**
Birchwoods B32: Bart G 3H **129**
Birchwood Wlk. DY6: K'wfrd 1C **92**
Birchy Cl. B90: Dic H 3F **163**
Birchy Leasowes La.
B90: Dic H 4E **163**
Bird Brook Cl. WS10: Darl 4C **46**
Birdbrook Rd. B44: Gt Barr 4G **67**
Birdcage Wlk. B38: King Nor 5B **146**
DY2: Dud 6F **77**
Bird End B71: W Brom 5D **64**
Birdie Cl. B38: King Nor 6H **145**
Birdlip Gro. B32: Quin 5A **114**
Birds Mdw. DY5: P'ntt 2F **93**
Bird St. DY3: Lwr G 4G **75**
Birdwell Cft. B13: Mose 1H **147**
Birkdale Av. B29: S Oak 4B **132**
Birkdale Cl. DY8: Stourb 4D **124**
WV1: Wolv 1C **44**
Birkdale Dr. B69: Tiv 2A **96**
Birkdale Gro. B29: S Oak 5C **132**
Birkdale Rd. WS3: Blox 4G **19**
Birkenshaw Rd. B44: Gt Barr 5G **67**
Birley Gro. B63: Hale 5E **127**
BIRMINGHAM 4E **5** (1G **117**)
BIRMINGHAM AIRPORT 1E **139**
Birmingham Alexander Sports Stadium **1F 83**
Birmingham & Solihull RFC **4B 138**
Birmingham Botanical Gdns. **4B 116**
Birmingham Bus. Est.
B37: Mars G 3G **123**
Birmingham City FC **2C 118**
Birmingham City University
Art & Design Institute - (Gosta Green Campus) **1G 5 (5H 101)**
Bournville Campus -
Linden Rd. **6A 132**
Sycamore Rd. **6A 132**
City North Campus **4G 83**
City South Campus **3C 116**
Hamstead Campus **4A 82**
School of Art **3C 4 (6F 101)**
School of Jewellery **1A 4 (5E 101)**
Birmingham Conservatoire ***4C 4***
(off Paradise Pl.)
Birmingham Crematorium
B42: P Barr 2E **83**
Birmingham Gymnastics & Martial Arts Cen. **1E 83**
Birmingham Hippodrome Theatre **6D 4 (2G 117)**
Birmingham International Station (Rail) **1F 139**
Birmingham Museum & Art Gallery **3C 4 (1F 117)**
Birmingham Museum of Transport **6G 161**
Birmingham Nature Cen. **1E 133**
Birmingham New Rd. DY1: Dud 6A **44**
DY4: Tip 6A **44**
WV4: Ett 6A **44**
WV14: Cose 6A **44**
Birmingham One Bus. Pk.
B1: Birm 6D **100**
Birmingham Railway Mus. **6F 119**
Birmingham Repertory Theatre **4A 4 (1E 117)**
Birmingham Rd. B31: Hopw 3F **159**
B36: Cas B 1E **105**
B37: K'hrst 4D **106**
B43: Gt Barr 5G **49**
B45: Rub 5C **156**
B46: Col 4E **107**
B46: Wat O 5B **88**
B48: Hopw 3F **159**
B61: Marlb, Rub 6C **156**
(not continuous)
B63: Hale 2B **128**
B65: Row R 1C **112**
B69: O'bry 2H **97**
B70: W Brom 6C **80**
B71: W Brom 6E **81**
B72: S Cold, W Grn 6H **69**
CV7: Mer 2D **140**
DY1: Dud 5G **77**
Birmingham Rd. DY9: Hag 6G **125**
WS1: Wals 2D **48**
WS5: Wals 4F **49**
(Lake Av.)
WS5: Wals 5G **49**
(Wellington Rd.)
WS9: A'rdge 4C **34**
WS14: Shen W 2G **37**
WV2: Wolv 5C **170** (2H **43**)
Birmingham St. B63: Hale 2B **128**
B69: O'bry 1G **97**
DY2: Dud 6F **77**
DY8: Stourb 6E **109**
DY9: Stourb 6E **109**
WS1: Wals 2D **48**
WS10: Darl 5E **47**
WV13: W'hall 1B **46**
Birmingham Town Hall **4C 4 (1F 117)**
Birmingham Trade Pk. B24: Erd 4B **86**
Birnham Cl. DY4: Tip 2F **77**
Birstall Way B38: King Nor 1G **159**
Bisbrook Cft. B91: Sol 1H **151**
Bisell Way DY5: Brie H 4H **109**
Bishbury Cl. B15: Edg 3A **116**
Bishop Asbury Cottage Mus. **5G 65**
Bishop Asbury Cres. B43: Gt Barr 5G **65**
Bishop Cl. B45: Fran 6E **143**
DY2: Dud 1G **95**
Bishop Rd. WS10: W'bry 3A **64**
Bishop Ryder Ho. B4: Birm 2G **5**
Bishops Cl. B23: Erd 5C **84**
B66: Smeth 5G **99**
Bishops Ct. B31: N'fld 4F **145**
B33: Kitts G 1H **121**
B37: Mars G 3G **123**
Bishops Ga. B31: N'fld 5E **145**
Bishopsgate St. B15: Birm 6A **4** (2D **116**)
Bishops Mdw. B75: R'ley 6C **38**
Bishops Rd. B73: S Cold 2H **69**
Bishop St. B5: Birm 3G **117**
Bishops Wlk. B64: Crad H 5A **112**
Bishops Way B74: Four O 3F **37**
Bishopton Cl. B90: Shir 6A **150**
Bishopton Rd. B67: Smeth 2D **114**
Bishton Gro. DY2: Neth 5F **95**
Bisley Gro. B24: Erd 5G **85**
Bismillah Bldg. B19: Birm 1C **4** (5F **101**)
Bissell Cl. B28: Hall G 1F **149**
Bissell Dr. WS10: W'bry 2H **63**
Bissell St. B5: Birm 3G **117**
B32: Quin 5G **113**
WV14: Bils 6H **45**
Bi-Tec Ind. Pk. WV1: Wolv 2C **44**
Biton Cl. B17: Harb 6F **115**
Bittell Cl. B31: Longb 2D **158**
WV10: Bush 3A **16**
Bittell Ct. B31: Longb 2D **158**
Bittell Farm Rd. B48: Hopw 6F **159**
Bitterne Dr. WV6: Wolv 5E **27**
Bittern Wlk. DY5: Brie H 5G **109**
Blackacre Rd. DY2: Dud 1F **95**
Blackberry Av. B9: Bord G 6G **103**
Blackberry Cl. DY1: Dud 1A **94**
Blackberry Gdns. B74: Four O 4E **37**
Blackberry La. B63: Hale 3A **128**
B65: Row R 4H **95**
B74: Four O 4E **37**
WS9: Wals W 3D **22**
Blackbird Cft. B36: Cas B 2C **106**
Blackbrook Cl. DY2: Neth 6C **94**
Blackbrook Rd. DY2: Dud, Neth 4C **94**
(not continuous)
Blackbrook Valley Ind. Est.
DY2: Dud 4C **94**
Blackbrook Way WV10: Bush 3A **16**
Blackburn Av. WV6: Tett 2C **26**
Blackburne Rd. B28: Hall G 1F **149**
Blackbushe Cl. B17: Harb 4D **114**
Blackcat Cl. B37: F'bri 6C **106**
Black Country Ho. B69: O'bry 2F **97**
Black Country Living Mus. **3F 77**
Black Country New Rd.
B70: W Brom 1D **78**
DY4: Tip 1D **78**
WS10: Darl, W'bry 5A **46**
WS10: Tip, W'bry 2D **62**
WV14: Bils 5A **46**

A-Z Birmingham 183

Black Country Route WS2: Wals 4B **46**
  WV13: W'hall 4B **46**
  WV14: Cose, Bils 2D **60**
Blackdown Cl. B45: Fran 5G **143**
Blackdown Rd. B93: Know 3D **166**
Blackenhall Community &
  Healthy Living Cen. 4G **43**
Blackett Ct. B73: S Cold 3G **69**
Blackfirs La. B37: Mars G 4E **123**
Blackford Cl. B63: Hale 3F **127**
Blackford Rd. B11: S'hll 1C **134**
  B90: Shir 2A **164**
Blackford St. B18: Win G 4A **100**
Blackhalve La. WV11: Wed, Ess 1D **28**
Blackham Dr. B73: Bold 6G **69**
Blackham Rd. WV11: Wed 1H **29**
Black Haynes Rd. B29: W Cas 1E **145**
BLACKHEATH 2C **112**
Blackheath Mkt. B65: B'hth 2D **112**
Blackheath Trad. Est. B65: Row R . .1E **113**
BLACKHILLS 2A **72**
Black Horse Cl. WS10: Darl 6D **46**
Blackhorse La. DY5: Brie H 2A **110**
BLACK LAKE 1H **79**
Black Lake B70: W Brom 1G **79**
Black Lake (Park & Tram) 2G **79**
Black Lake Ind. Est. B70: W Brom . .1H **79**
Black Lake Stop (Metro) 1G **79**
Blacklea Cl. B25: Yard 2B **120**
Black Mill DY1: Dud 3F **77**
Blackmoor Cft. B33: Kitts G 1H **121**
Blackpit La. WLr P 2E **57**
Blackrock Rd. B23: Erd 1B **84**
Blackroot Cl. WS7: Hamm 1F **11**
Blackroot Ho. B73: New O 3C **68**
  (off Welshmans Rd.)
Blackroot Rd. B74: S Cold 4G **53**
Blacksmith Dr. B75: R'ley 6C **38**
Blacksmith Way B70: W Brom 5A **80**
Blackthorn Cl. B30: B'vlle 1G **145**
Blackthorne Av. WS7: Chase 1B **10**
Blackthorne Cl. B91: Sol 3C **150**
  DY1: Dud 3B **76**
Blackthorne Rd. B67: Smeth 5B **98**
  DY1: Dud 3B **76**
  WS5: Wals 6D **48**
Blackthorn Rd. B30: B'vlle 1G **145**
  B36: Cas B 1G **105**
  DY8: Word 2D **108**
Blackwater Cl. DY5: P'ntt 3E **93**
Blackwell Rd. B72: W Grn 4B **70**
Blackwood Av. WV11: Wed 1D **28**
Blackwood Dr. B74: S'tly 3G **51**
Blackwood Rd. B74: S'tly 2G **51**
Blades Ho. B71: W Brom 5E **65**
Blades Rd. B70: W Brom 3D **78**
Blaenwern Dr. B63: Crad 4D **110**
Blagdon Rd. B63: Hale 5A **112**
Blair Gro. B37: Chel W 2F **123**
Blakedon Rd. WS10: W'bry 2E **63**
Blakedown Rd. B63: Hale 4G **127**
Blakedown Way B69: O'bry 5E **97**
Blake Hall Cl. DY5: Brie H 4G **109**
Blake Ho. WS2: Wals 3A **48**
  (off St Johns Rd.)
Blakeland Rd. B44: K'sdng 1G **83**
Blakeland St. B9: Bord G 1F **119**
Blake La. B9: Bord G 1F **119**
BLAKELEY 2F **73**
Blakeley Av. WV6: Tett 2D **26**
Blakeley Hall Gdns. B69: O'bry 2H **97**
Blakeley Hall Rd. B69: O'bry 2H **97**
Blakeley Heath Dr. WV5: Wom 2G **73**
Blakeley Ri. WV6: Tett 2D **26**
Blakeley Wlk. DY2: Neth 5E **95**
Blakeley Wood Rd. DY4: Tip 5C **62**
Blakemere Av. B25: Yard 3C **120**
Blakemore Cl. B32: Bart G 2D **130**
Blakemore Dr. B75: S Cold 5D **54**
Blakemore Rd. B70: W Brom 5G **79**
  WS9: Wals W 4C **22**
BLAKENALL HEATH 1B **32**
Blakenall Heath WS3: Blox 1B **32**
Blakenall La. WS3: Blox 2A **32**
Blakenall Row WS3: Blox 1B **32**
Blakeney Av. B17: Harb 4E **115**
  DY8: Woll 5B **108**

Blakeney Cl. DY3: Sed 5G **59**
Blakenhale Rd. B33: Sheld 2F **121**
BLAKENHALL 4G **43**
Blakenhall Gdns. WV2: Wolv 4G **43**
Blakenhall Ind. Est. WV2: Wolv 4F **43**
Blake Pl. B9: Bord G 1F **119**
Blakesley Cl. B76: Walm 2D **86**
Blakesley Gro. B25: Yard 2B **120**
Blakesley Hall 2C **120**
Blakesley M. B25: Yard 3B **120**
  B33: Stech 1C **120**
Blakesley Rd. B25: Yard 2A **120**
Blakesley Way B33: Stech 1B **120**
Blake St. B74: Four O 3E **37**
Blake Street Station (Rail) 3F **37**
Blakewood Cl. B34: S End 4G **105**
Blandford Av. B36: Cas B 6A **88**
Blandford Dr. DY8: Word 6C **92**
Blandford Rd. B32: Quin 6C **114**
Blanefield WV8: Pend 5C **14**
Blanning Ct. B93: Dorr 6A **166**
Blay Av. WS2: Wals 1H **47**
Blaydon Av. B75: R'ley 1C **54**
Blaydon Ct. B17: Harb 1H **131**
  (off Metchley La.)
Blaydon Rd. WV9: Pend 5E **15**
Blaythorn Av. B92: Olton 2E **137**
Blaze Hill Rd. DY6: W Hth 1G **91**
Blaze Pk. DY6: W Hth 1H **91**
Bleak Hill Rd. B23: Erd 3C **84**
Bleakhouse Rd. B68: O'bry 2A **114**
Bleak St. B67: Smeth 3D **98**
Blencathra Dr. B71: W Brom 1H **79**
Blenheim Cl. WS4: Rus 2H **33**
Blenheim Ct. B44: Gt Barr 5H **67**
  B91: Sol 3G **151**
Blenheim Dr. B43: Gt Barr 5H **65**
  WS10: W'bry 6E **47**
Blenheim Pl. B12: Bal H 5A **118**
  (off Ombersley Rd.)
Blenheim Rd. B13: Mose 4H **133**
  B90: Shir 5B **150**
  DY6: K'wfrd 3D **92**
  WS11: Nort C 1F **9**
  WV12: W'hall 3B **30**
Blenheim Way B35: Cas V 5F **87**
  B44: Gt Barr 5H **67**
  DY1: Dud 5A **76**
Bletchley Rd. B24: Erd 3C **86**
Blewitt Cl. B36: Cas B 5H **87**
Blewitt St. DY5: P'ntt 3G **93**
Blews St. B6: Birm 4G **101**
Blithe Cl. DY8: Amb 3E **109**
Blithfield Dr. DY5: Brie H 4F **109**
Blithfield Gro. B24: Erd 2A **86**
Blithfield Rd. WS8: Bwnhls 3F **9**
Blockall WS10: Darl 4D **46**
Blockall Cl. WS10: Darl 5C **46**
Bloom Cl. WV13: W'hall 6A **30**
BLOOMFIELD 6G **61**
Bloomfield Cl. WV5: Wom 1D **72**
Bloomfield Ct. B65: Row R 5C **96**
Bloomfield Dr. WV12: W'hall 6D **18**
Bloomfield Pk. DY4: Tip 1F **77**
Bloomfield Rd. B13: Mose 2B **134**
  DY4: Tip 1G **77**
Bloomfield St. Nth. B63: Hale 6H **111**
Bloomfield St. W. B63: Hale 1H **127**
Bloomfield Ter. DY4: Tip 1F **77**
Bloomsbury Gro. B14: King H 6E **133**
Bloomsbury St. B7: Nech 4B **102**
  WV2: Wolv 5A **170** (3G **43**)
Bloomsbury Wlk. B7: Nech 4B **102**
Blossom Av. B29: S Oak 3B **132**
BLOSSOMFIELD 5D **150**
Blossomfield Cl. B38: King Nor 1H **159**
  DY6: K'wfrd 1C **92**
Blossomfield Club 1E **165**
Blossomfield Ct. B38: King Nor 1H **159**
Blossomfield Gdns. B91: Sol 3E **151**
Blossomfield Rd. B91: Sol 6C **150**
Blossom Gro. B36: Hodg H 1C **104**
  B64: Old H 2H **111**
  (off Wright's La.)
Blossom Hill B24: Erd 3G **85**

Blossom Rd. B24: Erd 3A **86**
Blossom's Fold
  WV1: Wolv 3B **170** (1G **43**)
Blossomville Way B27: A Grn 1H **135**
Blounts Rd. B23: Erd 2C **84**
BLOWER'S GREEN 2D **94**
Blowers Grn. Cres. DY2: Dud 2D **94**
Blowers Grn. Pl. DY2: Dud 2D **94**
Blower's Grn. Rd. DY2: Dud 2D **94**
Bloxcidge St. B68: O'bry 5H **97**
BLOXWICH .6H **19**
Bloxwich Bus. Pk. WS2: Wals 2G **31**
Bloxwich Golf Course 3H **19**
Bloxwich La. WS2: Wals 5G **31**
Bloxwich Leisure Cen. 1A **32**
Bloxwich Library Theatre 6H **19**
Bloxwich North Station (Rail) 4F **19**
Bloxwich Rd. WS2: Wals 2A **32**
  WS3: Blox 2A **32**
Bloxwich Rd. Nth. WV12: W'hall . . .3D **30**
Bloxwich Rd. Sth. WV13: W'hall . . .6A **30**
Bloxwich Station (Rail) 6G **19**
Blucher St. B1: Birm 6C **4** (2F **117**)
Blue Ball La. B63: Crad 5E **111**
Blue Bell Cl. DY8: Word 1A **108**
Bluebell Cres. WV11: Wed 4F **29**
Bluebell Cft. B23: Erd 6C **68**
  B31: N'fld 3D **144**
Bluebell Dr. B37: Chel W 1F **123**
Bluebell La. WS6: Gt Wyr 4G **7**
Bluebell Rd. B64: Old H 6G **95**
  DY1: Dud 4D **76**
  WS9: Wals W 4D **22**
Bluebellwood Cl. B76: Walm 2E **71**
Blue Bird Pk. B62: Hunn 5A **128**
Bluebird Trad. Est. WV10: Wolv 4A **28**
Blue Cedar Dr. B74: S'tly 5H **51**
Blue Cedars DY8: Woll 5A **108**
Blue Lake Rd. B93: Dorr 6H **167**
Blue La. E. WS2: Wals 6B **32**
Blue La. W. WS2: Wals 1B **48**
Blue Rock Pl. B69: Tiv 2C **96**
Bluestone Ct. DY2: Dud 2G **95**
Blue Stone Wlk. B65: Row R 3C **96**
Blundell Rd. B11: S'hll 6D **118**
Blyth Ct. B92: Olton 6D **136**
Blythe Av. CV7: Bal C 6H **169**
Blythe Ct. B46: Col 2H **107**
  B73: S Cold 6H **53**
Blythefield Av. B43: Gt Barr 3G **65**
Blythe Gdns. WV8: Cod 3F **13**
Blythe Gro. B44: Gt Barr 6D **164**
Blythe Gro. B44: Gt Barr 2H **67**
Blythe Rd. B46: Col 2H **107**
BLYTHE VALLEY PARK 6D **164**
Blythe Valley Parkway B90: Bly P . .5D **164**
Blythe Way B91: Sol 4A **152**
Blythewood Cl. B91: Sol 6B **152**
Blythsford Rd. B28: Hall G 3F **149**
Blythswood Cl. B11: Tys 1G **135**
Blythswood Rd. B11: Tys 1G **135**
Blyton Cl. B16: Birm 6B **100**
Board School Gdns. DY3: Up Gor . . .1A **76**
Boar Hound Cl. B18: Hock 5C **100**
Boat La. WS14: Muck C 4H **11**
Boatmans La. WS9: A'rdge, Wals W . .5A **22**
Boatmans Reach B14: King H 3E **147**
Bobbin Cl. WS6: Gt Wyr 4F **7**
Bobbington Way DY2: Neth 4F **95**
Bob's Coppice Wlk. DY5: Quar B . . .4B **110**
Boddis Ind. Pk. B64: Old H 1H **111**
Boden Gdns. B28: Hall G 6G **135**
Bodenham Rd. B31: N'fld 5C **144**
  B68: O'bry 3H **113**
Boden Rd. B28: Hall G 6F **135**
Bodens La. WS9: A'rdge 4C **50**
Bodens Rd. WV6: Pert 6G **25**
Bodicote Gro. B75: R'ley 6C **38**
Bodington Rd. B75: Four O 6H **37**
Bodmin Cl. WS5: Wals 4H **49**
Bodmin Cl. DY5: Brie H 1H **109**
Bodmin Gro. B7: Birm 4B **102**
Bodmin Ri. WS5: Wals 4H **49**
Bodmin Rd. DY2: Neth 1F **111**
Bognop Rd. WV11: Ess 3E **17**
BOLDMERE .5F **69**
Boldmere Cl. B73: Bold 6G **69**

Boldmere Ct. *B43*: Gt Barr 6A *66*
(off South Vw.)
Boldmere Dr. B73: Bold 5G **69**
Boldmere Gdns. B73: Bold 5F **69**
Boldmere Golf Course 2E **69**
Boldmere Rd. B73: Bold 3F **69**
Boldmere Ter. B29: S Oak 4A *132*
Boleyn Cl. WS6: C Hay 3D **6**
Boleyn Rd. B45: Fran 6D *142*
Bolney Rd. B32: Quin 6C *114*
Bolton Ct. DY4: Tip 5C **62**
Bolton Ind. Cen. B19: Hock 3D *100*
Bolton Rd. B10: Small H 3B *118*
WV11: Wed 4E **29**
Bolton St. B9: Birm 1B *118*
Bolton Way WS3: Blox 4F **19**
Bomers Fld. B45: Redn 2A *158*
Bond, The B5: Birm 1A *118*
Bond Dr. B35: Cas V 4E **87**
Bondfield Rd. B13: Mose 1B *148*
Bond Gallery, The 1A *118*
Bond Sq. B18: Hock 5C *100*
Bond St. B19: Birm 1C **4** (1F *101*)
B30: Stir 6C *132*
B65: Row R 6E **97**
B70: W Brom 5A **80**
WV2: Wolv 5B *170* (2G **43**)
WV14: Cose 5C **60**
Bone Mill La. WV1: Wolv 5H **27**
Bonham Gro. B25: Yard 2B *120*
Boniface Cl. B66: Smeth 6G **99**
Boningale Way B93: Dorr 6H *165*
Bonner Dr. B76: Walm 2D **86**
Bonner Gro. WS9: A'rdge 4B **34**
Bonneville Cl. DY4: Tip 1F **77**
Bonnington Way B43: Gt Barr 1F **67**
Bonny Stile La. WV11: Wed 3D **28**
Bonsall Rd. B23: Erd 1G **85**
Bonville Gdns. WV10: Bush 3A **16**
Booth Cl. DY6: K'wfrd 3E **93**
WS3: Blox 1B **32**
Booth Ct. DY5: Brie H 1H *109*
Booth Ho. WS4: Wals 6D **32**
Booth Rd. WS10: W'bry 3A **64**
Booth's Farm Rd. B42: Gt Barr 6C **66**
Booth's La. B42: Gt Barr 4D **66**
(not continuous)
Booth St. B21: Hand 2G **99**
B66: Hand, Smeth 2G **99**
WS3: Blox 1A **32**
WS10: Darl 3D **48**
Bordeaux Cl. DY1: Dud 4A **76**
Borden Cl. WV8: Pend 1D **26**
BORDESLEY 1B *118*
Bordesley Cir. B10: Small H 2B *118*
Bordesley Cl. B9: Bord G 1G *119*
Bordesley Ct. B9: Birm 1B *118*
BORDESLEY GREEN 1E *119*
Bordesley Grn. B9: Bord G 1D *118*
Bordesley Grn. E. B9: Bord G 1H *119*
B33: Stech 1C *120*
Bordesley Grn. Rd. B8: Salt 1D *118*
B9: Bord G 1D *118*
Bordesley Grn. Trad. Est.
B9: Bord G 1E *119*
Bordesley Middleway B10: Small H . . .3A *118*
B11: S'brk 3A *118*
Bordesley Pk. Rd. B10: Small H 2B *118*
Bordesley Station (Rail) 2A *118*
Bordesley St. B5: Birm 4G **5** (1H *117*)
Bordesley Trad. Est. B8: Salt 6D *102*
Borneo St. WS4: Wals 5D **32**
Borough Cres. B69: O'bry 4E **97**
DY8: Stourb 6C *108*
Borrowdale Cl. DY5: Brie H 4F *109*
Borrowdale Gro. B31: N'fld 4B *144*
Borrowdale Rd. B31: N'fld 4A *144*
Borrow St. WV13: W'hall 6A **30**
Borwick Av. B70: W Brom 4G **79**
Bosbury Ter. B30: Stir 6D *132*
Boscobel Av. DY4: Tip 3H **77**
Boscobel Cl. DY1: Dud 4B **76**
Boscobel Cres. WV1: Wolv 5G **27**
Boscobel Rd. B43: Gt Barr 3H **65**
B90: Ches G 4B *164*
WS1: Wals 3F **49**
Boscombe Av. B11: S'brk 5C *118*

Boscombe Rd. B11: Tys 1E *135*
Bosmere Ct. B31: N'fld 4D *144*
Boss Dr. DY2: Dud 2E **95**
Bossgate Cl. WV5: Wom 3G **73**
Boston Gro. B44: K'sdng 5B **68**
Bosty La. WS9: A'rdge 4G **33**
Boswell Cl. WS10: Darl 6D **46**
WS10: W'bry 4C **62**
Boswell Rd. B44: K'sdng 1H **83**
B74: S Cold 5A **54**
WV14: Bils 4H **45**
Bosworth Cl. DY3: Sed 1B **76**
Bosworth Ct. B26: Sheld 6E *121*
Bosworth Dr. B37: Chel W, F'bri 1B *122*
Bosworth Rd. B26: Yard 1C *136*
Botany Dr. DY3: Up Gor 2H **75**
Botany Rd. WS5: Wals 6D **48**
Botany Wlk. B16: Birm 1C *116*
Botha Rd. B9: Bord G 6E *103*
Botteley Rd. B70: W Brom 1G **79**
BOTTERHAM 4E **73**
Botterham La. DY3: Swind 4E **73**
Bottetourt Rd. B29: W Cas 2E *131*
(not continuous)
Botteville Rd. B27: A Grn 3A *136*
Bott La. DY9: Lye 5H *109*
WS1: Wals 2D **48**
BOUCHALL 5F *109*
Boughton Rd. B25: Yard 4A *120*
Boulevard, The B5: Edg 6F *117*
B73: W Grn 5H **69**
DY5: Brie H 1A *110*
Boulevard Wlk. WS2: Wals 1B **48**
Boultbee Bus. Units B7: Nech 3C *102*
Boultbee Rd. B72: W Grn 6A **70**
Boulton Ho. B70: W Brom 6B **80**
Boulton Ind. Cen. B18: Hock 4D *100*
Boulton Middleway B18: Birm 4D *100*
B19: Birm 4D *100*
Boulton Retreat B21: Hand 2A *100*
Boulton Rd. B21: Hand 2A *100*
B66: Smeth 3H **99**
B70: W Brom 6B **80**
B91: Sol 6G *137*
Boulton Sq. B70: W Brom 6B **80**
Boulton Wlk. B23: Erd 3B **84**
Boundary Av. WV13: W'hall 2E **45**
Boundary Ct. B37: F'bri 1A *122*
Boundary Cres. DY3: Lwr G 4G **75**
Boundary Dr. B13: Mose 3F *133*
Boundary Hill DY3: Lwr G 4G **75**
Boundary Ho. B5: Edg 6E *117*
B47: Wyt 6G *161*
Boundary Ind. Est. WV10: F'hses 2G **15**
Boundary La. B90: Dic H 3G *163*
Boundary Pl. B21: Hand 6G **81**
Boundary Rd. B23: Erd 3E **85**
B74: S'tly 4H **51**
WS9: Wals W 4B **22**
Boundary Way WV4: Penn 6A **42**
WV6: Tett 1F **41**
Bourlay Cl. B45: Fran 5E *143*
Bourne Av. B31: N'fld 2C *144*
BOURNBROOK 3B *132*
Bournbrook Cl. B5: S Oak 2C *132*
Bournbrook Rd. B29: S Oak 2C *132*
Bourne Av. B62: Quin 1F *129*
DY4: Tip 6C **62**
Bournebrook Cl. DY2: Neth 4E **95**
Bournebrook Cres. B62: Quin 1G *129*
Bourne Cl. B13: Mose 1C *148*
B91: Sol 1A *152*
Bourne Grn. B32: Quin 5C *114*
Bourne Hill Cl. DY2: Neth 6G **95**
Bourne Rd. B6: Aston 2B *102*
Bournes Cl. B63: Hale 2H *127*
Bournes Cres. B63: Hale 1G *127*
Bournes Hill B63: Hale 1G *127*
Bourne St. DY2: Dud 6F **77**
DY3: Sed 6C **60**
WV14: Cose 6C **60**
Bourne Va. WS9: A'rdge 1D **48**
Bourne Wlk. B65: Row R 4H **95**
Bourne Way Gdns. B29: S Oak 5C *132*
Bourn Mill Dr. B6: Aston 3G *101*
BOURNVILLE .6A *132*

Bournville La. B30: B'vlle, Stir 6H *131*
Bournville Station (Rail) 6C *132*
Bourton Cl. WS5: Wals 2E **65**
Bourton Cft. B92: Olton 5D *136*
Bourton Rd. B92: Olton 5D *136*
Bovey Cft. B76: Walm 6E **71**
Bovingdon Rd. B35: Cas V 4E **87**
Bowater Av. B33: Stech 2B *120*
Bowater Ho. B19: Birm 4F *101*
(off Aldgate Gro.)
B70: W Brom 5A **80**
Bowater St. B70: W Brom 4A **80**
Bowbrook Av. B90: M'path 4E *165*
Bowcroft Gro. B24: Erd 1A **86**
Bowden Rd. B67: Smeth 3C **98**
Bowdler Rd. WV2: Wolv 6D *170* (3H **43**)
Bowen Av. WV4: Ett 2C **60**
Bowen Cl. B13: Mose 2B *134*
Bowen St. WV4: Ett 6A **44**
Bowercourt Cl. B91: Sol 6F *151*
Bower La. DY5: Quar B 3B *110*
Bowes Rd. B45: Rub 2E *157*
Bowfell Way B71: W Brom 1H **79**
Bowker St. WV13: W'hall 2E **45**
Bowlas Av. B74: Four O 3H **53**
BOWLING GREEN 6F **95**
Bowling Grn., The B76: Walm 1D **70**
Bowling Grn. Cl. B23: Erd 6E **69**
WS10: Darl 4D **46**
Bowling Grn. Dr. B67: Smeth 1C *114*
Bowling Grn. La. B20: Hand 1C *100*
Bowling Grn. Rd. B92: Neth 6F **95**
DY8: Stourb 6C *108*
Bowlplex
Birmingham 2C *116*
Dudley 4G **77**
Bowman Rd. B42: Gt Barr 4D **66**
Bowmans Ri. WV1: Wolv 6C **28**
Bowness Ct. WV12: W'hall 6B **18**
Bowness Ho. B69: O'bry 5D **96**
(off Lovett Av.)
Bowood Cres. B31: N'fld 5F *145*
Bowood Dr. WV6: Tett 3B **26**
Bowood End B76: Walm 5E **71**
Bowshot Cl. B36: Cas B 6H **87**
Bowstoke Rd. B43: Gt Barr 5G **65**
Bow St. B1: Birm 6D **4** (2F *117*)
WV13: W'hall 2B **46**
WV14: Bils 5G **45**
Bwyer Rd. B8: Salt 5E *103*
Bowyer St. B10: Small H 2A *118*
Boxhill Cl. B6: Aston 3H *101*
Box Rd. B37: Chel W 3E *123*
Box St. WS1: Wals 2D **48**
Box Trees Rd. B93: Dorr 6H *165*
Boyd Gro. B27: A Grn 3H *135*
Boydon Cl. WV2: Ett 5C **44**
Boyleston Rd. B28: Hall G 1G *149*
Boyne Rd. B26: Sheld 4E *121*
Boyton Gro. B44: Gt Barr 2H **67**
Brabazon Gro. B35: Cas V 4D **86**
Brabham Cres. B74: S'tly 5H **51**
Brabourne Av. WV10: F'hses 2H **15**
Bracadale Av. B24: Erd 3G **85**
Bracebridge Cl. CV7: Bal C 3H *169*
Bracebridge Dr. B17: Harb 6H *115*
Bracebridge Ho. B73: New O 3C **68**
(off Welshmans Hill)
Bracebridge Rd. B24: Erd 6F **85**
B74: Four O 3F **53**
Bracebridge St. B6: Aston 3G *101*
Braceby Av. B13: Mose 6C *134*
Brace St. WS1: Wals 3C **48**
(not continuous)
Brackenbury Rd. B44: K'sdng 5B **68**
Bracken Cl. WV8: Pend 6C **14**
Bracken Cft. B37: Chel W 6E *107*
Brackendale Dr. WS5: Wals 2F **65**
Brackendale Shop. Cen.
WV12: W'hall 5D **30**
Brackendale Way DY9: W'cte 1H *125*
Bracken Dr. B75: S Cold 6E **55**
Brackenfield Rd. B44: Gt Barr 3E **67**
B63: Hale 2G *127*
Brackenfield Vw. DY1: Dud 1H **93**
Bracken Pk. Gdns. DY8: Word 1D *108*

Bracken Rd. B24: Erd 5A **86**
Bracken Way B38: King Nor 2H **159**
 B74: S'tly 3H **51**
Bracken Wood WS5: Wals 6H **49**
Brackenwood Dr. WV11: Wed 4H **29**
Brackley Av. B20: Hand 6E **83**
Brackleys Way B92: Olton 3D **136**
Bracknell Cl. B31: N'fld 3G **145**
Bradbeer Ho. B16: Edg 2C **116**
Bradburne Way B7: Birm 4A **102**
Bradburn Rd. WV11: Wed 1D **28**
Bradbury Cl. WS8: Bwnhls 2B **22**
Bradbury Rd. B92: Olton 4D **136**
Braden Rd. WV4: Penn 2B **58**
Brades Cl. B63: Crad 4D **110**
Brades Ri. B69: O'bry 1D **96**
Brades Rd. B69: O'bry 6E **79**
BRADES VILLAGE 1D **96**
Bradewell Rd. B36: Cas B 6H **87**
Bradfield Ho. B26: Sheld 5A **122**
Bradfield Rd. B42: Gt Barr 6F **67**
Bradfield Way DY1: Dud 2E **77**
Bradford Cl. B43: Gt Barr 1A **66**
Bradford Ct. B12: Birm 3A **118**
Bradford La. WS1: Wals 2C **48**
Bradford Mall WS1: Wals 2C **48**
Bradford Pl. B11: S'brk 5A **118**
 WS1: Wals 2C **48**
Bradford Rd. B36: Cas B 1E **105**
 DY2: Dud 3B **94**
 WS8: Bwnhls 5A **10**
Bradford St. B5: Birm 6G 5 (2H **117**)
 B12: Birm 6G 5 (2H **117**)
 WS1: Wals 2C **48**
Bradgate Cl. WV12: W'hall 3C **30**
Bradgate Dr. B74: Four O 4E **37**
Bradgate Pl. B12: Bal H 6A **118**
BRADLEY 2G **61**
Bradley Cl. B31: Longb 6H **143**
Bradley Cft. CV7: Bal C 3H **169**
Bradley La. WV14: Bils 2H **61**
Bradley Lane Stop (Metro) 2A **62**
Bradleymore Rd. DY5: Brie H 6H **93**
Bradley Rd. B34: S End 3H **105**
 DY8: Stourb 5D **108**
 WV2: Wolv 4A **44**
Bradleys Cl. B64: Crad H 4G **111**
Bradley's La. DY4: Tip 5F **61**
 WV14: Cose 5F **61**
Bradley St. DY4: Tip 5H **77**
 DY5: P'ntt 2F **93**
 WV14: Bils 1H **61**
BRADMORE 3C **42**
Bradmore Cl. B91: Sol 1E **165**
Bradmore Gro. B29: W Cas 5E **131**
Bradmore Rd. WV3: Wolv 3D **42**
Bradnock Cl. B13: Mose 6C **134**
BRADNOCK'S MARSH 4E **155**
Bradnocks Marsh Bus. Cen.
 B92: H Ard 4E **155**
Bradnocks Marsh La. B92: H Ard ..6D **154**
Bradshaw Av. B38: King Nor 6H **145**
 WS10: Darl 6B **46**
Bradshaw Cl. B15: Birm 3E **117**
 DY4: Tip 4A **78**
Bradshawe Cl. B28: Hall G 4D **148**
Bradshaw Rd. B38: King Nor 3E **147**
Bradwell Cft. B75: R'ley 6C **38**
Braemar Av. DY8: Word 2A **108**
Braemar Cl. DY3: Sed 4G **59**
 WV12: W'hall 3B **30**
Braemar Dr. B23: Erd 2B **84**
Braemar Rd. B73: S Cold 3F **69**
 B92: Olton 4C **136**
 WS11: Nort C 1E **9**
Braeside Cft. B37: Chel W 1F **123**
Braeside Way WS3: Pels 4D **20**
Bragg Rd. B20: Hand 5F **83**
Braggs Farm La. B90: Dic H, Shir ..5F **163**
Braid Cl. B38: King Nor 6H **145**
Brailes Cl. B92: Sol 6A **138**
Brailes Dr. B76: Walm 2D **70**
Brailes Gro. B9: Bord G 2H **119**
Brailsford Cl. WV11: Wed 1G **29**
Brailsford Dr. B15: Edg 6A **116**
 B66: Smeth 4E **99**
Braithwaite Dr. DY6: K'wfrd 3B **92**

Braithwaite Rd. B11: S'brk 4B **118**
Bramah Way DY4: Tip 1C **78**
Bramall Cl. WV8: Cod 3E **13**
Bramber Dr. WV5: Wom 1F **73**
Bramber Ho. B31: Longb 1D **158**
Bramber Way DY8: Stourb 3D **124**
Bramble Cl. B6: Aston 2G **101**
 B31: N'fld 1D **144**
 B46: Col 2H **107**
 B64: Old H 5H **95**
 WS8: Clay 2A **22**
 WV12: W'hall 2C **30**
Bramble Dell B9: Bord G 6G **103**
Bramble Dr. B26: Sheld 5E **121**
Bramble Grn. DY1: Dud 2B **76**
Brambles, The B76: Walm 5E **71**
 DY9: W'cte 2H **125**
Brambleside DY8: Word 2D **108**
Bramble Way B74: Four O 5E **37**
Bramblewood WV5: Wom 6G **57**
Bramblewood Dr. WV3: Wolv 3C **42**
Bramblewoods B34: S End 4G **105**
Brambling Rd. B15: Edg 4E **117**
Brambling Wlk. DY5: Brie H 5G **109**
Bramcote Dr. B91: Sol 6G **137**
Bramcote Ri. B75: S Cold 4A **54**
Bramcote Rd. B32: Quin 5G **115**
Bramcote Way WS4: Rus 2E **33**
Bramdean Wlk. WV4: Penn 5A **42**
Bramerton Cl. WV11: Wed 3C **28**
Bramford Dr. DY1: Dud 1D **76**
Bramley Cl. B43: Gt Barr 2F **67**
 WS5: Wals 3H **49**
Bramley Cft. B90: Shir 5A **150**
Bramley Dr. B20: Hand 4D **82**
 B47: H'wd 3B **162**
Bramley M. Ct. B27: A Grn 6A **120**
Bramley Rd. B27: A Grn 6A **120**
 WS5: Wals 1F **65**
Brampton Av. B28: Hall G 1G **149**
Brampton Cres. B90: Shir 1H **149**
Bramshall Dr. B93: Dorr 6A **166**
Bramshaw Cl. B14: King H 5H **147**
Bramshill Ct. B15: Edg 3E **117**
Bramstead Av. WV6: Tett 1H **41**
Bramwell Dr. WS6: C Hay 4D **6**
Branchal Rd. WS9: A'rdge 6E **23**
Branch Rd. B38: King Nor 1A **160**
BRANDHALL 2H **113**
Brandhall Ct. B68: O'bry 1G **113**
Brandhall Golf Course 1G **113**
Brandhall La. B68: O'bry 2H **113**
Brandhall Rd. B68: O'bry 1H **113**
Brandon Cl. B70: W Brom 5G **79**
 DY3: Sed 6A **60**
 WS9: A'rdge 6H **35**
Brandon Gro. B31: Longb 2D **158**
Brandon Pk. WV3: Wolv 4C **42**
Brandon Pas. B16: Birm 6A **100**
Brandon Pl. B34: S End 2H **105**
Brandon Rd. B28: Hall G 3E **135**
 B62: B'hth 2E **113**
 B91: Sol 6G **137**
Brandon Thomas Ct. B6: Aston ..1B **102**
Brandon Way B70: W Brom 4G **79**
 DY6: Quar B 3A **110**
Brandon Way Ind. Est. B70: W Brom ..4F **79**
Brandwood Cres. B30: King Nor ...4F **147**
BRANDWOOD END 3F **147**
Brandwood Gro. B14: King H 2F **147**
Brandwood Ho. B14: King H 4F **147**
Brandwood Pk. Rd. B14: King H ...2D **146**
Brandwood Rd. B14: King H 4F **147**
Branfield Cl. WV14: Cose 5C **60**
Branksome Av. B21: Hand 1B **100**
Branscombe Cl. B14: King H 2F **147**
Bransdale Cl. WV6: Wolv 4E **27**
Bransdale Rd. WS8: Clay 6A **10**
Bransford Ri. B91: Cath B 2D **152**
Bransford Twr. B12: Birm 3H **117**
Branston Ct. B18: Birm 4E **101**
Branston St. B18: Birm 4E **101**
Branthill Cft. B91: Sol 6F **151**
Brantley Av. WV3: Wolv 2A **42**

Brantley Rd. B6: Witt 5A **84**
Branton Hill La. WS9: A'rdge 4E **35**
Brasshouse La. B66: Smeth 3D **98**
Brassie Cl. B38: King Nor 6H **145**
Brassington Av. B73: S Cold 1H **69**
BRATCH, THE 5F **57**
Bratch Cl. DY2: Neth 6E **95**
Bratch Comn. Rd. WV5: Wom 6E **57**
Bratch Hollow WV5: Wom 5G **57**
Bratch La. WV5: Wom 5F **57**
Bratch Pk. WV5: Wom 5F **57**
Bratt St. B70: W Brom 3A **80**
Braunston Cl. B76: Walm 3E **71**
Brawnes Hurst B26: Yard 2E **121**
Brayford Av. DY5: Brie H 4F **109**
Braymoor Rd. B33: Kitts G 2A **122**
Brays Rd. B26: Sheld 5E **121**
Bray St. WV13: W'hall 1B **46**
Bream Cl. B37: Chel W 1E **123**
Breamore Cres. DY1: Dud 4A **76**
Brean Av. B26: Yard 6D **120**
Brearley Cl. B19: Birm 4G **101**
Brearley St. B19: Birm 4F **101**
 B21: Hand 1H **99**
Breaside Wlk. B37: Chel W 6E **107**
Brecknock Rd. B71: W Brom 1G **79**
Brecon Dr. DY8: Amb 5F **109**
Brecon Rd. B20: Hand 1D **100**
Brecon Twr. B16: Birm 1C **116**
Bredon Av. DY9: Lye 6G **109**
Bredon Cl. B63: Hale 2A **128**
Bredon Cft. B18: Hock 4C **100**
Bredon Rd. B69: O'bry 4D **96**
 DY8: Amb 5E **109**
Bredon Ter. B18: Hock 4C **100**
 (off Brookfield Rd.)
Breech Cl. B74: S'tly 4G **51**
Breeden Dr. B76: Curd 1D **88**
Breedon Rd. B30: King Nor 2C **146**
Breener Ind. Est. DY5: Brie H 2F **109**
Breen Rydding Dr. WV14: Cose ...4D **60**
Breeze, The DY5: Brie H 1G **109**
Brelades Cl. DY1: Dud 5A **76**
Brennand Cl. B68: O'bry 3H **113**
Brennand Rd. B68: O'bry 2H **113**
Brentford Rd. B14: King H 2A **148**
 B91: Sol 4C **150**
Brentmill Cl. WV10: Bush 3B **16**
Brentnall Dr. B75: Four O 6H **37**
Brenton Rd. WV4: Penn 2D **58**
Brent Rd. B30: Stir 5F **133**
Brentwood Cl. B91: Sol 4C **150**
Brentwood Gro. B44: Gt Barr 5G **67**
Brenwood Cl. DY6: K'wfrd 2H **91**
Brereton Cl. DY2: Dud 1G **95**
Brereton Rd. WV12: W'hall 2C **30**
Bretby Cl. B93: Ben H 4B **166**
Bretby Gro. B23: Erd 1G **85**
Bretshall Cl. B90: M'path 4D **164**
Brett Dr. B32: Bart G 5A **130**
Brettell La. DY5: Brie H 3D **108**
 DY8: Amb 3D **108**
Brettell St. DY2: Dud 1D **94**
Bretton Gdns. WV10: Wolv 3B **28**
Bretton Rd. B27: A Grn 3B **136**
Brett St. B71: W Brom 2H **79**
Brett Young Cl. B63: Hale 2B **128**
Brevitt Rd. WV2: Wolv 5H **43**
Brewer's Dr. WS3: Pels 6E **21**
Brewers Sq. B16: Edg 6G **99**
Brewers Ter. WS3: Pels 5E **21**
Brewer St. WS2: Wals 5C **32**
Brewery St. WV1: Wolv 1F **43**
Brewery St. B6: Birm 4G **101**
 B21: Hand 1H **99**
 B67: Smeth 3D **98**
 DY2: Dud 6G **77**
 DY4: Tip 3H **77**
Brewins Way DY5: Brie H 5B **94**
Brewster St. DY2: Neth 4E **95**
Breydon Gro. WV13: W'hall 3H **45**
Brian Rd. B67: Smeth 3C **98**
Briar Av. B74: S'tly 2A **52**
Briarbeck WS4: S'fld 1G **33**
Briar Cl. B24: Erd 3G **85**

Briar Coppice B90: Ches G 5B **164**
Briar Ct. DY5: Brie H 1H **109**
(off Hill St.)
Briarfield Rd. B11: Tys 2G **135**
Briarley B71: W Brom 4D **64**
Briar Rd. DY1: Dud 2B **76**
Briars, The B23: Erd 1D **84**
WS9: A'rdge 2C **34**
Briars Cl. DY5: Brie H 5G **93**
Briar Way B38: King Nor 1C **160**
Briarwood Cl. B90: Ches G 5B **164**
WV2: Ett 4C **44**
Brickbridge La. WV5: Wom 2E **73**
Brickfield Rd. B25: Yard 5H **119**
Brickheath Rd. WV1: Wolv 6C **28**
Brickhill Dr. B37: F'bri 1C **122**
Brickhouse La. B70: W Brom 1E **79**
Brickhouse La. Sth. DY4: Tip 1D **78**
Brick Ho. M. B30: King Nor 3B **146**
Brickhouse Rd. B65: Row R 5A **96**
Brickiln Ct. DY5: Brie H 1H **109**
(off The Promenade)
Brickiln St. WS8: Bwnhls 6B **10**
Brick Kiln La. B44: Gt Barr 1G **83**
B47: Wyt 5H **161**
B91: Sol 1D **164**
DY3: Gorn 4E **75**
Brick Kiln Wlk. DY4: Tip 1G **77**
DY5: Brie H 4A **94**
DY5: Quar B 3C **110**
Brickkiln St. WV13: W'hall 2H **45**
Bricksmith Cl. B27: A Grn 1H **135**
Brick St. DY3: Sed 5H **59**
Brickyard Cl. CV7: Bal C 5H **169**
Brickyard Rd. WS9: A'rdge 6B **22**
Briddsland Rd. B33: Kitts G 1A **122**
Brides Wlk. B38: King Nor 2A **160**
Bridge, The WS1: Wals 2C **48**
Bridge Av. DY4: Tip 6C **62**
WS6: C Hay 1E **7**
Bridgeburn Rd. B31: N'fld 5C **130**
Bridge Cl. B11: S'hll 2B **134**
WS8: Clay 1A **22**
Bridge Ct. B64: Old H 3H **111**
(off Southbank Rd.)
WV11: Wed 2F **29**
Bridge Cft. B12: Bal H 5G **117**
Bridgefield Wlk. B65: Row R 4H **95**
Bridgefoot Wlk. WV8: Pend 6D **14**
Bridgeford Rd. B34: S End 3F **105**
Bridgehead Wlk. B76: Walm 6D **70**
Bridge Ho. B66: Smeth 3G **99**
(off Oakfield Cl.)
Bridge Ind. Est. B91: Sol 6G **137**
Bridgelands Way B20: Hand 6F **83**
Bridgeman Cft. B36: Cas B 1G **105**
Bridgeman St. WS2: Wals 2B **48**
Bridgemary Cl. WV10: Bush 3B **16**
Bridge Mdw. Dr. B93: Know 4B **166**
Bridgemeadow Ho. B36: Hodg H ...1C **104**
Bridgend Cft. DY5: P'ntt 3F **93**
Bridge Piece B31: N'fld 5F **145**
Bridge Rd. B8: Salt 5E **103**
DY4: Tip 1C **78**
WS4: S'fld 6F **21**
Bridges Cres. WS11: Nort C 1D **8**
Bridgeside Cl. WS8: Bwnhls 1B **22**
Bridges Rd. WS11: Nort C 1D **8**
Bridge St. B1: Birm 5B 4 (1E **117**)
B63: Crad 4E **111**
B69: O'bry 2G **97**
B70: W Brom 3H **79**
DY8: Word 2C **108**
WS1: Wals 1C **48**
WS8: Clay 1A **22**
WS10: W'bry 4F **63**
WV10: Wolv 4A **28**
WV13: W'hall 2H **45**
WV14: Bils 6G **45**
WV14: Cose 5E **61**
Bridge St. Ind. Est. WS10: W'bry ...4F **63**
Bridge St. Nth. B66: Smeth 3F **99**
Bridge St. Sth. B66: Smeth 3F **99**
Bridge St. W. B19: Hock 4F **101**
Bridge Trad. Cen., The B64: Crad H ..3F **111**
Bridge Trad. Est., The B66: Smeth ...3F **99**
Bridge Vw. B46: Col 2H **107**

Bridge Wlk. B27: A Grn 2B **136**
Bridgewater Av. B69: O'bry 5G **97**
Bridgewater Ct. B29: S Oak 4H **131**
Bridgewater Cres. DY2: Dud 6G **77**
Bridgewater Dr. WV5: Wom 6F **57**
WV14: Cose 3E **61**
Bridge Way WS8: Clay 1A **22**
Bridgnorth Av. WV5: Wom 3F **73**
Bridgnorth Gro. WV12: W'hall 3B **30**
Bridgnorth Rd. DY3: Himl 4H **73**
DY3: Swind 2A **72**
DY7: Stourt 4A **108**
(not continuous)
DY8: Woll 4A **108**
WV5: Wom 2E **73**
WV6: Pert, Tett, Tres 5A **40**
Bridgwater Cl. WS9: Wals W 4B **22**
Bridle Gro. B71: W Brom 5D **64**
Bridle La. B74: S'tly 4G **51**
WS9: A'rdge, S'tly 5E **51**
Bridle Mead B38: King Nor 1H **159**
Bridle Path, The B90: Shir 2H **149**
Bridle Rd. DY8: Woll 5B **108**
Bridlewood B74: S'tly 3H **51**
Bridport Ho. B31: N'fld 6C **130**
Brierley Ct. DY5: Quar B 2B **110**
BRIERLEY HILL 1H **109**
Brierley Hill Rd. DY5: Brie H 1C **108**
DY8: Brie H, Word 1C **108**
Brierley La. WV14: Bils, Cose 3G **61**
Brier Mill Rd. B63: Hale 2C **128**
Briery Cl. B64: Crad H 4H **111**
Briery Rd. B63: Hale 2G **127**
Briffen Ho. B16: Birm 1D **116**
Brigadoon Gdns. DY9: Pedm 3G **125**
Brigfield Cres. B13: Mose 2B **148**
Brigfield Rd. B13: Mose 2B **148**
Brighton Cl. WS2: Wals 6B **32**
Brighton Pl. WV3: Wolv 1E **43**
Brighton Rd. B12: Bal H 6H **117**
Bright Rd. B68: O'bry 4H **97**
Brightstone Cl. WV10: Bush 3B **16**
Brightstone Rd. B45: Fran 5H **143**
Bright St. DY8: Woll 5B **108**
WS10: Darl 6D **46**
WV1: Wolv 6F **27**
Brightwell Cres. B93: Dorr 6A **166**
Brimfield Pl. WV6: Wolv 5D **26**
(off Newbridge St.)
Brindle Cl. B26: Yard 6C **120**
Brindle Ct. B23: Erd 4B **84**
Brindlefields Way DY4: Tip 5A **78**
Brindle Rd. WS5: Wals 1G **65**
Brindley Av. WV11: Wed 6A **18**
Brindley Cl. DY8: Word 2C **108**
WS2: Wals 4F **31**
WV5: Wom 1D **72**
Brindley Ct. DY4: Tip 2G **77**
Brindley Dr. B1: Birm 4B 4 (1E **117**)
Brindley Ho. B3: Birm 2C 4 (6F **101**)
Brindley Pl. B1: Birm 5A 4 (1D **116**)
Brindley Point B16: Birm 1D **116**
Brindley Rd. B71: W Brom 5G **63**
Brindley Way B66: Smeth 4G **99**
Brineton Gro. B29: W Cas 4E **131**
Brineton Ind. Est. WS2: Wals 2A **48**
Brineton St. WS2: Wals 2A **48**
Bringewood Gro. B32: Bart G 5H **129**
Brinklow Cft. B34: S End 2H **105**
Brinklow Rd. B29: W Cas 3D **130**
Brinklow Twr. B12: Birm 4H **117**
Brinley Way DY6: K'wfrd 3A **92**
Brinsford Rd. WV10: F'hses 4G **15**
Brinsley Cl. B91: Sol 5F **151**
Brinsley Rd. B26: Sheld 3F **121**
Brisbane Rd. B67: Smeth 4C **98**
Briseley Cl. DY5: Brie H 3G **109**
Bristam Cl. B69: O'bry 3E **97**
BRISTNALL FIELDS 1H **113**
Bristnall Hall Cres. B68: O'bry 6A **98**
Bristnall Hall La. B68: O'bry 6A **98**
Bristnall Hall Rd. B68: O'bry 1H **113**
Bristol Ct. B29: W Cas 6G **131**
Bristol Rd. B5: Edg, S Oak 5H **131**
B23: Erd 4E **85**
B29: S Oak 6H **131**
DY2: Neth 1F **111**

Bristol Rd. Sth. B31: Longb, N'fld 1B **158**
B45: Redn 2G **157**
Bristol St. B5: Birm 6D 4 (3F **117**)
WV3: Wolv 3F **43**
Briston Cl. DY5: Brie H 3G **109**
Britannia Gdns. B65: Row R 6C **96**
Britannia Grn. DY3: Up Gor 2A **76**
Britannia M. B65: Row R 6C **96**
Britannia Pk. WS10: W'bry 2D **62**
Britannia Rd. B65: Row R 6C **96**
WS1: Wals 6B **48**
WV14: Bils 2H **61**
Britannia St. B69: Tiv 5C **78**
Britannic Gdns. B13: Mose 3F **133**
Britannic Pk. B13: Mose 3F **133**
Britford Cl. B14: King H 4H **147**
Briton Cl. B34: S End 3A **106**
Britton Dr. B72: W Grn 5A **70**
Britwell Rd. B73: W Grn 3G **69**
Brixfield Way B90: Dic H 4G **163**
Brixham Rd. B16: Edg 5H **99**
Broad Acres B31: N'fld 1C **144**
Broadcott Ind. Est. B64: Old H 2A **112**
Broad Cft. DY4: Tip 1C **78**
Broadfern Rd. B93: Know 1D **166**
Broadfield Cl. B71: W Brom 4D **64**
DY6: K'wfrd 4B **92**
Broadfield House Glass Mus. 4A **92**
Broad Fld. Rd. B31: Longb 5A **144**
B45: Fran 5H **143**
Broadfields Rd. B23: Erd 6H **69**
Broadfield Wlk. B16: Birm 2D **116**
Broad Gauge Way WV10: Wolv 1A **44**
Broadheath Dr. WS4: S'fld 1H **33**
Broadhidley Dr. B32: Bart G 4H **129**
Broadlands WV10: F'hses 2H **15**
Broadlands Cen. WV14: W'hall 4H **45**
Broadlands Dr. DY5: Brie H 4A **94**
Broad La. B14: King H 3F **147**
WS3: Blox 4F **19**
WS4: S'fld 6G **21**
WV3: Wolv 3C **42**
WV11: Ess 1C **18**
Broad La. Gdns. WS3: Blox 5G **19**
Broad La. Nth. WV12: W'hall 3B **30**
Broad Lanes WV14: Bils 2E **61**
Broad La. Sth. WV11: Wed 4H **29**
Broad Mdw. DY1: Dud 1A **94**
Broadmeadow DY6: K'wfrd 1C **92**
WS9: A'rdge 1D **34**
Broadmeadow Cl.
B30: King Nor 4D **146**
Broadmeadow Grn. WV14: Bils 4E **45**
Broadmeadow Ho. B32: Bart G 5B **130**
Broad Mdw. La. B30: King Nor 4D **146**
Broadmeadow La. WS6: Gt Wyr 3G **7**
Broadmeadows Cl. WV12: W'hall ...1E **31**
Broadmeadows Rd.
WV12: W'hall 1E **31**
Broadmede Ho. B67: Smeth 1C **114**
Broadmoor Av. B67: Smeth 1B **114**
B68: O'bry 1B **114**
Broadmoor Cl. WV14: Bils 1E **61**
Broadmoor Rd. WV14: Bils 1E **61**
Broadoaks B76: Walm 5E **71**
Broad Oaks Rd. B91: Sol 1D **150**
Broad Rd. B27: A Grn 2H **135**
Broads, The WV11: Wed 3A **30**
Broadstone Av. B63: Crad 1D **126**
WS3: Blox 3B **32**
Broadstone Cl. WV4: Penn 6H **43**
Broadstone Rd. B26: Yard 1D **120**
Broad St. B1: Birm 6A 4 (2D **116**)
B15: Birm 6A 4 (2D **116**)
B69: O'bry 4G **97**
DY5: P'ntt 3G **93**
DY6: K'wfrd 4B **92**
WV1: Wolv 2C 170 (1H **43**)
WV14: Bils 5E **45**
WV14: Cose 5E **61**
Broad St. Junc.
WV1: Wolv 2D 170 (1H **43**)
Broadwalk B1: Birm 6A 4 (2E **117**)
Broadwalk Retail Pk. WS1: Wals ...5B **48**
Broadwaters Av. WS10: Darl 1C **62**
Broadwaters Rd. WS10: Darl 1C **62**
Broad Way WS4: S'fld 5G **21**

Broadway B16: Birm 2D **116**
  B68: O'bry 2A **114**
  B90: Shir 3G **149**
  WS1: Wals 5D **48**
  WV3: Wolv 2A **42**
  WV8: Cod 4E **13**
  WV10: Bush 5A **16**
Broadway, The B20: Hand 5F **83**
  B71: W Brom 6G **63**
  DY1: Dud 4C **76**
  DY8: Stourb 3B **124**
          (not continuous)
  WV5: Wom 2G **73**
Broadway Av. B9: Bord G 1G **119**
  B63: Hale 3A **128**
Broadway Community Leisure Cen. . . .5G **83**
Broadway Cft. B26: Sheld 5E **121**
  B68: O'bry 2A **114**
Broadway Gdns. WV10: Bush 5A **16**
Broadway Nth. WS1: Wals 1D **48**
Broadway Plaza B16: Birm 2C **116**
Broadway W. WS1: Wals 5A **48**
Broadwell Rd. B69: O'bry 1G **97**
  B92: Olton 3E **137**
Broadwyn Trad. Est. B64: Old H 2A **112**
Broadyates Gro. B25: Yard 5A **120**
Broadyates Rd. B25: Yard 5A **120**
Brobury Cft. B91: Shir 3B **150**
Brochan Way B31: N'fld 1C **144**
Broches, The WS11: Nort C 1F **9**
Brock Cl. B45: Redn 6G **143**
Brockenhurst Ct. B73: W Grn 4H **69**
Brockeridge Cl. WV12: W'hall 6C **18**
Brockfield Ho. WV10: Wolv 5B **28**
Brockhall Gro. B37: K'hrst 4B **106**
Brockhill La. B48: A'chu 6D **160**
Brockhurst Cres. WS5: Wals 6C **48**
Brockhurst Dr. B28: Hall G 2G **149**
  WV6: Wolv 5E **27**
Brockhurst Ho. WS2: Wals 6B **32**
Brockhurst La. B75: Can 1F **39**
  B90: Dic H 3H **163**
Brockhurst Pl. WS5: Wals 6D **48**
  B75: R'ley 2B **54**
Brockhurst Rd. B36: Hodg H 3A **104**
  B75: R'ley 2B **54**
Brockhurst St. WS1: Wals 5C **48**
Brockley Cl. DY5: Brie H 6H **93**
Brockley Gro. B13: Mose 4E **133**
Brockley Pl. B7: Nech 2C **102**
BROCKMOOR 5G **93**
Brockmoor Cl. DY9: Pedm 3G **125**
Brockmoor Ind. Est. DY5: Brie H 6E **93**
Brock Rd. DY4: Tip 3C **78**
Brockswood 1G **75**
Brockton Rd. WV3: W Cas 4E **131**
Brockwell Gro. B44: Gt Barr 1G **67**
Brockwell Rd. B44: Gt Barr 1G **67**
Brockworth Rd. B14: King H 5E **147**
Brocton Cl. WS3: Blox 1G **31**
  WV14: Cose 2D **60**
Brogden Cl. B71: W Brom 5D **64**
Brolly Works, The B5: Birm 5F **5** (1H **117**)
Bromfield Cl. B6: Aston 2G **101**
Bromfield Ct. WV6: Tett 1H **41**
Bromfield Cres. WS10: W'bry 1A **64**
Bromfield Rd. WS10: W'bry 2A **64**
BROMFORD .1A **104**
Bromford Central B8: Hodg H 1H **103**
Bromford Cl. B20: Hand 6C **82**
  B23: Erd 2E **85**
Bromford Ct. B31: N'fld 6F **145**
Bromford Cres. B24: Erd 5G **85**
Bromford Dale WV6: Wolv 6E **27**
Bromford Dell B31: N'fld 3G **145**
Bromford Dr. B36: Hodg H 1H **103**
Bromford Gdns. B15: Edg 3G **115**
Bromford Ga. B24: Erd 1G **103**
Bromford Hill B20: Hand 4E **83**
Bromford Ho. B73: Bold 3F **69**
Bromford La. B8: W End 5G **85**
  B24: Erd 5G **85**
  B70: W Brom 6G **79**
Bromford Mere B92: Olton 5C **136**
Bromford Mills Ind. Est. B24: Erd 6G **85**
Bromford Pk. Ho. B13: Mose 3B **134**
         (off Wake Grn. Pk.)
Bromford Pk. Ind. Est. B70: W Brom . .6G **79**

Bromford Ri. WV3: Wolv 3F **43**
Bromford Rd. B36: Hodg H 2H **103**
  B69: O'bry 1G **97**
  B70: W Brom 1G **97**
  DY2: Dud 3C **94**
Bromford Rd. Ind. Est. B69: O'bry 6G **79**
Bromford Wlk. B43: Gt Barr 4B **66**
BROMLEY 4F **93**
Bromley DY5: P'ntt 4F **93**
Bromley Gdns. WV8: Cod 3G **13**
Bromley La. DY6: K'wfrd 5C **92**
Bromley Pl. WV4: Penn 6E **43**
Bromley St. B9: Birm 2A **118**
  DY9: Lye 5B **110**
  WV2: Wolv 4G **43**
Brompton Dr. DY5: Brie H 4F **109**
Brompton Lawns WV6: Tett 6G **25**
Brompton Pool Rd. B28: Hall G 4E **149**
Brompton Rd. B44: Gt Barr 1G **67**
Bromsgrove Rd. B62: Hunn, Roms . . .3A **142**
  B63: Hale 2C **128**
  DY9: Hag 6G **125**
Bromsgrove St. B5: Birm 6E **5** (2G **117**)
  B63: Hale 1C **128**
Bromwall Rd. B13: Mose 1B **148**
Bromwich Ct. B46: Col 5G **89**
Bromwich Dr. B75: S Cold 4A **54**
Bromwich La. DY9: Pedm 6F **125**
Bromwich Wlk. B9: Bord G 6G **103**
Bromwynd Cl. WV2: Wolv 5F **43**
Bromyard Av. B76: Walm 5E **71**
Bromyard Rd. B11: S'hll 2E **135**
Bronte Cl. B90: Shir 6B **150**
Bronte Ct. B90: Shir 6B **150**
Bronte Farm Rd. B90: Shir 6B **150**
Bronte Rd. WV2: Ett 5B **44**
Bronwen Rd. WV14: Cose 6E **61**
Brookbank Av. B34: S End 3H **105**
Brookbank Gdns. DY3: Gorn 5F **75**
Brookbank Rd. DY3: Gorn 5F **75**
Brook Cl. B33: Stech 5C **104**
  B90: Shir 6F **149**
  WS9: Wals W 4C **22**
Brook Cotts. B25: Yard 4G **119**
Brook Cres. DY6: W Hth 2A **92**
  DY9: W'cte 2B **126**
Brook Cft. B26: Sheld 4F **121**
  B37: Mars G 4D **122**
Brookdale DY3: Lwr G 4G **75**
Brookdale Cl. B45: Redn 6G **143**
Brookdale Dr. WV4: Penn 5C **42**
Brook Dr. B32: Bart G 4B **130**
Brook End WS7: Chase 1C **10**
Brookend Dr. B45: Rub 1F **157**
Brookes Cl. B69: Tiv 1B **96**
Brookes Ho. WS1: Wals 2D **48**
         (off Paddock La.)
Brookes Mdw. DY4: Tip 1A **78**
Brooke St. DY2: Dud 1E **95**
Brook Farm Wlk. B37: Chel W 6F **107**
Brookfield Cl. WS9: A'rdge 6C **22**
Brookfield Rd. B18: Hock 4C **100**
  B30: King Nor 4F **147**
  WS9: A'rdge 6C **22**
  WV8: Bilb 4H **13**
BROOKFIELDS 4D **100**
Brookfields Rd. B68: O'bry 5A **98**
Brookfield Ter. B18: Hock 4C **100**
Brookfield Way B92: Olton 6B **136**
  DY4: Tip 1A **78**
Brook Grn. La. B92: Bars 6A **154**
Brook Gro. WV8: Bilb 4H **13**
Brookhill Cl. WV12: W'hall 6C **18**
Brookhill Rd. B8: W End 5G **103**
Brookhill Way WV12: W'hall 6D **18**
Brook Holloway DY9: W'cte 1B **126**
Brook Ho. Cl. WV10: F'stne 1D **16**
Brook Ho. La. WV10: F'stne 1A **16**
Brookhouse Rd. WS5: Wals 4F **49**
Brookhus Farm Rd. B76: Walm 5E **71**
Brooking Cl. B43: Gt Barr 1F **67**
Brookland Gro. WS9: Wals W 5B **22**
Brookland Rd. WS9: Wals W 4B **22**
Brooklands DY3: Swind 6E **73**
  DY8: Word 2D **108**
  WS5: Wals 2F **65**
Brooklands Av. WS6: Gt Wyr 1F **7**

Brooklands Cl. B28: Hall G 4F **135**
Brooklands Dr. B14: King H 2G **147**
Brooklands Pde. WV1: Wolv 2C **44**
Brooklands Rd. B28: Hall G 4F **135**
Brooklands Way B37: Mars G 3D **122**
Brook La. B13: Mose 5A **134**
  B32: Harb 6D **114**
  B64: Old H 1G **111**
  B92: Olton 5B **136**
  WS6: Gt Wyr 2G **7**
  WS9: Wals W 4B **22**
Brooklea Gro. B38: King Nor 6C **146**
Brooklyn Av. B6: Aston 2H **101**
Brooklyn Gro. DY6: W Hth 1H **91**
  WV14: Cose 5F **61**
Brooklyn Rd. WS7: Chase 1C **10**
Brookmans Av. B32: Quin 1B **130**
Brook Mdw. Ct. B28: Hall G 1D **148**
Brook Mdw. Rd. B34: S End 3E **105**
  WS4: S'fld 1H **33**
Brook Mdws. WV8: Bilb 3H **13**
Brook Pk. Trad. Est. DY9: Lye 6B **110**
Brookpiece Ho. B14: King H 5G **147**
         (off Milston Cl.)
Brook Piece Wlk. B35: Cas V 4F **87**
Brook Rd. B15: Edg 4A **116**
  B45: Rub 2E **157**
  B68: O'bry 1G **113**
  DY8: Stourb 2F **125**
  WS6: C Hay 1E **7**
  WV5: Wom 1F **73**
  WV13: W'hall 2G **45**
Brooksbank Dr. B64: Old H 5H **95**
Brooksby Gro. B93: Dorr 6H **167**
Brooks Cft. B35: Cas V 5E **87**
Brookside B31: N'fld 2D **144**
  B43: Gt Barr 6H **65**
  B90: Ches G 6B **164**
  DY3: Gorn 5H **75**
  WS10: W'bry 2H **63**
Brookside Av. B13: Mose 6B **134**
Brookside Cl. B23: Erd 6C **68**
  B63: Hale 2F **127**
  WV5: Wom 1E **73**
Brookside Ind. Est. WS10: W'bry 2H **63**
Brookside Way DY6: W Hth 2H **91**
Brooks Rd. B72: W Grn 5A **70**
Brook St. B3: Birm 2B **4** (6E **101**)
  B66: Smeth 3F **99**
  B70: W Brom 4H **79**
  DY3: Gorn 4G **75**
  DY3: Sed 6C **60**
  DY4: Tip 1G **77**
  DY5: Quar B 3C **110**
  DY6: W Hth 6H **73**
  DY8: Stourb 6C **108**
  DY8: Word 2D **108**
  DY9: Lye 6B **110**
  WS2: Wals 2B **48**
  WV14: Bils 6G **45**
Brook St. Bus. Cen. DY4: Tip 1G **77**
Brook Ter. WV14: Bils 6G **45**
Brookthorpe Dr. WV12: W'hall 6C **30**
Brookvale Gro. B92: Olton 4B **136**
Brookvale M. B29: S Oak 3D **132**
Brookvale Pk. Rd. B23: Erd 2B **84**
Brookvale Rd. B6: Witt 5A **84**
  B23: Erd 5A **84**
  B92: Olton 4B **136**
Brookvale Trad. Est. B6: Witt 4A **84**
Brookview B67: Smeth 6D **98**
Brook Vw. Cl. B19: Hock 3E **101**
Brook Wlk. B32: Bart G 3B **130**
Brook Way B16: Edg 6G **99**
  B17: Edg 6G **99**
Brookwillow Rd. B63: Hale 4F **127**
Brookwood Av. B28: Hall G 2D **148**
Broomcroft Rd. B37: K'hrst 4B **106**
Broomdene Av. B34: S End 2E **105**
Broom Dr. B14: King H 3G **147**
Broome Av. B43: Gt Barr 6G **65**
Broome Cl. B63: Hale 2A **128**
Broome Ct. B36: Cas B 1G **105**
Broome Gdns. B75: S Cold 6A **54**
Broomehill Cl. DY5: Brie H 4G **109**
Broome Rd. WV10: Bush 2A **28**
Broomfield B67: Smeth 4D **98**

Broomfield Rd.—Burlington Pas.

Broomfield Rd. B23: Erd 5D **84**
Broomfields Av. B91: Sol 2H **151**
Broomfields Cl. B91: Sol 2H **151**
Broomfields Farm Rd.
B91: Sol 2H **151**
Broomhall Av. WV11: Wed 3F **29**
Broom Hall Cres. B27: A Grn 6H **135**
Broom Hall Gro. B27: A Grn 5A **136**
Broomhill Cl. B43: Gt Barr 5H **65**
Broomhill La. B43: Gt Barr 5H **65**
Broomhill Rd. B23: Erd 6B **68**
Broom Ho. B71: W Brom 4D **64**
Broomhurst B15: Edg 3A **116**
Broomie Cl. B75: S Cold 6B **54**
Broom La. B90: Dic H 3G **163**
Broomlea Cl. B74: S'tly 3G **51**
Broom Rd. DY1: Dud 2C **76**
WS5: Wals 2F **65**
Broom St. B12: Birm 3A **118**
Broomy Cl. B34: Stech 4E **105**
Broseley Av. B31: Longb 1F **159**
Broseley Brook Cl. B9: Bord G 2C **118**
Brosil Av. B20: Hand 4A **82**
Brougham St. B19: Loz 2D **100**
(not continuous)
Brough Cl. B7: Nech 3B **102**
WV4: Ett 2B **60**
Broughton Ct. WV6: Pert 6G **25**
Broughton Cres. B31: Longb 1B **158**
Broughton Rd. B20: Hand 1C **100**
DY9: W'cte 2H **125**
WV3: Wolv 2A **42**
Brownfield Rd. B34: S End 3G **105**
BROWNHILLS **6B 10**
Brownhills Bus. Pk. WS8: Bwnhls 2B **22**
BROWNHILLS COMMON **5A 10**
Brownhills Rd. WS8: Wals W 2B **22**
WS11: Nort C 1E **9**
BROWNHILLS WEST **3G 9**
Brownhills West Station
Chasewater Railway **2G 9**
Browning Cl. WV12: W'hall 2E **31**
Browning Cres. WV10: F'hses 5G **15**
Browning Gro. WV6: Pert 5E **25**
Browning Rd. DY3: Lwr G 3E **75**
Browning St. B16: Birm 1D **116**
Browning Twr. B31: N'fld 4G **145**
Brownley Rd. B90: Shir 2B **164**
Brown Lion St. DY4: Tip 6G **61**
Brown Rd. WS10: Darl 4C **46**
Brown's Coppice Av. B91: Sol 2B **150**
Browns Ct. B13: Mose 3B **134**
Brown's Dr. B73: Bold 5F **69**
Brownsea Cl. B45: Fran 6E **143**
Brownsea Dr. B1: Birm 6C **4** (2F **117**)
BROWN'S GREEN **4B 82**
Browns Grn. B20: Hand 4B **82**
Brownshore La. WV11: Ess 3A **18**
Browns La. B93: Know 3A **166**
Brownsover Cl. B36: Cas B 6F **87**
Brown St. WV2: Wolv 4H **43**
Brownswall Est. DY3: Sed 6F **59**
Brownswall Rd. DY3: Sed 6F **59**
Broxwood Pk. WV6: Tett 6H **25**
Brueton Av. B91: Sol 4H **151**
Brueton Dr. B24: Erd 4G **85**
Brueton Rd. WV14: Bils 4A **46**
Bruford Rd. WV3: Wolv 3E **43**
Brundard Cl. WS3: Blox 1B **32**
Brunel Cl. B12: Bal H 6A **118**
Brunel Ct. WS10: Darl 5F **47**
WV5: Wom 6G **57**
WV14: Cose 5G **61**
Brunel Dr. DY4: Tip 4G **61**
Brunel Gro. WV6: Pert 3E **25**
Brunel Rd. B69: O'bry 3D **96**
Brunel St. B1: Birm 5C **4** (1F **117**)
Brunel Wlk. WS10: Darl 5F **47**
Brunel Way WV2: Ett 4C **44**
Brunslow Cl. WV10: Oxl 6G **15**
WV13: W'hall 2C **46**
Brunswick Arc. *B1: Birm* *1D* ***116***
(off Brunswick St.)
Brunswick Ct. WS10: W'bry 2A **64**
Brunswick Gdns. B21: Hand 6B **82**
WS10: W'bry 1H **63**
Brunswick Ga. DY8: Stourb 4E **125**
Brunswick Ho. B34: S End 2E **105**
B37: Mars G 3B **122**
Brunswick Pk. Rd. WS10: W'bry 2G **63**
Brunswick Pl. *B12: Bal H* *5A* ***118***
(off Ombersley Rd.)
Brunswick Rd. B12: Bal H 6A **118**
B21: Hand 6B **82**
Brunswick Sq. B1: Birm 5A **4** (1D **116**)
Brunswick St. B1: Birm 5A **4** (1D **116**)
WS2: Wals 4A **48**
Brunswick Ter. WS10: W'bry 2F **63**
Brunton Rd. B10: Small H 4F **119**
Brushfield Rd. B42: Gt Barr 5F **67**
Brutus Dr. B46: Col 6G **89**
Bryan Av. WV4: Penn 1B **58**
Bryan Budd Cl. B65: Row R 5B **96**
Bryan Rd. WS2: Wals 5A **48**
Bryanston Ct. B91: Sol 6D **136**
Bryanston Rd. B91: Sol 6D **136**
Bryant St. B18: Win G 4A **100**
Bryce Rd. DY5: P'ntt 4E **93**
(not continuous)
Bryher Wlk. B45: Fran 6E **143**
Brylan Cft. B44: K'sdng 1H **83**
Brymill Ind. Est. DY4: Tip 6G **61**
Bryn Arden Rd. B26: Yard 6C **120**
Bryndale Av. B14: King H 2E **147**
Brynmawr Rd. WV14: Cose 2C **60**
Brynside Cl. B14: King H 5F **147**
Bryony *B74: Four O* *4F* ***37***
(off Badgers Bank Rd.)
Bryony Cft. B23: Erd 6B **68**
Bryony Gdns. WS10: Darl 4D **46**
Bryony Rd. B29: W Cas 6F **131**
BSA Bus. Pk. B11: Small H 5D **118**
Buchanan Av. WS4: Wals 6E **33**
Buchanan Cl. WS4: Wals 6E **33**
Buchanan Rd. WS4: Wals 6E **33**
Buckbury Cl. DY9: Pedm 4H **125**
Buckbury Cft. B90: M'path 3F **165**
Buckden Cl. B37: F'bri 2B **122**
Buckingham Cl. WS10: W'bry 1A **64**
Buckingham Ct. B29: S Oak 5A **132**
Buckingham Dr. WV12: W'hall 2B **30**
Buckingham Gro. DY6: K'wfrd 2A **92**
Buckingham M. B73: W Grn 2G **69**
Buckingham Ri. DY1: Dud 5A **76**
Buckingham Rd. B36: Cas B 2B **106**
B65: Row R 5D **96**
WV4: Penn 1E **59**
Buckingham St. B19: Birm 5F **101**
(not continuous)
BUCKLAND END **3D 104**
Buckland End B34: S End 3E **105**
Bucklands End La. B34: Hodg H 3D **104**
Buckle Cl. WS1: Wals 3D **48**
Buckley Ct. B13: King H 5H **133**
Buckley Rd. WV4: Penn 6B **42**
Bucklow Wlk. B33: Stech 5C **104**
Buckminster Dr. B93: Dorr 5A **166**
Bucknall Ct. B13: Mose 3B **134**
Bucknall Cres. B32: Bart G 5G **129**
Bucknall Ho. B14: King H 1G **147**
Bucknall Rd. WV11: Wed 6B **18**
Bucknell Cl. B91: Sol 2G **151**
BUCKPOOL **1D 108**
Buckpool & Fens Pools Local Nature Reserve
4G 93
Buckridge Cl. B38: King Nor 2H **159**
Buckridge La. B90: Dic H 4G **163**
(not continuous)
Buckthorn Av. B16: Edg 6G **99**
Buckton Cl. B75: R'ley 1C **54**
Budbrooke Gro. B34: S End 3A **106**
Budden Rd. WV14: Cose 6F **61**
Bude Rd. WS5: Wals 4H **49**
Budnam Brook Ct. DY5: Brie H 6F **93**
Buffery Rd. DY2: Dud 2F **95**
Bufferys Cl. B91: Sol 1F **165**
Buildwas Cl. WS3: Blox 5F **19**
Bulford Cl. B14: King H 5H **147**
Bulger Rd. WV14: Bils 4E **45**
Bullace Cft. B15: Edg 2H **131**
Buller St. WV4: Ett 6A **44**
Bullfields Cl. B65: Row R 4H **95**
Bullfinch Cl. DY1: Dud 1A **94**
Bullivents Cl. B93: Ben H 4B **166**
Bull La. B70: W Brom 4G **79**
WS10: Mox 2B **62**
WV5: Wom 5G **57**
WV14: Bils 2B **62**
Bull Mdw. La. WV5: Wom 5G **57**
Bullock's Row WS1: Wals 2D **48**
Bullock St. B7: Birm 4A **102**
B70: W Brom 1B **98**
Bullows Rd. WS8: Bwnhls 1G **21**
BULLRING, THE **5F 5 (1G 117)**
Bull Ring B63: Hale 2B **128**
DY3: Sed 5H **59**
WV13: W'hall *6A* ***30***
(off Bloxwich Rd. Sth.)
Bullring Shop. Cen.
B5: Birm 5E **5** (1G **117**)
Bull Ring Trad. Est.
B12: Birm 6H **5** (2H **117**)
Bull's La. B76: Walm, Wis 2F **71**
(not continuous)
Bull St. B4: Birm 3E **5** (6G **101**)
B17: Harb 5H **115**
B70: W Brom 4B **80**
DY1: Dud 1C **94**
DY3: Gorn 5G **75**
DY5: Brie H 2F **109**
(Goldencross Way)
DY5: Brie H 1E **109**
(Hawbush Rd.)
WS10: Darl 5E **47**
Bull St. Trad. Est. DY5: Brie H 1F **109**
Bulrush Cl. WS8: Bwnhls 6A **10**
Bulwell Cl. B6: Aston 2A **102**
BUMBLE HOLE **4G 95**
Bumble Hole Local Nature Reserve **4G 95**
Bumblehole Mdws. WV5: Wom 6F **57**
Bunbury Gdns. B30: King Nor 3G **145**
Bunbury Rd. B31: N'fld 3F **145**
Bundle Hill B63: Hale 2A **128**
Bungalows, The B70: W Brom 1F **79**
BUNKER'S HILL **4G 45**
Bunkers Hill La. WV14: Bils 3G **45**
Bunn's La. DY2: Dud 6H **77**
Burbage Cl. WV10: Wolv 3B **28**
Burberry Ct. DY4: Tip 5A **62**
Burberry Gro. CV7: Bal C 3G **169**
Burbidge Ind. Est. B9: Bord G 1D **118**
Burbidge Rd. B9: Bord G 6D **102**
Burbury St. B19: Loz 2E **101**
Burbury St. Sth. B19: Hock 3E **101**
Burcombe Twr. B23: Erd 1H **85**
Burcot Av. WV1: Wolv 1C **44**
Burcot Ct. B74: Four O 1F **53**
Burcote Rd. B24: Erd 4B **86**
Burcot Wlk. WV1: Wolv 1C **44**
Burdock Cl. WS5: Wals 2E **65**
Burdock Ho. B38: King Nor 6B **146**
Burdock Rd. B29: W Cas 1E **145**
Burdons Cl. B34: Stech 4E **105**
Bure Gro. WV13: W'hall 1D **46**
Burfield Rd. B63: Crad 5E **111**
Burford Cl. B92: Olton 2E **137**
WS5: Wals 2E **65**
Burford Ct. B13: Mose 3B **134**
Burford Pk. Rd. B38: King Nor 1A **160**
Burford Rd. B44: K'sdng 6H **67**
B47: H'wd 3H **161**
Burgess Cft. B92: Sol 6B **138**
Burghley Dr. B71: W Brom 3D **64**
Burghley Wlk. DY5: Brie H 3F **109**
Burgh Way WS2: Wals 4G **31**
Burhill Way B37: F'bri 4D **106**
Burke Av. B13: Mose 4D **134**
Burkitt Dr. DY4: Tip 5C **62**
Burland Av. WV6: Tett 2C **26**
Burleigh Cl. CV7: Bal C 2H **169**
WV12: W'hall 3B **30**
Burleigh Cft. WS7: Chase 1C **10**
Burleigh Rd. WV3: Wolv 4E **43**
Burleigh St. WS1: Wals 2E **49**
Burleton Rd. B33: Kitts G 1A **122**
Burley Cl. B90: Shir 5F **149**
Burley Way B38: King Nor 1G **159**
Burlington Arc. B2: Birm 4D **4**
Burlington Av. B70: W Brom 6C **80**
Burlington M. B10: Small H 2F **119**
Burlington Pas. B2: Birm 4D **4**

Burlington Rd. B10: Small H 2E 119
  B70: W Brom 6C 80
Burlington St. B6: Aston 3G 101
Burlish Av. B92: Olton 4D 136
Burman Cl. B90: Shir 5G 149
Burman Dr. B46: Col 4H 107
Burman Rd. B90: Shir 5F 149
Burmarsh Wlk. WV8: Pend 1D 26
Burmese Way B65: Row R 3H 95
Burnaston Cres. B90: M'path 3G 165
Burnaston Rd. B28: Hall G 4E 135
Burnbank Gro. B24: Erd 3H 85
Burn Cl. B66: Smeth 5E 99
Burncross Way WV10: Wolv 3B 28
Burnell Gdns. WV3: Wolv 3C 42
Burnel Rd. B29: W Cas 3E 131
Burnett Ho. B69: O'bry 4D 96
Burnett Rd. B74: Lit As 1B 52
Burney La. B8: W End 4A 104
Burnfields Way WS9: A'rdge 2C 34
Burnham Av. B25: Yard 5A 120
  WV10: Oxl 1F 27
Burnham Cl. DY6: K'wfrd 5D 92
Burnham Ct. B23: Erd 5C 84
  DY5: Brie H 1H 109
  (off Hill St.)
Burnham Mdw. B28: Hall G 1G 149
Burnham Rd. B44: Gt Barr 6G 67
Burnhill Gro. B29: W Cas 5E 131
Burnlea Gro. B31: N'fld 6G 145
Burnsall Cl. B37: F'bri 1B 122
  WV9: Pend 4E 15
Burns Av. DY4: Tip 5A 62
  WV10: F'hses 5H 15
Burns Cl. DY8: Amb 3E 109
Burns Gro. DY3: Lwr G 3E 75
Burnside Ct. B73: W Grn 4G 69
Burnside Gdns. WS5: Wals 5H 49
Burnside Way B31: Longb 2D 158
Burns Pl. WS10: Mox 6A 46
Burns Rd. WS10: Mox 6A 46
Burnthurst Cres. B90: M'path ...2E 165
Burnt Oak Dr. DY8: Stourb 6F 109
BURNT TREE 5H 77
Burnt Tree DY4: Tip 5H 77
Burnt Tree Ind. Est. DY4: Tip ...5B 78
BURNTWOOD JUNC. 2B 10
Burntwood Rd. WS7: Hamm 1F 11
Burrelton Way B43: Gt Barr 5H 65
Burrington Rd. B32: Bart G 5G 129
Burrow, The WV3: Wolv 2B 42
Burrowes St. WS2: Wals 6B 32
Burrow Hill Cl. B36: Cas B 1G 105
Burrows Ho. WS2: Wals 6B 32
  (off Green La.)
Burrows Rd. DY6: K'wfrd 5D 92
Burrs Dr. WS10: W'bry 4G 63
Bursledon Wlk. WV1: Wolv 3E 45
Burslem Cl. WS3: Blox 3G 19
Bursnips Rd. WV11: Ess 5B 18
Burton Av. WS4: Rus 1F 33
Burton Cres. WV10: Wolv 6A 28
Burton Farm Rd. WS4: Wals 6F 33
Burton Gro. B64: Old H 3G 111
Burton Rd. DY1: Dud 3B 76
  WV10: Wolv 6A 28
Burton Rd. E. DY1: Dud 3B 76
Burtons Pk. Rd. B36: Cas B 1B 106
Burtons Way B36: Cas B 2C 106
Burton Wood Dr. B20: Hand 5F 83
Buryfield Rd. B91: Sol 1E 151
Bury Hill Rd. B69: O'bry 2D 96
Bury Mound Ct. B90: Shir 5C 148
Bush Av. B66: Smeth 4G 99
BUSHBURY 6A 16
Bushbury Ct. WV10: Bush 5A 16
Bushbury Crematorium WV10: Bush ...4B 16
Bushbury Cft. B37: Chel W 6E 107
Bushbury La. WV10: Oxl, Bush ...3G 27
Bushbury Rd. B33: Stech 4E 105
  WV10: Wolv 3C 28
Bushell Dr. B91: Sol 3H 151
Bushey Cl. B74: S'tly 1H 51
Bushey Flds. Rd. DY1: Dud 1A 94
Bushfield Ct. WV14: Bils 6G 45
Bush Gro. B21: Hand 6G 81
  WS3: Pels 5E 21

Bushley Cft. B91: Sol 1F 165
Bushman Way B34: S End 4A 106
Bushmore Rd. B28: Hall G 1G 149
Bush Rd. DY2: Neth 1E 111
  DY4: Tip 3G 77
Bush St. WS10: Darl 4D 46
Bushway Cl. DY5: Brie H 1E 109
Bushwood Cl. B15: Edg 3E 117
  B29: S Oak 4F 131
Bushwood Dr. B93: Dorr 6C 166
Bushwood Rd. B29: S Oak 4F 131
  (not continuous)
Business Centre, The B11: Tys 5F 119
Bustleholme Av. B71: W Brom 4D 64
Bustleholme La. B71: W Brom 4C 64
Butchers La. B63: Crad 4E 111
Butchers Rd. B92: H Ard 1A 154
BUTCROFT 5E 47
Butcroft Gdns. WS10: Darl 5E 47
Bute Cl. B45: Fran 6E 143
  WV12: W'hall 3B 30
Butler Lane Station (Rail) 6G 37
Butlers Cl. B20: Hand 4C 82
  B23: Erd 4D 68
Butlers Courts La. B20: Hand ...4C 82
Butlers La. B74: Four O 6F 37
  B75: Four O 6F 37
Butlers Pct. WS1: Wals 1C 48
Butler's Rd. B20: Hand 4C 82
Butler St. B70: W Brom 3G 79
Butler Way B16: Edg 6G 99
Butlin St. B7: Nech 2C 102
Buttercup Cl. WS5: Wals 2E 65
Butterfield Cl. WV6: Pert 6D 24
Butterfield Ct. DY1: Dud 5C 76
Butterfield Rd. DY5: P'ntt 2F 93
Butterfly Way B64: Old H 2H 111
Buttermere Cl. DY5: Brie H 4F 109
  WV6: Tett 1B 26
Buttermere Dr. B32: Bart G 2D 130
  WV11: Ess 5A 18
Buttermere Gro. WV12: W'hall ...6B 18
Butterton Cl. WV6: Pert 5F 25
Butterworth Cl. WV14: Bils 4C 60
  WV14: Cose 4C 60
Buttery Rd. B67: Smeth 3C 98
Buttons Farm Rd. WV4: Penn 2B 58
Buttress Way B66: Smeth 3E 99
Butts, The WS4: Wals 6D 32
Butts Cl. WS11: Nort C 1C 8
Butts La. WS11: Nort C 1C 8
Butts Rd. WS4: Wals 6D 32
  WV4: Penn 1D 58
Butts St. WS4: Wals 6D 32
Butts Way WS11: Nort C 1C 8
Buxton Cl. WS3: Blox 4A 20
Buxton Rd. B23: Erd 1B 84
  B73: W Grn 4G 69
  DY2: Dud 3B 94
  WS3: Blox 4A 20
Byeways WS3: Blox 4A 20
Byfield Cl. B33: Kitts G 3A 122
Byfield Pas. B9: Bord G 1E 119
Byfield Vw. DY3: Sed 6A 60
Byfleet Cl. WV14: Cose 2C 60
Byford Way B37: Mars G 3D 122
Byland Way WS3: Blox 5F 19
By-Pass Link B91: Sol 4A 152
Byrchen Moor Gdns.
  DY5: P'ntt 2F 93
Byrne Rd. WV2: Wolv 4H 43
Byron Av. B23: Erd 4B 84
Byron Cl. B10: Small H 4D 118
Byron Ct. B74: Four O 4G 37
  B93: Know 3C 166
Byron Cres. DY1: Dud 2D 76
Byron Cft. B74: Four O 3F 37
  DY3: Lwr G 2E 75
Byron Gdns. B71: W Brom 2H 79
Byron Ho. B63: Crad 6D 110
Byron Rd. B10: Small H 4D 118
  WV10: Bush 1C 28
  WV12: W'hall 2E 31

Byron St. B71: W Brom 1H 79
  DY5: P'ntt 2H 93
Bywater Ho. WS1: Wals 2D 48
  (off Paddock La.)

C

Caban Cl. B31: N'fld 2C 144
Cable Dr. WS2: Wals 4A 32
Cable St. WV2: Wolv 3A 44
Cabot Gro. WV6: Pert 5E 25
Cadbury Dr. B35: Cas V 6E 87
Cadbury Ho. B19: Birm 4F 101
  (off Gt. Hampton Row)
Cadbury Rd. B13: Mose 1B 134
Cadbury Way B17: Harb 6F 115
Cadbury World 6B 132
Caddick Cres. B71: W Brom 6B 64
Caddick Rd. B42: Gt Barr 4D 66
Caddick St. WV14: Cose 5C 60
  (not continuous)
Cadet Dr. B90: Shir 4G 149
Cadgwith Gdns. WV14: Bils 3A 62
Cadine Gdns. B13: Mose 4E 133
Cadleigh Gdns. B17: Harb 2G 131
Cadle Rd. WV10: Bush 2A 28
Cadman Cres. WV10: Wolv 3C 28
Cadman's La. WS3: Blox 1B 20
  WS6: Gt Wyr 5A 8
Cadnam Cl. B17: Harb 2G 131
  WV13: W'hall 3B 46
Caernarvon Cl. WV12: W'hall ...2C 30
Caernarvon Way DY1: Dud 5A 76
Caesar Way B46: Col 6H 89
Cairn Dr. WS2: Wals 1F 47
Cairns St. WS2: Wals 6A 32
Caister Dr. WV13: W'hall 3H 45
Cakemore La. B68: O'bry 1F 113
Cakemore Rd. B65: Row R 1E 113
Cala Dr. B15: Edg 4D 116
Calcot Dr. WV6: Tett 2C 26
Calcutt Way B90: Dic H 3G 163
  (not continuous)
Caldecote Gro. B9: Bord G 2A 120
Caldeford Av. B90: M'path 2E 165
Calder Av. WS1: Wals 1E 49
Calder Dr. B76: Walm 5D 70
Calderfields Cl. WS4: Wals 6E 33
Calderfields Golf Course 1G 49
Calder Gro. B20: Hand 5B 82
Calder Ri. DY3: Sed 1B 76
CALDMORE 3C 48
Caldmore Grn. WS1: Wals 3C 48
Caldmore Rd. WS1: Wals 2C 48
Caldwell Cl. B91: Sol 2G 151
Caldwell Gro. B91: Sol 2G 151
Caldwell Ho. B70: W Brom 5A 80
Caldwell Rd. B9: Bord G 6H 103
Caldwell St. B71: W Brom 5B 64
Caldy Wlk. B45: Fran 6F 143
Caledonia DY5: Quar B 4H 109
Caledonia Cl. WS5: Wals 2G 65
Caledonia Rd. WV2: Wolv 3H 43
  (not continuous)
Caledonia St. WV14: Bils 5G 45
Caledon Pl. WS2: Wals 4A 48
Caledon St. WS2: Wals 4A 48
  (not continuous)
Calewood Rd. DY5: Quar B 4H 109
Calgary Ho. B5: Edg 4F 117
  (off Benmore Av.)
CALIFORNIA 2E 131
California Ho. B32: Bart G 3C 130
  (off Millmead Rd.)
California Rd. B69: Tiv 1B 96
California Way B32: Bart G 2D 130
Callaghan Dr. B69: Tiv 4C 78
Callcott Dr. DY5: Quar B 4H 109
Callear Rd. WS10: W'bry 4D 62
Calley Cl. DY4: Tip 4H 77
Callowbridge Rd. B45: Rub 2F 157
Callowbrook La. B45: Rub 1F 157
Calshot Rd. B42: Gt Barr 4B 66
Calstock Rd. WV12: W'hall 5D 30
Calthorpe Cl. WS5: Wals 5A 50
Calthorpe Mans. B15: Edg 2D 116

Calthorpe Rd. B15: Edg 3C 116
  B20: Hand 5E 83
  WS5: Wals 5H 49
Calver Cres. WV11: Wed 4H 29
Calver Gro. B44: Gt Barr 2F 67
Calverley Rd. DY6: K'wfrd 6H 145
Calverton Gro. B43: Gt Barr 5A 66
Calverton Wlk. WV6: Wolv 4F 27
Calves Cft. WV13: W'hall 6A 30
Calvin Cl. WV5: Wom 2F 73
  WV10: F'hses 4H 15
Camberley B71: W Brom 4D 64
Camberley Cres. WV4: Ett 3A 60
Camberley Dr. WV4: Penn 1E 59
Camberley Gro. B23: Erd 1E 85
Camberley Ri. B71: W Brom 4D 64
Camberley Rd. DY6: K'wfrd 6D 92
Camborne Cl. B6: Aston 2G 101
Camborne Ct. WS5: Wals 4H 49
Camborne Rd. WS5: Wals 4H 49
Cambourne Rd. B65: Row R 6C 96
Cambrai Dr. B28: Hall G 5E 135
Cambria Cl. B90: Maj G 2E 163
Cambrian Hall B1: Birm 3B 4
Cambridge Av. B73: W Grn 5H 69
  B91: Sol 4C 150
Cambridge Cl. WS9: A'rdge 1C 34
Cambridge Cres. B15: Edg 4E 117
Cambridge Dr. B37: Mars G 3B 122
Cambridge Rd. B13: Mose 4H 133
  B66: Smeth 2E 99
  DY2: Dud 2F 95
Cambridge St. B1: Birm 4A 4 (1E 117)
  B70: W Brom 5H 79
  WS1: Wals 4C 48
  WV10: Wolv 1G 43
Cambridge Twr. B1: Birm 4A 4 (6E 101)
Cambridge Way B27: A Grn 1B 136
Camden Cl. B36: Cas B 1E 105
  WS5: Wals 2F 65
Camden Dr. B1: Birm 2A 4 (6D 100)
Camden St. B1: Birm 5C 100
  B18: Hock 2A 4 (5C 100)
  WS1: Wals 3B 48
  WS9: Wals W 3A 22
Camden Way DY6: K'wfrd 6B 74
Camellia Cl. WS3: Blox 3C 32
Camellia Gdns. DY8: Word 1C 108
  WV9: Pend 4D 14
Camelot Way B10: Small H 3C 118
Cameo Dr. DY8: Amb 3D 108
Cameronian Cft. B36: Hodg H 1A 104
Cameron Rd. WS4: Wals 6E 33
Camford Gro. B14: King H 4H 147
Cam Gdns. DY5: P'ntt 3F 93
Camino Rd. B32: Bart G 2D 130
Camomile Cl. WS5: Wals 2E 65
Campbell Cl. WS4: Wals 6E 33
Campbells Grn. B26: Sheld 1F 137
Campbell St. DY5: Brie H 5G 93
Campden Grn. B92: Olton 2E 137
Camp Hill B12: Birm 3A 118
  DY8: Word 2C 108
Camp Hill Cir. B11: S'brk 3A 118
Camp Hill Ind. Est. B12: Birm 4A 118
Campians Av. WS6: C Hay 3D 6
Campion B74: Four O 4F 37
  (off Badgers Bank Rd.)
Campion Cl. B38: King Nor 1B 160
  WS5: Wals 2E 65
  WV5: Wom 1E 73
Campion Ct. DY4: Tip 2F 77
Campion Dr. WV10: F'stne 1C 16
Campion Gdns. B24: Erd 1A 86
Campion Gro. B63: Hale 2F 127
Campion Ho. B38: King Nor 1A 160
  WV10: Wolv 5B 28
Campion Way B90: Dic H 4G 163
Camp La. B21: Hand 6F 81
  B38: King Nor 4B 146
Camplea Cft. B37: F'bri 1C 122
Camplin Cres. B20: Hand 2A 82
Camp Rd. B75: R'ley 2H 37
  WS14: Lit H 2H 37
Camp St. B9: Bord G 2C 118
  WS10: W'bry 3F 63
  WV1: Wolv 1B 170 (6G 27)

Campville Cres. B71: W Brom 4C 64
Campville Gro. B37: K'hrst 4B 106
Camp Wood Cl. B30: B'ville 5A 132
Camrose Cft. B12: Bal H 6H 117
  B34: S End 3F 105
Camrose Gdns. WV9: Pend 4E 15
Camrose Twr. B7: Nech 3B 102
Canal Boat Trips 5D 108
Canal Cotts. DY2: Neth 6D 94
Canal Ct. B27: A Grn 2C 136
Canal La. B24: Erd 6G 85
Canal Side B30: King Nor 4C 146
  B48: Hopw 6G 159
  B69: O'bry 2F 97
  DY2: Neth 5G 95
Canalside Cl. WS3: Blox 6D 20
Canal Side Dr. B38: King Nor 6C 146
Canalside Ind. Est. DY5: Brie H 2G 109
Canal Sq. B16: Birm 1D 116
  (off Sherborne Wharf)
Canal St. B69: O'bry 2F 97
  DY4: Tip 3F 77
  DY5: Brie H 4A 94
  DY8: Amb 5D 108
  WS2: Wals 1B 48
  WV14: Cose 5E 61
Canal Vw. Ind. Est. DY5: Brie H 2F 109
  WS10: W'bry 3C 64
Canal Wlk. B1: Birm 6B 4
Canary Gro. B19: Loz 1E 101
Canberra Gdns. B34: S End 3A 106
Canberra Rd. WS5: Wals 6G 49
Canberra Way B12: Birm 3A 118
Canford Cl. B12: Birm 4H 117
Canford Cres. WV8: Cod 4E 13
Canning Cl. WS5: Wals 5H 49
Canning Gdns. B18: Win G 5A 100
Canning Rd. WS5: Wals 5H 49
Cannock Rd. WV1: Wolv 5H 27
  WV10: Bush, Wolv 5H 27
  WV10: F'stne, Share 2D 16
  WV12: W'hall 2C 30
Cannon Bus. Pk. WV14: Cose 4E 61
Cannon Dr. WV14: Cose 3E 61
Cannon Hill Gro. B12: Bal H 6G 117
Cannon Hill Pk. 1F 133
Cannon Hill Pl. B12: Bal H 6G 117
Cannon Hill Rd. B12: Bal H 6F 117
Cannon Raceway 4E 61
Cannon St. B2: Birm 4D 4 (1G 117)
  WS2: Wals 5C 32
  WV13: W'hall 1B 46
Cannon St. Nth. WS2: Wals 5C 32
Canterbury Av. WV13: W'hall 1D 46
Canterbury Cl. B23: Erd 5D 84
  B65: Row R 5E 97
  B71: W Brom 5C 64
  WS3: Pels 3E 21
Canterbury Dr. B37: Mars G 4C 122
  WV6: Pert 5D 24
Canterbury Pl. B92: Olton 2C 136
Canterbury Rd. B20: Hand 6F 83
  B71: W Brom 5B 64
  WV4: Penn 6C 42
Canterbury Twr. B1: Birm 2A 4
  (off St Marks St.)
Cantlow Ho. B13: Mose 4H 117
Cantlow Rd. B13: Mose 1A 148
Canton La. B46: Col 2H 89
Canute Cl. WS1: Wals 4D 48
Canvey Cl. B45: Fran 6E 143
CANWELL .4E 39
Canwell Av. B37: K'hrst 4B 106
Canwell Dr. B75: Can 4E 39
Canwell Gdns. WV14: Bils 1E 61
Canwell Ga. B75: R'ley 5C 38
Capcroft Rd. B13: Mose 1B 148
Cape Hill B66: Smeth 5F 99
Cape Hill Retail Cen. B66: Smeth 5F 99
Capener Rd. B43: Gt Barr 3C 66
Capern Gro. B32: Harb 6D 114
Cape St. B18: Win G 5H 99
  B70: W Brom 3E 79
Capethorn Rd. B66: Smeth 6E 99
Capilano Rd. B23: Erd 6C 68

Capponfield Cl. WV14: Cose 2D 60
Capstone Av. B18: Hock 5C 100
  WV10: Oxl 1F 27
Captain's Cl. WV3: Wolv 1B 42
Carcroft Rd. B25: Yard 3B 120
Cardale St. B65: B'hth 1D 112
Carden Cl. B70: W Brom 3F 79
Carder Cres. WV14: Bils 1F 61
Carder Dr. DY5: Brie H 1G 109
Cardiff Gro. B37: Mars G 2C 122
Cardiff St. WV3: Wolv 3F 43
Cardigan Cl. B71: W Brom 6A 64
Cardigan Dr. WV12: W'hall 3B 30
Cardigan St. B4: Birm 2H 5 (6H 101)
Cardinal Cl. B17: Edg 1E 115
Cardoness Pl. DY1: Dud 5B 76
Careless Grn. DY9: Lye, W'cte 1B 126
Careynon Ct. WS3: Blox 1H 31
Carhampton Rd. B75: S Cold 5E 55
Carillon Gdns. B65: Row R 6C 96
Carisbrooke Av. B37: Chel W 1E 123
Carisbrooke Cl. WS10: W'bry 3C 64
Carisbrooke Cres. WS10: W'bry 2C 64
Carisbrooke Dr. B62: Hale 1D 128
Carisbrooke Gdns. WV10: Bush 4A 16
Carisbrooke Ho. B31: Longb 1D 158
Carisbrooke Rd. B17: Edg 2F 115
  WS10: W'bry 3B 64
  WV6: Pert 6G 25
  WV10: Bush 4A 16
Carless Av. B17: Harb 4F 115
Carless St. WS1: Wals 3C 48
Carlisle St. B18: Win G 4A 100
Carlson Pk. B17: Harb 6F 115
Carl St. WS2: Wals 4B 32
Carlton Av. B21: Hand 6A 82
  B74: S'tly 1H 51
  DY9: W'cte 2A 126
  WV11: Wed 2C 28
  WV14: Bils 4H 45
Carlton Cl. B75: S Cold 4B 54
  DY1: Dud 1E 77
Carlton Cft. B74: S'tly 1A 52
Carlton M. B36: Cas B 1H 105
Carlton M. Flats B36: Cas B 1H 105
Carlton Rd. B9: Small H 2D 118
  B66: Smeth 1E 99
  WV3: Wolv 4E 43
Carlyle Bus. Pk. B70: W Brom 2F 79
Carlyle Gro. WV10: Bush 1C 28
Carlyle Rd. B16: Edg 2A 116
  B19: Loz 1E 101
  B65: Row R 1C 112
  WV10: Bush 1C 28
Carmel Gro. B32: Bart G 4H 129
Carmodale Av. B42: P Barr 1D 82
Carnation Av. DY4: Tip 3A 78
Carnegie Dr. WS10: W'bry 2G 63
Carnegie Rd. B65: Row R 1B 112
Carnelian Ct. B15: Edg 4F 117
  (off Stone Rd.)
Carnford Rd. B26: Sheld 5F 121
Carnforth Cl. DY6: K'wfrd 2H 91
Carnoustie Cl. B75: S Cold 3A 54
  WS3: Blox 4G 19
Carnwath Rd. B73: New O 3E 69
Carol Cres. B63: Hale 6H 111
  WV11: Wed 3G 29
Carol Gdns. DY8: Amb 3D 108
Caroline Pl. B13: Mose 2H 133
Caroline Point B3: Birm 1A 4
Caroline Rd. B13: Mose 1A 4
Caroline St. B3: Birm 1B 4 (5E 101)
  B70: W Brom 5H 79
  DY2: Dud 6G 77
Carpathian, The B18: Birm 1A 4
Carpathian Ct. B18: Birm 5E 101
Carpenter Glade B63: Crad 6F 111
Carpenter Pl. B12: Bal H 5A 118
Carpenter Rd. B15: Edg 4D 116
Carpenters Ct. B12: Birm 3H 117
  (off Vaughton St.)
Carpenter's Rd. B19: Loz 2E 101
Carriageway Wlk. B30: King Nor 4F 147
Carrick Cl. WS3: Pels 2E 21
Carriers Cl. WS2: Wals 2F 47

Carriers Fold—Central Arc.

Carriers Fold WV5: Wom 6H **57**
Carrington Rd. WS10: W'bry 3B **64**
CARROWAY HEAD **5G 39**
Carroway Head Hill B75: Bass P, Can . . . 6F **39**
Carrs La. B4: Birm 4F **5** (1G **117**)
Carshalton Gro. WV2: Wolv 4A **44**
Carshalton Rd. B44: K'sdng 3A **68**
Cartbridge Cres. WS3: Wals 3D **32**
Cartbridge La. WS4: Wals 4E **33**
Cartbridge La. Sth. WS4: Wals 5E **33**
Cartbridge Wlk. WS3: Wals 3E **33**
Carter Av. WV8: Bilb 4H **13**
Carter Rd. B43: Gt Barr 3B **66**
WV6: Wolv 4F **27**
Carters Cl. B37: Mars G 4C **122**
B76: Walm 2D **70**
Cartersfield La. WS9: Ston 1F **23**
Carters Grn. B70: W Brom 3H **79**
Carter's Hurst B33: Sheld 2F **121**
Carter's La. B62: Quin 6F **113**
Cartland Rd. B11: S'brk 4C **118**
B14: King H 5D **132**
B30: Stir 5D **132**
Cartmel Ct. B23: Erd 3B **84**
Cartway, The WV6: Pert 5D **24**
Cartwright Gdns. B69: Tiv 5C **78**
Cartwright Ho. WS3: Blox 6H **19**
Cartwright La. WV9: Coven 2C **14**
Cartwright Rd. B75: R'ley 6A **38**
Cartwright St. WV2: Wolv 6C **170** (3H **43**)
Carver Ct. B24: Erd 1A **86**
DY4: Tip 4A **62**
Carver Gdns. DY8: Stourb 3C **124**
Carver St. B1: Birm 5D **100**
Casern Vw. B75: S Cold 5E **55**
Casewell Rd. DY6: W Hth 1A **92**
Casey Av. B23: Erd 5D **68**
Cash Joynson Av. WS10: Darl 3C **46**
Caslon Cres. DY8: Stourb 1B **124**
Caslon Rd. B63: Crad 5E **111**
Caslow Flats B63: Crad 1E **127**
Cassandra Cl. DY5: P'ntt 6G **75**
Cassowary Rd. B20: Hand 4B **82**
Castello Dr. B36: Cas B 6H **87**
Castillo Ct. B14: King H 2A **148**
Castings, The WV14: Cose 3F **61**
Castle, The DY8: Stourb 2F **125**
Castlebridge Gdns. WV11: Wed 2H **29**
Castlebridge Rd. WV11: Wed 3H **29**
CASTLE BROMWICH **1F 105**
Castle Bromwich Bus. Pk.
B35: Cas V 6D **86**
Castle Bromwich Hall B36: Cas B 1E **105**
Castle Bromwich Hall Gdns. **1D 104**
Castle Cl. B64: Old H 2B **112**
B92: Olton 4F **137**
WS8: Bwnhls 3B **10**
Castle Ct. B29: W Cas 4E **131**
B34: S End 2A **106**
DY1: Dud 5G **77**
Castle Cres. B36: Cas B 1G **105**
CASTLECROFT **3G 41**
Castle Cft. B68: O'bry 3B **114**
Castlecroft WS11: Nort C 1C **8**
Castlecroft Av. WV3: Wolv 3G **41**
Castlecroft Gdns. WV3: Wolv 3A **42**
Castlecroft La. WV3: Wolv 3F **41**
Castlecroft Rd. WV3: Wolv 3F **41**
(not continuous)
WV14: Bils 4G **45**
Castle Dr. B46: Col 4H **107**
WV12: W'hall 4B **30**
Castleford Gro. B11: S'hll 1C **134**
Castleford Rd. B11: S'hll 1C **134**
Castlefort Rd. WS9: Wals W 4C **22**
Castlegate Dr. DY1: Dud 5G **77**
Castlegate Island DY1: Dud 5G **77**
Castlegate Way DY1: Dud 5G **77**
Castle Gro. DY8: Stourb 2F **125**
Castle Hgts. *B64: Old H* *3B* **112**
(off Granville Rd.)
Castle Hill DY1: Dud 5F **77**
Castlehill Rd. WS9: Wals W 4D **22**
Castlehills Dr. B36: Cas B 1E **105**
Castle La. B92: Olton 4D **136**
Castlemill DY4: Tip 5H **77**
Castle Mill Rd. DY1: Dud 3E **77**
Castle Rd. B29: W Cas 3E **131**
B30: King Nor 3B **146**
DY4: Tip 3F **77**
WS9: Wals W 5C **22**
Castle Rd. E. B68: O'bry 3B **114**
Castle Rd. W. B68: O'bry 3A **114**
Castle Sq. B29: W Cas 4E **131**
Castle St. B70: W Brom 5G **63**
DY1: Dud 6F **77**
DY3: Sed 5H **59**
DY4: Tip 2G **77**
WS8: Bwnhls 3B **10**
WS10: Darl 3D **46**
(not continuous)
WV1: Wolv 3C **170** (1H **43**)
WV14: Cose 5E **61**
Castle Swimming Pool, The **5E 87**
Castleton Rd. B42: Gt Barr 6F **67**
WS3: Blox 4A **20**
Castleton St. DY2: Neth 4E **95**
CASTLE VALE **4F 87**
Castle Va. Ent. Pk. B35: Cas V 4G **87**
Castle Va. Ind. Est. B76: Min 2E **87**
Castle Va. Retail Pk. B35: Cas V 4D **86**
Castle Vw. DY1: Dud 5D **76**
Castle Vw. Cl. WS10: Mox 1A **62**
Castle Vw. Ind. Est. DY4: Tip 4H **77**
Castle Vw. Rd. WS10: Bils 1A **62**
WV14: Bils 1B **62**
Castle Vw. Ter. WV14: Cose 5D **60**
Castle Yd. WV1: Wolv 3C **170** (1H **43**)
Caswell Rd. DY3: Sed 5G **59**
Catalpa Gro. B74: S'tly 4H **51**
Cat & Kittens La. WV10: F'stne 1A **16**
Cater Dr. B76: Walm 3D **70**
Caterham Dr. DY6: K'wfrd 6D **92**
Catesby Dr. DY6: K'wfrd 1B **92**
Catesby Ho. B37: K'hrst 4B **106**
Catesby Pk. B38: King Nor 4A **146**
Catesby Rd. B90: Shir 6H **149**
Cateswell Rd. B11: Tys 3F **135**
B28: Hall G 4F **135**
Cathcart Rd. DY8: Stourb 6C **108**
Cathedral Cl. DY4: Tip 2G **77**
Cathel Dr. B42: Gt Barr 6C **66**
Catherine Ct. B24: Erd 3A **86**
CATHERINE-DE-BARNES **2D 152**
Catherine de Barnes La.
B92: Bick, Cath B 1E **153**
Catherine Dr. B73: S Cold 5G **53**
Catherine Rd. WV14: Cose 4C **60**
Catherines Cl. B91: Cath B 3D **152**
Catherine St. B6: Aston 2A **102**
Catherton Cl. DY4: Tip 3C **62**
Catholic La. DY3: Sed 1G **75**
Catisfield Cres. WV8: Pend 6D **14**
Cat La. B34: S End 2F **105**
Caton Gro. B28: Hall G 6G **135**
Cato St. B7: Birm 5B **102**
Cato St. Nth. B7: Nech 4C **102**
CATSHILL **6C 10**
Catshill Rd. WS8: Bwnhls 6C **10**
Cattell Dr. B75: S Cold 6F **55**
Cattell Rd. B9: Bord G 2C **118**
Cattells Gro. B7: Nech 3C **102**
Cattermole Gro. B43: Gt Barr 2E **67**
Cattock Hurst Dr. B72: W Grn 6B **70**
Causeway B65: Row R 1C **112**
CAUSEWAY GREEN **6F 97**
Causeway Grn. Rd. B68: O'bry 6F **97**
Causeway Rd. WV14: Cose 5F **61**
Causey Farm Rd. B63: Hale 5E **127**
Cavalier Cir. WV10: Bush 3A **16**
Cavalier Dr. B63: Hale 2A **128**
Cavandale Av. B44: Gt Barr 4G **67**
Cavell Cl. WS2: Wals 1B **48**
Cavell Rd. DY2: Dud 6H **77**
Cavendish Cl. B38: King Nor 6D **146**
DY6: K'wfrd 5B **92**
Cavendish Ct. B17: Harb 3F **115**
B93: Dorr 6C **166**
Cavendish Gdns. WS2: Wals 5G **31**
WV1: Wolv 2E **45**
Cavendish Rd. B16: Edg 6H **99**
B62: Hale 1F **129**
WS2: Wals 4G **31**
WV1: Wolv 2D **44**
Cavendish Way WS9: A'rdge 4D **34**
Caversham Pl. B73: S Cold 1H **69**
Caversham Rd. B44: K'sdng 3A **68**
Cawdon Gro. B93: Dorr 6G **167**
Cawdor Cres. B16: Edg 2B **116**
Cawney Hill DY2: Dud 1G **95**
Caxton Gate B2: Birm 4E **5**
Caxton Gro. B44: K'sdng 4C **68**
Caynham Rd.
B32: Bart G 5H **129**
Cayton Gro. B23: Erd 1F **85**
Cearl Ct. B27: A Grn 3A **136**
Cecil Dr. B69: Tiv 5D **78**
Cecil Rd. B24: Erd 4F **85**
B29: S Oak 4E **133**
Cecil St. B19: Birm 5G **101**
DY8: Stourb 6D **108**
WS4: Wals 6D **32**
Cedar Av. B36: Cas B 1G **105**
WS8: Bwnhls 5C **10**
WV14: Cose 6D **60**
Cedar Bri. Cft. B74: Four O 3H **53**
Cedar Cl. B30: B'vlle 1A **146**
B68: O'bry 3A **114**
DY8: Stourb 3B **124**
WS5: Wals 1F **65**
Cedar Ct. B43: Gt Barr 5G **65**
Cedar Dr. B24: Erd 2A **86**
B31: Longb 2F **159**
B74: S'tly 2G **51**
Cedar Gro. WS6: Gt Wyr 1H **7**
WV3: Wolv 4D **42**
WV8: Bilb 4H **13**
WV14: Bils 4H **45**
Cedar Ho. B91: Sol 6D **150**
Cedarhurst B32: Harb 6E **115**
B91: Sol 4G **151**
Cedar Pk. Rd. WV12: W'hall 6C **18**
Cedar Rd. B30: B'vlle 1A **146**
DY1: Dud 4D **76**
(not continuous)
DY4: Tip 2F **77**
WS10: W'bry 3G **63**
WV13: W'hall 1G **45**
Cedars, The B25: Yard 2C **120**
B93: Know 5D **166**
WV6: Tett 4B **26**
WV6: Wolv 6D **26**
Cedars Av. B27: A Grn 1A **136**
DY6: K'wfrd 5B **92**
WV5: Wom 2G **73**
Cedar Tree B23: Erd 5E **85**
Cedar Wlk. *B37: Chel W* *1D* **122**
(within Chelmsley Wood Shop. Cen.)
Cedar Way B31: Longb 6D **144**
WV11: Wed 2E **29**
Cedarwood B74: Four O 3H **53**
Cedarwood Cft. B42: Gt Barr 5B **66**
Cedarwood Dr. CV7: Bal C 3H **169**
Cedarwood Rd. DY3: Up Gor 2H **75**
Ceefield Ct. B25: Yard 5A **120**
Celandine *B74: Four O* *4F* **37**
(off Badgers Bank Rd.)
Celandine Cl. DY6: K'wfrd 5A **92**
Celandine Rd. DY1: Dud 3C **76**
Celandines, The WV5: Wom 1E **73**
Celbury Way B43: Gt Barr 5H **65**
Celts Cl. B65: Row R 5C **96**
Cemetery La. B18: Birm 4D **100**
Cemetery Rd. B66: Smeth 3A **98**
B67: Smeth 5D **98**
B68: O'bry 3A **98**
B75: S Cold 5B **54**
DY9: Lye 6H **109**
WS10: Darl 3F **47**
WV13: W'hall 6A **30**
Cemetery St. WS6: C Hay 3C **6**
WV14: Bils 5E **45**
Cemetery Way WS3: Blox 6H **19**
Centenary Cl. B31: N'fld 6E **145**
Centenary Dr. B21: Hand 6A **82**
Centenary Plaza
B1: Birm 5B **4** (1E **117**)
Centenary Sq. B1: Birm 4B **4** (1E **117**)
Centenary Way *B1: Birm* *4B* **4**
(off Queensway)
Central Arc. WV1: Wolv 3B **170** (1G **43**)

192 A-Z Birmingham

Central Av. B31: Longb 1C **158**
B64: Crad H 4E **111**
B65: Row R 1C **112**
DY4: Tip 6H **61**
DY9: W'cte 2A **126**
WV14: Bils 4G **45**
Central Baths 2A **170** (1F **43**)
Central Blvd. B90: Bly P 6D **164**
Central Bus. Pk. B33: Kitts G 2H **121**
Central CI. WS3: Blox 6G **19**
Central Dr. DY3: Gorn 5G **75**
WS3: Blox 1F **31**
WV14: Cose 6E **61**
Central Gro. B27: A Grn 3A **136**
Central Links Ind. Est.
B7: Nech 3B **102**
Central Pk. DY2: Neth 6G **95**
Central Pk. Dr. B18: Win G 4B **100**
Central Sq. B1: Birm 5A **4**
B23: Erd 3G **85**
Central Trad. Est. DY6: K'wfrd 6D **74**
WV2: Wolv 3A **44**
Central Way DY5: Brie H 6A **94**
Centre City B5: Birm 6D **4**
Centre Ct. B63: Hale 2B **128**
Centre La. B63: Hale 2B **128**
Centreway, The B14: Yard W 3D **148**
Centurion CI. B46: Col 6H **89**
Centurion Dr. B74: S'tly 4H **51**
Century Dr. WV13: W'hall 3A **46**
Century Ho. B69: O'bry 3D **96**
Century Ind. Est. B44: Gt Barr 2G **67**
Century M. B64: Old H 1H **111**
Century Pk. B9: Bord G 1C **118**
B37: Mars G 5E **123**
Century Rd. B69: O'bry 1G **97**
Century Twr. B5: Edg 6E **117**
Century Way B63: Crad 5F **111**
Ceolmund Cres. B37: Chel W 6D **106**
Chaceley Gro. B23: Erd 6D **68**
Chadbrook Crest B15: Edg 4A **116**
Chadbury Rd. B63: Hale 2C **128**
Chaddersley CI. B45: Rub 6F **143**
Chaddesley CI. B69: O'bry 4D **96**
Chaddesley Ct. DY1: Dud 6D **76**
Chaddesley Dr. DY9: Pedm 4F **125**
Chaddesley Rd. B31: N'fld 5H **145**
B63: Hale 3H **127**
Chadley CI. B91: Sol 1E **151**
Chad Rd. B15: Edg 3B **116**
WV14: Cose 6C **60**
Chadshunt CI. B36: Cas B 5H **87**
Chadsmoor Ter. B7: Nech 3B **102**
Chad Sq. B15: Edg 4A **116**
Chadstone CI. B90: M'path 4F **165**
CHAD VALLEY 4A **116**
Chad Valley CI. B17: Harb 5H **115**
Chadwell Dr. B90: Shir 1H **149**
Chadwell Gdns. WV8: Cod 3F **13**
Chadwich La. B61: C'wich 2A **156**
Chadwick Av. B45: Redn 3H **157**
Chadwick CI. WV4: Penn 5A **42**
Chadwick Ct. B43: Gt Barr 5A **66**
Chadwick Ho. B45: Rub 2E **157**
B75: S Cold 5D **54**
Chadwick La. B93: Know 6A **168**
Chadwick Rd. B75: S Cold 6D **54**
Chadworth Av. B93: Dorr 5A **166**
Chafery Dr. WS10: Darl 1D **62**
Chaffcombe Rd. B26: Sheld 5G **121**
Chaffinch CI. DY3: Sed 3G **59**
Chaffinch Dr. B36: Cas B 2D **106**
Chaffinch Rd. DY9: W'cte 2H **125**
Chainmakers CI. WV14: Cose 3F **61**
Chain Wlk. B19: Loz 1F **101**
Chalcot Gro. B20: Hand 2A **82**
Chaldon CI. WV9: Pend 6E **15**
Chale Gro. B14: King H 4A **148**
Chalfont PI. DY9: W'cte 3A **126**
Chalfont Rd. B20: Hand 5D **82**
Chalford Rd. B23: Erd 5C **68**
Chalford Way B90: Shir 6A **150**
Chalgrove Av. B38: King Nor 6A **146**
Chalgrove Cres. B91: Sol 6F **151**
Challenge Way WV10: Wolv 4A **28**
Challenor Av. WV13: W'hall 1F **45**

Chalybeate CI. B45: Fran 6F **143**
Chamberlain CI. B69: Tiv 5D **78**
Chamberlain Ct. B14: King H 4G **133**
B18: Birm 5E **101**
Chamberlain Cres. B90: Shir 5G **149**
Chamberlain Hall B15: Edg 5C **116**
Chamberlain Health & Fitness Cen.
......................5H **117**
Chamberlain Ho. B16: Edg 2C **116**
Chamberlain Rd. B13: Mose 1H **147**
Chamberlains La. WV4: Penn 2C **58**
Chamberlain Sq.
B3: Birm 4C **4** (1F **117**)
Chamberlain Wlk. B46: Col 2H **107**
(off High St.)
B66: Smeth 4F **99**
Chance Cft. B68: O'bry 3H **113**
Chance Dr. B66: Smeth 1B **98**
Chancel Ct. B91: Sol 4G **151**
Chancel Ind. Est. DY6: K'wfrd 1C **92**
WS10: Darl 6D **46**
WV1: Wolv 2C **44**
WV13: W'hall 1B **46**
Chancellors CI. B15: Edg 3A **116**
Chancel Way B6: Witt 2H **83**
B62: Hale 5C **112**
Chancel Way Ind. Est. B6: Witt 2H **83**
Chancery Way DY5: Quar B 1B **110**
Chandler Dr. WV4: Penn 2B **58**
Chandler Ho. B69: O'bry 5D **96**
Chandlers CI. B18: Win G 4B **100**
WV9: Pend 6E **15**
Chandlers Keep WS8: Bwnhls 1B **22**
Chandos Av. B13: Mose 2H **133**
Chandos Rd. B12: Birm 3A **118**
Channon Dr. DY5: Brie H 3H **109**
Chanston Av. B14: King H 3G **147**
Chanterelle Gdns. WV4: Penn 1E **59**
Chantrey Cres. B43: Gt Barr 6G **51**
Chantry Av. WS3: Blox 1A **32**
Chantry CI. B47: H'wd 2A **162**
Chantry Cres. WV14: Bils 4H **45**
Chantry Dr. B62: Quin 5G **113**
Chantry Heath Cres. B93: Know 1E **167**
Chantry Ind. Est. B76: Curd 1D **88**
Chantry Rd. B13: Mose 1G **133**
B21: Hand 1B **100**
DY7: Stourt 4A **108**
Chapel Ash WV3: Wolv 3A **170** (1F **43**)
Chapel Ash Island
WV1: Wolv 3A **170** (1F **43**)
Chapel Av. WS8: Bwnhls 3A **10**
Chapel CI. B64: Old H 3B **112**
WV5: Wom 2F **73**
Chapel Ct. DY5: Brie H 1H **109**
(off Chapel St.)
DY5: P'ntt 2G **93**
(off Chapel St.)
Chapel Dr. B47: Wyt 6H **161**
CV7: Bal C 1H **169**
WS8: Bwnhls 3A **10**
Chapelfield M. B45: Rub 3F **157**
DY8: Stourb 1E **125**
Chapelfield Rd. B45: Redn 2G **157**
Chapel Flds. Rd. B92: Olton 3D **136**
Chapel Grn. WV13: W'hall 1B **46**
Chapelhouse La. B63: Crad 5E **111**
Chapelhouse Rd. B37: F'bri 1B **122**
Chapel Ho. St.
B12: Birm 6H **5** (2H **117**)
Chapel La. B29: S Oak 3A **132**
B43: Gt Barr 2A **66**
B47: Wyt 6G **161**
DY3: Swind 3C **72**
WV8: Cod 4E **13**
Chapel Pas. B69: O'bry 5G **97**
Chapel Ri. B45: Redn 1A **158**
Chapel Sq. WS6: C Hay 2D **6**
Chapel St. B21: Hand 2H **99**
B63: Hale 2A **128**
B70: W Brom 2A **80**
DY2: Neth 5F **95**
DY4: Tip 2G **77**
(not continuous)
DY5: P'ntt 2G **93**
DY5: Quar B 3C **110**
DY6: W Hth 1H **91**

Chapel St. DY8: Stourb 1E **125**
DY8: Word 6B **92**
DY9: Lye 6A **110**
WS3: Blox 1B **32**
WS3: Pels 4D **20**
WS8: Bwnhls 3A **10**
WS11: Nort C 1C **8**
WV2: Wolv 4H **43**
WV5: Wom 2F **73**
(not continuous)
WV14: Bils 6H **45**
Chapel Vw. B67: Smeth 5D **98**
Chapel Wlk. B30: King Nor 4C **146**
DY3: Gorn 5G **75**
Chapelwood Gro. B42: P Barr 2F **83**
Chapman Rd. B10: Small H 3C **118**
CHAPMAN'S HILL 6B **142**
Chapman's Hill B62: Roms 6B **142**
Chapmans Pas. B1: Birm 6C **4** (2F **117**)
Chapman St. B70: W Brom 4H **79**
Chapter Ct. B29: S Oak 3A **132**
Chapter Ho. B70: W Brom 2G **79**
Charfield CI. B30: B'ville 6H **131**
Charingworth Rd. B92: Sol 3G **137**
Charity Bick Way B70: W Brom 5A **80**
Charlbury Av. B37: F'bri 1B **122**
Charlbury Cres. B26: Yard 3D **120**
Charlbury Twr. B5: Birm 3G **117**
(off Southacre Av.)
Charlecote Cft. B90: Shir 1A **164**
Charlecote Dr. B23: Erd 6E **69**
DY1: Dud 4A **76**
Charlecote Gdns. B73: Bold 5G **69**
Charlecote Ri. WV13: W'hall 2H **45**
Charlecott CI. B13: Mose 6D **134**
CHARLEMONT 5C **64**
Charlemont Av. B71: W Brom 5C **64**
Charlemont CI. WS5: Wals 5G **49**
Charlemont Cres. B71: W Brom 5C **64**
Charlemont Gdns. WS5: Wals 5G **49**
Charlemont Rd. B71: W Brom 5C **64**
WS5: Wals 5F **49**
Charles Av. B65: Row R 5C **96**
WV4: Penn 6F **43**
WV11: Ess 3H **17**
Charles CI. B8: Salt 5D **102**
WS6: C Hay 4D **6**
Charles Ct. B13: Mose 3B **134**
B76: Walm 2D **70**
Charles Cres. WS3: Pels 2E **21**
Charlesdale Dr. WS9: A'rdge 5D **34**
Charles Dr. B7: Nech 3B **102**
Charles Edward Rd. B26: Yard 5B **120**
Charles Foster St. WS10: Darl 5C **46**
Charles Hayward Dr. WV4: Sed 2H **59**
Charles Henry St. B12: Birm 3H **117**
Charles Holland St. WV13: W'hall ...1B **46**
Charles Lanes Trust Ho's.
B28: Hall G 5G **135**
Charles Pearson Ct. B66: Smeth 4F **99**
(off Exeter Rd.)
Charles Rd. B6: Aston 6A **84**
B9: Small H 1E **119**
B10: Small H 3E **119**
B20: Hand 6E **83**
B63: Hale 1H **127**
B91: Sol 5C **150**
DY4: Tip 6A **62**
DY5: Quar B 2C **110**
DY8: Stourb 1C **124**
Charles St. B66: Smeth 2G **99**
B70: W Brom 2E **79**
WS2: Wals 1B **48**
WV13: W'hall 6C **30**
Charles St. Ind. Est. B70: W Brom ...2E **79**
Charles Wlk. B65: Row R 4C **96**
Charles Wesley Ct. WV3: Wolv 4E **43**
(off Claremont Rd.)
Charlesworth Av. B90: M'path 3F **165**
Charleville Rd. B19: Hock 2D **100**
Charlotte CI. B69: Tiv 5A **78**
Charlotte Gdns. B66: Smeth 4F **99**
B90: Shir 4G **149**
Charlotte Rd. B15: Edg 4E **117**
B30: Stir 1C **146**
WS10: W'bry 4C **62**

Charlotte St. B3: Birm 3B 4 (6E 101)
DY1: Dud .1D 94
WS1: Wals 1E 49
Charlton Dr. B64: Crad H 4F 111
Charlton Pl. B8: Salt 4D 102
Charlton Rd. B44: K'sdng 6A 68
Charlton St. DY1: Dud 6D 76
DY5: Brie H 6E 93
Charminster Av. B25: Yard 3B 120
Charnley Dr. B75: R'ley 1C 54
Charnwood Av. DY3: Sed 3H 59
Charnwood Bus. Pk. WV14: Bils 6E 45
Charnwood Cl. B45: Fran 4H 143
DY5: Brie H 4F 109
WV14: Bils 2B 62
Charnwood Cl. DY9: W'cte 3A 126
Charnwood Rd. B42: Gt Barr 6B 66
WS5: Wals 1E 65
Charter Cl. WS1: Nort C 1C 8
Charter Ct. WV10: F'hses 2H 15
Charter Cres. B64: Old H 3B 112
Charterfield Dr. DY6: K'wfrd 1B 92
Charterfield Shop. Cen.
DY6: K'wfrd 1C 92
Charter Ho. B66: Smeth 5F 99
Charterhouse Dr. B91: Sol 6F 151
Charter Pl. B68: O'bry 4H 113
Charter Rd. DY4: Tip 4C 62
Charters Av. WV8: Bilb 6H 13
Charter St. DY5: Brie H 4A 94
Chartist Rd. B8: Salt 3D 102
Chartley Cl. B93: Dorr 6A 166
WV6: Pert 5F 25
Chartley Rd. B23: Erd 6D 84
B71: W Brom 1B 80
Chartway, The WS3: Pels 3E 21
Chartwell Cl. DY1: Dud 1D 76
Chartwell Dr. B74: Four O 5D 36
B90: Ches G 4B 164
WV5: Wom 2F 73
WV10: Bush 6A 16
Chartwell Grange B64: Crad H 4A 112
Chase, The B76: Walm 6B 70
WV6: Wolv 3F 27
Chase Av. WS6: C Hay 2E 7
Chase Gro. B24: Erd 1B 86
Chase Link, The WS8: Bwnhls 4C 10
Chasepool Rd. DY3: Swind 2C 90
Chase Rd. DY3: Gorn 6F 75
DY5: P'ntt 6F 75
WS3: Blox 1G 31
WS8: Bwnhls 4C 10
Chase Sailing Club 1H 9
CHASETOWN 1A 10
Chasetown FC 1A 10
Chase Vw. WV4: Ett 3A 60
Chasewater Country Pk. 1G 9
Chasewater Innovation Cen. 2H 9
Chasewater Outdoor Education Cen. . . .1H 9
Chasewater Railway
  Brownhills West Station 2G 9
Chasewater Railway Museum &
  Heritage Cen. 2H 9
Chasewater Sports Cen. 2G 9
Chassieur Wlk. B46: Col 1H 107
Chater Dr. B76: Walm 4E 71
Chaters Cl. DY4: Tip 2G 77
Chatham Rd. B31: N'fld 4E 145
Chatsworth Av. B43: Gt Barr 4G 65
Chatsworth Cl. B72: W Grn 6B 70
B90: Ches G 4B 164
WV12: W'hall 4B 30
Chatsworth Cres. WS4: Rus 2H 33
Chatsworth Gdns. WV6: Tett 2G 25
Chatsworth M. DY8: Word 6H 91
Chatsworth Rd. B62: Hale 4A 112
Chatsworth Way B15: Birm 3E 117
Chattaway Dr. CV7: Bal C 3H 169
Chattaway St. B7: Nech 2C 102
CHATTLE HILL 5F 89
Chattle Hill B46: Col 5G 89
Chattock Av. B91: Sol 3A 152
Chattock Cl. B36: Hodg H 2C 104
Chatwell Gro. B29: S Oak 3F 131
Chatwin Pl. WV14: Bils 2G 61
Chatwin St. B66: Smeth 2D 98
Chatwins Wharf DY4: Tip 2H 77

Chaucer Av. DY3: Lwr G 2E 75
DY4: Tip .5B 62
WV12: W'hall 1E 31
Chaucer Cl. B23: Erd 4B 84
DY8: Amb 3E 109
WV14: Cose 5F 61
Chaucer Gro. B27: A Grn 3H 135
Chaucer Ho. B63: Crad 6D 110
Chaucer Rd. WS3: Blox 1C 32
Chauson Gro. B91: Sol 1E 165
Chavasse Rd. B72: S Cold 2A 70
CHAWN HILL 2G 125
Chawn Hill DY9: Pedm 2G 125
Chawn Hill Cl. DY9: Pedm 2G 125
Chawn Pk. Dr. DY9: Pedm 2G 125
Chaynes Gro. B33: Kitts G 6H 105
Cheadle Dr. B23: Erd 5D 68
Cheam Gdns. WV6: Tett 1C 26
Cheapside B5: Birm 6G 5 (2H 117)
  B12: Birm 6G 5 (2H 117)
  WV1: Wolv 3B 170 (1G 43)
  WV13: W'hall 2A 46
Cheapside Ind. Est. B12: Birm 2H 117
Cheatham St. B7: Nech 3C 102
Checketts St. WS2: Wals 1A 48
Checkley Cl. B90: Shir 3G 149
Checkley Cft. B76: Walm 5D 70
Cheddar Rd. B12: Bal H 5G 117
Chedworth Cl. B29: W Cas 6F 131
Chedworth Ct. B29: S Oak 5A 132
Cheedon Cl. B93: Dorr 6F 167
Chelford Cres. DY6: K'wfrd 6E 93
Chells Gro. B13: Mose 2B 148
Chelmar Cl. B36: Cas B 1B 106
Chelmar Dr. DY5: P'ntt 3E 93
Chelmarsh Av. WV3: Wolv 2G 41
Chelmorton Rd. B42: Gt Barr 6F 67
Chelmscote Rd. B92: Olton 4D 136
Chelmsley Av. B46: Col 3H 107
Chelmsley Circ. B37: Chel W 1D 122
Chelmsley Gro. B33: Kitts G 6A 106
Chelmsley La. B37: Mars G 3B 122
Chelmsley Rd. B37: Chel W, F'bri 6B 106
CHELMSLEY WOOD 1D 122
Chelmsley Wood Ind. Est.
  B37: F'bri 5D 106
Chelmsley Wood Shop. Cen.
  B37: Chel W 1D 122
Chelsea B37: K'hrst 1D 122
  (off Chilvers Gro.)
Chelsea Cl. B32: Quin 1D 130
Chelsea Ct. B29: W Cas 6F 131
Chelsea Dr. B74: Four O 5F 37
Chelsea Way DY6: K'wfrd 3B 92
Chelston Dr. WV6: Wolv 5C 26
Chelston Rd. B31: N'fld 5C 144
Cheltenham Cl. WV6: Wolv 3F 27
Cheltenham Dr. B36: Hodg H 1B 104
DY6: K'wfrd 3H 91
Cheltenham M. B74: Four O 2G 53
Chelthorn Way B91: Sol 5G 151
Cheltondale B90: Shir 1A 164
Cheltondale Rd. B91: Sol 1D 150
Chelveston Cres. B91: Sol 6F 151
Chelwood Gdns. WV14: Bils 6D 44
Chelworth Rd. B38: King Nor 5D 146
Chem Rd. WV14: Bils 6E 45
Cheniston Rd. WV12: W'hall 3C 30
Chepstow Cl. WV6: Pert 5F 25
Chepstow Gro. B45: Redn 3H 157
Chepstow Rd. WS3: Blox 1C 32
WV10: F'hses 2H 15
Chepstow Vs. B12: Bal H 6B 118
Chepstow Way WS3: Blox 6F 19
Chequerfield Dr. WV3: Wolv 5E 43
Chequers Av. WV5: Wom 4G 57
Chequer St. WV3: Wolv 5E 43
Cherhill Covert B14: King H 5E 147
Cherington Rd. B29: S Oak 5C 132
Cherish Ho. B12: Birm 2H 117
Cheriton Gro. WV6: Pert 6E 25
Cheriton Wlk. B23: Erd 4B 84
Cherrington Cl. B31: N'fld 6C 130
Cherrington Dr. WS6: Gt Wyr 1F 7
Cherrington Gdns. DY9: Pedm 6G 125
WV6: Tett 1H 41
Cherrington Way B91: Sol 6F 151

Cherry Arbour Ct. B11: S'hll 6C 118
  (off Stratford St.)
Cherry Brook WS11: Nort C 2D 8
Cherry Cres. B24: Erd 4F 85
Cherrydale Ct. DY1: Dud 5B 76
Cherry Dr. B9: Birm 2B 118
B64: Old H 2H 111
Cherry Gdns. B73: W Grn 6H 69
  (off Emscote Dr.)
Cherry Grn. DY1: Dud 3B 76
Cherry Gro. B66: Smeth 4G 99
  (off Rosedale Av.)
DY8: Stourb 1C 124
WV11: Wed 2E 29
Cherry Hill Wlk. DY1: Dud 1C 94
Cherry La. B73: Bold 6G 69
DY3: Himl 4A 74
WS10: W'bry 3G 63
Cherry Lea B34: S End 3F 105
CHERRY ORCHARD 2H 111
Cherry Orchard B64: Old H 2H 111
WV8: Cod 3F 13
Cherry Orchard Av. B63: Hale 6H 111
Cherry Orchard Cres. B63: Hale 5H 111
Cherry Orchard Rd. B20: Hand 2B 82
Cherry Rd. DY4: Tip 6H 61
Cherry St. B2: Birm 4E 5 (1G 117)
B63: Hale 6H 111
DY8: Stourb 1C 124
WV3: Wolv 2F 43
Cherry Tree Av. WS5: Wals 1E 65
Cherry Tree Cl. B75: S Cold 6D 54
Cherry Tree Ct. B30: King Nor 2B 146
DY9: W'cte 2A 126
WV11: Ess 4A 18
Cherry Tree Cft. B27: A Grn 6A 120
Cherry Tree Gdns. WV8: Bilb 4H 13
Cherry Tree La. B63: Hale 4F 127
WV8: Bilb 4H 13
Cherry Tree Rd. DY6: K'wfrd 1C 92
WS11: Nort C 1F 9
Cherry Wlk. B47: H'wd 4B 162
Cherrywood Cl. WV14: Cose 4E 61
Cherrywood Ct. B92: Olton 3E 137
Cherrywood Cres. B91: Sol 1G 165
Cherrywood Grn. WV14: Bils 3F 45
Cherrywood Ind. Est.
  B9: Bord G 6D 102
Cherrywood Rd. B9: Bord G 1D 118
B74: S'tly 2F 51
Cherrywood Way B74: Lit As 4D 36
Chervil Cl. B42: Gt Barr 6E 67
Chervil Ri. WV10: Wolv 6B 28
Cherwell Dr. B73: S Cold 6H 53
Cherwell Dr. B36: Cas B 1B 106
WS8: Bwnhls 3G 9
Cherwell Gdns. B6: Aston 1F 101
Cheshire Av. B90: Shir 4G 149
Cheshire Cl. DY8: Woll 3B 108
Cheshire Ct. B34: S End 2F 105
Cheshire Gro. WV6: Pert 5E 25
Cheshire Rd. B6: Witt 5A 84
B67: Smeth 5E 99
WS2: Wals 1F 47
Cheshunt Pl. B14: King H 5H 133
Cheslyn Dr. WS6: C Hay 2D 6
Cheslyn Gro. B14: King H 4A 148
CHESLYN HAY 3D 6
Cheslyn Hay Leisure Cen. 2C 6
Chessetts Gro. B13: Mose 1A 148
Chester Av. WV6: Tett 2D 26
Chester Cl. B37: F'bri 1C 122
WV13: W'hall 1D 46
Chester Ct. B29: W Cas 6F 131
  (off Abdon Av.)
B37: Chel W 1F 123
  (off Hedingham Gro.)
B73: Bold 6G 69
Chesterfield Cl. B31: N'fld 5F 145
Chesterfield Ct. B30: King Nor 3A 146
WS9: Wals W 3B 22
Chester Gdns. B73: New O 4E 69
Chester Hayes Ct. B24: Erd 2A 86
Chester Pl. WS2: Wals 2H 47
Chester Ri. B68: O'bry 3H 113
CHESTER ROAD 6H 69

Chester Rd. B23: Erd 4D 68
  B24: Erd .2A 86
  B35: Cas V 3C 86
  B36: Cas B 1E 105
  B37: Chel W, F'bri 4D 106
  B46: Col .4H 123
  B64: Crad H 3E 111
  B71: W Brom 4H 63
  B73: New O, Bold 4D 68
  B74: S'tly 4G 35
  CV7: Lit P 1B 140
  DY2: Neth 1F 111
  WS8: Bwnhls, Wals W 1C 22
  WS9: A'rdge, Wals W 1C 22
Chester Rd. Nth. B73: S'tly, New O . . .6A 52
  WS8: Bwnhls 4H 9
Chester Road Station (Rail) 6G 69
Chester St. B6: Aston 4H 101
  WV6: Wolv 5F 27
Chester St. Wharf B6: Aston 4H 101
Chesterton Av. B12: Bal H 6B 118
Chesterton Cl. B91: Sol 2C 150
Chesterton Rd. B12: Bal H 6A 118
  WV10: Bush 1C 28
Chester Wood WS9: A'rdge 1H 51
Chesterwood Rd. B13: Mose 1H 147
Chesterwoods Gdns. B20: Hand 5F 83
Chesterwood Rd. B13: Mose 1H 147
Chestnut Av. DY1: Dud 4E 77
  DY4: Tip .6H 61
Chestnut Cl. B27: A Grn 1A 136
  B74: S'tly 6A 36
  B92: Olton 5B 136
  DY8: Stourb 3B 124
  WV8: Cod 5F 13
Chestnut Ct. B36: Cas B 2A 106
Chestnut Cft. B29: W Cas 1E 145
Chestnut Dr. B24: Erd 3A 86
  B36: Cas B 1E 105
  B45: Coft H 5B 158
  WS4: S'fld 6F 21
  WS6: C Hay 2D 6
  WS6: Gt Wyr 2F 7
  WV5: Wom 2G 73
Chestnut Gro. B17: Harb 6H 115
  B46: Col .2H 107
  DY6: K'wfrd 2D 92
  WV11: Wed 2E 29
Chestnut Ho. B37: Chel W 1D 122
Chestnut Pl. WS3: Blox 3B 32
Chestnut Rd. B13: Mose 1A 134
  B68: O'bry 4A 114
  WS3: Blox 3C 32
  WS10: W'bry 4G 63
Chestnuts Av. B26: Sheld 4F 121
Chestnut Wlk. B37: Chel W 1D 122
  (within Chelmsley Wood Shop. Cen.)
Chestnut Way WV3: Wolv 3B 42
Chestom Rd. WV14: Bils 5D 44
Cheston Ct. B31: N'fld 5D 144
Cheston Ind. Est. B7: Nech 3A 102
Cheston Rd. B7: Nech 3A 102
Cheswell Cl. WV6: Tett 1H 41
Cheswick Cl. WV13: W'hall 3H 45
CHESWICK GREEN 5B 164
Cheswick Way B90: Ches G 5B 164
Cheswood Dr. B76: Walm 1F 87
Chetland Cft. B92: Sol 6B 138
Chettle Rd. WV14: Bils 2H 61
Chetton Grn. WV10: F'hses 4F 15
Chetwood Cl. WV6: Wolv 4E 27
Chetwynd Cl. WS2: Wals 6C 30
Chetwynd Rd. B8: W End 4H 103
  WV2: Wolv 5F 43
Cheveley Av. B45: Redn 2H 157
Chevening Cl. DY3: Sed 6A 60
Cheveridge Cl. B91: Sol 5F 151
Cheverton Rd. B31: N'fld 3C 144
Cheviot Rd. DY8: Amb 5E 109
  WV2: Ett .4B 44
Cheviot Way B63: Hale 2F 127
Cheylesmore Cl. B73: S Cold 1H 69
Cheyne Ct. B17: Harb 6H 133
  (off Greenfield Rd.)
Cheyne Gdns. B28: Hall G 4E 149
Cheyne Pl. B17: Harb 6H 115
Cheyne Wlk. DY5: Brie H 4G 109

Cheyne Way B17: Harb 6H 115
Cheyney Cl. WV6: Wolv 4E 27
Chichester Av. DY2: Neth 5F 95
Chichester Ct. B73: S Cold 6H 53
Chichester Dr. B32: Quin 6G 113
Chichester Gro. B37: Chel W 2C 122
  (not continuous)
Chigwell Cl. B35: Cas V 4E 87
Chilcote Cl. B28: Hall G 3F 149
Childs Av. WV14: Cose 3C 60
Childs Oak Cl. CV7: Bal C 3G 169
Chilgrove Gdns. WV6: Tett 4A 26
Chilham Dr. B37: Chel W 1E 123
Chillenden Ct. WV13: W'hall 1C 46
  (off Mill St.)
Chillinghome Rd. B36: Hodg H 1B 104
Chillington Cl. WS6: Gt Wyr 4F 7
Chillington Dr. DY1: Dud 4B 76
  WV8: Cod 3F 13
Chillington Flds. WV1: Wolv 2C 44
Chillington La. WV8: Cod 2D 12
Chillington Pl. WV14: Bils 6E 45
Chillington Rd. DY4: Tip 4C 62
Chillington St. WV1: Wolv 3B 44
Chillington Wlk. B65: Row R 6C 96
Chillington Works Ind. Est.
  WV1: Wolv 2B 44
Chilly Kiddy's 5E 109
Chiltern Cl. B63: Hale 3E 127
  DY3: Lwr G 4H 75
  WS6: C Hay 4D 6
Chiltern Dr. WV13: W'hall 2F 45
Chiltern Rd. DY8: Amb 5F 109
Chilterns, The B69: O'bry 4E 97
Chilton Ct. B23: Erd 5C 84
  (off North Pk. Rd.)
Chilton Rd. B14: Yard W 3D 148
Chilvers Gro. B37: K'hrst 4B 106
Chilwell Cl. B91: Sol 6F 151
Chilwell Cft. B19: Hock 4G 101
Chilworth Av. WV11: Wed 2H 29
Chilworth Cl. B6: Aston 3H 101
Chimes Cl. B33: Kitts G 2A 122
Chimney Rd. DY4: Tip 6D 62
Chingford Cl. DY8: Word 5A 92
Chingford Rd. B44: K'sdng 5A 68
Chinley Gro. B44: K'sdng 4C 68
Chinn Brook Rd. B13: Mose 2B 148
Chip Cl. B38: King Nor 5H 145
Chipperfield Rd. B36: Hodg H 1C 104
Chipstead Rd. B23: Erd 6D 68
Chipstone Cl. B91: Sol 1G 165
Chirbury Gro. B31: Longb 6F 145
Chirton Gro. B14: King H 1F 147
Chiseldon Cft. B14: King H 5A 148
Chisholm Gro. B27: A Grn 5A 136
Chiswell Rd. B18: Win G 5A 100
Chiswick Cl. B23: Erd 5E 85
Chiswick Ho. B15: Birm 3E 117
  (off Bell Barn Rd.)
Chiswick Wlk. B37: Chel W 1F 123
Chivenor Ho. B35: Cas V 5E 87
Chivington Cl. B90: M'path 3F 165
Chorley Av. B34: Hodg H 3D 104
Chorley Gdns. WV14: Bils 6D 44
Christchurch Cl. B15: Edg 3A 116
Christ Chu. Gro. WS1: Wals 4E 49
Christina Ct. B71: W Brom 3B 80
Christine Cl. DY4: Tip 3C 62
Christopher Ct. B23: Erd 5D 68
  (off Marshmont Way)
Christopher Rd. B29: S Oak 3G 131
  B62: Hale 2E 129
  WV2: Wolv 3A 44
Christopher Taylor Ct.
  B30: B'vlle 2A 146
Chubb St. WV1: Wolv 2D 170 (1H 43)
CHUCKERY, THE 2E 49
Chuckery Rd. WS1: Wals 2E 49
Chudleigh Gro. B43: Gt Barr 5H 65
Chudleigh Rd. B23: Erd 3E 85
Churchacre B23: Erd 5C 68
Church Av. B13: Mose 2H 133
  B20: Hand 1E 101
  B46: Wat O 4D 88
  DY8: Amb 4E 109
CHURCHBRIDGE 1G 7

Churchbridge B69: O'bry 4F 97
  (not continuous)
Churchbridge Ind. Est. B69: O'bry . . .4F 97
  (off Demuth Way)
Church Cl. B37: K'hrst 3C 106
  B47: Wyt .6A 162
Church Ct. B64: Old H 2G 111
Church Cres. WV11: Ess 4H 17
Church Cft. B63: Hale 1A 128
Churchcroft B17: Harb 1F 131
Church Cross Vw. DY1: Dud 1H 93
Churchdale Rd. B44: Gt Barr 2F 67
Churchdown Ct. B23: Erd 5C 84
  (off Dunlin Ct.)
Church Dr. B30: Stir 6D 132
CHURCHFIELD 1B 80
Churchfield Av. DY4: Tip 5H 61
Churchfield Cl. B7: Nech 3C 102
Churchfield Rd. WV10: Oxl 1F 27
Churchfields Rd. WS10: W'bry 1F 63
Churchfield St. DY2: Dud 1E 95
Churchfields Way B71: W Brom 1C 80
Church Gdns. B67: Smeth 5E 99
Churchgate Plaza B1: Birm 6A 4
Church Grn. B20: Hand 5B 82
  WV14: Bils 3E 45
Church Gro. B13: Mose 2C 148
  B20: Hand 6D 82
CHURCH HILL 2F 63
Church Hill B31: N'fld 4F 145
  (not continuous)
  B32: Fran 2G 143
  B46: Col .2H 107
  B72: S Cold 6A 54
  DY5: Brie H 1H 109
  WS1: Wals 2D 48
  WS10: W'bry 2F 63
  (not continuous)
  WV4: Penn 2C 58
  WV8: Cod 2F 13
Church Hill Cl. B91: Sol 5G 151
Church Hill Ct. WS10: W'bry 2F 63
Church Hill Dr. WV6: Tett 4C 26
Church Hill Rd. B20: Hand 6D 82
  B91: Sol .4G 151
  WV6: Tett 3B 26
Church Hill St. B67: Smeth 3D 98
Church Ho. WS2: Wals 4A 48
Church Ho. Dr. B72: S Cold 6A 54
Churchill Cl. B69: Tiv 5C 78
Churchill Dr. B65: Row R 1B 112
  DY8: Amb 4E 109
Churchill Gdns. DY3: Sed 6G 59
Churchill Pde. B75: S Cold 6E 55
Churchill Pl. B33: Sheld 2F 121
Churchill Rd. B9: Bord G 6F 103
  B63: Hale 3H 127
  B73: New O 2D 68
  B75: S Cold 6E 55
  WS2: Wals 1D 46
Churchill Shop. Cen., The
  DY2: Dud 6F 77
Churchill Wlk. DY4: Tip 5A 62
Church La. B6: Aston 1A 102
  B20: Hand 5B 82
  B33: Stech 6D 104
  B63: Hale 1B 128
  B71: W Brom 1H 79
  B76: Curd 1D 88
  B92: Bick .4F 139
  WS7: Hamm 2F 11
  WS9: Ston 3G 23
  WV2: Wolv 5A 170 (2G 43)
  WV5: Seis, Try 3A 56
  WV8: Cod 3F 13
  WV8: Cod W 1B 12
Church La. Ind. Est.
  B71: W Brom 1A 80
Church M. DY4: Tip 6H 61
Church Moat Way WS3: Blox 1H 31
Churchover Cl. B76: Walm 1B 86
Church Pl. B12: Bal H 6H 117
  WS3: Blox 1B 32
Church Rd. B6: Aston 2B 102
  B13: Mose 2H 133
  B15: Edg .4C 116
  B24: Erd .3F 85

Church Rd. B25: Yard 4B 120
  B26: Sheld 6F 121
  B31: N'fld 3E 145
  B33: Yard 3C 120
  B42: P Barr 2F 83
  B63: Crad 4E 111
  B65: Row R 6C 96
  B67: Smeth 5D 98
  B73: Bold 5F 69
  B73: S Cold 2H 69
  B90: Shir 5H 149
  DY2: Neth 4D 94
  DY3: Swind 4D 72
  DY8: Stourb 2F 125
  DY8: Word 1B 108
  DY9: Lye 6A 110
  WS3: Pels 4E 21
  WS8: Bwnhls 6B 10
  (not continuous)
  WS9: Ston 4G 23
  WS11: Nort C 1C 8
  WS3: Wolv 4C 42
  WV5: Wom 6H 57
  WV6: Pert 5E 25
  WV6: Tett 4C 26
  (Lower Grn.)
  WV6: Tett 6H 25
  (Richmere Ct.)
  WV8: Cod 3E 13
  (not continuous)
  WV10: Oxl 6G 15
  WV12: W'hall 3D 30
  WV14: Cose 4F 61
Churchside Way WS9: A'rdge 5D 22
Church Sq. B69: O'bry 2G 97
Church St. B3: Birm 3D 4 (6F 101)
  B19: Loz 2E 101
  B35: Cas V 3F 87
  B62: B'hth 2D 112
  B64: Old H 2G 111
  B69: O'bry 1G 97
  B70: W Brom 3A 80
  DY2: Dud 1E 95
  DY3: Lwr G 4H 75
  DY4: Tip 5A 78
  DY5: Brie H 2G 109
  DY5: P'ntt 2H 93
  DY5: Quar B 2B 110
  DY8: Stourb 6E 109
  WS1: Darl 2D 48
  WS3: Blox 1H 31
  WS7: Chase 1A 10
  WS8: Clay 1A 22
  WS10: Darl 4D 46
  (Bell St.)
  WS10: Darl 1B 62
  (Black Country New Rd.)
  WV2: Wolv 5A 170 (2G 43)
  WV10: Wolv 5C 28
  WV11: Wed 4E 29
  WV13: W'hall 1B 46
  (not continuous)
  WV14: Bils 6F 45
Church Ter. B33: Yard 2C 120
  B75: Four O 6H 37
Church Va. B20: Hand 6D 82
  B71: W Brom 1B 80
  WS11: Nort C 1C 8
Church Va. M. B71: W Brom 2B 80
Church Vw. B11: S'brk 5D 118
  B29: S Oak 4H 131
  WS9: A'rdge 4D 34
  WS9: Wals W 4B 22
Church Vw. Cl. WS3: Blox 1A 32
Church Vw. Dr. B64: Old H 2H 111
Church Wlk. B8: W End 3G 103
  B46: Col 3H 107
  B65: Row R 5C 96
  WS7: Chase 1A 10
  WV3: Wolv 4D 42
  WV6: Tett 4C 26
  WV13: W'hall 2B 46
Churchward Cl. DY8: Amb 5F 109
Churchward Gro. WV5: Wom 6G 57
Church Way WS4: S'fld 5F 21
Churchwell Cl. B63: Hale 2B 128
Churchwell Gdns. B71: W Brom 1B 80

Churchyard Rd. DY4: Tip 2B 78
Churnet Gro. WV6: Pert 5F 25
Churnhill Rd. WS9: A'rdge 5C 34
Churns Hill La. DY3: Himl 4H 73
Churston Cl. WS3: Blox 4G 19
Churwell Ct. WV5: Wom 1G 73
Cider Av. DY5: Quar B 3A 110
  (not continuous)
Cinder Bank DY2: Neth 2D 94
Cinder Bank Island DY2: Dud 2D 94
CINDER HILL 4B 60
Cinder Rd. DY3: Gorn 6F 75
Cinder Way WS10: W'bry 2E 63
Cineworld Cinema
  Birmingham 2D 116
  Solihull 4G 151
  Wolverhampton 5D 28
Cinquefoil Leasow DY4: Tip 1C 78
Circle, The B17: Harb 4G 115
Circuit Cl. WV13: W'hall 6B 30
Circular Rd. B27: A Grn 3A 136
Circus Av. B37: Chel W 1E 123
Citadel Junc. Way WV14: Bils 5A 46
City, The DY4: Tip 4A 78
City Arc. B2: Birm 4E 5
City Est. B64: Crad H 3F 111
City Ga. B24: Erd 6E 85
City Hgts. B4: Birm 1D 4
City Plaza B2: Birm 4E 5
City Rd. B16: Edg 2F 115
  B17: Edg 2F 115
  B69: Tiv 2B 96
City Trad. Est. B16: Birm 6C 100
City Vw. B8: Salt 5D 102
  B23: Erd 4E 85
City Wlk. B5: Birm 6E 5 (2G 117)
Civic Cl. B1: Birm 4A 4 (1E 117)
Civil Justice Cen.
  Birmingham 3E 5 (6G 101)
Claerwen Gro. B31: N'fld 2C 144
Claines Rd. B31: N'fld 3G 145
  B63: Crad 6F 111
Claire Ct. B26: Sheld 4G 121
Clairvaux Gdns. B92: Olton 2B 150
Clancey Way B63: Crad 5G 111
Clandon Cl. B14: King H 5E 147
Clanfield Av. WV11: Wed 1H 29
Clapgate Gdns. WV14: Cose 2C 60
Clap Ga. Gro. WV5: Wom 1E 73
Clapgate La. B32: Bart G 3G 129
Clap Ga. Rd. WV5: Wom 6E 57
Clapton Gro. B44: K'sdng 4B 68
Clare Av. WV11: Wed 6H 17
Clare Cres. WV14: Cose 3B 60
Clare Ct. B90: Shir 5D 148
Clare Dr. B15: Edg 3B 116
Clarel Av. B8: Salt 6C 102
Claremont Ct. B64: Old H 2G 111
Claremont M. WV3: Wolv 4E 43
Claremont Pl. B18: Hock 4B 100
Claremont Rd. B11: S'brk 4B 118
  B18: Hock 3D 100
  B66: Smeth 5F 99
  DY3: Sed 5A 60
  WV3: Wolv 4E 43
Claremont St. B64: Old H 2G 111
  WV14: Bils 5E 45
Claremont Way B63: Hale 2B 128
Claremont Av. B21: Hand 1G 99
Clarence Gdns. B74: Four O 1F 53
Clarence Gro. B90: Shir 3H 149
Clarence M. B17: Harb 5H 115
Clarence Rd. B11: S'hll 1C 134
  B13: King H, Mose 4A 134
  B17: Harb 5H 115
  B21: Hand 1G 99
  B23: Erd 4D 84
  B74: Four O 4E 37
  DY2: Dud 3D 95
  WV1: Wolv 2A 170 (1G 43)
  WV14: Bils 4G 45
Clarence St. DY3: Up Gor 1A 76
  WV1: Wolv 3A 170 (1G 43)
Clarendon Pl. B17: Harb 6G 115
Clarendon Dr. DY4: Tip 4D 62

Clarendon Pl. B62: Quin 4F 113
  WS3: Pels 3D 20
Clarendon Rd. B16: Edg 2A 116
  B67: Smeth 5D 98
  B75: R'ley 6A 38
  WS4: S'fld 5G 21
Clarendon St. WS3: Blox 6H 19
  WV3: Wolv 1E 43
Clarendon Way B91: Sol 4G 151
Clare Rd. WS3: Wals 3E 33
  WV10: Bush 2A 28
Clarewell Av. B91: Sol 1F 165
Clarke Ho. WS3: Blox 6H 19
Clarkes Gro. DY4: Tip 1C 78
Clarkes Ind. Est. B73: Bold 3G 69
Clarke's La. B71: W Brom 6A 64
  WV13: W'hall 6C 30
Clark Rd. WV3: Wolv 1D 42
Clarksland Gro. B37: Mars G 3C 122
Clarks La. B90: Dic H 3G 163
Clarkson Pl. DY5: Quar B 5A 110
Clarkson Rd. WS10: W'bry 1G 63
Clark St. B16: Birm 1B 116
  DY8: Stourb 6C 108
Clarry Dr. B74: Four O 3F 53
Clary Gro. WS5: Wals 2E 65
CLATTERBATCH 6F 109
Claughton Rd. DY2: Dud 6F 77
Claughton Rd. Nth. DY2: Dud 6F 77
Clausen Cl. B43: Gt Barr 1G 67
Clavedon Cl. B31: N'fld 6C 130
Claverdon Cl. B91: Sol 4C 150
  WS8: Bwnhls 5C 10
Claverdon Ct. B74: Lit As 6B 36
Claverdon Dr. B43: Gt Barr 5H 65
  B74: Lit As 5B 36
Claverdon Gdns. B27: A Grn 6H 119
Claverdon Ho. B13: Mose 6A 134
Claverley Ct. DY1: Dud 6D 76
Claverley Dr. WV4: Penn 6B 42
Claybrook St. B5: Birm 6E 5 (2G 117)
Claycroft Pl. DY9: Lye 6A 110
Claycroft Ter. DY1: Dud 1D 76
Claydon Gro. B14: King H 4A 148
Claydon Rd. DY6: W Hth 6A 74
Clay Dr. B32: Quin 6G 113
CLAYHANGER 1A 22
Clayhanger La. WS8: Bwnhls, Clay 6H 9
Clayhanger Rd. WS8: Bwnhls 1B 22
  B69: O'bry 5G 97
Claypit Cl. B70: W Brom 4G 79
Clay La. B26: Yard 6C 120
  B69: O'bry 5G 97
Claypit La. B90: Dic H 4G 163
  (not continuous)
Claypit La. B70: W Brom 4G 79
Clayton Cl. WV2: Wolv 4G 43
Clayton Dr. B36: Cas B 1G 105
Clayton Gdns. B45: Lick 6G 157
Clayton Ho. B16: Edg 2B 116
Clayton Rd. B8: Salt 4D 102
  WV14: Cose 6D 60
Clayton Wlk. B35: Cas V 5E 87
Clear Vw. DY6: K'wfrd 3H 91
Clearwell Gdns. DY1: Dud 4A 76
Clee Hill Dr. WV3: Wolv 2G 41
Clee Hill Rd. DY3: Lwr G 3G 75
Clee Rd. B31: Longb 1E 159
  B68: O'bry 5A 98
  DY2: Dud 2C 94
  DY8: Amb 5E 109
Cleeve Dr. B74: Four O 3F 37
Cleeve Ho. B24: Erd 5G 85
Cleeve Rd. B14: Yard W 3C 148
  WS3: Blox 4F 19
Clee Vw. Mdw. DY3: Sed 3H 59
Clee Vw. Rd. WV5: Wom 2E 73
Clematis Dr. WV9: Pend 4D 14
Clem Attlee Ct. WV14: Wolv 3E 45
Clement Pl. WV14: Bils 4F 45
Clement Rd. B62: B'hth 2D 112
  WV14: Bils 4F 45
Clements Cl. B69: O'bry 5F 97
Clements Rd. B25: Yard 3B 120
Clement St. B1: Birm 3A 4 (6D 100)
  WS2: Wals 2B 48
Clent Ct. DY1: Dud 6D 76

Clent Hill Dr. B65: Row R 4A **96**
Clent Ho. B63: Hale 3A **128**
Clent Rd. B21: Hand 6H **81**
  B45: Rub 1E **157**
  B68: O'bry 3A **114**
  DY8: Amb 5E **109**
Clent Vw. B66: Smeth 6F **99**
Clent Vw. Rd. B32: Bart G 4G **129**
  B63: Crad 1E **127**
  DY8: Stourb 2A **124**
          (not continuous)
Clent Vs. B12: Bal H 1B **134**
Clent Way B32: Bart G 5G **129**
  B94: Earls 4F **163**
Cleton St. DY4: Tip 4B **78**
Cleton St. Bus. Pk. DY4: Tip 4B **78**
Clevedon Av. B36: Cas B 1A **106**
Clevedon Rd. B12: Bal H 5G **117**
Cleveland Cl. WV11: Wed 6H **17**
  WV13: W'hall 2F **45**
Cleveland Ct. B13: Mose 3B **134**
  WV1: Wolv 6G **27**
Cleveland Pas. WV1: Wolv . .4B **170** (2G **43**)
Cleveland Rd. WV2: Wolv 5D **170** (2H **43**)
Cleveland St. DY1: Dud 6D **76**
  DY8: Stourb 1C **124**
  WV1: Wolv 4B **170** (2G **43**)
Cleveland Twr. B1: Birm 6D **4**
Cleves Cres. WS6: C Hay 4D **6**
Cleves Dr. B45: Rub 2E **157**
Cleves Rd. B45: Rub 1E **157**
Clewley Dr. WV9: Pend 4E **15**
Clewley Gro. B32: Quin 6H **113**
Clews Cl. WS1: Wals 4C **48**
Clewshaw La. B38: Head H 5D **160**
Cley Cl. B5: Edg 5F **117**
Cliff, The DY8: Stourb 5E **109**
Cliff Dr. DY4: Tip 5D **62**
Cliffe Dr. B33: Kitts G 6G **105**
Clifford Cl. DY4: Tip 6C **62**
Clifford Rd. B11: Tys 2F **135**
  B67: Smeth 2D **114**
  B70: W Brom 5G **79**
  B93: Ben H 5B **166**
Clifford St. B19: Loz 2F **101**
  DY1: Dud 1D **94**
  WV6: Wolv 6E **27**
Clifford Wlk. B19: Loz 2F **101**
          (not continuous)
Cliff Rock Rd. B45: Redn 2H **157**
Clift Cl. WV12: W'hall 3C **30**
Clifton Av. WS8: Bwnhls 6H **9**
  WS9: A'rdge 1E **35**
Clifton Cl. B6: Aston 2H **101**
  B69: O'bry 5G **97**
Clifton Cres. B91: Sol 6C **150**
Clifton Dr. B73: S Cold 5H **53**
Clifton Gdns. WV8: Bilb 4A **14**
Clifton Grn. B28: Hall G 2G **149**
Clifton Ho. B12: Bal H 6A **118**
Clifton La. B71: W Brom 5C **64**
Clifton Rd. B6: Aston 2H **101**
  B12: Bal H 6H **117**
  B36: Cas B 1A **106**
  B62: B'hth 3D **112**
  B67: Smeth 5D **98**
  B73: S Cold 1G **69**
  WV6: Tett 4B **26**
Clifton Rd. Ind. Est. B12: Bal H 6H **117**
          (off Clifton Rd.)
Clifton St. B64: Old H 2H **111**
  DY8: Stourb 1C **124**
  WV3: Wolv 1F **43**
  WV14: Cose 4B **60**
Clifton Ter. B23: Erd 3F **85**
Clinic Dr. DY9: Lye 6A **110**
Clinton Gro. B90: Shir 6C **150**
Clinton Rd. B46: Col 3H **107**
  B90: Shir 1B **164**
  WV14: Bils 4A **46**
Clinton St. B18: Win G 4A **100**
Clipper Vw. B16: Edg 2A **116**
Clipston Rd. B8: Salt 5F **103**
Clissold Cl. B12: Birm 4G **117**
Clissold Pas. B18: Hock 5C **100**
Clissold St. B18: Hock 5C **100**

Clive Cl. B75: R'ley 1B **54**
Cliveden Av. B42: P Barr 3E **83**
  WS9: A'rdge 6D **22**
Cliveden Coppice B74: Four O 2F **53**
Clivedon Way B62: Hale 4A **112**
Cleveland St. B19: Birm 1E **5** (5G **101**)
Clive Pas. B19: Birm 1D **4** (5F **101**)
Clive Rd. B32: Quin 4B **114**
  CV7: Bal C 6H **169**
Clive St. B71: W Brom 2A **80**
Clockfields Dr. DY5: Brie H 2E **109**
Clock La. B92: Bick 3F **139**
Clockmill Av. WS3: Pels 4C **20**
Clockmill Pl. WS3: Pels 4D **20**
Clockmill Rd. WS3: Pels 4C **20**
Clock Tower Vw. DY8: Word 6C **92**
Clodeshall Rd. B8: Salt 5E **103**
Cloister Dr. B62: Hale 2D **128**
Cloisters, The WS4: Wals 6D **32**
Clonmel Rd. B30: Stir 1C **146**
Clopton Cres. B37: F'bri 5D **106**
Clopton Rd. B33: Sheld 3G **121**
Close, The B17: Harb 4D **114**
  B29: S Oak 5H **131**
  B47: H'wd 4A **162**
  B62: Hunn 6A **128**
  B63: Crad 5F **111**
  B92: Olton 5D **136**
  DY3: Lwr G 3G **75**
  DY3: Swind 5E **73**
  WS10: W'bry 2E **63**
Close La. B32: Bart G 3G **129**
Closer to the Edge 6D **58**
Clothier Gdns. WV13: W'hall 6A **30**
Clothier St. WV13: W'hall 6A **30**
Cloudbridge Dr. B92: Sol 6B **138**
Cloudsley Gro. B92: Olton 2D **136**
Clover Av. B37: Chel W 1F **123**
Clover Ct. B38: King Nor 5H **145**
Cloverdale WV6: Pert 5D **24**
Clover Dr. B32: Bart G 3A **130**
Clover Hill WS5: Wals 3A **50**
Clover La. DY6: W Hth 2G **91**
Clover Lea Sq. B8: W End 3G **103**
Clover Ley WV10: Wolv 6B **28**
Clover Piece DY4: Tip 1C **78**
Clover Ridge WS6: C Hay 2C **6**
Clover Rd. B29: W Cas 6E **131**
Clover Wlk. B5: Edg 4F **117**
Club La. WV10: Cov H 1G **15**
Club Row DY3: Up Gor 2A **76**
Club Vw. B38: King Nor 5H **145**
Clunbury Cft. B34: S End 4F **105**
Clunbury Rd. B31: Longb 1E **159**
Clun Rd. B69: Tiv 6H **77**
Clun Rd. B31: N'fld 1D **144**
Clyde Av. B62: B'hth 3E **113**
Clyde Rd. B73: S Cold 6H **53**
Clyde M. DY5: P'ntt 3F **93**
Clyde Rd. B93: Dorr 6H **167**
Clydesdale B26: Sheld 6E **121**
Clydesdale Rd. B32: Quin 5H **113**
  DY2: Neth 6E **95**
  WS8: Clay 1A **22**
Clydesdale Twr. B1: Birm 6D **4**
Clyde St. B12: Birm 2A **118**
  B64: Old H 2G **111**
Clyde Twr. B19: Loz 1F **101**
C M T Ind. Est. B69: O'bry 1G **97**
COALBOURNBROOK 3D **108**
Coalbourn La. DY8: Amb 4D **108**
Coalbourn Way DY5: Brie H 6E **93**
Coalheath La. WS4: S'fld 1G **33**
Coalmeadow Cl. WS3: Blox 4F **19**
COAL POOL 3D **32**
Coalpool La. WS3: Wals 3D **32**
Coalpool Pl. WS3: Wals 3D **32**
Coalport Rd. WV1: Wolv 2C **44**
Coalway Av. B26: Sheld 1G **137**
  WV3: Penn 5E **43**
Coalway Gdns. WV3: Wolv 5B **42**
Coalway Rd. WS3: Blox 1G **31**
  WV3: Penn 5B **42**
Coatsgate Wlk. WV8: Pend 6D **14**
Cobbles, The B72: W Grn 6A **70**
Cobble Wlk. B18: Hock 4C **100**
Cobbs Wlk. B65: Row R 4H **95**

Cobden Cl. DY4: Tip 5H **61**
  WS10: Darl 5F **47**
Cobden Gdns. B12: Bal H 5G **117**
Cobden St. DY8: Woll 5B **108**
  WS1: Wals 4B **48**
  WS10: Darl 5F **47**
Cobham Bus. Cen. B9: Bord G 1D **118**
Cobham Cl. B35: Cas V 4D **86**
Cobham Ct. M. DY9: Hag 6H **125**
Cobham Rd. B9: Bord G 1D **118**
  B63: Hale 1B **128**
  DY8: Stourb 3E **125**
  WS10: W'bry 3C **64**
Cob La. B30: B'ville 6G **131**
Cobs Rd. B30: B'ville 1G **145**
Coburg Cft. DY4: Tip 1C **78**
Coburn Dr. B75: R'ley 1B **54**
Cochrane Cl. DY4: Tip 1C **78**
  DY9: Pedm 5G **125**
Cochrane Rd. DY2: Dud 3A **94**
COCK GREEN 5B **96**
Cock Hill La. B45: Redn, Rub 1F **157**
Cockshed La. B62: B'hth 3C **112**
Cockshut Hill B26: Yard 3E **121**
Cockshut Hill Sports & Fitness Cen.
  . . . . .3E **121**
Cockshutts La. WV2: Wolv 4H **43**
Cocksmead Cft. B14: King H 2F **147**
Cocksmoor Ho. B14: King H 6F **133**
Cocks Moors Woods Golf Course . .3H **147**
Cocks Moors Woods Leisure Cen. . .3H **147**
Cockthorpe Cl. B17: Harb 4D **114**
Cocoa Way B31: N'fld 1G **145**
Cocton Cl. WV6: Pert 4E **25**
CODSALL 3E **13**
Codsall Coppice Nature Reserve . .3G **111**
Codsall Gdns. WV8: Cod 3E **13**
Codsall Ho. WV8: Cod 3E **13**
Codsall Leisure Cen. 3G **13**
Codsall Rd. B64: Crad H 3G **111**
  WV6: Tett 6A **14**
  WV8: Tett 6A **14**
Codsall Station (Rail) 4E **13**
CODSALL WOOD 1B **12**
Codsall Wood Rd. WV8: Cod, Cod W . .1B **12**
Cofield Rd. B73: Bold 4F **69**
Cofton Chu. La. B45: Coft H 6A **158**
Cofton Ct. B45: Redn 2B **158**
Cofton Gro. B31: Longb 3C **158**
COFTON HACKETT 6A **158**
Cofton Lake Rd. B45: Coft H 6A **158**
Cofton Rd. B31: Longb 2E **159**
Cokeland Pl. B64: Crad H 3F **111**
Colaton Cl. WV10: Wolv 5A **28**
Colbourne Ct. B33: Stech 6B **104**
Colbourne Rd. DY4: Tip 3A **78**
Colbrand Gro. B15: Birm 3F **117**
Coldbath Rd. B13: Mose 5B **134**
Coldridge Cl. WV8: Pend 6D **14**
Coldstream Dr. DY8: Word 6C **92**
Coldstream Rd. B76: Walm 5C **70**
Cole Bank Rd. B13: Mose 5D **134**
  B28: Hall G 5E **135**
Colebourne Rd. B13: Mose 6C **134**
Colebridge Cres. B46: Col 1H **107**
Colebridge M. B46: Col 1H **107**
Colebrook Cft. B90: Shir 5F **149**
Colebrook Rd. B11: S'hll 6D **118**
  B90: Shir 5E **149**
COLE END .1H **107**
Coleford Cl. DY8: Word 1A **108**
Coleford Dr. B37: F'bri 1C **122**
Cole Grn. B90: Shir 6E **149**
COLEHALL .4E **105**
Cole Hall La. B33: Stech 5E **105**
  B34: S End 3E **105**
Cole Holloway B31: N'fld 5C **130**
Colehurst Cft. B90: M'path 3D **164**
Coleman Rd. WS10: W'bry 6G **47**
Coleman St. WV6: Wolv 5D **26**
Colemeadow Rd. B13: Mose 2B **148**
  B46: Col 2H **107**
Colenso Rd. B16: Edg 5H **99**
Coleraine Rd. B42: Gt Barr 1C **82**
Coleridge Cl. WS3: Pels 2E **21**
  WV12: W'hall 2E **31**

Coleridge Dr. WV6: Pert 5E 25
Coleridge Pas. B4: Birm 2F 5 (6G 101)
Coleridge Ri. DY3: Lwr G 3E 75
Coleridge Rd. B43: Gt Barr 6A 66
Cole River Pk. B11: Tys 1D 134
Colesbourne Av. B14: King H 5E 147
Colesbourne Rd. B92: Olton 2E 137
Coles Cres. WV4: Penn 6H 63
Colesden Wlk. WV4: Penn 5A 42
Coleshaven B46: Col 3H 107
COLESHILL 3H 107
Coleshill Freight Terminal B46: Col . . .5H 89
COLESHILL HEATH 2E 123
Coleshill Heath Rd.
    B37: Mars G, Chel W 4E 123
    B46: Col 4E 123
Coleshill Ind. Est. B46: Col 5G 89
    (not continuous)
Coleshill Leisure Cen. 3H 107
Coleshill Mnr. Office Campus
    B46: Col .2F 107
Coleshill Parkway Station (Rail) 5H 89
Coleshill Rd. B36: Hodg H 3B 104
    B37: Mars G 4C 122
    B46: Wat O 4D 88
    B75: S Cold 6A 54
    B76: Curd 1D 88
    (not continuous)
Coleshill St. B4: Birm 2G 5 (6H 101)
    B72: S Cold 6A 54
Coleshill Trad. Est. B46: Col 6H 89
Coleside Av. B13: Mose 6D 134
Coles La. B71: W Brom 6G 63
    B72: S Cold 1A 70
Cole St. DY2: Neth 6G 95
Cole Valley Rd. B28: Hall G 1D 148
Coleview Cres. B33: Kitts G 6A 106
Coleville Rd. B76: Walm 1F 87
Cole Way B34: S End 4G 105
Coley's La. B31: N'fld 5E 145
Colgreave Av. B11: Mose 3D 134
Colindale Rd. B44: K'sdng 2A 68
Colinwood Cl. WS6: Gt Wyr 4F 7
Collector Rd. B36: Cas B 6F 87
    B37: F'bri .6F 87
Colleen Av. B30: King Nor 4D 146
College Cl. WS10: W'bry 3G 63
College Ct. WV6: Tett 5B 26
College Dr. B20: Hand 5B 82
College Farm Dr. B23: Erd 5D 68
College Ga. B8: Salt 5E 103
College Gro. B20: Hand 2D 100
College High Community Leisure Centre, The
    . . . . .1B 84
College Hill B73: S Cold 1H 69
College Ho. B8: Salt 6E 103
College Rd. B8: Salt 6E 103
    B13: Mose 3C 134
    B20: Hand 5A 82
    B32: Quin 5G 113
    B44: P Barr, K'sdng 2G 83
    B73: New O 2G 83
    DY8: Stourb 1E 125
    WV6: Tett 5B 26
    (not continuous)
College St. B18: Hock 5C 100
College Vw. WV6: Tett 6B 26
College Wlk. B29: S Oak 5H 131
Collets Brook B75: Bass P 1F 55
Collett Cl. DY8: Amb 5E 109
Collett Rd. WV6: Pert 4E 25
Colletts Gro. B37: K'hrst 4B 106
Colley Av. WV10: Bush 1B 28
Colley Ga. B63: Crad 5E 111
Colley La. B63: Crad 4E 111
Colley Orchard B63: Crad 5E 111
Collier Cl. WS6: C Hay 3D 6
    WS8: Bwnhls 6G 9
Collier's Cl. WV12: W'hall 3B 30
Colliers Fold DY5: P'ntt 4F 93
Colliery Dr. WS3: Blox 4F 19
Colliery Rd. B71: W Brom 6E 81
    WV1: Wolv 1B 44
Collindale Ct. DY6: K'wfrd 6B 74
Collingbourne Av. B36: Hodg H 2B 104
Collingdon Av. B26: Sheld 5G 121
Collings Ho. B16: Edg 2C 116

Collingtree Ct. B92: Olton 3B 136
Colling Wlk. B37: K'hrst 3C 106
Collingwood Cen., The B43: Gt Barr . . .2F 67
Collingwood Dr. B43: Gt Barr 1E 67
Collingwood Rd. B30: King Nor 4F 147
    WV10: Bush 5A 16
Collins Cl. B32: Quin 6G 113
Collins Rd. WS8: Bwnhls 2C 22
    WS10: W'bry 2A 64
Collins St. B70: W Brom 4E 79
    WS1: Wals 4C 48
Collis St. DY8: Amb 3D 108
Collister Cl. B90: Shir 3H 149
Colly Cft. B37: K'hrst 4B 106
Collycroft Pl. B27: A Grn 6H 119
Colman Av. WV11: Wed 3H 29
Colman Cres. B68: O'bry 1A 114
Colman Hill B63: Crad 6F 111
Colman Hill Av. B63: Crad 5F 111
Colmers Community Leisure Cen. . . .1H 157
Colmers Wlk. B31: Longb 6B 144
Colmore Av. B14: King H 6F 133
Colmore Cir. Queensway
    B4: Birm 3E 5 (6G 101)
Colmore Cres. B13: Mose 4B 134
Colmore Dr. B75: S Cold 6E 55
Colmore Flats B19: Birm . . .1D 4 (5F 101)
Colmore Ga. B3: Birm 3E 5
Colmore Pl. B3: Birm 1C 4
Colmore Row B3: Birm 4C 4 (1F 117)
Colmore Sq. B4: Birm 3E 5 (6G 101)
Coln Cl. B31: N'fld 1D 144
Colonial Bus. Pk. B64: Crad H 4F 111
Colonial Rd. B9: Bord G 6F 103
Colshaw Rd. DY8: Stourb 1C 124
Colston Rd. B24: Erd 5H 85
Colsyll Gdns. DY1: Dud 1D 94
Colt Cl. B74: S'tly 4G 51
Coltham Rd. WV12: W'hall 3C 30
Coltishall Cl. B35: Cas V 5D 86
COLTON HILLS 1E 59
Colton Hills Sports Cen. 1F 59
Coltsfoot Cl. WV11: Wed 4G 29
Coltsfoot Vw. WS6: C Hay 3E 7
Columbia Cl. B5: Edg 5F 117
Columbine Cl. WS5: Wals 2E 65
Columbus Av. DY5: Brie H 6B 94
Colville Cl. DY4: Tip 5D 62
Colville Rd. B12: Bal H 6B 118
Colville Wlk. B12: Bal H 6B 118
Colwall Rd. DY3: Lwr G 3H 75
Colwall Wlk. B27: A Grn 1B 136
Colworth Rd. B31: N'fld 3C 144
Colyns Gro. B33: Stech 4D 104
Comber Cft. B13: Mose 5D 134
Comber Dr. DY5: P'ntt 3F 93
Comberford Ct. WS10: W'bry 3G 63
Comberford Dr. WS10: W'bry 6B 48
Comberton Rd. B26: Sheld 4F 121
Combine Cl. B75: R'ley 5B 38
Combined Court Cen.
    Wolverhampton 3D 170 (1H 43)
Combrook Grn. B34: S End 3H 105
Comet Rd. B26: Birm A 1E 139
Commercial Rd. WS2: Wals 2G 31
    WV1: Wolv .2A 44
Commercial St. B1: Birm . . .6B 4 (2E 117)
Commissary Rd. B26: Birm A 2C 138
Commonfield Cft. B8: Salt 4D 102
Common La. B8: Salt 3F 103
    B26: Sheld 6E 121
Common Rd. WV5: Wom 3F 73
COMMON SIDE .3E 9
Commonside DY5: P'ntt 3G 93
    WS3: Pels .5E 21
    WS8: Bwnhls 1C 22
Communication Row B15: Birm 2E 117
COMPTON 1A 42
Compton Cl. B91: Sol 3B 150
Compton Ct. B74: Four O 6F 37
    DY2: Neth .3E 95
    WV3: Wolv 1D 42
Compton Cft. B37: Chel W 2F 123
Compton Dr. B74: S'tly 4G 51
    DY2: Dud .1H 95
    DY6: K'wfrd 4B 92

Compton Grange B64: Crad H 3E 111
Compton Gro. B63: Crad 1E 127
    DY6: K'wfrd 4B 92
Compton Hill Dr. WV3: Wolv 1B 42
Compton Pk. WV3: Wolv 1C 42
Compton Rd. B24: Erd 6E 85
    B62: Quin .6F 113
    B64: Crad H 2E 111
    DY9: Pedm 4H 125
    WV3: Wolv 1C 42
Compton Rd. W. WV3: Wolv 1B 42
Comsey Rd. B43: Gt Barr 2D 66
Comwall Cl. WS3: Blox 3A 32
    (not continuous)
Conchar Cl. B72: W Grn 3A 70
Conchar Rd. B72: W Grn 3A 70
Concorde Dr. B35: Cas V 5D 86
Concorde Rd. B26: Birm A 1E 139
Condover Cl. WS2: Wals 6D 30
Condover Rd. B31: Longb 1F 159
Conduit Rd. WS11: Nort C 1E 9
Coneyford Rd. B34: S End 3G 105
Coneygre Community Cen. 3H 77
Coneygree Ind. Est. DY4: Tip 4H 77
Coney Grn. DY8: Stourb 6F 109
Coney Grn. Dr. B31: Longb 1D 158
Coney Grn. Ho. B31: Longb 1D 158
Coneygree Rd. DY4: Tip 5H 77
Congreve Pas. B3: Birm 4C 4 (1F 117)
Conifer Cl. DY5: Brie H 3G 109
Conifer Ct. B13: Mose 3G 133
Conifer Dr. B21: Hand 2A 100
    B31: N'fld .4F 145
Conifer Paddock B62: B'hth 3E 113
Conifer Rd. B74: S'tly 3G 51
Conington Gro. B17: Harb 6E 115
Coniston Av. B92: Olton 1D 136
Coniston Cl. B28: Hall G 6F 135
Coniston Cres. B43: Gt Barr 6B 66
Coniston Dr. DY6: K'wfrd 2H 91
Coniston Ho. B17: Harb 6H 115
    B69: O'bry 4D 96
Coniston Rd. B23: Erd 2D 84
    B74: S'tly .6H 35
    WV6: Tett .1B 26
Conker La. B93: Dorr 5A 166
Connaught Av. WS10: W'bry 2A 64
Connaught Cl. WS5: Wals 4G 49
Connaught Dr. WV5: Wom 4G 57
Connaught Gdns. B5: Edg 5G 117
Connaught Ho. WV1: Wolv 1E 43
Connaught Rd. WV1: Wolv 1E 43
    WV14: Bils .4H 45
Connect Bus. Pk. B9: Bord G 1D 118
Connops Way DY9: Lye 6A 110
Conolly Dr. B45: Redn 6H 143
Conrad Cl. B11: S'brk 4A 118
Consort Cres. DY5: P'ntt 3G 93
Consort Dr. WS10: Darl 3D 46
Consort Rd. B30: King Nor 4C 146
Constable Cl. B43: Gt Barr 2F 67
Constables, The B68: O'bry 1H 113
Constance Av. B70: W Brom 6B 80
Constance Rd. B5: Edg 6F 117
Constantine La. B46: Col 6H 89
Constantine Way WV14: Bils 3A 62
Constitution Hill B19: Birm . . .1C 4 (5F 101)
    DY2: Dud .1E 95
Constitution Hill E. DY2: Dud 1F 95
Containerbase B44: P Barr 2G 83
Convent Cl. WV2: Wolv 5C 170 (2H 43)
Conway Av. B32: Quin 5H 113
    B68: O'bry 1H 113
    B71: W Brom 4H 63
Conway Cl. B90: Shir 6B 150
    DY1: Dud .1E 77
    DY6: K'wfrd 5D 92
Conway Cres. WV12: W'hall 2C 30
Conway Dr. B65: Row R 1B 112
Conway Gro. B43: Gt Barr 6H 65
Conway Ho. WS3: Blox 3B 32
Conway Rd. B11: S'brk 5C 118
    B37: F'bri .6D 106
    B90: Shir .6B 150
    WV6: Pert .6F 25

Conwy Cl. WS2: Wals 5G **31**
Conybere St. B12: Birm 4H **117**
Conyworth Cl. B27: A Grn 1B **136**
Coockley Wharf Ind. Est.
 DY5: Brie H 5F **93**
Cook Av. DY2: Dud 2F **95**
Cook Cl. B93: Know 3E **167**
 WV6: Pert 5E **25**
Cookes Cft. B31: N'fld 5F **145**
Cookesley Cl. B43: Gt Barr 1F **67**
Cooke St. WV2: Wolv 4G **43**
Cookley Cl. B63: Hale 3H **127**
Cookley Way B69: O'bry 4E **97**
Cooknell Dr. DY8: Word 1C **108**
Cook Rd. WS3: Blox 5B **20**
Cooksey La. B44: Gt Barr 1G **67**
Cooksey Rd. B10: Small H 3B **118**
Cook's La. B37: K'hrst 6B **106**
Cookspiece Wlk. B33: Stech 6D **104**
Cook St. B7: Nech 2C **102**
 WS10: Darl 5F **47**
Coolshill Trade Pk. B46: Col 6H **89**
Coombe Cft. WV9: Pend 4E **15**
Coombe Hill B64: Old H 3B **112**
Coombe Pk. B74: Four O 4F **53**
Coombe Rd. B20: Hand 6G **83**
 B90: Shir 5A **150**
Coombes La. B31: Longb 3D **158**
COOMBESWOOD 3B **112**
Coombs Rd. B62: Hale 5B **112**
Coombswood Bus. Pk. B62: B'hth .3B **112**
Coombswood Ct. B62: Hale 4C **112**
Coombswood Way B62: B'hth 4B **112**
Cooperage Ct. DY4: Tip 5G **61**
Cooper Av. DY5: Brie H 1E **109**
Cooper Cl. B70: W Brom 5C **80**
COOPER'S BANK 6G **75**
Cooper's Bank Rd. DY3: Gorn 6G **75**
 DY5: P'ntt 6G **75**
Cooper's La. B67: Smeth 4D **98**
Coopers Rd. B20: Hand 4C **82**
Cooper St. B70: W Brom 4B **80**
 WV2: Wolv 3B **44**
Copeley Hill B23: Erd 6D **84**
Copenhagen M. B73: Bold 4F **69**
Copes Cres. WV10: Wolv 3C **28**
Copeshill Ct. B75: S Cold 1C **70**
Cope St. B18: Hock 6C **100**
 WS3: Blox 3A **32**
 WS10: Darl 5E **47**
Cophall St. DY4: Tip 2D **78**
Cophams Cl. B92: Sol 3G **137**
Coplow Cl. CV7: Bal C 3G **169**
Coplow Cotts. B16: Birm 6B **100**
Coplow St. B16: Birm 6B **100**
Coplow Ter. B16: Birm *6B 100*
 (off Coplow St.)
Copnor Gro. B26: Yard 5C **120**
Coppenhall Gro. B33: Kitts G 6E **105**
Copperbeech Cl. B32: Harb 6D **114**
Copper Beech Dr. DY6: K'wfrd 6B **74**
 WV5: Wom 1H **73**
Copperbeech Dr. B12: Bal H 6A **118**
Copper Beech Gdns. B20: Hand ...5B **82**
Copperbeech Gro. WS9: Wals W ...5B **22**
Copperfield Cl. B90: Dic H 4G **163**
Coppice, The B20: Hand 5C **82**
 B31: Longb 5A **144**
 B42: P Barr 4G **83**
 DY4: Tip 4C **62**
 WV12: W'hall 3C **30**
Coppice Ash Cft. B19: Loz 1F **101**
Coppice Av. DY9: W'cte 2B **126**
Coppice Cl. B24: Erd 4F **85**
 B45: Rub 2F **157**
 B90: Ches G 5A **164**
 B91: Sol 6E **137**
 DY3: Sed 6F **59**
 DY5: Quar B 2B **110**
 WS6: C Hay 1D **6**
 WV11: Wed 6A **18**
Coppice Cres. WS8: Bwnhls 6H **9**
Coppice Dr. B27: A Grn 3H **135**
Coppice Farm Way WV12: W'hall ...6B **18**
Coppice Gdns. B47: H'wd 2A **162**
Coppice Hollow B32: Bart G 4H **129**
Coppice Ho. B27: A Grn 3G **135**

Coppice La. B78: Midd 1G **55**
 DY5: Quar B 2B **110**
 WS6: C Hay 1D **6**
 WS7: Hamm 2H **11**
 WS8: Bwnhls 5G **9**
 WS9: A'rdge 6B **22**
 WV6: Tett 3H **25**
 (not continuous)
 WV12: W'hall 3C **30**
Coppice Oak B31: Mose 2A **134**
 WV12: W'hall 3C **30**
Coppice Ri. DY5: Quar B 1C **110**
Coppice Rd. B13: Mose 2A **134**
 B64: Crad H 4G **111**
 B92: Sol 6A **138**
 WS9: Wals W 3B **22**
 WV3: Wolv 3B **42**
 WV14: Cose 5C **60**
Coppice Side WS8: Bwnhls 5H **9**
Coppice Side Ind. Est. WS8: Bwnhls ..6G **9**
Coppice St. B70: W Brom 3G **79**
 DY4: Tip 3F **77**
 (Canal St.)
 DY4: Tip 1G **77**
 (Furnace Pde.)
Coppice Vw. Rd. B73: S'tly 1A **68**
Coppice Wlk. B90: Ches G 5A **164**
Coppice Way B37: Chel W *1D 122*
 (within Chelmsley Wood Shop. Cen.)
Copplestone Cl. B34: S End 3F **105**
Coppy Hall Gro. WS9: A'rdge 6D **22**
Coppy Nook La. WS7: Hamm 1D **10**
Copse, The B13: Mose 3B **134**
 B74: Four O 2F **53**
 B93: Dorr 6H **167**
Copse Cl. B31: N'fld 5E **145**
Copse Cres. WS3: Pels 3E **21**
Copse Rd. DY2: Neth 6D **94**
Copson Cl. B70: W Brom 4G **79**
Copstone Dr. B93: Dorr 6B **166**
Copston Gro. B29: W Cas 5F **131**
Copthall Rd. B21: Hand 5G **81**
COPT HEATH 6C **152**
Copt Heath Cft. B93: Know 1D **166**
Copt Heath Dr. B93: Know 2C **166**
Copt Heath Golf Course **1C 166**
Copt Heath Wharf B91: Sol 5D **152**
Copthorne Av. WS7: Chase 1B **10**
Copthorne Rd. B44: Gt Barr 2G **67**
 WV3: Wolv 4E **43**
Coralin Cl. B37: Chel W 1D **122**
Corbett Cres. DY8: Amb 4E **109**
Corbett Rd. B47: H'wd 2A **162**
 DY5: Brie H 2H **109**
Corbetts Cl. B92: H Ard 6B **140**
Corbett St. B66: Smeth 5F **99**
Corbridge Av. B44: Gt Barr 4H **67**
Corbridge Rd. B73: S Cold 3F **69**
Corbyn Rd. B9: Bord G 6H **103**
 DY1: Dud 1B **94**
Corbyn's Cl. DY5: P'ntt 2F **93**
Corbyn's Hall La. DY5: P'ntt 2F **93**
Corbyn's Hall Rd. DY5: P'ntt 2F **93**
Cordley St. B70: W Brom 3H **79**
Corfe Cl. B32: Harb 6D **114**
 WV6: Pert 6F **25**
Corfe Rd. WV14: Cose 5C **60**
Corfton Dr. WV6: Tett 5A **26**
Coriander Cl. B45: Fran 6H **143**
Corinne Cl. B45: Redn 3G **157**
Corisande Rd. B29: S Oak 3G **131**
Corley Av. B31: N'fld 4F **145**
Corley Cl. B90: Shir 6E **149**
Cormorant Cl. WS8: Bwnhls 6B **10**
Cornbow Cen. B63: Hale 2B **128**
Cornbrook Rd. B29: W Cas 6D **130**
Cornbury Gro. B91: Shir 3B **150**
Corncrake Cl. B72: S Cold 3B **70**
Corncrake Dr. B36: Cas B 1C **106**
Corncrake Rd. DY3: Lwr G 4A **76**
Cornel Cl. B37: Chel W 3E **123**
Cornerstone B13: Mose 2H **133**
Cornerstone Country Club
 B31: N'fld 2F **145**
Cornerway B38: King Nor 2B **160**

CORNETS END 1H **155**
Cornets End La. CV7: Mer 5E **141**
Cornfield WV8: Pend 6C **14**
Cornfield Cl. DY6: W Hth 1G **91**
Cornfield Cft. B37: Chel W 6F **107**
 B76: Walm 2D **70**
Cornfield Dr. B31: N'fld 1B **144**
Cornfield Pl. B65: Row R *5H 95*
 (off Doulton Rd.)
Cornfield Rd. B31: N'fld 3F **145**
 B65: Row R 5H **95**
 B76: Walm 4D **70**
Cornfields Cl. WV14: Bils 3G **61**
Cornflower Cl. WV10: F'stne 1C **16**
Cornflower Cres. DY2: Dud 1H **95**
Cornflower Rd. WS8: Clay 1H **21**
Corngreaves, The B34: S End 3G **105**
Corngreaves Rd. B64: Crad H 2F **111**
Corngreaves Trad. Est. B64: Crad H ..4F **111**
Corngreaves Wlk. B64: Crad H 4G **111**
Corn Hill WS5: Wals 3A **50**
 WV10: Wolv 3D **170** (1H **43**)
Cornhill Gro. B30: Stir 1E **147**
Corn Mill Cl. B32: Bart G 4C **130**
 B76: Walm 4D **70**
 WS1: Wals 4B **48**
Cornmill Gro. WV6: Pert 6D **24**
Cornovian Cl. WV6: Pert 4E **25**
Corns Gro. WV5: Wom 2F **73**
Corns Ho. WS10: Darl *5E 47*
 (off Birmingham St.)
Corns St. WS10: Darl 6E **47**
Cornwall Av. B68: O'bry 3H **113**
Cornwall Cl. DY6: K'wfrd 1B **92**
 WS9: A'rdge 6C **22**
 WS10: W'bry 2B **64**
Cornwall Ga. WV12: W'hall 4B **30**
Cornwall Ho. B90: Bly P 6D **164**
Cornwall Ind. Est. B8: Salt 5C **102**
Cornwallis Rd. B70: W Brom 6G **79**
Cornwall Pl. WS2: Wals 6E **31**
Cornwall Rd. B20: Hand 5B **82**
 B45: Fran 6E **143**
 B66: Smeth 2F **99**
 DY8: Woll 3B **108**
 WS5: Wals 4F **49**
 WV6: Tett 5A **26**
Cornwall Rd. Ind. Est. B66: Smeth ...2F **99**
Cornwall St. B3: Birm 3C **4** (6F **101**)
Cornwell Cl. DY4: Tip 2A **78**
Cornwood La. B90: Dic H 4G **163**
Cornyx La. B91: Sol 1H **151**
Coronation Av. WV13: W'hall 1D **46**
Coronation Rd. B8: Salt 3F **103**
 B29: S Oak 3B **132**
 B43: Gt Barr 1A **66**
 DY4: Tip 5A **62**
 WS4: S'fld 5F **21**
 WS9: Wals W 4C **22**
 WS10: W'bry 2A **64**
 WV10: Wolv 4C **28**
 WV14: Bils 6E **45**
Coronation Rd. DY2: Dud 5G **77**
Coronation Sq. B4: Birm ...3F **5** (6G **101**)
Coronation St. B2: Birm 4E **5** (1G **117**)
 B4: Birm 1F **5** (5H **101**)
 WS1: Wals 3C **48**
 WS10: W'bry 3G **63**
 WV1: Wolv 3A **170** (1G **43**)
Coronation St. W. WS1: Wals 3B **48**
 WS2: Wals 3B **48**
Corrie Cft. B26: Sheld 4F **121**
 B32: Bart G 5H **129**
Corrin Gro. DY6: W Hth 1A **92**
Corron Hill B63: Hale *1B 128*
 (off Cobham Rd.)
Corsers Cft. WV6: Pert 5E **25**
Corser St. DY1: Dud 5B **76**
 DY8: Stourb 2E **125**
 WV1: Wolv 2B **44**
Corser Street (Wolverhampton)
 (Park & Ride) **2B 44**
Corsican Cl. WV12: W'hall 2E **31**
Corvedale Rd. B29: W Cas 1E **145**
Corve Gdns. WV6: Tett 4C **26**
Corve Vw. DY3: Sed 4G **59**

Corville Gdns.—Crayford Rd.

Corville Gdns. B26: Sheld 1G 137
Corville Rd. B62: Quin 5F 113
Corwen Cft. B31: N'fld 1C 144
Cory Cft. DY4: Tip 2A 78
COSELEY 4F 61
Coseley Hall WV14: Cose 5E 61
Coseley Leisure Cen. 4D 60
Coseley Rd. WV14: Bils 6E 45
Coseley Station (Rail) 4E 61
Cosford Ct. WV6: Pert 4E 25
Cosford Cres. B35: Cas V 4E 87
Cosford Dr. DY2: Neth 5G 95
Cosgrove Wlk. WV8: Pend 6D 14
Cossington Rd. B23: Erd 6D 68
Costock Cl. B37: Mars G 3D 122
Cotford Rd. B14: King H 5A 148
Cotheridge Cl. B90: M'path 3G 165
Cot La. DY6: K'wfrd 3A 92
DY8: Word 4A 92
Cotleigh Gro. B43: Gt Barr 2G 67
Cotman Cl. B43: Gt Barr 2E 67
Coton Gro. B90: Shir 5E 149
Coton La. B23: Erd 3F 85
Coton Rd. WV4: Penn 6F 43
Cotsdale Rd. WV4: Penn 2C 58
Cotsford B91: Sol 4E 151
Cotswold Av. WS6: Gt Wyr 2F 7
Cotswold Cl. B45: Fran 5H 143
B69: O'bry 4E 97
WS9: A'rdge 6E 23
Cotswold Ct. *WV2: Penn 5F 43*
(off Goldthorn Hill)
Cotswold Cft. B63: Hale 4E 127
Cotswold Gro. WV12: W'hall 6B 18
Cotswold Rd. DY8: Amb 5F 109
WV2: Ett 4B 44
Cottage Cl. WV11: Wed 3E 29
(not continuous)
Cottage Gdns. B45: Rub 4F 157
Cottage La. B76: Min 1H 87
WV10: F'hses 4H 15
Cottage M. WS9: A'rdge 5G 35
Cottage St. DY5: Brie H 6H 93
DY6: K'wfrd 2B 92
Cottage Vw. WV8: Bilb 3H 13
Cottage Wlk. B70: W Brom 5B 80
COTTERIDGE 3B 146
Cotteridge Rd. B30: King Nor 3C 146
Cotterills Av. B8: W End 5A 104
Cotterills La. B8: W End 5H 103
Cotterills Rd. DY4: Tip 6B 62
Cottesbrook Rd. B27: A Grn 1B 136
Cottesfield Cl. B8: W End 5H 103
Cottesmore Cl. B71: W Brom 5D 64
Cottesmore Ho. B20: Hand 5B 82
Cottle Cl. WS2: Wals 6F 31
Cotton La. B13: Mose 3H 133
Cottrells Cl. B14: Yard W 3C 148
Cottrells M. B46: Wat O 5D 88
Cottrell St. B71: W Brom 3B 80
Cottsmeadow Dr. B8: W End 5A 104
COTWALL END 6H 59
Cotwall End Rd. DY3: Lwr G, Sed 3F 75
Cotwall End Valley Local Nature Reserve 3F 75
Cotysmore Rd. B75: S Cold 5B 54
Couchman Rd. B8: Salt 5E 103
Coulter Gro. WV6: Pert 5D 24
Council Cres. WV12: W'hall 5C 30
Counterfield Dr. B65: Row R 4H 95
Countess Dr. WS4: Rus 2H 33
Countess St. WS1: Wals 4B 48
Country Pk. Vw. B76: Walm 4D 70
COUNTY BRIDGE 1D 46
County Cl. B30: Stir 1D 146
B32: Bart G 2A 130
County Court
Dudley 5A 94
Walsall 1D 48
County La. DY8: I'ley 5B 124
WV8: Alb, Cod W 2A 12
County Pk. Av. B62: Hale 2C 128
Court, The B93: Know 4B 168
Court Cres. DY6: K'wfrd 4H 91
Courtenay Gdns. B43: Gt Barr 3A 66
Courtenay Rd. B44: Gt Barr 6G 67
Court Farm Rd. B23: Erd 1E 85
Court Farm Way B29: W Cas 6D 130
Courtland Rd. DY6: K'wfrd 1C 92
Courtlands, The WV6: Wolv 5C 26
Courtlands Cl. B5: Edg 5E 117
Court La. B23: Erd 5E 69
Court Oak Gro. B32: Harb 5D 114
Court Oak Rd. B17: Harb 5C 114
B32: Harb 5C 114
Court Pde. WS9: A'rdge 3D 34
Court Pas. DY1: Dud 6E 77
Court Rd. B11: S'hll 1C 134
B12: Bal H 5G 117
WV4: Ett 2C 60
WV6: Wolv 5D 26
Court St. B64: Old H 2H 111
DY8: Stourb 6E 109
Court Way WS2: Wals 1C 48
Courtway Av. B14: King H 6B 148
Courtway Ho. B29: S Oak 4F 131
Courtyard, The B46: Col 5H 89
B70: W Brom 4G 79
B91: Sol 3G 151
Cousins St. WV2: Wolv 4H 43
Coveley Gro. B18: Hock 4C 100
Coven Cl. WS3: Pels 2E 21
Coven Gro. B29: S Oak 3F 131
COVEN HEATH 1G 15
Coven La. WV9: Coven 2D 14
Coven St. WV10: Wolv 5H 27
Coventry Rd. B10: Small H 2A 118
B25: Yard 4G 119
B26: Yard, Sheld 6D 120
B46: Col 6H 107
B92: Bick 6D 120
CV7: Mer 3G 139
Coventry St. B5: Birm 5G 5 (1H 117)
DY8: Stourb 6E 109
WV1: Wolv 1C 44
Coverack Rd. WV14: Bils 3B 62
Cover Cft. B76: Walm 4E 71
Coverdale Rd. B92: Olton 1E 137
Covert, The WV8: Pend 6C 14
Covert La. DY8: Stourb 4B 124
Cowdrey Cl. DY8: Amb 5E 109
Cowles Cft. B25: Yard 2C 120
Cowley Cl. B36: Cas B 6B 88
Cowley Dr. B27: A Grn 1B 136
DY1: Dud 5B 76
Cowley Gro. B11: Tys 6E 119
Cowley Rd. B11: Tys 6E 119
Cowper Cl. WV12: W'hall 2E 31
Cowslip Cl. B29: W Cas 6E 131
B38: King Nor 1B 160
Cowslip Wlk. DY5: Brie H 5G 109
Coxcroft Av. DY5: Quar B 3B 110
Coxmoor Cl. WS3: Blox 4F 19
Cox Rd. WV14: Cose 4G 61
Cox's La. B64: Old H 1H 111
Cox St. B3: Birm 1C 4 (5F 101)
Coxwell Av. WV10: Wolv 3G 27
Coxwell Gdns. B16: Birm 1B 116
Coyne Cl. DY4: Tip 2F 77
Coyne Rd. B70: W Brom 5H 79
Crabbe St. DY9: Lye 6B 110
Crab La. DY6: K'wfrd 5E 93
WV12: W'hall 6D 18
Crabmill Cl. B38: King Nor 2A 160
B93: Know 2E 167
Crabmill La. B38: Head H 2E 161
Crabourne Rd. DY2: Neth 1D 110
Crabtree Cl. B31: N'fld 5G 145
B71: W Brom 5D 64
DY9: Hag 6F 125
WV4: Ett 1B 60
Crabtree Dr. B37: F'bri 1B 122
Crab Tree Ho. B33: Stech 6C 104
Crabtree Rd. B18: Hock 4C 100
WS1: Wals 1E 49
Crackley Way DY2: Dud 3C 94
Craddock Rd. B67: Smeth 3C 98
Craddock St. WV6: Wolv 5E 27
CRADLEY 4E 111
Cradley Cft. B21: Hand 4G 81
Cradley Ent. Cen. B63: Crad 4C 110
Cradley Flds. B63: Crad 6F 111
Cradley Forge DY5: Quar B 3C 110
CRADLEY HEATH 2G 111
Cradley Heath Factory Cen.
B64: Crad H 3E 111
Cradley Heath Station (Rail) 3D 110
Cradley Mill DY5: Quar B 4B 110
Cradley Pk. Rd. DY2: Neth 1E 111
Cradley Rd. B64: Crad H 3E 111
DY2: Neth 5F 95
Cradock Rd. B8: Salt 4E 103
Craig Cft. B37: Chel W 1F 123
Crail Gro. B43: Gt Barr 1D 66
Cramlington Rd. B42: Gt Barr 5C 66
Cramp Hill WS10: Darl 5D 46
Cranbourne Av. WV4: Ett 2A 60
Cranbourne Cl. B45: Fran 5G 143
Cranbourne Gro. B44: K'sdng 5A 68
Cranbourne Pl. B71: W Brom 3B 80
Cranbourne Rd. B44: K'sdng 5A 68
DY8: Stourb 1E 125
Cranbrook Ct. *WV13: W'hall 1C 46*
(off Walsall Rd.)
Cranbrook Gro. WV6: Pert 6F 25
Cranbrook Rd. B21: Hand 6G 81
Cranbrook Way B90: Shir 2D 164
Cranby St. B8: Salt 4C 102
Craneberry Rd. B37: F'bri 1A 122
Cranebrook Hill B78: Hints 4H 39
Cranebrook La. WS14: Hilt, Lynn 1H 23
Crane Ct. WS1: Wals 6E 33
Crane Dr. WS7: Chase 1C 10
Crane Hollow WV5: Wom 2E 73
Cranehouse Rd. B44: K'sdng 3B 68
Cranemoor Cl. B7: Nech 3C 102
Crane Rd. WV14: Bils 2H 61
Cranesbill Rd. B29: W Cas 1E 145
Cranes Pk. Rd. B26: Sheld 6G 121
Crane Ter. WV6: Tett 4C 26
Cranfield Gro. B26: Yard 3D 120
Cranfield Pl. WS5: Wals 1D 64
Cranford Gro. B91: Sol 6F 151
Cranford Rd. WV3: Wolv 3A 42
Cranford St. B66: Smeth 4G 99
Cranford Way B66: Smeth 4G 99
Cranham Dr. DY6: K'wfrd 4C 92
Cranhill Cl. B92: Olton 4F 137
Crankhall La. B71: W Brom 2H 63
WS10: W'bry 2H 63
Cranleigh Cl. WS9: A'rdge 4D 34
WV12: W'hall 6C 18
Cranleigh Ho. B23: Erd 1F 85
Cranleigh Pl. B44: P Barr 2G 83
Cranley Dr. WV8: Cod 3F 13
Cranmer Av. WV12: W'hall 2D 30
Cranmer Cl. WS6: C Hay 4D 6
Cranmere Av. WV6: Tett 3G 25
Cranmere Ct. WV6: Tett 3G 25
Cranmer Gro. B74: Four O 3F 37
Cranmoor WV8: Wrot P 4C 24
Cranmoor Cres. B63: Hale 6A 112
Cranmore Av. B21: Hand 2H 99
B90: Shir 1C 164
Cranmore Blvd. B90: Shir 2B 164
Cranmore Cl. DY4: Tip 5A 62
Cranmore Dr. B90: Shir 6C 150
Cranmore Rd. B36: Cas B 6H 87
B90: Shir 1B 164
WV3: Wolv 6D 26
Cransley Gro. B91: Sol 6E 151
Crantock Cl. WV11: Ess 6C 18
Crantock Rd. B42: P Barr 3E 83
Cranwell Grn. WV5: Wom 2F 73
Cranwell Gro. B24: Erd 4B 86
Cranwell Way B35: Cas V 4E 87
Crash Bang Wallop 2B 22
Crathorne Av. WV10: Oxl 6G 15
Craufurd Ct. DY8: Stourb 2E 125
Craufurd St. DY8: Stourb 2E 125
Craven Hgts. B92: H Ard 6A 140
Craven St. WV2: Ett 5B 44
Crawford Av. B67: Smeth 4D 98
WS10: Darl 4C 46
WV4: Ett 2B 60
Crawford Rd. B76: Walm 5D 70
WV3: Wolv 1E 43
Crawford St. B8: Salt 4C 102
Crawley Wlk. B64: Crad H 2F 111
Crawshaws Rd. B36: Cas B 6G 87
Crayford Rd. B44: K'sdng 4A 68

Craythorne Av. B20: Hand 2A 82
Creation Climbing Cen. 6H 117
    (off Moseley Rd.)
Crecy Cl. B76: Walm 1C 70
Credenda Rd. B70: W Brom 6G 79
Credon Gro. B15: Edg 1B 132
Creed Way B70: W Brom 3H 79
Cregoe St. B15: Birm 2E 117
Cremore Av. B8: Salt 4E 103
Cremorne Rd. B75: Four O 1H 53
Cremorne Wlk. B75: Four O 1H 53
Crendon Rd. B65: Row R 3A 96
Crescent, The B28: Hock 3D 100
  B37: Mars G 3G 123
  B43: Gt Barr 4C 66
    (Handsworth Dr.)
  B43: Gt Barr 2F 67
    (King's Rd.)
  B46: Wat O 4D 88
  B64: Crad H 4A 112
  B65: Row R 1B 112
  B90: Shir 3G 149
  B91: Sol 3F 151
  B92: H Ard 6B 140
  DY1: Dud 3G 77
  DY9: Lye 1G 125
  WS1: Wals 3E 49
  WS6: Gt Wyr 3G 7
  WS10: W'bry 1G 63
  WV6: Tett 6H 25
  WV13: W'hall 2C 46
  WV14: Bils 5F 45
Crescent Arc. B91: Sol 4G 151
    (within Touchwood)
Crescent Av. B18: Hock 3D 100
  DY5: Brie H 1G 109
Crescent Ind. Pk. DY2: Dud 2D 94
Crescent Rd. DY2: Neth 4D 94
  WS10: Darl 5D 46
  WV13: W'hall 1C 46
Crescent Studios B18: Hock 3D 100
Crescent Theatre 1D 116
Crescent, The Stop (Metro) 5F 45
Crescent Twr. B1: Birm 4A 4
Crescent Works Ind. Pk.
  WS10: Darl 2D 46
Cressage Av. B31: N'fld 6E 145
Cressett Av. DY5: Brie H 5F 93
Cressett La. DY5: Brie H 5G 93
Cressington Dr. B74: Four O 2G 53
Cresswell Ct. WV9: Pend 4E 15
Cresswell Cres. WS3: Blox 5F 19
Cresswell Gro. B24: Erd 3B 86
Cressy Cl. B14: King H 3D 146
Crest, The B31: Longb 2F 159
Crest Vw. B74: S'tly 3H 51
Crestview B14: King H 3B 148
Crestwood Dr. B44: Gt Barr 6G 67
Crestwood Glen WV6: Tett 2C 26
Creswell Rd. B28: Hall G 6H 135
Creswick Gro. B45: Redn 2A 158
Crew Dr. DY4: Tip 5A 78
Crew Rd. WS10: W'bry 1G 63
Creynolds Cl. B90: Ches G 6B 164
Creynolds La. B90: Ches G 6B 164
Cricket Cl. WS5: Wals 4F 49
Cricketers Mdw. B64: Crad H 4G 111
  WV10: F'hses 3H 15
Cricket St. B70: W Brom 6F 63
Crick La. B20: Hand 1C 100
Cricklewood Dr. B62: Hale 2D 128
Crimmond Ri. B63: Hale 6G 111
Crimscote Cl. B90: M'path 3D 164
Cripps Rd. WS2: Wals 6E 31
Criterion Works WV13: W'hall 3B 46
Crocketts Av. B21: Hand 2H 99
Crockett's La. B66: Smeth 4E 99
Crocketts Rd. B21: Hand 2G 99
Crockett St. DY1: Dud 5C 76
Crockford Dr. B75: Four O 6H 37
Crockford Rd. B71: W Brom 4A 64
Crockington La.
  WV5: Seis, Try 3A 56
Crocodile Ct. B19: Hock 3G 101
    (off Alma St.)
Crocus Cres. WV9: Pend 4E 15

Croft, The B31: N'fld 4F 145
  DY2: Dud 3B 94
  DY3: Sed 4A 60
  WS5: Wals 3A 50
  WS6: C Hay 3E 7
  WV5: Wom 2D 72
  WV12: W'hall 3D 30
Croft Apartments WV13: W'hall 1A 46
    (off Croft St.)
Croft Cl. B25: Yard 3C 120
Croft Ct. B36: Cas B 1F 105
Croft Cres. WS8: Bwnhls 6H 9
Croft Down Rd. B92: Sol 1H 137
Croftdown Rd. B17: Harb 5D 114
Crofters Ct. DY8: Stourb 1F 125
Crofters Cl. B15: Edg 5A 116
Crofters La. B75: R'ley 6C 38
Crofters Wlk. WV8: Pend 6C 14
Croft Ho. WS1: Wals 2D 48
    (off Paddock La.)
Croft Ind. Est. B37: Chel W 1F 123
  WV13: W'hall 1A 46
Croft La. WV10: Bush 2C 28
Croftleigh Gdns. B91: Sol 5C 150
Crofton Cen. B45: Coft H 4C 158
Crofton Pk. Cl. B31: Longb 3A 158
Crofton Pk. Dr. B31: Longb 3A 158
Croft Pde. WS9: A'rdge 3D 34
Croft Rd. B26: Yard 3C 120
Crofts, The B76: Walm 6E 71
Croft St. WS2: Wals 6B 32
  WV13: W'hall 1A 46
    (not continuous)
Croftway, The B20: Hand 1A 82
Croftwood Rd. DY9: W'cte 1H 125
Cromane Sq. B43: Gt Barr 6A 66
Cromdale Dr. B63: Hale 2F 127
Cromer Gdns. WV6: Wolv 4D 26
Crome Rd. B43: Gt Barr 2F 67
Cromer Rd. B12: Bal H 6H 117
Crompton Av. B20: Hand 6E 83
Crompton Cl. B7: Nech 1C 102
  WS2: Wals 4G 31
Crompton Ct. WV8: Bilb 3H 13
Crompton Rd. B7: Nech 1C 102
  B20: Hand 6E 83
  B45: Fran 6D 142
  DY4: Tip 3A 78
Cromwell Cl. B65: Row R 4H 95
  WS2: Wals 5E 31
Cromwell Ct. WS6: Gt Wyr 4G 7
Cromwell Dr. DY2: Dud 1H 95
Cromwell La. B31: N'fld 5B 130
Cromwell Rd. WV10: Bush 4A 16
Cromwell St. B7: Nech 4B 102
  B71: W Brom 3A 80
  DY2: Dud 1G 95
Crondal Pl. B15: Edg 4D 116
CRONEHILLS, THE 4A 80
Cronehills Linkway B70: W Brom 3B 80
Crooked Ho. La. DY3: Gorn, Himl 5D 74
Crookham Cl. B17: Harb 4D 114
Crookhay La. B71: W Brom 5G 63
Crook La. WS9: A'rdge 5C 50
Croome Cl. B11: S'hll 2B 134
Cropredy Rd. B31: Longb 1E 159
Cropthorne Dr. B47: H'wd 2B 162
Cropthorne Gdns. B90: Shir 4A 150
Cropthorne Rd. B90: Shir 4A 150
Crosbie Rd. B17: Harb 5F 115
Crosby Cl. B1: Birm 6D 100
  WV6: Wolv 4D 26
Cross, The DY6: K'wfrd 3B 92
Cross Cl. B64: Old H 1H 111
Cross Farm Mnr. B17: Harb 1H 131
    (off Cross Farm Rd.)
Cross Farm Rd. B17: Harb 1G 131
Cross Farms La. B45: Rub 6F 143
Crossfield Rd. B33: Kitts G 5F 105
Crossfield Way WV14: Bils 6G 45
Crossgate Rd. DY2: Dud 3B 94
Crossing, The B69: O'bry 1G 97
    (off Broadwell Rd.)
Crossings Ind. Est., The WS3: Blox 1H 31
    (off Fryer's Rd.)
Crosskey Cl. B33: Kitts G 1A 122
Cross Keys Bus. Pk. B69: Tiv 4B 78

Crossland Cres. WV6: Tett 3D 26
Cross La. B43: Gt Barr 4A 66
  DY3: Sed 5H 59
  WS14: Foot 1E 37
Crossley St. DY2: Neth 5F 95
Cross Pl. DY3: Sed 4A 60
Cross Quays Bus. Pk. B69: Tiv 5B 78
    (off Hallbridge Way)
Cross St. B21: Hand 1G 99
  B63: Hale 2A 128
  B65: B'hth 2C 112
  B66: Smeth 3E 99
  B68: O'bry 5G 97
  DY1: Dud 6D 76
  DY6: K'wfrd 3B 92
  DY6: W Hth 1H 91
  DY8: Stourb 6C 108
  DY8: Word 6B 92
  WS3: Pels 6E 21
  WS6: C Hay 2D 6
  WS10: Darl 4D 46
  WS10: W'bry 2E 63
  WV1: Wolv 2B 44
  WV13: W'hall 2A 46
  WV14: Bils 3H 61
Cross St. Nth. WV1: Wolv 5H 27
Cross St. Sth. WV2: Wolv 4G 43
Cross Wlk. B69: Tiv 1C 96
Cross Walks Rd. DY9: Lye 6A 110
Crossway La. B44: K'sdng 1H 83
Crossways Ct. B44: K'sdng 6B 68
Crossways Grn. B44: K'sdng 6B 68
Crossways Shop. Cen. WV10: Wolv 6C 28
Crosswells Rd. B68: O'bry 4H 97
Crowberry Cl. WS8: Clay 1H 21
Crowesbridge M. WV14: Cose 5D 60
Crowhurst Rd. B31: Longb 2C 158
Crowland Av. WV6: Pert 5E 25
Crowle Dr. DY9: Lye 6G 109
Crown Av. B20: Hand 5F 83
Crown Cen., The DY8: Stourb 6E 109
Crown Cl. B65: Row R 5D 96
  DY3: Sed 4H 59
Crown Court
  Birmingham 3F 5 (6G 101)
  WS10: Darl 3C 46
Crowngate Apartments B18: Birm 4E 101
Crown La. B74: Four O 6E 37
  DY8: Stourb 6A 124
  DY8: Stourb 6D 108
Crownmeadow Dr. DY4: Tip 6D 62
Crownoakes Dr. DY8: Word 1C 108
Crown Rd. B9: Bord G 1D 118
  B30: King Nor 3C 146
Crown St. B66: Smeth 6G 99
  WV1: Wolv 5H 27
Crown Wlk. DY4: Tip 5A 78
Crown Wharf Shop. Pk. WS2: Wals 1B 48
Crows Nest Cl. B76: Walm 2D 70
Crowther Gdns. B63: Crad 4E 111
Crowther Gro. WV6: Wolv 5D 26
Crowther Rd. B23: Erd 2C 84
  WV6: Wolv 5C 26
Crowther St. WV10: Wolv 5A 28
Croxall Way B66: Smeth 4F 99
Croxdene Av. WS3: Blox 6F 19
    (not continuous)
Croxley Gdns. WV13: W'hall 3H 45
Croxstalls Av. WS3: Blox 1G 31
Croxstalls Cl. WS3: Blox 6G 19
Croxstalls Pl. WS3: Blox 1G 31
Croxstalls Rd. WS3: Blox 6G 19
Croxton Gro. B33: Stech 5E 105
Croyde Av. B42: Gt Barr 6C 66
Croydon Rd. B29: W Cas 6G 131
    (off Abdon Av.)
Croydon Rd. B24: Erd 6F 85
  B29: S Oak 2B 132
Croy Dr. B35: Cas V 3F 87
Crucible, The WV14: Cose 3E 61
Crusader Cl. B69: O'bry 4E 97
Crychan Cl. B45: Fran 5H 143
Cryersoak Cl. B90: M'path 2F 165
Crystal Av. DY8: Word 2D 108
Crystal Dr. B66: Smeth 1A 98
Crystal Ho. B66: Smeth 3F 99

Crystal Leisure Cen. 6D 108
Cube East, The B1: Birm 6B 4
Cube West, The B1: Birm 6B 4
Cubley Rd. B28: Hall G 4E 135
Cuckoo Cl. B33: Stech 5D 104
Cuckoo Rd. B6: Aston 1C 102
  B7: Nech 1C 102
Cuckoo's Nook and The Dingle
  (Nature Reserve) 1B 50
Cuckoo Wharf B6: Aston 1C 102
Cuin Rd. B66: Smeth 4G 99
Cuin Wlk. B66: Smeth 4G 99
  (off Cuin Rd.)
Culey Gro. B33: Kitts G 1H 121
Culey Wlk. B37: Chel W 1F 123
Culford Dr. B32: Bart G 5A 130
Culham Cl. B27: A Grn 3B 136
Cullwick St. WV1: Wolv 4C 44
Culmington Rd. B31: Longb 1D 158
Culmore Cl. WV12: W'hall 5D 30
Culmore Rd. B62: B'hth 2E 113
Culverhouse Dr. DY5: Brie H 2E 109
Culverley Cres. B93: Know 3B 166
Culvert Way B66: Smeth 2B 98
Culwell Ind. Pk. WV10: Wolv 6A 28
Culwell St. WV10: Wolv 1D 170 (6H 27)
Culwell Trad. Est. WV10: Wolv 5B 28
Cumberford Av. B33: Kitts G 2A 122
Cumberland Av. B5: Birm 4G 117
Cumberland Cl. DY6: K'wfrd 5C 92
Cumberland Ho. WV1: Wolv 5G 27
  (off Lomas St.)
Cumberland St. B1: Birm 5A 4 (1D 116)
  B71: W Brom 1B 80
  WV13: W'hall 1D 46
  WV14: Bils 4F 45
Cumberland St. N. B1: Birm 5A 4 (2H 117)
Cumberland Wlk. B75: S Cold 6F 55
Cumbrian Ct. B63: Hale 3F 127
Cumbria Way B8: Salt 3D 102
Cunningham Rd. WS2: Wals 1E 47
  WV6: Pert 5E 25
Cupfields Av. DY4: Tip 5B 62
Cupfields Cres. DY4: Tip 6C 62
Curbar Rd. B42: Gt Barr 1E 83
Curdale Rd. B32: Bart G 5H 129
CURDWORTH 1D 88
Curlew Dr. WS8: Bwnhls 6A 10
Curlews Cl. B23: Erd 5C 68
Curral Rd. B65: Row R 6B 96
Curtin Dr. WS10: Mox 1B 62
Curtis Cl. B66: Smeth 5G 99
Curzon Circ. B4: Birm 6A 102
Curzon Gateway B4: Birm 6A 102
Curzon St. B4: Birm 3H 5 (6H 101)
  WV2: Wolv 4H 43
Cushman Av. WV5: Wom 6E 57
Custard Factory, The
  B9: Birm 6H 5 (2H 117)
Cuthbert Rd. B18: Win G 5A 100
Cutlass Ct. B1: Birm 6A 4 (2E 117)
Cutlers Rough Cl. B31: N'fld 2D 144
Cutler St. B66: Smeth 3F 99
Cutsdean Cl. B31: N'fld 1D 144
Cutshill Cl. B36: Cas B 1G 105
Cutting, The WS4: Wals 6D 32
Cuttle Pool La.
  B93: Know . . . . .5H 167 & 6A 168
Cutworth Cl. B76: Walm 2E 71
Cwerne Cl. DY3: Gorn 4G 75
Cygnet Cl. WV6: Tett 1A 42
Cygnet Ct. B66: Smeth 2C 98
  WV5: Wom 2F 73
Cygnet Dr. WS8: Bwnhls 6A 10
Cygnet Gro. B23: Erd 1A 84
Cygnet La. DY5: P'ntt 2G 93
Cygnet Rd. B70: W Brom 2G 79
Cygnus Bus. Pk. Ind. Cen.
  B70: W Brom 1F 79
Cygnus Way B70: W Brom 2F 79
Cypress Av. DY3: Up Gor 2H 75
Cypress Gdns. B74: S Cold 4G 53
  DY6: K'wfrd 5A 92
  WS5: Wals 1G 65
Cypress Gro. B31: Longb 6C 144
Cypress Rd. DY2: Dud 6H 77
  WS5: Wals 1G 65

Cypress Sq. B27: A Grn 6A 120
Cypress Way B31: Longb 1D 158
Cyprus Cl. B29: W Cas 6E 131
Cyprus St. B69: O'bry 1G 97
  (not continuous)
  WV2: Wolv 5G 43
Cyril Gro. B10: Small H 3C 118
Cyril Rd. B10: Small H 3C 118

D

Dacer Cl. B30: Stir 2D 146
Dace Rd. WV10: Wolv 5D 28
Dadford Vw. DY5: Brie H 1F 109
Dad's La. B13: Mose 4E 133
Daffodil Cl. DY3: Sed 6A 60
Daffodil Pl. WS5: Wals 3H 49
Daffodil Rd. WS5: Wals 3H 49
Daffodil Way B31: Longb 1C 158
Dagger La. B71: W Brom 3C 80
Dagnall Rd. B27: A Grn 2B 136
Dahlia Cl. WV1: Wolv 2E 45
Daimler Cl. B36: Cas B 6B 88
Daimler Rd. B14: Yard W 4D 148
Dain Ct. B29: S Oak 2B 132
Dainton Gro. B32: Bart G 4A 130
Dairy Cl. DY4: Tip 2B 78
Dairy Ct. B68: O'bry 4B 114
Dairy Way B21: Hand 6G 81
DAISY BANK 3H 49
Daisy Bank Cl. WS3: S'fld 5F 21
Daisy Bank Cres. WS5: Wals 3H 49
Daisy Dr. B23: Erd 2A 84
Daisy Farm Rd. B14: King H 5B 148
Daisy Mdw. DY4: Tip 1C 78
Daisy Rd. B16: Edg 1B 116
Daisy St. WV14: Cose 3F 61
Daisy Wlk. WV9: Pend 4E 15
Dakota Apartments B16: Birm 1D 116
  (off Grosvenor St. W.)
Dalbeg Cl. WV8: Pend 1C 26
Dalbury Rd. B28: Hall G 2E 149
Dalby Rd. WS3: Wals 3D 32
Dale Cl. B43: Gt Barr 4H 65
  B66: Smeth 6E 99
  DY4: Tip .2D 78
Dalecote Av. B92: Sol 5A 138
Dale End B4: Birm 4F 5 (6G 101)
  WS10: Darl 5D 46
  (not continuous)
Dale Mdw. Cl. CV7: Bal C 3H 169
Dale Rd. B29: S Oak 2A 132
  B62: B'hth 4E 113
  DY8: Stourb 3D 124
Dales Cl. WV6: Wolv 3F 27
Dales La. WS9: A'rdge 4G 33
Dalesman Cl. DY6: K'wfrd 2H 91
Dale St. B66: Smeth 6E 99
  WS1: Wals 4B 48
  (not continuous)
  WS10: W'bry 2E 63
  WV3: Wolv 2F 43
  WV14: Bils 6H 45
Dale Ter. B69: Tiv 1C 96
Daleview Rd. B14: Yard W 3C 148
Dale Wlk. B25: Yard 4G 119
Dalewood Cft. B26: Sheld 5D 120
Dalewood Rd. B37: K'hrst 4B 106
Daley Cl. B1: Birm 6D 100
Daley Rd. WV14: Bils 3H 61
Dalkeith Rd. B73: New O 3D 68
Dalkeith St. WS2: Wals 6A 32
Dallas Rd. B23: Erd 3C 84
Dallimore Cl. B92: Olton 2D 136
Dalloway Cl. B5: Edg 5F 117
Dalston Cl. DY2: Dud 3F 95
Dalston Rd. B27: A Grn 1A 136
Dalton Ct. WV5: Wom 6E 57
Dalton Pl. B92: Olton 3F 137
Dalton Rd. WS2: Wals 6G 31
Dalton St. B4: Birm 3F 5 (6G 101)
  WV3: Wolv 3F 43
Dalton Twr. B4: Birm 1G 5 (5H 101)
Dalton Way B4: Birm 3E 5 (6G 101)
Dalvine Rd. DY2: Neth 1D 110
Dalwood Cl. WV14: Cose 6D 60

Damar Cft. B14: King H 3F 147
Damian Cl. B67: Smeth 4D 98
Dam Mill Cl. WV8: Bilb 6A 14
Damson Cl. WV12: W'hall 3A 30
Damson La. B91: Sol 1A 152
  B92: Sol 2A 152
Damson Park 4B 138
Damson Parkway B91: Sol 2A 152
  B92: Sol 2B 138
Damson Wharf DY4: Tip 4A 78
Danbury Cl. B76: Walm 3E 71
Danbury Gdns. WV10: F'hses 5G 15
Danbury Rd. B90: Shir 5H 149
Danby Gro. B24: Erd 5H 85
Dando Rd. DY2: Dud 1F 95
Dandy Bank Rd. DY6: P'ntt 1E 93
Dandy's Wlk. WS1: Wals 2D 48
Dane Gro. B13: Mose 5F 133
Danehill Wlk. WV8: Pend 1D 26
Danesbury Cres. B44: K'sdng 5A 68
Danescourt Rd. WV6: Tett 3A 26
Danesmoor Ho. B25: Yard 4B 120
Daneswood Dr. WS9: Wals W 4B 22
Daneways Cl. B74: S'tly 3A 52
Danford Cl. DY8: Stourb 1E 125
Danford La. B91: Sol 5C 150
Danford Gdns. B10: Small H 3C 118
Danford La. B91: Sol 4C 150
Danford Rd. B47: H'wd 3H 161
Danford Way B43: Gt Barr 5H 65
Dangerfield Ho. B70: W Brom 6C 80
Dangerfield La. WS10: Darl 6C 46
Daniels La. WS9: A'rdge 5E 35
Daniels Rd. B9: Bord G 1G 119
Danks St. DY4: Tip 5A 78
Danzey Grn. Rd. B36: Cas B 6F 87
Danzey Gro. B14: King H 4E 147
Darby Cl. WV14: Cose 3C 60
DARBY END 5G 95
Darby End Rd. DY2: Neth 5G 95
Darby Rd. B68: O'bry 4A 98
  WS10: W'bry 2H 63
Darby's Hill Rd. B69: Tiv 1A 96
Darby St. B65: B'hth 2C 112
Darbys Way DY4: Tip 2B 78
Darell Cft. B76: Walm 2C 70
Daren Cl. B36: Cas B 1B 106
Dare Rd. B23: Erd 3E 85
Darfield Wlk. B12: Birm 3H 117
Darges La. WS6: Gt Wyr 1F 7
Darkhouse La. WV14: Cose 3E 61
Darkies, The B31: N'fld 4F 145
  (not continuous)
Dark La. B38: Head H 2E 161
  B47: H'wd 2E 161
  B62: Roms 3A 142
  WS6: Gt Wyr 4A 8
DARLASTON 4D 46
Darlaston Central Trad. Est.
  WS10: Darl 4E 47
DARLASTON GREEN 3D 46
Darlaston La. WV14: Bils 4A 46
Darlaston Rd. WS2: Wals 4F 47
  WS10: Darl, W'bry 6D 46
Darlaston Rd. Ind. Est.
  WS10: Darl 6D 46
Darlaston Row CV7: Mer 4H 141
Darlaston Swimming Pool 4E 47
Darley Av. B34: Hodg H 3D 104
Darleydale Av. B44: Gt Barr 4G 67
Darley Dr. WV6: Wolv 4F 27
Darley Ho. B69: O'bry 3D 96
Darley Mead Ct. B91: Sol 3A 152
Darley Way B74: S'tly 4A 52
Darlington St. WS10: Darl 6D 46
  WV1: Wolv 3A 170 (1G 43)
Darlston Cft. B10: Small H 2B 118
Darnel Hurst Rd. B75: R'ley 6A 38
Darnford Cl. B28: Hall G 2G 149
  B72: W Grn 6B 70
Darnick Rd. B73: New O 2D 68
Darnley Rd. B16: Birm 1C 116
Darris Rd. B29: S Oak 5C 132
Dartford Rd. WS3: Blox 6F 19
Dartmoor Cl. B45: Fran 5G 143

Dartmouth Av. DY8: Word 5B 92
  WS3: Wals 4C 32
  WV13: W'hall 1A 46
Dartmouth Cir. B6: Birm 4H 101
Dartmouth Cl. WS3: Wals 4C 32
Dartmouth Cres. WV14: Bils 4A 46
Dartmouth Dr. WS9: A'rdge 4B 34
Dartmouth Golf Course 1C 80
Dartmouth Ho. WS3: Wals 3D 32
  (off Ryecroft Pl.)
Dartmouth Middleway B6: Birm 4H 101
  B7: Birm 1H 5 (4H 101)
Dartmouth Pl. WS3: Wals 3D 32
Dartmouth Rd. B29: S Oak 3B 132
  B66: Smeth 1D 98
Dartmouth Sq. B70: W Brom 5B 80
Dartmouth St. B70: W Brom 4H 79
  WV2: Wolv 6D 170 (3H 43)
  (not continuous)
Dartmouth Street Stop (Metro) 4H 79
Dart St. B12: Birm 2B 118
Darvel Rd. WV12: W'hall 5D 30
Darwall St. WS1: Wals 1C 48
Darwin Ct. WV6: Pert 5E 25
Darwin Ho. B13: Mose 3B 134
  B37: Chel W 2E 123
Darwin Pl. WS2: Wals 3H 31
Darwin Rd. WS2: Wals 4H 31
Darwin St. B12: Birm 3H 117
  (not continuous)
Dassett Gro. B9: Bord G 1A 120
Dassett Rd. B93: Ben H 5B 166
Dauntsey Covert B14: King H 5F 147
Davena Dr. B29: W Cas 3C 130
Davena Gro. WV14: Cose 2F 61
Davenport Dr. B35: Cas V 4G 87
Davenport Rd. WV6: Tett 4H 25
  WV11: Wed 3G 29
Daventry Gro. B32: Quin 5B 114
Davey Rd. B20: Hand 6G 83
  B70: W Brom 2G 79
David Harman Dr. B71: W Brom 6D 64
David Lloyd Leisure
  Birmingham Club 2F 67
  Brierley Hill 5H 93
  Cranmore Club 2C 164
  Solihull South 3C 164
David Peacock Cl. DY4: Tip 2A 78
David Rd. B20: Hand 5D 82
  DY4: Tip 6A 62
Davids, The B31: N'fld 1G 145
Davies Av. WV14: Cose 2F 61
Davies Ho. B69: O'bry 2G 97
  WS3: Blox 5H 19
Davis Av. DY4: Tip 3G 77
Davis Gro. B25: Yard 5B 120
Davison Rd. B67: Smeth 6D 98
Davis Rd. WV12: W'hall 1D 30
Davy Cl. WS7: Chase 1B 10
Davy Rd. WS2: Wals 4G 31
Dawberry Cl. B14: King H 2F 147
Dawberry Flds. Rd. B14: King H 2E 147
Dawberry Rd. B14: King H 2E 147
DAW END .3G 33
Daw End WS4: Rus 3G 33
Daw End La. WS4: Rus 2F 33
Dawes Av. B70: W Brom 6A 80
Dawes La. WS8: Bwnhls 4C 10
Dawley Brook Rd. DY6: K'wfrd 2B 92
Dawley Cl. WS2: Wals 4H 47
Dawley Cres. B37: Mars G 2D 122
Dawley Rd. DY6: W Hth 1A 92
Dawley Trad. Est. DY6: K'wfrd 1B 92
Dawlish Rd. B29: S Oak 2B 132
  B66: Smeth 4F 99
  DY1: Dud 1D 76
Dawn Dr. DY4: Tip 3C 62
Dawney Dr. B75: Four O 5G 37
Dawn Rd. B31: N'fld 1C 144
Dawson Av. WV14: Cose 3C 60
Dawson Ct. B24: Erd 4F 85
Dawson Rd. B21: Hand 1A 100
Dawson Sq. WV14: Bils 6E 45
Dawson St. B66: Smeth 6E 99
  WS3: Blox 1B 32
Day Av. WV11: Wed 2G 29
Day Ho. DY4: Tip 5C 62

DAYHOUSE BANK 6B 142
Dayhouse Bank B62: Roms 6B 142
Daylesford Rd. B92: Olton 2E 137
Day St. WS2: Wals 6C 32
Deakin Av. WS8: Bwnhls 4B 10
Deakin Rd. B24: Erd 4F 85
  B75: S Cold 4C 54
Deakins Rd. B25: Yard 4H 119
Deal Dr. B69: Tiv 6A 78
Deal Gro. B31: N'fld 3E 145
Deanbrook Cl. B90: M'path 3E 165
Dean Cl. B44: K'sdng 5B 68
  B72: W'grn 6H 69
  DY8: Amb 5F 109
Dean Ct. DY5: Brie H 1H 109
  (off The Promenade)
  WV6: Pert 3E 25
Deanery Pl. WV1: Wolv 2B 170 (1G 43)
Deanery Row WV1: Wolv 1B 170 (6G 27)
Dean Ho. B5: Birm 6F 5 (2G 117)
Dean Rd. B23: Erd 2F 85
  WS4: Rus 2G 33
  WV5: Wom 2F 73
Deansbank Cen. WS1: Wals 3B 48
Deansfield Rd. WV1: Wolv 1C 44
Deans Ga. WV13: W'hall 1F 45
Deans Pl. WS3: Wals 3D 32
Dean's Rd. WV1: Wolv 6C 28
Dean St. B5: Birm 6F 5 (2G 117)
  DY3: Sed .5H 59
Dearman Rd. B11: S'brk 4B 118
Dearmont Rd. B31: Longb 2C 158
Dearne Ct. DY3: Sed 1C 76
Debden Cl. B93: Dorr 6F 167
Debenham Cres. B25: Yard 2B 120
Debenham Rd. B25: Yard 2B 120
Deblen Dr. B16: Edg 2H 115
Deborah Cl. WV2: Penn 5G 43
Dee Gro. B38: King Nor 1A 160
Deelands Rd. B45: Rub 1F 157
Deeley Cl. B15: Edg 4E 117
  B64: Crad H 4G 111
Deeley Pl. WS3: Blox 1H 31
Deeley St. DY5: Quar B 2A 110
  WS3: Blox 1H 31
Deepdale Av. B26: Sheld 1F 137
Deepdale La. DY3: Lwr G 4A 76
Deepdales WV5: Wom 1E 73
DEEPFIELDS 3D 60
Deeplow Cl. B72: S Cold 1A 70
Deepmoor Rd. B33: Yard 6D 104
Deepmore Av. WS2: Wals 6H 31
Deepwood Cl. WS4: S'fld 1F 33
Deepwood Gro. B32: Bart G 5H 129
Deerham Cl. B23: Erd 6D 68
Deerhurst Ct. B91: Sol 3H 151
Deerhurst Rd. B20: Hand 2B 82
  WS3: Blox 6C 20
Deer Pk. Gdns. B63: Crad 6D 110
Deer Pk. Way B91: Sol 6G 151
Deerstalker Sq. B16: Smeth 6G 99
Deers Way B16: Edg 6G 99
Deer Wlk. WV8: Pend 5D 14
Dee Wlk. B36: Cas B 1C 106
Defford Av. WS4: S'fld 6G 21
Defford Dr. B68: O'bry 5H 97
De Havilland Dr. B35: Cas V 5E 87
Deighton Rd. B25: Yard 1F 65
Delamere Cl. B36: Cas B 6H 87
Delamere Dr. WS5: Wals 2G 65
Delamere Rd. B28: Hall G 6F 135
  WV12: W'hall 2C 30
Delancey Keep B75: S Cold 6E 55
Delhurst Av. WV4: Ett 2A 60
Delhurst Rd. B44: Gt Barr 6G 67
Delingpole Wlk. B64: Old H 3G 111
Delius Ho. B16: Birm 1D 116
Dell, The B30: King Nor 3H 145
  B31: N'fld 1B 144
  B36: Cas B 6B 88
  B74: Four O 3G 53
  B92: Olton 4E 137
  DY8: Woll 5C 108
Della Dr. B32: Bart G 5B 130
Dell Farm Cl. B93: Know 3D 166

Dellows Cl. B38: King Nor 2H 159
Dell Rd. B30: King Nor 2C 146
  DY5: P'ntt 4F 93
Dell Stadium, The 4F 93
Delmore Way B76: Walm 1F 87
Delph Dr. DY5: Quar B 4A 110
Delphinium Cl. B9: Bord G 6F 103
Delph La. DY5: Brie H 3H 109
Delph Rd. DY5: Brie H 2G 109
Delph Rd. Ind. Est. DY5: Brie H 2G 109
Delrene Rd. B28: Hall G 4F 149
  B90: Shir 4F 149
Delta Point Ind. Pk. B70: W Brom 4F 79
DELVES, THE 6D 48
Delves Cres. WS5: Wals 6E 49
Delves Grn. Rd. WS5: Wals 5E 49
Delves Rd. WS1: Wals 4D 48
Delville Cl. WS10: W'bry 1F 63
Delville Rd. WS10: W'bry 1F 63
Delville Ter. WS10: W'bry 1F 63
De Marnham Cl. B70: W Brom 6C 80
De Montfort Ho. B37: K'hrst 4B 106
De Montfort M. B46: Col 3H 107
De Moram Gro. B92: Sol 6B 138
Demuth Way B69: O'bry 4F 97
Denaby Gro. B14: Yard W 3D 148
Denbigh Cl. DY1: Dud 5B 76
Denbigh Ct. B29: W Cas 6G 131
  (off Tugford Rd.)
Denbigh Cres. B71: W Brom 1H 79
Denbigh Dr. B71: W Brom 6G 63
  WS10: W'bry 1B 64
Denbigh Rd. DY4: Tip 2C 78
Denbigh St. B9: Bord G 1D 118
Denby Cl. B7: Birm 4B 102
Denby Cft. B90: M'path 3F 165
Dencer Cl. B45: Rub 1F 157
Dencil Cl. B63: Crad 6F 111
Dene Av. DY6: K'wfrd 5A 92
Dene Ct. Rd. B92: Olton 4D 136
Dene Cft. WS3: Blox 6G 19
Denegate Cl. B76: Walm 1F 87
Dene Hollow B13: Mose 1C 148
Dene Rd. DY8: Stourb 2D 124
  WV4: Lwr P 1F 57
Denewood Av. B20: Hand 5C 82
Denford Gro. B14: King H 2F 147
Dengate Dr. CV7: Bal C 2H 169
Denham Ct. B23: Erd 5C 84
  (off North Pk. Rd.)
Denham Gdns. WV3: Wolv 3H 41
Denham Rd. B27: A Grn 6H 119
Denholme Gro. B14: King H 4A 148
Denholm Rd. B73: New O 2D 68
Denise Dr. B17: Harb 1G 131
  B37: K'hrst 5B 106
  WV14: Cose 5D 60
Denleigh Rd. DY6: K'wfrd 5D 92
Denmark Cl. WV6: Wolv 5E 27
Denmead Dr. WV11: Wed 1H 29
Denmore Gdns. WV1: Wolv 1D 44
Dennfield Dr. WS6: C Hay 2C 6
Dennis Hall DY8: Amb 3D 108
Dennis Hall Rd. DY8: Amb 3E 109
Dennis Rd. B12: Bal H 1B 134
  (not continuous)
Dennis St. DY8: Amb 3D 108
Denshaw Rd. B14: King H 1F 147
Denstone Gdns. WV10: Bush 4B 16
Denton Cft. B93: Dorr 6H 165
Denton Gro. B33: Stech 1B 120
  B43: Gt Barr 6H 65
Denton Rd. DY9: W'cte 1C 126
Denver Rd. B14: King H 5A 148
Denville Cl. WV14: Bils 4G 45
Denville Cres. B9: Bord G 6H 103
Derby Av. WV6: Tett 2C 26
Derby Dr. B37: Chel W 1D 122
Derby St. B9: Birm 1A 118
  WS2: Wals 5B 32
Dereham Cl. B8: Salt 5D 102
Dereham Wlk. WV14: Bils 3G 61
Dereton Cl. DY1: Dud 1A 94
DERITEND 6H 5 (2H 117)
Derron Av. B26: Yard 6C 120
Derry Cl. B17: Harb 2E 131
Derrydown Cl. B23: Erd 4E 85

Derrydown Rd.—Dorsett Pl.

Derrydown Rd. B42: P Barr .2D **82**
Derry St. DY5: Brie H .1H **109**
WV2: Wolv .3H **43**
Derwent Cl. B74: S'tly .1H **51**
DY5: P'ntt .3F **93**
WV13: W'hall .1C **46**
Derwent Ct. B73: S Cold .6H **53**
Derwent Gro. B30: Stir .5E **133**
Derwent Ho. B17: Harb .6H **115**
B69: O'bry .4D **96**
Derwent Rd. B30: Stir .5E **133**
WV6: Tett .1B **26**
Desford Av. B42: Gt Barr .6E **67**
Dettonford Rd. B32: Bart G .5H **129**
Devereux Cl. B36: Cas B .1G **105**
Devereux Rd. B70: W Brom .6C **80**
B75: Four O .2A **54**
Devey Dr. DY4: Tip .1D **78**
Devey Rd. B66: Smeth .6G **99**
Deville M. WS8: Bwnhls .3A **10**
Devine Cft. DY4: Tip .2A **78**
Devitts Cl. B90: M'path .2D **164**
Devon Cl. B20: Hand .5B **82**
Devon Ct. *B29: W Cas .6F **131***
(off Holdgate Rd.)
Devon Cres. B71: W Brom .1A **80**
DY2: Dud .2B **94**
WS9: A'rdge .6C **22**
Devon Rd. B45: Fran .5E **143**
B67: Smeth .4C **114**
DY8: Woll .4C **108**
WS10: W'bry .1A **64**
WV1: Wolv .6F **27**
WV13: W'hall .1D **46**
Devonshire Av. B18: Hock .3B **100**
Devonshire Ct. B74: Four O .1G **53**
Devonshire Dr. B71: W Brom .4C **80**
Devonshire Rd. B20: Hand .5B **82**
B67: Smeth .3C **98**
Devonshire St. B18: Hock .3B **100**
Devonshire Vs. B10: Small H .3D **118**
Devon St. B7: Birm .5C **102**
Devon Way B31: Longb .1C **158**
Devoran Cl. WV6: Wolv .5F **27**
Dewberry Dr. WS5: Wals .2E **65**
Dewberry Rd. DY8: Word .2D **108**
Dewhurst Cft. B33: Kitts G .6F **105**
Dewsbury Cl. DY8: Word .6C **92**
Dewsbury Dr. WV4: Penn .2E **59**
Dewsbury Gro. B42: P Barr .2E **83**
Dexter Ho. B67: Smeth .3D **98**
Deykin Av. B6: Witt .5A **84**
Deykin Pk. Ind. Est. B6: Witt .5A **84**
Deyncourt Rd. WV10: Wolv .2C **28**
Dial Cl. B14: King H .5G **147**
Dial Glass Works .**3C 108**
Dial La. B70: W Brom .1F **79**
DY8: Amb .3C **108**
Diamond Pk. Dr. DY8: Word .2C **108**
Diana Cl. WS9: Wals W .4D **22**
Diana Way B45: Fran .5F **143**
Diane Cl. DY4: Tip .3B **62**
Dibble Cl. WV12: W'hall .4D **30**
Dibble Rd. B67: Smeth .3D **98**
Dibdale Ct. *DY3: Lwr G .4H **75***
(off Yorkdale Cl.)
Dibdale Rd. DY1: Dud .4B **76**
Dibdale Rd. W. DY1: Dud .4A **76**
Dibdale St. DY1: Dud .5B **76**
Dice Pleck B31: N'fld .5G **145**
Dickens Cl. DY3: Lwr G .2F **75**
DICKENS HEATH .**4G 163**
Dickens Heath Rd.
B90: Dic H, Tid G .5E **163**
Dickens Rd. WV10: Bush .1C **28**
WV14: Cose .3F **61**
Dickinson Av. WV10: Bush .1A **28**
Dickinson Dr. B76: Walm .1C **70**
WS2: Wals .5A **48**
Dickinson Rd. WV5: Wom .3G **73**
Dick Sheppard Av. DY4: Tip .5B **62**
Diddington Av. B28: Hall G .2G **149**
Diddington La.
B92: Bick, H Ard .5C **140**
CV7: Mer .5C **140**
Didgley Gro. B37: K'hrst .4C **106**
DIGBETH .**6G 5 (2H 117)**
Digbeth B5: Birm .5F **5 (1G 117)**
WS1: Wals .2C **48**
Digby Ct. B27: A Grn .2A **136**
Digby Cres. B46: Wat O .4D **88**
Digby Dr. B37: Mars G .5D **122**
Digby Ho. B37: K'hrst .5B **106**
Digby Rd. B46: Col .3H **107**
B73: S Cold .2G **69**
DY6: K'wfrd .1B **92**
Digby Wlk. B33: Sheld .3G **121**
Dilke Rd. WS9: A'rdge .4B **34**
Dilliars Wlk. B70: W Brom .2G **79**
Dillington Ho. B37: Chel W .1D **122**
Dilloway's La. WV13: W'hall .2G **45**
Dimmingsdale Bank B32: Quin .1A **130**
Dimmingsdale Rd.
WV4: Lwr P .6E **41**
Dimminsdale WV13: W'hall .2A **46**
Dimmocks Av. WV14: Cose .5F **61**
Dimmock St. WV4: Ett .6A **44**
Dimsdale Gro. B31: N'fld .4C **144**
Dimsdale Rd. B31: N'fld .4B **144**
Dingle, The B29: S Oak .3A **132**
B69: O'bry .1D **96**
B90: Ches G .4B **164**
WV3: Wolv .2B **42**
Dingle Av. B64: Crad H .3G **111**
Dingle Cl. B30: B'vlle .6H **131**
DY2: Dud .2G **95**
Dingle Ct. *B69: O'bry .1E **97***
(off Dingle St.)
B91: Sol .6D **150**
Dingle Hollow B69: O'bry .1D **96**
Dingle La. B91: Sol .5D **150**
WV13: W'hall .5A **30**
Dingle Mdw. Ct. B69: O'bry .1E **97**
Dingle Rd. DY2: Dud .2G **95**
DY6: K'wfrd .5E **93**
DY9: Pedm .3F **125**
WS8: Clay .1A **22**
WV5: Wom .1F **73**
Dingle St. B69: O'bry .1D **96**
Dingle Vw. DY3: Sed .6G **59**
Dingley Bells B70: W Brom .5A **80**
Dingley Rd. WS10: W'bry .6G **47**
Dinham Gdns. DY1: Dud .4A **76**
Dinmore Av. B31: N'fld .3F **145**
Dinsdale Wlk. WV6: Wolv .4E **27**
Dippons Dr. WV6: Tett .6G **25**
Dippons La. WV6: Pert .3E **25**
(not continuous)
WV6: Tett .3F **25**
Dippons Mill Cl. WV6: Tett .6G **25**
Direct 2 Industrial Est. B69: O'bry .6E **79**
Dirtyfoot La. WV4: Lwr P .6G **41**
Discovery Cl. DY4: Tip .2C **78**
Ditch, The WS1: Wals .2D **48**
Ditton Gro. B31: Longb .3D **158**
Dixon Cl. B35: Cas V .5E **87**
DY4: Tip .1C **78**
Dixon Ct. B10: Small H .3B **118**
Dixon Ho. B16: Edg .2C **116**
Dixon Rd. B10: Small H .3B **118**
DIXON'S GREEN .**1G 95**
Dixon's Grn. Ct. *DY2: Dud .1G **95***
(off Dixon's Grn. Rd.)
Dixon's Grn. Rd. DY2: Dud .1F **95**
Dixon St. WV2: Ett .5A **44**
Doal Trad. Est. B66: Smeth .3F **99**
Dobbins Oak Rd. DY9: W'cte .4H **125**
Dobbs Mill Cl. B29: S Oak .3D **132**
Dobbs St. WV2: Wolv .6B **170** (3G **43**)
Dock, The DY9: Lye .6B **110**
Dockar Rd. B31: N'fld .5C **144**
Dockers Cl. CV7: Bal C .5H **169**
Dock La. DY1: Dud .6D **76**
Dock La. Ind. Est. *DY1: Dud .6D **76***
(off Turner St.)
Dock Mdw. Dr. WV4: Ett .1C **60**
Dock Rd. DY8: Word .1D **108**
Doctors Hill DY9: Pedm .2G **125**
Doctors La. DY6: K'wfrd .4F **91**
Doctor's Piece WV13: W'hall .1B **46**
Doddington Gro. B32: Bart G .5H **129**
Dodford Cl. B45: Rub .2F **157**
DOE BANK .**3H 53**
Doe Bank Ct. B74: Four O .3H **53**
Doe Bank La. B43: A'rdge, Gt Barr .5E **51**
WS9: A'rdge .5E **51**
Doe Bank Rd. DY4: Tip .4C **62**
Dogge La. Cft. B27: A Grn .3H **135**
Dog Kennel La. B68: O'bry .4A **98**
B90: Shir .2A **164**
WS1: Wals .1D **48**
Dogkennel La. B63: Hale .2B **128**
Dogpool La. B30: Stir .4D **132**
Doidge Rd. B23: Erd .4D **84**
Dollery Dr. B5: Edg .6E **117**
Dollis Gro. B44: Gt Barr .2H **67**
Dollman St. B7: Birm .6B **102**
Dolman Rd. B6: Aston .1G **101**
Dolobran Rd. B11: S'brk .4B **118**
Dolphin Cl. WS3: Blox .6D **20**
Dolphin Ct. *WV12: W'hall .2D **30***
(off Huntington Rd.)
Dolphin Ho. WS3: Blox .1D **32**
Dolphin La. B27: A Grn .4H **135**
(not continuous)
Dolphin Rd. B11: S'hll .6D **118**
Dolton Way DY4: Tip .1G **77**
Dominic Dr. B30: King Nor .3H **145**
Doncaster Way B36: Hodg H .1A **104**
Don Cl. B15: Edg .3H **115**
Donegal Rd. B74: S'tly .6H **51**
Donibristle Cft. B35: Cas V .3E **87**
Donnington Ct. DY1: Dud .5B **76**
Donovan Dr. B73: S Cold .5G **53**
Dooley Cl. WV13: W'hall .1G **45**
Dora Herbert Ct. B12: Bal H .6G **117**
Doran Cl. B63: Hale .4F **127**
Doranda Way B71: W Brom .6D **80**
Doranda Way Ind. Pk.
B71: W Brom .6D **80**
Dora Rd. B10: Small H .3E **119**
B21: Hand .2A **100**
B70: W Brom .6A **80**
Dora St. WS2: Wals .4H **47**
Dorchester Cl. WV12: W'hall .1C **30**
Dorchester Ct. B91: Sol .3E **151**
Dorchester Dr. B17: Harb .1F **131**
Dorchester Rd. B91: Sol .3E **151**
DY9: W'cte .3H **125**
WV12: W'hall .1C **30**
Dordale Cl. B31: Longb .6A **144**
Dordon Cl. B90: Shir .6E **149**
Doreen Gro. B24: Erd .5G **85**
Doris Rd. B9: Bord G .1D **118**
B11: S'hll .1B **134**
B46: Col .1H **107**
Dorking Ct. *B29: W Cas .6G **131***
(off Abdon Av.)
Dorlcote Rd. B8: Salt .5G **103**
Dormie Cl. B38: King Nor .6H **145**
Dormington Rd. B44: Gt Barr .2G **67**
Dormston Cl. B91: Sol .2G **165**
Dormston Dr. B29: W Cas .3D **130**
DY3: Sed .5A **60**
Dormston Sports & Art Cen. .**5A 60**
Dormston Trad. Est. DY1: Dud .3B **76**
Dormy Dr. B31: Longb .2E **159**
Dorncliffe Av. B33: Sheld .4H **121**
Dornie Dr. B38: King Nor .6B **146**
Dornton Rd. B30: Stir .5E **133**
Dorothy Adams Cl. B64: Old H .3G **111**
Dorothy Gdns. B20: Hand .5C **82**
Dorothy Rd. B11: Tys .6H **119**
B67: Smeth .6E **99**
Dorothys Ga. B91: Sol .5G **151**
Dorothy St. WS1: Wals .4B **48**
DORRIDGE .**6B 166**
Dorridge Cft. B93: Dorr .6G **167**
Dorridge Rd. B93: Dorr .6H **167**
Dorridge Station (Rail) .**6G 167**
Dorrington Grn. B42: P Barr .2C **82**
Dorrington Rd. B42: P Barr .1C **82**
Dorset Cl. B45: Fran .5F **143**
Dorset Cotts. B30: Stir .1C **146**
Dorset Ct. *B29: W Cas .6F **131***
(off Abdon Av.)
Dorset Dr. WS9: A'rdge .6C **22**
Dorset Rd. B8: Salt .3D **102**
B17: Edg .6F **99**
DY8: Woll .4B **108**
Dorsett Pl. WS3: Blox .2A **32**

Dorsett Rd. WS10: Darl 5C 46
WS10: W'bry 3B 64
Dorsett Rd. Ter. WS10: Darl 5C 46
Dorsheath Gdns. B23: Erd 3F 85
Dorsington Rd. B27: A Grn 4B 136
Dorstone Covert B14: King H 5E 147
Dorville Cl. B38: King Nor 1H 159
Douay Rd. B24: Erd 1H 85
Double Row DY2: Neth 5G 95
Doug Ellis Sports Centre, The 4G 83
Doug Ellis Woodcock Sports Cen.
. . . . .1H 5 (5H 101)
Doughty Cl. DY4: Tip 2C 78
Douglas Av. B36: Hodg H 3B 104
B68: O'bry 4B 98
Douglas Davies Cl. WV12: W'hall 5C 30
Douglas Pl. WV10: Oxl 3G 27
Douglas Rd. B21: Hand 1A 100
B27: A Grn 1H 135
B47: H'wd 2A 162
B62: B'hth 2E 113
B68: O'bry 5B 98
B72: S Cold 2A 70
DY2: Dud 1F 95
WV14: Cose 5F 61
Douglas Turner Way WV3: Wolv 6C 26
Doulton Cl. B32: Quin 2D 130
Doulton Dr. B66: Smeth 3E 99
Doulton Rd. B64: Old H 6H 95
B65: Row R 6H 95
Doulton Trad. Est. B65: Row R 5H 95
Dovebridge Cl. B76: Walm 1D 70
Dove Cl. B25: Yard 3C 120
WS1: Wals 2E 49
WS10: W'bry 1G 63
Dovecote Cl. B91: Sol 5F 137
DY4: Tip 2C 78
WV6: Tett 5A 26
Dovecotes, The B75: Four O 6H 37
Dovedale Av. B90: Shir 6H 149
WS3: Pels 2F 21
WV12: W'hall 4A 30
Dovedale Cl. B29: W Cas 1G 145
B46: Wat O 4C 88
WV4: Ett 3B 60
Dovedale Dr. B28: Hall G 1F 149
Dovedale Rd. B23: Erd 6C 68
B44: K'sdng 5B 68
DY6: K'wfrd 1C 92
WV4: Ett 2A 60
WV14: Cose 2A 60
Dove Dr. DY8: Amb 3E 109
Dove Gdns. B38: King Nor 5D 146
Dove Hollow WS6: Gt Wyr 4F 7
Dove Ho. Ct. B91: Sol 6D 136
Dovehouse La. B91: Sol 6D 136
Dovehouse Pool Rd. B6: Aston 1G 101
Dover Cl. B32: Bart G 6G 129
Dover Ct. B29: W Cas 6G 131
(off Abdon Av.)
Dovercourt Rd. B26: Sheld 6G 121
Doverdale Cl. B63: Crad 6F 111
Dover Ho. WS3: Blox 2A 32
(off Providence Cl.)
Dove Ridge DY8: Amb 4E 109
Doveridge Cl. B91: Sol 6C 136
Doveridge Pl. WS1: Wals 3D 48
Doveridge Rd. B28: Hall G 2E 149
Doversley Rd. B14: King H 2E 147
Dover St. B18: Hock 3C 100
WV14: Bils 5F 45
Doveton Ho. DY8: Stourb 2E 125
Dove Way B36: Cas B 1B 106
Dovey Dr. B76: Walm 6E 71
Dovey Gro. B65: Row R 1B 112
Dovey Rd. B13: Mose 3D 134
B69: Tiv 1D 96
Dovey Twr. B7: Birm 5A 102
Dowar Rd. B45: Redn 2A 158
Dowells Cl. B13: Mose 3H 133
Dowells Gdns. DY8: Word 6B 92
Doweries, The B45: Rub 1F 157
Dower Rd. B75: Four O 2H 53
Dowles Cl. B29: W Cas 1F 145
Downcroft Av. B38: King Nor 5A 146
Downend Cl. WV10: Bush 3B 16
Downes Ct. DY4: Tip 2G 77

Downey Cl. B11: S'brk 4B 118
Downfield Cl. WS3: Blox 3G 19
Downfield Dr. DY3: Sed 1A 76
Downham Cl. WS5: Wals 2A 50
Downham Pl. WV3: Wolv 3D 42
Downham Wood WS5: Wals 3A 50
Downie Rd. WV8: Bilb 4A 14
Downing Cl. B65: B'hth 2C 112
B93: Know 5C 166
WV11: Wed 2A 30
Downing Cres. B70: W Brom 5A 80
Downing Ho. B37: Chel W 2D 122
Downing St. B63: Hale 6A 112
B66: Smeth 2F 99
Downing St. Ind. Est.
B66: Smeth 2G 99
Downland Cl. B38: King Nor 6B 146
Downside Rd. B24: Erd 6E 85
Downs Rd. WV13: W'hall 3C 46
Downton Cres. B33: Kitts G 6A 106
Dowry Ho. B45: Rub 1F 157
(off Rubery La. Sth.)
Dowty Way WV9: Pend 4E 15
Drainage Board Cotts. B24: Erd 6F 85
(off Saltley Cotts.)
Drake Cl. WS3: Blox 6H 19
Drake Cft. B37: Chel W 5F 107
Drake Rd. B23: Erd 4C 84
B66: Smeth 2C 98
WS3: Blox 6H 19
Drakes Cl. B47: H'wd, Wyt 4H 161
Drakes Ct. B23: Erd 6D 84
DRAKES CROSS 4A 162
Drakes Cross Pde. B47: H'wd 4A 162
Drakes Grn. WV14: Bils 2H 61
Drakes Hill Cl. DY8: Stourb 1A 124
Drake St. B71: W Brom 2A 80
Drancy Av. WV12: W'hall 3D 30
(not continuous)
Drawbridge Rd. B90: Maj G 1E 163
Draycote Cl. B92: Sol 6H 137
Draycott Av. B23: Erd 3D 84
Draycott Cl. WV4: Penn 6A 42
Draycott Dr. B31: N'fld 6C 130
Draycott Rd. B66: Smeth 2C 98
Drayman Cl. WS1: Wals 3D 48
Drayton Cl. B75: Four O 6H 37
Drayton Rd. B14: King H 5G 133
B66: Smeth 2E 115
B90: Shir 1C 164
Drayton St. WS2: Wals 1H 47
WV2: Wolv 6B 170 (3G 43)
Drayton St. E. WS2: Wals 1A 48
Dreadnought Rd. DY5: P'ntt 2F 93
Dreamwell Ind. Est. B11: Tys 5G 119
Dreel, The B15: Edg 4A 116
Dreghorn Rd. B36: Hodg H 1C 104
Drem Cft. B35: Cas V 5E 87
Dresden Cl. WV4: Ett 1C 60
Drew Cres. DY9: W'cte 3H 125
Drew Rd. DY9: W'cte 2H 125
Drew's Holloway B63: Crad 6F 111
Drew's Holloway Sth. B63: Crad 6F 111
Drews Ho. B14: King H 6F 147
(off Netheravon Cl.)
Drews La. B8: W End 3G 103
Drews Mdw. Cl. B14: King H 5E 147
DRIFFOLD 1H 69
Driffold B73: S Cold 1H 69
Driffold Vs. B73: S Cold 2H 69
Driftwood Cl. B38: King Nor 2H 159
Drive, The B20: Hand 5C 82
B23: Erd 5E 85
B48: Hopw 6F 159
B63: Crad 6F 111
B63: Hale 2A 128
DY5: Brie H 4G 93
WS3: Blox 5C 20
WS4: S'fld 6G 21
WS10: Darl 4E 47
WV6: Tett 4A 26
WV8: Cod 4F 13
Drive Flds. WV4: Lwr P 5H 41
Droicon Trad. Est. B65: Row R 4C 96

Droveway, The WV8: Pend 5C 14
WV9: Pend 5C 14
Droxford Wlk. WV8: Pend 6C 14
Druid Pk. Rd. WV12: W'hall 6C 18
Druids Av. B65: Row R 5D 96
WS9: A'rdge 6E 23
DRUID'S HEATH 6D 22
Druids Heath Golf Course 1E 35
Druids La. B14: King H 5E 147
Druids Wlk. WS9: Wals W 4C 22
Drumlin Wlk. B31: Longb 5A 144
Drummond Cl. WV11: Wed 5A 18
Drummond Gro. B43: Gt Barr 2E 67
Drummond Rd. B9: Bord G 1F 119
DY9: W'cte 6B 110
Drummond St. WV1: Wolv . .1A 170 (6G 27)
Drummond Way B37: Chel W 1E 123
Drury La. B91: Sol 4G 151
(not continuous)
DY8: Stourb 6E 109
DY8: Stourb 3F 13
Drybrook Cl. B38: King Nor 1A 160
Drybrooks Cl. CV7: Bal C 3H 169
Dryden Cl. DY4: Tip 6A 62
WV12: W'hall 1E 31
Dryden Gro. B27: A Grn 3H 135
Dryden Rd. WS3: Blox 2C 32
WV10: Bush 6B 16
Drylea Gro. B36: Hodg H 2D 104
Dubarry Av. DY6: K'wfrd 2A 92
Duchess Pde. B70: W Brom 4B 80
Duchess Pl. B16: Edg 2C 116
Duchess Rd. B16: Edg 2C 116
WS1: Wals 6B 48
Duckery Wood Wlk. B43: Gt Barr 2D 66
Duckhouse Rd. WV11: Wed 2F 29
Duck La. WV8: Bilb 5H 13
Duddeston Dr. B8: Salt 5D 102
Duddeston Mnr. Rd. B7: Birm 5A 102
Duddeston Mill Rd. B7: Birm 5B 102
B8: Birm, Salt 5B 102
Duddeston Mill Trad. Est.
B8: Salt 5C 102
Duddeston Station (Rail) 5B 102
Dudding Rd. WV4: Penn 6H 43
Dudhill Rd. B65: Row R 6A 96
Dudhill Wlk. B65: Row R 6H 95
DUDLEY 6E 77
Dudley Canal Trips 3F 77
Dudley Castle 5F 77
Dudley Central Trad. Est.
DY2: Dud 1E 95
Dudley Cl. B65: Row R 3A 96
Dudley Concert Hall 6E 77
Dudley Cres. WV11: Wed 3G 29
DUDLEY FIELDS 5G 93
Dudley Golf Course 3B 96
Dudley Gro. B18: Win G 5A 100
Dudley Innovation Cen.
DY6: P'ntt 2D 92
Dudley Leisure Cen. 6D 76
Dudley Museum & Art Gallery 6E 77
Dudley Pk. Rd. B27: A Grn 2A 136
DUDLEY PORT 3B 78
Dudley Port DY4: Tip 4A 78
Dudley Port Station (Rail) 3B 78
Dudley Priory 5E 77
Dudley Rd. B18: Win G 5H 99
B63: Hale 5B 112
B65: Row R 3H 95
B69: O'bry 6E 79
DY3: Himl 4A 74
DY3: Sed 6A 60
DY4: Tip 2F 77
DY5: Brie H 6H 93
DY6: K'wfrd 2D 92
DY6: W Hth 1A 92
DY9: Lye 5A 110
WV2: Wolv 6C 170 (3H 43)
Dudley Rd. E. B69: O'bry, Tiv 5C 78
Dudley Rd. W. B69: Tiv 5A 78
DY4: Tip 5A 78
Dudley Row DY2: Dud 6F 77
DUDLEY'S FIELDS 1G 31
Dudley St. B5: Birm 5E 5 (1G 117)
B70: W Brom 2F 79
DY3: Sed 5H 59

Dudley St. WS1: Wals 2C **48**
   WS10: W'bry 3E **63**
   WV1: Wolv 3B **170** (1G **43**)
   WV14: Bils 2C **44**
      (Carder Cres.)
   WV14: Bils 6F **45**
      (Pinfold St.)
Dudley Wlk. WV4: Penn 6G **43**
Dudley Wood Av. DY2: Neth 1E **111**
Dudley Wood Rd. DY2: Neth 2E **111**
Dudley Zoo .5F **77**
Dudmaston Way DY1: Dud 4A **76**
Dudnill Gro. B32: Bart G 5G **129**
Duffield Cl. WV8: Pend 6D **14**
Dufton Rd. B32: Quin 6C **114**
Dugdale Cres. B75: Four O 6A **38**
Dugdale Ho. B71: W Brom 5E **65**
Dugdale St. B18: Win G 5H **99**
Dukes Rd. B30: King Nor 3C **146**
Duke St. B65: Row R 1B **112**
   B70: W Brom 3H **79**
   B72: S Cold 1H **69**
   DY3: Up Gor 2H **75**
   DY8: Stourb 5E **109**
   WV1: Wolv 2A **44**
   WV3: Wolv 4E **43**
   WV11: Wed 4F **29**
Dulvern Gro. B14: King H 2F **147**
Dulverton Rd. B6: Witt 6A **84**
Dulwich Gro. B44: K'sdng 5B **68**
Dulwich Rd. B44: K'sdng 5A **68**
Dumbleberry Av. DY3: Sed 6G **59**
Dumbledery La. WS9: A'rdge 1A **34**
Dunard Rd. B90: Shir 4F **149**
Dunbar Cl. B32: Bart G 4B **130**
Dunbar Gro. B43: Gt Barr 1D **66**
Duncalfe Dr. B75: Four O 6H **37**
Duncan Edwards Cl. DY1: Dud 1C **94**
Duncan Edwards Way DY2: Dud 2C **94**
Duncan Ho. B73: W Grn 4H **69**
Duncan St. WV2: Wolv 4G **43**
Dunchurch Cl. CV7: Bal C 2H **169**
Dunchurch Cres. B73: New O 2C **68**
Dunchurch Dr. B31: N'fld 6C **130**
Dunchurch Ho. B5: Birm 3G **117**
Duncombe Grn. B46: Col 2H **107**
Duncombe Gro. B17: Harb 4D **114**
Duncombe St. DY8: Woll 5B **108**
Duncroft Rd. B26: Yard 3D **120**
Duncroft Wlk. DY1: Dud 1D **76**
Duncumb Rd. B75: S Cold 6E **55**
Dundalk La. WS6: C Hay 3D **6**
Dundas Av. DY2: Dud 1H **95**
Dunedin Ho. B32: Quin 1D **130**
Dunedin Rd. B44: Gt Barr 2G **67**
Dunham Cft. B93: Dorr 6H **165**
Dunkirk Av. B70: W Brom 3D **78**
Dunkley St. WV1: Wolv 1A **170** (6G **27**)
Dunley Ct. B23: Erd 5C **84**
      (off Dunlin Cl.)
Dunley Cft. B90: M'path 3D **164**
Dunlin Cl. B23: Erd 5C **84**
   DY6: K'wfrd 3E **93**
Dunlin Dr. WV10: F'stne 1C **16**
Dunlop Way B35: Cas V 6C **86**
Dunnerdale Rd. WS8: Clay 1H **21**
Dunnigan Rd. B32: Bart G 2D **130**
DUNN'S BANK 4B **110**
Dunns Bank DY5: Quar B 4B **110**
      (Montgomery Cres.)
   DY5: Quar B 4C **110**
      (Saltbrook Rd.)
Dunoon Dr. WV4: Ett 6B **44**
Dunsfold Cl. WV14: Cose 2C **60**
Dunsford Cl. DY5: Brie H 4F **109**
Dunsford Rd. B66: Smeth 1E **115**
Dunsink Rd. B6: Aston 6H **83**
Dunslade Cres. DY5: Quar B 3B **110**
Dunslade Rd. B23: Erd 6E **69**
Dunsley Dr. DY8: Word 6C **92**
Dunsley Gro. WV4: Penn 1E **59**
Dunsley Rd. DY8: Woll 1A **124**
Dunsmore Dr. DY5: Quar B 3B **110**
Dunsmore Gro. B91: Sol 6D **136**
Dunsmore Rd. B28: Hall G 3E **135**
Dunstall Av. WV6: Wolv 4G **27**

Dunstall Gro. B29: W Cas 5D **130**
DUNSTALL HILL 5F **27**
Dunstall Hill WV6: Wolv 4G **27**
Dunstall Hill Trad. Est. WV6: Wolv . . .4G **27**
Dunstall La. WV6: Wolv 4E **27**
Dunstall Park 3E **27**
Dunstall Rd. B63: Hale 2F **127**
   WV6: Wolv 5F **27**
Dunstan Cft. B90: Shir 1A **164**
Dunster Cl. B30: King Nor 3D **146**
Dunster Gro. WV6: Pert 6F **25**
Dunster Rd. B37: Chel W 6E **107**
Dunston Cl. DY6: K'wfrd 2B **92**
   WS6: Gt Wyr 5E **7**
Dunton Cl. B75: Four O 5G **37**
Dunton Hall Rd. B90: Shir 1G **163**
Dunton Rd. B37: K'hrst 5B **106**
Dunton Trad. Est. B7: Nech 2D **102**
Dunvegan Rd. B24: Erd 3G **85**
Durant Cl. B45: Fran 5D **142**
Durban Rd. B66: Smeth 5G **99**
D'Urberville Cl. WV2: Ett 5B **44**
      (off D'Urberville Rd.)
D'Urberville Rd. WV2: Ett 4B **44**
      (not continuous)
D'Urberville Rd. Ind. Est.
   WV2: Ett 4B **44**
Durham Av. WV13: W'hall 6C **30**
Durham Cl. B14: King H 5F **147**
Durham Ct. B29: W Cas 6G **131**
      (off Abdon Av.)
Durham Cft. B37: Chel W 1D **122**
Durham Dr. B71: W Brom 6B **64**
Durham Ho. WV1: Wolv 5G **27**
      (off Lomas St.)
Durham Pl. WS2: Wals 2H **47**
Durham Rd. B11: S'hll 1B **134**
   B65: Row R 5E **97**
   DY2: Neth 1F **111**
   DY8: Woll 3B **108**
   WS2: Wals 3H **47**
   WS10: W'bry 1B **64**
Durham Twr. B1: Birm 6D **100**
Durley Dean Rd. B29: S Oak 3G **131**
Durley Dr. B73: New O 2C **68**
Durley Rd. B25: Yard 5A **120**
Durlston Gro. B28: Hall G 5G **135**
Durnford Cft. B14: King H 6G **147**
Dursley Cl. B92: Olton 5F **137**
   WV12: W'hall 5D **30**
Dutton's La. B75: R'ley 5C **38**
Duxford Rd. B42: Gt Barr 5D **66**
Dwellings La. B32: Quin 6H **113**
Dyas Av. B42: Gt Barr 6B **66**
Dyas Rd. B44: Gt Barr 4G **67**
   B47: H'wd 2A **162**
Dyce Cl. B35: Cas V 3E **87**
Dymoke St. B12: Birm 3H **117**
Dynes Wlk. B67: Smeth 4E **99**
Dyott Rd. B13: Mose 4A **134**
Dyson Cl. WS2: Wals 6F **31**
Dyson Gdns. B8: Salt 4E **103**

E

Eachelhurst Rd. B24: Erd 3C **86**
   B76: Walm 3C **86**
Eachus Rd. WV14: Cose 5F **61**
EACHWAY 3F **157**
Eachway B45: Rub 3F **157**
Eachway Farm Cl. B45: Redn 3G **157**
Eachway La. B45: Redn 3G **157**
Eadgar Ct. B43: Gt Barr 6H **65**
Eagle Cl. Bus. Pk. B26: Sheld 1A **138**
Eagle Cft. B14: King H 5G **147**
Eagle Gdns. B24: Erd 5G **85**
Eagle Gro. B36: Cas B 1C **106**
Eagle Ind. Est. DY4: Tip 6E **63**
Eagle La. DY4: Tip 1D **78**
Eagle St. DY4: Tip 1C **78**
   WV2: Wolv 3A **44**
   WV3: Wolv 4E **43**

Eagle Trad. Est. B63: Hale 1A **128**
Eagleworks Dr. WS3: Blox 3B **32**
Ealing Gro. B44: K'sdng 4A **68**
Eanwulf Ct. B15: Edg 3E **117**
Earlsbury Gdns. B20: Hand 6F **83**
Earls Ct. Rd. B17: Harb 5E **115**
Earls Ferry Gdns.
   B32: Bart G 6H **129**
Earlsmead Rd. B21: Hand 1G **99**
Earls Rd. WS4: Rus 2G **33**
Earlston Way B43: Gt Barr 5H **65**
Earl St. B70: W Brom 3H **79**
   DY6: K'wfrd 5B **92**
   WS1: Wals 4B **48**
   WV14: Bils 6F **45**
   WV14: Cose 5F **61**
Earls Way B63: Hale 1B **128**
Earlswood Ct. B20: Hand 5C **82**
Earlswood Cres. WV9: Pend 4E **15**
Earlswood Dr. B74: S Cold 4A **54**
Earlswood Ho. B5: Birm 4G **117**
      (off Barrow Wlk.)
Earlswood Rd. B30: King Nor 4F **147**
   B93: Dorr 6F **167**
   DY6: K'wfrd 1C **92**
Easby Way B8: Salt 4E **103**
   WS3: Blox 5F **19**
Easenhall Cl. B93: Know 5C **166**
Easmore Cl. B14: King H 5F **147**
Eastacre WV13: W'hall 2A **46**
East Av. B69: Tiv 2C **96**
   WV3: Wed 3E **29**
Eastbourne Av. B34: Hodg H 3B **104**
Eastbourne St. WS4: Wals 6D **32**
Eastbrook Cl. B76: Walm 1B **70**
Eastbury Dri B92: Olton 2E **137**
Eastbury Dr. B92: Olton 2E **137**
East Car Pk. Rd.
   B40: Nat E C 1H **139**
EASTCOTE .4H **153**
Eastcote Cl. B90: Shir 4B **150**
Eastcote La. B92: H Ard 4H **153**
Eastcote Rd. B27: A Grn 4G **135**
   WV10: Wolv 4B **28**
Eastcroft Rd. WV4: Penn 1A **58**
Eastdean Cl. B23: Erd 1D **84**
East Dr. B5: Edg 1E **133**
Eastern Av. DY5: Brie H 1F **109**
Eastern Cl. WS10: Mox 2C **62**
Eastern Rd. B29: S Oak 2D **132**
   B73: W Grn 4H **69**
Easterton Cft. B14: King H 5G **147**
E. Farm Cft. B10: Small H 3D **118**
Eastfield Cl. WS9: A'rdge 3C **34**
Eastfield Dr. B92: Sol 5A **138**
Eastfield Gro. WV1: Wolv 1B **44**
Eastfield Retreat WV1: Wolv 1B **44**
Eastfield Rd. B8: W End 5A **104**
   B9: Bord G 5A **104**
   DY4: Tip 5A **62**
   WV1: Wolv 1B **44**
East Ga. B16: Edg 6A **100**
East Grn. WV4: Penn 5B **42**
Eastham Rd. B13: Mose 1C **148**
East Holme B9: Bord G 1C **118**
Eastlake Cl. B43: Gt Barr 2F **67**
Eastlands Rd. B13: Mose 4A **134**
Eastleigh DY3: Sed 5G **59**
Eastleigh Cft. B76: Walm 6E **71**
Eastleigh Dr. B62: Roms 3A **142**
Eastleigh Gro. B25: Yard 3B **120**
East Meadway B33: Kitts G 1H **121**
East M. B44: Gt Barr 3F **67**
Eastmoor Cl. B74: S'tly 1B **52**
Eastney Cres. WV8: Pend 1C **26**
Easton Gdns. WV11: Wed 4H **29**
Easton Gro. B27: A Grn 4A **136**
   B47: H'wd 2B **162**
East Pk. Trad. Est. WV1: Wolv 3B **44**
East Pk. Way WV1: Wolv 2D **44**
East Pathway B17: Harb 5G **115**
East Ri. B75: S Cold 5B **54**
East Rd. B24: Erd 5B **86**
   B35: Cas V 5B **86**
   DY4: Tip 5B **62**
   WV10: B'frd, F'stne 1C **16**

East St.—Ellerton Wlk.

East St. DY2: Dud 1G **95**
DY3: Gorn 4H **75**
DY5: Quar B 3C **110**
WS1: Wals 4D **48**
WV1: Wolv 2A **44**
East Vw. Rd. B72: S Cold 2B **70**
Eastville B31: N'fld 4F **145**
Eastward Glen WV8: Bilb 6A **14**
East Way B17: Harb 5G **115**
Eastway B40: Nat E C 2H **139**
B92: Bick 2H **139**
Eastwood Rd. B12: Bal H 6F **117**
B43: Gt Barr 5A **66**
DY2: Dud 3G **95**
Easyspace Bus. Cen. B21: Hand 6F **81**
Eatesbrook Rd. B33: Kitts G 6G **105**
Eathorpe Cl. B34: S End 3H **105**
Eaton Av. B70: W Brom 3G **79**
Eaton Ct. B74: S Cold 4H **53**
Eaton Cres. DY3: Gorn 4F **75**
Eaton Pl. DY6: K'wfrd 4C **92**
Eaton Ri. WV12: W'hall 3B **30**
Eaton Wood B24: Erd 4B **86**
Eaton Wood Dr. B26: Yard 6B **120**
Eaves Ct. Dr. DY3: Sed 4G **59**
Eaves Grn. Gdns. B27: A Grn 6H **119**
Ebenezer St. B70: W Brom 1F **79**
WV14: Cose 5D **60**
Ebley Rd. B20: Hand 3C **82**
Ebmore Dr. B14: King H 5F **147**
Eborne Cft. CV7: Bal C 1H **169**
Ebrington Av. B92: Sol 2F **137**
Ebrington Cl. B14: King H 3F **147**
Ebrington Rd. B71: W Brom 1B **80**
Ebrook Rd. B72: S Cold 1A **70**
EBSTREE **1C 56**
Ebstree Mdw. WV5: Seis 3A **56**
Ebstree Rd. WV4: Try 3A **56**
WV5: Seis, Try 3A **56**
Ebury Rd. B30: King Nor 3D **146**
Eccleshall Av. WV10: Oxl 1F **27**
Eccleston Cl. B75: S Cold 6D **54**
Ecclestone Rd. WV11: Wed 2A **30**
Echo Way WV4: Ett 1C **60**
Eckersall Rd. B38: King Nor 4A **146**
Eckington Wlk. B38: King Nor 2A **160**
Eclipse Trad. Est. DY4: Tip 2G **77**
Edale Cl. DY6: K'wfrd 2H **91**
WV4: Ett 2A **60**
Edale Rd. B42: Gt Barr 6E **67**
Eddish Rd. B33: Kitts G 6F **105**
Edelweiss Cl. WS5: Wals 2F **65**
Edenbridge Rd. B28: Hall G 5G **135**
Edenbridge Vw. DY1: Dud 4A **76**
Eden Cl. B31: Longb 1C **158**
B69: Tiv 5D **78**
Edencroft B15: Edg 3E **117**
Edendale Rd. B26: Sheld 5F **121**
Eden Gdns. B65: Row R 1B **112**
DY3: Sed 5A **60**
Eden Gro. B37: Chel W 2F **123**
B71: W Brom 2B **80**
Edenhall Rd. B32: Quin 5H **113**
Eden Ho. DY8: Stourb 6E **109**
Edenhurst Rd. B31: Longb 3D **158**
Eden Pl. B3: Birm 4C **4** (1F **117**)
Eden Rd. B92: Sol 2H **137**
Edensor Cl. WV10: Wolv 5A **28**
EDGBASTON **6C 116**
Edgbaston **6F 117**
Edgbaston Archery & Lawn Tennis Society **4B 116**
Edgbaston Cres. B5: Edg 6F **117**
Edgbaston Croquet Club **4B 116**
Edgbaston Golf Course **5D 116**
Edgbaston Pk. Rd. B15: Edg 6C **116**
Edgbaston Priory Club **6D 116**
Edgbaston Rd. B5: Edg 6F **117**
B12: Bal H 1G **133**
B66: Smeth 5E **99**
Edgbaston Rd. E. B12: Bal H 6H **117**
Edgbaston St. B5: Birm 6E **5** (2G **117**)
Edgcombe Rd. B28: Hall G 4F **135**
Edge Hill Av. WV10: Bush 5C **16**
Edge Hill Dr. DY3: Sed 3G **59**
WV6: Pert 6E **25**
Edge Hill Rd. B74: Four O 5D **36**
Edgehill Rd. B31: Longb 1E **159**
Edgemond Av. B24: Erd 3D **86**
Edge St. WV14: Cose 5F **61**
Edgeview Ct. B68: O'bry 4H **97**
Edgewood Cl. B64: Old H 3H **111**
Edgewood Rd. B38: King Nor 2A **160**
B45: Redn 2H **157**
Edgeworth Cl. WV12: W'hall 5C **30**
Edgware Rd. B23: Erd 2D **84**
Edinburgh Av. WS2: Wals 6E **31**
Edinburgh Ct. B24: Erd 3B **86**
Edinburgh Cres. DY8: Word 2A **108**
Edinburgh Dr. WS4: Rus 2H **33**
WV12: W'hall 3B **30**
Edinburgh La. WS2: Wals 5G **31**
Edinburgh Rd. B68: O'bry 3H **113**
DY2: Dud 3F **95**
WS5: Wals 3F **49**
WV14: Bils 2H **61**
Edison Ct. *WV12: W'hall* *2D 30*
(off Huntington Rd.)
Edison Gro. B32: Quin 6B **114**
Edison Rd. B46: Col 2H **89**
WS2: Wals 4G **31**
Edison Wlk. WS2: Wals 4H **31**
Edith Pope Ho. B42: Gt Barr 5F **67**
Edith Rd. B66: Smeth 6F **99**
Edith St. B70: W Brom 4H **79**
Edmonds Cl. B33: Kitts G 1F **121**
Edmonds Ct. B10: Small H 4D **118**
B26: Yard 4D **120**
Edmonds Rd. B68: O'bry 1A **114**
Edmonton Av. B44: K'sdng 4B **68**
Edmonton Ho. B5: Edg 4F **117**
Edmoor Cl. WV12: W'hall 3C **30**
Edmund Rd. B8: Salt 5D **102**
DY3: Up Gor 1A **76**
Edmund St. B3: Birm 3C **4** (6F **101**)
Ednam Cl. B71: W Brom 5D **64**
Ednam Gro. WV5: Wom 4G **57**
Ednam Rd. DY1: Dud 6E **77**
WV4: Penn 6G **43**
Edsome Way B36: Hodg H 1D **104**
Edstone Cl. B30: King Nor 4F **147**
B93: Dorr 5B **166**
Edstone M. B36: Hodg H 1D **104**
Edward Av. WS9: A'rdge 2C **34**
Edward Cl. WV14: Bils 2G **61**
Edward Ct. B16: Edg 2G **115**
B76: Walm 2D **70**
WS1: Wals 3E **49**
Edward Fisher Dr. DY4: Tip 2A **78**
Edwardian Cl. B90: Shir 2B **150**
Edward Lisle Gdns. WV6: Tett 4B **26**
Edward Rd. B5: Edg 5F **117**
B12: Bal H 5F **117**
B14: King H 6H **147**
B46: Wat O 4E **89**
B63: Hale 1H **127**
B67: Smeth 5D **98**
B68: O'bry 3A **114**
DY4: Tip 6A **62**
WV6: Pert 4E **25**
Edwards Rd. B24: Erd 2G **85**
B75: R'ley 6B **38**
DY2: Neth 5E **95**
Edward St. B1: Birm 4A **4** (1D **116**)
B68: O'bry 5G **97**
B70: W Brom 4A **80**
DY1: Dud 6D **76**
WS2: Wals 6H **31**
WS10: Darl 5E **47**
WV4: Ett 6B **44**
Edwin Phillips Dr. B71: W Brom 5H **63**
Edwin Rd. B30: Stir 6D **132**
Edwinstowe Cl. DY5: Quar B 1C **110**
Eel St. B69: O'bry 2F **97**
Effingham Rd. B13: Mose 6C **134**
Egbert Cl. B6: Aston 1B **102**
Egelwin Cl. WV6: Pert 4E **25**
Egerton Rd. B24: Erd 4B **86**
B74: S'tly 2H **51**
WV10: Bush 4A **16**
EGG HILL **4H 143**
Egghill La. B31: N'fld 3G **143**
B32: Fran 3G **143**
B45: Fran 3G **143**
Eggington Rd. DY8: Woll 4B **108**
Egginton Rd. B28: Hall G 2E **149**
Egmont Gdns. WV11: Wed 3H **29**
Eileen Gdns. B37: K'hrst 5B **106**
Eileen Rd. B11: S'hll 2B **134**
Elan Cl. DY3: Lwr G 4H **75**
Elan Rd. B31: Longb 5A **144**
DY3: Sed 5G **59**
Elbow St. B64: Old H 1H **111**
Elbury Cft. B93: Know 4B **166**
Elcock Dr. B42: P Barr 2F **83**
Eldalade Way WS10: W'bry 3A **64**
Elderberry Cl. DY8: Stourb 2A **124**
WS5: Wals 2D **64**
Elder Cl. B31: Longb 1D **158**
Elderfield B33: Sheld 3F **121**
Elderfield Rd. B30: King Nor 4D **146**
Elder Gro. WV5: Wom 1F **73**
WV11: Wed 3D **28**
Eldersfield Gro. B91: Sol 2F **165**
Elderside Cl. WS8: Bwnhls 5B **10**
Elder Way B23: Erd 5E **85**
Eldon Ct. *WS1: Wals* *2D 48*
(off Eldon St.)
Eldon Dr. B76: Walm 6C **70**
Eldon Rd. B16: Edg 2B **116**
B62: Quin 2G **129**
Eldon St. WS1: Wals 2D **48**
WS10: Darl 4D **46**
Eldridge Cl. WV9: Pend 5D **14**
Eleanor Rd. WV14: Bils 5F **45**
Electra Pk. B6: Witt 6B **84**
Electric Av. B6: Witt 6B **84**
Element Ct. WV10: F'stne 2D **16**
Elford Cl. B14: King H 2G **147**
B74: S'tly 1A **52**
Elford Gro. B37: Mars G 2D **122**
WV14: Bils 1E **61**
Elford Rd. B17: Harb 2F **131**
B29: W Cas 2F **131**
B71: W Brom 4C **64**
Elgar Ct. B15: Edg 4C **116**
Elgar Cres. DY5: P'ntt 2H **93**
Elgar Ho. B16: Birm 1D **116**
Elgin Cl. DY3: Sed 4A **60**
DY8: Amb 4E **109**
Elgin Ct. WV6: Pert 5E **25**
Elgin Gro. B25: Yard 4A **120**
Elgin Rd. WS3: Blox 3G **19**
Eliot Cft. WV14: Cose 3F **61**
Eliot St. B7: Nech 1C **102**
Elisabeth Ct. B74: Four O 6H **37**
Elizabeth Av. WS10: W'bry 2A **64**
WV4: Penn 6F **43**
WV14: Bils 2H **61**
Elizabeth Ct. *B17: Harb* *1H 131*
(off Metchley La.)
Elizabeth Cres. B68: O'bry 1B **114**
Elizabeth Gro. B90: Shir 5A **150**
DY2: Dud 2H **95**
Elizabeth Ho. B76: Walm 2D **70**
DY9: Lye 6H **109**
WS5: Wals 4H **49**
Elizabeth M. B69: Tiv 5A **78**
Elizabeth Prout Gdns. B65: B'hth 2B **112**
Elizabeth Rd. B13: Mose 3E **133**
B33: Stech 6A **104**
B63: Hale 2H **127**
B70: W Brom 3D **78**
B73: New O 4C **68**
WS5: Wals 4F **49**
Elizabeth Wlk. DY4: Tip 4A **62**
Elkington Cft. B90: M'path 4E **165**
Elkington St. B6: Aston 4G **101**
Elkstone Cl. B92: Olton 2F **137**
Elkstone Covert B14: King H 5E **147**
Elland Gro. B27: A Grn 3A **136**
Ellards Dr. WV11: Wed 4H **29**
Ellen St. B18: Hock 5C **100**
(not continuous)
Ellenvale Cl. WV14: Cose 5C **60**
Ellerby Gro. B24: Erd 3C **86**
Ellerside Gro. B31: N'fld 5D **144**
Ellerslie Cl. DY5: Quar B 3H **109**
Ellerslie Rd. B13: Mose 6C **134**
Ellerton Rd. B44: K'sdng 4B **68**
Ellerton Wlk. WV10: Wolv 4B **28**

Ellesboro' Rd. B17: Harb 3F **115**
Ellesmere Rd. B8: Salt 5D **102**
Ellice Dr. B36: Cas B 2D **106**
Elliot Dr. WS11: Gt Wyr 1E **7**
Elliott Gdns. B45: Redn 4A **158**
Elliott Rd. B29: S Oak 4A **132**
Elliotts La. WV8: Cod 4G **13**
Elliotts Rd. DY4: Tip 2G **77**
Elliott Way B6: Witt 3G **83**
Elliot Way B6: Witt 4H **83**
Ellis Av. DY5: Brie H 1E **109**
Ellison St. B70: W Brom 6A **80**
Ellis St. B1: Birm 6C **4** (2F **117**)
Elliston Av. B44: Gt Barr 5G **67**
Ellowes Rd. DY3: Lwr G 3G **75**
Elm Av. B12: Bal H 6A **118**
    WS10: W'bry 1F **63**
    WV11: Wed 1D **28**
    WV14: Bils 5F **45**
Elmay Rd. B26: Sheld 4E **121**
Elm Bank B13: Mose 2A **134**
Elmbank Gro. B20: Hand 2A **82**
Elmbank Rd. WS5: Wals 1G **65**
Elmbridge Cl. B63: Crad 6F **111**
Elmbridge Dr. B90: M'path 3F **165**
Elmbridge Rd. B44: K'sdng 1G **83**
Elmbridge Way B31: N'fld 5H **145**
    DY3: Sed 1A **76**
Elm Cl. DY3: Gorn 5F **75**
    DY8: Stourb 3B **124**
Elm Ct. B13: Mose 1H **133**
    B66: Smeth 1A **98**
    WS1: Wals 3E **49**
Elm Cres. DY4: Tip 1H **77**
Elm Cft. B68: O'bry 4A **114**
Elmcroft B66: Smeth 4G **99**
Elmcroft Av. B32: Bart G 4G **129**
Elmcroft Gdns. WV10: Bush 4A **16**
Elmcroft Rd. B26: Yard 4D **120**
Elmdale B62: Quin 4G **113**
Elmdale Cres. B31: N'fld 2C **144**
Elmdale Dr. WS9: A'rdge 1E **35**
Elmdale Gro. B31: N'fld 3C **144**
Elmdale Rd. WV4: Penn 6E **43**
    WV14: Cose 6C **60**
ELMDON 3A **138**
Elmdon Cl. B92: Sol 3H **137**
    WV10: Oxl 6E **15**
Elmdon Coppice B92: Sol 6B **138**
Elmdon Ct. B29: W Cas 6G **131**
                         (off Abdon Av.)
    B37: Mars G 4C **122**
ELMDON HEATH 1A **152**
Elmdon La. B26: Birm A 2C **138**
    B37: Mars G 4B **122**
Elmdon Park 3H **137**
Elmdon Pk. Rd. B92: Sol 3H **137**
Elmdon Rd. B27: A Grn 1B **136**
    B29: S Oak 3C **132**
    B37: Mars G 4C **122**
    WV10: Oxl 6E **15**
Elmdon Trad. Est. B37: Mars G 6E **123**
Elm Dr. B37: Longb 6A **144**
    B43: Gt Barr 4H **65**
    B62: B'hth 2E **113**
Elm Farm Av. B37: Mars G 4B **122**
Elm Farm Rd. WV2: Wolv 4H **43**
Elmfield Av. B24: Erd 3D **86**
Elmfield Cres. B13: Mose 3H **133**
Elmfield Rd. B36: Cas B 2A **106**
Elmfield Vw. DY1: Dud 4C **76**
Elm Grn. DY1: Dud 2C **76**
Elm Gro. B37: K'hrst 3B **106**
    CV7: Bal C 6H **169**
    WV8: Bilb 4G **13**
Elmhurst B15: Edg 3H **115**
Elmhurst Av. B65: Row R 6C **96**
Elmhurst Dr. DY6: K'wfrd 5D **92**
    WS7: Chase 1C **10**
Elmhurst Rd. B21: Hand 6A **82**
Elmley Cl. WV14: Cose 6D **60**
Elmley Gro. B30: King Nor 5D **146**
    WV6: Pert 4A **24**
Elm Lodge B92: H Ard 6A **140**
Elmore Cl. B37: F'bri 5C **106**
Elmore Grn. Cl. WS3: Blox 1H **31**
Elmore Grn. Rd. WS3: Blox 6G **19**

Elmore Rd. B33: Kitts G 6E **105**
Elmore Row WS3: Blox 6H **19**
Elm Rd. B30: B'vlle 5B **132**
    B76: Walm 3D **70**
    DY1: Dud 3E **77**
    DY6: K'wfrd 3C **92**
    WS3: Blox 3B **32**
    WS11: Nort C 1F **9**
Elms, The B16: Birm 6B **100**
Elms Cl. B38: King Nor 1G **159**
    B91: Sol 2H **151**
Elmsdale WV6: Tett 1G **41**
Elmsdale Ct. WS1: Wals 3D **48**
Elms Rd. B15: Edg 1B **132**
    B72: S Cold 2A **70**
Elmstead Av. B33: Sheld 4H **121**
Elmstead Cl. WS5: Wals 2A **50**
Elmstead Twr. B5: Birm 4G **117**
                         (off Berrington Wlk.)
Elmstead Wood WS5: Wals 2A **50**
Elmstone Cl. DY1: Dud 3B **76**
Elm St. WV3: Wolv 2E **43**
    WV13: W'hall 1C **46**
Elm Ter. B69: Tiv 6A **78**
Elm Tree Cl. WV5: Wom 2F **73**
Elm Tree Gro. B63: Crad 5F **111**
Elm Tree Ri. B92: H Ard 1A **154**
Elm Tree Rd. B17: Harb 5E **115**
    B30: Stir 1C **146**
Elmtree Rd. B74: S'tly 3F **51**
Elm Tree Way B64: Old H 2H **111**
Elmwood Av. WV11: Ess 4A **18**
Elmwood Cl. CV7: Bal C 6H **169**
Elmwood Ct. B5: Edg 5F **117**
    B73: S'tly 6A **52**
Elmwood Gdns. B20: Hand 5D **82**
Elmwood Gro. B47: H'wd 3A **162**
Elmwood Ri. DY3: Sed 4F **59**
Elmwood Rd. B24: Erd 5A **86**
    B74: S'tly 6A **52**
    DY8: Word 6A **92**
Elmwoods B32: Bart G 3H **129**
Elphinstone End B24: Erd 1A **86**
Elsma Rd. B92: H Ard 3A **114**
Elston Hall La. WV10: Bush 6H **15**
Elstree Rd. B23: Erd 2D **84**
Elswick Gro. B44: K'sdng 5B **68**
Elswick Rd. B44: K'sdng 4B **68**
Elsworth Gro. B25: Yard 5A **120**
Elsworth Rd. B31: N'fld 5H **145**
Eltham Gro. B44: K'sdng 4B **68**
Elton Cl. WV10: Bush 3A **16**
Elton Cft. B93: Dorr 5B **166**
Elton Gro. B27: A Grn 3G **135**
Eltonia Cft. B26: Sheld 5F **121**
Elva Cft. B36: Cas B 6B **88**
Elvaston Way B90: Dic H 4F **163**
Elvers Grn. La. B93: Know 3G **167**
Elvetham Rd. B15: Edg 4E **117**
Elvetham Rd. Nth. B15: Birm 3E **117**
Elviron Dr. WV6: Tett 4H **25**
Elwell Cres. DY1: Dud 1B **76**
Elwells Cl. WV14: Cose 2C **60**
Elwell St. B70: W Brom 2E **79**
    WS10: W'bry 2H **63**
Elwyn Rd. B73: S Cold 2G **69**
Ely Cl. B37: Chel W 1D **122**
    B65: Row R 5E **97**
Ely Cres. B71: W Brom 6H **63**
Ely Gro. B32: Quin 1D **130**
Ely Pl. WS2: Wals 2H **47**
Ely Rd. WS2: Wals 2H **47**
Emay Cft. B70: W Brom 5F **63**
Embankment, The DY5: Brie H 6A **94**
Embassy Dr. B15: Edg 3C **116**
    B69: O'bry 1E **97**
Embassy Ind. Est. DY9: Lye 6B **110**
Embassy Rd. B69: O'bry 1E **97**
Embleton Gro. B34: Hodg H 3E **105**
Emerald Ct. B8: W End 4A **104**
    B92: Olton 4D **136**
Emerson Cl. DY3: Lwr G 3E **75**
Emerson Gro. WV10: Bush 1B **28**
Emerson Rd. B17: Harb 5G **115**
    WV10: Bush 6B **16**
Emery Cl. B23: Erd 6D **84**
    WS1: Wals 3D **48**

Emery Ho. B23: Erd 1C **84**
Emery St. WS1: Wals 3D **48**
Emily Gdns. B16: Birm 6B **100**
Emily Rd. B26: Yard 5B **120**
Emily St. B12: Birm 3H **117**
    B70: W Brom 5H **79**
Emmanuel Rd. B73: W Grn 6H **69**
Emmeline St. B9: Birm 2B **118**
Emms Ct. DY5: Brie H 2F **109**
Emo Ct. B34: S End 3H **105**
Empire Cinema
    Great Park 1G **157**
    Sutton Coldfield 2H **69**
Empire Ind. Pk. WS9: A'rdge 1B **34**
Empress Way WS10: Darl 3D **46**
Emscote Dr. B73: W Grn 6H **69**
Emscote Grn. B91: Sol 5C **150**
Emscote Rd. B6: Aston 6H **83**
Emsworth Cres. WV9: Pend 5E **15**
Emsworth Gro. B14: King H 1F **147**
Enderby Cl. B93: Ben H 5B **166**
Enderby Dr. WV4: Penn 1D **58**
Enderley Cl. WS3: Blox 4H **19**
Enderley Dr. WS3: Blox 4H **19**
End Hall Rd. WV6: Tett 6G **25**
Endhill Rd. B44: K'sdng 1A **68**
Endicott Rd. B6: Aston 6H **83**
Endmoor Gro. B23: Erd 1D **84**
Endsleigh Gro. B28: Hall G 5G **135**
Endwood Ct. B20: Hand 5C **82**
Endwood Ct. Rd. B20: Hand 5C **82**
Endwood Dr. B74: Lit As 5C **36**
    B91: Sol 5D **150**
Energy Way B10: Small H 5F **119**
                         (not continuous)
Enfield Cl. B23: Erd 1F **85**
Enfield Ct. B29: W Cas 4F **59**
                         (off Abdon Av.)
Enfield Rd. B15: Edg 3D **116**
    B65: Row R 6D **96**
Enford Cl. B34: S End 3H **105**
Engine La. DY9: Lye 5H **109**
    WS8: Bwnhls 5F **9**
    WS10: Mox 1A **62**
Engine M. B92: H Ard 6A **140**
Engine St. B66: Smeth 3F **99**
    B69: O'bry 3G **97**
Englestede Cl. B20: Hand 4B **82**
Englewood Dr. B28: Hall G 5G **135**
Ennerdale Cl. WS8: Clay 6A **10**
Ennerdale Dr. B63: Hale 3F **127**
    WV6: Pert 5F **25**
Ennerdale Rd. B43: Gt Barr 1B **82**
    WV6: Tett 1B **26**
Ennersdale Bungs. B46: Col 6H **89**
Ennersdale Cl. B46: Col 6H **89**
Ennersdale Rd. B46: Col 6H **89**
Ensall Dr. DY8: Word 2C **108**
Ensbury Cl. WV12: W'hall 5D **30**
Ensdale Row WV13: W'hall 2A **46**
Ensdon Gro. B44: K'sdng 4B **68**
Ensford Cl. B74: Four O 4E **37**
Enstone Rd. B23: Erd 6G **69**
    DY1: Dud 1B **94**
Enterprise Dr. B74: S'tly 4G **51**
    DY9: Lye 5C **110**
Enterprise Ho. B23: Erd 2G **85**
Enterprise Trad. Est.
    DY5: Brie H 6B **94**
Enterprise Way B7: Birm 5H **101**
    WS3: Blox 4G **19**
Enville Cl. B37: Mars G 2D **122**
Enville Comn. Rd. DY3: Stourt 5A **90**
    DY7: Stourt 5A **90**
Enville Golf Course 3A **90**
Enville Gro. B11: S'brk 6D **118**
Enville Pl. DY8: Stourb 6D **108**
                         (off Short St.)
Enville Rd. DY3: Lwr G 3H **75**
    DY6: W Hth 1G **91**
    WV4: Penn 6A **58**
Enville St. DY8: Stourb 6D **108**
Epping Cl. B45: Fran 5H **143**
    WS3: Wals 3D **32**
Epping Gro. B44: K'sdng 6A **68**

Epsom Cl. WV6: Pert 5F 25
Epsom Ct. B29: W Cas 6G 131
Epsom Gro. B44: K'sdng 5B 68
Epwell Gro. B44: K'sdng 1H 83
Epwell Rd. B44: K'sdng 1H 83
Epworth Ct. DY5: P'ntt 4F 93
Equipoint B25: Yard 4B 120
Erasmus Rd. B11: S'brk 4A 118
Ercall Cl. B23: Erd 1A 84
ERDINGTON 3G 85
Erdington Court Bowls Club 5F 69
Erdington Fire Sta. B24: Erd 2G 85
(off Orphange Rd.)
Erdington Hall Rd. B24: Erd 5E 85
Erdington Ind. Pk. B24: Erd 3D 86
Erdington Rd. WS9: A'rdge 5D 34
Erdington Station (Rail) 2F 85
Erdington Swimming Pool & Turkish Suite
. . . . .3G 85
Erica Cl. B29: W Cas 5E 131
Erica Rd. WS5: Wals 2F 65
Ermington Cres.
B36: Hodg H 1C 104
Ermington Rd. WV4: Penn 6H 43
Ernest Clarke Cl.
WV12: W'hall 5C 30
Ernest Cl. B38: King Nor 6C 146
Ernest Rd. B12: Bal H 1B 134
B67: Smeth 3C 98
DY2: Dud 6H 77
Ernest St. B1: Birm 6C 4 (2F 117)
Ernsford Cl. B93: Dorr 6G 167
Erskine St. B7: Birm 5B 102
Esher Rd. B44: Gt Barr 1H 67
B71: W Brom 1B 80
Eskdale Cl. WV1: Wolv 1C 44
Eskdale Wlk. DY5: Brie H 3F 109
Esme Rd. B11: S'hll 1B 134
Esmond Cl. B30: B'vlle 2H 145
Essendon Gro. B8: W End 5H 103
Essendon Rd. B8: W End 5H 103
Essendon Wlk. B8: W End 5H 103
Essex Av. B71: W Brom 6A 64
DY6: K'wfrd 4H 91
WS10: W'bry 1A 64
Essex Ct. B29: W Cas 6G 131
Essex Gdns. DY8: Woll 4B 108
Essex Ho. WV1: Wolv 5G 27
(off Lomas St.)
Essex Rd. B75: R'ley 2B 54
DY2: Dud 3C 94
Essex St. B5: Birm 6D 4 (2G 117)
WS2: Wals 4C 32
ESSINGTON 4A 18
Essington Cl. DY8: Word 2C 108
Essington Ho. B8: W End 4G 103
Essington Ind. Est.
WV11: Ess 3H 17
Essington Rd. WV11: Ess 5B 18
WV12: W'hall 5B 18
Essington St. B16: Birm 2D 116
Essington Way WV1: Wolv 2D 44
Este Rd. B26: Yard 3E 121
Estone Cl. B8: Salt 5E 103
Estone Wlk. B6: Aston 2H 101
Estria Rd. B15: Edg 4D 116
Estridge La. WS6: Gt Wyr 3G 7
Fthelflieda Ter.
WS10: W'bry 2F 63
Ethelred Rd. B74: Four O 6G 37
Ethel Rd. B17: Harb 6H 115
Ethel St. B2: Birm 4D 4 (1F 117)
B67: Smeth 1D 114
B68: O'bry 5G 97
Etheridge Rd. WV14: Bils 4E 45
Etna St. B5: Birm 3G 5 (6H 101)
Eton Cl. DY3: Sed 6B 60
Eton Ct. B74: Four O 1F 53
(off Vesey Rd.)
Eton Dr. DY8: Stourb 2E 125
Eton Rd. B12: Bal H 1B 134
Etruria Way WV14: Bils 4G 45
Etta Gro. B44: Gt Barr 1H 67
ETTINGSHALL 6C 44
ETTINGSHALL PARK 2A 60
Ettingshall Pk. Farm La.
WV4: Ett 1A 60

Ettingshall Rd. WV2: Ett 4C 44
WV14: Cose 3C 60
Ettington Cl. B93: Dorr 6F 167
Ettington Rd. B6: Aston 1G 101
Ettymore Cl. DY3: Sed 5H 59
Ettymore Rd. DY3: Sed 5H 59
Ettymore Rd. W.
DY3: Sed 5G 59
Etwall Rd. B28: Hall G 2E 149
Euan Cl. B17: Harb 3G 115
Euro Bus. Pk. B69: O'bry 6D 78
Europa Av. B70: W Brom 5D 80
(not continuous)
European Bus. Pk. B69: O'bry 2E 97
Euroway Pk. B69: O'bry 1A 98
Evans Cl. DY4: Tip 2E 77
Evans Gdns. B29: S Oak 4H 131
Evans Pl. WV14: Bils 4G 45
Evans St. WV6: Wolv 5E 27
WV13: W'hall 2F 45
WV14: Cose 4B 60
Eva Rd. B18: Win G 3H 99
B68: O'bry 6A 98
Evason Ct. B6: Aston 6G 83
EVE HILL 5D 76
Eve La. DY1: Dud 2B 76
Evelyn Cft. B73: Bold 5G 69
Evelyn Rd. B11: S'hll 1C 134
Evenlode Cl. B92: Olton 2F 137
Evenlode Gro.
WV13: W'hall 2D 46
Evenlode Rd. B92: Olton 2E 137
Everene Ho. B27: A Grn 2A 136
Everest Rd. B20: Hand 4C 82
WS2: Wals 6F 31
Evergreen Cl. WV14: Cose 5D 60
Everitt Dr. B93: Know 3C 166
Eversley Dale B24: Erd 5G 85
Eversley Gro. DY3: Sed 3G 59
WV11: Wed 3E 29
Eversley Rd. B9: Small H 2D 118
(not continuous)
Evers St. DY5: Quar B 3C 110
Everton Rd. B8: W End 5A 104
Eves Cft. B32: Bart G 4A 130
Evesham Cres. WS3: Blox 4F 19
Evesham Ri. DY2: Neth 6F 95
Eveson Rd. DY8: Stourb 3B 124
Evington Pl. B25: Yard 4G 119
Evolution Dr. B8: Amb 3D 108
Ewart Rd. WS2: Wals 6E 31
Ewell Rd. B24: Erd 3H 85
Ewhurst Av. B29: S Oak 4B 132
(Birkdale Av.)
B29: S Oak 5C 132
(Birkdale Gro.)
Ewhurst Cl. WV13: W'hall 3H 45
Exbury Cl. WV9: Pend 5D 14
Excelsior Gro. WS3: Pels 2F 21
Exchange, The WS3: Blox 6H 19
Exchange Ct. WV10: F'hses 2H 15
Exchange St. DY5: Brie H 5H 93
WV1: Wolv 3B 170 (1G 43)
Exe Cft. B31: Longb 1F 159
Exeter Dr. B37: Mars G 3B 122
Exeter Pas. B1: Birm 2F 117
Exeter Pl. WS2: Wals 2H 47
Exeter Rd. B29: S Oak 3B 132
B66: Smeth 4F 99
DY2: Neth 1F 111
Exeter St. B1: Birm 6D 4 (2F 117)
Exford Cl. DY5: Brie H 4F 109
Exhall Cl. B91: Sol 5C 150
Exhall Ct. B23: Erd 5C 84
Exhibition Way B40: Nat E C 1F 139
Exmoor Grn. WV11: Wed 2E 29
Exon Ct. DY4: Tip 1H 77
Expressway, The B70: W Brom 3H 79
Expressway Ind. Est. B6: Aston 4H 101
Exton Cl. WV11: Wed 1H 29
Exton Gdns. B66: Smeth 3H 99
(off Foundry La.)
Exton Way B8: Salt 4D 102
Eyland Gro. WS1: Wals 1D 48
Eymore Cl. B29: W Cas 1F 145
Eyre St. B18: Hock 6C 100

Eyston Av. DY4: Tip 5D 62
Eyton Cft. B12: Birm 4H 117
Ezekiel La. WV12: W'hall 3C 30

F

F1 Karting
Kings Norton 2D 146
Fabian Cl. B45: Fran 5F 143
Fabian Cres. B90: Shir 6H 149
Facet Rd. B38: King Nor 5C 146
Factory Est. B44: P Barr 1G 83
Factory Rd. B18: Hock 3B 100
DY4: Tip 1G 77
Factory St. WS10: Darl 5C 46
Fairbourne Av. B44: Gt Barr 3G 67
B65: Row R 5E 97
Fairbourne Twr. B23: Erd 1G 85
Fairburn Cres. WS3: Pels 2F 21
Faircroft Av. B76: Walm 1D 86
Faircroft Rd. B36: Cas B 6H 87
Fairdene Way B43: Gt Barr 5H 65
Fairfax Dr. B31: Longb 1F 159
Fairfax Rd. B31: Longb 1E 159
B75: S Cold 6D 54
WV10: Bush 5H 15
Fairfield Dr. B62: B'hth 2E 113
WS3: Pels 3F 21
WV8: Cod 3E 13
Fairfield Gro. B62: B'hth 2E 113
Fairfield Mt. WS1: Wals 3D 48
Fairfield Pk. Ind. Est. B62: B'hth 2E 113
Fairfield Pk. Rd. B62: B'hth 2E 113
Fairfield Ri. CV7: Mer 4H 141
DY8: Woll 6A 108
Fairfield Rd. B14: King H 5G 133
B62: B'hth 2E 113
B63: Hale 3A 128
DY2: Dud 2F 95
DY8: Word 1D 108
Fairfold Lodge DY8: Word 5C 92
Fairford Cl. B91: Shir 2B 150
Fairford Gdns. DY8: Word 6C 92
Fairford Rd. B44: K'sdng 1H 83
Fairgreen Gdns. DY5: P'ntt 4G 93
Fairgreen Way B29: S Oak 4B 132
B74: S'tly 2A 52
Fairground Way WS1: Wals 3B 48
Fairhaven Cft. B62: B'hth 2E 113
Fairhills DY3: Sed 5H 59
Fairhill Way B11: S'brk 4B 118
Fairholme Rd. B36: Hodg H 2H 103
Fairlawn B15: Edg 4C 116
Fairlawn Cl. WV12: W'hall 6C 18
Fairlawn Dr. DY6: K'wfrd 5B 92
Fairlawns B26: Yard 2E 121
B76: Walm 5E 71
Fairlawn Way WV12: W'hall 6C 18
Fairlie Cres. B38: King Nor 6H 145
Fairlie Ho. B23: Erd 6G 69
Fairmead Ri. B38: King Nor 6A 146
Fairmile Rd. B63: Hale 5H 111
Fairoak Dr. WV6: Tett 6H 25
Fair Oaks Dr. WS6: Gt Wyr 5G 7
Fairview Av. B42: Gt Barr 1D 82
Fairview Cl. WS6: C Hay 3D 6
WV11: Wed 3D 28
Fairview Ct. WS2: Wals 1D 46
WS3: Blox 5G 19
Fairview Cres. DY6: K'wfrd 4D 92
WV11: Wed 2D 28
Fairview Gro. WV11: Wed 2D 28
Fairview Ind. Est. B76: Curd 1D 88
Fairview M. B46: Col 2H 107
Fairview Rd. DY1: Dud 4C 76
WV4: Penn 1A 58
WV11: Wed 2D 28
Fairway B31: N'fld 5C 144
WS4: S'fld 6H 21
Fairway, The B38: King Nor 5H 145
Fairway Av. B69: Tiv 1A 96
Fairway Dr. B45: Rub 3F 157
Fairway Grn. WV14: Bils 4F 45
Fairway Rd. B68: O'bry 1F 113
Fairways B93: Know 1C 166
Fairways, The B76: Walm 1D 86

Fairways Av. DY8: Stourb 3C 124
Fairways Cl. DY8: Stourb 3C 124
Fairyfield Av. B43: Gt Barr 4H 65
Fairyfield Ct. B43: Gt Barr 4H 65
Fakenham Cft. B17: Harb 4D 114
Falcon Cl. WS6: C Hay 3C 6
Falcon Cres. WV14: Cose 3B 60
Falcondale Rd. WV12: W'hall 6C 18
Falconhurst Rd. B29: S Oak 3G 131
FALCON LODGE 6E 55
Falcon Lodge Cres. B75: S Cold 6D 54
Falcon Pl. B69: Tiv 2C 96
Falcon Ri. DY8: Woll 5A 108
Falcon Rd. B68: O'bry 1F 113
Falcons, The B75: S Cold 6F 55
Falcon Vw. B30: King Nor 3C 146
Falcon Way DY1: Dud 6B 76
Falfield Cl. B65: Row R 3D 96
Falfield Gro. B31: Longb 2C 158
Falkland Cft. B30: Stir 1D 146
Falklands Cl. DY3: Swind 5E 73
Falkland Way B36: Cas B 4D 106
Falkwood Gro. B93: Know 3B 166
Fallindale Rd. B26: Sheld 5F 121
FALLINGS HEATH 5F 47
Fallings Heath Cl. WS10: Darl 4F 47
FALLINGS PARK 4B 28
Fallings Pk. Ind. Est. WV10: Wolv 4B 28
Fallow Fld. B74: Lit As 6B 36
Fallowfield B15: Edg 3A 116
      WV6: Pert 5D 24
      WV8: Pend 5C 14
Fallowfield Av. B28: Hall G 2F 149
Fallow Fld. Rd. B65: Row R 6A 96
Fallowfield Rd. B63: Hale 2F 127
      B92: Sol 3G 137
      WS5: Wals 3A 50
Fallows Ho. B19: Hock 4G 101
Fallows Rd. B11: S'brk 5C 118
Fallow Wlk. B32: Bart G 3G 129
Fallow Way B16: Edg 6G 99
Falmouth Rd. B34: Hodg H 4C 104
      WS5: Wals 4H 49
Falstaff Av. B47: H'wd 3A 162
Falstaff Cl. B76: Walm 6F 71
Falstaff Ct. B75: S Cold 6G 55
Falstaff Rd. B90: Shir 5H 149
Falstone Rd. B73: New O 3D 68
Family Courts
      Birmingham 3E 5 (6G 101)
Fancott Rd. B31: N'fld 2E 145
Fancourt Av. WV4: Penn 1B 58
Fane Rd. WV11: Wed 6A 18
Fanshawe Rd. B27: A Grn 4A 136
Faraday Av. B32: Quin 6B 114
      B46: Col, Curd 2H 89
      B76: Curd 2G 89
Faraday Ct. B32: Quin 6B 114
Faraday Ho. B15: Birm 3E 117
Faraday Rd. WS2: Wals 3H 31
Faraday Wharf B7: Birm 5H 101
Farbrook Way WV12: W'hall 3B 30
Farclose Ho. B15: Edg 4E 117
Farcroft Av. B21: Hand 1H 99
Farcroft Gro. B21: Hand 6H 81
Farcroft Rd. B21: Hand 6H 81
Fareham Cres. WV4: Penn 5A 42
Farfield Cl. B31: N'fld 5F 145
Far High Dr. DY4: Tip 2B 78
Far Highfield B76: Walm 1B 70
Farhill Cl. B71: W Brom 5D 64
Farlands Dr. DY8: Stourb 2E 125
Farlands Gro. B43: Gt Barr 6B 66
Farlands Rd. DY8: Stourb 2E 125
Farleigh Dr. WV3: Wolv 3G 41
Farleigh Rd. WV6: Pert 6G 25
Farley Cen. B70: W Brom 5B 80
Farley La. B62: Roms 5A 142
Farley Rd. B23: Erd 3B 84
      B70: W Brom 4E 79
Farley St. DY4: Tip 2D 78
Farlow Cft. B37: Mars G 3B 122
Farlow Rd. B31: N'fld 4G 145
Farmacre B9: Birm 1B 118
Farm Av. B68: O'bry 6G 97
Farmbridge Cl. WS2: Wals 6D 30
Farmbridge Rd. WS2: Wals 6D 30

Farmbridge Way WS2: Wals 6D 30
Farmbrook Av. WV10: F'hses 4H 15
Farm Cl. B92: Sol 3G 137
      DY3: Sed 6F 59
      WV8: Bilb 5H 13
Farmcote Rd. B33: Stech 5E 105
Farm Cft. B19: Hock 3E 101
Farmcroft Rd. DY9: W'cte 2A 126
Farmdale Gro. B45: Redn 3G 157
Farm End Cl. B71: W Brom 4D 64
Farmer Rd. B10: Small H 4G 119
Farmers Cl. B76: Walm 1C 70
Farmers Ct. B63: Hale 1H 127
Farmers Fold WV1: Wolv 3B 170
Farmers Wlk. B21: Hand 2H 99
Farmer Way DY4: Tip 4B 62
Farm Ho. La. B75: R'ley 6C 38
Farmhouse Rd. WV12: W'hall 4D 30
Farm Ho. Way B43: Gt Barr 1A 66
Farmhouse Way B90: M'path 2F 165
      WV12: W'hall 4E 31
Farmoor Gro. B34: S End 3A 106
Farmoor Way WV10: Bush 3A 16
Farm Rd. B11: S'brk 4B 118
      B65: Row R 5A 96
      B67: Smeth 6C 98
      B68: O'bry 6G 97
      DY2: Neth 6C 94
      DY4: Tip 6C 62
      DY5: Quar B 2A 110
      WV3: Wolv 3A 42
Farmside Cl. DY9: W'cte 2B 126
Farmside Grn. WV9: Pend 5D 14
Farmstead Cl. B75: R'ley 6B 38
      WS1: Wals 6C 48
Farmstead Rd. B92: Sol 3G 137
Farm St. B19: Hock 3E 101
      B70: W Brom 6A 80
      WS2: Wals 5C 32
Farnborough Ct. B75: Four O 1H 53
Farnborough Dr. B90: M'path 3D 164
Farnborough Rd. B35: Cas V 5E 87
Farnbury Cft. B38: King Nor 5D 146
Farn Cl. B33: Stech 6D 104
Farncote Dr. B74: Four O 6F 37
Farndale Av. WV6: Wolv 4D 26
Farndale Cl. DY5: Brie H 5F 109
Farndon Av. B37: Mars G 4D 122
Farndon Rd. B8: Salt 5F 103
Farndon Way B23: Erd 5D 68
Farnham Cl. B43: Gt Barr 5B 66
Farnham Rd. B21: Hand 5H 81
Farnhurst Rd. B36: Hodg H 2H 103
Farnol Rd. B26: Yard 3D 120
Farnworth Gro. B36: Cas B 6A 88
Farquhar Rd. B13: Mose 2H 133
      B15: Edg 5B 116
Farquhar Rd. E. B15: Edg 5B 116
Farran Way B43: Gt Barr 6A 66
Farran Rd. B31: Longb 6B 144
Farrier Cl. B76: Walm 5D 70
Farrier Rd. B43: Gt Barr 2F 67
Farriers, The B26: Sheld 6F 121
Farriers Mill WS3: Pels 3C 20
Farrier Way DY6: W Hth 2G 91
Farringdon Ho. WS2: Wals 6B 32
                                      (off Green La.)
Farringdon St. WS2: Wals 1B 48
Farrington Rd. B23: Erd 2B 84
      WV4: Ett 2H 59
Farrow Rd. B44: Gt Barr 2G 67
Farthing Ct. B1: Birm 2A 4
Farthing La. B72: S Cold 1H 69
      B76: Curd 1E 89
Farthings Pools Cl. B72: S Cold 1A 70
Farthings, The B17: Harb 5H 115
      DY2: Dud 1D 94
Farthings La. DY2: Dud 2C 94
Farvale Rd. B76: Min 1G 87
Far Vw. WS9: A'rdge 5D 22
Farway Gdns. WV8: Cod 5F 13
Far Wood Rd. B31: N'fld 5C 130
Fashoda Rd. B29: S Oak 4D 132
Fastlea Rd. B32: Bart G 4B 130
Fastmoor Oval B33: Kitts G 2A 122
Fast Pits Rd. B25: Yard 3H 119
Fatherless Barn Cres. B63: Crad 1E 127

Faulkland Cres.
      WV1: Wolv 1C 170 (6H 27)
Faulkner Cl. DY8: Stourb 1D 124
Faulkner Rd. B92: Olton 4F 137
Faulkners Farm Dr. B23: Erd 1B 84
Faversham Cl. WS2: Wals 6D 30
      WV8: Pend 1C 26
Fawdry Cl. B73: S Cold 6H 53
Fawdry St. B9: Birm 1A 118
      B66: Smeth 4G 99
      WV1: Wolv 6F 27
Fawley Cl. WV13: W'hall 2H 45
Fawley Gro. B14: King H 2D 146
Fazeley Cl. B91: Sol 3H 151
Fazeley Ind. Est. B5: Birm 4H 5 (1A 118)
Fazeley St. B5: Birm 4G 5 (1H 117)
                                      (not continuous)
Fazeley Studios B5: Birm 5H 5 (1A 118)
Fearon Pl. B66: Smeth 4E 99
FEATHERSTONE 1D 16
Featherstone Cl. B90: Shir 5B 150
Featherstone Cres. B90: Shir 5B 150
Featherstone Rd. B14: King H 1G 147
Featherston Rd. B74: S'tly 1A 52
FEIASHILL 6B 56
Feiashill Cl. WV5: Try 5B 56
Feiashill Rd. DY3: Try 5B 56
      WV5: Try 5B 56
Felbrigg Cl. DY5: Brie H 3G 109
Feldings, The B24: Erd 3A 86
Felgate Cl. B90: M'path 3E 165
Fellbrook Cl. B33: Stech 5D 104
Fell Gro. B21: Hand 5G 81
Fellmeadow Rd. B33: Yard 1E 121
Fellmeadow Way DY3: Sed 1A 76
Fellows Av. DY6: W Hth 1A 92
Fellows La. B17: Harb 5E 115
Fellows Pk. Gdns. WS2: Wals 5H 47
Fellows Rd. WV14: Bils 4F 45
Fellows St. WV2: Wolv 3G 43
Felsted Way B7: Birm 5A 102
Felstone Rd. B44: Gt Barr 4G 67
Feltham Cl. B33: Kitts G 2A 122
Felton Cft. B33: Kitts G 6E 105
Felton Gro. B91: Sol 6F 151
Fenbourne Cl. WS4: S'fld 1G 33
Fenchurch Cl. WS2: Wals 5B 32
Fencote Av. B37: F'bri 5C 106
FEN END 6E 169
Fen End Rd. CV8: Fen E 6E 169
Fen End Rd. W. B93: Know 4B 168
      CV8: Fen E 4B 168
Fenmere Cl. WV4: Penn 6H 43
Fennel Cl. WS6: C Hay 2D 6
Fennel Cft. B34: S End 2F 105
Fennel Gro. B74: S'tly 3H 51
Fennel Rd. DY5: Brie H 4G 109
Fennis Cl. B93: Dorr 6B 166
Fenn Ri. DY8: Word 6A 92
      WV12: W'hall 3B 30
Fenton Rd. B27: A Grn 6H 119
      B47: H'wd 2A 162
Fenton St. B66: Smeth 2C 98
      DY5: Brie H 6G 93
Fenton Way B27: A Grn 6H 119
Fereday Rd. WS9: Wals W 4D 22
Fereday's Cft. DY3: Sed 6H 59
Fereday St. DY4: Tip 5H 61
Ferguson Dr. DY4: Tip 1B 78
Ferguson Rd. B68: O'bry 4B 98
Ferguson St. WV11: Wed 6A 18
Fern Av. DY4: Tip 6H 61
Fernbank Cl. B63: Hale 3F 127
Fernbank Cres. WS5: Wals 1G 65
Fernbank Rd. B8: W End 5G 103

Ferncliffe Rd. B17: Harb 1F 131
Fern Cl. WS4: S'fld 6G 21
  WV14: Cose 5D 60
Ferndale Av. B43: Gt Barr 6B 66
Ferndale Ct. B17: Harb 1H 131
  (off Metchley La.)
  B46: Col 4H 107
Ferndale Cres. B12: Birm 3G 89
Ferndale M. B46: Col 4H 107
Ferndale Pk. DY9: Pedm 5F 125
Ferndale Rd. B28: Hall G 5F 135
  B46: Col 4H 107
  B68: O'bry 1G 113
  B74: S'tly 3H 51
  CV7: Bal C 3F 169
  WV11: Ess 4B 18
Ferndene Rd. B11: Tys 2F 135
Ferndown Av. DY3: Sed 6G 59
Ferndown Ct. B26: Yard 2E 121
  WS3: Blox 3H 19
Ferndown Gdns. WV11: Wed 4H 29
Ferndown Rd. B91: Sol 1F 151
Fern Dr. WS6: Gt Wyr 1G 7
Ferney Hills Cl. B43: Gt Barr 2D 66
Fernfail Ct. B23: Erd 2E 85
Fernhill Ct. B23: Erd 5C 84
Fernhill Gro. B44: Gt Barr 2H 67
Fernhill La. CV7: Bal C 5F 169
  CV8: Fen E 5E 169
Fernhill Rd. B92: Olton 3C 136
Fernhurst Dr. DY5: P'ntt 2F 93
Fernhurst Rd. B8: Salt 6G 103
Fernleigh Ct. B91: Sol 2G 151
Fernleigh Gdns. DY8: Word 6A 92
Fernleigh Rd. WS4: Wals 6F 33
Fernley Av. B29: S Oak 3D 132
Fernley Rd. B11: S'hll 1C 134
Fern Leys WV3: Wolv 2B 42
Fern Rd. B24: Erd 3G 85
  WV3: Wolv 3F 43
Fernside Gdns. B13: Mose 2B 134
Fernside Rd. WV13: W'hall 6F 29
Fernwood Cl. B73: Bold 4E 69
  DY4: Tip 3H 77
Fernwood Rd. B73: Bold 5E 69
Fernwoods B32: Bart G 3H 129
Ferrers Cl. B75: R'ley 1B 54
Ferrie Gro. WS8: Bwnhls 6A 10
Ferris Gro. B27: A Grn 4G 135
Festival Av. WS10: Darl 1C 62
Festival Ct. DY2: Neth 4E 95
Festival Way WV6: Wolv 4F 27
Fibbersley WV11: Wed 5H 29
  WV13: W'hall 5H 29
Fibbersley Bank WV13: W'hall 5H 29
Fiddlers Grn. B92: H Ard 6A 140
Field Av. B31: N'fld 2D 144
Field Cl. B26: Sheld 5E 121
  DY8: Word 1E 109
  WS3: Blox 1A 32
  WS4: S'fld 5F 21
  WV14: Bils 5E 45
Field Cott. Dr. DY8: Stourb 2F 125
Field Ct. WS4: S'fld 5F 21
Fieldfare WS7: Hamm 1F 11
Fieldfare Cl. B64: Old H 5H 95
Fieldfare Cft. B36: Cas B 1C 106
Fieldfare Rd. DY9: W'cte 1H 125
Fieldgate Trad. Est. WS1: Wals 2D 48
Field Head Pl. WV6: Tett 5H 25
Fieldhead Rd. B11: Tys 2G 135
Fieldhouse Rd. B25: Yard 3A 120
  WV4: Ett 1A 60
Fielding La B91: Sol 1F 165
Field La. B32: Bart G 4G 129
  B91: Sol 1C 152
  DY8: Stourb 2E 125
  WS4: S'fld 5F 21
  WS6: Gt Wyr 2F 7
Field Maple Rd. B74: S'tly 5H 51
Field M. DY2: Neth 6G 95
Fieldon Cl. B90: Shir 4A 150
Field Rd. DY2: Dud 6G 77
  DY4: Tip 5H 61
  WS3: Blox 1A 32
Field Rd. Ind. Est. WS3: Blox 1A 32

Fields, The WV8: Bilb 3H 13
Fieldside Wlk. WV14: Bils 3F 45
Fieldstone Vw. DY3: Lwr G 3H 75
Field St. WV10: Wolv 6A 28
  WV13: W'hall 1A 46
  WV14: Bils 2G 61
Fieldview Cl. WV14: Cose 3G 61
Field Vw. Dr. B65: Row R 6F 97
Field Wlk. WS9: A'rdge 2D 34
Fieldways Cl. B47: H'wd 2A 162
Fifield Gro. B33: Yard 6D 104
Fifth Av. B9: Bord G 1F 119
  DY5: Brie H 6B 94
  WV10: Bush 2H 27
Filbert Vw. B29: W Cas 1E 145
Filey Rd. WV10: Oxl 5F 15
Fillingham Cl. B37: Chel W 2F 123
Fillongley Rd. CV7: Mer 4H 141
Filton Cft. B35: Cas V 3E 87
Fimbrell Cl. DY5: Brie H 3E 109
Finbury Cl. B92: Olton 4D 136
Finchall Cft. B92: Sol 6A 138
Finch Cl. B65: Row R 5H 95
Finch Cft. CV7: Bal C 2H 169
Finchdene Gro. WV3: Wolv 2B 42
Finch Dr. B74: S'tly 6A 52
Finches End B34: S End 4G 105
Finchfield Cl. DY8: Stourb 1A 124
Finchfield Gdns. WV3: Wolv 2C 42
Finchfield Hill WV3: Wolv 1A 42
  (not continuous)
Finchfield La. WV3: Wolv 3A 42
Finchfield Rd. WV3: Wolv 2C 42
Finchfield Rd. W. WV3: Wolv 2B 42
Finch Ho. DY4: Tip 2G 77
  (off Chapel St.)
Finchley Av. B19: Loz 1E 101
Finchley Cl. DY3: Lwr G 5H 75
Finchley Rd. B44: K'sdng 3B 68
Finchmead Rd. B33: Kitts G 2A 122
Finchpath Rd. B70: W Brom 1G 79
Finch Rd. B19: Loz 1E 101
Findlay Rd. B14: King H 4G 133
Findon Rd. B8: W End 3H 103
Finery Rd. WS10: Darl 6D 46
Finford Cft. CV7: Bal C 3H 169
Fingerpost Dr. WS3: Pels 2E 21
Finlarigg Dr. B15: Edg 5B 116
Finmere Rd. B28: Hall G 5F 135
Finmere Way B90: Shir 4B 150
Finnemore Rd. B9: Bord G 1G 119
Finney Well Cl. WV14: Cose 2D 60
Finsbury Dr. DY5: Brie H 4G 109
Finsbury Gro. B23: Erd 1D 84
Finstall Cl. B7: Birm 5A 102
  B72: W Grn 4A 70
Finwood Cl. B92: Sol 5A 138
Fir Av. B12: Bal H 6A 118
Firbank Cl. B30: B'ville 6A 132
Firbank Way WS3: Pels 5D 20
Firbarn Cl. B76: Walm 2B 70
Firbeck Gro. B44: K'sdng 4A 68
Firbeck Rd. B44: K'sdng 4A 68
Fir Cft. DY5: Brie H 3G 109
Fircroft B31: N'fld 5D 130
  B91: Sol 1D 150
  WV14: Bils 2A 62
Fircroft Ho. B37: Chel W 1C 122
Firecrest Cl. B23: Erd 6B 68
Fire Station Rd. B26: Birm A 6C 122
Fir Gro. B14: King H 2H 147
  DY8: Woll 5A 108
  WV3: Wolv 2E 43
Firhill Cft. B14: King H 5F 147
Firmstone Ct. DY8: Woll 4C 108
Firmstone St. DY8: Woll 4C 108
Firs, The B11: S'brk 5C 118
  CV7: Mer 4H 141
Firsbrook Cl. WV6: Wolv 4D 26
Firsbrook Ho. WV6: Wolv 4E 27
Firsby Rd. B32: Quin 6C 114
Firs Dr. B90: Shir 6G 149
Firs Farm Dr. B36: Hodg H 1D 104
Firsholm Cl. B73: Bold 6G 69
Firs La. B67: Smeth 4E 99

Firs Rd. DY6: K'wfrd 3C 92
Firs St. DY2: Dud 6F 77
First Av. B6: Witt 5H 83
  B9: Bord G 2E 119
  B29: S Oak 2D 132
  B76: Min 2E 87
  DY6: P'ntt 6E 75
  WS8: Bwnhls 5C 10
  WV10: Bush 3A 28
First Mdw. Piece B32: Quin 1C 130
Fir St. DY3: Sed 6D 58
Firsvale Rd. WV11: Wed 4H 29
Firs Wlk. WS7: Burn 1D 10
Firsway WV6: Tett 1G 41
Firswood Rd. B33: Sheld 2G 121
Firth Dr. B14: Yard W 2B 148
  B62: B'hth 3E 113
Firth Pk. Cres. B62: B'hth 3E 113
Fir Tree Cl. B44: Gt Barr 6G 67
Fir Tree Dr. DY3: Sed 6A 60
  WS5: Wals 1F 65
Fir Tree Gro. B73: Bold 4F 69
Fir Tree Rd. WV3: Wolv 3B 42
Firtree Rd. B24: Erd 4H 85
Fisher Cl. B45: Fran 5E 143
Fisher Rd. B69: O'bry 2A 98
  WS3: Blox 5F 19
Fishers Dr. B90: Dic H 4F 163
Fisher St. DY2: Dud 6F 77
  DY4: Tip 2D 78
  (Great Bridge)
  DY4: Tip 4A 78
  (Imex Bus. Pk.)
  DY5: Brie H 1F 109
  WV3: Wolv 3F 43
  WV13: W'hall 1C 46
FISHLEY 4A 20
Fishley Cl. WS3: Blox 3A 20
Fishley La. WS3: Blox, Lit Wyr 4B 20
Fishley Park Golf Range 1B 20
Fish Ponds Way B43: Gt Barr 2D 66
Fishpool Cl. B36: Hodg H 1A 104
Fistral Gdns. WV3: Wolv 4D 42
Fithern Cl. DY3: Up Gor 2A 76
Fitness First
  Brierley Hill 6A 94
  Mere Green 1H 53
  Smethwick 2E 115
  Solihull 2F 137
  Stirchley 5D 132
  Walsall Wood 3C 22
  Wednesbury 3E 63
  Wolverhampton 6C 170 (3H 43)
Fitters Mill Cl. B5: Edg 5G 117
Fitton Av. DY6: K'wfrd 4E 93
Fitzgerald Pl. DY5: Brie H 5F 109
Fitzguy Cl. B70: W Brom 6C 80
Fitzmaurice Rd. WV11: Wed 2H 29
Fitz Roy Av. B17: Harb 4D 114
Fitzroy Rd. B31: N'fld 4A 144
Five Flds. Rd. WV12: W'hall 4A 30
Five Oaks Rd. WV13: W'hall 3G 45
FIVE WAYS 2D 116
Five Ways B15: Birm 2D 116
  B33: Stech 1B 120
  DY3: Lwr G 4H 75
  DY5: Brie H 1H 109
  WV1: Wolv 5G 27
  WV3: Penn 4A 42
Five Ways Ct. DY3: Lwr G 4H 75
Five Ways Shop. Cen. B15: Birm 2D 116
Five Ways Station (Rail) 3D 116
Flackwell Rd. B23: Erd 6E 69
Fladbury Cl. DY2: Neth 6F 95
Fladbury Cres. B29: S Oak 4H 131
Fladbury Gdns. B19: Hand 1E 101
Fladbury Pl. B19: Loz 2E 101
Flamborough Cl. B34: Hodg H 2E 105
Flamborough Way WV14: Cose 6D 60
Flamingo Gdns. B23: Erd 6C 68
Flanders Dr. DY6: K'wfrd 1B 92
Flash La. WV4: Lwr P 3E 57
Flash Rd. B69: O'bry 2G 97
Flatlea B31: N'fld 3D 144
Flatts, The WS10: Darl 4E 47
Flavell Av. WV14: Cose 4F 61
Flavell Cl. B32: Bart G 4H 129

Flavells La. B25: Yard 3A 120
  DY3: Gorn .5F 75
Flavell St. DY1: Dud 1D 76
Flax Cl. B47: H'wd 4A 162
Flax Gdns. B38: King Nor 1B 160
Flaxhall St. WS2: Wals 3H 47
Flaxley Cl. B33: Stech 6D 104
Flaxley Parkway B33: Stech 5C 104
Flaxley Rd. B33: Kitts G, Stech 5B 104
Flaxton Gro. B33: Kitts G 5E 105
Flaxton Wlk. WV6: Wolv 4E 27
Flecknoe Cl. B36: Cas B 6G 87
Fledburgh Dr. B76: Walm 1B 70
Fleet St. B3: Birm 3B 4 (6E 101)
  WV14: Bils .6F 45
Fleetwood Gro. B26: Yard 2E 121
Fleetwood Ho. B13: Mose 1H 133
Fleming Pl. WS2: Wals 3G 31
Fleming Rd. B32: Quin 6B 114
  WS2: Wals .3G 31
                (not continuous)
Fleming Way B45: Redn 1G 157
Flemmynge Cl. WV8: Cod 3E 13
Fletcher Gro. B93: Know 5C 166
Fletcher Rd. WV12: W'hall 6D 18
Fletcher's La. WV13: W'hall 1C 46
Fletcher St. DY9: Lye 5B 110
Fletchers Wlk. B3: Birm 4B 4 (1E 117)
Fletton Gro. B14: King H 4A 148
Flinkford Cl. WS5: Wals 5H 49
Flint Grn. Rd. B27: A Grn 2H 135
Flintham Cl. B27: A Grn 2C 136
Flint Ho. WV1: Wolv 5G 27
               (off Lomas St.)
Flintway, The B33: Stech 5C 104
Floodgate St. B5: Birm 6H 5 (2H 117)
Flood St. DY2: Dud 1F 95
Flood St. Island DY2: Dud 1F 95
Flora Rd. B25: Yard 4H 119
Florence Av. B11: S'hll 5C 118
  B73: W Grn 6H 69
  WV4: Ett 1B 60
Florence Bldgs. B29: S Oak 3B 132
Florence Dr. B73: W Grn 6H 69
Florence Gro. B18: Win G 5A 100
  B71: W Brom 4C 64
Florence Pl. B12: Bal H 5A 118
          (off Ombersley Rd.)
Florence Rd. B14: King H 5H 133
  B21: Hand .1H 99
  B27: A Grn .1B 136
  B66: Smeth .5F 99
  B69: O'bry 2D 96
  B70: W Brom 6C 80
  B73: W Grn 6H 69
  DY4: Tip 6A 62
  WV8: Bilb 4A 14
Florence St. B1: Birm 6C 4 (2F 117)
  WS1: Wals .2E 49
Florian Gro. WS10: Darl 4E 47
Florida Way DY6: K'wfrd 3E 93
Florins, The B72: S Cold 6A 54
              (off High St.)
Flowerdale Cl. WV14: Cose 5D 60
Floyd Gro. CV7: Bal C 5H 169
Floyds La. WS4: Rus 3G 33
Floyer Rd. B10: Small H 2E 119
Flyford Cft. B29: W Cas 3D 130
Foden Rd. B42: Gt Barr 5C 66
Foel Gro. B14: King H 1C 144
Foinavon Cl. B65: Row R 3H 95
Fold, The B38: King Nor 6C 146
  WS10: Darl .5D 46
  WV4: Penn .1D 58
  WV5: Seis 3A 56
  WV8: Oaken 5D 12
Fold St. WV1: Wolv 4A 170 (2G 43)
Foldyard Cl. B76: Walm 5E 71
Foley Av. WV6: Tett 5A 26
Foley Chu. Cl. B74: S'tly 1A 52
Foley Ct. B74: S'tly 2H 51
Foley Dr. WV6: Tett 6A 26
Foley Gro. WV5: Wom 2E 73
Foley Ho. B68: O'bry 3H 113
Foley Rd. B8: W End 4H 103
  DY9: Pedm .3F 125
Foley Rd. E. B74: S'tly 2H 51

Foley Rd. W. B74: S'tly 2F 51
Foley St. WS10: W'bry 2G 63
Foley Wood Cl. B74: S'tly 2G 51
Foliot Flds. B25: Yard 3B 120
Folkes Rd. DY9: Lye 5C 110
Folkestone Cft. B36: Hodg H 1C 104
Folliott Rd. B33: Kitts G 6E 105
Follyhouse Cl. WS1: Wals 4D 48
Follyhouse La. WS1: Wals 4D 48
Fontley Cl. B26: Yard 2D 120
Fontwell Rd. WV10: F'hses 3H 15
Footherley La. WS14: Foot, Shen W 1F 37
FORDBRIDGE .6C 106
Fordbridge Rd. B37: K'hrst 5B 106
Fordbrook La. WS3: S'fld 5F 21
Forder Gro. B14: King H 5A 148
Forde Way Gdns. B38: King Nor 2H 159
Fordfield Rd. B33: Kitts G 5G 105
Fordham Gro. WV9: Pend 4E 15
Fordhouse La. B30: Stir 1D 146
Fordhouse Rd. WV10: Bush 6H 15
Fordhouse Rd. Ind. Est.
  WV10: Bush 1H 27
FORDHOUSES .4G 15
Fordraught La. B62: Roms 6B 142
Fordrift B75: S Cold 6G 55
Fordrift, The B37: Mars G 6C 122
Fordrough B25: Yard 4F 119
Fordrough, The B31: N'fld 6F 145
  B74: Four O 2G 53
  B90: Maj G .1B 162
Fordrough Av. B9: Bord G 6E 103
Fordrough La. B9: Bord G 6E 103
Fordrough St. B90: Maj G 2E 163
Ford St. B18: Hock 4D 100
  B67: Smeth .3D 98
  WS2: Wals .4A 48
  B35: Cas V .1H 103
Fordwater Rd. B74: S'tly 5H 51
Fore 1 B90: M'path 4F 165
Foredraft Cl. B32: Bart G 3A 130
Foredraft St. B63: Crad 6F 111
Foredrove La. B92: Sol 1A 152
Forest Av. WS3: Blox 2B 32
Forest Cl. B66: Smeth 2C 98
  B74: S'tly 4G 51
Forest Ct. B13: Mose 2A 134
  B93: Dorr 6B 166
  WV12: W'hall 1C 30
Forest Dale B45: Redn 3H 157
Forest Dr. B17: Harb 5H 115
  B64: Old H .1H 111
Foresters Fold DY3: Lwr G 3G 75
Foresters Way B75: R'ley 6C 38
Forest Ga. WV12: W'hall 1D 30
Forest Glade WS6: C Hay 3F 7
Forest Hill Rd. B26: Sheld 6G 121
Forest La. WS2: Wals 4B 32
Forest Pk. B76: Walm 1C 70
Forest Pl. WS3: Wals 3C 32
Fore St. B2: Birm 4E 5 (1G 117)
Forest Rd. B13: Mose 2A 134
  B25: Yard 5A 120
  B68: O'bry 4A 114
  B93: Dorr 6C 166
  DY1: Dud 3E 77
Forest Way B47: H'wd 3B 162
  WS6: Gt Wyr 4G 7
Forfar Wlk. B38: King Nor 5H 145
Forge, The B63: Crad 3D 110
Forge Cl. WS7: Hamm 1F 11
  WV8: Pend .6C 14
Forge Cft. B76: Walm 1F 87
Forge La. B20: Hand 6E 65
  B62: Hale 6C 112
  B64: Crad H 3D 110
  B71: W Brom 6E 65
  B74: Foot, Lit As 3C 36
  B76: Min 1F 87
  DY6: W Hth .1G 91
  WS9: A'rdge .4C 34
                (Mill La.)
  WS9: A'rdge .4C 34
           (St Mary's Way)
  WS14: Foot .1B 36
Forge Leys WV5: Wom 1E 73
Forge Mill Farm 1F 81

Forge Mill Lake (Nature Reserve) 1G 81
Forge Mills Pk. B46: Col 5H 89
Forge Rd. DY8: Stourb 5D 108
             (not continuous)
  WS3: Pels 2D 20
  WS10: Darl .5C 46
  WV12: W'hall 5C 30
Forgers Wlk. B42: Gt Barr 5D 66
Forge St. WS10: Darl 1E 63
Forge Trad. Est. B62: Hale 6C 112
Forge Valley Way WV5: Wom 1E 73
Forge Way B69: O'bry 3E 97
FORHILL 5C 160
Forhill Ho. B38: Forh 5B 160
Forhill Mnr. B38: Forh 6B 160
Forman's Rd. B11: S'hll 2D 134
Forman Trad. Est. B11: S'hll 2D 134
Formby Av. WV6: Pert 5D 24
Formby Way WS3: Blox 4G 19
Forrell Gro. B31: Longb 2F 159
Forrest Av. WV11: Ess 3A 18
Forrester St. WS2: Wals 1A 48
Forrester St. Pct. WS2: Wals 1A 48
Forster St. B7: Birm 6A 102
  B67: Smeth .2C 98
Forsythia Cl. B31: N'fld 5D 130
Forsythia Gro. WV8: Bilb 4H 13
Fort Centre, The 5F 87
Fort Cres. WS9: Wals W 4C 22
Fort Dunlop B24: Erd 6B 86
Forth Dr. B37: F'bri 5D 106
Forth Gro. B38: King Nor 1A 160
Forth Way B62: B'hth 3E 113
Fort Ind. Park, The B35: Cas V 6C 86
Fortnum Cl. B33: Kitts G 1H 121
Forton Cl. WV6: Tett 1H 41
Fort Parkway B24: Erd 1H 103
  B35: Cas V .1H 103
Fort Shop. Pk., The B24: Erd 6H 85
Forum B40: Nat E C 2G 139
Forward Rd. B26: Birm A 2C 138
Fosbrooke Rd. B10: Small H 3G 119
Fosseway Dr. B23: Erd 5E 69
Fossil Dr. B45: Redn 2G 157
Foster Av. WV14: Cose 4D 60
Foster Gdns. B18: Hock 3B 100
Foster Grn. WV6: Pert 6E 25
Foster Pl. DY8: Woll 5C 108
Foster Rd. WV10: Bush 3A 28
Foster St. DY8: Stourb 6E 109
  WS3: Blox 1B 32
  WS10: Darl .4D 46
Foster St. E. DY8: Stourb 6E 109
Foster Way B5: Edg 6E 117
             (not continuous)
Fotherley Brook Rd. WS9: A'rdge 4H 35
Foundry La. B66: Smeth 2G 99
  WS3: Pels 4C 20
Foundry Rd. B18: Win G 4A 100
  DY6: W Hth .1H 91
Foundry St. DY4: Tip 5G 61
  DY6: W Hth .1A 92
  WV14: Bils 1A 62
  WV14: Cose .4E 61
Fountain Arc. DY1: Dud 6E 77
Fountain Cl. B31: Longb 3C 158
Fountain Ct. B4: Birm 2E 5
  B66: Smeth .5E 99
Fountain Ho. B63: Hale 2B 128
Fountain La. B69: O'bry 6F 79
  DY4: Tip 5F 61
  WV14: Cose .5F 61
Fountain Rd. B17: Edg 2F 115
Fountains Rd. WS3: Blox 5E 19
Fountains Way WS3: Blox 5E 19
Four Acres B32: Quin 1A 130
Four Ashes Golf Range 6H 165
Four Ashes Rd. B93: Ben H, Dorr 6H 165
Four Crosses Rd. WS4: S'fld 6G 21
Four Dwellings Leisure Cen. 1H 129
Fourlands Av. B72: W Grn 6B 70
Fourlands Rd. B31: N'fld 1C 144
FOUR OAKS 6E 37
Four Oaks Comn. Rd. B74: Four O 6E 37
Four Oaks Ct. B74: Four O 2H 53
FOUR OAKS PARK 3H 53
Four Oaks Rd. B74: Four O 1G 53

Four Oaks Station (Rail) 3H 53
Four Stones Cl. B91: Sol 6E 151
Four Stones Gro. B5: Edg 5G 117
Fourth Av. B9: Bord G 1F 119
  B29: S Oak 2E 133
  WS8: Bwnhls 4C 10
  (not continuous)
  WV10: Bush 3H 27
Fourways B64: Crad H 2F 111
Four Winds Rd. DY2: Dud 3G 95
Fowey Cl. B76: Walm 6E 71
Fowey Rd. B34: Hodg H 3D 104
Fowgay Dr. B91: Sol 6D 150
Fowler Cl. B66: Smeth 1E 99
  WV6: Pert 3E 25
Fowler Rd. B75: S Cold 6E 55
Fowler St. B7: Nech 4B 102
  WV2: Wolv 5G 43
Fowlmere Rd. B42: Gt Barr 5D 66
Fox & Goose Shop. Cen.
  B8: W End 4A 104
Foxbury Dr. B93: Dorr 6C 166
Fox Cl. B75: S Cold 4D 54
FOXCOTE 2C 126
Foxcote Av. B21: Hand 2A 100
Foxcote Cl. B90: Shir 1B 164
Foxcote Dr. B90: Shir 1B 164
Foxcote La. B63: Crad 2D 126
Fox Cres. B11: S'hll 1D 134
Foxdale Dr. DY5: Brie H 6F 93
Foxdale Gro. B33: Kitts G 1G 121
Foxes Mdw. B30: King Nor 3B 146
  B76: Walm 5E 71
Foxes Ridge B64: Crad H 3G 111
Foxes Way CV7: Bal C 3H 169
Foxfield B31: N'fld 3D 144
Foxfield Dr. DY8: Stourb 2E 125
Fox Foot Dr. DY5: Brie H 5G 93
Foxford Cl. B36: Cas B 6H 87
  B72: W Grn 6B 70
Foxglove Cl. B27: A Grn 4H 135
  WS3: Pels 2E 21
  WV11: Wed 4G 29
Foxglove Cres. B37: K'hrst 6A 106
Foxglove Rd. DY1: Dud 3B 76
Foxglove Way B21: Hand 2H 99
  B23: Erd .6B 68
Fox Grn. Cres. B27: A Grn 4G 135
Fox Gro. B27: A Grn 3G 135
Fox Hill B29: S Oak 5C 131
Fox Hill Cl. B29: S Oak 5G 131
Fox Hill Rd. B75: R'ley 1C 54
  (not continuous)
Foxhills Pk. DY2: Neth 5E 95
Foxhills Rd. DY8: Word 2B 108
  WV4: Penn 2A 58
Foxhollies Dr. B63: Hale 1G 127
Fox Hollies Leisure Cen. 4G 135
Fox Hollies Rd. B27: A Grn 2H 135
  B28: Hall G 6F 135
  B76: Walm 5D 70
  (not continuous)
Fox Hollow WV6: Tett 1A 42
Fox Hollow Cl. B45: Redn 2A 158
Foxhope Cl. B38: King Nor 5E 147
Foxhunt Rd. B63: Hale 3G 127
Foxland Av. B45: Redn 2A 158
  WS6: Gt Wyr 2G 7
Foxland Cl. B37: Chel W 1F 123
  B90: Ches G 5B 164
Foxlands Av. WV4: Penn 2B 58
Foxlands Cres. WV4: Penn 2A 58
Foxlands Dr. B72: W Grn 6B 70
  DY3: Up Gor 2H 75
  WV4: Penn 2A 58
Foxlea Rd. B63: Hale 4F 127
Foxley Dr. B91: Cath B 2D 152
Foxmeadow Cl. DY3: Sed 6A 60
Fox Mill Est. B11: S'hll 2D 134
Foxoak Ent. Cen. *B64: Crad H* 2F 111
  (off Foxoak St.)
Foxoak St. B64: Crad H 3E 111
Fox's La. WV1: Wolv 5G 27
Fox St. B5: Birm 3G 5 (6H 101)
  DY1: Dud 1E 77

Foxtail Wlk. B5: Edg 4F 117
Foxton Rd. B8: Salt 4F 103
Fox Wlk. WS9: Wals W 4D 22
Foxwell Gro. B9: Bord G 6A 104
Foxwell Rd. B9: Bord G 6H 103
Foxwood Av. B43: Gt Barr 3D 66
Foxwood Gro. B37: K'hrst 4B 106
Foxyards Rd. DY4: Tip 2F 77
Foyle Rd. B38: King Nor 6A 146
Fozdar Cres. WV14: Cose 4D 60
Fradley Cl. B30: King Nor 3H 145
Framefield Dr. B91: Sol 1A 152
Framlingham Gro. WV6: Pert 6G 25
Frampton Cl. B30: B'vlle 6H 131
  B37: Chel W 6F 107
Frampton Way B43: Gt Barr 1F 67
Frances Dr. WS3: Blox 1H 31
Frances Rd. B19: Loz 1E 101
  B23: Erd 4D 84
  B30: King Nor 2C 146
Franchise Gdns. WS10: W'bry 5F 47
Franchise St. B42: P Barr 5G 83
  WS10: W'bry 6E 47
Francis Cl. B74: S'tly 3H 51
  DY6: K'wfrd 1B 92
Francis Rd. B16: Edg 2C 116
  B25: Yard 5G 119
  B27: A Grn 6B 120
  B33: Stech 1B 120
  B67: Smeth 4B 98
  DY8: Woll 6A 108
Francis St. B7: Birm 5A 102
  B70: W Brom 6B 80
  WV1: Wolv 5G 27
Francis Wlk. B31: Longb 2E 159
Francis Ward Cl. B71: W Brom 5G 63
Frankburn Rd. B74: S'tly 3G 51
Frank Fisher Way
  B70: W Brom 5A 80
Frankfort St. B19: Hock 3F 101
Frankholmes Dr. B90: M'path 3D 164
FRANKLEY 2H 143
Frankley Av. B62: Quin 6F 113
FRANKLEY BEECHES 3G 143
Frankley Beeches Rd.
  B31: Longb, N'fld 5A 144
Frankley Community Leisure Cen. . .6F 143
FRANKLEY GREEN 2G 143
Frankley Grn. B32: Fran 2D 142
Frankley Grn. La. B32: Fran 2E 143
FRANKLEY HILL 4F 143
Frankley Hill La. B32: Fran 4F 143
Frankley Hill Rd. B45: Fran 4F 143
Frankley Ind. Pk. B45: Fran 5H 143
Frankley La. B31: N'fld 1B 144
  B32: Bart G, N'fld 1A 144
Frankley Lodge Rd. B31: Fran 3B 144
Frankley Rd. B68: O'bry 3H 113
FRANKLEY SERVICE AREA 6F 129
Frankley Ter. B17: Harb 6F 115
Franklin Cl. B47: Wyt 5C 162
Franklin Rd. B30: B'vlle 2A 146
Franklin St. B18: Win G 4A 100
Franklin Way B30: B'vlle 1B 146
Franklyn Cl. WV6: Pert 4E 25
Frank Rd. B67: Smeth 3C 98
Frank St. B12: Birm 4H 117
Franks Way B33: Stech 1C 120
Frayne Av. DY6: K'wfrd 2A 92
Freasley Cl. B90: Shir 5B 150
Freasley Rd. B34: S End 3A 106
Freda Ri. B69: Tiv 1D 96
Freda Rd. B70: W Brom 6B 80
Freda's Gro. B17: Harb 6E 115
Frederick Rd. B6: Aston 1G 101
  B11: S'hll 1C 134
  B15: Edg 3D 116
  B23: Erd .5D 84
  B29: S Oak 3H 131
  B33: Stech 6B 104

Frederick Rd. B68: O'bry 4B 114
  B73: W Grn 3G 69
  WV11: Wed 4E 29
Fredericks Cl. DY8: Stourb 1C 124
Frederick St. B1: Birm 1A 4 (5E 101)
  B70: W Brom 3A 80
  WS2: Wals 1B 48
  WV2: Wolv 6B 170 (3G 43)
Frederick William St.
  WV13: W'hall 1B 46
Fred Smith Cl. WS10: W'bry 6H 47
Freeland Gro. DY6: K'wfrd 5D 92
Freeman Dr. B76: Walm 1D 70
Freeman Pl. WV14: Bils 3G 45
Freeman Rd. B7: Nech 3B 102
  WS10: W'bry 2A 64
Freeman St. B5: Birm 4F 5 (1G 117)
  WV10: Wolv 1B 44
Freemount Sq. B43: Gt Barr 6A 66
Freer Rd. B6: Aston 1F 101
Freer St. WS1: Wals 1C 48
Freeth Rd. WS8: Bwnhls 4C 10
Freeth St. B16: Birm 1B 116
  B69: O'bry 1F 97
Freezeland St. WV14: Bils 5D 44
Fremantle Dr. B34: S End 3A 106
Fremont Dr. DY1: Dud 4A 76
French Rd. DY2: Dud 6G 77
French Walls B66: Smeth 4G 99
Frensham Cl. B37: Chel W 1E 123
  WS6: C Hay 1E 7
Frensham Way B17: Harb 5G 115
Frenshaw Gro. B44: Gt Barr 5H 67
Freshwater Dr. DY5: Brie H 3F 109
Friardale Cl. WS10: W'bry 2B 64
FRIAR PARK 3A 64
Friar Pk. Farm WS10: W'bry 1B 64
Friar Pk. Rd. WS10: W'bry 2A 64
Friars, The B28: Hall G 1E 149
Friars Cl. DY8: Word 6A 92
Friars Gorse DY7: Stourt 4A 108
Friar St. WS10: W'bry 2H 63
Friars Wlk. B37: Chel W 1F 123
Friary Av. B90: M'path 3E 165
Friary Cl. B20: Hand 4B 82
Friary Cres. WS4: Rus 3G 33
Friary Dr. B74: Four O 6F 37
Friary Gdns. B21: Hand 5H 81
Friary Rd. B20: Hand 5A 82
Friday Bri. B1: Birm 6A 4
Friday La. B92: Cath B, H Ard 2E 153
Friesland Dr. WV1: Wolv 6D 28
Friezeland Rd. WS2: Wals 1H 47
Friezland La. WS8: Bwnhls 2B 22
Friezland Way WS8: Bwnhls 2C 22
Frinton Gro. B21: Hand 2G 99
Friston Av. B16: Birm 2D 116
Frobisher Cl. WS6: Gt Wyr 4F 7
Frobisher Rd. B66: Smeth 2B 98
Frodesley Rd. B26: Sheld 3F 121
Froggatt Rd. WV14: Bils 4F 45
Froggatts Ride B76: Walm 2D 70
Frog Hall Cotts. DY7: I'ley 2A 124
Fog La. CV7: Bal C 4G 169
Frogmill Rd. B45: Fran 6H 143
Frogmoor Ho. B25: Yard 4C 120
Frogmore La. CV8: Fen E 6F 169
Frome Cl. DY3: Lwr G 5H 75
Frome Dr. WV11: Wed 1E 29
Frome Way B14: King H 1E 147
Frost St. WV2: Ett 5C 44
Froxmere Cl. B91: Sol 1F 165
Froyle Cl. WV6: Tett 4A 26
Froysell St. WV13: W'hall 1B 46
Fryer Rd. B31: Longb 2F 159
Fryer's Cl. WS3: Blox 2H 31
Fryer's Rd. WS2: Wals 3G 31
  WS3: Blox 3G 31
Fryer St.
  WV1: Wolv 2C 170 (1H 43)
Fuchsia Dr. WV9: Pend 4D 14
Fugelmere Cl. B17: Harb 4D 114
Fulbrook Gro. B29: W Cas 5D 130
Fulbrook Rd. DY1: Dud 6C 76
Fulford Cl. B47: Wyt 4C 162
Fulford Dr. B76: Min 2F 87
Fulford Gro. B26: Sheld 5G 121

Fulford Hall Rd. B90: Tid G 6D 162
  B94: Earls 6D 162
FULFORD HEATH 6D 162
Fulford Heath Golf Course 6B 162
Fulham Rd. B11: S'hll 6B 118
FULLBROOK 5D 48
Fullbrook Cl. B90: M'path 4E 165
Fullbrook Rd. WS5: Wals 6C 48
Fullelove Rd. WS8: Bwnhls 6C 10
Fullerton Cl. WV8: Pend 6C 14
Fullwood Cres. DY2: Dud 3A 94
Fullwoods End WV14: Cose 4E 61
Fulmer Wlk. B18: Hock 6C 100
Fulwell Gro. B44: K'sdng 6A 68
Fulwell M. B37: Mars G 3D 122
Fulwood Av. B62: B'hth 3F 113
Funky Monkeys
  Birmingham 6B 86
Furber Pl. DY6: K'wfrd 3D 92
Furlong, The WS10: W'bry 6E 47
Furlong Ct. B63: Crad 5E 111
Furlong La. B63: Crad 5E 111
Furlong Mdw. B31: N'fld 5G 145
Furlongs, The DY8: Stourb 2F 125
  WV11: Wed 4D 28
Furlongs Rd. DY3: Sed 1H 75
Furlong Wlk. DY3: Lwr G 3H 75
Furnace Cl. WV5: Wom 2E 73
Furnace Coppice B63: Hale 5B 112
Furnace Hill B63: Hale 5B 112
Furnace La. B63: Hale 6B 112
Furnace Pde. DY4: Tip 1G 77
Furnace Rd. DY2: Dud 1E 95
Furness Cl. WS3: Blox 4F 19
Furst St. WS8: Bwnhls 5C 10
Furzebank Way WV12: W'hall 5E 31
Furze Way WS5: Wals 3A 50

G

Gables, The B24: Erd 3B 86
  DY6: W Hth 1H 91
  WV5: Try 4C 56
  WV11: Ess 3A 18
Gaddesby Rd. B14: King H 5H 133
Gadds Dr. B65: Row R 5D 96
Gadsby Av. WV11: Wed 2A 30
Gads Grn. DY2: Neth 4G 95
Gads Grn. Cres. DY2: Dud 3G 95
Gads La. B70: W Brom 5G 79
  DY1: Dud 6E 77
Gadwall Cft. B23: Erd 4B 84
Gaiety Ho. B66: Smeth 4E 99
             (off Regent St.)
Gail Cl. WS9: Wals W 3D 22
Gailey Cft. B44: Gt Barr 2G 67
Gail Pk. WV3: Wolv 4B 42
Gainford Cl. WV8: Pend 6D 14
Gainford Rd. B44: K'sdng 4C 68
Gainsborough Cres. B43: Gt Barr .6F 51
  B93: Know 3C 166
Gainsborough Dr. WV6: Pert 5F 25
Gainsborough Hill DY8: Stourb ...2D 124
Gainsborough Pl. DY1: Dud 5A 76
Gainsborough Rd. B42: Gt Barr ...1D 82
Gainsborough Trad. Est. DY9: Lye .1G 125
Gainsford Dr. B62: Hale 5B 112
Gains La. WS3: Lit Wyr 3A 8
  WS11: Lit Wyr 3A 8
Gairloch Rd. WV12: W'hall 6B 18
Gaitskell Ter. B69: Tiv 5D 78
Gaitskell Way B66: Smeth 2D 98
Gala Bingo
  Great Park 6H 143
  Harborne 6G 115
  Stockland Green 2D 84
  Tower Hill 1D 82
  Tyburn 4C 86
  Walsall 2B 48
  Wednesbury 4F 47
  Wednesfield 2A 30
  Wolverhampton 1H 27
Gala Casino
  Birmingham 5D 4 (1F 117)
Galahad Way WS10: W'bry 3G 63
Galbraith Cl. WV14: Cose 5F 61

Galena Way B6: Aston 3G 101
Galeno Pl. B36: Cas B 6C 88
Gale Wlk. B65: Row R 4H 95
Gallagher Ct. B13: Mose 3B 134
          (off Wake Grn. Pk.)
Gallery, The WV1: Wolv ...4B 170 (2G 43)
Gallery Sq. WS2: Wals 1B 48
Galloway Av. B34: Hodg H 3D 104
Galton Cl. B24: Erd 3D 86
  DY4: Tip 1C 78
Galton Dr. B43: Gt Barr 4B 66
  DY2: Dud 3D 94
Galton Rd. B67: Smeth 1D 114
Galton Twr. B1: Birm 4A 4 (1E 117)
Galton Valley Canal Heritage Cen. .2D 98
Gamesfield Grn. WV3: Wolv 2D 42
Gammage St. DY2: Dud 1D 94
Gandy Rd. WV12: W'hall 3A 30
Gannah's Farm Cl. B76: Walm 2D 70
Gannaway B93: Know 5D 166
GANNOW GREEN 6D 142
Gannow Grn. La. B45: Rub 6C 142
Gannow Mnr. Cres. B45: Fran 5E 143
Gannow Mnr. Gdns. B45: Fran 6F 143
Gannow Rd. B45: Rub 2E 157
Gannow Shop. Cen. B45: Fran 6E 143
Gannow Wlk. B45: Rub 2E 157
Ganton Rd. WS3: Blox 3G 19
Ganton Wlk. WV8: Pend 1D 26
Garden Cl. B8: W End 4G 103
  B45: Fran 5G 143
  B93: Know 3B 166
Garden Ct. B16: Birm 2D 116
       (off Ladywood Middleway)
Garden Cres. WS3: Pels 4D 20
Garden Cft. WS9: A'rdge 2D 34
Gardeners Wlk. B91: Sol 4G 151
Gardeners Way WV5: Wom 3F 73
Garden Gro. B20: Hand 1A 82
Gardens, The B23: Erd 4E 85
  B72: W Grn 4H 69
Garden St. WS2: Wals 6C 32
Garden Wlk. DY2: Dud 6E 77
  DY3: Gorn 5G 75
        (not continuous)
  WV14: Bils 5H 45
Garfield Rd. B26: Sheld 3F 121
Garland Cres. B62: B'hth 3E 113
Garlands, The WV11: Wed 2E 29
Garland St. B9: Birm 6C 102
Garland Way B31: N'fld 2F 145
        (not continuous)
Garman Cl. B43: Gt Barr 3A 66
Garner Cl. WV14: Cose 2F 61
Garnet Av. B43: Gt Barr 1D 66
Garnet Cl. WS9: Ston 3G 23
Garnet Ct. B92: Olton 4D 136
Garnett Dr. B75: S Cold 5C 54
Garrard Gdns. B73: S Cold 6H 53
Garratt Cl. B68: O'bry 5A 98
Garratt's La. B64: Old H 1H 111
Garratt St. B71: W Brom 2H 79
  DY5: Brie H 4A 94
Garret Cl. DY6: K'wfrd 1B 92
GARRETT'S GREEN 2G 121
Garrett's Grn. Ind. Est.
  B33: Sheld 2G 121
Garretts Grn. La. B26: Sheld 4D 120
  B33: Sheld 3F 121
Garretts Wlk. B14: King H 5G 147
Garrick Cl. DY1: Dud 4B 76
Garrick St. WV1: Wolv 4C 170 (2H 43)
Garrington St. WS10: Darl 4C 46
Garrison Centre, The B9: Birm 1B 118
Garrison Cir. B9: Birm 1A 118
Garrison Ct. B9: Birm 1B 118
       (off Barwell Rd.)
Garrison La. B9: Birm, Bord G 1B 118
Garrison St. B9: Birm 1B 118
Garston Way B43: Gt Barr 5H 65
Garth, The B14: Yard W 3D 148
Garway Gro. B25: Yard 5H 119
Garwood Rd. B26: Yard 1D 120
Gas St. B1: Birm 5A 4 (1E 117)
Gatacre St. DY3: Gorn 4H 75
Gatcombe Cl. WV10: Bush 3B 16
Gatcombe Rd. DY1: Dud 5A 76

Gatehouse Fold DY2: Dud 6F 77
       (off Birmingham St.)
Gatehouse Trad. Est. WS8: Bwnhls ...4D 10
Gate La. B73: Bold 3F 69
  B93: Dorr 5F 165
  B94: H'ley H 5F 165
Gateley Rd. B68: O'bry 4C 114
Gate St. B8: Salt 4D 102
  DY3: Sed 6A 60
  DY4: Tip 5A 78
Gateway, The DY5: Brie H 5B 94
Gatis St. WV6: Wolv 5E 27
Gatwick Rd. B35: Cas V 3G 87
Gauden Rd. DY9: W'cte 4H 125
Gavin Way B6: Witt 3H 83
Gawne La. B64: Old H 6H 95
Gaydon Cl. WV6: Pert 4E 25
Gaydon Gro. B29: S Oak 3E 131
Gaydon Pl. B73: S Cold 1H 69
Gaydon Rd. B92: Sol 2H 137
  WS9: A'rdge 5C 34
Gayfield Av. DY5: Brie H 2H 109
GAY HILL 2E 161
Gay Hill Golf Course 1A 162
Gayhill La. B38: Head H 6D 146
Gayhurst Dr. B25: Yard 3C 120
Gayle Gro. B27: A Grn 5A 136
Gayton Rd. B71: W Brom 1B 80
Geach St. B19: Hock 3F 101
Geach Twr. B19: Birm 4F 101
       (off Uxbridge St.)
Gedney Cl. B90: Shir 4C 148
Geeson Cl. B35: Cas V 3F 87
Gee St. B19: Hock 3F 101
Gem Ho. B4: Birm 1G 5 (6H 101)
Gems Sports Hall 2G 5
Gem Vs. B11: S'brk 4C 118
Geneva Rd. DY4: Tip 2F 77
Genge Av. WV4: Ett 1A 60
Genners App. B31: N'fld 5B 130
Genners La. B31: N'fld 6B 130
  B32: Bart G, N'fld 5A 130
Genthorn Cl. WV4: Ett 1B 60
Gentian B74: Four O 5F 37
Gentian Cl. B31: N'fld 1D 144
Gentleshaw La. B91: Sol 5B 152
Geoffrey Cl. B76: Walm 6F 71
Geoffrey Pl. B11: S'hll 2C 134
Geoffrey Rd. B11: S'hll 2C 134
  B90: Shir 4F 149
George Arthur Rd. B8: Salt 5D 102
George Av. B65: Row R 1D 112
George Bird Cl. B66: Smeth 3E 99
George Cl. DY2: Dud 1G 95
George Frederick Rd. B73: S'tly ...1A 68
George Henry Rd. DY4: Tip 6E 63
George Rd. B15: Edg 3D 116
  B23: Erd 3B 84
  B25: Yard 5G 119
  B29: S Oak 2A 132
  B43: Gt Barr 3B 66
  B46: Wat O 4E 89
  B63: Hale 1H 127
  B68: O'bry 1H 113
  B73: New O 4D 68
  B91: Sol 4G 151
  DY4: Tip 1F 77
  WV14: Cose 4F 61
George Rose Gdns. WS10: Darl 5C 46
George St. B3: Birm 3A 4 (6E 101)
  B12: Bal H 6G 117
  B19: Loz 2D 100
  B21: Hand 1G 99
  B70: W Brom 5B 80
  DY1: Dud 1D 76
  DY8: Word 2D 108
  WS1: Wals 2C 48
  WV2: Ett 4C 44
  WV2: Wolv 5C 170 (2H 43)
  WV13: W'hall 5A 30
George St. West B18: Hock 5C 100
George Wood Av. B69: O'bry 6D 78
Georgian Gdns. WS10: W'bry 2F 63
Georgina Av. WV14: Cose 2F 61
Geraldine Rd. B25: Yard 4H 119
Gerald Rd. DY8: Woll 4C 108
Geranium Gro. B9: Bord G 6F 103

Geranium Rd. DY2: Dud 1H 95
Gerardsfield Rd. B33: Kitts G 6H 105
Germander B74: Four O 4F 37
Germander Dr. WS5: Wals 2F 65
Gerrard Cl. B19: Loz 2F 101
Gerrard Rd. WV13: W'hall 2G 45
Gerrards Dr. B19: Loz 2F 101
Gerrard St. B19: Loz 2E 101
Gertrude Pl. B18: Hock 4C 100
Gervase Dr. DY1: Dud 4E 77
Geston Rd. DY1: Dud 1B 94
Gibbet Hill B69: Tiv 2A 96
Gibbet La. DY7: Kinv 1A 124
Gibbins Rd. B29: S Oak 4G 131
Gibbons Gro. WV6: Wolv 5D 26
Gibbons Hill Rd. DY3: Sed 3H 59
Gibbons Ind. Pk. DY6: K'wfrd 2E 93
Gibbon's La. DY5: P'ntt 2E 93
Gibbons Rd. B75: Four O 6H 37
  WV6: Wolv 5D 26
Gibbs Hill Rd. B31: Longb 6F 145
Gibb Sq. B9: Birm 6H 5 (2A 118)
Gibbs Rd. DY9: Lye 6C 110
Gibbs St. WV6: Wolv 5E 27
Gibb St. B9: Birm 6H 5 (2H 117)
GIB HEATH 3C 100
Gibson Dr. B20: Hand 1D 100
  B66: Smeth 3E 99
Gibson Rd. B20: Hand 1D 100
  WV6: Pert .6E 25
Gideon Cl. B25: Yard 5B 120
Gideons Cl. DY3: Up Gor 2H 75
Giffard Rd. WV1: Wolv 4D 44
  WV10: Bush 4A 16
Gifford Ct. DY5: Brie H 1H 109
  (off Hill St.)
Giffords Way B70: W Brom 6A 80
GIGGETTY .1E 73
Giggetty La. WV5: Wom 1E 73
Gigmill Way DY8: Stourb 1C 124
Gilbanks Rd. DY8: Woll 4B 108
Gilberry Cl. B93: Know 4C 166
Gilbert Av. B69: Tiv 2B 96
Gilbert Cl. WV11: Wed 2A 30
Gilbert Ct. WS4: Wals 5E 33
  (off Lichfield Rd.)
Gilbert Ent. Pk. WV12: W'hall 5B 30
Gilbert La. WV5: Wom 6H 57
Gilbert Rd. B66: Smeth 5F 99
GILBERTSTONE 4C 120
Gilbertstone Av. B26: Yard 6C 120
Gilbert St. DY4: Tip 5H 77
Gilbeys Cl. DY8: Word 2C 108
Gilby Rd. B16: Birm 1C 116
Gilchrist Dr. B15: Edg 3A 116
Gildas Av. B38: King Nor 6C 146
Giles Cl. B33: Stech 6C 104
  B92: Sol 6B 138
Giles Cl. Ho. B33: Stech 6C 104
Giles Hill DY8: Stourb 5E 109
Giles Rd. B68: O'bry 4H 97
Gilldown Pl. B15: Edg 4D 116
Gill Dr. B68: O'bry 4H 97
Gillespie Dr. B6: Aston 2H 101
Gillhurst Rd. B17: Harb 4F 115
Gillies Cl. B33: Stech 6B 104
Gilling Gro. B34: Hodg H 3E 105
Gillingham Cl. WS10: W'bry 6B 48
Gillity Av. WS5: Wals 3F 49
Gillity Cl. WS5: Wals 3F 49
Gillity Cl. WS5: Wals 4H 49
Gilliver Rd. B90: Shir 5H 149
Gillman Cl. B26: Sheld 1H 137
Gillott Cl. B91: Sol 4A 152
Gillott Rd. B16: Edg 2G 115
Gillows Cft. B90: M'path 2E 165
Gillscroft Rd. B33: Kitts G 5E 105
Gill St. B70: W Brom 6A 80
  DY2: Neth 5G 95
Gilmorton Cl. B17: Harb 4F 115
  B91: Sol 6G 151
Gilpin Cl. B8: W End 2A 104
Gilpin Cres. WS3: Pels 3E 21
Gilpins Cft. WS6: C Hay 4D 6
GILSON 6F 89
Gilson Dr. B46: Col 2F 107
Gilson Rd. B46: Col 6F 89

Gilson St. DY4: Tip 5C 62
Gilson Way B37: K'hrst 4C 106
Gilwell Rd. B34: S End 3A 106
Gimble Wlk. B17: Harb 3E 115
  (not continuous)
Gipsy Cl. CV7: Bal C 4H 169
Gipsy La. B23: Erd 2A 84
  CV7: Bal C .4H 169
  WV13: W'hall 2B 46
Girton Ho. B36: Cas B 1B 106
Gisborn Cl. B10: Small H 3B 118
GK Davies Trad. Est.
  B63: Crad 5C 110
Glade, The B26: Sheld 1H 137
  B74: S'tly 2G 51
  DY9: Lye 6A 110
  WV8: Pend 6C 14
Glades, The WS9: A'rdge 2D 34
Gladeside Cl. WS4: S'fld 1H 33
Gladstone Dr. B69: Tiv 5C 78
  DY8: Woll 6B 108
Gladstone Gro. DY6: K'wfrd 1B 92
Gladstone Rd. B11: S'brk 5B 118
  B23: Erd 4D 84
  B26: Yard 5B 120
  B93: Dorr 6H 167
  DY8: Woll 5B 108
Gladstone St. B6: Aston 1A 102
  B71: W Brom 1A 80
  WS2: Wals 5B 32
  WS10: Darl .5E 47
Gladys Rd. B25: Yard 4H 119
  B67: Smeth .1D 114
Gladys Ter. B67: Smeth 1E 115
Glaisdale Gdns. WV6: Wolv 4E 27
Glaisdale Rd. B28: Hall G 5G 135
Glaisedale Gro. WV13: W'hall 1C 46
Glaisher Dr. WV10: Wolv 3G 27
Glamis Rd. WV12: W'hall 2B 30
Glanville Dr. B75: Four O 5G 37
Glasbury Cft. B38: King Nor 2A 160
Glascote Cl. B90: Shir 3G 149
Glascote Gro. B34: S End 2G 105
Glaslyn Av. B65: Row R 1B 112
Glassford Dr. WV6: Tett 3C 26
Glasshouse, The B16: Birm 1D 116
Glasshouse Hill DY8: Stourb 2F 125
Glastonbury Cres. WS3: Blox 5E 19
Glastonbury Rd. B14: Yard W 3C 148
  B71: W Brom 4B 64
Glastonbury Way WS3: Blox 6E 19
Glaston Dr. B91: Sol 6E 151
Gleads Cft. B62: Quin 2G 129
Gleaston Wlk. WV1: Wolv 3E 45
Gleave Rd. B29: S Oak 4A 132
Glebe Dr. B73: Bold 4G 69
Glebe Farm Rd. B33: Stech 4E 105
Glebe Flds. B76: Curd 1D 88
Glebefields Rd. DY4: Tip 5A 62
Glebeland Cl. B16: Birm 2D 116
Glebe La. DY8: Stourb 1C 124
Glebe Pl. WS10: Darl 5B 46
Glebe Rd. B91: Sol 2H 151
  WV13: W'hall 3H 45
Glebe St. WS1: Wals 3C 48
Glebe Way CV7: Bal C 2G 169
Glenavon Rd. B14: King H 4H 147
Glen Cl. WS4: Wals 6E 33
Glencoe Rd. B16: Edg 5G 99
Glen Ct. WV3: Wolv 1C 42
  WV8: Cod 3G 13
Glencroft Rd. B92: Sol 1H 137
Glendale Cl. B63: Hale 1B 128
  WV3: Wolv 3A 42
Glendale Dr. B33: Stech 6D 104
  WV5: Wom 1G 73
Glendale Twr. B23: Erd 1H 85
Glendene Cres. B38: King Nor 2G 159
Glendon Dr. B43: Gt Barr 5H 65
Glen Devon Cl. B45: Fran 5G 143
Glendon Rd. B23: Erd 1D 84
Glendon Way B93: Dorr 6H 165
Glendower Rd. B42: P Barr 3E 83
  WS9: A'rdge .6D 22
Gleneagles Dr. B43: Gt Barr 2A 66
  B69: Tiv 2A 96
  B75: S Cold .4A 54

Gleneagles Rd. B26: Yard 3E 121
  WS3: Blox 4F 19
  WV6: Pert 4D 24
Glenelg Dr. DY8: Stourb 3F 125
Glenelg M. WS5: Wals 6H 49
Glenfern Rd. WV14: Cose 5C 60
Glenfield WV8: Pend 5C 14
Glenfield Cl. B76: Walm 2C 70
  B91: Sol 1G 165
Glenfield Gro. B29: S Oak 4C 132
Glengarry Cl. B32: Bart G 6H 129
Glengarry Gdns. WV3: Wolv 2D 42
Glenhill Dr. B38: King Nor 1C 160
Glenhurst Cl. WS2: Wals 6D 30
Glenmead Rd. B44: Gt Barr 5F 67
Glenmore Cl. WV3: Wolv 4C 42
Glenmore Dr. B38: King Nor 5H 145
Glen Pk. Rd. DY3: Gorn 5H 75
Glenpark Rd. B8: Salt 4E 103
Glen Ri. B13: Mose 1C 148
Glen Rd. DY3: Up Gor 1A 76
  DY8: Stourb .2D 124
Glenroyde B38: King Nor 2A 160
Glen Side B32: Bart G 3B 130
Glenside Av. B92: Sol 2G 137
Glenthorne Dr. WS6: C Hay 2E 7
Glenthorne Rd. B24: Erd 5G 85
Glentworth B76: Walm 3E 71
Glentworth Gdns. WV6: Wolv 4F 27
Glenville Dr. B23: Erd 2E 85
Glenwood Cl. DY5: Quar B 3H 109
Glenwood Dr. B90: Ches G 5B 164
Glenwood Ri. WS9: Ston 4F 23
Glenwood Rd. B38: King Nor 1H 159
Globe St. WS10: W'bry 4F 63
Gloucester Flats B65: Row R 5E 97
Gloucester Ho. WV1: Wolv 5G 27
  (off Lomas St.)
Gloucester Pl. WV13: W'hall 1D 46
Gloucester Rd. DY2: Neth 1F 111
  WS5: Wals 3F 49
  WS10: W'bry 2A 64
Gloucester St. B5: Birm 6E 5 (2G 117)
  WV6: Wolv 5F 27
Gloucester Way B37: Mars G 2C 122
Glover Cl. B28: Hall G 1F 149
Glover Rd. B75: S Cold 6D 54
Glovers Cft. B37: F'bri 6B 106
Glovers Fld. Dr. B7: Nech 2C 102
Glover's Rd. B10: Small H 3C 118
Glover St. B9: Birm 1A 118
  B70: W Brom 6B 80
Glovers Trust Homes B73: Bold 5F 69
Glyme Dr. WV6: Tett 4C 26
Glyn Av. WV14: Bils 2B 62
Glyn Dr. WV14: Bils 2B 62
Glyne Ct. B73: S Cold 6H 53
Glyn Farm Rd. B32: Quin 6A 114
Glynne Av. DY6: K'wfrd 5B 92
Glyn Rd. B32: Quin 5B 114
Glynside Av. B32: Quin 5B 114
Goals Soccer Cen.
  Birmingham 1E 103
  Perry Barr 2G 83
  Rowley Regis 1E 113
  Walsall 4B 46
Godrich Ho. B13: Mose 2A 134
Goffs Cl. B32: Bart G 2D 130
Goldborough Cl. WV14: Cose 2F 61
Goldby Dr. WS10: W'bry 1E 63
Gold Crest Cl. DY2: Neth 1F 111
Goldcrest Cft. B36: Cas B 1C 106
Goldcrest Dr. B69: O'bry 1E 97
Golden Cft. B20: Hand 6B 82
Goldencross Way DY5: Brie H 2F 109
GOLDEN END 3F 167
Golden End Dr. B93: Know 3F 167
Golden Hillock Rd.
  B10: Small H 4D 118
  B11: S'brk, Small H 6D 118
  DY2: Neth 6E 95
Golden Orchard B63: Hale 4B 112
Goldfinch Cl. B30: B'vlle 5H 131
Goldfinch Rd. DY9: W'cte 2G 125
Goldicroft Rd. WS10: W'bry 1G 63
Goldieslie Cl. B73: W Grn 3H 69

Goldieslie Rd.—Grant Ct.

Goldieslie Rd. B73: W Grn 3H 69
GOLDS GREEN 6E 63
Golds Hill Gdns. B21: Hand 2B 100
Golds Hill Rd. B21: Hand 1B 100
Golds Hill Way DY4: Tip 6D 62
Goldsmith Rd. B14: King H 5H 133
WS3: Blox 2C 32
Goldstar Way B33: Kitts G 1G 121
Goldthorn Av. WV4: Penn 5F 43
Goldthorn Cres. WV4: Penn 5E 43
Goldthorne Av. B26: Sheld 1G 137
GOLDTHORN HILL 5F 43
Goldthorn Hill WV2: Penn 5E 43
GOLDTHORN PARK 6H 43
Goldthorn Rd. WV2: Wolv 5F 43
Goldthorn Ter. WV2: Wolv 4F 43
Goldthorn Wlk. DY5: Brie H 3H 109
Golf Club Dr. WS1: Wals 5E 49
Golf La. WV14: Bils 4F 45
Golson Cl. B75: S Cold 5D 54
Gomeldon Av. B14: King H 4H 147
Gomer St. WV13: W'hall 1A 46
Gomer St. W. WV13: W'hall 1A 46
Gonville Ho. B36: Cas B 1B 106
Gooch Cl. DY8: Amb 5E 109
Gooch St. B5: Birm 3G 117
Gooch St. Nth. B5: Birm 2G 117
Goodall Gro. B43: Gt Barr 6G 51
Goodall St. WS1: Wals 2D 48
Goodby Rd. B13: Mose 2F 133
Goode Av. B18: Hock 4C 100
Goode Cl. B68: O'bry 5A 98
Goodeve Wlk. B75: S Cold 6F 55
Goodison Gdns. B24: Erd 2H 85
Goodleigh Av. B31: Longb 3C 158
Goodman Cl. B28: Hall G 1F 149
Goodman St. B1: Birm 6D 100
Goodrest Av. B62: Quin 6F 113
Goodrest Cft. B14: Yard W 3C 148
Goodrest La. B38: Head H 3B 160
Goodrich Av. WV6: Pert 6G 25
Goodrich Covert B14: King H 5E 147
Goodrich M. DY3: Up Gor 3A 76
Goodrick Way B7: Nech 3B 102
Goodway Ct. B4: Birm 1E 5 (off Shadwell St.)
Goodway Rd. B44: Gt Barr 5G 67
B92: Sol 2A 138
Goodwood Cl. B36: Hodg H 1B 104
Goodwood Dr. B74: S'tly 4H 51
Goodwyn Av. B68: O'bry 4B 114
Goodyear Av. WV10: Bush 1A 28
Goodyear Rd. B67: Smeth 1B 114
Goosemoor La. B23: Erd 6E 69
Gopsal St. B4: Birm 2H 5 (6A 102)
Gorcott La. B90: Dic H 4G 163
Gordon Av. B19: Loz 2F 101
B71: W Brom 5A 64
WV4: Ett 2B 60
Gordon Cl. B69: Tiv 5D 78
Gordon Ct. B33: Stech 6B 104
Gordon Cres. DY5: Brie H 4A 94
Gordon Dr. DY4: Tip 1C 78
Gordon Pl. WV14: Bils 6E 45
Gordon Rd. B17: Harb 5H 115
B19: Loz 1E 101
Gordon St. B9: Birm 1B 118 (off Garrison La.)
WS10: Darl 5D 46
WV2: Wolv 6D 170 (3H 43)
Gorey Cl. WV12: W'hall 1B 30
Gorge Rd. DY3: Sed 5A 60
WV14: Cose 5A 60
Gorleston Gro. B14: King H 5B 148
Gorleston Rd. B14: King H 5B 148
GORNALWOOD 4G 75
Gornal Wood Crematorium
DY3: Gorn 5G 75
Gorsebrook Rd. WV6: Wolv 4F 27
WV10: Wolv 4F 27
Gorse Cl. B29: W Cas 5E 131
B37: F'bri 1B 122
Gorse Farm Rd. B43: Gt Barr 5A 66
Gorse Farm Wood Nature Reserve 5B 66
Gorsefield Rd. B34: S End 4G 105
Gorse La. WV5: Try 1A 72
Gorsemoor Way WV11: Ess 4B 18
Gorse Rd. DY1: Dud 3C 76
WV11: Wed 1A 30
Gorsey La. B46: Col 5G 89
B47: Wyt 5A 162
WS3: Lit Wyr 3B 8
WS6: Gt Wyr 4F 7
Gorsey Way B46: Col 5G 89
WS9: A'rdge 4A 34
Gorsly Piece B32: Quin 1A 130
Gorstie Cft. B43: Gt Barr 5A 66
Gorsty Av. DY5: Brie H 6G 93
Gorsty Cl. B71: W Brom 5D 64
Gorsty Hayes WV8: Cod 4F 13
Gorsty Hill Rd. B65: B'hth 3B 112
Gorsymead Gro. B31: Longb 5A 144
Gorsy Rd. B32: Quin 1B 130
Gorton Cft. CV7: Bal C 2H 169
Gorway Cl. WS1: Wals 4D 48
Gorway Gdns. WS1: Wals 4E 49
Gorway Rd. WS1: Wals 4D 48
GOSCOTE 5C 20
Goscote Cl. WS3: Wals 2D 32
Goscote Ind. Est. WS3: Blox 6C 20
Goscote La. WS3: Blox, Wals 6C 20
Goscote Lodge Cres. WS3: Wals 2E 33
Goscote Pl. WS3: Wals 2E 33
Goscote Rd. WS3: Pels 6D 20
Gosford St. B12: Bal H 5H 117
Gosford Wlk. B92: Olton 4F 137
Gosmoor Ho. B26: Yard 4C 120
GOSPEL END 5E 59
Gospel End Rd. DY3: Sed 5E 59
Gospel End St. DY3: Sed 6H 59
Gospel Farm Rd. B27: A Grn 5H 135
Gospel La. B27: A Grn 6A 136
Gospel Oak Rd. DY4: Tip 4B 62
Gosport Cl. WV1: Wolv 4D 44
Goss, The DY5: Brie H 2H 109
Goss Cft. B29: S Oak 4H 131
Gossey La. B33: Kitts G 1G 121
Gosta Grn. B4: Birm 1G 5 (5H 101)
Gotham Rd. B26: Yard 5C 120
GOTHERSLEY 6E 91
Gothersley La. DY7: Stourt 6D 90
Goths Cl. B65: Row R 5C 96
Gough Av. WV11: Wed 1D 28
Gough Dr. DY4: Tip 2C 78
Gough Rd. B11: S'brk 6D 118
B15: Edg 4E 117
WV14: Cose 4E 61
Gough St. B1: Birm 6C 4 (2F 117)
WV1: Wolv 1A 44
WV13: W'hall 6C 30
Gould Firm La. WS9: A'rdge 3G 35
Gowan Rd. B8: Salt 5E 103
Gower Av. DY6: K'wfrd 5D 92
Gower Ho. B62: Quin 5F 113 (off Lockington Cft.)
Gower Rd. B62: Quin 5E 113
DY3: Sed 5F 59
Gower St. B19: Loz 2F 101
WS2: Wals 4H 47
WV2: Wolv 3A 44 (not continuous)
WV13: W'hall 1A 46
Gowshall Dr. B69: O'bry 3A 98
Gozzard St. WV14: Bils 6G 45
Gracechurch Shop. Cen.
B72: S Cold 6H 53
Gracemere Cres. B28: Hall G 4E 149
Grace Rd. B11: S'brk 4C 118
B69: Tiv 1C 96
DY4: Tip 6A 62
Gracewell Ct. B28: Hall G 2G 149
Gracewell Homes B13: Mose 4D 134
Gracewell Rd. B13: Mose 4D 134
Grafton Ct. B23: Erd 5C 84
WV6: Wolv 5D 26
Grafton Dr. WV13: W'hall 3F 45
Grafton Gdns. DY3: Lwr G 4F 75
Grafton Gro. B19: Loz 2E 101
Grafton Pl. WV14: Bils 4G 45
Grafton Rd. B11: S'brk 4B 118
B21: Hand 6H 81
B68: O'bry 2F 113
B71: W Brom 3B 80
B90: Shir 5C 148
Graham Cl. DY4: Tip 4B 62
Graham Cres. B45: Rub 2G 157
Graham Rd. B8: Salt 6F 103
B25: Yard 5A 120
B62: B'hth 3C 112
B71: W Brom 3B 80
DY8: Word 5B 92
Graham St. B1: Birm 2A 4 (6E 101)
B19: Loz 2E 101
Grainger Cl. DY4: Tip 1D 78
Graingers La. B64: Crad H 3E 111
Grainger St. DY2: Dud 2F 95
Graiseley Ct. WV3: Wolv 5A 170
Graiseley Hill WV2: Wolv 6A 170 (3G 43)
Graiseley La. WV11: Wed 4D 28
Graiseley Row WV2: Wolv 6A 170 (3G 43)
Graiseley St. WV3: Wolv 5A 170 (2F 43)
Graith Cl. B28: Hall G 4E 149
Grammar School La. B63: Hale 1A 128
Grampian Rd. DY8: Amb 5E 109
Granada Ind. Est. B69: O'bry 3F 97
Granary, The WS9: A'rdge 2D 34
Granary Cl. DY6: W Hth 1G 91
Granary La. B76: Walm 2D 70
Granary Rd. WV8: Pend 6C 14
Granbourne Rd. WS2: Wals 5D 30
Granby Av. B33: Sheld 2G 121
Granby Bus. Pk. B33: Sheld 2H 121
Granby Cl. B92: Olton 6C 136
Grandborough Dr. B91: Sol 6E 151
Grand Cl. B66: Smeth 6F 99
Grand Junc. Way WS1: Wals 5B 48
Grand Prix Karting 6C 102
Grand Theatre
Wolverhampton 3C 170 (1H 43)
Grandys Cft. B37: F'bri 6B 106
Grange, The B20: Hand 3B 82
B62: Quin 5F 113
WV5: Wom 6G 57
Grange Av. B8: W End 3H 103
B75: Four O 6A 38
WS9: A'rdge 5C 22
Grange Ct. DY1: Dud 6C 76
DY9: Lye 2G 125
WS2: Wals 1D 46
WV3: Wolv 2F 43
Grange Cres. B45: Rub 1E 157
B63: Hale 2B 128
WS4: S'fld 1F 33
Grange Dr. B74: S'tly 1H 51
GRANGE ESTATE 1G 125
Grange Farm Dr. B38: King Nor 6H 145
Grangefield Cl. WV8: Pend 6D 14
Grange Golf Course 2G 49
Grange Hill B62: Hale 3C 128
Grange Hill Rd. B38: King Nor 6A 146
Grange La. B75: R'ley 6A 38
DY6: K'wfrd 5D 92
DY9: Lye 2G 125
Grange Ri. B38: King Nor 2B 160
Grange Rd. B6: Aston 1G 101
B10: Small H 2D 118
B14: King H 5F 133
B24: Erd 2H 85
B29: S Oak 2B 132
B63: Hale 2B 128
B64: Old H 2A 112
B66: Smeth 6E 99
B70: W Brom 4H 79
B91: Sol 6C 136
B93: Dorr 6F 167
CV7: Bal C 2F 169
DY1: Dud 6D 76
DY9: Lye 1G 125
WV2: Wolv 5F 43
WV6: Tett 4A 26
WV14: Cose 6D 60
Grange St. DY1: Dud 6D 76
WS1: Wals 4D 48
Grange Wlk. B31: Longb 2G 159
Grangewood Ct. B73: Bold 6G 69
B92: Olton 6C 136
Granmore Ho. B90: Shir 6C 150
Granshaw Cl. B38: King Nor 6B 146
Grant Cl. B71: W Brom 2A 80
DY6: K'wfrd 1B 92
Grant Ct. B30: King Nor 2C 146

Grantham Rd. B11: S'brk 5B 118
  B66: Smeth 6F 99
Grantley Cres. DY6: K'wfrd 3A 92
Grantley Dr. B37: F'bri 6D 106
Granton Cl. B14: King H 2F 147
Granton Rd. B14: King H 2F 147
Grantown Gro. WS3: Blox 3G 19
Grant St. B15: Birm 3F 117
  WS3: Blox 1H 31
Granville Cl. WV2: Wolv 6D 170 (3H 43)
Granville Ct. B15: Birm 6A 4 (2E 117)
Granville Dr. DY6: K'wfrd 4D 92
Granville Rd. B64: Old H 3B 112
  B93: Dorr 6H 167
Granville Sq. B15: Birm 6A 4 (2E 117)
Granville St. B1: Birm 6A 4 (2E 117)
  WV2: Wolv 6D 170 (3H 43)
  WV13: W'hall 6A 30
Graphic Cl. WS1: Wals 3B 48
Grasdene Gro. B17: Harb 1G 131
Grasmere Av. B74: Lit As 1A 52
  WV6: Pert 6F 25
Grasmere Cl. B43: Gt Barr 6B 66
  DY6: K'wfrd 2H 91
  WV6: Tett 1C 26
  WV11: Wed 2E 29
Grasmere Ho. B69: O'bry 5D 96
Grasmere Rd. B21: Hand 2B 100
Grassington Dr. B37: F'bri 2B 122
Grassmere Ct. WS6: C Hay 2D 6
Grassmere Dr. DY8: Stourb 1D 124
Grassmoor Rd. B38: King Nor 5A 146
Grassy La. WV10: Wed 6D 16
Graston Cl. B16: Birm 1C 116
Gratham Cl. DY5: Brie H 4F 109
Grattidge Rd. B27: A Grn 3B 136
Gravel Bank B32: Bart G 2B 130
Gravel Hill WV5: Wom 1H 73
GRAVELLY HILL 5E 85
Gravelly Hill B23: Erd 6D 84
Gravelly Hill Nth. B23: Erd 5E 85
Gravelly Hill Station (Rail) 5E 85
Gravelly Ind. Pk. B24: Erd 1F 103
                 (Hanover Dr.)
  B24: Erd 1F 103
                  (Jarvis Way)
Gravelly La. B23: Erd 2F 85
  WS9: Ston 5G 23
Gravity M. B68: O'bry 6A 98
Graydon Ct. B74: S Cold 4H 53
Grayfield Av. B13: Mose 2A 134
Grayland Cl. B27: A Grn 3H 135
Grayling Cl. WS10: Mox 2B 62
Grayling Rd. DY9: Lye 5G 109
Grayling Wlk. B37: Chel W 6E 107
  WV10: Wolv 5D 28
Grayshott Cl. B23: Erd 2E 85
Grays Rd. B17: Harb 5H 115
Gray St. B9: Birm 1B 118
Grayswood Pk. Rd. B32: Quin 5A 114
Grayswood Rd. B31: Longb 2D 158
Grazebrook Cft. B32: Bart G 5B 130
Grazebrook Ind. Pk. DY2: Dud 3D 94
Grazebrook Rd. DY2: Dud 2E 95
Grazewood Cl. WV12: W'hall 1B 30
Greadier St. WV12: W'hall 4C 30
Gt. Arthur St. B66: Smeth 2D 98
GREAT BARR 1A 66
Gt. Barr Bus. Pk. B42: P Barr 2C 82
Great Barr Golf Course 1B 66
Great Barr Leisure Cen. 4F 67
Gt. Barr St. B9: Birm 1A 118
Gt. Brickkiln St. WV3: Wolv . . .5A 170 (2E 43)
GREAT BRIDGE 1E 79
Great Bridge DY4: Tip 2D 78
Gt. Bridge Cen., The B70: W Brom . . .2E 79
Gt. Bridge Ind. Est. DY4: Tip 6C 62
Gt. Bridge Rd. WV14: Bils 1A 62
Gt. Bridge St. B70: W Brom 2E 79
Gt. Bridge W. Ind. Cen. DY4: Tip 1D 78
Gt. Brook St. B7: Birm 1H 5 (5A 102)
Gt. Charles St. WS8: Bwnhls 5B 10
Gt. Charles St. Queensway
  B3: Birm 3C 4 (6F 101)
Gt. Colmore St. B15: Birm 3F 117
Great Cornbow B63: Hale 2B 128
              (not continuous)

Gt. Croft Ho. WS10: Darl 5D 46
         (off St Lawrence Way)
Gt. Farley Dr. B31: Longb 6A 144
Gt. Francis St. B7: Birm 5B 102
Gt. Gable Rd. B71: W Brom 1A 80
Gt. Hampton Row B19: Birm 5E 101
Gt. Hampton St. B18: Birm 4E 101
  WV1: Wolv 6F 27
            (not continuous)
Great Hill DY1: Dud 6D 76
Gt. King St. B19: Birm 4E 101
Gt. King St. Nth. B19: Hock 3E 101
Gt. Lister St. B7: Birm 5H 101
Gt. Moor Rd. WV6: Patt 1A 40
Gt. Oaks B26: Sheld 6F 121
Greatorex Ct. B71: W Brom 5H 63
GREAT PARK 6H 143
Gt. Stone Rd. B31: N'fld 4E 145
Gt. Tindal St. B16: Birm 1C 116
Gt. Western Arc. B2: Birm 3E 5 (6G 101)
Gt. Western Cl. B18: Win G 3A 100
Gt. Western Ct. B27: A Grn 1A 136
Gt. Western Dr. B64: Old H 2A 112
Gt. Western Ind. Est.
  B18: Win G 3A 100
Gt. Western St. WS10: W'bry 3E 63
  WV1: Wolv 1C 170 (6H 27)
Gt. Western Way DY4: Tip 1D 78
Gt. Wood Rd. B10: Small H 2C 118
GREAT WYRLEY 3E 7
Greaves, The B76: Min 1B 88
Greaves Av. WS5: Wals 4G 49
Greaves Cl. WS5: Wals 3G 49
Greaves Cres. WV12: W'hall 1C 30
Greaves Rd. DY2: Neth 4F 95
Greaves Sq. B38: King Nor 6D 146
Grebe Cl. B23: Erd 4B 84
Greek Cathedral 3A 4 (6D 100)
Green, The B23: Erd 2G 85
  B31: Longb 5A 144
  B32: Quin 5G 113
  B36: Cas B 2F 105
  B38: King Nor 5B 146
  B68: O'bry 1H 113
  B72: W Grn 4B 70
  B91: Sol .2H 151
  CV7: Mer 4H 141
  DY8: Word 1B 108
  WS3: Blox 6H 19
            (not continuous)
  WS6: Gt Wyr 5E 7
  WS9: A'rdge 3D 34
            (not continuous)
  WS10: Darl 4D 46
  WV5: Try 5C 56
Greenacre Dr. WV8: Bilb 5H 13
Greenacre Rd. DY4: Tip 4A 62
Green Acres B27: A Grn 3H 135
  WV5: Wom 2F 73
Greenacres B32: Bart G 4C 130
  B76: Walm 5E 71
  DY3: Sed 4F 59
  WV6: Tett 4H 25
Greenacres Av. WV10: Bush 5D 16
Greenacres Cl. WS9: A'rdge 1G 51
Green Acres Rd. D30: King Nor 1H 159
Greenaleigh Rd. B14: Yard W 3D 148
Green Av. B28: Hall G 4E 135
Greenaway Cl. B43: Gt Barr 2E 67
Greenaway Ct. WV10: F'stne 1E 17
          (off The Avenue)
Green Bank Av. B28: Hall G 4E 135
Greenbank Gdns. DY8: Word 1C 108
Greenbank Rd. CV7: Bal C 3H 169
Green Barns La. WS14: Lit H 1A 38
Greenbush Dr. B63: Hale 6A 112
Green Cl. B47: Wyt 6A 162
Green Ct. B24: Erd 5E 85
  B28: Hall G 5F 135
Greencft. B97: Bord G 6G 103
Greencroft DY6: K'wfrd 5B 92
  WV14: Bils 5F 45
Green Dr. B32: Bart G 4A 130
  WV10: Oxl 2G 27
Greenend Rd. B13: Mose 1H 133
Greenfels Ri. DY2: Dud 1H 95

Greenfield Av. B64: Crad H 2D 110
  CV7: Bal C 2G 169
  DY8: Stourb 6D 108
Greenfield Cres. B15: Edg 3C 116
Greenfield Cft. WV14: Cose 3F 61
Greenfield Ho. B26: Sheld 5A 122
Greenfield La. WV10: Bush, F'hses 2H 15
Greenfield Rd. B17: Harb 6G 115
  B43: Gt Barr 6G 65
  B67: Smeth 5C 98
Green Flds. WS9: A'rdge 2C 34
Greenfields Rd. DY6: K'wfrd 4B 92
  WS4: S'fld 5H 21
  WV5: Wom 2G 73
Greenfield Vw. DY3: Sed 6F 59
Greenfinch Cl. B36: Cas B 2C 106
Greenfinch Rd. B36: Cas B 1C 106
  DY9: W'cte 2H 125
Greenford Ho. B23: Erd 1B 84
  B70: W Brom 1C 98
            (off Maria St.)
Greenford Rd. B14: King H 4C 148
Green Gables B74: S Cold 4H 53
Green Gables Dr. B47: H'wd 2A 162
Greenhill WV5: Wom 1H 73
Green Hill Av. B14: King H 4H 133
Greenhill Cl. WV12: W'hall 4B 30
Greenhill Ct. WV5: Wom 2H 73
Greenhill Dr. B29: S Oak 4G 131
Greenhill Gdns. B43: Gt Barr 3A 66
  B62: Hale 5D 112
  WV5: Wom 2H 73
Greenhill Rd. B13: Mose 4H 133
  B21: Hand 5H 81
  B62: B'hth 4D 112
  B72: W Grn 5H 69
  DY3: Up Gor 2A 76
Greenhill Wlk. WS1: Wals 3D 48
Green Hill Way B90: Shir 2H 149
Greenholm Rd. B44: Gt Barr 6G 67
Greening Dr. B15: Edg 4C 116
Greenland Av. B31: N'fld 5E 145
Greenland Cl. DY6: K'wfrd 1C 92
Greenland Ct. B8: Salt 3E 103
Greenland Ri. B92: Sol 6H 137
Greenland Rd. B29: S Oak 4D 132
Greenlands WV5: Wom 6F 57
Greenlands Rd. B37: Chel W 1D 122
Green La. B9: Small H 2C 118
  B21: Hand 1G 99
  B32: Quin 5A 114
  B36: Cas B 1H 105
  B38: King Nor 1A 160
  B43: Gt Barr 5H 65
  B46: Col .4H 107
       (Castle Dr., not continuous)
  B46: Col .1D 106
           (Collector Rd.)
  B46: Col .5F 107
            (Drake Cft.)
  B62: B'hth 2D 112
  B62: Roms 1B 156
  B90: Shir 6E 149
  CV7: Bal C 2H 169
  DY3: Up Gor 2B 76
  DY6: K'wfrd 2B 92
  DY9: Lye 6H 109
  WS2: Wals 1B 48
  WS3: Blox, Wals 2A 32
  WS3: Pels 3E 21
  WS4: S'fld 6G 21
  WS7: Hamm 3C 10
  WS9: A'rdge 4G 35
  WS9: Wals W 6D 22
  WV6: Tett 2C 26
Green La. Ind. Est. B9: Bord G 2E 119
GREEN LANES 4E 45
Green Lanes B73: W Grn 4E 45
  WV14: Bils 4E 45
Green La. Wlk. B38: King Nor 1B 160
Greenlawns DY4: Tip 5B 62
Greenleas Gdns. B63: Hale 2C 128
Green Leigh B23: Erd 5F 69
Greenleighs DY3: Sed 2H 59
Greenly Rd. WV4: Ett 6H 43
Green Man Entry DY1: Dud 6F 77

Green Mdw. DY9: Pedm 5F 125
WV11: Wed 4G 29
Green Mdw. Cl. WV5: Wom 2E 73
Green Mdw. Rd. B29: W Cas 6E 131
WV12: W'hall 2B 30
Greenoak Cres. B30: Stir 5E 133
WV14: Cose 6C 60
Green Oak Rd. WV8: Bilb 5H 13
Greenock Cres. WV4: Ett 6A 44
Green Pk. Av. WV14: Bils 3E 45
Green Pk. Dr. WV14: Bils 3E 45
Green Pk. Rd. B31: N'fld 5C 144
DY2: Dud 1H 95
Greenridge Rd. B20: Hand 2A 82
Green Rd. B13: Mose 4D 134
B28: Hall G 4D 134
DY2: Dud 2F 95
Green Rock La. WS3: Blox 6B 20
Greenroyde DY9: Pedm 4F 125
Greens, The WV6: Pert 6E 25
(off Edge Hill Dr.)
Greensand Dr. WV14: Cose 3F 61
GREENSFORGE 3E 91
Greensforge La. DY7: Stourt 6E 91
Greens Health & Fitness Club
Great Park 1H 157
Greenside B17: Harb 6G 115
B90: Ches G 5B 164
Greenside Gdns. WS5: Wals 1F 65
Greenside Rd. B24: Erd 2A 86
Greenside Way WS5: Wals 1D 64
Greensill Av. DY4: Tip 5H 61
Greenslade Cft. B31: N'fld 5E 145
Greenslade Rd. B90: Shir 5C 148
DY3: Sed 3F 59
WS5: Wals 4G 49
Greensleeves B74: Four O 2G 53
Greenstead Rd. B13: Mose 4D 134
Green St. B12: Birm 6H 5 (2H 117)
B67: Smeth 4D 98
B69: O'bry 2G 97
B70: W Brom 6C 80
DY8: Stourb 6D 108
WS2: Wals 6A 32
WV14: Cose 5E 61
Greensway WV11: Wed 1D 28
Greenvale B31: N'fld 2D 144
Greenvale Av. B26: Sheld 5H 121
Green Wlk. B17: Harb 4D 114
Greenway B20: Hand 1B 82
DY3: Sed 4A 60
WS9: A'rdge 5D 22
Greenway, The B37: Mars G 5C 122
B73: S'tly 2B 68
Greenway Av. DY8: Word 2C 108
Greenway Dr. B73: S'tly 2B 68
Greenway Gdns. B38: King Nor 2A 160
DY3: Sed 4A 60
Greenway Rd. WV14: Bils 1G 61
Greenways B31: N'fld 5D 130
B63: Crad 6E 111
DY8: Word 2A 108
Greenway St. B9: Bord G 2C 118
Greenway Wlk. B33: Kitts G 2A 122
Green Wickets B14: King H 1H 147
Greenwood B25: Yard 3B 120
Greenwood Av. B27: A Grn 3G 135
B65: Row R 6D 96
B68: O'bry 4H 97
Greenwood Cl. B14: King H 2G 147
Greenwood Cotts. DY1: Dud 2C 76
(off Maple Grn.)
Greenwood Pk. WS9: A'rdge 5E 23
Greenwood Pl. B44: K'sdng 4B 68
Greenwood Rd. B71: W Brom 5H 63
WS9: A'rdge 5C 22
WV10: Oxl 2F 27
Greenwoods, The DY8: Stourb 6C 108
Greenwood Sq. B37: Chel W 1D 122
(within Chelmsley Wood Shop. Cen.)
Greenwood Way B37: Chel W 1D 122
(within Chelmsley Wood Shop. Cen.)
GREET .6D 118
Greethurst Dr. B13: Mose 3C 134
GREETS GREEN 4F 79
Greets Grn. Ind. Est. B70: W Brom 3F 79
Greets Grn. Rd. B70: W Brom 4F 79

Greetville Cl. B34: Stech 4E 105
Gregg Ct. B12: Bal H 1H 133
Gregory Av. B29: W Cas 5D 130
Gregory Cl. WS10: W'bry 3F 63
Gregory Ct. WV11: Wed 4F 29
Gregory Dr. DY1: Dud 5C 76
Gregory Rd. DY8: Woll 6A 108
Gregston Ind. Est. B69: O'bry 2H 97
Grendon Dr. B73: New O 2D 68
Grendon Gdns. WV3: Penn 5B 42
Grendon Rd. B14: King H 4A 148
B92: Olton 5C 136
Grenfell Ct. B72: W Grn 4H 69
Grenfell Dr. B15: Edg 3B 116
Grenfell Rd. WS3: Blox 4B 20
Grenville Cl. WS2: Wals 6D 30
Grenville Dr. B23: Erd 4B 84
B66: Smeth 1B 98
Grenville Pl. B70: W Brom 4E 79
Grenville Rd. B90: Shir 5H 149
DY1: Dud 6A 76
Gresham Rd. B28: Hall G 1F 149
B68: O'bry 3A 98
Gresham Twr. B12: Birm 3H 117
Gresley Cl. B75: Four O 5G 37
Gresley Gro. B23: Erd 5C 84
Gressel La. B33: Kitts G 6G 105
Grestone Av. B20: Hand 3A 82
Greswolde Dr. B24: Erd 3H 85
Greswolde Pk. Rd. B27: A Grn 1H 135
Greswolde Rd. B11: S'hll 2C 134
B91: Sol 1C 150
Greswold Gdns. B34: Stech 4E 105
Greswold St. B71: W Brom 2H 79
Gretton Cres. WS9: A'rdge 4A 34
Gretton Rd. B23: Erd 6D 68
WS9: A'rdge 4B 34
Greville Dr. B15: Edg 5E 117
Grevis Cl. B13: Mose 1H 133
Grevis Rd. B25: Yard 2C 120
Greyfort Cres. B92: Olton 4D 136
Greyfriars Cl. B92: Olton 1B 150
DY1: Dud 4A 76
Greyhound La. DY8: Stourb 3B 124
WV4: Lwr P 6E 41
Greyhurst Cft. B91: Sol 1G 165
Grey Mill Cl. B90: M'path 3D 164
Greystoke Av. B36: Hodg H 2B 104
Greystoke Dr. DY6: K'wfrd 3B 92
Greystone Pas. DY1: Dud 6D 76
Greystone St. DY1: Dud 6E 77
Greytree Cres. B93: Dorr 6A 166
Grice St. B70: W Brom 1A 98
Griffin Cl. B31: N'fld 1F 145
Griffin Ct. B5: Edg 6E 117
(off West Dr.)
Griffin Gdns. B17: Harb 1H 131
Griffin Ind. Est. B65: Row R 6F 97
Griffin La. B90: Dic H 4G 163
Griffin Rd. B23: Erd 2C 84
Griffin's Brook Cl. B30: B'vlle 6H 131
Griffin's Brook La. B30: B'vlle 1G 145
Griffins Cres. WS4: Wals 4E 33
Griffin St. DY2: Neth 5E 95
WV1: Wolv 2B 44
Griffiths Dr. WV5: Wom 2G 73
WV11: Wed 1H 29
Griffiths Lodge DY8: Word 6C 92
Griffiths Rd. B71: W Brom 4A 64
DY1: Dud 1C 76
WV12: W'hall 1D 30
Griffiths St. DY4: Tip 2G 77
Grigg Gro. B31: Longb 6C 144
Grimley Rd. B31: N'fld 1H 145
Grimpits La. B38: Head H 2C 160
Grimshaw Rd. B27: A Grn 4G 135
Grimstock Hill B46: Col 6G 89
Grimstone St. WV10: Wolv . . .1D 170 (6H 27)
Grindleford Rd. B42: Gt Barr 6F 67
Gristhorpe Rd. B29: S Oak 4C 132
Grizedale Cl. B45: Fran 5H 143
Grocott Rd. WS10: Mox 1B 62
Grosmont Av. B12: Bal H 5A 118
Grosvenor Av. B20: Hand 5E 83
B74: S'tly 2H 51
Grosvenor Cl. B75: R'ley 2A 54
WV10: Bush 5H 15

Grosvenor Ct. B20: Hand 5E 83
B38: King Nor 5B 146
DY3: Lwr G 5H 75
DY9: Pedm 4F 125
(off Redlake Rd.)
WV3: Wolv 5A 170
WV11: Wed 4F 29
Grosvenor Cres. WV10: Bush 5H 15
Grosvenor Ho. B23: Erd 2G 85
Grosvenor Pk. WV4: Penn 6D 42
Grosvenor Rd. B6: Aston 1B 102
B17: Harb 5E 115
B20: Hand 5E 83
B68: O'bry 6G 97
B91: Sol 6D 150
DY3: Lwr G 5H 75
WV4: Ett 2A 60
WV10: Bush 5H 15
Grosvenor Rd. Sth. DY3: Gorn 5H 75
Grosvenor Shop. Cen. B31: N'fld 3E 145
Grosvenor Sq. B28: Hall G 2F 149
Grosvenor St. B5: Birm 3G 5 (6H 101)
WV10: Wolv 6B 28
Grosvenor St. W. B16: Birm 2D 116
Grosvenor Ter. B15: Birm 2D 116
Grosvenor Way DY5: Quar B 4A 110
Grotto La. WV6: Tett 4C 26
Groucott St. WV14: Cose 5E 61
Grounds Dr. B74: Four O 6F 37
Grounds Rd. B74: Four O 6F 37
Groundwork Environment Cen.
DY4: Tip 1G 77
Grout St. B70: W Brom 3E 79
Grove, The 1A 128
Grove, The B8: Salt 5C 102
B31: Longb 1F 159
B43: Gt Barr 1A 66
B45: Coft H 5B 158
B46: Col 5H 107
B65: Row R 1C 112
B74: Lit As 4D 36
B92: H Ard 4A 140
DY5: Brie H 3G 109
WS5: Wals 2F 65
WV4: Ett 6A 44
WV11: Wed 3D 28
Grove Av. B13: Mose 3A 134
B21: Hand 1B 100
B27: A Grn 2H 135
B29: S Oak 4A 132
B63: Hale 2H 127
B91: Sol 2G 151
Grove Cott. Rd. B9: Small H 1D 118
Grove Cotts. WS3: Blox 1H 31
Grove Ct. B42: Gt Barr 1B 82
Grove Cres. B70: W Brom 6C 80
DY5: Brie H 4G 93
WS3: Pels 4D 20
Grove Farm Dr. B75: S Cold 6D 54
Grovefield Cres. CV7: Bal C 1H 169
Grove Gdns. B20: Hand 5B 82
Grove Hill WS5: Wals 3A 50
Grove Hill Rd. B21: Hand 6B 82
Groveland Rd. DY4: Tip 4A 78
Grovelands Cres. WV10: F'hses 4H 15
Grove La. B17: Harb 1G 131
B20: Hand 5B 82
B21: Hand 1B 100
B66: Smeth 4G 99
(not continuous)
WS3: Lit Wyr 4C 8
WV6: Tett 1H 41
Groveley La. B31: Longb 3C 158
B45: Coft H 5A 158
Grove M. B31: Longb 1F 159
Grove Pk. DY6: W Hth 1A 92
Grove Rd. B11: S'hll 2C 134
B14: King H 6F 133
B68: O'bry 2B 114
B91: Sol 2G 151
B93: Know 5C 166
DY9: W'cte 1B 126
Groveside Way WS3: Pels 2E 21
Grove St. B66: Smeth 5H 99
DY2: Dud 1G 95
WV2: Wolv 6C 170 (3H 43)
WV10: Wolv 6B 28

Grove Ter. WS1: Wals 2D **48**
GROVE VALE .4H **65**
Grove Va. Av. B43: Gt Barr 4G **65**
Grove Vs. B64: Crad H 4F **111**
Grove Way B74: S'tly 4H **51**
Grovewood Dr. B38: King Nor 6A **146**
Guardian Ct. B26: Yard 4D **120**
  B31: N'fld .4B **144**
  B91: Sol 4H **151**
Guardian Ho. B68: O'bry 4A **114**
Guardians Wlk. DY8: Word 6C **92**
Guardians Way B31: N'fld 5C **130**
Guernsey Dr. B36: Cas B 3D **106**
Guest Av. WV11: Wed 1E **29**
Guest Gro. B19: Hock 3E **101**
Guild Av. WS3: Blox 2B **32**
Guild Cl. B16: Birm 1C **116**
Guild Cft. B19: Hock 3F **101**
Guildford Ct. B29: W Cas 6G **131**
  (off Abdon Av.)
Guildford Cl. B37: Mars G 3B **122**
Guildford Dr. B19: Hock 3F **101**
Guildford St. B19: Loz 2F **101**
Guildhall Mews, The WS1: Wals 2D **48**
  (off Goodall St.)
Guillemard Ct. B37: Chel W 2D **122**
Guillimot Gro. B23: Erd 5C **68**
Guiting Rd. B29: W Cas 6E **131**
Gullane Cl. B38: King Nor 6H **145**
Gullswood Cl. B14: King H 5F **147**
Gumbleberrys Cl. B8: W End 5A **104**
Gun Barrel Ind. Cen.
  B64: Crad H 5H **111**
Gunmakers Wlk. B19: Loz 2F **101**
Gunner Gro. B75: S Cold 5E **55**
Gunner La. B45: Rub 2D **156**
Gunns Way B92: Olton 6B **136**
Guns La. B70: W Brom 3H **79**
Gunstock Cl. B74: S'tly 4G **51**
GUNSTONE .1G **13**
Gunstone La. WV8: Cod, Cod W 2F **13**
  (not continuous)
GUNS VILLAGE 3H **79**
Guns Village Stop (Metro) 3H **79**
Gunter Rd. B24: Erd 4C **86**
Gupta Trad. Est. B69: O'bry 6F **79**
Gurnard Cl. WV12: W'hall 6B **18**
Gurney Pl. WS2: Wals 4G **31**
Gurney Rd. WS2: Wals 4G **31**
Guthram Cl. B23: Erd 5E **69**
Guthrie Cl. B19: Hock 3F **101**
Guthrum Cl. WV6: Pert 4F **25**
Guy Av. WV10: Bush 3H **27**
Guy Motors Ind. Pk. WV10: Wolv 4B **28**
Guys Cliffe Av. B76: Walm 4D **70**
Guy's La. DY3: Gorn 5F **75**
Gwalia Gro. B23: Erd 3F **85**
Gwendoline Way WS9: Wals W 3D **22**
GWS Ind. Est. WS10: W'bry 4D **62**
Gypsy La. B46: Wat O 5F **89**

H

Habberley Cft. B91: Sol 6F **151**
Habberley Rd. B65: Row R 1D **112**
Habitat Ct. B24: Erd 2A **86**
  D76: Walm 2D **70**
Hackett Cl. WV14: Cose 4B **60**
Hackett Ct. B69: O'bry 2G **97**
  (off Church Sq.)
Hackett Dr. B66: Smeth 2B **98**
  DY1: Dud .3E **77**
Hackett Rd. B65: Row R 6E **97**
Hackett St. DY4: Tip 6C **62**
Hackford Rd. WV4: Ett 1B **60**
Hack St. B9: Birm 2A **118**
Hackwood Ho. B69: O'bry 4D **96**
Hackwood Rd. WS10: W'bry 3H **63**
Hadcroft Grange DY9: W'cte 1H **125**
Hadcroft Rd. DY9: Lye 1G **125**
Haddock Rd. WV14: Bils 4E **45**
Haddon Cres. WV12: W'hall 2C **30**
Haddon Cft. B63: Hale 4E **127**
Haddon Rd. B42: Gt Barr 1F **83**
Haden Arch Ct. B63: Hale 5A **112**
Haden Cir. B12: Birm 4H **117**

Haden Cl. B64: Crad H 4H **111**
  DY8: Word 1B **108**
Haden Cres. WV11: Wed 3A **30**
Haden Cross Dr. B64: Crad H 4A **112**
Hadendale B64: Crad H 4A **112**
Haden Hill WV3: Wolv 1E **43**
Haden Hill House 3H **111**
Haden Hill Leisure Cen. 3H **111**
Haden Hill Rd. B63: Hale 5A **112**
Haden Pk. Rd. B64: Crad H 4G **111**
Haden Rd. B64: Old H 1G **111**
  DY4: Tip 4A **62**
Haden St. B12: Bal H 5H **117**
Haden Wlk. B65: Row R 6C **96**
Haden Way B12: Bal H 5H **117**
Hadfield Cft. B19: Birm 4E **101**
Hadfield Way B37: F'bri 5C **106**
Hadland Rd. B33: Sheld 2F **121**
Hadleigh Cft. B76: Walm 1E **87**
Hadley Cl. B47: Wyt 4A **162**
Hadley Ct. B16: Edg 2H **115**
Hadley Cft. B66: Smeth 2E **99**
Hadley Pl. WV14: Bils 4E **45**
Hadley Rd. WS2: Wals 3F **31**
  WV14: Bils 4E **45**
Hadleys Cl. DY2: Neth 5G **95**
Hadley Stadium 6E **99**
Hadley St. B68: O'bry 5G **97**
Hadley Way WS2: Wals 3F **31**
Hadlow Cft. B33: Sheld 4H **121**
Hadrian Dr. B46: Col 6H **89**
Hadyn Gro. B26: Sheld 5F **121**
Hadzor Rd. B68: O'bry 3B **114**
Hafren Cl. B45: Fran 5H **143**
Hafton Gro. B9: Small H 2D **118**
Haggar St. WV2: Wolv 5G **43**
HAGLEY 6G **125**
Hagley C'way. DY9: Hag 6B **126**
Hagley Cl. DY9: Hag 6G **125**
Hagley Country Club Golf Course . . .5C **126**
Hagley Ct. DY3: Lwr G 4H **75**
Hagley Grange DY9: Hag 6F **125**
Hagley Hall Gdns. DY9: Hag 6H **125**
Hagley Hill DY9: Hag 6A **126**
Hagley Mall B63: Hale 2B **128**
Hagley Park 6A **126**
Hagley Pk. Dr. B45: Redn 3G **157**
Hagley Rd. B16: Edg 2C **116**
  B17: Edg .2E **115**
  B63: Hale .5E **127**
  B66: Edg .2E **115**
  DY8: Pedm, Stourb 1E **125**
  DY9: Pedm 4G **125**
Hagley Rd. W. B17: Edg, Harb 5G **113**
  B32: Quin 5G **113**
  B62: Quin 5G **113**
  B67: Harb 5G **113**
  B68: O'bry 5G **113**
Hagley St. B63: Hale 2B **128**
Hagley Vw. Rd. DY2: Dud 1E **95**
Hagley Vs. B12: Bal H 3H **134**
  (off Taunton Rd.)
Hagley Wood La. DY9: Hag 5D **126**
Haig Cl. B75: S Cold 4A **54**
Haig Pl. B13: Mose 6A **134**
Haig Rd. DY2: Dud 6H **77**
Haig St. B71: W Brom 2A **80**
Hailes Pk. Cl. WV4: Wolv 5A **44**
Hailsham Rd. B23: Erd 2F **85**
Hailstone Cl. B65: Row R 4A **96**
Hailwood Dr. B43: Gt Barr 4A **66**
Haines Cl. DY4: Tip 3B **78**
Haines St. B70: W Brom 5B **80**
Hainfield Dr. B91: Sol 2A **152**
Hainge Rd. B69: Tiv 6C **78**
Hainge Rd. B69: Tiv 5C **78**
Hainult Cl. DY8: Word 5B **92**
Halas Ind. Est. B62: Hale 6B **112**
Halberton St. B66: Smeth 5H **99**
Haldane Cl. B33: Yard 1F **121**
Haldon Gro. B31: Longb 2C **158**
Halecroft Av. WV11: Wed 4F **29**
Hale Gro. B24: Erd 3B **86**
Halesbury Ct. B63: Hale 3H **127**
  (off Ombersley Rd.)
Hales Cres. B67: Smeth 6C **98**

Halescroft Sq. B31: N'fld 1C **144**
Hales Gdns. B23: Erd 5C **68**
Hales La. B67: Smeth 5C **98**
Halesmere Way B63: Hale 2C **128**
HALESOWEN 2B **128**
Halesowen Abbey 3D **128**
Halesowen By-Pass B62: Hale 2D **128**
  B62: Roms, Hale 4G **127**
Halesowen Golf Course 6D **112**
Halesowen Golf Range 4A **128**
Halesowen Ind. Pk. B62: Hale 5B **112**
  (Coombs Rd.)
  B62: Hale .5C **112**
  (Hereward Ri.)
Halesowen Leisure Cen. 2B **128**
Halesowen Rd. B61: L Ash 6C **156**
  B62: Quin 5E **113**
  B64: Crad H 3H **111**
  B64: Old H 1G **111**
  DY2: Neth 4E **95**
  (Baptist End Rd.)
  DY2: Neth 5F **95**
  (Cradley Rd.)
Halesowen St. B65: B'hth 3C **112**
  B69: O'bry 2F **97**
Halesowen Town FC 6A **112**
Hales Rd. B63: Hale 2A **128**
  (not continuous)
  WS10: W'bry 1G **63**
Hales Way B69: O'bry 2F **97**
Halesworth Rd. WV9: Pend 6E **15**
Hale Trad. Est. DY4: Tip 2B **78**
Halewood Gro. B28: Hall G 6G **135**
Haley St. WV12: W'hall 4C **30**
Halfcot Av. DY9: Pedm 2G **125**
Halford Cres. WS3: Wals 4D **32**
Halford Gro. B24: Erd 3C **86**
Halford Rd. B91: Sol 1C **150**
Halford's La. B66: Smeth 2E **99**
  B71: W Brom 2E **99**
Halford's La. Ind. Est.
  B66: Smeth 1E **99**
Halfords Pk. B66: Smeth 1E **99**
Halfpenny Fld. Wlk. B35: Cas V 5E **87**
Halfway Cl. B44: Gt Barr 1G **83**
Halifax Gro. B18: Win G 5A **100**
Halifax Ho. B5: Edg 4F **117**
Halifax Rd. B90: Shir 4H **149**
Haliscombe Gro. B6: Aston 1G **101**
Halkett Glade B33: Stech 6B **104**
Halladale B38: King Nor 6B **146**
Hallam Cl. B71: W Brom 2C **80**
Hallam Ct. B71: W Brom 2C **80**
Hallam Cres. WV10: Wolv 3A **28**
Hallam Dr. B71: W Brom 2C **80**
Hallam St. B12: Bal H 6B **117**
  B71: W Brom 3B **80**
Hallbridge Cl. WS3: Pels 5D **20**
Hallbridge Way B69: Tiv 5B **78**
Hallchurch Rd. DY2: Dud 2B **94**
Hall Cres. B71: W Brom 1A **80**
Hallcroft Cl. B72: W Grn 6A **70**
Hallcroft Way B93: Know 3C **166**
  WS9: A'rdge 4E **35**
Hall Dale Cl. B28: Hall G 2F **149**
Hall Dr. B37: Mars G 4C **122**
HALL END 1B **80**
Hall End WS10: W'bry 2F **63**
Hallens Dr. WS10: W'bry 2D **62**
Hallett Dr. WV3: Wolv 5A **170** (2F **43**)
Hallewell Rd. B16: Edg 6H **99**
HALL GREEN
  B28 . . . . .5F **135**
  B71 . . . . .4B **64**
  WV14 . . . . .3G **61**
Hall Green Greyhound Stadium 4F **135**
Hall Green Little Theatre 3G **135**
Hall Grn. Rd. B71: W Brom 4A **64**
Hall Green Station (Rail) 4F **135**
Hallgreen St. WV14: Bils 2G **61**
Hall Grn. Wharf B71: W Brom 4A **64**
Hall Grn. WV14: Cose 5E **61**
Hall Hays Rd. B34: S End 2A **106**
Hall La. DY2: Neth 3E **95**
  DY4: Tip 5B **62**
  DY9: Hag .6H **125**
  WS3: Pels 4D **20**

Hall La.—Hargrave Rd.

Hall La. WS6: Gt Wyr 1F **7**
WS7: Hamm 1F **11**
(not continuous)
WS9: Wals W 3A **22**
WS14: Muck C 3H **11**
WV14: Cose 4B **60**
Hall Mdw. DY9: Hag 6H **125**
Hallmeadow Rd. CV7: Bal C 6H **155**
Hallmoor Rd. B33: Kitts G 6F **105**
Hall of Memory, The 4B 4 (1E 117)
Hallot Cl. B23: Erd 5D **68**
Halloughton Rd. B74: S Cold 4G **53**
Hallow Cl. B31: N'fld 5H **145**
Hall Pk. St. WV14: Bils 5D **44**
Hall Rd. B8: Salt 5D **102**
B20: Hand 1C **100**
B36: Cas B 1E **105**
B67: Smeth 5C **98**
Hall Rd. Av. B20: Hand 1C **100**
Hallstead Rd. B13: Mose 2B **148**
Hall St. B18: Birm 1B **4** (5E **101**)
B64: Old H 1H **111**
B68: O'bry 4H **97**
B70: W Brom 5A **80**
DY2: Dud 6F **77**
DY3: Sed 5H **59**
DY4: Tip 2G **77**
DY8: Stourb 2E **125**
WS2: Wals 6B **32**
WS10: Darl 4B **46**
WV11: Wed 4E **29**
WV13: W'hall 2B **46**
WV14: Bils 6G **45**
Hall St. E. WS10: Darl 4C **46**
Hall St. Sth. B70: W Brom 1B **98**
Hallswelle Gro. B43: Gt Barr 1G **67**
Hall Wlk. B46: Col 4G **107**
(Birmingham Rd.)
B46: Col 5H **107**
(The Grove)
Halsbury Gro. B44: K'sdng 5B **68**
Halstead Gro. B91: Sol 1E **165**
Halton Rd. B73: New O, S Cold 2D **68**
Halton St. DY2: Neth 4E **95**
Hamar Way B37: Mars G 2D **122**
Hamberley Ct. B18: Win G 5H **99**
Hamble Cl. B36: Cas B 1B **106**
DY5: P'ntt 3E **93**
Hamble Ct. B73: S Cold 6H **53**
Hambledon Cl. WV9: Pend 5E **15**
Hamble Gro. WV6: Pert 6E **25**
Hamble Rd. B42: Gt Barr 4B **66**
WV4: Penn 5A **42**
Hambleton Rd. B63: Hale 3F **127**
Hambletts Rd. B70: W Brom 4G **79**
Hambrook Cl. WV6: Wolv 4E **27**
Hambury Dr. B14: King H 6F **133**
Hamilton Av. B17: Harb 3E **115**
B62: Hale 2C **128**
DY8: Woll 5B **108**
Hamilton Cl. DY3: Sed 6G **59**
DY8: Word 1A **108**
Hamilton Ct. B13: Mose 1H **133**
B30: King Nor 3A **146**
Hamilton Dr. B29: S Oak 5H **131**
B69: Tiv .5C **78**
DY8: Word 1A **108**
Hamilton Gdns. WV10: Bush 4A **16**
Hamilton Ho. B66: Smeth 4G **99**
WS3: Blox 6A **20**
Hamilton Rd. B21: Hand 1H **99**
B67: Smeth 1C **114**
DY4: Tip 1C **78**
Hamilton St. B68: O'bry 4H **113**
WS3: Blox 6A **20**
Ham La. DY6: K'wfrd 6C **74**
DY9: Pedm 4G **125**
Hamlet, The WS11: Nort C 1C **8**
Hamlet Gdns. B28: Hall G 5F **135**
Hamlet Rd. B28: Hall G 5F **135**
Hammer Bank DY5: Quar B 3C **110**
Hammersley Cl. B63: Crad 4D **110**
HAMMERWICH 1F 11
Hammerwich La. WS7: Hamm 2H **11**
Hammond Av. WV10: Bush 1A **28**
Hammond Dr. B23: Erd 2F **85**
Hammond Way DY8: Amb 4E **109**
Hampden Cl. DY5: Quar B 3C **110**
Hampden Retreat B12: Bal H 5G **117**
Hampshire Ct. B29: W Cas 6F **131**
Hampshire Dr. B15: Edg 3A **116**
Hampshire Rd. B71: W Brom 5G **63**
Hampson Cl. B11: S'brk 5B **118**
Hampstead Glade B63: Hale 3C **128**
Hampton Cl. B73: New O 3C **68**
Hampton Ct. *B15: Edg 3D 116*
(off George Rd.)
B71: W Brom 4A **64**
B92: H Ard 1B **154**
WV10: Bush 5D **16**
Hampton Ct. Rd. B17: Harb 5D **114**
Hampton Dr. B74: Four O 3H **53**
Hampton Gdns. DY9: Pedm 2G **125**
Hampton Grange CV7: Mer 4H **141**
Hampton Gro. WS3: Pels 3D **20**
HAMPTON IN ARDEN 1A 154
Hampton in Arden Station (Rail) 6B 140
Hampton La. B91: Cath B, Sol 3H **151**
(not continuous)
B92: Cath B 3A **152**
CV7: Mer 5E **141**
Hampton Pl. WS10: Darl 3C **46**
Hampton Rd. B6: Aston 6F **83**
B23: Erd .3D **84**
B93: Know 2E **167**
WV10: Oxl 6F **15**
Hamptons, The B93: Know 3E **167**
Hampton St. B19: Birm 1C **4** (5F **101**)
DY2: Neth 4E **95**
WV14: Cose 5D **60**
Hampton Vw. WV10: Wolv 5B **28**
Hampton Wlk. WV1: Wolv 3B **170**
HAMS HALL .3H 89
Hams Hall Distribution Pk. B46: Col . . .2H **89**
Hams La. B46: Lea M 2G **89**
B76: Lea M 2G **89**
Hams Rd. B8: Salt 5D **102**
HAMSTEAD .6B 66
Hamstead Cl. WV11: Wed 3F **29**
Hamstead Hall Av. B20: Hand 2A **82**
Hamstead Hall Rd. B20: Hand 3A **82**
Hamstead Hill B20: Hand 4B **82**
Hamstead Ho. B43: Gt Barr 6B **66**
Hamstead Ind. Est. B42: P Barr 2C **82**
Hamstead Rd. B19: Hock 2D **100**
B20: Hand 6D **82**
B43: Gt Barr 5G **65**
Hamstead Station (Rail) 1B 82
Hamstead Ter. WS10: W'bry 3G **63**
Hanam Cl. B75: S Cold 5D **54**
Hanbury Cl. B63: Hale 3H **127**
Hanbury Ct. *DY8: Stourb 1E 125*
(off College Rd.)
Hanbury Cres. WV4: Penn 5C **42**
Hanbury Cft. B27: A Grn 2C **136**
Hanbury Dr. B69: O'bry 5E **97**
Hanbury Hill DY8: Stourb 1E **125**
Hanbury Pas. DY8: Stourb 6E **109**
Hanbury Rd. B70: W Brom 4G **79**
B93: Dorr 5B **166**
WS8: Bwnhls 3A **10**
Hanch Pl. WS1: Wals 3D **48**
Hancock Rd. B8: Salt 5F **103**
Hancox St. B68: O'bry 1H **113**
Handley Gro. B31: Longb 5A **144**
Handley St. WS10: W'bry 1G **63**
HANDSWORTH 6A 82
Handsworth Booth Street Stop (Metro)
. . . . . .2G 99
Handsworth Cl. B21: Hand 2H **99**
Handsworth Dr. B43: Gt Barr 2C **66**
Handsworth Golf Course 3A 82
Handsworth Horticultural Institute *5A 82*
(off Oxhill Rd.)
Handsworth Leisure Cen. 6B 82
Handsworth New Rd. B18: Win G 3A **100**
Handsworth Park 6B 82
HANDSWORTH WOOD 5C 82
Handsworth Wood Rd. B20: Hand 4B **82**
Hangar Rd. B26: Birm A 2C **138**
Hanging La. B31: N'fld 5C **144**
Hangleton Dr. B11: S'brk 5D **118**
Hanley Cl. B63: Hale 1G **127**
Hanley St. B19: Birm 1E **5** (5G **101**)
Hannafore Rd. B16: Edg 6H **99**
Hannah Rd. WV14: Bils 2A **62**
Hanney Hay Rd. WS7: Chase, Hamm . . .1C **10**
WS8: Hamm 2D **10**
Hannon Rd. B14: King H 2G **147**
Hanover Cl. B6: Aston 2G **101**
Hanover Ct. WS2: Wals 2E **47**
WV6: Tett 5A **26**
Hanover Dr. B24: Erd 1F **103**
Hanover Gdns. B68: O'bry 1H **113**
Hanover Rd. B65: Row R 5C **96**
Hansell Dr. B93: Dorr 6F **167**
Hansom Rd. B32: Quin 6A **114**
Hanson Cl. B66: Smeth 2E **99**
Hanson Gro. B92: Olton 6D **120**
Hansons Bri. Rd. B24: Erd 2D **86**
Hanwell Cl. B76: Walm 6F **71**
Hanwood Cl. B12: Birm 3H **117**
Harald Cl. WV6: Pert 4E **25**
Harbeck Av. B44: Gt Barr 5H **67**
Harbet Dr. B40: Nat E C 1G **139**
Harbinger Rd. B38: King Nor 5D **146**
HARBORNE .6G 115
Harborne Church Farm Golf Course
. . . . . .6F 115
Harborne Cotts. B67: Smeth 4D **98**
Harborne Ct. B17: Harb 1G **131**
Harborne Golf Course 6E 115
Harborne Ho. B17: Harb 1E **131**
Harborne La. B17: Harb, S Oak 2H **131**
B29: S Oak 2H **131**
Harborne Pk. Rd. B17: Harb 6G **115**
Harborne Pool & Fitness Cen. 6F 115
Harborne Rd. B15: Edg 5A **116**
B68: O'bry 2B **114**
Harborough Ct. B74: Four O 1G **53**
Harborough Dr. B36: Cas B 6H **87**
WS9: A'rdge 4C **34**
Harborough Wlk. DY9: Pedm 3G **125**
Harbours Hill B61: Wild 4A **156**
Harbury Cl. B76: Walm 1F **87**
Harbury Rd. B12: Bal H 6F **117**
Harby Cl. B37: Mars G 3D **122**
Harcourt Dr. B74: Four O 5F **37**
DY3: Gorn 5H **75**
Harcourt Rd. B23: Erd 1E **85**
B64: Crad H 3H **111**
WS10: W'bry 1F **63**
HARDEN 2C 32
Harden Cl. WS3: Blox 2C **32**
Harden Ct. B31: N'fld 6C **144**
Harden Gro. WS3: Blox 2C **32**
Harden Keep B66: Smeth 5E **99**
Harden Mnr. Ct. B63: Hale 2C **128**
Harden Rd. WS3: Blox, Wals 2B **32**
Harden Va. B63: Hale 6G **111**
Harding St. WV14: Cose 3F **61**
Hardon Rd. WV4: Ett 6B **44**
HARDWICK .2G 51
Hardwick Ct. B74: S'tly 1H **51**
DY9: Lye 6H **109**
Hardwick Dr. B62: Hale 4A **112**
Hardwicke Wlk. B14: King H 5F **147**
Hardwicke Way DY9: Lye 6H **109**
Hardwick Rd. B74: S'tly 1H **51**
B92: Olton 1C **136**
Hardy Ct. B13: Mose 1H **133**
Hardy Rd. WS3: Blox 1C **32**
WS10: W'bry 2G **63**
Hardy Sq. WV2: Ett 5B **44**
Harebell Cl. WS5: Wals 2E **65**
Harebell Cres. DY1: Dud 3C **76**
Harebell Gdns. B38: King Nor 1B **160**
Harebell Wlk. B37: Chel W 1F **123**
Hare Gro. B31: N'fld 4B **144**
Haresfield B90: Dic H 4G **163**
Hare St. WV14: Bils 6H **45**
(not continuous)
Harewell Dr. B75: R'ley 2A **54**
Harewood Av. B43: Gt Barr 3G **65**
WS10: W'bry 2A **64**
Harewood Cl. B28: Hall G 2E **149**
Harford St. B19: Birm 5E **101**
Hargate La. B70: W Brom 3A **80**
B71: W Brom 3A **80**
Hargrave Cl. B46: Wat O 4D **88**
Hargrave Rd. B90: Shir 5C **148**

220 A-Z Birmingham

Hargreave Cl. B76: Walm 6D 70
Hargreaves St. WV1: Wolv 4C 44
Harland Rd. B74: Four O 6G 37
Harlech Cl. B32: Bart G 6G 129
  B69: Tiv 6A 78
Harlech Ho. WS3: Blox 3A 32
                      (off Providence Cl.)
Harlech Rd. WV12: W'hall 3C 30
Harlech Twr. B23: Erd 1G 85
Harlech Way DY1: Dud 5B 76
Harlequin Dr. B13: Mose 3G 133
Harleston Rd. B44: Gt Barr 5H 67
Harley Cl. WS8: Bwnhls 1C 22
Harley Dr. WV14: Bils 1D 60
Harley Grange DY2: Dud 1G 95
                      (off Dixon's Grn. Rd.)
Harlow Gro. B28: Hall G 1G 149
Harlstones Cl. DY8: Amb 3E 109
Harlyn Cl. WV14: Bils 3A 62
Harman Rd. B72: W Grn 6H 69
Harmer St. B18: Hock 4C 100
Harmon Rd. DY8: Woll 6A 108
Harmony Ho. B10: Small H 2C 118
Harnall Cl. B90: Shir 2C 164
Harness Cl. WS5: Wals 1D 64
Harold Rd. B16: Edg 2B 116
  B67: Smeth 6C 98
Harold Ter. B19: Loz 1E 101
Harper Av. WV11: Wed 2E 29
Harper Gro. DY4: Tip 1F 77
Harper Rd. WV14: Bils 5F 45
Harpers Rd. B14: King H 6A 148
  B31: N'fld 6E 145
Harper St. WV13: W'hall 1A 46
Harpur Cl. WS4: Wals 5E 33
Harpur Rd. WS4: Wals 5E 33
Harrier Rd. B27: A Grn 3B 136
Harriet Cl. DY5: P'ntt 4F 93
Harringay Dr. DY8: Stourb 2C 124
Harringay Rd. B44: K'sdng 3A 68
Harrington Cft. B71: W Brom 6D 64
Harringworth Ct. WS4: S'fld 1G 33
Harriots Hayes La.
  WV8: Cod W 1A 12
Harris Cl. B18: Hock 3C 100
Harris Dr. B42: Gt Barr 5C 66
  B66: Smeth 6F 99
Harrison Cl. WS3: Blox 6A 20
  WS6: C Hay 4D 6
Harrison Ct. DY8: Amb 2E 109
Harrison Ho. B14: King H 4H 147
Harrison Rd. B24: Erd 3F 85
  B74: Four O 4E 37
  DY8: Word 2E 109
  WS4: S'fld 5G 21
Harrison's Fold DY2: Neth 4E 95
Harrisons Grn. B15: Edg 5A 116
Harrisons Pleck B13: Mose 2H 133
Harrison's Rd. B15: Edg 5A 116
Harrison St. WS3: Blox 6H 19
Harrold Av. B65: Row R 6E 97
Harrold Rd. B65: Row R 6E 97
Harrold St. DY4: Tip 6C 62
Harrop Way DY8: Amb 3C 108
Harrowby Dr. DY4: Tip 3A 78
Harrowby Pl. WV13: W'hall 2D 46
  WV14: Bils 1A 62
Harrowby Rd. WV10: F'hses 4F 15
  WV14: Bils 1A 62
Harrow Cl. DY9: Hag 6E 125
Harrowfield Rd. B33: Stech 5C 104
Harrow Rd. B29: S Oak 2B 132
  DY6: K'wfrd 6B 74
Harrow St. WV1: Wolv 5F 27
Harry Mitchell Leisure Cen. 4D 98
Harry Perks St.
  WV13: W'hall 6A 30
Harry Price Ho. B69: O'bry 4D 96
Hart Dr. B73: Bold 5G 69
Hartfield Cres. B27: A Grn 3G 135
Hartfields Way B65: Row R 4H 95
Hartford Cl. B17: Harb 4E 115
Hartill Rd. WV4: Penn 2B 58
Hartill St. WV13: W'hall 3B 46
Hartington Cl. B93: Dorr 6A 166
Hartington Rd. B19: Loz 1F 101
Hartland Av. WV14: Cose 5C 60

Hartland Rd. B31: Longb 3C 158
  B71: W Brom 5D 64
  DY4: Tip 2F 77
Hartland St. DY5: P'ntt 2H 93
Hartlebury Cl. B93: Dorr 6B 166
Hartlebury Rd. B63: Hale 3H 127
  B69: O'bry 4D 96
Hartledon Rd. B17: Harb 6F 115
Hartley Dr. WS9: A'rdge 5D 34
Hartley Gro. B44: K'sdng 2B 68
Hartley Pl. B15: Edg 3B 116
Hartley Rd. B44: K'sdng 2B 68
Hartley St. WV3: Wolv 1E 43
Harton Way B14: King H 2E 147
Hartopp Cl. B74: Four O 3H 53
                      (off Lichfield Rd.)
Hartopp Rd. B8: Salt 5E 103
  B74: Four O 2F 53
Hart Rd. B24: Erd 2G 85
  WV11: Wed 5F 29
Hartsbourne Dr. B62: Hale 1D 128
Harts Cl. B17: Harb 5H 115
HARTS GREEN 6E 115
Harts Grn. Rd. B17: Harb 6E 115
HART'S HILL 4A 94
Hartshill Cl. B34: S End 3E 105
Hartshill Rd. B27: A Grn 3B 136
  B34: S End 3E 105
Hartshorn St. WV14: Bils 6F 45
Hartside Cl. B63: Hale 3F 127
Harts Rd. B8: Salt 4E 103
Hart St. WS1: Wals 3C 48
Hartswell Dr. B13: Mose 1H 147
Hartwell Cl. B91: Sol 6F 151
Hartwell La. WS6: Gt Wyr 2G 7
Hartwell Rd. B24: Erd 5H 85
Hartwood Cres. WV4: Penn 6D 42
Harvard Cl. DY1: Dud 3B 76
Harvard Rd. B92: Olton 1F 137
Harvest Cl. B30: Stir 1D 146
  DY3: Up Gor 2A 76
Harvest Ct. B65: Row R 5A 96
Harvesters Cl. WS9: A'rdge 1G 51
Harvesters Rd. WV12: W'hall 4D 30
Harvesters Wlk. B65: Row R 6C 14
Harvesters Way WV12: W'hall 4D 30
Harvester Way DY6: W Hth 1G 91
Harvest Flds. B65: Row R 6A 96
Harvest Flds. Way B75: R'ley 5B 38
Harvest Gdns. B68: O'bry 5G 97
Harvest Rd. B65: Row R 5A 96
  B67: Smeth 6B 98
Harvest Wlk. B65: Row R 5A 96
Harvey Ct. B33: Kitts G 6H 105
Harvey Dr. B75: R'ley 1A 54
Harvey M. B30: B'vlle 6A 132
Harvey Rd. B26: Yard 4B 120
  WS2: Wals 4H 31
Harvey's Ter. DY2: Neth 5F 95
HARVILLS HAWTHORN 1F 109
Harvills Hawthorn B70: W Brom 6F 63
Harvine Wlk. DY8: Stourb 2C 124
Harvington Dr. B90: M'path 3F 165
Harvington Rd. B29: W Cas 5E 131
  B63: Hale 3H 127
  B68: O'bry 4G 113
  WV14: Cose 5D 60
Harvington Wlk. B65: Row R 6C 96
Harvington Way B76: Walm 5E 71
Harwin Cl. WV6: Tett 2D 26
Harwood Gro. B90: Shir 1A 164
Harwood St. B70: W Brom 4H 79
HASBURY 3G 127
Hasbury Cl. B63: Hale 3G 127
Hasbury Rd. B32: Bart G 5G 129
Haseley Rd. B21: Hand 2A 100
  B91: Sol .1C 150
Haselor Rd. B73: New O 4E 69
Haselour Rd. B37: K'hrst 4B 106
Haselwell Dr. B30: King Nor 4F 147
Haskell St. WS1: Wals 3C 48
Haslingden Cres. DY3: Lwr G 3H 75
Haslucks Cl. B90: Shir 4G 149
Haslucks Cft. B90: Shir 4G 149
HASLUCKS GREEN 6E 149
Haslucks Grn. Rd. B90: Maj G, Shir . .2E 163
Hassop Rd. B42: Gt Barr 6F 67

Hastings Ct. DY1: Dud 5A 76
Hastings Rd. B23: Erd 6B 68
Hastingwood Ind. Pk. B24: Erd 6H 85
Haswell Rd. B63: Hale 2F 127
Hatcham Rd. B44: K'sdng 3C 68
Hatchett St. B19: Birm 4G 101
Hatchford Av. B92: Sol 2G 137
Hatchford Brook Golf Course 1A 138
Hatchford Brook Rd. B92: Sol 2G 137
Hatchford Ct. B92: Sol 2G 137
Hatchford Wlk. B37: Chel W 2D 122
Hatchford Way B26: Sheld 1A 138
Hatch Heath Cl. WV5: Wom 6F 57
Hateley Dr. WV4: Ett 1A 60
HATELEY HEATH 6A 64
Hatfield Cl. B23: Erd 6D 68
Hatfield Rd. B19: Loz 1F 101
  DY9: Lye 1G 125
Hathaway Cl. CV7: Bal C 2H 169
  WV13: W'hall 3H 45
Hathaway M. B97: Word 6H 91
Hathaway Rd. B75: Four O 5G 37
  B90: Shir .6H 149
Hatherden Dr. B76: Walm 3E 71
Hathersage Rd. B42: Gt Barr 6F 67
Hatherton Gdns. WV10: Bush 5A 16
Hatherton Gro. B29: W Cas 4D 130
Hatherton Pl. WS9: A'rdge 2C 34
Hatherton Rd. WS1: Wals 1C 48
  WV14: Bils 5H 45
Hatherton St. WS1: Wals 1C 48
  WS4: Wals 1C 48
  WS6: C Hay 3C 6
Hattersley Gro. B11: Tys 2G 135
Hatton Cres. WV10: Wolv 2C 28
Hatton Gdns. B42: Gt Barr 6D 66
Hatton Rd. WV6: Wolv 6D 26
Hattons Gro. WV8: Bilb 5H 13
Hatton St. WV14: Bils 1G 61
Haughton Rd. B20: Hand 6F 83
Haunch Cl. B13: Mose 2A 148
Haunch La. B13: Mose 1H 147
Haunchwood Dr. B76: Walm 6D 70
Havacre La. WV14: Cose 3E 61
Havelock Cl. WV3: Wolv 3D 42
Havelock Rd. B8: Salt 4D 102
  B11: Tys .1E 135
  B20: Hand 6E 83
Haven, The B14: Yard W 3D 148
  B23: Erd 4E 85
  DY8: Word 1B 108
  WV2: Wolv 3G 43
Haven Caravan Pk. B92: Bick 3E 139
Haven Cft. B43: Gt Barr 5H 65
Haven Dr. B27: A Grn 2H 135
Haverford Dr. B45: Redn 3H 157
Havergal Wlk. B63: Crad 1D 126
Haverhill Cl. WS3: Blox 4G 19
Hawbridge Cl. B90: M'path 3F 165
HAWBUSH .1F 109
Hawbush Gdns. DY5: Brie H 2E 109
Hawbush Rd. DY5: Brie H 6F 93
  WS3: Blox 3B 32
Hawcroft Gro. B34: S End 3G 105
Hawes Cl. WS1: Wals 5D 48
Hawes La. B65: Row R 5B 96
Hawes Rd. WS1: Wals 5D 48
Haweswater Dr. DY6: K'wfrd 3B 92
Hawfield Cl. B69: Tiv 2C 96
Hawfield Gro. B72: W Grn 6A 70
Hawfield Rd. B69: Tiv 2C 96
Hawker Dr. B35: Cas V 5D 86
Hawkesbury Rd. B90: Shir 6F 149
Hawkes Cl. B30: Stir 5C 132
Hawkesford Cl. B36: Cas B 1E 105
  B74: Four O 2H 53
Hawkesford Rd. B33: Kitts G 6H 105
Hawkes La. B70: W Brom 6G 63
HAWKESLEY 2A 160
Hawkesley Cres. B31: Longb 6D 144
Hawkesley Dr. B31: Longb 1D 158
Hawkesley End B38: King Nor 2A 160
Hawkesley Mill La. B31: N'fld 5D 144
Hawkesley Rd. DY1: Dud 1B 94
Hawkesley Sq. B38: King Nor 2A 160
Hawkes St. B10: Small H 3D 118

Hawkestone Cres.—Heather Dr.

Hawkestone Cres. B70: W Brom 1F **79**
Hawkestone Rd. B29: W Cas 6E **131**
Hawkeswell Cl. B92: Olton 4C **136**
Hawkeswell Dr. DY6: K'wfrd 6B **74**
Hawkesyard Rd. B24: Erd 6E **85**
Hawkhurst Rd. B14: King H 5H **147**
Hawkinge Dr. B35: Cas V 4E **87**
Hawkins Cl. B5: Edg 5G **117**
Hawkins Cft. DY4: Tip 4A **78**
Hawkins Dr. WS11: Cann 1C **6**
Hawkins Pl. WV14: Bils 2H **61**
Hawkins St. B70: W Brom 5G **63**
Hawkley Cl. WV1: Wolv 1D **44**
Hawkley Rd. WV1: Wolv 1D **44**
Hawkmoor Gdns. B38: King Nor 1C **160**
Hawks Cl. WS6: C Hay 3D **6**
Hawksford Cres. WV10: Bush 2H **27**
Hawkshead Dr. B93: Know 3B **166**
Hawksmill Ind. Est. B9: Small H 2C **118**
Hawksmoor Dr. WV6: Pert 6D **24**
Hawkstone Ct. WV6: Pert 4D **24**
Hawkswell Av. WV5: Wom 2G **73**
Hawkswell Dr. WV13: W'hall 2H **45**
Hawkswood Dr. CV7: Bal C 2H **169**
WS10: Mox 2B **62**
Hawkswood Gro. B14: King H 4B **148**
Hawksworth Cres. B37: Chel W 6F **107**
Hawley Cl. WS4: Wals 5D **32**
Hawley Ct. B43: Gt Barr 4A **66**
Hawnby Gro. B76: Walm 3E **71**
HAWNE **5G 111**
Hawne Cl. B63: Hale 5G **111**
Hawnelands, The B63: Hale 6H **111**
Hawne La. B63: Hale 5G **111**
Hawthorn Brook Way B23: Erd 5E **69**
Hawthorn Cl. B9: Birm 2B **118**
B23: Erd 6F **69**
Hawthorn Coppice B30: King Nor 3A **146**
Hawthorn Cft. B68: O'bry 4B **114**
Hawthornden Ct. B76: Walm 6B **70**
Hawthorn Dr. B29: S Oak 4G **131**
B47: H'wd .3B **162**
CV7: Bal C 1H **169**
Hawthorne Av. WS6: Gt Wyr 4G **7**
Hawthorne Cft. B30: King Nor 2H **145**
Hawthorne Gdns. B13: Mose 5B **134**
Hawthorne Gro. DY3: Gorn 5H **75**
Hawthorne Ho. WV10: Wolv 6B **28**
Hawthorne La. WV8: Cod 5F **13**
Hawthorne Rd. B15: Edg 4A **116**
B30: King Nor 3H **145**
B36: Cas B 2A **106**
B63: Hale .3G **127**
DY1: Dud 3E **77**
WS5: Wals .6D **48**
WS6: C Hay .1E **7**
WV2: Wolv .5H **43**
WV11: Ess .3A **18**
WV11: Wed 4H **29**
WV12: W'hall 2D **30**
Hawthorn Gro. B19: Loz 1E **101**
Hawthorn Pk. B20: Hand 4A **82**
Hawthorn Pk. Dr. B20: Hand 4B **82**
Hawthorn Pl. WS2: Wals 6E **31**
Hawthorn Rd. B44: K'sdng 5H **67**
B72: W Grn 4A **70**
B74: S'tly .2A **52**
DY4: Tip 5A **62**
DY5: Quar B 3A **110**
WS4: S'fld .6F **21**
WS10: W'bry 1F **63**
WV1: Wolv .3D **44**
Hawthorns, The **6F 81**
Hawthorns, The B13: Mose 2H **133**
B68: O'bry 4B **114**
Hawthorns Bus. Cen. B66: Smeth 1E **99**
Hawthorns Ind. Est. B21: Hand 6F **81**
Hawthorns, The (Park & Tram) 1E **99**
Hawthorns, The Station (Rail & Metro)
. . . . .1F **99**
Hawthorn Ter. WS10: W'bry 1F **63**
Haxby Av. B34: Hodg H 3E **105**
Haybarn, The B76: Walm 5E **71**
Hay Brook Dr. B11: Tys 1F **135**
Haycock Pl. WS10: Darl 4C **46**
Haycroft Av. B8: Salt 4E **103**
Haycroft Dr. B74: Four O 5G **37**
Haydn Sanders Sq. *WS1: Wals* *3C* ***48***
(off Brace St.)
Haydock Cl. B36: Hodg H 1A **104**
WV6: Wolv .3F **27**
Haydon Cl. B93: Dorr 6G **167**
Haydon Cft. B33: Kitts G 6E **105**
Haye Ho. Gro. B36: Hodg H 2C **104**
HAYES, THE **5C 110**
Hayes, The B31: Longb 2G **159**
DY9: Lye .6B **110**
WV12: W'hall 4B **30**
Hayes Bus. Pk. DY9: Lye 5B **110**
Hayes Cres. B68: O'bry 4B **98**
Hayes Cft. B38: King Nor 2B **160**
Hayes Dr. B24: Erd 2B **86**
Hayes Gro. B24: Erd 1B **86**
Hayes La. DY9: Lye 5C **110**
Hayes Mdw. B72: W Grn 6B **70**
Hayes Rd. B68: O'bry 4B **98**
Hayes St. B70: W Brom 3G **79**
Hayes Trad. Est., The DY9: Lye 5C **110**
Hayes Vw. Dr. WS6: C Hay 1E **7**
Hayfield Ct. B13: Mose 3B **134**
Hayfield Gdns. B13: Mose 3C **134**
Hayfield Gro. WS9: A'rdge 5D **34**
Hayfield Rd. B13: Mose 3B **134**
HAY GREEN **6H 109**
Hay Green DY9: Lye 6H **109**
Hay Grn. Cl. B30: B'vlle 1H **145**
Hay Grn. La. B30: B'vlle 2G **145**
Hay Gro. WS8: Bwnhls 5B **10**
Hay Hall Rd. B11: Tys 6F **119**
Hay Head Wood (Nature Reserve) **6A 34**
Hay Hill WS5: Wals 3A **50**
Hayland Rd. B23: Erd 1E **85**
Hay La. B90: M'path 3D **164**
Hayle Cl. B38: King Nor 5D **146**
Hayley Ct. B24: Erd 1A **86**
HAYLEY GREEN **4F 127**
Hayley Grn. Rd. B32: Bart G 5H **129**
Hayley Pk. Rd. B63: Hale 5E **127**
Hayling Cl. B45: Fran 6F **143**
Hayling Gro. WV2: Wolv 5F **43**
Haylofts, The B63: Hale 4E **127**
Haymarket, The WV8: Pend 6C **14**
HAY MILLS **5H 119**
Hay Mills B25: Yard 5F **119**
Haynes La. WS5: Wals 1F **65**
Hay Pk. B5: Edg 5F **117**
Haypits Cl. B71: W Brom 6C **64**
Hayrick Dr. DY6: W Hth 2G **91**
Hay Rd. B25: Yard 4G **119**
Hayseech B64: Crad H 4H **111**
Hayseech Rd. B63: Hale 5H **111**
Hays Kents Moat, The
B26: Yard 2E **121**
Haytor Av. B14: King H 2F **147**
Haywain Cl. WV9: Pend 5E **15**
Hayward Ind. Pk. WS9: A'rdge 2C **34**
Hayward Rd. B75: S Cold 4A **54**
Haywards Cl. B23: Erd 2E **85**
WS3: Pels .4D **20**
Haywards Ind. Est. B35: Cas V 6F **87**
Hayward St. WV14: Cose 5D **60**
Hayway, The WS2: Wals 6G **31**
Haywharf Rd. DY5: P'ntt 4F **93**
Haywood Dr. B62: B'hth 3C **112**
WV6: Tett .5A **26**
Haywood Rd. B33: Kitts G 1A **122**
Haywood's Farm B71: W Brom 3D **64**
Hazel Av. B73: New O 4C **68**
WS10: W'bry 1G **63**
Hazelbank B38: King Nor 5A **146**
Hazelbeach Rd. B8: Salt 4F **103**
Hazelbeech Rd. B70: W Brom 5H **79**
Hazel Cft. B31: N'fld 4E **145**
B37: Chel W 2D **122**
Hazeldene Gro. B6: Aston 1G **101**
Hazeldene Rd. B33: Sheld 4H **121**
B63: Hale .3G **127**
Hazel Dr. B29: W Cas 6D **130**
B47: H'wd .4B **162**
Hazeley Cl. B17: Harb 4D **114**
Hazel Gdns. B27: A Grn 1A **136**
WV8: Cod 3G **13**
Hazelglen Gro. *B18: Win G* *5A* ***100***
(off Heath Grn. Rd.)
Hazel Gro. B70: W Brom 6A **80**
DY8: Stourb 2A **124**
WV5: Wom .6G **57**
WV11: Wed 2E **29**
WV14: Bils 4G **45**
Hazelhurst Rd. B14: King H 1G **147**
B36: Cas B 2A **106**
Hazel La. WS6: Gt Wyr 3H **7**
Hazelmead Ct. B73: Bold 6G **69**
Hazelmere Dr. WS7: Chase 1B **10**
WV3: Wolv .2G **41**
Hazelmere Rd. B28: Hall G 4F **135**
Hazeloak Rd. B90: Shir 6G **149**
Hazel Rd. B45: Rub 3F **157**
DY1: Dud 5E **77**
DY4: Tip 4C **62**
DY6: K'wfrd 4C **92**
WV3: Wolv .4C **42**
Hazelton Cl. B91: Sol 6F **151**
Hazeltree Cft. B27: A Grn 3H **135**
Hazeltree Dr. B75: Four O 6H **37**
Hazeltree Gro. B93: Dorr 6A **166**
Hazelville Gro. B28: Hall G 1G **149**
Hazelville Rd. B28: Hall G 1G **149**
Hazelwell Cres. B30: Stir 1D **146**
Hazelwell Dr. B14: King H 1F **147**
Hazelwell Fordrough B30: Stir 6D **132**
Hazelwell La. B30: Stir 6D **132**
Hazelwell Rd. B30: Stir 1C **146**
Hazelwell St. B30: Stir 6C **132**
Hazelwood Cl. WS6: C Hay 3D **6**
Hazelwood Dr. WV11: Wed 4C **28**
Hazelwood Gro. WV12: W'hall 4D **30**
Hazelwood Rd. B27: A Grn 3H **135**
B74: S'tly .2F **51**
DY1: Dud 2B **76**
Hazlemere Dr. B74: Four O 3G **53**
Hazlitt Gro. B30: King Nor 3H **145**
Headborough Wlk. WS9: A'rdge 6D **22**
Headingley Rd. B21: Hand 5A **82**
Headland Dr. B8: Salt 4D **102**
Headland Rd. WV3: Wolv 2F **41**
Headlands, The B74: Lit As 6C **36**
Headley Cft. B38: King Nor 1H **159**
HEADLEY HEATH **3D 160**
Headley Heath La. B38: Head H 2D **160**
Headley Ri. B90: Shir 5B **150**
Headway Rd. WV10: F'hses 4G **15**
Heale Cl. B63: Crad 4C **110**
Heanor Cft. B6: Aston 1B **102**
Heantum Cft. WV10: Wolv 4C **28**
Heantun Ho. WV3: Wolv 4A **170**
Heantun Mill Ct. WS10: W'bry 4D **62**
Heantun Ri. WV1: Wolv 5G **27**
Heantun Row WV11: W'hall 5B **18**
Heartland Cl. B18: Hock 3B **100**
Heartland M. B65: Row R 1B **112**
Heartlands Parkway B7: Erd 4C **102**
B7: Nech .4C **102**
Heartlands Pl. B8: Salt 5E **103**
HEATH **1D 124**
Heath Acres WS10: Darl 1C **62**
Heath Bri. Cl. WS4: Rus 1E **33**
Heathbrook Av. DY6: W Hth 2H **91**
Heathcliff Rd. B11: Tys 1F **135**
DY2: Dud 2H **95**
Heath Cl. B30: B'vlle 2H **145**
B75: S Cold 5D **54**
DY4: Tip 2B **78**
WS9: Ston .2G **23**
Heathcote Av. B91: Sol 4C **150**
Heathcote Ho. *B17: Harb* *6G* ***115***
(off Vivian Cl.)
Heathcote Rd. B30: King Nor 2C **146**
Heath Ct. B12: Bal H 6H **117**
Heath Cft. B31: Longb 2E **159**
Heath Cft. Rd. B75: R'ley 2A **54**
HEATH END **6E 21**
Heather Av. WS5: Wals 1F **65**
Heather Cl. B36: Cas B 1C **106**
WS3: Blox .1G **31**
WV11: Wed 4G **29**
Heather Ct. B13: Mose 2F **133**
Heather Ct. Gdns. B74: Four O 3H **53**
Heather Cft. B44: Gt Barr 4H **67**
Heather Dale B13: Mose 3E **133**
Heather Dr. B45: Rub 3F **157**

Heather Gro. B91: Sol 1A 152
WV12: W'hall 5E 31
Heather Ho. B38: King Nor 6B 146
Heatherleigh Rd. B36: Cas B 1B 106
Heather Rd. B10: Small H 4F 119
B43: Gt Barr 5G 65
B67: Smeth 3C 98
WS3: Blox 1G 31
Heath Farm Rd. DY8: Stourb 3B 124
WV8: Bilb 5H 13
Heathfield Av. B20: Hand 1D 100
Heathfield Cl. B64: Old H 1H 111
B93: Know 4C 166
Heathfield Ct. B19: Loz 2D 100
Heathfield Dr. WS3: Blox 5H 19
Heathfield Gdns. DY8: Stourb 1D 124
WV11: Wed, W'hall 4A 30
Heathfield La. WS10: Darl 5C 46
Heathfield La. W. WS10: Darl 6B 46
Heathfield Rd. B14: King H 5G 133
B19: Hand 1D 100
B63: Hale 2G 127
B74: Four O 6F 37
Heathfields WV8: Cod 6E 13
Heath Gdns. B91: Sol 1H 151
Heath Grn. DY1: Dud 2B 76
Heathgreen Cl. B37: Chel W 6F 107
Heath Grn. Gro. B18: Win G 5A 100
(off Heath Grn. Rd.)
Heath Grn. Rd. B18: Win G 5A 100
Heath Gro. WV8: Bilb 4H 13
Heath Hill Rd. WV6: Tett 2E 41
Heath Ho. B14: King H 5H 147
Heath Ho. Dr. WV5: Wom 2D 72
Heath Ho. La. WV8: Cod 1E 25
Heathland Av. B34: S End 2E 105
Heathlands, The B65: B'hth 2C 112
DY8: Stourb 1F 125
WS2: Wals 6G 31
WV5: Wom 2D 72
Heathlands Cl. DY6: K'wfrd 1C 92
Heathlands Cres. B73: Bold 4F 69
Heathlands Gro. B31: N'fld 6E 145
Heathlands Rd. B73: Bold 3F 69
Heath La. B71: W Brom 6B 64
DY8: Stourb 1E 125
Heathleigh Rd. B38: King Nor 1G 159
Heathmere Av. B25: Yard 3B 120
Heathmere Dr. B37: F'bri 1B 122
Heath Mill Bus. Cen. WV5: Wom 4D 72
Heath Mill Cl. WV5: Wom 3D 72
Heath Mill La. B9: Birm 6H 5 (2A 118)
Heath Mill Rd. WV5: Wom 3D 72
Heath Pk. WV10: Cov H 1G 15
Heath Ri. B14: King H 6A 148
Heath Rd. B30: B'vlle 2G 145
B47: H'wd 2A 162
B91: Sol 1H 151
DY2: Neth 1D 110
WS10: Darl 3E 47
WV12: W'hall 1C 30
Heath Rd. Sth. B31: N'fld 3E 145
Heathside Dr. B38: King Nor 6D 146
WS3: Pels 3E 21
Heath St. B18: Win G 4H 99
B65: B'hth 2C 112
B66: Smeth 4H 99
DY8: Stourb 6D 108
Heath St. Ind. Est. B66: Smeth ...4H 99
Heath St. Sth. B18: Win G 5B 100
HEATH TOWN 5C 28
Heath Trad. Pk. B66: Smeth 4H 99
Heath Vw. WS2: Wals 6F 31
Heath Way B34: Hodg H, S End 2D 104
Heathway Cl. B34: S End 3E 105
Heathy Farm Cl. B32: Bart G 4H 129
Heathy Ri. B32: Bart G 3G 129
Heaton Cl. WV10: Bush 2A 16
Heaton Dr. B15: Edg 3A 116
B74: Four O 3F 53
Heaton Rd. B91: Sol 1D 150
Heaton St. B18: Hock 4D 100
Hebden Gro. B28: Hall G 4E 149
WV12: W'hall 6B 18
Heddon Pl. B7: Birm 6A 102
Hedera Cl. WS5: Wals 2F 65
Hedgefield Gro. B63: Crad 1E 127

Hedgerow Dr. DY6: K'wfrd 6B 74
Hedgerows, The B62: Roms 3A 142
Hedgerow Wlk. WV8: Pend 6C 14
Hedges, The WV5: Wom 1E 73
Hedgetree Cft. B37: Chel W 1E 123
Hedgings, The B34: S End 3F 105
(off Meadow Rd.)
Hedgley Gro. B33: Stech 5E 105
Hedingham Gro. B37: Chel W 1F 123
Hedley Cft. B35: Cas V 3F 87
Hednesford Rd. WS8: Bwnhls 2G 9
Heeley Rd. B29: S Oak 3A 132
Heer Ct. B43: Gt Barr 2F 67
Hefford Dr. B66: Smeth 3E 99
Heights, The B4: Birm 1F 5 (5G 101)
B71: W Brom 4C 64
Helena Cl. B66: Smeth 2A 98
Helena St. B1: Birm 3A 4 (6E 101)
Helenny Cl. WV11: Wed 4C 28
Helford Cl. DY4: Tip 2F 77
Hellaby Cl. B72: S Cold 1H 69
Hellaby Cl. B73: Bold 6G 69
Hellaby Ho. B74: Four O 6F 37
Hellier Av. DY4: Tip 3B 78
Hellier Dr. WV5: Wom 6A 72
Hellier Rd. WV10: Bush 5A 16
Hellier St. DY2: Dud 1E 95
Helming Dr. WV1: Wolv 6D 28
Helmsdale Way DY3: Sed 6C 60
Helmsley Cl. DY5: Brie H 3G 109
Helmsley Rd. WV11: Wed 1E 29
Helmswood Dr. B37: Chel W 3E 123
Helston Cl. DY8: Word 1A 108
WS5: Wals 4H 49
Helstone Gro. B11: Tys 2G 135
Helston Rd. WS5: Wals 4H 49
Helvellyn Way B71: W Brom 1H 79
Hembs Cres. B43: Gt Barr 5G 65
Hemisphere B5: Edg 1F 133
Hemlingford Cft. B37: Mars G 4C 122
Hemlingford Rd. B37: K'hrst 3A 106
B76: Walm 6E 71
Hemmings Cl. DY8: Stourb 6D 108
WV10: Wolv 6A 28
Hemmings St. WS10: Darl 3C 46
Hemplands Rd. DY8: Stourb 6D 108
Hempole La. DY4: Tip 6D 62
Hemyock Rd. B29: W Cas 5F 131
Henbury Dr. B37: Chel W 5E 107
Henbury Rd. B27: A Grn 2B 136
Henderson Ct. B68: O'bry 3H 113
Henderson Wlk. DY4: Tip 5B 62
Henderson Way B65: B'hth 2C 112
Hendon Cl. DY3: Lwr G 5H 75
WV10: Bush 1A 28
Hendon Rd. B11: S'hll 6B 118
Heneage Pl. B7: Birm 5A 102
Heneage St. B7: Birm 5A 102
Heneage St. W. B7: Birm 1H 5 (5H 101)
(not continuous)
Henfield Cl. WV11: Wed 2F 29
Hengham Rd. B26: Yard 2E 121
Henley Cl. B73: W Grn 5H 69
DY4: Tip 2D 78
WS3: Blox 6C 20
Henley Cres. B91: Sol 6F 137
Henley Dr. B75: Four O 6G 37
Henley Rd. WV10: Oxl 6F 15
Henley St. B11: S'brk 4A 118
Henley Vs. B12: Bal H 6B 118
(off Chesterton Rd.)
Henlow Cl. DY4: Tip 2F 77
Henlow Rd. B14: King H 5H 147
Hennalls, The B36: Hodg H 2D 104
Henn Dr. DY4: Tip 5G 61
Henne Dr. WV14: Cose 4E 61
Henn St. DY4: Tip 5A 62
Henrietta St. B19: Birm 1C 4 (5F 101)
Henry Rd. B25: Yard 4A 120
Henry St. WS2: Wals 2B 48
Hensborough B90: Dic H 4G 163
Hensel Dr. WV3: Wolv 3A 42
Henshaw Gro. B10: Small H 3C 118
B25: Yard 4A 120
Henshaw Rd. B10: Small H 3D 118
Henstead St. B5: Birm 3F 117
Henwood Cl. WV6: Tett 6A 26

Henwood La. B91: Cath B 2D 152
Henwood Rd. WV6: Tett 1A 42
Henzel Cft. DY5: Brie H 6G 93
Hepburn Cl. WS9: A'rdge 5C 34
Hepburn Edge B24: Erd 3H 85
Hepworth Cl. WV6: Pert 5F 25
Herald Cl. DY1: Dud 6E 77
Herald Rd. B26: Birm A 1E 139
Herbert Rd. B10: Small H 2C 118
B21: Hand 6B 82
B67: Smeth 2E 115
B91: Sol 4F 151
WS9: A'rdge 6C 22
Herberts Pk. Rd. WS10: Darl 5B 46
Herbert St. B70: W Brom 4B 80
WV1: Wolv 1C 170 (6H 27)
WV14: Bils 5D 44
Herbhill Cl. WV4: Penn 1H 59
Hereford Av. B12: Bal H 5A 118
Hereford Cl. B45: Fran 5G 143
WS9: A'rdge 1C 34
Hereford Ho. WV1: Wolv 6G 27
(off Lomas Cl.)
Hereford Pl. B71: W Brom 6H 63
Hereford Rd. B68: O'bry 4H 113
DY2: Neth 6G 95
Hereford St. WS2: Wals 5C 32
Hereford Wlk. B37: Mars G 2B 122
Hereward Ri. B62: Hale 6B 112
Heritage, The WS1: Wals 3C 48
(off Wednesbury Rd.)
Heritage Cl. B68: O'bry 5A 98
Heritage Ct. B18: Birm 1A 4
DY5: Quar B 2C 110
Heritage Way B33: Kitts G 6H 105
DY4: Tip 2B 78
Hermes Ct. B74: Four O 6F 37
Hermitage, The B91: Sol 1G 151
Hermitage Dr. B76: Walm 2D 70
Hermitage Rd. B15: Edg 2G 115
B23: Erd 4D 84
B91: Sol 2G 151
Hermit St. DY3: Up Gor 2H 75
Hermon Row B11: S'brk 6D 118
Hernall Cft. B26: Sheld 4E 121
Herne Cl. B18: Hock 5C 100
Hernefield Rd. B34: S End 2E 105
Hernehurst B32: Quin 6H 113
Hern Rd. DY5: Brie H 5G 109
Heroes Way B15: Edg 1A 132
Heron Cl. B90: Ches G 5B 164
WS8: Bwnhls 6A 10
Heron Ct. B73: W Grn 6H 69
(off Emscote Dr.)
Herondale Cres. B78: Stourb 1A 124
Herondale Rd. B26: Sheld 5D 120
DY8: Stourb 1A 124
Heronfield Dr. B31: Longb 3D 158
Heronfield Way B91: Sol 2A 152
Heron Ho. DY4: Tip 2G 77
Heron Mill WS3: Pels 4C 20
Heron Rd. B68: O'bry 1G 113
Heronry, The WV6: Tett 1F 41
Herons Way B29: S Oak 2G 131
Heronswood Dr. DY5: Brie H 2H 109
Heronswood Rd. B45: Redn 3H 157
Heronville Dr. B70: W Brom 6G 63
Heronville Ho. DY4: Tip 4A 78
Heronville Rd. B70: W Brom 1F 79
Heron Way B45: Rub 2F 157
Herrick Rd. B8: Salt 4E 103
Herringshaw Cft. B76: Walm 2C 70
Hertford St. B12: Bal H 6A 118
Hertford Way B93: Know 5D 166
Hervey Gro. B24: Erd 1B 86
Hesket Av. B68: O'bry 2A 114
Hesketh Cres. B23: Erd 2C 84
Hessian Cl. WV14: Cose 3D 60
Hestia Dr. B29: S Oak 5A 132
Heston Av. B42: Gt Barr 5C 66
Hever Av. B44: K'sdng 4A 68
Hever Cl. DY1: Dud 4A 76
Hewell Cl. B31: Longb 2D 158
DY6: K'wfrd 6B 74
Hewitson Gdns. B67: Smeth 1D 114
Hewitt St. WS10: Darl 5C 46
Hexham Cft. B36: Hodg H 1A 104

Hexham Way DY1: Dud 5B 76
Hexton CI. B90: Shir 5D 148
Heybarnes Cir. B10: Small H 4F 119
Heybarnes Rd. B10: Small H 4F 119
Heycott Gro. B38: King Nor 5E 147
Heydon Rd. DY5: P'ntt 4F 93
Heyford Gro. B91: Sol 1G 165
Heyford Way B35: Cas V 2F 87
Heygate Way WS9: A'rdge 5D 22
Heyland Cnr. B10: Small H 2F 119
Heynesfield Rd. B33: Kitts G 6G 105
Heythrop Gro. B13: Mose 5D 134
Hickman Av. WV1: Wolv 2C 44
Hickman Gdns. B16: Edg 2B 116
Hickman Pl. WV14: Bils 5E 45
Hickman Rd. B11: S'brk 5B 118
     DY4: Tip 5H 61
     DY5: Brie H 5G 93
     WV14: Bils 6E 45
Hickman's Av. B64: Old H 1G 111
Hickmans CI. B62: Quin 5G 113
Hickman St. DY9: Lye 5G 109
Hickmerelands DY3: Sed 3H 59
Hickmerelands La. DY3: Sed 5H 59
Hickory Dr. B17: Edg 1E 115
Hickory Way B29: W Cas 1E 145
Hidcote Av. B76: Walm 5E 71
Hidcote Gro. B33: Sheld 3G 121
     B37: Mars G 4C 122
Hidson Rd. B23: Erd 2C 84
Higgins Av. WV14: Cose 3F 61
Higgins La. B32: Quin 6A 114
Higgins Wlk. B66: Smeth 3F 99
Higgs Fld. Cres. B64: Old H 2B 112
Higgs Rd. WV11: Wed 6A 18
Highams CI. B65: Row R 6B 96
Higham Way WV10: Wolv 3A 28
High Arcal Dr. DY3: Sed 6B 60
High Arcal Rd. DY3: Lwr G 4D 74
High Av. B64: Crad H 3H 111
High Beeches B43: Gt Barr 4H 65
HIGHBRIDGE 2E 21
Highbridge Rd. B73: Bold, W Grn 4F 69
     DY2: Neth 6C 94
High Brink Rd. B46: Col 2H 107
Highbrook CI. WV9: Pend 5E 15
High Brow B17: Harb 4F 115
High Bullen WS10: W'bry 2F 63
Highbury Av. B21: Hand 1B 100
     B65: Row R 6D 96
Highbury CI. B65: Row R 6D 96
Highbury Ct. B13: Mose 6G 133
Highbury Little Theatre 6G 69
Highbury Rd. B14: King H 5F 133
     B66: Smeth 2B 98
     B68: O'bry 4H 97
     B74: Four O 6C 36
High Clere B64: Crad H 4A 112
Highcrest CI. B31: Longb 2E 159
Highcroft WS9: A'rdge 5D 22
Highcroft B43: Gt Barr 4G 65
     WS3: Pels 2F 21
Highcroft Av. DY8: Word 6A 92
Highcroft CI. B92: Sol 3G 137
Highcroft Dr. B74: Four O 6E 37
Highcroft Hall B23: Erd 4E 85
Highcroft Rd. B23: Erd 4E 85
Highcroft Vs. B23: Erd 3E 85
Highdown Cres. B90: M'path 3E 165
HIGH ERCAL 1G 109
High Ercal Av. DY5: Brie H 1G 109
High Farm Rd. B62: B'hth 3F 113
     B63: Hale 2G 127
Highfield CV7: Mer 4H 141
Highfield Av. WS4: S'fld 1G 33
     WV10: Bush 5C 16
Highfield CI. B28: Hall G 2D 148
Highfield Ct. B73: W Grn 4H 69
     DY2: Dud 5H 77
Highfield Cres. B63: Crad 5F 111
     B65: B'hth 3B 112
     WV11: Wed 3D 28
Highfield Dr. B73: Bold 6F 69
Highfield La. B32: Quin 5H 113
     B63: Hale 2H 127
Highfield M. B63: Crad 5F 111
Highfield Pas. WS1: Wals 3C 48

Highfield PI. B14: Yard W 2D 148
Highfield Rd. B8: Salt 5E 103
     B13: Mose 2B 134
     B14: Yard W 2D 148
     B15: Edg 3C 116
     B28: Hall G 2D 148
     B43: Gt Barr 6G 65
     B63: Crad 6F 111
     B65: B'hth 2B 112
     B67: Smeth 4D 98
     DY2: Dud 6G 77
     DY3: Sed 4H 59
     DY4: Tip 6A 62
     DY8: Word 1E 109
     WS3: Pels 3E 21
Highfield Rd. Nth. WS3: Pels 2D 20
HIGHFIELDS 1B 10
Highfields B23: Erd 3C 84
Highfields, The WV6: Tett 1G 41
Highfields Av. WV14: Bils 1G 61
Highfields Ct. WV4: Penn 5A 42
Highfields Dr. WV5: Wom 2G 73
     WV14: Cose 2F 61
Highfields Grange WS6: C Hay 4D 6
Highfields Pk. WS6: C Hay 4D 6
Highfields Rd. WS7: Chase 1B 10
Highfield Ter. B18: Hock 4C 100
Highfield Way WS9: A'rdge 5D 22
HIGHGATE 4H 117
Highgate B74: S'tly 2A 52
     DY3: Up Gor 2A 76
Highgate Av. WS1: Wals 3D 48
     WV4: Penn 5B 42
Highgate Bus. Cen. B12: Bal H 5B 118
Highgate CI. B12: Birm 4H 117
     WS1: Wals 4D 48
Highgate Common Country Pk. 1A 90
Highgate Comn. E.
     DY3: Stourt, Swind 2A 90
     DY7: Stourt 2A 90
Highgate Dr. WS1: Wals 4D 48
Highgate Ho. B5: Birm 3G 117
                                    (off Southace Av.)
Highgate Middleway B12: Birm 4H 117
Highgate PI. B12: Birm 4A 118
Highgate Retail Est. B12: Birm 4A 118
Highgate Rd. B12: Bal H 5A 118
     DY2: Dud 3B 94
     WS1: Wals 3D 48
Highgate Sq. B12: Birm 4H 117
Highgate St. B12: Birm 4H 117
     B64: Old H 1H 111
                                    (not continuous)
Highgrove WV6: Tett 6A 26
Highgrove CI. WV12: W'hall 2B 30
Highgrove PI. DY1: Dud 5B 76
High Haden Cres.
     B64: Crad H, Old H 3A 112
High Haden Rd. B64: Crad H, Old H . .3A 112
HIGH HEATH 3F 55
     B75 . . . . .3F 55
     WS4 . . . . .5G 21
High Heath CI. B30: B'vlle 2H 145
High Hill WV11: Ess 5A 18
High Holborn DY3: Sed 6H 59
High Ho. Dr. B45: Lick 6F 157
Highland Ho. B62: B'hth 3C 112
Highland M. WV14: Cose 4F 61
Highland Ridge B62: Quin 6E 113
High Land Rd. WS9: Wals W 4D 22
Highland Rd. B23: Erd 2F 85
     B43: Gt Barr 2A 66
     B64: Old H 1G 111
     DY1: Dud 4C 76
Highlands Ct. B90: Shir 1C 164
Highlands Ind. Est., The B90: Shir . . .1C 164
Highlands Rd. B90: Shir 1C 164
     WV3: Wolv 3B 42
High Leasowes B63: Hale 1A 128
High Lodge B46: Col 1F 107
                                    (off Coventry Rd.)
High Mdw. Rd. B38: King Nor 5C 146
High Mdws. WV5: Wom 1G 73
     WV6: Tett 6A 26
Highmoor CI. WV12: W'hall 2B 30
     WV14: Cose 2F 61

Highmoor Rd. B65: Row R 6B 96
Highmore Dr. B32: Bart G 5A 130
High Oak DY5: P'ntt 2G 93
Highover Dr. B75: Four O 5G 37
High Pk. Av. DY8: Woll 6B 108
High Pk. CI. B66: Smeth 4F 99
     DY3: Sed 4H 59
High Pk. Cres. DY3: Sed 4H 59
HIGH PARK ESTATE 6B 108
High Pk. Rd. B63: Crad 6E 111
High Pk. St. B7: Nech 3B 102
High Point B15: Edg 5A 116
High Ridge WS9: A'rdge 4B 34
High Ridge CI. WS9: A'rdge 4A 34
     WS10: Mox 1A 62
High Rd. WV12: W'hall 4C 30
High St. B2: Birm 4E 5 (1G 117)
     B4: Birm 4E 5 (1G 117)
     B6: Aston 2G 101
     B8: Salt 4C 102
     B14: King H 5G 133
     B17: Harb 6G 115
     B23: Erd 2G 85
                                    (not continuous)
     B32: Quin 5G 113
     B35: Cas V 4F 87
     B46: Col 1H 107
     B63: Hale 1B 128
     B64: Crad H 3E 111
     B65: B'hth 2B 112
     B66: Smeth 3D 98
     B70: W Brom 3H 79
                                    (not continuous)
     B72: S Cold 5A 54
     B90: Shir 5C 148
     B91: Sol 3G 151
     B92: H Ard 1A 154
     B93: Know 3E 167
     DY1: Dud 6E 77
     DY3: Sed 4H 59
     DY3: Swind 5E 73
     DY4: Tip 2G 77
                                    (Castle St.)
     DY4: Tip 5G 61
                                    (Short St.)
     DY5: Brie H 5F 93
                                    (School La.)
     DY5: Brie H 1H 109
                                    (Venture Way)
     DY5: P'ntt 2E 93
     DY5: Quar B 2B 110
     DY6: K'wfrd 3B 92
     DY6: W Hth 1H 91
     DY8: Stourb 6E 109
     DY8: Woll 5C 108
     DY8: Word 6C 92
     DY9: Lye 6A 110
     WS1: Wals 2C 48
     WS3: Blox 6H 19
     WS3: Pels 3E 21
     WS6: C Hay 3D 6
     WS7: Chase 1B 10
                                    (not continuous)
     WS8: Bwnhls 6B 10
     WS8: Clay 1A 22
     WS9: A'rdge 3D 34
                                    (not continuous)
     WS9: Wals W 4B 22
     WS10: Mox 1A 62
     WS11: Nort C 1F 9
     WV5: Wom 1H 73
     WV6: Tett 5B 26
     WV11: Wed 4E 29
     WV14: Bils 6F 45
High St. Amblecote DY8: Amb 3D 108
High St. Bordesley B12: Birm 2A 118
High St. Deritend B12: Birm . . .6H 5 (2H 117)
Highters CI. B14: King H 5B 148
HIGHTER'S HEATH 5H 147
Highter's Heath La. B14: King H 6A 148
Highters Rd. B14: King H 4A 148
High Timbers B45: Fran 6F 143
High Twr. B7: Birm 4B 102
Hightown B63: Crad 5E 111
                                    (not continuous)
Hightree CI. B32: Bart G 4H 129
High Trees B20: Hand 4B 82

High Trees Rd.—Hobacre Cl.

High Trees Rd. B93: Know 2C 166
High Vw. WV14: Cose 4B 60
Highview *WS1: Wals 3D 48*
(off Highgate Rd.)
Highview Dr. DY6: K'wfrd 5D 92
Highview St. DY2: Dud 6G 77
Highwood Av. B92: Olton 4E 137
High Wood Cl. DY6: K'wfrd 3A 92
Highwood Cft. B38: King Nor 6H 145
Hiker Gro. B37: Chel W 1F 123
Hilary Cres. DY1: Dud 1D 76
Hilary Dr. B76: Walm 2E 71
WS9: A'rdge 4C 34
WV3: Wolv 4B 42
Hilary Gro. B31: N'fld 3D 144
Hilden Rd. B7: Birm 5A 102
Hilderic Cres. DY1: Dud 2B 94
Hilderstone Rd. B25: Yard 5A 120
Hildicks Cres. WS3: Wals 2D 32
Hildicks Pl. WS3: Wals 2D 32
HILL 5G 37
Hill, The B32: Bart G 3C 130
Hillaire Cl. B38: King Nor 5E 147
Hillaries Rd. B23: Erd 5D 84
Hillary Av. WS10: W'bry 2A 64
Hillary Crest DY3: Up Gor 2A 76
Hillary St. WS2: Wals 4A 48
Hill Av. WV4: Ett 2B 60
Hill Bank DY9: Lye 6B 110
Hillbank B69: Tiv 6D 78
Hill Bank Dr. B33: Stech 5B 104
Hill Bank Rd. B38: King Nor 5C 146
B63: Crad 5F 111
Hillborough Rd. B27: A Grn 3C 136
Hillbrook Gro. B33: Stech 6D 104
Hillbrow Cres. B62: B'hth 3F 113
Hillbury Dr. WV12: W'hall 1B 30
Hill Cl. B31: N'fld 6F 145
DY3: Sed 4A 60
Hillcrest DY3: Lwr G 3G 75
Hillcrest Av. B43: Gt Barr 3A 66
B63: Crad 4D 110
DY5: Brie H 2G 109
WV10: Bush 6A 16
Hillcrest Bus. Pk. DY2: Neth 2E 95
Hillcrest Cl. DY2: Neth 4E 95
Hillcrest Community Leisure Cen. 4E 95
Hillcrest Gdns. WV12: W'hall 4D 30
Hill Crest Gro. B44: K'sdng 6A 68
Hillcrest Ind. Est. B64: Crad H 3F 111
Hillcrest Ri. WS7: Burn 1D 10
Hill Crest Rd. B13: Mose 3G 133
Hillcrest Rd. B43: Gt Barr 3A 66
B62: Roms 3A 142
B72: W Grn 5A 70
DY2: Dud 6G 77
Hillcroft Ho. B14: King H 5H 147
Hill Cft. Rd. B14: King H 1E 147
Hillcroft Rd. DY6: K'wfrd 2C 92
Hillcross Wlk. B36: Hodg H 1D 104
(not continous)
Hilldene Rd. DY6: K'wfrd 5A 92
Hilldrop Gro. B17: Harb 2H 131
Hilleys Cft. B37: F'bri 6B 106
HILLFIELD 6F 151
Hillfield Hall Ct. B91: Sol 6G 151
Hillfield M. B91: Sol 1F 165
Hillfield Rd. B11: S'hll 2D 134
B91: Sol 5G 151
Hillfields B67: Smeth 6B 98
Hillfields Rd. DY5: Brie H 4F 109
Hillfield Wlk. B65: Row R 4H 95
Hill Gro. B20: Hand 5E 83
Hillhampton Cl. B92: Sol 4G 137
HILL HOOK 4E 37
Hill Hook Nature Reserve 4F 37
Hill Hook Rd. B74: Four O 4E 37
Hill Ho. *B66: Smeth 3G 99*
(off Oakfield Cl.)
Hill Ho. La. B33: Stech 6D 104
(not continuous)
Hillhurst Gro. B36: Cas B 6H 87
Hillhurst Rd. B73: New O 2B 68
Hilliards Cft. B42: Gt Barr 5C 66
Hillingford Av. B43: Gt Barr 2E 67
Hill La. B43: Gt Barr 3A 66
B75: Bass P 1F 55
Hillman Dr. DY2: Dud 2G 95
Hillman Gro. B36: Cas B 6A 88
Hillmeads Dr. DY2: Dud 2G 95
Hillmeads Rd. B38: King Nor 6C 146
Hillmorton B74: Four O 6F 37
Hillmorton Rd. B74: Four O 5F 37
B93: Know 4C 166
Hillmount Cl. B28: Hall G 3E 135
Hill Pk. WS9: Wals W 3C 22
Hill Pas. B64: Old H 1G 111
Hill Pl. WV11: Wed 6A 18
Hill Rd. B69: Tiv 5A 78
DY9: Lye 6A 110
WV13: W'hall 2F 45
Hillside DY3: Lwr G 3G 75
WS8: Bwnhls 1C 22
WV5: Wom 6E 57
Hillside Av. B63: Crad 5F 111
B65: B'hth 3B 112
DY5: Quar B 3C 110
Hillside Cl. B32: Bart G 5G 129
WS8: Bwnhls 1C 22
Hillside Ct. B43: Gt Barr 3H 65
Hillside Cres. WS3: Pels 5D 20
Hillside Cft. B92: Sol 1A 138
Hillside Dr. B37: K'hrst 5B 106
B42: Gt Barr 1C 82
B74: S'tly 4H 51
Hillside Gdns. B37: K'hrst 5B 106
WV1: Wolv 6C 20
Hillside Ho. B45: Rub 1F 157
Hillside Rd. B23: Erd 5D 84
B43: Gt Barr 3H 65
B74: Four O 5G 37
DY1: Dud 2C 76
Hillside Wlk. WV1: Wolv 6C 28
Hillstone Gdns. WV10: Bush 1B 28
Hillstone Rd. B34: S End 4H 105
Hill St. B2: Birm 4C 4 (1F 117)
B5: Birm 4C 4 (1F 117)
B63: Hale 2A 128
B66: Smeth 3E 99
DY2: Neth 4D 94
DY3: Up Gor 2H 75
DY4: Tip 3H 77
DY5: Brie H 1H 109
DY5: Quar B 3C 110
DY8: Amb 3D 108
DY8: Stourb 1D 124
DY9: Lye 6B 110
WS1: Wals 2D 48
WS6: C Hay 3C 6
WS10: Darl 5E 47
WV11: Ess 4H 17
WV14: Bils 2G 61
HILL TOP 6G 63
Hill Top B70: W Brom 5G 63
DY9: W'cte 2A 126
Hill Top Av. B62: B'hth 4E 113
Hill Top Cl. B44: Gt Barr 1G 83
Hilltop Dr. B36: Hodg H 1B 104
Hilltop Golf Course 3G 81
Hill Top Ind. Est. B70: W Brom 5F 63
(not continuous)
Hill Top Rd. B31: N'fld 4D 144
B68: O'bry 1A 114
Hilltop Rd. DY2: Dud 1G 95
Hill Top Wlk. WS9: A'rdge 6E 23
Hillview WS9: A'rdge 5D 22
Hillview Cl. B63: Hale 5G 111
Hillview Rd. B45: Rub 1E 157
Hill Village Rd. B75: Four O 4G 37
Hillville Gdns. DY8: Stourb 2F 125
HILL WOOD 5A 38
Hillwood WS3: Pels 5D 20
Hillwood Av. B90: M'path 3E 165
Hillwood Cl. DY6: K'wfrd 5A 92
Hillwood Comn. Rd. B75: Four O 5H 37
Hillwood Rd. B31: N'fld 6C 130
B62: B'hth 4C 112
B75: Four O, R'ley 5H 37
Hillyfields Rd. B23: Erd 3C 84
Hilly Rd. WV14: Bils 3G 61
Hilsea Cl. WV8: Pend 6D 14
Hilston Av. B63: Hale 1H 127
WV4: Penn 1A 58
HILTON 5H 11
Hilton Av. B28: Hall G 3E 149
Hilton Cl. WS3: Blox 5F 19
Hilton Cross WV10: F'stne 2D 16
Hilton Cross Bus. Pk. WV10: F'stne 1D 16
Hilton Dr. B72: W Grn 5A 70
Hilton La. WS6: Gt Wyr 3F 7
WV11: Ess 6A 6
Hilton Main Ind. Est. WV11: F'stne 2E 17
Hilton Pk. WV11: Ess 1G 17
HILTON PARK SERVICE AREA 6A 6
Hilton Pl. WV14: Bils 6H 45
Hilton Rd. B69: Tiv 1C 96
WV4: Ett 6B 44
WV10: F'stne 1D 16
WV12: W'hall 1C 30
Hilton St. B70: W Brom 4G 79
WV10: Wolv 6A 28
Hilton Trad. Est. WV4: Ett 6B 44
Hilton Way WV12: W'hall 1C 30
Himbleton Cft. B90: M'path 2E 165
HIMLEY 4H 73
Himley Av. DY1: Dud 5B 76
Himley By-Pass DY3: Himl 4G 73
Himley Cl. B43: Gt Barr 3G 65
WV12: W'hall 4B 30
WV14: Bils 1G 61
Himley Ct. *DY3: Lwr G 4A 76*
(off Peak Dr.)
Himley Cres. WV4: Penn 6F 43
Himley Gdns. DY3: Lwr G 3D 74
Himley Gro. B45: Redn 3H 157
Himley Hall 3B 74
Himley Hall Golf Course 3C 74
Himley Hall Sailing Club 4A 74
Himley La. DY3: Himl, Swind 5E 73
(not continuous)
Himley Pk. 2B 74
Himley Plantation 4G 73
Himley Ri. B90: Ches G 5C 164
Himley Rd. DY1: Dud 5G 75
DY3: Gorn 4E 75
Himley St. DY1: Dud 6C 76
Hinbrook Rd. DY1: Dud 6A 76
Hinchliffe Av. WV14: Cose 3D 60
Hinchwick Ct. B93: Dorr 6B 166
Hinckes Rd. WV6: Tett 4H 25
Hinckley St. B5: Birm 6D 4 (2F 117)
Hincks St. WV2: Ett 4C 44
Hindhead Rd. B14: Yard W 3C 148
Hindlip Cl. B63: Hale 3H 127
Hindlow Cl. B7: Birm 5B 102
Hindon Gro. B27: A Grn 6A 136
Hindon Sq. B15: Edg 3B 116
Hindon Wlk. B32: Bart G 3A 130
Hingeston St. B18: Hock 5D 100
Hingley Ct. *B64: Old H 1G 111*
(off Hill Pas.)
Hingley Cft. WS9: A'rdge 6H 35
Hingley Ind. Pk. B64: Crad H 2E 111
Hingley Rd. B63: Crad 5C 110
Hingley St. B64: Crad H 2F 111
HINKSFORD 1E 91
Hinksford Gdns. DY3: Swind 5E 73
Hinksford La. DY3: Swind 5E 73
DY6: K'wfrd 1F 91
Hinksford Pk. Res. Mobile Homes
DY6: K'wfrd 1E 91
Hinsford Cl. DY6: K'wfrd 1C 92
Hinstock Cl. WV4: Penn 1E 59
Hinstock Rd. B20: Hand 6B 82
Hintlesham Av. B15: Edg 6H 115
Hinton Gro. WV11: Wed 4H 29
Hintons Coppice B93: Know 3A 166
Hipkins St. DY4: Tip 6G 61
Hiplands Rd. B62: Hale 1F 129
Hipsley Cl. B36: Cas B 6G 87
Hipsmoor Cl. B37: K'hrst 6B 106
Hirdemonsway B90: Dic H 4G 163
Histons Dr. WV8: Cod 5F 13
Histons Hill WV8: Cod 5F 13
Hitchcock Cl. B67: Smeth 4B 98
Hitches La. B15: Edg 4D 116
Hitherside B90: Dic H 4H 163
Hive Development Cen.
B18: Hock 2C 100
HMP Birmingham B18: Win G 4A 100
Hobacre Cl. B45: Rub 1G 157

A-Z Birmingham 225

Hobart Ct. B74: Four O 6G 37
Hobart Cft. B7: Birm 5A 102
Hobart Dr. WS5: Wals 5G 49
Hobart Rd. DY4: Tip 4G 61
Hobbis Ho. B38: King Nor 2G 159
HOBBLE END .6H 7
Hobble End La. WS6: Gt Wyr 1G 19
Hobgate Cl. WV10: Wolv 5B 28
Hobgate Rd. WV10: Wolv 5B 28
Hob Grn. Rd. DY9: W'cte 3A 126
Hobhouse Cl. B42: Gt Barr 6B 66
Hob La. B92: Bars 3A 168
Hobley St. WV13: W'hall 1C 46
Hob Moor Cl. B10: Bord G 2G 119
Hobmoor Cft. B25: Yard 4B 120
Hob Moor Rd. B10: Small H 2F 119
B25: Yard 3A 120
Hobnock Rd. WV11: Ess 3A 18
Hobs Hole La. WS9: A'rdge 2D 34
Hob's Mdw. B92: Olton 3E 137
Hobs Moat Rd. B92: Olton, Sol 3F 137
Hobson Cl. B18: Hock 4C 100
Hobson Rd. B29: S Oak 4D 132
Hobs Rd. WS10: W'bry 1G 63
HOCKLEY 4D 100
Hockley Brook Cl. B18: Hock 4C 100
Hockley Brook Trad. Est. B18: Hock . .3C 100
Hockley Centre, The B18: Birm 1A 4
Hockley Cir. B18: Hock 3D 100
Hockley Cl. B19: Hock 3F 101
Hockley Flyover B18: Hock 3D 100
B19: Hock 3D 100
Hockley Hill B18: Birm 4D 100
Hockley Hill Ind. Est. B18: Hock 4D 100
Hockley Ind. Est. B18: Hock 4D 100
Hockley La. DY2: Neth 6D 94
Hockley Pool Cl. B18: Hock 4D 100
Hockley Rd. B23: Erd 3D 84
WV14: Cose 6C 60
Hockley St. B18: Birm 5E 101
B19: Birm 5E 101
Hodder Gro. B71: W Brom 6D 64
HODGEHILL .3B 104
Hodge Hill Av. DY9: W'cte 2A 126
Hodge Hill Comn. B34: Hodg H 3C 104
B36: Hodg H 2C 104
Hodgehill Ct. B36: Hodg H 2C 104
Hodge Hill Rd. B34: Hodg H 3C 104
Hodges Dr. B69: Tiv 6B 78
Hodgetts Cl. B67: Smeth 6B 98
Hodgetts Dr. B63: Hale 5F 127
Hodgkins Cl. WS8: Bwnhls 1C 22
Hodgkiss Cl. WS10: W'bry 1E 63
Hodgson Twr. B19: Hock 3F 101
Hodnell Cl. B36: Cas B 6G 87
Hodnet Cl. WV14: Bils 6D 44
Hodnet Dr. DY5: P'ntt 3G 93
Hodnet Gro. B5: Birm 3G 117
Hodson Av. WV13: W'hall 2C 46
Hodson Cl. WV11: Wed 1H 29
Hoff Beck Ct. B9: Birm 1B 118
Hogarth Cl. B43: Gt Barr 6F 51
WV13: W'hall 1G 45
Hogarth Ho. B15: Birm 3E 117
Hogg's La. B31: N'fld 3C 144
HOLBEACHE .6A 74
Holbeache La. DY6: K'wfrd 6A 74
Holbeache Rd. DY6: W Hth 1A 92
Holbeach Rd. B33: Yard 1F 121
Holbeche Rd. B75: S Cold 6F 55
B93: Know 2C 166
Holberg Gro. WV11: Wed 4H 29
Holborn Cen., The DY3: Sed 6H 59
Holborn Hill B6: Aston 1B 102
B7: Nech 1B 102
Holbrook Gro. B37: Mars G 2D 122
Holbrook Twr. B36: Hodg H 1A 104
Holbury Cl. WV9: Pend 5E 15
Holcombe Rd. B11: Tys 1G 135
Holcroft Rd. B63: Crad 6E 111
DY6: W Hth 6A 74
DY9: Lye 1G 125
Holcroft St. DY4: Tip 5A 78
WV2: Ett 4C 44
Holden Cl. B23: Erd 5E 85
Holden Cres. WS3: Wals 4C 32
Holden Cft. DY4: Tip 4A 78

Holden Pl. WS3: Wals 5C 32
Holden Rd. WS10: W'bry 3G 63
WV4: Penn 2B 58
Holdens, The B28: Hall G 1E 149
Holden Way B74: Four O 1H 53
Holder Rd. B11: S'brk 5C 118
B25: Yard 4A 120
Holders Gdns. B13: Mose 3E 133
Holders La. B13: Mose 3E 133
Holdford Rd. B6: Witt 5H 83
Holdgate Rd. B29: W Cas 6F 131
Hole Farm Rd. B31: N'fld 3G 145
Hole Farm Way B38: King Nor 2B 160
Hole La. B31: N'fld 1G 145
Holendene Way WV5: Wom 6E 57
Holford Av. WS2: Wals 5A 48
Holford Dr. B6: Witt 3G 83
B42: P Barr 3G 83
Holford Ind. Pk. B6: Witt 4H 83
Holford Way B6: Witt 3H 83
Holifast Rd. B72: W Grn 6H 69
Holland Av. B68: O'bry 5B 98
B93: Know 1D 166
Holland Ho. B19: Birm 4F 101
(off Gt. Hampton Row)
Holland Ind. Pk. WS10: Darl 3D 46
HOLLAND PARK 4A 10
Holland Rd. B43: Gt Barr 6H 65
B72: S Cold 2H 69
WV14: Bils 4G 45
Holland Rd. E. B6: Aston 3A 102
Holland Rd. W. B6: Aston 3H 101
Hollands Pl. WS3: Blox 6B 20
Hollands Rd. WS3: Blox 6B 20
Holland St. B3: Birm 3A 4 (6E 101)
B72: S Cold 1H 69
DY1: Dud 1D 94
DY4: Tip 6C 62
Hollands Way WS3: Pels 3D 20
Hollemeadow Av. WS3: Blox 2B 32
Holliars Gro. B37: K'hrst 4B 106
Holliday Pas. B1: Birm 6B 4 (2E 117)
Holliday Rd. B21: Hand 2B 100
B24: Erd 3G 85
Holliday St. B1: Birm 6A 4 (2E 117)
Holliday Wharf B1: Birm 6B 4 (2E 117)
Hollie Lucas Rd. B13: Mose 6H 133
Hollies, The B6: Aston 1B 102
B16: Birm 6B 100
B66: Smeth 5G 99
(off Montague Rd.)
WS6: Gt Wyr 5E 7
WV2: Wolv 6A 170 (3G 43)
WV3: Wolv 5E 43
WV6: Wolv 6H 57
Hollies Cft. B5: Edg 6E 117
Hollies Dr. B62: Hale 5D 112
WS10: W'bry 2F 63
Hollies Ind. Est.
WV2: Wolv 6A 170 (3G 43)
Hollies La. WV6: Patt 5A 24
Hollies Ri. B64: Crad H 3H 111
Hollies St. DY5: P'ntt 2H 93
Hollin Brow Cl. B93: Know 6D 166
Hollinberry La. B76: Walm 2D 70
Hollings Gro. B91: Sol 1F 165
Hollington Cres. B33: Stech 5E 105
Hollington Rd. WV1: Wolv 3D 44
Hollington Way B90: M'path 2G 165
Hollinwell Ct. WS3: Blox 4G 19
Hollister Dr. B32: Bart G 2D 130
Hollow, The B13: Mose 1G 133
Holloway B31: N'fld 1C 144
Holloway, The DY3: Swind 6D 72
DY8: Amb 4D 108
WV6: Tett 1A 42
Holloway Bank B70: W Brom 4F 63
WS10: W'bry 4F 63
Holloway Bank Trad. Est.
WS10: W'bry 4F 63
Holloway Cir. Queensway
B1: Birm 6D 4 (2F 117)
Holloway Ct. B63: Crad 6F 111
WV5: Wom 2E 73
Holloway Dr. WV5: Wom 2E 73
HOLLOWAY END 5F 109

Holloway Head B1: Birm 6C 4 (2F 117)
Holloway St. DY3: Lwr G, Up Gor 3H 75
WV1: Wolv 4C 44
Holloway St. W. DY3: Lwr G 2H 75
Hollow Cft. B31: N'fld 4F 145
Hollowcroft Rd. WV12: W'hall 1B 30
Hollowmeadow Ho. B36: Hodg H 1B 104
Holly Av. B12: Bal H 6B 118
B29: S Oak 4D 132
HOLLY BANK 4C 22
Hollybank Av. WV11: Ess 4A 18
Hollybank Cl. WS3: Blox 5G 19
Hollybank Gro. B63: Hale 4F 127
Hollybank Rd. B13: Mose 6A 134
Hollyberry Av. B91: Sol 1E 165
Hollyberry Cl. B63: Hale 2A 128
Hollyberry Cft. B34: S End 3G 105
Hollybrow B29: W Cas 6E 131
Hollybush Garden Centre Miniature Railway
. . . . .3A 6
Holly Bush Gro. B32: Quin 4B 114
Holly Bush La. WV10: Share 5A 6
Hollybush La. DY8: Amb 4D 108
WV4: Penn 1B 58
WV8: Oaken 5D 12
Holly Bush Wlk. B64: Crad H 2F 111
Holly Cl. B76: Walm 3D 70
WV12: W'hall 3C 30
Hollycot Gdns. B12: Bal H 5H 117
Holly Ct. B23: Erd 2G 85
WS5: Wals 1E 65
Hollycroft Gdns. WV6: Tett 4H 25
Hollycroft Rd. B21: Hand 6H 81
Hollydale Rd. B24: Erd 4A 86
B65: Row R 6D 96
Holly Dell B38: King Nor 5D 146
Holly Dr. B27: A Grn 3H 135
B47: H'wd 2B 162
Hollyfaste Rd. B33: Sheld 2F 121
Hollyfield Av. B91: Sol 4C 150
Hollyfield Ct. B75: S Cold 6C 54
Hollyfield Cres. B75: S Cold 1C 70
Hollyfield Dr. B75: S Cold 6C 54
Hollyfield Rd. B75: S Cold 6C 54
Hollyfield Rd. Sth. B76: Walm 1D 70
Holly Grange B66: Smeth 2B 98
Holly Gro. B19: Hand 1D 100
B29: S Oak 3B 132
(Exeter Rd.)
B29: S Oak 3B 132
(Tiverton Rd.)
B30: B'vlle 5B 132
DY8: Stourb 6D 108
WV3: Wolv 4D 42
Holly Hall Rd. DY2: Dud 3C 94
Hollyhedge Cl. B31: N'fld 1B 144
WS2: Wals 1A 48
Hollyhedge La. WS2: Wals 6A 32
Hollyhedge Rd. B71: W Brom 6C 64
Holly Hill B45: Fran 6F 143
WS6: Gt Wyr 5E 7
(off Holly La.)
Holly Hill Rd. B45: Fran 5G 143
Holly Hill Shop. Cen. B45: Fran 6G 143
Hollyhock Rd. B27: A Grn 4F 135
DY2: Dud 6H 77
Hollyhurst B46: Wat O 4E 89
Hollyhurst Caravan Pk. B62: Hunn . . .1B 142
Hollyhurst Dr. DY8: Word 6B 92
Hollyhurst Gro. B26: Yard 5C 120
B90: Shir 1H 163
Hollyhurst Rd. B73: S'tly 2B 68
Holly La. B24: Erd 2H 85
B37: Mars G 3B 122
B66: Smeth 2C 98
B67: Smeth 4B 98
B75: Four O 6G 37
B76: Wis 2H 71
CV7: Bal C 4H 169
WS6: Gt Wyr 5E 7
WS9: A'rdge 1H 35
WS9: Wals W 3C 22
Holly Lodge Wlk. B37: F'bri 1B 122
Hollymoor Point B31: Longb 6A 144
Hollymoor Way B31: Longb 5A 144
Holly Mt. B16: Edg 2H 115
Hollymount B62: Quin 4G 113

Hollyoak Cft. B31: Longb 1F 159
Hollyoake Cl. B68: O'bry 1G 113
Hollyoak Gro. B91: Sol 6E 151
Hollyoak Rd. B74: S'tly 5H 51
Holly Pk. Dr. B24: Erd 3H 85
Holly Pk. Ind. Est. B24: Erd 5A 86
Hollypiece Ho. B27: A Grn 3G 135
Holly Pl. B6: Aston 1G 101
B29: S Oak 3D 132
Holly Rd. B16: Edg 2G 115
B20: Hand 1B 100
B30: King Nor 3C 146
B65: B'hth 2B 112
B68: O'bry 3A 114
B71: W Brom 5C 64
DY1: Dud 4C 76
WS10: W'bry 6F 47
Holly St. B67: Smeth 4D 98
DY1: Dud 3A 94
Holly Vw. WV11: Ess 4A 18
Hollywell Rd. B26: Sheld 5F 121
B93: Know 4C 166
Hollywell St. WV14: Cose 4C 60
HOLLYWOOD 1A 162
Holly Wood B43: Gt Barr 4C 66
Hollywood Bowl
Great Park 1H 157
Wolverhampton 5D 28
Hollywood By-Pass B38: Head H . . .3G 161
B47: Wyt 3G 161
Hollywood Cl. B42: Gt Barr 5B 66
Hollywood Dr. B47: H'wd 1A 162
Hollywood Gdns. B47: H'wd 1A 162
Hollywood La. B47: H'wd 1A 162
Holly Wood Nature Reserve 4C 66
Holman Cl. WV13: W'hall 1G 45
Holman Rd. WV13: W'hall 1F 45
Holman Way WV13: W'hall 1G 45
Holmbridge Gro. WS4: S'fld 5G 21
Holme Mill WV10: F'hses 3H 15
Holmes, The WV10: F'hses 4H 15
Holmes Cl. B43: Gt Barr 6A 66
Holmes Dr. B45: Rub 3F 157
Holmesfield Rd. B42: Gt Barr 6E 67
Holmes Rd. WV12: W'hall 2D 30
Holme Way WS4: Rus 2F 33
Holmwood Rd. B10: Small H 2D 118
Holt Cl. Nth. B7: Birm 1H 5 (5H 101)
Holt Cl. Sth. B7: Birm 1H 5 (5H 101)
Holte Dr. B75: R'ley 1B 54
Holte Rd. B6: Aston 6A 84
B11: S'brk 6D 118
Holtes Wlk. B6: Aston 1B 102
Holt Rd. B62: B'hth 2E 113
Holtshill La. WS1: Wals 1D 48
Holt St. B7: Birm 1G 5 (5H 101)
Holyhead Community Leisure Cen. . . .1H 99
Holyhead Rd. B21: Hand 6F 81
WS10: Darl 1C 62
WS10: W'bry 2D 62
WV7: Alb 6A 12
WV8: Cod, Oaken 6A 12
Holyhead Rd. Ind. Est. WS10: W'bry . .2D 62
Holyhead Way B21: Hand 1H 99
Holyoak Cl. B6: Aston 6H 83
Holyrood Gro. B6: Aston 1G 101
Holy Well Cl. B16: Edg 1C 116
Holywell La. B45: Rub 3D 156
Home Cl. B28: Hall G 1F 149
Homecroft Rd. B25: Yard 3C 120
Homedene Rd. B31: N'fld 6C 130
Homefield Rd. WV8: Bilb 4H 13
Homelands B42: Gt Barr 6D 66
Homelands Pk. WV10: Cov H 1G 15
Homelea Rd. B25: Yard 3B 120
Homemead Gro. B45: Rub 2F 157
Home Mdw. Ct. B13: Mose 2B 148
Home Mdw. Ho. B27: A Grn 3G 135
Home Peal Ho. B14: King H 1G 147
HOMER HILL 4D 110
Homer Hill Rd. B63: Crad 4E 111
Homer Rd. B75: R'ley 1A 54
B91: Sol 4F 151
Homers Fold WV14: Bils 6F 45
Homer St. B12: Bal H 6H 117
Homerton Rd. B44: K'sdng 4B 68

Homestead Cl. DY3: Up Gor 2A 76
Homestead Dr. B75: R'ley 6A 38
Homestead Rd. B33: Sheld 2F 121
Home Twr. B7: Birm 4B 102
Homewood Cl. B76: Walm 2C 70
Honesty Cl. WS8: Clay 1H 21
Honeswode Cl. B20: Hand 1C 100
Honeyborne Rd. B75: S Cold 4B 54
Honeybourne Cl. B63: Hale 2A 128
Honeybourne Cres. WV5: Wom 2F 73
Honeybourne Rd. B33: Sheld 3G 121
B63: Hale 2C 128
Honeybourne Way WV13: W'hall 1C 46
Honeycomb Way B31: N'fld 4C 144
Honeysuckle Av. DY6: K'wfrd 2C 92
Honeysuckle Cl. B32: Quin 6H 113
Honeysuckle Dr. WS5: Wals 2E 65
Honeysuckle Gro. B27: A Grn 6A 120
Honeysuckle Way WS6: Gt Wyr 1H 7
Honeytree Cl. DY6: K'wfrd 6D 92
Honiley Dr. B73: New O 3C 68
Honiley Rd. B33: Yard 1E 121
Honister Cl. DY5: Quar B 2B 110
Honiton Cl. B31: N'fld 3C 144
Honiton Cres. B31: N'fld 3C 144
Honiton Wlk. B66: Smeth 4F 99
Honiton Way WS9: A'rdge 4B 34
Honnington Ct. B29: W Cas 4D 130
Honor Av. WV4: Penn 6G 43
Hood Gro. B30: King Nor 3H 145
Hook Dr. B74: Four O 5F 37
HOOK END 2B 154
Hooper St. B18: Win G 5B 100
Hoosen Cl. B62: Quin 5G 113
Hopedale Rd. B32: Quin 6A 114
Hope Pl. B29: S Oak 3B 132
Hope Rd. DY4: Tip 1C 78
Hope St. B5: Birm 3F 117
B62: B'hth 3D 112
B70: W Brom 5C 80
DY2: Dud 1E 95
DY8: Word 6B 92
WS1: Wals 3C 48
Hope Ter. DY2: Neth 4E 95
Hopkins Cl. WS10: W'bry 2G 63
Hopkins Dr. B71: W Brom 6C 64
Hopkins St. DY4: Tip 5A 78
Hop Leasow B31: Longb 5A 144
Hopstone Gdns. WV4: Penn 6D 42
Hopstone Rd. B29: W Cas 4E 131
Hopton Cl. DY4: Tip 1C 78
WV6: Pert 6F 25
Hopton Cres. WV11: Wed 3G 29
Hopton Gdns. DY1: Dud 4C 76
Hopton Gro. B13: Mose 2C 148
Hopwas Gro. B37: K'hrst 4B 106
HOPWOOD 6F 159
Hopwood Cl. B63: Hale 3A 128
Hopwood Gro. B31: Longb 3C 158
Hopyard Cl. DY3: Gorn 4F 75
Hopyard Gdns. WV14: Cose 2D 60
Hopyard La. DY3: Gorn 4F 75
Hopyard Rd. WS2: Wals 1E 47
Horace Partridge Rd. WS10: Mox 6A 46
Horace St. WV14: Cose 5C 60
Horatio Dr. B13: Mose 1H 133
Hordern Cl. WV6: Wolv 4D 26
Hordern Cres. DY5: Quar B 3H 109
Hordern Gro. WV6: Wolv 4D 26
Hordern Pk. WV10: Cov H 1G 15
Hordern Rd. WV6: Wolv 4D 26
Horizon, The B26: Sheld 6D 120
Hornbeam Cl. B29: W Cas 6F 131
Hornbeam Wlk. WV3: Wolv 2E 43
Hornbrook Gro. B92: Olton 6A 136
Hornby Gro. B14: Yard W 3C 148
Hornby Rd. WV4: Penn 1G 59
Horner Way B65: B'hth 2C 112
Horne Way B34: S End 4A 106
Horning Dr. WV14: Bils 2E 61
Hornsey Gro. B44: K'sdng 3A 68
Hornsey Rd. B44: K'sdng 3A 68
Hornton Cl. B74: Lit As 4D 36
Horrell Rd. B26: Sheld 4E 121
B90: Shir 5F 149
Horsecroft Dr. B71: W Brom 5E 65
(off Tompstone Rd.)

Horse Fair B1: Birm 6D 4 (2F 117)
Horsehills Dr. WV3: Wolv 1C 42
Horselea Cft. B8: W End 5A 104
Horseley Flds. WV1: Wolv . .3D 170 (1H 43)
Horseley Heath DY4: Tip 3B 78
Horseley Rd. DY4: Tip 1C 78
Horseshoe, The B68: O'bry 1A 114
Horseshoe Cl. WS2: Wals 4H 47
(off Narrow La.)
Horseshoe Cres. B43: Gt Barr 2D 66
Horse Shoes La. B26: Sheld 6F 121
Horseshoe Wlk. DY4: Tip 2G 77
(off Owen St.)
Horsfall Rd. B75: S Cold 6E 55
Horsham Av. DY8: Word 6A 92
Horsley Rd. B43: Gt Barr 1F 67
B74: Lit As 1B 52
Horton Cl. DY3: Sed 5G 59
WS10: Darl 4D 46
Horton Gro. B90: M'path 4E 165
Horton Pl. WS10: Darl 4D 46
Horton Sq. B12: Birm 4G 117
Horton St. B70: W Brom 5A 80
DY4: Tip 2D 78
WS10: Darl 4D 46
Hospital La. B69: Tiv 5B 78
WS6: C Hay 2B 6
WV14: Cose 6D 60
Hospital Rd. WS7: Burn 1C 10
Hospital St. B19: Birm, Hock . .1D 4 (4F 101)
(not continuous)
B23: Erd 3E 85
WS2: Wals 5B 32
WV2: Wolv 5D 170 (2H 43)
Hospital Way B15: Edg 1A 132
Hothersall Dr. B73: Bold 5F 69
Hotspur Rd. B44: K'sdng 4H 67
Hough Pl. WS2: Wals 4H 47
Hough Rd. B14: King H 1F 147
WS2: Wals 4G 47
Houghton Ct. B28: Hall G 3D 148
Houghton St. B69: O'bry 3F 97
B70: W Brom 1B 98
Hough Way WV11: Ess 4A 18
Houldey Rd. B31: N'fld 6F 145
Houliston Cl. WS10: W'bry 6H 47
Houndel Gro. WV5: Wom 6F 57
Houndsfield Cl. B47: H'wd 3C 162
Houndsfield Cl. B47: Wyt 4A 162
Houndsfield Gro. B47: Wyt 4A 162
(not continuous)
Houndsfield Ind. Est. B47: Wyt 3C 162
Houndsfield La. B47: H'wd 3C 162
B47: Wyt 3C 162
B90: Dic H 3C 162
Houndsfield La. Caravan Site
B47: H'wd 3D 162
Houndsfield M. B47: Wyt 4B 162
House Mdw. DY4: Tip 1A 78
House of York B3: Birm 2B 4 (6E 101)
Houx, The DY8: Amb 3C 108
Hove Rd. B27: A Grn 4A 136
Howard Ho. B92: H Ard 1B 154
Howard Rd. B14: King H 6F 133
B20: Hand 5D 82
B25: Yard 4A 120
B43: Gt Barr 5G 65
B92: Olton 2C 136
WV11: Wed 1H 29
WV14: Bils 2H 61
Howard Rd. E. B13: Mose 6H 133
Howard St. B19: Birm 1C 4 (5F 101)
B70: W Brom 6F 63
DY4: Tip 6F 63
WV2: Wolv 6C 170 (3H 43)
Howard St. Ind. Est. B70: W Brom 6F 63
Howarth Cl. B46: Wat O 5D 88
Howarth Way B6: Aston 2A 102
Howden Pl. B33: Stech 4E 105
Howdle's La. WS8: Bwnhls 3B 10
Howe Cres. WV12: W'hall 3C 30
Howell Rd. WV2: Wolv 4A 44
Howes Cft. B35: Cas V 5E 87
Howe St. B4: Birm 2H 5 (6H 101)
Howford Gro. B7: Birm 5B 102
Howland Cl. WV9: Pend 5D 14

Howley Av.—Instow Cl.

Howley Av. B44: Gt Barr 4G **67**
Howley Grange Rd. B62: Quin 6F **113**
Howl Pl. DY4: Tip 2H **77**
Hoylake Cl. WS3: Blox 4H **19**
Hoylake Dr. B69: Tiv 2A **96**
Hoylake Rd. WV6: Pert 4D **24**
Hoyland Way B30: B'vlle 5A **132**
HRS Ind. Pk. B33: Sheld 2G **121**
Hub, The B19: Birm 1D **4**
B69: O'bry 2G **97**
Hubert Cft. B29: S Oak 3B **132**
Hubert Rd. B29: S Oak 3B **132**
Hubert St. B6: Aston 4H **101**
Hucker Cl. WS2: Wals 4G **47**
Hucker Rd. WS2: Wals 4G **47**
Huddesford Dr. CV7: Bal C 1H **169**
Huddlestone Cl. WV10: F'stne 1D **16**
Huddleston Way B29: S Oak 4G **131**
Huddocks Vw. WS3: Pels 2D **20**
Hudson Av. B46: Col 3H **107**
Hudson Gro. WV6: Pert 4E **25**
Hudson Ind. Est. WV2: Ett 4B **44**
Hudson Rd. B20: Hand 3B **82**
DY4: Tip .3C **78**
Hudson's Dr. B30: King Nor 3C **146**
Hudsons Vw. B30: King Nor 3C **146**
Hudswell Dr. DY5: Brie H 3H **109**
Huggins Cl. CV7: Bal C 5H **169**
Hughes Av. WV3: Wolv 3D **42**
Hughes Pl. WV14: Bils 4F **45**
Hughes Rd. WS10: Mox 6A **46**
WV14: Bils 4F **45**
Hugh Gaitskell Ct. WV14: Wolv 3E **45**
Hugh Porter Way WV6: Tett 2D **26**
Hugh Rd. B10: Small H 2E **119**
B67: Smeth 4B **98**
Hugh Vs. B10: Small H 2E **119**
Hulbert Dr. DY2: Dud 3D **94**
Hulbert Ind. Est. DY2: Dud 3D **94**
Hulland Pl. DY5: Brie H 6G **93**
Hullbrook Rd. B13: Mose 2C **148**
Humara Ghar WS1: Wals 3C **48**
Humber Av. B76: Walm 6E **71**
Humber Gdns. B63: Crad 6E **111**
Humber Gro. B36: Cas B 6B **88**
Humber Rd. WV3: Wolv 2E **43**
Humberstone Rd. B24: Erd 3C **86**
Humber Twr. B7: Birm 5A **102**
Humpage Rd. B9: Bord G 1E **119**
Humphrey Middlemore Dr.
B17: Harb 1H **131**
Humphrey St. DY3: Lwr G 4H **75**
Humphries Cres. WV14: Bils 4H **61**
Humphries Ho. WS8: Bwnhls 6B **10**
Humphries Rd. WV10: Bush 2H **27**
Hundred Acre Rd. B74: S'tly 4H **51**
Hungary Cl. DY9: Lye 6G **109**
Hungary Hill DY9: Lye 6G **109**
Hungerfield Rd. B36: Cas B 6G **87**
Hungerford Rd. DY8: Stourb 3C **124**
Hunningham Gro. B91: Sol 1F **165**
HUNNINGTON **6B 128**
Hunnington Cl. B32: Bart G 4G **129**
Hunnington Cres. B63: Hale 3B **128**
Hunscote Cl. B90: Shir 6F **149**
Hunslet Cl. B32: Quin 1D **130**
Hunslet Rd. B32: Quin 1D **130**
Hunstanton Av. B17: Harb 4D **114**
Hunstanton Cl. DY5: Brie H 4G **109**
Hunter Ct. B5: Edg 6F **117**
Hunter Cres. WS3: Blox 3D **32**
Hunters Cl. WV14: Bils 4A **46**
Hunters Ride DY7: Stourt 6H **91**
Hunters Ri. B63: Hale 4F **127**
Hunter's Rd. B19: Hock 2D **100**
Hunter St. WV6: Wolv 5E **27**
Hunter's Va. B19: Hock 3E **101**
Hunters Wlk. B23: Erd 5C **68**
Huntingdon Ho. B23: Erd 1B **84**
Huntingdon Rd. B71: W Brom 1H **79**
Huntington Rd. WV12: W'hall 2D **30**
Huntingtree Rd. B63: Hale 1G **127**
Huntlands Rd. B63: Hale 3G **127**
Huntley Dr. B91: Sol 5F **151**
Huntly Rd. B16: Edg 2C **116**
Hunton Ct. *B23: Erd 5E* ***85***
(off Gravelly Hill Nth.)
Hunton Hill B23: Erd 4D **84**
Hunton Rd. B23: Erd 4E **85**
Hunt's La. WV12: W'hall 3D **30**
Huntsman Cl. WV14: Cose 3F **61**
Hunts Mill Dr. DY5: P'ntt 6G **75**
Hunt's Rd. B30: Stir 6C **132**
Hurdis Rd. B90: Shir 4G **149**
Hurdlow Av. B18: Hock 4D **100**
Hurley Cl. B72: W Grn 3A **70**
WS5: Wals 5H **49**
Hurley Gro. B37: K'hrst 4B **106**
Hurley's Fold DY2: Neth 4D **94**
Hurlingham Rd. B44: K'sdng 3A **68**
Hurricane Pk. B7: Erd 1G **103**
Hurricane Way B35: Cas V 5E **87**
Hursey Dr. DY4: Tip 2A **78**
Hurst, The B13: Mose 6C **134**
B47: H'wd 3A **162**
Hurstbourne Cres.
WV1: Wolv 2D **44**
Hurst Bus. Pk. DY5: Brie H 5C **94**
Hurst Cl. B36: Cas B 2A **106**
Hurst Ct. DY9: Lye 6B **110**
Hurstcroft Rd. B33: Kitts G 6F **105**
HURST GREEN **3F 113**
Hurst Grn. Rd. B62: B'hth 2E **113**
B76: Min .1H **87**
B93: Ben H 5B **166**
Hurst Grn. Shop. Cen.
B62: B'hth 3F **113**
HURST HILL **5C 60**
Hurst Hill Ct. WV14: Cose 5C **60**
(not continuous)
Hurst La. B34: S End 3H **105**
DY4: Tip .2F **77**
DY5: Brie H 6B **94**
Hurst La. Nth. B36: Cas B 2A **106**
Hurst Rd. B67: Smeth 6B **98**
WV14: Cose 4C **60**
Hurst St. B5: Birm 6E **5** (2G **117**)
(not continuous)
Hurstway, The B23: Erd 5C **68**
Hurstwood Rd. B23: Erd 5C **68**
Huskison Cl. B69: Tiv 6B **78**
Huskisson Way B90: M'path 5E **165**
Husphins La. WV8: Cod, Cod W 2A **12**
Hussey Rd. WS8: Bwnhls 5A **10**
Hutchings La. B90: Dic H 4G **163**
Hut Hill La. WS6: Gt Wyr 1G **7**
Hutton Av. B8: Salt 4D **102**
Hutton Rd. B8: Salt 4D **102**
B20: Hand 6D **82**
Huxbey Dr. B92: Sol 5B **138**
Huxley Cl. WV9: Pend 4E **15**
Hyacinth Cl. WS5: Wals 2D **64**
Hyatt Sq. DY5: Brie H 4G **109**
Hyatts Wlk. B65: Row R 4H **95**
Hyde, The DY9: W'cte 3H **125**
Hyde Rd. WV11: Wed 2F **29**
Hydes Rd. B71: W Brom 4A **64**
WS10: W'bry 2G **63**
Hyett Way WV14: Bils 3B **62**
Hylda Rd. B20: Hand 6D **82**
Hylstone Cres. WV11: Wed 3F **29**
Hylton St. B18: Birm 4E **101**
Hyperion Dr. WV4: Penn 2E **59**
Hyperion Rd. B36: Hodg H 6C **86**
DY7: Stourt 4A **108**
Hyron Hall Rd. B27: A Grn 3A **136**
Hyssop Cl. B7: Birm 4A **102**
Hytall Rd. B90: Shir 5C **148**
Hythe Gro. B25: Yard 3B **120**

I

Ibberton Rd. B14: King H 4B **148**
Ibis Gdns. DY6: K'wfrd 3E **93**
Ibstock Dr. DY8: Stourb 1E **125**
Icknield Cl. B74: S'tly 2A **52**
Icknield Port Rd. B16: Birm 5A **100**
Icknield Sq. B16: Birm 6C **100**
Icknield St. B18: Birm 5D **100**
B18: Hock 4D **100**
B38: Forh, Head H, King Nor
. . . . .1C **160**
(not continuous)
Ida Rd. B70: W Brom 6B **80**
WS2: Wals 2H **47**
Idbury Rd. B44: K'sdng 6A **68**
Ideal Works DY9: Lye 5C **110**
Idmiston Cft. B14: King H 5H **147**
Idonia Rd. WV6: Pert 4E **25**
Ikon Gallery . . . .**5A 4 (1E 117)**
Ilford Rd. B23: Erd 1D **84**
Iliffe Way B17: Harb 1H **131**
Ilkley Gro. B37: F'bri 1B **122**
ILLEY **5E 129**
Illeybrook Sq. B32: Bart G 3B **130**
Illey Cl. B31: Longb 6H **143**
Illey La. B32: Fran 5E **129**
B62: Hunn, Hale 4C **128**
Illshaw WV9: Pend 4F **15**
Illshaw Heath Rd.
B94: H'ley H 6B **164**
Illshaw Path B90: Bly P 6D **164**
Ilmington Dr. B73: New O 2C **68**
Ilmington Rd. B29: W Cas 4D **130**
Ilsham Gro. B31: Longb 3C **158**
Ilsley Dr. B27: A Grn 3H **135**
Ilsley Rd. B23: Erd 3E **85**
IMAX Theatre . . . .**2H 5 (6H 101)**
Imex Auto Cen. DY4: Tip 4A **78**
Imex Bus. Pk. B9: Bord G 1D **118**
B33: Stech 5C **104**
DY4: Tip .4A **78**
WV2: Wolv 4G **43**
I-Mex Bus. Pk. B11: Tys 5F **119**
Imperial Ri. B46: Col 5G **89**
Imperial Rd. B9: Bord G 1E **119**
Impey Rd. B31: N'fld 6D **144**
Impsley Cl. B36: Cas B 1F **105**
Ince Rd. WS10: Darl 4C **46**
Inchcape Av. B20: Hand 4C **82**
Inchford Rd. B92: Sol 6A **138**
Inchlaggan Rd. WV10: Wolv 3B **28**
Infantry Pl. B75: S Cold 5E **55**
Infield, The B63: Crad 4F **111**
Ingatestone Dr. DY8: Word 6A **92**
Ingestre Cl. WS3: Blox 4F **19**
Ingestre Dr. B43: Gt Barr 4H **65**
Inge St. B5: Birm 6D **4** (2G **117**)
Ingestre Rd. B28: Hall G 6F **135**
WV10: Oxl 6G **15**
Ingham Way B17: Harb 3E **115**
Ingleby Gdns. WV6: Wolv 4D **26**
Ingledew Cl. WS2: Wals 6D **30**
Inglefield Rd. B33: Stech 6D **104**
Inglemere Gro. B29: W Cas 6D **130**
Inglenook Dr. B20: Hand 5D **82**
Ingleside Vs. *B11: S'hll 6C* ***118***
(off Warwick Rd.)
Ingleton Rd. B8: W End 2G **103**
Inglewood Av. WV3: Wolv 3D **42**
Inglewood Cl. DY6: K'wfrd 4B **92**
Inglewood Gro. B74: S'tly 1H **51**
Inglewood Rd. B11: S'hll 6C **118**
Ingoldsby Ct. B13: Mose 3B **134**
Ingoldsby Rd. B31: N'fld 3G **145**
Ingot Cl. WS2: Wals 3H **31**
Ingram Dr. B43: Gt Barr 5G **65**
Ingram Gro. B27: A Grn 3G **135**
Ingram Pl. WS3: Blox 6B **20**
Ingram Rd. WS3: Blox 6A **20**
Inhedge, The DY1: Dud 6E **77**
Inhedge St. DY3: Up Gor 2A **76**
Inkberrow Cl. B69: O'bry 5E **97**
Inkberrow Rd. B63: Hale 3H **127**
Inkerman Gro. WV10: Wolv 1B **44**
Inkerman Ho. *B19: Hock 3G* ***101***
(off Newtown Shop. Cen.)
Inkerman St. B7: Birm 6B **102**
(not continuous)
WV10: Wolv 6B **28**
Inland Rd. B24: Erd 5H **85**
Innage, The B47: H'wd 4A **162**
Innage Rd. B31: N'fld 3F **145**
Innisfree Cl. B47: Wyt 5C **162**
Innovation Dr. WV9: Coven 3F **15**
Innsworth Dr. B35: Cas V 3E **87**
Inshaw Cl. B33: Stech 6C **104**
Institute Rd. B14: King H 5H **133**
Instone Rd. B63: Hale 2H **127**
Instow Cl. WV12: W'hall 1B **30**

Insull Av. B14: King H 6B **148**
Intended St. B63: Crad 4E **111**
Interlux Bus. Pk.
   B70: W Brom 4F **79**
International Conference Cen. (ICC)
   . . . . .4A **4** (1E **117**)
International Ho. B37: Mars G 6F **123**
International Sq. B37: Mars G 5E **123**
Intown WS1: Wals 1D **48**
Intown Row WS1: Wals 1D **48**
Invention Av. B21: Hand 6A **82**
Inverclyde Dr. WV4: Ett 6B **44**
Inverclyde Rd. B20: Hand 4C **82**
Inverkip Wlk. WV4: Ett 6B **44**
Inverness Ho. WV1: Wolv 6G **27**
   (off Lomas St.)
Inverness Rd. B31: N'fld 4C **144**
Inworth WV9: Pend 4F **15**
Ionic Bus. Pk. DY1: Dud 5G **77**
Ipsley Gro. B23: Erd 2A **84**
Ipstones Av. B33: Stech 5D **104**
Ipswich Cres. B42: Gt Barr 6D **66**
Ipswich Wlk. B37: Chel W 1D **122**
Ireland Grn. Rd.
   B70: W Brom 5H **79**
Ireton Rd. B20: Hand 3C **82**
   WV10: Bush 4A **16**
Iris Cl. B29: W Cas 5F **131**
   DY2: Dud 6H **77**
Iris Dr. B14: King H 4F **147**
Irnham Rd. B74: Four O 1G **53**
Iron Bri. Wlk. DY9: Pedm 5F **125**
Iron La. B33: Stech 5B **104**
Iron Mill Way WS10: Darl 6D **46**
Irvan Av. B70: W Brom 2F **79**
Irvine Cl. WS3: Blox 2H **31**
Irvine Rd. WS3: Blox 1H **31**
Irving Cl. DY3: Lwr G 3E **75**
Irving Rd. B92: Sol 1A **138**
   DY4: Tip 4A **62**
Irving St. B1: Birm 2F **117**
Irwin Av. B45: Redn 3A **158**
Isaac Walton Pl.
   B70: W Brom 6E **63**
Isbourne Way B9: Birm 1B **118**
Isis Gro. B36: Cas B 1B **106**
   WV13: W'hall 1C **46**
Island Rd. B21: Hand 6G **81**
Islington B63: Hale 1A **128**
Islington Row Middleway
   B15: Birm 2D **116**
Ismere Rd. B24: Erd 5H **85**
Itchen Gro. WV6: Pert 6E **25**
Ithon Gro. B38: King Nor 1A **160**
Ivanhoe Rd. B43: Gt Barr 2D **66**
   WV2: Ett 5C **44**
Ivanhoe St. DY2: Dud 2C **94**
Ivatt Cl. WS4: Rus 2F **33**
IVERLEY 5B **124**
Iverley Rd. B63: Hale 1C **128**
Iverley Wlk. DY9: Pedm 3G **125**
Ivor Rd. B11: S'hll 1B **134**
Ivy Av. B12: Bal H 6A **118**
   (Chesterton Rd.)
   B12: Bal H 6A **118**
   (Runcorn Rd.)
Ivybridge Gro. B42: P Barr 4E **83**
Ivy Cft. WV9: Pend 4D **14**
Ivydale Av. B26: Sheld 6G **121**
Ivydene Way WV13: W'hall 6H **29**
Ivyfield Rd. B23: Erd 2B **84**
Ivy Gro. B18: Win G 5A **100**
   (off Heath Grn. Rd.)
   WS8: Wals W 3C **22**
Ivyhouse La. WV14: Cose 5D **60**
Ivy Ho. Rd. B38: King Nor 1G **159**
   B69: O'bry 3D **96**
Ivy Lodge Cl. B37: Mars G 4C **122**
Ivy Pl. B29: S Oak 3B **132**
Ivy Rd. B21: Hand 2C **100**
   B30: Stir 1C **146**
   B73: Bold 3F **69**
   DY1: Dud 3C **76**
   DY4: Tip 6H **61**
Ivy Way B90: Dic H 3G **163**
Ivywood Dr. B93: Ben H 4A **166**
Izons Ind. Est. B70: W Brom 6F **79**

Izons La. B70: W Brom 6F **79**
Izons Rd. B70: W Brom 4A **80**

J

Jacamar Av. B33: Stech 5D **104**
Jacey Rd. B16: Edg 1H **115**
   B90: Shir 3H **149**
Jack David Ho. DY4: Tip 2D **78**
Jackdaw Cl. DY3: Sed 3G **59**
Jackdaw Dr. B36: Cas B 1C **106**
Jackdaw Rd. B23: Erd 6C **68**
Jack Hayward Way
   WV1: Wolv 1B **170** (6G **27**)
Jack Holden Av. WV14: Cose 3C **60**
Jack Newell Ct. WV14: Cose 5E **61**
   (off Jevon St.)
Jack O Watton Ind. Est. B46: Wat O . . .4F **89**
Jackson Av. B8: Salt 5F **103**
Jackson Cl. B11: S'brk 4B **118**
   B68: O'bry 4H **97**
   DY4: Tip 4B **62**
   WS11: Nort C 1C **8**
   WV10: F'stne 1C **16**
Jackson Ct. DY5: Quar B 2B **110**
Jackson Dr. B67: Smeth 4B **98**
Jackson Ho. B69: O'bry 2G **97**
Jackson Rd. B8: Salt 5F **103**
Jackson St. B68: O'bry 5H **97**
   DY9: Lye 6A **110**
   WV6: Wolv 5F **27**
Jackson Wlk. B35: Cas V 5E **87**
Jackson Way B32: Quin 6G **113**
Jacob's Hall La. WS6: Gt Wyr 4G **7**
Jacobean La. B91: Sol 6C **152**
   B93: Know 6C **152**
Jacoby Pl. B5: Edg 6E **117**
Jaffray Cl. B23: Erd 4E **85**
Jaffray Cres. B24: Erd 4F **85**
Jaffray Rd. B24: Erd 4F **85**
Jakeman Rd. B12: Bal H 6G **117**
Jamaica Row B5: Birm 6F **5** (2G **117**)
James Beattie Ho. WV6: Tett 5H **25**
James Bri. Cl. WS2: Wals 4H **47**
James Brindley Wlk.
   B1: Birm 4A **4** (1E **117**)
James Clift Ho. B69: O'bry 4D **96**
James Cl. B67: Smeth 4E **99**
   WS10: Darl 5F **47**
James Ct. B13: Mose 3B **134**
   B38: King Nor 5B **146**
James Dee Cl. DY5: Quar B 2C **110**
James Eaton Cl. B71: W Brom 2A **80**
James Ho. B17: Harb 6F **115**
   (off Cadbury Way)
   B19: Hock 3E **101**
   (off Newtown Dr.)
James Lloyd Trust Flats B30: B'vlle . . .2G **145**
James Memorial Homes B7: Nech 2C **102**
   (off Stuart St.)
Jameson Rd. B6: Aston 1C **102**
Jameson St. WV6: Wolv 5F **27**
James Rd. B11: Tys 5F **119**
   B43: Gt Barr 6A **66**
   B46: Col 1H **107**
James Row B69: O'bry 1D **96**
James Samuel Pl. B12: Birm 4H **117**
James Scott Rd. B63: Crad 5E **110**
James St. B3: Birm 2B **4** (6E **101**)
   WV13: W'hall 6A **30**
   WV14: Bils 5G **45**
James Turner St. B18: Win G 3A **100**
James Watt Dr. B19: Hand 1D **100**
   WS10: W'bry 1H **63**
James Watt Ho. B66: Smeth 4F **99**
James Watt Ind. Pk. B66: Smeth 3G **99**
James Watt Queensway
   B4: Birm 2F **5** (6G **101**)
James Watt St. B4: Birm 3F **5**
   B71: W Brom 5H **63**
   (not continuous)
Jane La. Cl. WS2: Wals 5F **31**
Janice Gro. B14: Yard W 3C **148**
Janie Ct. B13: Mose 3C **134**
Janine Av. WV11: Wed 2G **29**

Jaques Cl. B46: Wat O 5D **88**
Jardine Cl. DY8: Amb 5E **109**
Jardine Rd. B6: Aston 6H **83**
Jarratt Hall B29: S Oak 2A **132**
Jarvis Av. B23: Erd 1F **85**
Jarvis Cres. B69: O'bry 5F **97**
Jarvis Rd. B23: Erd 1E **103**
Jarvis Way B24: Erd 1E **103**
J A S Ind. Pk. B65: Row R 5E **97**
Jasmin Cft. B14: King H 3G **147**
Jasmine Cl. WV9: Pend 4D **14**
Jasmine Gro. WV8: Bilb 4H **13**
Jasmine Rd. DY2: Dud 6H **77**
Jasmine Way WS10: Darl 4D **46**
Jason Rd. DY9: W'cte 1B **126**
Javelin Av. B35: Cas V 4F **87**
Javelin Pk. WS10: W'bry 3D **62**
Jayne Cl. B71: W Brom 4C **64**
   WV11: Wed 2F **29**
Jay Rd. DY6: K'wfrd 1B **92**
Jay's Av. DY4: Tip 3B **78**
Jayshaw Av. B43: Gt Barr 4A **66**
Jeal Cl. B47: Wyt 6G **161**
Jean Dr. DY4: Tip 1D **78**
Jean Hasketh Cl. WV14: Bils 4A **46**
Jeavons Pl. WV14: Bils 6E **45**
Jedburgh Av. WV6: Pert 5E **25**
Jeddo St. WV2: Wolv 6A **170** (3G **43**)
Jeffcock Rd. WV3: Wolv 3D **42**
Jefferson Cl. B71: W Brom 5H **63**
Jefferson Pl. B71: W Brom 2B **80**
Jeffrey Av. WV4: Ett 6B **44**
Jeffrey Rd. B65: Row R 6E **97**
Jeffries Ho. B69: O'bry 2G **97**
Jeffs Av. WV2: Wolv 6D **170** (3H **43**)
Jenkins Cl. WV14: Bils 6E **45**
Jenkinson Rd. WS10: W'bry 4D **62**
Jenkins St. B10: Small H 3C **118**
Jenks Av. WV10: Bush 1A **28**
Jenks Rd. WV5: Wom 2F **73**
Jenna Ho. B24: Erd 4F **85**
   (off Wood End Rd.)
Jennens Ct. B5: Birm 3G **5**
Jennens Rd. B4: Birm 6H **101**
   B5: Birm 3G **5** (6H **101**)
   B7: Birm 2H **5** (6H **101**)
Jenner Cl. WS2: Wals 3G **31**
Jenner Ct. B45: Redn 1G **157**
Jenner Ho. WS2: Wals 3F **31**
Jenner Rd. WS2: Wals 3F **31**
Jenner St. WV2: Wolv 2A **44**
Jennifer Wlk. B25: Yard 3C **120**
Jennings St. B64: Old H 1H **111**
Jenny Cl. WV14: Bils 4G **61**
Jennyns Ct. WS10: W'bry 2F **63**
Jenny Walkers La. WV6: Pert 3D **40**
Jensen Av. B36: Cas B 6A **88**
Jephcott Gro. B8: Salt 5G **103**
Jephcott Rd. B8: Salt 5G **103**
Jephson Dr. B26: Yard 4D **120**
Jeremiah Rd. WV10: Wolv 6B **28**
Jeremy Gro. B92: Sol 1F **137**
Jeremy Rd. WV4: Penn 6G **43**
Jerome Ct. B74: S'tly 2H **51**
Jerome Retail Pk. WS1: Wals 2B **48**
Jerome Rd. B72: S Cold 1B **70**
   WS2: Wals 2H **47**
Jerrard Ct. B75: S Cold 6A **54**
Jerrard Dr. B75: S Cold 6A **54**
Jerrard M. B75: S Cold 6A **54**
Jerry's La. B23: Erd 6D **68**
Jersey Cft. B36: Cas B 3D **106**
Jersey Rd. B8: Salt 5D **102**
Jervis Cl. DY5: P'ntt 2G **93**
Jervis Ct. WS1: Wals 1D **48**
   (off Dog Kennel La.)
Jervis Cres. B74: Four O 6D **36**
Jervis Pk. B74: Lit As 5C **36**
Jervis Ter. B21: Hand 1H **99**
Jervoise Dr. B31: N'fld 2F **145**
Jervoise La. B71: W Brom 4C **64**
Jervoise Rd. B29: W Cas 4D **130**
Jervoise St. B70: W Brom 3G **79**
Jesmond Gro. B24: Erd 3C **86**
Jessel Rd. WS2: Wals 1A **48**
Jessie Rd. WS9: A'rdge 6C **22**
Jesson Cl. WS1: Wals 4E **49**
Jesson Ct. WS1: Wals 3E **49**

Jesson Rd. B75: S Cold 6E **55**
DY3: Sed 1C **76**
WS1: Wals 3D **48**
Jesson St. B70: W Brom 5C **80**
Jetstream Dr. B26: Birm A 2F **139**
Jevons Dr. DY4: Tip 2B **78**
Jevons Rd. B73: New O 2C **68**
Jevon St. WV14: Cose 5D **60**
(not continuous)
JEWELLERY QUARTER 1A **4** (5D **100**)
Jewellery Quarter Station (Rail & Metro)
. . . . .5D **100**
Jew's La. DY3: Up Gor 3A **76**
Jews La. Ind. Est. DY3: Up Gor . .3A **76**
Jiggin's La. B32: Bart G 5A **130**
Jill Av. B43: Gt Barr 4G **65**
Jillcot Rd. B92: Sol 2F **137**
Jinnah Cl. B12: Birm 3H **117**
Joan St. WV2: Ett 5A **44**
Jockey Fld. DY3: Up Gor 1A **76**
Jockey La. WS10: W'bry 1G **63**
Jockey Rd.
B73: Bold, New O, W Grn 3D **68**
Joe Jones Ct. DY3: Sed 4A **60**
Joey's La. WV8: Bilb 3A **14**
John Bright Cl. DY4: Tip 5H **61**
John Bright St. B1: Birm 5D **4** (1F **117**)
John Corbett Dr. DY8: Amb 4D **108**
John F Kennedy Wlk. DY4: Tip 5A **62**
John Fletcher Cl. WS10: W'bry 1H **63**
John Harper St. WV13: W'hall 1B **46**
John Howell Dr. DY4: Tip 2A **78**
John Kempe Way B12: Birm 4A **118**
John Padden Cl. B65: Row R 2B **112**
John Riley Dr. WV12: W'hall 1C **30**
John Rd. B62: Hale 2F **129**
John Rudge Ct. WV5: Wom 2E **73**
(off Brickbridge La.)
Johns Gro. B43: Gt Barr 5G **65**
Johns La. B69: Tiv 4C **78**
DY4: Tip 3B **78**
WS6: Gt Wyr 2F **7**
John Smyth Ho. B1: Birm 3A **4** (6E **101**)
Johnson Av. WV11: Wed 2H **29**
Johnson Cl. B8: W End 3A **104**
B11: S'hll 6C **118**
WS10: Darl 6D **46**
Johnson Dr. B35: Cas V 4D **86**
Johnson Pl. WV14: Bils 4H **45**
Johnson Rd. B23: Erd 2F **85**
WS10: Darl 6D **46**
WS10: W'bry 3A **64**
WV12: W'hall 2D **30**
Johnsons Bri. Rd. B71: W Brom . . .1A **80**
Johnsons Gro. B68: O'bry 3A **114**
Johnson St. B7: Nech 3C **102**
WV2: Wolv 4H **43**
(not continuous)
WV14: Cose 4B **60**
Johnstone St. B19: Loz 1F **101**
Johnston St. B70: W Brom 6B **80**
John St. B19: Loz 2D **100**
B65: B'hth 2C **112**
B69: O'bry 2G **97**
B70: W Brom 2F **79**
(Victoria St.)
B70: W Brom 3H **79**
(Winkle St.)
DY5: Brie H 5H **93**
DY8: Word 2D **108**
WS2: Wals 6C **32**
WV2: Ett 5C **44**
WV13: W'hall 2B **46**
John St. Nth. B71: W Brom 2H **79**
John Wesley Way WS10: W'bry . . .4G **63**
John Willmott Leisure Cen. 1D **70**
John Wooton Ho. WS10: Darl 5D **46**
(off St Lawrence Way)
Joiners Cl. B92: Sol 5A **138**
Joinings Bank B68: O'bry 5H **97**
Jonah Dr. DY4: Tip 1C **78**
Jonesfield Cres. WV1: Wolv 1C **44**
Jones Ho. WS2: Wals 6B **32**
Jones Rd. WV10: Oxl 3G **27**
WV12: W'hall 6D **18**
Jones's La. WS6: Gt Wyr 4G **7**
Jones Wood Cl. B76: Walm 6D **70**

Jonfield Gdns. B43: Gt Barr 4B **66**
Jonquil Cl. B23: Erd 6C **68**
Jordan Cl. B66: Smeth 4F **99**
B75: Four O 2H **53**
Jordan Ho. B36: Hodg H 1B **104**
Jordan Leys DY4: Tip 2B **78**
Jordan Pl. WV14: Bils 2G **61**
Jordan Rd. B75: Four O 2H **53**
Jordan Way WS9: A'rdge 6D **22**
Joseph Hall Dr. DY4: Tip 6G **61**
Joseph St. B69: O'bry 3F **97**
Josiah Rd. B31: N'fld 5B **144**
Jowett's La. B71: W Brom 5H **63**
Joyberry Dr. DY8: Stourb 2D **124**
Joynson St. WS10: Darl 6E **47**
Jubilee Av. B71: W Brom 6H **63**
Jubilee Bus. Pk. DY9: Lye 6C **110**
Jubilee Cl. WS3: Wals 3C **32**
WS6: Gt Wyr 3F **7**
Jubilee Ct. B27: A Grn 3A **136**
B31: N'fld 6F **145**
Jubilee Dr. B20: Hand 6C **82**
Jubilee Gdns. B23: Erd 6B **68**
Jubilee Rd. B45: Fran 5E **143**
DY4: Tip 6A **62**
WV14: Bils 1A **62**
Jubilee St. B71: W Brom 6B **64**
Jubilee Trade Cen. B5: Birm 2G **117**
Judge Cl. B69: O'bry 2G **97**
Judge Rd. DY5: Quar B 4B **110**
Julia Av. B24: Erd 2D **86**
Julia Gdns. B71: W Brom 5D **64**
Julian Cl. WS6: Gt Wyr 2G **7**
WV1: Wolv 1D **44**
Julian Rd. WV1: Wolv 1D **44**
Julie Cft. WV14: Bils 4G **61**
Juliet Gro. WV10: Bush 2A **28**
Juliet Rd. B62: Hale 2F **129**
Julius Dr. B46: Col 6H **89**
Junction, The DY8: Word 3C **108**
Junction 6 Ind. Pk. B6: Witt 6B **84**
Junction Ind. Est. B66: Smeth 1D **98**
Junction Rd. B21: Hand 1G **99**
DY8: Stourb 1F **125**
DY8: Word 3C **108**
DY9: Stourb 1F **125**
WV2: Ett 4D **44**
Junction St. B69: O'bry 6E **79**
DY2: Dud 1D **94**
WS1: Wals 3B **48**
Junction St. Sth. B69: O'bry 4G **97**
Junction Two Ind. Est. B69: O'bry 4F **97**
(off Demuth Way)
June Cft. B26: Sheld 6H **121**
Juniper Cl. B27: A Grn 6H **119**
B76: Walm 6E **71**
WS5: Wals 1F **65**
Juniper Ho. B20: Hand 4B **82**
Juniper Ri. B63: Crad 6E **111**
Jupiter B16: Birm 2D **116**
Jury Rd. DY5: Quar B 4B **110**
Jutland Rd. B13: Mose 6B **134**

K

Kalum Dr. B70: W Brom 6G **63**
Karen Way DY5: Brie H 3H **109**
Karma Ct. B68: O'bry 6F **97**
KATE'S HILL 6G **77**
Katherine Ho. B17: Harb 6F **115**
(off Cadbury Way)
Katherine Rd. B67: Smeth 1D **114**
Kathleen Rd. B25: Yard 4A **120**
B72: S Cold 1A **70**
Katie Rd. B29: S Oak 4A **132**
Katsura Cl. B74: S'tly 4H **51**
Kayne Cl. DY6: K'wfrd 3A **92**
Keanscott Dr. B68: O'bry 5A **98**
Keasden Gro. WV13: W'hall 6C **30**
Keating Gdns. B75: Four O 5G **37**
Keatley Av. B33: Kitts G 1A **122**
Keats Av. B10: Small H 4D **118**
Keats Cl. B74: Four O 3F **37**
DY3: Lwr G 2E **75**
DY8: Amb 3E **109**

Keats Dr. WV14: Cose 3F **61**
Keats Gro. B27: A Grn 4H **135**
WV10: Bush 1C **28**
Keats Ho. B68: O'bry 5A **98**
Keats Rd. WS3: Blox 2C **32**
WV10: Bush 5C **16**
WV12: W'hall 2E **31**
Keble Gro. B26: Sheld 5F **121**
WS1: Wals 4E **49**
Keble Ho. B37: F'bri 1C **122**
Kedleston Cl. WS3: Blox 4G **19**
Kedleston Ct. B28: Hall G 3F **149**
Kedleston Rd. B28: Hall G 2F **149**
Keegan Wlk. WS2: Wals 5F **31**
Keel Dr. B13: Mose 4D **134**
Keele Ho. B37: F'bri 5D **106**
Keeley St. B9: Birm 1B **118**
Keelinge St. DY4: Tip 2B **78**
Keen St. B66: Smeth 5H **99**
Keepers Cl. B18: Win G 4B **100**
B46: Col 5H **107**
DY6: W Hth 1H **91**
WS9: Wals W 4B **22**
Keepers Ga. B37: Chel W 1E **123**
Keepers Ga. Cl. B74: S Cold 4A **54**
Keepers Ho. B73: New O 3C **68**
(off Welshmans Hill)
Keepers La. WV6: Tett 5G **13**
WV8: Cod, Tett 5G **13**
Keepers Rd. B74: Lit As 4C **36**
Keer Ct. B9: Birm 1B **118**
Kegworth Rd. B23: Erd 5C **84**
Keir Hardie Wlk. B69: Tiv 5D **78**
Keir Pl. DY8: Amb 3C **108**
Keir Rd. WS10: W'bry 3A **64**
Kelby Cl. B31: N'fld 3C **144**
Kelby Rd. B31: N'fld 3D **144**
Keldy Cl. WV6: Wolv 4D **26**
Kelfield Av. B17: Harb 1F **131**
Kelham Pl. B92: Olton 4F **137**
Kelia Dr. B67: Smeth 3D **98**
Keller Wlk. DY8: Amb 3C **108**
Kellett Rd. B7: Birm 5A **102**
Kelling Cl. DY5: Brie H 3G **109**
Kellington Cl. B8: W End 5F **103**
Kellner Gdns. B69: O'bry 1G **97**
Kelmarsh Dr. B91: Sol 6F **151**
Kelmscott Rd. B17: Harb 4F **115**
Kelsall Cl. WV1: Wolv 1D **44**
Kelsall Cft. B1: Birm 6D **100**
Kelsey Cl. B7: Birm 5B **102**
Kelso Gdns. WV6: Pert 5D **24**
Kelsull Cft. B37: F'bri 1C **122**
Kelton Ct. B15: Edg 4C **116**
Kelvedon Gro. B91: Sol 3G **151**
Kelverdale Gro. B14: King H 3E **147**
Kelverley Gro. B71: W Brom 4E **65**
Kelvin Dr. B66: Smeth 5G **99**
Kelvin Ho. DY1: Dud 5F **77**
Kelvin Pl. WS2: Wals 3H **31**
Kelvin Rd. B31: N'fld 6E **145**
WS2: Wals 3G **31**
Kelvin Way B70: W Brom 6H **79**
Kelvin Way Trad. Est. B70: W Brom . . .6H **79**
Kelway Av. B43: Gt Barr 2D **66**
Kelwood Dr. B63: Hale 6A **112**
Kelynmead Rd. B33: Yard 1E **121**
Kemberton Cl. WV3: Wolv 2A **42**
Kemberton Rd. B29: S Oak 3E **131**
WV3: Wolv 2A **42**
Kemble Cl. WV12: W'hall 6D **30**
Kemble Cft. B5: Edg 4G **117**
Kemble Dr. B35: Cas V 4E **87**
Kemelstowe Cres. B63: Hale 5E **127**
Kemerton Way B90: M'path 4D **164**
Kempe Rd. B33: Kitts G 5E **105**
Kempsey Cl. B63: Hale 1G **127**
B69: O'bry 5E **97**
B92: Olton 2E **137**
Kempsey Covert B38: King Nor 2A **160**
Kempsey Ho. B32: Bart G 5G **129**
Kemps Grn. Rd. CV7: Bal C 3H **169**
Kempson Av. B71: W Brom 2H **79**
B72: W Grn 4A **70**
Kempson Rd. B36: Hodg H 1C **104**
Kempsons Gro. WV14: Cose 2D **60**
Kempthorne Av. WV10: Bush 6A **16**

Kempthorne Gdns. WS3: Blox 5G 19
Kempthorne Rd. WV14: Bils 5H 45
Kempton Dr. WS6: Gt Wyr 3F 7
Kempton Pk. Rd. B36: Hodg H 1B 104
Kempton Way DY8: Stourb 2C 124
Kemsey Dr. WV14: Bils 2H 61
Kemshead Av. B31: Longb 1C 158
Kemsley Rd. B14: King H 5H 147
Kendal Av. B45: Redn 2H 157
    B46: Col 2H 107
Kendal Cl. WV6: Tett 3D 26
Kendal Ct. B23: Erd 4B 84
    B29: W Cas 6G 131
    WS9: Wals W 3B 22
Kendal Gro. B92: Sol 5B 138
Kendal Ho. B69: O'bry 5D 96
Kendall Ri. DY6: K'wfrd 4D 92
Kendal Ri. B68: O'bry 6H 97
    WV6: Tett 3D 26
Kendal Ri. Rd. B45: Redn 2H 157
Kendal Rd. B11: S'brk 4B 118
Kendal Twr. B17: Harb 6H 115
Kendrick Av. B34: S End 4A 106
Kendrick Cl. B92: Sol 1B 152
Kendrick Gro. B28: Hall G 6E 135
Kendrick Pl. WV14: Bils 1A 62
Kendrick Rd. B76: Walm 2D 86
    WV10: Bush 3A 28
    WV14: Bils 1A 62
Kendricks Rd. WS10: Darl 4F 47
Kendrick St. WS10: W'bry 2G 63
Keneggy M. B29: S Oak 3B 132
Kenelm Ct. B73: S Cold 1H 69
Kenelm Rd. B10: Small H 3E 119
    B68: O'bry 6G 97
    B73: S Cold 1H 69
    WV14: Cose 4E 61
Kenelm's Ct. B62: Roms 3A 142
Kenilworth Cl. B74: Four O 3G 53
    CV7: Bal C 3G 169
    DY4: Tip .3F 77
    DY8: Word 1B 108
Kenilworth Ct. B16: Edg 3B 116
    B24: Erd .5E 85
    DY1: Dud 1B 94
Kenilworth Cres. WS2: Wals 5G 31
    WV4: Ett .1A 60
Kenilworth Ho. B13: Mose 1A 148
    WS3: Blox 3A 32
                                (off Providence La.)
Kenilworth Rd. B20: Hand 6G 83
    B46: Col 2H 123
    B68: O'bry 3B 114
    B92: H Ard, Mer 1D 154
    B93: Know 3F 167
    CV7: Bal C 2E 155
    CV7: Mer 3C 140
    WV6: Pert 5F 25
Kenley Gro. B30: King Nor 4D 146
Kenley Way B91: Shir 3B 150
Kenmare Way WV11: Wed 5E 29
Kenmure Rd. B33: Sheld 4G 121
Kennedy Cl. B72: S Cold 1A 70
Kennedy Ct. DY8: Stourb 6D 108
Kennedy Cres. DY3: Lwr G 3H 75
    WS10: Darl 4C 46
Kennedy Cft. B26: Sheld 4E 121
Kennedy Gro. B30: Stir 1D 146
Kennedy Rd. WV10: Wolv 6H 27
Kennedy Twr. B4: Birm 2E 5
Kennerley Rd. B25: Yard 5B 120
Kennet Cl. WS8: Bwnhls 3G 9
Kennet Gro. B36: Cas B 1B 106
Kenneth Gro. B23: Erd 2A 84
Kennford Cl. B65: Row R 3C 96
Kennington Rd. WV10: Wolv 4B 28
Kenrick Cft. B35: Cas V 5E 87
Kenrick Ho. B70: W Brom 6C 80
Kenrick Park Stop (Metro) 6C 80
Kenrick Way B70: W Brom 1B 98
    B71: W Brom 6D 80
Kensington Av. B12: Bal H 1A 134
Kensington Dr. B74: Four O 4F 37
Kensington Gdns. DY8: Word 2A 108
Kensington Rd. B29: S Oak 3C 132
    WV12: W'hall 2B 30
Kensington St. B19: Hock 3F 101

Kenswick Dr. B63: Hale 3A 128
Kent Av. WS2: Wals 6H 31
Kent Cl. B71: W Brom 6H 63
    WS2: Wals 4C 32
    WS9: A'rdge 6D 22
Kent Dr. B21: Hand 1G 99
Kentmere Twr. B23: Erd 1H 85
Kenton Av. WV6: Wolv 5D 26
Kenton Wlk. B29: S Oak 3B 132
Kent Pl. DY2: Dud 3C 94
Kent Rd. B45: Fran 6F 143
    B62: Quin 5E 113
    DY8: Woll 4B 108
    WS2: Wals 6F 31
    WS10: W'bry 1A 64
    WV2: Wolv 4A 44
Kents Cl. B92: Olton 2D 136
Kent St. B5: Birm 3G 117
    DY3: Up Gor 2A 76
    WS2: Wals 4C 32
Kent St. Nth. B18: Hock 4B 100
Kenward Cft. B17: Harb 4D 114
Kenway B47: H'wd 2A 162
Kenwick Rd. B17: Harb 1F 131
Kenwood Rd. B9: Bord G 6H 103
Kenyon Cl. DY8: Amb 4E 109
Kenyon St. B3: Birm 1B 4 (5E 101)
    B18: Birm 1B 4 (5E 101)
Kerby Rd. B23: Erd 3C 84
Kererwin Cl. B64: Old H 2A 112
Keresley Cl. B91: Sol 2G 151
Keresley Gro. B29: W Cas 3D 130
Kernthorpe Rd. B14: King H 3F 147
Kerr Dr. DY4: Tip 5G 61
Kerria Ct. B15: Birm 3F 117
Kerridge Cl. WV9: Pend 5E 15
Kerrison Ride B73: Bold 4F 69
Kerr La. B90: Dic H 3G 163
Kerry Cl. B31: N'fld 1D 144
    DY5: Brie H 5G 93
Kerry Ct. WS1: Wals 3E 49
Kersley Gdns. WV11: Wed 3H 29
Kerswell Dr. B90: M'path 4D 164
Kesterton Rd. B74: Four O 4E 37
Kesteven Cl. B15: Edg 5D 116
Kesteven Rd. B71: W Brom 6A 64
Keston Rd. B44: Gt Barr 1H 67
Kestrel Av. B25: Yard 3H 119
Kestrel Cl. B23: Erd 1D 84
    B35: Cas V 4F 87
Kestrel Dr. B74: Four O 4F 37
Kestrel Gro. B30: B'ville 5H 131
    WV12: W'hall 1C 30
Kestrel Ho. DY4: Tip 2G 77
                                   (off Owen St.)
Kestrel Ri. WV6: Tett 2D 26
Kestrel Rd. B63: Crad 4D 110
    B68: O'bry 1F 113
    DY1: Dud 1B 94
Kestrel Way WS6: C Hay 3C 6
Keswick Dr. DY6: K'wfrd 3B 92
Keswick Gro. B74: S'tly 1H 51
Keswick Ho. B69: O'bry 5D 96
Keswick Rd. B92: Olton 1D 136
Ketley Cft. B12: Birm 4H 117
Ketley Flds. DY6: K'wfrd 4E 93
Ketley Hill Rd. DY1: Dud 1B 94
Ketley Rd. DY6: K'wfrd 3D 92
                               (not continuous)
Kettlebrook Rd. B90: M'path 3F 165
Kettlehouse Rd. B44: Gt Barr 2H 67
Kettlesbank Rd. DY3: Gorn 5G 75
Kettles Wood Dr. B32: Bart G 3H 129
Kettlewell Way B37: F'bri 1B 122
Ketton Gro. B33: Sheld 4H 121
Kew Cl. B37: K'hrst 6B 106
Kew Dr. DY1: Dud 5C 76
Kew Gdns. B33: Stech 2B 120
Kewstoke Cl. WV12: W'hall 6B 18
Kewstoke Cft. B31: N'fld 1C 144
Kewstoke Rd. WV12: W'hall 6B 18
Key Bus. Pk. B24: Erd 4C 86
Keyes Dr. DY6: K'wfrd 6B 74
Key Gdns. WV10: Wolv 6B 28
Key Hill B18: Birm 4D 100
Key Hill Cir. B18: Birm 4D 100
Key Hill Dr. B18: Birm 4D 100

Key Ind. Pk. WV13: W'hall 6F 29
Keynell Covert B30: King Nor 5E 147
Keynes Dr. WV14: Bils 5G 45
Keys Cres. B71: W Brom 1A 80
Keyse Rd. B75: S Cold 4D 54
Keysmith Cl. WV13: W'hall 2C 46
Keyte Cl. DY4: Tip 2A 78
Keyway, The WV13: W'hall 2H 45
Keyway Retail Pk. WV13: W'hall 3B 46
Keyworth Cl. DY4: Tip 2A 78
Khalsa Ind. Est. B66: Smeth 5H 99
Khyber Cl. WS10: Darl 4C 46
Kidd Cft. DY4: Tip 3C 62
Kidderminster Rd.
    DY6: K'wfrd, W Hth 6G 91
    DY7: I'ley 6A 124
    DY7: Stourt 6G 91
    DY9: Hag 6G 125
    DY10: I'ley 6A 124
Kielder Cl. WS5: Wals 2G 65
Kielder Gdns. DY9: Pedm 4F 125
Kier's Bri. Cl. DY4: Tip 4A 78
Kilburn Dr. DY6: K'wfrd 6C 74
Kilburn Gro. B44: Gt Barr 2H 67
Kilburn Pl. DY2: Dud 3F 95
Kilburn Rd. B44: Gt Barr 2H 67
Kilby Av. B16: Birm 1C 116
Kilbys Gro. B20: Hand 5B 82
Kilcote Rd. B90: Shir 5C 148
Kilderkin Ct. B66: Smeth 5G 99
Kilmet Wlk. B67: Smeth 4E 99
Kilmore Cft. B36: Hodg H 6C 86
Kilmorie Rd. B27: A Grn 6A 120
Kiln Cl. B65: Row R 5A 96
Kiln La. B25: Yard 5H 119
    B90: Dic H 4G 163
Kilsby Gro. B91: Sol 1G 165
Kilvert Rd. WS10: W'bry 3H 63
Kimbells Wlk. B93: Know 3E 167
Kimberley Av. B8: Salt 4E 103
Kimberley Cl. B74: S'tly 6A 36
Kimberley Pl. WV14: Cose 6D 60
Kimberley Rd. B66: Smeth 2E 99
    B92: Olton 3E 137
Kimberley St. WV3: Wolv 2E 43
Kimberley Wlk. B76: Min 1H 87
Kimble Gro. B24: Erd 4B 86
Kimbley Ri. B71: W Brom 6G 63
Kimpton Cl. B14: King H 5G 147
Kimsan Cft. B74: S'tly 4A 52
Kinchford Cl. B91: Sol 1G 165
Kineton Cft. B32: Bart G 5B 130
    B92: Olton 5B 136
Kineton Grange B92: Olton 5B 136
Kineton Grn. Rd. B92: Olton 5B 136
Kineton Ho. B13: Mose 1A 148
Kineton Ri. DY3: Sed 3G 59
Kineton Rd. B45: Rub 2E 157
    B73: New O 4E 69
King Charles Av. WS2: Wals 1E 47
King Charles Ct. B44: K'sdng 3B 68
King Charles Rd. B62: Quin 1F 129
King Edmund St. DY1: Dud 5D 76
                                       (Nith Pl.)
    DY1: Dud 5D 76
                                   (The Parade)
King Edward VI Ho. B4: Birm 6H 101
                                  (off Aston St.)
King Edward Ct. B63: Hale 1A 128
King Edward Rd. B13: Mose 2H 133
King Edwards Cl. B20: Hand 1D 100
King Edwards Dr. B16: Birm 1D 116
King Edwards Gdns. B20: Hand 2D 100
King Edwards Rd.
    B1: Birm 4A 4 (1D 116)
                                     (Edward St.)
    B1: Birm 6C 100
                                  (St Marks Cres.)
King Edward's Row WV2: Wolv 3G 43
King Edwards Sq. B73: S Cold 5A 54
King Edward St. WS10: Darl 5D 46
King Edwards Wharf
    B16: Birm 1D 116
Kingfield Rd. B90: Shir 5C 148

Kingfisher Cl.—Kittiwake Dr.

Kingfisher Cl. B26: Sheld 5E **121**
DY3: Sed 3G **59**
WS8: Bwnhls 6A **10**
Kingfisher Ct. WV13: W'hall 1C **46**
Kingfisher Dr. B36: Cas B 1C **106**
DY8: Stourb 1A **124**
Kingfisher Gro. WV12: W'hall 1B **30**
Kingfisher Ho. *DY4: Tip* *2G* ***77***
(off Kingfisher Way)
Kingfisher Ind. Est. B70: W Brom 3F **79**
Kingfisher Rd. B23: Erd 6C **68**
Kingfisher Vw. B34: Stech 4E **105**
Kingfisher Way B30: B'vlle 5H **131**
DY4: Tip 2G **77**
King George VI Av. WS1: Wals 3G **49**
King George Cres. WS4: Rus 3F **33**
King George Pl. WS4: Rus 3F **33**
Kingham Cl. DY3: Gorn 5G **75**
Kingham Covert B14: King H 5F **147**
Kings Av. B69: Tiv 5B **78**
Kingsbridge Ho. B23: Erd 1B **84**
Kingsbridge Rd. B32: Bart G 4B **130**
Kingsbridge Wlk. B66: Smeth 4F **99**
Kingsbrook Dr. B91: Sol 1F **165**
Kingsbury Av. B24: Erd 4B **86**
Kingsbury Bus. Pk. B76: Min 1A **88**
Kingsbury Cl. B76: Min 2H **87**
WS4: Wals 5F **33**
Kingsbury Community Leisure Cen. **5F 85**
Kingsbury Pl. B24: Erd 3H **85**
Kingsbury Rd. B24: Erd 5E **85**
B35: Cas V 5B **86**
B76: Min, Curd 2G **87**
(not continuous)
DY4: Tip 5A **62**
Kings Bus. Pk. B44: Gt Barr 2G **67**
Kingsclere Wlk. WV4: Penn 5A **42**
Kingscliff Rd. B10: Small H 3G **119**
Kings Cl. B14: King H 1E **147**
B30: King Nor 5C **146**
Kingscote Rd. B15: Edg 5H **115**
B93: Dorr 6F **167**
Kings Ct. B1: Birm 6B **4** (2E **117**)
B3: Birm 1C **4** (5E **101**)
B37: Mars G 2G **123**
B68: O'bry 4G **113**
B75: Four O 6H **37**
DY4: Tip 3A **78**
DY8: Woll 6C **108**
Kings Ct. Plazas B1: Birm 3A **4**
Kings Cft. B26: Sheld 6E **121**
B36: Cas B 2B **106**
Kingscroft Cl. B74: S'tly 4A **52**
Kingscroft Rd. B74: S'tly 3A **52**
Kingsdene Av. DY6: K'wfrd 5A **92**
Kingsdown Av. B42: Gt Barr 1B **82**
Kingsdown Rd. B31: N'fld 4D **130**
Kingsfield Rd. B14: King H 5G **133**
Kingsford Cl. B36: Cas B 6H **87**
Kingsford Ct. B92: Olton 2F **137**
Kingsford Nouveau DY6: K'wfrd 4E **93**
Kings Gdns. B30: King Nor 3A **146**
Kings Ga. B14: King H 5G **133**
B38: King Nor 6A **146**
Kingsgate Ho. B37: Chel W 1C **122**
Kings Grn. Av. B38: King Nor 5B **146**
Kings Hall *B13: Mose* *3A* ***134***
(off The Academy)
Kingshayes Rd. WS9: A'rdge 5D **22**
KING'S HEATH **5G 133**
King's Heath Park **5F 133**
KING'S HILL **6D 46**
Kings Hill Bus. Pk. WS10: W'bry 1E **63**
Kings Hill Cl. WS10: Darl 6E **47**
Kingshill Dr. B38: King Nor 5B **146**
Kings Hill Fld. WS10: Darl 6E **47**
Kings Hill M. WS10: Darl 6D **46**
KINGSHURST **4B 106**
Kingshurst Ho. B37: K'hrst 4B **106**
Kingshurst Rd. B31: N'fld 4E **145**
B90: Shir 6F **149**
Kingshurst Way B37: K'hrst 5B **106**
Kingsland Dr. B93: Dorr 6A **166**
Kingsland Rd. B44: Gt Barr 1G **67**
WV1: Wolv 6F **27**
Kingslea Rd. B91: Sol 5C **150**
Kingsleigh Cft. B75: Four O 1H **53**
Kingsleigh Dr. B36: Cas B 1E **105**
Kingsleigh Rd. B20: Hand 5D **82**
Kingsley Av. WV6: Tett 5H **25**
Kingsley Bank Way B26: Sheld 4F **121**
Kingsley Ct. B25: Yard 3C **120**
Kingsley Gdns. WV8: Cod 4E **13**
Kingsley Gro. DY3: Lwr G 2E **75**
Kingsley Rd. B12: Bal H 5A **118**
B30: King Nor 3H **145**
DY6: K'wfrd 4H **91**
Kingsley St. DY2: Neth 4E **95**
WS2: Wals 4H **47**
Kings Lodge B38: King Nor 5B **146**
Kingslow Av. WV4: Penn 5B **42**
Kingsmere Cl. B24: Erd 5E **85**
KINGS NORTON **5B 146**
King's Norton Bus. Cen.
B30: King Nor 3C **146**
Kings Norton Community Leisure Cen.
1B 160
King's Norton Golf Course **6E 161**
Kings Norton Nature Reserve **4H 145**
Kings Norton Station (Rail) **3B 146**
Kings Oak Ct. B75: S Cold 1D **70**
Kingsoak Gdns. DY2: Dud 2G **95**
Kings Pde. B4: Birm 4F **5**
Kings Pk. W. B38: King Nor 1G **159**
Kingspiece Ho. B36: Hodg H 1C **104**
Kings Rd. B11: Tys 6G **119**
B14: King H 1E **147**
B23: Erd 3C **84**
B25: Yard 6G **119**
B44: Gt Barr, K'sdng 2G **67**
B73: New O 3A **68**
DY3: Sed 5A **60**
WS4: Rus 2G **33**
Kings Rd. Ind. Est. B11: Tys 5G **119**
Kings Sq. B70: W Brom 4B **80**
WV14: Cose 5C **60**
King's Standing Ancient Monument **1H 67**
KINGSTANDING **5A 68**
Kingstanding Cen., The B44: Gt Barr 2H **67**
Kingstanding Leisure Cen. **5B 68**
Kingstanding Rd. B44: K'sdng 1H **83**
King's Ter. B14: King H 1F **147**
Kingsthorpe Rd. B14: King H 4A **148**
Kingston Ct. B29: W Cas 6F **131**
B74: S Cold 4H **53**
Kingston Ind. Est. *B9: Birm* *2B* ***118***
(off Glover St.)
Kingston Rd. B9: Birm 2B **118**
B75: S Cold 5D **54**
Kingston Row B1: Birm 4A **4** (1E **117**)
Kingston Way DY6: K'wfrd 2A **92**
King St. B11: S'brk 4A **118**
B63: Hale 1A **128**
B64: Old H 2H **111**
B66: Smeth 2F **99**
DY2: Dud 1E **95**
DY5: Quar B 3C **110**
DY8: Woll 5C **108**
DY9: Lye 1B **126**
WS1: Wals 4B **48**
WS7: Chase 1B **10**
WS9: Wals W 5B **22**
WS10: W'bry 3E **63**
WV1: Wolv 3B **170** (1H **43**)
WV13: W'hall 1B **46**
WV14: Bils 2G **61**
WV14: Cose 5C **60**
King St. Pas. DY2: Dud 6E **77**
DY5: Quar B 3C **110**
King St. Pct. WS10: Darl 5D **46**
Kingsway B68: O'bry 4G **113**
DY8: Woll 3B **108**
WV10: Wolv 3C **28**
WV11: Ess 3A **18**
Kingsway Av. DY4: Tip 5A **62**
Kingsway Dr. B38: King Nor 5B **146**
Kingsway Nth. WS9: A'rdge 3A **34**
Kingsway Rd. WV10: Wolv 3C **28**
Kingsway Sth. WS9: A'rdge 3A **34**
Kingswear Av. WV6: Pert 6F **25**
KINGSWINFORD **3B 92**
Kingswinford Rd. DY1: Dud 2A **94**
KING'S WOOD **1G 161**
KINGSWOOD **5A 12**
Kingswood Cl. B30: King Nor 4G **147**
B90: Shir 6B **150**
Kingswood Cft. B7: Nech 2C **102**
Kingswood Dr. B30: King Nor 4E **147**
B74: S'tly 1H **67**
WS6: Gt Wyr 1G **7**
Kingswood Gdns. WV4: Penn 5D **42**
Kingswood Ho. B14: King H 5G **147**
Kingswood Rd. B13: Mose 1A **134**
B31: Longb 3D **158**
DY6: K'wfrd 5A **92**
Kingswood Ter. *B25: Yard* *4H* ***119***
(off Berkeley Rd. E.)
Kingswood Wlk. B31: Longb 2D **158**
Kington Cl. WV12: W'hall 1B **30**
Kington Gdns. B37: F'bri 2B **122**
Kington Way B33: Stech 1B **120**
King William St. DY8: Amb 3D **108**
Kiniths Cres. B71: W Brom 2C **80**
Kiniths Way B62: B'hth 2E **113**
B71: W Brom 3C **80**
Kinlet Av. B31: N'fld 5G **145**
Kinlet Cl. WV3: Wolv 3G **41**
Kinloch Dr. DY1: Dud 4B **76**
Kinnerley St. WS1: Wals 2E **49**
Kinnersley Cres. B69: O'bry 4D **96**
Kinnerton Cres. B29: W Cas 3D **130**
Kinross Cres. B43: Gt Barr 1D **66**
Kinsall Ct. *WV1: Wolv* *5G* ***27***
(off Boscobel Cres.)
Kinsey Gro. B14: King H 3H **147**
Kinsey Rd. B66: Smeth 5G **99**
Kinsham Dr. B91: Sol 1F **165**
Kintore Cft. B32: Bart G 6H **129**
Kintyre Cl. B45: Fran 6E **143**
Kinvara Hgts. B12: Birm 3A **118**
Kinver Av. WV12: W'hall 4B **30**
Kinver Cres. WS9: A'rdge 6E **23**
Kinver Cft. B12: Bal H 4G **117**
B76: Walm 5E **71**
Kinver Dr. DY9: Hag 6G **125**
WV4: Penn 6A **42**
Kinver M. B37: Mars G 3C **122**
Kinver Rd. B31: N'fld 5H **145**
Kinver St. DY8: Word 2B **108**
Kinwarton Cl. B25: Yard 5B **120**
Kipling Av. WV14: Cose 4D **60**
Kipling Cl. DY4: Tip 5A **62**
Kipling Rd. B30: King Nor 3G **145**
DY3: Lwr G 2E **75**
WV10: F'hses 5H **15**
WV12: W'hall 2E **31**
Kirby Cl. WV14: Bils 2G **61**
Kirby Dr. DY1: Dud 4A **76**
Kirby Rd. B18: Win G 3A **100**
Kirkby Grn. B73: S Cold 2H **69**
Kirkham Gdns. DY5: P'ntt 3G **93**
Kirkham Gro. B33: Stech 5D **104**
Kirkham Way DY4: Tip 2A **78**
Kirklands Est. DY2: Dud 2E **95**
Kirk Patrick Dr. DY8: Word 5C **92**
Kirkside Gro. WS8: Bwnhls 6B **10**
Kirkside M. WS8: Bwnhls 6B **10**
Kirkstall Cl. WS3: Blox 5F **19**
Kirkstall Cres. WS3: Blox 5F **19**
Kirkstone Ct. DY5: Brie H 4F **109**
Kirkstone Cres. B43: Gt Barr 1B **82**
WV5: Wom 1F **73**
Kirkstone Way DY5: Brie H 4F **109**
Kirkwall Rd. B32: Bart G 4B **130**
Kirkwood Av. B23: Erd 6F **69**
Kirmond Wlk. WV6: Wolv 4F **27**
Kirstead Gdns. WV6: Tett 6H **25**
Kirton Gro. B33: Stech 5E **105**
B91: Sol 6E **151**
WV6: Tett 4A **26**
Kitchener Rd. B29: S Oak 4D **132**
DY2: Dud 6H **77**
Kitchener St. B66: Smeth 3H **99**
Kitchen La. WV11: Wed 6H **17**
Kitebrook Cl. B90: M'path 2E **165**
Kitegreen Cl. B37: Chel W 5F **107**
Kitsland Rd. B34: S End 3A **106**
(not continuous)
Kitswell Gdns. B32: Bart G 5G **129**
Kittermaster Rd. CV7: Mer 4H **141**
Kittiwake Dr. DY5: Brie H 4G **109**

Kittoe Rd. B74: Four O 6F **37**
KITT'S GREEN 6G **105**
Kitts Grn. B33: Kitts G 6F **105**
Kitts Grn. Rd. B33: Kitts G 5E **105**
Kitwell La. B32: Bart G 5G **129**
Kitwood Dr. B92: Sol 6H **137**
Kixley La. B93: Know 3E **167**
Klaxon Ind. Est. B11: Tys 1F **135**
Knarsdale Cl. DY5: Brie H 3G **109**
Knaves Castle Av. WS8: Bwnhls 3B **10**
Knebworth Cl. B44: Gt Barr 5G **67**
Knightcote Dr. B91: Sol 1F **165**
Knight Ct. B75: S Cold 6G **55**
Knightley Rd. B91: Sol 5D **150**
Knightlow Rd. B17: Harb 3E **115**
Knighton Cl. B74: Four O 6F **37**
Knighton Dr. B74: Four O 1F **53**
Knighton Rd. B31: N'fld 3G **145**
   B74: Four O 4D **36**
   DY2: Neth .5F **95**
Knights Av. WV6: Tett 3B **26**
Knightsbridge Cl. B74: Four O 5F **37**
Knightsbridge Rd. B37: K'hrst 4B **106**
Knightsbridge La. WV12: W'hall 3C **30**
Knightsbridge Rd. B92: Olton 4E **137**
Knights Cl. B23: Erd 5E **85**
   WV13: W'hall 1C **46**
Knights Ct. WS11: Nort C 1E **9**
Knights Cres. WV6: Tett 2C **26**
Knightsfield Cl. B73: New O 2C **68**
Knights Hill WS9: A'rdge 6D **34**
Knight's Rd. B11: Tys 1G **135**
Knightstone Av. B18: Hock 5C **100**
Knightswood Cl. B75: S Cold 4B **54**
Knightwick Cres. B23: Erd 2C **84**
Knipersley Rd. B73: Bold 1G **85**
Knoll, The B32: Bart G 4A **130**
   DY6: K'wfrd 4C **92**
Knoll Cl. WS7: Chase 1C **10**
Knoll Cft. B90: Ches G 5B **164**
   WS9: A'rdge 6E **23**
Knollcroft B16: Birm 1C **116**
Knott Ct. DY5: Brie H 1H **109**
Knottsall La. B68: O'bry 6H **97**
Knotts Farm Rd. DY6: K'wfrd 5E **93**
Knowlands Rd. B90: M'path 2E **165**
KNOWLE 3E **167**
Knowle Cl. B45: Redn 2B **158**
KNOWLE GROVE 6D **166**
Knowle Hill Rd. DY2: Neth 5D **94**
Knowle Rd. B11: S'hll 2D **134**
   B65: Row R .5H **95**
   B92: H Ard .6G **153**
Knowles Dr. B74: Four O 4G **53**
Knowles Rd. WV1: Wolv 2B **44**
Knowles St. WS10: W'bry 2G **63**
Knowle Wood Rd. B93: Dorr 6D **166**
Knox Rd. WV2: Wolv 5H **43**
Knoyle Ct. DY8: Stourb 5D **108**
                        (off Scott's Rd.)
Knutsford St. B12: Bal H 5H **117**
Knutswood Cl. B13: Mose 6D **134**
Kohima Dr. DY8: Stourb 6C **108**
Kossuth Rd. WV14: Cose 4C **60**
Kyle Cl. WV10: Oxl 6F **15**
Kyles Way B32: Bart G 6H **129**
Kynance Gro. WV14: Bils 3A **62**
Kynaston Cres. WV8: Cod 5H **13**
Kynaston Ho. B71: W Brom 5A **64**
Kyngsford Rd. B33: Kitts G 6H **105**
Kyngston Rd. B71: W Brom 1C **80**
Kyotts Lake Rd. B11: S'brk 4A **118**
Kyrwicks La. B11: S'brk 5A **118**
   B12: Birm .5A **118**
Kyter La. B36: Cas B 1F **105**

L

Laburnum Av. B37: K'hrst 3B **106**
   B67: Smeth 5C **98**
Laburnum Cl. B37: K'hrst 3B **106**
   B47: H'wd .4A **162**
   DY8: Woll .4C **108**
   WS3: Pels .5E **21**
Laburnum Cotts. B21: Hand 1A **100**
Laburnum Dr. B69: S'brk 5B **78**

Laburnum Dr. B76: Walm 2E **71**
Laburnum Gro. B13: Mose 2H **133**
   WS2: Wals .6F **31**
Laburnum Ho. B30: B'vlle 6B **132**
Laburnum Rd. B30: B'vlle 5B **132**
   DY1: Dud .3D **76**
   DY4: Tip 6H **61**
   DY6: K'wfrd 3C **92**
   WS5: Wals .1G **65**
   WS9: Wals W 4C **22**
   WS10: W'bry 1H **63**
   WV1: Wolv 3D **44**
   WV4: Ett 2A **60**
Laburnum St. DY8: Woll 4C **108**
   WV3: Wolv .2E **43**
Laburnum Trees B47: H'wd 3A **162**
                        (off May La.)
Laburnum Vs. B11: S'hll 6C **118**
Laburnum Way B31: Longb 6E **145**
Laceby Gro. B13: Mose 4D **134**
Ladbroke Dr. B76: Walm 3D **70**
Ladbroke Gro. B27: A Grn 5A **136**
Ladbrook Gro. DY3: Lwr G 4E **75**
Ladbrook Rd. B91: Sol 4G **151**
Ladbury Gro. WS5: Wals 1D **64**
Ladbury Rd. WS5: Wals 1E **65**
Ladeler Gro. B33: Kitts G 1A **122**
Ladies Wlk. DY3: Sed 5H **59**
Lady Bank B32: Bart G 6H **129**
Lady Bracknell M. B31: N'fld 3G **145**
Lady Byron La. B93: Know 2B **166**
Ladycroft B16: Birm 1C **116**
Lady Grey's Wlk. DY8: Stourb 6B **108**
Lady La. B90: Shir 6G **163**
   B94: Earls .6G **163**
Ladymoor Rd. WV14: Bils 2E **61**
Ladypool Av. B11: S'brk 5B **118**
Ladypool Cl. B62: Hale 1C **128**
   WS4: Wals .4E **33**
Ladypool Rd. B11: S'brk 1A **134**
   B12: Bal H .1A **134**
Ladysmith Rd. B63: Crad 5E **111**
Ladywell Cl. WV5: Wom 5G **57**
Ladywell Wlk. B5: Birm 6E **5** (2G **117**)
LADYWOOD 1D **116**
Ladywood Arts & Leisure Cen. 1B **116**
Ladywood Cir. B16: Birm 1C **116**
                (off Ladywood Middleway)
Ladywood Cl. DY5: Quar B 2B **110**
Ladywood Cft. B74: Four O 2H **53**
                (off Lichfield Rd.)
Ladywood Middleway B1: Birm 1C **116**
   B16: Birm .1C **116**
Ladywood Rd. B16: Edg 2C **116**
   B74: Four O 4G **53**
LA Fitness
   Birmingham 4E **5**
   Kings Heath 6G **133**
   Longbridge 1C **158**
   Sutton Coldfield 6G **69**
Laing Ho. B69: O'bry 4D **96**
Lake Av. WS5: Wals 4F **49**
Lake Cl. WS5: Wals 4G **49**
Lakedown Cl. B14: King H 6G **147**
Lakefield B31: N'fld 3D **144**
Lakefield Cl. B28: Hall G 6H **135**
Lakefield Rd. WV11: Wed 4G **29**
Lakehouse Ct. B23: Erd 5E **69**
Lakehouse Gro. B38: King Nor 4H **145**
Lakehouse Rd. B73: Bold 5E **69**
Laker Cl. DY8: Amb 4E **109**
Lakeside B74: Lit As 4B **36**
Lakeside Centre, The
   B30: King Nor 4C **146**
Lakeside Cl. WV13: W'hall 6G **29**
Lakeside Ct. DY5: Brie H 3F **109**
Lakeside Dr. B23: Erd 1B **84**
   B90: M'path 2D **164**
Lakeside Ind. Pk. B46: Wat O 3E **89**
Lakeside Residences
   B4: Birm 2F **5** (6H **101**)
Lakeside Rd. B70: W Brom 1G **79**
Lakeside Wlk. B23: Erd 3B **84**
Lakes Rd. B23: Erd 2A **84**
Lake St. DY3: Lwr G 4H **75**
Lake Vw. Cl. B30: B'vlle 2A **146**
Lake Vw. Ct. B23: Erd 5C **84**

Lakewood Dr. B45: Redn 6H **143**
Lakey La. B28: Hall G 5G **135**
Lambah Cl. WV14: Bils 4H **45**
Lamb Cl. B34: S End 4A **106**
Lamb Cres. WV5: Wom 1F **73**
                        (not continuous)
Lambert Cl. B23: Erd 1D **84**
Lambert Ct. DY6: K'wfrd 1B **92**
Lambert End B70: W Brom 4H **79**
Lambert Fold DY2: Dud 1G **95**
Lambert Rd. WV10: Wolv 3B **28**
LAMBERT'S END 4H **79**
Lambert St. B70: W Brom 4H **79**
Lambeth Cl. B37: F'bri 5D **106**
Lambeth Rd. B44: Gt Barr 2G **67**
   WV14: Bils .4D **44**
Lambourn Cl. WS3: Blox 5A **20**
Lambourne Cl. WS6: Gt Wyr 2F **7**
Lambourne Gro. B37: F'bri 1B **122**
Lambourne Way DY5: Brie H 3F **109**
   WS11: Nort C 1E **9**
Lambourn Rd. B23: Erd 3D **84**
   WV13: W'hall 2D **46**
Lambscote Cl. B90: Shir 5C **148**
Lammas Cl. B92: Sol 4G **137**
Lammas Rd. DY8: Word 6A **92**
Lammermoor Av. B43: Gt Barr 3B **66**
Lamont Av. B32: Bart G 2D **130**
Lamorna Cl. WV3: Wolv 3H **41**
Lanark Cl. DY6: K'wfrd 4D **92**
Lanark Cft. B35: Cas V 4D **86**
Lancaster Av. B45: Rub 1G **157**
   WS9: A'rdge 1D **34**
   WS10: W'bry 2A **64**
Lancaster Cir. Queensway
   B4: Birm 1F **5** (5G **101**)
Lancaster Cl. B30: B'vlle 1C **146**
Lancaster Dr. B35: Cas V 5F **87**
Lancaster Gdns. WV4: Penn 6C **42**
Lancaster Ho. B65: Row R 5E **97**
Lancaster Pl. WS3: Blox 5A **20**
Lancaster Rd. DY5: Brie H 1G **109**
Lancaster St. B4: Birm 1F **5** (5G **101**)
Lancelot Cl. B8: Salt 6E **103**
Lancelot Pl. B70: W Brom 3E **79**
Lanchester Rd. B38: King Nor 6C **146**
Lanchester Way B36: Cas B 6A **88**
Lander Cl. B45: Rub 3G **157**
Landgate Rd. B21: Hand 5G **81**
Land La. B37: Mars G 4C **122**
Landor Rd. B93: Know 3C **166**
Landor St. B8: Birm, Salt 6B **102**
Landport Rd. WV2: Wolv 3B **44**
Landrail Wlk. B36: Cas B 1C **106**
                        (not continuous)
Landrake Rd. DY6: K'wfrd 4D **92**
Landseer Gro. B43: Gt Barr 1F **67**
Landsgate DY8: Stourb 4E **125**
Landswood Cl. B44: K'sdng 4A **68**
Landswood Rd. B68: O'bry 5A **98**
LANDYWOOD .3G **7**
Landywood Ent. Pk. WS6: Gt Wyr 5F **7**
Landywood Grn. WS6: C Hay 3E **7**
Landywood La. WS6: C Hay, Gt Wyr . .3D **6**
Landywood Station (Rail) 3F **7**
Lane Av. WS2: Wals 6H **31**
Lane Cl. WS2: Wals 6H **31**
Lane Ct. WV1: Wolv 5G **27**
                    (off Boscobel Cres.)
Lane Cft. B76: Walm 5E **71**
LANE GREEN .4A **14**
Lane Grn. Av. WV8: Bilb 4A **14**
Lane Grn. Ct. WV8: Bilb 4H **13**
Lane Grn. Rd. WV8: Bilb 4H **13**
Lane Grn. Shop. Pde. WV8: Bilb 4H **13**
LANE HEAD 3C **30**
Lane Rd. WV4: Ett 2C **60**
Lanes Cl. WV5: Wom 2E **73**
LANESFIELD 3C **60**
Lanesfield Dr. WV4: Ett 1C **60**
Lanesfield Ind. Est. WV4: Ett 1C **60**
Laneside Av. B74: S'tly 4H **51**
Laneside Gdns. WS2: Wals 1H **47**
Lanes Shop. Cen., The B72: W Grn . . .6H **69**
Lane St. WV14: Bils, Cose 2F **61**
LANEY GREEN 3A **6**
Langcomb Rd. B90: Shir 1G **163**

Langdale Cl. WS8: Clay 1A 22
Langdale Cft. B21: Hand 2A 100
Langdale Dr. WV14: Bils 4F 45
Langdale Rd. B43: Gt Barr 6B 66
Langdale Way DY9: W'cte 1H 125
Langdon St. B9: Birm 1B 118
Langdon Wlk. B26: Yard 1C 136
Langer's Apartments
   DY8: Stourb 6D 108
                            (off Enville St.)
Langfield Rd. B93: Know 2C 166
Langford Av. B43: Gt Barr 5A 66
Langford Cl. WS1: Wals 2E 49
Langford Cft. B91: Sol 5G 151
Langford Gro. B17: Harb 2G 131
Langham Cl. B26: Sheld 4E 121
Langham Grn. B74: S'tly 2H 51
Langholm Dr. B44: K'sdng 4D 68
Langland Dr. DY3: Sed 5G 59
LANGLEY 4G 97
Langley Av. WV3: Wolv 5E 61
Langley Cl. WS9: Wals W 3C 22
Langley Ct. B69: O'bry 4G 97
   WV4: Penn 5B 42
Langley Cres. B68: O'bry 5H 97
Langley Dr. B35: Cas V 6E 87
Langley Gdns. B68: O'bry 5H 97
   WV3: Wolv 4B 42
LANGLEY GREEN 5H 97
Langley Grn. Rd. B69: O'bry 5G 97
Langley Green Station (Rail) 4H 97
Langley Gro. B10: Small H 3D 118
Langley Hall Dr. B75: S Cold 6F 55
Langley Hall Rd. B75: S Cold 6F 55
   B92: Olton 6A 136
Langley Heath Dr. B76: Walm 2D 70
Langley High St. B69: O'bry 4G 97
Langley Mede B68: O'bry 4H 97
LANGLEY MILL JUNC.
   Falcon Lodge 5H 55
   Littleworth End 2G 55
Langley Pk. Way B75: S Cold 5D 54
Langley Point B15: Birm 2E 117
                           (off Langley Wlk.)
Langley Ri. B92: Sol 2A 138
Langley Rd. B10: Small H 3D 118
   B68: O'bry 5H 97
   WV3: Penn 6E 41
   WV4: Lwr P, Penn 6E 41
Langleys Rd. B29: S Oak 4A 132
Langley Swimming Cen. 5H 97
Langley Wlk. B15: Birm 2E 117
Langmead Cl. WS2: Wals 6D 30
Langsett Rd. WV10: Wolv 5A 28
Langstone Rd. B14: King H 5B 148
   DY1: Dud .6A 76
Langton Cl. B36: Cas B 3D 106
Langton Pl. WV14: Bils 5A 46
Langton Rd. B8: Salt 5E 103
Langtree Av. B91: Sol 6F 151
Langwood Ct. B36: Cas B 1F 105
Langworth Av. B27: A Grn 6A 120
Lannacombe Rd.
   B31: Longb 3C 158
Lansbury Av. WS10: Darl 1C 62
Lansbury Grn. B64: Old H 3B 112
Lansbury Rd. B64: Old H 3B 112
Lansbury Wlk. DY4: Tip 5A 62
Lansdale Av. B92: Sol 5B 138
Lansdowne Av. WV8: Cod 5E 13
Lansdowne Cl. DY2: Dud 3H 95
   WV14: Cose 6C 60
Lansdowne Ct. DY9: Pedm 4F 125
Lansdowne Ho. B15: Birm 3F 117
Lansdowne Rd. B21: Hand 2C 100
   B24: Erd 4F 85
   B62: B'hth 3F 113
   B63: Hale .3F 127
   WV1: Wolv 1A 170 (6F 27)
   WV14: Bils 4G 45
Lansdowne St. B18: Win G 5B 100
Lansdown Pl. B18: Hock 4B 100
Lantern Rd. DY2: Neth 1E 111
Lanton Cl. WS3: Blox 5G 19
LAPAL 2E 129
Lapal La. B32: Bart G 3F 129
Lapal La. Nth. B62: Hale 2E 129

Lapal La. Sth. B62: Hale 2E 129
Lapal Mnr. Ct. B32: Bart G 3F 129
Lapley Cl. WV1: Wolv 1D 44
Lappath Ho. B32: Bart G 5B 130
Lapper Av. WV4: Ett 2B 60
Lapwing Cl. WS6: C Hay 4C 6
   WS8: Bwnhls 6A 10
Lapwing Cft. B23: Erd 6C 68
Lapwing Dr. B92: H Ard 6B 140
Lapwood Av. DY6: K'wfrd 3D 92
Lapworth Dr. B73: New O 2C 68
Lapworth Gro. B12: Bal H 5H 117
Lapworth Ho. B5: Birm 4G 117
Lapworth Mus. 2B 132
Lara Cl. B17: Harb 3F 115
Lara Gro. DY4: Tip 5A 78
Larch Av. B21: Hand 5H 81
Larch Cft. B37: Chel W 1D 122
   B69: Tiv 5B 78
Larch Dr. B31: Longb 6A 144
Larches La. WV3: Wolv 1E 43
Larches St. B11: S'brk 5A 118
Larchfield Cl. B20: Hand 4D 82
Larch Gdns. WV14: Bils 1H 61
Larch Gro. DY3: Sed 6A 60
Larch Ho. B20: Hand 4B 82
Larchmere Dr. B28: Hall G 5F 135
   WV11: Ess .4B 18
Larch Rd. DY6: K'wfrd 3C 92
Larch Wlk. B25: Yard 3H 119
Larchwood Cres. B74: S'tly 3G 51
Larchwood Grn. WS5: Wals 1F 65
Larchwood Rd. WS5: Wals 1E 65
Larcombe Dr. WV4: Penn 6H 43
Large Av. WS10: Darl 1C 62
Lark Cl. B14: King H 5A 148
Larkfield Av. B36: Cas B 1F 105
Larkhill Rd. DY8: Stourb 1A 124
Larkhill Wlk. B14: King H 6F 147
Larkin Cl. WV10: Bush 6C 16
Lark Mdw. Dr. B37: K'hrst 6A 106
Larksfield B66: Smeth 5F 99
                           (off Windmill La.)
Larksfield M. DY5: Brie H 4G 109
Larks Mill WS3: Pels 3C 20
Larkspur Ct. B62: Quin 4F 113
Larkspur Cft. B36: Hodg H 1B 104
Larkspur Rd. DY2: Dud 1H 95
Larkspur Way WS8: Clay 1H 21
Larkswood Dr. DY3: Sed 6H 59
   WV4: Penn 2A 58
Larne Rd. B26: Sheld 4E 121
Lashbrooke Ho. B45: Rub 2F 157
Latches Cl. WS10: Darl 5E 47
Latelow Rd. B33: Yard 1E 121
Latham Av. B43: Gt Barr 6A 66
Latham Cres. DY4: Tip 4A 78
Lath La. B66: Smeth 1B 98
Lathom Gro. B33: Stech 4D 104
Latimer Gdns. B15: Edg 4F 117
Latimer Pl. B18: Win G 3A 100
Latimer St. WV13: W'hall 6B 30
Latitude B5: Birm 6E 5 (2G 117)
Latymer Cl. B76: Walm 6E 71
Lauder Cl. DY3: Sed 4G 59
   WV13: W'hall 2F 45
Lauderdale Cl. WS8: Clay 1A 22
Lauderdale Gdns.
   WV10: Bush 4A 16
Laughton Cl. B31: Longb 2F 159
Launceston Cl. WS5: Wals 4H 49
Launceston Rd. WS5: Wals 4H 49
Launde, The B28: Hall G 4E 149
Laundry Rd. B66: Smeth 6G 99
Laureates Wlk. B74: Four O 2G 53
Laurel Av. B12: Bal H 6A 118
Laurel Cl. DY1: Dud 4C 76
Laurel Ct. B13: Mose 3H 133
Laurel Dr. B66: Smeth 1E 99
   B74: S'tly .3G 51
Laurel Gdns. B21: Hand 6A 82
Laurel Gro. B30: B'vlle 1A 146
   WV3: Wolv 5C 42
   WV14: Bils .1A 62
Laurel La. B63: Hale 2B 128

Laurel Rd. B21: Hand 6A 82
   B30: King Nor 3C 146
   DY1: Dud .3B 76
   DY4: Tip 6H 61
   WS5: Wals 1F 65
Laurel Road Community Sports Cen.
                         . . . . .6A 82
Laurels, The B16: Birm 6B 100
                         (off Marroway St.)
   B24: Erd 5G 85
   B26: Sheld 6G 121
   B30: King Nor 4G 147
   B66: Smeth 5G 99
                         (off Montague Rd.)
Laurels Cres. CV7: Bal C 6H 169
Laurel Ter. B6: Aston 6H 83
Laurence Ct. B31: N'fld 2F 145
Laurence Gro. WV6: Tett 2C 26
Lauriston Cl. DY1: Dud 4B 76
Lavender Cl. B14: King H 3G 147
   WS5: Wals 2D 64
   WV9: Pend 4D 14
Lavender Ct. B71: W Brom 6A 64
                            (off Sussex Av.)
Lavender Gdns. B23: Erd 6B 68
Lavender Gro. WS3: Wals 4C 32
   WV14: Bils 5H 45
Lavender Hall La. CV7: Bal C, Berk . . .1H 169
Lavender Ho. B38: King Nor 1B 160
Lavender La. DY8: Stourb 2B 124
Lavender Rd. DY1: Dud 4D 76
Lavendon Rd. B42: P Barr 2D 82
Lavinia Rd. B62: Hale 2E 129
Law Cliff Rd. B42: Gt Barr 1D 82
Law Cl. B69: Tiv 5D 78
Lawden Rd. B10: Small H 3B 118
Lawford Cl. B7: Birm 6A 102
Lawford Gro. B5: Birm 3G 117
   B90: Shir .5D 148
Lawfred Av. WV11: Wed 4F 29
Lawley, The B63: Hale 4F 127
Lawley Cl. WS4: S'fld 6F 21
Lawley Middleway B4: Birm 5A 102
Lawley Rd. WV14: Bils 5D 44
Lawley St. B70: W Brom 4F 79
   DY1: Dud .6C 76
Lawn Av. DY8: Stourb 1C 124
Lawn La. WV9: Coven 2D 14
Lawnoaks Cl. WS8: Bwnhls 3H 9
Lawn Rd. WV2: Ett 5B 44
Lawnsdale Cl. B46: Col 2H 107
Lawnsdown Rd. DY5: Quar B 4B 110
Lawnsfield Gro. B23: Erd 1D 84
Lawnside Grn. WV14: Bils 3F 45
Lawn St. DY8: Stourb 1C 124
LAWNS WOOD 6G 91
Lawnswood B76: Walm 5E 71
   DY7: Stourt 5G 91
Lawnswood Av. B90: Shir 4B 150
   DY8: Word 5A 92
   WS7: Chase 1B 10
   WV4: Ett 1A 60
   WV6: Tett .1C 26
Lawnswood Dr. DY7: Stourt 6G 91
   WS9: Wals W 4C 22
Lawnswood Gro. B21: Hand 6G 81
Lawnswood Ri. WV6: Tett 1D 26
Lawnswood Rd. DY3: Up Gor 2H 75
   DY8: Word 6A 92
Lawnwood Rd. DY2: Neth 1D 110
Lawrence Av. WV10: Wolv 5C 28
   WV11: Wed 3H 29
Lawrence Ct. B68: O'bry 3H 113
Lawrence Dr. B76: Min 1H 87
Lawrence La. B64: Old H 2G 111
Lawrence St. DY9: Lye 5G 109
   WV13: W'hall 6A 30
Lawrence Twr. B4: Birm 2G 5
Lawrence Wlk. B43: Gt Barr 1F 67
Lawson Cl. WS9: A'rdge 5D 34
Lawson St. B4: Birm 1F 5 (5G 101)
Law St. B71: W Brom 2A 80
Lawton Av. B29: S Oak 3D 132
Lawton Cl. B65: Row R 3D 96
Lawyers Wlk. WS1: Wals 2D 48
Laxey Rd. B16: Edg 6H 99
Laxford Cl. B12: Bal H 5G 117

Laxton Cl. DY6: K'wfrd 4E 93
Laxton Gro. B25: Yard 2B 120
  B91: Sol 6G 137
Lazy Hill B38: King Nor 5D 146
  WS9: Ston 4F 23
Lazy Hill Rd. WS9: A'rdge 1D 34
Lea, The B33: Yard 1E 121
Lea Av. WS10: W'bry 4D 62
Lea Bank WV3: Wolv 1A 42
Leabank Rd. DY2: Neth 6D 94
Leabon Gro. B17: Harb 1G 131
Leabrook B26: Yard 3D 120
Leabrook Rd. DY4: Tip 4C 62
  WS10: W'bry 4C 62
Leabrook Rd. Nth.
  WS10: W'bry 4D 62
Leach Grn. La. B45: Redn 2G 157
Leach Heath La. B45: Rub 2F 157
Leacliffe Way WS9: A'rdge 6H 35
Leacote Dr. WV6: Tett 5A 26
Leacroft WV12: W'hall 2C 30
Leacroft Cl. WS9: A'rdge 6D 22
Leacroft Gro. B71: W Brom 5H 63
Leacroft La. WS11: Cann 1F 7
Leacroft Rd. DY6: K'wfrd 1C 92
Leadbeater Ho. WS3: Blox 1H 31
  (off Somerfield Rd.)
Lea Dr. B26: Sheld 5E 121
LEA END 6B 160
Lea End La. B38: Forh 5G 159
  B48: Hopw 5G 159
Leafield Cres. B33: Stech 4E 105
Leafield Gdns. B62: B'hth 3D 112
Leafield Rd. B92: Sol 4F 137
Lea Ford Rd. B33: Kitts G 5G 105
Leaford Way DY6: K'wfrd 4D 92
Leafy Glade B74: S'tly 6A 36
Leafy Ri. DY3: Lwr G 3H 75
Lea Gdns. WV3: Wolv 3F 43
Lea Grn. Av. DY4: Tip 2E 77
Lea Grn. Dr. B47: Wyt 5C 162
Lea Grn. La. B47: Wyt 3C 162
Lea Hall Rd. B33: Yard 6E 105
Lea Hall Station (Rail) 1F 121
Leah Cl. B37: Mars G 3E 123
Leahill Cft. B37: F'bri 1B 122
Lea Hill Rd. B20: Hand 5E 83
Leaholme Gdns. DY9: Pedm 3F 125
Leahouse Gdns. B68: O'bry 6G 97
Lea House Rd. B30: Stir 6C 132
Leahouse Rd. B68: O'bry 6G 97
Leahurst Cres. B17: Harb 1G 131
Lea La. WS6: Gt Wyr 2G 7
Lea Mnr. Dr. WV4: Penn 2C 58
Leam Cres. B92: Sol 4F 137
Lea M. B33: Yard 6E 105
Leamington Rd. B12: Bal H 6A 118
LEAMORE 4H 31
Leamore Cl. WS2: Wals 2G 31
Leamore Ent. Pk. WS2: Wals 2G 31
  (Commercial Rd.)
  WS2: Wals 3G 31
  (Fryer's Rd.)
Leamore Ind. Est. WS2: Wals 3H 31
Leamore La. WS2: Blox, Wals 2G 31
  WS3: Blox 2G 31
Leamount Dr. B44: K'sdng 3C 68
Leander Cl. WS6: Gt Wyr 4F 7
Leander Gdns. B14: King H 2H 147
Leander Rd. DY9: W'cte 1B 126
Leandor Dr. B74: S'tly 4A 52
Lea Rd. B11: S'hll 1D 134
  WV3: Wolv 6A 170 (4E 43)
Lear Rd. WV5: Wom 5H 57
Leasemaster Ho. B1: Birm 2A 4
Leason La. WV10: Bush 1C 28
Leasow, The WS9: A'rdge 4A 34
Leasow Dr. B15: Edg 2H 131
Leasowe Dr. WV6: Pert 5D 24
Leasowe Rd. B45: Rub 1F 157
  DY4: Tip 3G 77
Leasowes, The DY4: Tip 2C 78
Leasowes Cl. B63: Hale 3A 128
Leasowes Dr. WV4: Penn 5B 42
Leasowes La. B62: Hale 6D 112
Leasowes Park 1D 128

Leasowes Rd. B14: King H 4H 133
Leasowes Sports Cen. 5E 113
Leatherhead Cl. B6: Aston 3H 101
Leather Museum, The 6C 32
Lea Va. Rd. DY8: Stourb 3D 124
Leavesden Gro. B26: Sheld 6E 121
Lea Vw. WS9: A'rdge 4A 34
  WV12: W'hall 4A 30
Lea Village B33: Kitts G 1F 121
Lea Yield Cl. B30: Stir 6C 132
Lechlade Rd. B43: Gt Barr 5A 66
Leckie Rd. WS2: Wals 5C 32
Ledbury Cl. B16: Birm 1C 116
  WS9: A'rdge 6E 23
Ledbury Ct. B29: W Cas 6G 131
  (off Ruthall Cl.)
Ledbury Dr. WV1: Wolv 2D 44
Ledbury Ho. B33: Kitts G 1A 122
Ledbury Way B76: Walm 5E 71
Ledene Golf Cen. 2B 12
Ledsam Gro. B32: Harb 5D 114
Ledsam St. B16: Birm 1C 116
Ledwell B90: Dic H 3G 163
LEE BANK 3E 117
Lee Bank Middleway
  B15: Birm 3E 117
Leebank Rd. B63: Hale 3G 127
Leech St. DY4: Tip 2C 78
Lee Ct. WS9: Wals W 4B 22
Lee Cres. B15: Edg 3E 117
Lee Gdns. B67: Smeth 4C 98
Lee Rd. B47: H'wd 2A 162
  B64: Crad H 3H 111
Leeson Wlk. B17: Harb 1H 131
Lees Av. WV14: Bils 2H 61
Lees St. B18: Hock 4B 100
Lees Ter. WV14: Bils 2H 61
Lee St. B70: W Brom 5G 63
Legge La. B1: Birm 2A 4 (6D 100)
  WV14: Cose 3F 61
Legge St. B4: Birm 5H 101
  B70: W Brom 4B 80
  WV2: Ett 5A 44
Legion Rd. B45: Rub 2E 157
Legs La. WV10: Bush 3A 16
Leicester Cl. B67: Smeth 2C 114
Leicester Pl. B71: W Brom 6A 64
Leicester Sq. WV6: Wolv 5E 27
Leicester St. WS1: Wals 1C 48
  WV6: Wolv 5E 27
Leigham Dr. B17: Harb 4E 115
Leigh Cl. WS4: Wals 5E 33
Leigh Ct. B23: Erd 5C 84
  WS4: Wals 6E 33
Leigh Rd. B8: Salt 3E 103
  B75: S Cold 5F 55
  WS4: Wals 6E 33
Leighs Cl. WS4: S'fld 6G 21
Leighs Rd. WS4: S'fld 6F 21
LEIGHSWOOD 1C 34
Leighswood Av. WS9: A'rdge 2C 34
Leighswood Ct. WS9: A'rdge 3D 34
Leighswood Gro. WS9: A'rdge 2C 34
Leighswood Ind. Est.
  WS9: A'rdge 6B 22
  (Brickyard Rd.)
  WS9: A'rdge 2C 34
  (Phoenix Dr.)
Leighswood Rd. WS9: A'rdge 2C 34
Leighton Cl. B43: Gt Barr 2E 67
  DY1: Dud 5A 76
Leighton Rd. B13: Mose 3H 133
  WV4: Penn 5D 42
  WV14: Bils 1A 62
Leith Gro. B38: King Nor 1A 160
Lelant Gro. B17: Harb 6E 115
Lellow St. B71: W Brom 5H 63
Lemar Ind. Est. B30: Stir 4D 132
Le More B74: Four O 1G 53
Lemox Rd. B70: W Brom 5G 63
Lench Cl. B62: B'hth 2C 112
Lenches, The B69: O'bry 4E 97
  (off Shelsley Av.)
Lench's Cl. B13: Mose 3H 133
Lenchs Grn. B5: Edg 4G 117
Lench St. B4: Birm 1F 5 (5G 101)

Lench's Trust Ho's. B12: Birm 3A 118
  (Camp Hill Cir.)
  B12: Birm 4H 117
  (Ketley Cft.)
Len Davis Rd. WV12: W'hall 2B 30
Lennard Gdns. B66: Smeth 3H 99
Lennox Gdns. WV3: Wolv 3E 43
Lennox Gro. B73: Bold 6G 69
Lennox St. B19: Hock 3F 101
Lenton Cft. B26: Yard 1C 136
Lenwade Rd. B68: O'bry 3B 114
Leofric Cl. B15: Edg 3E 117
Leominster Ct. B45: Rub 1F 157
  (off Deelands Rd.)
Leominster Rd. B33: Kitts G 1A 122
Leominster Rd. B11: S'hll 2E 135
Leominster Wlk. B45: Rub 1F 157
Leona Ind. Est. B62: B'hth 2D 112
Leonard Av. B19: Loz 1F 101
Leonard Gro. B19: Loz 1E 101
Leonard Rd. B19: Loz 1E 101
  DY8: Woll 6A 108
Leopold Av. B20: Hand 2A 82
Leopold St. B12: Birm 3H 117
Lepid Gro. B29: S Oak 3H 131
Lerryn Cl. DY6: K'wfrd 4D 92
Lerwick Cl. DY6: K'wfrd 4D 92
Lesley Dr. DY6: K'wfrd 5C 92
Leslie Bentley Ho. B1: Birm 3A 4
Leslie Dr. DY4: Tip 4A 62
Leslie Ri. B69: Tiv 1C 96
Leslie Rd. B16: Edg 1B 116
  B20: Hand 5F 83
  B74: Lit As 1B 52
  WV10: Wolv 4B 28
Lesscroft Cl. WV9: Pend 4E 15
Lester Gro. WS9: A'rdge 1G 51
Lester St. WV14: Bils 6H 45
Levante Gdns. B33: Stech 1B 120
Leve La. WV13: W'hall 1B 46
Level St. DY5: Brie H 6H 93
Leven Cft. B76: Walm 6E 71
Leven Dr. WV12: W'hall 6B 18
Levenwick Way DY6: K'wfrd 4E 93
Leverretts, The B21: Hand 5G 81
Lever St. WV2: Wolv 6C 170 (3H 43)
Leverton Ga. B91: Sol 6C 150
Leverton Ri. WV10: Oxl 3G 27
Leveson Av. WS6: C Hay 3E 7
Leveson Cl. DY2: Dud 1G 95
Leveson Ct. WV13: W'hall 1A 46
Leveson Cres. CV7: Bal C 3H 169
Leveson Dr. DY4: Tip 1G 77
Leveson Rd. WV11: Wed 1H 29
Leveson St. WV13: W'hall 1A 46
Leveson Wlk. DY2: Dud 1G 95
Levington Cl. WV6: Pert 5F 25
Leviss Trad. Est. B33: Stech 5B 104
Lewis Av. WV1: Wolv 6D 28
Lewis Cl. WV12: W'hall 4D 30
Lewis Gro. WV11: Wed 3F 29
Lewisham Ind. Est. B66: Smeth 2E 99
Lewisham Rd. B66: Smeth 2E 99
  WV10: Oxl 5F 15
Lewisham St. B71: W Brom 3B 80
Lewis Rd. B30: Stir 6E 133
  B68: O'bry 4H 113
  DY9: Lye 6H 109
Lewis St. DY4: Tip 2D 78
  WS2: Wals 5D 32
  WV14: Bils 5G 45
Lewthorn Ri. WV4: Penn 1H 59
Lexington Grn. DY5: Brie H 4G 109
Leybourne Cres. WV9: Pend 5D 14
Leybrook Rd. B45: Redn 1H 157
Leyburn Cl. WS2: Wals 6D 30
Leyburn Rd. B16: Edg 2C 116
Leycester Cl. B31: Longb 2E 159
Leycroft Av. B33: Kitts G 5H 105
Leydon Cft. B38: King Nor 5D 146
LEY HILL 2G 53
Ley Hill Farm Rd. B31: N'fld 2C 144
Ley Hill Rd. B75: Four O 2A 54
Leylan Cft. B13: Mose 6C 134
Leyland Av. WV3: Wolv 2D 42

Leyland Cft. WS3: Pels 3D 20
Leyland Dr. DY2: Dud 1F 95
Leyman Cl. B14: Yard W 3C 148
Ley Ri. DY3: Sed 4G 59
Leys, The B31: N'fld 2F 145
  DY5: Brie H 6F 93
  WS10: Darl .5C 46
Leys Cl. DY9: Pedm 3G 125
Leys Cres. DY5: Brie H 6F 93
Leysdown Gro. B27: A Grn 5A 136
Leysdown Rd. B27: A Grn 5A 136
Leys Rd. DY5: Brie H 6E 93
Leys Wood Cft. B26: Sheld 5E 121
Leyton Cl. DY5: Brie H 3G 109
Leyton Gro. B44: K'sdng 4A 68
Leyton Rd. B21: Hand 1B 100
LG Arena 2G 139
Liana Gdns. WV2: Ett 4D 44
Libbards Ga. B91: Sol 1G 165
Libbards Way B91: Sol 1F 165
Liberty Ct. WS6: C Hay 2D 6
Liberty Pl. B16: Birm 1D 116
Library Theatre
  Birmingham 4B 4 (1F 117)
Library Way B45: Rub 2F 157
Lich Av. WV11: Wed 2G 29
Lichen Gdns. B38: King Nor 2H 159
Lichfield Cl. WS6: Gt Wyr 4G 7
Lichfield Ct. B90: Shir 5D 148
  WS4: K'sdng 5E 33
    (off Lichfield Rd.)
Lichfield Pas. WV1: Wolv . . .2C 170 (1H 43)
Lichfield Rd. B6: Aston 2A 102
  B46: Col, Wat O 3F 89
  B74: Four O, S Cold 4F 37
  B76: Curd, Wis 2F 89
  WS3: Blox .5H 19
  WS3: Pels .2E 21
  WS4: Rus, S'fld, Wals 5E 33
  WS8: Bwnhls 5B 10
  WS9: Wals W, Bwnhls 4B 22
  WV11: Wed 4F 29
  WV12: Wed, W'hall 3G 29
  WV12: W'hall 1C 30
Lichfield St. DY4: Tip 5H 61
  WS1: Wals .1D 48
  WS4: Wals .6D 32
  WV1: Wolv 3B 170 (1G 43)
  WV14: Bils .5F 45
Lich Gates WV1: Wolv 2B 170 (1G 43)
Lichwood Rd. WV11: Wed 2H 29
LICKEY 6G 157
Lickey Coppice B45: Coft H 5A 158
Lickey Hills Country Pk. 6H 157
Lickey Hills Country Pk. Vis. Cen. . .6H 157
Lickey Hills Golf Course 5G 157
Lickey Rd. B45: Coft H 4H 157
  DY8: Amb .5F 109
Liddiard Ct. DY8: Woll 5C 108
Liddon Gro. B27: A Grn 5A 136
Liddon Rd. B27: A Grn 5A 136
LIFFORD 2D 146
Lifford Cl. B14: King H 2D 146
Lifford La. B30: King Nor 2C 146
Lifton Cft. DY6: K'wfrd 4D 92
Lightfields Wlk. B65: Row R 4A 96
Lighthorne Av. B16: Birm 1C 116
Lighthorne Rd. B91: Sol 1G 151
Light House .2C 170
Lightning Way B31: Longb 2F 159
Lightwood Cl. B93: Know 1D 166
Lightwood Rd. DY1: Dud 4C 76
Lightwoods Hill B67: Smeth 3C 114
Lightwoods Rd. B67: Smeth 1E 115
  DY9: Pedm 4G 125
Lilac Av. B12: Bal H 6A 118
  B44: Gt Barr 6G 67
  B74: S'tly 3G 51
  DY4: Tip 6G 61
  WS5: Wals .1E 65
Lilac Dr. WV5: Wom 1F 73
Lilac Gro. WS2: Wals 6E 31
  WS10: W'bry 3G 63
Lilac La. WS6: Gt Wyr 5F 7
Lilac Rd. DY1: Dud 3D 76
  WV1: Wolv .3D 44
  WV12: W'hall 2E 31

Lilac Way B62: B'hth 3F 113
Lilian Gro. WV14: Bils 4G 61
Lilleshall Cres. WV2: Wolv 4H 43
Lilleshall Rd. B26: Sheld 4F 121
Lilley La. B31: Longb 1F 159
Lillington Cl. B75: S Cold 1E 71
Lillington Gro. B34: S End 4H 105
Lillington Rd. B90: Shir 1H 163
Lillycroft La. B38: Head H 2C 160
Lily Rd. B26: Yard 5B 120
Lily St. B71: W Brom 2A 80
Limberlost Cl. B20: Hand 4C 82
Limbrick Cl. B90: Shir 5F 149
Limbury Gro. B92: Sol 5B 138
Lime Av. B29: S Oak 3B 132
  WS2: Wals .6E 31
Lime Cl. B47: H'wd 4A 162
  B70: W Brom 3G 79
  DY4: Tip 2G 77
  WS2: Wals .6E 31
  WS6: Gt Wyr 1F 7
Lime Ct. B11: S'hll 1C 134
Lime Gro. B10: Small H 3D 118
  B12: Bal H .6H 117
  B19: Loz 2E 101
  B26: Yard 5B 120
  B37: Chel W 2D 122
  B66: Smeth .6F 99
    (Edith Rd.)
  B66: Smeth .5F 99
    (Windmill La.)
  B73: W Grn .6H 69
  WS4: Rus 3G 33
  WV14: Bils .4E 45
Limehurst Av. WV3: Wolv 3A 42
Limehurst Rd. WS4: Rus 4G 33
Lime Kiln Cl. B38: King Nor 2H 159
Limekiln La. B14: King H 3A 148
Lime Kiln Wlk. DY1: Dud 5F 77
Limepit La. DY1: Dud 4C 76
Limerick Cl. DY3: Gorn 5F 75
Lime Rd. DY3: Sed 4B 60
  WS10: W'bry 1F 63
Limes, The B11: S'brk 5C 118
  B16: Birm .6B 100
  B24: Erd 4F 85
  DY3: Himl 4H 73
  WS1: Wals .1E 49
  WS4: Rus 2H 33
Limes Av. B65: Row R 1C 112
  DY5: Brie H .4G 93
Limescroft Cl. WS4: Rus 2F 33
Limes Rd. DY1: Dud 4D 76
  WV6: Tett 5A 26
Lime St. WS1: Wals 2D 48
  WV3: Wolv .3E 43
  WV14: Cose 5C 60
Limes Vw. DY3: Sed 6H 59
Lime Ter. B6: Aston 6H 83
Lime Tree Av. WV6: Tett 6G 25
Lime Tree Gdns. WV8: Bilb 4H 13
Lime Tree Gro. B31: N'fld 5F 145
Lime Tree Rd. B8: Salt 5G 103
  B27: A Grn .6A 120
  WS5: Wals .1E 65
  W8: Bilb 4H 13
Limetree Rd. B74: S'tly 3F 51
  WV8: Bilb 4H 13
Linacre Ho. B37: F'bri 1B 122
Linchmere Rd. B21: Hand 5G 81
Lincoln Av. WV13: W'hall 6D 30
Lincoln Cl. B27: A Grn 2C 136
  B28: W Cas 6G 131
    (off Tugford Rd.)
Lincoln Grn. WV10: Bush 5H 15
Lincoln Gro. B37: Mars G 2C 122
Lincoln Ho. WV10: Wolv 6A 28
Lincoln Rd. B27: A Grn 3B 136
  B67: Smeth 1C 114
  B71: W Brom 4B 64
  DY2: Neth 6F 95
  WS1: Wals .1E 49
Lincoln Rd. Nth. B27: A Grn 2C 136
Lincoln Rd. Wharf
  B27: Olton .3C 136

Lincoln St. B12: Bal H 6G 117
  WV10: Wolv 6A 28
Lincoln Twr. B16: Birm 2C 116
    (off Gilby Rd.)
Lindale Av. B36: Hodg H 3A 104
Lindale Cres. DY5: Brie H 5F 109
Lindale Dr. WV5: Wom 1F 73
Linden Av. B43: Gt Barr 5H 65
  B62: B'hth .4E 113
  B69: Tiv 1D 96
Linden Cl. WS2: Wals 1D 46
Linden Dr. DY8: Stourb 2E 125
Linden Glade B63: Hale 1A 128
Linden Ho. WV3: Wolv 3F 43
    (off Pennant Ct.)
Linden La. WV12: W'hall 2E 31
Linden Lea WV3: Wolv 2C 42
Linden Rd. B30: B'vlle 5A 132
  B66: Smeth 1E 115
  DY1: Dud 4D 76
Linden Road Instruction Pool 6B 132
Lindens, The B32: Harb 4C 114
  WV6: Wolv .6C 26
Lindens Dr. B74: S'tly 6H 51
Lindenwood B73: S Cold 5H 53
Lindford Way B38: King Nor 5D 146
Lindley Av. DY4: Tip 4H 77
Lindon Cl. WS8: Bwnhls 1C 22
Lindon Dr. WS8: Bwnhls 6B 10
Lindon Rd. WS8: Bwnhls 2B 22
Lindon Vw. WS8: Bwnhls 2C 22
Lindrick Cl. WS3: Blox 4F 19
Lindridge Dr. B76: Min 1G 87
Lindridge Rd. B23: Erd 3B 84
  B75: S Cold 3D 54
  B90: Shir 6F 149
Lindrosa Rd. B74: S'tly 6H 35
Lindsay Rd. B42: Gt Barr 4D 66
Lindsey Av. B31: N'fld 3G 145
Lindsey Pl. DY5: Brie H 6G 93
Lindsey Rd. B71: W Brom 6A 64
Lindsworth App.
  B30: King Nor 4E 147
Lindsworth Cl. B30: King Nor 4F 147
Lindsworth Ct. B30: King Nor 4F 147
Lindsworth Rd. B30: King Nor 4D 146
Linfield Gdns. DY3: Sed 4G 59
Linford Gro. B25: Yard 2B 120
Linforth Dr. B74: S'tly 4A 52
Lingard Cl. B7: Nech 4B 102
Lingard Ho. B76: Walm 5D 70
Lingard Rd. B75: S Cold 6D 54
Lingfield Av. B44: Gt Barr 4G 67
  WV10: F'hses 2H 15
Lingfield Cl. WS6: Gt Wyr 3F 7
Lingfield Ct. B43: Gt Barr 6H 65
Lingfield Dr. WS6: Gt Wyr 3F 7
Lingfield Gdns. B34: S End 3F 105
Lingfield Grange B74: S'tly 2A 52
Lingfield Gro. WV6: Pert 5F 25
Lingfield Rd. WS11: Nort C 1E 9
Lingfield Way DY6: K'wfrd 4B 92
Lingham Cl. B92: Sol 6H 137
Ling Ho. WV10: Wolv 6B 28
Lingmoor Gro. WS9: A'rdge 2C 34
Lingwood Hall DY1: Dud 5E 77
Linhope Dr. DY6: K'wfrd 4E 93
Link, The B27: A Grn 4G 135
Link One Ind. Pk. DY4: Tip 1E 79
Link Rd. B16: Edg 6A 100
  WS9: Wals W 4D 22
  WV5: Wom .6G 57
Links Av. WV6: Tett 2B 26
Links Cres. B68: O'bry 3H 113
Links Dr. B45: Rub 4G 157
  B91: Sol 1F 151
  DY8: Stourb 3C 124
Links Rd. B14: King H 6A 148
  B68: O'bry .3H 113
  WV4: Penn .2E 59
Links Side Way WS9: A'rdge 1E 35
Links Vw. B62: Hale 1D 128
  B74: S'tly 6A 36
Linkswood Cl. B13: Mose 4B 134
Linkwood Ind. Est. DY8: Woll 5C 108
Linley Cl. WS9: A'rdge 4A 34
Linley Dr. WV10: Bush 6A 16

Linley Gro. B14: King H 1E **147**
DY3: Gorn .5F **75**
Linley Lodge Ind. Est. WS9: A'rdge 2A **34**
Linley Rd. WS4: Rus 2H **33**
Linley Wood Rd. WS9: A'rdge 4A **34**
Linnet Cl. B30: B'vlle 5A **132**
B62: Hale 5B **112**
(Lodgefield Rd.)
B62: Hale 4G **127**
(Uffmoor La.)
Linnet Gro. B23: Erd 1B **84**
WV12: W'hall 1B **30**
Linpole Wlk. B14: King H 5F **147**
Linsey Rd. B92: Sol 3G **137**
Linslade Cl. WV4: Penn 1H **59**
Linthouse La. WV11: Wed 1F **29**
Lint Mdw. B47: H'wd 2B **162**
Linton Av. B91: Sol 6E **151**
Linton Cl. B63: Crad 6F **111**
Linton Cft. WV14: Bils 6F **45**
Linton Rd. B11: Tys 1G **135**
B43: Gt Barr 1E **67**
B64: Old H 6H **95**
WV4: Penn 6C **42**
Linton Wlk. B23: Erd 4B **84**
Linwood Ct. B23: Erd 4E **85**
Linwood Rd. B21: Hand 1A **100**
B91: Sol 2B **150**
DY1: Dud 2D **76**
Lion Ct. *B18: Birm* 5D **100**
(off Warstone La.)
Lionel St. B3: Birm 3B **4** (6E **101**)
Lion Ind. Pk. WS9: A'rdge 1C **34**
Lion Pas. DY8: Stourb 6D **108**
Lion Rd. B64: Old H 2A **112**
Lion's Den WS7: Hamm 3G **11**
Lion St. DY8: Stourb 6D **108**
Liskeard Rd. WS5: Wals 4H **49**
Lisko Cl. DY5: Brie H 3E **109**
Lismore Cl. B45: Fran 6E **143**
Lismore Dr. B17: Harb 2E **131**
Lissimore Dr. DY4: Tip 5A **78**
(not continuous)
Lissimore Ho. *B70: W Brom* 1C **98**
(off Maria St.)
Lisson Gro. B44: Gt Barr 1H **67**
Listelow Cl. B36: Cas B 1F **105**
Lister Cl. DY4: Tip 3A **78**
WS2: Wals 4H **31**
Lister Dr. B45: Redn 1G **157**
Lister Rd. DY2: Dud 2E **95**
WS2: Wals 4H **31**
Lister St. B7: Birm 1G **5** (5B **101**)
WV13: W'hall 2B **46**
Listowel Rd. B14: King H 1F **147**
Lisures Dr. B76: Walm 1B **70**
Lit. Ann St. B5: Birm 5H **5** (1H **117**)
LITTLE ASTON 4C **36**
Little Aston Golf Course 5C **36**
Lit. Aston Hall Dr. B74: Lit As 4A **36**
Lit. Aston La. B74: Lit As 3C **36**
Lit. Aston Pk. Rd. B74: Lit As 6A **36**
Lit. Aston Rd. WS9: A'rdge 3D **34**
Lit. Barr St. B9: Birm 1A **118**
Little Birches WV3: Wolv 3D **42**
LITTLE BLOXWICH 4B **20**
Lit. Brick Kiln St.
WV3: Wolv 5A **170** (2G **43**)
LITTLE BROMWICH 1F **119**
Lit. Bromwich Rd. B9: Bord G 2H **119**
Lit. Broom St. B12: Birm 3A **118**
Little Caldmore WS1: Wals 3C **48**
Lit. Checkhill La. DY7: Stourt 5D **90**
Lit. Clothier St. WV13: W'hall 6A **30**
Lit. Clover Cl. B7: Nech 3C **102**
Little Comn. WS3: Pels 3E **21**
Little Cornbow B63: Hale 2B **128**
Littlecote Cft. B14: King H 4A **148**
Littlecote Dr. B23: Erd 6F **69**
Lit. Cottage St. DY5: Brie H 6H **93**
Little Cft. B43: Gt Barr 4G **65**
Lit. Cross St. WS10: Darl 4C **46**
Lit. Edward St. B9: Birm 1A **118**
Lit. Fields Way B69: O'bry 2F **97**
Lit. Francis Gro. B7: Birm 4B **102**
Little Gorway WS1: Wals 4D **48**
Lit. Green La. B9: Small H 2C **118**

Lit. Green Lanes B73: W Grn 6H **69**
Lit. Hall Rd. B7: Birm 5B **102**
Lit. Hardwick Rd. WS9: A'rdge 1E **51**
LITTLE HAY 1H **37**
Lit. Hay La.
WS14: Lit H, W'frd 2H **37**
Lit. Heath Cft. B34: S End 2F **105**
Little Hill WS10: W'bry 2F **63**
Littlehill Cres. B63: Crad 4E **111**
Little Hill Gro. B38: King Nor 6C **146**
Lit. Hill Ho. B24: Erd 1B **86**
Lit. Hill Way B32: Bart G 3B **130**
Lit. Island Dr. WV13: W'hall 1C **46**
Lit. Johnson's La.
WS9: A'rdge 2D **50**
Lit. John St. DY5: Brie H 5H **93**
Little La. B71: W Brom 2B **80**
WV12: W'hall 2D **30**
Lit. Lawns Cl. WS8: Wals W 3C **22**
LITTLE LONDON 6A **30**
Little London WS1: Wals 4C **48**
Lit. London Ho. WS1: Wals 4D **48**
Littlemead Av. B31: N'fld 6G **145**
Lit. Meadow Cft. B31: N'fld 3D **144**
Lit. Meadow Wlk.
B33: Stech 6C **104**
Littlemead Rd. B90: Maj G 1E **163**
Lit. Moor Hill B67: Smeth 4D **98**
Lit. Newport St. *WS1: Wals* 2C **48**
(off Caldmore Rd.)
Lit. Oaks Rd. B6: Aston 1G **101**
Lit. Orchard Cl. WS4: S'fld 6G **21**
Littleover Av. B28: Hall G 1F **149**
Lit. Owl Cl. B23: Erd 5C **68**
Little Park B32: Quin 1H **129**
Lit. Park St. WV1: Wolv 3D **170** (1H **43**)
Lit. Pitts Cl. B24: Erd 2B **86**
Lit. Potter St. DY5: Brie H 1H **109**
Lit. Pountney St.
WV2: Wolv 6B **170** (3G **43**)
Lit. Shadwell St. B4: Birm 1E **5** (5G **101**)
Littleshaw Cft. B47: Wyt 5C **162**
Littleshaw La. B47: Wyt 5C **162**
Little's La. WV1: Wolv 1C **170** (6H **27**)
(not continuous)
Lit. Station St. WS2: Wals 1C **48**
Little St. DY2: Dud 6F **77**
LITTLE SUTTON 1B **54**
Lit. Sutton La.
B75: R'ley, S Cold 4A **54**
Lit. Sutton Rd. B75: R'ley 1A **54**
Littleton Cl. B76: Walm 3E **71**
Littleton Cft. B91: Sol 4H **153**
Littleton Rd. WV12: W'hall 2C **30**
Littleton St. E. WS1: Wals 1D **48**
Littleton St. W. WS2: Wals 1C **48**
LITTLEWOOD 1E **7**
Littlewood Cl. B91: Sol 1F **165**
Littlewood La. WS6: C Hay 1E **7**
Littlewood Rd. WS6: C Hay 1E **7**
Lit. Wood St. WV13: W'hall 1A **46**
Littleworth Av. DY1: Dud 1D **76**
LITTLEWORTH END 3G **55**
Littleworth Gro. B76: Walm 1D **70**
LITTLE WYRLEY 5C **8**
Liveridge Cl. B93: Know 3B **166**
Liverpool Cft. B37: Mars G 3B **122**
Liverpool St. B9: Birm 1A **118**
Livery St. B3: Birm 1C **4** (5F **101**)
(not continuous)
Livingstone Av. WV6: Pert 4E **25**
Livingstone Rd. B14: King H 1G **147**
B20: Hand 6E **83**
B70: W Brom 6H **79**
WS3: Blox 5C **20**
WV14: Bils 6D **44**
LivingWell Health Club
National Exhibition Centre 1G **139**
Lizafield Ct. B66: Smeth 2C **98**
Lloyd Dr. WV4: Penn 3A **58**
Lloyd Hill WV4: Penn 2A **58**
Lloyd Ho. *B19: Hock* 3E **101**
(off Sampson Rd.)
Lloyd Rd. B20: Hand 3C **82**
WV6: Tett 4B **26**
Lloyd Sq. B15: Edg 3B **116**
Lloyds Rd. B62: B'hth 3C **112**

Lloyd St. B10: Small H 3D **118**
B71: W Brom 3C **80**
DY2: Dud 1F **95**
WS10: W'bry 2E **63**
WV6: Wolv 5D **26**
Locarno Rd. DY4: Tip 2H **77**
Lochalsh Gro. WV12: W'hall 6B **18**
Lochranza Cft. B43: Gt Barr 3A **66**
Lock Basin Cl. WS11: Gt Wyr 1F **7**
Lock Dr. B33: Stech 6B **104**
Locke Pl. B7: Birm 6A **102**
Locket Cl. WS2: Wals 5F **31**
Lockfield Cl. DY8: Word 2D **108**
Lockhart Dr. B75: R'ley 2A **54**
Lock House, The B19: Birm . . .1D **4** (5F **101**)
Locking Cft. B35: Cas V 4F **87**
Lockington Cft. B62: Quin 5F **113**
Lock Keepers Cl. WS11: Nort C 1D **8**
Lockley Cl. WV10: Wolv 5B **28**
Lock Side DY4: Tip 2G **77**
Lockside WS9: A'rdge 2B **34**
WS11: Gt Wyr 1F **7**
WV5: Wom 6E **57**
Lockside Cl. DY5: Brie H 2H **109**
Locksmith Cl. WV13: W'hall 1B **46**
Lock St. WV1: Wolv 1D **170** (6H **27**)
(not continuous)
Locks Vw. DY8: Word 2C **108**
Lockton Rd. B30: Stir 5E **133**
Lockwood Rd. B31: N'fld 3D **144**
LODE HEATH 2H **151**
Lode La. B91: Sol 3F **151**
B92: Olton, Sol 4F **137**
Lode Mill Ct. B92: Olton 5F **137**
Lodge Cl. B62: Hale 2E **129**
WS5: Wals 5H **49**
Lodge Cres. DY2: Neth 5C **94**
Lodge Cft. B31: N'fld 1C **144**
B93: Know 3D **166**
Lodge Dr. B26: Yard 3D **120**
Lodge Farm Cl. B76: Walm 2D **70**
Lodgefield Rd. B62: Hale 5B **112**
Lodge Forge Rd. B64: Crad H 4E **111**
Lodge Forge Trad. Est. B64: Crad H 4E **111**
Lodge Gro. B31: N'fld 2C **144**
WS9: A'rdge 4C **34**
LODGE HILL 3F **131**
Lodge Hill Crematorium
B29: S Oak 4F **131**
Lodge Hill Rd. B29: S Oak 4H **131**
Lodge La. DY6: K'wfrd 3G **91**
WS11: Cann 1C **6**
Lodge Pool Cl. B44: Gt Barr 1G **83**
Lodge Rd. B6: Aston 1G **101**
B18: Hock 4D **100**
B18: Hock, Win G 4A **100**
B67: Smeth 2C **98**
B70: W Brom 4H **79**
B93: Know 3D **166**
WS4: S'fld 6F **21**
WS5: Wals 6H **49**
(not continuous)
WS10: Darl 6D **46**
WV10: Oxl 1F **27**
WV14: Bils 1H **61**
Lodge St. B69: O'bry 2G **97**
WV12: W'hall 4C **30**
Lodge Ter. B17: Harb 6G **115**
Lodge Vw. WS6: C Hay 2C **6**
Loeless Rd. B33: Kitts G 6E **105**
Lofthouse Cres. B31: N'fld 4D **144**
Lofthouse Gro. B31: N'fld 4D **144**
Lofthouse Rd. B20: Hand 4A **82**
Loftus Cl. B29: W Cas 5D **130**
Logan Cl. WV10: Oxl 3G **27**
Lomaine Dr. B30: King Nor 3A **146**
Lomas Dr. B31: N'fld 4C **144**
Lomas St. WV1: Wolv 5G **27**
Lombard Av. DY2: Neth 6F **95**
Lombard St. B12: Birm 3H **117**
B70: W Brom 4A **80**
Lombard St. W. B70: W Brom 4A **80**
B12: Birm 3H **117**
Lombardy Cft. B62: Quin 5G **113**
Lombardy Gdns. WV12: W'hall 2E **31**
Lomond Cl. B34: S End 3A **106**
Lomond Rd. DY3: Sed 4G **59**
LONDONDERRY 5B **98**

Londonderry Gro. B67: Smeth 4D 98
Londonderry Ho. B4: Birm 3F 5
Londonderry La. B67: Smeth 5B 98
Londonderry Rd. B68: O'bry 5B 98
London Dr. WV13: W'hall 6A 30
LONDON FIELDS 5C 76
London Hgts. DY1: Dud 5C 76
London Ho. WV3: Wolv 4A 170 (2G 43)
London Rd. B20: Hand 5G 83
    B75: Bass P 6F 39
    B75: Can 4E 39
    B78: Midd 6F 39
    WS14: W'frd, Can 1D 38
London St. B66: Smeth 4G 99
London St. Ind. Est. B66: Smeth 4H 99
Lones Rd. B71: W Brom 1F 99
Long Acre B7: Nech 3B 102
    WV8: Cod 5F 13
Longacre WV3: W'hall 3A 46
Long Acre Ind. Est. B7: Nech 1C 102
                                    (Plume St.)
    B7: Nech 2B 102
                              (Thimble Mill La.)
Longacres B74: Lit As 5C 36
Long Acre St. WS2: Wals 6B 32
Longbank Rd. B69: Tiv 1C 96
Longboat La. DY8: Word 3C 108
Longboat Quay DY2: Neth 5F 95
Longbow Rd. B29: W Cas 6D 130
LONGBRIDGE 1D 158
Longbridge La. B31: Longb 1C 158
Longbridge Station (Rail) 1C 158
Longbrook La. CV7: Bal C 3E 169
    CV8: Fen E 3E 169
Long Cl. Wlk. B35: Cas V 4F 87
Long Comn. WV5: Try 2A 72
Longcroft, The B63: Hale 2G 127
    WS4: Rus 2G 33
Longcroft Av. WS10: W'bry 2G 63
Longcroft Cl. B35: Cas V 5D 86
Longdales Rd. B38: King Nor 2H 159
Longdon Av. WV4: Penn 6H 43
Longdon Cft. B93: Know 1C 166
Longdon Dr. B74: Four O 5E 37
Longdon Rd. B93: Know 3C 166
Longfellow Rd. B30: King Nor 3H 145
    DY3: Lwr G 2E 75
Longfield Cl. B28: Hall G 1F 149
Longfield Dr. B74: Lit As 5C 36
Longfield Ho. WV10: Wolv 6B 28
Longfield Rd. B31: N'fld 5C 130
    DY9: Lye 6H 109
Longford Cl. B32: Bart G 5G 129
    B93: Dorr 6D 166
    WV5: Wom 2D 72
Longford Gro. B44: K'sdng 2A 68
Longford Rd. B44: K'sdng 2A 68
    WV10: Wolv 5B 28
Long Furrow WV8: Pend 6C 14
Long Grn. Cl. B31: N'fld 5E 145
Longham Cft. B32: Harb 1D 130
Longhurst Cft. B31: Longb 2F 159
Long Hyde Rd. B67: Smeth 2D 114
Long Innage B63: Crad 5D 110
Long Knowle La. WV11: Wed 1D 28
Long Lake Av. WV6: Tett 6G 25
Longlands, The WV5: Wom 1G 73
Longlands Cl. B38: King Nor 1G 159
                                (off Nearhill Rd.)
Longlands Rd. B62: Hale 2E 129
Long La. B62: B'hth 2D 112
    B65: B'hth 2D 112
    WS6: Gt Wyr 2D 18
    WS11: Nort C 1D 8
    WV11: Ess 2G 61
Long La. Trad. Est. B62: B'hth 3D 112
Long Leasow B29: W Cas 6E 131
Longleat B43: Gt Barr 3H 65
Longleat Av. B15: Birm 2E 117
Longleat Dr. B90: Ches G 4C 164
    DY1: Dud 5A 76
Longleat Rd. WS9: A'rdge 6C 22
Long Ley WV10: Wolv 6B 28
Longley Av. B76: Min 2H 87
Longley Cres. B26: Yard 1C 136
Long Leys Ct. B46: Wat O 5D 88
Long Leys Cft. B46: Wat O 5D 88

Longley Wlk. B37: Chel W 2F 123
                                        (Blair Gro.)
    B37: Chel W 1E 123
                                  (Carisbrooke Av.)
    B37: Chel W 2F 123
                                   (Compton Cft.)
Long Meadow B65: Row R 6C 96
Longmeadow Cl. B75: S Cold 6D 54
Longmeadow Cres. B34: S End 3A 106
Longmeadow Dr. DY3: Sed 3F 59
Longmeadow Gro. B31: Longb 3E 159
Longmeadow Rd. WS5: Wals 3A 50
Long Mill Av. WV11: Wed 2D 28
Long Mill Nth. WV11: Wed 2D 28
Long Mill Sth. WV11: Wed 2D 28
Longmoor Cl. WV11: Wed 4H 29
Longmoor Rd. B63: Hale 2G 127
    B73: S'tly 2B 68
Longmore Av. WS2: Wals 2F 47
Longmore Cl. B73: S'tly 6A 52
Longmore Rd. B90: Shir 5A 150
Longmore St. B12: Bal H 4G 117
    WS10: W'bry 2F 63
Long Mynd B63: Hale 4F 127
Long Mynd Cl. WV12: W'hall 6B 18
Long Mynd Rd. B31: N'fld 1C 144
Long Nuke Rd. B31: N'fld 6C 130
Long Saw Dr. B31: Longb 6B 144
Longshaw Gro. B34: S End 3H 105
Longstone Cl. B90: M'path 3F 165
Longstone Rd. B42: Gt Barr 6E 67
Long St. B11: S'brk 5A 118
    WS2: Wals 2B 48
    WV1: Wolv 2C 170 (1H 43)
Long Wood B30: B'vlle 2A 146
Longwood La. WS4: Wals 1A 50
    WS5: Wals 1A 50
Longwood Pathway B34: S End 4G 105
Longwood Ri. WV12: W'hall 4D 30
Longwood Rd. B45: Redn 2G 157
    WS9: A'rdge 6D 34
Lonicera Cl. WS5: Wals 2F 65
Lonsdale Cl. B33: Stech 1B 120
    WV12: W'hall 4B 30
Lonsdale Ct. B17: Harb 5G 115
Lonsdale Rd. B17: Harb 5F 115
    B66: Smeth 2B 98
    WS5: Wals 5G 49
    WV3: Wolv 4F 43
    WV14: Bils 5H 45
Loom Cl. WS6: Gt Wyr 4F 7
Lords B17: Harb 5F 115
Lordsmore Cl. WV14: Cose 4G 61
Lord St. B7: Birm 5H 101
    WS1: Wals 4B 48
                                  (not continuous)
    WV3: Wolv 1F 43
                                  (not continuous)
    WV14: Bils 2G 61
Lord St. W. WV14: Bils 2G 61
Lordswood Rd. B17: Harb 3E 115
Lordswood Sq. B17: Harb 4F 115
Lorien Cl. WV4: Penn 5A 42
Lorimer Way B43: Gt Barr 6F 51
Loriners Gro. WS1: Wals 2F 49
Lorne Ct. B13: Mose 3A 134
Lorne St. DY4: Tip 5H 61
Lorrainer Av. DY5: Brie H 3E 109
Lothians Rd. WS3: Pels 2E 21
    WV6: Tett 3C 26
Lottie Rd. B29: S Oak 4A 132
Lotus Ct. B16: Edg 2A 116
Lotus Cft. B67: Smeth 5D 98
Lotus Dr. B64: Old H 1H 111
Lotus Wlk. B36: Cas B 6B 88
Lotus Way B65: Row R 5A 96
Loughton Gro. B63: Hale 1H 127
Louisa Pl. B18: Hock 4C 100
Louisa St. B1: Birm 3A 4 (6E 101)
Louis Ct. B67: Smeth 4D 98
Louise Ct. B27: A Grn 2A 136
    B91: Sol .6C 150
Louise Cft. B14: King H 5G 147
Louise Lorne Rd. B13: Mose 1H 133
Louise Rd. B21: Hand 2B 100
Louise St. DY3: Gorn 4F 75
Lount Wlk. B19: Hock 4G 101

Lovatt Cl. DY4: Tip 4C 62
Loveday St. B4: Birm 1E 5 (5G 101)
                                  (not continuous)
Lovelace Av. B91: Sol 1H 165
Love La. B7: Birm 5H 101
    B47: H'wd 2G 161
    B69: Tiv 6A 78
    DY8: Stourb 2E 125
    DY9: Lye 6A 110
    WS1: Wals 4C 48
    WS6: Gt Wyr 2G 7
    WV6: Tett 3F 26
Lovell Cl. B29: W Cas 1F 145
Loveridge Cl. WV8: Cod 4E 13
Lovers Wlk. B6: Aston 1B 102
    WS10: W'bry 2F 63
Lovett Av. B69: O'bry 4D 96
Low Av. B43: Gt Barr 3B 66
Lowbridge Cl. WV12: W'hall 4C 30
Lowbridge Wlk. WV14: Bils 5E 45
Lowbrook La. B90: Tid G 5D 162
Lowcroft Gdns. WV10: Bush 1A 28
Lowden Cft. B26: Yard 1C 136
Lowe Av. WS10: Darl 4B 46
Lowe Dr. B73: New O 2D 68
    DY6: K'wfrd 5C 92
Lwr. Beeches Rd. B31: Longb 5A 144
LOWER BRADLEY 2A 62
Lwr. Chapel St. B69: Tiv 5C 78
Lwr. Church La. DY4: Tip 2B 78
Lwr. City Rd. B69: Tiv 6C 78
Lwr. Comball DY4: Tip 1A 78
Lowercroft Way B74: Four O 3E 37
Lwr. Dartmouth St. B9: Birm 1B 118
Lwr. Darwin St. B12: Birm 3H 117
Lwr. Derry St. DY5: Brie H 1H 109
Lwr. Essex St. B5: Birm 2G 117
Lwr. Forster St. WS1: Wals 1D 48
LOWER GORNAL 4H 75
Lower Grn. DY4: Tip 2G 77
    WS10: Darl 3D 46
    WV6: Tett 4C 26
Lwr. Ground Cl. B6: Aston 6H 83
                                (off Emscote Rd.)
Lwr. Hall La. WS1: Wals 2C 48
Lwr. Hall St. WV13: W'hall 2B 46
                                (off Walsall St.)
Lwr. High St. B64: Crad H 3E 111
    DY8: Stourb 5D 108
    WS10: W'bry 3F 63
Lwr. Higley Cl. B32: Quin 1C 130
Lwr. Hill Barn B32: Fran 4F 143
Lwr. Horseley Flds. WV1: Wolv 1A 44
Lwr. Lapwing Pl. DY4: Tip 1A 78
Lwr. Lichfield St. WV13: W'hall 1A 46
Lwr. Loveday St. B4: Birm . . .1D 4 (5F 101)
    B19: Birm 1D 4 (5F 101)
Lower Mall B5: Birm 5F 5
Lower Moor B30: B'vlle 5A 132
Lwr. North St. WS4: Wals 6D 32
Lower Pde., The B72: S Cold 6A 54
LOWER PENN 1G 57
Lwr. Prestwood Rd. WV11: Wed 2E 29
Lwr. Queen St. B72: S Cold 1A 70
Lwr. Reddicroft B73: S Cold 6A 54
Lwr. Rushall St. WS1: Wals 1D 48
Lwr. Severn St. B1: Birm 5D 4 (1F 117)
Lowerstack Cft. B37: F'bri 6B 106
LOWER STONNALL 3H 23
Lower St. WV6: Tett 4C 26
Lwr. Temple St. B2: Birm 4D 4 (1F 117)
Lwr. Tower St. B19: Birm 4G 101
Lwr. Trinity St. B9: Birm 2A 118
    B70: W Brom 6B 80
                                (off Glover St.)
Lwr. Valley Rd. DY5: Brie H 1E 109
Lower Vauxhall WV1: Wolv 1E 43
Lwr. Villiers St. WV2: Wolv 4G 43
Lwr. Walsall St. WV1: Wolv 2A 44
Lwr. White Rd. B32: Quin 6B 114
Lowesmoor Rd. B26: Sheld 4G 121
Lowe St. B12: Birm 3A 118
    WV6: Wolv 5E 27
Loweswater Dr. DY3: Lwr G 4H 75
Loweswater Ho. B38: King Nor 6C 146
Low Field Av. B45: Fran 5H 143
Lowfield Cl. B62: Quin 2G 129

LOW HILL 2A 28
Low Hill Cres. WV10: Bush 1A 28
Lowhill La. B31: Redn 3A 158
Lowland Cl. B64: Old H 2H 111
Lowlands Av. B74: S'tly 3F 51
 WV6: Tett 3C 26
Lowlands Ct. WV6: Tett 3C 26
Lowndes Rd. DY8: Woll 5C 108
Lowrey Ct. B68: O'bry 6A 98
Lowry Cl. B67: Smeth 3D 98
 WV6: Pert 5F 25
 WV13: W'hall 1F 45
Low St. WS6: C Hay 2D 6
Low Thatch B38: King Nor 2A 160
Lowther Ct. DY5: Brie H 1H 109
Low Town B69: O'bry 2G 97
Low Wood Rd. B23: Erd 2D 84
Loxdale Ind. Est. WV14: Bils 1G 61
Loxdale Sidings WV14: Bils 1H 61
Loxdale Stop (Metro) 1H 61
Loxdale St. WS10: W'bry 3F 63
 WV14: Bils 1H 61
Loxley Av. B14: Yard W 4C 148
 B90: Shir .6F 149
Loxley Cl. B31: N'fld 5C 130
Loxley Rd. B67: Smeth 2D 114
 B75: R'ley 5B 38
Loxley Sq. B92: Olton 5B 136
Loxton Cl. B74: Lit As 4D 36
Loxton Ct. B7: Birm 4B 102
Loynells Rd. B45: Redn 2H 157
Loyns Cl. B37: F'bri 6B 106
LOZELLS .2D 100
Lozells Rd. B19: Loz 2D 100
Lozells St. B19: Loz 2E 101
Lozells Wood Cl. B19: Loz 2D 100
Luanne Cl. B64: Old H 2A 112
Lucas Cir. B19: Birm 4E 101
Lucas Ri. WS11: Gt Wyr 1F 7
Luce Cl. B35: Cas V 3F 87
Lucerne Ct. B23: Erd 1D 84
Luce Rd. WV10: Bush 3A 28
Lucknow Rd. WV12: W'hall 4B 30
Lucton Ho. B30: B'vlle 2A 146
Luddington Rd. B92: Sol 5A 138
Ludford Cl. B75: S Cold 4C 54
Ludford Rd. B32: Bart G 4G 129
Ludgate Cl. B46: Wat O 4C 88
 B69: Tiv 1B 96
Ludgate Ct. WS5: Wals 4H 49
Ludgate Hill B3: Birm 2C 4 (6F 101)
Ludgate Ho. B13: Mose 1H 133
Ludgate Loft Apartments
 B3: Birm .2C 4
Ludgate St. DY1: Dud 6D 76
Ludlow Cl. B37: Chel W 1E 123
 WV12: W'hall 3B 30
Ludlow Ct. B11: S'brk 5B 118
Ludlow Ho. B13: Mose 1A 148
 WS3: Blox 3A 32
 (off Providence La.)
Ludlow La. WS2: Wals 5G 31
Ludlow Rd. B8: Salt 6F 103
Ludlow Way DY1: Dud 5A 76
Ludmer Way B20: Hand 5E 83
Ludstone Av. WV4: Penn 6B 42
Ludstone Rd. B29: W Cas 4D 130
Ludworth Av. B37: Mars G 2D 122
Lugtrout La. B91: Sol, Cath B 1A 152
 (not continuous)
Lukes, The DY2: Neth 2E 111
Lulworth Cl. B63: Crad 5E 111
Lulworth Rd. B28: Hall G 5G 135
Lulworth Wlk. WV4: Penn 5A 42
Lumley Gro. B37: Chel W 1F 123
Lumley Rd. WS1: Wals 2E 49
Lundy Vw. B36: Cas B 4D 106
LUNT, THE 4A 46
Lunt Gro. B32: Quin 6B 114
Lunt Pl. WV14: Bils 5A 46
Lunt Rd. WV14: Bils 5H 45
Lupin Gro. B9: Bord G 6F 103
 WS5: Wals 1F 65
Lupin Rd. DY2: Dud 6H 77
Lusbridge Cl. B63: Crad 1D 126
LUTLEY 2D 126
Lutley Av. B63: Hale 1F 127

Lutley Cl. WV3: Wolv 4C 42
Lutley Dr. DY9: Pedm 2G 125
Lutley Gro. B32: Bart G 4H 129
Lutley La. B63: Hale, Lutley 2D 126
Lutley Mill Rd. B63: Hale 1G 127
Luton Rd. B29: S Oak 2B 132
Luttrell Ct. B74: Four O 3H 53
 (off Lichfield Rd.)
Luttrell Rd. B74: Four O 3F 53
Lyall Gdns. B45: Fran 6E 143
Lyall Gro. B27: A Grn 3G 135
Lychgate Av. B33: Sheld 4H 121
 DY9: Pedm 4G 125
Lydate Rd. B62: Quin 1F 129
Lydbrook Covert B38: King Nor 1A 160
Lydbury Gro. B33: Kitts G 5E 105
Lyd Cl. WV11: Wed 4D 28
Lyddington Dr. B62: Hale 4B 112
Lyde Grn. B63: Crad 4D 110
Lydford Dro. B24: Erd 5G 85
Lydford Rd. WS3: Blox 5H 19
Lydgate Rd. DY6: K'wfrd 3D 92
Lydget Gro. B23: Erd 6D 68
Lydham Cl. B44: K'sdng 1A 84
 WV14: Bils 1D 60
Lydia Cft. B74: Four O 3E 37
Lydian Cl. WV6: Wolv 5F 27
LYDIATE ASH 6C 156
Lydiate Ash Rd. B61: L Ash 6B 156
 (not continuous)
Lydiate Av. B31: Longb 6B 144
Lydiates Cl. DY3: Sed 6F 59
Lydney Cl. WV12: W'hall 6D 30
Lydney Gro. B31: N'fld 4D 144
Lydon Ct. B92: Sol 1G 137
LYE 6A 110
Lye Av. B32: Bart G 3G 129
Lye Bus. Cen. DY9: Lye 5B 110
Lye By-Pass DY9: Lye 5A 110
Lye Cl. La. B32: Bart G 3F 129
 B62: Hale .3F 129
Lyecroft Av. B37: Chel W 1F 123
Lye Cross Rd. B69: Tiv 2B 96
Lye Station (Rail) 5A 110
Lye Valley Ind. Est. DY9: Lye 5B 110
Lygon Cl. B62: Hale 5B 112
Lygon Gro. B32: Quin 1C 130
Lymedene Rd. B42: P Barr 2D 82
Lyme Grn. Rd. B33: Stech 5D 104
Lymer Rd. WV10: Oxl 6G 15
Lymington Ct. B73: W Grn 4H 69
Lymington Rd.
 WV13: W'hall 1D 46
Lymsey Cft. DY8: Word 6A 92
Lynbrook Cl. B47: H'wd 2A 162
 DY2: Neth 3F 95
Lyncourt Gro. B32: Quin 5H 113
Lyncroft Rd. B11: Tys 3F 135
Lyndale Dr. WV11: Wed 3G 29
Lyndale Rd. DY2: Dud 3G 95
 DY3: Sed .3F 59
Lyndhurst Dr. DY8: Word 2D 108
Lyndhurst Rd. B24: Erd 5F 85
 B71: W Brom 6C 64
 WV3: Wolv 4E 43
LYNDON 2B 80
Lyndon B71: W Brom 2B 80
Lyndon Cl. B20: Hand 5E 83
 B36: Cas B 1G 105
 B63: Hale .1G 127
 DY3: Sed .4A 60
Lyndon Cft. B37: Mars G 4D 122
 B92: Olton 3E 137
LYNDON GREEN 4E 121
Lyndon Gro. B71: W Brom 3B 80
 DY6: W Hth 1H 91
Lyndon Ho. B31: N'fld 4F 145
Lyndon Rd. B33: Stech 6C 104
 B45: Rub .2E 157
 B73: S Cold 6H 53
 B92: Olton 3D 136
Lyndworth Rd. B30: Stir 6E 133
Lyneham Gdns. B76: Walm 1E 87
Lyneham Way B35: Cas V 4D 86
Lynfield Cl. B38: King Nor 2B 160
Lynfield Ct. B28: Hall G 1E 149

Lyng La. B70: W Brom 4A 80
 (not continuous)
Lynmouth Cl. WS9: A'rdge 4C 34
LYNN 2H 23
Lynn Gro. B29: S Oak 2G 131
Lynn La. WS14: Lynn 2H 23
Lynton Av. B66: Smeth 3E 99
 B71: W Brom 6A 64
 WV6: Tett 2C 26
Lynton Ho. B23: Erd 1B 84
Lynton Rd. B6: Aston 2A 102
Lynval Rd. DY5: Quar B 4B 110
Lynwood Av. DY6: W Hth 2H 91
Lynwood Cl. WV12: W'hall 1E 31
Lynwood Wlk. B17: Harb 1H 131
Lynwood Way B45: Lick 6G 157
Lyon Ct. B46: Col 2H 107
 (off Parkfield Rd.)
 B75: S Cold 6A 54
 (off Rectory Rd.)
Lyons Gro. B11: S'hll 2C 134
Lysander Rd. B45: Fran 5G 143
Lysander Way B35: Cas V 5F 87
Lysways St. WS1: Wals 3D 48
Lytham Cl. B76: Walm 1F 87
 DY8: Stourb 3E 125
Lytham Cft. B15: Birm 2F 117
Lytham Gro. WS3: Blox 3G 19
Lytham Rd. WV6: Pert 5D 24
 DY8: Stourb 3E 125
Lythwood Dr. DY5: Brie H 3G 109
Lyttelton Rd. B16: Edg 2H 115
 B33: Stech 1B 120
 DY8: Stourb 6B 108
Lyttleton Av. B62: B'hth 4E 113
Lyttleton Cl. DY2: Neth 5E 95
Lyttleton Ho. B63: Hale 3A 128
Lyttleton St. B70: W Brom 5A 80
Lytton Av. WV4: Penn 1B 58
Lytton Gro. B27: A Grn 4H 135
Lytton La. B32: Bart G 2D 130

M

Maas Rd. B31: N'fld 4E 145
Macarthur Rd. B64: Crad H 3E 111
Macaulay Ho. B70: W Brom 6B 80
McBean Rd. WV6: Wolv 5D 26
McClaren Ct. B74: Four O 6E 37
Macdonald Cl. B69: Tiv 5D 78
Macdonald St. B5: Birm 3G 117
 B12: Birm 3G 117
McDougall Rd. WS10: W'bry 2A 64
Mace St. B64: Old H 2G 111
McGregor Cl. B6: Aston 6H 83
Machin Rd. B23: Erd 3F 85
Mackadown La.
 B33: Kitts G, Sheld 1H 121
Mackay Rd. WS3: Blox 5B 20
McKean Rd. B69: O'bry 6G 79
McKen Ct. B70: W Brom 6A 80
Mackenzie Ct. B31: N'fld 5C 130
Mackenzie Rd. B11: S'hll 3C 134
Mackmillan Rd. B65: Row R 1B 112
McLean Rd. WV10: Oxl 5G 15
Macmillan Cl. B69: Tiv 5C 78
Macrome Rd. WV6: Tett 1C 26
Madams Hill Rd. B90: Shir 2B 164
Maddocks Hill B72: W Grn 3A 70
Madehurst Rd. B23: Erd 1E 85
Madeira Av. WV8: Cod 5G 13
Madeline Ho. B33: Stech 6C 104
Madeley Rd. B11: S'brk 6C 118
 DY6: K'wfrd 5D 92
Madin Rd. DY4: Tip 3G 77
Madison Av. B36: Hodg H 3B 104
 DY5: Brie H 6B 94
 WS2: Wals 1H 47
Madley Cl. B45: Rub 1E 157
Madresfield Dr. B63: Hale 3B 128
Maer Cl. B65: Row R 5C 96
Mafeking Rd. B66: Smeth 2E 99
Magdala St. B18: Win G 4A 100
Magdalen Cl. DY1: Dud 5C 76
Magdalen Ct. B16: Edg 2A 116
 (off Vernon Cl.)
Magdalene Rd. WS1: Wals 4E 49

Magistrates' Court
Aldridge 3D 34
Birmingham 2F 5 (6G 101)
Dudley 6E 77
Solihull 4F 151
Walsall 6C 32
Warley (Oldbury) 2G 97
Wolverhampton 3A 170 (1G 43)
Magna Cl. WS6: C Hay 2E 7
Magness Cres. WV12: W'hall 4C 30
Magnet Wlk. B23: Erd 4C 84
Magnolia Cl. B29: W Cas 6E 131
Magnolia Dr. WS5: Wals 1D 64
Magnolia Gro. WV8: Bilb 4G 13
WV12: W'hall 5B 30
Magnolia Way DY8: Word 3D 108
Magnum Cl. B74: S'tly 4H 51
Magpie Cl. DY2: Neth 6G 95
Magpie La. CV7: Bal C 2E 169
Magreal Ind. Est. B16: Birm 6B 100
Maiden Cl. WV13: W'hall 1C 46
Maidendale Rd. DY6: K'wfrd 2H 91
Maidensbridge Dr. DY6: W Hth 1A 92
Maidensbridge Gdns. DY6: W Hth . . .6H 73
Maidensbridge Rd. DY6: W Hth 6H 73
Maidstone Dr. DY8: Word 6C 92
Maidstone Rd. B20: Hand 6G 83
Maidwell Dr. B90: Shir 1C 164
Mailbox, The B1: Birm 6C 4 (1F 117)
Mailbox Sq. B1: Birm 5C 4 (1F 117)
Main Rd. CV7: Mer 4H 141
Mainstream Ind. Pk. B7: Birm 4C 102
Mainstream Way B7: Birm 5C 102
Main St. B11: S'brk 4A 118
B90: Dic H 4G 163
WS9: Ston 4F 23
Main Ter. B11: S'brk 4A 118
Mainwaring Dr. B75: R'ley 1C 54
Maitland Dr. B34: S End 3A 106
Maitland Ho. B36: Cas B 6H 87
Maitland Rd. B8: Salt 5F 103
DY1: Dud 6A 76
Majestic Way B65: Row R 5C 96
Major Ct. B13: Mose 3B 134
Major's Fold DY3: Lwr G 3D 74
MAJOR'S GREEN 1D 162
Major St. WV2: Wolv 3A 44
Majuba Rd. B16: Edg 5G 99
Malcolm Av. B24: Erd 1A 86
Malcolm Ct. B26: Sheld 6E 121
WV1: Wolv 6E 27
Malcolm Gro. B45: Redn 2G 157
Malcolm Rd. B90: Shir 6H 149
Malcolmson Cl. B15: Edg 3B 116
Malfield Dr. B27: A Grn 2C 136
Mali Jenkins Ho. WS1: Wals 2F 49
Malins Rd. B17: Harb 6H 115
WV4: Ett 6A 44
Malkit Cl. WS2: Wals 5F 31
Mallaby Cl. B90: Shir 1G 163
Mallard Cl. B27: A Grn 2A 136
DY5: Brie H 4G 109
WS3: Pels 1E 21
Mallard Dr. B23: Erd 4B 84
B69: O'bry 5F 97
Mallards Reach B92: Olton 5C 136
Mallender Dr. B93: Know 3B 166
Mallen Dr. B69: Tiv 6B 78
Mall, The (Gracechurch Shop. Cen.)
B72: S Cold 6H 53
Mallin Gdns. DY1: Dud 1A 94
Mallin St. B66: Smeth 2B 98
Mallory Cres. WS3: Blox 5B 20
Mallory Ri. B13: Mose 4C 134
Mallory Rd. WV6: Pert 6E 25
Mallow Cl. WS5: Wals 2E 65
Mallow Ct. WV6: Wolv 4F 27
Mallow Ri. B23: Erd 6B 68
Mallows Cl. WS10: Darl 5D 46
Malmesbury Pk. B15: Edg 4A 116
Malmesbury Rd. B10: Small H 5E 119
Malpas Dr. B32: Bart G 5A 130
Malpas Gdns. WV8: Cod 3E 13
Malpas Rd. DY5: Quar B 4B 110
Malpas Wlk. WV10: Wolv 4C 28
Malt Cl. B17: Harb 5H 115
Malthouse B66: Smeth 2C 98

Malthouse Ct. DY3: Sed 5A 60
Malthouse Cft. B6: Aston 1G 101
Malthouse Dr. DY1: Dud 5C 76
Malthouse Gdns. B19: Loz 2F 101
Malthouse Gro. B25: Yard 2C 120
Malt Ho. La. WV13: W'hall 1A 46
Malthouse La. B8: Salt 3E 103
B42: Gt Barr 5F 67
B61: C'wich 4B 156
WV6: Tett 3C 26
Malthouse Mdw. B91: Sol 6G 151
Malthouse Rd. DY4: Tip 2G 77
Malthouse Row B37: Mars G 3C 122
Maltings, The B1: Birm 6B 4 (2E 117)
WS9: A'rdge 2A 128
WV1: Wolv 1C 170 (6H 27)
WV5: Wom 1G 73
Malt Mill La. B62: B'hth 3C 112
Malton Av. B69: O'bry 3D 96
Malton Gro. B13: Mose 6B 134
Malvern Av. DY9: Lye 6G 109
Malvern Cl. B15: Edg 3G 115
B71: W Brom 2B 80
WV12: W'hall 5B 30
Malvern Ct. B27: A Grn 1A 136
WV10: Bush 1H 27
Malvern Cres. DY2: Dud 3B 94
Malvern Dr. B76: Walm 5E 71
WS9: A'rdge 6E 23
WV1: Wolv 2D 44
Malvern Hill Rd. B7: Nech 2C 102
Malvern Ho. B63: Hale 2A 128
(off Pickersleigh Cl.)
Malvern Pk. Av. B91: Sol 4H 151
Malvern Rd. B21: Hand 6G 81
B27: A Grn 1B 136
B45: Lick 6G 157
B68: O'bry 3H 113
CV7: Bal C 6H 169
Malvern St. B12: Bal H 6A 118
Malvern Vw. Rd. DY3: Lwr G 3H 75
Mamble Rd. DY8: Stourb 6C 108
Mammoth Dr. WV10: Wolv 4H 27
Manby Cl. WV6: Wolv 5F 27
Manby Rd. B35: Cas V 3E 87
Manby St. DY4: Tip 5H 61
Mancetter Rd. B90: Shir 4A 150
Manchester St. B6: Birm 4G 101
B69: O'bry 2H 97
Mancroft Cl. DY6: K'wfrd 2H 91
Mancroft Gdns. WV6: Tett 4A 26
Mancroft Rd. WV6: Tett 4A 26
Mandale Rd. WV10: Wolv 3B 28
Mander Cen. WV1: Wolv . . .3B 170 (1G 43)
Manderley Cl. DY3: Sed 3G 59
Manders Ind. Est. WV1: Wolv 6B 28
Mander Sq. WV1: Wolv 4B 170
Manderston Cl. DY1: Dud 4A 76
Mander St. WV3: Wolv 6A 170 (3F 43)
Manderville Gdns. DY6: K'wfrd 3A 92
Manderville Ho. B31: Longb 1D 158
Mandeville Gdns. WS1: Wals 3D 48
MANEY 1A 70
Maney Cnr. B72: S Cold 1H 69
Maney Hill Rd. B72: W Grn 2H 69
Manlove St. WV3: Wolv 3E 43
Manningford Cl. B14: King H 5H 147
Manningford Rd. B14: King H 5G 147
Mnr. Abbey Rd. B62: Hale 2E 129
Manor Abbey Stadium 3C 128
Manor Av. WS6: Gt Wyr 1G 7
Manor Cl. WV4: Penn 1D 58
WV8: Bilb 3H 13
WV13: W'hall 6A 30
Manor Ct. B27: A Grn 3B 136
B30: King Nor 5C 146
B62: Quin 4G 113
(off Binswood Rd.)
B93: Dorr 6G 167
DY2: Neth 5E 95
WS2: Wals 1A 48

Manor Dr. B31: N'fld 6F 131
B46: Col 2F 107
B73: S Cold 1H 69
DY3: Gorn 4F 75
DY3: Swind 5E 73
Mnr. Farm Dr. WV12: W'hall 4D 30
Mnr. Farm Rd. B11: Tys 1E 135
Manor Fold WV8: Oaken 5D 12
Manorford Av. B71: W Brom 4E 65
Manor Gdns. B33: Stech 1B 120
WS10: W'bry 1F 63
WV5: Wom 6H 57
Manor Hill B73: S Cold 1H 69
Manor Ho. B31: N'fld 6F 131
Manor House, The B44: Gt Barr 3G 67
(off Amblecote Av.)
Manor Ho. Cl. B29: W Cas 4D 130
Manorhouse Cl. WS1: Wals 6C 48
Manor Ho. Dr. B31: N'fld 6F 131
Manor Ho. La. B26: Sheld, Yard 5D 120
B46: Wat O 4D 88
Manor Ho. Pk. WV8: Bilb 3H 13
Manor Ho. Rd. WS10: W'bry 2F 63
Manor Ho. Way B46: Wat O 4D 88
Manorial Rd. B75: R'ley 6C 38
Manor Ind. Est. WS2: Wals 2A 48
Manor La. B61: C'wich, L Ash 4C 156
B62: Hale 2E 129
DY8: Stourb 2B 124
Manor Pk. DY6: K'wfrd 3B 92
Manor Pk. Cl. B13: Mose 3A 134
Manor Pk. Gro. B31: Longb 6A 144
Manor Pk. Rd. B36: Cas B 2H 105
Manor Rd. B6: Aston 6H 83
B16: Edg 2H 115
B33: Stech 6C 104
B47: Wyt 6A 162
B67: Smeth 4B 98
B73: S Cold 6H 53
B74: S'tly 3A 52
B91: Sol 2F 151
B93: Dorr 6A 166
DY4: Tip 3H 77
DY8: Word 1C 108
WS2: Wals 1A 48
WS10: W'bry 3B 64
WV4: Ett 6C 44
WV4: Penn 1D 58
WV10: Oxl 2G 27
Manor Rd. Nth. B16: Edg 2H 115
Manor Rd. Pct. WS2: Wals 1A 48
Manor Sq. B91: Sol 4G 151
Manor St. WV6: Tett 4A 26
Manor Wlk. B91: Sol 4G 151
Manor Way B62: Hale, Roms 4G 127
B73: S Cold 1H 69
Mansard Cl. WV3: Wolv 3D 42
WV10: Bush 1D 28
Mansard Ct. B46: Col 2H 107
Mansell Cl. B63: Crad 4D 110
Mansell Rd. DY4: Tip 5A 62
Mansel Rd. B10: Small H 3E 119
Mansfield Ho. B37: Chel W 6E 107
Mansfield Rd. B6: Aston 1F 101
B25: Yard 6A 120
Mansion Cl. DY1: Dud 4C 76
Mansion Ct. WV5: Wom 2D 72
(off Heath Ho. Dr.)
Mansion Cres. B67: Smeth 5C 98
Mansion Dr. DY4: Tip 2C 78
WS7: Hamm 1F 11
Mansions Mews, The B74: Four O . . .2G 53
Manson Dr. B64: Old H 2A 112
Manston Dr. WV6: Pert 4E 25
Manston Rd. B26: Sheld 4F 121
Manton Cft. B93: Dorr 6A 166
Manton Ho. B19: Loz 2G 101
Manway Cl. B20: Hand 2B 82
Manwoods Cl. B20: Hand 5D 82
Maple Av. WS10: W'bry 1A 64
Maple Bank B15: Edg 4C 116
Maplebeck Ct. B91: Sol 3G 151
Maple Bus. Pk. B7: Nech 3B 102
Maple Cen. WS10: Mox 2B 62
Maple Cl. B21: Hand 6A 82
DY8: Stourb 3B 124
WV14: Cose 6C 60

Maple Ct. B24: Erd 4F **85**
(off Coppice Cl.)
B66: Smeth 1B **98**
Maple Cft. B13: Mose 1H **147**
Mapledene B13: Mose 3B **134**
Mapledene Rd. B26: Sheld 5H **121**
Maple Dr. B44: K'sdng 5B **68**
DY3: Gorn 5F **75**
WS4: S'fld 1F **33**
WS5: Wals 1F **65**
WS10: Mox 1B **62**
Maple Grn. DY1: Dud 2C **76**
Maple Gro. B19: Loz 1E **101**
B37: K'hrst 3B **106**
DY6: K'wfrd 3C **92**
WV3: Wolv 1A **42**
WV14: Bils 1H **61**
Maple Leaf Dr. B37: Mars G 3D **122**
Maple Leaf Ind. Est. WS2: Wals 6G **31**
Maple Leaf Rd. WS10: W'bry 4C **62**
Maple Ri. B68: O'bry 1A **114**
Maple Rd. B30: B'vlle 5A **132**
B45: Rub 3F **157**
B62: B'hth 3D **112**
B72: S Cold 2A **70**
DY1: Dud 4E **77**
WS3: Pels 5D **20**
WV3: Wolv 4C **42**
Maple Row DY5: Brie H 1H **109**
Maple St. WS3: Blox 5B **20**
Mapleton Gro. B28: Hall G 6H **135**
Mapleton Rd. B28: Hall G 6H **135**
Mapletree La. B63: Crad 5E **111**
Maple Wlk. B37: Chel W 1D **122**
(within Chelmsley Wood Shop. Cen.)
Maple Way B31: Longb 6D **144**
Maplewood B76: Walm 5E **71**
Mapperley Gdns. B13: Mose 2E **133**
Mappleborough Rd. B90: Shir 6E **149**
Mapps Cl. B63: Crad 5E **111**
Marans Cft. B38: King Nor 2H **159**
Marbury Cl. B38: King Nor 5H **145**
Marbury Dr. WV14: Bils 5A **46**
Marbury M. DY5: Brie H 2H **109**
Marchant Rd. WV3: Wolv 1D **42**
WV14: Bils 4E **45**
March Cl. WS6: C Hay 4D **6**
MARCH END 4G **29**
March End Rd. WV11: Wed 4F **29**
(not continuous)
Marchmont Rd. B9: Bord G 1G **119**
Marchmount Rd. B72: W Grn 5A **70**
March Way WS9: A'rdge 6E **23**
Marcliff Cres. B90: Shir 5C **148**
Marcos Dr. B36: Cas B 6B **88**
Marcot Rd. B92: Olton 6D **120**
Marden Cl. WV13: W'hall 2H **45**
Marden Gro. B31: Longb 2E **159**
Mardon Rd. B26: Sheld 6G **121**
Maree Gro. WV12: W'hall 6B **18**
Marfield Cl. B76: Walm 1E **87**
Margam Cres. WS3: Blox 5F **19**
Margam Ter. WS3: Blox 5F **19**
Margam Way WS3: Blox 5F **19**
Margaret Av. B63: Hale 1H **127**
Margaret Cl. DY5: Quar B 3A **110**
Margaret Dr. DY8: Stourb 1F **125**
Margaret Gdns. B67: Smeth 4C **98**
Margaret Gro. B17: Harb 4G **115**
Margaret Ho. B17: Harb 6F **115**
Margaret Rd. B17: Harb 6G **115**
B73: New O 4D **68**
WS2: Wals 6E **31**
WS10: Darl 1C **62**
Margarets Ho. B76: Walm 2D **70**
Margaret St. B3: Birm 3C **4** (6F **101**)
B70: W Brom 5H **79**
Margaret Va. WV4: E'shll 4C **62**
Margaret Vine Ct. B62: B'hth 2F **113**
Marholm Cl. WV9: Pend 5D **14**
Marian Cft. B26: Sheld 6H **121**
Maria St. B70: W Brom 1C **98**
Marie Dr. B27: A Grn 5H **135**
Marigold Cres. DY1: Dud 3C **76**
Marine Cres. DY8: Word 2C **108**
Marine Dr. B44: K'sdng 1G **83**

Marine Gdns. DY8: Word 2C **108**
Mariner Av. B16: Edg 2A **116**
Marion Cl. DY5: Quar B 1B **110**
Marion Rd. B67: Smeth 4C **98**
Marion Way B28: Hall G 6E **135**
Marita Cl. DY2: Neth 6G **95**
Marjoram Cl. B38: King Nor 1B **160**
Marjorie Av. B30: King Nor 4D **146**
Mark Av. WS10: W'bry 2E **63**
Markby Rd. B18: Win G 3A **100**
Mark Ct. WS1: Wals 1C **48**
Market Hall WV3: Wolv 4A **170** (2G **43**)
Market La. WV4: Lwr P 5F **41**
Market Pl. B65: B'hth 2C **112**
B69: O'bry 1G **97**
(off Market St.)
DY2: Dud 6E **77**
DY2: Neth 4E **95**
DY4: Tip 2D **78**
WS3: Blox 6H **19**
WS10: W'bry 3F **63**
WV13: W'hall 2A **46**
Market Sq. B64: Crad H 3E **111**
WV3: Wolv 4A **170** (2G **43**)
Market St. B69: O'bry 1G **97**
DY6: K'wfrd 3B **92**
DY8: Stourb 6E **109**
WV1: Wolv 3C **170** (1H **43**)
WV14: Bils 6F **45**
Market Way DY9: Hag 6G **125**
WV14: Bils 6F **45**
Markfield Rd. B26: Sheld 3F **121**
Markford Wlk. B19: Hock 3F **101**
Markham Cres. B92: Sol 4B **138**
Markham Cft. WV9: Pend 5E **15**
Markham Dr. DY6: K'wfrd 5C **92**
Markham Rd. B73: New O 2C **68**
Marklew Cl. WS8: Bwnhls 2C **22**
Marklin Av. WV10: Oxl 6H **15**
Mark Rd. WS10: W'bry 2E **63**
Marksbury Cl. WV6: Wolv 4E **27**
Marlbank Rd. DY8: Word 2E **109**
Marlborough Cl. B74: Four O 3E **37**
Marlborough Ct. B36: Cas B 1G **105**
B74: Four O 1F **53**
(off Vesey Cl.)
Marlborough Dr. DY8: Stourb 2E **125**
Marlborough Gdns. DY8: Word 1A **108**
WV6: Wolv 5C **26**
Marlborough Gro. B25: Yard 2B **120**
Marlborough Ind. Est. WV2: Wolv 4H **43**
Marlborough Rd. B10: Small H 2E **119**
B36: Cas B 1G **105**
B66: Smeth 6E **99**
DY3: Sed 1B **76**
Marlborough St. WS3: Blox 6H **19**
Marlbrook Cl. B92: Sol 1G **137**
Marlbrook Dr. WV4: Penn 5F **43**
Marlbrook La. B60: Marlb 6D **156**
Marlburn Way WS5: Wom 1E **73**
Marlcliff Gro. B13: Mose 1A **148**
Marldon Rd. B14: King H 1G **147**
Marlene Cft. B37: Chel W 2E **123**
Marley Hgts. B27: A Grn 1B **136**
Marley Rd. DY6: K'wfrd 5E **93**
Marling Cft. B92: Sol 6A **138**
Marlin Office Village B35: Cas V 6D **86**
Marlow Cl. DY2: Neth 6G **95**
Marlowe Dr. WV12: W'hall 2A **30**
Marlow Rd. B23: Erd 2D **84**
Marlow St. B65: B'hth 2B **112**
WS2: Wals 5C **32**
Marlpit La. B75: R'ley 1B **54**
Marlpit Ri. B75: R'ley 6C **38**
Marlpool Dr. WS3: Pels 6E **21**
Marlpool Gdns. WS3: Pels 6E **21**
Marl Rd. DY2: Neth 5D **94**
Marl Top B38: King Nor 5B **146**
Marmion Gro. DY1: Dud 1C **94**
Marmion Ho. B70: W Brom 1F **79**
Marmion Way B70: W Brom 1F **79**
Marnel Dr. WV3: Wolv 3B **42**
Marner Rd. B70: W Brom 1C **80**
Marquis Dr. B62: Hale 4A **112**
Marriott Rd. B66: Smeth 2B **98**
DY2: Neth 5E **95**

Marroway St. B16: Birm 6B **100**
Marrowfat La. B21: Hand 2B **100**
Mars Cl. WV14: Cose 4C **60**
Marsden Cl. B92: Olton 4C **136**
Marsh, The WS10: W'bry 2E **63**
Marshall Cl. WS9: A'rdge 5D **34**
Marshall Cres. DY8: Word 5C **92**
Marshall Gro. B44: Gt Barr 6H **67**
Marshall Lake Rd. B90: Shir 1B **164**
Marshall Rd. B68: O'bry 2A **114**
WV13: W'hall 2E **45**
Marshalls Ind. Est. WV2: Wolv 4G **43**
Marshall St. B1: Birm 6C **4** (2F **117**)
B67: Smeth 2B **98**
Marsham Ct. Rd. B91: Sol 6D **136**
Marsham Rd. B14: King H 4H **147**
Marshbrook Cl. B24: Erd 3C **86**
Marshbrook Rd. B24: Erd 3B **86**
Marsh Cl. B23: Erd 2F **85**
Marsh Cres. DY8: Word 6A **92**
Marsh End B38: King Nor 1C **160**
Marshfield B90: Dic H 4H **163**
Marshfield Gdns. B24: Erd 5E **85**
Marsh Gro. DY3: Swind 5E **73**
Marsh Hill B23: Erd 3B **84**
Marsh Ho. Farm La. B92: H Ard 4D **154**
Marshland Way WS2: Wals 2E **47**
Marsh La. B23: Erd 2D **84**
B46: Wat O 4D **88**
B71: W Brom 6A **64**
B76: Curd 2E **89**
B91: Sol 3A **152**
B92: H Ard 1A **154**
(not continuous)
WS2: Wals 1B **48**
WV10: F'hses 4F **15**
Marsh La. Pde. WV10: Oxl 5G **15**
Marshmont Way B23: Erd 5D **68**
Marsh St. WS2: Wals 1B **48**
Marshwood Cft. B62: Quin 2G **129**
Marsland Cl. B17: Edg 2G **115**
Marsland Rd. B92: Olton 6C **136**
Marston Av. WS10: Darl 5C **46**
Marston Cl. DY8: Stourb 1B **124**
Marston Cft. B37: Mars G 4B **122**
Marston Dr. B37: K'hrst 4C **106**
MARSTON GREEN 3B **122**
Marston Green Station (Rail) 4B **122**
Marston Gro. B43: Gt Barr 5G **65**
Marston Rd. B29: W Cas 5D **130**
B73: Bold 6G **69**
DY1: Dud 1H **93**
WV2: Wolv 4F **43**
Marston Rd. Ind. Est. WV2: Wolv 4G **43**
Marston St. WV13: W'hall 1C **46**
WV14: Cose 6F **61**
Martham Dr. WV6: Tett 1H **41**
Martin Cl. B25: Yard 5B **120**
WV14: Cose 6F **61**
Martin Gro. WS6: Gt Wyr 2G **7**
Martin Hill St. DY2: Dud 1E **95**
Martin Ri. B37: Mars G 3B **122**
Martin Rd. DY4: Tip 2A **78**
WS5: Wals 3G **49**
WV14: Bils 2H **61**
Martin St. WV4: Ett 6B **44**
Martlesham Sq. B35: Cas V 3E **87**
Martley Cft. B32: Quin 1C **130**
B91: Sol 1F **165**
Martley Dr. DY9: Lye 1G **125**
Martley Rd. B69: O'bry 3D **96**
WS4: S'fld 6G **21**
Marton Cl. B7: Nech 3B **102**
Martyn Smith Cl. B43: Gt Barr 4G **65**
Marwood Cft. B74: S'tly 1A **52**
Mary Ann St. B3: Birm 1C **4** (5F **101**)
WV1: Wolv 2A **44**
(off Walsall St.)
Maryland Av. B34: Hodg H 4C **104**
Maryland Dr. B31: N'fld 2F **145**

Maryland Rd.—Meaton Gro.

Maryland Rd. DY5: Quar B 4B 110
Marylebone Cl. DY8: Amb 4E 109
Mary Macarthur Dr.
B64: Crad H 2E 111
Mary Rd. B21: Hand 2A 100
B33: Stech 6B 104
B69: Tiv 1C 96
B70: W Brom 6B 80
Mary Rose Cl. WS6: C Hay 4D 6
Mary Stevens Cl. DY8: Stourb 2D 124
Mary Stevens Pk. 2D 124
Mary St. B3: Birm 1B 4 (5E 101)
B12: Bal H 6G 117
WS2: Wals 6B 32
Maryvale Ct. WS1: Wals 2C 48
Mary Va. Rd. B30: B'vlle, Stir 1A 146
Marywell Cl. B32: Bart G 6H 129
Masefield Av. DY1: Dud 6E 61
Masefield Cl. WV14: Bils 3H 61
Masefield M. WV10: Bush 6C 16
Masefield Ri. B62: Hale 2D 128
Masefield Rd. DY3: Lwr G 3E 75
WS3: Blox 2C 32
WV10: Bush 6C 16
Masefield Sq. B31: N'fld 3G 145
Masham Cl. B33: Stech 1C 120
Mashie Gdns. B38: King Nor 6H 145
Maslen Pl. B63: Hale 2B 128
Maslin Dr. WV14: Cose 4C 60
Mason Ct. B27: A Grn 3C 136
Mason Cres. WV4: Penn 6C 42
Mason Hall B15: Edg 5C 116
Mason Ho. B90: Shir 6E 149
Masonleys Rd. B31: N'fld 4B 144
Mason Rd. B24: Erd 3G 85
WS2: Wals 4H 31
Masons Cl. B63: Crad 5E 111
B92: Olton 3C 136
Masons Cotts. B24: Erd 2H 85
Mason St. B70: W Brom 3H 79
WV2: Wolv 4G 43
WV14: Cose 6D 60
Masons Vw. B24: Erd 5G 85
Mason's Way B92: Olton 3C 136
Mason Way B15: Birm 2E 117
Massbrook Gro. WV10: Wolv 3B 28
Massbrook Rd. WV10: Wolv 3B 28
Masshouse La. B5: Birm 3G 5 (6H 101)
B38: King Nor 6B 146
Masshouse Plaza B5: Birm 3G 5 (6H 101)
Masters La. B62: B'hth 2E 113
Matchlock Cl. B74: S'tly 4G 51
Matfen Av. B73: S Cold 3F 69
Math Mdw. B32: Harb 6D 114
Matlock Cl. DY2: Neth 6F 95
WS3: Blox 4A 20
Matlock Rd. B11: Tys 2F 135
WS3: Blox 4A 20
Matlock Vs. *B12: Bal H 6B 118*
(off Chesterton Rd.)
Matthews Cl. B65: B'hth 2B 112
Mattox Rd. WV11: Wed 3F 29
Matty Rd. B68: O'bry 5H 97
Maud Rd. B46: Wat O 4F 89
B70: W Brom 6A 80
Maughan St. DY1: Dud 6C 76
DY5: Quar B 3B 110
Maurice Gro. WV10: Wolv 3C 28
Maurice Rd. B14: King H 2G 147
B67: Smeth 1C 114
Mavis Gdns. B68: O'bry 3H 113
Mavis Rd. B31: N'fld 6C 144
Maw St. WS1: Wals 5D 48
Maxholm Rd. B74: S'tly 3G 51
Max Rd. B32: Quin 6B 114
Maxstoke Cl. B32: Bart G 6G 129
B73: New O 3E 69
CV7: Mer 4H 141
WS3: Blox 4G 19
Maxstoke Cft. B90: Shir 1A 164
Maxstoke La. CV7: Mer 3H 141
(not continuous)
Maxstoke Rd. B73: New O 3E 69
Maxstoke St. B9: Birm 1B 118
Maxted Rd. B23: Erd 5C 68
Maxwell Av. B20: Hand 6D 82
Maxwell Rd. WV2: Wolv 6D 170 (3H 43)
Mayall Dr. B75: R'ley 5A 38
May Av. B12: Bal H 6A 118
Maybank B9: Bord G 6F 103
Maybank Pl. B44: P Barr 1G 83
Maybank Rd. DY2: Neth 6E 95
Mayberry Cl. B14: King H 5B 148
Maybridge Dr. B91: Sol 1F 165
Maybrook Bus. Pk. B76: Min 1E 87
Maybrook Ho. B63: Hale 1A 128
Maybrook Ind. Est.
WS8: Bwnhls 2B 22
(not continuous)
Maybrook Rd. B76: Min 2E 87
WS8: Bwnhls 3B 22
Maybury Cl. WV8: Cod 3E 13
Maybush Gdns. WV10: Oxl 6G 15
Maydene Cft. B12: Bal H 5H 117
MAYERS GREEN 3C 80
Mayfair *B37: K'hrst 4B 106*
(off Haselour Rd.)
DY9: W'cte 3H 125
Mayfair Cl. B44: K'sdng 6B 68
DY1: Dud 5C 76
Mayfair Dr. DY6: K'wfrd 2A 92
Mayfair Gdns. DY4: Tip 3A 78
WV3: Wolv 1B 42
Mayfair Pde. B44: K'sdng 6B 68
May Farm Cl. B47: H'wd 3A 162
Mayfield Av. B29: S Oak 3D 132
Mayfield Cl. B91: Sol 6G 151
Mayfield Ct. B13: Mose 3A 134
Mayfield Cres. B65: Row R 6A 96
Mayfield Rd. B11: Tys 1G 135
B13: Mose 3A 134
B19: Hand 1E 101
B27: A Grn 1G 135
B30: Stir 1C 146
B62: B'hth 2F 113
B63: Hale 3F 127
B73: W Grn 3G 69
B74: S'tly 3H 51
DY1: Dud 2D 76
WV1: Wolv 2D 44
Mayfields Dr. WS8: Bwnhls 3F 9
Mayflower Cl. B19: Loz 3F 101
Mayflower Dr. DY5: P'ntt 2E 93
Mayford Gro. B13: Mose 1B 148
Maygrove Rd. DY6: K'wfrd 2A 92
Mayhurst Cl. B47: H'wd 2C 162
DY4: Tip 5A 62
Mayhurst Rd. B47: H'wd 2B 162
Mayland Dr. B74: S'tly 6H 51
Mayland Rd. B16: Edg 1G 115
May La. B14: King H 2H 147
B47: H'wd 2A 162
Maynard Av. DY8: Stourb 2B 124
Maynard Rd. B16: Smeth 6G 99
Mayou Ct. WS3: Pels 3E 21
Maypole Cl. B14: King H 6A 148
B64: Crad H 3D 110
Maypole Ct. WV5: Wom 1G 73
Maypole Dr. DY8: Stourb 6C 108
Maypole Flds. B63: Crad 4C 110
Maypole Gro. B14: King H 5B 148
Maypole Hill B63: Crad 3C 110
Maypole La. B14: King H 5H 147
Maypole Rd. B68: O'bry 2H 113
Maypole St. WV5: Wom 6H 57
May St. WS3: Blox 3A 32
Mayswood Dr. WV6: Tett 2F 41
Mayswood Gro. B32: Quin 1B 130
Mayswood Rd. B92: Sol 3G 137
Maythorn Av. B76: Walm 1E 87
Maythorn Gdns. WV6: Tett 6A 26
WV8: Bilb 3G 13
Maythorn Gro. B91: Sol 1F 165
Maytree Cl. B37: F'bri 1C 122
May Tree Gro. B20: Hand 4B 82
May Trees B47: H'wd 3H 161
Maywell Dr. B92: Sol 5B 138
Maywood Cl. DY6: K'wfrd 3A 92
Meaburn Cl. B29: W Cas 6E 131
Mead, The DY3: Sed 5F 59
Mead Av. B16: Edg 6G 99
Mead Cl. WS9: A'rdge 3D 34
Mead Cres. B9: Bord G 6H 103
Meadfoot Av. B14: King H 4H 147
Meadfoot Dr. DY6: K'wfrd 2H 91
Meadlands, The WV5: Wom 1E 73
Meadow Av. B71: W Brom 4D 64
Meadowbank Dr. B46: Col 6F 89
Meadowbank Grange
WS6: Gt Wyr 1E 7
Meadowbrook Gdns.
WV8: Bilb 3H 13
Meadow Brook Rd. B31: N'fld 2D 144
Meadowbrook Rd. B63: Hale 2F 127
Meadow Cl. B17: Harb 3F 115
B74: S'tly 1H 51
B76: Walm 4D 70
B90: Shir 1B 164
WS4: S'fld 1G 33
Meadow Ct. B17: Edg 2F 115
B30: King Nor 5D 146
Meadow Cft. B47: Wyt 6A 162
WV6: Pert 6D 24
Meadow Dr. B92: H Ard 1B 154
Meadowfield Rd. B45: Rub 2G 157
Meadowfields Cl. DY8: Word 1C 108
Meadow Ga. B31: N'fld 5C 144
Meadow Grange Dr.
WV12: W'hall 2C 30
Meadow Gro. B92: Olton 4B 136
WS6: Gt Wyr 3G 7
Meadow Hill Dr. DY8: Word 1C 108
Meadow Hill Rd. B38: King Nor 5A 146
Meadowlands Dr. WS4: S'fld 1H 33
Meadow La. WV5: Wom 5G 57
WV10: Cov H 1G 15
WV12: W'hall 4A 30
WV14: Cose 3D 60
(not continuous)
Meadow Pk. Rd. DY8: Woll 3B 108
Meadow Pleck La. B90: Dic H 3G 163
Meadow Rise B30: B'vlle 6H 131
CV7: Bal C 5H 169
Meadow Rd. B17: Harb 2F 115
B32: Quin 5G 113
B47: Wyt 6A 162
B62: B'hth 3C 112
B67: Smeth 5E 99
B68: O'bry 1H 113
DY1: Dud 3C 76
WS9: A'rdge 5C 34
WV3: Wolv 3A 42
Meadows, The DY9: Pedm 6F 125
WS9: A'rdge 4A 34
Meadows Gro. WV8: Bilb 3G 13
Meadowside Cl. B43: Gt Barr 4A 66
Meadowside Rd. B74: Four O 5F 37
Meadow St. B64: Old H 3H 111
WS1: Wals 3B 48
WV1: Wolv 1F 43
Meadowsweet Av.
B38: King Nor 1B 160
Meadowsweet Way DY6: K'wfrd 3D 92
Meadow Va. WV8: Bilb 5H 13
Meadow Vw. B13: Mose 5C 134
DY3: Sed 4G 59
WV6: Tett 5C 26
WV11: Ess 4H 17
Meadow Vw. Mobile Home Pk.
WV10: Cov H 1G 15
Meadow Vw. Ter. WV6: Tett 5C 26
Meadow Vw. Wharf WV6: Tett 5C 26
Meadow Wlk. B14: King H 6G 147
B64: Crad H 3F 111
Meadow Way DY8: Word 1A 108
WV8: Cod 5E 13
Mead Ri. B15: Edg 5B 116
Meadthorpe Rd. B44: Gt Barr 5F 67
Meadvale Rd. B45: Redn 3H 157
Meadway B33: Kitts G, Yard 1D 120
Meadway, The WV6: Tett 4G 25
Meadwood Ind. Est. WV14: Bils 6G 45
Mears Cl. B23: Erd 5D 68
Mears Coppice DY5: Quar B 5A 110
DY9: Lye 5A 110
Mears Dr. B33: Stech 5B 104
Mearse Cl. B18: Hock 4C 100
Mease Cft. B9: Birm 1B 118
Measham Gro. B26: Yard 6C 120
Measham Way WV11: Wed 2G 29
Meaton Gro. B32: Bart G 5H 129

Mecca Bingo
Acocks Green 1H 135
Bilston 1E 61
Birmingham 2H 67
Brierley Hill 1H 109
Oldbury 2F 97
Wednesbury 3E 63
West Bromwich 4A 80
Medcroft Av. B20: Hand 3A 82
Medina Cl. WV10: Bush 3B 16
Medina Rd. B11: Tys 1E 135
Medina Way DY6: K'wfrd 3A 92
Medley Gdns. DY4: Tip 3D 78
Medley Rd. B11: S'brk 6D 118
Medlicott Rd. B11: S'brk 5C 118
Medway Cl. DY5: P'ntt 3E 93
Medway Ct. B73: S Cold 6H 53
Medway Cft. B36: Cas B 2B 106
Medway Gro. B38: King Nor 1A 160
Medway Rd. WS8: Bwnhls 3G 9
Medway Twr. B7: Nech 4B 102
Medway Wlk. WS8: Bwnhls 3G 9
Medwin Gro. B23: Erd 6D 68
Meerash La. WS7: Hamm 2D 10
Meer End B38: King Nor 2H 159
Meerhill Av. B90: M'path 3E 165
Meeting Ho. La. B31: N'fld ...3E 145
  CV7: Bal C 5H 169
Meeting La. DY5: Brie H 2F 109
  (not continuous)
Meeting St. DY2: Neth 4E 95
  DY4: Tip 1D 78
  WS10: W'bry 2E 63
Mehdi Rd. B69: O'bry 1E 97
Melbourne Av. B19: Hock 3E 101
  B66: Smeth 2F 99
Melbourne Cl. B70: W Brom 6G 63
  DY6: K'wfrd 5C 92
Melbourne Gdns. WS5: Wals ...5F 49
Melbourne Rd. B34: S End 3A 106
  B63: Hale 6B 112
  B73: S Cold 2E 99
Melbury Cl. WV3: Wolv 2E 43
Melbury Gro. B14: King H 2G 147
Melchett Rd. B30: King Nor ...4B 146
Melcote Gro. B44: Gt Barr 5G 67
Meldon Dr. WV14: Bils 3A 62
Melford Cl. DY3: Sed 3G 59
Melford Hall Rd. B91: Sol 6D 136
Melfort Gro. B14: King H 4A 148
Melia Dr. WS10: W'bry 2H 63
Melksham Sq. B35: Cas V 4E 87
Mellis Gro. B23: Erd 2A 84
Mellish Av. B71: W Brom 1C 80
Mellish Cl. WS4: Wals 6E 33
  (off Mellish Rd.)
Mellish Dr. WS4: Wals 6F 33
Mellish Rd. WS4: Wals 6E 33
Mellor Dr. B74: Four O 6E 37
Mellors Cl. B17: Harb 2F 131
Mellowdew Rd. DY8: Word 6A 92
Mell Sq. B91: Sol 3G 151
Melplash Av. B91: Sol 3E 151
Melrose Av. B11: S'hll 5C 118
  (off Walford Rd.)
  B12: Bal H 5A 118
  B71: W Brom 5B 64
  B73: S Cold 3E 69
  DY8: Stourb 3D 124
Melrose Cl. B38: King Nor 6B 146
Melrose Cotts. WS14: Muck C ...4H 11
Melrose Dr. WV6: Pert 5D 24
Melrose Gro. B19: Loz 2D 100
Melrose Pl. B66: Smeth 1B 98
Melrose Rd. B20: Hand 6G 83
Melstock Cl. DY4: Tip 2F 77
Melstock Rd. B14: King H 6F 133
Melton Av. B92: Olton 1E 137
Melton Dr. B15: Edg 4E 117
Melton Rd. B14: King H 5H 133
Melverley Gro. B44: K'sdng ...5H 67
Melverton Av. WV10: Bush 1H 27
Melville Hall B16: Edg 2G 115
Melville Rd. B16: Edg 2G 115
Melvina Rd. B7: Birm 5B 102
Membury Rd. B8: Salt 3D 102

Memorial Cl. WV13: W'hall 1A 46
Memory La. WS10: Darl 3D 46
  WV11: Wed 4D 28
Menai Cl. WV12: W'hall 3C 30
Menai Wlk. B37: F'bri 5D 106
Mendip Av. B8: Salt 4E 103
Mendip Cl. B63: Hale 4F 127
  DY3: Lwr G 4H 75
  WV2: Ett 5B 44
Mendip Rd. B8: Salt 5E 103
  B63: Hale 4F 127
  DY8: Amb 5F 109
Menin Cres. B13: Mose 6B 134
Menin Rd. B13: Mose 5B 134
Menin Pas. B13: Mose 5B 134
Menin Rd. B13: Mose 5B 134
  DY4: Tip 2F 77
Mentone Ct. B20: Hand 4A 82
Meon Gro. B33: Sheld 3F 121
  WV6: Pert 5E 25
Meon Ri. DY9: Pedm 2G 125
Meon Way WV11: Wed 2H 29
Meranti Cl. WV12: W'hall 1C 30
Mercer Av. B46: Wat O 4C 88
Mercer Gro. WV11: Wed 2G 29
Merchants Way WS9: A'rdge 2C 34
Mercia Dr. B14: King H 1F 147
  WV6: Pert 4E 25
Mercote Hall La. CV7: Mer ...2G 155
Mercury Dr. WV10: Oxl 2G 27
Mere Av. B35: Cas V 4E 87
Mere Cl. WV12: W'hall 4A 30
Merecote Rd. B92: Olton 6B 136
Mere Cft. WS11: Nort C 1D 8
Meredith Rd. DY3: Lwr G 2E 75
  WV11: Wed 1E 29
Merediths Pool Cl. B18: Hock ..3B 100
Meredith St. B64: Crad H 2F 111
Mere Dr. B75: Four O 1H 53
Mere Grn. Cl. B75: Four O 1A 54
Mere Grn. Rd. B75: Four O 1H 53
Mere Oak Rd. WV6: Pert 4E 25
Mere Pool Rd. B75: R'ley 1B 54
Mere Rd. B23: Erd 4D 84
  DY8: Stourb 2C 124
Mereside Way B92: Olton 5C 136
Meres Rd. B63: Crad 6E 111
Mere St. B23: Erd 4E 85
Merevale Rd. B92: Sol 3F 137
Mere Vw. WS4: S'fld 1G 33
Mereways B90: Dic H 4G 163
Mereworth Cl. B26: Sheld 6F 121
Meriden Av. DY8: Woll 5B 108
Meriden Cl. B25: Yard 4H 119
  DY8: Woll 5B 108
Meriden Dr. B37: K'hrst 3C 106
Meriden Ri. B92: Sol 2H 137
Meriden Rd. B92: H Ard 6B 140
  CV7: Mer 6B 140
  WV10: Oxl 1E 27
Meriden St. B5: Birm 6G 5 (1H 117)
Merino Av. B31: Longb 1E 159
Merlin Cl. B35: Cas V 4E 87
  DY1: Dud 1B 94
  WS8: Bwnhls 1C 22
Merlin Gro. B26: Sheld 6F 121
Merlin Wlk. B35: Cas V 3F 87
  (off Merlin Way)
Merlin Way B35: Cas V 3F 87
Merrick Cl. B63: Hale 3F 127
Merrick Rd. WV11: Wed 3A 30
MERRIDALE 2D 42
Merridale Av. WV3: Wolv 2D 42
Merridale Ct. WV3: Wolv 2D 42
Merridale Cres. WV3: Wolv 1E 43
Merridale Gdns. WV3: Wolv 2E 43
Merridale Gro. WV3: Wolv 2C 42
  (not continuous)
Merridale La. WV3: Wolv 1E 43
Merridale Rd. WV3: Wolv 2D 42
Merridale St. WV3: Wolv ...5A 170 (2F 43)
Merridale St. W. WV3: Wolv ...3E 43
Merrill Cl. WS6: C Hay 3E 7
Merrill's Hall La. WV11: Wed ..5G 29
Merrington Cl. B91: Sol 1G 165
Merrions Cl. B43: Gt Barr 1A 66
Merrions Wood (Nature Reserve) 1A 66

Merrishaw Rd. B31: Longb 1E 159
Merritts Brook Cl. B29: W Cas ..2E 145
Merritt's Brook La. B31: N'fld ..3C 144
Merritt's Hill B31: N'fld 1B 144
  (not continuous)
Merrivale Rd. B62: B'hth 3F 113
  B66: Smeth 1E 115
Merryfield Cl. B92: Sol 6H 137
Merryfield Gro. B17: Harb 1G 131
Merryfield Rd. DY1: Dud 1H 93
MERRY HILL
  DY5 ....6A 94
  WV3 ....4B 42
Merry Hill DY5: Brie H, Quar B ..2B 110
Merry Hill Cen. DY5: Brie H ...6B 94
Merry Hill Ct. B66: Smeth 3H 99
Merryhill Dr. B18: Hock 3B 100
Merryhills Ent. Pk. WV10: Wolv ..4B 28
Mersey Gro. B38: King Nor 1A 160
Mersey Pl. WS3: Blox 6C 20
Mersey Rd. WS3: Blox 6C 20
Merstal Dr. B92: Sol 6B 138
Merstone Cl. B37: Mars G 3E 123
  WV14: Bils 5E 45
Merstowe Cl. B27: A Grn 2H 135
Merton Cl. B68: O'bry 1H 113
Merton Ho. B37: F'bri 1B 122
Merton Rd. B13: Mose 2B 134
Merton Way WS2: Wals 4A 48
Mervyn Pl. WV14: Bils 2H 61
Mervyn Rd. B21: Hand 6A 82
  WV14: Bils 2H 61
Meryhurst Rd. WS10: W'bry 6G 47
Messenger Rd. B66: Smeth 3F 99
MESTY CROFT 2H 63
Metchley Abbey B17: Harb 6H 115
Metchley Ct. B17: Harb 1H 131
Metchley Cft. B90: M'path 3D 164
Metchley Dr. B17: Harb 6G 115
Metchley Gro. B18: Win G 5A 100
  (off Heath Grn. Rd.)
Metchley Ho. B17: Harb 6H 115
Metchley La. B15: Harb 1H 131
  B17: Harb 1H 131
Metchley Pk. Rd. B15: Edg 6A 116
Metchley Ri. B17: Harb 6G 115
Meteor Pk. B7: Nech 1D 102
Meteor Way B7: Nech 1C 102
Metfield Cft. B17: Harb 1H 131
  DY6: K'wfrd 3D 92
Metlin Gro. B33: Kitts G 6A 106
Metric Wlk. B67: Smeth 4E 99
Metropolitan Ho. B16: Birm 2D 116
  (off Hagley Rd.)
Metropolitan Lofts DY1: Dud 6E 77
  (off Parson's St.)
Metro Triangle B7: Nech 2D 102
Metro Way B66: Smeth 2G 99
Mews, The B27: A Grn 2H 135
  B44: K'sdng 6B 68
  B65: Row R 1B 112
  B66: Smeth 5E 99
Mey Coppice B36: Cas B 2B 106
Meynell Ho. B20: Hand 4B 82
Meyrick Rd. B70: W Brom 1G 79
Meyrick Wlk. B16: Edg 2B 116
Miall Pk. Rd. B91: Sol 2C 150
Miall Rd. B28: Hall G 5G 135
Michael Blanning Gdns. B93: Dorr ..5A 166
Michael Blanning Ho. B13: Mose ..3B 134
  (off Wake Grn. Pk.)
Michael Blanning Pl. CV7: Bal C ..2H 169
Michael Ct. B5: Edg 5F 117
Michael Dr. B15: Edg 4E 117
Michael Rd. B67: Smeth 3C 98
  WS10: Darl 4B 46
Michelle Cl. B13: Mose 2A 148
Micklehill Dr. B90: Shir 1H 163
Mickle Mdw. B46: Wat O 4D 88
Mickleover Rd. B8: W End 4A 104
Mickleton Av. B33: Sheld 3G 121
Mickleton Rd. B92: Olton 5B 136
Mickley Av. WV10: Wolv 4A 28
Midacre WV13: W'hall 2A 46
Middle Acre Rd. B32: Bart G ..3C 130
Middle Av. WV13: W'hall 3G 45
Middle Bickenhill La. B92: Bick ..1A 140

Middle College Ho. B8: Salt 6E 103
Middle Cres. WS3: Wals 2E 33
Middle Cross
  WV1: Wolv 4D 170 (2H 43)
Middle Dr. B45: Coft H 5B 158
Middlefield WV8: Pend 5C 14
Middlefield Av. B62: B'hth 3F 113
  B93: Know 5D 166
Middlefield Cl. B62: B'hth 2F 113
Middlefield Gdns. B62: B'hth 3F 113
                                    (off Hurst Grn. Rd.)
Middlefield Ho. B14: King H 4H 147
                                    (off Britford Cl.)
Middle Fld. Rd. B31: N'fld 5G 145
Middlefield Rd. B69: Tiv 1A 96
MIDDLE HILL 1B 6
MIDDLE HILL JUNC. 1A 6
Middlehill Ri. B32: Bart G 3B 130
Middle La. B38: Head H 3E 161
  B47: Wyt 3E 161
  WV8: Oaken 5C 12
  WV9: Coven 3D 14
Middle Leaford B34: Stech 4E 105
Middle Leasow B32: Quin 1A 130
Middle Mall B5: Birm 5F 5
Middle Mdw. DY4: Tip 2B 78
Middle Mdw. Av. B32: Quin 6A 114
Middlemist Gro. B43: Gt Barr 1B 82
Middlemore Ind. Est. B21: Hand 1F 99
Middlemore La. WS9: A'rdge 3B 34
Middlemore La. W. WS9: A'rdge 3H 33
Middlemore Rd. B21: Hand 2F 99
  B31: N'fld 5F 145
  B66: Smeth 2F 99
  B71: W Brom 2F 99
Middle Pk. Cl. B29: W Cas 5F 131
Middlepark Dr. B31: N'fld 1F 145
Middle Pk. Rd. B29: W Cas 5F 131
Middlepark Rd. DY1: Dud 1A 94
Middle Piece Way WV13: W'hall 1B 46
Middle Rd. B61: Wild 5A 156
Middleton Cl. WS5: Wals 6D 48
                                    (not continuous)
  WS7: Hamm 1F 11
Middleton Gdns. B30: King Nor 3H 145
Middleton Grange B31: N'fld 3G 145
Middleton Hall Rd. B30: King Nor . . .3H 145
Middleton Rd. B14: King H 6G 133
  B74: S'tly 2A 52
  B90: Shir 5G 149
  WS8: Bwnhls 4C 10
Middleton Trad. Est.
  WV13: W'hall 2G 45
Middle Tree Rd. B63: Crad 4E 111
Middle Vauxhall WV1: Wolv 1E 43
Middleway Av. DY8: Word 6A 92
Middleway Grn. WV14: Bils 3E 45
Middleway Ind. Est. B12: Birm 4H 117
                                    (off Moseley Rd.)
Middleway Rd. WV14: Bils 3E 45
Middleway Vw. B18: Hock 6C 100
Middlewood Cl. B91: Sol 1H 151
Midford Gro. B15: Birm 3E 117
Midgley Dr. B74: Four O 1G 53
Midhill Dr. B65: Row R 3C 96
Midhurst Gro. WV6: Tett 4A 26
Midhurst Rd. B30: King Nor 4D 146
Midland Cl. B21: Hand 2C 100
Midland Ct. B3: Birm 1B 4
Midland Cft. B33: Kitts G 6H 105
Midland Dr. B72: S Cold 6A 54
Midland Rd. B30: King Nor 2B 146
  B74: S Cold 4G 53
  WS1: Wals 2B 48
  WS10: Darl 3C 46
Midland Sailing Club 6A 100
Midlands Arts Cen. 1F 133
Midland St. B8: Birm 6C 102
  B9: Birm .6C 102
Midpoint Blvd. B76: Min 2G 87
Midpoint Pk. B76: Min 3G 87
Midpoint Way B76: Min 3H 87
Midvale Dr. B14: King H 5F 147
Milburn Rd. B44: K'sdng 2A 68
Milcote Dr. B73: New O 2C 68
  WV13: W'hall 2F 45

Milcote Rd. B29: W Cas 5E 131
  B67: Smeth 1D 114
  B91: Sol .3F 151
Milcote Way DY6: K'wfrd 2H 91
Mildenhall Rd. B42: Gt Barr 4C 66
Mildred Rd. B64: Old H 1G 111
Mildred Way B65: Row R 3C 96
Milebrook Gro. B32: Bart G 5H 129
Mile Flat DY6: K'wfrd 3E 91
Mile Oak Ct. B66: Smeth 3F 99
Milesbush Av. B36: Cas B 6H 87
Miles Druce Way
  B4: Birm 3H 5 (6A 102)
Miles Gro. DY2: Dud 2H 95
Miles Mdw. Cl. WV12: W'hall 1C 30
Milestone Ct. WV6: Tett 6G 25
Milestone Cft. B63: Crad 6E 111
Milestone La. B21: Hand 1H 99
Milestone Way WV12: W'hall 1B 30
Milford Av. B12: Bal H 5A 118
  WV12: W'hall 4A 30
Milford Cl. DY8: Word 6C 92
Milford Copse B17: Harb 6F 115
Milford Cft. B19: Birm 4F 101
  B65: Row R 3H 95
Milford Gro. B90: M'path 2G 165
Milford Ho. B23: Erd 3C 84
Milford Pl. B14: King H 5G 133
Milford Rd. B17: Harb 6F 115
  WV2: Wolv 4G 43
Milholme Grn. B92: Sol 5H 137
MILKING BANK 5A 76
Milk St. B5: Birm 6H 5 (2H 117)
Milking Bank DY1: Dud 5H 75
Mill, The WV1: Wolv 1A 44
Millard Ind. Est. B70: W Brom 6G 79
Millard Rd. WV14: Cose 4D 60
Millbank Gro. B23: Erd 1B 84
                                    (not continuous)
Millbank St. WV11: Wed 6H 17
Mill Brook Dr. B31: Longb 1C 158
Millbrook Gdns. B13: Mose 5B 134
Millbrook Rd. B14: King H 1E 147
Millbrook Way B75: Brie H 3F 109
Mill Burn Way B9: Birm 1B 118
Mill Cl. B47: H'wd 2A 162
Mill Cft. WV14: Bils 5G 45
Millcroft Cl. B32: Bart G 3C 130
Millcroft Rd. B74: S'tly 3A 52
Milldale Cres. WV10: F'hses 3H 15
Mill Dr. B66: Smeth 4F 99
Millennium Apartments B3: Birm . . .2C 4
Millennium Cl. WS3: Pels 4E 21
Millennium Gdns. B64: Old H 1H 111
Millennium Pk. B70: W Brom 2G 79
Millennium Point 3H 5 (6H 101)
Millennium Way WV8: Bilb 3H 13
Miller Ct. B33: Stech 6C 104
Miller Cres. WV14: Cose 4C 60
Millers Cl. WS2: Wals 2F 47
Millers Ct. B66: Smeth 4F 99
                                    (off Corbett St.)
  B90: Shir 5F 149
Millersdale Dr. B71: W Brom 3D 64
Millers Grn. Dr. DY6: W Hth 1G 91
Miller St. B6: Aston 4G 101
Millers Va. WV5: Wom 2D 72
Millers Wlk. WS3: Pels 4C 20
Mill Farm Rd. B17: Harb 2G 131
Millfield B31: N'fld 3E 145
Millfield Av. WS3: Blox 5B 20
  WS4: S'fld 6F 21
Millfield Ct. DY1: Dud 5C 76
                                    (off Pelham Dr.)
Millfield Rd. B20: Hand 2A 82
  WS8: Bwnhls 6C 10
Millfields B33: Kitts G 6C 104
                                    (not continuous)
Millfields Cl. B71: W Brom 4H 63
Millfields Rd. B71: W Brom 4H 63
  WV4: Ett .6C 44
  WV14: Bils 6C 44
Millfields Way WV5: Wom 1E 73
Millfield Vw. B63: Hale 1G 127
Millford Cl. B28: Hall G 2G 149

Mill Gdns. B14: Yard W 2D 148
  B67: Smeth 6D 98
MILL GREEN 2A 36
Mill Grn. WV10: F'hses 3H 15
Mill Gro. WV8: Bilb 4A 14
Millhaven Av. B30: Stir 1D 146
Mill Hill B67: Smeth 6D 98
Mill Ho. B8: W End 5B 104
Mill Ho., The B30: King Nor 3C 146
Mill Ho. La. B75: Can 1D 38
Millhouse Rd. B25: Yard 3H 119
Millicent Pl. B12: Bal H 5A 118
Millichip Rd. WV13: W'hall 2G 45
Millington Rd. B36: Hodg H 1C 104
  DY4: Tip .4H 61
  WV10: Bush 3A 28
Millison Gro. B90: M'path 1E 165
Mill La. B5: Birm 6G 5 (2H 117)
  B31: N'fld 6D 144
  B32: Bart G 3B 130
  B61: Wild 6A 156
  B63: Hale 1C 128
  B69: O'bry 5G 97
  B91: Sol .4G 151
  B93: Ben H, Dorr 5A 166
  DY7: Stourt 6A 90
  WS3: Wals 5D 32
  WS4: Wals 5D 32
  WS7: Hamm 2F 11
  WS9: A'rdge 2H 35
  WS9: Ston 3H 23
  WV5: Swind 4D 72
  WV5: Wom 6H 57
  WV6: Tett 1G 41
  WV8: Cod 1E 13
  WV11: Wed 2C 28
  WV12: W'hall 4C 30
Mill La. Arc. B91: Sol 4G 151
                                    (within Touchwood)
Millmead Lodge B13: Mose 5D 134
Mill Mdw. DY8: Amb 5E 109
Millmead Rd. B32: Bart G 3C 130
Millpool, The WV5: Seis 3A 56
Mill Pool Cl. WV5: Wom 2D 72
Millpool Gdns. B14: King H 4H 147
Millpool Hill B14: King H 3H 147
Millpool Way B66: Smeth 5E 99
Millport Rd. WV4: Ett 6B 44
Mill Race La. DY8: Amb 5E 109
Mill Rd. B64: Crad H 4G 111
  WS4: S'fld 6F 21
  WS8: Bwnhls 6C 10
Mills Av. B76: Walm 1C 70
Mills Cl. WV11: Wed 1D 28
Mills Ct. B74: Four O 1H 53
Mills Cres. WV2: Wolv 3A 44
Millside B28: Hall G 4E 149
  WV5: Wom 2E 73
Millside Ct. WV2: Wolv 3A 44
Millstone Cl. B76: Walm 4D 70
Mill Stream Cl. WV8: Bilb 3H 13
Mill St. B6: Birm 4H 101
  B63: Crad 4E 111
  B70: W Brom 3A 80
  B72: S Cold 6A 54
  DY4: Tip .2D 78
  DY5: Brie H 1H 109
  DY8: Word 1C 108
  WS2: Wals 6C 32
  WS10: Darl 5C 46
  WV13: W'hall 1C 46
  WV14: Bils 6E 45
Millsum Ho. WS1: Wals 2D 48
                                    (off Paddock La.)
Mills Wlk. DY4: Tip 6H 61
Millthorpe Cl. B8: W End 4F 103
Mill Vw. B33: Kitts G 5G 105
Mill Wlk., The B31: N'fld 6D 144
Millwalk Dr. WV9: Pend 4E 15
Millward St. B9: Small H 2C 118
  B70: W Brom 4G 79
Millwright Cl. DY4: Tip 2B 78
Milner Rd. B29: S Oak 4C 132
Milner Way B13: Mose 5D 134
Milnes Walker Ct. B44: Gt Barr 3G 67
Milsom Gro. B34: S End 3H 105

Milstead Rd. B26: Yard 2E 121
Milston Cl. B14: King H 6G 147
Milton Av. B12: Bal H 5A 118
Milton Cl. B93: Ben H 5B 166
  DY8: Amb 4E 109
  WS1: Wals 5B 48
  WV12: W'hall 2E 31
Milton Ct. B66: Smeth 2E 115
  WV6: Pert 5E 25
Milton Cres. DY3: Lwr G 2E 75
Milton Dr. DY9: Hag 6H 125
Milton Gro. B21: Hand 1G 99
              (off Wattville Rd.)
  B29: S Oak 2B 132
Milton Pl. WS1: Wals 5B 48
Milton Rd. B67: Smeth 4B 98
  B93: Ben H 5B 166
  WV10: Wolv 4C 28
  WV14: Cose 5F 61
Milton St. B19: Hock 3G 101
  B71: W Brom 2H 79
  DY5: P'ntt 3H 93
  WS1: Wals 3B 48
Milverton Cl. B63: Hale 5A 112
  B76: Walm 6D 70
Milverton Ct. B62: Quin 4G 113
           (off Binswood Rd.)
Milverton Rd. B23: Erd 3E 85
  B93: Know 4E 167
Mimosa Cl. B29: W Cas 5F 131
Mimosa Wlk. DY6: K'wfrd 1C 92
Mincing La. B65: Row R 6D 96
Mindelsohn Cres. B15: Edg 2A 132
Mindelsohn Way B15: Edg 1H 131
Minden Gro. B29: S Oak 4F 131
Minehead Rd. DY1: Dud 1H 93
  WV10: Oxl 5F 15
Miner St. WS2: Wals 6A 32
Minerva Cl. WV12: W'hall 5E 31
Minerva La. WV1: Wolv 2A 44
Minewood Cl. WS3: Blox 4F 19
Minith Rd. WV14: Cose 5F 61
Miniva Dr. B76: Walm 4E 71
Minivet Dr. B12: Bal H 5G 117
Minley Av. B17: Harb 4A 114
Minories B4: Birm 3E 5 (6G 101)
Minories, The DY2: Dud 6E 77
Minstead Rd. B24: Erd 6D 84
Minster, The WV3: Wolv 4D 42
Minster Cl. B65: Row R 6E 97
  B93: Know 1D 166
Minster Ct. B13: Mose 1A 134
  B29: W Cas 6G 131
           (off Abdon Av.)
Minster Dr. B10: Small H 4D 118
Minsterley Cl. WV3: Wolv 3C 42
Mintern Rd. B25: Yard 3A 120
Minto Ho. B12: Bal H 6G 117
Minton Cl. WV1: Wolv 2C 44
Minton Rd. B32: Quin 1D 130
MINWORTH 2H 87
Minworth Ind. Est. 1E 87
Minworth Ind. Pk. B76: Min 1G 87
Minworth Parkway B76: Min 2H 87
Minworth Rd. B46: Wat O 4C 88
Miraj Av. B11: S'hll 2B 134
Miranda Cl. B45: Fran 4G 143
Mirbeck Cl. WV3: Wolv 2A 42
Mirfield Cl. WV9: Pend 4E 15
Mirfield Rd. B33: Kitts G 1F 121
  B91: Sol 1E 151
Mission Cl. B64: Old H 2A 112
Mission Dr. DY4: Tip 4A 78
Mistletoe Dr. WS5: Wals 2F 65
Mitcham Ct. B29: W Cas 6G 131
           (off Abdon Av.)
Mitcham Gro. B44: K'sdng 4B 68
Mitcheldean Covert
  B14: King H 5F 147
Mitchell Av. WV14: Cose 4D 60
Mitchells Art & Craft Cen. 1C 54
Mitchel Rd. DY6: K'wfrd 5D 92
Mitford Dr. B92: Sol 6H 137
Mitre Cl. WV11: Ess 4A 18
  WV12: W'hall 2D 30
Mitre Ct. B74: S Cold 5A 54
Mitre Fold WV1: Wolv 2A 170 (1G 43)

Mitre Rd. DY9: Lye 6A 110
  WS6: C Hay 3C 6
Mitten Av. B45: Fran 6F 143
Mitton Rd. B20: Hand 5A 82
Moatbrook Av. WV8: Cod 3E 13
Moatbrook La. WV8: Cod 2C 12
Moat Coppice B32: Bart G 4H 129
Moat Cft. B37: F'bri 1C 122
  B76: Walm 6F 71
Moat Dr. B34: Hodg H 3E 105
  B77: S Cold 2E 113
Moat Farm Dr. B32: Bart G 4G 129
Moat Farm Way WS3: Pels 2E 21
Moatfield Ter. WS10: W'bry 2G 63
Moat Grn. Av. WV11: Wed 2G 29
Moat Ho. B31: Longb 1D 158
Moathouse La. E. WV11: Wed 2F 29
Moathouse La. W. WV11: Wed 2F 29
Moat Ho. Rd. B8: W End 5G 103
Moat La. B5: Birm 6F 5 (2G 117)
  B26: Yard 4C 120
  B91: Sol 1G 151
  WS6: Gt Wyr 3G 7
Moat Mdws. B32: Quin 1C 130
Moatmead Wlk. B36: Hodg H 1C 104
Moat Rd. B68: O'bry 1H 113
  DY4: Tip 6A 62
  WS2: Wals 1H 47
Moatside Cl. WS3: Pels 2E 21
Moat St. WV13: W'hall 1A 46
Moatway, The B38: King Nor 2A 160
Mobberley Rd. WV14: Cose 4C 60
Mob La. WS4: S'fld 5G 21
Mockley Wood Rd. B93: Know 2D 166
Modbury Av. B32: Bart G 4B 130
Moden Cl. DY3: Up Gor 2H 75
Moden Hill DY3: Sed 1G 75
Mogul La. B63: Crad 4C 110
Moilliett Ct. B66: Smeth 3G 99
Moilliett St. B18: Win G 5H 99
Moira Cres. B14: Yard W 3C 148
Moises Hall Rd. WV5: Wom 6H 57
Moland St. B4: Birm 5G 101
Mole St. B11: S'brk 5B 118
Molhay Gdns. B42: Gt Barr 5C 66
Molineux 1A 170 (6G 27)
Molineux All. WV1: Wolv . . .1A 170 (6G 27)
           (not continuous)
Molineux St. WV1: Wolv . . .1B 170 (6G 27)
Mollington Cres. B90: Shir 4A 150
Molyneux Rd. DY2: Neth 1G 111
Monaco Ho. B5: Birm 3F 117
Monarch Dr. WS10: Darl 5F 47
Monarch Dr. DY4: Tip 1C 78
Monarch Ind. Est. B11: Tys 5G 119
Monarchs Ga. B91: Sol 2A 152
Monarch Way DY2: Neth 5E 95
Mona Rd. B23: Erd 2F 85
Monastery Dr. B23: Erd 5C 84
  B91: Sol 1B 150
Monckton Rd. B68: O'bry 4G 113
Moncrieffe Cl. DY2: Dud 1G 95
Moncrieffe St. WS1: Wals 2E 49
Money La. B61: C'wich 4A 156
Monica Rd. B10: Small H 4F 119
Monins Av. DY4: Tip 4A 78
Monk Cl. DY4: Tip 4B 78
Monkgate Dr. B71: W Brom 1A 80
Monk Rd. B8: W End 4H 103
Monks Cl. WV5: Wom 1E 73
Monkseaton Rd. B72: W Grn 3H 69
Monksfield Av. B43: Gt Barr 4H 65
Monkshood M. B23: Erd 6B 68
Monkshood Retreat B38: King Nor . . .1B 160
Monks Kirby Rd. B76: Walm 2D 70
MONKSPATH 3E 165
Monkspath B76: Walm 5D 70
Monkspath Bus. Pk. B90: Shir 1D 164
Monkspath Cl. B90: Shir 2B 164
Monkspath Hall (Park & Ride) 4F 151
Monkspath Hall Rd. B90: M'path 3D 164
  B91: Sol 1F 165
Monkspath Leisure Pk. 2C 164
Monksway B38: King Nor 6D 146
Monkswell Cl. B10: Small H 4D 118
  DY5: Brie H 2H 109
Monkswood Av. B31: N'fld 5G 145

Monkton Rd. B29: W Cas 2E 131
Monmar Ct. WV12: W'hall 4B 30
Monmer Cl. WV13: W'hall 6B 30
Monmer Cl. Ind. Est. WV13: W'hall 6B 30
Monmore Bus. Pk. WV2: Wolv 4B 44
MONMORE GREEN 6D 170 (3A 44)
Monmore Green Stadium 3C 44
Monmore Pk. Ind. Est. WV2: Ett 4B 44
Monmore Rd. WV1: Wolv 3C 44
Monmouth Dr. B71: W Brom 6H 63
  B73: New O, S Cold 2C 68
Monmouth Ho. B33: Kitts G 1A 122
Monmouth Rd. B32: Bart G 5B 130
  B67: Smeth 3C 114
  WS2: Wals 6E 31
Monsal Av. WV10: Wolv 5A 28
Monsaldale Cl. WS8: Clay 1H 21
Monsal Rd. B42: Gt Barr 6E 67
Mons Hill .1D 76
Mons Rd. DY2: Dud 6G 77
Montague Rd. B16: Edg 2A 116
  B21: Hand 1B 100
  B24: Erd 6G 85
  B66: Smeth 6F 99
Montague St. B6: Aston 1B 102
  B9: Birm 1A 118
Montana Av. B42: P Barr 2C 82
Montano Dr. WV10: Bush 3A 28
Monteagle Dr. DY6: K'wfrd 6B 74
Montford Gro. DY3: Sed 6H 59
Montfort Rd. B46: Col 4H 107
  WS2: Wals 5H 47
Montfort Wlk. B32: Bart G 3G 129
Montgomery Cres. DY5: Quar B 4B 110
Montgomery Cft. B11: S'brk 4C 118
Montgomery Rd. WS2: Wals 1E 47
Montgomery St. B11: S'brk 4B 118
Montgomery St. Bus. Cen.
  B11: S'brk 4C 118
Montgomery Wlk. B71: W Brom 3B 80
Montgomery Way B8: Salt 5G 103
Montpelier Rd. B24: Erd 6G 85
Montpellier Gdns. DY1: Dud 5A 76
Montpellier St. B12: Birm 5A 118
Montreal Ho. B5: Edg 4F 117
Montrose Dr. B35: Cas V 4E 87
  DY1: Dud 1C 94
Montsford Cl. B93: Know 3B 166
Monument Av. DY9: W'cte 1A 126
Monument La. B45: Lick 5F 157
  DY3: Sed 4A 60
  DY9: Hag 6H 125
Monument Rd. B16: Birm, Edg 2B 116
           (not continuous)
Monway Bldgs. WS10: W'bry 2E 63
Monway Ind. Est. WS10: W'bry 2E 63
Monway Ter. WS10: W'bry 2E 63
Monwood Gro. B91: Sol 5D 150
Monyhull Hall Rd.
  B30: King Nor 5D 146
Moodyscroft Rd. B33: Kitts G 6G 105
Moons La. WS6: C Hay 3D 6
Moor, The B76: Walm 5E 71
Moor Cen., The DY5: Brie H 6H 93
Moor Ct. B24: Erd 4F 85
Moorcroft WV14: Bils 2A 62
Moorcroft Dr. WS10: W'bry 3C 62
Moorcroft Nine WS10: W'bry 3C 62
Moorcroft Pl. B7: Birm 5A 102
Moorcroft Rd. B13: Mose 2G 133
Moordown Av. B92: Olton 3E 137
Moore Cl. B74: Four O 3F 37
  WV6: Pert 5F 25
Moore Ct. B92: Olton 4C 136
Moore Cres. B68: O'bry 6A 98
Moorend Av.
  B37: Chel W, F'bri, Mars G 3B 122
Moor End La. B24: Erd 3G 85
Moore Rd. WV12: W'hall 1D 30
Moore's Row B5: Birm 6H 5 (2H 117)
Moore St. WV1: Wolv 2B 44
Moorfield Av. B93: Know 3A 166
Moorfield Dr. B63: Hale 5H 111
  B73: Bold 5F 69
Moorfield Rd. B34: S End 3E 105
  WV2: Wolv 4G 43

Moorfields Cl.—Mucklow Office Pk.

Moorfields Cl. WS9: A'rdge 2C **34**
Moorfoot Av. B63: Hale 4E **127**
MOOR GREEN 4E **133**
Moor Grn. La. B13: Mose 4E **133**
Moor Hall Dr. B75: R'ley 3A **54**
Moor Hall Golf Course 2B **54**
Moor Hall Way B75: R'ley 2B **54**
Moorhen Cl. WS8: Bwnhls 6A **10**
Moorhills Cft. B90: Shir 1H **163**
Moor Ho. *B14: King H 5E **147***
(off Druids La.)
Moorings, The B18: Win G 4B **100**
B19: Birm 1D **4** (5G **101**)
B69: O'bry 1E **97**
DY5: Brie H 5B **94**
WV9: Pend 5D **14**
Moorland Av. WV10: Oxl 3G **27**
Moorland Rd. B16: Edg 2H **115**
WS3: Blox 1G **31**
Moorlands, The B74: Four O 3F **53**
Moorlands Cl. B75: S Cold 5D **54**
Moorlands Ct. B65: Row R 5D **96**
Moorlands Dr. B90: Shir 4A **150**
Moorlands Rd. B71: W Brom 4A **64**
Moor La. B6: Witt 1H **83**
B65: Row R 1A **112**
Moor La. Ind. Est. B6: Witt 3A **84**
Moor La. Trad. Est. B6: Witt 3H **83**
Moor Leasow B31: N'fld 5G **145**
Moor Mdw. Rd. B75: S Cold 4B **54**
Moor Pk. WS3: Blox 4H **19**
WV6: Pert 4D **24**
Moorpark Rd. B31: Longb 6E **145**
Moor Pool Av. B17: Harb 5G **115**
Moorpool Ter. B17: Harb 5G **115**
Moors, The B36: Hodg H 1D **104**
Moors Cft. B32: Bart G 4H **129**
Moorside Gdns. WS2: Wals 6H **31**
Moorside Rd. B14: Yard W 3C **148**
Moor's La. B31: N'fld 5C **130**
Moors Mill La. DY4: Tip 6D **62**
Moorsom St. B6: Aston 4G **101**
MOOR STREET 3G **129**
Moor St. B5: Birm 5F **5**
B70: W Brom 5A **80**
DY5: Brie H 6E **93**
WS10: W'bry 3H **63**
Moor St. Ind. Est. DY5: Brie H 1G **109**
(Bague Wlk.)
DY5: Brie H 6E **93**
(Leys Rd.)
Moor St. Queensway
B4: Birm 4F **5** (1G **117**)
Moor St. Sth. WV2: Wolv 4G **43**
Moor Street Station (Rail) 4F **5** (1G **117**)
Moorville Wlk. B11: S'brk 4A **118**
Morar Cl. B35: Cas V 3G **87**
Moray Cl. B62: B'hth 3E **113**
Morcom Rd. B11: Tys 6E **119**
Mordaunt Dr. B75: R'ley 1C **54**
Morden Rd. B33: Stech 6B **104**
Moreland Cft. B76: Walm 1F **87**
Morelands, The B31: N'fld 6F **145**
Morestead Av. B26: Sheld 6G **121**
Moreton Av. B43: Gt Barr 2E **67**
WV4: Ett 1A **60**
Moreton Cl. B25: Yard 4H **119**
B32: Harb 6D **114**
(not continuous)
DY4: Tip 3B **62**
Moreton Rd. B90: Shir 5A **150**
WV10: Bush 6H **15**
Moreton St. B1: Birm 5D **100**
Morford Rd. WS9: A'rdge 2C **34**
Morgan Cl. B64: Old H 3G **111**
B69: O'bry 1D **96**
WV12: W'hall 5B **30**
Morgan Ct. B24: Erd 1A **86**
Morgan Dr. WV14: Cose 5D **60**
Morgan Gro. B36: Cas B 6B **88**
Morgans Bus. Pk. WS11: Nort C 1D **8**
Morgrove Av. B93: Know 3B **166**
Morjon Dr. B43: Gt Barr 3B **66**
Morland Pl. B31: N'fld 6D **144**
Morland Rd. B43: Gt Barr 1E **67**
Morley Cl. B47: Wyt 5C **162**
Morley Gro. WV6: Wolv 5G **27**
Morley Rd. B8: W End 3H **103**
Morlich Ri. DY5: Brie H 3F **109**
Morning Pines DY8: Stourb 1C **124**
Morningside B73: S Cold 5H **53**
Mornington Ct. B46: Col 2H **107**
Mornington Ind. Pk. B66: Smeth 2F **99**
Mornington Rd. B66: Smeth 2F **99**
Morris Av. WS2: Wals 1E **47**
Morris Cl. B27: A Grn 1B **136**
Morris Ct. DY5: Brie H 2F **109**
Morris Cft. B36: Cas B 6A **88**
Morris Fld. Cft. B28: Hall G 3E **149**
Morrison Av. WV10: Bush 1H **27**
Morrison Rd. DY4: Tip 3C **78**
Morris Rd. B8: W End 3H **103**
Morris St. B70: W Brom 6A **80**
Morris Way B37: Mars G 6F **123**
B40: Mars G 6F **123**
Mortimers Cl. B14: King H 6B **148**
Morton Rd. DY5: Quar B 4H **109**
Morvale Gdns. DY9: Lye 6A **110**
Morvale St. DY9: Lye 6A **110**
Morven Rd. B73: S Cold 3F **69**
Morville Cl. B93: Dorr 6H **165**
Morville Cft. WV14: Bils 1D **60**
Morville Rd. DY2: Neth 5F **95**
Morville St. B16: Birm 2C **116**
(not continuous)
Mosborough Cres. B19: Birm 4E **101**
Mosedale Dr. WV11: Wed 4H **29**
Mosedale Way B15: Birm 3F **117**
MOSELEY
B13 2H **133**
WV1 1E **45**
WV10 3B **16**
Moseley Bog Nature Reserve 4C **134**
Moseley Ct. B13: Mose 3B **134**
WV11: Ess 4H **17**
WV13: W'hall 2F **45**
Moseley Dovecote 2G **133**
Moseley Dr. B37: Mars G 3B **122**
Moseley Ga. B13: Mose 2H **133**
Moseley Golf Course 5A **134**
Moseley Old Hall 2C **16**
Moseley Old Hall La. WV10: F'stne 2C **16**
Moseley Rd. B12: Bal H 6H **117**
B12: Birm 3A **118**
WV10: Bush 2B **16**
WV13: W'hall 2F **45**
WV14: Bils 2F **45**
Moseley Road Swimming Pool 6H **117**
Moseley RUFC 6B **134**
Moseley School Health & Fitness Cen.
3C **134**
Moseley St. B5: Birm 2H **117**
B12: Birm 2H **117**
DY4: Tip 6C **62**
WV10: Wolv 5G **27**
Moss Cl. WS4: Wals 6E **33**
WS9: A'rdge 4C **34**
Mossdale Way DY3: Sed 6A **60**
Moss Dr. B72: W Grn 2A **70**
Mossfield Rd. B14: King H 6G **133**
Moss Gdns. WV14: Cose 2D **60**
Moss Gro. B14: King H 1F **147**
DY6: K'wfrd 2B **92**
Moss Ho. Cl. B15: Birm 2D **116**
Mossley Cl. WS3: Blox 6F **19**
Mossley La. WS3: Blox 5F **19**
Mossvale Cl. B64: Old H 2H **111**
Mossvale Gro. B8: Salt 4F **103**
Moss Way B74: S'tly 4H **51**
Mostyn Cres. B71: W Brom 6H **63**
Mostyn Rd. B16: Edg 1B **116**
B21: Hand 1B **100**
Mostyn St. WV1: Wolv 5F **27**
Mother Teresa Ho. *B70: W Brom 4H **79***
(off Dartmouth St.)
Motorway Trad. Est. B6: Birm 4H **101**
Mott Cl. DY4: Tip 5C **62**
Mottram Cl. B70: W Brom 5G **79**
Mottrams Cl. B72: W Grn 3A **70**
Mott St. B19: Birm 1C **4** (5F **101**)
Mott St. Ind. Est. B19: Birm 5F **101**
Motts Way B46: Col 4H **107**
Mounds, The B38: King Nor 1A **160**
Moundsley Gro. B14: King H 4A **148**
Moundsley Ho. B14: King H 5G **147**
Mount, The B23: Erd 6D **84**
B64: Old H 2A **112**
B76: Curd 1E **89**
Mountain Ash Dr. DY9: Pedm 3G **125**
Mountain Ash Rd. WS8: Clay 2A **22**
Mount Av. DY5: Brie H 5G **93**
Mountbatten Cl. B70: W Brom 5D **80**
Mountbatten Rd. WS2: Wals 1F **47**
Mount Cl. B13: Mose 1H **133**
DY3: Gorn 5G **75**
WS6: C Hay 3E **7**
WV5: Wom 6G **57**
Mount Ct. WV6: Tett 1H **41**
Mount Dr. WV5: Wom 6G **57**
Mountfield Cl. B14: King H 5A **148**
Mountford Cl. B65: Row R 6C **96**
Mountford Cres. WS9: A'rdge 1E **35**
Mountford Dr. B75: Four O 3H **53**
Mountford Ho. *B70: W Brom 6C **80***
(off Glover St.)
Mountford La. WV14: Bils 4F **45**
Mountford Rd. B90: Shir 6D **148**
Mountford St. B11: S'hll 6D **118**
Mount Gdns. WV8: Cod 3F **13**
Mountjoy Cres. B92: Sol 2G **137**
Mount La. DY3: Gorn 5G **75**
Mt. Pleasant B10: Small H 2B **118**
B14: King H 4H **133**
DY5: Quar B 2A **110**
DY6: K'wfrd 4H **91**
WS6: C Hay 3D **6**
WV14: Bils 5G **45**
Mt. Pleasant Av. B21: Hand 6A **82**
WV5: Wom 6F **57**
Mt. Pleasant Ct. B10: Small H 2B **118**
Mt. Pleasant St. B70: W Brom 5A **80**
WV14: Cose 5D **60**
Mountrath St. WS1: Wals 2C **48**
Mount Rd. B21: Hand 1H **99**
B65: Row R 6E **97**
B69: Tiv 1C **96**
DY8: Stourb 6F **109**
DY8: Word 1B **108**
WS3: Pels 3E **21**
WV4: Ett 3B **60**
WV4: Penn 6E **43**
WV5: Wom 6G **57**
WV6: Tett 1G **41**
WV13: W'hall 3G **45**
Mounts Rd. WS10: W'bry 3F **63**
Mount St. B7: Nech 3C **102**
B63: Hale 3A **128**
DY4: Tip 1C **78**
DY8: Stourb 6E **109**
WS1: Wals 3C **48**
Mount St. Bus. Cen. B7: Nech 3C **102**
Mount St. Bus. Pk. B7: Nech 2D **102**
Mounts Way B7: Nech 2C **102**
Mount Vw. B75: S Cold 1C **70**
Mountwood Covert WV6: Tett 6H **25**
Mousehall Farm Rd. DY5: Quar B 3H **109**
Mouse Hill WS3: Pels 4D **20**
MOUSESWEET 6G **95**
Mousesweet Brook Nature Reserve
2D **110**
Mousesweet Cl. DY2: Neth 5G **95**
Mousesweet La. DY2: Neth 6G **95**
Mousesweet Wlk. B64: Crad H 3D **110**
Mowbray Cl. B45: Fran 5G **143**
Mowbray St. B5: Birm 3G **117**
Mowe Cft. B37: Mars G 4C **122**
Moxhull Cl. WV12: W'hall 6C **18**
Moxhull Dr. B76: Walm 5C **70**
Moxhull Gdns. WV12: W'hall 6C **18**
Moxhull Rd. B37: K'hrst 4C **106**
MOXLEY 1B **62**
Moxley Ct. WS10: Mox 1A **62**
Moxley Ind. Cen. WS10: Mox 1C **62**
Moxley Rd. WS10: Darl 1B **62**
Moyle Dr. B63: Crad 4D **110**
Moyses Cft. B66: Smeth 1E **99**
Muchall Rd. WV4: Penn 6E **43**
MUCKLEY CORNER 4H **11**
Mucklow Hill B62: Hale 1C **128**
Mucklow Hill Trad. Est. B62: Hale 6C **112**
Mucklow Office Pk. B62: Hale 5D **112**

Muirfield Cl. WS3: Blox 4G **19**
Muirfield Cres. B69: Tiv 2A **96**
Muirfield Gdns. B38: King Nor 6H **145**
Muirhead Ho. B5: Edg 5E **117**
Muirville Cl. DY8: Word 6B **92**
Mulberry Ct. B44: K'sdng 3C **68**
   B90: Shir 2B **164**
Mulberry Dr. B13: Mose 4B **134**
Mulberry Grn. DY1: Dud 2B **76**
Mulberry Pl. WS3: Blox 6F **19**
Mulberry Rd. B30: B'vlle 2G **145**
   WS3: Blox 6F **19**
Mulberry Wlk. B74: S'tly 3G **51**
Mull Cl. B45: Fran 6E **143**
Mull Cft. B36: Cas B 2C **106**
Mullein B74: Four O 4F **37**
Mullensgrove Rd. B37: K'hrst 4C **106**
Mullett Rd. WV11: Wed 2D **28**
Mullett St. DY5: P'ntt 4F **93**
Mulliners Cl. B37: Chel W 1E **123**
Mullion Cft. B38: King Nor 6A **146**
Mullion Dr. WV14: Bils 3B **62**
Mulroy Rd. B74: S Cold 5H **53**
Mulwych Rd. B33: Kitts G 6A **106**
Munslow Gro. B31: Longb 1D **158**
Muntz Ho. B16: Edg 2C **116**
Muntz St. B10: Small H 3D **118**
Murcroft Rd. DY9: W'cte 4H **125**
Murdock Dr. DY6: K'wfrd 2A **92**
Murdock Rd. WV14: Bils 5A **46**
Murdock Ct. WV12: W'hall 2D **30**
      (off Huntington Rd.)
Murdock Gro. B21: Hand 2A **100**
Murdock Pl. B66: Smeth 5F **99**
      (off Corbett St.)
Murdock Rd. B21: Hand 1A **100**
   B66: Smeth 3H **99**
Murdock Way WS2: Wals 3F **31**
Murray Ct. B73: S Cold 2G **69**
Murrell Cl. B5: Edg 4F **117**
Musborough Cl. B36: Cas B 6G **87**
Muscott Gro. B17: Harb 6F **115**
Muscovy Rd. B23: Erd 4C **84**
Museum of the Jewellery Quarter ...4E **101**
      (off Vyse St.)
Musgrave Cl. B76: Walm 2C **70**
Musgrave Rd. B18: Hock 3B **100**
MUSHROOM GREEN 2D **110**
Mushroom Grn. DY2: Neth 2D **110**
Mushroom Hall Rd. B68: O'bry 4H **97**
Musk La. DY3: Lwr G 4F **75**
Musk La. Trad. Est. DY3: Lwr G ...4G **75**
Musk La. W. DY3: Lwr G 4F **75**
Musson Cl. B37: Mars G 3D **122**
Muswell Cl. B91: Sol 2H **151**
Muxloe Cl. WS3: Blox 4G **19**
Myatt Av. WS9: A'rdge 4B **34**
   WV2: Ett 5A **44**
Myatt Cl. WV2: Ett 5A **44**
Myatt Way WS9: A'rdge 4B **34**
Myddleton St. B18: Hock 5C **100**
Myles Ct. DY5: Brie H 5H **93**
Mynors Cres. B47: H'wd 4A **162**
Myring Dr. B75: S Cold 5D **54**
Myrtle Av. B12: Bal H 6A **118**
   B14: King H 5H **147**
Myrtle Cl. WV12: W'hall 2E **31**
Myrtle Glade WS11: Gt Wyr 1F **7**
Myrtle Gro. B19: Loz 1E **101**
   WV3: Wolv 5C **42**
Myrtle Pl. B29: S Oak 3D **132**
Myrtle Rd. DY1: Dud 4D **76**
Myrtle St. WV2: Ett 5B **44**
Myrtle Ter. DY4: Tip 3B **62**
Myton Dr. B90: Shir 5D **148**
Mytton Cl. DY2: Dud 6G **77**
Mytton Gro. DY4: Tip 2G **77**
Mytton Rd. B30: B'vlle 2G **145**
   B46: Wat O 4C **88**
Myvod Rd. WS10: W'bry 6G **47**

N

Naden Rd. B19: Hock 3D **100**
Nadin Rd. B73: W Grn 5G **69**
Nafford Gro. B14: King H 5H **147**

Nagersfield Rd. DY5: Brie H 6E **93**
Nailers Cl. B32: Bart G 3F **129**
Nailers Row WV5: Wom 2F **73**
Nailors Fold WV14: Cose 3F **61**
Nailstone Cres. B27: A Grn 5A **136**
Nairn Cl. B28: Hall G 2F **149**
Nairn Rd. WS3: Blox 3G **19**
Nally Dr. WV14: Cose 3C **60**
Nanaimo Way DY6: K'wfrd 5E **93**
Nansen Rd. B8: Salt 4E **103**
   B11: S'hll 2C **134**
Nantmel Gro. B32: Bart G 5A **130**
Naomi Way WS9: Wals W 3D **22**
Napier Dr. DY4: Tip 1C **78**
Napier Rd. WS2: Wals 4G **31**
   WV2: Wolv 4H **43**
Napton Gro. B29: W Cas 3D **130**
Narel Sharpe Cl. B66: Smeth 2B **98**
Narraway Gro. DY4: Tip 5D **62**
Narrowboat Way DY2: Dud 5C **94**
   DY5: Brie H 5C **94**
Narrow La. B62: B'hth 3E **113**
   WS2: Wals 4H **47**
   WS8: Bwnhls 5B **10**
Naseby Dr. B63: Hale 3F **127**
Naseby Rd. B8: Salt 4F **103**
   B91: Sol 1F **151**
Nash Av. WV6: Pert 6E **25**
Nash Cl. B65: B'hth 2C **112**
Nash Cft. B37: Mars G 3D **122**
Nash Ho. B15: Birm 3F **117**
Nash Sq. B42: P Barr 3F **83**
Nash Wlk. B66: Smeth 4G **99**
      (off Windmill La.)
Nately Gro. B29: S Oak 3G **131**
Nathan Cl. B75: S Cold 3H **53**
National Exhibition Cen. 6F **123**
National Indoor Arena 4A **4** (1D **116**)
National Motorcycle Mus. 3A **140**
National Sea Life Cen. 4A **4** (1D **116**)
Naunton Cl. B29: W Cas 6E **131**
Naunton Rd. WS2: Wals 6G **31**
Navenby Cl. B90: Shir 4C **148**
Navigation Dr. B30: King Nor 4F **147**
   DY5: Brie H 5C **94**
Navigation La. B71: W Brom 3D **64**
   WS10: W'bry 3D **64**
Navigation Point DY4: Tip 1E **62**
Navigation Rdbt. DY4: Tip 1E **79**
Navigation St. B2: Birm 5D **4** (1F **117**)
   B5: Birm 5C **4** (1F **117**)
   WS2: Wals 1B **48**
   WV1: Wolv 2A **44**
Navigation Way B18: Win G 4B **100**
   B70: W Brom 5F **79**
Navigators Rd. B27: A Grn 2B **136**
Nayland Cft. B28: Hall G 2G **149**
Naylors Gro. DY3: Up Gor 3A **76**
NEACHELL 5F **29**
Neachells Ct. WV13: W'hall 2G **45**
Neachells La. WV11: Wed 4F **29**
   WV13: W'hall 1F **45**
Neachells La. Ind. Est. WV11: Wed ..5F **29**
Neachless Av. WV5: Wom 2G **73**
Neachley Gro. B33: Stech 5D **104**
Neale Ho. B70: W Brom 6B **80**
Neale St. WS2: Wals 1A **48**
Near High Dr. DY4: Tip 2B **78**
Nearhill Rd. B38: King Nor 1G **159**
Near Lands Cl. B32: Quin 1H **129**
Nearmoor Rd. B34: S End 3H **105**
Near Oak Ho. B32: Bart G 5B **130**
Neasden Gro. B44: K'sdng 5B **68**
Neath Rd. WS3: Blox 5F **19**
Neath Way WS3: Sed 1C **76**
   WS3: Blox 5F **19**
Nebsworth Cl. B90: Shir 2B **150**
NECHELLS 2C **102**
Nechells Bus. Cen. B7: Nech 5B **102**
Nechells Community Sports Cen. ..4A **102**
NECHELLS GREEN 4A **102**
Nechells Pk. Rd. B7: Nech 3B **102**
Nechell's Parkway B7: Birm 5A **102**
Nechells Pl. B7: Nech 3B **102**
NEC House B40: Nat E C 6F **123**
Needham St. B7: Nech 2C **102**

Needhill Cl. B93: Know 3B **166**
NEEDLERS END 2H **169**
Needlers End La. CV7: Bal C 3F **169**
Needlers End Rd. CV7: Bal C 2F **169**
Needless All. B2: Birm 4D **4** (1F **117**)
Needwood Cl. WV2: Wolv 5F **43**
Needwood Dr. WV4: Ett 1B **60**
Needwood Gro. B71: W Brom 4C **64**
Needwood Ho. B27: A Grn 2B **136**
Nelson Av. WV14: Bils 4E **45**
Nelson Ct. B13: Mose 1H **133**
Nelson Ho. DY4: Tip 6A **62**
Nelson Rd. B6: Aston 6H **83**
   DY1: Dud 6D **76**
Nelson St. B1: Birm 6D **100**
   B69: O'bry 3H **97**
   B71: W Brom 2A **80**
   WV2: Wolv 6B **170** (3G **43**)
   WV13: W'hall 6B **30**
Nene Cl. DY8: Stourb 1E **125**
Nene Way B36: Cas B 1B **106**
Neptune Health Pk. DY4: Tip 2G **77**
Neptune Ind. Est. WV13: W'hall ...3B **46**
Neptune St. DY4: Tip 2G **77**
Nesbit Gro. B9: Bord G 6H **103**
Nesfield Cl. B38: King Nor 6G **145**
Nesfield Gro. B92: H Ard 6B **140**
Nesscliffe Gro. B23: Erd 6D **68**
Nest Comn. WS3: Pels 2D **20**
      (not continuous)
Neston Gro. B33: Stech 1A **120**
Netheravon Cl. B14: King H 5F **147**
Netherby Rd. DY3: Sed 5G **59**
Nethercote Gdns. B90: Shir 4E **149**
Netherdale Cl. B72: W Grn 6A **70**
Netherdale Rd. B14: King H 6A **148**
NETHEREND 4C **110**
Netherend Cl. B63: Crad 4C **110**
Netherend La. B63: Crad 4D **110**
Netherend Sq. B63: Crad 4C **110**
Netherfield Gdns. B27: A Grn 2H **135**
Nethergate DY3: Up Gor 2B **76**
Netherhouse Cl. B44: Gt Barr 2G **67**
      (off Privet Cl.)
Netherstone Gro. B74: Four O 4F **37**
NETHERTON 4E **95**
Netherton Arts Cen. 4F **95**
      (Chapel St.)
Netherton Bus. Pk. DY2: Neth 5F **95**
      (Marlow St.)
   DY2: Neth 6G **95**
Netherton Gro. B33: Kitts G 6H **105**
Netherton Hill DY2: Neth 4E **95**
Netherton Lodge DY2: Neth 4E **95**
Netherwood Cl. B91: Sol 1C **150**
Nethy Dr. WV6: Tett 4H **25**
Netley Gro. B11: Tys 2F **135**
Netley Ho. B32: Harb 6D **114**
Netley Rd. WS3: Blox 5E **19**
Netley Way WS3: Blox 5E **19**
Nettlefolds Way WV14: Bils 6F **45**
Network Pk. B8: Salt 5C **102**
Nevada Way B37: Chel W 2E **123**
Neve Av. WV10: Bush 6B **16**
Neve's Opening WV1: Wolv 1B **44**
Neville Av. WV4: Penn 6H **43**
Neville Rd. B23: Erd 4C **84**
   B36: Cas B 6A **88**
   B90: Shir 6F **149**
Neville Wlk. B35: Cas V 5E **87**
Nevin Gro. B42: P Barr 2E **83**
Nevis Ct. WV3: Wolv 1C **42**
Nevis Gro. WV12: W'hall 6B **18**
Nevison Gro. B43: Gt Barr 1D **66**
Newark Cft. B26: Sheld 5F **121**
Newark Rd. DY2: Neth 1F **111**
   WV12: W'hall 2C **30**
New Art Gallery Walsall, The 1C **48**
Newbank Gro. B9: Bord G 6H **103**
New Bartholomew St.
   B5: Birm 4G **5** (1H **117**)
New Birmingham Rd. B69: Tiv 5H **77**
   DY2: Dud 5H **77**
Newbold Cl. B93: Ben H 4B **166**
Newbold Ct. B63: Hale 2B **128**
Newbold Cft. B7: Birm 4B **102**

NEWBOLDS. WV10: Wolv 3C 28
Newbolds Rd. WV10: Wolv 3C 28
Newbolt Rd. WV14: Bils 5G 45
Newbolt St. WS5: Wals 6C 48
New Bond St. B9: Birm 2B 118
DY2: Dud 1F 95
Newborough Gro. B28: Hall G 3F 149
Newborough Rd. B28: Hall G 3F 149
B90: Shir .3F 149
NEWBRIDGE .5D 26
Newbridge Av. WV6: Wolv 6C 26
Newbridge Cres. WV6: Wolv 5C 26
Newbridge Dr. WV6: Wolv 5C 26
Newbridge Gdns. WV6: Wolv 5C 26
Newbridge M. WV6: Wolv 5D 26
Newbridge Rd. B9: Bord G 3H 119
DY6: W Hth 1A 92
Newbridge St. WV6: Wolv 5D 26
New Bldgs. WV10: Cov H 1G 15
Newburn Cft. B32: Quin 6H 113
Newbury Cl. B62: Hale 2D 128
WS6: Gt Wyr 2F 7
Newbury Ho. B69: O'bry 4D 96
Newbury La. B69: O'bry 3C 96
Newbury Rd. B19: Hock 2G 101
DY8: Word 1A 108
WS11: Nort C 1E 9
WV10: F'hses 5G 15
Newbury Wlk. B65: Row R 3C 96
Newby Gro. B37: F'bri 4D 106
New Canal St. B5: Birm 4G 5 (1H 117)
(not continuous)
New Cannon Pas. B2: Birm 4E 5 (1G 117)
Newcastle Cft. B35: Cas V 4G 87
Newchurch Gdns. B24: Erd 5E 85
New Church Rd. B73: Bold, W Grn 5G 69
New Cole Hall La. B34: Stech 4F 105
New College Cl. WS1: Wals 4E 49
Newcombe Rd. B21: Hand 5H 81
Newcome Cl. B24: Erd 3B 86
Newcomen Cl. WS4: Rus 2F 33
Newcomen Dr. DY4: Tip 4H 77
Newcott Cl. WV9: Pend 5D 14
New Ct. DY5: Brie H 1H 109
(off Chapel St.)
New Coventry Rd. B26: Sheld 6D 120
New Cft. B19: Loz 2G 101
Newcroft Gro. B26: Yard 4C 120
NEW CROSS .4D 28
New Cross Av. WV11: Wed, Wolv 5D 28
New Cross Ind. Est. WV1: Wolv 6C 28
New Cross St. DY4: Tip 2G 77
WS10: Darl .6D 46
New Crown St. DY1: Dud 1D 94
Newdigate Rd. B75: S Cold 6E 55
New Dudley Rd. DY6: W Hth 1A 92
Newells Dr. DY4: Tip 6D 62
Newells Rd. B26: Yard 3E 121
New England B62: B'hth 4E 113
New England Cl. B69: O'bry 6E 79
Newent Cl. WV12: W'hall 6D 30
New Ent. Cen. WV1: Wolv 4C 44
New Ent. Workshops B18: Hock 4C 100
Newent Rd. B31: N'fld 3G 145
Newey Bus. Pk. DY4: Tip 1F 77
Newey Cl. B45: Redn 3G 157
Newey Rd. B28: Hall G 1F 149
WV11: Wed 1A 30
Newey St. DY1: Dud 5C 76
New Farm Rd. DY9: Lye 6G 109
Newfield Cl. B91: Sol 1H 151
WS2: Wals .3A 32
Newfield Cres. B63: Hale 6A 112
Newfield Dr. DY6: K'wfrd 5C 92
Newfield La. B63: Hale 6A 112
Newfield Rd. B69: O'bry 1F 97
New Forest Rd. WS3: Wals 4C 32
New Fosse Way B15: Edg 2A 132
New Gas St. B70: W Brom 2G 79
Newhall Ct. B3: Birm 2A 4 (6E 101)
New Hall Dr. B75: S Cold 1B 70
B76: Walm 2C 70
Newhall Farm Cl. B76: Walm 1B 70
Newhall Hill B1: Birm 2A 4 (6E 101)
Newhall Ho. WS1: Wals 3C 48
(off Newhall St.)
New Hall Lodge B75: S Cold 6D 54

New Hall Pl. WS10: W'bry 2G 63
Newhall Pl. B3: Birm 2A 4
Newhall Rd. B65: Row R 6C 96
Newhall Sq. B3: Birm 2B 4 (6E 101)
Newhall St. B3: Birm 2B 4 (6E 101)
B70: W Brom 5A 80
DY4: Tip 5G 61
WS1: Wals .3C 48
WV13: W'hall 1A 46
New Hall Valley Country Pk. 2B 70
Newhall Wlk. B3: Birm 3B 4 (6E 101)
B72: S Cold 1A 70
Newhampton Arts Cen. 1A 170 (6G 27)
Newhampton Ho. WV1: Wolv 1A 170
New Hampton Lofts B18: Birm 4E 101
Newhampton Rd. E.
WV1: Wolv 1A 170 (6F 27)
Newhampton Rd. W. WV6: Wolv 5D 26
Newhaven Cl. B7: Birm 5A 102
Newhay Cft. B19: Loz 2E 101
New Heath Cl. WV11: Wed 4D 28
New Henry St. B68: O'bry 5G 97
Newhome Way WS3: Blox 1B 32
Newhope Cl. B15: Birm 3F 117
New Hope Rd. B66: Smeth 5G 99
New Horse Rd. WS6: C Hay 2E 7
Newhouse Cft. CV7: Bal C 3H 169
Newhouse Farm Cl. B76: Walm 2D 70
New Ho. Farm Dr. B31: N'fld 1F 145
Newick Av. B74: Lit As 6B 36
Newick Gro. B14: King H 3E 147
Newick St. DY2: Neth 5E 95
New Imperial Cres. B11: Tys 2F 135
Newington Rd. B37: Mars G 3D 122
New Inn Rd. B19: Loz 6F 83
New Inns Cl. B21: Hand 1H 99
New Inns La. B45: Fran, Rub 6E 143
NEW INVENTION 1D 30
New John St. B6: Birm 4G 101
B62: B'hth 2C 112
New John St. W. B19: Birm, Hock 3E 101
New King St. DY2: Dud 6E 77
Newland Cl. WS4: S'fld 5G 21
Newland Ct. B23: Erd 4B 84
Newland Gdns. B64: Crad H 4G 111
Newland Gro. DY2: Dud 2B 94
Newland Rd. B9: Small H 2F 119
Newlands, The B34: S End 2G 105
Newlands Cl. DY9: Hag 6G 125
WV13: W'hall 2A 46
Newlands Dr. B62: B'hth 4E 113
Newlands Grn. B66: Smeth 5E 99
Newlands La. B37: Mars G 5C 122
B76: Curd .2G 89
Newlands Rd. B30: Stir 6D 132
B93: Ben H 5B 166
Newlands Wlk. B68: O'bry 5H 97
(off Jackson St.)
New Landywood La. WV11: Ess 1E 19
New Leasow B76: Walm 6E 71
Newlyn Rd. B31: N'fld 4D 144
B64: Crad H 3F 111
Newman Av. WV4: Ett 1B 60
Newman Coll. Cl. B32: Bart G 5A 130
Newman Ct. B21: Hand 6A 82
Newman Pl. WV14: Bils 4H 45
Newman Rd. B24: Erd 3F 85
DY4: Tip 4C 62
WV10: Bush 6C 16
Newmans Cl. B66: Smeth 5G 99
Newman University College 5A 130
Newman Way B45: Redn 2G 157
Newmarket Cl. WV6: Wolv 4E 27
New Market Rd. WS11: Nort C 1E 9
New Market St. B3: Birm 3C 4 (6F 101)
Newmarket Way B36: Hodg H 1H 103
Newmarsh Rd. B76: Walm 1E 87
New Meadow Cl. B31: N'fld 5F 145
New Meeting St. B4: Birm 4F 5 (1G 117)
B69: O'bry .1G 97
New Mills St. WS1: Wals 4B 48
New Mill St. DY2: Dud 6E 77
Newmore Gdns. WS5: Wals 6G 49
New Moseley Rd. B12: Birm 3A 118
Newnham Gro. B23: Erd 1E 85
Newnham Ho. B36: Cas B 4D 106
Newnham Ri. B90: Shir 4B 150

Newnham Rd. B16: Edg 1G 115
NEW OSCOTT .4C 68
New Oscott Village B23: Erd 5E 69
New Pool Rd. B64: Crad H 3D 110
Newport Rd. B12: Bal H 1A 134
B36: Hodg H 1D 104
Newport St. WS1: Wals 2C 48
WV10: Wolv 5A 28
Newquay Cl. WS5: Wals 4A 50
Newquay Rd. WS5: Wals 4H 49
New Railway St. WV13: W'hall 1B 46
New Rd. B18: Win G 3A 100
B45: Rub .2F 157
B46: Wat O 4D 88
B47: H'wd .1H 161
B63: Hale .1B 128
B91: Sol 4G 151
DY2: Dud, Neth 3E 95
DY3: Swind .4A 72
DY4: Tip 1D 78
DY8: Stourb 6E 109
WS8: Bwnhls 6B 10
WS9: A'rdge 4C 34
WS10: Darl .5D 46
WV6: Wolv .5C 26
WV10: Bush 1D 28
WV13: W'hall 2A 46
New Rowley Rd. DY2: Dud 2G 95
New Shipton Cl. B76: Walm 4D 70
New Spring Gdns. B18: Hock 5C 100
New Spring St. B18: Hock 5C 100
New Spring St. Nth. B18: Hock 4C 100
Newstead Rd. B44: K'sdng 2A 68
New St. B2: Birm 4D 4 (1F 117)
B23: Erd 1D 84
B36: Cas B 1F 105
B45: Fran .5F 143
B66: Smeth .3E 99
B70: W Brom 6G 63
(Adelaide Av.)
B70: W Brom 4B 80
(High St.)
DY1: Dud 6E 77
DY3: Gorn .4G 75
DY4: Tip 2H 77
DY5: Quar B 3C 110
DY6: K'wfrd 5B 92
DY6: W Hth 1A 92
DY8: Stourb 6D 108
DY8: Word 1B 108
WS1: Wals .2D 48
WS3: Blox .6H 19
WS4: Rus 2F 33
WS4: S'fld .6H 21
WS6: Gt Wyr .3G 7
WS10: Darl .5D 46
WS10: W'bry 4F 63
WV2: Ett 5C 44
WV3: Wolv .4B 42
WV4: Ett 6A 44
WV11: Ess .4A 18
WV13: W'hall 2G 45
New St. Nth. B71: W Brom 4B 80
New Street Station (Rail) 5D 4 (1F 117)
New Summer St. B19: Birm 5F 101
New Swan La. B70: W Brom 2G 79
New Swinford Hall DY9: Lye 1G 125
NEWTON 5G 65
Newton Av. B74: S Cold 4H 53
Newton Chambers B2: Birm 4D 4
(off Cannon St.)
Newton Cl. B43: Gt Barr 4G 65
Newton Ct. WV9: Pend 4D 14
Newton Gdns. B43: Gt Barr 5G 65
Newton Gro. B29: S Oak 3B 132
Newton Ho. WV13: W'hall 2B 46
Newton Ind. Est. B9: Bord G 1D 118
Newton Mnr. Cl. B43: Gt Barr 5H 65
Newton Pk. M. B43: Gt Barr 4A 66
Newton Pl. B18: Hock 2B 100
WS2: Wals .3H 31
Newton Rd. B11: S'hll 6B 118
B43: Gt Barr 1C 80
B71: W Brom 1C 80
B93: Know .2D 166
WS2: Wals .4H 31
Newton Sq. B43: Gt Barr 4A 66

Newton St. B4: Birm 2F **5** (6G **101**)
  B71: W Brom 6C **64**
NEW TOWN
  B70 . . . . .3E **79**
  WS8 . . . . .3D **10**
NEWTOWN
  B19 . . . . .3F **101**
  B64 . . . . .2F **111**
  WS6 . . . . .2G **19**
New Town DY5: Brie H 5G **93**
Newtown DY2: Neth 2E **111**
Newtown Dr. B19: Hock 3E **101**
Newtown La. B62: Roms 6C **142**
  B64: Crad H 2F **111**
Newtown Middleway B6: Birm . . .4G **101**
Newtown Pool & Fitness Cen. 3G **101**
NEW TOWN ROW 3G **101**
New Town Row
  B6: Aston, Birm 3G **101**
Newtown Shop. Cen. B19: Hock . . .3G **101**
Newtown St. B64: Crad H 1F **111**
New Village DY2: Neth 2E **111**
New Villas WV11: Wed 4C **28**
New Wood DY7: Stourt 4A **108**
New Wood Cl. DY7: Stourt 3A **108**
New Wood Dr. B31: Longb 6B **144**
New Wood Gro. WS9: Wals W 4C **22**
Ney Ct. DY4: Tip 5H **77**
Niall Cl. B15: Edg 3A **116**
Nicholas Rd. B74: S'tly 3G **51**
Nicholds Cl. WV14: Cose 4D **60**
Nicholls Fold WV11: Wed 4F **29**
Nicholls Rd. DY4: Tip 4G **61**
Nicholls St. B70: W Brom 5C **80**
Nichols Cl. B92: Sol 6B **138**
Nigel Av. B31: N'fld 2E **145**
Nigel Ct. B16: Edg 2A **116**
Nigel Rd. B8: Salt 3E **103**
  DY1: Dud 5C **76**
Nightingale Av. B36: Cas B 1C **106**
Nightingale Cl. B15: Edg 4E **117**
  B23: Erd 6C **68**
Nightingale Cres. DY5: Brie H 4H **109**
  WV12: W'hall 1B **30**
Nightingale Dr. DY4: Tip 2C **78**
Nightingale Gro. B45: Redn 1G **157**
Nightingale Pl. WV9: Pend 3D **14**
  WV14: Bils 5F **45**
Nightjar Gro. B23: Erd 1C **84**
Nighwood Dr. B74: S'tly 4H **51**
Nijon Cl. B21: Hand 6G **81**
Nimmings Cl. B31: Longb 3D **158**
Nimmings Rd. B62: B'hth 3D **112**
Nineacres Dr. B37: F'bri 1C **122**
Nine Elms La. WV10: Wolv 4A **28**
Nine Leasowes B66: Smeth 2C **98**
Nine Locks Ridge DY5: Brie H 1H **109**
Nine Pails Wlk. B70: W Brom 6B **80**
Nineveh Av. B21: Hand 2B **100**
Nineveh Rd. B21: Hand 2A **100**
Ninfield Gdns. B27: A Grn 1H **135**
Ninfield Rd. B27: A Grn 2G **135**
Nith Pl. DY1: Dud 5D **76**
Noah's Ark Apartments DY2: Neth . .5E **95**
Noakes Ct. WS10: Darl 4F **47**
Nobel Way B6: Witt 4G **83**
Nocke Rd. WV11: Wed 6H **17**
Nock St. DY4: Tip 6C **62**
Noddy Pk. WS9: A'rdge 2D **34**
Noddy Pk. Rd. WS9: A'rdge 2D **34**
Noel Av. B12: Bal H 5A **118**
Noele Gordon Gdns. WS1: Wals 3C **48**
Noel Rd. B16: Edg 2B **116**
Nolton Cl. B43: Gt Barr 5H **65**
Nook, The DY5: P'ntt 4F **93**
  WS6: C Hay 4C **6**
Nooklands Cft. B33: Yard 1E **121**
Noose Cres. WV13: W'hall 1G **45**
Noose La. WV13: W'hall 1G **45**
Nora Rd. B11: S'hll 2C **134**
Norbiton Rd. B44: K'sdng 5A **68**
Norbreck Cl. B43: Gt Barr 4H **65**
Norbury Av. WS3: Pels 4D **20**
Norbury Cres. WV4: Ett 1B **60**
Norbury Dr. DY5: Brie H 2H **109**
Norbury Gro. B92: Olton 2E **137**

Norbury Rd. B44: Gt Barr 2H **67**
  B70: W Brom 6G **63**
  WV10: Wolv 3B **28**
  WV14: Bils 5H **45**
Norcombe Gro. B90: M'path 4E **165**
Nordley Rd. WV11: Wed 4E **29**
Nordley Wlk. WV11: Wed 3E **29**
Norfolk Av. B71: W Brom 6B **64**
Norfolk Cl. B30: Stir 1D **146**
Norfolk Ct. B16: Edg 2H **115**
  B29: W Cas 6F **131**
Norfolk Cres. WS9: A'rdge 1D **34**
  WS10: W'bry 1B **64**
Norfolk Gdns. B75: S Cold 3H **53**
Norfolk Gro. WS6: Gt Wyr 4F **7**
Norfolk Ho. B23: Erd 2F **85**
  B30: King Nor 4C **146**
Norfolk New Rd. WS2: Wals 5G **31**
Norfolk Pl. WS2: Wals 4B **32**
Norfolk Rd. B15: Edg 4H **115**
  B23: Erd 2F **85**
  B45: Fran 5F **143**
  B68: O'bry 4H **113**
  B75: S Cold 4H **53**
  DY2: Dud 2C **94**
  DY8: Woll 3B **108**
  WV3: Wolv 3E **43**
Norfolk Twr. B18: Hock 4D **100**
Norgrave Rd. B92: Sol 3G **137**
Norlan Dr. B14: King H 4H **147**
Norland Rd. B27: A Grn 4A **136**
Norley Gro. B13: Mose 6C **134**
Norley Trad. Est. B33: Sheld 2G **121**
Norman Av. B32: Harb 4C **114**
  B23: Erd 2F **85**
Normandy Rd. B20: Hand 6G **83**
Norman Green Athletics Cen. 4E **151**
Norman Rd. B31: N'fld 4F **145**
  B67: Smeth 2B **114**
  WS5: Wals 3G **49**
Norman St. B18: Win G 4A **100**
  DY2: Dud 1F **95**
Norman Ter. B65: Row R 5C **96**
Normanton Av. B26: Sheld 6H **121**
Normanton Twr. B23: Erd 1G **85**
Norma Rose Cl. B66: Smeth 5E **99**
Normid Ct. *B31: N'fld* *3G 145*
(off Bunbury Rd.)
Norrington Gro. B31: N'fld 4A **144**
Norrington Rd. B31: N'fld 4A **144**
Norris Dr. B33: Stech 6D **104**
Norris Rd. B6: Aston 6H **83**
Norris Way B75: S Cold 6B **54**
Northampton St. B18: Birm 5E **101**
Northanger Rd. B27: A Grn 3H **135**
North Av. B40: Nat E C 6G **123**
  WV11: Wed 3E **29**
Northbrook Ct. B90: Shir 2A **150**
Northbrook Rd. B90: Shir 2A **150**
Northbrook St. B16: Birm 5B **100**
Northcote Rd. B33: Stech 5B **104**
Northcote St. WS2: Wals 5B **32**
Northcott Rd. DY2: Neth 5F **95**
  WV14: Bils 1H **61**
North Cres. WV10: F'stne 1D **16**
Northcroft Way B23: Erd 3D **84**
Northdale WV6: Tett 5H **25**
Northdown Rd. B91: Sol 6D **150**
North Dr. B5: Edg 6E **117**
  B20: Hand 1D **100**
  B75: S Cold 5A **54**
NORTHFIELD 4E **145**
Northfield Gro. WV3: Wolv 4A **42**
Northfield Pool & Fitness Cen. 4E **145**
Northfield Rd. B17: Harb 2E **131**
  B30: King Nor 3H **145**
  DY2: Neth 4F **95**
Northfield Station (Rail) 5E **145**
Northfields Way WS8: Clay 1H **21**
North Gate B17: Harb 4G **115**
Northgate B64: Crad H 3F **111**
  WS9: A'rdge 5C **22**
Northgate Cl. DY1: Dud 5D **76**
Northgate Way WS9: A'rdge 1C **34**
North Grn. WV4: Penn 5B **42**
North Holme B9: Bord G 1C **118**

Northland Rd. B90: Shir 6C **150**
Northlands Rd. B13: Mose 4A **134**
Northleach Av. B14: King H 5F **147**
Northleigh Rd. B8: W End 3G **103**
Northmead B33: Yard 1E **121**
Northmoor Ind. Est. DY5: Brie H . . .1H **109**
Northolt Dr. B35: Cas V 4E **87**
Northolt Gro. B42: Gt Barr 4B **66**
North One M. DY3: Sed 4G **59**
North Oval DY3: Up Gor 2A **76**
Northover Cl. WV9: Pend 5E **15**
North Pk. Rd. B23: Erd 3B **84**
North Pathway B17: Harb 4F **115**
North Rd. B17: Harb 5H **115**
  B20: Hand 5G **83**
  B29: S Oak 2B **132**
  DY4: Tip 5B **62**
  WV1: Wolv 5G **27**
North Rd. Halls WV1: Wolv 5G **27**
North Roundhay B33: Kitts G 5E **105**
Northside Bus. Cen. B18: Win G . . .4A **100**
Northside Dr. B74: S'tly 3H **51**
North Solihull Sports Cen. 6C **106**
North Springfield DY3: Sed 4A **60**
North St. B67: Smeth 4D **98**
  DY2: Dud 6F **77**
  DY5: Brie H 1G **109**
  WS2: Wals 5C **32**
  WS10: W'bry 1F **63**
  WV1: Wolv 2B **170** (1G **43**)
(not continuous)
North St. Ind. Est. DY5: Brie H 1G **109**
Northumberland St. B7: Birm 6B **102**
North Vw. Dr. DY5: Brie H 4H **93**
North Wlk. B31: N'fld 6G **145**
North Warwickshire Golf Course . . .5F **141**
Nth. Warwick St. B9: Small H 2D **118**
Northway B40: Nat E C 5H **123**
  DY3: Sed 2G **59**
Nth. Western Arc. B2: Birm . . .3E **5** (6G **101**)
Nth. Western Rd. B66: Smeth 3D **98**
Nth. Western Ter. B18: Hock 2B **100**
Northwick Cres. B91: Sol 6F **151**
Northwood Ct. DY5: Brie H 1H **109**
Northwood Pk. Cl. WV10: Bush 4H **15**
Northwood Pk. Rd. WV10: Bush 4A **16**
Northwood St. B3: Birm 2B **4** (5E **101**)
Northwood Way DY5: Brie H 3F **109**
North Worcestershire Golf Course . .4C **144**
North Yd. B9: Birm 6H **5**
Northycote Farm 4C **16**
Northycote Farm Country Pk. 4C **16**
Northycote La. WV10: Bush 3B **16**
NORTON 2B **124**
Norton Canes Bus. Pk.
  WS11: Nort C 1D **8**
NORTON CANES SERVICE AREA 2E **9**
Norton Cl. B30: King Nor 4F **147**
  B31: N'fld 4E **145**
  B66: Smeth 4G **99**
  WV4: Penn 2A **58**
Norton Ct. B15: Edg 6H **115**
Norton Cres. B9: Bord G 6H **103**
  DY2: Neth 6G **95**
  WV14: Cose 4F **61**
Norton Dr. B47: Wyt 5C **162**
Norton East Rd. WS11: Nort C 1E **9**
Norton Ga. B38: King Nor 6A **146**
Norton Grange WS11: Nort C 1D **8**
Norton Grange Cres.
  WS11: Nort C 1D **8**
NORTON GREEN 2D **8**
Norton Grn. La. B93: Know 6E **167**
  WS11: Nort C 1C **8**
Norton Hall La. WS11: Nort C 1B **8**
Norton La. B47: Tid G, Wyt 5C **162**
  B90: Tid G 5C **162**
  B94: Earls 5C **162**
  WS6: Gt Wyr 1G **7**
  WS11: Cann, Nort C 1B **8**
Norton Rd. B46: Col 6H **89**
  DY8: Stourb 4B **124**
  WS3: Pels 1E **21**
Norton St. B18: Hock 4C **100**
Norton Ter. *B30: Stir* *1D 146*
(off Warren Rd.)

Norton Twr. B1: Birm 4A 4
Norton Vw. B14: King H 6F 133
Norton Wlk. B23: Erd 4C 84
Nortune Cl. B38: King Nor 5H 145
Norwich Cft. B37: Mars G 2B 122
Norwich Dr. B17: Harb 3D 114
Norwich Rd. DY2: Neth 1F 111
   WS2: Wals 2H 47
Norwood Av. B64: Crad H 4G 111
Norwood Gro. B19: Hock 2D 100
Norwood Rd. B9: Bord G 1E 119
   DY5: Brie H 6G 93
Nottingham Dr. WV12: W'hall 2C 30
Nottingham New Rd.
   WS2: Wals 4G 31
Nottingham Way DY5: Quar B 1B 110
Nova Ct. B43: Gt Barr 4D 66
Nova Scotia St. B4: Birm ...3G 5 (6H 101)
Nowell St. WS10: Darl 6E 47
Nugent Cl. B6: Aston 2G 101
Nugent Gro. B90: Ches G 5B 164
Number 9 The Gallery 5A 4
Nursery, The B29: S Oak 4C 132
Nursery Av. B12: Bal H 6H 117
   WS9: A'rdge 4D 34
Nursery Cl. B30: King Nor 2B 146
Nursery Dr. B20: Hand 6C 82
   B30: King Nor 2B 146
   WV5: Wom 3F 73
Nursery Gdns. B90: Maj G 1E 163
   DY8: Word 2D 108
   WV8: Cod 3F 13
Nursery La. B74: Four O 1G 53
Nursery Rd. B15: Edg 5H 115
   B19: Loz 3D 100
   WS3: Blox 1H 31
Nursery St. WV1: Wolv 1B 170 (6G 27)
Nursery Vw. Cl. WS9: A'rdge 1G 51
Nursery Wlk. WV6: Tett 5B 26
NURTON 6A 24
Nurton Bank WV6: Patt 6A 24
Nutbush Dr. B31: N'fld 1B 144
Nutfield Wlk. B32: Harb 6D 114
Nutgrove Cl. B14: King H 6H 133
Nuthatch Dr. DY5: Brie H 4G 109
Nuthurst B75: S Cold 1F 71
Nuthurst Dr. WS11: Cann 1F 7
Nuthurst Gro. B14: King H 5H 147
   B93: Ben H 5C 166
Nuthurst Rd. B31: Longb 3D 158
Nutley Dr. DY4: Tip 5D 62
Nutmeg Gro. WS1: Wals 1E 49
Nutmeg Wlk. B29: W Cas 1E 145
Nuttall Gro. B21: Hand 2G 99

O

Oak Av. B12: Bal H 6A 118
   B70: W Brom 4H 79
   WS2: Wals 6E 31
   WS6: Gt Wyr 4G 7
Oak Bank B18: Hock 3C 100
Oak Barn Rd. B62: B'hth 3E 113
Oak Cl. B17: Harb 5E 115
   DY4: Tip 4A 62
Oak Cotts. B7: Birm 6B 102
Oak Ct. B45: Redn 2A 158
   B63: Hale 3H 127
   B66: Smeth 1A 98
   DY8: Stourb 1E 125
   WS5: Wals 1E 65
Oak Cres. B69: Tiv 6B 78
   WS3: Blox 3B 32
Oak Cft. B37: F'bri 6B 106
Oakcroft Rd. B13: Mose 6B 134
Oakdale Cl. B68: O'bry 1G 113
   DY5: P'ntt 2E 93
Oakdale Rd. B36: Hodg H 1C 104
   B68: O'bry 1G 113
Oakdale Trad. Est.
   DY6: K'wfrd 6B 74
Oakdene Cl. WS6: C Hay 3D 6
Oak Dr. B23: Erd 6C 68
   WV5: Seis 3A 56
OAKEN 5D 12
Oaken Covert WV8: Cod 5E 13

Oaken Dr. B91: Sol 2D 150
   WV8: Cod, Oaken 5D 12
   WV12: W'hall 2E 31
Oaken Grange WS6: Gt Wyr 4F 7
Oaken Gro. WV8: Cod 5E 13
Oakenhayes Cres. B76: Min 2G 87
   WS8: Bwnhls 4B 10
Oakenhayes Dr.
   WS8: Bwnhls 4B 10
Oaken La. WV8: Oaken 4C 12
Oaken Lanes WV8: Cod 4E 13
OAKEN LAWN 4A 12
Oaken Pk. WV8: Cod 5G 13
Oakenshaw Rd. B90: Shir 6B 150
Oakeswell St. WS10: W'bry 2G 63
Oakeywell St. DY2: Dud 6F 77
OAKFARM 6C 74
Oak Farm Cl. B76: Walm 6E 71
Oak Farm Rd. B30: B'ville 2H 145
Oakfield Av. B11: S'brk 5C 118
   B12: Bal H 5A 118
   B21: Hand 2H 99
   DY1: Dud 6D 60
   DY6: K'wfrd 4C 92
Oakfield Cl. B66: Smeth 3G 99
   DY8: Word 2D 108
Oakfield Ct. DY5: Brie H 1H 109
   (off The Promenade)
Oakfield Dr. B45: Coft H 5B 158
   WS3: Pels 2F 21
Oakfield Rd. B12: Bal H 6G 117
   B24: Erd 4F 85
   B29: S Oak 2C 132
   B66: Smeth 3G 99
   DY8: Word 2E 109
   DY9: W'cte 3B 126
   WV8: Bilb 5H 13
Oakfields Way B91: Cath B 2D 152
Oak Grn. DY1: Dud 2C 76
   WV5: Wom 6H 25
Oak Grn. Way B68: O'bry 5G 97
   B69: O'bry 5G 97
Oak Gro. B31: Longb 6C 144
   WV11: Wed 2D 28
Oakhall Dr. B93: Dorr 5B 166
OAKHAM 2B 96
Oakham Av. DY2: Dud 2G 95
Oakham Ct. DY2: Dud 1G 95
Oakham Cres. DY2: Dud 2G 95
Oakham Dr. DY2: Dud 1H 95
Oakham Rd. B17: Harb 4F 115
   B69: Tiv 1G 95
   DY2: Dud 1G 95
Oakham Way B92: Olton 4E 137
Oak Hill WV3: Wolv 3A 42
Oakhill Cl. B17: Harb 3F 115
Oakhill Cres. B27: A Grn 5H 135
Oak Hill Dr. B15: Edg 4A 116
Oakhill Dr. DY5: Brie H 4F 109
Oak Ho. WS6: Gt Wyr 4G 7
Oak House Mus. 5H 79
Oakhurst Rd. B27: A Grn 4H 135
   B72: W Grn 5H 69
Oak Ind. Pk. DY6: K'wfrd 6C 74
Oakington Dr. B35: Cas V 4E 87
Oakland Cl. B91: Sol 3A 152
Oakland Dr. DY3: Gorn 5F 75
Oakland Ho. B74: Four O 5G 37
Oakland Rd. B13: Mose 2A 134
   B21: Hand 1H 99
   (not continuous)
   WS3: Blox 2C 32
Oaklands B31: N'fld 3D 144
   B62: Quin 1G 129
   B76: Curd 1D 88
   WV5: Wom 1E 73
Oaklands, The B37: Mars G 4C 122
   WV3: Wolv 3F 43
Oaklands Av. B17: Harb 6F 115
Oaklands Cft. B76: Walm 6F 71
Oaklands Dr. B20: Hand 5B 82
   B74: S'tly 2H 51
Oaklands Grn. WV14: Bils 3F 45
Oaklands Rd. B74: Four O 3H 53
   WV3: Wolv 3F 43
Oaklands Way B31: Longb 6A 144
   WS3: Pels 4F 21

Oak La. B70: W Brom 4H 79
   B92: Bars 6B 154
   DY6: K'wfrd 6C 74
Oak La. Caravan Pk. DY6: K'wfrd 5C 74
Oaklea Dr. B64: Old H 1H 111
Oakleaf Cl. B32: Bart G 3B 130
Oak Leaf Dr. B13: Mose 2A 134
Oak Leasow B32: Quin 1H 129
Oakleigh B31: N'fld 5G 145
Oakleigh Dr. DY3: Sed 6G 59
   WV8: Bilb 4G 13
Oakleigh Rd. DY8: Stourb 3E 125
Oakleigh Wlk. DY6: K'wfrd 1C 92
Oakleighs DY8: Word 2A 108
Oakleigh Trad. Est. WV14: Cose 3E 61
Oakley Av. DY4: Tip 1A 78
   WS9: A'rdge 4C 34
Oakley Ct. B15: Edg 6A 116
Oakley Gro. WV4: Penn 6B 42
Oakley Ho. B66: Smeth 3G 99
   (off Oakfield Cl.)
Oakley Rd. B10: Small H 4C 118
   (not continuous)
   B30: Stir 2D 146
   WV4: Penn 6B 42
Oak Leys WV3: Wolv 2A 42
Oakley Wood Dr. B91: Sol 3A 152
Oakmeadow Av. B24: Erd 4B 86
Oakmeadow Cl. B33: Kitts G 1H 121
Oakmeadow Way B24: Erd 4B 86
Oakmount Cl. WS3: Pels 4D 20
Oakmount Rd. B74: S'tly 4A 52
Oak Pk. Ct. B74: Four O 6E 37
   (off Walsall Rd.)
Oak Park Leisure Cen. 3B 22
Oak Pk. Rd. DY8: Word 2D 108
Oakridge Cl. WV12: W'hall 5C 30
Oakridge Dr. WS6: C Hay 3F 7
   WV12: W'hall 5C 30
Oakridge Rd. B31: N'fld 5H 145
Oak Ri. B46: Col 4H 107
Oak Rd. B68: O'bry 4H 113
   B70: W Brom 5H 79
   DY1: Dud 4E 77
   DY4: Tip 6G 61
   WS3: Pels 2D 20
   WS4: S'fld 6G 21
   WS9: Wals W 4C 22
   WV13: W'hall 1G 45
Oaks, The B17: Harb 3F 115
   B34: S End 2F 105
   B38: King Nor 2B 160
   B67: Smeth 4D 98
   B72: W Grn 6H 69
   B76: Walm 2E 71
   DY4: Tip 4B 62
   WS3: Blox 6G 19
   WV3: Wolv 1E 43
Oaks Cres. WV3: Wolv 2E 43
Oaks Dr. B75: Four O 1H 53
   WV3: Wolv 1E 43
   WV5: Wom 2G 73
Oakslade Dr. B92: Sol 5A 138
Oak St. B64: Crad H 2F 111
   DY2: Neth 5G 95
   DY5: Quar B 2B 110
   DY6: K'wfrd 4A 92
   WV3: Wolv 2E 43
   WV14: Cose 6D 60
Oak St. Ind. Est. B64: Crad H 2F 111
   (off Newton St.)
Oak St. Trad. Est. DY5: Quar B 2B 110
Oakthorpe Dr. B37: K'hrst 4B 106
Oakthorpe Gdns. B69: Tiv 5A 78
Oak Tree Cl. B93: Ben H 5A 166
Oak Tree Ct. B28: Hall G 2G 149
   B70: W Brom 4H 79
   B92: Olton 1E 137
Oak Tree Cres. B62: Quin 5F 113
Oak Tree Dr. B8: Salt 3D 102
Oak Tree Gdns. B28: Hall G 4E 149
   DY8: Word 2E 109
Oak Tree La. B29: S Oak 4A 132
   B30: B'ville 6A 132
   B47: H'wd 3B 162
Oaktree Ri. WV8: Cod 3E 13

Oaktree Rd. WS10: W'bry 2H 63
Oak Trees B47: H'wd 3H 161
Oak Turn Dr. B38: King Nor 1H 159
Oak Vw. WS2: Wals 6E 31
Oak Wlk., The B31: Longb 6E 145
Oak Way B76: Walm 3D 70
Oakwood Cl. WS9: Wals W 3A 22
    WV11: Ess 4B 18
Oakwood Ct. B63: Hale 1A 128
Oakwood Cres. DY2: Dud 3B 94
Oakwood Cft. B71: W Brom 4B 64
    B91: Sol .6G 151
Oakwood Dr. B14: King H 3F 147
    B74: S'tly 3G 51
Oakwood Pl. B11: S'hll 3E 135
Oakwood Rd. B11: S'hll 2C 134
    B47: H'wd 3A 162
    B67: Smeth 5D 98
    B73: Bold 3E 69
    WS3: Blox 2C 32
Oakwood St. B70: W Brom 2H 79
Oast Ho. B8: W End 5A 104
Oasthouse Cl. DY6: W Hth 2G 91
Oaston Rd. B36: Cas B 1H 105
Oatfield Cl. WS7: Chase 1C 10
Oatfield Ct. *B43: Gt Barr 5G 65*
    (off Hamstead Rd.)
Oatlands Wlk. B14: King H 5E 147
Oatlands Way WV6: Pert 6D 24
Oatmill Cl. WS10: Darl 6E 47
Oban Rd. B92: Olton 4D 136
Oberon Cl. B45: Fran 5G 143
Oberon Dr. B90: Shir 6G 149
Oberon Gro. WS10: Darl 3E 47
Occupation Rd. WS8: Wals W 3C 22
Occupation St. DY1: Dud 5C 76
Ocean Dr. WS10: W'bry 4D 62
Ockam Cft. B31: N'fld 5G 145
OCKER HILL 5C 62
Ocker Hill Rd. DY4: Tip 4B 62
O'Connell Wlk. *WS10: W'bry 2H 61*
    (off Camp St.)
O'Connor Dr. DY4: Tip 4C 62
Octagon Bus. Cen. B6: Aston 4G 101
Oddingley Cl. B23: Erd 4C 84
Oddingley Rd. B31: N'fld 5G 145
Odell Cres. WS3: Blox 2A 32
Odell Pl. B5: Edg 6E 117
Odell Rd. WS3: Blox 2H 31
Odell Way WS3: Blox 2H 31
Odensil Grn. B92: Sol 3F 137
Odeon Cinema
    Birmingham 5E 5 (1G 117)
    Brierley Hill 1A 110
Offa's Dr. WV6: Pert 4E 25
Offenham Covert B38: King Nor 1A 160
Offini Cl. B70: W Brom 5D 80
Offlow M. DY4: Tip 4H 61
Offmoor Rd. B32: Bart G 5H 129
Ogbury Cl. B14: King H 5E 147
Ogley Cres. WS8: Bwnhls 6C 10
Ogley Dr. B75: S Cold 6D 54
Ogley Hay Rd. WS7: Chase 1D 10
    WS8: Bwnhls, Chase 3C 10
Ogley Rd. WS8: Bwnhls 6C 10
O'Hare Ho. WS4: Wals 6D 32
O'Keeffe Cl. B11: S'brk 5B 118
Okehampton Dr. B71: W Brom 1A 80
Okement Dr. WV11: Wed 4D 28
Old Abbey Gdns. B17: Harb 1H 131
Oldacre Cl. B76: Walm 1B 86
Old Acre Dr. B21: Hand 2A 100
Oldacre Rd. B8: O'bry 3G 113
Old Bank Bldgs. *B64: Crad H 2F 111*
    (off Up. High St.)
Old Bank Pl. B72: S Cold 6A 54
Old Bank Top B31: N'fld 5F 145
Old Barn Rd. B30: B'vlle 1H 145
    DY8: Word 2E 109
Old Beeches B23: Erd 5C 68
Old Bell Rd. B23: Erd 1H 85
Oldberrow Cl. B90: M'path 3E 165
Old Birchills WS2: Wals 6A 32
Old Birmingham Rd.
    B45: Lick, Marlb 6F 157
Old Bridge St. B19: Hock 3E 101
Old Bridge Wlk. B65: Row R 4H 95

Old Bromford La. B8: W End 2H 103
Old Brookside B33: Stech 1C 120
Old Buffery Gdns. DY2: Dud 1F 95
OLDBURY 1G 97
OLDBURY GREEN 2F 97
Oldbury Grn. Retail Pk.
    B69: O'bry 1F 97
Oldbury Leisure Cen. 2E 97
Oldbury Pk. B69: O'bry 3H 97
Oldbury Ringway B69: O'bry 1F 97
Oldbury Rd. B65: Row R 1D 112
    B66: Smeth 2A 98
    B70: W Brom 4E 79
Oldbury Rd. Ind. Est. B66: Smeth . . .2B 98
    B70: W Brom 5F 79
Oldbury St. WS10: W'bry 2H 63
Old Bush St. DY5: Brie H 6A 94
Old Bush Trad. Est. DY5: Brie H 6A 94
Old Camp Hill B12: S'brk 3A 118
Old Canal Wlk. DY4: Tip 2B 78
Old Castle Gro. WS8: Bwnhls 3B 10
Old Chapel, The B3: Birm 2C 4 (6F 101)
Old Chapel Rd. B67: Smeth 6D 98
Old Chapel Wlk. B68: O'bry 5G 97
Old Church Av. B17: Harb 6G 115
Old Church Ct. B17: Harb 6F 115
Old Church Grn. B33: Stech 1C 120
Old Church Rd. B17: Harb 6F 115
    B46: Wat O 4D 88
Old College Dr. WS10: W'bry 4G 63
Old College Rd. B33: Sheld 3F 121
Old Court Cft. B9: Bord G 2C 118
Old Court House, The *DY1: Dud 6E 77*
    (off Priory St.)
Old Croft La. B34: S End 1F 105
    B36: Cas B 1F 105
Old Cross St. B4: Birm 2G 5
Old Cross St. DY4: Tip 2G 77
Old Crown Cl. B32: Bart G 4H 129
Old Damson La. B92: Sol 3B 138
Old Dickens Heath Rd.
    B90: Dic H 4G 163
Old Edwardians Sports Club 1A 150
Olde Hall La. WS6: Gt Wyr 1F 7
Olde Hall Rd. WV10: F'stne 1E 17
Old End La. WV14: Cose 6E 61
OLD FALLINGS 1B 28
Old Fallings Cres. WV10: Bush 2A 28
Old Fallings La. WV10: Bush 6B 16
Old Falls Cl. WS6: C Hay 2D 6
Old Farm Dr. WV8: Bilb 3G 13
Old Farm Gro. B14: Yard W 2D 148
Old Farm Mdw. WV3: Wolv 3A 42
Old Farm Rd. B33: Stech 5C 104
Old Fire Station, The B17: Harb 5H 115
Old Flour Mills B70: W Brom 5A 80
Old Fordrove B76: Walm 2B 70
Old Forest Way B34: S End 3F 105
Old Forge Cl. WS1: Wals 3D 48
Old Forge Trad. Est. DY9: Lye 5A 110
Old Grange Rd. B11: S'hll 1C 134
Old Green La. B93: Know 6B 168
Old Gro. Gdns. DY9: W'cte 2H 125
Old Hall Cl. DY8: Amb 3E 109
Old Hall Gdns. B90: M'path 3D 164
Old Hall Ind. Est. WS3: Blox 1A 32
Old Hall La. WS9: A'rdge 6D 50
Old Hall St. WV1: Wolv 4C 170 (2H 43)
Old Ham La. DY9: Pedm 3G 125
Old Hampton La. WV10: Bush 5D 16
Old Hawne La. B63: Hale 6A 112
Old Heath Cres. WV1: Wolv 2C 44
Old Heath Rd. WV1: Wolv 2C 44
Old High St. DY5: Quar B 2B 110
OLD HILL 1H 111
Old Hill WV6: Tett 4B 26
Old Hill By-Pass B64: Old H 1H 111
Old Hill Station (Rail) 3A 112
Old Hobicus La. B68: O'bry 4H 97
Old Horns Cres. B43: Gt Barr 3E 67
Oldhouse Farm Cl. B28: Hall G 1F 149
Old House La. B62: Roms 6B 142

Oldington Gro. B91: Sol 1F 165
Old Kingsbury Rd. B76: Min 2G 87
Oldknow Rd. B10: Small H 5E 119
Old Landywood La.
    WV11: Ess 1C 18
Old La. WS3: Blox 2A 32
    WV6: Tett .1F 41
Old Langley Hall B75: S Cold 1F 71
Old Level Way DY2: Neth 5F 95
Old Lime Gdns. B38: King Nor 1A 160
Old Lindens Cl. B74: S'tly 4G 51
Old Lode La. B92: Sol 1F 137
Old Manor, The WV6: Tett 4B 26
Old Masters Cl. WS1: Wals 2E 49
Old Meadow Rd. B31: Longb 2G 159
Old Meeting Rd. WV14: Cose 5E 61
Old Meeting St. B70: W Brom 2H 79
    (not continuous)
Old Mill Cl. B90: Shir 5D 148
Old Mill Cl. B46: Col 2H 107
Old Mill Gdns. B33: Stech 1C 120
    WS4: S'fld 5G 21
Old Mill Gro. B20: Hand 5E 83
Old Mill House Cl. WS4: S'fld 6F 21
Old Mill Rd. B46: Col 2H 107
Old Moat Dr. B31: N'fld 4F 145
Old Moat Way B8: W End 3H 103
OLD MOXLEY 1A 62
Oldnall Cl. DY9: W'cte 1B 126
Oldnall Rd. B63: Crad 1B 126
    DY9: W'cte 1B 126
Old Oak Cl. WS9: A'rdge 1D 34
Old Oak Rd. B38: King Nor 5C 146
OLD OSCOTT 4G 67
Old Oscott Hill B44: Gt Barr 4G 67
Old Oscott La. B44: Gt Barr 5G 67
Old Park B29: N'fld 2E 145
Old Park Cl. B6: Aston 2G 101
Old Park La. B69: O'bry 4G 97
Old Park Rd. DY1: Dud 3B 76
    WS10: Darl, W'bry 5E 47
Old Park Trad. Est. WS10: W'bry 1E 63
Old Park Wlk. B6: Aston 2G 101
Old Parkway DY3: Swind 5E 73
Old Penns La. *B46: Col 2H 107*
    (off High St.)
Old Pl. WS3: Blox 1A 32
Old Pleck Rd. WS2: Wals 3H 47
Old Port Cl. DY4: Tip 5B 78
Old Portway B38: King Nor 2A 160
Old Postway B19: Loz 2F 101
Old Pump House, The DY9: Lye 6H 109
Old Quarry Cl. B45: Rub 1F 157
Old Quarry Dr. DY3: Up Gor 2H 75
Old Rectory Farm 5G 121
Old Rectory Gdns. WS9: A'rdge 3E 35
Old Repertory Theatre, The 5D 4 (1F 117)
Old School Cl. WV13: W'hall 1A 46
Old School La. WV14: Bils 2E 61
Old School Dr. B65: Row R 6B 96
Old Scott Cl. B33: Kitts G 1G 121
Old Smithy Pl. B18: Hock 4C 100
Old Snow Hill B4: Birm 1D 4 (5F 101)
Old Square B4: Birm 3F 5 (6G 101)
Old Square Shop. Cen.
    WS1: Wals 2C 48
Old Stables Wlk. B7: Nech 2C 102
Old Station M. B74: Lit As 1B 52
Old Station Rd. B33: Stech 5B 104
    B92: H Ard 3H 139
Old Stone Cl. B45: Fran 6F 143
Old Stowheath La. WV1: Wolv 2E 45
OLD SWINFORD 3E 125
Old Tokengate B17: Harb 5H 115
Old Town Cl. B38: King Nor 5B 146
Old Town La. WS3: Pels 4D 20
Old Union Mill B16: Birm 1D 116
Old Vicarage Cl. WS3: Pels 5E 21
    WV5: Wom 6H 57
Old Walsall Rd. B42: P Barr 1B 82
Old Warstone La. WV11: Ess 5B 6
Old Warwick Ct. B92: Olton 4C 136
Old Warwick Rd. B92: Olton 4C 136
Oldway Dr. B91: Sol 5A 152
Old Well Cl. WS4: Rus 2F 33
Old Wharf Rd. DY8: Amb 5D 108
Olga Dr. DY4: Tip 4B 62

Olinthus Av. WV11: Wed 2G 29
Olive Av. WV4: Ett 6A 44
Olive Dr. B62: B'hth 3C 112
Olive Hill Rd. B62: B'hth 3D 112
Olive La. B62: B'hth 3C 112
Olive Mt. B69: O'bry 1D 96
Olive Pl. B14: King H 6H 133
Oliver Cl. DY2: Dud 1G 95
Oliver Ct. B65: Row R 1B 112
Oliver Cres. WV14: Bils 3G 61
Oliver Rd. B16: Birm 1B 116
  B23: Erd 1F 85
  B66: Smeth 6G 99
Oliver St. B7: Birm 4A 102
Ollerton Rd. B26: Yard 4D 120
Ollison Dr. B74: S'tly 1H 51
Olliver Cl. B62: Quin 2G 129
Olorenshaw Rd.
  B26: Sheld 6H 121
OLTON 4C 136
Olton Blvd. E. B27: A Grn 3G 135
Olton Blvd. W. B11: Tys 2F 135
Olton Cft. B27: A Grn 2B 136
Olton Golf Course 6E 137
Olton Mere B92: Olton 4C 136
Olton Mere Sailing Club 5C 136
Olton Rd. B90: Shir 3H 149
Olton Station (Rail) 4C 136
Olton Wharf B92: Olton 3C 136
Olympus Dr. DY4: Tip 1D 78
Ombersley Cl. B69: O'bry 4D 96
Ombersley Rd. B12: Bal H 5A 118
  B63: Hale 3H 127
Ombersley Way B31: N'fld 5H 145
One Stop Retail Pk.
  B42: P Barr 4F 83
Onibury Rd. B21: Hand 6H 81
Onslow Cres. B92: Olton 4E 137
Onslow Rd. B11: Tys 1G 135
Ontario Cl. B38: King Nor 1C 160
Oozells Sq. B1: Birm 5A 4 (1E 117)
Oozells St. B1: Birm 5A 4 (1E 117)
Oozells St. Nth.
  B1: Birm 5A 4 (1D 116)
Opal Gdns. B68: O'bry 4H 97
Opal One B5: Edg 4F 117
                                       (off Bristol Rd.)
Open Fld. Cl. B31: N'fld 5F 145
Openfield Cft. B46: Wat O 5E 89
Ophelia Gdns. WV10: Bush 3A 28
Oracle Bldg. B90: Bly P 6E 165
Oracle Dr. B90: Bly P 6E 165
Oratory, The 2B 116
Orchard, The B37: Mars G 3B 122
  B68: O'bry 5A 98
  B73: W Grn 6H 69
  WS3: Blox 5B 20
  WV6: Tett 3C 26
  WV14: Bils 6G 45
Orchard Av. B91: Sol 2H 151
Orchard Blythe B46: Col 3H 107
Orchard Cl. B21: Hand 5B 82
  B46: Col 2H 107
  B63: Crad 5E 111
  B65: Row R 6A 96
  B73: Bold 5G 69
  B76: Curd 1D 88
  WS4: Rus 4G 33
  WS6: C Hay 2E 7
  WV3: Wolv 4H 41
  WV13: W'hall 2B 46
Orchard Ct. B23: Erd 2G 85
                                       (Grosvenor Ho.)
  B23: Erd 3B 84
                                       (Waterford Ct.)
  B65: Row R 6B 96
  DY6: K'wfrd 3B 92
Orchard Cres. WV3: Wolv 4H 41
Orchard Dr. B31: Longb 2D 158
Orchard Gro. B74: Four O 6F 37
  DY3: Lwr G 4F 75
  WS9: A'rdge 5D 34
  WV4: Penn 1E 59
Orchard Ho. B24: Erd 2G 85
Orchard La. WV8: Bilb 4H 13
Orchard Mdw. Wlk. B35: Cas V 4F 87
Orchard Ri. B26: Yard 4D 120

Orchard Rd. B12: Bal H 5H 117
  B24: Erd 2G 85
  DY2: Neth 1E 111
  WS5: Wals 2F 65
  WV11: Wed 2E 29
  WV13: W'hall .2B 46
Orchards, The B47: H'wd 2A 162
  B74: Four O 3G 53
  B90: Ches G 5B 164
Orchard St. DY4: Tip 5H 77
  DY5: Brie H 5G 93
Orchards Way B12: Bal H 5G 117
Orchard Way B27: A Grn 1H 135
  B43: Gt Barr 4B 66
  B47: H'wd 1A 162
  B64: Old H 2H 111
Orcheston Wlk. B14: King H 6F 147
Orchid Cl. B66: Smeth 2B 98
Orchid Ct. B44: Gt Barr 4H 67
Orchid Dr. B19: Hock 3F 101
Oregon Cl. DY6: K'wfrd 3D 92
Oregon Dr. WV12: W'hall 2E 31
Orford Gro. B21: Hand 1G 99
Oriel Cl. DY1: Dud 5A 76
Oriel Dr. WV10: F'hses 4H 15
Oriel Ho. B37: F'bri 6C 106
Oriel Vs. B11: S'hll 6C 118
                                       (off Warwick Rd.)
Orion Bldg. B5: Birm 5C 4 (1F 117)
Orion Cl. B8: W End 5H 103
  WS6: Gt Wyr 4F 7
Orkney Av. B34: Hodg H 3D 104
Orkney Cft. B36: Cas B 2D 106
Orlando Cl. WS1: Wals 3C 48
Orlando Ho. WS1: Wals 3D 48
                                       (off Barleyfield Row)
Orme Cl. DY5: Brie H 3E 109
Ormes La. WV6: Tett 6A 26
Ormonde Cl. B63: Crad 4D 110
Ormond Pl. WV14: Bils 5H 45
Ormsby Ct. B15: Edg 4A 116
Ormsby Gro. B27: A Grn 6H 135
Ormscliffe Rd. B45: Redn 3H 157
Orphanage Rd. B24: Erd 2G 85
  B72: W Grn 2G 85
Orpington Rd. B44: Gt Barr 2G 67
Orpwood Rd. B33: Yard 1E 121
Orslow Wlk. WV10: Wolv 4C 28
ORTON 2F 57
Orton Av. B76: Walm 1D 86
Orton Cl. B46: Wat O 4C 88
Orton Gro. WV4: Penn 1B 58
Orton La. WV4: Lwr P 2F 57
  WV5: Wom 2F 57
Orton Way B35: Cas V 6E 87
Orwell Cl. DY8: Stourb 1B 124
  WV11: Wed 4H 29
Orwell Dr. B38: King Nor 1F 159
  B71: W Brom 1B 80
Orwell Pas. B5: Birm 5F 5 (1G 117)
Orwell Rd. WS1: Wals 3F 49
Osberton Dr. DY1: Dud 5B 76
Osborn Ct. B73: W Grn 4H 69
Osborne Dr. WS10: Darl 3D 46
Osborne Gro. B19: Loz 2E 101
Osborne Rd. B21: Hand 1B 100
  B23: Erd 2F 85
  B70: W Brom 4A 80
  WV4: Penn 6D 42
Osborne Rd. Sth. B23: Erd 3F 85
Osborne Twr. B6: Aston 1A 102
Osborn Rd. B11: S'brk 5C 118
Osbourne Cl. B6: Aston 2A 102
  DY5: Quar B 3B 110
Osbourne Cft. B90: Ches G 4B 164
Oscott Cl. B23: Erd 5E 69
Oscott Gdns. B42: P Barr 4G 83
Oscott Rd. B42: P Barr 4G 83
Oscott School La. B44: Gt Barr 3G 67
Osier Gro. B23: Erd 1B 84
Osier Pl. WV1: Wolv 1B 44
Osier St. WV1: Wolv 1B 44
Osler St. B16: Birm 1B 116
Osmaston Rd. B17: Harb 2E 131
  DY8: Stourb 3C 124
Osmington Gro. B63: Crad 5F 111

Osprey Dr. DY1: Dud 6B 76
Osprey Rd. B23: Erd 1C 84
  B27: A Grn 3B 136
Ostler Cl. DY6: W Hth 2G 91
Oswestry Ct. B11: S'brk 5B 118
Oswin Pl. WS3: Wals 4D 32
Oswin Rd. WS3: Wals 4D 32
Othello Rd. WV10: Bush 2A 28
Otley Gro. B9: Bord G 6A 104
Ottawa Twr. B5: Edg 4F 117
Otter Cft. B34: S End 4H 105
Otterstone Cl. DY3: Sed 3G 59
Oughton Rd. B12: Birm 4A 118
Oulsnam Ct. B13: Mose 3B 134
Oulton Bri. B92: Olton 5D 136
Oundle Rd. B44: K'sdng 6H 67
OUNSDALE 1F 73
Ounsdale Cres. WV5: Wom 6G 57
Ounsdale Dr. DY2: Neth 6E 95
Ounsdale Rd. WV5: Wom 6E 57
Ounty John La. DY8: Stourb 5E 125
Outfields B14: King H 1G 147
Outmore Rd. B33: Sheld 2F 121
Out Wood Dr. B31: Longb 6B 144
Oval, The B67: Smeth 6C 98
  DY1: Dud 1A 94
  WS10: W'bry 1F 63
Oval Dr. WV10: F'hses 3H 15
Oval Rd. B24: Erd 6E 85
  DY4: Tip 6H 61
Overbrook Cl. DY3: Gorn 5G 75
Over Brunton Cl. B31: N'fld 5F 145
Overbury Cl. B31: N'fld 4G 145
  B63: Hale 3B 128
Overbury Rd. B31: N'fld 3G 145
Overdale Av. B76: Walm 2D 86
Overdale Cl. WS2: Wals 6C 30
Overdale Ct. B13: Mose 1H 133
Overdale Dr. WS2: Wals 6C 30
Overdale Rd. B32: Quin 1C 130
Overend Rd. B63: Crad 4F 111
  B64: Crad H 4F 111
Overend St. B70: W Brom 4B 80
Overfield Dr. WV14: Cose 2D 60
Overfield Rd. B32: Bart G 4C 130
  DY1: Dud 1A 94
Over Grn. Dr. B37: K'hrst 3B 106
Overhill Rd. WS7: Burn 1C 10
Overlea Av. B27: A Grn 2H 135
Overman Cl. DY9: Lye 6H 109
Over Mill Dr. B29: S Oak 3D 132
Over Moor Cl. B19: Loz 2E 101
Over Pool Rd. B8: W End 3G 103
Overseal Rd. WV11: Wed 1G 29
Overslade Rd. B91: Sol 5D 150
Oversley Rd. B76: Walm 1E 87
Overstrand WV9: Pend 3D 14
Overton Cl. B28: Hall G 1G 149
Overton Dr. B46: Wat O 4E 89
Overton Gro. B27: A Grn 5A 136
Overton La. WS7: Hamm 1E 11
Overton Pl. B7: Birm 6A 102
  B71: W Brom 1B 80
Overton Rd. B27: A Grn 5H 135
Overton Wlk. WV4: Penn 5A 42
Over Wood Cft. B8: Salt 6D 102
Owen Ct. B75: S Cold 1D 70
Owen Pl. WV14: Bils 5F 45
Owen Rd. WV3: Wolv 2E 43
  WV13: W'hall 2C 46
  WV14: Bils 4F 45
Owen Rd. Ind. Est. WV13: W'hall 2C 46
Owens Cft. B38: King Nor 6C 146
Owen St. DY2: Dud 1G 95
  DY4: Tip 2G 77
  WS10: Darl 4D 46
Owens Way B64: Old H 2A 112
Ownall Rd. B34: S End 3G 105
Oxbarn Av. WV3: Wolv 5C 42
Oxenton Cft. B63: Hale 3F 127
Oxford Cl. B8: W End 4H 103
  WS6: Gt Wyr 2F 7
Oxford Ct. B29: W Cas 6G 131
Oxford Dr. B27: A Grn 1B 136
  DY8: Stourb 1D 124
Oxford Gro. B37: Chel W 2C 122
Oxford Pas. DY1: Dud 6D 76

Oxford Rd.—Parkes Av.

Oxford Rd. B13: Mose 2H **133**
B23: Erd 3F **85**
B27: A Grn 2A **136**
B66: Smeth 1E **99**
(not continuous)
B70: W Brom 4H **79**
Oxford St. B5: Birm 6G **5** (2H **117**)
B30: Stir 6C **132**
DY1: Dud 6D **76**
WS2: Wals 4A **48**
WS10: W'bry 2H **63**
WV1: Wolv 2A **44**
WV14: Bils 6G **45**
Oxford St. Ind. Est. WV14: Bils 6H **45**
Oxford Ter. WS10: W'bry 3H **63**
Oxford Way DY4: Tip 3F **77**
Oxhayes Cl. CV7: Bal C 6H **169**
Oxhill Rd. B21: Hand 5G **81**
B90: Shir 5C **148**
Ox Leasow B32: Bart G 3A **130**
OXLEY 1E **27**
Oxley Av. WV10: Oxl 3G **27**
Oxley Cl. DY2: Neth 1D **110**
WS6: Gt Wyr 4F **7**
Oxley Ct. Caravan Pk. WV10: Oxl 1E **27**
Oxley Gro. B29: W Cas 5E **131**
Oxley La. WV1: Wolv 6G **27**
Oxley Links Rd. WV10: Oxl 1F **27**
Oxley Moor Rd. WV9: Pend 1E **27**
WV10: Oxl 1E **27**
Oxley Park Golf Course **2G 27**
Ox Leys Rd. B75: S Cold 1F **71**
B76: Walm, Wis 1F **71**
Oxley St. WV1: Wolv 5G **27**
Oxlip Cl. WS5: Wals 2E **65**
Oxpiece Dr. B36: Hodg H 1B **104**
Oxstall Cl. B76: Min 2H **87**
Ox St. DY3: Up Gor 2H **75**
Oxted Cl. WV11: Wed 4H **29**
Oxted Cft. B23: Erd 4E **85**
Oxwood La. B32: Fran 3D **142**
B62: Hunn 3D **142**

P

Pace Cres. WV14: Bils 3A **62**
Pacific Av. WS10: W'bry 4D **62**
Packhorse La. B38: Head H 3F **161**
B47: H'wd 3F **161**
Packington Av. B34: S End 4G **105**
Packington Ct. B74: Four O 5E **37**
Packmores B90: Dic H 4G **163**
Packwood Cl. B20: Hand 5C **82**
B93: Ben H 5A **166**
WV13: W'hall 3H **45**
Packwood Cotts. B93: Dorr 6G **167**
Packwood Ct. B29: W Cas 4D **130**
B91: Sol 2G **151**
Packwood Dr. B43: Gt Barr 4H **65**
PACKWOOD GULLET **6F 167**
Packwood Rd. B26: Sheld 3F **121**
B69: Tiv 6A **78**
Padarn Cl. DY3: Sed 4G **59**
Padbury WV9: Pend 4F **15**
Paddington Rd. B21: Hand 6G **81**
Paddington Wlk. WS2: Wals 5F **31**
Paddock WS1: Wals 2D **48**
Paddock, The B31: N'fld 3G **145**
B76: Curd 1E **89**
B76: Walm 1E **71**
DY3: Up Gor 2A **76**
DY9: Pedm 4F **125**
WV4: Penn 5F **43**
WV5: Wom 1E **73**
WV6: Pert 5D **24**
WV8: Cod 5F **13**
WV14: Cose 4F **61**
Paddock Dr. B26: Sheld 4E **121**
B93: Dorr 6H **167**
Paddock Gdns. WS5: Wals 5F **49**
Paddock La. WS1: Wals 2D **48**
(not continuous)
WS6: Gt Wyr 2G **7**
WS9: A'rdge 4C **34**
Paddocks, The B15: Edg 3D **116**
CV7: Bal C 1H **169**
Paddocks Grn. B18: Hock 4C **100**
Paddocks Rd. B47: H'wd 3H **161**
Paddock Vw. WV6: Wolv 3F **27**
Paddys Wide Water Ind. Est.
DY5: Brie H 4G **93**
Padgate Cl. B35: Cas V 4F **87**
Padstow Rd. B24: Erd 3B **86**
Paganal Dr. B70: W Brom 6C **80**
Paganel Dr. DY1: Dud 4E **77**
Paganel Rd. B29: W Cas 3E **131**
Pagan Pl. B9: Birm 6H **5**
Pageant Ct. B12: Bal H 6G **117**
Pages Cl. B75: S Cold 6A **54**
Pages Ct. B43: Gt Barr 4A **66**
Page's Cft. DY1: Dud 4G **77**
Pages La. B43: Gt Barr 4A **66**
Paget Cl. WV14: Cose 5D **60**
Paget Ho. DY4: Tip 4B **78**
Paget M. B76: Walm 3D **70**
Paget Rd. B24: Erd 3B **86**
(not continuous)
WV6: Wolv 1D **42**
Paget St. WV1: Wolv 6F **27**
Pagham Cl. WV9: Pend 5D **14**
Pagnell Gro. B13: Mose 1C **148**
Pagoda Cl. B74: S'tly 4H **51**
Paignton Rd. B16: Edg 6H **99**
Pailton Gro. B29: W Cas 4F **131**
Pailton Rd. B90: Shir 2H **149**
Painswick Cl. WS5: Wals 2F **65**
Painswick Rd. B28: Hall G 6E **135**
Paint Cup Row DY2: Neth 1E **111**
Painters Cnr. *B66: Smeth* *4G* ***99***
(off Woodlands St.)
Painters Cft. WV14: Cose 4G **61**
Pakefield Rd. B30: King Nor 4E **147**
Pakenham Cl. B76: Walm 5D **70**
Pakenham Dr. B76: Walm 5D **70**
Pakenham Ho. B76: Walm 5D **70**
Pakenham Rd. B15: Edg 4E **117**
Pakenham Village *B15: Edg* *4E* ***117***
(off Gilldown Pl.)
Pakfield Wlk. B6: Aston 6H **83**
Palace Cl. B65: Row R 5D **96**
Palace Dr. B66: Smeth 1B **98**
Palace Rd. B9: Small H 1E **119**
Palefield Rd. B90: M'path 3D **164**
Pale La. B17: Harb 3D **114**
Pale St. DY3: Up Gor 2A **76**
Palethorpe Rd. DY4: Tip 5A **62**
PALFREY **4A 48**
Palfrey Rd. DY8: Stourb 6B **108**
Pallasades Shop. Cen., The
B2: Birm 5D **4** (1F **117**)
Palmcourt Av. B28: Hall G 6E **135**
Palm Cft. DY5: Brie H 3G **109**
Palmer Cl. WV11: Wed 6H **17**
Palmers Cl. B90: Shir 2H **149**
WV8: Bilb 6A **14**
PALMERS CROSS **1B 26**
Palmers Gro. B36: Hodg H 1C **104**
Palmerston Dr. B69: Tiv 5D **78**
Palmerston Rd. B11: S'brk 5B **118**
Palmer St. B9: Birm 1A **118**
(not continuous)
Palmer's Way WV8: Bilb 6A **14**
Palm Ho. B20: Hand 4B **82**
Palmvale Cft. B26: Sheld 5E **121**
Palomino Pl. B16: Birm 1B **116**
Pamela Rd. B31: N'fld 5E **145**
Pan Cft. B36: Hodg H 2A **104**
Panjab Gdns. B67: Smeth 3D **98**
Pannel Cft. Village B19: Hock 3F **101**
Panther Cft. B34: S End 4H **105**
Paper Mill End B44: Gt Barr 1F **83**
Paper Mill End Ind. Est. B44: Gt Barr 1F **83**
Papyrus Way B36: Hodg H 6D **86**
Parade B1: Birm 3A **4** (6E **101**)
B72: S Cold 1H **69**
Parade, The B37: K'hrst 3C **106**
B64: Crad H 3G **111**
B72: S Cold 1H **69**
DY1: Dud 5D **76**
DY6: W Hth 2H **91**
WS8: Bwnhls 4A **10**
Parade Vw. WS8: Bwnhls 5A **10**
PARADISE **1F 95**
Paradise DY2: Dud 1F **95**
Paradise Cir. Queensway
B1: Birm 3B **4** (6E **101**)
Paradise Ct. B28: Hall G 1D **148**
Paradise Gro. WS3: Pels 4D **20**
Paradise La. B28: Hall G 1E **149**
WS3: Pels 4D **20**
Paradise Pl. B3: Birm 4B **4** (1E **117**)
Paradise St. B1: Birm 4C **4** (1F **117**)
Par Ct. WS3: Blox 4H **19**
Pardington Cl. B92: Sol 5A **138**
Pargeter Ct. WS2: Wals 1A **48**
Pargeter Rd. B67: Smeth 1D **114**
Pargeter St. DY8: Stourb 1D **124**
WS2: Wals 1A **48**
Par Grn. B38: King Nor 6H **145**
Parish Ct. WS3: Blox 1B **32**
Parish Gdns. DY9: Pedm 4F **125**
Park & Ride
Corser Street (Wolverhampton)
2B 44
Monkspath Hall **4F 151**
Plascom Road (Wolverhampton)
2C 44
Science Park (Wolverhampton)
3G 27
Tettenhall Pall (Wolverhampton)
4B 26
Park & Tram
Black Lake **2G 79**
Priestfield **4C 44**
The Hawthorns **1E 99**
Wednesbury Parkway **3D 62**
Park App. B23: Erd 5C **84**
Park Av. B12: Bal H 6H **117**
B18: Hock 2C **100**
B30: King Nor 2C **146**
B46: Col 3H **107**
B65: Row R 6C **96**
B67: Smeth 5D **98**
B68: O'bry 6H **97**
B91: Sol 4H **151**
DY4: Tip 2G **77**
WV1: Wolv 1A **170** (6F **27**)
WV4: Penn 6G **43**
WV5: Wom 2F **73**
WV13: W'hall 1H **45**
Park Bldgs. *DY3: Lwr G* *3G* ***75***
(off Park Rd.)
Park Cir. B6: Aston 2H **101**
Park Cl. B24: Erd 2B **86**
B69: Tiv 2C **96**
B92: Sol 3H **137**
DY1: Dud 6D **60**
WS6: C Hay 2E **7**
WS8: Bwnhls 5B **10**
WV11: Ess 4A **18**
Park Ct. B46: Col 2H **107**
B65: Row R *6C* ***96***
(off Rowley Village)
B73: Bold 4F **69**
Park Cres. B71: W Brom 3B **80**
WV1: Wolv 1F **43**
Park Cft. B47: H'wd 4A **162**
PARK DALE **6E 27**
Park Dale WS5: Wals 5G **49**
Parkdale DY3: Sed 5H **59**
Parkdale Av. WS10: W'bry 1G **63**
Parkdale Cl. B24: Erd 5F **85**
Park Dale Ct. WV1: Wolv 6E **27**
Parkdale Ct. WS10: W'bry 1G **63**
Parkdale Dr. B31: Longb 2E **159**
Park Dale E. WV1: Wolv 6E **27**
Parkdale Rd. B26: Sheld 6G **121**
Park Dale W. WV1: Wolv 6E **27**
Park Dr. B74: Four O 1G **53**
B74: Lit As 5C **36**
WV4: Penn 6G **43**
Park Edge B17: Harb 4G **115**
Park End B32: Bart G 4B **130**
Parker Ho. B14: King H 4H **147**
Parker Paul Ind. Est.
WV2: Wolv 4G **43**
Parker Rd. WV11: Wed 6H **17**
Parker St. B16: Edg 2B **116**
WS3: Blox 6G **19**
Parkes Av. WV8: Cod 5H **13**

Parkes' Hall Rd. DY1: Dud 1C 76
Parkes Ho. B69: O'bry 2G 97
Parkes La. DY3: Sed 6C 60
  DY4: Tip 5H 61
Parkes St. B67: Smeth 5D 98
  DY5: Brie H 6H 93
  WV13: W'hall 2B 46
Parkeston Cres. B44: K'sdng 4C 68
Park Farm Rd. B43: Gt Barr 1D 66
PARKFIELD 5A 44
Parkfield Chalet Land
  WV2: Wolv 5H 43
Parkfield Cl. B15: Edg 4E 117
  B62: Quin 6G 113
Parkfield Colliery WV4: Ett 6B 44
Parkfield Ct. B46: Col 2H 107
  (Birmingham Rd.)
  B46: Col 3H 107
  (Sumner Rd.)
Parkfield Cres. WV2: Ett 5A 44
Parkfield Dr. B36: Cas B 6G 87
Parkfield Gro. WV2: Ett 5A 44
Parkfield Ho. B23: Erd 6E 85
  DY8: Stourb 6E 109
Parkfield Rd. B8: Salt 6E 103
  B46: Col 2H 107
  B68: O'bry 6G 97
  DY2: Dud 3F 95
  DY8: Stourb 6E 109
  WV4: Ett 5H 43
Parkfields B74: Four O 5E 37
Park Gdns. DY9: W'cte 2B 126
Park Gro. B10: Small H 3D 118
  B46: Wat O 4E 89
Park Hall Cl. WS5: Wals 5G 49
Park Hall Cres. B36: Cas B 1F 105
Parkhall Cft. B34: S End 2G 105
Park Hall Rd. WS5: Wals 4G 49
  WV4: Penn 1H 59
Parkhead Cres. DY2: Dud 1D 94
Parkhead Rd. DY2: Dud 1D 94
Park Hill B13: Mose 1G 133
  B65: B'hth 2B 112
  WS10: W'bry 1H 63
Park Hill Dr. B20: Hand 3B 82
Park Hill Rd. B17: Harb 5G 115
Parkhill Rd. B67: Smeth 4D 98
  B76: Walm 1D 86
Parkhill St. DY2: Dud 1G 95
Park Ho. B66: Smeth 4G 99
Parkhouse Av. WV11: Wed 3D 28
Parkhouse Dr. B23: Erd 2A 84
Parkhouse Gdns. DY3: Lwr G 3G 75
Parkhouse Gro. WS9: A'rdge 4C 34
Park Inn DY4: Tip 3A 78
Parklands B45: Redn 1G 157
  B91: Sol 4E 151
Parklands, The B23: Erd 1D 84
  DY9: Pedm 2G 125
  WV3: Wolv 2B 42
Parklands Av. B20: Hand 1C 100
Parklands Ct. B45: Redn 1G 157
  WS3: Blox 6H 19
Parklands Dr. B74: Four O 3F 53
Parklands Gdns. WS1: Wals 3E 49
Parklands Rd. WS10: Darl 6E 47
  WV1: Wolv 2C 44
  WV14: Cose 3F 61
Park La. B6: Aston 2G 101
  B20: Hand 2F 81
  B21: Hand 2F 81
  B35: Cas V 3F 87
  B63: Crad 5C 110
  B69: O'bry 3G 97
  B76: Min 3G 87
  CV7: Bal C 5G 155
  DY6: K'wfrd 2C 92
  WS6: Gt Wyr 2F 7
  WS10: Darl, W'bry 4F 47
  WV10: Bush, Wolv 3A 28
Park La. E. DY4: Tip 3A 78
Park La. Ind. Est. B69: O'bry 2G 97
  B71: W Brom 6F 81
Park La. Trad. Est. WV10: Wolv 4A 28
Park La. W. DY4: Tip 2G 77
Park Lime Dr. WS4: Wals 5F 33

Park Lime Pitts Local Nature Reserve
  ....4G 33
Park Mall WS1: Wals 1C 48
Park Mdw. Av. WV14: Bils 3E 45
Park M. B29: S Oak 4F 131
  B67: Smeth 5B 98
Park Mill Wlk. B7: Nech 2C 102
Park Moor Gdns. DY1: Dud 4G 77
Park Pl. B7: Nech 2C 102
  WS1: Wals 1C 48
Park Retreat B66: Smeth 5F 99
Park Ridge B74: S Cold 4G 53
Park Ridge Dr. B63: Crad 5D 110
Parkridge Cen. 5A 152
Park Ri. WV3: Wolv 1C 42
Park Rd. B6: Aston 2A 102
  B11: S'hll 2C 134
  B13: Mose 1H 133
  B18: Hock 3B 100
  B23: Erd 5C 84
  B46: Col 3H 107
  B63: Crad 6C 110
  B67: Smeth 1D 114
  B69: Tiv 1C 96
  B73: S Cold 6H 53
  B91: Sol 4G 151
  DY1: Dud 1D 76
  DY2: Neth 3E 95
  DY3: Lwr G 3G 75
  DY5: Quar B 3B 110
  DY8: Woll 6B 108
  WS3: Blox 6H 19
  (not continuous)
  WS4: Rus 4G 33
  WS5: Wals 6H 49
  WS10: Darl 5C 46
  WV13: W'hall 6H 29
  WV14: Bils 6E 45
Park Rd. E. WV1: Wolv 6F 27
Park Rd. Nth. B6: Aston 2A 102
Park Rd. Sth. B18: Hock 4D 100
Park Rd. W. DY8: Woll 6A 108
  WV1: Wolv 6E 27
Parkrose Ind. Est. B66: Smeth 1F 99
Parks Cres. WV11: Ess 3A 18
Parkside B16: Edg 6H 99
  B32: Bart G 3A 130
  B37: Mars G 4F 123
Parkside Av. WV13: W'hall 1G 45
Parkside Cl. WS10: W'bry 2H 63
Parkside Ind. Est.
  WV1: Wolv 2B 44
Parkside Pl. B70: W Brom 5G 63
Parkside Rd. B20: Hand 2A 82
  B63: Crad 6F 111
Parkside Vw. B66: Smeth 5E 99
  (off Bearwood Rd.)
Parkside Way B31: Longb 6A 144
  B74: S'tly 2A 52
Park Sq. B37: Mars G 3F 123
Parkstone Cl. WS4: S'fld 1G 33
Park St. B5: Birm 3G 5 (6H 101)
  (not continuous)
  B6: Aston 2A 102
  (not continuous)
  B64: Crad H 1G 111
  B65: B'hth 2D 112
  B69: O'bry 3F 97
  B70: W Brom 4B 80
  DY1: Dud 3B 94
  DY4: Tip 2A 78
  DY6: K'wfrd 3B 92
  DY8: Amb 3D 108
  DY8: Stourb 6E 109
  DY9: Lye 6B 110
  WS1: Wals 1C 48
  WS6: C Hay 2E 7
  WS10: Darl 6C 46
  WS10: W'bry 2F 63
Park St. Arc. WS1: Wals 1C 48
  (off Park St.)
Park St. Sth. WV2: Wolv 5G 43
Park St. Sth. B65: B'hth 2D 112
Park Ter. B21: Hand 1A 100
  WS10: Darl 5B 46
Park Trad. Est. B18: Hock 3C 100
Parktree Wlk. B24: Erd 3B 86

Park Vw. B10: Small H 4D 118
  B18: Win G 5A 100
  B36: Cas B 6A 88
  B73: S Cold 5G 53
  B91: Sol 5F 151
  DY8: Stourb 2E 125
  WS10: Darl 5C 46
Park View Community Leisure Cen.
  ....4F 103
Parkview Ct. DY6: W Hth 1H 91
Parkview Cres. WS2: Wals 5G 31
Parkview Dr. B8: W End 3G 103
  WS8: Bwnhls 3B 10
Park Vw. Rd. B31: N'fld 4C 144
  B74: Four O 6D 36
  DY9: W'cte 1B 126
Parkview Rd. WV14: Bils 3E 45
Park Vw. Trad. Est. B30: King Nor .4B 146
PARK VILLAGE 4B 28
Park Village Youth Media Activity Cen.
  ....4B 28
Park Vs. B9: Birm 1B 118
Parkville Av. B17: Harb 2G 131
Park Wlk. DY5: Quar B 3B 110
Park Way B45: Redn 6H 143
  WV11: Wed 6A 18
Parkway B8: W End 4G 103
Parkway, The DY4: Tip 4D 62
  WS4: S'fld 1G 33
  WV6: Pert 3D 24
Parkway Ind. Cen. B7: Birm ..1H 5 (5A 102)
Parkway Ind. Est., The WS10: W'bry ..3E 63
Parkway Rd. DY1: Dud 5C 76
Parkway Rdbt. WS10: W'bry 4E 63
Parkwood Cl. WS8: Wals W 2C 22
Park Wood Ct. B74: Four O 1F 53
Parkwood Cft. B43: Gt Barr 4D 66
Parkwood Dr. B73: New O 3C 68
Parkyn St. WV2: Wolv 3A 44
Parliament St. B6: Aston 3H 101
  B10: Small H 3C 118
  B70: W Brom 6B 80
Parlows End B38: King Nor 2H 159
Parnell Av. WV11: Wed 1A 30
Parry Rd. WV11: Wed 4F 29
Parsonage Dr. B45: Coft H 5B 158
  B73: S Cold 4C 110
Parsonage St. B69: O'bry 2H 97
  B70: W Brom 1B 80
Parsons Hill B30: King Nor 5C 146
  B68: O'bry 2H 113
Parsons M. B30: King Nor 5D 146
Parson's St. DY1: Dud 6E 77
Parsons Way WS2: Wals 3F 31
Partons Rd. B14: King H 1F 147
Partridge Av. WS10: Darl 5B 46
Partridge Cl. B37: Chel W 6E 107
Partridge Ct. B4: Birm 1E 5
  WS10: W'bry 2F 63
Partridge Mill WS3: Pels 4C 20
Partridge Rd. B26: Yard 2E 121
  DY8: Stourb 1A 124
Passey Rd. B13: Mose 3D 134
Passfield Rd. B33: Yard 6E 105
Pastures, The WV6: Pert 5D 24
Pastures Vw. DY3: Swind 5E 73
Pastures Wlk. B38: King Nor 2H 159
Pasture Vw. WS3: Pels 5D 20
Patent Dr. WS10: W'bry 3C 62
Patent Shaft Rdbt. WS10: W'bry ...2D 62
Paternoster Row B5: Birm 4F 5 (1G 117)
  WV1: Wolv 2A 170 (1G 43)
Paterson Ct. B93: Know 3E 167
Paterson Pl. WS8: Bwnhls 2D 22
Pathlow Cres. B90: Shir 6G 149
Pathway, The B14: King H 2D 146
Patina Cl. DY5: Quar B 3B 110
Patman Gdns. B16: Edg 2G 115
Paton Gro. B13: Mose 3H 133
Patricia Av. B14: Yard W 3C 148
  WV4: Penn 6G 43
Patricia Cres. DY1: Dud 1D 76
Patricia Dr. DY4: Tip 5A 78
Patrick Gregory Rd. WV11: Wed ...2H 29
Patrick Rd. B26: Yard 4C 120
Patricks Farm Barn B92: H Ard ...6D 140
Patriot Cl. WS1: Wals 5B 48
Patshull Av. WV10: F'hses 4F 15

Patshull Cl. B43: Gt Barr 4H 65
Patshull Gro. WV10: F'hses 4F 15
Patshull Pl. B19: Loz 2E 101
Pattenham Cl. WV12: W'hall 5D 30
Patterdale Rd. B23: Erd 3D 84
Patterdale Way DY5: Brie H 3F 109
Patterton Dr. B76: Walm 5E 71
Pattingham Rd. WV6: Pert, Tett 6A 24
Pattison Gdns. B23: Erd 5D 84
Pattison St. WS5: Wals 6C 48
Paul Byrne Ct. B20: Hand 6D 82
Paul Pursehouse Rd.
      WV14: Cose 2F 61
Pauls Coppice WS8: Bwnhls 2B 22
Paul St. WS10: W'bry 3G 63
      WV2: Wolv 6A 170 (3G 43)
      WV14: Cose 4C 60
Paul Va. DY4: Tip 2B 78
Pavenham Dr. B5: Edg 1E 133
Pavilion B40: Nat E C 1G 139
Pavilion Av. B67: Smeth 6B 98
Pavilion Dr. B6: Witt 4H 83
Pavilion Gdns. DY2: Neth 1E 111
Pavilion Lodge DY8: Word 6C 92
      (off Marshall Cres.)
Pavilion Rd. B6: Witt 4H 83
Pavilions, The B4: Birm 4F 5 (1G 117)
      B37: Mars G 3F 123
Pavillion Cl. WS9: A'rdge 2D 34
Pavior's Rd. WS7: Chase 1A 10
Paxford Way B31: N'fld 1D 144
Paxton Av. WV6: Pert 6E 25
Paxton Rd. B18: Hock 4C 100
      DY9: W'cte 1C 126
Payne St. B65: B'hth 2C 112
Payton Cl. B69: O'bry 6E 79
Payton Rd. B21: Hand 1H 99
PDH Ind. Est. WS10: Mox 1C 62
Peace Cl. WS6: C Hay 2E 7
Peace Wlk. B37: Chel W 2D 122
Peach Av. WS10: Darl 5C 46
Peachley Cl. B63: Hale 2B 128
Peach Ley Rd. B29: W Cas 6D 130
Peach Rd. WV12: W'hall 3A 30
Peacock Av. WV11: Wed 1A 30
Peacock Cl. DY4: Tip 3B 78
Peacock Rd. B13: Mose 1H 147
      WS10: Darl 4B 46
Peacocks Est. B64: Crad H 2E 111
Peak Cft. B36: Hodg H 1B 104
Peak Dr. DY3: Lwr G 4H 75
Peake Cres. WS8: Bwnhls 2B 22
Peake Dr. DY4: Tip 3B 78
Peake Rd. WS8: Bwnhls 2C 22
Peak Ho. Rd. B43: Gt Barr 2A 66
Peakman Cl. B45: Redn 3G 157
Peak Rd. DY8: Amb 5F 109
Peal St. WS1: Wals 2D 48
Pearce Cl. DY1: Dud 1A 94
Pearl Gro. B18: Win G 5A 100
      B27: A Grn 2H 135
Pearman Rd. B45: Fran 6D 142
      B66: Smeth 6E 99
Pearmans Cft. B47: H'wd 3A 162
Pearsall Dr. B69: O'bry 1E 97
Pearson Ct. WV12: W'hall 5D 30
Pearson St. B64: Old H 2G 111
      B70: W Brom 3H 79
      DY5: Brie H 6H 93
      DY9: Lye 1B 126
      WV2: Wolv 6B 170 (3G 43)
Pear Tree Av. DY4: Tip 2H 77
Peartree Av. WV13: W'hall 2B 46
Pear Tree Cl. B33: Stech 1B 120
      B43: Gt Barr 4F 65
Peartree Cl. B90: Shir 5D 148
Pear Tree Cl. B43: Gt Barr 5G 65
      B65: Row R 6D 96
Peartree Cres. B90: Shir 4C 148
Pear Tree Dr. B43: Gt Barr 5F 65
      B65: Row R 6D 96
      DY8: Stourb 3E 125
Peartree Gro. B90: Shir 5C 148
Peartree Ho. B68: O'bry 4A 98
Peartree Ind. Est. DY2: Dud 3C 94
Pear Tree La. WS8: Bwnhls 3G 9
      WV11: Wed 6D 16

Peartree La. B64: Old H 2G 111
      DY2: Dud 4B 94
      WV14: Cose 5F 61
Pear Tree Rd. B34: S End 3G 105
      B43: Gt Barr 4F 65
      B67: Smeth 5C 98
Peascroft La. WV14: Bils 5G 45
Peasefield Cl. B21: Hand 1G 99
Pebble Cl. DY8: Stourb 6F 109
Pebble Mill Rd. B5: Edg 1E 133
Pebworth Av. B90: M'path 3F 165
Pebworth Cl. B29: S Oak 3D 132
Pebworth Gro. B33: Sheld 3G 121
      DY1: Dud 4C 76
Pecan Pl. B29: W Cas 1E 145
Peckham Rd. B44: K'sdng 3A 68
Peckingham St. B63: Hale 2B 128
Peckover Cl. B65: B'hth 2C 112
Peddimore La. B76: Min 6G 71
      B76: Walm 1F 87
PEDMORE 4G 125
Pedmore Ct. Rd. DY8: Stourb 4F 125
Pedmore Gro. B44: Gt Barr 3H 67
Pedmore Hall La. DY9: Pedm 5G 125
Pedmore La. DY9: Hag, Pedm 4G 125
Pedmore M. DY8: Stourb 4F 125
Pedmore Rd. DY2: Dud 5B 94
      DY5: Brie H 5B 94
      DY9: Lye 6H 109
Pedmore Rd. Ind. Est.
      DY5: Brie H 5B 94
Pedmore Wlk. B69: O'bry 4D 96
Peel Cl. B92: H Ard 1B 154
      WS10: Darl 3D 46
      WV13: W'hall 2A 46
Peel St. B18: Win G 4A 100
      B71: W Brom 2A 80
      DY2: Dud 1G 95
      DY4: Tip 3A 78
      WV3: Wolv 4A 170 (2G 43)
      WV13: W'hall 2A 46
Peel Wlk. B17: Harb 4D 114
Peel Way B69: Tiv 5C 78
Pegasus Ct. B62: Quin 6F 113
      B75: Four O 6G 37
      B90: Shir 5A 150
Pegasus Wlk. B29: S Oak 4H 131
Pegleg Wlk. B14: King H 5E 147
Pei Cres. B69: O'bry 2A 98
Pelham Dr. DY1: Dud 5C 76
Pelham Rd. B8: W End 5H 103
Pelham St. WV3: Wolv 2E 43
PELSALL 4E 21
Pelsall La. WS3: Blox 4B 20
      (not continuous)
      WS4: Rus 1E 33
Pelsall North Common (Nature Reserve)
      ....1D 20
Pelsall Rd. WS8: Bwnhls 1G 21
PELSALL WOOD 3D 20
Pemberley Rd. B27: A Grn 3G 135
Pemberton Cl. B66: Smeth 6F 99
Pemberton Cres. WS10: W'bry 1A 64
Pemberton Rd. B70: W Brom 1G 79
      WV14: Cose 4F 61
Pemberton St. B18: Birm 5D 100
Pembridge Cl. B32: Bart G 6G 129
      B93: Dorr 6H 165
Pembroke Av. WV2: Ett 4C 44
Pembroke Cl. B71: W Brom 4H 63
      (off Pembroke Rd.)
      WV12: W'hall 3C 30
Pembroke Cft. B28: Hall G 2G 149
Pembroke Gdns. DY8: Word 2A 108
Pembroke Ho. B36: Cas B 2C 106
      WS3: Blox 3A 32
      (off Providence Cl.)
Pembroke Rd. B12: Bal H 1A 134
      B71: W Brom 5H 63
Pembroke Way B8: Salt 4C 102
      B28: Hall G 2G 149
      B71: W Brom 6H 63
Pembrook Dr. B31: N'fld 1C 144
Pembury Cl. B74: S'tly 5H 51
Pembury Cft. B44: K'sdng 4A 68
Pencombe Dr. WV4: Penn 6H 43

Pencroft Rd. B34: S End 2F 105
Penda Ct. B20: Hand 1C 100
Penda Gro. WV6: Pert 4F 25
Pendeen Rd. B14: Yard W 3B 148
PENDEFORD 4E 15
Pendeford Av. WV9: Tett 1C 26
Pendeford Bus. Pk. WV9: Pend 3D 14
Pendeford Cl. WV6: Tett 1C 26
Pendeford Hall La.
      WV9: Coven, Pend 2H 13
Pendeford Hall Mobile Home Pk.
      WV9: Pend 3C 14
Pendeford La. WV9: Pend 3E 15
Pendeford Mill La. WV8: Bilb 4H 13
Pendeford Pl. WV9: Pend 4D 14
Pendene Ct. WV4: Penn 6E 43
Pendennis Cl. B30: B'vlle 2H 145
Pendennis Dr. B69: Tiv 1A 96
Penderel Cl. WV10: F'stne 1C 16
Penderel St. WS3: Blox 1A 32
Pendigo Way B40: Nat E C 1G 139
      (not continuous)
Pendinas Dr. WV8: Bilb 4H 13
Pendlebury Cl. WS2: Wals 2F 47
Pendleton Gro. B27: A Grn 5H 135
Pendragon Rd. B42: P Barr 3E 83
Pendrel Cl. WS6: Gt Wyr 5F 7
Pendrell Cl. B37: F'bri 6C 106
      WV8: Cod 4G 13
Pendrell Ct. WV8: Cod 4G 13
Pendrill Rd. WV10: Bush 4A 16
Penfields Rd. DY8: Amb 5E 109
Penge Gro. B44: Gt Barr 2G 67
Penhallow Dr. WV4: Ett 6A 44
Penkridge Cl. WS2: Wals 5B 32
Penkridge Gro. B33: Stech 5D 104
Penkridge St. WS2: Wals 6B 32
Penk Ri. WV6: Tett 5G 25
Penleigh Gdns. WV5: Wom 6F 57
Penley Gro. B8: W End 3H 103
Penmakers Ct. B66: Smeth 5E 99
Penmire Gro. WS4: Wals 4E 33
PENN 1D 58
Pennant Ct. B65: Row R 6B 96
      WV3: Wolv 6A 170 (3F 43)
Pennant Gro. B29: W Cas 3E 131
Pennant Rd. B64: Crad H 2F 111
      B65: Row R 6B 96
Pennard Gro. B32: Quin 1D 130
Penn Cl. WS3: Blox 1A 32
PENN COMMON 3D 58
Penn Comn. Rd. WV4: Penn 4C 58
Penncricket Ct. B65: Row R 6F 97
      (off Penncricket La.)
Penncricket La. B65: Row R 6E 97
      B68: O'bry 6F 97
Penncroft La. WV4: Penn 4D 58
Penndale Cl. B24: Erd 1A 86
PENN FIELDS 5E 43
Penn Golf Course 3E 59
Penn Gro. B29: W Cas 3F 131
Pennhouse Av. WV4: Penn 6D 42
Penn Ind. Est. B64: Crad H 2F 111
Pennine Dr. DY3: Lwr G 4H 75
Pennine Way B8: Salt 4C 102
      DY8: Amb 5E 109
      WV12: W'hall 4D 30
Pennington Cl. B70: W Brom 5G 79
Penn Rd. B65: Row R 6E 97
      DY3: Sed 6H 59
      WV2: Wolv 6A 170 (4F 43)
      WV3: Wolv 4F 43
      WV4: Penn 2B 58
      WV4: Sed 4D 58
Penn Rd. Island
      WV2: Wolv 5A 170 (2G 43)
Penn Rd. Retail Pk.
      WV3: Wolv 3G 43
Penns Cl. B76: Walm 6D 70
Penns Lake Rd. B76: Walm 5C 70
Penns La. B46: Col 2H 107
      B72: W Grn 6H 69
      B76: Walm 6H 69
Penn St. B4: Birm 2H 5 (6A 102)
      B64: Old H 3H 111
      WV3: Wolv 3F 43
Penns Wood Cl. DY3: Sed 3G 59

Penns Wood Dr. B76: Walm 6D 70
Pennwood Ct. WV4: Penn 5B 42
Pennwood La. WV4: Penn 2D 58
Pennyacre Rd. B14: King H 5F 147
Penny Ct. WS6: Gt Wyr 5F 7
Pennycress Grn. WS11: Nort C 1D 8
Pennycroft Ho. B33: Stech 6C 104
Penny Farthing Arc. DY3: Sed 5H 59
(off Bilston St.)
Pennyfield Cft. B33: Stech 6C 104
Pennyhill La. B71: W Brom 6C 64
Penny Royal Cl. DY3: Lwr G 5H 75
Pennyroyal Cl. WS5: Wals 2F 65
Penrice Dr. B69: O'bry 6H 77
Penrith Cl. DY5: Brie H 3F 109
Penrith Cft. B32: Bart G 5B 130
Penrith Gro. B37: Chel W 1E 123
Penryn Cl. WS5: Wals 4H 49
Penryn Rd. WS5: Wals 4H 49
Pensby Cl. B13: Mose 5D 134
Pens Cl. B66: Smeth 5E 99
Pensford Rd. B31: N'fld 4G 145
Pensham Cft. B90: M'path 3B 165
Penshaw Cl. WV9: Pend 4E 15
Penshaw Gro. B13: Mose 4D 134
Penshurst Av. B20: Hand 6F 83
PENSNETT .2G 93
Pensnett Rd. DY1: Dud 2A 94
DY5: Brie H 4G 93
Pensnett Trad. Est. DY6: P'ntt 1D 92
Penstock Dr. B69: O'bry 5G 97
Penstone La. WV4: Lwr P 1E 57
Pentland Cft. B12: Birm 4H 117
Pentland Gdns. WV3: Wolv 1C 42
Pentos Dr. B11: S'hll 1D 134
Pentridge Cl. B76: Walm 2D 86
Penwood Gdns. WV14: Cose 5E 61
Penzer St. DY6: K'wfrd 2B 92
Peolsford Rd. WS3: Pels 3E 21
Peony Wlk. B23: Erd 4B 84
Peplins Way B30: King Nor 4D 146
Peplow Rd. B33: Stech 5E 105
Pepperbox Dr. DY4: Tip 2A 78
Peppercorn Pl. B70: W Brom 3A 80
Pepper Wood Dr. B31: Longb 6A 144
Pepys Ct. B43: Gt Barr 6A 66
Perch Av. B37: F'bri 6C 106
Perch Cl. WV10: Wolv 5D 28
Perch Rd. WS2: Wals 5G 31
Percival Rd. B16: Edg 2G 115
Percy Bus. Pk. B69: O'bry 2F 97
Percy Rd. B11: S'hll 2D 134
Peregrine Cl. DY1: Dud 6B 76
Pereira Rd. B17: Harb 4G 115
Perimeter Rd. B40: Nat E C 1F 139
Perivale Gro. WV14: Cose 5F 61
Perivale Way DY8: Amb 3E 109
Periwinkle Cl. WS8: Clay 1H 21
Perkins Cl. DY1: Dud 1E 77
Perks Rd. WV11: Wed 6A 18
Perott Dr. B75: R'ley 1B 54
Perrins Gro. B8: W End 3G 103
Perrins La. DY9: W'cte 1B 126
Perrins Ri. DY9: W'cte 1B 126
Perrott Gdns. DY5: Brie H 2E 109
Perrott's Folly 2B 116
Perrott St. B18: Win G 3H 99
PERRY 1G 83
Perry Av. B42: P Barr 2E 83
WV10: Bush 1B 28
PERRY BARR 2C 82
Perry Barr Locks 1E 83
Perry Barr Stadium (Greyhound) 4F 83
Perry Barr Station (Rail) 5F 83
PERRY BEECHES 6D 66
Perry Cl. DY2: Dud 1F 95
PERRY COMMON 5D 68
Perry Comn. Rd. B23: Erd 6B 68
Perry Ct. B68: O'bry 4H 113
Perryford Dr. B91: Sol 1G 165
Perry Hall Dr. WV12: W'hall 4B 30
Perry Hall Rd. WV11: Wed 3H 29
Perry Hill Cres. B68: O'bry 4H 113
Perry Hill Ho. B68: O'bry 3A 114
Perryhill La. B68: O'bry 4H 113
Perry Hill Rd. B68: O'bry 4H 113

Perry Pk. Cres. B42: P Barr 1E 83
Perry Pk. Ind. Est. B42: P Barr 1E 83
Perry Pk. Rd. B64: Old H 2B 112
B65: B'hth 2B 112
Perry St. B66: Smeth 2D 98
DY4: Tip .3A 78
WS10: Darl 3D 46
(not continuous)
WS10: W'bry 3F 63
WV14: Bils 2G 61
Perry St. Trad. Est. WV14: Bils 2G 61
Perry Villa Dr. B42: P Barr 2F 83
Perry Wlk. B23: Erd 1B 84
Perry Well Dr. B6: Witt 3H 83
Perry Well Rd. B6: Witt 2H 83
Perrywood Rd. B42: Gt Barr 5C 66
Persehouse St. WS1: Wals 1D 48
Pershore Av. B29: S Oak 3D 132
Pershore Cl. WS3: Blox 5F 19
Pershore Rd. B5: Edg 3C 146
B29: S Oak 3C 146
B30: King Nor, Stir 3C 146
B63: Hale 3A 128
WS3: Blox 5F 19
Pershore Rd. Sth.
B30: King Nor 3B 146
Pershore St. B5: Birm 6E 5 (2G 117)
Pershore Way WS3: Blox 5F 19
Perth Rd. WV12: W'hall 3B 30
PERTON 5E 25
Perton Brook Va. WV6: Tett 1F 41
Perton Gro. B29: W Cas 4E 131
WV6: Tett 1F 41
Perton Park Golf Course 6C 24
Perton Rd. WV6: Tett 1E 41
Petchells Cl. DY5: P'ntt 4F 93
Peterdale Dr. WV4: Penn 2D 58
Peterhouse M. B13: Mose 3A 134
Peters Av. B31: N'fld 5D 144
Petersbourne Ct. B28: Hall G 5F 135
Petersfield Ct. B28: Hall G 5F 135
Petersfield Dr. B65: Row R 6E 97
Petersfield Rd. B28: Hall G 5E 135
Petersham Pl. B15: Edg 5A 116
Petersham Rd. B44: K'sdng 4C 68
Peter's Hill Rd. DY5: Brie H 4G 109
Petershouse Dr. B74: Four O 4F 37
Peters St. B70: W Brom 6G 63
Petford St. B64: Old H 2G 111
Pettitt Cl. B14: King H 5G 147
Pettyfield Cl. B26: Sheld 5F 121
Pettyfields Cl. B93: Know 4B 166
Petworth Cl. WV13: W'hall 3H 45
Petworth Gro. B26: Yard 5C 120
Peveral Dr. B28: Hall G 6F 135
Pevensey Cl. B69: Tiv 1H 95
Peverell Dr. B28: Hall G 6F 135
Peverill Gro. B76: Walm 1C 70
Peverill Rd. WV4: Ett 2A 60
WV6: Pert 5F 25
Peveril Way B43: Gt Barr 3B 66
Pheasant Cft. B36: Cas B 1C 106
Pheasant Rd. B67: Smeth 1B 114
Pheasant St. DY5: Brie H 6G 93
PHEASEY 1F 67
Philip Ct. B76: Walm 2D 70
Philip Rd. B63: Hale 2H 127
DY4: Tip .2D 78
Philip Sidney Rd. B11: S'hll 2C 134
Philip St. WV14: Cose 4F 61
Philip Victor Rd. B20: Hand 6B 82
Phillimore Rd. B8: Salt 4D 102
Phillip Rd. WS2: Wals 5A 48
Phillips Av. WV11: Wed 6H 17
Phillips St. B6: Aston 3G 101
Phillips St. Ind. Est. B6: Aston 3H 101
Phipson Rd. B11: S'hll 1B 134
Phoenix, The B90: Bly P 6D 164
Phoenix Bus. Pk. B7: Nech 3A 102
Phoenix Cl. B5: Edg 6E 117
(off West Dr.)
B35: Cas V 4D 86
Phoenix Dr. WS9: A'rdge 2C 34

Phoenix Grn. B15: Edg 4A 116
Phoenix Ind. Est. WV14: Bils 1H 61
Phoenix Intl. Ind. Est.
B70: W Brom 2F 79
Phoenix Pk. B65: Row R 1E 113
Phoenix Pas. DY2: Dud 6F 77
(off Trindle Rd.)
Phoenix Ri. B23: Erd 6B 68
WS10: Darl 1D 62
WV14: Wolv 4G 43
Phoenix Rd. DY4: Tip 1H 77
WV11: Wed 6F 29
Phoenix Rd. Ind. Est. WV11: Wed 6F 29
Phoenix St. B70: W Brom 3F 79
WV2: Wolv 5H 43
Phoenix Works Ind. Est.
WS10: Darl 4E 47
Piccadilly Arc. B2: Birm 4D 4
Piccadilly Cl. B37: Chel W 2E 123
Pickenham Rd. B14: King H 6A 148
Pickering Cft. B32: Bart G 4A 130
Pickering Rd. WV11: Wed 4F 29
Pickersleigh Cl. B63: Hale 2A 128
Pickford St. B5: Birm 5H 5 (1H 117)
Pickrell Rd. WV14: Cose 4D 60
Pickwick Cl. B13: Mose 3B 134
Pickwick Gro. B13: Mose 3C 134
Pickwick Pl. WV14: Bils 1G 61
Picton Cft. B37: Chel W 1F 123
Picton Gro. B13: Mose 2B 148
Picturedrome Way WS10: Darl 5D 46
Piddock Rd. B66: Smeth 4E 99
Pierce Av. B92: Olton 2C 136
Piercy St. B70: W Brom 4G 79
Piers Rd. B18: Hock 2C 100
B21: Hand 2C 100
Pier St. WS8: Bwnhls 6B 10
Piggotts Cft. B37: F'bri 6B 106
Pike Cl. B20: Hand 6B 82
Pike Dr. B37: Chel W 6E 107
Pikehelve St. B70: W Brom 6E 63
Pikehorne Cft. B36: Cas B 5H 87
Pike Rd. WS2: Wals 5G 31
Pikes, The B45: Rub 1F 157
Pikewater Rd. B9: Bord G 1E 119
Pilkington Av. B72: W Grn 2H 69
Pilson Cl. B36: Hodg H 1D 104
Pimbury Rd. WV12: W'hall 2D 30
Pimlico Ct. DY3: Lwr G 4H 75
Pimpernel Dr. WS5: Wals 2E 65
Pinbury Cft. B37: Mars G 2D 122
Pineapple Cl. B14: King H 1E 147
Pineapple Gro. B30: Stir 5E 133
Pineapple Pl. B14: King H 1F 147
Pineapple Rd. B30: Stir 6E 133
Pine Av. B66: Smeth 2C 98
WS10: W'bry 6F 47
Pine Cl. B91: Sol 5D 150
DY6: K'wfrd 4B 92
WS6: Gt Wyr 1F 7
WV3: Wolv 2E 43
Pine Gro. B14: King H 2A 148
Pinehurst Dr. B38: King Nor 4B 146
Pine Leigh B74: Four O 2H 53
Pineneedle Cft. WV12: W'hall 5E 31
Pine Rd. B69: Tiv 1A 96
Pines, The B45: Redn 6G 143
B90: Ches G 4B 164
WS1: Wals 3D 48
WV3: Wolv 2B 42
Pine Sq. B37: Chel W 1D 122
Pine St. WS3: Blox 5B 20
Pine Tree Cl. WS7: Burn 1D 10
Pinetree Dr. B74: S'tly 2F 51
Pineview B31: N'fld 5D 144
Pine Wlk. B31: N'fld 4F 145
DY9: W'cte 2H 125
WV8: Cod 5F 13
Pinewall Av. B38: King Nor 6C 146
Pineways B74: Four O 6C 36
DY8: Word 1A 108
Pineways, The B69: O'bry 4C 96
Pineways Dr. WV6: Wolv 5C 26
Pinewood Bus. Pk.
B37: Mars G 3D 122

Pinewood Cl. B44: Gt Barr 6G 67
  B45: Rub 1D 156
  WS5: Wals 6E 49
  WS8: Bwnhls 3A 10
  WV3: Wolv 3G 41
  WV5: Wom 1G 73
  WV12: W'hall 3D 30
Pinewood Ct. B37: Mars G 3D 122
Pinewood Dr. B32: Bart G 4G 129
Pinewood Gro. B91: Sol 5D 150
Pine Woods B32: Bart G 3G 129
Pinewoods B31: N'fld 5D 130
  B62: Quin 4G 113
Pinewood Wlk. DY6: K'wfrd 1C 92
Pinfold, The WS3: Blox 1A 32
Pinfold Ct. WS10: Darl 6C 46
Pinfold Cres. WV4: Penn 5B 42
Pinfold Gdns. WV11: Wed 4F 29
Pinfold Gro. WV4: Penn 5B 42
Pinfold Ind. Est. WS3: Blox 1A 32
Pinfold La. WS6: C Hay 3C 6
  WS9: A'rdge 4D 50
  WS11: Nort C 1C 8
  WV4: Penn 5B 42
Pinfold Rd. B91: Sol 2A 152
Pinfold St. B2: Birm 4C 4 (1F 117)
  B69: O'bry 1G 97
  WS10: Darl 6C 46
                            (not continuous)
  WV14: Bils 6F 45
Pinfold St. Extension WS10: Darl 6C 46
Pingle Cl. B71: W Brom 4D 64
Pingle La. WS7: Hamm 1F 11
Pinkney Pl. B68: O'bry 6A 98
Pinley Gro. B43: Gt Barr 2E 67
Pinley Way B91: Sol 1E 165
Pinner Ct. B17: Harb 5G 115
Pinner Gro. B32: Quin 1C 130
Pinson Gdns. WV13: W'hall 1H 45
Pinson Rd. WV13: W'hall 1H 45
Pintail Dr. B23: Erd 5C 84
Pinto Cl. B16: Birm 1B 116
Pinza Cft. B36: Hodg H 1B 104
Pioli Pl. WS2: Wals 4B 32
Pioneer Way B35: Cas V 5F 87
Piper Cl. WV6: Pert 5F 25
Piper Pl. DY8: Amb 3D 108
Piper Rd. WV3: Wolv 3A 42
Pipers Grn. B28: Hall G 2F 149
Piper's Row
  WV1: Wolv 3D 170 (1H 43)
Pipes Mdw. WV14: Bils 6G 45
Pippin Av. B63: Crad 4D 110
Pirbright Cl. WV14: Bils 2G 61
Pirrey Cl. WV14: Cose 4G 61
Pitcairn Cl. B30: Stir 1D 146
Pitcairn Dr. B62: Hale 6B 112
Pitcairn Rd. B67: Smeth 2B 114
Pitchwood Cl. WS10: Darl 5C 46
Pitclose Rd. B31: N'fld 6F 145
Pitfield Rd. B33: Kitts G 2A 122
Pitfield Row DY1: Dud 6D 76
Pitfields Cl. B68: O'bry 3G 113
Pitfields Rd. B68: O'bry 3G 113
Pitfield St. DY1: Dud 6E 77
Pithall Rd. B34: S End 4H 105
Pit Leasow Cl. B30: Stir 5D 132
Pitman Rd. B32: Quin 6A 114
Pitts Farm Rd. B24: Erd 2A 86
Pitt St. B4: Birm 6A 102
  WV3: Wolv 4A 170 (2G 43)
Pixall Dr. B15: Edg 4D 116
Pixhall Wlk. B35: Cas V 4F 87
                            (not continuous)
Plainview Cl. WS9: A'rdge 1G 51
Plaistow Av. B36: Hodg H 2A 104
Plane Gro. B37: Chel W 2D 122
Planetary Bus. Cen.
  WV13: W'hall 6E 29

Planetary Ind. Est. WV13: W'hall 6E 29
Planetary Rd. WV13: W'hall 5D 28
Plane Tree Rd. WS5: Wals 1F 65
Planetree Rd. B74: S'tly 3F 51
Planet Rd. DY5: Brie H 5H 93
Planks La. B46: Wat O 5C 88
Planks La. WV5: Wom 1F 73
Plantation, The DY5: P'ntt 2F 93
Plantation Dr. B75: S Cold 5D 54
Plantation La. DY3: Himl 3H 73
Plantation Rd. WS5: Wals 1E 65
Plant Ct. DY5: Brie H 1H 109
                            (off Lwr. Derry St.)
Plants Brook Cres. B24: Erd 4B 86
Plantsbrook Local Nature Reserve 2D 86
Plants Cl. B73: New O 4D 68
Plants Gro. B24: Erd 2B 86
Plants Hollow DY5: Brie H 2A 110
Plant St. B64: Old H 2F 111
  DY8: Word 1C 108
Plant Way WS3: Pels 3D 20
Plascom Rd. WV1: Wolv 2C 44
Plascom Road (Wolverhampton)
  (Park & Ride) 2C 44
Platt Brook Way B26: Sheld 4G 121
Platts Cres. DY8: Amb 3C 108
Platts Dr. DY8: Amb 3C 108
Platts Rd. DY8: Amb 3C 108
Platt St. WS10: Darl 6D 46
Playdon Gro. B14: King H 4A 148
Pleasant Cl. DY6: K'wfrd 5A 92
Pleasant St. B70: W Brom 5G 63
                                 (Castle St.)
  B70: W Brom 5A 80
                               (Newhall St.)
Pleasant Vw. DY3: Gorn 5H 75
PLECK 3H 47
Pleck Bus. Pk. WS2: Wals 2A 48
Pleck Ho. B14: King H 6E 147
                  (off Winterbourne Cft.)
Pleck Ind. Est. WS2: Wals 3A 48
Pleck Rd. WS2: Wals 3A 48
Pleck Wlk. B38: King Nor 6C 146
Plestowes Cl. B90: Shir 2H 149
Plimsoll Gro. B32: Quin 6A 114
Plough & Harrow Rd.
  B16: Edg 2B 116
Plough Av. B32: Bart G 3A 130
Plough Ct. B75: R'ley 6C 38
Ploughmans Pl. B75: R'ley 5B 38
Ploughmans Wlk. DY6: W Hth 2G 91
  WV8: Pend 6C 14
Plover Cl. WV10: F'stne 1D 16
Ploverdale Cres. DY6: K'wfrd 2E 93
Plowden Rd. B33: Stech 5D 104
Plume St. B6: Aston 1C 102
Plummers Ho. B6: Aston 2G 101
Plumstead Rd. B44: K'sdng 5A 68
Plym Cl. WV11: Wed 4E 29
Plymouth Cl. B31: Longb 2E 159
Plymouth Rd. B30: Stir 6D 132
Plympton M. B71: W Brom 1A 80
Poets Cnr. B10: Small H 4D 118
Poets Ct. B70: W Brom 2H 79
Point, The B12: Birm 3H 117
Point 3 B3: Birm 2B 4 (6E 101)
Pointon Cl. WV14: Cose 3C 60
Polden Cl. B63: Hale 4E 127
Polesworth Gro. B34: S End 3F 105
Pollard Rd. B27: A Grn 4A 136
Pollards, The B23: Erd 5E 69
Polly Brooks Yd. DY9: Lye 6A 110
Polo Flds. DY9: Pedm 4F 125
Pomeroy Rd. B32: Bart G 4A 130
  B43: Gt Barr 1F 67
Pommel Cl. WS5: Wals 1D 64
Pond Cres. WV2: Wolv 4A 44
Pond Gro. WV2: Wolv 4A 44
Pond La. WV2: Wolv 3H 43
Pool Cotts. WS7: Chase 1A 10
Poole Cres. B17: Harb 2G 131
  WS8: Bwnhls 3G 9
  WV14: Cose 3F 61
Poole Ho. Rd. B43: Gt Barr 2A 66
Pool End Cl. B93: Know 3B 166

Pooles La. WV12: W'hall 1E 31
Poole St. DY8: Stourb 1C 124
Pool Farm Rd. B27: A Grn 4H 135
Pool Fld. Av. B31: N'fld 6C 130
Poolfield Dr. B91: Sol 4D 150
POOL GREEN 4B 34
Pool Grn. WS9: A'rdge 4C 34
Pool Grn. Ter. WS9: A'rdge 4C 34
Pool Hall Cres. WV3: Wolv 3F 41
Pool Hall Rd. WV3: Wolv 3F 41
Pool Hayes La. WV12: W'hall 4A 30
Poolhouse Rd. WV5: Wom 1D 72
Pool La. B69: O'bry 5F 97
Pool Mdw. B76: Walm 5E 71
  WS6: C Hay 4D 6
Pool Mdw. Cl. B13: Mose 4C 134
  B91: Sol .6B 152
Pool Mdw. Ho. B91: Sol 6B 152
Pool Rd. B63: Hale 2B 128
  B66: Smeth 4F 99
  WS7: Chase 1A 10
                            (not continuous)
  WS8: Bwnhls 3A 10
  WV11: Wed 3A 30
Pool St. B6: Aston 3H 101
  DY1: Dud .1C 76
  WS1: Wals 2D 48
  WV2: Wolv 6A 170 (3G 43)
                            (not continuous)
Pooltail Wlk. B31: Longb 6B 144
Pool Vw. WS4: Rus 2H 33
  WS6: Gt Wyr 1G 7
Pool Way B33: Yard 2E 121
Pope Rd. WV10: Bush 1C 28
Popes La. B30: King Nor 3H 145
  B38: King Nor 3H 145
  B69: O'bry 3H 97
  WV6: Tett .3G 25
Pope St. B1: Birm 6D 100
  B66: Smeth 2F 99
Poplar Arc. B91: Sol 3G 151
                          (within Touchwood)
Poplar Av. B11: S'brk 5B 118
  B12: Bal H 1A 134
  B14: King H 5H 133
  B17: Edg .2E 115
  B19: Loz .1E 101
  B20: Hand 6E 83
  B23: Erd .3F 85
  B37: Chel W 3E 123
  B69: O'bry 5G 97
  B69: Tiv 1B 96
  B70: W Brom 5C 80
  B75: S Cold 4D 54
  DY4: Tip 2F 77
  WS2: Wals 6D 30
  WS5: Wals 1E 65
  WS8: Bwnhls 5C 10
  WV11: Wed 2D 28
Poplar Cl. B69: Tiv 6C 78
  WS2: Wals 5E 31
  WV5: Wom 1H 73
Poplar Cres. DY1: Dud 4D 76
  DY8: Stourb 2C 124
Poplar Dr. B6: Witt 2H 83
  B8: Salt .3D 102
Poplar Grn. DY1: Dud 1C 76
Poplar Gro. B19: Loz 1E 101
  B66: Smeth 6F 99
  B70: W Brom 6C 80
Poplar La. B62: Roms 3A 142
Poplar Ri. B42: Gt Barr 6D 66
  B69: Tiv 1C 96
  B74: Lit As 3D 36
Poplar Rd. B11: S'hll 6B 118
  B14: King H 5G 133
  B66: Smeth 2E 115
  B69: O'bry 1G 97
  B91: Sol .3G 151
  B93: Dorr 5B 166
  DY6: K'wfrd 4C 92
  DY8: Stourb 2C 124
  WS6: Gt Wyr 4G 7
  WS8: Bwnhls 5C 10
  WS10: W'bry 5G 47
  WV3: Wolv 5E 43
  WV14: Bils 4H 45

Poplars, The B11: S'brk 5C **118**
B16: Birm 5B **100**
B66: Smeth *5G 99*
(off Montague Rd.)
DY5: P'ntt 2F **93**
DY8: Word 1D **108**
Poplars Dr. B36: Cas B 1F **105**
WV8: Cod 5F **13**
Poplars Ind. Est., The B6: Witt 2H **83**
Poplar St. B66: Smeth 4G **99**
WV2: Wolv 5H **43**
Poplar Trees *B47: H'wd* *3A 162*
(off May Farm Cl.)
Poplar Way B91: Sol 3G **151**
Poplarwoods B32: Bart G 3H **129**
Poppy Cl. B73: Bold 3F **69**
Poppy Dr. WS5: Wals 2D **64**
Poppy Gro. B8: Salt 5F **103**
Poppy La. B24: Erd 2A **86**
Poppymead B23: Erd 5B **68**
Porchester Cl. WS9: Wals W 4C **22**
Porchester Dr. B19: Hock 3F **101**
Porchester St. B19: Hock 3F **101**
Porlock Cres. B31: N'fld 4B **144**
Porlock Rd. DY8: Amb 5E **109**
Portal Rd. WS2: Wals 1F **47**
Portchester Dr. WV11: Wed 4F **29**
Porter Cl. B72: W Grn 6H **69**
Porters Cft. B17: Harb 3E **115**
Porters Dr. B14: King H 3E **147**
Porter's Fld. DY2: Dud 6F **77**
Portersfield Ind. Est. B64: Crad H . . .4F **111**
Portersfield Rd. B64: Crad H 3E **111**
Portershill Dr. B90: Shir 6A **150**
Porters Lodge *DY8: Word* *6C 92*
(off Clock Tower Vw.)
Porter St. DY2: Dud 6F **77**
Porter St. Sth. DY2: Dud 6F **77**
Porters Way B9: Bord G 1E **119**
Portfield Dr. DY4: Tip 4A **78**
Portfield Gro. B23: Erd 1G **85**
Porthkerry Gro. DY3: Sed 5F **59**
Port Hope Rd. B11: S'brk 4A **118**
Porthouse Gro. WV14: Cose 2D **60**
Portia Av. B90: Shir 5H **149**
Portland Av. WS9: A'rdge 4D **34**
Portland Cl. WS9: A'rdge 4D **34**
Portland Cres. DY9: Pedm 4F **125**
Portland Dr. B69: Tiv 5D **78**
DY9: Pedm 4F **125**
Portland Pl. WV14: Cose 6D **60**
Portland Rd. B16: Edg 6F **99**
B17: Edg 6F **99**
WS9: A'rdge 3D **34**
Portland St. B6: Aston 2A **102**
WS2: Wals 6C **32**
Portland Ter. *B18: Hock* *4C 100*
(off Crabtree Rd.)
Port La. WV9: Coven 1H **13**
Portman Rd. B13: Mose 6H **133**
PORTOBELLO .3G **45**
Portobello Cl. WV13: W'hall 2F **45**
Portobello Rd. B70: W Brom 5G **63**
Portrush Av. B38: King Nor 6G **145**
Portrush Rd. WV6: Pert 5D **24**
Portsdown Cl. WV10: Bush 2B **28**
Portsdown Rd. B63: Hale 4E **127**
Portsea St. WS3: Blox 3A **32**
Portswood Cl. WV9: Pend 6D **14**
PORTWAY 4C **96**
Portway, The DY6: K'wfrd 4C **92**
Portway Cl. B91: Sol 6C **150**
DY6: K'wfrd 4C **92**
Portway Hill B65: Row R 3B **96**
Portway Rd. B65: Row R 5B **96**
B69: O'bry 2E **97**
WS10: W'bry 2E **63**
WV14: Bils 4G **45**
Portway Rd. Ind. Est. B69: O'bry . . .2E **97**
Portway Wlk. B65: Row R 3C **96**
Posey Cl. B21: Hand 4H **81**
Post Office Rd. WV5: Seis 2A **56**
Poston Cft. B14: King H 3F **147**
Potter Cl. B23: Erd 5D **68**
Potter Ct. *DY5: Brie H* *1H 109*
(off The Promenade)
Potters Brook DY4: Tip 2B **78**

Potters La. B6: Aston 3G **101**
WS10: W'bry 3E **63**
Potterton Way B66: Smeth 1D **98**
Pottery Rd. B66: Smeth 2E **99**
B68: O'bry 2A **114**
Pouk Hill Cl. WS2: Wals 6G **31**
Pouk La. WS14: Hilt 5G **11**
Poultney St. B70: W Brom 6F **63**
Poulton Cl. B13: Mose 3A **134**
Pound Cl. B68: O'bry 6F **97**
Pound Grn. B8: Salt 3F **103**
Pound La. B32: Fran 4F **143**
B46: Col 5H **107**
Pound La. Ind. Est. B63: Crad 4C **110**
Pound La. Units DY5: Brie H 6H **93**
Poundley Cl. B36: Cas B 1G **105**
Pound Rd. B14: King H 6G **147**
B68: O'bry 6F **97**
(not continuous)
WS10: W'bry 6F **47**
Pountney St. WV2: Wolv 6A **170** (3G **43**)
Powell Av. B32: Quin 5G **113**
Powell Pl. DY4: Tip 2C **78**
WV14: Bils 2G **61**
Powells Cl. B72: W Grn 3A **70**
Powells Ho. B73: New O 3C **68**
Powell St. B1: Birm 6D **100**
B63: Hale 2B **128**
WV10: Wolv 5B **28**
Power Cres. B16: Birm 1C **116**
Powerleague
Birmingham 6C **84**
Birmingham South 2D **120**
Halesowen 6D **110**
Power Way DY4: Tip 5D **62**
Powick Pl. B19: Loz 2E **101**
Powick Rd. B23: Erd 6D **84**
Powis Av. DY4: Tip 1A **78**
Powke La. B64: Old H 6H **95**
B65: Row R 1A **112**
Powke La. Ind. Est. B65: Row R 1A **112**
Powlers Cl. DY9: W'cte 3A **126**
Powlett St. WV2: Wolv 5D **170** (2H **43**)
Poxon Rd. WS9: Wals W 3C **22**
Poynings, The WV6: Tett 4A **26**
Precinct, The WV12: W'hall 4B **30**
Premier Bus. Cen. DY9: Lye 6B **110**
Premier Bus. Pk. WS2: Wals 2B **48**
Premier Cl. B30: King Nor 4E **147**
Premier Pk. B73: New O 3D **68**
Premier Partnership Ind. Est.
DY6: K'wfrd 6F **93**
Premier Trad. Est. B7: Birm 4H **101**
Prescot Rd. DY9: Lye 1G **125**
Prescott St. B18: Hock 5D **100**
Prestbury Rd. B6: Aston 1G **101**
Preston Av. B76: Walm 2C **70**
Preston Ho. *WS1: Wals* *2D 48*
(off Paddock La.)
Preston Rd. B18: Win G 3A **100**
B26: Yard 5B **120**
Prestons Row WV14: Cose 2C **60**
Prestwick Cl. B75: S Cold 3A **54**
Prestwick Rd. B35: Cas V 3F **87**
DY6: K'wfrd 3A **92**
Prestwood Av. WV11: Wed 2F **29**
Prestwood Dr. DY7: Stourt 4A **108**
Prestwood Rd. B29: W Cas 5F **131**
WV11: Wed 4C **28**
Prestwood Rd. W. WV11: Wed 3D **28**
Pretoria Rd. B9: Bord G 6E **103**
Priam Gro. WS3: Pels 1F **21**
Price Cres. WV14: Bils 4F **45**
Price Rd. DY9: Lye 5B **110**
WS10: W'bry 2A **64**
Price St. DY3: Gorn 4G **75**
B4: Birm 1E **5** (5G **101**)
B66: Smeth 4F **99**
B70: W Brom 4A **80**
DY2: Dud 1G **95**
WV14: Bils 6H **45**
PRIESTFIELD .4C **44**
Priestfield (Park & Tram) 4C **44**
Priestfield Cl. B44: Gt Barr 3E **67**
Priestfield Stop (Metro) 4C **44**

Priestfield St. WV14: Bils 5D **44**
Priestland Rd. B34: S End 2F **105**
Priestley Cl. B20: Hand 6C **82**
B63: Crad 5D **110**
Priestley Rd. B11: S'brk 4A **118**
WS2: Wals 4G **31**
Priestly Wharf B7: Birm 1H **5** (5H **101**)
Priest St. B64: Old H 2H **111**
Primley Av. B36: Hodg H 2B **104**
WS2: Wals 2H **47**
Primley Cl. WS2: Wals 1H **47**
Primrose Av. B11: S'hll 5C **118**
DY4: Tip 5C **62**
WV10: F'hses, Bush 4H **15**
Primrose Bank B68: O'bry 5H **97**
Primrose Cl. B64: Crad H 3D **110**
WS3: Pels 2E **21**
Primrose Cotts. B19: Loz 2D **100**
Primrose Cft. B23: Erd 6C **68**
B28: Hall G 2F **149**
Primrose Gdns. B38: King Nor 1B **160**
WS8: Cod 4G **13**
PRIMROSE HILL 5F **95**
Primrose Hill B38: King Nor 6B **146**
(not continuous)
B67: Smeth 5B **98**
DY8: Word 2C **108**
Primrose Hill Trad. Est. DY2: Neth . . .5F **95**
Primrose La. B28: Hall G 2F **149**
B90: Dic H 4G **163**
WV10: Bush 3A **16**
(Cromwell Rd.)
WV10: Bush 1B **28**
(Emerson Gro.)
Primrose Pk. DY5: P'ntt 2G **93**
Primrose Rd. DY2: Neth 5E **95**
Primroses, The WS5: Wals 1F **65**
Primrose Woods B32: Bart G 3H **129**
Primsland Cl. B90: M'path 2G **165**
Prince Albert St. B9: Small H 2D **118**
(not continuous)
Prince Andrew Cres. B45: Fran 5E **143**
Prince Charles Cl. B45: Fran 5E **143**
Prince Charles Rd. WV14: Bils 2H **61**
Prince Edward Dr. B45: Fran 5E **143**
Prince George Rd. WS10: W'bry 6G **47**
Prince of Wales La.
B14: King H, Yard W 5C **148**
Prince of Wales Way
B66: Smeth 4G **99**
Princep Cl. B43: Gt Barr 1F **67**
Prince Philip Cl. B45: Fran 5E **143**
Prince Rd. B30: King Nor 4B **146**
Princes Av. WS1: Wals 3E **49**
Princes Cl. B14: Yard W 5C **148**
Princes Dr. WV8: Cod 4G **13**
PRINCES END 5H **61**
Princes End Ind. Est. DY4: Tip 4G **61**
Princes Gdns. WV8: Cod 4F **13**
Princes Ga. B70: W Brom 5C **80**
B91: Sol 3F **151**
Princes Rd. B69: Tiv 5A **78**
DY8: Stourb 3B **124**
Princess Alice Dr. B73: New O 3D **68**
Princess All.
WV1: Wolv 3C **170** (1H **43**)
Princess Anne Dr. B45: Fran 5E **143**
Princess Anne Rd. WS2: Wals 6F **31**
WV14: Bils 2H **61**
Princess Ct. WV10: Wolv 3C **28**
Princess Cres. B63: Hale 5G **111**
Princess Diana Way B45: Fran 5E **143**
Princess Gro. B71: W Brom 5B **64**
Princess Pde. B70: W Brom 4B **80**
Princess Sq. WV1: Wolv 2C **170** (1H **43**)
Princess Rd. B5: Edg 5G **117**
B68: O'bry 1B **114**
Princess Sq. WV14: Bils 2H **61**
Princess St.
WV1: Wolv 3C **170** (1H **43**)
Princess Way WS10: Darl 3C **46**
Prince St. B64: Crad H 3F **111**
DY2: Neth 3E **95**
WS2: Wals 3A **48**
WS9: Wals W 5B **22**
Princes Way B68: O'bry 4H **113**
B91: Sol 3F **151**

Princethorpe Cl. B34: S End 2H **105**
  B90: Shir 5G **149**
Princethorpe Rd. B29: W Cas 4E **131**
  WV13: W'hall 3B **46**
Princeton Gdns. WV9: Pend 5D **14**
Prince William Cl. B23: Erd 5D **84**
Principal Ct. B67: Smeth 4E **99**
Princip St. B4: Birm 1E 5 (5G **101**)
Printing Ho. St. B4: Birm ..2E 5 (6G **101**)
Priors Cl. CV7: Bal C 3H **169**
Priors Mill DY3: Up Gor 2A **76**
Priors Way B23: Erd 5C **68**
Priory, The DY3: Sed 5H **59**
Priory Av. B29: S Oak 3D **132**
Priory Chambers DY1: Dud 6E **77**
  (off Priory St.)
Priory Cl. B46: Col 4H **107**
  B66: Smeth 5G **99**
  B70: W Brom 5D **80**
  DY1: Dud 5D **76**
  DY8: Stourb 2F **125**
Priory Ct. B5: Edg 6E **117**
  B90: M'path 2F **165**
  DY1: Dud 6E **77**
  DY8: Stourb 2F **125**
  WS9: Wals W 3C **22**
  WV1: Wolv 1A 170 (6G **27**)
Priory Courts
  Birmingham 3E 5 (6G **101**)
Priory Dr. B68: O'bry 4A **98**
Priory Fld. Cl. WV14: Cose 4B **60**
Priory Fields Nature Reserve 5D **148**
Priory Gdns. B28: Hall G 3D **148**
Priorygate Way B9: Bord G 1E **119**
Priory Ho. B63: Hale 6H **111**
Priory Ho. Ind. Est. B18: Hock 4C **100**
Priory La. DY3: Sed 6H **59**
Priory New Way Ind. Est.
  B6: Aston 4G **101**
Priory Queensway, The
  B4: Birm 3E 5 (6G **101**)
Priory Rd. B5: Edg 5D **116**
  B6: Aston 1B **102**
  B14: King H 6E **133**
  B15: Edg 5D **116**
  B28: Hall G 2D **148**
  B62: Hale 1E **129**
  B90: Shir 2D **148**
  DY1: Dud 2E **77**
  DY8: Stourb 2F **125**
Priory Sq. B4: Birm 3F **5**
Priory St. DY1: Dud 6E **77**
Priory Wlk. B4: Birm 3F 5 (6G **101**)
  B72: W Grn 6A **70**
Priory Woods Nature Reserve 4E **81**
Pritchard Av. WV11: Wed 3G **29**
Pritchard Cl. B66: Smeth 4F **99**
Pritchard St. DY5: Brie H 6F **93**
  WS10: W'bry 2G **63**
Pritchatts Rd. B15: Edg 6A **116**
Pritchett Av. WV4: Ett 2B **60**
Pritchett Rd. B31: Longb 2F **159**
Pritchett St. B6: Birm 4G **101**
Pritchett Twr. B10: Small H 2C **118**
Private Way B45: Coft H 5A **158**
Privet Cl. B44: Gt Barr 2G **67**
Probert Rd. WV10: Oxl 1E **27**
Proctor St. B7: Birm 4A **102**
Proffitt Cl. WS2: Wals 5C **32**
  WS8: Bwnhls 2C **22**
Proffitt St. WS2: Wals 5C **32**
Prole St. WV10: Wolv 5A **28**
Prologis Pk. B76: Min 3H **87**
  (not continuous)
Promenade, The DY5: Brie H 1H **109**
Prospect Gdns. DY8: Stourb 1E **125**
Prospect Hill DY8: Stourb 1E **125**
Prospect La. B91: Sol 2B **150**
Prospect Pl. B12: Bal H 6H **117**
Prospect Rd. B13: Mose 4H **133**
  B62: Hale 6C **112**
  DY3: Gorn 5F **75**
Prospect Row DY2: Dud 2F **95**
  DY8: Stourb 2E **125**
Prospect St. DY4: Tip 4C **62**
  WV14: Bils 5G **45**
Prospect Trad. Est. B1: Birm 3A **4**

Prosper Mdw. DY6: K'wfrd 2C **92**
Prospero Cl. B45: Fran 5G **143**
Prosser St. WV10: Wolv 4A **28**
  WV14: Bils 6F **45**
Prossers Wlk. B46: Col 2H **107**
Prouds La. WV14: Bils 3F **45**
Provence Cl. WV10: Wolv 5B **28**
Providence Cl. WS3: Blox 2A **32**
  (not continuous)
Providence Dr. DY9: Lye 5B **110**
Providence Ind. Est. DY9: Lye 5A **110**
Providence La. WS3: Blox 3A **32**
Providence Row WV14: Cose 5D **60**
Providence St. B64: Crad H 2F **111**
  DY4: Tip 2C **78**
  DY9: Lye 5A **110**
Pruden Av. WV4: Ett 2B **60**
Pryor Rd. B68: O'bry 6A **98**
Public, The 4B **80**
Puddlers Dr. DY4: Tip 6G **61**
Puddlers Gro. WS10: Darl 1D **62**
Pudsey Dr. B75: Four O 6A **38**
Pugh Cres. WS2: Wals 1E **47**
Pugh Rd. B6: Aston 2A **102**
  WV14: Bils 2G **61**
  WV14: Cose 3B **60**
Pugin Cl. WV6: Pert 6D **24**
Pugin Gdns. B23: Erd 5D **68**
Pulley Cl. WS3: Blox 5H **19**
Pumphouse Way B69: O'bry 5F **97**
Pump St. WV2: Ett 4C **44**
Puppy Grn. DY4: Tip 2A **78**
Purbeck Cl. B63: Hale 4F **127**
Purbeck Cft. B32: Harb 6D **114**
Purbrook Rd. WV1: Wolv 3C **44**
Purcell Rd. WV10: Bush 1H **27**
  (not continuous)
Purdy Rd. WV14: Bils 3G **61**
Purefoy Rd. B13: Mose 2C **148**
Purley Gro. B23: Erd 2A **84**
Purlin Wharf DY2: Neth 5G **95**
Purnells Way B93: Know 4C **166**
Purslet Rd. WV1: Wolv 2C **44**
Purslow Gro. B31: N'fld 5E **145**
Putney Av. B20: Hand 6E **83**
Putney La. B62: Roms 5A **142**
Putney Rd. B20: Hand 6D **82**
Putney Wlk. B37: F'bri 6D **106**
Pype Hayes Cl. B24: Erd 3B **86**
Pype Hayes Golf Course 1D **86**
Pype Hayes Rd. B24: Erd 3B **86**
Pype Marshbrook Rd. B24: Erd 3B **86**
Pytchley Ho. B20: Hand 4B **82**
Pytman Dr. B76: Walm 6E **71**

Q

Quadrangle, The B30: B'vlle 1B **146**
  B90: Shir 1C **164**
Quadrant, The DY3: Sed 4H **59**
Quadrille Lawns WV9: Pend 5D **14**
Quail Grn. WV6: Tett 1F **41**
Qualcast Rd. WV1: Wolv 1B **44**
Qualcast Rd. Ind. Est.
  WV1: Wolv 1B **44**
Quantock Cl. B45: Fran 5H **143**
  B63: Hale 3F **127**
  WS8: Wals W 3C **22**
Quantock Rd. DY8: Amb 5F **109**
Quantry La. DY9: Belb 1A **156**
Quarrington Gro. B14: King H 4A **148**
QUARRY BANK 2B **110**
Quarry Brow DY3: Up Gor 2A **76**
Quarry Cl. WS6: C Hay 2E **7**
Quarry Hill B63: Hale 3H **127**
Quarry Ho. B45: Rub 1F **157**
Quarry Ho. Cl. B45: Fran 6F **143**
Quarry La. B31: N'fld 4D **144**
  B63: Hale 3H **127**
Quarry Pk. Rd. DY8: Stourb 5E **125**
Quarry Ri. B69: Tiv 1H **95**
Quarry Rd. B29: W Cas 4D **130**
  DY2: Neth 1D **110**
Quarry Wlk. B45: Redn 2G **157**
Quartz Point DY3: Sed 3H **59**
Quatford Gdns. WV10: Wolv 4A **28**

Quayle Gro. DY8: Word 6B **92**
Quayside B18: Win G 4C **100**
Quayside Cl. B69: O'bry 1E **97**
Quayside Dr. WS2: Wals 3A **48**
Quayside Wlk. DY2: Neth 5G **95**
Qube B1: Birm 3A **4**
Queen Eleanors Dr. B93: Know 1D **166**
Queen Elizabeth Av. WS2: Wals 6F **31**
Queen Elizabeth Ct. B19: Hock 3D **100**
Queen Elizabeth Rd. B45: Fran 5E **143**
Queen Mary St. WS1: Wals 5B **48**
Queen Mother Cl. B30: B'vlle 5A **132**
Queen Mother Gdns. B17: Harb 5E **115**
Queen's
  WV1: Wolv 3B 170 (1G **43**)
Queens Av. B14: King H 5G **133**
  B18: Hock 3B **100**
  B69: Tiv 6B **78**
  B90: Shir 6H **149**
Queensbridge Rd. B13: Mose 3F **133**
Queens Cl. B24: Erd 5F **85**
  B67: Smeth 4E **99**
Queens Ct. B1: Birm 6B 4 (2E **117**)
  B3: Birm 1C 4 (5F **101**)
  B17: Harb 6E **115**
  B32: Harb 6E **115**
  B91: Sol 3H **151**
  DY5: P'ntt 3G **93**
  WV10: Wolv 3C **28**
Queens Ct. Trad. Est.
  B70: W Brom 4F **79**
Queens Cres. DY8: Amb 4E **109**
  WV14: Cose 4C **60**
Queen's Cross DY1: Dud 1D **94**
Queens Dr. B5: Birm 5D 4 (1F **117**)
  B30: King Nor 3C **146**
  B65: Row R 5D **96**
  WS7: Chase 1B **10**
Queens Dr., The B62: Hale 6C **112**
Queens Gdns. B23: Erd 6B **68**
  DY2: Neth 5E **95**
  WS10: W'bry 2E **63**
  WV8: Cod 4F **13**
  WV14: Bils 4F **45**
Queensgate Bus. Cen. B1: Birm 6C **4**
Queens Hall DY1: Dud 5E **77**
Queen's Head Rd. B21: Hand 2A **100**
Queens Hospital Cl. B15: Birm 2E **117**
Queens Lea WV12: W'hall 4C **30**
Queenslett Rd. B43: Gt Barr 4B **66**
Queens Pde. WS3: Blox 6H **19**
Queen's Pk. Rd. B32: Harb 5D **114**
Queen Sq. WV1: Wolv 3B 170 (1G **43**)
Queen's Ride B5: Edg 1E **133**
Queensridge Ct. B68: O'bry 3H **113**
Queens Rd. B6: Aston 1A **102**
  B23: Erd 4C **84**
  B26: Yard 2D **120**
  B67: Smeth 5B **98**
  DY3: Sed 5A **60**
  DY4: Tip 2H **77**
  DY8: Stourb 5D **108**
  WS4: Rus 2G **33**
  WS5: Wals 5F **49**
Queens Sq. B70: W Brom 4B **80**
Queens Twr. B7: Birm 4B **102**
Queen St. B12: Bal H 6B **118**
  B63: Hale 1A **128**
  B64: Crad H 2F **111**
  B69: O'bry 1G **97**
  B72: S Cold 1A **70**
  DY4: Tip 5H **61**
  DY5: P'ntt 2H **93**
  (Church St.)
  DY5: P'ntt 3G **93**
  (Commonside)
  DY5: Quar B 3C **110**
  (not continuous)
  DY6: K'wfrd 2B **92**
  DY8: Stourb 6D **108**
  DY8: Word 6B **92**
  WS2: Wals 2B **48**
  WS6: C Hay 2D **6**
  WS7: Chase 1B **10**
  WS9: Wals W 5B **22**
  WS10: Darl 3D **46**
  WS10: Mox 1B **62**

Queen St. WS10: W'bry 2E 63
WV1: Wolv 3C 170 (1H 43)
(not continuous)
WV14: Bils 6G 45
(Fraser St.)
WV14: Bils 1B 62
(Tudor Rd.)
Queen St. Ind. Est. WS7: Chase 1B 10
Queen St. Pas. DY5: Quar B 3C 110
Queensway B4: Birm 2D 4 (6F 101)
B6: Witt 4H 83
B63: Hale 2A 128
B68: O'bry 2H 113
B74: S'tly 3A 52
DY9: W'cte 3A 126
Queensway Cl. B68: O'bry 2H 113
Queensway Mall B63: Hale 2B 128
(off Hagley Mall)
Queensway Trad. Est. B5: Birm 3G 5
Queenswood Rd. B13: Mose 1A 134
B75: Four O 2H 53
Quenby Dr. DY1: Dud 4C 76
Quendale WV5: Wom 1E 73
Quentin Dr. DY1: Dud 1B 94
Queslade Cl. B43: Gt Barr 4C 66
QUESLETT 3E 67
Queslett Rd. B43: Gt Barr 4B 66
Queslett Rd. E. B43: Gt Barr 6G 51
B74: S'tly 6G 51
Quicksand La. WS9: A'rdge 5B 34
Quigley Av. B9: Birm 1B 118
Quillets Rd. DY8: Word 6A 92
Quilter Cl. WS2: Wals 6F 31
WV14: Cose 5C 60
Quilter Rd. B24: Erd 5H 85
Quinborne Fitness Cen. 5B 114
Quincey Dr. B24: Erd 4A 86
Quincy Ri. DY5: Brie H 4G 109
QUINTON 5G 113
Quinton Av. WS6: Gt Wyr 2F 7
Quinton Bus. Pk. B32: Quin 6G 113
Quinton Cl. B92: Sol 2H 137
Quinton Ct. B68: O'bry 4A 114
Quintondale B90: Shir 1A 164
Quinton Expressway B32: Quin . . .1H 129
Quinton La. B32: Quin 5A 114
Quinton Pl. WS11: Nort C 1E 9
Quinton Rd. B17: Harb 2E 131
Quinton Rd. W. B32: Quin 6H 113
Quorn Cres. DY8: Word 6A 92
Quorn Gro. B24: Erd 5H 85
Quorn Ho. B20: Hand 4B 82

R

Rabone La. B66: Smeth 3F 99
Rabone Pk. B66: Smeth 3G 99
Raby Cl. B69: Tiv 1H 95
Raby St. WV2: Wolv 6D 170 (3H 43)
Racecourse Dr. DY8: Stourb 3C 124
Racecourse Rd. WV6: Wolv 4E 27
Racecourse Rd. Ind. Est. WV6: Wolv . .4E 27
Racemeadow Cres. DY2: Neth 2E 111
Rachael Gdns. WS10: W'bry 1H 63
Rachel Cl. DY4: Tip 4C 62
Rachel Gdns. B29: S Oak 3H 131
Radbourne Dr. B74: S Cold 4A 54
Radbourne Dr. B63: Crad 4C 110
Radbourne Rd. B90: Shir 4B 150
Radcliffe Dr. B62: Quin 5E 113
Radcliffe Twr. B12: Birm 3H 117
Raddens Rd. B62: Hale 2F 129
Raddington Dr. B92: Olton 5B 136
Raddlebarn Farm Dr.
B29: S Oak 4B 132
Raddlebarn Rd. B29: S Oak 4A 132
Radford Cl. WS5: Wals 2E 65
Radford Dr. WS4: S'fld 5G 21
Radford La. WV3: Lwr P, Wolv 5F 41
WV4: Lwr P 5F 41
Radford Ri. B91: Sol 2A 152
Radford Rd. B29: W Cas 1E 145
Radley Cl. B26: Sheld 4G 121
Radley Gro. B29: W Cas 3E 131
Radley Rd. DY9: W'cte 1B 126
WS4: Rus 2G 33

Radleys, The B33: Kitts G, Sheld 4G 121
Radley's Wlk. B33: Sheld 4G 121
Radlow Cres. B37: Mars G 3D 122
Radnall Ho. B69: O'bry 3D 96
Radnor Cl. B45: Fran 5H 143
Radnor Ct. WS9: Wals W 3B 22
Radnor Cft. WS5: Wals 2G 65
Radnor Grn. B71: W Brom 6A 64
Radnor Rd. B20: Hand 1D 100
B68: O'bry 4H 113
DY3: Sed 5G 59
Radnor St. B18: Hock 3C 100
Radstock Av. B36: Hodg H 2A 104
Radstock Rd. WV12: W'hall 6C 18
Radway Ind. Est. B90: Shir 2C 164
Radway Rd. B90: Shir 2C 164
Raeburn Rd. B43: Gt Barr 1E 67
Raford Rd. B23: Erd 1D 84
Ragdene Rd. B33: Sheld 3H 121
Ragged Rd. DY6: K'wfrd 5D 92
Raglan Av. B66: Smeth 5G 99
WV6: Pert 6F 25
Raglan Cl. DY3: Sed 6F 59
WS9: A'rdge 6H 35
Raglan Rd. B5: Edg 5F 117
B21: Hand 1G 99
B66: Smeth 5G 99
Raglan St. DY5: Brie H 5G 93
WV3: Wolv 4A 170 (1F 43)
(not continuous)
Raglan Way B37: Chel W 2F 123
Ragley Cl. B93: Know 2D 166
WS3: Blox 6G 19
Ragley Dr. B26: Sheld 5G 121
B43: Gt Barr 3H 65
WV13: W'hall 3H 45
Ragley Wlk. B65: Row R 6C 96
Ragnall Av. B33: Sheld 4H 121
Ragstone Cl. WS2: Wals 6G 31
Rail Bri. Est. B70: W Brom 6G 79
Railswood Dr. WS3: Pels 4E 21
Railway Dr. WV1: Wolv 2D 170 (1H 43)
WV14: Bils 6G 45
Railway La. WV13: W'hall 2A 46
Railway Rd. B20: Hand 5H 83
B73: S Cold 6H 53
Railwayside Cl. B66: Smeth 2C 98
(off Forest Cl.)
Railway St. B70: W Brom 3H 79
DY4: Tip 2C 78
WV1: Wolv 2D 170 (1H 43)
WV14: Bils 6G 45
Railway Ter. B7: Nech 3B 102
B42: Gt Barr 1B 82
WS10: W'bry 3F 63
Railway Vw. B10: Small H 4C 118
Railway Wlk. WS11: Nort C 1E 9
Railwharf Sidings DY2: Neth 5F 95
Rainbow Bus. Pk. WV13: W'hall 6C 30
Rainbow St. WV2: Wolv 3G 43
WV14: Cose 6C 44
Rainford Way B38: King Nor 1G 159
(off Nearhill Rd.)
Rainham Cl. DY4: Tip 2F 77
Rainsbrook Dr. B90: M'path 3D 164
Rakegate Cl. WV10: Oxl 6F 15
Rake Way B15: Birm 6A 4 (2D 116)
Raleigh Cl. B21: Hand 6F 81
Raleigh Cft. B43: Gt Barr 2A 66
Raleigh Ind. Est. B21: Hand 6F 81
Raleigh Rd. B9: Bord G 6D 102
WV14: Bils 2H 61
Raleigh St. B71: W Brom 3A 80
WS2: Wals 1A 48
Ralph Barlow Gdns.
B44: K'sdng 5B 68
Ralph Gdns. B44: K'sdng 5B 68
Ralph Rd. B8: Salt 5D 102
B90: Shir 3H 149
Ralphs Mdw. B32: Bart G 3B 130
Ralston Cl. WS3: Blox 3G 19
Ramblers Way B75: R'ley 6C 38
Ramillies Cres. WS6: Gt Wyr 4F 7
Ramp Rd. B26: Birm A 6E 123
Ramsay Rd. B68: O'bry 2A 114
DY4: Tip 6G 61
WS2: Wals 4G 31

Ramsden Cl. B29: W Cas 6F 131
Ramsey Cl. B45: Fran 6E 143
B71: W Brom 5D 64
Ramsey Ho. WS2: Wals 4A 48
Ramsey Rd. B7: Nech 2C 102
Randall Cl. DY6: K'wfrd 5D 92
Randall Lines Ho. WV1: Wolv 6G 27
Randle Dr. B75: R'ley 6A 38
Randle Rd. DY9: Lye 1G 125
Randwick Gro. B44: Gt Barr 4F 67
Ranelagh Rd. WV2: Wolv 5G 43
Range, The B74: S'tly 4G 51
Range, The (Golf Range) 3E 19
Rangeways Rd. DY6: K'wfrd 5D 92
Rangoon Rd. B92: Sol 1A 138
Ranleigh Av. DY6: K'wfrd 5D 92
Rann Cl. B16: Birm 2C 116
Rannoch Cl. DY5: Brie H 3F 109
Ranscombe Dr. DY3: Gorn 5H 75
Ransom Rd. B23: Erd 3C 84
Ranworth Ri. WV4: Penn 1H 59
Ratcliffe Av. B30: King Nor 4F 147
Ratcliffe Cl. DY3: Sed 6B 60
Ratcliffe Dr. WV13: W'hall 3B 46
Ratcliffe Rd. B91: Sol 6G 137
WV11: Wed 3A 30
Ratcliff Wlk. B69: O'bry 2G 97
Ratcliff Way DY4: Tip 1D 78
Rathbone Cl. B5: Edg 4G 117
WV14: Bils 6F 45
Rathbone Rd. B67: Smeth 1D 114
Rathlin Cl. WV9: Pend 4E 15
Rathlin Cft. B36: Cas B 3D 106
Rathmore Cl. DY8: Stourb 3B 124
Rathwell Cl. WV9: Pend 5E 15
Rattle Cft. B33: Stech 6C 104
Ravenall Cl. B34: S End 2F 105
Raven Cl. WS6: C Hay 3D 6
Raven Ct. DY5: Brie H 1H 109
(off Lit. Potter St.)
Raven Cres. WV11: Wed 1H 29
Ravenfield Cl. B8: W End 4F 103
Ravenhayes La. B32: Fran 6G 129
Raven Hays Rd. B31: Longb 5A 144
Ravenhill Dr. WV8: Cod 4G 13
Ravenhurst Dr. B43: Gt Barr 2A 66
Ravenhurst M. B23: Erd 4E 85
Ravenhurst Rd. B17: Harb 4G 115
Ravenhurst St. B12: Birm 3A 118
Raven Rd. WS5: Wals 5F 49
Ravensbourne Gro. WV13: W'hall 1C 46
Ravens Ct. WS8: Bwnhls 6B 10
Ravenscroft DY8: Woll 5A 108
Ravenscroft Rd. B92: Olton 5E 137
WV12: W'hall 4B 30
Ravensdale Cl. WS5: Wals 4F 49
Ravensdale Gdns. WS5: Wals 5F 49
Ravensdale Rd. B10: Small H 4F 119
Ravenshaw B91: Sol 5D 152
Ravenshaw La. B91: Sol 3C 152
(not continuous)
Ravenshaw Rd. B16: Edg 1G 115
Ravenshaw Way B91: Sol 5C 152
Ravenshill Rd. B14: Yard W 3C 148
Ravensholme WV6: Tett 1F 41
Ravenside Retail Pk. B24: Erd 4C 86
Ravensitch Wlk. DY5: Brie H 2A 110
Ravenswood B15: Edg 3A 116
Ravenswood Cl. B74: Four O 3H 53
Ravenswood Dr. B91: Sol 6D 150
Ravenswood Dr. Sth. B91: Sol 6C 150
Ravenswood Hill B46: Col 2H 107
Rawdon Gro. B44: K'sdng 5B 68
Rawlings Rd. B67: Smeth 1D 114
Rawlins Cft. B35: Cas V 4G 87
Rawlins St. B16: Birm 2C 116
Rawnsley Dr. B45: Redn 3G 157
Rayboulds Bri. Rd. WS2: Wals 5A 32
Raybould's Fold DY2: Neth 4E 95
Rayford Dr. B71: W Brom 3D 64
Ray Hall La. B43: Gt Barr 4E 65
Rayleigh Ho. B27: A Grn 2B 136
Rayleigh Rd. WV3: Wolv 3E 43
Raymond Av. B42: Gt Barr 1D 82
Raymond Cl. WS2: Wals 4B 32
Raymond Gdns. WV11: Wed 4G 29

Raymond Rd. B8: Salt 5E **103**
Raymont Gro. B43: Gt Barr 1D **66**
Rayners Cft. B26: Yard 2D **120**
Raynor Rd. WV10: Wolv 3B **28**
RBSA Gallery 2B **4** (6E **101**)
Rea Av. B45: Rub 1E **157**
Reabrook Rd. B31: Longb 1D **158**
Rea Bus. Pk. B7: Birm 5C **102**
Rea Cl. B31: Longb 2E **159**
Rea Ct. B5: Birm 5H **5** (1H **117**)
 B12: Birm 3A **118**
Readers Wlk. B43: Gt Barr 4B **66**
Rea Fordway B45: Fran 6F **143**
Reansway Sq. WV6: Wolv 5E **27**
Reapers Cl. WV12: W'hall 4D **30**
Reapers Wlk. WV8: Pend 6D **14**
Rea Pl. B12: Birm 3A **118**
 (off Cheapside)
Rea Rd. B31: N'fld 6D **144**
Reaside Cres. B14: King H 2D **146**
Reaside Cft. B12: Bal H 5G **117**
Reaside Dr. B45: Redn 1H **157**
Rea St. B5: Birm 6G **5** (2H **117**)
Rea St. Sth. B5: Birm 3G **117**
Rea Ter. B5: Birm 5H **5** (1H **117**)
Rea Twr. B19: Birm 4E **101**
 (off Mosborough Cres.)
Rea Valley Dr. B31: N'fld 5F **145**
Reaview Dr. B29: S Oak 3D **132**
Reaymer Cl. WS2: Wals 3H **31**
Reay Nadin Dr. B73: S'tly 1B **68**
Rebecca Dr. B29: S Oak 3A **132**
Rebecca Gdns. WV4: Penn 1D **58**
Recreation St. DY2: Neth 4F **95**
Rectory Av. WS10: Dar'l 5D **46**
Rectory Cl. DY8: Stourb 2F **125**
Rectory Flds. DY8: Word 1C **108**
Rectory Gdns. B36: Cas B 1E **105**
 B68: O'bry 4H **97**
 B91: Sol 4G **151**
 DY8: Stourb 2F **125**
Rectory Gro. B18: Win G 3A **100**
Rectory La. B36: Cas B 1E **105**
Rectory Pk. Av. B75: S Cold 1C **70**
Rectory Pk. Cl. B75: S Cold 1C **70**
Rectory Pk. Ct. B75: S Cold 5D **54**
Rectory Pk. Rd. B26: Sheld 6F **121**
Rectory Rd. B31: N'fld 4F **145**
 B75: S Cold 6A **54**
 B91: Sol 4G **151**
 DY8: Stourb 2F **125**
Rectory St. DY8: Word 6B **92**
Redacre Rd. B73: Bold 3F **69**
Redacres WV6: Tett 3C **26**
Red Admiral Apartments
 DY8: Stourb 6D **108**
Redbank Av. B23: Erd 4C **84**
Redbourn Rd. WS3: Blox 3G **19**
Red Brick Cl. B64: Crad H 4F **111**
Redbrooke Covert B38: King Nor 1A **160**
Red Brook Ho. WS2: Wals 4G **31**
Redbrooks Cl. B91: Sol 6E **151**
Redburn Dr. B14: King H 5F **147**
Redcar Cft. B36: Hodg H 1A **104**
Redcar Rd. WV10: F'hses 3H **15**
Redcliffe Dr. WV5: Wom 1H **73**
Redcott's Cl. WV10: Bush 1C **28**
Redcroft Dr. B24: Erd 2A **86**
Redcroft Rd. DY2: Dud 3G **95**
Red Cross Wlk. WV1: Wolv 6G **27**
 (off North Rd.)
Reddal Hill Rd. B64: Old H 2G **111**
REDDICAP HEATH 1C **70**
Reddicap Heath Rd.
 B75: S Cold 6B **54**
Reddicap Hill B75: S Cold 1C **70**
Reddicap Trad. Est.
 B75: S Cold 6B **54**
Reddicroft B73: S Cold 6A **54**
Reddings, The B47: H'wd 4A **162**
Reddings La. B11: Tys 3E **135**
 B28: Hall G 3E **135**
Reddings Rd. B13: Mose 3F **133**
Redditch Ho. B33: Kitts G 1A **122**
Redditch Rd. B31: Longb 3G **159**
 B38: King Nor 2G **159**
 B48: Hopw 6G **159**

Redfern Cl. B92: Olton 4F **137**
Redfern Dr. WS7: Burn 1D **10**
Redfern Pk. Way B11: Tys 6G **119**
Redfern Rd. B11: Tys 6F **119**
Redfly La. DY5: P'ntt 3G **93**
Redford Cl. B13: Mose 3B **134**
Redgate Cl. B38: King Nor 5H **145**
Redhall Rd. B32: Harb 4C **114**
 DY3: Gorn 5G **75**
Redhill DY2: Dud 1F **95**
 DY8: Stourb 1F **125**
Redhill Av. WV5: Wom 1G **73**
Redhill Cl. DY8: Stourb 1F **125**
Redhill Ct. DY8: Stourb 2F **125**
Redhill Gdns. B38: King Nor 1G **159**
Red Hill Gro. B38: King Nor 2B **160**
Redhill La. B45: Rub 4C **156**
 B61: C'wich 4C **156**
Redhill Pl. B62: Hunn 6A **128**
Redhill Rd. B25: Yard 5G **119**
 B31: Longb 1F **159**
 B38: King Nor, Head H 1F **159**
Red Hill St. WV1: Wolv 6G **27**
Redholme Ct. DY8: Stourb 1E **125**
Red Ho. Av. WS10: W'bry 2H **63**
Redhouse Cl. B93: Ben H 4A **166**
Red House Glass Cone Mus. 1C **108**
Redhouse Ind. Est. WS9: A'rdge 3H **33**
Redhouse La. WS9: A'rdge 4A **34**
Red Ho. Pk. Rd. B43: Gt Barr 3A **66**
Redhouse Rd. WV6: Tett 4G **25**
Redhouse St. WS1: Wals 4C **48**
Redhurst Dr. WV10: F'hses 4H **15**
Red Kite Dr. DY1: Dud 1A **94**
Redlake Dr. DY9: Pedm 5F **125**
Redlake Rd. DY9: Pedm 4F **125**
Redlands Cl. B91: Sol 2H **151**
Redlands Rd. B91: Sol 2G **151**
Redlands Way B74: S'tly 2A **52**
Red La. DY3: Sed 5F **59**
 WV11: Ess 6C **18**
Red Leasowes Rd. B63: Hale 2H **127**
Redliff Av. B36: Cas B 6H **87**
Red Lion Av. WS11: Nort C 1E **9**
Red Lion Cl. B69: Tiv 1A **96**
Red Lion Cres. WS11: Nort C 1E **9**
Red Lion La. WS11: Nort C 1E **9**
Red Lion St. WS2: Wals 6C **32**
 WV1: Wolv 2A **170** (1G **43**)
Redmead Cl. B30: King Nor 3G **145**
Redmires Cl. WS4: Rus 3F **33**
Redmoor Gdns. WV4: Penn 6E **43**
Redmoor Way B76: Min 1H **87**
REDNAL 2A **158**
Rednal Hill La. B45: Rub 3F **157**
Rednall Dr. B75: R'ley 6A **38**
Rednal Mill Dr. B45: Redn 2B **158**
Rednal Pk. Ct. B38: King Nor 5B **146**
Rednal Rd. B38: King Nor 1G **159**
Redoak Ho. WV10: Wolv 6B **28**
Redpine Crest WV12: W'hall 5D **30**
Redpoint Climbing Cen. 5G **101**
Red River Rd. WS2: Wals 4G **31**
Red Rock Dr. WV8: Cod 5F **13**
Red Rooster Ind. Est.
 WS9: A'rdge 3H **33**
Redruth Cl. DY6: K'wfrd 1B **92**
 WS5: Wals 4H **49**
Redruth Rd. WS5: Wals 4H **49**
Redstone Dr. WV11: Wed 4H **29**
Redstone Farm Rd. B28: Hall G 1H **149**
Redstone Way DY3: Lwr G 3H **75**
Redthorn Gro. B33: Stech 6B **104**
Redvers Rd. B9: Small H 2E **119**
Redway Ct. B75: S Cold 1C **70**
Redwing Cl. WS7: Hamm 1F **11**
Redwing Gro. B23: Erd 6B **68**
Red Wing Wlk. B36: Cas B 1C **106**
Redwood Av. DY1: Dud 2B **76**
Redwood Bus. Pk. B66: Smeth 2A **98**
Redwood Cl. B30: King Nor 3A **146**
 B74: S'tly 1H **51**
Redwood Ct. B14: King H 6G **133**
Redwood Dr. B69: Tiv 5B **78**
Redwood Gdns. B27: A Grn 6H **119**
Redwood Ho. B37: K'hrst 4C **106**

Redwood Rd. B30: King Nor 3A **146**
 WS5: Wals 1F **65**
 WV14: Cose 3F **61**
Redwood Way WV12: W'hall 1B **30**
Redworth Ho. B45: Rub 1F **157**
 (off Deelands Rd.)
Reedham Gdns. WV4: Penn 6B **42**
Reedly Rd. WV12: W'hall 6C **18**
Reedmace Cl. B38: King Nor 1B **160**
Reedswood Cl. WS2: Wals 6A **32**
Reedswood Gdns. WS2: Wals 6A **32**
 (not continuous)
Reedswood La. WS2: Wals 6A **32**
Reedswood Retail Pk. WS2: Wals 5H **31**
Reedswood Way WS2: Wals 5G **31**
Rees Dr. WV5: Wom 6H **57**
Reeves Cl. DY4: Tip 5B **78**
Reeves Gdns. WV8: Cod 3G **13**
Reeves Rd. B14: King H 1E **147**
Reeves St. WS3: Blox 1H **31**
Reflex Ind. Pk. WV13: W'hall 6H **29**
Reform St. B70: W Brom 4B **80**
 B71: W Brom 4B **80**
Regal Cl. B15: Birm 6A **4**
Regal Cft. B36: Hodg H 1H **103**
Regal Dr. WS2: Wals 3A **48**
Regan Av. B90: Shir 6G **149**
Regan Ct. B75: S Cold 6G **55**
Regan Cres. B23: Erd 1E **85**
Regan Dr. B69: O'bry 1D **96**
Regency Cl. B9: Small H 2D **118**
Regency Ct. DY1: Dud 4A **76**
 WV1: Wolv 1A **170** (6G **27**)
Regency Dr. B38: King Nor 5B **146**
Regency Gdns. B14: Yard W 4C **148**
Regency Pl. DY6: K'wfrd 4B **92**
Regency Wlk. B74: Four O 4D **36**
Regent Av. B69: Tiv 6A **78**
Regent Cl. B5: Edg 5F **117**
 B63: Hale 1A **128**
 B69: Tiv 1A **96**
 DY6: K'wfrd 3B **92**
Regent Ct. B62: Quin 4G **113**
 (off Binswood Rd.)
 B66: Smeth 4E **99**
Regent Dr. B69: Tiv 6A **78**
Regent Ho. B72: W Grn 6H **69**
 WS2: Wals 6B **32**
 (off Green La.)
 WV1: Wolv 2A **170** (6F **27**)
Regent Pde. B1: Birm 1A **4** (5E **101**)
Regent Pk. Rd. B10: Small H 3C **118**
Regent Pl. B1: Birm 1A **4** (5E **101**)
 B69: Tiv 5B **78**
Regent Rd. B17: Harb 5H **115**
 B21: Hand 1H **99**
 B69: Tiv 1A **96**
 WV4: Penn 6C **42**
Regent Row B18: Birm 1A **4** (5E **101**)
Regents, The B15: Edg 3H **115**
Regent St. B1: Birm 1A **4** (5E **101**)
 B30: Stir 6C **132**
 B64: Old H 1H **111**
 B66: Smeth 3E **99**
 DY1: Dud 1E **77**
 DY4: Tip 5G **61**
 WV13: W'hall 6A **30**
 WV14: Bils 5F **45**
Regents Way B75: S Cold 5D **54**
Regent Wlk. B8: W End 2H **103**
Regina Av. B44: Gt Barr 5G **67**
Regina Cl. B45: Fran 5E **143**
Regina Cres. WV6: Tett 5H **25**
Regina Dr. B42: P Barr 4E **83**
 WS4: Wals 5F **33**
Reginald Rd. B8: Salt 5D **102**
 B67: Smeth 1D **114**
Regis Beeches WV6: Tett 4A **26**
Regis Gdns. B65: Row R 1C **112**
Regis Heath Rd. B65: Row R 1D **112**
Regis Rd. B65: Row R 2C **112**
 WV6: Tett 4H **25**
Regus Bldg. B90: Bly P 6D **164**
Reid Av. WV12: W'hall 3D **30**
Reid Rd. B68: O'bry 2A **114**
Reigate Av. B8: W End 5H **103**
Reliance Trad. Est. WV14: Bils 5D **44**

Reliant Av.—Riverway

Reliant Av. B36: Cas B ... 6A 88
Relko Dr. B36: Hodg H ... 2A 104
Remembrance Rd.
WS10: W'bry ... 2A 64
Remington Pl. WS2: Wals ... 4A 32
Remington Rd. WS2: Wals ... 3H 31
Renaissance Ct. B12: Birm ... 2H 117
Renfrew Cl. DY8: Word ... 6A 92
Renfrew Sq. B35: Cas V ... 3F 87
Rennie Gro. B32: Quin ... 6B 114
Rennison Dr. WV5: Wom ... 1G 73
Renown Cl. DY5: P'ntt ... 1F 93
Renton Gro. WV10: Oxl ... 6E 15
Renton Rd. WV10: Oxl ... 6E 15
Repington Way B75: S Cold ... 5F 55
Repton Av. WV6: Pert ... 6E 25
Repton Gro. B9: Bord G ... 6H 103
Repton Ho. B23: Erd ... 1F 85
Repton Rd. B9: Bord G ... 6H 103
Reservoir Cl. B31: N'fld ... 2B 144
WS2: Wals ... 3H 47
Reservoir Pas. WS10: W'bry ... 2F 63
Reservoir Pl. WS2: Wals ... 3H 47
Reservoir Retreat B16: Edg ... 2B 116
Reservoir Rd. B16: Edg ... 1B 116
B23: Erd ... 3D 84
B29: S Oak ... 2F 131
B45: Coft H ... 6A 158
B65: Row R ... 6C 96
B68: O'bry ... 5A 98
B92: Olton ... 5D 136
Reservoir St. WS2: Wals ... 3H 47
Retallack Cl. B66: Smeth ... 1F 99
Retford Dr. B76: Walm ... 1C 70
Retford Gro. B25: Yard ... 5A 120
Retreat, The B64: Crad H ... 4G 111
Retreat Gdns. DY3: Sed ... 6A 60
Retreat St. WV3: Wolv ... 6A 170 (3F 43)
Revesby Wlk. B7: Birm ... 5A 102
Revival St. WS3: Blox ... 6H 19
Reynards Cl. DY3: Sed ... 6C 60
Reynolds Cl. DY3: Swind ... 5E 73
Reynolds Gro. WV6: Pert ... 4F 25
Reynolds Ho. *B19: Loz ... 2G 101*
(off Newbury Rd.)
Reynolds Rd. B21: Hand ... 2A 100
Reynoldstown Rd. B36: Hodg H ... 1A 104
Reynolds Wlk. WV11: Wed ... 1B 30
Rhayader Rd. B31: N'fld ... 2C 144
Rhodes Cl. DY3: Lwr G ... 3E 75
Rhone Cl. B11: S'hll ... 2C 134
Rhoose Cft. B35: Cas V ... 4F 87
Rhys Thomas Cl. WV12: W'hall ... 5D 30
Rian Ct. B64: Crad H ... 3F 111
Ribbesford Av. WV10: Oxl ... 1F 27
Ribbesford Cl. B63: Crad ... 6F 111
Ribbesford Cres. WV14: Cose ... 4F 61
Ribble Ct. B73: S Cold ... 6H 53
Ribblesdale Rd. B30: Stir ... 6C 132
Ribble Wlk. B36: Cas B ... 1B 106
Richard Bradley Way DY4: Tip ... 6G 61
Richard Lighton Ho. B1: Birm ... 3B 4
Richard Parkes Ho.
WS10: W'bry ... 2E 63
Richard Pl. WS5: Wals ... 3G 49
Richard Rd. WS5: Wals ... 3G 49
Richards Cl. B31: Longb ... 3D 158
B65: Row R ... 5E 97
Richards Ho. B69: O'bry ... 5D 96
WS2: Wals ... 6B 32
(off Burrowes St.)
Richardson Dr. DY8: Amb ... 3C 108
Richards Rd. DY4: Tip ... 4H 61
Richards St. WS10: Darl ... 3D 46
Richard St. B6: Aston ... 4H 101
B7: Birm ... 4H 101
B70: W Brom ... 4H 79
Richard St. Sth. B70: W Brom ... 5A 80
Richard St. W. B70: W Brom ... 5H 79
Richard Wattis Dr. WS10: W'bry ... 6F 47
Richard Williams Rd.
WS10: W'bry ... 3H 63
Richborough Dr. DY1: Dud ... 3A 76
Riches Ho. *WV6: Wolv ... 6D 26*
(off Riches St.)
Riches St. WV6: Wolv ... 6D 26
Richford Gro. B33: Kitts G ... 1H 121
Richmere Ct. WV6: Tett ... 6H 25
Richmond Aston Dr. DY4: Tip ... 2A 78
Richmond Av. B12: Bal H ... 6H 117
WV3: Wolv ... 2D 42
Richmond Cl. B20: Hand ... 4C 82
B47: H'wd ... 2B 162
Richmond Ct. *B15: Edg ... 3D 116*
(off George Rd.)
B29: W Cas ... 6G 131
B63: Hale ... 2G 127
B68: O'bry ... 4A 98
B72: W Grn ... 6H 69
DY9: Pedm ... 4F 125
(off Redlake Rd.)
Richmond Cft. B42: Gt Barr ... 1B 82
Richmond Dr. B75: S Cold ... 5D 54
WV3: Wolv ... 2C 42
WV6: Pert ... 5F 25
Richmond Gdns. DY8: Amb ... 4D 108
WV5: Wom ... 2G 73
Richmond Gro. DY8: Woll ... 3C 108
Richmond Hill B68: O'bry ... 4A 98
Richmond Hill Gdns. B15: Edg ... 4A 116
Richmond Hill Rd. B15: Edg ... 5A 116
Richmond Ho. B37: Chel W ... 2E 123
Richmond Pk. DY6: W Hth ... 1A 92
Richmond Pl. B14: King H ... 5H 133
Richmond Rd. B18: Hock ... 3D 100
B33: Stech ... 1B 120
B45: Rub ... 2E 157
B66: Smeth ... 1E 115
B73: S Cold ... 5H 53
B92: Olton ... 4C 136
DY2: Dud ... 1E 95
DY3: Sed ... 6A 60
WV3: Wolv ... 1C 42
Richmond St. B63: Hale ... 1A 128
B70: W Brom ... 1F 79
WS1: Wals ... 2D 48
Richmond St. Sth. B70: W Brom ... 2E 79
Richmond Way B37: Chel W ... 6E 107
Rickard Cl. B93: Know ... 4A 166
Rickman Dr. B15: Birm ... 3F 117
Rickyard Cl. B25: Yard ... 2B 120
B29: W Cas ... 1E 145
Rickyard Piece B32: Quin ... 1C 130
Riddfield Rd. B36: Hodg H ... 1C 104
Ridding La. WS10: W'bry ... 3F 63
Riddings, The B33: Stech ... 5C 104
B76: Walm ... 5F 71
DY9: W'cte ... 3H 125
WV10: Bush ... 2C 28
Riddings Cres. WS3: Pels ... 3D 20
Riddings Hill CV7: Bal C ... 5H 169
RIDGACRE ... 5B 114
Ridgacre Ent. Pk.
B71: W Brom ... 1H 79
Ridgacre La. B32: Quin ... 6A 114
Ridgacre Rd. B32: Quin ... 5H 113
B71: W Brom ... 1H 79
Ridgacre Rd. W. B32: Quin ... 5G 113
Ridge Cl. B13: Mose ... 1C 148
WS2: Wals ... 6D 30
Ridgefield Rd. B62: B'hth ... 3C 112
Ridge Gro. DY9: Lye ... 6G 109
Ridge Hill DY8: Word ... 6D 92
Ridge La. WV11: Wed ... 2F 29
Ridgemount Dr. B38: King Nor ... 2H 159
Ridge Rd. DY6: K'wfrd ... 4H 91
Ridge St. DY8: Woll ... 5A 108
Ridgewater Cl. B45: Redn ... 3H 157
Ridgeway B17: Edg ... 1F 115
B32: Quin ... 1G 129
WS9: A'rdge ... 5D 34
Ridgeway, The B23: Erd ... 1A 84
DY3: Sed ... 1H 75
WS7: Burn ... 1C 10
Ridgeway Av. B62: Quin ... 5G 113
Ridgeway Ct. B6: Aston ... 1H 101
WS2: Wals ... 2F 47
Ridgeway Dr. WV4: Penn ... 2D 58
Ridgeway Rd. DY4: Tip ... 5A 62
DY8: Word ... 1D 108
Ridgewood B34: S End ... 3F 105
Ridgewood Av. DY8: Woll ... 4A 108
Ridgewood Cl. WS1: Wals ... 3D 48
Ridgewood Dr. B75: Four O ... 2H 53
Ridgewood Gdns. B44: Gt Barr ... 6H 67
Ridgmont Cft. B32: Quin ... 6C 114
Riding Cl. B71: W Brom ... 5D 64
Riding Way WV12: W'hall ... 3D 30
Ridley St. B1: Birm ... 6B 4 (2E 117)
Ridpool Rd. B33: Kitts G ... 6F 105
Rifle St. WV14: Cose ... 5C 60
Rigby St. WS10: W'bry ... 4F 63
Riland Av. B75: S Cold ... 6B 54
Riland Ct. B72: W Grn ... 6A 70
B75: S Cold ... 6A 54
Riland Gro. B75: S Cold ... 6A 54
Riland Ind. Est. B75: S Cold ... 6B 54
Riland Rd. B75: S Cold ... 6B 54
Riley Cres. WV3: Wolv ... 5D 42
Riley Dr. B36: Cas B ... 6C 88
Riley Rd. B14: Yard W ... 4D 148
Riley St. WV13: W'hall ... 1B 46
Rilstone Rd. B32: Harb ... 6D 114
Rindleford Av. WV4: Penn ... 5A 42
Ring, The B25: Yard ... 3A 120
Ringhills Rd. WV8: Bilb ... 5H 13
Ringinglow Rd. B44: Gt Barr ... 3E 67
Ringmere Av. B36: Cas B ... 1F 105
Ring Rd. Nth. B15: Edg ... 1B 132
Ring Rd. St Andrews
WV1: Wolv ... 3A 170 (1F 43)
Ring Rd. St Davids
WV1: Wolv ... 2D 170 (1H 43)
Ring Rd. St Georges
WV2: Wolv ... 5C 170 (2H 43)
Ring Rd. St Johns
WV2: Wolv ... 5A 170 (2G 43)
Ring Rd. St Marks
WV3: Wolv ... 4A 170 (2F 43)
Ring Rd. St Patricks
WV1: Wolv ... 1C 170 (6H 27)
Ring Rd. St Peters
WV1: Wolv ... 2A 170 (1G 43)
Ring Rd. Sth. B15: Edg ... 1B 132
Ringswood Rd. B92: Olton ... 1C 136
Ring Way B70: W Brom ... 3B 80
Ringway Bus. Pk. B7: Birm ... 4A 102
Ringwood Av. WS9: A'rdge ... 4D 34
Ringwood Dr. B45: Fran ... 6G 143
Ringwood Rd. WV10: Bush ... 6H 15
Ripley Cl. B69: Tiv ... 1H 95
Ripley Gro. B23: Erd ... 2B 84
DY1: Dud ... 3B 76
Ripon Dr. B71: W Brom ... 4B 64
Ripon Rd. B14: Yard W ... 3C 148
WS2: Wals ... 1H 47
WV10: Oxl ... 2G 27
Rippingille Rd. B43: Gt Barr ... 1E 67
Ripple Rd. B30: Stir ... 6D 132
Risborough Ho. B31: Longb ... 1D 158
Rischale Way WS4: Rus ... 1H 33
Rise, The B37: Mars G ... 4C 122
B42: Gt Barr ... 5C 66
B48: Hopw ... 5F 159
B69: Tiv ... 6A 78
DY6: K'wfrd ... 4C 92
Rise Av. B45: Redn ... 2G 157
Riseley Cres. B5: Edg ... 5F 117
Rising Brook WV6: Tett ... 5H 25
Rissington Av. B29: S Oak ... 5C 132
Ritchie Cl. B13: Mose ... 4A 134
Rivendell Ct. B28: Hall G ... 4E 135
Rivendell Gdns. WV6: Tett ... 4H 25
Riverbank Rd. WV13: W'hall ... 1D 46
River Brook Dr. B30: Stir ... 5D 132
River Lee Rd. B11: Tys ... 6E 119
Rivermead Pk. B34: S End ... 4E 105
Riverpark Way B31: N'fld ... 6D 144
Riversdale Rd. B14: Yard W ... 4D 148
Riverside Ct. B38: King Nor ... 4H 145
B46: Col ... 2H 107
(off Prossers Wlk.)
Riverside Cres. B28: Hall G ... 3D 148
Riverside Dr. B29: S Oak ... 2E 133
B33: Stech ... 5B 104
B91: Sol ... 5A 152
Riverside Gdns. WV8: Bilb ... 3H 13
Riversleigh Dr. DY8: Word ... 3C 108
River St. B5: Birm ... 5H 5 (1A 118)
River Wlk. WS10: W'bry ... 4G 63
Riverway WS10: W'bry ... 3H 63

Rivington Cl. DY8: Stourb 1C 124
Rivington Cres. B44: K'sdng 4C 68
Roach Cl. B37: Chel W 6E 107
  DY5: Brie H 4H 93
Roach Cres. WV11: Wed 1H 29
Roach Pool Cft. B16: Edg 1G 115
Robert Av. B23: Erd 1E 85
Robert Ct. B13: Mose 3B 134
Robert Lucas Pl. B67: Smeth 5D 98
Robert Rd. B20: Hand 6D 82
  DY4: Tip 1H 77
Roberts Cl. WS9: Wals W 5B 22
  WS10: Mox 1B 62
Roberts Ct. B24: Erd 1A 86
Roberts Grn. Rd. DY3: Up Gor 3A 76
Robertson Knoll B36: Hodg H 2D 104
Robertsons Gdns. B7: Nech 2C 102
Roberts Rd. B27: A Grn 2A 136
  WS3: Wals 4D 32
  WS10: W'bry 2C 64
Robert St. DY3: Lwr G 3H 75
Robert Wynd WV14: Cose 4B 60
Robeson Cl. DY4: Tip 2F 77
Robin Cl. B36: Cas B 1C 106
  DY6: K'wfrd 3E 93
Robin Gro. WV11: Wed 2E 29
Robin Hood Crematorium
  B90: Shir 2H 149
Robin Hood Cres. B28: Hall G 6E 135
Robin Hood Cft. B28: Hall G 1F 149
Robin Hood Golf Course 1A 150
Robin Hood Island B28: Hall G 2G 149
  (off Stratford Rd.)
Robin Hood La. B28: Hall G 6D 134
Robin Hood Rd. DY5: Quar B 1B 110
Robin Rd. B23: Erd 3E 85
Robins Bus. Pk. DY4: W Brom 6E 63
Robins Cl. DY8: Stourb 2E 125
  WS6: C Hay 4D 6
Robins Ct. B14: King H 4H 133
Robinsfield Dr. B31: Longb 2E 159
Robinsons M. B74: Four O 6E 37
Robinsons Way B76: Min 2H 87
Robin Wlk. WS2: Wals 6F 31
Robottom Cl. WS2: Wals 3H 31
Robson Cl. WS8: Bwnhls 2C 22
Rocester Av. WV11: Wed 2G 29
Rochdale Wlk. B10: Small H 4C 118
Rochester Cft. WS2: Wals 5G 31
Rochester Rd. B31: N'fld 3E 145
Roche Way WS3: Blox 6F 19
Rochford Cl. B45: Rub 2E 157
  B63: Hale 3H 127
  B76: Walm 5E 71
  WS2: Wals 4A 48
Rochford Ct. B90: M'path 3E 165
Rochford Gro. WV4: Penn 6B 42
Rock, The WV6: Tett 4B 26
Rock Av. B45: Redn 2A 158
Rocket Pool Dr. WV14: Bils 3H 61
Rockford Rd. B42: Gt Barr 6C 66
Rock Gro. B92: Olton 2C 136
Rockingham Cl. B93: Dorr 6H 165
  DY3: Gorn 4F 75
  WS3: Blox 6H 19
Rockingham Dr. WV6: Pert 6F 25
Rockingham Gdns. B74: S Cold 5H 53
Rockingham Hall Gdns. DY9: Hag ...6H 125
Rockingham Rd. B25: Yard 3B 120
Rockland Dr. B33: Stech 5C 104
Rockland Gdns. WV13: W'hall 3H 45
Rocklands Dr. B75: S Cold 3H 53
Rockley Gro. B45: Redn 2H 157
Rockley Rd. B65: Row R 3A 96
Rockmead Av. B44: Gt Barr 3H 67
Rockmoor Cl. B37: K'hrst 6A 106
Rock Rd. B92: Olton 2C 136
  WV14: Cose 5B 60
Rockrose Gdns. WV10: F'stne 1D 16
Rocks Hill DY5: Brie H 2H 109
Rock St. DY3: Up Gor 2A 76
Rockville Rd. B8: Salt 5G 103
Rocky La. B6: Aston 3A 102
  B7: Nech 3B 102
  B42: Gt Barr, P Barr 1C 82

Rocky La. & Chelsea Trad. Ests.
  B7: Nech 3A 102
Rodborough Rd. B26: Sheld 5F 121
  B93: Dorr 6F 167
Rodbourne Rd. B17: Harb 2G 131
Roddis Cl. B23: Erd 5D 68
Roderick Dr. WV11: Wed 2F 29
Roderick Rd. B11: S'brk 6C 118
Rodlington Av. B44: Gt Barr 4H 67
Rodman Cl. B15: Edg 3H 115
Rodney Cl. B16: Birm 1C 116
  B92: Olton 4F 137
Rodney Rd. B92: Olton 4F 137
Rodway Cl. B19: Loz 2G 101
  DY5: Quar B 4H 109
  WV4: Ett 2H 59
Rodwell Gro. B44: K'sdng 5A 68
Roebuck Cl. B34: S End 4A 106
Roebuck Glade WV12: W'hall 5E 31
Roebuck La. B66: Smeth 2C 98
  B70: W Brom 6C 80
Roebuck Pl. WS3: Blox 3C 32
Roebuck Rd. B16: Edg 6G 99
  B17: Edg 6G 99
  WS3: Blox 3C 32
Roebuck St. B70: W Brom 6D 80
Roedean Cl. B44: K'sdng 6B 68
Roford Ct. DY3: Up Gor 1A 76
Rogerfield Rd. B23: Erd 1G 85
Rogers Cl. WV11: Wed 6A 18
Rogers Rd. B8: W End 4H 103
Rokeby Cl. B76: Walm 1C 70
Rokeby Rd. B43: Gt Barr 3B 66
Rokeby Wlk. B34: Hodg H 3D 104
Rokewood Cl. DY6: K'wfrd 6B 74
Roland Gdns. B19: Loz 1E 101
Roland Dr. B19: Loz 1E 101
Rolan Dr. B90: Maj G 1E 163
Roland Rd. B19: Loz 1E 101
Roland Ter. B19: Loz 1F 101
Roland Vernon Way DY4: Tip 6C 62
Rolfe St. B66: Smeth 3E 99
Rollason Rd. B24: Erd 4G 85
  DY2: Dud 1F 95
Rollers Way DY4: Tip 6G 61
Rollesby Dr. WV13: W'hall 3H 45
Rollingmill Bus. Pk. WS2: Wals 2A 48
Rolling Mill Cl. B5: Edg 4G 117
Rolling Mill Rd. WS11: Nort C 2E 9
Rollingmill St. WS2: Wals 2A 48
Rollswood Dr. B91: Sol 3D 150
Roman Cl. WS8: Bwnhls 3A 10
Roman Ct. B38: King Nor 1C 160
Roman Grange B74: Lit As 4C 36
Roman La. B74: Lit As 5B 36
Roman Pk. B46: Col 6H 89
  B74: Lit As 5B 36
Roman Pl. B74: Lit As 1B 52
Roman Rd. B74: Lit As 4C 36
  DY7: Stourb 3A 124
  DY8: Stourb 2A 124
Roman Vw. WS11: Cann 1F 7
Roman Way B15: Edg 2H 131
  B46: Col 5G 89
  B65: Row R 5C 96
Romany Rd. B45: Fran 6D 142
Romany Way DY8: Stourb 2A 124
Roma Rd. B11: Tys 6E 119
Romford Cl. B26: Sheld 5F 121
Romilly Av. B20: Hand 5D 82
Romilly Cl. B76: Walm 1E 71
  DY8: Woll 5C 108
Romney Cl. B28: Hall G 6F 135
Romney Ho. Ind. Est. WS10: Darl 4B 46
  (off Wolverhampton St.)
Romney Way B43: Gt Barr 1F 67
Romsey Gro. WV10: F'hses 4G 15
Romsey Rd. WV10: F'hses 4G 15
Romsey Way WS3: Blox 4F 19
ROMSLEY 3A 142
Romsley Cl. B45: Rub 1E 157
  B63: Hale 3B 128
  WS4: S'fld 5G 21
ROMSLEY HILL 5A 142
Romsley Rd. B32: Bart G 5H 129
  B68: O'bry 1H 113
  DY9: Lye 6G 109

Romulus Cl. B20: Hand 4D 82
Ronald Gro. B36: Cas B 6H 87
Ronald Pl. B9: Bord G 1E 119
Ronald Rd. B9: Bord G 1D 118
Ron Davis Cl. B66: Smeth 4F 99
ROOD END 3A 98
Rood End Rd. B68: O'bry 3A 98
  B69: O'bry 2A 98
Rooker Av. WV2: Ett 4A 44
Rooker Cres. WV2: Ett 5B 44
Rookery, The B62: Quin 3G 129
Rookery Av. DY5: Brie H 1E 109
  WV4: Ett 2C 60
Rookery La. WS9: A'rdge 3D 34
  WV2: Wolv 5E 43
Rookery Pde.
  WS9: A'rdge 3D 34
Rookery Pk. DY5: P'ntt 4F 93
Rookery Ri. WV5: Wom 1H 73
Rookery Rd. B21: Hand 1A 100
  B29: S Oak 3B 132
  WV4: Ett 2C 60
  WV5: Wom 1H 73
  WV14: Ett 2C 60
Rookery St. WV11: Wed 4E 29
Rookwood Dr. WV6: Tett 1F 41
Rookwood Rd. B27: A Grn 1H 135
Rooth St. WS10: W'bry 1H 63
Roper Wlk. DY3: Sed 1B 76
Roper Way DY3: Sed 1B 76
Rope Wlk. WS1: Wals 2E 49
Rosafield Av. B62: Quin 5F 113
Rosalind Av. DY1: Dud 6D 60
Rosalind Gro. WV11: Wed 4A 30
Rosamond St. WS1: Wals 4B 48
Rosary Rd. B23: Erd 4D 84
Rosary Vs. B11: S'hll 6C 118
Rosco Ho. B24: Erd 4F 85
  (off Wood End Rd.)
Rose Av. B68: O'bry 4B 114
  DY6: K'wfrd 4D 92
Rose Bank B74: Lit As 4C 36
Rose Bank Dr. WS3: Wals 5C 32
Rosebay Av. B38: King Nor 1B 160
Rosebay Gro. WV5: Wom 1E 73
Rosebery Rd. B66: Smeth 5G 99
Rosebery St. B18: Hock 5C 100
  WV3: Wolv 2F 43
Rosebriars B90: Maj G 2E 163
Rose Cl. B66: Smeth 4G 99
Rose Cott. Dr. DY8: Word 6B 92
  (off Barnett La.)
Rose Cotts. B29: S Oak 3B 132
  B30: Stir 1C 146
Rose Ct. CV7: Bal C 1H 169
Rosecroft Rd. B26: Sheld 5G 121
Rosedale Av. B23: Erd 4E 85
  B66: Smeth 4G 99
Rosedale Gro. B25: Yard 3A 120
Rosedale Pl. WV13: W'hall 3A 46
Rosedale Rd. B25: Yard 3A 120
Rosedale Wlk. DY6: K'wfrd 1C 92
  (off Pinewood Wlk.)
Rosedene Dr. B20: Hand 5B 82
Rose Dr. WS8: Clay 1A 22
Rosefield Ct. B67: Smeth 5E 99
Rosefield Cft. B6: Aston 2H 101
Rosefield Rd. B67: Smeth 5E 99
Rosefields B31: N'fld 2F 145
Rosegardens, The B63: Hale 3G 127
Rosehall Cl. B91: Sol 6D 150
Rose Hill B45: Coft H, Lick 6G 157
  DY5: Quar B 2C 110
  WV13: W'hall 3A 46
Rose Hill Cl. B36: Cas B 1F 105
Rosehill Ct. DY1: Dud 6E 77
  (off Wolverhampton St.)
Rose Hill Gdns. WV13: W'hall 2A 46
Rose Hill Rd. B21: Hand 2C 100
Roseship Cl. WS5: Wals 2E 65
Roseland Av. DY2: Dud 6H 77
Roseland Way B15: Birm 2D 116
Rose La. B69: Tiv 5C 78
Roseleigh Rd. B45: Redn 3H 157
Rosemary Av. WS6: C Hay 2D 6
  WV4: Penn 5G 43
  WV14: Bils 5H 45

Rosemary Cl. WS8: Clay 1H 21
   WV11: Ess 4A 18
Rosemary Ct. WV11: Wed 2H 29
Rosemary Cres. DY1: Dud 1B 76
   WV4: Penn 6G 43
Rosemary Cres. W. WV4: Penn 6F 43
Rosemary Dr. B74: Lit As 6C 36
Rosemary Hill Rd. B74: Four O 6C 36
Rosemary La. DY8: Stourb 2B 124
Rosemary Nook B74: Lit As 4D 36
Rosemary Rd. B33: Stech 1D 120
   B63: Hale 3F 127
   WS6: C Hay 1D 6
Rosemoor Dr. DY5: Brie H 4F 109
Rosemount B32: Quin 1C 130
Rose Pl. B18: Birm 1A 4 (5E 101)
Rose Rd. B17: Harb 5H 115
   B46: Col 1H 107
Rose St. WV14: Bils 3H 61
Rosetone Pl. B65: B'hth 2D 112
                       (off Park St.)
ROSEVILLE 6D 60
Roseville Ct. WV14: Cose 5E 61
                   (off Green St.)
Roseville Gdns. WV8: Cod 3G 13
Roseville Pct. WV14: Cose 5E 61
       (off Castle St., not continuous)
Rosewood Cl. B74: Lit As 4D 36
Rosewood Ct. WV14: Cose 5E 61
                  (off Bayer St.)
Rosewood Dr. B23: Erd 5D 84
   WV12: W'hall 1B 30
Rosewood Gdns. WV11: Ess 4B 18
Rosewood Pk. WS6: C Hay 3D 6
Rosewood Rd. DY1: Dud 2D 76
Roshven Rd. B12: Bal H 1A 134
Roslin Gro. B19: Hock 3E 101
Roslyn Cl. B66: Smeth 3E 99
Rosneath Cl. WV4: Ett 6B 44
Ross B65: Row R 1B 112
Ross Cl. WV3: Wolv 1C 42
Ross Dr. DY6: K'wfrd 2A 92
Rosse Ct. B92: Sol 5B 138
Rossendale Cl. B63: Crad 5F 111
Ross Hgts. B65: Row R 6B 96
Rosslyn Rd. B76: Walm 1D 86
Ross Rd. WS3: Wals 3D 32
Rostrevor Rd. B10: Small H 2F 119
Rotary Ho. DY1: Dud 6B 76
Rotherby Gro. B37: Mars G 4D 122
Rotherfield Rd. B26: Sheld 3F 121
Rothesay Cft. B32: Bart G 6H 129
Rothesay Dr. DY8: Word 6A 92
Rothesay Gdns. WV4: Ett 6A 44
Rothesay Way WV12: W'hall 3B 30
Rothley Wlk. B38: King Nor 1G 159
Rothwell Dr. B91: Shir 2B 150
Rotton Pk. Rd. B16: Edg 5H 99
               (not continuous)
Rotton Pk. St. B16: Birm 6B 100
ROTTON ROW 5E 167
Rough Brook Rd. WS4: Rus 2E 33
Rough Coppice Wlk.
   B35: Cas V .5E 87
ROUGH HAY 4C 46
Rough Hay Pl. WS10: Darl 4C 46
Rough Hay Rd. WS10: Darl 4C 46
Rough Hill Dr. B65: Row R 3H 95
Rough Hills Cl. WV2: Ett 5B 44
Rough Hills Rd. WV2: Ett 5B 44
Roughlea Av. B36: Hodg H 2D 104
ROUGHLEY 1A 54
Roughley Dr. B75: R'ley 1A 54
Roughley Farm Rd. B75: R'ley 6C 38
Rough Rd. B44: K'sdng 2A 68
Rough Wood (Nature Reserve) 3E 31
Rouncil Cl. B92: Sol 6H 137
Roundabout, The B31: Longb 6B 144
Round Cl. B90: Dic H 3G 163
Round Cft. WV13: W'hall 1A 46
Round Hill DY3: Sed 3H 59
Round Hill Av. DY9: Pedm 4G 125
Roundhill Cl. B76: Walm 2C 70
Roundhill Ho. DY6: K'wfrd 6B 74
Roundhills Rd. B62: B'hth 3F 113
Roundhill Ter. B62: B'hth 2E 113
Roundhill Way WS8: Bwnhls 3B 10

Roundhouse Rd. DY3: Up Gor 3A 76
Roundlea Cl. WV12: W'hall 1B 30
Roundlea Rd. B31: N'fld 5C 130
Round Moor Wlk. B35: Cas V 4E 87
ROUND OAK 6A 94
Round Rd. B24: Erd 5H 85
Round Saw Cft. B45: Rub 1F 157
ROUND'S GREEN 2E 97
Round's Grn. Rd. B69: O'bry 2E 97
Rounds Hill Rd. WV14: Cose 5F 61
Rounds Rd. WV14: Cose 2F 61
Round St. DY2: Neth 3E 95
Rounds Wharf DY4: Tip 2G 77
Roundway Down WV6: Pert 6E 25
Rounton Cl. B74: Four O 5D 36
Rousay Cl. B45: Fran 6F 143
Rousdon Gro. B43: Gt Barr 5H 65
Rover Dr. B27: A Grn 1B 136
   B36: Cas B .6B 88
Rovex Bus. Pk. B11: Tys 6F 119
Rowallan Rd. B75: R'ley 5A 38
Rowan Cl. B47: H'wd 4B 162
   B76: Walm 3D 70
Rowan Ct. B10: Small H 3C 118
   B30: King Nor 5C 146
   B66: Smeth .1B 98
Rowan Cres. WV3: Wolv 4C 42
   WV14: Cose .4D 60
Rowan Dr. B28: Hall G 2G 149
   WV11: Ess 4B 18
Rowan Ri. DY6: K'wfrd 3C 92
Rowan Rd. B72: S Cold 3A 70
   DY3: Sed 4B 60
   WS5: Wals 1D 64
Rowantrees B45: Redn 4H 157
Rowan Way B31: Longb 6D 144
   B37: Chel W 2E 123
Roway La. B69: O'bry 6E 79
Rowberrie Cl. B45: Redn 2A 158
Rowbrook Cl. B90: Maj G 1E 163
Rowchester Ct. B4: Birm 2E 5
Rowcroft Covert B14: King H 4E 147
Rowdale Rd. B42: Gt Barr 6E 67
Rowden Dr. B23: Erd 1G 85
   B91: Sol 5C 150
Rowena Gdns. DY3: Sed 3G 59
Rowheath Ho. B30: B'vlle 1A 146
Rowheath Rd. B30: King Nor 3B 146
Rowington Av. B65: Row R 6D 96
Rowington Rd. B34: S End 3A 106
Rowington Ter. B25: Yard 4H 119
Rowland Gdns. WS2: Wals 6A 32
Rowland Hill Dr. DY4: Tip 2C 78
Rowlands Av. WS2: Wals 6E 31
   WV1: Wolv 1D 44
Rowlands Cl. WS2: Wals 5E 31
Rowlands Cres. B91: Sol 5F 137
Rowlands Rd. B26: Yard 4C 120
Rowland St. WS2: Wals 6A 32
Rowley Gro. B33: Kitts G 6H 105
Rowley Hall Av. B65: Row R 5C 96
Rowley Hall Vw. B64: Crad H 3H 111
Rowley Pl. WS4: Rus 2F 33
ROWLEY REGIS 6C 96
Rowley Regis Crematorium
   B65: Row R 1A 112
Rowley Regis Golf Course 5B 96
Rowley Regis Station (Rail) 1E 113
Rowley St. WS1: Wals 1D 48
Rowley Vw. B70: W Brom 4H 79
   WS10: Darl 1C 62
   WV14: Bils 2A 62
Rowley Village B65: Row R 6C 96
Rowney Cft. B28: Hall G 3E 149
Rowood Dr. B91: Sol 6G 137
   B92: Sol 6H 137
Rowthorn Cl. B74: S'tly 4A 52
Rowthorn Dr. B90: M'path 3E 165
Rowton Av. WV6: Pert 6E 25
Rowton Dr. B74: S'tly 6H 51
Roxburgh Gro. B43: Gt Barr 1E 67
Roxburgh Rd. B73: S Cold 2G 69
Roxby Gdns. WV6: Wolv 4E 27
Royal Arch Apartments B1: Birm 6B 4
Royal Cl. B65: Row R 4E 96
   DY5: Brie H 3G 109
Royal Ct. B72: W Grn 3H 69

Royal Ct. Apartments
   B74: S Cold .4A 54
Royal Gro. B23: Erd 6B 68
Royal Mdw. Way B74: S'tly 4G 51
Royal Oak Rd. B62: Quin 1F 129
   B65: Row R .4H 95
Royal Rd. B72: S Cold 6A 54
Royal Scot Gro. WS1: Wals 6C 48
Royal Star Cl. B33: Kitts G 1G 121
Royal, The Stop (Metro) 2A 44
Royal Way DY4: Tip 5A 78
Roydon Rd. B27: A Grn 5A 136
Roylesden Cres. B73: New O 3C 68
Royston Chase B74: Lit As 6A 38
Royston Cl. B13: Mose 3B 134
             (off Wake Grn. Pk.)
Royston Cft. B12: Bal H 5H 117
Royston Way DY3: Sed 5G 59
Rubens Cl. DY3: Up Gor 2H 75
RUBERY 2F 157
Rubery By-Pass B45: Rub 2E 157
Rubery Ct. WS10: Darl 4C 46
Rubery Farm Gro. B45: Rub 1F 157
Rubery Fld. Cl. B45: Redn 6G 143
Rubery La. B45: Fran, Redn 6F 143
Rubery La. Sth. B45: Rub 1F 157
Rubery St. WS10: Darl 3D 46
Ruckley Av. B19: Loz 2E 101
Ruckley Rd. B29: W Cas 5E 131
Rudd Gdns. WV10: Wolv 5D 28
Ruddington Way B19: Hock 4G 101
Rudge Av. WV1: Wolv 6D 28
Rudge Cl. WV12: W'hall 5C 30
Rudge Cft. B33: Kitts G 6E 106
Rudge Wlk. B18: Hock 6C 100
Rudgewick Cft. B6: Aston 3H 101
Rudyard Cl. WV10: Bush 3A 16
Rudyard Gro. B33: Kitts G 6F 105
Rudyngfield Dr. B33: Stech 6D 104
Rufford Cl. B23: Erd 5D 68
Rufford Rd. DY9: Lye 1G 125
Rufford St. DY9: Lye 5H 109
Rufford Way WS9: A'rdge 2A 34
Rugby Rd. DY8: Woll 4B 108
Rugby St. WV1: Wolv 6F 27
Rugeley Av. WV12: W'hall 1D 30
Rugeley Cl. DY4: Tip 2B 77
Rugeley Gro. B7: Nech 3B 102
Ruislip Cl. B35: Cas V 3E 87
RUITON 3H 75
Ruiton St. DY3: Lwr G 3H 75
Rumbow B63: Hale 1B 128
RUMBUSH 6E 163
Rumbush La. B90: Dic H 3G 163
              (not continuous)
   B90: Dic H, Tid G 6E 163
   B94: Earls 6E 163
Runcorn Cl. B37: F'bri 5E 107
Runcorn Rd. B12: Bal H 6H 117
Runnymede Dr. CV7: Bal C 6H 169
Runnymede Rd. B11: S'hll 2E 135
Rupert St. B7: Birm, Nech 4A 102
   WV3: Wolv 1E 43
RUSHALL 2F 33
Rushall Cl. DY8: Word 3C 108
   WS4: Wals 5F 33
Rushall Ct. B43: Gt Barr 6A 66
               (off West Rd.)
Rushall Mnr. Cl. WS4: Wals 5F 33
Rushall Mnr. Rd. WS4: Wals 5F 33
Rushall Rd. WV10: Bush 5A 16
Rushbrook Cl. B92: Olton 3C 136
   WS8: Clay 1A 22
Rushbrooke Cl. B13: Mose 1H 133
Rushbrooke Dr. B73: New O 2C 68
Rushbrook Gro. B14: King H 4E 147
Rushbury Cl. B90: Shir 3B 150
   WV14: Bils 6D 44
Rushden Cft. B44: K'sdng 4H 67
Rushes Mill WS3: Pels 4C 20
Rushey La. B11: Tys 6G 119
Rushford Av. WV5: Wom 1G 73
Rushford Cl. B90: M'path 2E 165
Rush Grn. B32: Bart G 3C 130
Rushlake Grn. B34: S End 4F 105
Rushleigh Rd. B90: Maj G 1E 163
Rushmead Gro. B45: Redn 2G 157

Rushmere Rd. DY4: Tip 5A 62
Rushmoor Cl. B74: S Cold 5H 53
Rushmore Ho. B45: Rub 1F 157
Rushton Cl. CV7: Bal C 5H 169
Rushwater Cl. WV5: Wom 1E 73
Rushwick Cft. B34: S End 3H 105
Rushwick Gro. B90: M'path 3E 165
Rushwood Cl. WS4: Wals 6E 33
Rushy Piece B32: Bart G 2B 130
Ruskin Av. B65: Row R 1D 112
   DY3: Lwr G 2E 75
   WV4: Ett 3B 60
Ruskin Cl. B6: Aston 2H 101
Ruskin Glass Cen. 4D 108
Ruskin Gro. B27: A Grn 3H 135
Ruskin Hall Gro. B6: Aston 2H 101
Ruskin Pl. B66: Smeth 2B 98
Ruskin Rd. WV10: Bush 1B 28
Ruskin St. B71: W Brom 2A 80
Russell Bank Rd. B74: Four O 5E 37
Russell Cl. B69: Tiv 5D 78
   DY4: Tip 4C 62
   WV11: Wed 6H 17
Russell Ct. B74: Four O 6D 36
   WV3: Wolv 2F 43
Russell Ho. WS10: W'bry 3F 63
   WV8: Cod 3E 13
Russell Rd. B13: Mose 2F 133
   B28: Hall G 3E 135
   WV14: Bils 4H 45
Russells, The B13: Mose 2F 133
RUSSELL'S HALL 6B 76
Russells Hall Rd. DY1: Dud 6A 76
Russell St. DY1: Dud 6D 76
   WS10: W'bry 3F 63
   WV3: Wolv 2F 43
   WV13: W'hall 1B 46
Russett Cl. WS5: Wals 3A 50
Russett Way DY5: P'ntt 2F 93
Russet Wlk. WV8: Pend 6C 14
Russet Way B31: N'fld 1C 144
Ruston St. B16: Birm 2D 116
Ruthall Cl. B29: W Cas 6G 131
Ruth Cl. DY4: Tip 3C 62
Rutherford Rd. B23: Erd 6E 69
   WS2: Wals 3G 31
Rutland Av. WV4: Penn 1B 58
Rutland Cl. B29: W Cas 6G 131
Rutland Cres. WS9: A'rdge 6D 22
   WV14: Bils 4G 45
Rutland Dr. B26: Yard 4C 120
Rutland Pas. DY1: Dud 6E 77
Rutland Pl. DY8: Woll 3D 108
Rutland Rd. B66: Smeth 2E 115
   B71: W Brom 6A 64
   WS10: W'bry 1A 64
Rutland St. WS3: Wals 4C 32
Rutland Ter. B18: Hock 4C 100
   (off Crabtree Rd.)
Rutley Gro. B32: Quin 1D 130
Rutters Mdw. B32: Quin 1H 129
Rutter St. WS1: Wals 4B 48
Ryan Av. WV11: Wed 1A 30
Ryan Pl. DY2: Neth 3E 95
Rycroft Gro. B33: Kitts G 1G 121
Rydal Cl. B74: S'tly 1H 51
   WV11: Wed 2E 29
Rydal Dr. WV6: Pert 5F 25
Rydal Ho. B69: O'bry 4D 96
Rydal Way B28: Hall G 6F 135
Rydding La. B71: W Brom 5H 63
Rydding Sq. B71: W Brom 5H 63
Ryde Gro. B27: A Grn 4G 135
Ryde Pk. Rd. B45: Redn 3A 158
Ryders Grn. Rd. B70: W Brom 3E 79
Ryders Hayes La. WS3: Pels 3E 21
Ryder St. B4: Birm 2F 5 (6G 101)
   B70: W Brom 2F 79
   DY8: Word 1B 108
Ryebank Cl. B30: B'vlle 2G 145
Ryeclose Cft. B37: Chel W 6F 107
RYECROFT 5B 32
Rye Cft. B27: A Grn 6A 120
   B47: H'wd 4A 162
   DY9: W'cte 2A 126
Ryecroft Av. WV4: Penn 6F 43
Ryecroft Cl. DY3: Sed 5G 59

Ryecroft Pk. WS2: Wals 6C 32
Ryecroft Pl. WS3: Wals 3D 32
Ryecroft St. WS2: Wals 6C 32
Ryefield WV8: Pend 5C 14
Ryefield Cl. B91: Sol 2C 150
Ryefield Way DY6: K'wfrd 3A 92
Rye Grass Wlk. B35: Cas V 4F 87
Rye Gro. B11: Tys 1F 135
Ryemarket DY8: Stourb 6E 109
Ryhope Wlk. WV9: Pend 5D 14
   (Howland Cl.)
WV9: Pend 4E 15
   (Penshaw Cl.)
Ryknild Cl. B74: Four O 3F 37
Ryknild Dr. B74: S'tly 4A 52
Ryland Cl. B63: Hale 3G 127
   DY4: Tip 2B 78
Ryland Ho. B19: Birm 4F 101
   (off Gt. Hampton Row)
Ryland Rd. B11: S'hll 1D 134
   B15: Edg 4E 117
   B24: Erd 6F 85
Rylands Dr. WV4: Penn 1D 58
Ryland St. B16: Birm 2D 116
Ryle St. WS3: Blox 5B 20
Rymond Rd. B34: Hodg H 3C 104
Ryton Cl. B73: S Cold 6H 53
   WV10: Wolv 4C 28
Ryton End La. B92: Bars 6C 154
Ryton Gro. B34: S End 2H 105

S

Sabell Rd. B67: Smeth 3D 98
Sabrina Rd. WV6: Tett 2E 41
Saddlers Cen. WS1: Wals 2C 48
Saddlers Cl. B63: Crad 6D 110
Saddlers Ct. WS2: Wals 4H 47
Saddlers Ct. Ind. Est.
   WS2: Wals 2G 31
Saddlers M. B91: Sol 6G 151
Saddleworth Rd. WS3: Blox 3G 19
Sadler Cres. B11: S'hll 1D 134
   (off Lea Rd.)
Sadler Ho. B19: Hock 3E 101
Sadler Rd. B75: S Cold 4D 54
   WS8: Bwnhls 6C 10
Sadlers Mill WS8: Bwnhls 6C 10
Sadlers Wlk. B16: Edg 2C 116
Saffron Gdns. WV4: Penn 1E 59
Saffron Ho. B38: King Nor 1A 160
Sage Cft. B31: N'fld 2U 144
St Agatha's Rd. B8: W Fnd 4H 103
St Agnes Cl. B13: Mose 3B 134
St Agnes Rd. B13: Mose 3B 134
St Aidans Wlk. B10: Small H 3C 118
St Albans Cl. B67: Smeth 3C 98
   WV11: Wed 1A 30
St Albans Gro. WV13: W'hall 2G 45
St Albans Ho. B32: Harb 6D 114
St Albans Rd. B13: Mose 2A 134
   B67: Smeth 3C 98
St Alphege Cl. B91: Sol 4G 151
St Ambrose Cl. B65: B'hth 3B 112
St Andrew's Av. WS3: Pels 2E 21
St Andrews Cl. B32: Bart G 2E 131
   DY3: Lwr G 5H 59
   DY8: Stourb 3D 124
   WV6: Wolv 5E 27
St Andrews Dr. B69: Tiv 2B 96
   WV6: Pert 4D 24
St Andrew's Ho. WV6: Wolv 5F 27
St Andrews Ind. Est. B9: Bord G 1C 118
St Andrews Rd. B9: Birm 1B 118
   B75: S Cold 4A 54
St Andrews Stadium 2C 118
St Andrews St. B9: Birm 1B 118
St Annes Cl. B20: Hand 3B 82
   DY2: Neth 4E 95
St Annes Ct. B13: Mose 1G 133
   B44: K'sdng 4H 67
   B64: Crad H 2E 111
   WV13: W'hall 2B 46
St Annes Gro. B93: Know 3C 166
St Annes Ind. Est. WV13: W'hall 6B 30

St Annes Rd. B64: Crad H 2E 111
   DY2: Crad H 2E 111
   WV10: Oxl 6F 15
   WV13: W'hall 6B 30
St Anne's Way B44: K'sdng 1A 84
St Ann's Ter. WV13: W'hall 6B 30
St Anthony's Dr. WS3: Pels 2F 21
St Athan Cft. B35: Cas V 4F 87
St Audries Ct. B91: Sol 5D 150
St Augustine's Rd. B16: Edg 2H 115
St Augustus Cl. B70: W Brom 5D 80
St Austell Rd. WS5: Wals 4A 50
St Bartholomew's Ter.
   WS10: W'bry 2F 63
St Benedict Cl. DY1: Dud 3E 77
St Benedict's Cl. B70: W Brom 5D 80
St Benedicts Rd. B10: Small H 4F 119
   WV5: Wom 1G 73
St Bernards Rd. B72: W Grn 3A 70
   B92: Olton 2B 150
St Blaise Av. B46: Wat O 5D 88
St Blaise Rd. B75: R'ley 6B 38
St Brades Cl. B69: Tiv 2C 96
St Brides Cl. DY3: Sed 5G 59
   WV5: Wom 1F 73
Saintbury Dr. B91: Sol 2G 165
St Caroline Cl. B70: W Brom 5D 80
St Catharines Cl. WS1: Wals 4E 49
St Catherines Cl. B15: Birm 2F 117
   B75: S Cold 4D 54
   DY2: Dud 6A 78
St Catherine's Ct. B91: Sol 3F 151
St Catherine's Cres. WV4: Penn 1D 58
St Cecilia's WV11: Wed 4E 29
St Chads WV14: Cose 6D 60
St Chads Cir. B4: Birm 2D 4 (6F 101)
St Chad's Cl. DY3: Lwr G 4F 75
St Chads Ind. Est. B19: Brom 4F 101
St Chad's Queensway
   B4: Birm 1E 5 (5G 101)
St Chad's RC Cathedral 1D 4 (5G 101)
St Chads Rd. B45: Rub 2F 157
   B75: S Cold 6C 54
   WV10: Bush 1B 28
   WV14: Bils 4H 45
St Christopher Cl. B70: W Brom 5D 80
St Christopher Dr. WS10: W'bry 2C 64
St Christophers B20: Hand 3B 82
St Clements Av. WS3: Blox 2B 32
St Clements Cl. B63: Hale 2A 128
St Clements Ho. B71: W Brom 3B 80
   (off Hallam St)
St Clements La. B71: W Brom 3B 80
St Clements Rd. B7: Nech 3C 102
St Columbas Dr. B45: Redn 2A 158
St Cuthbert's Cl. B70: W Brom 5D 80
St Cuthbert's Cl. B35: Cas V 4F 87
St David Dr. WS10: W'bry 2C 64
St David's Cl. B70: W Brom 5D 80
   WS3: Pels 2F 21
St Davids Ct. B69: O'bry 2G 97
St Davids Dr. B32: Quin 6H 113
St Davids Gro. B20: Hand 3B 82
St Davids Pl. WS3: Blox 5B 20
St Denis Rd. B29: W Cas 1E 145
St Dennis Ho. B16: Edg . . . .
   (off Melville Rd.)
St Dominic's Rd. B24: Erd 6E 85
   (not continuous)
St Edburgh's Rd. B25: Yard 2C 120
St Edmund Cl. DY1: Dud 3E 77
St Edmund's Cl. B70: W Brom 5D 80
   WV6: Wolv 6D 26
St Edwards Rd. B29: S Oak 3B 132
St Eleanors Cl. B70: W Brom 5D 80
St Eugenes Ct.
   B5: Birm 6G 5 (2H 117)
St Francis Av. B91: Sol 1C 150
St Francis' Cl. WS3: Pels 2F 21
St Francis Dr. B30: King Nor 4F 147
St Francis Factory Est.
   B70: W Brom 5B 80
St George Dr. B66: Smeth 2E 99
St Georges Av. B23: Erd 2G 85
St Georges Cl. B15: Edg 4C 116
   B75: S Cold 5D 54
   WS10: Darl 4D 46

St Georges Ct. *B1:* Birm 6D **100**
(off Albion St.)
B30: B'ville 6A **132**
B74: Four O 4E **37**
WS1: Wals 1D **48**
(off Persehouse St.)
WS10: Darl 4D **46**
(off St George's Cl.)
St George's Pde.
WV2: Wolv 4C **170** (2H **43**)
St Georges Pl. B70: W Brom 4A **80**
WS1: Wals 1D **48**
St Georges Rd. B90: Shir 1B **164**
DY2: Dud 3F **95**
DY8: Stourb 3B **124**
St George's Stop (Metro) 4C **170** (2H **43**)
St George's St. B19: Birm 5F **101**
WS10: Darl 4D **46**
St Gerards Cl. B91: Sol 5C **150**
St Gerards Rd. B91: Sol 5C **150**
St Giles Av. B65: Row R 5B **96**
St Giles Cl. B65: Row R 5C **96**
St Giles Ct. B65: Row R 6D **96**
WV13: W'hall 2B **46**
St Giles Cres. WV1: Wolv 1C **44**
St Giles Rd. B33: Kitts G 1H **121**
WV1: Wolv 1C **44**
WV13: W'hall 2B **46**
St Giles Row *DY8: Stourb* 5E **109**
(off Lwr. High St.)
St Giles St. DY2: Neth 4E **95**
St Helens Av. DY4: Tip 2C **78**
St Helens Pas. B1: Birm 1A **4** (6E **101**)
St Helens Rd. B91: Sol 1E **151**
St Helier Ho. *B16: Edg* 2H **115**
(off Melville Rd.)
St Heliers Rd. B31: N'fld 3C **144**
St Ives Rd. WS5: Wals 4H **49**
St James Av. B65: Row R 5B **96**
St James Cl. B70: W Brom 5D **80**
WS3: Pels 2F **21**
St James Gdns.
B68: O'bry 6G **97**
WS8: Bwnhls 6B **10**
St James Pl. B7: Birm 6A **102**
B15: Edg 3D **116**
B90: Shir 5H **149**
WS11: Nort C 1C **8**
St James Rd. B15: Edg 3D **116**
B21: Hand 1H **99**
B69: O'bry 1D **96**
B75: Four O 1A **54**
St James's Rd. DY1: Dud 5D **76**
St James's Ter. DY1: Dud 5C **76**
St James St. DY3: Lwr G 4H **75**
WS10: W'bry 3E **63**
WV1: Wolv 2A **44**
St James Wlk. *WS8: Bwnhls* 6B **10**
(off Church Rd.)
St John Bosco Cl. B71: W Brom 6H **63**
St John Cl. B75: R'ley 5B **38**
St John's Arc.
WV1: Wolv 3B **170** (1G **43**)
St Johns Av. B65: Row R 5B **96**
St John's Cl. B70: W Brom 5D **80**
B93: Know 3D **166**
DY3: Swind 5D **72**
WS9: Wals W 4B **22**
St Johns Ct. B17: Harb 5F **115**
B31: N'fld 6F **145**
DY5: Brie H 1H **109**
(off Lwr. Derry St.)
WS3: Blox 6H **19**
WS10: W'bry 3F **63**
St Johns Gro. B37: K'hrst 6B **106**
St John's Ho. B70: W Brom 5A **80**
St Johns Retail Pk.
WV2: Wolv 6B **170** (2G **43**)
St Johns Rd. B11: S'hll 6C **118**
B17: Harb 5H **115**
B63: Hale 1G **127**
B68: O'bry 4A **98**
DY2: Dud 1G **95**
DY4: Tip 6H **61**
DY8: Stourb 5E **109**
WS2: Wals 3H **47**
WS3: Pels 2F **21**

St Johns Rd. WS8: Bwnhls 2C **22**
WS10: Darl 6C **46**
WV11: Ess 4A **18**
St John's Sq.
WV2: Wolv 5B **170** (2G **43**)
St John's St. DY2: Neth 4E **95**
WV1: Wolv 3B **170**
B42: P Barr 3F **83**
St John's Way B93: Know 3E **167**
St Johns Wlk. B5: Birm 6E **5** (2G **117**)
B42: P Barr 3F **83**
St Johns Wood B45: Redn 4H **157**
St Joseph's Av. B31: N'fld 3F **145**
St Josephs Cl. WS3: Pels 3E **21**
St Joseph's Ct. WV4: Penn 5A **42**
St Joseph's Rd. B8: W End 4A **104**
St Joseph St. DY2: Dud 6F **77**
St Judes Cl. B14: King H 5H **147**
B75: S Cold 5D **54**
St Judes Pas.
B5: Birm 6D **4** (2F **117**)
St Jude's Rd. WV6: Wolv 6D **26**
St Jude's Rd. W. WV6: Wolv 6D **26**
St Katherines Rd. B68: O'bry 1H **113**
St Kenelms Av. B63: Hale 4G **127**
St Kenelm's Cl.
B70: W Brom 5D **80**
St Kenelm's Rd. B62: Roms 3A **142**
St Kilda's Rd. B8: Salt 5E **103**
St Laurence M. B31: N'fld 4E **145**
St Laurence Rd. B31: N'fld 2F **145**
St Lawrence Cl. B5: Edg 4F **117**
B93: Know 4D **166**
St Lawrence Ho. *B16: Edg* 2H **115**
(off Melville Rd.)
St Lawrence Way WS10: Darl 4D **46**
St Leonard's Cl. B37: Mars G 4C **122**
St Loye's Cl. B62: B'hth 3D **112**
St Lukes Cl. B65: Row R 5B **96**
St Luke's Rd. B5: Birm 3F **117**
(not continuous)
WS10: W'bry 2G **63**
St Lukes St. B64: Crad H 2F **111**
St Luke's Ter. DY1: Dud 1C **94**
St Margaret's Rd. B74: Four O 6C **36**
St Margarets Av. B8: W End 3H **103**
St Margaret's Ct. B92: Olton 4C **136**
St Margarets Dr. B63: Hale 3H **127**
St Margarets Rd. B8: W End 3G **103**
B43: Gt Barr 3B **66**
B92: Olton 4C **136**
WS3: Pels 3E **21**
St Marks Cl. WS6: Gt Wyr 1F **7**
St Marks Cres. B1: Birm 6C **100**
St Mark's Factory Cen.
DY9: Lye 6H **109**
St Marks Rd. B67: Smeth 6B **98**
DY2: Dud 5H **77**
DY4: Tip 5H **61**
DY9: Lye 6H **109**
WS3: Pels 3E **21**
WS8: Bwnhls 2C **22**
WV3: Wolv 2E **43**
(not continuous)
St Marks St. B1: Birm 6D **100**
WV3: Wolv 4A **170** (2F **43**)
St Martin's Church 5F **5** (1G **117**)
St Martins Cl. B70: W Brom 5D **80**
WV2: Ett 5A **44**
St Martin's Dr. DY4: Tip 2A **78**
St Martin's Ga. B2: Birm 5E **5**
St Martins Ind. Est. B69: O'bry 3H **97**
St Martin's Queensway
B2: Birm 5E **5** (1G **117**)
St Martin's Rd. B75: S Cold 6D **54**
St Martins Sq. B5: Birm 5F **5** (1G **117**)
St Martin's St. B15: Birm 2D **116**
St Martin's Ter. WV14: Bils 1G **61**
St Marys Cl. B24: Erd 3B **86**
B27: A Grn 2H **135**
DY3: Sed 5B **60**
St Marys Ct. DY5: Brie H 1H **109**
WV13: W'hall 1A **46**
(off Wolverhampton St.)
St Mary's Hall WV2: Wolv 5C **170**
St Mary's La. DY8: Stourb 2F **125**
St Mary's Pk. B47: Wyt 6G **161**

St Mary's Rd. B17: Harb 6G **115**
B67: Smeth 2D **114**
WS10: W'bry 2F **63**
St Marys Row B4: Birm 2E **5** (6G **101**)
B13: Mose 2H **133**
St Mary's St. WV1: Wolv 2C **170** (1H **43**)
St Marys Vw. B23: Erd 5D **68**
St Marys Way WS9: A'rdge 4C **34**
St Mathews St. WV1: Wolv 2B **44**
St Matthews Cl. WS1: Wals 2D **48**
WS3: Pels 2F **21**
St Matthews Rd. B66: Smeth 4G **99**
B68: O'bry 1G **113**
(not continuous)
St Mawes Rd. WV6: Pert 6F **25**
St Mawgan Cl. B35: Cas V 3G **87**
St Michael Ho. *B16: Edg* 2H **115**
(off Melville Rd.)
St Michaels Cl. WS3: Pels 5E **21**
St Michaels Ct. *B18: Birm* 5D **100**
(off Warstone Pde. E.)
B68: O'bry 5G **97**
(off Causeway Grn. Rd.)
B70: W Brom 4A **80**
WV6: Tett 4C **26**
St Michaels Cres. B69: O'bry 5F **97**
St Michael's Gro. DY2: Dud 6A **78**
St Michael's Hill B18: Hock 2C **100**
St Michael's M. B69: Tiv 5A **78**
St Michael's Rd. B18: Hock 2C **100**
B73: Bold 5F **69**
DY3: Lwr G 2D **74**
St Michael St. B70: W Brom 4A **80**
WS1: Wals 3C **48**
St Michaels Way DY4: Tip 4A **78**
St Nicholas Cl. WS3: Pels 3E **21**
St Nicholas Wlk. B76: Curd 1D **88**
St Nicolas Gdns. B38: King Nor 5B **146**
St Oswald's Ct. B10: Small H 3E **119**
St Oswald's Rd. B10: Small H 3E **119**
St Patricks Cl. B14: King H 2G **147**
St Paul's Av. B12: Bal H 6A **118**
St Paul's Cl. WS1: Wals 1C **48**
St Pauls Ct. B46: Wat O 4D **88**
B65: B'hth 2D **112**
St Paul's Cres. B46: Col 2H **107**
B70: W Brom 6E **63**
WS3: Pels 3F **21**
St Pauls Dr. B62: B'hth 2D **112**
DY4: Tip 3B **78**
St Paul's Pl. B3: Birm 1B **4**
St Paul's Rd. B12: Bal H 5H **117**
B66: Smeth 2B **98**
DY2: Neth 4F **95**
WS10: W'bry 6H **47**
St Paul's Sq. B3: Birm 2B **4** (6E **101**)
St Pauls Stop (Metro) 1C **4** (5F **101**)
St Paul's St. WS1: Wals 1C **48**
St Pauls Ter. B3: Birm 1B **4** (5E **101**)
St Peter Cft. WS10: W'bry 2C **64**
St Peters Cl. B28: Hall G 1D **148**
B46: Wat O 5D **88**
B72: W Grn 2H **69**
DY4: Tip 3D **78**
WS9: Ston 3G **23**
WV1: Wolv 2B **170** (1G **43**)
St Peters Ct. B6: Aston 1A **102**
WS3: Blox 6H **19**
St Peter's Cft. B73: S Cold 2H **69**
St Peter's Dr. WS3: Pels 3E **21**
St Peters La. B92: Bick 4F **139**
St Peters Rd. B17: Harb 6F **115**
B20: Hand 6E **83**
DY2: Dud, Neth 3F **95**
DY9: Pedm 4G **125**
St Peter's Sq. WV1: Wolv . . .2B **170** (1G **43**)
St Philips Av. WV3: Wolv 4D **42**
St Philips Cathedral 3D **4** (6F **101**)
St Philips Gro. WV3: Wolv 4D **42**
St Philips Pl. B3: Birm 3E **5** (6G **101**)
St Phillips Ct. B46: Col 2H **107**
St Quentin St. WS2: Wals 3A **48**
St Saviours Cl. WV2: Ett 5B **44**
St Saviour's Rd. B8: Salt 5D **102**
St Silas' Sq. B19: Loz 2D **100**
St Simons Cl. B75: S Cold 5D **54**

St Stephens Av. WV13: W'hall 1H 45
St Stephen's Cen. B21: Hand 3A 100
St Stephens Gdns. WV13: W'hall 1A 46
St Stephens Rd. B29: S Oak 5D 132
  B71: W Brom 6F 81
St Stephens St. B6: Aston 3G 101
St Thomas Cl. B75: S Cold 6D 54
  WS3: Wals 3C 32
  WS9: A'rdge 6D 22
St Thomas' Rd. B23: Erd 4D 84
St Thomas St. DY2: Neth 4E 95
St Valentines Cl. B70: W Brom 5D 80
St Vincent Cres. B70: W Brom 1F 79
St Vincent St. B16: Birm 1D 116
St Vincent St. W. B16: Birm 1C 116
Saladin Av. B69: O'bry 4E 97
Salcombe Av. B26: Sheld 6G 121
Salcombe Dr. DY5: Brie H 4G 109
Salcombe Gro. WV14: Cose 4F 61
Salcombe Rd. B66: Smeth 4F 99
Saldavian Ct. WS2: Wals 5H 47
Salem St. DY4: Tip 2D 78
Salford Bri. Wharf B24: Erd 6D 84
Salford Circ. B6: Aston 6D 84
Salford St. B6: Aston 1C 102
Salford Trad. Est. B6: Aston 1C 102
Salisbury Cl. B13: Mose 1G 133
  DY1: Dud 4B 76
Salisbury Ct. B91: Sol 3G 151
Salisbury Dr. B46: Wat O 4E 89
Salisbury Gro. B72: W Grn 6A 70
Salisbury Pl. Ind. Est.
  WV3: Wolv 2F 43
           (off Rosebery St.)
Salisbury Rd. B8: Salt 4E 103
  B13: Mose 1G 133
  B19: Loz 1F 101
  B66: Smeth 5F 99
  B70: W Brom 6C 80
Salisbury St. WS10: Darl 4E 47
  WV3: Wolv 2F 43
Salisbury Twr. B18: Hock 6C 100
Sallow Gro. WS8: Bwnhls 4C 10
Sally Ward Dr. WS9: Wals W 3C 22
Salop Cl. B71: W Brom 1H 79
Salop Dr. B68: O'bry 1A 114
Salop Rd. B68: O'bry 6A 98
Salop St. B12: Birm 3H 117
  B69: O'bry 6E 79
  DY1: Dud 5D 76
  WV3: Wolv 4A 170 (2G 43)
  WV14: Bils 1G 61
Salstar Cl. B6: Aston 3G 101
Saltash Gro. B25: Yard 2A 120
Saltbrook Rd. B63: Crad 4C 110
  DY9: Lye 4B 110
Saltbrook Trad. Est. B63: Crad 4C 110
Salter Rd. DY4: Tip 6H 61
Salter's La. B71: W Brom 3C 80
Salter's Rd. WS9: Wals W 3C 22
Salter St. B94: Earls, H'ley H 6A 164
Salters Va. B70: W Brom 6C 80
SALTLEY .4D 102
Saltley Bus. Pk. B8: Salt 3D 102
Saltley Cotts. B24: Erd 6F 85
Saltley Ga. B8: Salt 4D 102
Saltley Ind. Cen. B8: Salt 5C 102
Saltley Leisure Cen. 6G 103
Saltley Rd. B7: Birm 4B 102
Saltley Trad. Est. B8: Salt 3D 102
Saltley Viaduct B7: Birm 4C 102
  B8: Salt 4C 102
Saltney Cl. B24: Erd 2B 86
SALTWELLS 1D 110
Saltwells La. DY2: Neth 1B 110
  DY5: Brie H, Quar B 1B 110
Saltwells Local Nature Reserve 1C 110
Saltwells Rd. DY2: Neth 1D 110
Salwarpe Gro. B29: W Cas 3D 130
Sambourn Cl. B91: Sol 1A 152
Sambourne Dr. B34: S End 2H 105
Sambrook Rd. WV10: Wolv 3C 28
  B69: Tiv 2C 96
Sampson Cl. B21: Hand 6G 81
Sampson Rd. B11: S'brk 4B 118
Sampson Rd. Nth. B11: S'brk 3B 118
Sampson St. WS10: W'bry 2H 63

Sams La. B70: W Brom 5A 80
Samuels Rd. B32: Quin 6G 113
Samuel St. WS3: Blox 6H 19
Sanda Cft. B36: Cas B 3D 106
Sandalls Cl. B31: Longb 6B 144
Sandal Ri. B91: Sol 4A 152
Sandals Ri. B62: Hale 2D 128
Sandalwood Cl. WV12: W'hall 1B 30
Sandbank WS3: Blox 6G 19
Sandbarn Cl. B90: M'path 3D 164
Sandbeds Rd. WV12: W'hall 5C 30
Sandbourne Rd. B8: W End 5G 103
Sanderling Ri. DY6: K'wfrd 3E 93
Sanders Cl. DY2: Dud 2G 95
Sandfield B66: Smeth 2C 98
Sandfield Cl. B90: Shir 1G 163
Sandfield Bri. DY5: P'ntt 6F 75
Sandfield Farm Home Pk.
  WS8: Bwnhls 4D 10
Sandfield Gro. DY3: Gorn 5F 75
Sandfield Rd. B71: W Brom 4C 64
  DY8: Word 1D 108
Sandfields Av. B10: Small H 3B 118
Sandfields Rd. B68: O'bry 1A 114
Sandford Av. B65: Row R 6C 96
Sandford Ri. WV6: Tett 3C 26
Sandford Rd. B13: Mose 1A 134
  DY1: Dud 6A 76
Sandgate Rd. B28: Hall G 3F 149
  DY4: Tip 5A 62
Sandham Grange B34: Hodg H 2E 105
Sandhill Farm Cl. B19: Loz 2F 101
Sandhills Cres. B91: Sol 1F 165
Sandhill St. WS3: Blox 6G 19
Sandhurst Av. B36: Hodg H 3B 104
  DY9: W'cte 3H 125
Sandhurst Ct. B66: Smeth 1E 115
          (off Bearwood Rd.)
Sandhurst Dr. WV4: Penn 1E 59
Sandhurst Gro. DY8: Word 6C 92
Sandhurst Ho. B38: King Nor 6C 146
Sandhurst Rd. B13: Mose 3G 133
  B74: Four O 4F 37
  DY6: K'wfrd 5E 93
Sandland Cl. WV14: Bils 1G 61
Sandland Rd. WV12: W'hall 1D 30
Sandmartin Cl. DY2: Neth 1E 111
Sandmeadow Pl. DY6: K'wfrd 4A 92
Sandmere Gro. B14: Yard W 4D 148
Sandmere Ri. WV10: Bush 6A 16
Sandmere Rd. B14: Yard W 4D 148
Sandon Gro. B24: Erd 3H 85
Sandon Rd. B17: Edg 1E 115
  B66: Smeth 1E 115
  DY9: W'cte 1B 126
  WV10: F'hses 5F 15
Sandown Av. WS6: C Hay 2E 7
Sandown Cl. B29: W Cas 6G 131
Sandown Dr. WV6: Pert 5F 25
Sandown Rd. B36: Hodg H 1B 104
Sandown Twr. B31: N'fld 6E 145
Sandpiper Cl. DY9: W'cte 6B 110
Sandpiper Gdns. B38: King Nor 2B 160
Sandpiper Way B23: Erd 1C 84
Sandpit Cl. WS10: W'bry 3C 64
Sand Pits B1: Birm 3A 4 (6D 100)
Sandpits, The B30: B'ville 5A 132
Sandpits Cl. B76: Curd 1D 88
Sandpits Ind. Est. B1: Birm 6D 100
Sandpits Trad. Est. B47: H'wd 3D 162
Sandra Cl. WS9: A'rdge 4D 34
Sandringham Av. WV12: W'hall 2B 30
Sandringham Ct. B42: Gt Barr 4B 66
Sandringham Dr. B65: Row R 5C 96
  WS9: A'rdge 6D 22
Sandringham Ho. WV3: Wolv 3F 43
          (off Pennant Ct.)
Sandringham Pl. DY8: Word 2B 108
Sandringham Rd. B14: Yard W 4C 148
  B42: P Barr 1D 82
  B62: Hale 4B 112
  DY8: Word 2A 108
  WV4: Penn 1E 59
  WV5: Wom 1F 73
Sandringham Way
  DY5: Brie H 3G 109
Sandstone Av. B45: Rub 1G 157

Sandstone Cl. DY3: Lwr G 3H 75
Sand St. B70: W Brom 3E 79
Sandway Gdns. B8: Salt 3D 102
Sandway Gro. B13: Mose 6C 134
SANDWELL 1E 99
Sandwell Av. WS10: Darl 6B 46
Sandwell Business & Technology Cen.
  B68: O'bry 6G 97
      (off Wolverhampton Rd.)
Sandwell Bus. Development Cen.
  B66: Smeth 2A 98
Sandwell Bus. Pk. B66: Smeth 1A 98
Sandwell Cen. B70: W Brom 4B 80
Sandwell Ct. B21: Hand 1H 99
  B69: O'bry 2A 98
Sandwell & Dudley Station (Rail) . . .6G 79
Sandwell Gro. B64: Crad H 2E 111
Sandwell Ind. Est. B66: Smeth 1A 98
Sandwell Park Farm 4D 80
Sandwell Park Golf Course 6D 80
Sandwell Pl. B66: Smeth 1E 99
  WV12: W'hall 2D 30
Sandwell Rd. B21: Hand 6H 81
  B70: W Brom 3A 80
  WV10: Oxl 6F 15
Sandwell Rd. Nth. B71: W Brom 3B 80
Sandwell Rd. Pas. B70: W Brom 3A 80
Sandwell St. WS1: Wals 3D 48
Sandwell Valley Country Pk. 1G 81
Sandwell Valley Crematorium
  B71: W Brom 6E 65
Sandwell Valley Nature Reserve 1G 81
Sandwell Valley Sailing Club 2F 81
Sandwell Valley Vis. Cen. 1G 81
Sandwell Wlk. WS1: Wals 3D 48
Sandwood Dr. B44: Gt Barr 5H 67
Sandyacre Way DY8: Stourb 6F 109
Sandy Cres. WV11: Wed 1A 30
Sandy Cft. B13: Mose 6C 134
  B72: W Grn 2A 70
Sandyfields Rd.
  DY3: Lwr G, Sed 2D 74
Sandy Gro. WS8: Bwnhls 4B 10
Sandy Hill Ri. B90: Shir 3G 149
Sandy Hill Rd. B90: Shir 3G 149
Sandy Hollow WV6: Tett 1A 42
Sandy La. B6: Aston 2B 102
  B42: Gt Barr 5E 67
  B61: L Ash, Wild 4A 156
  DY8: Stourb 1B 124
  WS10: W'bry 2D 64
  WV6: Tett 3C 26
  WV8: Cod 2F 13
  WV10: Bush 6A 16
Sandy Mt. WV5: Wom 6H 57
Sandymount Rd. WS1: Wals 3D 48
Sandy Rd. DY8: Stourb 4B 124
Sandys Gro. DY4: Tip 2G 77
Sandy Way B15: Birm 6A 4 (2D 116)
Sangwin Rd. WV14: Cose 6E 61
Sannders Cres. DY4: Tip 2B 78
Sansome Ri. B90: Shir 5F 149
Sansome Rd. B90: Shir 5F 149
Sanstone Cl. WS3: Blox 4A 20
Sanstone Rd. WS3: Blox 4H 19
Santolina Dr. WS5: Wals 2E 65
Sant Rd. B31: Longb 2F 159
Sapcote Bus. Pk. B10: Small H 5E 119
Sapcote Trad. Cen. B6: Witt 5A 84
  B64: Old H 6H 95
Saplings, The B76: Walm 5E 71
Sapphire Ct. B3: Birm 1B 4 (5E 101)
  B92: Olton 4D 136
Sapphire Hgts. B1: Birm 6D 100
Sapphire Ho. E. B91: Sol 3E 151
Sapphire Ho. W. B91: Sol 3E 151
Sapphire Twr. B6: Aston 3H 101
          (off Thomas St.)
Saracen Dr. B75: S Cold 5D 54
  CV7: Bal C 3E 169
Sara Cl. B74: Four O 6G 37
Sarah Cl. WV14: Bils 4G 61
Sarah Ct. B73: New O 4D 68
Sarah Gdns. WS5: Wals 1D 64
Sarah St. B9: Birm 1B 118
Saredon Cl. WS3: Pels 6E 21
Saredon Gdns. DY1: Dud 3E 77

Saredon Rd. WS6: C Hay 1B **6**
   WV10: Share 1A **6**
   (not continuous)
Sarehole Mill 5D **134**
Sarehole Mill Gdns. B13: Mose 1H **133**
Sarehole Rd. B28: Hall G 6D **134**
Sargent Cl. B43: Gt Barr 1F **67**
Sargent Ho. B16: Birm 1D **116**
Sargent's Hill WS5: Wals 5G **49**
Sargent Turner Trad. Est.
   DY9: Lye 5B **110**
Sark Dr. B36: Cas B 3D **106**
Satellite Ind. Pk. WV11: W'hall 5F **29**
Saturday Bri. B1: Birm 6B **4**
Saturn Centre, The B5: Birm 3G **117**
Saunton Rd. WS3: Blox 4G **19**
Saunton Way B29: S Oak 4G **131**
Saveker Dr. B76: Walm 1C **70**
Savernake Cl. B45: Fran 5G **143**
Saville Cl. B45: Redn 2H **157**
Savoy Cl. B32: Harb 6D **114**
Saw Mill Cl. WS4: Wals 6C **32**
Saxelby Cl. B14: King H 5G **147**
   (not continuous)
Saxelby Ho. B14: King H 5G **147**
Saxon Cl. WS6: Gt Wyr 3G **7**
Saxon Cl. B31: Longb 1D **158**
   B31: N'fld 6D **144**
   WV6: Tett 4A **26**
Saxondale Av. B26: Sheld 5D **120**
Saxon Dr. B65: Row R 5C **96**
Saxonfields WV6: Tett 4A **26**
Saxons Way B14: King H 5A **148**
Saxon Way B37: K'hrst 6B **106**
Saxon Wood Cl. B31: N'fld 3E **145**
Saxon Wood Rd. B90: Ches G 4B **164**
Saxton Dr. B74: Four O 3F **37**
Scafell Dr. B23: Erd 2D **84**
   WV14: Bils 4H **45**
Scafell Rd. DY8: Amb 5F **109**
Scafell Way B71: W Brom 1A **80**
Scampton Cl. WV6: Pert 4E **25**
Scarborough Cl. WS2: Wals 3H **47**
Scarborough Rd. WS2: Wals 3H **47**
Scarecrow La. B75: R'ley 5C **38**
Scarsdale Rd. B42: Gt Barr 5F **67**
Schofield Av. B71: W Brom 5H **63**
Schofield Rd. B37: K'hrst 4C **106**
Scholars Cl. B21: Hand 2C **100**
Scholars Ga. B1: Birm 6C **4**
   B33: Kitts G 1F **121**
Scholars Ground, The 1A **10**
Scholars Wlk. WS4: Rus 2F **33**
Scholefield Twr. *B19: Birm* 4F **101**
   (off Uxbridge St.)
Schoolacre Ri. B74: S'tly 2G **51**
Schoolacre Rd. B34: S End 3F **105**
School Av. WS3: Blox 1A **32**
   WS8: Bwnhls 5B **10**
School Cl. B31: N'fld 5C **144**
   B35: Cas V 4F **87**
   B37: K'hrst 3C **106**
   B69: Tiv .2C **96**
   WV3: Wolv 4H **41**
   WV5: Try 5C **56**
   WV8: Cod 3G **13**
School Dr. B34: S End 4A **106**
   B47: Wyt 6A **162**
   DY8: Amb 3D **108**
   WV14: Bils 3A **62**
School Dr., The DY2: Dud 2F **95**
School Ga. Cl. B8: W End 3G **103**
Schoolgate Cl. WS4: S'fld 6H **21**
School Grn. WV14: Bils 3E **45**
Schoolhouse Cl.
   B38: King Nor 5D **146**
School La. B33: Yard 2D **120**
   B34: S End 3F **105**
   B63: Hale 3H **127**
   B91: Sol 2H **151**
   DY5: Brie H 5F **93**
   DY9: Hag 6H **125**
   WS3: Lit Wyr 3C **8**
   WS3: Pels 3D **20**
   WS11: Lit Wyr 3C **8**
   WV10: Bush 5H **15**
School Pas. DY5: Quar B 2C **110**

School Rd. B13: Mose 4H **133**
   B14: Yard W 3B **148**
   B28: Hall G 5F **135**
   B45: Rub 3E **157**
   B90: Shir 5H **149**
   DY3: Himl 4H **73**
   DY5: Quar B 1C **110**
   WS10: W'bry 3B **64**
   WV5: Try 5C **56**
   WV5: Wom 6H **57**
   WV6: Tett 5G **25**
   WV11: Wed 3D **28**
School St. B64: Crad H 2F **111**
   DY1: Dud 6D **76**
   (not continuous)
   DY3: Sed 5A **60**
   DY5: P'ntt 2H **93**
   DY8: Stourb 5D **108**
   WS4: S'fld 6H **21**
   WS10: Darl 5C **46**
   (Alma St.)
   WS10: Darl 6E **47**
   (Nowell St., not continuous)
   WV1: Wolv 4A **170** (2G **43**)
   WV3: Wolv 4A **170** (2G **43**)
   WV13: W'hall 1H **45**
   WV14: Cose 5E **61**
School St. W. WV14: Cose 5E **61**
School Ter. B29: S Oak 3B **132**
School Wlk. WV14: Bils 3E **45**
Science Park (Wolverhampton)
   (Park & Ride) 3G **27**
Scorers Cl. B90: Shir 1H **149**
Scotchings, The B36: Hodg H 1C **104**
Scotland La. B32: Bart G 5H **129**
Scotland Pas. B70: W Brom 4B **80**
SCOTLANDS 1C **28**
Scotland St. B1: Birm 3A **4** (6E **101**)
Scott Arms Shop. Cen.
   B42: Gt Barr 4B **66**
Scott Av. WS10: W'bry 3H **63**
   WV4: Penn 1C **58**
Scott Cl. B71: W Brom 2B **80**
Scott Gro. B92: Olton 2C **136**
Scott Ho. B43: Gt Barr 6B **66**
Scott Rd. B43: Gt Barr 3B **66**
   B92: Olton 2C **136**
   WS5: Wals 5H **49**
SCOTT'S GREEN 1C **94**
Scotts Grn. Cl. DY1: Dud 1B **94**
Scotts Grn. Island DY1: Dud 2B **94**
Scott's Rd. DY8: Stourb 5D **108**
Scott St. DY4: Tip 2C **78**
Scotwell Cl. B65: Row R 6B **96**
Scout Cl. B33: Kitts G 1G **121**
Scribbans Cl. B66: Smeth 5F **99**
Scriber's La. B28: Hall G 3D **148**
   (not continuous)
Scribers Mdw. B28: Hall G 3E **149**
Seacroft Av. B25: Yard 2C **120**
Seafield Cl. DY6: K'wfrd 5C **92**
Seaforth Gro. WV12: W'hall 6B **18**
Seagar St. B71: W Brom 3C **80**
Seagers La. DY5: Brie H 1H **109**
Seagull Bay Dr. WV14: Cose 4F **61**
Seal Cl. B76: Walm 1C **70**
Seals Grn. B38: King Nor 2H **159**
Seamless Dr. WV11: Wed 5F **29**
Sear Hills Cl. CV7: Bal C 3H **169**
Sears Retail Pk. B90: Shir 6B **150**
Seaton Cl. WV11: Wed 4H **29**
Seaton Gro. B13: Mose 4F **133**
Seaton Pl. DY8: Word 1A **108**
Seaton Rd. B66: Smeth 4F **99**
Second Av. B6: Witt 4H **83**
   B9: Bord G 2E **119**
   B29: S Oak 2D **132**
   DY6: P'ntt 2D **92**
   WS8: Bwnhls 4C **10**
   WV10: Bush 2A **28**
Sedge Av. B38: King Nor 4B **146**
Sedgeberrow Covert
   B38: King Nor 1A **160**
Sedgeberrow Rd. B63: Hale 3A **128**
Sedgebourne Way B31: Longb 6A **144**
Sedgefield Cl. DY1: Dud 4A **76**
Sedgefield Gro. WV6: Pert 5F **25**

Sedgeford Cl. DY5: Brie H 3H **109**
Sedgehill Av. B17: Harb 1F **131**
Sedgemere Gro. CV7: Bal C 6H **169**
   WS4: S'fld 1G **33**
Sedgemere Rd. B26: Yard 2D **120**
Sedgfield Way WS11: Nort C 1E **9**
SEDGLEY 5H **59**
Sedgley Golf Course 1F **75**
Sedgley Gro. B20: Hand 3A **82**
Sedgley Hall Av. DY3: Sed 5G **59**
Sedgley Hall Est. DY3: Sed 4G **59**
Sedgley Rd. DY1: Dud 1D **76**
   DY4: Tip 1D **76**
   WV4: Penn 2C **58**
Sedgley Rd. E. DY4: Tip 3A **78**
Sedgley Rd. W. DY4: Tip 1F **77**
Sedgley St. WV2: Wolv 4G **43**
Seedhouse Ct. B64: Old H 3A **112**
Seeds La. WS8: Bwnhls 5B **10**
Seeleys Pk. B11: S'brk 6D **118**
Seeleys Rd. B11: Tys 6D **118**
Sefton Dr. B65: Row R 3H **95**
Sefton Gro. DY4: Tip 3C **62**
Sefton Rd. B16: Edg 1B **116**
Segbourne Rd. B45: Rub 1E **157**
Segundo Cl. WS5: Wals 1D **64**
Segundo Rd. WS5: Wals 1D **64**
SEISDON 2A **56**
Seisdon Hollaway WV5: Seis 2A **56**
Seisdon Rd. WV5: Seis, Try 3A **56**
Sela Ho. B70: W Brom 5C **80**
Selborne Cl. WS1: Wals 2E **49**
Selborne Gro. B13: Mose 2C **148**
Selborne Rd. B20: Hand 5C **82**
   DY2: Dud 2F **95**
Selborne St. WS1: Wals 2E **49**
Selbourne Cres. WV1: Wolv 2D **44**
Selby Cl. B26: Yard 2D **120**
Selby Ho. B69: O'bry 3D **96**
Selby Way WS3: Blox 5E **19**
Selcombe Way B38: King Nor 2B **160**
Selco Way B76: Min 2E **87**
Selcroft Av. B32: Harb 6D **114**
Selecta Av. B44: Gt Barr 3F **67**
Selkirk Cl. B71: W Brom 1A **80**
Selly Av. B29: S Oak 3C **132**
Selly Cl. B29: S Oak 3D **132**
Selly Hall Cft. B30: B'vlle 1C **146**
Selly Hill Rd. B29: S Oak 3B **132**
Selly Manor 5B **132**
SELLY OAK .4A **132**
Selly Oak Ind. Est. B29: S Oak 4A **132**
Selly Oak New Rd. B15: Edg 3A **132**
   B29: S Oak 3A **132**
Selly Oak Rd.
   B30: B'vlle, King Nor 6A **132**
Selly Oak Station (Rail) 3A **132**
SELLY PARK 3C **132**
Selly Pk. Rd. B29: S Oak 3C **132**
Selly Wharf B29: S Oak 3A **132**
Selly Wick Dr. B29: S Oak 3D **132**
Selly Wick Rd. B29: S Oak 3C **132**
Sellywood Rd. B30: B'vlle 6H **131**
Selma Gro. B14: Yard W 2D **148**
Selman's Hill WS3: Blox 4A **20**
Selman's Pde. WS3: Blox 5A **20**
Selsdon Cl. B47: Wyt 4C **162**
Selsdon Rd. WS3: Blox 4F **19**
Selsey Av. B17: Edg 6F **99**
Selsey Rd. B17: Edg 6F **99**
Selston Rd. B6: Aston 2G **101**
Selvey Av. B43: Gt Barr 2D **66**
Selworthy Rd. B36: Cas B 2B **106**
Selwyn Cl. WV2: Wolv 4G **43**
Selwyn Ho. B37: Chel W 6F **107**
Selwyn Rd. B16: Edg 6H **99**
   WV14: Bils 5H **45**
Selwyn Wlk. B74: Lit As 5C **36**
Senior Cl. WV11: Ess 4A **18**
Senneley's Pk. Rd. B31: N'fld 5C **130**
Sennen Cl. WV13: W'hall 2H **45**
Sensall Rd. DY9: W'cte 2B **126**
Sentry Way B75: S Cold 5D **54**
Serpentine Rd. B6: Aston 6A **84**
   B17: Harb 5G **115**
   B29: S Oak 2C **132**

Servite Ct. B14: King H 5A 148
Servite Ho. B44: Gt Barr 3H 67
B46: Col 2H 107
B92: Olton .6B 136
Settle Av. B34: Hodg H 3E 105
Settle Cft. B37: F'bri 2B 122
Setton Dr. DY3: Sed 6A 60
Seven Acres WS9: A'rdge 4D 34
Seven Acres Rd. B31: N'fld 6G 145
B62: Quin .6G 113
Sevendwellings Vw. DY5: Brie H 2G 109
Seven Star Rd. B91: Sol 2E 151
Seven Stars Rd. B69: O'bry 2G 97
Severn Cl. B36: Cas B 2B 106
DY4: Tip 2H 77
WV12: W'hall 2A 30
Severn Ct. B23: Erd 4B 84
B73: S Cold 6H 53
Severn Dr. DY5: P'ntt 2F 93
WV6: Pert 5E 25
Severne Gro. B27: A Grn 4A 136
Severne Rd. B27: A Grn 5A 136
Severn Gro. B11: S'brk 5C 118
B19: Loz 2E 101
(not continuous)
Severn Ri. B65: Row R 1B 112
Severn Rd. B63: Crad 6D 110
DY8: Stourb 2D 124
WS3: Blox .6C 20
WS8: Bwnhls 3G 9
Severn St. B1: Birm 6C 4 (2F 117)
Severn St. Pl. B1: Birm 6C 4
Severn Twr. B7: Nech 4B 102
Severn Way B47: Wyt 6G 161
Sevington Cl. B91: Sol 1G 165
Seymour Cl. B29: S Oak 3C 132
WS6: C Hay .4D 6
Seymour Gdns. B74: Four O 6E 37
Seymour Rd. B69: O'bry 2A 98
DY4: Tip 4C 62
DY9: W'cte 6B 110
Shackleton Dr. WV6: Pert 4E 25
Shackleton Hall B15: Edg 5C 116
Shackleton Rd. WS3: Blox 5B 20
Shadowbrook La. B92: H Ard 5F 139
Shadwell Dr. DY3: Lwr G 4H 75
Shadwell St. B4: Birm 1D 4 (5F 101)
Shady La. B44: Gt Barr 3F 67
Shadymoor Dr. DY5: Brie H 3G 109
Shaftesbury Av. DY9: Pedm 2G 125
Shaftesbury Rd. WS10: W'bry 3H 63
Shaftesbury Sq. B71: W Brom 2A 80
Shaftesbury St. B70: W Brom 3A 80
B71: W Brom 3A 80
Shaftmoor Ind. Est. B28: Hall G 3F 135
Shaftmoor La. B27: A Grn 3E 135
B28: Hall G 3E 135
Shaftsbury Av. B63: Crad 4D 110
Shaftsbury Rd. B26: Sheld 6G 121
Shahjalal Rd. B8: Salt 4D 102
Shakespeare Cl. WV14: Cose 3F 61
Shakespeare Cres. B18: Hock 4C 100
WS3: Blox .2D 32
(Harden Rd.)
WS3: Blox .1C 32
(Tennyson Rd.)
Shakespeare Dr. B90: Shir 6G 149
Shakespeare Ho. B31: Longb 1E 159
Shakespeare Rd. B23: Erd 4B 84
B67: Smeth .5C 98
B90: Shir .6B 150
DY3: Lwr G .3E 75
DY4: Tip 5A 62
Shakespeare St. B11: S'hll 6C 118
WV1: Wolv .2A 44
Shaldon Wlk. B66: Smeth 4F 99
Shales, The WV5: Wom 2E 73
Shale St. WV14: Bils 6E 45
Shalford Rd. B92: Olton 1C 136
Shallcross La. DY3: Lwr G 4H 75
Shalnecote Gro. B14: King H 2E 147
Shambles, The WS10: W'bry 3F 63
Shandon Cl. B32: Bart G 2D 130
Shanklin Cl. WS6: Gt Wyr 2F 7
Shannon Dr. WS8: Bwnhls 3G 9
Shannon Rd. B38: King Nor 2H 159

Shannon Wlk. WS8: Bwnhls 3G 9
Shanti Niketan WV2: Wolv 4H 43
(off Johnson St.)
Shapinsay Dr. B45: Fran 6F 143
SHARD END .3G 105
Shard End Community Centre & Sports Hall
. . . . .3H 105
Shard End Cres. B34: S End 3G 105
Shardlow Rd. WV11: Wed 1G 29
Shardway, The B34: S End 4G 105
Sharesacre St. WV13: W'hall 6B 30
Sharington Cl. DY2: Dud 1F 95
Sharman Rd. WV10: Bush 3A 28
SHARMANS CROSS 3C 150
Sharmans Cross Rd. B91: Sol 3C 150
Sharon Cl. WV4: Ett 6A 44
Sharps Cl. B45: Redn 2G 157
Sharrat Fld. B75: R'ley 1B 54
Sharrocks St. WV1: Wolv 2A 44
SHAVER'S END 5D 76
Shawberry Av. B35: Cas V 4E 87
Shawberry Rd. B37: K'hrst 4B 106
SHAWBROOK 5H 161
Shawbrook Gro. B14: King H 4A 148
Shawbury Gro. B12: Birm 3H 117
WV6: Pert 4E 25
Shawbury Rd. WV10: Wolv 4B 28
Shaw Dr. B33: Yard 1C 120
Shawfield B47: H'wd 4A 162
Shaw Hall La. WV10: Cov H 1F 15
Shawhellier Av. DY5: Brie H 1A 110
Shaw Hill Gro. B8: W End 5G 103
Shaw Hill Rd. B8: W End 5G 103
Shawhurst Cft. B47: H'wd 2A 162
Shawhurst Gdns. B47: H'wd 2B 162
Shawhurst La. B47: H'wd 4A 162
Shaw La. WV6: Tett 6H 25
Shawley Cft. B27: A Grn 1C 136
Shaw Pk. Bus. Village
WV10: Bush 3H 27
Shaw Rd. DY2: Dud 2D 94
(not continuous)
DY4: Tip 3C 78
WV2: Wolv .5G 43
WV10: Bush 3G 27
WV14: Cose 4D 60
Shawsdale Rd. B36: Hodg H 2D 104
Shaws La. WS6: Gt Wyr 3G 7
Shaw's Pas. B5: Birm 5G 5 (1H 117)
Shaw St. B70: W Brom 5E 63
WS2: Wals .1B 48
Shayler Gro. WV2: Wolv 4H 43
Sheaf La. B26: Sheld 6F 121
Sheapecote Ho. B71: W Brom 3D 64
Shearers Pl. B75: R'ley 6C 38
Shearwater Cl. B45: Rub 3F 157
Shearwater Dr. DY5: Brie H 4G 109
Shearwater Wlk. B23: Erd 6B 68
Sheaves Cl. WV14: Cose 2D 60
Shedden St. DY2: Dud 1F 95
Sheddington Rd. B23: Erd 6D 68
Sheen Rd. B44: Gt Barr 1G 67
Sheepclose Dr. B37: F'bri 6C 106
Sheepcote St. B16: Birm 6A 4 (1D 116)
Sheepfold Cl. B65: Row R 5A 96
Sheepmoor Cl. B17: Harb 3D 114
Sheepwash La. DY4: Tip 2D 78
Sheepwash Nature Reserve 3D 78
Sheffield Rd. B73: Bold 6G 69
Sheffield St. DY5: Quar B 2C 110
Shefford Rd. B6: Aston 4H 101
Sheila Av. WV11: Wed 2G 29
Shelah Rd. B63: Hale 5H 111
Shelbourne Cl. B69: Tiv 5D 78
SHELDON 6H 121
Sheldon Av. WS10: W'bry 1G 63
Sheldon Cl. WV14: Bils 2F 61
Sheldon Country Pk. 4H 121
Sheldon Dr. B31: Longb 5B 144
Sheldonfield Rd. B26: Sheld 6H 121
Sheldon Gro. B26: Sheld 6F 121
Sheldon Hall Av. B33: Kitts G 6H 105
Sheldon Heath Leisure Cen. 3G 121
Sheldon Heath Rd.
B26: Yard, Sheld 2E 121
Sheldon Rd. B71: W Brom 5C 64
WV10: Oxl 6E 15

Sheldon Wlk. B33: Sheld 2G 121
SHELFIELD 6G 21
Shelfield Rd. B14: King H 4E 147
Shelley Av. DY4: Tip 5A 62
Shelley Cl. DY3: Lwr G 2E 75
DY8: Amb .3E 109
Shelley Dr. B23: Erd 4B 84
B74: Four O 3F 37
Shelley Rd. WV10: F'hses 5H 15
WV12: W'hall 2E 31
Shelley Twr. B31: N'fld 4G 145
Shelly Cl. B37: F'bri 1B 122
Shelly Cres. B90: M'path 2F 165
Shelly Cft. B33: Kitts G 6E 105
Shelly Ho. B68: O'bry 5H 97
Shelly La. B90: M'path 3F 165
Shelly Shop. Cen. B90: M'path 2F 165
Shelsley Av. B69: O'bry 4D 96
Shelsley Dr. B13: Mose 4B 134
Shelsley Way B91: Sol 6F 151
Shelton Cl. WS10: W'bry 6A 48
Shelton La. B63: Crad 6G 111
Shelwick Gro. B93: Dorr 5A 166
Shenley Av. DY1: Dud 1D 76
Shenley Court Community Leisure Cen.
. . . . .6D 130
SHENLEY FIELDS 6C 130
Shenley Flds. Dr. B31: N'fld 5C 130
Shenley Flds. Rd.
B29: S Oak, W Cas 6D 130
Shenley Gdns. B29: W Cas 6E 131
SHENLEY GREEN 1D 144
Shenley Hill B31: N'fld 1C 144
Shenley La. B29: W Cas 4D 130
Shenley Lane Community & Sports Cen.
. . . . .1E 145
Shenstone Av. B62: Hale 6E 113
DY8: Stourb 2B 124
Shenstone Cl. B74: Four O 3E 37
Shenstone Ct. B90: Shir 5D 148
WV3: Wolv .5E 43
Shenstone Dr. CV7: Bal C 3G 169
WS9: A'rdge .1C 34
Shenstone Flats B62: Quin 6F 113
Shenstone Rd. B14: King H 6A 148
B16: Edg 6G 99
B43: Gt Barr 5A 66
Shenstone Trad. Est. B63: Hale 1C 128
Shenstone Valley Rd. B62: Quin 5E 113
Shenstone Wlk. B62: Hale 6D 112
SHENSTONE WOODEND 1G 37
Shonton Wlk. B37: K'hrst 4C 106
Shepheard Rd. B26: Sheld 6H 121
Shepherd Dr. WV12: W'hall 4C 30
Shepherds Brook Rd. DY9: Lye 6H 109
Shepherds Fold B65: Row R 1B 112
Shepherds Gdns. B15: Birm 2D 116
Shepherds Grn. Rd. B24: Erd 5F 85
B90: Shir 2A 164
Shepherds La. CV7: Mer 2G 141
Shepherds Pool Rd. B75: R'ley 1C 54
Shepherds Standing B34: S End 3F 105
Shepherds Wlk. WV8: Pend 5D 14
Shepherds Way B23: Erd 5C 68
Shepley Rd. B45: Redn 3H 157
Sheppey Dr. B36: Cas B 4D 106
SHEPWELL GREEN 1C 46
Shepwell Grn. WV13: W'hall 2C 46
Sherard Cft. B36: Cas B 3D 106
Sheraton Cl. WS9: A'rdge 3D 34
Sheraton Grange DY8: Stourb 3D 124
Sherborne Cl. B46: Col 5H 107
WS3: Blox .2A 32
Sherborne Gdns. WV8: Cod 4G 13
Sherborne Gro. B1: Birm 6C 100
Sherborne Lofts B16: Birm 1D 116
Sherborne Rd. WV10: Bush 6H 15
Sherborne St. B16: Birm 1D 116
Sherborne Wharf B16: Birm 1D 116
Sherbourne Ct. B27: A Grn 1A 136
Sherbourne Dr. B27: A Grn 1A 136
Sherbourne Rd. B12: Bal H 4G 117
B27: A Grn 1A 136
B64: Old H .3A 112
DY8: Stourb 1F 125
Sherbourne Rd. E. B12: Bal H 5H 117
Sherdmore Cft. B90: M'path 3E 165

Sheridan Cl. WS2: Wals 4H 47
Sheridan Gdns. DY3: Lwr G 2D 74
Sheridan St. B71: W Brom 3B 80
  WS2: Wals .4H 47
Sheriff Dr. DY5: Quar B 1B 110
Sherifoot La. B75: Four O 5H 37
Sheringham B15: Edg 3A 116
Sheringham Rd. B30: King Nor 4D 146
Sherington Dr. WV4: Penn 6H 43
Sherlock Cl. WV12: W'hall 4D 30
Sherlock St. B5: Birm 3G 117
Sherrans Dell WV4: Ett 2A 60
Sherratt Cl. B76: Walm 5D 70
Sherringham Dr. WV11: Ess 6C 18
Sherron Gdns. B12: Bal H 6H 117
Sherston Covert B30: King Nor 5E 147
Shervale Cl. WV4: Penn 5E 43
Sherwin Av. WV4: Cose 3C 60
Sherwood Av. DY4: Tip 3H 77
Sherwood Cl. B28: Hall G 2F 149
  B92: Olton 6D 136
Sherwood Dr. DY5: Quar B 2B 110
Sherwood M. B28: Hall G 1E 149
Sherwood Rd. B28: Hall G 6E 135
  B67: Smeth 2E 115
  DY8: Woll .4C 108
Sherwood St. WV1: Wolv 6G 27
Sherwood Wlk. B45: Fran 4H 143
  WS9: A'rdge 2A 34
Shetland Cl. B16: Birm 1B 116
  WV6: Wolv .4F 27
Shetland Dr. B66: Smeth 2B 98
Shetland Wlk. B36: Cas B 3D 106
Shidas La. B69: O'bry 2E 97
Shifnal Wlk. B31: Longb 1D 158
Shifrall Way B75: S Cold 4D 54
Shillcock Gro. B19: Birm 4G 101
Shilton Cl. B90: M'path 3D 164
Shilton Gro. B29: W Cas 5D 130
Shinglers Dr. DY4: Tip 6G 61
Shinwell Cres. B69: Tiv 5D 78
Shipbourne Cl. B32: Harb 6D 114
Shipley Flds. B24: Erd 4G 85
Shipley Gro. B29: W Cas 5E 131
Shipleys Luxury Bingo 3D 130
Shipston Rd. B31: N'fld 6F 145
Shipton Cl. DY1: Dud 4A 76
Shipton Rd. B72: S Cold 2A 70
Shipway Rd. B25: Yard 4G 119
Shire Brook Cl. B6: Aston 1G 101
Shire Brook Ct. B19: Loz 1F 101
Shire Cl. B16: Birm 1B 116
  B68: O'bry .1H 113
Shireland Brook Gdns.
  B18: Win G .5H 99
Shireland Cl. B20: Hand 4A 82
Shireland Rd. B66: Smeth 5F 99
Shire Lea WS8: Bwnhls 1D 22
SHIRE OAK .2B 22
Shire Oak Cl. WS9: Wals W 2D 22
Shire Oak Park (Nature Reserve) 3D 22
Shire Ridge WS9: Wals W 3C 22
Shirestone Rd. B33: Kitts G 1H 121
Shireview Gdns. WS3: Pels 3F 21
Shireview Rd. WS3: Pels 3E 21
Shirland Rd. B37: Mars G 2C 122
SHIRLEY 5H 149
Shirleydale B90: Shir 6A 150
Shirley Dr. B72: S Cold 1A 70
Shirley Golf Course 5D 164
SHIRLEY HEATH 1H 163
Shirley Pk. Rd. B90: Shir 5H 149
Shirley Rd. B27: A Grn 4H 135
  B28: Hall G 1G 149
  B30: King Nor 2C 146
  B68: O'bry .3A 98
  DY2: Dud 1G 95
Shirley Station (Rail) 6F 149
SHIRLEY STREET 5A 150
Shirley Trad. Est. B90: Shir 1D 164
Shirrall Dr. B75: Dray B 5G 39
  B78: Dray B 5G 39
Shirrall Gro. B37: K'hrst 4B 106
Sholing Cl. WV8: Pend 6D 14
Shooters Cl. B5: Edg 5F 117
Shooters Hill B72: S Cold 3B 70

Shop La. WV6: Tres 4B 40
  WV8: Oaken 6C 12
Shopton Rd. B34: S End 2E 105
Shoreham Cl. WV13: W'hall 2F 45
Short Acre St. WS2: Wals 6B 32
SHORT CROSS 6H 111
Shorters Av. B14: King H 3B 148
Shortfield Cl. CV7: Bal C 2H 169
SHORT HEATH
  B23 . . . . .1D 84
  WV12 . . . . .4D 30
Short Heath Ct. B23: Erd 2F 85
Short Heath Rd. B23: Erd 1D 84
Shortland Cl. B93: Know 2C 166
Shortlands Cl. B30: King Nor 5C 146
Shortlands La. WS3: Pels 3D 20
Short La. WS6: C Hay 2E 7
Short Rd. B67: Smeth 6B 98
  WV10: Bush 6A 16
Short St. B63: Hale 1H 127
  B65: B'hth 2C 112
  B65: B'hth, Row R 1C 112
            (not continuous)
  B90: Dic H .4G 163
  DY1: Dud 5C 76
  DY4: Tip 5G 61
  DY8: Stourb 6D 108
  WS2: Wals .2B 48
  WS8: Bwnhls 5B 10
  WS10: Darl 4F 47
  WS10: W'bry 2E 63
  WV1: Wolv 2C 170 (1H 43)
  WV12: W'hall 4C 30
  WV14: Bils .5F 45
Shorwell Pl. DY5: Brie H 3G 109
Shottery Cl. B76: Walm 4D 70
Shottery Gro. B76: Walm 4D 70
Shotteswell Rd. B90: Shir 2H 163
Showcase Cinema
  Birmingham 5B 86
  Dudley 5G 77
  Walsall 2G 47
Showell Cir. WV10: Bush 2A 28
SHOWELL GREEN 1B 134
Showell Grn. La. B11: S'hll 2B 134
Showell Ho. B69: O'bry 2G 97
Showell La. WV4: Lwr P 2G 57
Showell Rd. WV10: Bush 2H 27
Showell Rd. Ind. Est.
  WV10: Wolv 3H 27
Showells Gdns. B7: Nech 2C 102
Shrawley Av. B31: N'fld 5G 145
Shrawley Cl. B45: Rub 2F 157
  B63: Hale .3A 128
Shrewley Cres. B33: Kitts G 2A 122
Shrewsbury Cl. WS3: Blox 6F 19
Shrewsbury Pl. DY1: Dud 3E 77
Shrewton Av. B14: King H 6F 147
Shropshire Way B71: W Brom 6A 64
Shrubbery, The B16: Birm 6B 100
  DY1: Dud 5D 76
  DY4: Tip 1C 78
Shrubbery Av. DY4: Tip 2F 77
Shrubbery Cl. B76: Walm 1B 86
  WS1: Wals .2F 49
Shrublands Av. B68: O'bry 4H 113
Shrub La. B24: Erd 3H 85
Shugborough Cl. WS3: Blox 6H 19
Shugborough Dr. DY1: Dud 5A 76
Shustoke La. WS5: Wals 1F 65
Shustoke Rd. B34: S End 3G 105
  B91: Sol 2H 151
SHUT END 6E 75
Shutlock La. B13: Mose 4F 133
Shyltons Cft. B16: Birm 1C 116
Sibdon Gro. B31: Longb 1E 159
Sidaway Cl. B65: Row R 3C 96
Sidaway St. B64: Old H 2G 111
Sidbury Gro. B93: Dorr 6A 166
Sidcup Cl. WV14: Cose 2D 60
Sidcup Rd. B44: K'sdng 4A 68
Siddeley Wlk. B36: Cas B 6B 88
Siddons Factory Est.
  B70: W Brom 5F 63
Siddons Rd. WV14: Cose 3F 61
Siddons Way B70: W Brom 6G 63

Sidenhill Cl. B90: Shir 1H 163
Sidestrand WV9: Pend 4D 14
Sidford Gdns. B24: Erd 4A 86
Sidford Gro. B23: Erd 6E 69
Sidings, The B17: Harb 5G 115
  B20: Hand 1E 101
  B23: Erd 4E 85
  B70: W Brom 5A 80
Sidings Cl. WV11: Wed 5E 29
Sidlaw Cl. B63: Hale 3F 127
  WV10: Oxl .3G 27
Sidney St. WV2: Wolv 6A 170 (3G 43)
Sidwick Cres. WV2: Ett 5D 44
Sigmund Cl. WV1: Wolv 6D 28
Signal Gro. WS3: Blox 6G 19
Signal Hayes Rd. B76: Walm 3D 70
            (not continuous)
Silesbourne Cl. B36: Cas B 1G 105
Silhill Hall Rd. B91: Sol 1E 151
Silva Av. DY6: K'wfrd 5D 92
Silver Birch Cl. B8: Salt 3D 102
Silver Birch Coppice B74: Four O 4D 36
Silverbirch Ct. B24: Erd 1H 85
Silver Birch Dr. B47: H'wd 3B 162
Silver Birch Rd. B24: Erd 1H 85
  B37: K'hrst 3B 106
  B74: S'tly 2H 51
  WS11: Nort C 1F 9
  WV2: Wolv .4A 44
Silverbirch Rd. B91: Sol 4A 152
Silver Ct. WS8: Bwnhls 6B 10
Silver Ct. Gdns. WS8: Bwnhls 6B 10
Silvercroft Av. B20: Hand 4G 81
Silverdale Dr. WV10: Wolv 5A 28
Silverdale Gdns. DY8: Word 6A 92
Silverdale Rd. B24: Erd 2B 86
SILVER END .2F 109
Silver End Bus. Pk. DY5: Brie H 2G 109
Silver End Ind. Est. DY5: Brie H 2F 109
Silverfield Cl. B14: King H 5G 133
Silver Innage B63: Crad 4E 111
Silverlands Av. B68: O'bry 6H 97
Silverlands Cl. B28: Hall G 4F 135
Silvermead Ct. B47: Wyt 4H 161
Silvermead Rd. B73: W Grn 4G 69
Silvermere Rd. B26: Sheld 5H 121
Silvers Cl. WS3: Pels 2D 20
Silverstone Cl. WS2: Wals 6D 30
Silverstone Cl. B30: Stir 5E 133
Silverstone Dr. B74: S'tly 5H 51
SILVER STREET 4G 161
Silver St. B14: King H 5G 133
  B38: Head H 4F 161
  B47: Wyt 4G 161
  DY5: Brie H 2G 109
  WS8: Bwnhls 6A 10
Silverthorne Av. DY4: Tip 2F 77
Silverthorne La. B64: Crad H 2D 110
Silverton Cres. B13: Mose 4D 134
Silverton Hgts. B67: Smeth 3D 98
Silverton Rd. B67: Smeth 3C 98
Silverton Way WV11: Wed 4H 29
Silvertrees Rd. DY4: Tip 2G 77
Silverwood WV5: Wom 6E 57
Silvester Cl. B70: W Brom 4B 80
Silvester Rd. WV14: Bils 5G 45
Silvester Way DY5: Brie H 3F 109
Silvington Cl. B29: W Cas 6G 131
Simcox Gdns. B32: Bart G 3B 130
Simcox Rd. WS10: W'bry 6F 47
Simeon Bissell Cl. DY4: Tip 2A 78
Simeon's Wlk. DY5: Quar B 4B 110
Simkins Cl. WS9: Wals W 4C 22
Simmonds Cl. WS3: Blox 4B 20
Simmonds Pl. WS3: Blox 4B 20
  WS10: Darl 4E 47
Simmonds Way WS8: Bwnhls 2C 22
Simmons Dr. B32: Quin 1A 130
Simmons Leasow B32: Bart G 3B 130
Simmons Rd. WV11: Wed 6B 18
Simms La. B47: H'wd 4A 162
            (not continuous)
  DY2: Neth 4E 95
Simon Cl. B71: W Brom 4C 64
Simon Rd. B47: H'wd 2A 162
Simpson Gro. WV10: Bush 3A 28

Simpson Rd. B72: W Grn 4A 70
  WS2: Wals 4H 31
  WV10: Bush 3A 28
Simpson St. B69: O'bry 2G 97
Sinclair Ct. B13: Mose 1G 133
Singer Cft. B36: Cas B 6B 88
Singh Cl. B21: Hand 6A 82
Sion Cl. DY5: Brie H 6H 93
Sir Alfred's Way B76: Walm 2C 70
Sir Harrys Rd. B5: Edg 5D 116
  B15: Edg 5D 116
Sir Herbert Austin Way
  B31: N'fld 4D 144
Sir Hilton's Rd. B31: Longb 2F 159
Sir Johns Rd. B29: S Oak 2E 133
Sir Richards Dr. B17: Harb 4D 114
Sisefield Rd. B38: King Nor 6C 146
Siskin Cl. B68: O'bry 1A 114
  WS7: Hamm 1F 11
Siskin Dr. B12: Bal H 5G 117
Siskin Rd. DY9: W'cte 2H 125
Sister Dora Bldgs. WS1: Wals 2C 48
  (off The Bridge)
Sister Dora Gdns. WS1: Wals 2C 48
Siviters Cl. B65: Row R 6C 96
Siviters La. B65: Row R 6B 96
Siviter St. B63: Hale 1B 128
Six Acres B32: Quin 1A 130
Sixes Football Cen. 6C 74
Six Foot Rd. DY2: Neth 4E 95
Six Towers Rd. WS2: Wals 5A 32
Six Ways B23: Erd 3F 85
Skelcher Rd. B90: Shir 3G 149
Skemp Cl. WV14: Bils 2F 61
Sketchley Cl. B66: Smeth 4E 99
Skiddaw Dr. B71: W Brom 1A 80
Skidmore Av. WV3: Wolv 3D 42
Skidmore Dr. B70: W Brom 4G 79
Skidmore Rd. WV14: Cose 3F 61
Skinner La. B5: Birm 2G 117
Skinner St. WV1: Wolv . . .3A 170 (1G 43)
Skip La. WS5: Wals 6H 49
Skipton Grn. WV6: Wolv 4E 27
Skipton Rd. B16: Edg 2C 116
Skomer Cl. B45: Fran 6E 143
Skye Cl. B36: Cas B 3D 106
Skye Wlk. B64: Old H 2G 111
Skylark Cl. B23: Erd 6C 68
  DY5: P'ntt 6G 75
Skyline B15: Birm 6B 4 (2E 117)
Skywalk B40: Nat E C 1F 139
Slack La. B20: Hand 5A 82
Slacky La. WS3: Blox 6C 20
Slade Cl. B71: W Brom 3D 64
Sladefield Rd. B8: W End 4G 103
Slade Gdns. WV8: Cod 3G 13
Slade Gro. B93: Know 3B 166
Slade Hill WV6: Wolv 6D 26
Slade La. B28: Hall G 4E 149
  B75: R'ley 6E 39
Slade Lanker B34: Stech 4E 105
Sladepool Farm Rd. B14: King H 4H 147
Slade Rd. B23: Erd 3D 84
  B63: Crad 5E 111
  B75: R'ley, Can 6C 38
  WV10: F'hses 4G 15
Slaithwaite Rd. B71: W Brom 3C 80
Slaney Ct. WS2: Wals 4A 48
Slaney Rd. WS2: Wals 5H 47
Slatch Ho. Rd. B67: Smeth 1C 114
Slate La. WV8: Cod 2D 12
Slateley Cres. B90: M'path 3E 165
Slater Cl. B64: Old H 2H 111
Slater Row WS3: Pels 4E 21
Slater Rd. B93: Ben H 5A 166
Slater's La. WS2: Wals 4H 47
Slater's Pl. WS2: Wals 4H 47
Slater St. DY4: Tip 3A 78
  (Crompton Rd.)
  DY4: Tip 2D 78
  (Sheepwash La.)
  WS10: Darl 4D 46
  WV13: W'hall 6C 30
  WV14: Bils 2G 61
Sleaford Gro. B28: Hall G 6G 135
Sleaford Rd. B28: Hall G 6H 135
Sledmore Rd. DY2: Dud 2F 95

Slieve, The B20: Hand 4C 82
Slim Av. WV14: Bils 2G 61
Slimbridge Cl. B90: M'path 3E 165
Slim Rd. WS2: Wals 1E 47
Slims Ga. B63: Hale 1A 128
Sling, The DY2: Neth 3E 95
Slingfield Rd. B31: N'fld 5G 145
Slitting Mill Cl. B21: Hand 1G 99
Sloane Ho. B1: Birm 2A 4
Sloane St. B1: Birm 2A 4 (6E 101)
Slough La. B38: Head H 1G 161
  B47: H'wd 1G 161
Smallbrook La. WV5: Wom 6H 57
Smallbrook Queensway
  B5: Birm 6D 4 (2F 117)
Small Cl. B67: Smeth 4B 98
Smalldale Rd. B42: Gt Barr 6F 67
SMALL HEATH 3D 118
Small Heath Bri. B10: Small H 4B 118
  B11: S'brk 4B 118
Small Heath Bus. Pk.
  B10: Small H 4F 119
Small Heath Highway
  B10: Small H 3B 118
Small Heath Leisure Cen. 3D 118
Small Heath Station (Rail) 4D 118
Small Heath Trad. Est.
  B11: Small H 5D 118
Smallshire Cl. WV11: Wed 4H 29
Smallshire Way DY8: Word 3B 108
Small St. B71: W Brom 1H 79
  WS1: Wals 3C 48
Smallwood Cl. B24: Erd 4B 86
  B76: Walm 2C 70
Smallwood Rd. WV8: Pend 5C 14
Smalman Cl. DY8: Word 5C 92
Smarts Av. WS14: Shen W 2G 37
Smeaton Gdns. B18: Win G 5A 100
Smeed Gro. B24: Erd 4H 85
SMESTOW 3C 72
Smestow Ga. DY3: Swind 2B 72
Smestow La. DY3: Swind 3C 72
Smestow St. WV10: Wolv 5H 27
Smestow Valley Local Nature Reserve
  . . . . .3D 26
SMETHWICK 3D 98
Smethwick Galton Bridge Station (Rail)
  . . . . .2C 98
Smethwick New Ent. Cen.
  B66: Smeth 3E 99
Smethwick Rolfe Street Station (Rail)
  . . . . .3E 99
Smethwick Swimming Cen. 1D 114
Smirrells Rd. B28: Hall G 2E 149
Smith Av. WS10: Darl 6C 46
Smith Cl. B67: Smeth 6B 98
  WV14: Cose 4C 60
Smithfield Rd. WS3: Blox 6B 20
Smithfields DY8: Stourb 6E 109
Smithfield St. B5: Birm 6G 5 (2G 117)
Smith Ho. WS3: Blox 4A 20
Smithmoor Cres. B71: W Brom 5D 64
Smith Pl. DY4: Tip 3B 78
Smith Rd. WS2: Wals 5A 48
  WS10: W'bry 4E 63
Smiths Cl. B32: Bart G 3H 129
Smiths La. B93: Know 3A 166
Smith St. B19: Birm 4E 101
  DY2: Dud 2F 95
  WV14: Bils 6F 45
Smiths Way B46: Wat O 4C 88
SMITH'S WOOD 2C 106
Smithy, The B26: Sheld 5G 121
Smithy Dr. WS3: Pels 3E 21
Smithy La. DY5: P'ntt 2F 92
Smout Cres. WV14: Cose 3B 60
Snapdragon Dr. WS5: Wals 2D 64
Snape Rd. WV11: Wed 6A 18
Sneyd Hall Cl. WS3: Blox 1G 31
Sneyd Hall Rd. WS3: Blox 6G 19
Sneyd La. WS3: Blox 6G 19
  WS3: Ess 5C 18
  WV11: Ess 5C 18
Snitterfield Dr. B90: Shir 6A 150
Snowberry Dr. DY5: P'ntt 5G 75
Snowberry Gdns. B27: A Grn 6A 120
Snowdon Gro. B63: Hale 4F 127

Snowdon Ri. DY3: Sed 1H 75
Snowdon Rd. DY8: Amb 5F 109
Snowdon Way WV10: Oxl 3F 27
  WV12: W'hall 6B 18
Snowdrop Cl. WS8: Clay 1H 21
Snowford Cl. B90: Shir 6F 149
Snow Hill WV1: Wolv 4C 170 (2H 43)
  WV2: Wolv 4C 170 (2H 43)
Snow Hill Junc.
  WV2: Wolv 5C 170 (2H 43)
Snow Hill Queensway
  B4: Birm 2D 4 (6F 101)
Snow Hill Station (Rail & Metro)
  . . . . .3E 5 (6G 101)
Snowshill Dr. B90: Ches G 4B 164
Snowshill Gdns. DY1: Dud 3B 76
Soberton Cl. WV11: Wed 2H 29
SOHO 2G 99
Soho Av. B18: Hock 2C 100
Soho Benson Road Stop (Metro) 3B 100
Soho Cl. B66: Smeth 4G 99
Soho Hill B19: Hock 2C 100
Soho House 2C 100
Soho Ho. B66: Smeth 4G 99
Soho Pool Way B18: Hock 3C 100
Soho Rd. B21: Hand 1A 100
Soho St. B66: Smeth 3G 99
Soho Way B66: Smeth 3F 99
Solari Cl. DY4: Tip 5C 62
Solent Cl. WV9: Pend 5D 14
Solent Ct. B73: S Cold 6H 53
SOLIHULL 4G 151
Solihull Arden Club 3D 150
Solihull Arts Complex 4G 151
Solihull Bus. Pk. B90: Shir 2D 164
Solihull By-Pass B91: Sol 2G 151
Solihull Gate Retail Pk.
  B90: Shir 6A 150
Solihull Ice Rink 2F 137
Solihull Indoor Bowls Club 1D 164
Solihull La. B28: Hall G 1G 149
SOLIHULL LODGE 5C 148
Solihull Municipal Bowls Club 6D 150
Solihull Parkway
  B37: Mars G 3F 123
Solihull Retail Pk. B90: Shir 6B 150
Solihull Rd. B11: S'hll 2D 134
  B90: Shir 4A 150
  B92: Cath B, H Ard 1E 153
Solihull Station (Rail) 3E 151
Solly Gro. DY4: Tip 6D 62
Solva Cl. WV1: Wolv 2D 44
Solway Cl. WS10: W'bry 1A 64
Soma Ho. B75: S Cold 6G 55
Somerby Dr. B91: Sol 1E 165
Somercotes Rd. B42: Gt Barr 5F 67
Somerdale Rd. B31: N'fld 3G 145
Somerfield Cl. WS4: S'fld 6G 21
Somerfield Rd. WS3: Blox 1H 31
Somerford Cl. WS6: Gt Wyr 4E 7
Somerford Gdns. WV10: Bush 5A 16
Somerford Pl. WV13: W'hall 2H 45
Somerford Rd. B29: W Cas 5D 130
Somerford Way WV14: Cose 5D 60
Somerland Rd. B26: Yard 2E 121
Somerset Cres. WS10: W'bry 1H 64
Somerset Dr. B31: Longb 2D 158
  DY8: Woll 4B 108
Somerset Rd. B15: Edg 5A 116
  B20: Hand 5B 82
  B23: Erd 1F 85
  B71: W Brom 1B 80
  WS4: Wals 5E 33
  WV13: W'hall 1D 46
Somers Rd. B62: Hale 6C 112
  CV7: Mer 4F 141
  WS2: Wals 4G 47
Somers Wood Caravan & Camping Pk.
  CV7: Mer 4F 141
Somerton Ct. B23: Erd 1C 84
Somerton Dr. B23: Erd 1G 85
  B37: Mars G 4C 122
Somerville Ct. B73: S Cold 3G 69
Somerville Dr. B73: S Cold 1G 69
Somerville Ho. B37: Chel W 6F 107
Somerville Rd. B10: Small H 3D 118
  B73: S Cold 1G 69

Somery Rd. B29: W Cas 3E **131**
  DY1: Dud 4E **77**
Sommerfield Rd. B32: Bart G 3A **130**
Sonning Dr. WV9: Pend 5D **14**
Sophie Gdns. B43: Gt Barr 1A **66**
Sopwith Cft. B35: Cas V 5E **87**
Sorrel Cl. B69: Tiv 5B **78**
Sorrel Dr. WS5: Wals 2E **65**
Sorrel Gro. B24: Erd 4B **86**
Sorrel Ho. B24: Erd 4B **86**
Sorrell Dr. B27: A Grn 3H **135**
Sorrel Wlk. DY5: Brie H 5F **109**
Sorrento Ct. B13: Mose 2A **134**
Sot's Hole Nature Reserve 2C **80**
Souters Ho. B32: Bart G 5B **130**
Southacre Av. B5: Birm 3G **117**
  (not continuous)
Southall Cres. WV14: Cose 4E **61**
Southall Rd. WV11: Wed 1A **30**
Southalls La. DY1: Dud 6D **76**
Southam Cl. B28: Hall G 5E **135**
Southam Dr. B73: W Grn 4H **69**
Southam Ho. B13: Mose 6A **134**
Southampton St.
  WV1: Wolv 1D **170** (6H **27**)
Southam Rd. B28: Hall G 5E **135**
South Av. DY8: Stourb 1D **124**
  WV11: Wed 4E **29**
Southbank Rd. B64: Old H 2G **111**
Southbank Vw. DY6: K'wfrd 5C **92**
Southbourne Av. B34: Hodg H 3B **104**
  WS2: Wals 2H **47**
Southbourne Cl. B29: S Oak 3C **132**
Southbourne Rd. WV10: F'hses 4G **15**
South Car Pk. Rd. B40: Nat E C ..2G **139**
Sth. College Ho. B8: Salt 6E **103**
Southcote Gro. B38: King Nor 6H **145**
Southcott Av. DY5: Brie H 3H **109**
South Cres. WV10: F'stne 1D **16**
Southcroft Rd. B23: Erd 4E **85**
South Dene B67: Smeth 4D **98**
Southdown Av. B18: Hock 3C **100**
South Dr. B5: Edg 1E **133**
  B46: Col 2F **107**
  B75: S Cold 5A **54**
Southern Cl. DY6: K'wfrd 6D **92**
Southerndown Rd. DY3: Sed 6F **59**
Southern Dr. B30: King Nor 4F **147**
Southern Rd. B8: W End 4A **104**
Southern Way WS10: Mox 2C **62**
Southey Cl. B91: Sol 1F **165**
  WV12: W'hall 1E **31**
Southfield Av. B16: Edg 6H **99**
  B36: Cas B 1E **105**
Southfield Cl. WS9: A'rdge 3C **34**
Southfield Dr. B28: Hall G 2G **149**
Southfield Gro. WV3: Wolv 4A **42**
Southfield Rd. B16: Edg 6H **99**
  WV11: Wed 4H **29**
Southfields Cl. B46: Col 5H **107**
Southfields Rd. B91: Sol 6D **150**
Southfield Way WS6: Gt Wyr 3F **7**
Southgate B64: Crad H 3F **111**
  WV1: Wolv 1F **43**
Southgate Rd. B44: Gt Barr 3G **67**
Southgate Way DY1: Dud 5D **76**
South Grn. WV4: Penn 6B **42**
South Gro. B6: Aston 1F **101**
  B19: Hand 1D **100**
  B23: Erd 2F **85**
South Holme B9: Bord G 1C **118**
Southlands Rd. B13: Mose 4A **134**
Southmead Way WS2: Wals 5B **32**
Southminster Dr. B14: King H 1G **147**
South Oval DY3: Up Gor 2A **76**
South Pde. B72: S Cold 6A **54**
South Pk. M. DY5: Brie H 1G **109**
South Range B11: Bal H 5B **118**
South Rd. B11: S'brk 4B **118**
  B14: King H 5G **133**
  B18: Hock 2C **100**
  B23: Erd 3F **85**
  B31: N'fld 5D **144**
  B67: Smeth 4D **98**
  DY4: Tip 5B **62**
  DY8: Stourb 1B **124**
South Rd. Av. B18: Hock 3C **100**

South Roundhay B33: Kitts G 6E **105**
Southside B5: Birm 6E **5**
  (not continuous)
Southside Bus. Cen. *B12: Bal H 6A 118*
  (off Ladypool Rd.)
Sth. Staffordshire Bus. Pk.
  WS11: Cann 1C **6**
South Staffordshire Golf Course **3A 26**
South St. B17: Harb 6H **115**
  DY5: Brie H 1G **109**
  WS1: Wals 3B **48**
  WV10: Oxl 3G **27**
  WV13: W'hall 2H **45**
South St. Gdns. WS1: Wals 3B **48**
South Twr. B7: Birm 5B **102**
South Vw. B43: Gt Barr 6A **66**
South Vw. Cl. WV8: Bilb 5H **13**
  WV10: F'stne 1D **16**
Southview Ridge DY5: Brie H 4H **109**
Southview Rd. DY3: Sed 5G **59**
Southville Bungs. B14: King H 3B **148**
South Wlk. B31: N'fld 6G **145**
South Way B40: Nat E C 2H **139**
Southway Ct. DY6: K'wfrd 5D **92**
Southwell Wlk. B70: W Brom 5A **80**
Southwick Pl. WV14: Bils 4F **45**
Southwick Rd. B62: B'hth 3D **112**
Southwold Av. B30: King Nor 4E **147**
Southwood Av. B34: S End 2F **105**
Southwood Cl. DY6: K'wfrd 4C **92**
Southwood Covert B14: King H ..5F **147**
SOUTH YARDLEY 5B **120**
Sovereign Ct. B1: Birm 2A **4** (6E **101**)
Sovereign Dr. DY1: Dud 5A **76**
Sovereign Hgts. B31: Longb 6A **144**
Sovereign Rd. B30: King Nor 3B **146**
Sovereign Wlk. WS1: Wals 1E **49**
Sovereign Way B13: Mose 1H **133**
Sowerby March B24: Erd 3B **86**
Sowers Cl. WV12: W'hall 4D **30**
Sowers Ct. B75: R'ley 5B **38**
Sowers Gdns. WV12: W'hall 4D **30**
Spa Gro. B30: Stir 5E **133**
SPARKBROOK 4B **118**
SPARKHILL 1C **134**
Spark St. B11: S'brk 4A **118**
Sparrey Dr. B30: Stir 5C **132**
Sparrow Cl. WS10: W'bry 6H **47**
Sparrowhawk Fold DY1: Dud 1A **94**
Spartan Ind. Cen. B70: W Brom ..1E **79**
Speakers Cl. B69: Tiv 2B **96**
Spectacle Works *B18: Birm 4D 100*
  (off Hylton St.)
Speed Rd. DY4: Tip 1G **77**
Speedwell Cl. B25: Yard 5G **119**
  WS9: A'rdge 4B **34**
  WV11: Wed 4G **29**
Speedwell Dr. CV7: Bal C 3G **169**
Speedwell Gdns. DY5: Brie H 5F **109**
Speedwell Ho. B38: King Nor 6C **146**
Speedwell Rd. B5: Edg 5F **117**
  B25: Yard 5G **119**
Speedwell Trad. Est. B11: Tys 5G **119**
Spelter Works WS3: Blox 2G **31**
Spencer Av. WV14: Cose 5E **61**
Spencer Cl. B24: Erd 3B **86**
  B69: Tiv 1B **96**
  B71: W Brom 5D **64**
  DY3: Lwr G 3E **75**
Spencer St. B18: Birm 1A **4** (4E **101**)
  (not continuous)
Spenser Av. WV6: Pert 5F **25**
Spernall Gro. B29: W Cas 4E **131**
Spey Cl. B5: Edg 5F **117**
Spiceal St. B5: Birm 5F **5** (1G **117**)
Spiceland Rd. B31: N'fld 1D **144**
Spicer Lodge DY8: Stourb 6D **108**
Spiers Cl. B93: Know 3C **166**
Spies La. B62: Quin 6F **113**
Spills Mdw. DY3: Up Gor 2A **76**
Spilsbury Cft. B91: Sol 1E **165**
Spindle La. B90: Dic H 3G **163**
  (not continuous)
Spindles, The WS6: Gt Wyr 4F **7**
Spindle Tree Ri. WV12: W'hall 4D **30**
Spinners End Dr. B64: Crad H 2F **111**

Spinners End Ind. Est. B64: Crad H ..3F **111**
Spinney, The B15: Edg 6A **116**
  B20: Hand 3A **82**
  B38: King Nor 6B **146**
  B47: Wyt 5B **162**
  B74: Lit As 4B **36**
  B91: Sol 1G **165**
  DY3: Gorn 5G **75**
  WV3: Wolv 2B **42**
Spinney Cl. B31: N'fld 4E **145**
  DY8: Word 6A **92**
  WS3: Pels 5E **21**
Spinney Dr. B90: Ches G 5B **164**
Spinney La. DY6: K'wfrd 2B **92**
Spinney Wlk. B76: Walm 6D **70**
Spiral Cl. B62: B'hth 3E **113**
Spiral Ct. B24: Erd 5E **85**
  B76: Walm 2D **70**
  DY3: Lwr G *4H 75*
  (off Yorkdale Cl.)
  DY8: Stourb 1E **125**
  WV11: Wed 2F **29**
Spiral Grn. B24: Erd 3A **86**
Spires, The B73: Bold 5F **69**
Spirit M. WS10: Darl 5F **47**
Spitfire Pk. B24: Erd 5B **86**
Spitfire Rd. B24: Erd 5B **86**
Spitfire Way B35: Cas V 5E **87**
Spondon Gro. B34: S End 4G **105**
Spondon Rd. WV11: Wed 1G **29**
Spon La. B70: W Brom 6B **80**
Spon La. Ind. Est. B66: Smeth 1B **98**
Spon La. Sth. B66: Smeth 1B **98**
  B70: Smeth, W Brom 1B **98**
Spon La. Trad. Est. B70: W Brom ..5B **80**
Spon Rd. B38: King Nor 5H **145**
Spooner Cft. B5: Birm 3G **117**
Spooners Cl. B92: Sol 6B **138**
Spouthouse La. B43: Gt Barr 6A **66**
Spout La. WS1: Wals 4C **48**
  (not continuous)
Spreadbury Cl. B17: Harb 3D **114**
Sprig Cft. B36: Hodg H 1A **104**
Spring Av. B65: Row R 1C **112**
Springavon Cft. B17: Harb 5F **115**
SPRING BANK 6B **30**
Spring Bank Ho. WV13: W'hall 6A **30**
Spring Bank Rd. B15: Edg 4E **117**
Springbrook Cl. B36: Cas B 6H **87**
Spring Cl. B91: Sol 4D **150**
  WS4: S'fld 5G **21**
Spring Coppice Dr. B93: Dorr 6C **166**
Spring Ct. B66: Smeth 4G **99**
  B70: W Brom 5B **80**
  WS1: Wals 4E **49**
Spring Cres. B64: Crad H 4H **111**
Springcroft Rd. B11: Tys 3F **135**
Spring Dr. WS6: Gt Wyr 3G **7**
SPRINGFIELD
  B13 ....4D **134**
  B65 ....4A **96**
  WV10 ....5A **28**
Springfield B23: Erd 4D **84**
Springfield Av. B12: Bal H 5A **118**
  B68: O'bry 5A **98**
  DY3: Sed 4A **60**
  DY9: W'cte 1A **126**
Springfield Cl. B65: Row R 4A **96**
Springfield Ct. B28: Hall G 5F **135**
  B75: S Cold 6G **55**
Springfield Cres. B70: W Brom 6C **80**
  B76: Walm 1E **71**
  B92: Sol 2G **137**
  DY2: Dud 1H **95**
Springfield Dr. B14: King H 4G **133**
  B62: B'hth 4D **112**
Springfield Grn. DY3: Sed 4A **60**
Springfield Gro. DY3: Sed 4H **59**
Springfield Ind. Est. B69: O'bry 2H **97**
Springfield La. B65: Row R 4A **96**
  WV10: F'hses 3H **15**
Springfield Rd. B13: Mose 4D **134**
  B14: King H 5H **133**
  B36: Cas B 1H **105**
  B62: B'hth 4D **112**
  B68: O'bry 5A **98**

Springfield Rd. B75: S Cold 1F 71
B76: Walm 3D 70
DY5: Brie H 1F 109
WV10: Wolv 5A 28
WV14: Bils 4G 45
Springfields B46: Col 4H 107
WS4: Rus .2F 33
Springfield St. B18: Hock 6C 100
Springfield Ter. B65: Row R 4H 95
Spring Gdns. B21: Hand 2A 100
B66: Smeth 6F 99
DY2: Dud .1F 95
DY3: Gorn 5G 75
Spring Gro. B19: Hock 3D 100
Spring Gro. Gdns. B18: Hock 3B 100
Spring Head WS10: W'bry 3F 63
SPRING HILL 1A 58
SPRINGHILL
WS14 . . . . .6G 11
WV11 . . . . .2D 18
Spring Hill B1: Birm 6D 100
B18: Hock 5C 100
B24: Erd .4F 85
Springhill Av. WV4: Penn 2A 58
Springhill Cl. WS4: S'fld 6H 21
WV12: W'hall 2D 30
Springhill Ct. WS1: Wals 3D 48
Springhill Gro. WV4: Penn 1A 58
Spring Hill Ind. Est. B18: Hock 6C 100
Springhill La. WV4: Lwr P 6F 41
WV4: Penn 2A 58
Springhill Pk. WV4: Penn 2H 57
Spring Hill Pas. B18: Hock 6C 100
Springhill Rd. WS1: Wals 2D 48
WS8: Bwnhls 6C 10
WV11: Wed 1G 29
Spring Ho. B37: K'hrst 4D 106
Spring La. B24: Erd 4G 85
WS4: S'fld 5G 21
WV12: W'hall 5B 30
Spring Mdw. B63: Hale 3H 127
B64: Old H 2H 111
DY4: Tip .1C 78
WS6: C Hay 4D 6
Springmeadow Gro. B19: Hock 3F 101
Spring Mdw. Rd. DY2: Neth 1E 111
Springmeadow Rd. B15: Edg 4F 117
Spring Mdws. Cl. WV8: Bilb 3H 13
Spring Parklands DY1: Dud 1C 94
Spring Rd. B11: Tys 2F 135
B15: Edg 4F 117
B66: Smeth 1B 98
DY2: Neth 3F 95
WS4: S'fld 6H 21
WV4: Ett .6C 44
Spring Rd. Ind. Est. WV4: Ett 1C 60
(not continuous)
Spring Road Station (Rail) 3G 135
Springs, The B64: Old H 2A 112
Springslade B32: Harb 6D 114
Springslade Dr. B24: Erd 4B 86
SPRINGS MIRE 1A 94
Spring St. B15: Birm 3F 117
B63: Crad 5E 111
DY4: Tip .2A 78
(Alexandra Rd.)
DY4: Tip .5C 62
(Thompson Ho.)
DY9: Lye .1A 126
Springthorpe Grn. B24: Erd 3A 86
Springthorpe Rd. B24: Erd 3B 86
(Varley Rd.)
B24: Erd .3B 86
(Windfall Ct.)
SPRING VALE 1D 60
Springvale Av. WS5: Wals 4G 49
WV14: Bils 1D 60
Springvale Bus. Pk. WV14: Bils 1D 60
Springvale Cl. WV14: Cose 4C 60
Springvale Ind. Pk. WV14: Bils 6E 45
Spring Vale Rd. B65: Row R 4A 96
Springvale St. WV13: W'hall 6B 30
Springvale Way WV14: Bils 1E 61
Spring Vs. B63: Hale 2A 128
Spring Wlk. B63: Hale 4F 127
B69: O'bry 4G 97
WS2: Wals 6H 31

Sproat Av. WS10: Darl 6C 46
Spruce Gro. B24: Erd 5H 85
Spruce Rd. WS5: Wals 2F 65
Spruce Way WV3: Wolv 2B 42
Spur Tree Av. WV3: Wolv 2G 41
Squadron Cl. B35: Cas V 3G 87
Square, The B15: Birm 2D 116
B17: Harb 6G 115
(off High St.)
B17: Harb 5F 115
(St Johns Ct.)
B91: Sol .4G 151
DY2: Dud .3B 94
DY4: Tip .6D 62
WS9: A'rdge 3D 34
WV2: Wolv 6D 170 (3H 43)
WV8: Cod 3F 13
WV12: W'hall 1D 30
Square Cl. B32: Bart G 2A 130
Square on the Square, The B3: Birm . . .1B 4
Squires Cl. DY5: Brie H 3G 109
Squires Cft. B76: Walm 4E 71
Squires Ga. Rd. WV13: W'hall 1B 46
Squires Ga. Wlk. B35: Cas V 4E 87
Squires Gro. WV12: W'hall 2D 30
Squires Wlk. WS10: W'bry 2F 63
Squirrel Hollow B76: Walm 3E 71
Squirrels Hollow B68: O'bry 4B 114
Squirrel Wlk. B74: Lit As 4C 36
WV4: Penn 1E 59
Stable Ct. DY3: Sed 1A 76
Stable Cft. B71: W Brom 6D 64
Stableford Cl. B32: Bart G 2D 130
Stable Lodge DY8: Word 6C 92
Stables, The B29: S Oak 3C 132
Stablewood Gro. WS1: Wals 4E 49
Stacey Cl. B64: Old H 2G 111
Stacey Dr. B13: Mose 2A 148
Stacey Grange Gdns. B45: Redn 3G 157
Stackhouse Cl. WS9: Wals W 3C 22
Stackhouse Dr. WS3: Pels 3E 21
Staddlestones, The WV6: Pert 5D 24
Stadium Cl. WV13: W'hall 6B 30
Stadium Dr. DY2: Neth 2E 111
Stadium Way B42: P Barr 2E 83
Stafford Cl. WS3: Blox 5H 19
Stafford Ct. B43: Gt Barr 6A 66
(off West Rd.)
WV10: F'hses 2G 15
Stafford Dr. B71: W Brom 1H 79
Stafford Ho. B33: Kitts G 1A 122
Stafford La. WV8: Cod 6D 12
Stafford Rd. B21: Hand 1B 100
WS3: Blox 1G 19
WS6: Gt Wyr 1G 19
WS10: Darl 5C 46
WV10: Cov H, F'hses, Oxl, Wolv . . .1H 15
Staffordshire Pool Cl. B6: Aston 6H 83
(off Emscote Rd.)
Stafford St. DY1: Dud 6D 76
WS2: Wals 6C 32
WS10: W'bry 3D 46
WV1: Wolv 1C 170 (5G 27)
WV13: W'hall 1A 46
(not continuous)
WV14: Bils 6F 45
Stafford St. Junc.
WV1: Wolv 1B 170 (6H 27)
Stafford Twr. B4: Birm 2G 5 (6H 101)
Stafford Way B43: Gt Barr 6A 66
Staff Way B23: Erd 3E 85
Stag Cres. WS3: Blox 3C 32
Stag Hill Rd. WS3: Blox 2C 32
Stag Ind. Est. WV14: Bils 1H 61
Stag Rd. B16: Edg 6G 99
Stag Wlk. B76: Walm 6B 70
Stainsby Av. B19: Birm 4E 101
Stainsby Cft. B90: M'path 4F 165
Stallings La. DY6: K'wfrd 1B 92
Stambermill Cl. DY9: Lye 6H 109
Stambermill Ho. DY9: Lye 6A 110
Stambermill Ind. Est. DY9: Lye 5G 109
Stamford Cft. B91: Sol 5F 151
Stamford Gro. B20: Hand 6E 83
Stamford Rd. B20: Hand 6E 83
DY5: Brie H 4G 109
DY8: Amb 6F 109

Stamford St. DY8: Amb 4D 108
Stamford Way WS9: A'rdge 5D 22
Stamping Way WS3: Blox 5H 19
Stanbrook Rd. B90: M'path 3E 165
Stanbury Av. WS10: Darl 5B 46
Stanbury Rd. B14: King H 3B 148
Stancroft Gro. B26: Yard 3E 121
Standard Way B24: Erd 1F 103
Standbridge Way DY4: Tip 2A 78
Standhills Rd. DY6: K'wfrd 3C 92
Standlake Av. B36: Hodg H 2B 104
Standleys Twr. B23: Erd 1G 85
Stanfield Rd. B32: Quin 4C 114
B43: Gt Barr 6F 51
Stanford Av. B42: Gt Barr 6C 66
Stanford Dr. B65: Row R 5B 96
Stanford Gro. B63: Hale 4E 127
Stanford Rd. WV2: Wolv 4G 43
Stanford Way B69: O'bry 5E 97
(off Kempsey Cl.)
Stanham Cl. WV5: Wom 6G 57
Stanhoe Cl. DY5: Brie H 3H 109
Stanhope Rd. B67: Smeth 6D 98
Stanhope St. B12: Birm 4H 117
DY2: Neth 5G 95
Stanhope Way B43: Gt Barr 1F 67
B46: Col .6H 89
Stanhurst Way B71: W Brom 3E 65
Stanier Cl. WS4: Rus 2F 33
Stanier Gro. B20: Hand 5D 82
Staniforth St. B4: Birm 1F 5 (5G 101)
Stanley Av. B32: Harb 4C 114
B75: S Cold 1D 70
B90: Shir .3H 149
Stanley Cl. B28: Hall G 2G 149
WV11: Wed 1H 29
Stanley Ct. B13: Mose 3B 134
(off Wake Grn. Pk.)
WV6: Pert .5E 25
Stanley Dr. DY3: Swind 5E 73
Stanley Gro. B11: S'brk 5B 118
Stanley Pl. B13: Mose 2H 133
WS4: Rus .3F 33
WV14: Bils 6D 44
Stanley Rd. B7: Nech 2C 102
B14: King H 6F 133
B68: O'bry 3A 114
B71: W Brom 6C 64
DY8: Stourb 2D 124
WS4: Rus .3F 33
WS10: Darl 6D 46
WV10: Bush 6H 15
(not continuous)
Stanley St. WS3: Blox 1A 32
Stanmore Gro. B62: Quin 2G 129
Stanmore Rd. B16: Edg 2G 115
Stanton Av. DY1: Dud 1B 76
Stanton Gro. B26: Yard 3D 120
B90: Shir .3G 149
DY4: Tip .2A 78
Stanton Ho. B71: W Brom 4D 64
Stanton Rd. B43: Gt Barr 6H 65
B90: Shir .3G 149
WV1: Wolv 1B 44
Stanville Rd. B26: Sheld 5G 121
Stanway Gdns. B71: W Brom 1B 80
Stanway Gro. B44: Gt Barr 2H 67
Stanway Rd. B71: W Brom 1B 80
B90: Shir .4H 149
Stanwell Gro. B23: Erd 1E 85
Stanwick Av. B33: Kitts G 6A 106
Stapenhall Rd. B90: M'path 3E 165
Stapleford Cft. B14: King H 5E 147
Stapleford Gro. DY8: Word 6C 92
Staple Hall Rd. B31: N'fld 5F 145
Staplehurst Rd. B28: Hall G 5F 135
Staple Lodge Rd. B31: N'fld 5F 145
Stapleton Cl. B76: Walm 1F 87
Stapleton Dr. B37: F'bri 6D 106
Stapleton Rd. WS9: A'rdge 4B 34
Stapylton Av. B17: Harb 6F 115
Stapylton Ct. B17: Harb 6F 115
(off Old Church Rd.)
Starbank Rd. B10: Small H 3G 119
Starbold Cl. B93: Know 3D 165
Starbold Cres. B93: Know 4C 166
Star City 1D 102

Star Cl. DY4: Tip 2C 78
   WS2: Wals 5F 31
Starcrest Ind. Est. DY5: Brie H 2A 110
Starcross Rd. B27: A Grn 3A 136
Star Foundry Dr. WV14: Bils 3G 61
Star Hill B15: Edg 3D 116
Starkey Cft. B37: Chel W 1E 123
Starkie Dr. B68: O'bry 5A 98
Starley Ct. B27: A Grn 1B 136
Starley Way B37: Mars G 5E 123
Starling Gro. B36: Cas B 2C 106
Star St. DY9: Lye 6B 110
   WV3: Wolv 3C 42
Start Point Trad. Est. B11: S'hll 1D 134
Statham Dr. B16: Edg 1G 115
Station App. B73: S Cold 5H 53
   B74: Four O 1F 37
   B91: Sol 3E 151
   B93: Dorr 6G 167
Station Av. B16: Edg 2G 115
Station Bldgs. B46: Wat O 4D 88
          (off Birmingham Rd.)
Station Cl. WS3: Blox 1H 31
   WV8: Cod 4E 13
Station Dr. B28: Hall G 4F 135
   B46: Wat O 4D 88
   B74: Four O 3H 53
   B92: Olton 4C 136
   DY4: Tip 3B 78
   DY5: Brie H 2F 109
           (Meeting La.)
   DY5: Brie H 5A 110
           (The Boulevard)
   DY9: Lye 5A 110
Station Link Rd. B26: Birm A 1F 139
   B40: Nat E C 1F 139
Station M. B17: Harb 5G 115
Station Pl. WS3: Blox 1H 31
Station Rd. B6: Aston 6H 83
   B14: King H 5F 133
   B17: Harb 5G 115
   B21: Hand 1G 99
   B23: Erd 2F 85
   B27: A Grn 2A 136
   B30: King Nor 2A 146
   B31: N'fld 5E 145
   B33: Stech 5B 104
   B37: Mars G 3B 122
   B38: King Nor 2A 146
   B46: Col 5H 89
   B47: Wyt 4A 162
   B64: Old H 2H 111
   B65: Row R 1D 112
   B69: O'bry 4G 97
   B73: Bold, W Grn 4G 69
   B91: Sol 3F 151
   B92: H Ard 6B 140
   B93: Dorr, Know 6C 166
   CV7: Bal C 3G 169
   DY5: Brie H 5G 93
   DY9: Lye 5A 110
   WS3: Pels 4E 21
   WS4: Rus 3E 33
   WS6: Gt Wyr 1F 7
   WS7: Hamm 2G 11
   WS9: A'rdge 4C 34
   WV5: Wom 5G 57
   WV8: Cod 4E 13
   WV14: Bils 6G 45
Station Rd. Ind. Est. B46: Col 6H 89
   B65: Row R 1D 112
Station St. B5: Birm 6D 4 (2F 117)
   B64: Crad H 3E 111
   B73: S Cold 6H 53
   DY4: Tip 2B 78
   WS2: Wals 2B 48
   WS3: Blox 1H 31
   WS6: C Hay 2E 7
   WS10: Darl 5E 47
Station Ter. WV14: Cose 4E 61
Station Way B37: Mars G 2F 139
   B40: Nat E C 1F 139
Staulton Grn. B69: O'bry 5E 97
Staveley Rd. B14: King H 1F 147
   WV1: Wolv 5G 27
Stead Cl. DY4: Tip 4B 62
   WS2: Wals 4A 32

Steadman Cft. DY4: Tip 5D 62
Stechford Cascades 6C 104
Stechford La. B8: W End 4A 104
Stechford Retail Pk. B33: Stech 5C 104
Stechford Rd. B34: Hodg H 4B 104
Stechford Station (Rail) 6B 104
Stechford Trad. Est. B33: Stech 6C 104
Steel Bright Rd. B66: Smeth 3G 99
Steel Dr. WV10: Bush 1H 27
Steel Gro. B25: Yard 4A 120
Steelhouse La. B4: Birm 2E 5 (6G 101)
   WV2: Wolv 2A 44
Steelmans Rd. WS10: Darl 4F 47
Steelpark Rd. B62: Hale 4B 112
Steelpark Way WV11: Wed 5F 29
Steel Rd. B31: N'fld 5D 144
Steel Rdbt. WS10: W'bry 3E 63
Steelway Gdns. B31: N'fld 4B 144
Steep Bri. Way WS9: Wals W 5A 22
Steeples, The DY8: Stourb 2F 125
Steepwood Cft. B30: King Nor 3H 145
Stella Cft. B37: Chel W 1E 123
Stella Gro. B43: Gt Barr 5F 65
Stella Rd. DY4: Tip 1H 77
Stenbury Cl. WV10: Bush 3B 16
Stencills Dr. WS4: Wals 6F 33
Stencills Rd. WS4: Wals 5F 33
Stennels Av. B62: Hale 1E 129
Stephens Cl. WV11: Wed 1H 29
Stephens Ind. Est. B11: Tys 1F 135
Stephenson Av. WS2: Wals 3G 31
Stephenson Dr. B37: Chel W 6D 106
   WV6: Pert 4E 25
Stephenson Pl. B2: Birm 4E 5 (1G 117)
Stephenson Sq. WS2: Wals 4H 31
Stephenson St. B2: Birm 4D 4 (1F 117)
   WV3: Wolv 2F 43
Stephens Rd. B76: Walm 1E 71
Stepping Stone Cl. WS2: Wals 5F 31
Stepping Stones DY8: Stourb 6F 109
Steppingstone St. DY1: Dud 6D 76
Sterling Pk. DY5: Brie H 5B 94
Sterndale Rd. B42: Gt Barr 1E 83
Steven Dr. WV14: Bils 4G 61
Stevens Av. B32: Bart G 3B 130
Stevens Ga. WV2: Wolv 6B 170 (3G 43)
Stevens Rd. DY9: W'cte 3H 125
Stevens Ter. B3: Birm 2B 4
Stewards Fld. Dr. B43: Gt Barr 2D 66
Steward St. B18: Hock 6C 100
Stewart Rd. DY6: K'wfrd 5B 92
   WS9: Wals W 4C 22
Stewarts Rd. B62: B'hth 4D 112
Stewart St. WV2: Wolv 6B 170 (3G 43)
Stewkins DY8: Word 3C 108
Steyning Rd. B26: Yard 6C 120
St Georges Stop (Metro) 4C 170 (2H 43)
Stickley La. DY3: Lwr G 3G 75
Stilehouse Cres. B65: Row R 1C 112
Stillhouse Gro. B45: Redn 2G 157
Stillhouse Gro. B45: Redn 2G 157
STIRCHLEY 1C 146
Stirchley Indoor Bowls Cen. 6B 132
Stirchley Trad. Est. B30: Stir 6D 132
Stirling Cl. B16: Edg 2B 116
Stirling Cres. WV12: W'hall 3B 30
Stirling Rd. B16: Edg 2A 116
   B73: New O 3D 68
   B90: Shir 1C 164
   DY2: Dud 3G 95
   WV14: Bils 2H 61
Stirrup Cl. WS5: Wals 1D 64
Stockbridge Cl. WV6: Tett 1F 41
Stockdale Pl. B15: Edg 3H 115
Stock Exchange Bldg. B3: Birm 3C 4
STOCKFIELD 6B 120
Stockfield Rd. B25: Yard 1H 135
   B27: A Grn 1H 135
Stockhill Dr. B45: Rub 3F 157
Stocking St. DY9: Lye 6B 110
Stockland Ct. B74: S'tly 3A 52
STOCKLAND GREEN 3C 84
Stockland Green Community Leisure Cen.
   . . . . .3C 84
Stockland Rd. B23: Erd 3D 84
Stockley Cres. B90: Shir 4B 150

Stockmans Cl. B38: King Nor 1A 160
Stocks Wood B30: B'vlle 5B 132
Stockton Cl. B76: Min 2F 87
   B93: Know 5D 166
   WS2: Wals 5B 32
Stockton Ct. WV14: Cose 5D 60
Stockton Gro. B33: Kitts G 2H 121
Stockwell Av. DY5: Quar B 3H 109
STOCKWELL END 4B 26
Stockwell End WV6: Tett 3B 26
Stockwell Ri. B92: Sol 6H 137
Stockwell Rd. B21: Hand 5A 82
   WV6: Tett 3B 26
Stokes Av. DY4: Tip 5A 62
   WV13: W'hall 3H 45
Stokesay Av. WV6: Pert 6F 25
Stokesay Cl. B69: Tiv 1A 96
Stokesay Gro. B31: Longb 1D 158
Stokesay Ho. B23: Erd 1F 85
Stokesay Ri. DY1: Dud 4A 76
Stokes St. WS3: Blox 1H 31
Stoke Way B15: Birm 6A 4 (2E 117)
Stom Rd. WV14: Bils 6D 44
Stoneacre Cl. WV3: Wolv 2G 41
Stone Av. B75: S Cold 6E 55
Stonebow Av. B91: Sol 1F 165
STONEBRIDGE 3C 140
Stonebridge Cres. B37: K'hrst 4B 106
Stonebridge Golf Course 4F 141
Stonebridge Rd. B46: Col 2H 107
          (not continuous)
Stonebrook Way B29: W Cas 3D 130
Stonebury B15: Edg 3H 115
Stonechat Dr. B23: Erd 5C 84
Stone Cl. B38: King Nor 5B 146
Stonecroft Av. B45: Redn 2G 157
Stonecrop Cl. B38: King Nor 1B 160
   WS8: Clay 1H 21
Stonecross B46: Wat O 4D 88
Stonedown Cl. WV14: Cose 2C 60
Stonefield Dr. DY5: P'ntt 2E 93
Stonefield Wlk. WV14: Bils 6F 45
Stoneford Rd. B90: Shir 3G 149
Stonehaven Gro. B28: Hall G 5H 135
Stonehenge Cft. B14: King H 6F 147
Stonehill Cft. B90: M'path 3D 164
Stonehouse Av. WV13: W'hall 5H 29
Stonehouse Cres. WS10: W'bry 3H 63
Stonehouse Dr. B74: Lit As 5C 36
Stonehouse Gro. B32: Bart G 3B 130
Stonehouse Hill B29: W Cas 2E 131
Stonehouse La. B32: Bart G 3B 130
Stonehouse Rd. B73: S Cold 2F 69
Stonehurst Rd. B43: Gt Barr 1E 67
Stone Lea WS9: A'rdge 4D 34
Stonelea Cl. B71: W Brom 5C 64
Stoneleigh Cl. B74: Four O 3F 53
Stoneleigh Gdns. WV8: Cod 3F 13
Stoneleigh Ho. B32: Harb 6C 114
Stoneleigh Rd. B20: Hand 6C 82
   B91: Sol 2B 150
Stoneleigh Way DY3: Up Gor 1H 75
Stonepine Pl. DY3: Up Gor 1A 76
Stone Rd. B15: Edg 4F 117
Stonerwood Av. B28: Hall G 5E 135
          (not continuous)
Stones Grn. B23: Erd 1F 85
Stone St. B69: O'bry 2G 97
   DY1: Dud 6E 77
Stoneton Cres. CV7: Bal C 3G 169
Stoneton Gro. B29: W Cas 5E 131
Stone Yd. B12: Birm 6H 5 (2H 117)
   B64: Crad H 3E 111
Stoneybrook Leys WV5: Wom 2E 73
Stoney Cl. B92: Sol 6A 138
Stoneyford Gro. B14: Yard W 3B 148
Stoneyhurst Rd. B24: Erd 6F 85
Stoney La. B12: Bal H 6B 118
   B25: Yard 3C 120
   B32: Quin 5H 113
   B71: W Brom 3B 80
   DY2: Neth 6E 95
   WS3: Blox 4H 19
          (not continuous)
   WV4: Penn 6F 43
Stoney Leasow B72: W Grn 3H 69

Stoneymoor Dr. B36: Cas B 6G 87
Stoneythorpe Cl. B91: Sol 6F 151
Stonnal Gro. B23: Erd 1G 85
STONNALL 3G 23
Stonnall Ga. WS9: A'rdge 1E 35
Stonnall Rd. WS9: A'rdge 1E 35
Stonor Pk. Rd. B91: Sol 2D 150
Stonor Rd. B28: Hall G 2G 149
Stony La. B67: Smeth 4D 98
Stony St. B67: Smeth 3D 98
Stornoway Rd. B35: Cas V 3F 87
Storrs Cl. B9: Small H 2D 118
Storrs Pl. B10: Small H 2D 118
Storrs Way, The B32: Bart G 6H 129
Stotfold Rd. B14: King H 5H 147
STOURBRIDGE 6E 109
Stourbridge Crematorium
    DY8: Stourb 1B 124
Stourbridge FC 4D 108
Stourbridge Golf Course 4E 125
Stourbridge Ind. Est. DY8: Amb ...5E 109
Stourbridge Junction Station (Rail)
    ....2F 125
Stourbridge Lawn Tennis & Squash Club
    ....4A 124
Stourbridge Rd. B63: Hale 6G 111
    DY1: Dud 4A 94
    DY3: Himl 3A 74
    DY5: Brie H 4A 94
    DY9: Hag 6G 125
    DY9: Lye 6G 109
    WV4: Penn, Wom 4B 58
    WV5: Himl, Wom 2H 73
Stourbridge RFC 5A 108
Stourbridge Town Station (Rail) 6E 109
Stour Cl. B63: Hale 5G 111
Stour Ct. B63: Hale 6B 112
Stourdale Rd. B64: Crad H 4E 111
Stourdell Rd. B63: Crad 5G 111
Stour Hill DY5: Quar B 4C 110
Stourmore Cl. WV12: W'hall 3D 30
Stour St. B18: Hock 6C 100
    B70: W Brom 4E 79
Stourton Cl. B76: Walm 1D 70
    B93: Know 2D 166
Stourton Dr. WV4: Penn 6A 42
Stourton Park 5A 108
Stourton Rd. B32: Quin 6H 113
Stour Va. Rd. DY9: Lye 5B 110
Stourvale Trad. Est. B63: Crad ...5G 111
Stour Valley Cl. DY5: Quar B 4H 109
Stourville Ind. Est. DY9: Lye 5B 110
Stow Dr. DY5: Brie H 5F 109
Stowell Rd. B44: K'sdng 6H 67
Stowe St. WS3: Blox 2A 32
Stow Gro. B36: Hodg H 2C 104
STOW HEATH 4D 44
Stowheath La. WV1: Wolv 4D 44
Stowheath Pl. WV1: Wolv 4D 44
STOW LAWN 3E 45
Stowmans Cl. WV14: Cose 2D 60
St Pauls Stop (Metro) 1C 4 (5F 101)
Straight Rd. WV12: W'hall 3C 30
STRAITS, THE 3E 75
Straits, The DY3: Lwr G 2D 74
Straits Est. DY3: Lwr G 3E 75
Straits Grn. DY3: Lwr G 3F 75
Straits Ho. DY3: Lwr G 3E 75
Straits Rd. DY3: Lwr G 4F 75
Stratford Cl. DY1: Dud 5A 76
Stratford Ct. B72: S Cold 2H 69
    B90: Shir 1B 164
Stratford Dr. WS9: A'rdge 1E 35
Stratford Pl. B12: Birm 3A 118
Stratford Rd.
    B11: Hall G, S'brk, S'hll 4A 118
    B28: Hall G 3E 135
    B90: M'path, Shir 1A 164
    B94: H'ley H 6F 165
Stratford St. B11: S'hll 6C 118
Stratford St. Nth. B11: S'brk 3A 118
Stratford Wlk. B36: Hodg H 2A 104
Strathdene Gdns. B29: S Oak 4G 131
Strathdene Rd. B29: S Oak 3G 131
Strathern Dr. WV14: Cose 4C 60
Strathfield Wlk. WV4: Penn 5A 42
Strathmore Cres. WV5: Wom 4G 57

Strathmore Rd. DY4: Tip 5A 62
Stratton St. WV10: Wolv 5A 28
Strawberry Cl. B69: Tiv 2C 96
Strawberry Flds. CV7: Mer 4H 141
Strawberry La. WS6: Gt Wyr 5E 7
    WV13: W'hall 6E 29
Strawberry La. Ind. Est.
    WV13: W'hall 1E 45
Strawmoor La. WV8: Oaken, Cod 5B 12
Stray, The DY5: P'ntt 3G 93
Stream Mdw. WS4: S'fld 6H 21
Stream Pk. DY6: K'wfrd 5C 92
Stream Rd. DY6: K'wfrd 4B 92
    (not continuous)
    DY8: Word 4B 92
Streamside Way B92: Sol 1H 137
    WS4: S'fld 1H 33
Streatham Gro. B44: K'sdng 3A 68
Streather Rd. B75: R'ley 2A 54
STREETLY 2H 51
Streetly Crematorium
    WS9: A'rdge 1F 51
Streetly Cres. B74: Four O 6D 36
Streetly Dr. B74: Four O 6D 36
Streetly La. B74: Four O 1C 52
Streetly Rd. B23: Erd 2D 84
Streetly Wood B74: S'tly 1A 52
Streetly Youth & Sports Cen. 2A 52
Streetsbrook Rd. B90: Shir, Sol ..1H 149
    B91: Sol 2C 150
Streets Cnr. Gdns. WS9: Wals W ...3C 22
Streets La. WS6: Gt Wyr 5G 7
Strensham Ct. B13: Mose 1G 133
Strensham Hill B13: Mose 1G 133
Strensham Rd. B12: Bal H 1G 133
Stretton Cl. B24: Erd 5E 85
Stretton Gdns. WV8: Cod 3F 13
Stretton Gro. B8: W End 3A 104
    B11: S'brk 5C 118
    (off Sydenham Rd.)
    B19: Loz 2E 101
Stretton Pl. DY2: Neth 5F 95
    WV14: Cose 4C 60
Stretton Rd. B90: Shir 1H 163
    WV12: W'hall 1C 30
Stringer Cl. B75: Four O 5G 37
Stringes Cl. WV13: W'hall 6C 30
Stringes La. WV13: W'hall 1B 46
Strode Rd. WV2: Wolv 5G 43
Stronsay Cl. B45: Fran 6F 143
Stroud Av. WV12: W'hall 5C 30
Stroud Cl. WV12: W'hall 5C 30
Stroud Rd. B90: Shir 5H 149
Strutt Cl. B15: Edg 3H 115
Strykers Bowling 3G 27
Stuart Cres. DY2: Dud 6G 77
Stuart Rd. B62: Quin 6F 113
    B65: Row R 5C 96
Stuarts Dr. B33: Stech 2B 120
Stuarts Grn. DY9: Pedm 5F 125
Stuarts Rd. B33: Stech 1B 120
Stuart St. B7: Nech 2C 102
    WS3: Blox 1H 31
Stuarts Way B32: Bart G 6G 129
STUBBERS GREEN 1A 34
Stubbers Grn. Rd. WS4: A'rdge 6H 21
    WS9: A'rdge 6H 21
Stubbington Cl. WV13: W'hall 2F 45
Stubbs Rd. WV3: Wolv 4E 43
Stubby La. WV11: Wed 3H 29
Stubley Dr. WV10: Wolv 3A 28
Studland Rd. B28: Hall G 5G 135
Stud La. B33: Stech 6D 104
Studley Cft. B92: Sol 1H 137
Studley Dr. DY5: Brie H 3G 109
Studley Ga. DY8: Stourb 1B 124
Studley Rd. WV3: Wolv 1A 42
Studley St. B12: Bal H 5B 118
Studley Twr. B12: Birm 4H 5
    (off Canford Cl.)
Sturman Dr. B65: B'hth 2B 112
Suckling Grn. La. WV8: Cod 5F 13
Sudbury Cl. WV11: Wed 1G 29
Sudbury Gro. B44: K'sdng 3B 68
Sudeley Cl. B36: Cas B 6F 87
Sudeley Gdns. DY1: Dud 5H 75
Suffield Gro. B23: Erd 2B 84

Suffolk Cl. B68: O'bry 5H 97
    WV1: Wed 3E 29
Suffolk Dr. DY5: Brie H 4G 109
Suffolk Gro. WS9: A'rdge 1D 34
Suffolk Ho. B23: Erd 2F 85
Suffolk Pl. B1: Birm 6D 4 (2F 117)
    WS2: Wals 4B 32
Suffolk Rd. DY2: Dud 2C 94
    WS10: W'bry 2A 64
Suffolk St. Queensway
    B1: Birm 5C 4 (1F 117)
Suffrage St. B66: Smeth 4F 99
Sugar Loaf La. DY7: I'ley 5A 124
Sugden Gro. B5: Birm 3G 117
Sulgrave Cl. DY1: Dud 4B 76
Sumburgh Cft. B35: Cas V 4E 87
Summercourt Dr. DY6: K'wfrd 3A 92
Summercourt Ho. B29: S Oak 4F 131
Summercourt Sq. DY6: K'wfrd 4A 92
Summer Cft. B19: Hock 3F 101
Summer Dr. DY3: Lwr G 4G 75
Summerfield Av. B70: W Brom 3A 80
    (not continuous)
    DY6: W Hth 2A 92
Summerfield Ct. B15: Edg 3G 115
Summerfield Cres. B16: Edg 6A 100
Summerfield Dr. B29: W Cas 6E 131
Summerfield Gro. B18: Win G 5A 100
Summerfield Ind. Est.
    B18: Win G 5C 100
Summerfield Rd. B16: Edg 6A 100
    B92: Olton 3E 137
    DY2: Dud 2F 95
    WV1: Wolv 1F 43
Summerfields Av. B62: B'hth 3F 113
Summergate DY3: Lwr G 4G 75
SUMMER HILL 5A 62
SUMMERHILL 4G 11
Summer Hill B63: Hale 2B 128
    (not continuous)
Summerhill DY6: K'wfrd 3A 92
Summer Hill Ind. Pk. B1: Birm 6D 100
    (off Anderton St.)
Summer Hill Rd. B1: Birm 6D 100
    WV4: Tip 6H 61
    WV14: Cose 4F 61
Summer Hill St. B1: Birm 6D 100
Summer Hill Ter. B1: Birm ...3A 4 (6D 100)
Summerhouse Rd. WV14: Cose 4C 60
Summer La.
    B19: Birm, Hock 1D 4 (5F 101)
    B76: Min 1H 87
    DY3: Lwr G 4G 75
    WS4: S'fld 5G 21
Summerlee Rd. B24: Erd 5H 85
Summer Rd. B15: Edg 4E 117
    B23: Erd 2F 85
    B27: A Grn 3G 135
    B65: Row R 6D 96
    DY1: Dud 3C 76
Summer Row B3: Birm 38 4 (6E 101)
    WV2: Wolv 4B 170 (2G 43)
Summer St. B71: W Brom 3B 80
    DY6: K'wfrd 3B 92
    DY8: Stourb 6D 108
    DY9: Lye 6D 108
    WV13: W'hall 1H 45
Summerton Rd. B69: O'bry 6D 78
Summerville Ter. B17: Harb 6G 115
Summit, The DY9: W'cte 1H 125
Summit Cres. B66: Smeth 1C 98
Summit Gdns. B63: Hale 2H 127
Summit Pl. DY3: Gorn 5F 75
Sumner Rd. B46: Col 3H 107
Sunbeam Cl. B36: Cas B 6B 88
Sunbeam Dr. WS6: Gt Wyr 2F 7
Sunbeam St. WV2: Wolv 4G 43
Sunbeam Way B33: Kitts G 1G 121
Sunbury Cl. WV14: Cose 4G 61
Sunbury Cotts. B31: N'fld 3E 145
Sunbury Rd. B31: Longb 2C 158
    B63: Hale 1H 127
Suncroft B32: Quin 6A 114
Sundbury Ri. B31: N'fld 2F 145
Sunderland Dr. DY8: Amb 3E 109
Sunderton Rd. B14: King H 2G 147
Sundew Cft. B36: Hodg H 1B 104

Sundial La. B43: Gt Barr	.4B 66
Sundour Cres. WV11: Wed	.6D 16
Sundridge Ct. B44: Gt Barr	.2G 67
Sundridge Rd. B44: Gt Barr	.1G 67
Sundridge Wlk. WV4: Penn	.5A 42
Sun Ho. B2: Birm	.4D 4
Sunleigh Gro. B27: A Grn	.1C 136
Sunningdale B62: Hale	.1E 129
Sunningdale Av. WV6: Pert	.4D 24
Sunningdale Cl. B20: Hand	.3A 82
B73: W Grn	.3G 69
DY8: Stourb	.3D 124
Sunningdale Ct. B73: W Grn	.4H 69
Sunningdale Dr. B69: Tiv	.2A 96
Sunningdale Rd. B11: Tys	.2G 135
DY3: Sed	.5F 59
Sunningdale Way WS3: Blox	.4G 19
Sunny Av. B12: Bal H	.6A 118
Sunnybank Av. B44: K'sdng	.6B 68
Sunnybank Cl. WS9: A'rdge	.1G 51
Sunnybank Ct. B68: O'bry	.4A 114
Sunnybank Rd. B68: O'bry	.4A 114
B73: Bold, W Grn	.5G 69
DY3: Up Gor	.2B 76
Sunnydale Wlk. B71: W Brom	.3A 80
Sunnydene B8: W End	.4G 103
Sunny Hill Cl. WV5: Wom	.1H 73
Sunnymead Rd. B26: Sheld	.5D 120
Sunnymead Way B74: S'tly	.4H 51
Sunnymede Rd. DY6: K'wfrd	.5E 93
Sunnyside B69: Tiv	.2B 96
WS9: Wals W	.5C 22
Sunnyside Av. B23: Erd	.4E 85
Sunnyside Cl. CV7: Bal C	.5H 169
Sunnyside La. CV7: Bal C	.5H 169
Sunnyside Ter. CV7: Bal C	.5H 169
Sunridge Av. B19: Hock	.3F 101
WV5: Wom	.6G 57
Sunrise Bus. Pk. DY8: Amb	.4D 108
Sunrise Ct. B15: Edg	.4F 117
Sunrise Wlk. B68: O'bry	.6A 98
Sunset Cl. WS6: Gt Wyr	.2F 7
Sunset Pl. WV4: Ett	.2B 60
Sun St. DY5: Quar B	.2B 110
WS1: Wals	.4B 48
WV10: Wolv	.1A 44
(not continuous)	
Surfeit Hill Rd. B64: Crad H	.3F 111
Surrey Cres. B71: W Brom	.5G 63
Surrey Dr. DY6: K'wfrd	.5D 92
WV3: Wolv	.2C 42
Surrey Rd. B44: Gt Barr	.1G 67
DY2: Dud	.2C 94
Surrey Wlk. WS9: A'rdge	.6C 22
Sussex Av. B71: W Brom	.1A 80
WS9: A'rdge	.1C 34
WS10: W'bry	.1B 64
Sussex Ct. B29: W Cas	.6G 131
Sussex Dr. WV3: Wolv	.2C 42
Sutherland Av. B90: Shir	.4A 150
WV2: Wolv	.3B 44
Sutherland Cl. B43: Gt Barr	.1F 67
Sutherland Dr. B13: Mose	.1H 133
WV5: Wom	.5G 57
Sutherland Gro. WV6: Pert	.5F 25
Sutherland Ho. WV1: Wolv	.1E 43
Sutherland Pl. WV2: Wolv	.5D 170 (2H 43)
Sutherland Rd. B64: Old H	.3G 111
WS6: C Hay	.2E 7
WV4: Penn	.6F 43
Sutherland St. B6: Aston	.1B 102
Sutton App. B8: W End	.5G 103
Sutton Arts Theatre	.1A 70
SUTTON COLDFIELD	.6H 53
Sutton Coldfield By-Pass	
B75: Bass P, S Cold	.1F 55
B76: Min, Wis	.6G 71
Sutton Coldfield Crematorium	
B75: S Cold	.1E 55
Sutton Coldfield Golf Course	.2B 52
Sutton Coldfield Station (Rail)	.6H 53
Sutton Coldfield Tennis & Squash Club	
	.3H 69
Sutton Ct. B23: Erd	.1H 85
B43: Gt Barr	.6A 66
B75: S Cold	.4A 54
WV4: Ett	.3A 60

Sutton Cres. B70: W Brom	.4G 79
Sutton Lodge B91: Sol	.4E 151
Sutton New Rd. B23: Erd	.3F 85
Sutton Oak Cnr. B74: S'tly	.6A 52
Sutton Oak Rd. B73: S'tly	.1A 68
Sutton Pk. B'rm	.4E 53
Sutton Pk. Ct. B72: W Grn	.3H 69
Sutton Park Visitors Cen.	.6G 53
Sutton Rd. B23: Erd	.2G 85
WS1: Wals	.3D 48
WS5: Wals	.3F 49
WS9: A'rdge	.3F 49
WS10: Mox	.6A 46
Sutton Sailing Club	.2E 69
Suttons Dr. B43: Gt Barr	.1B 66
Sutton Sq. B76: Min	.1A 88
Sutton St. B1: Birm	.2F 117
B6: Aston	.3H 101
DY8: Word	.2C 108
Swains Gro. B44: Gt Barr	.1h 67
Swale Gro. B38: King Nor	.6B 146
WV13: W'hall	.1D 46
Swale Rd. B76: Walm	.4E 71
Swallow Av. B36: Cas B	.1C 106
Swallow Cl. B12: Bal H	.6B 118
DY2: Neth	.1F 111
WS10: W'bry	.1h 63
Swallow Ct. WV10: Bush	.2H 27
Swallowdale WS9: Wals W	.3D 22
WV6: Tett	.1F 41
Swallowfall Av. DY8: Stourb	.1A 124
Swallow Flds. DY4: Tip	.2G 77
Swallowfields Rd. DY3: Sed	.3G 59
Swallows Cl. WS3: Pels	.2E 21
Swallows Ind. Est., The B90: Shir	.1B 164
Swallows Mdw. B90: Shir	.1B 164
(not continuous)	
Swallows Rise Bus. Pk. DY5: Brie H	.1A 64
Swallow St. B1: Birm	.5C 4 (1F 117)
B70: W Brom	.3G 79
Swanage Rd. B10: Small H	.3D 118
Swan Av. B66: Smeth	.2C 98
Swan Bank WV4: Penn	.1D 58
Swan Cen. B26: Yard	.5B 120
Swan Cl. B8: Salt	.3F 103
WS6: C Hay	.3D 6
Swan Copse B25: Yard	.6A 120
Swancote Dr. WV4: Penn	.5A 42
Swancote Rd. B33: Stech	.4D 104
DY1: Dud	.6D 76
Swancote St. DY1: Dud	.1C 94
Swan Courtyard B26: Yard	.5B 120
Swan Cres. B69: O'bry	.5F 97
Swancroft Rd. DY4: Tip	.5H 61
Swan Dr. WS8: Bwnhls	.6A 10
Swanfield Rd. DY8: Word	.2D 108
Swan Gdns. B23: Erd	.3F 85
Swanhurst Community Leisure Cen.	
	.6A 134
Swan Island B25: Yard	.5B 120
Swan La. B70: W Brom	.2G 79
DY8: Word	.1D 108
Swan La. Ind. Est. B70: W Brom	.2G 79
Swanley Cl. B62: Quin	.2G 129
Swanmore Cl. WV3: Wolv	.3C 42
Swann Rd. WV14: Cose	.3C 60
Swann Wlk. DY4: Tip	.5A 62
Swan Pool Gro. WS4: S'fld	.6H 21
Swansbrook Gdns. B38: King Nor	.5E 147
Swanshurst La. B13: Mose	.5C 134
Swan St. DY2: Neth	.3E 95
DY5: P'ntt	.2G 93
DY8: Stourb	.6C 108
WV1: Wolv	.1B 44
Swanswell Rd. B92: Olton	.5B 136
Swanswood Gro. B37: Chel W	.6E 107
SWAN VILLAGE	
B70	.2G 79
WV14	.6D 60
Swan Village B70: W Brom	.2G 79
Swan Village Ind. Est. B70: W Brom	.2G 79
Swarthmore Rd. B29: W Cas	.6E 131
Sweetbriar La. WV12: W'hall	.4D 30
Sweetbriar Rd. WV2: Ett	.4C 44
Sweetbrier Dr. DY8: Word	.2C 108
Sweetman Pl. WV6: Wolv	.6E 27

Sweetman St. WV6: Wolv	.5D 26
(not continuous)	
Sweetmoor Cl. B36: Cas B	.1G 105
Swift Cl. B36: Cas B	.1C 106
Swinbrook Gro. B44: Gt Barr	.4G 67
Swinbrook Way B90: Shir	.3B 150
Swincross Rd. DY8: Stourb	.1F 125
Swindell Rd. DY9: Pedm	.4G 125
SWINDON	.5E 73
Swindon Golf Course	.3A 72
Swindon Rd. B17: Edg	.6F 99
DY6: K'wfrd	.1F 91
Swinford Gro. B93: Dorr	.6A 166
Swinford Leys WV5: Wom	.2D 72
Swinford Rd. B29: W Cas	.2E 131
DY8: Stourb	.3E 125
WV10: Wolv	.4A 28
Swin Forge Way DY3: Swind	.5E 73
Swiss Dr. DY8: Word	.1D 108
Swynnerton Dr. WV11: Ess	.3H 17
Sycamore Av. B12: Bal H	.6A 118
Sycamore Cl. B24: Erd	.4F 85
B76: Walm	.3D 70
DY2: Dud	.1D 94
DY8: Stourb	.3B 124
WS4: S'fld	.1F 33
Sycamore Ct. B23: Erd	.6C 68
B30: King Nor	.3A 146
Sycamore Cres. B24: Erd	.4F 85
B37: Mars G	.3C 122
Sycamore Dr. B47: H'wd	.4A 162
WV3: Wolv	.2B 42
(not continuous)	
Sycamore Grn. DY1: Dud	.2B 76
Sycamore Ho. B13: Mose	.2A 134
B31: N'fld	.4F 145
(off Rectory Rd.)	
Sycamore Ind. Est. B21: Hand	.2H 99
Sycamore Paddock DY8: Word	.2E 109
Sycamore Pl. B67: Smeth	.5D 98
WV14: Bils	.2A 62
Sycamore Rd. B6: Aston	.1A 102
B21: Hand	.2H 99
B23: Erd	.6F 69
B30: B'ville	.6B 132
B43: Gt Barr	.2A 66
B66: Smeth	.6F 99
B69: O'bry	.5G 97
DY4: Tip	.6H 61
DY6: K'wfrd	.3C 92
WS4: S'fld	.1F 33
WS5: Wals	.6D 48
WS10: W'bry	.3G 63
Sycamores, The WV10: Bush	.1B 28
Sycamore Ter. B14: King H	.1E 147
Sycamore Way B27: A Grn	.1A 136
Sydenham Rd. B11: S'brk	.5C 118
B66: Smeth	.2E 99
WV1: Wolv	.1D 44
Sydney Cl. B70: W Brom	.6G 63
Sydney Rd. B9: Bord G	.1C 118
B64: Crad H	.2E 111
B67: Smeth	.1C 114
Sydney Way B34: S End	.3A 106
Sylvan Av. B31: N'fld	.4D 144
Sylvan Grn. B62: Hale	.6D 112
Sylvan Gro. B90: Shir	.2H 149
Sylvia Av. B31: Longb	.1F 159
Symphony Ct. B16: Birm	.1D 116
(off Sheepcote St.)	
Symphony Hall	.4A 4 (1E 117)
Sytch La. WV5: Wom	.2G 73

T

Tack Farm Rd. DY8: Word	.2B 108
Tackford Cl. B36: Cas B	.6G 87
Tackley Cl. B90: Shir	.1H 163
Tadmore Cl. WV14: Bils	.6E 45
Tadworth Cl. WV1: Wolv	.1C 44
Tait Cft. B92: Sol	.5B 138
Talaton Cl. WV9: Pend	.5E 15
Talbot Av. B74: Lit As	.6B 36
Talbot Cl. B23: Erd	.5D 68
WS2: Wals	.3A 32
Talbot Ho. WS10: W'bry	.2F 63

Talbot Pas.—Terrace, The

Talbot Pas. *DY8: Stourb* 6E 109
(off High St.)
Talbot Pl. WV14: Bils 5E 45
Talbot Rd. B66: Smeth 6E 99
DY2: Neth 5D 94
WV2: Wolv 5G 43
Talbots La. DY5: Brie H 2A 110
Talbots La. Trad. Est. DY5: Brie H 2B 110
Talbot St. B18: Hock 3B 100
B63: Crad 5E 111
DY5: Brie H 6H 93
(Adelaide St.)
DY5: Brie H 6H 93
(Albion St.)
DY8: Stourb 6E 109
DY9: Lye 6B 110
Talbot Way B10: Small H 4F 119
Talfourd St. B9: Small H 2D 118
Talgarth Covert B38: King Nor 2A 160
Talke Rd. WS5: Wals 6D 48
Talladale B32: Bart G 6H 129
Tallington Rd. B33: Sheld 4G 121
Tall Trees Cl. B74: Four O 5D 36
WV12: W'hall 3D 30
Tall Trees Dr. DY9: Pedm 3H 125
Talton Cl. B90: M'path 4E 165
Tamar Cl. WS8: Bwnhls 3G 9
Tamar Dr. B36: Cas B 1B 106
B76: Walm 6F 71
DY3: Sed 1B 76
Tamar Gro. WV6: Pert 5E 25
WV13: W'hall 1C 46
Tamarisk Cl. B29: W Cas 5F 131
Tamar Ri. DY8: Amb 3E 109
Tame Av. B36: Cas B 1C 106
WS10: W'bry 1H 63
Tame Bri. WS5: Wals 1D 64
Tame Bri. Factory Est. WS5: Wals 3F 65
Tamebridge Ind. Est. B42: P Barr 3G 83
Tame Bridge Parkway Station (Rail) **3D 64**
Tamebrook Way DY4: Tip 1A 78
Tame Cl. WS1: Wals 5C 48
Tame Cres. B71: W Brom 1A 80
Tame Crossing WS10: W'bry 4G 63
Tame Dr. WS3: Pels 6E 21
Tame Ri. B68: O'bry 3H 113
Tame Rd. B6: Witt 5A 84
B68: O'bry 3G 113
DY4: Tip 2C 78
Tame Rd. Ind. Est. B6: Witt 6A 84
Tamerton Rd. B32: Bart G 4B 130
Tameside Cl. WV13: W'hall 2H 45
Tameside Dr. B6: Witt 3H 83
B35: Cas V 6D 86
Tameside Way B42: P Barr 2G 83
Tame St. B70: W Brom 5F 63
WS1: Wals 5C 48
WV14: Bils 6H 45
Tame St. E. WS1: Wals 5D 48
Tamworth Cl. WS8: Bwnhls 3B 10
Tamworth Rd. B75: Bass P 1F 55
B75: Bass P, S Cold 4A 54
Tanacetum Dr. WS5: Wals 2F 65
Tandy Ct. B14: King H 4H 147
Tandy Dr. B14: King H 4H 147
Tanfield Cl. WV6: Tett 6H 25
Tanfield Rd. B33: Stech 6D 104
DY2: Dud 2D 94
Tanford Rd. B92: Sol 2G 137
Tanglewood Cl. B32: Quin 6H 113
B34: S End 4G 105
Tanglewood Gro. DY3: Sed 3G 59
Tangmere Cl. WV6: Pert 4E 25
Tangmere Dr. B35: Cas V 5D 86
Tangmere Sq. B35: Cas V 4D 86
Tanhouse Av. B43: Gt Barr 6G 65
Tanhouse Farm Rd. B92: Sol 3G 137
Tanhouse La. B63: Crad 5D 110
Tanners Cl. B75: S Cold 4D 54
Tanners Ct. WS1: Wals 3C 48
Tannery Cl. WS2: Wals 6B 32
Tansey B74: Four O 4F 37
Tansey Ct. DY5: P'ntt 2F 93
TANSEY GREEN **2F 93**
Tansey Grn. Rd. DY5: P'ntt 6E 75
DY6: P'ntt 6E 75
Tansey Grn. Trad. Est.
DY5: P'ntt 1F 93
Tansley Cl. B93: Dorr 5B 166
Tansley Gro. B44: K'sdng 4H 67
Tansley Hill Av. DY2: Dud 1H 95
Tansley Hill Rd. DY2: Dud 1G 95
Tansley Rd. B44: K'sdng 5H 67
Tansley Vw. WV2: Wolv 4H 43
Tantallon Dr. B32: Bart G 4B 130
Tantany La. B71: W Brom 3A 80
Tantarra St. WS1: Wals 2D 48
(not continuous)
Tanwood Cl. B91: Sol 1F 165
Tanworth Gro. B12: Bal H 5H 117
Tanworth La. B90: Shir 2H 163
Tanyard, The WS7: Hamm 2F 11
Tanyards B27: A Grn 2A 136
Tapestries Av. B70: W Brom 3G 79
Tapton Cl. WS3: Blox 4A 20
Tara La. B21: Hand 2A 100
Tarmac Rd. WV4: Ett 6D 44
Tarragon Gdns. B31: Longb 5A 144
Tarrant Gro. B32: Harb 6D 114
Tarrington Covert
B38: King Nor 1A 160
Tarry Hollow Rd. DY5: P'ntt 1F 93
Tarry Rd. B8: Salt 5E 103
Tarvin M. DY5: Brie H 2H 109
Taryn Dr. WS10: Darl 4D 46
Tasker St. B70: W Brom 3E 79
WS1: Wals 3B 48
Tasman Gro. WV6: Pert 4E 25
TAT BANK **3H 97**
Tat Bank Rd. B68: O'bry 2G 97
B69: O'bry 2G 97
Tattenhall Ga. WV3: Wolv 1E 43
Taunton Av. WV10: F'hses 3H 15
Taunton Cl. B31: Longb 4A 144
Taunton Rd. B12: Bal H 1A 134
Taverners Cl. WV12: W'hall 6C 18
Taverners Grn. B20: Hand 4B 82
Tavistock Rd. B27: A Grn 6A 136
Taw Cl. B36: Cas B 1B 106
Tay Cft. B37: F'bri 5E 107
Tay Gro. B38: King Nor 1B 160
B62: B'hth 3E 113
Taylor Rd. B13: Mose 2H 147
DY2: Neth 1G 111
WV4: Ett 6B 44
Taylors La. B67: Smeth 4D 98
B69: O'bry 2E 97
B71: W Brom 3B 80
Taylors Orchard B23: Erd 3B 84
Taylor St. WV11: Wed 4F 29
Taylor Way B69: Tiv 1B 96
Taynton Covert B30: King Nor 4E 147
Tay Rd. B45: Fran 6H 143
Taysfield Rd. B31: N'fld 1C 144
Taywood Dr. B10: Small H 4C 118
Tealby Gro. B29: S Oak 4C 132
Teal Dr. B23: Erd 4B 84
Teal Gro. WS10: Mox 2B 62
Teall Ct. B27: A Grn 2A 136
Teall Rd. B8: Salt 4E 103
Teamworks Karting
Birmingham **1A 118**
Tean Cl. B11: Tys 2G 135
Teasdale Way DY9: W'cte 1H 125
Teasel Rd. WV11: Wed 4G 29
Teazel Av. B30: B'vlle 1H 145
Tebworth Cl. WV9: Pend 5D 14
Tedbury Cres. B23: Erd 1E 85
Tedder Rd. WS2: Wals 1F 47
Teddesley Gro. B33: Kitts G 5G 105
Teddesley St. WS4: Wals 6D 32
Teddington Cl. B73: S Cold 3G 69
Teddington Gro. B42: P Barr 4F 83
Tedstone Rd. B32: Quin 6C 114
Teesdale Av. B34: Hodg H 3D 104
Teesdale Cl. WV1: Wolv 1C 44
Tees Gro. B38: King Nor 1B 160
Teignmouth Rd. B29: S Oak 3B 132
Telford Av. WS6: Gt Wyr 2F 7
Telford Cl. B67: Smeth 2B 114
B71: W Brom 5G 63
WS2: Wals 4G 31
Telford Gdns. WV3: Wolv 4B 42
Telford Rd. WS2: Wals 4G 31
Telford Way B66: Smeth 2D 98
Teme Gro. WV13: W'hall 1D 46
Teme Rd. B63: Crad 6D 110
DY8: Stourb 2D 124
Tempest St. WV2: Wolv 4C 170 (2H 43)
Templars, The B69: O'bry 4E 97
Templars Wlk. WV13: W'hall 6A 30
Temple Av. B28: Hall G 1G 149
CV7: Bal C 3F 169
TEMPLE BALSALL **5B 168**
Temple Bar WV13: W'hall 1A 46
Temple Ct. B46: Col 6H 89
Templefield Gdns. B9: Bord G 2C 118
Templefield Sq. B15: Edg 4D 116
Templefield St. B9: Bord G 2C 118
Temple Ho. *B2: Birm* *4D 4*
(off Temple St.)
Temple La. B93: Know 6A 168
Temple Mdws. Rd.
B71: W Brom 2C 80
Templemore Dr. B43: Gt Barr 6A 66
Temple Pas. B2: Birm 4D 4 (1F 117)
Temple Rd. B93: Dorr 6C 166
WV13: W'hall 6A 30
Temple Row B2: Birm 4D 4 (1F 117)
Temple Row W. B2: Birm 3D 4 (1F 117)
Temple Sq. WV13: W'hall 6B 30
Temple St. B2: Birm 4D 4 (1F 117)
B70: W Brom 3A 80
DY3: Lwr G 4H 75
WV2: Wolv 4B 170 (2G 43)
WV14: Bils 6G 45
Templeton Cl. B93: Dorr 6C 166
Templeton Rd. B44: Gt Barr 3G 67
Temple Way B46: Col 6G 89
B69: Tiv 5C 78
Tempus Dr. WS2: Wals 2G 47
Tempus Ten WS2: Wals 2G 47
Tenacre La. DY3: Up Gor 1A 76
Ten Acre M. B30: Stir 5D 132
TEN ACRES **5D 132**
Ten Acres End B30: Stir 5D 132
Ten Ashes La. B45: Coft H 5A 158
Tenbury Cl. WS2: Wals 6D 30
WS9: A'rdge 1E 35
Tenbury Ct. WV4: Penn 6B 42
Tenbury Gdns. WV4: Penn 1B 58
Tenbury Ho. *B63: Hale* *2A 128*
(off Highfield La.)
Tenbury Rd. B14: King H 1F 147
Tenby Ct. *B29: W Cas* *6G 131*
(off Tugford Rd.)
Tenby Rd. B13: Mose 4D 134
Tenby St. B1: Birm 1A 4 (5D 100)
Tenby St. Nth. B1: Birm 1A 4 (5D 100)
Tenby Twr. B31: N'fld 6E 145
Tenlands Rd. B63: Hale 2H 127
Tennal Dr. B32: Harb 5D 114
Tennal Gro. B32: Harb 5D 114
Tennal La. B32: Harb 6C 114
Tennal Rd. B32: Harb 5C 114
Tennant St. B15: Birm 6A 4 (2D 116)
Tennis Ct. B15: Edg 6C 116
B30: King Nor 3H 145
Tennis Ct. Flats B15: Edg 6C 116
Tennscore Av. WS6: C Hay 2E 7
Tennyson Av. B74: Four O 3F 37
Tennyson Ho. B31: Longb 1E 159
B68: O'bry 5A 98
Tennyson Rd. B10: Small H 4E 119
DY3: Lwr G 2E 75
WS3: Blox 1C 32
WV10: Bush 6C 16
WV12: W'hall 1E 31
Tennyson St. DY5: P'ntt 3H 93
Tenpin
Birmingham ***1D 102***
(within Star City)
Tenter Ct. B63: Hale 1B 128
Tenter Dr. B63: Hale 1B 128
Tenterfields B63: Hale 1B 128
Terminal Rd. B26: Birm A 2B 138
Tern Cl. WV4: Ett 2H 59
Tern Gro. B38: King Nor 6A 146
Terrace, The B64: Crad H 3G 111
WV3: Wolv 2A 42

A-Z Birmingham 277

Terrace Rd. B15: Edg 2B **132**
B19: Hock 2C **100**
Terrace St. B65: Row R 2B **112**
DY5: Brie H 4A **94**
WS10: W'bry 2G **63**
Terret Cl. WS1: Wals 1D **48**
Terry Dr. B76: Walm 4D **70**
Terrys La. B24: Erd 4A **86**
Terry St. DY2: Dud 6F **77**
Tessall La. B31: Longb 4A **144**
(not continuous)
Tetbury Gro. B31: N'fld 4B **144**
Tetley Av. WS4: Wals 5F **33**
Tetley Rd. B11: S'hll 2E **135**
Tetnall St. DY2: Dud 1F **95**
TETTENHALL 4B **26**
Tettenhall Rd. WV1: Wolv 5C **26**
WV3: Wolv 5C **26**
WV6: Wolv 5C **26**
TETTENHALL WOOD 6H **25**
Tettenhal Pool (Wolverhampton)
(Park & Ride) 4B **26**
Teviot Gdns. DY5: P'ntt 3E **93**
WV8: Bilb 2G **13**
Teviot Gro. B38: King Nor 1B **160**
Teviot Twr. B19: Birm 4E **101**
(off Mosborough Cres.)
Tewkesbury Dr. DY2: Neth 6F **95**
Tewkesbury Rd. B20: Hand 6G **83**
WS3: Blox 5E **19**
Tew Pk. Rd. B21: Hand 2A **100**
Thackeray Rd. B30: B'vlle 2H **145**
Thames Cl. DY5: P'ntt 2F **93**
Thames Ct. B47: Wyt 6G **161**
(off Trent Cres.)
B73: S Cold 6H **53**
Thames Gdns. WV14: Cose 4C **60**
Thames Rd. WS3: Blox 1B **32**
Thames Twr. B7: Nech 4B **102**
Thanet Cl. DY6: K'wfrd 3A **92**
Thanet Gro. B42: P Barr 3E **83**
Thatchers, The B62: B'hth 3E **113**
Thatchway Gdns. B38: King Nor 2A **160**
Thaxted Rd. B33: Kitts G 6A **106**
The . . . .
Names prefixed with 'The' for example
'The Academy' are indexed under the
main name such as 'Academy, The'
Theatre App. B5: Birm 6E **5** (2G **117**)
Thelbridge Rd. B31: Longb 3C **158**
Thelma Dr. DY4: Tip 2G **77**
Thelma St. WS1: Wals 4B **48**
Thelsford Way B92: Sol 5H **137**
Theodore Cl. B17: Harb 1H **131**
B69: O'bry 6E **79**
Theresa Rd. B11: S'brk 4B **118**
Thetford Cl. DY4: Tip 2F **77**
Thetford Gdns. WV11: Wed 3F **29**
Thetford Rd. B42: Gt Barr 6D **66**
Thetford Way WS5: Wals 2G **65**
Thickett Cl. WS2: Wals 3H **47**
Thicknall Dr. DY9: Pedm 3F **125**
THIMBLE END 3E **71**
Thimble Dr. B76: Walm 4D **70**
Thimble End Ct. B76: Walm 3E **71**
Thimble End Rd. B76: Walm 2D **70**
Thimble La. B93: Know 3E **167**
Thimble Mill La. B6: Aston 2B **102**
B7: Nech 2B **102**
Thimblemill Rd. B67: Smeth 5B **98**
Thinktank 3H **5** (6H **101**)
Third Av. B6: Witt 4H **83**
B9: Bord G 1F **119**
B29: S Oak 2E **133**
DY6: P'ntt 1D **92**
WS8: Bwnhls 4C **10**
WV10: Bush 2A **28**
Third Rd. B61: Wild 5A **156**
Thirlmere Cl. WV6: Tett 1B **26**
Thirlmere Dr. B13: Mose 5C **134**
WV11: Ess 5A **18**
Thirlmere Gro. WV6: Pert 5F **25**
Thirlmere Ho. B15: Edg 2H **131**
Thirlmere Rd. WV6: Tett 1B **26**
Thirlmere Wlk. DY5: Brie H 4F **93**
Thirsk Cft. B36: Hodg H 1A **104**
Thirston Cl. WV11: Wed 4A **30**

Thistle Cl. DY3: Sed 1B **76**
Thistle Cft. WV11: Wed 4F **29**
Thistle Down Cl. B74: S'tly 1A **52**
Thistledown Rd. B34: S End 2G **105**
Thistledown Wlk. DY3: Sed 4G **59**
Thistle Grn. B38: King Nor 2A **160**
Thistlegreen Cl. B65: Row R 4H **95**
Thistlegreen Rd. DY2: Neth 5G **95**
Thistle Ho. B36: Hodg H 1B **104**
Thistle La. B32: Bart G 5H **129**
Thomas Benson Pl. B12: Birm 4H **117**
Thomas Cres. B66: Smeth 4G **99**
Thomas Guy Rd. B70: W Brom 6E **63**
Thomas Ho. B24: Erd 4F **85**
(off Wood End Rd.)
WS3: Blox 4B **20**
Thomas Mason Cl. WV11: Wed 2F **29**
Thomas St. B6: Aston 3H **101**
B66: Smeth 4F **99**
B70: W Brom 5B **80**
WS2: Wals 1C **48**
WV2: Wolv 6B **170** (3G **43**)
Thomas Wlk. B35: Cas V 4F **87**
Thompson Av. WV2: Wolv 4H **43**
Thompson Cl. DY2: Neth 1D **110**
WV13: W'hall 6A **30**
Thompson Dr. B24: Erd 1F **103**
Thompson Gdns. B67: Smeth 5D **98**
Thompson Ho. DY4: Tip 5C **62**
Thompson Rd. B67: Smeth 5D **98**
B68: O'bry 5H **97**
Thompson St. WV13: W'hall 6A **30**
WV14: Bils 6F **45**
Thomson Av. B38: King Nor 6G **145**
Thoresby Cft. DY1: Dud 4B **76**
Thornberry Dr. DY1: Dud 1H **93**
Thornberry Wlk. B7: Nech 3C **102**
Thornbridge Av. B42: Gt Barr 6E **67**
Thornbridge Gro. WS9: Wals W 4B **22**
Thorn Brook Ct. WS4: Wals 6D **32**
(off Lwr. North St.)
Thornbury Ct. WV6: Pert 6G **25**
Thornbury Rd. B20: Hand 5F **83**
WS2: Wals 5B **32**
Thornby Av. B91: Sol 2F **151**
Thornby Rd. B23: Erd 5C **68**
Thorncliffe Rd. B44: Gt Barr 3G **67**
Thorn Cl. WS10: W'bry 1F **63**
Thorncroft Way WS5: Wals 1F **65**
Thorne Av. WV10: Bush 2A **28**
Thorne Pl. B65: Row R 1C **112**
Thorne Rd. WV13: W'hall 6A **30**
THORNES .4G **23**
Thornes Cft. WS9: Ston 3G **23**
Thorne St. WV2: Ett 4C **44**
Thorneycroft La. WV10: Wolv 4C **28**
Thorneycroft Pl. WV14: Bils 2B **62**
Thorneycroft Rd. WV14: Bils 2A **62**
Thorney Rd. B74: S'tly 2H **51**
Thornfield Cft. DY3: Sed 6A **60**
Thornfield Rd. B27: A Grn 3A **136**
Thorngrove Av. B91: Sol 1G **165**
Thornham Way B14: King H 6F **147**
Thornhill Gro. B21: Hand 1B **100**
Thornhill Pk. B74: S'tly 3A **52**
Thornhill Rd. B11: S'hll 2D **134**
B21: Hand 2B **100**
B63: Hale 2B **128**
B74: S'tly 5A **52**
B91: Sol 6G **137**
DY5: Quar B 2A **110**
Thornhurst Av. B32: Quin 4C **114**
Thornleigh DY3: Up Gor 2H **75**
Thornleigh Trad. Est. DY2: Dud 2C **94**
Thornley Cl. B13: Mose 4A **134**
WV11: Wed 6H **17**
Thornley Cft. WS6: C Hay 4D **6**
Thornley Gro. B76: Min 1G **87**
Thornley Rd. WV11: Wed 6H **17**
Thornley St. WV1: Wolv 2C **170** (1H **43**)
Thorn Rd. B30: B'vlle 6A **132**
Thorns Av. DY5: Quar B 2A **110**
Thornsett Gro. B90: Shir 1H **149**
Thorns Leisure Cen. 3A **110**
Thorns Rd. DY5: Quar B 4A **110**
Thornthwaite Cl. B45: Fran 5H **143**
Thornton Cl. B69: Tiv 5C **78**

Thornton Dr. DY5: Brie H 2A **110**
Thornton Ho. B19: Hock 4G **101**
(off Ruddington Way)
Thornton Rd. B8: W End 4H **103**
B90: M'path 3D **164**
WV1: Wolv 2D **44**
Thornwood Cl. B68: O'bry 4A **98**
Thornyfield Cl. B90: Shir 4A **150**
Thornyfield Rd. B90: Shir 4A **150**
Thornyhurst La.
WS14: Hilt, Lynn . . . . . . .6H **11** & 1H **23**
Thorpe Cl. B75: S Cold 3A **54**
Thorpe Ct. B91: Sol 1D **150**
Thorpe Rd. WS1: Wals 1C **48**
Thorp St. B5: Birm 6D **4** (2F **117**)
Three Acres La. B90: Dic H 3F **163**
Three Cnr. Cl. B90: Maj G 1E **163**
THREE MAYPOLES 2H **163**
Three Oaks Rd. B47: Wyt 5B **162**
Three Shires Oak Rd.
B67: Smeth 1D **114**
Three Tuns La. WV10: Oxl 5G **15**
Three Tuns Pde. WV10: Oxl 5G **15**
Threshers Dr. WV12: W'hall 3D **30**
Threshers Way WV12: W'hall 3D **30**
Throne Cl. B65: Row R 4C **96**
Throne Cres. B65: Row R 4D **96**
Throne Rd. B65: Row R 4C **96**
Throstles Cl. B43: Gt Barr 6A **66**
Thrushel Wlk. WV11: Wed 4E **29**
Thrush Rd. B68: O'bry 1F **113**
Thruxton Cl. B14: King H 4H **147**
Thunderbolt Way DY4: Tip 1F **77**
Thurcroft Cl. B8: W End 5F **103**
Thuree Rd. B67: Smeth 1C **114**
Thurleigh Cl. DY9: Pedm 3G **125**
Thurlestone Rd. B31: Longb 2C **158**
Thurloe Cres. B45: Fran 6E **143**
Thurlston Av. B92: Olton 1D **136**
Thurlstone Rd. WV4: Penn 1D **58**
Thurlstone Rd. WS3: Blox 4H **19**
Thursfield Rd. B71: W Brom 5C **64**
Thurston Av. B69: O'bry 3F **97**
Thynne St. B70: W Brom 5C **80**
Tibbats Cl. B32: Bart G 2A **130**
Tibberton Cl. B63: Hale 2C **128**
B91: Sol 1E **165**
WV3: Wolv 4B **42**
Tibbets La. B17: Harb 1E **131**
Tibbetts Rd. B64: Crad H 2E **111**
Tibbington Rd. DY4: Tip 6G **61**
Tibbington Ter. DY4: Tip 6G **61**
Tibbits Ho. WS2: Wals 6B **32**
(off Burrowes St.)
Tibblestone B90: Dic H 4G **163**
Tiberius Cl. B46: Col 6H **89**
Tibland Rd. B27: A Grn 4A **136**
TIDBURY GREEN 5E **163**
Tidbury Green Golf Course 4D **162**
Tiddington Cl. B36: Cas B 6F **87**
Tideswell Rd. B42: Gt Barr 1E **83**
Tidmarsh Cl. CV7: Bal C 3G **169**
Tidworth Cft. B14: King H 4A **148**
Tierney Dr. DY4: Tip 1C **78**
Tiffany La. WV9: Pend 5D **14**
Tiffield Rd. B25: Yard 6A **120**
Tigley Av. B32: Bart G 4B **130**
Tilbury Cl. WV3: Wolv 3G **41**
Tilbury Gro. B13: Mose 4F **133**
Tildasley St. B70: W Brom 2H **79**
Tildesley Dr. WV12: W'hall 4B **30**
Tile Croft DY9: Lye 6G **109**
TILE CROSS 1G **121**
Tile Cross Rd. B33: Kitts G 2H **121**
Tile Cross Trad. Est. B33: Kitts G 2H **121**
Tiled Ho. La. DY5: P'ntt 3F **93**
Tile Gro. B37: K'hrst 4C **106**
TILEHOUSE GREEN 2B **166**
Tilehouse Grn. La. B93: Know 2B **166**
Tilehouse La. B90: Dic H, Tid G 5E **163**
Tilesford Cl. B90: M'path 4E **165**
Tiller Gro. B75: R'ley 5B **38**
Tilley St. WS10: Darl 5E **47**
Tillyard Cft. B29: S Oak 4G **131**
Tilshead Cl. B14: King H 4G **147**
Tilsley Gro. B23: Erd 2B **84**
Tilston Dr. DY5: Brie H 2H **109**

Tilton Rd. B9: Bord G 2C 118
   (not continuous)
Timba Ct. B46: Col 5H 89
Timbercombe Way B21: Hand 1H 99
Timberdine Cl. B63: Crad 5F 111
Timberlake Cl. B90: M'path 3F 165
Timberley Cft. B34: S End 2H 105
Timberley La. B34: S End 3G 105
   (not continuous)
Timber Mill Ct. B17: Harb 5F 115
Timbers Way B11: S'brk 5A 118
   B24: Erd 3D 86
Timbertree Cres. B64: Crad H 4G 111
Timbertree Rd. B64: Crad H 4G 111
Timber Way, The B34: S End 3G 105
Times Sq. Av. DY5: Brie H 1A 110
Timmins Cl. B91: Sol 2A 152
Timmis Cl. WV14: Cose 2D 60
Timmis Rd. DY9: Lye 5G 109
Timothy Rd. B69: Tiv 2C 96
Tinacre Hill WV6: Tett 1E 41
Tinchbourne St. DY1: Dud 6E 77
Tindal St. B12: Bal H 6H 117
Tinker's Farm Gro. B31: N'fld 4C 144
Tinker's Farm Rd. B31: N'fld 4C 144
Tinmeadow Cres. B45: Redn 2A 158
Tinsley Av. B64: Old H 2G 111
Tinsley St. DY4: Tip 2E 79
Tintagel Cl. WV6: Pert 6F 25
Tintagel Dr. DY1: Dud 5A 76
Tintagel Way WS9: A'rdge 3A 34
Tintern Cl. B74: S'tly 4A 52
Tintern Ct. WV6: Pert 5E 25
Tintern Cres. WS3: Blox 4F 19
Tintern Ho. B32: Harb 6D 114
Tintern Rd. B20: Hand 6G 83
Tintern Vs. B12: Bal H 6B 118
   (off Chesterton Rd.)
Tintern Way WS3: Blox 5F 19
Tipperary Cl. B36: Hodg H 1C 104
Tipperary Wlk. B69: O'bry 2F 97
Tipper Trad. Est. B63: Lye 6C 110
Tippity Grn. B65: Row R 5B 96
Tipps Stone Cl. DY4: Tip 3G 77
TIPTON 2F 77
Tipton Heritage Cen. 2H 77
   (off Owen St.)
Tipton Ind. Est. WV14: Cose 6F 61
Tipton Rd. B69: Tiv 4B 78
   DY1: Dud 3G 77
   DY3: Sed 6A 60
   DY4: Tiv 4B 78
Tipton Sports Academy 4B 62
Tipton Station (Rail) 1H 77
Tipton St. DY3: Sed 6A 60
Tipton Swimming Cen. 2H 77
Tipton Trad. Est. WV14: Cose 6F 61
Tirley Rd. B33: Stech 4E 105
Titania Cl. B45: Fran 4H 143
Titchfield Cl. WV10: Bush 3A 16
Titford Cl. B69: O'bry 5F 97
Titford La. B65: Row R 5E 97
Titford Rd. B69: O'bry 5F 97
   (not continuous)
Tithe Cft. WV10: Wolv 6B 28
Tithe Rd. WV11: Wed 3F 29
Titterstone Rd. B31: Longb 1E 159
Tiverton Cl. DY6: K'wfrd 6D 92
Tiverton Dr. B71: W Brom 1A 80
Tiverton Gro. B67: Smeth 3D 98
   (off Dibble Rd.)
Tiverton Pool & Fitness Cen. 3B 132
Tiverton Rd. B29: S Oak 3B 132
   B66: Smeth .4F 99
TIVIDALE 6A 78
Tividale Rd. B69: Tiv 5H 77
   DY4: Tip 5H 77
Tividale St. DY4: Tip 4A 78
Tixall Rd. B28: Hall G 2E 149
Toadnest La. WV6: Pert 6A 24
Toberland WS2: Wals 2H 31
Tobruk Wlk. DY5: Brie H 6H 93
   WV13: W'hall 2G 45
Toll End Rd. DY4: Tip 1C 78
Tollgate Cl. B31: Longb 1D 158
Tollgate Dr. B20: Hand 2C 100
Tollgate Shop. Pct. B67: Smeth 3D 98

Toll Ho. Rd. B45: Redn 2A 158
Tollhouse Way B66: Smeth 2D 98
   WV5: Wom .6E 57
Tolworth Gdns. WV2: Wolv 4A 44
Tolworth Hall Rd. B24: Erd 4H 85
Tomey Rd. B11: S'brk 6D 118
Tom La. DY3: Swind 2A 72
Tomlan Rd. B31: Longb 2G 159
Tomlinson Rd. B36: Cas B 6H 87
Tompstone Rd. B71: W Brom 5D 64
Tonadine Cl. WV11: Wed 6A 18
Tonbridge Rd. B24: Erd 6G 85
Tong Ct. WV1: Wolv 5G 27
   (off Boscobel Cres.)
Tong St. WS1: Wals 2E 49
Topcroft Rd. B23: Erd 6F 69
Topfield Ho. B14: King H 6G 147
Top Fld. Wlk. B14: King H 5F 147
Topland Gro. B31: Longb 5A 144
Top Rd. B61: Wild 4A 156
Topsham Cft. B14: King H 2F 147
Topsham Rd. B67: Smeth 3C 98
Torfield WV8: Pend 5C 14
Tor Lodge Dr. WV6: Tett 1H 41
Toronto Gdns. B32: Harb 5C 114
Torre Av. B31: N'fld 5C 144
Torrey Rd. B8: W End 5A 104
Torridge Dr. WV11: Wed 4E 29
Torridon Cft. B13: Mose 2F 133
Torridon Rd. WV12: W'hall 6B 18
Torvale Rd. WV6: Tett 1G 41
Tor Way WS3: Pels 4D 20
Totnes Gro. B29: S Oak 3B 132
Totnes Rd. B67: Smeth 3D 98
Tottenham Cres. B44: K'sdng 3B 68
Touchwood B91: Sol 4G 151
Touchwood Hall Cl. B91: Sol 3G 151
Tourist Info. Cen.
   Birmingham, Corporation St.
   . . . . .4E 5 (1G 117)
   Birmingham, Paradise Cir. Queensway
   . . . . .4C 4 (1F 117)
   Birmingham Airport 1E 139
   Solihull 4G 151
   Wolverhampton 2B 170 (1H 43)
Towcester Cft. B36: Hodg H 1B 104
Tower Cft. B37: F'bri 5D 106
TOWER HILL 1D 82
Tower Hill B42: Gt Barr 1C 82
Tower Lodge DY8: Word 5C 92
Tower Ri. B69: Tiv 2C 96
Tower Rd. B6: Aston 2H 101
   (not continuous)
   B23: Erd 4E 85
   B69: Tiv 2C 96
   B75: Four O 6H 37
Tower St. B19: Birm 4F 101
   DY1: Dud 6E 77
   DY3: Sed 4H 59
   WS1: Wals .1C 48
   WV1: Wolv 3C 170 (1H 43)
Tower Vw. Rd. WS6: Gt Wyr 5F 7
Townend St. WS2: Wals 1C 48
Townfold WS3: Pels 3E 21
Town Gate Retail Pk. DY1: Dud 5H 77
Town Hall Stop (Metro) 4A 80
Town Hill WS1: Wals 2D 48
Townley Gdns. B6: Aston 6G 83
Townsend Av. DY3: Sed 5H 59
Townsend Dr. B76: Walm 6D 70
Townsend Pl. DY6: K'wfrd 3B 92
Townsend Way B1: Birm 3A 4 (6D 100)
Townshend Gro. B37: K'hrst 5B 106
Townson Rd. WV11: Wed 1A 30
Townwell Fold WV1: Wolv 3A 170 (1G 43)
Town Wharf Bus. Pk. WS2: Wals 2B 48
Town Yd. WV13: W'hall 2A 46
Towpath Cl. B9: Birm 1B 118
Towpath Way B14: King H 3E 147
Towyn Rd. B13: Mose 3D 134
Toy's La. B63: Crad 6E 111
Tozer St. DY4: Tip 6H 61
Traceys Mdw. B45: Redn 2G 157
Tractor Spares Ind. Est.
   WV13: W'hall 1F 45
Trafalgar Ct. B69: Tiv 6B 78

Trafalgar Gro. B25: Yard 5G 119
Trafalgar Rd. B13: Mose 2H 133
   B21: Hand .1A 100
   B24: Erd 4F 85
   B66: Smeth .5F 99
   B69: Tiv 6B 78
Trafalgar Ter. B66: Smeth 5F 99
Trajan Hill B46: Col 6H 89
Tram Way B66: Smeth 2A 98
Tramway Cl. WS10: Darl 4E 47
   WV14: Bils .4H 45
Tranter Rd. B8: W End 4G 103
Tranwell Cl. WV9: Pend 5D 14
Traquain Dr. DY1: Dud 4C 76
Travellers Way B37: Chel W 6F 107
Treaford La. B8: W End 5H 103
Treddles La. B70: W Brom 4B 80
Tredington Cl. B29: W Cas 6E 131
Tree Acre Gro. B63: Crad 1E 127
Treeford Cl. B91: Sol 6D 150
Treeside Way B31: N'fld 5E 145
Trees Rd. WS1: Wals 5D 48
Treeton Cft. B33: Yard 1E 121
Tree Tops WV5: Wom 5E 57
Treetops Dr. WV12: W'hall 4E 31
Trefoil Cl. B29: W Cas 6E 131
   (not continuous)
Trefoil Gdns. DY8: Amb 5E 109
Tregaron Dr. B31: N'fld 1C 144
Tregarron Rd. B63: Crad 6E 111
Tregea Ri. B43: Gt Barr 6G 65
Trehern Cl. B93: Know 4C 166
Trehernes Dr. DY9: Pedm 4F 125
Trehurst Av. B42: Gt Barr 5E 67
Trejon Rd. B64: Crad H 3G 111
Tremaine Gdns. WV10: Wolv 5H 27
Tremont Ho. WV10: Wolv 6B 28
Tremont St. WV10: Wolv 6A 28
Trenchard Cl. B75: S Cold 6D 54
Trent Cl. DY8: Stourb 1E 125
   WV6: Pert 5E 25
Trent Ct. B73: S Cold 6H 53
Trent Cres. B47: Wyt 6G 161
Trent Dr. B36: Cas B 1B 106
Trentham Av. WV12: W'hall 4A 30
Trentham Gro. B26: Yard 6C 120
Trentham Ri. WV2: Ett 4B 44
Trent Pl. WS3: Blox 1B 32
Trent Rd. WS3: Pels 6E 21
Trent St. B5: Birm 5H 5 (1H 117)
Trent Twr. B7: Birm 5A 102
Trenville Av. B11: S'hll 6B 118
   B12: Bal H .6B 118
Tresco Cl. B45: Fran 6E 143
TRESCOTT 4B 40
Trescott Rd. B31: N'fld 4B 144
Tresham Rd. B44: Gt Barr 4H 67
   DY6: K'wfrd 1B 92
Trevanie Av. B32: Quin 5A 114
Trevelyan Ho. B37: Chel W 2E 123
Trevor Av. WS6: Gt Wyr 2G 7
Trevorne Cl. B12: Bal H 5H 117
Trevor Rd. WS3: Pels 3D 20
Trevor St. B7: Nech 3C 102
Trevor St. Ind. Est. B7: Nech 3C 102
Trevor St. W. B7: Nech 3C 102
Trevose Cl. WS3: Blox 4F 19
Trevose Retreat B12: Bal H 6H 117
Trewman Cl. B76: Walm 5D 70
Treyamon Rd. WV5: Wals 4H 49
Treynham Cl. WV1: Wolv 2E 45
TRIANGLE 1D 10
Triangle, The B18: Hock 3A 100
Trickley Dr. B75: S Cold 5D 54
Tricorn Ho. B16: Edg 2C 116
Trident Blvd. B35: Cas V 5F 87
Trident Cen. DY1: Dud 6E 77
Trident Cl. B23: Erd 6G 69
   B76: Walm .6D 70
Trident Ct. B20: Hand 4C 82
   B37: Mars G 3G 123
Trident Dr. B68: O'bry 4H 97
   WS10: W'bry 2D 62
Trident Ho. B15: Birm 6A 4 (2E 117)
Trident Retail Pk. B9: Birm 1A 118
Trident Rd. B26: Birm A 1E 139
Trigen Ho. B90: Bly P 6D 164

Trigo Cft.—Ullswater Cl.

Trigo Cft. B36: Hodg H 1C **104**
Trillenium B46: Col 5H **89**
Trimpley Cl. B93: Dorr 6A **166**
Trimpley Gdns. WV4: Penn 2C **58**
Trimpley Rd. B32: Bart G 5H **129**
Trinder Rd. B67: Smeth 1B **114**
Trindle Cl. DY2: Dud 6F **77**
Trindle Rd. DY2: Dud 6F **77**
Tring Ct. WV6: Wolv 5D **26**
Trinity Cen. B64: Old H 1G **111**
Trinity Cl. B19: Loz 6F **83**
B92: Olton 4F **137**
DY8: Word 1B **108**
Trinity Ct. B6: Aston 6F **83**
B13: Mose 3B **134**
B64: Old H 2G **111**
WV3: Wolv 1E **43**
WV10: F'hses 2A **16**
Trinity Gro. WS10: W'bry 2G **63**
Trinity Hill B72: S Cold 6A **54**
Trinity Ho. B1: Birm 6C **4**
B6: Aston 6F **83**
*B70: W Brom 6C **80***
(off Florence Rd.)
Trinity Pk. B37: Mars G 2F **139**
Trinity Pl. B72: S Cold 6A **54**
Trinity Rd. B6: Aston 6F **83**
B75: Four O 2H **53**
DY1: Dud 6E **77**
DY8: Amb 3E **109**
WV12: W'hall 3D **30**
WV14: Bils 6H **45**
Trinity Rd. Nth. B70: W Brom 6B **80**
(not continuous)
Trinity Rd. Sth. B70: W Brom 6B **80**
Trinity St. B64: Old H 2G **111**
B67: Smeth 3E **99**
B69: O'bry 4G **97**
B70: W Brom 5B **80**
DY5: Brie H 6H **93**
Trinity Ter. B11: S'brk 3A **118**
Trinity Way B20: Hand 6D **82**
B70: W Brom 6B **80**
Trinity Way Stop (Metro) **6B 80**
Trippleton Av. B32: Bart G 5H **129**
Tristram Av. B31: N'fld 6F **145**
Triton Cl. WS6: Gt Wyr 4F **7**
Trittiford Rd. B13: Mose 1B **148**
Triumph Wlk. B36: Cas B 6C **88**
Tromans Cl. B64: Crad H 4G **111**
Tromans Ind. Est. DY2: Neth 6F **95**
Troon Cl. B75: S Cold 3B **54**
WS3: Blox 4G **19**
Troon Ct. WV6: Pert 4D **24**
Troon Pl. DY8: Word 6A **92**
Trostrey Rd. B30: King Nor 4F **147**
Trotter's La. B71: W Brom 6G **63**
Trouse La. WS10: W'bry 2E **63**
Troutbeck Dr. DY5: Brie H 3F **109**
Troy Gro. B14: King H 3F **147**
Truck Stop Bus. Pk. B11: Tys 6H **119**
Truda St. WS1: Wals 4B **48**
TRUEMAN'S HEATH **2C 162**
Trueman's Heath La. B47: H'wd 2B **162**
B90: Maj G 2B **162**
Trundalls La. B90: Dic H 4G **163**
Truro Cl. B65: Row R 5E **97**
Truro Rd. WS5: Wals 4H **49**
Truro Twr. B16: Birm 1C **116**
Truro Wlk. B37: Chel W 1C **122**
Trustin Cres. B92: Sol 5A **138**
Tryon Pl. WV14: Bils 5G **45**
TRYSULL **4C 56**
Trysull Av. B26: Sheld 1G **137**
Trysull Gdns. WV3: Wolv 4B **42**
Trysull Holloway WV5: Try 1C **56**
Trysull Rd. WV3: Wolv 4B **42**
WV5: Wom 5E **57**
Trysull Way DY2: Neth 6E **95**
Tudbury Rd. B31: N'fld 3B **144**
Tudman Cl. B76: Walm 6E **71**
Tudor Cl. B13: Mose 1H **147**
B14: King H 6A **148**
B73: New O 3D **68**
CV7: Bal C 3G **169**
WS6: C Hay 2E **7**
Tudor Coppice B91: Sol 5F **151**
Tudor Ct. B1: Birm 3A **4**
B72: S Cold 6A **54**
B74: Four O 1G **53**
DY4: Tip 3A **78**
WV11: Ess 4H **17**
Tudor Cres. WV2: Wolv 5F **43**
Tudor Cft. B37: F'bri 2B **122**
Tudor Eaves B17: Harb 6G **115**
Tudor Gdns. B23: Erd 4E **85**
DY8: Stourb 6C **108**
Tudor Grange Leisure Cen. **4F 151**
Tudor Grange Pk. **4E 151**
Tudor Gro. B74: S'tly 3A **52**
TUDOR HILL **5H 53**
Tudor Hill B73: S Cold 5G **53**
Tudor Ind. Est. B11: Tys 6H **119**
Tudor Pk. Ct. B74: Four O 6F **37**
Tudor Pl. DY3: Up Gor 1A **76**
Tudor Rd. B13: Mose 3H **133**
B65: Row R 4C **96**
B68: O'bry 5A **98**
B73: S Cold 6H **53**
DY3: Up Gor 1A **76**
WV10: Wolv 5C **28**
WV14: Bils 1B **62**
Tudors Cl. B10: Small H 3C **118**
Tudor St. B18: Win G 5H **99**
DY4: Tip 3A **78**
Tudor Ter. B17: Harb 5G **115**
DY2: Dud 6G **77**
Tudor Va. DY3: Up Gor 1A **76**
Tudor Way B72: W Grn 3H **69**
WS6: C Hay 4D **6**
Tufnell Gro. B8: W End 2G **103**
Tugford Rd. B29: W Cas 6G **131**
Tulip Gdns. B29: W Cas 6D **130**
Tulip Gro. B74: S'tly 4H **51**
Tulip Wlk. B37: Chel W 3E **123**
Tulsi Cen. B19: Birm 5E **101**
Tulyar Cl. B36: Hodg H 1A **104**
Tumble Jungle **2D 146**
Tumbler Gro. WV10: Wolv 6B **28**
Tunnel La. B14: King H 3E **147**
B30: King Nor, King H 3D **146**
Tunnel Rd. B70: W Brom 5G **63**
Tunnel St. WV14: Cose 5E **61**
Tunstall Rd. DY6: K'wfrd 4E **93**
Turchill Dr. B76: Walm 5E **71**
Turf Cl. WS11: Nort C 1E **9**
Turfpits La. B23: Erd 1D **84**
Turf Pitts La. B75: Can 6D **38**
(not continuous)
Turks Head Way B70: W Brom 5A **80**
Turley St. DY1: Dud 1C **76**
Turls Hill Rd. DY3: Sed 5A **60**
WV14: Cose 6A **60**
Turls St. DY3: Sed 5A **60**
Turnberry Cl. WV6: Pert 4D **24**
Turnberry Rd. B42: Gt Barr 5D **66**
WS3: Blox 4F **19**
Turner Av. WV14: Cose 3B **60**
Turner Dr. DY5: Quar B 4H **109**
Turner Gro. WV6: Pert 5G **25**
Turners Cft. B71: W Brom 5E **65**
Turners Gro. DY3: Lwr G 3G **75**
TURNER'S HILL **3B 96**
Turner's Hill B65: Row R 3B **96**
Turners Hill Rd. DY3: Lwr G 3G **75**
Turner's La. DY5: Brie H 3G **109**
Turner St. B11: S'brk 5A **118**
B70: W Brom 3G **79**
DY1: Dud 1D **94**
DY3: Lwr G 4H **75**
DY4: Tip 6H **61**
Turney Rd. DY8: Stourb 5D **108**
Turnham Grn. WV6: Pert 6E **25**
Turnhouse Rd. B35: Cas V 3F **87**
Turnley Rd. B34: S End 3G **105**
Turnpike Cl. B11: S'brk 5A **118**
CV7: Bal C 2H **169**
Turnpike Dr. B46: Wat O 4E **89**
Turnstone Dr. WV10: F'stne 1D **16**
Turton Cl. WS3: Blox 3G **19**
Turton Rd. B70: W Brom 5H **79**
DY4: Tip 4H **61**
Turtons Cft. WV14: Cose 2D **60**
TURVES GREEN **1E 159**
Turves Grn. B31: Longb, N'fld 2D **158**
Turves Green Community Leisure Cen. **6E 145**
Turville Rd. B20: Hand 6E **83**
Tustin Gro. B27: A Grn 5A **136**
Tutbury Av. WV6: Pert 6F **25**
Tuxford Cl. WV10: Wolv 5A **28**
Twatling Rd. B45: B Grn, Lick 6G **157**
Tweeds Well B32: Bart G 6H **129**
Twickenham Ct. DY8: Woll 4A **108**
Twickenham Dr. B13: Mose 3G **133**
Twickenham Rd. B44: K'sdng 4B **68**
Two Gates B63: Crad 6D **110**
Two Gates La. B63: Crad 6E **111**
Two Locks DY5: Brie H 5B **94**
Two Woods La. DY5: Brie H 2A **110**
Twycross Gro. B36: Hodg H 2B **104**
Twydale Av. B69: Tiv 5C **78**
Twyford Cl. WS9: A'rdge 4D **34**
Twyford Gro. WV11: Wed 2H **29**
Twyford Rd. B8: W End 4A **104**
Twyning Rd. B16: Edg 5H **99**
B30: Stir 6D **132**
Tybalt Cl. WV10: Bush 3A **28**
Tyber Dr. B20: Hand 4D **82**
Tyberry Cl. B90: Shir 6G **149**
TYBURN **4D 86**
Tyburn Av. B24: Erd 4B **86**
Tyburn Gro. B24: Erd 4B **86**
Tyburn Ind. Est. B24: Cas V 5B **86**
Tyburn Rd. B24: Erd 6D **84**
WV1: Wolv 2E **45**
Tyburn Sq. B24: Erd 4B **86**
Tyebeams B34: S End 4G **105**
Tye Gdns. DY9: Pedm 4F **125**
Tyler Ct. B24: Erd 4F **85**
Tyler Gdns. WV13: W'hall 2B **46**
Tyler Gro. B43: Gt Barr 4C **66**
Tyler Rd. WV13: W'hall 3A **46**
Tylers Grn. B38: King Nor 5D **146**
Tylers Gro. B90: M'path 3D **164**
Tylney Cl. B5: Edg 4F **117**
Tyndale Cres. B43: Gt Barr 2E **67**
Tyndall Wlk. B32: Bart G 3G **129**
Tyne Cl. B37: F'bri 5D **106**
WS8: Bwnhls 3G **9**
Tyne Ct. B73: S Cold 6H **53**
Tynedale Cres. WV4: Ett 2A **60**
Tynedale Rd. B11: Tys 2F **135**
Tyne Gro. B25: Yard 3B **120**
Tyne Pl. DY5: Quar B 1B **110**
Tyning Cl. WV9: Pend 5E **15**
Tyninghame Av. WV6: Tett 3B **26**
Tynings La. WS9: A'rdge 4C **34**
Tyrley Cl. WV6: Tett 1H **41**
Tyrol Cl. DY8: Woll 6B **108**
TYSELEY **1G 135**
Tyseley Hill Rd. B11: Tys 1G **135**
Tyseley Ind. Est. B11: Tys 6E **119**
Tyseley La. B11: Tys 1G **135**
Tyseley Station (Rail) **6G 119**
Tysoe Dr. B76: Walm 1D **70**
Tysoe Rd. B44: K'sdng 6H **67**
Tythebarn Dr. DY6: W Hth 2G **91**
Tythe Barn La. B90: Dic H 3E **163**
(not continuous)
Tyzack Cl. DY5: Brie H 1G **109**

U

Udall Rd. WV14: Cose 2F **61**
Uffculme Rd. B30: Stir 5F **133**
Uffmoor Est. B63: Hale 3G **127**
Uffmoor La. B62: Roms, Hale 6F **127**
B63: Hale 4G **127**
Ufton Cl. B90: Shir 4C **150**
Ufton Cres. B90: Shir 4B **150**
Ullenhall Rd. B76: Walm 4D **70**
B93: Know 3C **166**
Ullenwood B21: Hand 2H **99**
Ulleries Rd. B92: Olton 3D **136**
Ullrik Grn. B24: Erd 5F **85**
Ullswater Cl. B32: Bart G 3D **130**

Ullswater Gdns. DY6: K'wfrd 3B 92
Ullswater Ho. B69: O'bry 4D 96
Ullswater Ri. DY5: Brie H 4H 93
Ullswater Rd. WV12: W'hall 6B 18
Ulster Dr. DY6: K'wfrd 5C 92
Ulverley Cl. B92: Olton 5D 136
Ulverley Cres. B92: Olton 5D 136
ULVERLEY GREEN 5D 136
Ulverley Grn. Rd. B92: Olton 4C 136
Umberslade Rd. B29: S Oak 4B 132
  B30: Stir .6C 132
Uncle Ben's Cl. B69: O'bry 5F 97
Underhill La. WV10: Bush 4B 16
Underhill Rd. B8: Salt 6F 103
  DY4: Tip .1C 78
Underhill St. B69: O'bry 4G 97
Underhill Wlk. B69: O'bry 4G 97
Underley Cl. DY6: W Hth 2H 91
Underpass, The B40: Nat E C 1F 139
Underwood Cl. B15: Edg 2H 131
  B23: Erd 3C 84
Underwood Rd. B20: Hand 2A 82
Unett Ct. B66: Smeth 4G 99
Unett St. B19: Birm 4E 101
  B66: Smeth 5G 99
Unett St. Nth.
  B19: Birm, Hock 4E 101
Unett Wlk. B19: Birm 4E 101
Union Dr. B73: Bold 3F 69
Union La. WV5: Try 4D 56
Union Mill St. WV1: Wolv 1A 44
Union Pas. B2: Birm 4E 5 (1G 117)
Union Pl. B29: S Oak 3D 132
Union Rd. B6: Aston 1B 102
  B69: O'bry .6E 79
  B70: W Brom 5F 79
  B90: Shir .5A 150
  B91: Sol 3G 151
Union Row B21: Hand 1B 100
Union St. B2: Birm 4E 5 (1G 117)
  B65: B'hth 2C 112
  B70: W Brom 1B 98
  DY2: Dud .6E 77
  DY4: Tip 2H 77
    (Albion St.)
  DY4: Tip 5H 61
    (Greensill Av.)
  DY8: Stourb 1E 125
  DY9: Lye .6A 110
  WS1: Wals 1D 48
  WS10: W'bry 3F 63
  WV1: Wolv 3D 170 (1H 43)
  WV13: W'hall 1A 46
  WV14: Bils .6E 45
Unisant Trad. Est.
  B64: Old H 1H 111
Unitt Dr. B64: Old H 3G 111
Unity Cl. WS10: Darl 1C 62
Unity Pl. B29: S Oak 3B 132
  B69: O'bry .1G 97
Unity Wlk. DY4: Tip 2G 77
University College Birmingham
  Lionel St. 3B 4 (6F 101)
  Newhall St. 3C 4
  Postgraduate Centre . . .2B 4 (6E 101)
University of Birmingham
  Edgbaston Campus 1B 132
  Selly Oak Campus 5H 131
University of Wolverhampton
  City Campus 2B 170 (1G 43)
  Compton Pk. Campus 1B 42
  Molineux St. 1B 170 (6G 27)
  Walsall Campus 4E 49
University Rd. E. B15: Edg 1B 132
University Rd. W. B15: Edg 1B 132
University Station (Rail) 1A 132
Unketts Rd. B67: Smeth 6C 98
Unwin Cres. DY8: Stourb 6C 108
Upavon Cl. B35: Cas V 3E 87
Upland Rd. B29: S Oak 3C 132
Uplands B63: Hale 3F 127
Uplands, The B67: Smeth 4D 98
Uplands Av. B65: Row R 6D 96
  WV3: Wolv .3B 42
  WV13: W'hall 2F 45
Uplands Cl. DY2: Dud 2H 95

Uplands Dr. DY3: Sed 5H 59
  WV3: Wolv .3C 42
  WV5: Wom .1G 73
Uplands Gro. WV13: W'hall 2E 45
Uplands Rd. B21: Hand 5H 81
  DY2: Dud .2G 95
  WV13: W'hall 2E 45
Up. Ashley St. B62: B'hth 2C 112
Up. Balsall Heath Rd. B12: Bal H . . .5H 117
Up. Brook St. WS2: Wals 2B 48
Up. Castle St. WS10: Darl 3D 46
Up. Chapel St. B69: Tiv 5B 78
Up. Church La. DY4: Tip 5H 61
Up. Clifton Rd. B73: S Cold 6H 53
Upper Cl. B32: Bart G 2B 130
Up. Conybere St. B12: Birm 4H 117
Up. Dean St. B5: Birm 6E 5 (2G 117)
Up. Ettingshall Rd. WV14: Cose 5C 60
Up. Forster St. WS4: Wals 6D 32
UPPER GORNAL 2A 76
Up. Gough St. B1: Birm 6C 4 (2F 117)
Upper Grn. WV6: Tett 4B 26
Up. Grosvenor Rd. B20: Hand 5D 82
Upper Hall La. WS1: Wals 2C 48
Up. Highgate St. B12: Birm 4H 117
Up. High St. B64: Crad H 2F 111
  WS10: W'bry 2F 63
Up. Holland Rd. B72: S Cold 1A 70
UPPER LANDYWOOD 5E 7
Up. Landywood La.
  WS6: C Hay, Gt Wyr 4D 6
Up. Lichfield St. WV13: W'hall 1A 46
Upper Mall B5: Birm 5E 5
Up. Mall E. B5: Birm 5F 5 (1G 117)
Up. Mall W. B5: Birm 5E 5 (1G 117)
Up. Marshall St. B1: Birm 6C 4
Up. Meadow Rd. B32: Quin 6A 114
Up. Navigation St. WS2: Wals 1B 48
Up. Portland St. B6: Aston 2A 102
Up. Rushall St. WS1: Wals 2D 48
Up. Russell St. WS10: W'bry 3F 63
Up. St Mary's Rd. B67: Smeth 2D 114
Up. Short St. WS2: Wals 2B 48
Up. Sneyd Rd. WV11: Ess 5B 18
Up. Stone Cl. B76: Walm 1C 70
Upper St. WV6: Tett 4B 26
Up. Sutton St. B6: Aston 2H 101
Up. Thomas St. B6: Aston 2H 101
    (not continuous)
Up. Trinity St. B9: Birm 2A 118
Upper Vauxhall WV1: Wolv 1E 43
Up. Villiers St. WV2: Wolv 5G 43
Up. William St. B1: Birm 6A 4 (2E 117)
Up. Zoar St. WV3: Wolv 3F 43
Upton Ct. B23: Frd 4B 84
    (off Alwynn Wlk.)
Upton Gdns. WV14: Bils 6E 45
Upton Gro. WV10: F'hses 4F 15
Upton Gro. B33: Stech 2A 120
Upton Rd. B33: Stech 1A 120
Upton St. DY2: Neth 4E 95
Upwey Av. B91: Sol 3E 151
Urban Ga. B23: Erd 3D 84
USAM Trad. Est. WV10: F'hses 5H 15
Usk Cl. WS3: Blox 1B 32
Usk Way B36: Cas B 1B 106
Uttoxeter Cl. WV6: Wolv 3F 27
Uxbridge Cl. DY3: Lwr G 4H 75
Uxbridge St. WS7: Chase 1A 10
Uxbridge St. B19: Birm 4F 101

Valentine Rd. B14: King H 4G 133
  B68: O'bry .1A 114
Valepits Rd. B33: Sheld 2G 121
Valerian B74: Four O 5F 37
Valerie Gro. B43: Gt Barr 5G 65
Vale Rd. DY2: Neth 5G 95
Vale Row DY3: Up Gor 2H 75
Vales Cl. B76: Walm 6C 70
Vale St. B71: W Brom 1C 80
  DY3: Up Gor 2H 75
  DY8: Amb .3E 109
  WV2: Ett 5C 44
Vale Vw. WS9: A'rdge 6D 34
VALE VILLAGE, THE 5C 116
Valiant Ho. B35: Cas V 2F 87
Valiant Way B92: Sol 5G 137
Valley Farm Rd. B45: Rub 3F 157
Valley Grn. WS6: C Hay 3E 7
Valley Rd. B43: Gt Barr 6G 65
  B62: B'hth .3F 113
  B64: Crad H 4G 111
  B67: Smeth 6D 98
  B74: S'tly 4H 51
  B92: Sol 2G 137
  DY3: Up Gor 1A 76
  DY9: Lye .6B 110
  WS3: Blox .1A 32
  WV10: Wolv 4B 28
Valleyside WS3: Pels 5D 20
Valley Vw. WS8: Bwnhls 6C 10
Vallian Cft. B36: Hodg H 2D 104
Valliant Way WV9: Coven 3F 15
Vanborough Wlk. DY1: Dud 5C 76
Vanbrugh Ct. WV6: Pert 6E 25
Van Diemans Rd. WV5: Wom 2E 73
Vanguard Cl. B36: Hodg H 1C 104
Vanguard Rd. B26: Birm A 1E 139
Vann Cl. B10: Small H 3C 118
    (not continuous)
Vantage Point B70: W Brom 5A 80
    (off Blacksmith Way)
Vantage Way B24: Erd 6B 86
Varden Cft. B5: Edg 4F 117
Vardon Way B38: King Nor 6H 145
Varley Rd. B24: Erd 3B 86
Varley Va. B24: Erd 3B 86
Varlins Way B38: King Nor 2H 159
Varney Av. B70: W Brom 5B 80
Varney Bus. Pk. B70: W Brom 5B 80
    (off Varney Av.)
Vaughan Cl. B74: Four O 3F 37
Vaughan Gdns. WV8: Cod 3F 13
Vaughan Rd. WV13: W'hall 2F 45
Vaughan Trad. Est. DY4: Tip 3B 78
Vaughton Dr. B75: S Cold 5C 54
Vaughton Ho. B15: Edg 4E 117
Vaughton St. B12: Birm 3H 117
Vaughton St. Sth. B5: Birm 3G 117
  B12: Birm .3G 117
VAUXHALL 4C 102
Vauxhall Av. WV1: Wolv 1E 43
Vauxhall Bus. Pk. B/: Birm 4C 102
Vauxhall Cres. B36: Cas B 6B 88
Vauxhall Gdns. DY2: Dud 2G 95
Vauxhall Gro. B7: Birm 6B 102
Vauxhall Ho. WV1: Wolv 1E 43
    (off Upper Vauxhall)
Vauxhall Pl. B7: Birm 6A 102
Vauxhall Rd. B7: Birm 6A 102
  DY8: Stourb 6E 109
Vauxhall St. DY1: Dud 1D 94
Vauxhall Ter. B7: Birm 5B 102
Vauxhall Trad. Est. B7: Birm 5B 102
Vector Ind. Pk. B71: W Brom 1A 80
Velsheda Rd. B90: Shir 5G 149
Venetia Rd. B9: Bord G 1C 118
Venice Ct. B13: Mose 3B 134
Venning Gro. B43: Gt Barr 6H 65
Ventnor Av. B19: Hock 2E 101
  B36: Hodg H 2B 104
Ventnor Cl. B68: O'bry 4A 114
Ventnor Rd. B92: Sol 2G 137
Venture Ct. WV10: F'hses 2H 15
Venture Way B7: Birm 1H 5 (5H 101)
  DY5: Brie H .6H 93
Vera Rd. B26: Yard 4C 120

V

Valbourne Rd. B14: King H 3E 147
Vale, The B11: S'hll 3C 134
  B15: Edg .5C 116
    (not continuous)
Vale Av. DY3: Up Gor 1H 75
  WS9: A'rdge 6F 35
Vale Cl. B32: Bart G 2D 130
Vale Ct. B64: Crad H 4F 111
Vale Head Dr. WV6: Tett 1G 41
Valencia Cft. B35: Cas V 3F 87
Valentine Cl. B74: S'tly 5H 51
Valentine Ct. B14: King H 4H 133

Verbena Gdns. B7: Birm 4A **102**
Verbena Rd. B31: N'fld 1D **144**
Vercourt B74: Lit As 6B **36**
Verdun Cres. DY2: Dud 5H **77**
Vere St. B5: Birm 3F **117**
Verity Wlk. DY8: Word 2C **108**
Verney Av. B33: Sheld 4H **121**
Vernier Av. DY6: K'wfrd 4E **93**
Vernolds Cft. B5: Birm 3G **117**
Vernon Av. B20: Hand 3B **82**
   DY4: Tip .3G **77**
   WS8: Bwnhls 5C **10**
Vernon Cl. B62: B'hth 3C **112**
   B74: Four O 4E **37**
   WV11: Ess 3H **17**
   WV13: W'hall 2G **45**
Vernon Ct. B16: Edg 2A **116**
Vernon Pk. WV10: F'stne 2E **17**
Vernon Rd. B16: Edg 2H **115**
   B62: B'hth 3C **112**
   B68: O'bry 3A **98**
   WV14: Bils 5H **45**
Vernon St. B70: W Brom 4E **79**
Vernon Trad. Est. B62: B'hth 3C **112**
Vernon Way WS3: Blox 6D **18**
Verona Ct. WV10: Wolv 5C **28**
Veronica Av. WV4: Ett 6A **44**
Veronica Cl. B29: W Cas 1D **144**
Veronica Rd. DY6: K'wfrd 3E **93**
Verstone Cft. B31: N'fld 4E **145**
Verstone Rd. B90: Shir 3A **150**
Verwood Cl. WV13: W'hall 2F **45**
Vesey Cl. B46: Wat O 5D **88**
   B74: Four O 1F **53**
Vesey Rd. B73: W Grn 4H **69**
Vesey St. B4: Birm 1E **5** (5G **101**)
Vestry Cl. B64: Old H 2H **111**
Vestry Ct. DY8: Woll 5C **108**
Viaduct Dr. WV6: Wolv 3F **27**
Viaduct St. B7: Birm 6A **102**
Vibart Rd. B26: Yard 3D **120**
Vicarage Cl. B30: Stir 6E **133**
   B42: Gt Barr 6F **67**
   DY4: Tip .2G **77**
   DY5: Brie H 3G **109**
   WS8: Bwnhls 6C **10**
   (not continuous)
Vicarage Gdns. B62: B'hth 2D **112**
   B65: B'hth 2C **112**
   B76: Walm 6D **70**
Vicarage Gro. B27: A Grn 5H **135**
Vicarage La. B46: Wat O 5D **88**
   DY5: P'ntt 1H **93**
Vicarage Pl. WS1: Wals 2C **48**
Vicarage Prospect
   DY1: Dud 6D **76**
Vicarage Ri. B43: Gt Barr 1A **66**
Vicarage Rd. B6: Aston 2A **102**
   (not continuous)
   B14: King H 1E **147**
   B15: Edg 3B **116**
   B17: Harb 6F **115**
   B18: Hock 2C **100**
   B33: Yard 2C **120**
   B62: B'hth 2C **112**
   B67: Smeth 4D **98**
   B68: O'bry 5H **97**
   B71: W Brom 1B **80**
   B94: Earls 6A **164**
   DY3: Up Gor 2B **76**
   DY5: Brie H 4G **109**
   DY8: Amb 4E **109**
   DY8: Woll 4A **108**
   DY9: Lye 6B **110**
   WS3: Pels 5E **21**
   WS8: Bwnhls 6B **10**
   WS10: W'bry 2F **63**
   WV2: Wolv 6D **170** (3H **43**)
   WV4: Penn 2B **58**
   WV11: Wed 3D **28**
   WV14: Cose 6E **61**
Vicarage Rd. Sth. DY9: Lye 6A **110**
Vicarage Rd. W. DY1: Dud 1D **76**
Vicarage St. B68: O'bry 4H **97**
Vicarage Ter. WS2: Wals 3A **48**
Vicarage Wlk. WS1: Wals 2C **48**

Vicar St. DY2: Dud 6E **77**
   DY3: Sed 5H **59**
   WS10: W'bry 2G **63**
Vicars Wlk. DY9: W'cte 3A **126**
Viceroy Cl. B5: Edg 5E **117**
   DY6: K'wfrd 4E **93**
Victor Cl. WV2: Ett 5D **44**
Victoria Arc. WV1: Wolv 3B **170**
Victoria Av. B10: Small H 3D **118**
   B21: Hand 1B **100**
   B62: Quin 5F **113**
   B66: Smeth 4E **99**
   WS3: Blox 6H **19**
Victoria Bldgs. *B16: Birm* 6A **100**
   (off Barford Rd.)
Victoria Ct. B11: S'brk 5C **118**
   B13: Mose 1H **133**
   B62: Quin .4G **113**
   (off Binswood Rd.)
   B66: Smeth 3F **99**
   DY5: Brie H 6H **93**
   WS11: Nort C 1F **9**
Victoria Fold
   WV1: Wolv 4A **170** (2G **43**)
Victoria Gdns. B64: Old H 1H **111**
Victoria Gro. B18: Win G 5A **100**
   WV5: Wom 5G **57**
Victoria Hall B29: S Oak 2B **132**
Victoria Ho. *B16: Birm* 1D **116**
   (off Bellcroft)
   WS3: Blox 1B **32**
   WS10: Darl 5C **46**
   (off Wolverhampton St.)
Victoria M. B69: O'bry 6F **97**
   WS4: Wals 6E **33**
Victoriana Way B20: Hand 6C **82**
Victoria New Works WS10: Darl 3D **46**
Victoria Pk. Rd. B66: Smeth 4F **99**
Victoria Pas. DY8: Stourb 6E **109**
   WV1: Wolv 3B **170** (1G **43**)
Victoria Pl. WS10: W'bry 2G **63**
Victoria Rd. B6: Aston 2G **101**
   (not continuous)
   B17: Harb 6F **115**
   B21: Hand 2A **100**
   B23: Erd 4D **84**
   B27: A Grn 3A **136**
   (not continuous)
   B30: Stir 6C **132**
   B33: Stech 6B **104**
   B62: B'hth 2D **112**
   B64: Old H 1H **111**
   B68: O'bry 3A **98**
   B72: S Cold 6A **54**
   DY3: Sed 5A **60**
   DY4: Tip .2H **77**
   DY5: Quar B 2C **110**
   WS3: Pels 4E **21**
   WS10: Darl 5D **46**
   WV3: Wolv 4C **42**
   WV6: Tett 4C **26**
   WV10: Wolv 4B **28**
   WV11: Wed 3D **28**
Victoria Sq. B1: Birm 1F **117**
   B3: Birm 4C **4** (1F **117**)
   WV1: Wolv 3C **170**
Victoria St. B9: Small H 2D **118**
   B63: Hale 1A **128**
   B70: W Brom 2F **79**
   (John St.)
   B70: W Brom 4A **80**
   (Price St.)
   DY5: Brie H 6H **93**
   DY5: P'ntt 2G **93**
   DY6: W Hth 6H **73**
   DY8: Stourb 6E **109**
   WS10: W'bry 3E **63**
   WV1: Wolv 4B **170** (2G **43**)
   WV13: W'hall 6A **30**
Victoria Ter. WS4: Wals 6E **33**
Victoria Way B46: Col 4H **107**
Victor Rd. B18: Win G 3A **100**
   B92: Sol 2H **137**
Victor St. WS1: Wals 4C **48**
   WS3: Pels 6E **21**
Victor Twr. B7: Nech 3B **102**

Victory Av. B65: Row R 1B **112**
   WS10: Darl 1C **62**
Victory Ho. B13: Mose 1H **133**
Victory La. WS2: Wals 5G **31**
Victory Ri. B71: W Brom 2A **80**
View Dr. DY2: Dud 1G **95**
Viewfield Cres. DY3: Sed 6H **59**
Viewlands Dr. WV6: Tett 1G **41**
View Point B69: Tiv 1B **96**
VIGO **5B 22**
Vigo Cl. WS9: Wals W 5B **22**
Vigo Pl. WS9: A'rdge 1B **34**
Vigo Rd. WS9: Wals W 5B **22**
Vigo Ter. WS9: Wals W 5B **22**
Viking Ri. B65: Row R 5C **96**
Villa Cotts. *B19: Loz* 2D **100**
   (off Wills St.)
Villa Cross B19: Loz 2D **100**
VILLAGE, THE **2C 92**
Village, The DY6: K'wfrd 2C **92**
Village M. B32: Quin 5G **113**
Village M., The WV6: Tett 4A **26**
Village Rd. B6: Aston 6A **84**
Village Sq. B31: Longb 5A **144**
Village Wlk. WS10: W'bry 2H **63**
Village Way B76: Walm 5D **70**
   WS2: Wals 1G **47**
   WV14: Bils 6E **45**
Villa Park **6H 83**
Villa Rd. B19: Hock 2C **100**
Villa St. B19: Hock, Loz 2D **100**
   (not continuous)
   DY8: Amb 3E **109**
Villa Wlk. B19: Hock 3E **101**
Villette Gro. B14: Yard W 3C **148**
Villiers Av. WV14: Bils 4F **45**
Villiers Pl. WV14: Bils 4F **45**
Villiers Sq. WV14: Bils 4F **45**
Villiers St. B18: Win G 4A **100**
   WS1: Wals 4C **48**
   WV13: W'hall 1A **46**
Villiers Trad. Est.
   WV2: Wolv 4F **43**
Vimy Rd. B13: Mose 5B **134**
   WS10: W'bry 1G **63**
Vimy Ter. WS10: W'bry 1G **63**
Vincent Cl. B12: Bal H 5H **117**
Vincent Dr. B15: Edg 2H **131**
   (Roman Way)
   B15: Edg 1A **132**
   (Westgate)
Vincent Pde. B12: Bal H 5H **117**
Vincent Rd. B75: S Cold 4C **54**
Vincent St. B12: Bal H 6H **117**
   (not continuous)
   WS1: Wals 4D **48**
Vince St. B66: Smeth 6E **99**
Vinculum Way WV13: W'hall 3B **46**
Vine Av. B12: Bal H 6A **118**
Vine Cl. WV10: F'hses 4H **15**
Vine Cres. B71: W Brom 1B **80**
Vine Gdns. B64: Old H 1H **111**
Vine La. B27: A Grn 2B **136**
   B63: Hale 2B **128**
Vineries, The B27: A Grn 1B **136**
Vine St. B6: Aston 2B **102**
   DY5: Brie H 4A **94**
   DY8: Word 2C **108**
Vine Ter. B17: Harb 6G **115**
Vineyard Cl. B18: Hock 2B **100**
Vineyard Rd. B31: N'fld 2D **144**
Vinnall Gro. B32: Bart G 5H **129**
Vintage Cl. B34: Stech 4E **105**
Violet Cft. DY4: Tip 4C **62**
Virgin Active
   Solihull 6D **164**
   Birmingham, Broadway Plaza
   . . . . .2C **116**
   Birmingham, Star City 1D **102**
   (within Star City)
   Wolverhampton 2H **15**
Virginia Dr. WV4: Penn 1D **58**
Viscount Cl. B35: Cas V 5E **87**
Viscount Dr. B35: Cas V 5F **87**
Viscount Ho. B26: Birm A 1E **139**
Vista, The DY3: Sed 4H **59**

Vista Grn. B38: King Nor 6C **146**
Vittoria St. B1: Birm **1A 4** (5E **101**)
  B66: Smeth 3H **99**
Vivian Cl. B17: Harb 6G **115**
Vivian Rd. B17: Harb 6G **115**
Vixen Cl. B76: Walm 6B **70**
Vowles Rd. B71: W Brom 1B **80**
Vue Cinema
  Birmingham *1D* **102**
  (within Star City)
Vulcan Ind. Est. WS2: Wals 3A **32**
Vulcan Rd. B91: Sol 1G **151**
  WV14: Bils 6H **45**
Vulcan Rd. Ind. Est. B91: Sol 1G **151**
Vyrnwy Gro. B38: King Nor 1A **160**
Vyse St. B6: Aston 1B **102**
  B18: Birm **1A 4** (4E **101**)

W

Wadbarn B90: Dic H 4G **163**
Waddell Cl. WV14: Cose 3B **60**
Waddens Brook La. WV11: Wed 4G **29**
Waddens Brook (Nature Reserve) . . .5H **29**
Waddington Av. B43: Gt Barr 4A **66**
Wades Cl. DY4: Tip 2G **77**
Wadesmill Lawns WV10: Bush 3A **16**
Wadham Cl. B65: Row R 3C **96**
Wadham Ho. B37: Chel W 6E **107**
Wadham's Fold WV1: Wolv 2B **170**
Wadhurst Rd. B17: Edg 1F **115**
Wadley's Rd. B91: Sol 1D **150**
Waen Cl. DY4: Tip 5B **62**
Waggoners La. B78: Hints 2H **39**
Waggon St. B64: Old H 1H **111**
Waggon Wlk. B38: King Nor 1G **159**
  (not continuous)
Wagoners Cl. B8: Salt 3F **103**
Wagon La. B26: Sheld 6E **121**
  B92: Olton 1D **136**
Wagstaff Cl. WV14: Cose 5F **61**
Waine Ho. WS8: Bwnhls 1C **22**
Wainwright Dr. DY6: W Hth 1G **91**
  WV14: Bils 3G **61**
Wainwright St. B6: Aston 2A **102**
Waite Rd. WV13: W'hall 3G **45**
Wakefield Cl. B73: Bold 3G **69**
Wakefield Ct. B13: Mose 3B **134**
  B29: W Cas 6D **131**
  (off Abdon Av.)
Wakefield Gro. B46: Wat O 4D **88**
Wakeford Rd. B31: N'fld 6G **145**
WAKE GREEN 3B **134**
Wake Grn. Pk. B13: Mose 3B **134**
Wake Grn. Rd. B13: Mose 2H **133**
  DY4: Tip 4A **62**
Wakelam Gdns. B43: Gt Barr 4H **65**
Wakelams Fold DY3: Gorn 4G **75**
Wakeley Hill WV4: Penn 1D **58**
Wakelin Rd. B90: Shir 2H **163**
Wakeman Ct. WV11: Ess 4H **17**
Wakeman Dr. B69: Tiv 1B **96**
Wakeman Gro. B33: Sheld 4H **121**
Wakes Cl. WV13: W'hall 2B **46**
Wakes Rd. WS10: W'bry 3G **63**
Walcot Cl. B75: Four O 6H **37**
Walcot Dr. B43: Gt Barr 1B **82**
Walcot Gdns. WV14: Bils 1D **60**
Walcot Grn. B93: Dorr 6H **167**
Waldale Cl. WV11: Ess 6C **18**
Walden Gdns. WV4: Penn 5C **42**
Walden Rd. B11: Tys 2G **135**
Waldeve Gro. B92: Sol 5B **138**
Waldley Gro. B24: Erd 4A **86**
Waldon Wlk. B36: Cas B 1B **106**
Waldron Av. DY5: Brie H 1F **109**
Waldron Cl. WS10: W'bry 5F **47**
Waldrons Moor B14: King H 2E **147**
Walford Av. WV3: Wolv 3D **42**
Walford Dr. B92: Sol 2H **137**
Walford Grn. B32: Bart G 6H **129**
Walford Rd. B11: S'brk 5B **118**
Walford St. B69: Tiv 5A **78**

Walhouse Cl. WS1: Wals 1D **48**
Walhouse Rd. WS1: Wals 1D **48**
  (not continuous)
Walk, The DY3: Sed 4H **59**
Walker Av. B69: Tiv 2C **96**
  DY5: Quar B 4H **109**
  DY9: W'cte 2H **125**
  WV10: Bush 1A **28**
Walker Dr. B24: Erd 1E **103**
Walker Grange DY4: Tip 6H **61**
Walker Pl. WS3: Blox 1C **32**
Walker Rd. WS3: Blox 1B **32**
Walkers Fold WV12: W'hall 3D **30**
WALKER'S HEATH 5D **146**
Walkers Heath Rd.
  B38: King Nor 6D **146**
Walker St. DY2: Neth 5E **95**
  DY4: Tip 6B **62**
Walk La. WV5: Wom 6G **57**
Walkmill La. WS11: Cann 1D **6**
Wallace Cl. B69: O'bry 3D **96**
  WS11: Nort C 1D **8**
Wallace Ct. WS6: C Hay 4D **6**
Wallace Ho. B69: O'bry 4D **96**
Wallace Ri. B64: Crad H 4G **111**
Wallace Rd. B29: S Oak 3D **132**
  B69: O'bry 3D **96**
  WS8: Bwnhls 5A **10**
  WV14: Bils 2A **62**
Wall Av. B46: Col 4H **107**
Wallbank Cl. B8: W End 3G **103**
Wallbank Rd. B8: W End 3G **103**
WALLBROOK 5F **61**
Wallbrook St. WV14: Cose 5F **61**
Wall Cl. B67: Smeth 5B **98**
Wallcroft WS9: A'rdge 2D **34**
Wall Dr. B74: Four O 5F **37**
Wall End Cl. WS2: Wals 2G **31**
Wallface B71: W Brom 6G **63**
WALL HEATH 1H **91**
Wallheath Cres. WS11: Ston 2G **23**
Wallheath La. WS9: Ston 2H **23**
Walling Cft. WV14: Cose 2D **60**
Wallington Cl. WS3: Blox 5H **19**
WALLINGTON HEATH 5H **19**
Wallington Heath WS3: Blox 5H **19**
Wallis Ct. B13: Mose 3B **134**
Wallows Ind. Est., The DY5: Brie H 4H **93**
Wallows La. WS1: Wals 5A **48**
  WS2: Wals 5A **48**
Wallows Pl. DY5: Brie H 4G **93**
Wallows Rd. DY5: Brie H 5G **93**
Wallows Wood DY3: Lwr G 3E **75**
Wall St. WV1: Wolv 1D **44**
Wall Well B63: Hale 2H **127**
Wall Well La. B63: Hale 2H **127**
Walmead Cft. B17: Harb 4D **114**
Walmer Ct. B16: Edg 1H **115**
Walmer Gro. B23: Erd 2B **84**
Walmer Mdw. WS9: A'rdge 2D **34**
Walmers, The WS9: A'rdge 2D **34**
Walmer Wlk., The B31: Longb 6B **144**
Walmer Way B37: Chel W 6E **107**
Walmesley Way B31: N'fld 4C **144**
WALMLEY 5D **70**
WALMLEY ASH 2D **86**
Walmley Ash Cl. B76: Walm 5D **70**
Walmley Ash La. B76: Min, Walm 1F **87**
Walmley Ash Rd.
  B76: Walm, Min 6D **70**
Walmley Cl. B63: Crad 4D **110**
  B76: Walm 5D **70**
Walmley Golf Course 5A **70**
Walmley Pk. Ct. B76: Walm 5D **70**
Walmley Rd. B76: Walm 1C **70**
Walnut Av. WV8: Bilb 4G **13**
Walnut Cl. B37: Chel W 2D **122**
  DY9: Pedm 4F **125**
Walnut Dr. B66: Smeth 4F **99**
  WV3: Wolv 2B **42**
Walnut Ho. B20: Hand 4B **82**
Walnut La. WS10: W'bry 3G **63**
Walnut M. B29: W Cas 1E **145**
Walnut Rd. WS5: Wals 1E **65**
Walnut Way B31: Longb 1D **158**
Walpole St. WV6: Wolv 6E **27**

Walpole Wlk. B70: W Brom 6B **80**
WALSAL END 4A **154**
Walsal End La. B92: H Ard 4H **153**
WALSALL 2D **48**
Walsall Business Pk.
  WS9: A'rdge 6A **34**
Walsall Enterprise Pk. WS2: Wals 3A **48**
Walsall FC .5B **48**
Walsall Gala Baths 1D **48**
Walsall Golf Course 5E **49**
Walsall Local History Cen. 4C **32**
Walsall Mus. 1D **48**
Walsall New Firms Cen., The
  WS1: Wals 3B **48**
Walsall Rd. B42: Gt Barr, P Barr 4B **66**
  B71: W Brom 6B **64**
  B74: Four O 5D **36**
  B74: Lit As 3C **36**
  WS3: Pels 5E **21**
  WS5: Wals 1D **64**
  WS6: Gt Wyr 1F **7**
  WS9: A'rdge 6A **34**
  WS9: S'fld, Wals W 6H **21**
  WS10: Darl 5D **46**
  WS10: W'bry 3C **64**
  WS11: Nort C 2D **8**
  WS14: Hilt, Lynn, Muck C 6F **11**
  WV13: W'hall 1B **46**
Walsall Station (Rail) 2C **48**
Walsall St. B70: W Brom 4B **80**
  WS10: Darl 4D **46**
  WS10: W'bry 2F **63**
  WV1: Wolv 2A **44**
  WV13: W'hall 2A **44**
  WV14: Bils 5F **45**
WALSALL WOOD 3C **22**
Walsall Wood Rd. WS9: A'rdge 5C **22**
Walsgrave Cl. B92: Sol 1H **151**
Walsgrave Dr. B92: Sol 6H **137**
Walsham Cft. B34: S End 4G **105**
Walsh Dr. B76: Walm 1D **70**
Walsh Gro. B23: Erd 5D **68**
Walsingham St. WS1: Wals 2E **49**
Walstead Cl. WS5: Wals 6G **49**
Walstead Rd. WS5: Wals 6D **48**
Walstead Rd. W. WS5: Wals 6C **48**
Waltdene Cl. B43: Gt Barr 3A **66**
Walter Burden Ho. B66: Smeth 6G **99**
Walter Cobb Dr. B73: W Grn 4G **69**
Walter Rd. B67: Smeth 3C **98**
  WV14: Bils 2G **61**
Walters Cl. B31: Longb 3D **158**
Walters Row DY1: Dud 6C **76**
Walter St. B7: Nech 3B **102**
  B70: W Brom 5C **80**
  WS3: Pels 6E **21**
Waltham Gro. B44: K'sdng 3B **68**
Waltham Ho. B38: King Nor 6C **146**
  B70: W Brom 4B **80**
Walthamstow Ct. DY5: Brie H 2H **109**
Walton Av. B65: B'hth 3B **112**
Walton Cl. B63: Hale 3H **127**
  B65: Row R 5A **96**
Walton Ct. B63: Hale 2H **127**
Walton Cres. WV4: Ett 6A **44**
Walton Cft. B91: Sol 6F **151**
Walton Dr. DY9: Lye 6G **109**
Walton Gdns. WV8: Cod 3F **13**
Walton Gro. B30: King Nor 5D **146**
Walton Heath WS3: Blox 4F **19**
Walton Ho. B16: Birm 1D **116**
Walton Rd. B68: O'bry 1H **113**
  DY8: Amb 5E **109**
  WS9: A'rdge 6C **22**
  WS10: W'bry 3A **64**
  WV4: Ett .6A **44**
Walton St. DY4: Tip 2H **77**
Wanderers Av. WV2: Wolv 5G **43**
Wanderer Wlk. B36: Hodg H 6C **86**
Wandle Gro. B11: Tys 2G **135**
Wandsworth Rd. B44: Gt Barr 1G **67**
Wansbeck Gro. B38: King Nor 1A **160**
Wansbeck Wlk. DY3: Sed 1B **76**
Wanstead Gro. B44: K'sdng 4A **68**
Wantage Rd. B46: Col 6G **89**

Ward Cl. B8: W End 4G 103
Warden Av. B73: Bold 5F 69
WARD END 4F 103
Ward End Cl. B8: Salt 3F 103
Ward End Ho. B8: Salt 3G 103
Ward End Hall Gro. B8: W End . .3G 103
Ward End Pk. Rd. B8: Salt 4F 103
Wardend Rd. B8: W End 3G 103
Warden Rd. B73: Bold 5F 69
Ward Gro. WV4: Ett 2A 60
Wardle Cl. B75: Four O 5G 37
Wardlow Cl. WV4: Penn 5F 43
Wardlow Rd. B7: Birm 4B 102
Wardour Dr. B37: Chel W 1E 123
Wardour Gro. B44: K'sdng 5C 68
Ward Rd. WV4: Penn 6H 43
 WV8: Cod 4F 13
Ward St. B19: Birm 5G 101
 B23: Erd 3E 85
 WS1: Wals 1D 48
 WV1: Wolv 1A 44
 (not continuous)
 WV2: Ett 4D 44
 WV13: W'hall 6B 30
 WV14: Cose 5D 60
Wareham Cl. WS3: Wals 4D 32
Wareham Ho. B28: Hall G 4E 149
Wareham Rd. B45: Fran 5H 143
Wareing Dr. B23: Erd 5D 68
Warewell Cl. WS1: Wals 1D 48
Warewell St. WS1: Wals 2D 48
Waring Cl. DY4: Tip 5G 61
Waring Rd. DY4: Tip 5A 62
Warings, The WV5: Wom 3F 73
War La. B17: Harb 6F 115
Warley Ct. B68: O'bry 1H 113
Warley Cft. B68: O'bry 3C 114
Warley Hall Rd. B68: O'bry 3B 114
Warley Rd. B68: O'bry 4A 98
WARLEY WOODS 2C 114
Warley Woods Golf Course 3C 114
War Memorial Athletic Ground 5D 108
Warmington Dr. B73: S Cold 1G 69
Warmington Rd. B26: Sheld 6G 121
 B47: H'wd 3A 162
Warmley Cl. B91: Sol 2H 151
 WV6: Wolv 4F 27
Warner Dr. DY5: Brie H 2H 109
Warner Pl. WS3: Wals 3D 32
Warner Rd. WS3: Wals 3D 32
 WS10: W'bry 3A 64
 WV8: Cod 4F 13
Warner St. B12: Birm 3A 118
Warners Wlk. B10: Small H 3C 118
Warnford Wlk. WV4: Penn 5A 42
Warple Rd. B32: Quin 6A 114
Warren Av. B13: Mose 3H 133
 WV10: Wolv 4B 28
Warren Cl. DY4: Tip 6H 61
Warren Dr. B65: Row R 4H 95
 B93: Dorr 6C 166
 DY3: Sed 4G 59
Warren Farm Rd. B44: K'sdng 5H 67
Warren Gdns. DY6: K'wfrd 3A 92
Warren Gro. B8: Salt 3E 103
Warren Hill Rd. B44: K'sdng 1H 83
Warren Ho. Ct. B76: Walm 4D 70
Warren Ho. Wlk. B76: Walm 4D 70
Warren La. B45: Lick 6H 157
Warren Pl. WS8: Bwnhls 6C 10
Warren Rd. B8: Salt 3E 103
 B30: Stir 6C 132
 B44: K'sdng 6A 68
Warrens Cft. WS5: Wals 6H 49
Warrens End B38: King Nor 1B 160
Warrens Hall Nature Reserve 3G 95
Warrens Hall Rd. DY2: Dud 2F 95
Warrington Cl. B76: Walm 4E 71
Warrington Dr. B23: Erd 5D 68
Warsash Cl. WV1: Wolv 3D 44
WARSTOCK 4B 148
Warstock Cl. B91: Sol 2E 151
Warstock La. B14: King H 2A 148
Warstock Rd. B14: King H 4A 148
Warston Av. B32: Bart G 3B 130

WARSTONE 5B 6
Warstone Ct. B18: Birm 1A 4 (5E 101)
Warstone Dr. B71: W Brom 3C 80
Warstone La. B18: Birm 1A 4 (5D 100)
Warstone M. B18: Birm 1A 4
Warstone Pde. E. B18: Birm 5D 100
Warstone Rd. WV10: Share 3A 6
 WV11: Ess 3A 6
Warstones Cres. WV4: Penn 6B 42
Warstones Dr. WV4: Penn 5A 42
Warstones Gdns. WV4: Penn 5A 42
Warstones Ho. WV4: Penn 5B 42
Warstones Rd. WV4: Penn 2A 58
Warstone Ter. B21: Hand 1A 100
Warstone Twr. B36: Hodg H 1A 104
Wartell Bank DY6: K'wfrd 2B 92
Wartell Bank Ind. Est.
 DY6: K'wfrd 2C 92
Warwards La. B29: S Oak 4C 132
Warwell La. B26: Yard 5B 120
Warwick Av. WS10: W'bry 1A 64
 WV6: Pert 6F 25
 WV13: W'hall 1D 46
Warwick Cl. B68: O'bry 1H 113
 B70: W Brom 6E 63
 DY3: Lwr G 4H 75
Warwick Ct. B13: Mose 3A 134
 B29: W Cas 6F 131
 B37: Chel W 1F 123
 B91: Sol 2F 151
Warwick Crest B15: Edg 4D 116
Warwick Cft. B36: Hodg H 1A 104
Warwick Dr. WV8: Cod 3E 13
Warwick Gdns. B28: Hall G 2E 149
 B69: Tiv 5C 78
Warwick Grange B91: Sol 6D 136
Warwick Gro. B92: Olton 4C 136
Warwick Mnr. B91: Sol 2F 151
Warwick Pk. Ct. B92: Olton 5D 136
Warwick Pas. B2: Birm 4E 5 (1G 117)
Warwick Rd. B11: S'hll, Tys 6C 118
 B27: A Grn 6C 118
 B68: O'bry 4B 114
 B73: New O 3C 68
 B91: Sol 2E 151
 B92: Olton 5D 136
 B93: Know 6C 152
 (Jacobean La.)
 B93: Know 4E 167
 (Milverton Rd.)
 DY2: Neth 6G 95
 DY8: Word 2B 108
Warwick Rd. Trad. Est. B11: S'hll . .6D 118
Warwickshire County Cricket Club . .6F 117
Warwick St. B12: Birm 2A 118
 WS4: Wals 6D 32
 WV1: Wolv 2A 44
 WV14: Bils 6G 45
Warwick Way WS9: A'rdge 6C 22
Wasdale Dr. DY6: K'wfrd 3C 92
Wasdale Rd. B31: N'fld 3D 144
 WS8: Clay 1H 21
Waseley Hills Country Pk.
 . . . . .6C 142
Waseley Hills Country Pk. Vis. Cen.
 . . . . .6C 142
Waseley Rd. B45: Rub 1E 157
Washbrook La. WS11: Nort C . .1A 8 & 1C 8
Washbrook Rd. B8: W End 3G 103
Washford Gro. B25: Yard 3H 119
Washington Cen. DY2: Neth 6F 95
Washington Cl. B1: Birm 6B 4
 DY1: Dud 3C 76
 WV3: Wolv 2B 42
Washington Dr. B20: Hand 4D 82
Washington St. B1: Birm 6B 4 (2F 117)
 DY2: Neth 6F 95
Washington Sth. Ind. Est. DY2: Neth 6F 95
Washington Wharf B1: Birm . .6B 4 (2E 117)
Wash La. B25: Yard 4A 120
WASHWOOD HEATH 3E 103
Washwood Heath Rd.
 B8: Salt, W End 4D 102
Wasperton Cl. B36: Cas B 1F 105
Wassell Cl. B63: Hale 3G 127
Wassell Gro. Bus. Cen. DY9: Hag . .3C 126
Wassell Gro. La. DY9: Hag 5B 126

Wassell Rd. B63: Hale 3G 127
 DY9: W'cte 3B 126
 WV14: Bils 4F 45
Wast Hills Golf Cen. 2H 159
Wast Hill Gro. B38: King Nor 2B 160
Wasthill La. B38: Hopw 5H 159
 B48: Hopw 5H 159
Wastwater Ct. WV6: Pert 5F 25
Watchbury Cl. B36: Cas B 6G 87
Watchman Av. DY5: Quar B 4B 110
Watchbridge La. WV5: Wom 6E 57
Waterdale B90: Ches G 4B 164
 WV3: Wolv 1C 42
 WV5: Wom 2E 73
Waterfall Cl. B66: Smeth 2C 98
Waterfall La. B64: Old H 2A 112
 B65: B'hth 2A 112
Waterfall La. Trad. Est.
 B64: Old H 2A 112
Waterfall Rd. DY5: Brie H 4G 109
Waterfield Cl. DY4: Tip 2E 77
Waterfield Ho. WV5: Wom 6H 57
Waterfield Way B26: Sheld 4G 121
Waterford Ct. B23: Erd 3B 84
Waterford Pl. B33: Kitts G 6G 105
Waterford Rd. DY6: K'wfrd 2B 92
Waterfront, The DY5: Brie H 5A 94
Waterfront Bus. Pk. DY5: Brie H . . .5H 93
Waterfront E. DY5: Brie H 5A 94
Waterfront Point DY5: Brie H 6H 93
 (off Dudley Rd.)
Waterfront Wlk. B1: Birm 6B 4 (2E 117)
Waterfront Way DY5: Brie H 5A 94
 WS2: Wals 1B 48
Waterfront W. DY5: Brie H 5A 94
Water Gardens, The
 WV4: Lwr P, Penn 2A 58
Waterglade La. WV13: W'hall 2A 46
Waterhaynes Cl. B45: Redn 3G 157
Waterhead Cl. WV10: Bush 5C 16
Waterhead Dr. WV10: Bush 5C 16
Water La. B71: W Brom 6D 64
Water Lily Gro. WS8: Bwnhls 6A 10
Waterlinks Blvd. B6: Aston 2A 102
Waterlinks Ho. B7: Birm 4H 101
 (off Richard St.)
Waterloo Av. B37: F'bri 5D 106
Waterloo Ind. Est. B37: F'bri 4D 106
Waterloo Pas. B2: Birm 4D 4
 B25: Yard 5H 119
 B66: Smeth 6E 99
 WV1: Wolv 2A 170 (1G 43)
Waterloo Rd. Junc.
 WV1: Wolv 2A 170 (1G 43)
Waterloo St. B2: Birm 4C 4 (1F 117)
 DY1: Dud 1D 94
 DY4: Tip 2G 77
Waterloo St. E. DY4: Tip 2H 77
Waterloo Ter. WV1: Wolv 6F 27
Watermarque B71: Birm 1D 116
Watermead Grange WS8: Bwnhls . .6A 10
Watermeadow Dr. WS4: S'fld 6H 21
Watermere WS4: S'fld 1H 33
Water Mill Cl. B29: S Oak 2H 131
Watermill Cl. WV10: F'hses 4H 15
Water Mill Cres. B76: Walm 4D 70
WATER ORTON 4D 88
Water Orton La. B76: Min 2H 87
Water Orton Rd. B36: Cas B 1G 105
Water Orton Station (Rail) 4C 88
Water Reed Gro. WS3: Blox 2H 31
Water Rd. DY3: Gorn 5G 75
Waters Dr. B74: Four O 6D 36
Waters Edge, The B1: Birm . . .5A 4 (1E 117)
Waterside B15: Birm 2E 117
 B43: Gt Barr 6A 66
 B90: Dic H 4G 163
Waterside Av. WS10: W'bry 4G 63
Waterside Bus. Pk. DY5: Brie H 2F 109
Waterside Cl. B9: Birm 1C 118
 B24: Erd 2E 87
 B69: O'bry 5F 97
 WV2: Wolv 4H 43
Waterside Ct. B16: Birm 1D 116
 (off Vincent St.)

Waterside Dr. B18: Win G 4B **100**
(not continuous)
Waterside Est. DY2: Neth 6E **95**
Waterside Ind. Est. B65: Row R 5H **95**
WV2: Ett 5C **44**
Waterside Orchard B38: Hopw 6F **159**
Waterside Pk. DY4: Tip 6D **62**
Waterside Vw. B18: Hock 4C **100**
DY5: Brie H 3F **109**
Waterside Way WS8: Bwnhls 3G **9**
WV9: Pend 4E **15**
Waterson Cft. B37: Chel W 6F **107**
Water St. B3: Birm 2C **4** (6F **101**)
B70: W Brom 5B **80**
DY6: K'wfrd 2B **92**
WV10: Wolv 6H **27**
Waters Vw. WS3: Pels 2F **21**
Waterward Cl. B17: Harb 6G **115**
Waterway Ct. B14: Yard W 4C **148**
Waterways Dr. B69: O'bry 6E **79**
Waterways Dr. DY8: Word 2C **108**
Waterworks Cotts. B71: W Brom 6C **64**
Waterworks Dr. B31: N'fld 2B **144**
Waterworks Rd. B16: Edg 2B **116**
Waterworks St. B6: Aston 1B **102**
Watery La. B32: Quin 2G **129**
B48: A'chu, Hopw 6A **160**
B67: Smeth 4E **99**
B93: Know 5G **167**
B94: Earls 5A **164**
DY4: Tip 2H **77**
(not continuous)
DY8: Word 1C **108**
WS1: Wals 4B **48**
(not continuous)
WV8: Cod 3G **13**
WV13: W'hall 6F **29**
Watery La. Ind. Est. WV13: W'hall ...6G **29**
Watery La. Middleway B9: Birm ...1B **118**
WATFORD GAP 2G **37**
Watford Gap Rd. WS14: Lit H 2G **37**
Watford Rd. B30: King Nor 2B **146**
Wathan Av. WV14: Cose 4B **60**
Watkins Gdns. B31: N'fld 4F **145**
Watkins Rd. WV12: W'hall 4C **30**
Watland Grn. B34: Stech 4E **105**
Watling St. WS7: Muck C 3E **11**
WS8: Bwnhls, Muck C 3E **9**
WS11: Cann 1F **7**
WS14: Muck C 3E **11**
Watling St. Bus. Pk. WS11: Bwnhls ...3E **9**
Watney Bus. B44: K'sdng 5C **68**
Watson Cl. B72: W Grn 3A **70**
Watson Rd. B7: Nech 1D **102**
B8: W End 4F **103**
WS10: Mox 6A **46**
WV10: F'hses 5F **15**
WV14: Cose 3C **60**
Watson Rd. E. B7: Nech 2D **102**
Watsons Cl. DY2: Dud 1G **95**
Watson's Grn. Flds. DY2: Dud 1H **95**
Watson's Grn. Rd. DY2: Dud 6G **77**
Watson Way CV7: Bal C 1H **169**
Wattisham Sq. B35: Cas V 3E **87**
Wattis Rd. B67: Smeth 1E **115**
Wattle Grn. B70: W Brom 4F **79**
Wattle Rd. B70: W Brom 4F **79**
Watton Cl. WV14: Cose 4C **60**
Watton Ct. B6: Aston 1G **101**
Watton Grn. B35: Cas V 5E **87**
(not continuous)
Watton La. B46: Wat O 5E **89**
Watton St. B70: W Brom 5B **80**
Watt Rd. B23: Erd 3E **85**
DY4: Tip 5B **62**
Watts Cl. DY4: Tip 2E **77**
Watt's Rd. B10: Small H 3D **118**
Watt St. B21: Hand 6D **82**
B66: Smeth 3F **99**
Wattville Av. B21: Hand 1G **99**
Wattville Rd. B21: Hand 1G **99**
B66: Hand, Smeth 2F **99**
Wattville Rd. Ind. Est. B66: Smeth ...2F **99**
Watwood Rd. B28: Hall G 4F **149**
B90: Shir 4F **149**
Waugh Cl. B37: Chel W 1D **122**

Waugh Dr. B63: Hale 5F **127**
Wave Cl. WS2: Wals 1B **48**
Wavell Rd. B8: Salt 4E **103**
DY5: Quar B 4B **110**
WS2: Wals 1E **47**
Waveney Av. WV6: Pert 5E **25**
Waveney Cft. B36: Cas B 1B **106**
Wavenham Cl. B74: Four O 4E **37**
Waverhill Rd. B21: Hand 2B **100**
Waverley Av. B43: Gt Barr 1D **66**
Waverley Cres. B62: Roms 3A **142**
WV2: Penn 5F **43**
WV4: Ett 2B **60**
Waverley Gdns. WV5: Wom 6H **57**
Waverley Gro. B91: Sol 4D **150**
Waverley Rd. B10: Small H 4D **118**
WS3: Blox 5F **19**
WS10: Darl 5D **46**
Waverley St. DY2: Dud 1C **94**
Wavers Marston B37: Mars G 3C **122**
Waxland Rd. B63: Hale 3B **128**
Wayfield Cl. B90: Shir 4A **150**
Wayfield Rd. B90: Shir 4A **150**
Wayford Dr. B72: W Grn 6B **70**
Wayford Glade WV13: W'hall 3H **45**
Wayford Gro. B8: W End 5H **103**
Waynecroft Rd. B43: Gt Barr 3A **66**
Wayside B37: Mars G 3B **122**
WV8: Pend 5C **14**
Wayside Acres WV8: Cod 5C **13**
Wayside Dr. B74: Lit As 6C **36**
B75: R'ley 6C **38**
Wayside Gdns. WV12: W'hall 5E **31**
Wayside Wlk. WS2: Wals 6G **31**
Wealden Hatch WV10: Bush 3A **16**
Wealdstone Dr. DY3: Lwr G 5H **75**
Weaman St. B4: Birm 2E **5** (6G **101**)
Weates Yd. B27: A Grn 1A **136**
Weatheroak Rd. B11: S'hll 6C **118**
Weather Oaks B17: Harb 6F **115**
Weatheroaks B62: Quin 4G **113**
WS9: Wals W 3D **22**
Weaver Av. B26: Sheld 5F **121**
B76: Walm 4E **71**
Weaver Cl. DY5: P'ntt 3A **92**
Weaver Ct. B75: R'ley 6C **38**
Weaver Gro. WV13: W'hall 1D **46**
Weavers Ri. DY2: Neth 6F **95**
Weaves Cl. WS6: Gt Wyr 4F **7**
Webb Av. WV6: Pert 4E **25**
Webb Ct. DY8: Stourb 6D **108**
(off Drury La.)
Webbcroft Rd. B33: Stech 5C **104**
Webb La. B28: Hall G 1E **149**
Webb Rd. DY4: Tip 6C **62**
Webb St. WV13: W'hall 1H **45**
WV14: Cose 3E **61**
Webley Gro. DY1: Dud 3E **77**
Webley Ri. WV10: Bush 3B **16**
Webner Ind. Est. WV2: Ett 5C **44**
Webster Cl. B11: S'brk 5B **118**
B72: W Grn 6H **69**
Webster Rd. WS2: Wals 4B **32**
WV13: W'hall 6A **30**
Webster Way B76: Walm 4E **71**
Weddell Wynd WV14: Bils 4G **61**
Wedgbury Cl. WS10: W'bry 4G **63**
Wedgbury Way DY5: Brie H 2F **109**
Wedge Cl. WS1: Wals 2D **48**
(off Union St.)
Wedge St. WS1: Wals 1D **48**
Wedgewood Av. B70: W Brom 6F **63**
Wedgewood Cl. WS4: S'fld 6G **21**
(off Green La.)
Wedgewood Ho. B37: F'bri 5D **106**
Wedgewood Pl. B70: W Brom 6F **63**
Wedgewood Rd. B32: Quin 6A **114**
Wedgwood Cl. WV1: Wolv 2C **44**
WV5: Wom 6F **57**
Wedgwood Dr. B20: Hand 5D **82**
Wedmore Rd. B73: Bold 4F **69**
WEDNESBURY 3F **63**
Wednesbury Great Western Street Stop
(Metro) 3E **63**
Wednesbury Leisure Cen. 2E **63**
Wednesbury Museum & Art Gallery ..3F **63**

Wednesbury New Ent. Cen.
WS10: Mox 2C **62**
Wednesbury Oak Rd. DY4: Tip 4A **62**
Wednesbury One WS10: W'bry 2D **62**
Wednesbury Parkway (Park & Tram)
...........................3D **62**
Wednesbury Parkway Stop (Metro) ..3D **62**
Wednesbury Rd. WS1: Wals 4A **48**
WS2: Wals 4A **48**
Wednesbury Trad. Est.
WS10: W'bry 1E **63**
WEDNESFIELD 4F **29**
Wednesfield Rd.
WV1: Wolv 1D **170** (6H **27**)
WV10: Wolv 1D **170** (6H **27**)
WV13: W'hall 6A **30**
Wednesfield Way WV10: Wolv 5C **28**
WV11: Wed 5F **29**
Wednesfield Way Ind. Est.
WV11: Wed 5F **29**
Weeford Dell B75: R'ley 6C **38**
Weeford Dr. B20: Hand 3B **82**
Weeford Rd. B75: R'ley 1C **54**
Weirbrook Cl. B29: W Cas 6F **131**
Weland Cl. B46: Wat O 5D **88**
Weland Ct. B46: Wat O 5D **88**
Welbeck Av. WV10: Bush 2H **27**
Welbeck Cl. B62: Quin 6E **113**
Welbeck Dr. WS4: Rus 2H **33**
Welbeck Gro. B23: Erd 2B **84**
Welbury Gdns. WV6: Wolv 4D **26**
Welby Ga. CV7: Bal C 4H **169**
Welby Rd. B28: Hall G 4F **135**
Welch Cl. DY4: Tip 6B **62**
Welches Cl. B31: N'fld 2F **145**
Welcombe Dr. B76: Walm 6D **70**
Welcombe Gro. B91: Sol 4D **150**
Welcome Centre, The 4E **5**
(off New St.)
Welford Av. B26: Yard 3D **120**
Welford Gro. B74: Four O 6F **37**
Welford Rd. B20: Hand 1C **100**
B73: New O 4E **69**
B90: Shir 3A **150**
Welham Cft. B90: M'path 3E **165**
Welland Dr. DY8: Amb 3E **109**
Welland Gro. B24: Erd 4A **86**
WV13: W'hall 1C **46**
Welland Rd. B63: Hale 3A **128**
Welland Way B76: Walm 6E **71**
Well Cl. B36: Hodg H 1C **104**
Wellcroft Rd. B34: S End 2E **105**
Wellcroft St. WS10: W'bry 2F **63**
Weller Ct. WV3: Wolv 2B **42**
Wellesbourne Cl. WV3: Wolv 3H **41**
Wellesbourne Dr. WV14: Cose 6D **60**
Wellesbourne Rd. B20: Hand 6D **82**
Wellesbourne Twr. B5: Birm 3G **117**
Wellesley Dr. DY4: Tip 2H **77**
Wellesley Gdns. B13: Mose 4D **134**
Wellesley Rd. B68: O'bry 3H **97**
Wellfield Gdns. DY2: Dud 3G **95**
Wellfield Rd. B28: Hall G 1H **149**
WS9: A'rdge 1D **34**
Wellhead La. B42: P Barr 5G **83**
Wellington Av. WV3: Wolv 4D **42**
Wellington Cl. DY6: K'wfrd 5C **92**
Wellington Ct. B20: Hand 5E **83**
B32: Harb 6D **114**
B64: Old H 1H **111**
(off Wellington Rd.)
Wellington Cres. B20: Hand 5D **82**
Wellington Gro. B91: Sol 1D **150**
Wellington Ho. B32: Quin 1D **130**
Wellington Ind. Est.
WV14: Cose 6E **61**
(not continuous)
Wellington Pas. B2: Birm 4D **4**
Wellington Pl. WV13: W'hall 6H **29**
Wellington Rd. B15: Edg 5D **116**
B20: Hand 5D **82**
B67: Smeth 6E **99**
DY1: Dud 1D **94**
DY4: Tip 3A **78**
WS5: Wals 5G **49**
WV14: Bils 4D **44**

Wellington St.—Westland Av.

Wellington St. B18: Win G ...3H **99**
B64: Old H ...1H **111**
B66: Smeth ...3H **99**
B69: O'bry ...3H **97**
B71: W Brom ...3A **80**
WS2: Wals ...4H **47**
Wellington St. Sth.
B70: W Brom ...3A **80**
Wellington Ter. B19: Loz ...2D **100**
WV13: W'hall ...6H **29**
Wellington Twr. B31: N'fld ...6E **145**
Wellington Way B35: Cas V ...5F **87**
Well La. B5: Birm ...5F **5** (1H **117**)
WS3: Blox ...2C **32**
WS6: Gt Wyr ...4G **7**
WV11: Wed ...5E **29**
Wellman Cft. B29: S Oak ...4H **131**
Wellman's Rd. WV13: W'hall ...2C **46**
Well Mdw. B45: Redn ...3G **157**
Wellmeadow Gro. B92: H Ard ...6A **140**
Wellmead Wlk. B45: Rub ...1F **157**
Well Pl. WS3: Blox ...1C **32**
Wells Av. WS10: Darl ...5B **46**
Wells Cl. DY4: Tip ...4A **62**
WV6: Pert ...5D **24**
Wells Ct. B71: W Brom ...5B **64**
DY2: Neth ...4E ***95***
(off Meeting St.)
Wellsford Av. B92: Olton ...1E **137**
WELLS GREEN ...**6F 121**
Wells Grn. Rd. B92: Olton ...1D **136**
Wells Grn. Shop. Cen.
B26: Sheld ...1F **137**
Wells Rd. B65: Row R ...5E **97**
B92: Sol ...1G **137**
DY5: Brie H ...6F **93**
WV4: Penn ...6D **42**
WV14: Bils ...2G **61**
Wells Twr. B16: Birm ...1C **116**
Well St. B19: Birm ...4E **101**
WS10: Darl ...5E **47**
Wells Wlk. B37: Mars G ...2C **122**
Welney Gdns. WV9: Pend ...4E **15**
Welsby Av. B43: Gt Barr ...6A **66**
Welsh Ho. Farm Rd.
B32: Quin, Harb ...1D **130**
Welshmans Hill B73: New O ...3B **68**
Welton Cl. B76: Walm ...3E **71**
Welwyndale Rd. B72: W Grn ...1A **86**
Wembley Gro. B25: Yard ...3A **120**
Wem Gdns. WV11: Wed ...3F **29**
Wendell Crest WV10: Bush ...3B **16**
Wendover Ho. B31: Longb ...1D **158**
Wendover Rd. B23: Erd ...6C **68**
B65: Row R ...4A **96**
WV4: Ett ...3B **60**
Wendron Gro. B14: King H ...3F **147**
Wenlock Av. WV3: Wolv ...3C **42**
Wenlock Cl. B63: Hale ...3F **127**
DY3: Sed ...6G **59**
Wenlock Gdns. WS3: Wals ...4C **32**
Wenlock Rd. B20: Hand ...6H **83**
DY8: Amb ...5F **109**
Wenman St. B12: Bal H ...5H **117**
Wensley Cft. B90: Shir ...1H **149**
Wensleydale Rd. B42: P Barr ...1C **82**
Wensley Rd. B26: Sheld ...5D **120**
Wentbridge Rd. WV1: Wolv ...2E **45**
Wentworth Av. B36: Cas B ...1F **105**
Wentworth Ct. B24: Erd ...5F **85**
B74: Four O ...2H **53**
Wentworth Dr. B69: Tiv ...2A **96**
Wentworth Ga. B17: Harb ...5F **115**
Wentworth Gro. WV6: Pert ...4D **24**
Wentworth Pk. Av. B17: Harb ...5F **115**
Wentworth Ri. B62: Hale ...1D **128**
Wentworth Rd. B17: Harb ...5F **115**
B74: Four O ...4G **53**
B92: Olton ...2D **136**
DY8: Woll ...4B **108**
WS3: Blox ...3F **19**
WV10: Bush ...5A **16**
Wentworth Way B32: Bart G ...2D **130**
Wenyon Cl. DY4: Tip ...3B **78**
Weoley Av. B29: S Oak ...3G **131**
WEOLEY CASTLE ...**4E 131**
Weoley Castle ...**3E 131**
Weoley Castle Rd. B29: W Cas ...4D **130**
Weoley Hill B29: S Oak ...5G **131**
Weoley Pk. Rd. B29: S Oak ...4F **131**
WERGS ...**3F 25**
Wergs Dr. WV6: Tett ...2G **25**
Wergs Golf Course ...**2G 25**
Wergs Hall WV8: Tett ...2F **25**
Wergs Hall Rd. WV6: Tett ...6F **13**
WV8: Cod, Tett ...6F **13**
Wergs Rd. WV6: Tett ...3G **25**
Werneth Gro. WS3: Blox ...3G **19**
Wesley Av. B63: Crad ...3D **110**
WS6: C Hay ...2D **6**
WV8: Bilb ...5H **13**
Wesley Cl. B64: Old H ...2H **111**
WV5: Wom ...2F **73**
Wesley Ct. B16: Edg ...6H **99**
B64: Old H ...3H **111**
Wesley Gro. WS10: W'bry ...2E **63**
Wesley Pl. DY4: Tip ...6C **62**
Wesley Rd. B23: Erd ...2F **85**
DY5: P'ntt ...4F **93**
WV8: Bilb ...5H **13**
WV12: W'hall ...3C **30**
Wesley's Fold WS10: Darl ...5D **46**
Wesley St. B69: O'bry ...1G **97**
B70: W Brom ...4H **79**
WV2: Ett ...5C **44**
WV14: Bils ...3G **61**
Wessex Cl. WS8: Bwnhls ...6B **10**
Wessex Rd. WV2: Ett ...5B **44**
Wesson Gdns. B63: Hale ...2A **128**
Wesson Rd. WS10: Darl ...3C **46**
Westacre WV13: W'hall ...2H **45**
Westacre Cres. WV3: Wolv ...2A **42**
Westacre Dr. DY5: Quar B ...3B **110**
Westacre Gdns. B33: Stech ...6D **104**
West Av. B20: Hand ...3B **82**
B36: Cas B ...1H **105**
B69: Tiv ...2B **96**
WV11: Wed ...3E **29**
West Blvd. B32: Quin, Bart G ...5C **114**
Westbourne Av. B34: Hodg H ...3C **104**
WS6: C Hay ...1E **7**
Westbourne Ct. *WS4: Wals ...6E* ***33***
(off Lichfield Rd.)
Westbourne Cres. B15: Edg ...3C **116**
Westbourne Gdns. B15: Edg ...4C **116**
Westbourne Gro. B21: Hand ...2A **100**
Westbourne Ho. B21: Hand ...6H **81**
Westbourne Rd. B15: Edg ...4B **116**
B21: Hand ...6H **81**
B62: B'hth ...4E **113**
B70: W Brom ...5H **79**
B92: Olton ...5D **136**
WS4: Wals ...5D **32**
WS10: Darl ...4F **47**
WV4: Penn ...6E **43**
Westbourne St. WS4: Wals ...6D **32**
WEST BROMWICH ...**4B 80**
West Bromwich Albion FC ...**6F 81**
West Bromwich Central Stop (Metro)
...**5A 80**
W. Bromwich Parkway B70: W Brom ...4H **79**
(Edith St.)
B70: W Brom ...6C **80**
(Springfield Cres.)
W. Bromwich Ringway B70: W Brom ...4A **80**
W. Bromwich Rd. WS1: Wals ...5C **48**
(not continuous)
WS5: Wals ...5C **48**
W. Bromwich St. B69: O'bry ...6F **79**
WS1: Wals ...3C **48**
Westbrook Av. WS9: A'rdge ...4A **34**
Westbrook Way WV5: Wom ...2F **73**
Westbury Av. WS10: W'bry ...5F **47**
Westbury Ct. *DY5: Brie H ...1H* ***109***
(off Lit. Potter St.)
Westbury Rd. B17: Edg ...6F **99**
WS10: W'bry ...5F **47**
Westbury St. WV1: Wolv ...2C **170** (1H **43**)
Westcliffe Pl. B31: N'fld ...3D **144**
Westcombe Gro. B32: Bart G ...4G **129**
W. Coppice Rd. WS8: Bwnhls ...5G **9**
Westcote Av. B31: Longb ...4A **144**
Westcote Cl. B92: Olton ...3E **137**
Westcott Cl. DY6: K'wfrd ...6D **92**
Westcott Rd. B26: Yard ...3E **121**
WESTCROFT ...**6C 16**
Westcroft Av. WV10: Bush ...6C **16**
Westcroft Gro. B38: King Nor ...4G **145**
Westcroft Rd. DY3: Sed ...3F **59**
WV6: Tett ...3F **25**
Westcroft Way B14: King H ...6B **148**
W. Cross Shop. Cen. B66: Smeth ...2B **98**
Westdean Cl. B62: Hale ...1C **128**
West Dr. B5: Edg ...6E **117**
B20: Hand ...1D **100**
West End Av. B66: Smeth ...2B **98**
Westerdale Cl. DY3: Sed ...6C **60**
Westerham Cl. B93: Know ...3B **166**
Westeria Cl. B36: Cas B ...1G **105**
Westering Parkway
WV10: Bush ...3A **16**
Westerings B20: Hand ...5E **83**
Western Av. B19: Loz ...2E **101**
B62: Hale ...1E **129**
DY3: Sed ...5F **59**
DY5: Brie H ...1F **109**
WS2: Wals ...6D **30**
Western Bus. Pk. B62: Hale ...4B **112**
Western Cl. WS2: Wals ...6D **30**
Western Ct. *B9: Birm ...2A* ***118***
(off Bromley St.)
Western Rd. B18: Win G ...5B **100**
B24: Erd ...4G **85**
B64: Crad H ...3G **111**
B69: O'bry ...4H **97**
B73: W Grn ...4G **69**
DY8: Stourb ...1D **124**
Western Way WS10: Mox, W'bry ...1C **62**
Westfield Av. B14: King H ...6B **148**
Westfield Cl. B93: Dorr ...6F **167**
Westfield Dr. WS9: A'rdge ...3C **34**
WV5: Wom ...6F **57**
Westfield Grange B14: King H ...4G **133**
Westfield Gro. WV3: Wolv ...3A **42**
Westfield Hall B16: Edg ...2G **115**
Westfield Ho. B36: Cas B ...2C **106**
Westfield Mnr. B75: Four O ...5G **37**
Westfield Rd. B14: King H ...5F **133**
B15: Edg ...3H **115**
B27: A Grn ...2H **135**
B62: B'hth ...2E **113**
B67: Smeth ...5D **98**
DY2: Dud ...2F **95**
DY3: Sed ...4H **59**
DY5: Quar B ...3B **110**
WV13: W'hall ...3G **45**
WV14: Bils ...4D **44**
Westford Gro. B28: Hall G ...4E **149**
West Gate B16: Edg ...6A **100**
Westgate B1: Birm ...2A **4** (6D **100**)
B15: Edg ...1A **132**
B69: O'bry ...5E **97**
WS9: A'rdge ...2H **33**
Westgate Cl. DY3: Sed ...6A **60**
Westgate Pk. Ind. Est. WS9: A'rdge ...3A **34**
West Ga. Plaza B70: W Brom ...5A **80**
Westgate Trad. Est. WS9: A'rdge ...3A **34**
West Grn. WV4: Penn ...6A **42**
West Green Cl. B15: Edg ...3D **116**
Westgrove Av. B90: M'path ...4D **164**
Westhall Ct. B26: Yard ...1E **121**
Westhall Ga. WS3: Blox ...5H **19**
Westham Ho. B37: F'bri ...5D **106**
Westhaven Dr. B31: N'fld ...6C **130**
Westhaven Rd. B72: S Cold ...5A **54**
Westhay Rd. B28: Hall G ...6H **135**
WEST HEATH ...**1F 159**
W. Heath Rd. B18: Win G ...5H **99**
B31: N'fld ...5F **145**
Westhill WV3: Wolv ...1A **42**
Westhill Cl. B29: S Oak ...4H **131**
B92: Olton ...5C **136**
West Hill Ct. B14: King H ...3E **147**
Westhill Rd. B38: King Nor ...4B **146**
West Holme B9: Birm ...1C **118**
Westholme Cft. B30: B'vlle ...6A **132**
Westhouse Gro. B14: King H ...3F **147**
Westland Av. WV3: Wolv ...1D **42**

Westland Cl. B23: Erd 2F 85
Westland Gdns. DY8: Amb 4D 108
  WV3: Wolv .1E 43
Westland Rd. WV3: Wolv 1D 42
Westlands Est. DY8: Word 2C 108
Westlands Rd. B13: Mose 4A 134
  B76: Walm 1D 86
Westland Wlk. B35: Cas V 5D 86
Westleigh Rd. WV5: Wom 2F 73
Westley Brook Cl. B26: Sheld 6F 121
Westley Cl. B28: Hall G 1H 149
Westley Ct. B71: W Brom 1B 80
Westley Rd. B27: A Grn 2H 135
Westley St. B9: Birm 1A 118
  DY1: Dud 1D 94
West Mall B37: Chel W 1D 122
  (within Chelmsley Wood Shop. Cen.)
Westmead Cres. B24: Erd 3A 86
W. Mead Dr. B14: King H 1G 147
Westmead Dr. B68: O'bry 5H 97
West M. B44: Gt Barr 3F 67
W. Midlands Freeport B26: Birm A . . .2B 138
West Midlands Golf Course 4C 154
W. Mill Cft. B38: King Nor 2A 160
Westminster B37: K'hrst 4B 106
Westminster Av. WV4: Penn 6F 43
Westminster Cl. DY1: Dud 5C 76
Westminster Ct. B20: Hand 5D 82
Westminster Cres. B20: Hand 6E 83
Westminster Dr. B14: King H 1G 147
Westminster Ind. Est. DY2: Neth 1F 111
Westminster Pl. B31: Longb 1F 159
  WS4: Rus 2F 33
Westminster Rd. B20: Hand 5E 83
  B29: S Oak .4C 132
  B71: W Brom .4B 64
  DY8: Word .1A 108
  WS4: Rus 2F 33
Westmore Way WS10: W'bry 6B 48
Westmorland Ct. B71: W Brom 6B 64
Westmorland Rd. B71: W Brom 6B 64
Weston Av. B11: S'brk 5C 118
  B69: Tiv 6B 78
Weston Cl. B93: Dorr 6H 167
  WS1: Wals 5C 48
Weston Ct. WV1: Wolv 5G 27
  (off Boscobel Cres.)
Weston Cres. WS9: A'rdge 4D 34
Weston Dr. DY4: Tip 3C 62
  WS6: Gt Wyr .5E 7
  WV14: Bils .1D 60
Weston Ho. B19: Hock 3G 101
Weston Ind. Est. B11: Tys 1E 135
Weston La. B11: Tys 1E 135
Weston Rd. B19: Hock 2D 100
  B67: Smeth .1D 114
Weston St. WS1: Wals 5C 48
Weston Ter. B19: Loz 4H 101
  (off New Inn Rd.)
Westover Rd. B20: Hand 3A 82
West Pk. Av. B31: N'fld 5C 144
West Pk. Cl. WS9: A'rdge 4A 34
West Pk. Ct. WV1: Wolv 1E 43
West Pk. Rd. B67: Smeth 2B 98
West Pathway B17: Harb 5G 115
West Point B15: Edg 3G 115
Westport Cres. WV11: Wed 4H 29
Westray Cl. B45: Fran 6E 143
Westridge DY3: Sed 5G 59
Westridge Rd. B13: Mose 6C 134
West Ri. B75: S Cold 5A 54
West Rd. B43: Gt Barr 6A 66
  B63: Crad .5D 110
  DY4: Tip 5B 62
West Rd. Sth. B63: Crad 5D 110
Westside Dr. B32: Bart G 4B 130
WEST SMETHWICK 2B 98
Weststrand WV9: Pend 4D 14
West St. B65: B'hth 2C 112
  DY3: Gorn 4H 75
  DY5: Quar B .3B 110
  DY8: Stourb .6D 108
  WS3: Blox 2A 32
  WV10: Wolv .4G 27
Westthorpe Gro. B19: Birm 4E 101
West Vw. B8: W End 5A 104

West Vw. Ct. B75: S Cold 5C 54
West Vw. Dr. DY6: K'wfrd 4C 92
West Vw. Rd. B75: S Cold 5C 54
Westville Rd. WS2: Wals 6G 31
Westward Cl. B44: K'sdng 5H 67
West Way B31: Longb 2F 159
Westway WS4: S'fld 5F 21
Westwick Cl. WS9: Ston 3G 23
Westwood Av. B11: Tys 1D 134
  DY8: Stourb .2A 124
Westwood Bus. Pk. B6: Witt 6B 84
Westwood Ct. B73: S'tly 1B 68
Westwood Dr. B45: Redn 6H 143
Westwood Gro. B91: Sol 5D 150
Westwood Rd. B6: Witt 6A 84
  B73: S'tly 1A 68
Westwood St. DY5: Brie H 2E 109
Westwood Vw. B24: Erd 4A 86
Wetherby Cl. B36: Hodg H 1B 104
  WV10: F'hses .3H 15
Wetherby Rd. B27: A Grn 3A 136
  WS3: Blox 3G 19
Wetherfield Rd. B11: Tys 2G 135
Wexford Cl. DY1: Dud 5B 76
Wexler Lofts B1: Birm 2A 4
Weybourne Rd. B44: Gt Barr 3G 67
Weycroft Rd. B23: Erd 6B 68
Weyhill Cl. WV9: Pend 5D 14
Weymoor Rd. B17: Harb 2E 131
Weymouth Dr. B74: Four O 5F 37
Wharf, The B1: Birm 5B 4 (1E 117)
Wharf App. WS9: A'rdge 2B 34
Wharfdale Rd. B11: Tys 6G 119
Wharfedale Cl. DY6: W Hth 2H 91
Wharfedale St. WS10: W'bry 3F 63
Wharf La. B18: Hock 3C 100
  B91: Sol 6H 137
  WS7: Chase .2C 10
Wharf Rd. B11: Tys 6H 119
  B30: King Nor 5C 146
Wharf Rd. Ind. Est. B11: Tys 6H 119
Wharfside B69: O'bry 2F 97
Wharfside Leisure Complex
  B30: King Nor 2D 146
Wharfside St. B1: Birm 6B 4 (2E 117)
  (not continuous)
Wharf St. B6: Aston 2A 102
  B18: Hock 3C 100
  WS2: Wals 2A 48
  WV1: Wolv 2A 44
Whar Hall Rd. B92: Sol 5A 138
Wharton Av. B92: Sol 6A 138
Wharton Rd. B66: Smeth 2G 99
Wharton St. B7: Nech 1D 102
Wharton St. Ind. Est. B7: Nech 1D 102
Wharwell La. WS6: Gt Wyr 4G 7
Whatcote Grn. B92: Sol 5H 137
Whatecroft, The B17: Harb 5F 115
Whateley Av. WS3: Wals 3D 32
Whateley Cres. B36: Cas B 1H 105
Whateley Grn. B36: Cas B 1G 105
  B74: Four O 3G 53
Whateley Hall Cl. B93: Know 2E 167
Whateley Hall Rd. B93: Know 2D 166
Whateley Lodge Dr. B36: Cas B 1G 105
Whateley Pl. WS3: Wals 3D 32
Whateley Rd. B21: Hand 1A 100
  WS3: Wals 3D 32
Wheatcroft Cl. B62: B'hth 3F 113
  B75: R'ley 6C 38
Wheatcroft Dr. B37: Chel W 2E 123
Wheatcroft Gro. DY2: Dud 6H 77
Wheatcroft Rd. B33: Yard 1D 120
Wheaten Cl. B37: Chel W 6F 107
Wheatfield Cl. B36: Cas B 2C 106
Wheatfield Vw. B31: N'fld 1B 144
Wheat Hill WS5: Wals 3A 50
Wheathill Cl. WV4: Penn 2C 58
Wheatland Gro. WS9: A'rdge 5D 34
Wheatlands, The WV6: Pert 6D 24
Wheatlands Cft. B33: Kitts G 6A 106
Wheatley Cl. B68: O'bry 3B 114
  B75: Four O 6A 38
  B92: Sol 5A 138
Wheatley Grange B46: Col 3H 107
Wheatley Gro. WS6: Gt Wyr 3G 7

Wheatley Rd. B68: O'bry 3A 114
Wheatley St. B70: W Brom 4G 79
  WV2: Ett 5A 44
Wheatmoor Ri. B75: S Cold 5C 54
Wheatmoor Rd. B75: S Cold 4D 54
Wheatmore Gro. B75: S Cold 4D 54
Wheaton Cl. WV10: Oxl 2G 27
Wheaton Va. B20: Hand 4A 82
Wheatridge Cl. DY6: W Hth 1G 91
Wheats Av. B17: Harb 2F 131
Wheatsheaf Cl. B75: R'ley 5C 38
Wheatsheaf Rd. B16: Edg 1H 115
  B69: Tiv 1A 96
  WV8: Pend 6C 14
Wheatstone Cl. DY3: Sed 1A 76
Wheatstone Gro. B33: Stech 4D 104
WHEATSTONE PARK 2D 12
Wheel Av. WV8: Cod 4F 13
Wheel Cl., The WV8: Cod 4F 13
Wheeldon Ho. B26: Yard 1C 136
Wheeler Cl. WV8: Cod 3E 13
Wheeler Ho. B69: O'bry 2G 97
Wheeler Rd. WV11: Wed 1E 29
Wheeler's Fold
  WV1: Wolv 3C 170 (1H 43)
Wheeler's Hill DY8: Stourb 5D 108
  (off Lwr. High St.)
Wheeler's La. B13: Mose 1G 147
Wheeler St. B19: Hock, Loz 3F 101
  DY8: Stourb .6D 108
Wheeler St. Shop. Cen.
  B19: Birm 3F 101
Wheeley Moor Rd. B37: K'hrst 4C 106
Wheeley Rd. B92: Sol 6H 137
Wheeley's La. B15: Birm 3E 117
Wheeley's Rd. B15: Edg 4D 116
Wheelfield WV8: Cod 4F 13
Wheelock Cl. B74: S'tly 4H 51
Wheels Park .1C 118
Wheelwright Cl. WS10: Darl 5C 46
Wheelwright Ct. B24: Erd 5E 85
Wheelwright Rd. B24: Erd 5E 85
Wheldrake Av. B34: S End 4G 105
Whernside Dr. WV6: Wolv 4E 27
Wherretts Well La. B91: Sol 2A 152
Whetstone Cl. B15: Edg 6B 116
Whetstone Grn. WV10: Bush 6H 15
Whetstone Gro. WV10: Bush 1H 27
Whetstone La. WS9: A'rdge 5D 34
Whetstone Rd. WV10: Bush 1H 27
Whetty Bri. Rd. B45: Rub 3E 157
Whetty La. B45: Rub 2E 157
Whichbury Ct. B65: Row R 5D 96
Whichford Cl. B76: Walm 1B 86
Whichford Gro. B9: Bord G 1H 119
While Rd. B72: S Cold 1H 69
Whilmot Cl. WV10: F'stne 1D 16
Whinberry Ri. DY5: P'ntt 6G 75
Whisley Brook La. B28: Hall G 3F 135
Whistler Gro. WV10: Bush 1C 28
Whiston Av. WV11: Wed 2A 30
Whiston Gro. B29: W Cas 5F 131
Whiston Ho. WS1: Wals 2D 48
Whitacre La. WS14: Lynn 6G 11
Whitacre Rd. B9: Bord G 6E 103
  B93: Know 2D 166
Whitbourne Cl. B12: Bal H 6B 118
Whitburn Av. B42: P Barr 2C 82
Whitburn Cl. WV9: Pend 5E 15
Whitby Cl. WS3: Blox 4F 19
Whitby Rd. B12: Bal H 1A 134
Whitchurch La. B90: Dic H 3F 163
Whitcot Gro. B31: Longb 1D 158
Whitebeam Cl. DY3: Lwr G 3G 75
  WS8: Clay 1A 22
Whitebeam Cft. B38: King Nor 6A 146
Whitebeam Rd. B37: Chel W 3E 123
White City Rd. DY5: Quar B 2C 110
White Cl. DY9: Pedm 3G 125
Whitecrest B43: Gt Barr 3B 66
Whitecroft Rd. B26: Sheld 6H 121
White Falcon Ct. B91: Sol 4D 150
White Farm Rd. B74: Four O 4E 37
White Fld. Av. B17: Harb 5E 115
Whitefield Cl. WV8: Bilb 5H 13
Whitefields Cres. B91: Sol 5F 151

Whitefields Ga. B91: Sol 6E 151
Whitefields Rd. B91: Sol 6E 151
(not continuous)
Whitefriars B91: Sol 2H 151
Whitefriars Dr. B63: Hale 1A 128
Whitegates Rd. WV14: Cose 2F 61
Whitehall Dr. B63: Hale 1B 128
DY1: Dud 5C 76
Whitehall Ind. Pk. DY4: Tip 2E 79
Whitehall Rd. B9: Small H 1D 118
B21: Hand 2C 100
B63: Hale 1B 128
B64: Crad H 2E 111
B70: W Brom 2E 79
DY4: Tip 2D 78
DY6: K'wfrd 3A 92
DY8: Stourb 3F 125
WS1: Wals 4C 48
(not continuous)
WV4: Penn 1F 59
White Hart, The WS1: Wals 3C 48
(off Caldmore Grn.)
Whitehead Dr. B76: Min 1H 87
Whitehead Gro. CV7: Bal C 2H 169
Whitehead Rd. B6: Aston 2G 101
Whiteheath Ct. B69: O'bry 5E 97
(off Birchfield La.)
White Hill B31: N'fld 2F 145
Whitehill La. B29: W Cas 2E 145
White Hollies WS3: Pels 3D 20
Whitehorse Rd. WS8: Bwnhls 3A 10
Whitehouse Av. WS10: Darl 4B 46
WS10: W'bry 2F 63
WV3: Wolv 3B 42
WV11: Wed 2H 29
White Ho. Cl. B91: Sol 4D 150
WHITEHOUSE COMMON 4C 54
Whitehouse Comn. Rd. B75: S Cold 3C 54
Whitehouse Ct. B75: S Cold 6D 54
Whitehouse Cres. B75: S Cold 3C 54
WV11: Wed 6H 17
Whitehouse Dr. B66: Smeth 2E 99
WHITEHOUSE GATE 5D 97
White Ho. Grn. B91: Sol 4D 150
Whitehouse La. DY3: Stourt, Swind 6A 72
DY7: Stourt 6A 72
WV8: Cod, Cod W 1B 12
Whitehouse Pl. B45: Rub 3F 157
White Ho's. La. WV10: F'stne 1C 16
(not continuous)
Whitehouse St. B6: Aston 3H 101
DY4: Tip .5A 78
WS2: Wals 6B 32
WV14: Cose 5E 61
White Ho. Way B91: Sol 4E 151
Whitehouse Way WS9: A'rdge 5B 34
Whitemoor Dr. B90: M'path 2E 165
White Oak Dr. DY6: K'wfrd 3A 92
WV3: Wolv 3A 42
Whitepoplars Cl. DY5: Brie H 5G 93
White Rd. B11: S'brk 4C 118
B32: Quin 5B 114
B67: Smeth 3C 98
White Row WV5: Try 4C 56
Whites Dr. DY3: Sed 5A 60
Whiteslade Cl. B93: Know 2C 166
Whitesmiths Cl. DY3: Sed 5H 59
Whitesmiths Cft. B14: King H 5G 133
Whites Rd. B71: W Brom 1A 80
WHITE STITCH 1H 141
Whitestitch La. CV7: Mer 2H 141
Whitestone Rd. B63: Hale 5A 112
White St. B12: Bal H 6A 118
WS1: Wals 3C 48
Whites Wood WV5: Wom 2G 73
Whitethorn Cres. B74: S'tly 2F 51
Whitethorn Rd. DY8: Stourb 2E 109
Whitewood Glade WV12: W'hall 5E 31
Whitford Dr. B90: M'path 2F 165
Whitgreave Av. WV10: Bush 1A 28
WV10: F'stne 1D 16
Whitgreave Ct. B70: W Brom 4E 79
WV10: F'stne 1D 16
Whitgreave St. B70: W Brom 4E 79
Whitland Cl. B45: Redn 3H 157
Whitland Dr. B14: King H 4H 147

Whitley Cl. WV6: Tett 1H 41
Whitley Ct. B20: Hand 4A 82
Whitley Ct. Rd. B32: Quin 5A 114
Whitley Dr. B74: S'tly 3A 52
Whitley St. WS10: W'bry 2E 63
Whitlock Gro. B14: King H 4A 148
WHITLOCK'S END 3E 163
Whitlock's End Station (Rail) 2E 163
Whitminster Av. B24: Erd 4H 85
Whitminster Cl. WV12: W'hall 5D 30
Whitmore Hill WV1: Wolv 2A 170 (6G 27)
Whitmore Ho. WV6: Wolv 5E 27
WHITMORE REANS 5E 27
Whitmore Rd. B10: Small H 3C 118
DY8: Stourb 6B 108
Whitmore St. B18: Hock 4D 100
WS1: Wals 4B 48
WV1: Wolv 2C 170 (1H 43)
Whitnash Cl. CV7: Bal C 3G 169
Whitney Av. DY8: Woll 5B 108
Whittaker St. WV2: Ett 5A 44
Whittall St. B4: Birm 2E 5 (6G 101)
Whittimere St. WS1: Wals 1D 48
Whittingham Gro. WV11: Wed 3H 29
Whittingham Rd. B63: Hale 6H 111
Whittington Cl. B14: King H 2G 147
B71: W Brom 5D 64
Whittington Gro. B33: Yard 1D 120
Whittington Hall La. DY7: Kinv 1A 124
Whittington Oval B33: Yard 1E 121
Whittington Rd. DY8: Stourb 2B 124
Whittle Cft. B35: Cas V 4D 86
Whittleford Gro. B36: Cas B 6G 87
Whitton St. WS10: Darl 5E 47
Whitwell Cl. B90: M'path 4E 165
Whitworth Cl. WS10: Darl 4E 47
Whitworth Dr. B71: W Brom 4C 64
Whitworth Ind. Pk. B9: Bord G 1C 118
Wholesale Markets Pct.
B5: Birm 6F 5 (2G 117)
Whyle St. B63: Hale 1B 128
Whyley St. B70: W Brom 3G 79
Whyley Wlk. B69: O'bry 4G 97
Whynot St. B63: Crad 6D 110
Wibert Cl. B29: S Oak 4C 132
Wichnor Rd. B92: Olton 6D 120
Wickets, The DY5: Brie H 6G 93
Wickets Twr. B5: Edg 6E 117
Wickham Gdns. WV11: Wed 3C 28
Wickham Sq. B70: W Brom 5H 79
Wicklow Cl. B63: Hale 4F 127
Wideacre Dr. B44: Gt Barr 6G 67
Wide Acres B45: Fran 6F 143
Widney Av. B29: S Oak 3G 131
WS9: A'rdge 6D 22
Widney Cl. B93: Ben H 4B 166
Widney La. B91: Sol 6C 150
Widney Manor Golf Course 2G 165
Widney Mnr. Rd. B91: Sol 5G 151
B93: Know 5G 151
Widney Manor Station (Rail) 1G 165
Widney Rd. B93: Ben H, Know 4A 166
Wiggin Cotts. B17: Harb 6G 115
Wiggin Ho. WS3: Blox 4A 20
Wiggins Cft. B76: Walm 2D 70
Wiggins Hill Rd. B76: Min, Wis 1B 88
Wigginsmill Rd. WS10: W'bry 4D 62
Wiggin St. B16: Birm 6B 100
Wight Cft. B36: Cas B 3D 106
WIGHTWICK 2E 41
Wightwick Bank WV6: Tett 2G 41
Wightwick Cl. WS3: Blox 6H 19
Wightwick Ct. WV6: Tett 1G 41
Wightwick Gro. WV6: Tett 1G 41
Wightwick Hall Rd. WV6: Tett 2E 41
Wightwick Leys WV6: Tett 1F 41
Wightwick Manor 2F 41
Wigland Way B38: King Nor 6C 146
Wigmore Gro. B44: K'sdng 5B 68
Wigmore La. B71: W Brom 5E 65
(not continuous)
Wigorn La. DY9: Pedm 5F 125
Wigorn Rd. B67: Smeth 2D 114
Wilberforce Way B92: Sol 6B 138
Wilcote Gro. B27: A Grn 5A 136

Wildacres DY8: Woll 5A 108
Wilday Cl. DY4: Tip 2A 78
Wilde Cl. B14: King H 3F 147
Wilderley Cl. B31: N'fld 4A 144
Wilderness La. B43: Gt Barr 3H 65
Wildfell Rd. B27: A Grn 3B 136
WILDMOOR 5A 156
Wildmoor La. B61: Cats, Wild 6A 156
Wildmoor Rd. B90: Shir 2H 149
Wildside Activity Cen. 4D 26
Wildtree Av. WV10: Bush 5C 16
Wiley Av. WS10: Darl 5C 46
Wiley Av. Sth. WS10: Darl 6C 46
Wilford Gro. B76: Walm 1F 87
B91: Sol 5F 151
Wilford Rd. B71: W Brom 1B 80
Wilkes Av. WS2: Wals 1F 47
Wilkes Cl. WS3: Pels 4C 20
Wilkes Cft. DY3: Sed 6H 59
Wilkes Rd. WV8: Cod 3F 13
Wilkes St. B71: W Brom 6C 64
WV13: W'hall 2A 46
Wilkin, The WS8: Bwnhls 3G 9
Wilkin Rd. WS8: Bwnhls 3G 9
Wilkins Ho. WS3: Blox 1H 31
(off Sandbank)
Wilkinson Av. WV14: Bils 2G 61
Wilkinson Cl. B73: W Grn 3H 69
Wilkinson Cft. B8: W End 3A 104
Wilkinson Ho. DY4: Tip 6G 61
Wilkinson Rd. WS10: Mox 6A 46
Wilkinson Rd. WV14: Bils 4F 45
Wilks Grn. B21: Hand 4H 81
Willard Rd. B25: Yard 5A 120
Willaston Rd. B33: Sheld 4H 121
Willclare Rd. B26: Sheld 5E 121
Willcock Rd. WV2: Wolv 4A 44
WILLENHALL 1B 46
Willenhall Ind. Est.
WV13: W'hall 6B 30
Willenhall La. WS2: Wals 2F 31
WS3: Blox .2F 31
Willenhall La. Ind. Est.
WS3: Blox .1G 31
Willenhall Mus. 2B 46
Willenhall Rd. WS10: Darl 2D 46
WV1: Wolv .2C 44
WV13: W'hall 2C 44
WV14: Bils .5H 45
Willenhall St. WS10: Darl 3C 46
Willenhall Trad. Est. WV13: W'hall 2H 45
Willerby Fold WV10: Bush 3B 16
Willersey Rd. B13: Mose 5D 134
Willes Ct. B62: Quin 4G 113
(off Binswood Rd.)
Willes Rd. B18: Win G 3A 100
Willett Av. WS7: Chase 1A 10
Willett Rd. B71: W Brom 5C 64
Willetts Dr. B63: Crad 1D 126
Willetts Lodge DY8: Word 6C 92
Willetts Rd. B31: N'fld 6E 145
Willetts Way B64: Old H 1H 111
Willey Gro. B24: Erd 5H 85
William Barrows Way DY4: Tip 6G 61
William Bentley Ct. WV11: Wed 4E 29
William Booth La. B4: Birm . . .1D 4 (5F 101)
William Cook Rd. B8: W End 4H 103
William Ct. B13: Mose 1H 133
B16: Edg 2B 116
William Edward St. B12: Birm 3H 117
William Grn. Rd. WS10: W'bry 2A 64
William Harper Rd. WV13: W'hall 2B 46
William Henry St. B7: Nech 3A 102
William Kerr Rd. DY4: Tip 2C 78
William Lench Ct. B32: Quin 5B 114
William Paget Ho. WS10: W'bry 2E 63
William Rd. B31: N'fld 6D 144
B67: Smeth 6B 98
William Savage Way B66: Smeth 5G 99
William's Cl. WV12: W'hall 4C 30
Williamson St. WV3: Wolv 6A 170 (3F 43)
William St. B15: Birm 6A 4 (2E 117)
B70: W Brom 2E 79
DY5: Brie H 6G 93
WS4: Wals .6D 32
William St. Nth. B19: Birm 5F 101

William St. W. B66: Smeth 2F 99
William Wiggin Av. WS3: Blox 5H 19
Willingsworth Rd.
    WS10: W'bry 4C 62
Willingworth Cl. WV14: Cose 2C 60
Willis Pearson Av. WV14: Bils 3H 61
Willmore Gro. B38: King Nor 1B 160
Willmore Rd. B20: Hand 5F 83
Willmott Cl. B75: R'ley 6B 38
Willmott Rd. B75: R'ley 6B 38
Willoughby Ct. B76: Walm 3D 70
    (off Springfield Rd.)
Willoughby Dr. B91: Sol 6F 151
Willoughby Gro. B29: W Cas 4E 131
Willow Av. B17: Edg 1E 115
    WS10: W'bry 1F 63
    WV11: Wed 1C 28
Willow Bank WV3: Wolv 2A 42
Willowbank Rd. B93: Know 3B 166
Willow Cl. B21: Hand 1H 99
    B64: Old H 2G 111
Willow Coppice B32: Bart G 4A 130
Willow Ct. B13: Mose 2A 134
    B66: Smeth 1B 98
    DY9: Lye 6H 109
Willowdale Grange WV6: Tett 4C 26
Willow Dr. B21: Hand 6G 81
    B69: Tiv 2C 96
    B90: Ches G 5B 164
    WV8: Bilb .4H 13
Willow End DY9: W'cte 2H 125
Willowfields WV14: Cose 5E 61
Willow Gdns. B16: Birm 5B 100
Willow Gro. WV11: Ess 4B 18
    WV13: W'hall 2B 46
Willow Hgts. B64: Crad H 3A 112
Willowherb Cl. WS5: Wals 2E 65
Willowherb Way B90: Dic H 4G 163
Willow Ho. B7: Birm 5A 102
    (off Vauxhall Rd.)
    B71: W Brom 4E 65
Willow M. B29: S Oak 4F 131
Willow Pk. Dr. DY8: Stourb 3E 125
Willow Ri. DY5: Brie H 2G 109
Willow Rd. B30: B'vlle 5B 132
    B43: Gt Barr 4B 66
    B91: Sol 5C 150
    DY1: Dud 3C 76
    WV3: Wolv .3B 42
Willows, The B27: A Grn 3H 135
    B47: H'wd .3A 162
    B74: Four O 1F 53
    B76: Walm .3D 70
    DY2: Neth .4G 95
    WV5: Wom .2F 73
Willowsborough Rd. B62: B'hth 3F 113
Willows Cres. B12: Bal H 6F 117
Willowside WS4: S'fld 1G 33
Willows Rd. B12: Bal H 6G 117
    WS1: Wals .2E 49
    WS4: S'fld .1G 33
Willow Wlk. B76: Walm 6D 70
Willow Way B37: Chel W 1D 122
Wills Av. B71: W Brom 5H 63
Willsbridge Covert
    B14: King H 5F 147
Wills Ho. B70: W Brom 5A 80
Willson Cft. B28: Hall G 4D 148
Wills St. B19: Loz 2D 100
Wills Way B66: Smeth 5G 99
Wilmcote Cl. B12: Bal H 5G 117
Wilmcote Dr. B75: Four O 6H 37
Wilmcote Rd. B91: Sol 1D 150
Wilmcote Twr. B12: Birm 4H 117
Wilmington Rd. B32: Quin 5H 113
Wilmore La. B47: Wyt 6G 161
Wilmot Av. B46: Col 3H 107
Wilmot Cl. CV7: Bal C 1H 169
Wilmot Dr. B23: Erd 1G 85
    DY4: Tip 1G 77
Wilmot Gdns. DY1: Dud 5C 76
Wilnecote Gro. B42: P Barr 3F 83
Wilner's Vw. WS3: Pels 2D 20
Wilsford Cl. B14: King H 6F 147
    WS4: S'fld .1G 33
Wilsford Grn. B15: Edg 4A 116

Wilson Dr. B69: Tiv 4C 78
    B75: S Cold 6E 55
    (not continuous)
Wilson Rd. B19: Loz 1F 101
    B66: Smeth 6F 99
    B68: O'bry .3B 114
    DY5: Brie H 5G 93
    WV14: Cose 6E 61
Wilsons Rd. B93: Know 3E 167
Wilson St. DY4: Tip 2A 78
    WV1: Wolv .6H 27
Wilton Cl. DY3: Sed 6A 60
Wilton Rd. B11: S'hll 6B 118
    B20: Hand .6D 82
    B23: Erd 2G 85
    CV7: Bal C .3H 169
Wilton St. B19: Loz 1F 101
Wiltshire Cl. WS2: Wals 5B 32
Wiltshire Dr. B29: W Cas 6G 131
    (off Tugford Rd.)
Wiltshire Dr. B63: Crad 4D 110
Wiltshire Way B71: W Brom 6A 64
Wimberger Ho. B71: W Brom 3B 80
    (off Hallam St.)
Wimbledon Dr. DY8: Stourb 3F 125
Wimborne Rd. WV10: Wolv 3C 28
Wimbourne Rd. B16: Edg 6H 99
    B76: Walm .1E 71
Wimhurst Mdw. WV10: Bush 3B 16
Wimperis Way B43: Gt Barr 1E 67
Wimpole Gro. B44: K'sdng 6B 68
Wincanton Cft. B36: Hodg H 1A 104
Winceby Rd. WV6: Pert 6F 25
Winchcombe Cl. B92: Olton 3F 137
    DY1: Dud 4A 76
Winchcombe Rd. B92: Olton 3F 137
Winchester Cl. B65: Row R 5E 97
    DY9: Hag 6E 125
Winchester Ct. B74: Four O 1F 53
    (off Vesey Cl.)
Winchester Dr. B37: Chel W 1C 122
    DY8: Stourb 2E 125
Winchester Gdns. B31: N'fld 4E 145
Winchester Gro. B21: Hand 1G 99
Winchester M. WS9: A'rdge 5D 34
Winchester Ri. DY1: Dud 5C 76
Winchester Rd. B20: Hand 6F 83
    B71: W Brom 5H 63
    WV10: F'hses 4G 15
Winchester Works B62: B'hth 3D 112
Winchfield Dr. B17: Harb 3D 114
Wincote Dr. WV6: Tett 5A 26
Wincrest Way B34: S End 4G 105
Windermere Dr. B74: S'tly 6H 35
    DY6: K'wfrd 3B 92
Windermere Ho. B15: Edg 2F 117
    (off Vincent Dr.)
    B69: O'bry .4D 96
Windermere Rd. B13: Mose 4B 134
    B21: Hand .5A 82
    WV6: Tett 1B 26
Windfall Ct. B24: Erd 3B 86
Winding Mill Nth. DY5: Quar B 4A 110
Winding Mill Sth. DY5: Quar B 4A 110
Windlass Cft. B31: N'fld 2D 144
Windleaves Rd. B36: Cas B 1A 106
Windley Cl. B19: Birm 4E 101
Windley Ho. B73: New O 3C 68
Windmill Av. B45: Rub 1E 157
    B46: Col 2H 107
Windmill Bank WV5: Wom 6G 57
Windmill Cl. B31: N'fld 2G 145
Windmill Cres. B66: Smeth 4G 99
    WV3: Wolv .2G 41
Windmill End DY2: Neth 5G 95
Windmill Fold WV5: Wom 6G 57
Windmill Gro. DY6: W Hth 1H 91
Windmill Hill B31: N'fld 2F 145
    B63: Crad .5E 111
Windmill Ind. Pk. DY2: Dud 3D 94
Windmill La. B66: Smeth 5F 99
    WV3: Wolv .2G 41
Windmill Pct. B66: Smeth 4F 99
Windmill Rd. B90: Shir 5E 149
Windmills Shop. Cen.
    B66: Smeth 5F 99

Windmill St. B1: Birm 6D 4 (2F 117)
    DY1: Dud 5C 76
    DY3: Up Gor 2H 75
    WS1: Wals .3C 48
    WS10: W'bry 2G 63
Windmill Ter. WS10: W'bry 2G 63
Windmill Vw. DY1: Dud 6D 60
Windridge Cres. B92: Sol 5B 138
Windrow, The WV6: Pert 5D 24
Windrush Cl. B92: Olton 3E 137
    WS3: Pels .6E 21
Windrush Gro. B15: Birm 3F 117
    B29: S Oak .5C 132
Windrush Rd. B47: H'wd 2B 162
Windsor Arc. B2: Birm 3E 5 (6G 101)
Windsor Av. B68: O'bry 6G 97
    WV4: Penn .5C 42
Windsor Cl. B31: Longb 3E 159
    B45: Fran 5G 143
    B63: Hale 2H 127
    B65: Row R 5C 96
    DY3: Gorn .6F 75
Windsor Ct. B38: King Nor 6B 146
Windsor Cres. DY2: Dud 3F 95
Windsor Dr. B24: Erd 2A 86
    B92: Sol 2F 137
Windsor Gdns. WV3: Wolv 4G 41
    WV8: Cod 4F 13
Windsor Gate WV12: W'hall 5C 30
Windsor Gro. DY8: Word 2C 108
    WS4: S'fld .5G 21
Windsor Ho. B23: Erd 1F 85
    WV3: Wolv .3F 43
    (off Pennant Ct.)
Windsor Ind. Est. B7: Birm 4A 102
Windsor Lodge B92: Olton 5B 136
Windsor Pl. B7: Birm 6A 102
    B23: Erd 4E 85
Windsor Rd. B30: Stir 2D 146
    B36: Cas B .2B 106
    B63: Hale 1H 127
    B65: Row R 5C 96
    B68: O'bry .6G 97
    B71: W Brom 5H 63
    B73: New O 4D 68
    DY4: Tip 5A 62
    DY8: Stourb 2B 124
    WS6: C Hay 1E 7
    WV4: Ett 6B 44
    WV5: Wom .1F 73
Windsor St. B7: Birm 4H 101
    WS1: Wals .4C 48
    WV14: Bils .5E 45
Windsor St. Sth. B7: Birm 5A 102
Windsor Ter. B16: Edg 2B 116
Windsor Vw. B32: Bart G 6H 129
Windsor Wlk. WS10: Darl 3D 46
Windsor Way WS4: Rus 2H 33
Winds Point DY9: Hag 6E 125
Windward Way B36: Cas B 1B 106
Windward Way Ind. Est.
    B36: Cas B 1B 106
Windyridge Rd. B76: Walm 1D 86
Winford Av. DY6: K'wfrd 5C 92
Wingate Cl. B30: King Nor 3B 146
Wingate Ct. B74: Four O 5E 37
Wingate Rd. WS2: Wals 1E 47
Wing Cl. WS2: Wals 5F 31
Wingfield Cl. B37: F'bri 6B 106
Wingfield Ho. B37: K'hrst 4B 106
Wingfield Rd. B42: Gt Barr 6E 67
    B46: Col 4H 107
Wingfoot Av. WV10: Bush 1A 28
Wingfoot Cl. B24: Erd 6A 86
Wingfoot Way B24: Erd 6A 86
Wing Yip Cen. B7: Nech 3B 102
Winifride Ct. B17: Harb 6F 115
Winkle St. B70: W Brom 3H 79
Winleigh Rd. B20: Hand 5B 82
Winnall Cl. WV14: Cose 3F 61
Winn Ho. WS2: Wals 6B 32
    (off Burrowes St.)
Winnie Rd. B29: S Oak 4A 132
Winnington Rd. B8: W End 2G 103
Winnipeg Rd. B38: King Nor 1C 160
Winrush Cl. DY3: Gorn 4H 75

Winscar Cft. DY3: Lwr G 4A 76
Winsford Cl. B63: Hale 5A 112
  B76: Walm .2C 70
  CV7: Bal C 3G 169
Winsham Gro. B21: Hand 1A 100
Winslow Av. B8: W End 5H 103
Winslow Dr. WV6: Wolv 5D 26
Winslow Ho. B29: S Oak 4F 131
WINSON GREEN 4A 100
Winson Green / Outer Circle Stop (Metro)
  . . . . .2A 100
Winson Grn. Rd. B18: Win G 4A 100
Winson St. B18: Win G 5H 99
Winspear Cl. CV7: Ner 4H 141
Winstanley Rd. B33: Stech 1B 120
Winster Av. B93: Dorr 5A 166
Winster Gro. B44: Gt Barr 3F 67
Winster Gro. Ind. Est.
  B44: Gt Barr 3F 67
Winster Rd. B43: Gt Barr 5H 65
  WV1: Wolv .2D 44
Winston Churchill Ct.
  WV14: Bils .3E 45
Winston Dr. B20: Hand 6D 82
  B62: Roms 3A 142
Winston Rd. DY3: Swind 5E 73
Winterbourne Cft. B14: King H 6E 147
Winterbourne House & Garden 1C 132
Winterbourne Rd. B91: Sol 3D 150
Winterdene CV7: Bal C 2H 169
Winterley Gdns. DY3: Sed 1A 76
Winterley La. WS4: Rus 2G 33
Winterton Rd. B44: K'sdng 2A 68
Winthorpe Dr. B91: Sol 1G 165
Wintney Cl. B17: Harb 4E 115
Winton Gro. B76: Walm 1E 87
Winwood Rd. B65: Row R 6E 97
Winwoods Gro. B32: Bart G 5G 129
Wiremill Cl. B44: Gt Barr 1G 83
Wirral Rd. B31: N'fld 1D 144
Wiseacre Cft. B90: Shir 5E 149
Wiseman Gro. B23: Erd 4D 68
Wisemeadows B90: Shir 5E 149
Wisemore WS1: Wals 1C 48
  WS2: Wals .1C 48
Wishaw Cl. B90: Shir 5E 149
Wishaw Golf Course 3G 71
Wishaw Gro. B37: K'hrst 4B 106
Wishaw La. B76: Curd 1D 88
  B76: Min, Wis 1H 87
Wisley Way B32: Harb 6D 114
Wistaria Cl. B31: N'fld 1E 145
Wisteria Dr. WS5: Wals 1D 64
  WS8: Bwnhls 3G 9
Wisteria Gro. B44: Gt Barr 3G 67
Wistmans Cl. DY1: Dud 5A 76
Wistwood Hayes WV10: Bush 3B 16
Witham Cl. B76: Walm 4E 71
Witham Cft. B91: Sol 6G 151
Withdean Cl. B11: S'brk 6D 118
Witherford Cl. B29: S Oak 5G 131
Witherford Cft. B91: Sol 5B 150
Witherford Way B29: S Oak 5G 131
Withern Way DY3: Gorn 4G 75
Withers Rd. WV8: Bilb 4H 13
Withers Way B71: W Brom 3B 80
Withington Covert B14: King H 5F 147
Withington Gro.
  B93: Ben H, Dorr 5A 166
Withybrook Rd. B90: Shir 1H 163
Withy Gro. B37: K'hrst 4B 106
Withy Hill Rd.
  B75: Bass P, S Cold 4D 54
Withymere La. WV5: Wom 5A 58
Withymoor Rd. DY2: Neth 5G 95
  DY8: Amb .4E 109
WITHYMOOR VILLAGE 2H 109
Withy Rd. WV14: Bils 2E 61
Withy Rd. Ind. Est. WV14: Bils 2E 61
Withywood CV12: W'hall 6C 18
Witley Av. B63: Hale 1G 127
  B91: Sol 5G 151
Witley Cres. B69: O'bry 4E 97
Witley Farm Cl. B91: Sol 5G 151
Witley Rd. B31: N'fld 5H 145
Witney Dr. B37: F'bri 1B 122

Witney Gro. WV10: F'hses 4F 15
Wittersham Ct. WV13: W'hall 1B 46
  (off Walsall Rd.)
WITTON 6H 83
Witton Bank B62: Quin 4F 113
Witton La. B6: Aston 6H 83
  B71: W Brom 5G 63
Witton Lodge Rd. B23: Erd 6B 68
Witton Rd. B6: Aston, Witt 1G 101
  WV4: Penn .5E 43
Witton Station (Rail) 6H 83
Witton St. B9: Birm 1B 118
  DY8: Stourb 1C 124
Wixford Cft. B34: S End 2E 105
Wixford Gro. B90: Shir 5B 150
Wizards Wlk. B13: Mose 3G 133
Wobaston Rd. WV9: Pend 4B 14
  WV10: F'hses 3E 15
Woburn Av. WV12: W'hall 3B 30
Woburn Cres. B43: Gt Barr 4H 65
Woburn Dr. B62: Hale 4B 112
  DY5: Brie H 4F 109
Woburn Gro. B27: A Grn 4A 136
Wodehouse Cl. WV5: Wom 1E 73
Wodehouse La. DY3: Sed 5A 58
  WV5: Wom .5A 58
Woden Av. WV11: Wed 3E 29
Woden Cl. WV5: Wom 6F 57
Woden Cres. WV11: Wed 3E 29
Woden Pas. WS10: W'bry 3F 63
Woden Rd. WV10: Wolv 5A 28
Woden Rd. E. WS10: W'bry 1H 63
Woden Rd. Nth. WS10: W'bry 6E 47
Woden Rd. Sth.
  WS10: W'bry 4F 63
Woden Rd. W. WS10: Darl 1D 62
Wodensfield Twr. WV11: Wed 4E 29
Woden Way WV11: Wed 3E 29
Wolcot Gro. B6: Witt 2H 83
Wold Wlk. B13: Mose 1B 148
Wolf Mountain 6C 26
Wolfsbane Dr. WS5: Wals 2E 65
WOLLASTON 5B 108
Wollaston Ct. DY8: Woll 5A 108
  WS1: Wals .1D 48
  (off Lwr. Rushall St.)
Wollaston Cres. WV11: Wed 3F 29
Wollaston Rd. DY7: Stourt 4A 108
  DY8: Amb .4C 108
Wollerton Gro. B75: S Cold 5D 54
WOLLESCOTE 6B 110
Wollescote Bus. Pk.
  DY9: Lye .6B 110
Wollescote Dr. B91: Sol 6F 151
  (not continuous)
Wollescote Rd. DY9: W'cte 2G 125
  (not continuous)
Wolmer Rd. WV11: Wed 5H 17
Wolseley Av. B27: A Grn 1B 136
Wolseley Bank WV10: Bush 2B 28
Wolseley Cl. B36: Cas B 6C 88
  WV10: Bush 2B 28
Wolseley Dr. B8: W End 2G 103
Wolseley Ga. WV10: Bush 2B 28
Wolseley Rd. B70: W Brom 6E 63
  WV14: Bils .4D 44
Wolseley St. B9: Birm 1B 118
  (not continuous)
Wolston Cl. B90: Shir 2H 149
WOLVERHAMPTON 4D 170 (1G 43)
Wolverhampton Art Gallery 2C 170
Wolverhampton Bus. Pk.
  WV10: F'hses 2H 15
Wolverhampton Race Course 3E 27
Wolverhampton Rd. B68: O'bry 5F 97
  B69: O'bry .2D 96
  DY3: Sed 4H 59
  DY6: W Hth 6A 74
  WS2: Wals .1G 47
  (not continuous)
  WS3: Blox .6H 19
  WS3: Pels .4C 20
  WS6: C Hay .4B 6
  WS11: Cann .1B 6
  (not continuous)
  WV4: Sed 2H 59
  WV6: Patt 6A 24

Wolverhampton Rd. WV8: Cod 4F 13
  (Gorsty Hayes)
  WV8: Cod 3F 13
  (The Square)
  WV10: Share .4B 6
  (Hospital La.)
  WV10: Share .3A 6
  (Warstone Rd., not continuous)
  WV10: Wolv .6B 28
  WV11: Ess .4H 17
  WV11: Wed .5C 28
Wolverhampton Rd. E. WV4: Penn 6H 43
Wolverhampton Rd. Sth. B32: Quin . . .4C 114
Wolverhampton Rd. W. WS2: Wals 1C 46
  WV13: W'hall 1C 46
Wolverhampton Science Pk.
  WV10: Wolv .3G 27
Wolverhampton Sports Arena 4E 27
Wolverhampton Station (Rail)
  . . . . .2D 170 (1H 43)
Wolverhampton St. DY1: Dud 5D 76
  WS2: Wals .1B 48
  WS10: Darl .4B 46
  WV13: W'hall 2H 45
  WV14: Bils .5E 45
Wolverhampton Swimming & Fitness Cen.
  . . . . .5D 28
Wolverhampton Wanderers FC
  . . . . .1A 170 (6G 27)
Wolverley Av. DY8: Woll 5A 108
  WV4: Penn .6B 42
Wolverley Cres. B69: O'bry 4D 96
Wolverley Rd. B32: Bart G 5H 129
  B63: Hale .3H 127
  B92: Sol 3H 137
Wolverson Cl. WV12: W'hall 5C 30
Wolverson Rd. WS9: Wals W 3C 22
Wolverton Rd. B37: Mars G 4D 122
  B45: Redn .3A 158
  DY2: Dud 6G 77
WOMBOURNE 1H 73
Wombourne Cl. DY3: Sed 5G 59
Wombourne Ent. Pk. WV5: Wom 2D 72
Wombourne Leisure Cen. 6F 57
Wombourne Pk. WV5: Wom 2F 73
Wombourne Rd. DY3: Swind 5E 73
Wombrook Bus. Cen. WV5: Wom 1E 73
Wombrook Ct. WV5: Wom 1G 73
Wombrook Dale WV5: Wom 1D 72
Woodacre Rd. B24: Erd 3A 86
Woodall Rd. B6: Aston 6H 83
Woodall St. B64: Crad H 2E 111
  WS3: Blox 6A 20
  (not continuous)
Woodard Rd. DY4: Tip 6C 62
Wood Av. DY3: Lwr G 3G 75
  WV11: Wed .3F 29
Wood Bank Rd. WV3: Wolv 3G 41
Woodbank Rd. DY3: Sed 6G 59
Woodberry Dr. B76: Walm 3E 71
Woodberry Wlk. B27: A Grn 2B 136
Woodbine Av. B10: Small H 3D 118
Woodbine Cft. B26: Sheld 5E 121
Woodbine Wlk. B37: Chel W 1F 123
Woodbourne B15: Edg 3H 115
  (not continuous)
Woodbourne Rd. B15: Edg 3G 115
  B17: Harb .3G 115
  B67: Smeth 1C 114
Woodbridge Cl. WS3: Blox 4G 19
  WS4: S'fld 6H 21
Woodbridge Rd. B13: Mose 2H 133
Woodbrooke Rd. B30: B'ville 6H 131
Woodbrooke Gro. B31: N'fld 1G 145
Woodbrooke Ho. B37: Chel W 1D 122
Woodburn Rd. B66: Smeth 2H 99
Woodbury Cl. B34: Hodg H 3E 105
  B62: B'hth .3F 113
  DY5: Brie H 1A 110
Woodbury Gro. B91: Sol 1F 165
Woodbury Rd. B62: B'hth 3F 113
  B62: Quin .4F 113
Woodchester Rd. B93: Dorr 6F 167
Woodchurch Grange B73: Bold 5F 69
Wood Cl. B46: Col 2H 107
Woodclose Rd. B37: F'bri 6B 106

Woodcock Cl. B31: Longb 6A **144**
WOODCOCK HILL 6C **130**
Woodcock La. B27: A Grn 2B **136**
    (not continuous)
  B31: N'fld 6C **130**
Woodcock La. Nth. B26: Yard 1B **136**
  B27: A Grn 1B **136**
Woodcock St. B7: Birm 1G **5** (5H **101**)
Woodcombe Cl. DY5: Brie H 4F **109**
Wood Comn. Grange WS3: Pels 3D **20**
Woodcote Dr. B8: Salt 4F **103**
  B93: Dorr 6H **167**
Woodcote Pl. B19: Loz 2E **101**
Woodcote Rd. B24: Erd 2B **86**
  WV6: Tett 5A **26**
Woodcote Way B18: Hock 4C **100**
  B74: S'tly 5H **51**
Wood Ct. B20: Hand 5C **82**
Wood Cft. B47: H'wd 3B **162**
Woodcroft Av. B20: Hand 4A **82**
  DY4: Tip 2E **77**
Woodcroft Cl. B64: Old H 3H **111**
  WS3: Pels 3E **21**
Woodcroft Ct. WS3: Blox 3C **32**
WOODCROSS 3B **60**
Woodcross La. WV14: Cose 3C **60**
Woodcross St. WV14: Cose 3B **60**
Woodcutter Cl. WS1: Wals 2B **48**
WOOD END 2E **29**
Woodend B20: Hand 1A **82**
Wood End Farm WS5: Wals 2H **49**
Wood End La. B24: Erd 4F **85**
Woodend Pl. WV6: Tett 5H **25**
Wood End Rd. B24: Erd 4F **85**
  WV11: Wed 6E **17**
Woodend Rd. WS5: Wals 3H **49**
Woodend Way WS9: A'rdge 6D **22**
Woodfall Av. B30: King Nor 2B **146**
Woodfield Av. B64: Crad H 3F **111**
  B69: O'bry 5G **97**
  DY5: P'ntt 2F **93**
  DY9: W'cte 3B **126**
  WV4: Penn 5D **42**
Woodfield Cl. B74: Four O 3H **53**
  WS5: Wals 6A **50**
Woodfield Cres. B12: Bal H 5A **118**
Woodfield Hgts. WV6: Tett 5B **26**
Woodfield Rd. B12: Bal H 5A **118**
  B13: King H 5H **133**
  B91: Sol 1F **151**
  DY3: Lwr G 3G **75**
Woodfield Social and Sports Club 5E **43**
Woodfold Cft. WS9: A'rdge 2D **34**
Woodford Av. B36: Cas B 1F **105**
Woodford La. WV9: Pend 5E **15**
Woodford Grn. Rd. B28: Hall G 5G **135**
Woodford La. WV5: Try, Wom 5C **56**
Woodford Way WV5: Wom 1D **72**
Woodfort Rd. B43: Gt Barr 6A **66**
WOODGATE 5H **129**
Woodgate Bus. Pk.
  B32: Bart G 1H **129**
    (not continuous)
Woodgate Dr. B32: Bart G 4G **129**
Woodgate Gdns. B32: Bart G 3G **129**
Woodgate La. B32: Bart G 3G **129**
Woodgate Valley Country Pk. 2A **130**
Woodgate Valley Country Pk. Vis. Cen.
  . . . . .3H **129**
Woodgate Valley Urban Farm 3G **129**
Woodglade Cft. B38: King Nor 5A **146**
WOOD GREEN 6H **47**
Wood Grn. WS6: C Hay 1E **7**
Woodgreen Cft. B68: O'bry 4A **114**
Wood Grn. Rd. B18: Win G 5H **99**
  WS10: W'bry 2G **63**
Woodgreen Rd. B68: O'bry 4A **114**
Woodhall Cl. DY4: Tip 5A **62**
Woodhall Cft. B92: Olton 2D **136**
Woodhall Ho. WS3: Blox 1A **32**
    (off Woodhall St.)
Woodhall Rd. WV4: Penn 1C **58**
Woodham Cl. B45: Fran 6E **143**
Woodhaven WS4: S'fld 6H **21**
WOOD HAYES 6E **17**
Wood Hayes Cft. WV10: Bush 5E **17**

Wood Hayes Rd. WV10: Bush, Wed 5D **16**
  WV11: Wed 5D **16**
Woodhill Cl. WV5: Wom 1F **73**
Woodhill Dr. WV5: Wom 2F **73**
Wood Ho. WS1: Wals 4D **48**
Woodhouse Ct. DY5: Quar B 2C **110**
Woodhouse Fold WV11: Wed 4F **29**
Woodhouse Rd. B32: Quin 5C **114**
  WV6: Tett 5H **25**
Woodhouse Rd. Nth. WV6: Tett 5H **25**
Woodhouse Way B64: Crad H 2E **111**
Woodhurst Rd. B13: Mose 1A **134**
Wooding Cres. DY4: Tip 4B **62**
Woodington Rd. B75: S Cold 6E **55**
Woodland Av. DY1: Dud 4E **77**
  DY5: Quar B 2C **110**
  WV6: Tett 6H **25**
Woodland Cl. DY9: Pedm 4H **125**
  WV12: W'hall 3D **30**
Woodland Ct. WS14: Shen W 2G **37**
Woodland Cres. WV3: Wolv 4B **42**
Woodland Dr. B66: Smeth 2C **98**
  WS6: C Hay 1E **7**
Woodland Gro. B43: Gt Barr 2A **66**
  DY3: Gorn 4F **75**
Woodland Ri. B64: Crad H 3H **111**
  B73: S Cold 1H **69**
Woodland Rd. B21: Hand 1G **99**
  B31: N'fld 4F **145**
  B62: B'hth 3D **112**
  WV3: Wolv 4B **42**
Woodlands, The B64: Crad H 4A **112**
  B75: S Cold 5E **55**
  DY8: Stourb 3E **125**
  WV8: Cod 5G **13**
Woodlands Av. B46: Wat O 5D **88**
  WS5: Wals 6A **50**
Woodlands Cen., The WV12: W'hall . . .2E **31**
Woodlands Cotts. WV5: Wom 1C **58**
Woodlands Crematorium
  B46: Col 4F **107**
Woodlands Cres. WS3: Pels 2D **20**
Woodlands Farm Rd. B24: Erd 3D **86**
Woodlands La. B90: Shir 1H **163**
Woodlands Paddock WV4: Penn 1C **58**
Woodlands Pk. Rd.
  B30: B'vlle, King Nor 1G **145**
Woodlands Rd. B8: Salt 5F **103**
  B11: S'hll 2B **134**
  B45: Rub 2D **156**
  WV5: Wom 2G **73**
Woodlands St. B66: Smeth 4G **99**
Woodlands Wlk. WV4: Penn 6C **42**
Woodlands Way B37: Chel W 6F **107**
Wood La. B17: Harb 5E **115**
  B20: Hand 5C **82**
  B24: Erd 6G **85**
  B32: Bart G 4G **129**
  B37: Mars G 3C **122**
  B70: W Brom 4G **79**
  B74: S'tly 2G **51**
  B92: Bars 5G **153**
  WS3: Pels 2D **20**
  WS9: A'rdge 6H **23**
  WS14: Foot 6H **23**
  WV10: F'hses 6H **15**
  WV12: W'hall 2E **31**
Wood La. Cl. WV12: W'hall 2E **31**
Woodlawn B91: Sol 3A **152**
Woodlawn Dr. DY6: K'wfrd 4B **92**
Woodlea Dr. B24: Erd 5F **85**
  B91: Sol 2C **150**
Wood Leasow B32: Bart G 3B **130**
Woodleaves B47: H'wd 1H **161**
Woodleigh Av. B17: Harb 1H **131**
Woodleigh Cl. B63: Hale 5A **112**
Woodleigh Ct. B38: King Nor 6B **146**
Woodleigh Rd. B72: W Grn 4A **70**
Woodleys, The B14: King H 3B **148**
Woodloes Rd. B90: Shir 1H **163**
Woodman Cl. B63: Hale 2C **128**
  WS10: W'bry 1H **63**
Woodman Gro. B75: R'ley 6C **38**
Woodman La. WS6: C Hay 1E **7**
Woodman Rd. B14: King H 6A **148**
  B63: Hale 2C **128**

Woodman Wlk. B23: Erd 2A **84**
Woodmeadow Rd. B30: King Nor 4D **146**
Woodnorton Dr. B13: Mose 3G **133**
Woodnorton Rd. B65: Row R 1F **113**
Woodpecker Gro. B36: Cas B 2C **106**
Woodpecker Rd. B33: Stech 5D **104**
Woodperry Av. B91: Sol 6G **151**
Woodridge B6: Aston 6G **83**
Woodridge Av. B32: Quin 1H **129**
Woodridge Rd. B63: Hale 6A **112**
Wood Rd. DY3: Lwr G 4G **75**
  WV5: Wom 5H **57**
  WV6: Tett 6H **25**
  WV8: Cod 2D **12**
Woodrough Dr. B13: Mose 3H **133**
Woodrow Cres. B93: Know 4C **166**
Woodrow La. B61: Cats 6B **156**
Woodruff Way WS5: Wals 1D **64**
Woodrush Dr. B47: H'wd 4A **162**
WOODS, THE 1A **64**
Woods, The B14: King H 4H **133**
WOODS BANK 5D **46**
Woods Bank Est., The WS10: Darl 1D **62**
Woodsbank Ter. WS10: Darl 6C **46**
Woods Cres. DY5: Quar B 2C **110**
WOODSETTON 1B **76**
Woodsetton Cl. DY1: Dud 1D **76**
Woodshires Rd. B92: Olton 6C **136**
WOODSIDE 3B **94**
Woodside B37: K'hrst 4A **106**
  B74: Four O 1E **53**
  WV11: Wed 1A **30**
Woodside Cl. WS5: Wals 5H **49**
Woodside Cres. B93: Know 5D **166**
Woodside Dr. B74: Lit As 4C **36**
Woodside Gro. WV8: Bilb 4H **13**
Woodside Ho. B34: S End 4A **106**
Woodside Ind. Est. DY5: Brie H 4B **94**
Woodside Rd. B29: S Oak 4C **132**
    (not continuous)
  DY2: Dud 3B **94**
  WS5: Wals 5H **49**
Woodside Way B32: Bart G 5G **129**
  B91: Sol 2C **150**
  WS9: A'rdge 4D **34**
  WV12: W'hall 2E **31**
Woods La. B64: Crad H 3E **111**
  DY5: Brie H 4H **109**
Woodsome Gro. B23: Erd 6C **68**
Woodsorrel Rd. DY1: Dud 3B **76**
Woodstile Cl. B75: R'ley 6B **38**
Woodstile Way B34: S End 3F **105**
Woodstock Cl. DY1: Dud 1C **94**
  DY8: Word 2A **108**
  WS5: Wals 2E **65**
Woodstock Cres. B93: Dorr 6B **166**
Woodstock Dr. B74: Four O 5D **36**
  DY8: Word 2A **108**
Woodstock Ho. B13: Mose 6A **134**
Woodstock Rd. B13: Mose 1A **134**
  B21: Hand 1B **100**
  WV1: Wolv 2D **44**
Woodston Gro. B91: Sol 1G **165**
Wood St. B16: Birm 1C **116**
  DY2: Dud 3B **94**
  DY4: Tip 1G **77**
  DY8: Woll 4B **108**
  DY9: Lye 6B **110**
  WS10: Darl 5F **47**
  WV4: Ett 2C **60**
  WV10: Wolv 4B **28**
  WV13: W'hall 1A **46**
  WV14: Bils 6F **45**
Woodthorne WV6: Tett 3H **25**
Woodthorne Cl. DY3: Gorn 5H **75**
Woodthorne Rd. WV6: Tett 3G **25**
Woodthorne Rd. Sth. WV6: Tett 5G **25**
Woodthorpe Av. DY6: K'wfrd 1C **92**
    (off Oakleigh Wlk.)
Woodthorpe Dr. DY9: W'cte 2H **125**
Woodthorpe Gdns. B14: King H 2G **147**
Woodthorpe Rd. B14: King H 2F **147**
Woodvale Dr. B28: Hall G 3E **149**
Woodvale M. B14: King H 1B **148**
Woodvale Rd. B28: Hall G 3E **149**
  B32: Bart G 4G **129**

Woodview Dr. B15: Edg 4E **117**
Woodville Ct. *B23: Erd* *5E **85***
(off Gravelly Hill)
Woodville Gdns. DY3: Sed 4B **60**
Woodville Rd. B14: King H 5H **133**
B17: Harb 5E **115**
Woodward Pl. DY9: Lye 1G **125**
Woodwards Cl. WS2: Wals 3H **47**
Woodwards Pl. WS2: Wals 3H **47**
Woodwards Rd. WS2: Wals 3H **47**
Woodward St. B71: W Brom 3C **80**
Woodway B24: Erd 2H **85**
Woodwells Rd. B8: W End 4G **103**
Woody Bank WS6: C Hay 3E **7**
Woolacombe Lodge Rd.
B29: S Oak 3G **131**
Woolmore Rd. B23: Erd 3C **84**
Woolpack All. WV1: Wolv 3B **170**
Woolpack Cl. B65: Row R 5A **96**
Woolpack St. WV1: Wolv . . .3B **170** (1G **43**)
Wootton Av. B44: K'sdng 5C **68**
Wootton Av. WV11: Wed 2F **29**
Wootton Cl. DY5: Brie H 3F **109**
WOOTTON GREEN 6G **155**
Wootton Grn. La. CV7: Bal C 6G **155**
Wootton La. CV7: Bal C 6E **155**
Wootton Rd. B31: Longb 2E **159**
WV3: Wolv 4B **42**
Woottons Sq. WV14: Bils 3G **61**
Worcester Arc. *B2: Birm* *5E **5***
(off New St.)
Worcester Bar B1: Birm 5A **4** (1E **117**)
Worcester Cl. B75: R'ley 6B **38**
Worcester Ct. WV3: Wolv 5E **43**
Worcester Grn. B71: W Brom 6A **64**
Worcester Gro. WV6: Pert 5D **24**
Worcester Ho. *B63: Hale* *2A **128***
(off Hill St.)
Worcester La. B75: R'ley 1B **54**
DY8: Stourb 4F **125**
DY9: Hag, Pedm 4F **125**
Worcester Ri. B29: S Oak 4D **132**
Worcester Rd. B68: O'bry 3G **113**
DY2: Neth 6G **95**
DY9: Hag 6F **125**
WV13: W'hall 1D **46**
Worcester St. B2: Birm 5E **5**
DY8: Stourb 1D **124**
WV2: Wolv 5A **170** (2G **43**)
Worcester Wlk. B2: Birm . . .5E **5** (1G **117**)
B37: Mars G 3B **122**
Worcester Way B90: Shir 2A **164**
Word Hill B17: Harb 4D **114**
WORDSLEY 1B **108**
Wordsley Ct. DY8: Word 6B **92**
Wordsley Grn. DY8: Word 1B **108**
(not continuous)
Wordsley Grn. Shop. Cen.
DY8: Word 1B **108**
Wordsworth Av. WV4: Ett 1A **60**
WV6: Pert 5E **25**
Wordsworth Cl. DY4: Tip 5A **62**
Wordsworth Ho. B31: Longb 1E **159**
B68: O'bry 5A **98**
Wordsworth Rd. B10: Small H 4D **118**
DY3: Lwr G 2F **75**
WV10: Bush 1C **28**
WV12: W'hall 2E **31**
Wordsworth St. B71: W Brom 2A **80**
Worfield Cl. WS4: Wals 5E **33**
Worfield Gdns. WV3: Wolv 5D **42**
Works Rd. B26: Birm A 2C **138**
WORLDS END 6D **136**
Worlds End Av. B32: Quin 5B **114**
Worlds End La. B32: Quin 5B **114**
Worlds End Rd. B20: Hand 4C **82**
Worleys Wharf Av. WS10: W'bry 3C **64**
Worsey Dr. DY4: Tip 1D **78**
Worthen Gro. B31: Longb 1E **159**
Worthings, The B30: Stir 1D **146**
Worthy Down WV11: Wed 4H **29**
Worthy Down Wlk. B35: Cas V 4F **87**
Wortley Av. WV10: Wolv 3A **28**
Worton Rd. DY9: W'cte 3A **126**
Wragby Cl. WV9: Pend 4F **15**
Wrekin Cl. B63: Hale 4E **127**

Wrekin Dr. DY9: W'cte 1H **125**
WV3: Wolv 3C **42**
WV6: Tett 4G **25**
Wrekin Gro. WV12: W'hall 6B **18**
Wrekin La. WV6: Tett 4G **25**
Wrekin Rd. B44: K'sdng 1H **83**
B73: Bold 4G **69**
Wrekin Vw. WS8: Bwnhls 2C **22**
WV1: Wolv 2A **170** (1G **43**)
Wrekin Vw. Rd. DY3: Sed 5G **59**
(not continuous)
Wren Av. WV6: Pert 6D **24**
Wrenbury Dr. WV14: Bils 4A **46**
Wrens Av. DY4: Tip 2E **77**
DY6: K'wfrd 5E **93**
Wrens Ct. B72: S Cold 6A **54**
Wrens Hill Rd. DY1: Dud 2C **76**
WREN'S NEST 3C **76**
Wren's Nest Cl. B90: Dic H 4G **163**
Wren's Nest National Nature Reserve
. . . . .3D **76**
Wrens Nest Pl. DY1: Dud 2D **76**
Wrens Nest Rd. DY1: Dud 2C **76**
Wrens Pk. Av. B76: Walm 6C **70**
Wren St. DY1: Dud 1D **94**
DY2: Neth 4D **94**
Wrentham St. B5: Birm 3F **117**
Wretham Ct. B19: Hock 2D **100**
Wretham Rd. B19: Hock 3D **100**
Wrexham Av. WS2: Wals 2F **47**
Wright Av. WV11: Wed 2F **29**
Wrighton Cl. WV12: W'hall 1C **30**
Wrighton Dr. DY5: P'ntt 6G **75**
Wright Rd. B8: Salt 4E **103**
Wright's La. B64: Old H 1H **111**
Wright St. B10: Small H 3D **118**
B63: Hale 1B **128**
WV10: Wolv 5H **27**
WV14: Bils 1G **61**
Wrottesley Golf Course 1C **24**
Wrottesley Pk. Rd. WV6: Pert 1D **40**
WV8: Pert, Wrot P 6D **24**
Wrottesley Rd. B43: Gt Barr 4H **65**
WV6: Tett 4H **25**
Wrottesley Rd. W. WV6: Tett 3F **25**
Wrottesley St. B5: Birm 6E **5** (2G **117**)
Wroxall Cl. DY5: Brie H 3F **109**
Wroxall Gro. B13: Mose 1A **148**
Wroxall Rd. B91: Sol 1C **150**
Wroxham Glen WV13: W'hall 4H **45**
Wroxton Rd. B26: Yard 3C **120**
WS2 Ind. Est. WS2: Wals 4B **32**
Wulfruna Ct. WV3: Wolv 2F **43**
Wulfruna Gdns. WV3: Wolv 2D **42**
Wulfruna St. WV1: Wolv . . .2B **170** (1G **43**)
Wulfrun Cen. WV1: Wolv . . .4B **170** (2G **43**)
Wulfrun Sq. WV1: Wolv 4C **170** (2H **43**)
Wulfrun Trad. Est. WV10: Wolv 4G **27**
Wulfrun Way WV1: Wolv 4B **170** (2G **43**)
Wyatt Cl. B5: Edg 6E **117**
Wyatt Rd. B75: S Cold 5F **55**
Wychall Dr. WV10: Bush 3A **16**
Wychall La. B38: King Nor 5H **145**
Wychall Pk. Gro. B38: King Nor 5H **145**
Wychall Rd. B31: N'fld 4F **145**
Wychbold Cl. WV12: W'hall 6D **18**
Wychbold Ct. DY9: Pedm 5G **125**
Wychbold Cres. B33: Kitts G 6G **105**
Wychbold Way WV12: W'hall 6D **18**
Wychbury B76: Walm 4E **71**
Wychbury Ct. B63: Hale 2A **128**
Wychbury Dr. DY9: Hag 6G **125**
Wychbury Grange DY9: Pedm 4F **125**
Wychbury Rd. B32: Bart G 5G **129**
DY5: Quar B 3A **110**
DY9: W'cte 4H **125**
WV3: Wolv 4A **42**
Wyche Av. B14: King H 3F **147**
Wychelm Farm Rd. B14: King H 6A **148**
Wych Elm Rd. WS8: Clay 2A **22**
Wycherley Way B64: Old H 3G **111**
Wychnor Gro. B71: W Brom 3C **64**
Wychwood Av. B93: Know 1D **166**
Wychwood Cres. B26: Sheld 5D **120**
Wyckham Cl. B17: Harb 1E **131**
Wyckham Rd. B36: Cas B 1A **106**

Wycliffe Gro. WS2: Wals 3A **48**
Wycome Rd. B28: Hall G 1F **149**
Wye Cliff Rd. B20: Hand 1D **100**
Wye Cl. B76: Walm 6E **71**
WV6: Pert 5F **25**
Wyegate Cl. B36: Cas B 1B **106**
Wyemanton Cl. B43: Gt Barr 4G **65**
Wye Rd. WS3: Blox 6C **20**
Wykeham Gro. WV6: Pert 6D **24**
Wyken Cl. B93: Dorr 6F **167**
Wyld Cl. B71: W Brom 5G **63**
Wylde Cres. B65: Row R 5C **96**
WYLDE GREEN 4A **70**
Wylde Grn. Rd. B72: W Grn 4A **70**
B76: Walm 4A **70**
Wylde Green Station (Rail) 4H **69**
Wymering Av. WV11: Wed 2H **29**
Wynall La. DY9: W'cte 1B **126**
Wynall La. Sth. DY9: W'cte 2C **126**
Wynbrook Gro. B90: M'path 3F **165**
Wynchcombe Av. WV4: Penn 1B **58**
Wynd, The DY3: Sed 4H **59**
Wyndcliff Rd. B9: Small H 2D **118**
Wyndham Gdns. B30: King Nor 3H **145**
Wyndham Rd. B16: Edg 2B **116**
Wyndhurst Rd. B33: Stech 5C **104**
Wyndley Cl. B74: Four O 3F **37**
Wyndley Dr. B73: S Cold 1H **69**
Wyndley Gro. B72: W Grn 3A **70**
Wyndley La. B73: S Cold 1G **69**
Wyndley Leisure Cen. 6G **53**
Wyndley Mnr. B74: Four O 3G **37**
Wyndley Swimming Baths 1G **69**
Wyndmill Cres. B71: W Brom 4D **64**
Wynds Covert B14: King H 5F **147**
Wynds Point B31: N'fld 2F **145**
Wynfield Gdns. B14: King H 2H **147**
Wynford Rd. B27: A Grn 6A **120**
Wynford Rd. Ind. Est. B27: A Grn . . .6A **120**
Wynne Cres. WV4: Penn 2A **58**
Wynn-Griffith Dr. DY4: Tip 4A **78**
Wynn Rd. WV4: Penn 5D **42**
Wynn St. B15: Birm 3F **117**
Wynstead Covert B14: King H 5E **147**
Wyntor La. B71: W Brom 5H **63**
Wyre Cl. B45: Fran 6H **143**
WS9: Wals W 3B **22**
Wyre Rd. DY8: Woll 5C **108**
Wyrley Cl. WS8: Bwnhls 2B **10**
WV12: W'hall 2D **30**
Wyrley Ho. B23: Erd 1D **84**
DY4: Tip 4B **78**
Wyrley La. WS3: Lit Wyr 4C **8**
Wyrley Rd. B6: Witt 4A **84**
B75: R'ley 2B **54**
WV11: Wed 3A **30**
Wyrley St. WV10: Wolv 1B **44**
Wyrley Trad. Est. B6: Witt 5A **84**
Wyrley Way B23: Erd 1A **84**
WYTHALL .6A **162**
Wythall Grn. Way B47: Wyt 5G **161**
Wythall Rd. B63: Hale 3A **128**
Wythall Station (Rail) 5C **162**
Wythwood Cl. DY9: Pedm 4H **125**
Wythwood Gro. B47: H'wd 3C **162**
DY4: Tip 5A **62**
Wythwood Rd. B47: H'wd 3B **162**
Wyton Av. B68: O'bry 1A **114**
Wyvern Cl. B68: O'bry 5H **97**
B74: S Cold 4H **53**
WV11: Wed 2A **30**
Wyvern Gro. B29: S Oak 3G **131**
Wyvern Rd. B74: S Cold 4H **53**
Wyvis Cl. WV3: Wolv 1C **42**

Y

Yale Dr. WV11: Wed 4G **29**
Yale Rd. WV13: W'hall 3A **46**
YARDLEY 2B **120**
Yardley Cl. B68: O'bry 2H **113**
Yardley Crematorium B25: Yard 6B **120**
Yardley Flds. Rd. B33: Stech 1B **120**
Yardley Grn. Rd. B9: Bord G 2F **119**
B33: Stech 2F **119**

Yardley Rd. B25: Yard 1A 136
  B27: A Grn 1A 136
Yardleys School Sport & Fitness Cen.
  . . . . .1F 135
Yardley St. DY9: Lye 5G 109
  WS10: Darl 4C 46
YARDLEY WOOD 4C 148
Yardley Wood Rd. B13: Mose 2B 134
  B14: Yard W 2B 148
  B90: Shir 2B 148
Yardley Wood Station (Rail) 2D 148
Yardley Works DY9: Lye 6G 109
Yare Gro. WV13: W'hall 1D 46
Yarnborough Hill DY8: Stourb 3E 125
Yarnbury Cl. B14: King H 6G 147
Yarn Cl. B47: H'wd 4A 162
Yarner Cl. DY1: Dud 5A 76
Yarnfield Rd. B11: Tys 2G 135
Yarningale Cl. B30: King Nor 4F 147
Yarningale Rd. B14: King H 3E 147
Yarningdale B90: Shir 6A 150
Yarn La. B90: Dic H 3G 163
Yarrow Cl. WS3: Pels 2E 21
  WV11: Wed 4H 29
Yarrow Dr. B38: King Nor 1B 160
Yarwell Cl. WV10: Wolv 5H 27
Yateley Av. B42: Gt Barr 6C 66
Yateley Cres. B42: Gt Barr 6C 66
Yateley Rd. B15: Edg 4H 115
Yatesbury Av. B35: Cas V 4D 86
Yates Cft. B74: Four O 3F 37
Yates La. B65: Row R 1F 113
Yeadon Gdns. WV3: Wolv 3B 42
Yeames Cl. B43: Gt Barr 1E 67
Yelverton Cl. WS3: Blox 3H 19
Yelverton Dr. B15: Edg 3A 116
Yeman Rd. B68: O'bry 6B 98
Yems Cft. WS4: Rus 3E 33
Yemscroft WS6: Gt Wyr 5G 7
Yemscroft Flats WS4: Rus 3E 33
Yenton Ct. B24: Erd 1H 85
Yenton Gro. B24: Erd 1A 86
Yeomanry Cl. B75: S Cold 5E 55
Yeomans Grange B75: S Cold 5D 54
  (off Yeomans Way)

Yeomans Way B75: S Cold 5D 54
Yeovil Ct. DY5: Brie H 1H 109
  (off Hill St.)
Yerbury Gro. B23: Erd 3B 84
Yew Cft. Av. B17: Harb 5E 115
Yewdale B17: Harb 1G 131
Yewhurst Rd. B91: Sol 3C 150
Yew St. WV3: Wolv 2E 43
Yew Tree Av. B26: Yard 4C 120
YEW TREE 1F 65
Yew Tree Gdns. WS5: Wals 1F 65
  WV8: Cod 3G 13
Yew Tree Hills DY2: Neth 5E 95
Yew Tree La. B26: Yard 4C 120
  B32: Fran 4D 142
  B65: Row R 1B 112
  B91: Sol 2A 152
  WS10: W'bry 3G 63
  WV6: Tett 3G 25
  WV14: Cose 4F 61
Yew Tree Pl. B62: Roms 2A 142
  WS3: Blox 4B 20
Yew Tree Retail Pk.
  B25: Yard 3B 120
Yew Tree Ri. B76: Walm 2D 70
Yew Tree Rd. B6: Aston 6A 84
  B13: Mose 3F 133
  B15: Edg 3E 117
  B36: Cas B 1A 106
  B63: Hale 2H 127
  B67: Smeth 5C 98
  B73: Bold 6G 69
  DY2: Neth 5E 95
  WS4: S'fld 6F 21
  WS5: Wals 6E 49
Yewtree Rd. B74: S'tly 3F 51
Yew Tree Vs. B73: Bold 6G 69
Yew Wlk. B37: Chel W 1D 122
Yockleton Rd. B33: Kitts G 6G 105
York Av. WS2: Wals 1H 47
  WV3: Wolv 2C 42
  WV13: W'hall 1D 46
Yorkbrook Dr. B26: Sheld 6F 121
York Cl. B30: B'ville 2C 146
  DY4: Tip 3F 77

York Cres. B34: S End 4A 106
  B70: W Brom 1G 79
  DY8: Woll 4B 108
  WS10: Darl 5D 46
  WV3: Wolv 2C 42
Yorkdale Cl. DY3: Lwr G 4H 75
York Dr. B36: Hodg H 1H 103
Yorke Av. DY5: Brie H 2E 109
York Gdns. WV3: Wolv 2C 42
York Ho. B73: W Grn 2H 69
Yorklea Cft. B37: F'bri 1B 122
York M. B17: Harb 5H 115
Yorkminster Dr.
  B37: Chel W 1E 123
York Rd. B14: King H 5G 133
  B16: Edg 2A 116
  B21: Hand 1B 100
  B23: Erd 3F 85
  B28: Hall G 3F 135
  B65: Row R 6E 97
  DY2: Neth 6G 95
  WS4: Rus 2H 33
  WV3: Wolv 3H 41
Yorks Pk. DY2: Dud 2D 94
York St. B17: Harb 5H 115
  WV1: Wolv 2A 44
Yorks Wood Dr. B37: K'hrst 3B 106
Yorkswood Rd. B34: S End 4G 105
York Ter. B18: Birm 4E 101
Young St. B70: W Brom 4G 79
Youth Court
  Birmingham 3E 5 (6G 101)
Yoxall Gro. B33: Kitts G 6E 105
Yoxall Rd. B90: Shir 5B 150

Zaria Ct. DY8: Word 6C 92
Zion Cl. WS6: C Hay 2D 6
Zions Cl. B64: Old H 2H 111
Zion St. DY4: Tip 5H 61
Zoar St. DY3: Gorn 4G 75
  WV3: Wolv 2F 43
Zouche Cl. DY8: Amb 3C 108

MIX
From responsible
sources
FSC
www.fsc.org
FSC® C015185

The representation on the maps of a road, track or footpath is no evidence of the existence of a right of way.

The Grid on this map is the National Grid taken from Ordnance Survey® mapping with the permission of the Controller of Her Majesty's Stationery Office.

Copyright of Geographers' A-Z Map Company Ltd.

No reproduction by any method whatsoever of any part of this publication is permitted without the prior consent of the copyright owners.

SAFETY CAMERA INFORMATION

PocketGPSWorld.com's CamerAlert is a self-contained speed and red light camera warning system for SatNavs and Android or Apple iOS smartphones/tablets. Visit www.cameralert.co.uk to download.

Safety camera locations are publicised by the Safer Roads Partnership which operates them in order to encourage drivers to comply with speed limits at these sites. It is the driver's absolute responsibility to be aware of and to adhere to speed limits at all times.

By showing this safety camera information it is the intention of Geographers' A-Z Map Company Ltd., to encourage safe driving and greater awareness of speed limits and vehicle speed. Data accurate at time of printing.

HOSPITALS, HOSPICES and selected HEALTHCARE FACILITIES covered by this atlas.

N.B. Where it is not possible to name these facilities on the map, the reference given is for the road in which they are situated.

ACORNS CHILDREN'S HOSPICE (SELLY OAK) 5A **132**
103 Oak Tree Lane
Selly Oak
BIRMINGHAM
B29 6HZ
Tel: 0121 2484850

ACORNS CHILDREN'S HOSPICE (WALSALL) 6D **48**
Walstead Road
WALSALL
WS5 4NL
Tel: 01922 422500

BARBERRY, THE 2A **132**
25 Vincent Drive
BIRMINGHAM
B15 2FG
Tel: 0121 3012002

BIRMINGHAM CHEST CLINIC 3C **4** (6F **101**)
151 Gt. Charles Street
Queensway
BIRMINGHAM
B3 3HX
Tel: 0121 4241950

BIRMINGHAM CHILDREN'S HOSPITAL 2F **5** (6G **101**)
Steelhouse Lane
BIRMINGHAM
B4 6NH
Tel: 0121 3339999

BIRMINGHAM DENTAL HOSPITAL 1E **5** (6G **101**)
St Chad's Queensway
BIRMINGHAM
B4 6NN
Tel: 0121 2368611

BIRMINGHAM HEARTLANDS HOSPITAL 1H **119**
Bordesley Green East
BIRMINGHAM
B9 5SS
Tel: 0121 4242000

BIRMINGHAM ST MARY'S HOSPICE 4C **132**
176 Raddlebarn Road
BIRMINGHAM
B29 7DA
Tel: 0121 4721191

BIRMINGHAM TREATMENT CENTRE (B.T.C.) 5B **100**
Dudley Road
BIRMINGHAM
B18 7QH
Tel: 0121 5076180

BIRMINGHAM WOMEN'S HOSPITAL 1H **131**
Mindelsohn Way
BIRMINGHAM
B15 2TG
Tel: 0121 4721377

BLOXWICH HOSPITAL 1H **31**
Reeves Sreet
WALSALL
WS3 2JJ
Tel: 01922 858600

BUSHEY FIELDS HOSPITAL 2A **94**
Bushey Fields Road
DUDLEY
DY1 2LZ
Tel: 01384 456111

CITY HOSPITAL (BIRMINGHAM) 5B **100**
Dudley Road
BIRMINGHAM
B18 7QH
Tel: 0121 554 3801

COMPTON HOSPICE 1A **42**
4 Compton Road West
WOLVERHAMPTON
WV3 9DH
Tel: 0845 2255497

CORBETT HOSPITAL 4E **109**
Vicarage Road
STOURBRIDGE
DY8 4JB
Tel: 01384 456111

DOROTHY PATTISON HOSPITAL 2H **47**
Alumwell Close
WALSALL
WS2 9XH
Tel: 01922 607000

EDGBASTON BMI HOSPITAL 6B **116**
22 Somerset Road
Edgbaston
BIRMINGHAM
B15 2QQ
Tel: 0121 4562000

EDWARD STREET HOSPITAL 4A **80**
Edward Street
WEST BROMWICH
B70 8NL
Tel: 0845 146 1800

FAIR OAKS DAY HOSPICE 1D **32**
Goscote Lane
WALSALL
WS3 1SJ
Tel: 01922 602580

GOOD HOPE HOSPITAL 5B **54**
Rectory Road
SUTTON COLDFIELD
B75 7RR
Tel: 0121 4242000

GREET URGENT CARE CENTRE 1D **134**
50 Percy Road
BIRMINGHAM
B11 3ND
Tel: 0345 111 1310

GUEST HOSPITAL 4G **77**
Tipton Road
DUDLEY
DY1 4SE
Tel: 01384 456111

HALLAM STREET HOSPITAL 2C **80**
Hallam Street
WEST BROMWICH
B71 4NH
Tel: 0121 612 8628

ST GILES HOSPICE 4D **54**
Lindridge Road
Sutton Coldfield
SUTTON COLDFIELD
B75 6JB
Tel: 0121 37806290

ST GILES WALSALL HOSPICE 1D **32**
Goscote Lane
WALSALL
WS3 1SJ
Tel: 01922 602540

SANDWELL GENERAL HOSPITAL 2B **80**
Lyndon
WEST BROMWICH
B71 4HJ
Tel: 0121 553 1831

SHELDON UNIT 6B **144**
11 Sheldon Drive
BIRMINGHAM
B31 5EJ
Tel: 0121 475 6100

SOLIHULL HOSPITAL 3G **151**
Lode Lane
SOLIHULL
B91 2JL
Tel: 0121 4242000

THE MARY STEVENS HOSPICE 3F **125**
221 Hagley Road
STOURBRIDGE
DY8 2JR
Tel: 01384 443010

URGENT CARE CENTRE (SUMMERFIELD) 5A **100**
134 Heath Street
Winson Green
BIRMINGHAM
B18 7AL
Tel: 0345 245 0769

URGENT CARE CENTRE (WARREN FARM) 5A **68**
Warren Farm Road
Kingstanding
BIRMINGHAM
B44 0PU
Tel: 0121 4655613

URGENT CARE CENTRE (WASHWOOD HEATH
Clodeshall Road
Saltley
BIRMINGHAM
B8 3SW

WEST HEATH HOSPITAL . . . .
Rednal Road
BIRMINGHAM
B38 8HR
Tel: 0121 46604100

WEST MIDLANDS PRIVATE HOSPITAL . . . .
Colman Hill
HALESOWEN
B63 2AH
Tel: 01384 560123

WEST PARK REHABILITATION HOSPITAL 1
Park Road West
WOLVERHAMPTON
WV1 4PW
Tel: 01902 444000

WOLVERHAMPTON NUFFIELD HEALTH HOSPITAL 5B **26**
Wood Road
WOLVERHAMPTON
WV6 8LE
Tel: 01902 212208

WOODBOURNE PRIORY HOSPITAL 3G **115**
21 Woodbourne Road
Harborne
BIRMINGHAM
B17 8BY
Tel: 0121 4344343

ZINNIA CENTRE 2C **134**
100 Showell Green Lane
BIRMINGHAM
B11 4HL
Tel: 0121 3015300

Direct
Customer Service

If you experience difficulty obtaining
any of our 300 titles, please contact
us direct for help and advice.

www./az.co.uk

Tel: 01732 783422   Fax: 01732 780677

L 6B **64**

CH
8470

PITAL 3D **84**
oir Road
HAM
V
21 6235500

LOR HOSPICE 2A **86**
range Road
ngton
RMINGHAM
24 0DF
el: 0121 4652000

GS HILL DAY UNIT 6E **47**
School Street
WEDNESBURY
WS10 9JB
Tel: 0121 526 4405

LITTLE ASTON SPIRE HOSPITAL 4A **36**
Little Aston Hall Drive
Little Aston
SUTTON COLDFIELD
B74 3UP
Tel: 0121 353 2444

MANOR HOSPITAL (WALSALL) 2A **48**
Moat Road
WALSALL
WS2 9PS
Tel: 01922 721172

MARIE CURIE HOSPICE, SOLIHULL 3H **151**
911-913 Warwick Road
SOLIHULL
B91 3ER
Tel: 0121 2547800

OSELEY HALL HOSPITAL 2G **133**
Alcester Road
BIRMINGHAM
B13 8JL
Tel: 0121 4666000

OSSLEY DAY UNIT 6G **19**
Sneyd Lane
WALSALL
WS3 2LW
Tel: 01922 607500

N CROSS HOSPITAL (WOLVERHAMPTON) 4D **28**
Wolverhampton Road
Heath Town
WOLVERHAMPTON
WV10 0QP
Tel: 01902 307999

WALK-IN CENTRE (BIRMINGHAM) 4E **5** (1G **117**)
Boots The Chemist
66 High Street
BIRMINGHAM
B4 7TA
Tel: 0121 255 4500

WALK-IN CENTRE (ERDINGTON) 3F **85**
196 High Street
Erdington
BIRMINGHAM
B23 6SJ
el: 0121 6868011

ALK-IN CENTRE PHOENIX HEALTH CENTRE 5H **43**
kfield Road
LVERHAMPTON
6ED
01902 444015

NHS WALK-IN CENTRE SHOWELL PARK HEALTH CENTRE . . .2A **28**
Fifth Avenue
WOLVERHAMPTON
WV10 9ST
Tel: 01902 446711

NHS WALK-IN CENTRE (WALSALL) 2C **48**
The Market Square
Unit 19-21 Digbeth
WALSALL
WS1 1QZ
Tel: 01922 605730

OLEASTER, THE 2A **132**
6 Mindelsohn Crescent
BIRMINGHAM
B15 2SY
Tel: 0121 3012201

PARKWAY SPIRE HOSPITAL 2A **152**
1 Damson Parkway
SOLIHULL
B91 2PP
Tel: 0845 8501451

PENN HOSPITAL 1C **58**
Penn Road
WOLVERHAMPTON
WV4 5HN
Tel: 01902 444141

PERRY TREE REHABILITATION CENTRE 5C **68**
Dovedale Road
Perry Common
BIRMINGHAM
B23 5BX
Tel: 0121 675 5598

PRIORY BMI HOSPITAL 6D **116**
Priory Road
Edgbaston
BIRMINGHAM
B5 7UG
Tel: 0121 4402323

QUEEN ELIZABETH HOSPITAL 1A **132**
Edgbaston
BIRMINGHAM
B15 2TH
Tel: 0121 627 2000

QUEEN ELIZABETH HOSPITAL BIRMINGHAM 1A **132**
Mindelsohn Way
Edgbaston
BIRMINGHAM
B15 2WB
Tel: 0121 6272000

ROWLEY REGIS HOSPITAL 1B **112**
Moor Lane
ROWLEY REGIS
B65 8DA
Tel: 0121 553 1831

ROYAL ORTHOPAEDIC HOSPITAL 2F **145**
Bristol Road South
Northfield
BIRMINGHAM
B31 2AP
Tel: 0121 685 4000

RUSSELLS HALL HOSPITAL 2H **93**
Pensnett Road
DUDLEY
DY1 2HQ
Tel: 01384 456111

ST DAVID'S HOUSE (DAY HOSPITAL) 1F **73**
Planks Lane
Wombourne
WOLVERHAMPTON
WV5 8DU
Tel: 01902 326001